Europe, 1914

W9-DIH-110

SWEDEN

Torneälven

Umeälven

Gulf of Bothnia

Åbo

Vyborg

Helsingfors

Petrograd

Lake Ladoga

Lake Onega

Volkhov

Stockholm

Lake Vänern

Saaremaa

Gotland

Öland

Baltic Sea

(Bornholm (Denmark))

Dvina

Neman

Minsk

Vistula

Warsaw

Bug

Vistula

Oder

Carpathian Mts.

AUSTRIA-HUNGARY

Budapest

Tisza

Maros (Mures)

Dráva

Sava

Belgrade

SERBIA

Dinaric Alps

MONTENEGRO

ALBANIA

GREECE

Ionian Sea

Athens

Crete

Dniester

Prut

Siret

Morava

Vardar

Balkan Mts.

BULGARIA

Maritsa

ROMANIA

Bucharest

Danube

Constantinople

Sea of Marmara

Aegean Sea

Kiev

Dnieper

Southern Bug

Moscow

RUSSIA

Volga

Don

Donets

Kuban'

Volga

Black Sea

Caspian Sea

CAUCASUS MTS.

URAL MTS.

PERSIA

OTTOMAN EMPIRE

Cyprus

40°E

N

0   200   400 mi.

0   200   400 km

EUROPE

SINCE 1914

ENCYCLOPEDIA OF THE AGE OF WAR AND RECONSTRUCTION

EDITORIAL BOARD

EUROPE
SINCE 1914
ENCYCLOPEDIA OF THE AGE OF WAR AND RECONSTRUCTION

Volume 4

Nagy to Switzerland

John Merriman and Jay Winter

EDITORS IN CHIEF

CHARLES SCRIBNER'S SONS

An imprint of Thomson Gale, a part of The Thomson Corporation

Detroit • New York • San Francisco • New Haven, Conn. • Waterville, Maine • London • Munich

Europe since 1914: Encyclopedia of the Age of War and Reconstruction

John Merriman
Jay Winter
Editors in Chief

LIBRARY OF CONGRESS CATALOGING-IN-PUBLICATION DATA

Europe since 1914: encyclopedia of the age of war and reconstruction / edited by John Merriman and Jay Winter.
    p. cm. — (Scribner library of modern Europe)
    Includes bibliographical references and index.
    ISBN 0-684-31365-0 (set : alk. paper) — ISBN 0-684-31366-9 (v. 1 : alk. paper) — ISBN 0-684-31367-7 (v. 2 : alk. paper) — ISBN 0-684-31368-5 (v. 3 : alk. paper) — ISBN 0-684-31369-3 (v. 4 : alk. paper) — ISBN 0-684-31370-7 (v. 5 : alk. paper) — ISBN 0-684-31497-5 (e-book)
    1. Europe–History–20th century–Encyclopedias. 2. Europe–Civilization–20th century–Encyclopedias. I. Merriman, John M. II. Winter, J. M.
    D424.E94 2006
    940.503–dc22
                                                    2006014427

This title is also available as an e-book and as a ten-volume set with Europe 1789 to 1914: Encyclopedia of the Age of Industry and Empire.
E-book ISBN 0-684-31497-5
Ten-volume set ISBN 0-684-31530-0
Contact your Gale sales representative for ordering information.

Printed in the United States of America
10 9 8 7 6 5 4 3 2 1

CONTENTS OF THIS VOLUME

CONTENTS OF OTHER VOLUMES

VOLUME 5

MAPS OF EUROPE SINCE 1914

The maps in this section illuminate some of the major events of European history in the twentieth and early twenty-first centuries, including World War I and World War II, the Holocaust, the breakup of Yugoslavia, and the formation of the European Union.

WWI in Europe

- Allies, 1918
- Central Powers
- Neutral nations
- Farthest advance by Central Powers
- 1914 border

ATLANTIC OCEAN

NORWAY

SWEDEN

Baltic Sea

DENMARK

North Sea

UNITED KINGDOM

London

NETH.

BELG.

Berlin

GERMANY

Eastern Front

RUSSIA

Paris

LUX.

Western Front

FRANCE

SWITZ.

Italian Front

Vienna

Budapest

AUSTRIA-HUNGARY

Belgrade

ROMANIA

Black Sea

ITALY

MONT.

SERBIA

BULGARIA

ALBANIA

Constantinople

SPAIN

PORTUGAL

Lisbon

Salonika Front

GREECE

Athens

OTTOMAN EMPIRE

Mediterranean Sea

0   250   500 mi.
0   250   500 km

Versailles Settlement

Newly-formed nations

Boundaries, 1923

ICELAND

0   200   400 mi.
0   200   400 km

ATLANTIC OCEAN

NORWAY

SWEDEN

FINLAND

Christiania (Oslo)

Stockholm

Helsinki

Tallinn

Petrograd

ESTONIA

North Sea

DENMARK

Copenhagen

Baltic Sea

Riga

LATVIA

Moscow

LITH.

Danzig

East Prussia (Ger.)

Kaunas

UNION OF SOVIET SOCIALIST REPUBLICS

IRISH FREE STATE

UNITED KINGDOM

London

Amsterdam

NETH.

Berlin

GERMANY

Warsaw

POLAND

Brussels

BELG.

LUX.

Paris

Saar

Prague

Krakow

CZECHOSLOVAKIA

FRANCE

Bern

SWITZ.

Vienna

AUSTRIA

Budapest

HUNGARY

ROMANIA

Venice

Bucharest

PORTUGAL

ANDORRA

Madrid

ITALY

Belgrade

YUGOSLAVIA

Black Sea

BULGARIA

Lisbon

SPAIN

Rome

Sofia

Constantinople

Tangier (International Territory)

Gibraltar

Tiranë

ALBANIA

GREECE

TURKEY

Spanish Morocco

Athens

Morocco (Fr.)

Algeria (Fr.)

Tunisia (Fr.)

Mediterranean Sea

WWII in Europe

- Axis Powers
- Maximum Axis Control
- Neutral countries
- Allied Powers
- ─── Farthest German advance as of Dec. 1941
- ─── 1937 borders

N

0   200   400 mi.
0   200   400 km

ATLANTIC OCEAN

North Sea

SWEDEN

NORWAY

FINLAND

EST.

LATVIA

LITH.

DENMARK

East Prussia

IRELAND

GREAT BRITAIN

London

Berlin

• Warsaw

GERMANY

Sudetenland

POLAND

UNION OF SOVIET SOCIALIST REPUBLICS

• Moscow

NETH.

Dunkirk

BELG.

Rhineland

LUX.

CZECHOSLOVAKIA

Paris

AUSTRIA

HUNGARY

ROMANIA

FRANCE

Vichy •

SWITZ.

YUGOSLAVIA

Black Sea

BULGARIA

PORTUGAL

SPAIN

ITALY

Rome •

ALBANIA

GREECE

TURKEY

Tangier (International Territory)

Spanish Morocco

Mediterranean   Sea

Tunisia (Fr.)

Morocco (Fr.)

Algeria (Fr.)

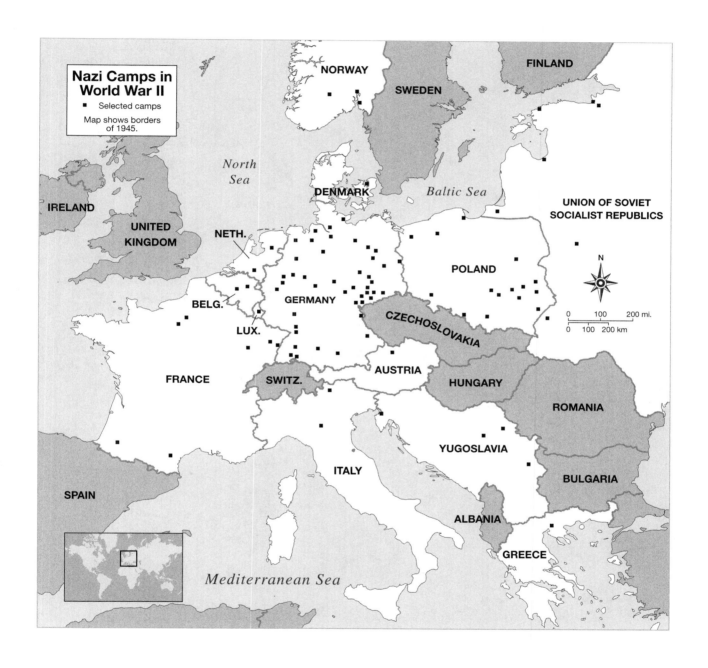

Nazi Camps in World War II
- ■ Selected camps
- Map shows borders of 1945.

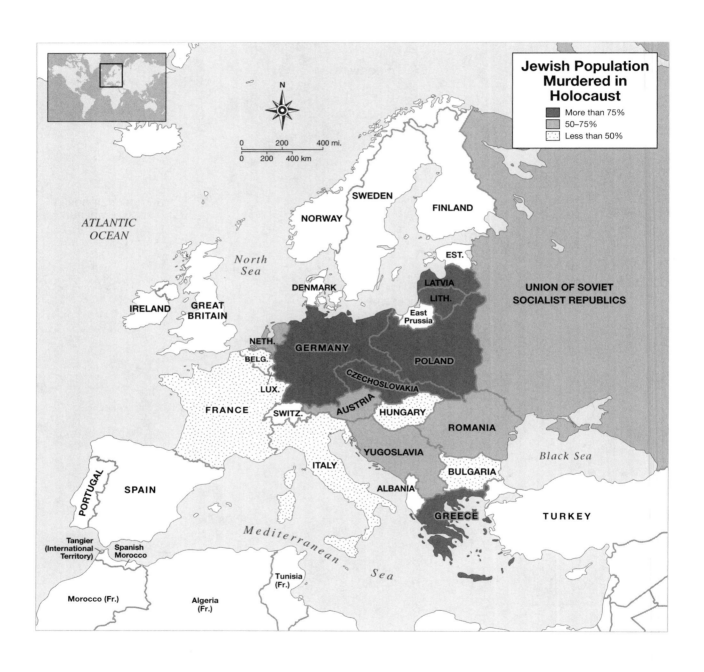

Post 1945 Europe

Communist nations ······ Iron Curtain ———

Non-Communist nations ★ Capital

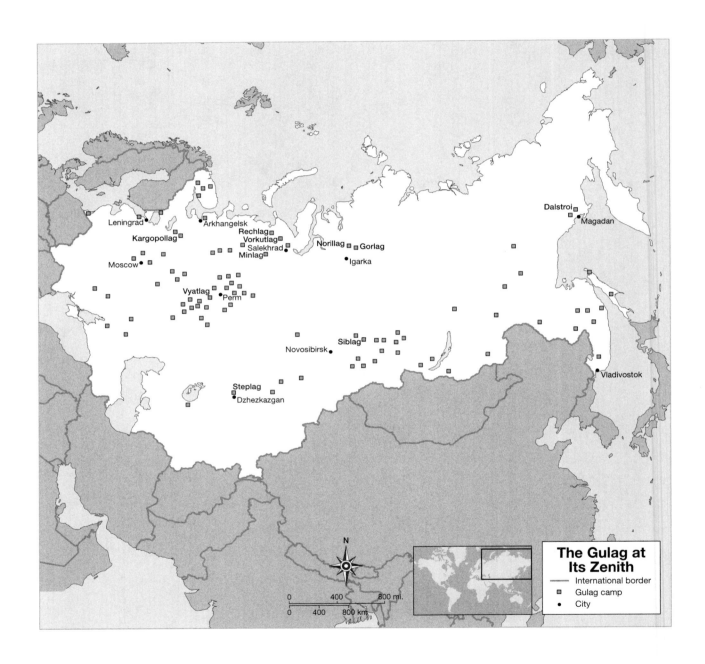

The Gulag at
Its Zenith

International border
☐ Gulag camp
● City

AUSTRIA

HUNGARY

ITALY

ROMANIA

Ljubljana
Slovenia

Zagreb

Croatia

Vojvodina
Novi Sad

Belgrade

Bosnia and
Herzegovina

Sarajevo

Serbia

Adriatic Sea

Montenegro

Priština
Kosovo

BULGARIA

Titograd

Skopje

ITALY

Macedonia

N

ALBANIA

GREECE

**Yugoslavia Before
the Breakup**

——	International border
—·—·—	Republic border
— — —	Autonomous area border
✪	National capital
•	Republic or autonomous area capital

0   40   80 mi.
0   40   80 km

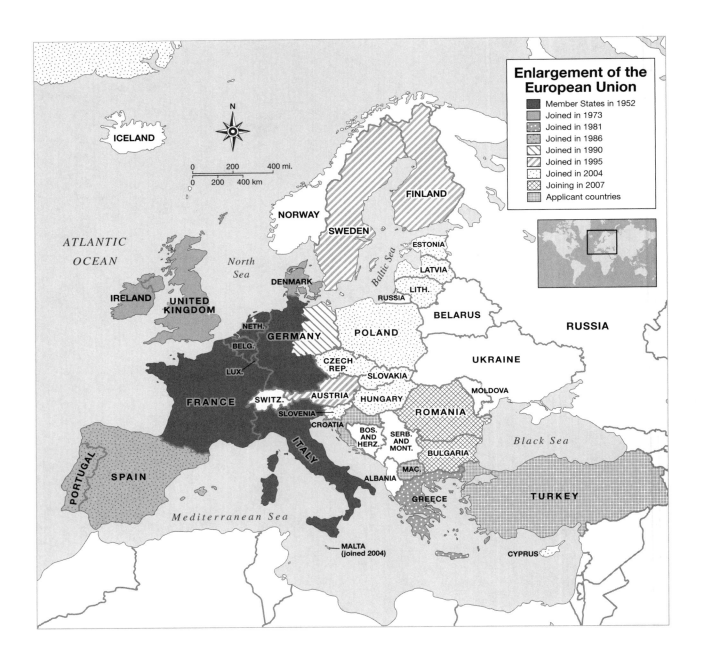

Enlargement of the European Union

- Member States in 1952
- Joined in 1973
- Joined in 1981
- Joined in 1986
- Joined in 1990
- Joined in 1995
- Joined in 2004
- Joining in 2007
- Applicant countries

NAGY, IMRE (1896–1958), Hungarian statesman, premier of the 1956 revolutionary government.

A lifelong communist, Nagy paradoxically became the symbol of courageous resistance to communist repression as a leader of the Hungarian revolution of 1956.

Nagy was born to a peasant family in the provincial town of Kaposvár in western Hungary. After four years of high school education he was apprenticed as a locksmith. In 1915 he was drafted and fought on the Russian front, until he was captured in the following year and became a prisoner of war. At the time of the Russian Civil War he joined the Communist Party and fought in the Red Army. In 1921 he returned to Hungary and participated in the work of the Social Democratic Party, until he was expelled as a communist. In 1927 he was briefly jailed for illegal organizational activities and, on being freed, he left the country first for Austria and then in 1929 for the Soviet Union. He spent the next fourteen years in exile, where he trained himself to be a specialist on agrarian issues. He worked in the Agricultural Institute of the Comintern and the Central Statistical Institute, and during World War II he was an editor of the Hungarian language broadcasts of Radio Moscow.

He was among the first communists to return to Hungary in October 1944. Even though he had not been among the best-known leaders, he was chosen to play a major role because, unlike the other top communists, he was not Jewish. The fact that he was an agrarian economist also recommended him at a time when the issue of land reform had great political significance. Nagy served as minister of agriculture in the provisional government and in that capacity became responsible for the radical land reform that was carried out in 1945. After the elections in November 1945 he served briefly as minister of the interior but was removed by the communists, who saw him as weak. Between 1947 and 1949 he was speaker of the Parliament. He opposed the party's agrarian policy, the extremely unpopular forced collectivization, and for his views was excluded from the leadership.

At the death of Stalin in 1953, on Soviet initiative Nagy was made prime minister. What recommended him for this job in the eyes of the Soviet leadership was once again that he was not Jewish and had not been part of the leadership at the time of the worst terror. Also as a major organizer planning the land reform, he had acquired a degree of popularity. Nagy initiated "a new course," which meant increased investment in consumer goods in order to raise the disastrously low standard of living of the people along with the lessening of terror. Nagy's patron in the Soviet government was Georgy Malenkov. It was Nagy's misfortune that Nikita Khrushchev defeated his patron, which in turn allowed Mátyás Rákosi, the Hungarian Stalin, to remove Nagy and replace him with his own man, András Hegedüs.

Imre Nagy addresses the Hungarian parliament, 1955.
Seated next to him is Hungarian Communist Party chief Mátyás
Rákosi. ©BETTMANN/CORBIS

Rákosi saw Nagy as a dangerous opponent and succeeded in excluding him from the party. In spite of pressure Nagy refused to exercise self-criticism. Khrushchev's speech at the Twentieth Party Congress undermined the standing of the Stalinist leaders in Eastern Europe, in particular in Hungary. The revolution that followed on 23 October 1956 made Nagy premier once again. This was not a revolution that Nagy made or desired; rather than doing away with the communist system, he hoped to improve it. In fact, during the short period of the revolution the demands of its leaders went much further than Premier Nagy would have liked. However, when presented with the choice of turning against his own people or remaining faithful to his communist convictions, Nagy made the morally correct choice and thereby became a hero and later a martyr. He called for the removal of Soviet troops from Hungary, accepted the reintroduction of the multiparty system as well as freedom of speech and organization, took the country out of the Warsaw Pact, and declared Hungary's neutrality.

When Soviet troops reentered Budapest and suppressed the revolution on 4 November 1956, Nagy took refuge at the Yugoslav embassy. On receiving a promise of safe conduct, he left the embassy on 22 November. Soviet troops immediately captured him and his fellow leaders and deported them to Romania. Nagy could have saved his life by repudiating the revolution and endorsing the new János Kádár government imposed by Soviet troops, but he refused. He was returned to Hungary, sentenced to death on 15 June 1958, and executed on the following day.

On 16 June 1989 Nagy's reburial became a celebration of the martyrs of the revolution and at the same time, fittingly, represented the end of the communist regime in Hungary.

See also **Eastern Bloc; Hungary; Khrushchev, Nikita.**

BIBLIOGRAPHY

Meray, Tibor. *Imre Nagy, l'homme trahi. Traduit du hongrois.* Paris, 1960.

Unwin, Peter. *Voice in the Wilderness: Imre Nagy and the Hungarian Revolution.* London, 1991.

PETER KENEZ

NATIONAL FRONT. On 21 April 2002 a political earthquake rocked France. In the first round of the presidential elections, the National Front candidate, Jean-Marie Le Pen, came in second, behind the sitting president, Jacques Chirac, and ahead of the favorite, the Socialist Party candidate, Prime Minister Lionel Jospin. In response to this disappointing result, Jospin immediately announced his retirement from political life. The result of the (run-off) second round, following massive anti–National Front street demonstrations, was admittedly an overwhelming victory for Chirac, who obtained 82.2 percent of votes cast as compared with Le Pen's 17.8 percent. But it still meant that in a country much given to advertising itself as a model of democracy, the Far Right could garner almost a fifth of French votes. Nor was this a new development: over the previous twenty years the National Front had become a significant player among political forces in France, and France by extension had acquired one of the largest far-right constituencies in a European

Jean-Marie Le Pen, leader of the National Front, speaks in front of the Place de l'Opera, September 1986.
©Jacques Langevin & Thierry Orban/Sygma/Corbis

country. The National Front's leader was certainly a talented individual, but it took him a very long time to translate that talent into ballots. Suffice it to recall that the Front, over which Le Pen had presided from its foundation in 1972, failed for over ten years to cull more than 1 percent of votes cast in elections; indeed, in the presidential elections of 1981, Le Pen could not even gather the five hundred signatures required by law for him to run.

It was only in 1984 that the National Front began its rapid ascent. A harbinger of things to come was Le Pen's performance in the 1982 municipal elections, when he collected 11.3 percent of the votes in the working-class 20th arrondissement (or district) of Paris. In 1984, at the national level, the party obtained 10.95 percent of votes cast in the European parliamentary elections. In presidential contests, the Front's share of votes reached 14.39 percent in 1988 and 15 percent in 1995, while in the legislative elections of 1997 it came to 15.24 percent. These percentages represent millions of French citizens—more than 4.5 million in 1995. All French political parties have a high turnover of supporters, but this trait is even more marked in the case of the National Front, in view of which one can but conclude that a very significant proportion of the French people have voted at least once since the 1980s for the Far Right. The Front has become a permanent feature of France's political landscape.

How is this to be explained? One consideration is the National Front's propensity to attract protest votes. For a portion of the electorate, a vote for the Front has been no more than an expression of dissatisfaction, cast in the confident expectation that the party would not come to power. It is noteworthy, however, that the French Communist Party long antedated the Front as a recipient of protest votes. The rise of Le Pen's party was in inverse proportion to the decline of the Communists: at least to some extent the two parties were like communicating vessels. In the 1984 European elections the National

Front was just behind the Communists, and in the legislative elections of 1986 it overtook them. Of course this is not to say that Communist voters went over en masse to the Front; many, indeed, defected instead to the Socialists or to small far-left parties. Yet a time eventually came when many more workers were voting for the National Front than for the Communist Party. The Soviet model no longer held out any promise, and many working-class voters were seduced by Le Pen's denunciation of "immigration, insecurity, unemployment" and by his trumpeting of the purported solution: "French people first." The failure of the Socialist Party to fulfill its promise to "change life" after its triumphant victory in 1981 merely strengthened the appeal of the Front, especially since the Socialists were vulnerable to the charge that they neglected the issues of public safety and immigration.

There can be no doubt, in any case, that the growth of the National Front resulted from the addition of a large number of solidly working-class voters to the party's traditional constituency of conservative Catholics and rightists motivated by nostalgia for Vichy France or French Algeria. The Front's composition accounts for the fact that, twenty years after it first burst onto the French political scene, it is still a factor to be reckoned with and has several times thrown French political institutions into turmoil. The National Front has survived the more or less long-term electoral impact of many controversial issues, among them Le Pen's verbal excesses and the naked racism they betray, the party's support for Saddam Hussein in the first Gulf War, the profaning of the Jewish cemetery in Carpentras (widely attributed to the Front), and above all the split of 1998, when a portion of the party's supporters left under the leadership of Bruno Mégret and formed the National and Republican Movement (MNR). Only time will tell whether the National Front can survive the departure of its aging chief, who was seventy-six years old in 2004.

See also **Immigration and Internal Migration; Le Pen, Jean-Marie; Riots in France.**

BIBLIOGRAPHY

Becker, Jean-Jacques, and Pascal Ory. *Crises et alternances, 1974–2000.* New ed. Paris, 2002.

Le Pen, Jean-Marie. *Les Français d'abord.* Paris, 1984.

Mayer, Nonna, and Pacal Perrineau, eds. *Le Front national à découvert.* Rev. ed. Paris, 1996.

Perrineau, Pascal. *Le symptôme Le Pen, radiographie des électeurs du Front national.* Paris, 1997.

JEAN-JACQUES BECKER

NATO. A creation of the early Cold War, the North Atlantic Treaty Organization (NATO) has surprised many commentators by outlasting the conflict that produced it.

THE ESTABLISHMENT OF NATO
NATO was established by the North Atlantic Treaty in Washington, D.C., on 4 April 1949, after over a year's negotiations. Although the treaty referred to cultural and political cooperation (Article 2), the operative clause was Article 5. In it, the twelve signatories—the United States, Canada, Iceland, Denmark, Norway, Belgium, Netherlands, Luxembourg, France, Great Britain, Portugal, and Italy—pledged that an attack on one was an attack on all and would lead to them taking whatever measures they deemed necessary, including armed action.

In the minds of those whose initiatives led to the establishment of NATO—most especially British Foreign Secretary Ernest Bevin—the major problem that faced Western Europe in 1948–1949 was not an immediate invasion by the Soviet army as such, but the possibility that fear of Soviet power would hinder recovery from the traumas of the war period, bringing economic stagnation and poor morale and reducing resistance to the subversive methods that the Soviets were believed to prefer. Bevin argued to the Americans that Europeans needed a sense of security if they were to complete the economic recovery that was the aim of the U.S. Marshall Plan begun in 1947. There are revisionist historians, indeed, who have argued that the establishment of NATO was mainly to provide the necessary preconditions for the Marshall Plan to succeed and for American markets in Western Europe to be revived. Certainly, in its first year or so, NATO had little capacity to actually defend its European members; what it had done, however, was effectively to place them under a guarantee of American nuclear protection. While military planners were initially skeptical of the defensive capabilities of the alliance, for the politicians the main point was to increase the Western European sense of security. Again, revisionists have argued that this may well have had the opposite effect: by provoking Soviet responses and making the Cold War into a more overtly military confrontation, it may well have institutionalized insecurity.

In any event, at the start the treaty was less like a collective defense arrangement between equals than a protectorate of the weak by the strong. The treaty formalized the American intention to remain engaged in European affairs, but the reality was that the U.S. Congress was clear that the U.S. contribution should be strategic air power while the European allies provided the foot-soldiers: no additional U.S. troops were initially assigned to Europe (and indeed U.S. strategic air forces themselves remained outside NATO command). Mutual resentments over "burden-sharing" were to plague NATO throughout its history.

NATO was transformed after the outbreak of the Korean War in June 1950. Elements of organization were put in place to focus it on defense—to move from a fairly loose alliance of like-minded nations (with a central core of Anglo-American strategic coordination) intended to provide a generalized "sense of security" into an integrated military alliance focused on defense against a specific threat. The Korean War moved the U.S. government firmly in the direction of rearmament—and because the communist attack in Korea seemed to suggest a Soviet grand design in which the next target would be Europe, much of this was directed toward strengthening the defensive capabilities of NATO and thereafter the defense function of the alliance was the most prominent—and for many, indeed, the sole reason for the organization's existence. Congress authorized nearly one billion dollars to upgrade NATO's capabilities. At the end of 1950, General Dwight Eisenhower was named first NATO Supreme Commander (SACEUR), followed in 1951 by the establishment of Supreme Headquarters Allied Powers Europe (SHAPE) at Roquencourt, near Paris. The high-profile appointment of Eisenhower was as clear a sign of American commitment as the concurrent dispatch of American ground forces and B-29 bombers to Europe. Greece and Turkey, which had been under

NATO guarantees from the start, were admitted to membership in 1952 (underlining the anti-Soviet as opposed to "North Atlantic community" nature of the alliance). Permanent political and military structures were finalized on 25 February 1952.

However, with the growth of U.S. commitments elsewhere, especially in Asia, it was expected that European contributions to their own defense would increase—and to many Americans this had to involve the Germans, who were, after all, being accorded protection by the alliance. France was concerned to ensure that German economic recovery took place within a structure that prevented a resurgence of the German military threat. On the other hand, NATO's strategy was to fight on a defensive line as far east as possible—any other strategy would alienate key members such as Norway and the Netherlands. This meant fighting in Germany, and France shared the desire of its allies to find a way of bringing German military potential into the balance. The way forward had been suggested in the French Pleven Plan in the autumn of 1950. This proposed the establishment of a European army, in which the Germans would participate in small integrated units, which meant there would be no German General Staff or defense ministry. By May 1952, the plan had developed into the European Defense Community (EDC), and the proposed German contribution had been raised to regimental level. However, neither the British nor Americans would join the EDC, merely offering pledges of aid. The French army, heavily engaged outside Europe in the French Empire, was not itself keen on being submerged in the EDC, but also feared that with only the small nations as counterbalance, it would become dominated by the German military. As a consequence, the French Assembly rejected the European Defense Treaty in May 1954. However, the allies had become accustomed by now to think in terms of West German involvement, and under the initiative of British Foreign Secretary Anthony Eden, West Germany and Italy were brought into the Western Union that had been established by the Brussels Treaty (1948) by Britain, France, and the Benelux countries, with German troops to be wholly part of the forces of this renamed Western European Union (WEU). On this basis, France accepted West Germany as the fifteenth member of NATO

French foreign minister Pierre Mendès-France signs the treaties that admitted Germany to NATO at a meeting in Paris, 22 October 1954. ©BETTMANN/CORBIS

(in the name of all Germany). West Germany was scheduled to contribute twelve divisions, under WEU command, though it pledged not to manufacture nuclear, chemical, or bacteriological weapons. The Soviets had long feared West German rearmament and responded by drawing its satellites together in the Warsaw Pact.

TENSIONS WITHIN THE ALLIANCE

Although NATO celebrated its tenth anniversary in style at its new headquarters in Porte Dauphiné, Paris, trouble was brewing. Charles de Gaulle had returned to power in France, and viewed NATO as an instrument of Anglo-American hegemony. At the same time, some in the United States believed that since Western Europe had now recovered so well and was taking steps toward integration, the Europeans should shoulder a greater share of their own defense, with a reduction of American

commitments. These tensions came to a head with the American offer of Polaris nuclear missiles to the British in 1962—de Gaulle declined a similar offer and saw this as final proof that the British were too closely under U.S. influence to fit into his vision of Europe as a "third force" between the United States and the Soviet Union. This feeling was reinforced when President John Fitzgerald Kennedy acted during the Cuban missile crisis in October 1962 without coordinating with his NATO allies (except informal contacts with Britain). The Kennedy administration's rejection of the doctrine of massive nuclear retaliation in favor of "flexible response" also caused problems with America's allies, who feared the expense of competing with the Soviets in conventional forces, and worried that the American nuclear guarantee was being softened. Conversely, the U.S. desire to share the burden of NATO's defenses more equally led the Americans to press for European increases in conventional armaments. Some in the Kennedy administration favored a Multilateral Force as the means of achieving this, but this scheme foundered on unwillingness on both sides of the Atlantic to go far along the route of removing forces from national command and a preference to maintain NATO as essentially an intergovernmental alliance. The thaw in East-West relations that followed the Cuban crisis allowed many Europeans to be drawn to de Gaulle's concept. At the same time, U.S. actions in Vietnam were alienating many younger European voters. In addition, the direct nuclear threat to U.S. cities posed by Soviet intercontinental ballistic missiles (ICBMs) raised doubts whether the United States would actually risk destruction in the event of an attack on Western Europe by Soviet conventional forces. In 1966 de Gaulle withdrew the French from NATO's military command structures, protesting the dominance of American commanders. The military headquarters of NATO was moved to Mons and the political one to Brussels.

In response, an initiative by the smaller allies produced the Harmel Report, *The Future Tasks of the Alliance* (1967), which many have claimed redefined the nature of NATO in such a way that enabled it to survive the disappearance of the threat that brought it into being. There is a case, however, for arguing that Pierre Charles Harmel (Belgian foreign minister) was reiterating the security (as opposed to defense) motivations that were the driving force for those who founded it back in 1949. What the report did was to address the changed situation of the 1960s, which some Gaullists were claiming had made NATO redundant. While committing NATO to engage actively in the process of détente—reducing tensions with the Warsaw Pact—it also, most significantly in the long term, stated in firm terms the case for NATO to be seen as an organization serving the security needs of its members, rather than a purely defensive military alliance whose existence was dependent on a level of threat from a particular foe.

Under the impetus of the Harmel Report, NATO followed a twin-track policy of détente and modernization. Détente meant constructive dialogue with the Warsaw Pact, based on a recognition of their common interest in stability in

Europe and restraint in the use of nuclear weapons. This in turn meant that NATO could consider reduction of forces and their adaptation to a wider range of uses in line with the flexible response at the heart of Harmel—even though NATO had but recently expressed its commitment to a strategy of first use of nuclear weapons as a defense against a conventional threat from Soviet forces. In 1970 it was announced that reduction in nuclear or conventional forces would only come if the Soviet Union reduced its forces; dialogue began on conventional forces reduction on 5 October 1971. Simultaneously, the Soviet Union and United States were discussing reduction of numbers of warheads and limitations to antiballistic missile systems in the Strategic Arms Limitation Talks, and signed the SALT I Treaty on 26 May 1972. On 30 May the NATO Council agreed to participate in the Conference on Security and Cooperation in Europe (CSCE) in Helsinki, in which balanced force reductions were to be discussed with the Warsaw Pact. Despite the final act of the CSCE that called for force reductions and peaceful conflict resolution, and progress in slowing the nuclear arms race, in 1976 NATO reaffirmed its nuclear first use policy and rejected demands to restrict itself to a doctrine of nuclear usage only in response to nuclear aggression. Within NATO, some tensions remained: in 1974 Greece withdrew from the integrated military structures, citing a desire for military independence similar to that of the French. This was connected to the Cyprus crisis and Greek internal politics; with changes in the Greek government, Greece rejoined the military structures in 1980. A year later, NATO added its sixteenth member with the accession of Spain, which now had a democratic government.

By this time détente had given way to increased tension between the United States and the Soviet Union. SALT II was not ratified and U.S. presidents Jimmy Carter and Ronald Reagan sought European cooperation in isolating the Soviet Union in punishment for its 1979 invasion of Afghanistan. While some European leaders, such as Britain's Margaret Thatcher, supported Reagan, others had reservations about the revival of Cold War attitudes. Some of the structures set up in the détente period therefore endured, though NATO's withdrawal of 1,400 nuclear warheads from Europe in October 1983 was overshadowed by the

deployment of intermediate-range nuclear weapons that were not covered in the SALT agreement. Fears that Europe would be the battleground for a "limited" nuclear exchange of cruise missiles and Soviet SS-20s led to a revival of antinuclear protests in many Western European countries. The tension was eased after Reagan's reelection in November 1984 and the coming to power of Mikhail Gorbachev in the Soviet Union in March 1985. Talks on intermediate-range nuclear forces (INF) were restarted. The United States and Soviet Union agreed at Geneva in November 1985 to cuts of up to 50 percent in their nuclear arsenals. In this atmosphere, relations between NATO and the Warsaw Pact warmed once more and in 1986 the Conference on Disarmament in Europe agreed to mutual observation of military maneuvers, and in February 1987 talks on reducing conventional forces were resumed. In December the United States and Soviet Union agreed to eliminate all land-based INF missiles.

NATO was in a sense a passive observer of the dramatic changes that followed in Europe. The Soviet Union announced 15 percent force reductions in Europe in January 1989 and began a process of disengagement from its Eastern European satellites, which resulted in the rapid disappearance of their communist regimes, the destruction of the Berlin Wall, and in 1990 the reunification of Germany. At a stroke, NATO's frontiers were moved significantly eastward. In 1991, the Soviet Union itself ceased to exist.

NATO AFTER THE COLD WAR

These events posed a huge challenge to NATO. Many argued that with the disappearance of the Warsaw Pact and the Soviet Union itself, NATO had won its struggle, and therefore had no reason to continue to exist. Isolationism returned to the political agenda in the United States, and U.S. congressmen once more raised the issue of burden sharing. As we have seen, however, NATO had already redefined itself as an organization designed to promote security through stability and collective action as much as a defensive alliance against a particular threat, and generally NATO leaders, faced with the uncertainties of these startling changes in Europe, clung to NATO as an element of stability—or at least as an instrument

to manage change. NATO reiterated the role laid out by Harmel. In July 1990 at its London summit, NATO declared it would be a pillar of European and Transatlantic security, while also, by stating that it was extending the hand of friendship to Eastern European countries, attempting to show its concern with stability and the control of nuclear weapons in the context of the demise of the Warsaw Pact. At Rome in 1991 a new Strategic Concept was announced, declaring that the greatest threat to security was instability, often through the activities of nationalist or terrorist groups. It was recognized that the Organization of Security and Cooperation in Europe (the former CSCE) had a role in bringing stability to Europe. The North Atlantic Cooperation Council was set up, with 16 NATO countries and 9 others, becoming in 1997 the Euro-Atlantic Partnership Council with 40 members (46 by 2001). At Brussels in 1994, the Partnership for Peace was formed to promote defense cooperation.

However, while NATO made progress in defining a future for itself, the strains and tensions with the organization, which had always been present, were naturally increased as the common threat from the Soviet Union vanished. The first test of the reality of NATO's commitment to its new role was in the long crisis as Yugoslavia disintegrated. It was in Bosnia, in January 1996, that NATO troops fired their first shots in action. Deep divisions were revealed between the Europeans and Americans over the attitude to take toward the Serbs (the Americans wanted more forthright condemnation) and what action to take (the Europeans resented American reluctance to send troops as part of the peacekeeping mission). Many began to question NATO's future when it could not coordinate a policy toward events in the heart of Europe.

Finally, in 1997, the idea of the Partnership for Peace apparently offered progress on two of the most thorny questions for NATO as it approached its fiftieth birthday: could former Warsaw Pact countries become members (without damaging relations with Russia, which were already sensitive because of the Serbian situation), and what should NATO's relationship to United Nations (UN) peacekeeping efforts be? The Partnership provided

British NATO soldiers arrive at the airport in Sarajevo in preparation for the beginning of ground operations there, December 1995. ©AP/WORLDWIDE PHOTOS

for greater contributions to the latter, beginning with missions to the former Yugoslav republics. It also made possible the NATO-Russia Founding Act signed in Paris in 1997, establishing the NATO-Russia Permanent Joint Council (PJC). This reduced Russian hostility to the expansion of NATO eastward, which duly happened with the membership of Poland, Hungary, and the Czech Republic in 1999. Through the PJC, Russian troops took part in peacekeeping forces in Bosnia (Implementation Force [IFOR] and Stabilization Force [SFOR]). Tensions remained with the Russians, especially when the crisis flared up in Kosovo in 1999, but this was resolved eventually by the Russians joining the peacekeeping forces there (Kosovo Force [KFOR]).

There was a show of solidarity by NATO members after the September 2001 terrorist attacks on the United States, with Secretary-General George Robertson invoking Article 5, but this crumbled in the face of the determination of the George W. Bush administration to take whatever actions it felt necessary, regardless of the opinion of allies, in its "war on terror." While NATO was not directly involved as a body in the operations in Afghanistan, it became

involved subsequently in the efforts to pacify the country in the wake of the overthrow of the Taliban, taking control in August 2003 of the International Security Assistance Force (ISAF), in its first major operation outside Europe. Germany and France, however, had deep misgivings about Bush's approach and opposed the attack on Iraq in 2003. This became a NATO issue when they vetoed American requests to strengthen Turkey in advance of the attack. To many observers, expecting it since 1990, NATO at last seemed to be coming apart at the seams. This has not, as of 2005, happened, and it may be that the habits of cooperation, and the level of integration of military forces, including intelligence (despite NATO's remaining essentially an intergovernmental organization), are strong enough to prevent an actual breakup. Some argue that NATO had more the appearance of an alliance than the reality by the turn of the twenty-first century, but it has proved itself an adaptable instrument for articulating and advancing the security interests of its members, and must in consequence be seen as one of the more enduring, and successful, alliances in history. Tensions remain, especially between the United

States and Great Britain on one hand and Germany and France on the other, with moves to develop defense structures for the European Union seen by the Americans as threatening the integrity of the alliance. On the other hand, NATO has continued to expand, with seven new members joining formally in 2004—Bulgaria, Estonia, Lithuania, Latvia, Romania, Slovakia, and Slovenia. NATO forces and command structures have been adapted to provide rapid reaction forces to be deployed anywhere in the world.

See also **Bevin, Ernest; Cold War; Eastern Bloc; Soviet Union; Warsaw Pact.**

BIBLIOGRAPHY

Baylis, John. *The Diplomacy of Pragmatism: Britain and the Formation of NATO, 1942–1949.* Kent, Ohio, 1993.

Cyr, Arthur. *U.S. Foreign Policy and European Security.* London, 1987.

Duke, Simon. *The Burdensharing Debate: A Reassessment.* New York, 1993.

Haftendorn, Helga. *NATO and the Nuclear Revolution: A Crisis of Credibility, 1966–1967.* Oxford, U.K., 1996.

Ireland, Timothy P. *Creating the Entangling Alliance.* Westport, Conn., 1981.

Kaplan, Lawrence S. *The Long Entanglement: NATO's First Fifty Years.* Westport, Conn., 1999.

Kugler, Richard L. *Commitment to Purpose: How Alliance Partnership Won the Cold War.* Santa Monica, Calif., 1993.

Papacosma, S. Victor, Sean Kay, and Mark R. Rubin, eds, *NATO After Fifty Years.* Wilmington, Del., 2001.

Rudd, David, and Jim Hanson, eds. *NATO at Fifty: Successes, Challenges, Prospects.* Toronto, 1999.

Schmidt, Gustav, ed. *A History of NATO: The First Fifty Years.* 3 vols. Basingstoke, U.K., 2001.

Smith, Joseph, ed. *The Origins of NATO.* Exeter, U.K., 1990.

Smith, Martin A. *NATO in the First Decade after the Cold War.* Boston, 2000.

MARTIN H. FOLLY

NAZISM. Nazism constitutes one of the most studied phenomena of twentieth-century Europe. Philosophers, historians, and sociologists have all theorized on the causes of this multifaceted movement whose concrete dimensions unfolded on various planes. But trying to describe Nazism is like trying to fit the pieces together of a complex puzzle: How to account for a phenomenon whose nature concerned ideology, political militancy, and government practice all at the same time? How to encapsulate in these three poles its militant activism, the reactionary nature of German society, and the regime-driven policy choices that resulted in the Nazi rise to power in 1933? How, finally, to write the history of what began as a *völkisch* minor mass movement from Munich in the aftermath of World War I that would later grow to encompass all of Europe, from the Pyrenees to the Arctic Circle, from the Caucasus Mountains to the Atlantic Ocean?

Reconstructing the story in chronological order necessarily begins with an image of Nazism as a belief-system open to ever-increasing numbers of militants, who made it their own in extremely diverse ways. Next, attention would need to be drawn to understanding how the militant movements that drew on these ideas were regulated by a fundamentally racist ideology into an organization whose quest for power in Germany was launched in the late 1920s. Only then would an exploration begin of state-sponsored Nazism bent on European conquest, and whose main objective was to build a thousand-year reign out of iron, fire, conquest, domination, and extermination.

NAZISM: A BELIEF-SYSTEM
The root of Nazism as a belief-system was racial determinism. Nazi racism was determinist because it endowed the factor of biology with the power to create reality; racism served as a filter conditioning its entire outlook. Nazism was a biological grid for reading history, the world, and one's self.

The reference point for this Nazi reading of the world was furnished by the racial theories of Hans F. K. Günther (1891–1968), the Jena anthropologist whose system for describing European phenotypes was adopted by the Nazi Party in the early 1930s, after a series of debates whose intensity is worth noting. Güntherian analysis was made using racial types, which were identifiable based on groupings of both "intellectual and physical" characteristics shared by the individuals belonging to them. After having identified the concept, Günther immediately deduced that it was virtually impossible to pinpoint an actually existing "impervious human group" with a racially pure lineage: "All the peoples of the West," he wrote, "are composed of racially mixed populations in which all, or at least many, of the races of Europe are present in fixed proportions" (pp. 10–11). According to Günther, therefore, the difference between nations was grounded in the combinations that resulted from miscegenation, which produced a clear-cut hierarchical scale: each nation had its strengths and its weaknesses, each people a vocation. The world was thus an aggregate of races whose (conflictual) relations formed the stage of global history. In this sense Nazism would not rest content to merely read the world—it became its own historical tale to tell: a tale of racial conflict and the emergence thereby of the superior race.

Nazi racial fundamentalism produced a historical discourse whose importance has often been grossly underestimated. Indeed even though some historians seek the origins of Nazism in ancient history, the sharply honed analysis the Nazis themselves made of World War I and its consequences has been largely passed over in silence, despite the fact that it constitutes the heart of the Nazi belief-system itself. Nazi racial scientists viewed World War I as an unprecedented demographic catastrophe for Germany. The nation's Nordic racial core was slowly being endangered by neighboring races that comprised the world of enemies exposed by World War I. In this sense, Nazism fashioned itself into an apocalyptic discourse that fostered the spread of anxiety throughout German society about the threat posed by other, hostile races.

Nazism, however, was not destined to remain an anxiety-provoking discourse on history. Clearly its discourse explained Germany's World War I defeat in terms of racial hatred, but it also lent the movement a mission: to finally purge Germany of the scourge of encirclement, to reverse the world order laid out in the Treaty of Versailles (1919), and to forge a new society based on hope and racial fraternity out of the ruins of enemy states organized into a Europe-wide racial empire. Racial fundamentalism, the core of the Nazi belief-system, thus assumed a dual-role in the minds of its activists: on the one hand it mobilized and gave expression to a powerful political anxiety, but it

also lent credence to a utopian vision by giving direction to history and making it possible to envision the future of the Thousand-Year Reich. Perhaps it was this transformation of an unspeakable anxiety into an ineffable utopia that explains the sheer force of the belief this ideology engendered in its activists' minds.

NAZISM AS MILITANT ACTIVISM

The structure of Nazi ideology may be viewed through lenses other than the work of philosophers and historians, although this approach already gave some indication of the extent to which its dogmas were refashioned in numerous and diverse ways by the activist individuals and groups who adhered to the Nazi system of thought. In fact as this dogma was progressively realized, it devolved into a series of diverse militant organizations that played a fundamental part in the evolution of the political role Nazism would eventually assume. Founded in the early 1920s, the National Socialist German Workers Party, or NSDAP, long remained a small movement among thousands of others, in a nebulous underground of *völkische* groups that testified to both an extreme vitality and a certain form of clandestine practice. Although the NSDAP's emergence as a mass movement drew initially from its reserves among the ethno-nationalist elites, it was nonetheless a watershed event in the evolution of the *völkische* forces, to which it lent a structure and strategy for the acquisition of power. The NSDAP brought these radical nationalist forces together under the same federal umbrella by driving them to internalize the different elements of the Nazi belief-system, and thereby structured the movement to be able in due course to encompass the whole of German society.

The NSDAP in the early years of its creation remained one small group among many, and the chaotic and futile challenge to power, known as the Munich *putsch* of 1923, could have spelled total disaster for it. But the method Adolf Hitler (1889–1945) developed, during his time in prison after the *putsch*, of seeking power through legal means, and the party's electoral successes during the years 1927–1931, rendered the Nazi strategy ever more attractive. Originally conceived as a mass movement, the NSDAP began to spawn local and national institutions headed by general and regional leadership

Adolf Hitler presides over a meeting of the NSDAP, Munich, 1925. ©BETTMANN/CORBIS

committees, known as *Reichsleitung* and *Gauleitungen* respectively, which were run by the party's dignitaries. In Berlin for example, Josef Goebbels forged the party's regional direction and made it into one of the movement's power centers. However at the most local level, the NSDAP nourished a mass of activist functionaries whose recruitment and propaganda work became part and parcel of everyday social life in a host of towns and villages. From 1928 to 1933, Party membership went from 150,000 to 500,000 members. In 1935, the NSDAP numbered 2.5 million and had grown to 5.4 million on the eve of World War II. Although the party remained in certain respects an organ of militant activism in 1933, it soon became a tool for the supervision, management, and mobilization of German society. Before 1933 it had spearheaded the electoral campaigns that served as the Nazis' primary

means for acquiring political power. After the Nazis came to power in 1933, the party was transformed into a simple conduit for the transmission of mass mobilization slogans issued by the propaganda ministry. This transformation was also true of the first Nazi paramilitary organization, the SA (Sturmabteilung). Despite the fact that it was the primary means for winning the battle with communists and others in working-class neighborhoods, the SA, which counted more than 500,000 members in 1933 and more than 3 million one year later, grew to a point that it was far too dangerous for the party to leave as it was. The outcome was the massacre of 30 June 1934, marked by the execution of virtually all the leaders of its paramilitary corps. Instead, the SA was transformed into an agency limited primarily to crowd control. Thus in the space of just a few short years during the period of the Nazi rise to power, the militant organizations whose effectiveness had been so legendary at silencing opponents and securing a stage for the party's expression—including through the use of violent combat in the streets—were changed into agencies of supervision, surveillance, and mobilization once that acquisition was complete.

The fact also remains that National Socialism styled itself as a reformist movement, with the goal of creating a racially purified *Volksgemeinschaft* (racial community) where the "class struggle" would be overcome, and whose core values of brotherhood and mutual aid would be the principles of social interaction. This plan was embodied in a second and relatively more widespread form of activism that went beyond formal membership in the NSDAP. Two groups, the National Socialist Volunteers (Nationalsozialistische Volkswohlfahrt, or NSV) and the National Socialist Winter Aid Society (Winter Hilfswerk, or WHW), along with a multitude of satellite organizations, produced the image of a society that cared for the poor, that came together in corporate entities and, in short, forged a set of social bonds. No doubt the drive toward supervision was a factor in the work of these Nazi organizations. However the fact remains that the large sums collected by NSV campaigns, and the sheer number of its members, demonstrate that this idea of mutual aid and solidarity (put into effect in a society in which racial purity had come to represent an obvious and indispensable prerequisite), went beyond the framework of political adherence, and constituted a locus of activism in its own right whose sources should not be underestimated. By 1939 some 16 million people had already participated in NSV campaigns redistributing nearly 2.5 billion reichsmarks.

Finally there was a third and lasting form of militant activism evident in the National Socialist movement. This form was represented by the SS (Schutzstaffel), founded in 1925. It was an organization that grew rapidly, particularly after the party assumed power in 1933. Nevertheless its leader Heinrich Himmler kept a strong hand on its growth, and issued recruitment guidelines that were both racial and social in nature. Although these criteria were not adhered to strictly, they did serve to preserve an image of the SS as the Third Reich's elite.

Whereas the NSDAP and the SA constituted working class–dominated mass movements, the SS was composed mainly of middle-class and upper-class men. In a way it was a cultural elite; in another respect, it was a body to represent German racial purity. The SS drew, throughout the Third Reich's history, on a reserve of young graduates from the bourgeoisie and middle classes, who were university educated and almost without exception won over by Nazi and *völkische* views.

Thus Nazi militant activism came to be embodied in a multitude of organizations that each enjoyed a measure of relative success, and that recruited from different elements of the German social body. The NSDAP, the SA, and the corporatist organizations attracted and funneled the working-class and rural masses, drawn to the Nazi discourse of fraternity and solidarity that animated its charity organizations. The incontestable success of these groups indicates the degree to which this version of Nazism reached an audience composed of a much larger fraction of the German population, stretching well beyond the conservative and *völkische* militant activists.

NAZISM AS STATE-SPONSORED MURDER

The NSDAP's formal rise to power on 30 January 1933 was not the result of a legislative victory, but of truly political calculations intended to allow career-members of the Weimar Republic's ministries to remain part of the new regime. The NSDAP had been the largest party in the Reichstag since 1931 in terms of numbers of representatives, and the Conservatives were attempting to limit its influence by associating it with a regime in which the Nazis were not in the majority. Hitler played the part of the inexperienced Führer, and the conservatives thought they had tricked him into playing into their hands. One year later however, anything Germany might have called a potential opposition force had been destroyed, and the NSDAP was the sole arbiter of the instruments of state. Historians of the functionalist school have carefully studied the dynamics of Nazi governmental policies, including the role of the dictator, the charismatic aspect of his domination, the phenomenon of anticipatory obedience it generated, the proliferation of extraordinary institutions, and the

Girls waving swastika pennants are among thousands lining the streets to greet Adolf Hitler's motorcade, Berlin, September 1938. ©BETTMANN/CORBIS

Nazi propensity to transform institutions from their traditional functions.

The result of these fundamental elements of Hitlerian state-sponsored governance when taken as a whole is what historians, following Hans Mommsen, have dubbed "cumulative radicalization"—a state practice founded on racial ideology, claiming for itself the mission of regenerating Germany and offering it the space it needed to forge an empire of a thousand years. To move these two axes of development forward however, the Nazis first needed to lift the fatal curse of World War I. Every policy of the new German regime was oriented toward this obsession and its prerequisites.

The first order of business therefore, once the assumption of power was assured and society had been effectively controlled by the militant organizations, was to undo the consequences of the Treaty of Versailles. This task was dependent on the foreign secretary, Joachim von Ribbentrop, and a diplomatic corps staffed by the traditional German elites, although they received almost all their direction from the impulses and opportunism of Hitler himself. From 1935 to 1939 the Nazis remilitarized the Rhineland; annexed Austria, the Sudetenland, and Czechoslovakia without firing a shot; and laid plans to recover the western provinces lost to a reconstituted Poland in 1918. As is well known it was this final episode, this last bluff, that led Britain and France to declare war against Germany. For the Nazis however this was a direct continuation of World War I, a war that drove the Nazi imaginary to its zenith—and the lay of the land in early 1941, after massive victories in the west, suggested indeed that the curse of 1918 had been lifted. Poland and France had been brought to their knees, Paris was occupied, Great Britain seemed to be in no condition to cause any serious harm. The hour appeared to have arrived for the realization of Germany's regeneration, for the utopia itself to be completed.

That meant occupying the eastern territories and invading the Soviet Union (USSR). In the eyes of the Nazi racist fundamentalists, the USSR was the place where the confrontation with the Reich's apocalyptic enemies would take place, because it was there that its racial and political enemies were the most completely fused. It was there as well that the vital space needed for the Nazi Empire's Thousand-Year Reich was to be conquered.

This conjunction of a racialized apocalyptic image of the enemy and utopian war objectives led the Nazi hierarchy to conceive the war with the Soviet Union from the outset as a war of annihilation. For the Nazis, whose occupation policies in the already acquired Polish territories aimed at Germanification, and whose murderous nature was being carried out on the ground every day, the Soviet population would henceforth have to be subjected to wholesale decimation. The demographic catastrophe would be so complete that the Soviet territories would be emptied and made available to Nordic colonization. According to the Wehrmacht's logistical calculations, which agreed with those made by SS demographers and the officers of the Reich Security Main Office (Reichssicherheitshauptamt, or RSHA), "dozens of millions of individuals" would have to be starved to death. Even in its early planning stages, Nazi policies envisaged extermination, and it was in the Soviet Union that the practices used to exhaustively eliminate Jewish populations were first put into effect. Shortly after the invasion of the Soviet Union on 22 June 1941, the Einsatzgruppen, or special killing groups, began massacring Russian Jewish women and children. By December 1941, a sizable portion of these communities had already disappeared behind enormous firing lines such as the one at Babi Yar on the outskirts of Kiev.

The cumulative radicalization of the Nazi regime was marked by the decision Hitler took in 1941, at a date historians still debate, to exterminate all of the Jews of Europe. Following an initial planning phase involving experimentation with different methods of extermination by gas, the Nazi genocidal machine went into full gear in early May 1942. The program culminated at its highest point with the killing of ten thousand Jews per day in the gas chambers of Auschwitz in the summer of 1944. All told, more than five million Jews fell victim to Nazi state-sponsored extermination.

However by the summer of 1944 the situation on the ground had also developed in a way the Nazis had always feared. They were now fighting a war on two fronts: on the west with the United States and Britain, who invaded in June, and on the east, the de facto main front, with the Soviet army, which had already decisively pierced through German lines and was inexorably headed toward its territory. From the Nazi standpoint the accomplishment of a utopia was no longer in question, but what was more likely was the physical disappearance of the Nordic race under the blows of the "Asiatic hordes." Immense waves of apocalyptic thinking and fear engulfed the final months of the Nazi state's existence, months during which the Wehrmacht raised an increasingly hopeless resistance against the advancing Red Army, which was little disposed to spare the German civilian populations it encountered, given the heavy losses it had suffered and the savagery of the Germans' own occupation policies in the East. Instead of the dream of colonizing the territories of the East, there unfolded the nightmare of an exodus of German populations whom the national sanctuary could no longer safeguard.

The nightmare ended on 8 May 1945, with the capitulation of the German armed forces. The Third Reich had been decimated, and its primary leaders were either dead, on the run, or in prison and awaiting trial. In these trials, the Allies judged an ideology of racial determinism, a militant activism with totalitarian aims, and state-sponsored policies of extermination that were without a doubt responsible for the deaths of more than twenty-five million civilians and soldiers, men, women, children, Jews, Slavs, Gypsies, and Western Europeans, by war, famine, and genocide.

See also **Einsatzgruppen; Fascism; Germany; Goebbels, Josef; Hitler, Adolf; Holocaust; Operation Barbarossa; Totalitarianism; World War II.**

BIBLIOGRAPHY

Aly, Götz. *"Endlösung": Völkerverschiebung und der Mord an den europäischen Juden*. Frankfurt, 1996.

Bartov, Omer. *Hitler's Army: Soldiers, Nazis, and War in the Third Reich*. Oxford, U.K., 1991.

Bracher, Karl Dietrich. *Die deutsche Diktatur: Entstehung, Struktur, Folgen des Nationalsozialismus*. Cologne, 1980.

Broszat, Martin. *Der Staat Hitlers: Grundlegung und Entwicklung seiner inneren Verfassung*. Munich, 1992.

Essner, Cornelia, and Edouard Conte. *La quête de la race: Une anthropologie du nazisme*. Paris, 1995.

Gerlach, Christian. *Krieg, Ernährung, Völkermord: Forschungen zur deutschen Vernichtungspolitik*. Hamburg, 1998.

Günther, Hans F. K. *Kleine Rassenkunde des deutschen Volkes*. Munich, 1933.

Jäckel, Eberhard. *Hitlers Weltanschauung: Entwurf einer Herrschaft*. Tubingen, Germany, 1969.

———. *Hitlers Herrschaft: Vollzug einer Weltanschauung*. Stuttgart, 1986.

Kershaw, Ian. *Qu'est-ce que le nazisme?: Problèmes et perspectives d'interprétation*. Translated by Jacqueline Carnaud. Paris, 1997.

———. *Hitler: 1889–1936, Hubris*. Paris, 1999.

———. *Hitler: 1936–1945, Némésis*. Paris, 2000.

Koehl, Robert Lewis. *The Black Corps: The Structure and Power Struggles of the Nazi SS*. Madison, Wis., 1983.

Reichardt, Sven. *Faschistische Kampfbünde: Gewalt und Gemeinschaft im italienischen Squadrismus und in der deutschen SA*. Cologne, 2002.

Rhodes, James. *The Hitler Movement: A Modern Millenarian Revolution*. Stanford, Calif., 1980.

CHRISTIAN INGRAO

NEGRITUDE. In the 1930s the poet and politician Aimé Césaire (b. 1913), a Martinican who later led his home colony to assimilation as a French department, coined the term *negritude*. Negritude corresponded to an intellectual movement that emerged during the interwar years in France and promoted culture as a political mode of expression for black identity within the context of Europe's relationship to its colonies. Scholars have traditionally credited Césaire, Léopold Sédar Senghor (1906–2001, the first president of Senegal), and the French Guianan Léon-Gontran Damas (1912–1978) with developing negritude. However, in the intellectually and politically turbulent Paris of the 1920s and 1930s, many people contributed to elaborating a set of ideas that are neither clearly defined nor completely obvious in their repercussions. The origins and influences of negritude should be understood within their cultural, intellectual, and political contexts. Among the sociopolitical conditions providing a backdrop for this movement were the arrival of colonial men in France during World War I; ensuing anti-imperialism across Europe; and the printing of African- and Caribbean-run newspapers in interwar Paris.

WORLD WAR I AND THE ORIGINS OF ANTICOLONIALISM

World War I transformed France's relationship with its African and Caribbean colonies. For the first time black men were invited to discover the metropole at the center of their empire. Approximately 250,000 conscripted soldiers from Sudan and Senegal were joined by 30,000 from the Caribbean and Madagascar. Moreover, French men called upon to fight were replaced in factories by 200,000 colonial workers.

Colonial soldiers were admired for their fighting skills and suffered high casualty rates. Some of those who survived remained in France after the war as workers, often in exploitative jobs, or students. Remembering fallen comrades and knowing that they had helped France out of a severe crisis in manpower, many from Africa and the Caribbean believed the nation owed them a blood debt. Yet the social prospects momentarily revealed by the war, including possibilities for interracial relationships with French women and the promise of equality as citizens, disappeared during the postwar years. Convinced that France owed them suffrage and freedom, some black men and women organized associations that demanded assimilation as French departments or an end to French colonialism.

Proponents of anticolonialism congregated in port cities across France and Europe, including Bordeaux, Marseille, Toulon, and Le Havre, but played to France's centralized political system by placing headquarters in Paris. A series of organizations succeeded one another, including the Committee for the Defense of the Negro Race (1926), the League for the Defense of the Negro Race (1927), and the Negro Workers' Union (1932). These associations were carefully observed by undercover informants who reported to the police and the Ministry of Colonies, and as a result were divided by paranoia about how to escape the French government's scrutiny. Uncertain to what extent they should allow themselves to be funded by the Communist Party and influenced by directives from Moscow, they fell victim to bickering that broke down along class lines, as well as lines of geographical origin. Intellectuals and workers from the Caribbean and Africa, were often at loggerheads over whether they could trust one another. Nonetheless, these organizations maintained an ongoing presence in Paris and contacts with likeminded European groups throughout the 1920s and 1930s.

EARLY DEFINITIONS OF NEGRITUDE

Police informants were more concerned with members of radical anticolonialist associations than with individuals who are usually credited with elaborating black nationalism through negritude. They made few references to Senghor or Césaire, preferring to comment upon debates within all three associations about whether to describe themselves as Negro or black. *Nègre*, or Negro, the word that forms the base for negritude, was considered a powerful statement about the desire to take control of a pejorative descriptive previously employed by Europeans in an attempt to affirm white superiority. The January 1927 issue of *La race nègre* (The Negro race), an organ for the Committee, included an article entitled "The Word *Negro*." The author explicitly placed the word in opposition to others less charged with race and class, such as men of color or blacks. The scholar Christopher Miller suggests that this article marks the beginning of an attempt to recapture blackness through language, one that has been associated traditionally with the writings of Senghor and Césaire. Repeated references to the divide between black and Negro in newspapers and police notes suggests that cultural and intellectual attempts to redefine the parameters of a debate on race predated those usually associated with negritude.

WOMEN AND NEWSPAPERS IN PARIS

This historiographical development in the understanding of negritude's origins has emerged alongside a growing interest in the women who were part of a movement traditionally associated with men. Senghor and Césaire had few contacts with their radical anticolonialist counterparts, even though they were also fleetingly intrigued by communism. In contrast, there were exchanges between these groups and a woman named Paulette Nardal. The eldest of seven Martinican sisters, Paulette and her sister Jane held a salon that connected Africans, Antilleans, and African Americans. Negritude developed in Paris largely because the city facilitated interracial and intercultural contacts, and the salon encouraged such exchanges.

The Nardal sisters contributed to newspapers linked with their salon that challenged black intellectuals to find their place in Europe while coming to terms with their identity, both essential components of negritude. In a 15 October 1928 article for *La dépêche africaine* (The black dispatch), Jane explored the dangers of allowing Europeans to project their negrophilia—or passion for all things black—upon colonial men and women who would be reduced to mere "Exotic Puppets." Writing for *La revue du monde noir* (The review of the black world) in April 1932, Paulette added that women were the first to be truly challenged by their blackness because they were the focal points for exotic gazes projected by Europeans. *L'etudiant noir* (The black student) appeared only once, in March 1935, but gathered writings by Paulette Nardal, Césaire, and Senghor in a paper that has often been considered the immediate catalyst for negritude. Articles focused, in the vein of Jane and Paulette Nardal's work, upon establishing an identity as both European and black by rejecting stereotyping and defending blackness.

NEGRITUDE'S FOUNDERS ON ITS DEFINITION

Negritude, anticipated in the writings of anti-imperialist blacks and Antillean women, was finally embodied by Césaire's term. But what did it mean? In *L'etudiant noir*, Césaire wrote that before World War I black men wished to become European and assimilated, but the blood debt and France's stern dealings with its colonies in postwar years changed their hopes. This concurrence inspired negritude, which was voiced by black men educated in elite French institutions including the Ecole Normale Supérieure. Senghor emphasized in negritude a cultural heritage common to Africans around the world. Césaire took control of blackness by reclaiming the word *nègre* in his 1939 work *Cahier d'un retour au pays natal* (*Notebook of a Return to the Native Land*). As poets and politicians, both men sought to explore black consciousness through the French language, inspired by the writings of African Americans Claude McKay (1889–1948), Langston Hughes (1902–1967), and Countee Cullen (1903–1946), as well as by some of the French avant-garde artists known as surrealists. They were stirred, like the Nardal sisters, by a sense of alienation that they saw spreading to an entire race. They answered by articulating fundamental differences between Europeans and Africans. Female, emotional, and rhythmic Africa, all components of a black essence, contrasted in their writings with male, technical, and cold Europe. However their expression of negritude differed slightly since Senghor emphasized the essentialist approach while Césaire argued that differences defining people of African descent were cultural rather than genetic. For Césaire negritude meant the recognition of one's cultural heritage and the communications of that legacy to others in the African diaspora.

NEGRITUDE AND DECOLONIZATION

World War II marked a turning point for colonialism. During the war Césaire resisted in the Vichy-dominated West Indies with the journal *Tropiques*. Senghor saw service in the French army and was taken prisoner before eventually being released. After the war Senghor and Césaire became increasingly involved in politics. They also continued to write about negritude, encouraging others to find a black consciousness.

Their project and the term *negritude* were recognized when the French philosopher Jean-Paul Sartre (1905–1980) wrote in a 1948 preface for an anthology of African and Caribbean poetry edited by Senghor. In it he described the movement as an inner experience and a philosophy in its own right that depended upon the black poets' ability to recapture European languages.

Many reacted to negritude after Sartre helped reveal it to a broad public. Negritude was attacked by communists, who believed it withdrew attention from the class struggle. Others believed negritude was racist because it established black men as different, not only physically but also in their essence, through their souls. Some who saw a fundamental break between poet-politicians and their increasingly anti-imperialist people attacked the idea for its elitism. The final criticism appeared in the 1960s: most Africans in France's past and present colonies did not read French and hence could never discover negritude. These critiques suggested an important post–World War II development: politics, not culture, were supposed to lead Africans toward their desired independence.

Negritude was a literary and cultural movement that identified a shift in the relationship between black and French identity. Although not the first expression of black nationalism, since several 1920s organizations presaged its ideas, negritude was the most articulate rejection of white European supremacy. Contrasting Africa's emotive intuition with European rationalism and individualism allowed a cultural movement to reinvent itself politically and inspire others after World War II in their African nationalism. The movement died down in the 1960s because decolonization had largely succeeded and because of internal inconsistencies. Nonetheless, negritude marked a seminal moment in Europe's changing relationship with its colonies, one in which Africans and Antilleans found articulate and passionate voices in defense of their blackness.

See also **Colonialism; French Empire; Racism; Senghor, Léopold Sédar.**

BIBLIOGRAPHY

Primary Sources

Césaire, Aimé. *Notebook of a Return to the Native Land.* Translated and edited by Clayton Eshleman and Annette Smith. Middletown, Conn., 2001.

Sartre, Jean-Paul. *Black Orpheus.* Translated by S.W. Allen. Paris, 1976. Translation of *Orphée Noir*, originally the preface to *Anthologie de la nouvelle poésie nègre et malgache de langue française*, edited by L. S. Senghor (1948).

Senghor, Léopold Sédar. *Liberté.* Paris, 1964. Contains most of Senghor's cultural works from reviews and journals published between 1937 and 1964.

Secondary Sources

Dewitte, Philippe. *Les Mouvements nègres en France 1919–1939*. Paris, 1985. A thorough text portraying, using police archives, the black men who were politically engaged in interwar France.

Edwards, Brent Hayes. *The Practice of Diaspora: Literature, Translation, and the Rise of Black Internationalism*. Cambridge, Mass., 2003. An investigation of the links between African American writers and their French counterparts.

Kesteloot, Lilyan. *Black Writers in French: A Literary History of Negritude*. Translated by Ellen Conroy Kennedy. Washington, D.C., 1991. A classic reference work that includes a number of interviews with negritude's founding thinkers.

Miller, Christopher L. *Nationalists and Nomads: Essays on Francophone African Literature and Culture*. Chicago, 1998. A collection of essays on the interwar context in which negritude developed.

Sharpley-Whiting, T. Denean. *Negritude Women*. Minneapolis, Minn., 2002. The most complete study of women who claimed negritude for themselves. Includes translations of primary works.

JENNIFER ANNE BOITTIN

NEOLIBERALISM. Neoliberalism is a set of economic policies that have become widespread since the last quarter of the twentieth century. However neoliberalism is not just about economics; it is a social and moral philosophy too. It is, in brief, the desire to intensify and expand the market mechanism to all areas of life. The emergence of neoliberalism is associated with the way in which a new social formation has arisen out of the liberal international order established by the Bretton Woods Conference near the end of World War II. This will be done here, first, by establishing the key features of global structural transformation as they have taken shape since the late 1970s, and second, by identifying the political consequences of this transformation. For many, neoliberalism is often seen as the driving force behind, if not directly synonymous with, the effects of contemporary globalization. Thus contemporary globalization is characterized by two interlinked processes: the material transnationalization of finance and production; and the ideological movement toward neoliberalism. Changes in material factors have been mirrored by a transformation in ideas and thinking

with neoliberalism replacing Keynesianism as the dominant paradigm of economic policy. This is driving, and driven by, what Stephen Gill has termed *disciplinary neoliberalism*, illustrated through the interplay among the international and domestic structures and institutions of the global political economy. This interaction among ideas, institutions, and material capabilities is crucial in attempting to understand the changes that have occurred since the 1970s as a distinct constellation of neoliberal practices, techniques, and modes of organization in the global economy.

GLOBAL STRUCTURAL TRANSFORMATION SINCE THE 1970S

To begin to make sense of the emergence of neoliberalism, we must go back at least to the 1970s. The crises of Fordism, the Keynesian welfare state, and the oil price rises of the 1970s, in tandem with new transport, communication, and information technologies, were the catalysts for the rapid internationalization of financial and production capital. Successive state-led liberalizations and deregulations have subordinated national economies to the discipline of the market and the global economy. The process that emerged in response to the crisis resulted in the triumph of neoliberalism. The key feature of the postwar order was the compromise between economic liberalism and national intervention that John G. Ruggie terms *embedded liberalism*. Embedded liberalism consisted of two main characteristics: first, broad agreement on multilateralism and tariff reduction that, through the General Agreement on Tariffs and Trade (GATT) negotiations, encouraged free trade; and second, national governments maintaining capital controls and the right to intervene to ensure domestic stability. Embedded liberal hegemony was based on a Fordist regime of accumulation that rested on the organization of social relations of production at a national level, characterized by mass production of consumer goods and mass consumption. The architects of this system were critical of money capital and sought articles in the International Monetary Fund (IMF) agreements to reduce the role of cross-border capital flows to lubricants of international trade and the movement of factors of production. Speculative movements of capital were considered to be profoundly destabilizing. Finance was, according to the U.S. Treasury, to be the servant rather than the master of production. However, the original intentions for imposing state control on international finance were diluted by financial interests associated with Wall Street and their counterparts in Europe.

The embedded liberal world order, based on compromise, corporatism, and Keynesian macroeconomic management, was hegemonic at its core, with left- and right-wing extremism marginalized and the political center consolidated. The balance between these forces began to break up during the 1970s in response to the recessions of the late 1970s and early 1980s that provoked a mercantilist reaction throughout the capitalist world. The recessions helped to activate a reappraisal of the role of the public sector and of the correct mix of intervention and market in the economy. The relationship between developed and developing states was recast, and with accelerating declines in real commodity prices and high interest rates, indebted nations were forced to turn to the IMF. The IMF prescription was to press for liberalization and the curtailment of the public sector. In the short term, the recessions had a purgative effect associated with a downswing in the business cycle, promoting a general restructuring of capital and capital-labor relations. The recession and the links between different aspects of global restructuring facilitated the material and ideological reemergence of U.S. hegemony with the boom of 1982 under President Ronald Reagan. The combination of financial stimulus through expanded military expenditure and supply-side tax cuts stimulated investment and improved productivity and competitiveness in certain sectors of the U.S. economy. Reagan's stress on a "strong America" complemented the deregulation of industry and banking, tax cuts, attacks on union power, and the speculative short-term mentality in the United States. By the late 1980s the United States appeared to have succeeded in restructuring the major sectors of its economy more successfully than elsewhere, especially Western Europe.

Key to the neoliberal triumph was the propagation of monetarism in policy circles. (Largely unpopular since the 1920s, monetarism continued to attract the support of some economists, journalists, and government officials, particularly in the United States and Britain, reemerging after 1945 in a number of private international groups such as the Mont Pelerin Society inspired by Friedrich Hayek and Milton Friedman.) By making money scarce, the monetarists argued, inflation could be combated and sound microeconomic reasoning could be forced upon state and society as a whole. As the 1970s crisis deepened, monetarist arguments grew more convincing, winning over more and more influential bodies. Crucial neoliberal victories were scored in Chile (with the rise to prominence in 1975 of General Pinochet's regime) and Britain (with Prime Minister Margaret Thatcher's emergence in 1979). A significant turning point came in 1979 when Paul Volcker was appointed chairman of the U.S. Federal Reserve Board and initiated a strict monetarist regime that drove up real interest rates in the United States and in the world economy. This rapid shift toward monetarist policies resulted in moves away from the preceding corporate-liberal pattern to an individualist one in which the interests of mobile capital were predominant. Stock ownership was popularized through privatization, and bank profits increased relative to those of industry. Investment banking and financial services became the leading sectors. In reaction to the Keynesian corporate-liberal consensus of the post-1945 years, neoliberalism ushered in an era extolling the virtues of the free market and the withdrawal of the state from the management of the economy. The core neoliberal values of liberalization, privatization, deregulation, and internationalization and the new individualist ethic, so memorably captured in Thatcher's 1987 statement that "there is no such thing as society," eclipsed traditional forms of social democracy. Since then agents such as the World Economic Forum and others have carried forward the neoliberal agenda.

The rise to hegemony of neoliberalism during the 1970s and 1980s occurred primarily in the developed capitalist parts of the world if not globally. However, since the crisis of the 1970s, a range of other states have subscribed to the neoliberal project. These neoliberal projects have taken a number of different forms—*salinismo* in Mexico, "shock therapy" in Poland, Reaganomics in the United States, or Thatcherism in Britain—but they have all been characterized by the state's attempt to engender processes of depoliticization, liberalization, and deregulation, forcing adaptation in areas including labor relations, competitiveness, welfare, and corporate governance. While these policies might not eliminate differences in the face of local or national "embeddedness" and "path-dependency," there are progressively more common global and regional neoliberal forces at work and a common direction of change. In an abstract sense neoliberalism is the outcome of liberal internationalist representations of cosmopolitan money and industry capital that has outgrown its national confines. The paradigmatic scale of operation of industrial capital in the early twenty-first century is global in tendency. Simultaneously there is the relative disintegration of national state frameworks into a multiplicity of local and regional frameworks. However, these projects or programs are never simply put into practice: they are shaped and continuously reshaped in a process of struggle, compromise, and readjustment. The ultimate goal is, therefore, to decompose labor within national spaces, facilitating to the fullest degree possible the capability of capital to perform in a vision of a truly competitive world market in which capital has complete access to the global population and is able to compete in the labor market for its means of reproduction on a global scale. Despite the toll such a strategy exacts upon the populations of states, whether in the form of increased job insecurity or the ratcheting down of welfare regimes, neoliberal state policies are increasingly presented as "common sense" and necessary because "there is no alternative."

CONSEQUENCES OF NEOLIBERAL CONSOLIDATION

The outcome of this common sense has been the global consolidation of neoliberalism, and not just in the advanced industrial states. Any notion of an alternative to the rule of footloose global capital has become unrealistic and discredited as neoliberal changes have been locked in and normalized. Since the collapse in 1989–1990 of existing state socialism as the only alternative economic and social system, any incentive for capitalists in the West to accommodate workers has disappeared, and instead, the opportunity for carving out ever greater political space for the radical overhaul of the structures of postwar corporate liberalism has materialized. The strategy that has emerged is, as noted above, centrally concerned with the depoliticization of

the economy and society by the weakening and, where possible, removal of historically accumulated forms of social protection. Existing forms of non-market coordination and state regulation have been abandoned as enterprises have been encouraged or, indeed, compelled to look to their own devices rather than to the state. Collective organizations such as unions have been weakened, and ever-increasing amounts of discipline have been enforced through the direct dependence on profit as the sole means of accounting for or evaluating successful employment or economic development. Demands on public services are resisted on the grounds of the need to reduce state spending to increase competitiveness.

These main characteristics of what has become a global consensus regarding the requirements and necessities of the world economy within a common ideological framework have been translated into a general interest. The implications are far-reaching. To theoretically grasp the new structure of the global political economy and the nature of neoliberalism, a convenient point of departure is Robert Cox's concept of the internationalization of the state. Cox analyzes the mechanisms for maintaining hegemony in the era of Pax Americana and argues that the internationalization of the state is associated with the expansion of international production and the process through which "the nation state becomes part of a larger and more complex political structure that is the counterpart to international production" (p. 253). In this process of change the internal structures of states are adjusted so that each can best transform the neoliberal global consensus into national policy and practice. At the apex of this emerging global structure is the transnational managerial class situated in the higher echelons of the Trilateral Commission, the World Bank and IMF, and the Organisation for Economic Co-operation and Development (OECD). The members develop a common framework of thought and guidelines for policies that are disseminated through the process of the internationalization of the state. In peripheral areas the financial power exercised by the IMF and the World Bank, which was intensified after the debt crisis of the 1980s, serves to impose or restore the discipline of the market where it is lacking or weakening. The collapse of the Soviet Union and the subsequent transformation of the global state system have eliminated many obstacles to the further expansion of markets through the enhanced global reach of transnational capital.

The priorities of economic and social policies worldwide have been recast to reflect the new dominance of investors. International institutions (such as OECD, IMF, World Bank, and World Trade Organization, or WTO) and groupings of dominant states (G7) are engaged in the legal and political reproduction of this *disciplinary neoliberalism* and ensure through a variety of regulatory, surveillance, and policing mechanisms that neoliberal reforms are *locked in* (Gill). In the core areas of the world economy this discipline appears in the shape of "voluntary" programs of competitiveness, deregulation, and austerity that are codified in such arrangements as the Economic and Monetary Union (EMU) stability pact or the WTO liberalization regime. Gill refers to the erosion of democratic control implied in this process as "New Constitutionalism," the move toward construction of legal or constitutional devices to remove or insulate substantially the new economic institutions from popular scrutiny or democratic accountability (Gill, 1995). Despite an increasingly homogeneous formal governance framework, indicated by membership of intergovernmental bodies and adherence to their rules and norms, and despite the almost universal national presence of electoral democracy and market-regulated consumption, the unequal distribution of wealth and power both within and among nations is staggering and arguably increasing (Cammack).

See also **Bretton Woods Agreement; Fordism; Keynes, J. M.; Thatcher, Margaret.**

BIBLIOGRAPHY

Cammack, Paul. "Making the Poor Work for Globalisation?" *New Political Economy* 6, no. 3 (2001): 397–408.

Cox, Robert W. *Production, Power, and World Order: Social Forces in the Making of History.* New York, 1987.

Gill, Stephen. "Globalisation, Market Civilisation, and Disciplinary Neoliberalism." *Millennium: Journal of International Studies* 24, no. 3 (1995): 399–423.

Polanyi, Karl. "Evolution of the Market Pattern." In his *The Great Transformation: The Political and Economic Origins of Our Time*, 56–67. Boston, 1944.

Radice, Hugo. "Globalisation and National Capitalisms: Theorising Convergence and Differentiation." *Review of International Political Economy* 7, no. 4 (2000): 719–742.

Ruggie, John G. "International Regimes, Transactions, and Change: Embedded Liberalism in the Post-war Order." *International Organization* 36, no. 2 (1982): 379–415.

Rupert, Mark. "The Hegemonic Project of Liberal Globalization." In his *Ideologies of Globalization*, 42–64. London, 2000.

Weiss, Linda. "Globalization and the Myth of the Powerless State." *New Left Review* 225 (1997): 3–27.

STUART SHIELDS

NETHERLANDS. The Netherlands was fortunate enough to remain neutral during World War I and hence escaped the bloodshed experienced by its neighbors. That is not to say, however, that the country remained altogether unscathed; the economic problems arising from the disturbance of the European economy did cause considerable hardship in the Netherlands, not least because the division of available supplies was dismally managed by local and national governments. Rioting, and even an attempt at socialist revolution, ensued in 1917 and 1918, although neither truly threatened the existing order. In international politics, the pre-1940 Netherlands was particularly conflict averse. Internally, however, the first two decades of the twentieth century were rife with conflict. While, as in most countries at the time, there was disagreement about the economic role of governments, voting rights, and many other issues, there also was a particularly problematic conflict related to diversity.

The population of the Netherlands had for centuries been divided between roughly equally large numbers of Catholics and Protestants, of which the latter were divided into several smaller denominations. The last decades of the nineteenth century had seen the emancipation of Catholics and the restoration of Episcopal structure. The relative ease with which several centuries of discrimination against Catholics had been ended owed much to the fact that the Netherlands, since 1848, had been ruled by consecutive bourgeois liberal governments. Yet the Catholics had not been the only ones to emancipate. Orthodox Protestantism also rose to political prominence, forming a power adverse to liberal political hegemony. The orthodox Protestants considered themselves the true heirs of the Dutch state. The eighty years' struggle for independence (1568 to 1648) by what they saw as a pious, Protestant nation against Catholic Spain, under the leadership of the Prince of Orange, played a crucial role in their self-perception as a section of Dutch society. Their popular slogan *God, Nederland en Oranje* (God, the Netherlands, and Orange) reflected their political ideology—the state was to be inexorably linked to Protestant Christianity and headed by a Protestant monarch.

While (orthodox) Protestants thus strove for a more outspokenly Protestant state, Catholics desired a strict separation of church and state. As such, Dutch Catholic politics differed from Catholic political movements elsewhere in Europe. The geographical concentration of Catholics in the south of the country, notably the provinces of Limburg and Brabant, offered the church ample opportunity to exert influence over its flock there, especially on the subject of public education. North of the Rhine, Catholics were a minority and felt a much stronger desire to distance themselves from the dominant secular or Protestant culture. Education in particular was a difficult issue in those areas where Catholics could not, through sheer numerical dominance, change the character of public education. Both north and south, the Rooms-Katholieke Staatspartij (Roman-Catholic State Party) could, more than other parties, count on a stable electoral base and support from the church hierarchy.

The solution to the tensions among liberal, Catholic, and Protestant forces was found in the "Pacification" of 1917. Under the Pacification, suffrage was made universal (effective as of 1917 for men and 1920 for women), and denominational schools were granted the same level of financial support as public ones. The extension of the suffrage ended liberal political hegemony and the rise to power of religious political parties so that Liberal parties were relegated to, at best, a secondary place in Dutch society and politics. The liberals did continue to regard themselves as the "thinking part of society" and were generally opposed to division along (especially) denominational lines. While Catholics, Protestants, and Socialists were forming broadcasting societies, published papers, etc., that were specifically aimed at their own section of the population, liberal organs were stubbornly named *algemeen* (general) or otherwise claimed to be directed at the population as a whole, rather than at their own supporters.

The extension of suffrage also allowed for the strong rise of a fourth, Socialist, political bloc. Socialist parties were on the rise in the early decades of the twentieth century. Socialist, anarchist, and other left-wing movements had existed in the nineteenth century as well, but only in the course of the twentieth century did they develop a stable and coherent political force. Although fringe groups had always existed, Socialist power came to center mostly on the Sociaal-Democratische Arbeiderspartij (Social Democratic Labour Party), founded in 1894, and after 1946 on the Partij van de Arbeid (PvdA; Labour Party). The consecutive communist parties and various left-wing movements always disputed Social Democratic leadership of the left wing, but were too electorally weak to muster significant opposition until very late in the twentieth century.

Thus, Dutch political power had become divided among four so-called pillars, which were to remain central to both politics and society for decades to come. Not only politics but also public broadcasting, unions, press, and education became rigidly divided along pillar lines. Perhaps paradoxically, the fourfold division of Dutch society became the basis of a remarkably stable social and political order. Although the relative size of the pillars could vary as a consequence of demographic developments or defection of individuals to another pillar, such cases were relatively rare, and the loyalty of people to their pillar was strong. As noted by the political scientist Arend Lijphart in 1967, pillarization ensured political stability in a deeply divided country. The leaders of each pillar generally were not particularly hostile toward their counterparts in other pillars and hence were willing to cooperate (and form parliamentary coalitions). They could, moreover, count on a stable share of the vote from the members of their pillar. The combination of unflagging pillar loyalty at the base and willingness to cooperate at the top made pillarization a stabilizing factor in Dutch politics and also enabled pillarized institutions to survive throughout the twentieth century. Although the traditional view of pillarization has been criticized in the early twenty-first century, notably by J. C. H. Blom and J. Talsma (2000), it remains central to the history of and historiography about the Netherlands in the twentieth century. At least until 1970, and in many ways up to the twenty-first century, pillarization remained central to Dutch political life.

Newly found political stability, however, could not ward off a period of economic hardship during the 1930s. Being a small, open economy, heavily dependent on export, the Netherlands was hard hit by the world economic crisis. A series of governments under Protestant premier Hendrikus Colijn, confronted with the difficult circumstances of economic crisis, were unwilling to leave the gold standard and allow the guilder to devaluate. The late recovery of the Netherlands from the crisis (about 1936) is commonly attributed to the stubborn attachment of the Colijn governments to the hard guilder. High unemployment and low exports marked the 1930s. Even though the Colijn governments principally adhered to balanced budgets, the 1930s were an era of rising government interference in economic matters, especially in agriculture. The rise of a more economically intrusive state would prove to be an important asset during World War II.

Any Dutch hopes of remaining neutral during World War II were quashed on 10 May 1940, when Germany attacked the Netherlands. The Netherlands capitulated after five days of fighting and the bombardment of Rotterdam, which left over two thousand civilians dead and the city center in ruins. Five years of Nazi occupation ensued, which without any doubt was the most disastrous period to befall the Netherlands in the twentieth century. Unlike most other occupied countries, the Netherlands was placed under civilian German rule, headed by the Austrian Nazi Arthur Seyss-Inquart. During the first occupation years Seyss aimed to win over the Dutch to the National Socialist cause, an attempt that by and large failed. The "soft approach" did, however, help to establish a relatively high degree of cooperation (later often denounced as collaboration) from much of the Dutch civil service. This allowed everyday life to go on as usual, at least during the first years of occupation. Added to the relatively restrained attitude of the occupying authorities was the reasonably good supply of basic goods. Through well-prepared economic controls, executed largely by the civil servants who had been enrolled to come to the aid of agriculture during the crisis of the 1930s, the population was at least reasonably well fed during the occupation years. Perhaps because of the relatively favorable economic circumstances, resistance, while not absent, was limited. Only the illegal press was large in comparison to other occupied nations.

The Netherlands stands out among the occupied countries as the one that, proportionally, lost most of its citizens in the Holocaust. Exact numbers cannot be given, but some 104,000 out of 140,000 Jews did not survive Nazi persecution. There has been extensive debate about why the Netherlands lost so much more, proportionally, of its Jewish population than other Western European countries. The publication of Presser's watershed study *Ondergang* (1965; *The Destruction of the Dutch Jews,* 1969) did much to dispel the contented self-image the Dutch held with regard to their role during the war. Still, it would be wrong to claim that the disastrous outcome can be blamed entirely on cowardice or anti-Semitism on the part of the Dutch, even though such claims surface regularly in the Netherlands. A number of other factors, such as Seyss-Inquart's approach to his genocidal task, which combined great sophistication with uncanny ruthlessness, also played an important, if not decisive, role. Other factors include the very orderly and law-abiding nature of Dutch society and the lack of a readily accessible safe country nearby.

In the end phase of World War II, the front came to lie within the Netherlands. After D-Day, the Allied forces relatively quickly made their way north, but their advance halted at the Rhine after the fiasco of operation Market Garden in September 1944, and the front froze on the great rivers. Due to a gradual erosion of relations between German and indigenous officials, a railroad strike, and a relatively harsh winter, food could no longer reach the western cities of the Netherlands, causing a grave famine to break out.

Rotterdam, Netherlands, following bombing by German forces, May 1940. German bombers attacked the city after the Dutch ignored a German ultimatum. Approximately 30,000 residents of the city were killed. ©CORBIS

Somewhere between twenty thousand and twenty-five thousand deaths ensued, a consequence of both hunger and disease. Being relatively well-documented, short-lived, and severe, the Dutch hunger winter has become a popular test case for medical research into the consequences of periods of malnourishment, especially in (unborn) children.

After the complete liberation of the Netherlands in early May 1945, a period of rather frenzied political activity began. During the occupation, dissatisfaction with prewar political structures, especially with pillarization, had become very vocal. Everybody, it seemed—the queen, the Resistance, the political elite—agreed that there was a need for radical change. A new political party was formed, the aforementioned PvdA, which was to be the incarnation of unified, modern politics.

In practice, however, all the opponents of prewar politics turned out to have very different views on what the new order was to be like. The *Doorbraak*, or "breakthrough," failed completely and quickly. The PvdA came to be little more than the heir of the Sociaal-Democratische Arbeiderspartij, and disappointed liberals, many of whom had originally joined the PvdA, formed a new liberal party, the Volkspartij voor Vrijheid en Democratie (People's Party for Freedom and Democracy). If anything, pillarization was stronger than ever during the postwar years and was only to wane when the Netherlands rapidly desecularized in the 1960s and 1970s.

While the *Doorbraak* failed miserably, one radical change was taking place, namely, the decolonization of the Dutch Indies. On 17 August 1945, the nationalist leader Sukarno proclaimed the republic of Indonesia, to the horror of the Dutch and the Dutch political elite. The fact that Sukarno had cooperated with the Japanese after they had invaded the Dutch Indies only aggravated the dismay of the Dutch at the perceived disloyalty of its Asian colony. Moreover, many believed that Indonesia was indispensable to the Dutch economy, especially as reconstruction was under way. The slogan *indië verloren, rampspoed geboren* (Indies lost, disaster born) became commonplace. The Dutch were not going to give up their empire without putting up a fight.

During the periods July 1947 and December 1948, the Netherlands waged war on the guerrilla army fighting for independence. This struggle ended in a bloody deadlock, much like the war in Vietnam later would. The Dutch, with their superior military technology, could retain a firm grip on the colonial cities but were almost powerless in the countryside. Because the guerrilleros could become invisible among the indigenous population, and because they could rely on the cover of the immense tropical rainforests, they were impossible to beat. It nevertheless required considerable international (American) pressure to make the Dutch accept their defeat and officially confer sovereignty over most of Indonesia to the rebels. Only New Guinea was to remain Dutch, and a source of dispute between the newborn republic and the stubborn colonizer, until 1962. After the transfer of New Guinea to Indonesia, relations between the countries improved markedly.

The independence of Indonesia had a massive impact on Dutch society, not least because it brought about a wave of immigration. Not only did the former white colonial elite return to the Netherlands between roughly 1947 and 1957, but so did many people of mixed ethnicity, as well as many indigenous people previously employed in the colonial army. With the influx of people from the former Dutch Indies, Dutch society was for the first time confronted with a very visible form of ethnic diversity. The arrival of a large "Indo" community changed the appearance of Dutch society, which had before had only a handful of non-European inhabitants. Among the immigrants were large numbers of Ambonese soldiers and their families. The Ambonese community, and initially many Dutch citizens as well, cherished the hope of establishing an independent republic on the Isle of Ambon. After Indonesia had all but crushed Nationalist resistance there and began a policy of ethnic dilution through so-called transmigration, the Republic of the Southern Moluccas, or RMS, flourished in the Netherlands under the leadership of their president-in-exile Manusama. As the Dutch government refused to support the Ambonese independence even diplomatically, relations between the Ambonese and Dutch society deteriorated. During the 1970s, small groups of young Ambonese tried (unsuccessfully) to force their way by hijacking trains, taking hostages in a school, and numerous other violent actions.

Another consequence of World War II was that it ended the Dutch preference for neutrality. The country wholeheartedly joined the Atlantic bloc. The Netherlands was among the first and most loyal members of the North Atlantic Treaty Organization (NATO), the United Nations, and various European organizations (and eventually, of course, the European Union). Economically, the 1950s and 1960s, as in most other northwestern European countries, were an era of strong economic growth and relative prosperity. The combination of wage moderation and relative social peace provided for a highly successful economic model. In this and other respects, the postwar Netherlands often seemed, at least from an economic point of view, to be a mere annex of the Federal Republic of Germany.

Full employment, the spread of mass media, and increased leisure impacted Dutch culture in many ways, not least by leading to a new influx of immigrants. Moroccans and Turks in particular were invited to work in Dutch factories in great numbers. In spite of expectations that their presence would be temporary, many of them settled permanently in the Netherlands, forming large Moroccan and Turkish communities, especially in the large cities. In the mid-1970s, after the independence of Surinam, they were followed by thousands of Surinamese who, for various reasons, preferred the Dutch to the Surinamese nationality. The Netherlands were rapidly becoming a colorful country.

Religiousness came under increasing pressure, especially during the 1960s. Although pillarization in the form of separate parties, broadcasting societies, and schools continued more or less unabated, church attendance and loyalty to church teachings declined sharply. Moreover, the rise of second-wave feminism and modernist literature, later followed by modern drugs, sexual libertarianism, and many other new phenomena, besieged the otherwise stable political order. The presence of large numbers of relatively young people (the period after 1936, especially the immediate postwar years, had experienced very high birth rates) added much to the progressive storm that seemed to wash over the country. The old political order fought a losing battle against the onslaught of modernity during the postwar decades and was perhaps quicker to give way than in many other countries. One could speculate that the culture of pillarization, which could exist only as long as people were willing to ignore those whose worldview they despised, helped establish the famous Dutch tolerance, but such explanations have yet to rise above the level of speculation.

As in many other countries, the first decades after the war also saw the gradual expansion of the Dutch welfare state. In 1956 a Social Democratic–Catholic coalition government introduced state pensions; many other social arrangements were to follow. A great leap in the expansion of the welfare state was made after the discovery of one of the world's greatest reserves of natural gas at Slochteren in 1959. The immediate cash flow to the government resulting from this find helped consecutive governments to build the relatively generous Dutch welfare state. Yet the natural gas reserves also resulted in what has come to be known as "Dutch disease": searing inflation driven by balance-of-payment problems resulting from the sale of expensive natural resources during the 1970s. More generally, the 1970s were an era of relative decline for the Netherlands. Stagflation, the combination of recession and high inflation, hit hard and was stubbornly fought with fiscally expansionist measures. During the 1980s seemingly endless cuts were made in public expenditure by right-wing governments under the Christian Democrat Ruud Lubbers. Only in the prosperous 1990s, when the country was ruled for the first time by a coalition of liberals and Socialists, without confessional parties, did rapid economic growth cause both a sharp upturn in wealth and a slight expansion in government spending.

At the end of the 1990s, however, economic growth fell back once more and popular discontent rose markedly. The presence of numerous foreigners, many of whom were Muslims, increasingly awakened widespread discontent. The rise of Pim Fortuyn, a right-wing politician with a strongly anti-Islam agenda, and his consequent murder by a left-wing activist seemed to consolidate feelings of discontent into a viable political movement. Remarkably, one of the main reasons why the "new Right" is attacking immigrants, especially Muslims, is because it finds them to be too conservative. There have been reported calls for a more thorough "integration," or rather assimilation, of first-, second-, and third-generation immigrants, including the adoption of Dutch liberal views. The early twenty-first century did see the adoption of more extreme anti-immigration legislation and widespread anti-Muslim sentiments, even among mainstream parties. The Netherlands, in 2004, found itself once more ill at ease with the very diverse people within its borders. A pacification, however, does not as yet appear to be at hand.

See also **Amsterdam; Fortuyn, Pim; Frank, Anne.**

BIBLIOGRAPHY

Blom, J. C. H., and J. Talsma, eds. *De verzuiling voorbij: godsdienst, stand en natie in de lange negentiiende eeuw.* Amsterdam, 2000.

De Rooy, Piet. *Republiek van rivaliteiten: Nederland sinds 1813.* Amsterdam, 2002.

Kossman, Ernst H. *De lage landen 1780–1980: Twee eeuwen Nederland en België.* Amsterdam, 1986

Presser, Jacob. *The Destruction of the Dutch Jews.* New York, 1969.

Van Galen Last, Dick, and Rolf Wolfswinkel. *Anne Frank and After: Dutch Holocaust Literature in Historical Perspective.* Amsterdam, 1996.

Van Zanden, Jan L. *The Economic History of the Netherlands 1914–1995: A Small Open Economy in the "Long" Twentieth Century.* New York, 1998.

Woltjer, Jan Juliaan. *Recent verleden: De geschiedenis van Nederland in de twintigste eeuw.* Amsterdam, 1992.

RALF FUTSELAAR

NEW ECONOMIC POLICY (NEP).

In the historiography of the USSR the term *New Economic Policy* (NEP) can refer specifically to the economic policy changes initiated by the Tenth Congress of the Communist Party in March 1921 or generally to the entire period of 1921 to 1927. As economic policy, NEP involved legalization of some private trade, as well as concessions to peasant farmers aimed at increasing agricultural output. But the term *NEP* has also become part of the periodization of Soviet history. Most scholars accept a division of early Soviet history into the periods of civil war (1918–1921), the New Economic Policy (1921–1927), and the First Five-Year Plan (1928–1932). In this schema NEP is often presented as a time of economic decentralization and relative cultural pluralism sandwiched between the more repressive eras of the civil war and the First Five-Year Plan.

INITIATION OF THE NEW ECONOMIC POLICY

During the Russian Civil War the Bolsheviks cobbled together a set of economic policies known as war communism. These included the forced confiscation of grain from peasants, a ban on private trade, and an attempt at state control of the entire economy, including distribution of food and consumer goods. In the chaos of the civil war, government coordination of production and rationing frequently failed, and the populace had to engage in illegal private economic activity on a massive scale in order to survive.

By 1921 the civil war and war communism had devastated the economy and depopulated many cities. Soviet rubles were nearly valueless. Confiscation of peasant grain supplies contributed to catastrophic declines in harvests and widespread famine. In industry and mining, production dropped to around one-fifth of prewar totals. Urban population dropped as unemployed factory workers and others fled the cities in search of food. By the end of the civil war, Bolshevik leaders were deeply worried by the decline in the urban working class, which they considered their base of support.

Economic disaster bred widespread resentment of Bolshevik rule. Even as the Red Army defeated the last major White forces in late 1920, peasant rebellions broke out in Tambov, Ukraine, western Siberia, Belarus, and several provinces along the Volga River. In the cities workers struck for better rations, more political freedom, and more control over their factories. In sympathy with strikers in Petrograd (now St. Petersburg), sailors mutinied and seized control of the Kronstadt naval base in the Gulf of Finland in March 1921. The Kronstadt rebellion revealed that the regime had even lost support in the navy, one of their key political bases since 1917. The stage was set for radical policy changes.

At the Tenth Party Congress Vladimir Lenin announced the replacement of coercive grain requisitions with an agricultural tax in kind set at a level much lower than the requisitions. This was the beginning of the New Economic Policy, a series of measures intended to revive the Soviet economy and conciliate the peasants. NEP policies developed gradually throughout 1921–1922. One important provision was legalization of small-scale trade. Together with the end of grain requisitioning, this would encourage peasants to increase the amount of land they sowed and market their surplus production. The Soviet government also allowed private individuals to lease factories from the state in certain branches of industry. And in an effort to stabilize the Soviet currency, the government introduced a mandate (never fully implemented) that state-run enterprises balance their budgets.

Lenin described NEP as a temporary retreat necessary before advancing further down the road to socialism. Although some communist leaders, such as Nikolai Bukharin, apparently came to view NEP as a long-term solution to the problems of constructing socialism, most continued to view it with suspicion. Party commentators frequently complained that NEP "coddled class enemies" such as private entrepreneurs and well-off peasants (kulaks). Opponents of NEP feared it would lead to a renaissance of capitalism and ultimately to the overthrow of the Soviet government.

POLITICAL DISCIPLINE AND STALIN'S RISE TO POWER

In the view of most party leaders, the party had to maintain tight discipline to prevent the NEP retreat from turning into a rout. In response to the rise of contending factions within the party, notably the so-called Workers Opposition, the Tenth Party Congress banned the organization of such groupings. Joseph Stalin used this ban to great effect in his battles for political domination, regularly accusing opponents of factionalism.

In spite of the ban on factionalism, the 1920s saw fierce political struggles as Stalin established a personal dictatorship over the party. Using his initial base as Central Committee secretary in charge of personnel decisions, along with the ban on factionalism, Stalin defeated several challenges to his policies and his personal rule. Following Lenin's final incapacitation by stroke in March 1923, he defeated a movement led by Commissar of Defense Leon Trotsky against the increasing "bureaucratism" of Soviet society and the decline of democracy within the party. In 1926–1927 he vanquished the so-called United Opposition that united Trotsky with Politburo members Lev Kamenev and Grigory Zinoviev against Stalin. At the end of this battle, in December 1927 the Fifteenth Party Congress expelled Trotsky from the party and exiled him to Central Asia. Finally, in 1928–1929 Stalin defeated a challenge to his personal rule by "rightists" opposed to the forced collectivization of the peasantry, led by his erstwhile ally Nikolai Bukharin.

CULTURAL "PLURALISM" AND MASS ENLIGHTENMENT

Literature and the arts during the NEP years were less subordinated to an overt party agenda and more open to experimentation than under the high Stalinism that followed. Some private publishing houses continued to function early in the period. Newspapers presented some information in a neutral tone and published limited policy debates.

The situation in literature exemplifies that in other arts. Writers tended to sort themselves self-consciously into literary schools. Some writers, most notably the group known as the Serapion Brothers (among the Brothers were Yevgeny Zamyatin and Mikhail Zoshchenko), rejected the notion of writing to serve the party's political agenda. Other groups that sought to work with the party, such as the Left Front of Art, founded by the poet Vladimir Mayakovsky, experimented with modernist and futurist literary techniques. "Proletarian" writers such as Fyodor Gladkov and

Mikhail Sholokhov sought to develop literature by and for the working class. Throughout the period various literary groups competed fiercely with one another for state patronage.

In the 1980s and 1990s there was significant scholarly debate about whether NEP could be called a period of "pluralism," at least in culture. Certainly there was much artistic experimentation. However, the party allowed this not out of a commitment to pluralism per se but rather out of the sense that artists and writers would serve the Bolshevik agenda best if allowed to try new approaches. During NEP, party officials hoped to use the arts, literature, and journalism to "enlighten the masses"—to teach them to be model citizens of socialist society and work for the party's goals. It was this hope, rather than any commitment to pluralism, that motivated the relative freedom of artistic expression during the NEP years.

END OF NEP

The winter of 1927–1928 may be regarded as the end of NEP. Throughout 1927 party/state officials had been shutting down private trade and cooperative producers. That winter Joseph Stalin, whose supporters now clearly dominated the party leadership, returned to a policy of forced grain requisitions in districts of the USSR where the government could not procure enough grain through purchase. At the Fifteenth Party Congress in December 1927 Stalin's supporters crushed the United Opposition, and by the spring of 1928 they had begun a campaign against "rightist" opponents of coercing the peasantry. This was the last open opposition movement within the party in Stalin's lifetime. In the winter of 1927–1928 the economic planning agency, Gosplan, formulated the first formal central economic plan. Finally, in the early spring of 1928 the party Central Committee began a campaign to force journalists and writers to promote the party's agenda actively in their work. Taken together, these developments suggest the end of an era.

A variety of considerations seem to have motivated the end of NEP. Among party leaders the conviction was growing that the Soviet Union needed a crash industrialization program to increase its military capacity in a threatening international environment. Stalin and his lieutenants concluded that the only way to finance such a program was to squeeze more grain out of the peasants at below-market prices. In general, party leaders may have despaired of the possibility of winning voluntary cooperation from the peasants. Overall suspicion of NEP policies as soft on "capitalism" and Stalin's drive to dominate the party/state also probably helped to catalyze policy changes.

SCHOLARLY DEBATE ABOUT NEP

Debate about NEP has revolved around the question of whether it constituted a viable "soft" communist alternative to Stalinism. Throughout the world communist reformers disillusioned with Stalinism's repression and failure to improve living standards have looked to the NEP period for alternatives. NEP-inspired reform efforts began in Eastern Europe in the 1950s and included the Soviet leader Mikhail Gorbachev's reform efforts (perestroika) in the late 1980s. Most reformers focused on NEP as a model for making command economies more efficient by integrating small-scale market activity. A few, including Gorbachev, were also interested in allowing more freedom of expression in order to build popular support and make government more effective.

In U.S. scholarship the interpretation of NEP as a real alternative emerged in the 1960s and 1970s as a challenge to the then widespread view of the Soviet system as static, totalitarian, and essentially Stalinist. In 1971 U.S. political scientist Stephen Cohen published a biography of Nikolai Bukharin that argued that NEP could have been a stable alternative developmental model for the USSR. The literary scholar Edward J. Brown emphasized the relative openness of NEP culture as early as 1963.

After about 1990, however, a number of scholars tried to qualify the developing view of the NEP years as a "soft," tolerant period of Soviet history and as a viable economic alternative. Christopher Read and Matthew Lenoe argued that party policy on culture had never been in any way "pluralistic." Michael David-Fox contended that party policy in higher education during the 1920s was never "soft-line" or tolerant, but rather aimed at revolutionary transformation of human consciousness. Vladimir Brovkin collected evidence of political repression throughout NEP. And the Hungarian economist Janos Kornai concluded (*The Socialist System,* 1992) that mixed economies of the NEP type were in the long run incompatible with single-party communist dictatorships.

See also **Communism; Lenin, Vladimir; Russian Civil War; Stalin, Joseph.**

BIBLIOGRAPHY

Ball, Alan M. *Russia's Last Capitalists: The Nepmen, 1921–1929.* Berkeley, Calif., 1987.

Brovkin, Vladimir. *Russia after Lenin: Politics, Culture, and Society, 1921–1929.* New York, 1998.

Carr, Edward Hallett. *A History of Soviet Russia: Foundations of a Planned Economy, 1926–1929.* 2 vols. London, 1969–1971.

Cohen, Stephen F. *Bukharin and the Bolshevik Revolution: A Political Biography, 1888–1938.* Oxford, U.K., 1971.

David-Fox, Michael. *Revolution of the Mind: Higher Learning among the Bolsheviks, 1918–1929.* Ithaca, N.Y., 1997.

Fitzpatrick, Sheila, Alexander Rabinowitch, and Richard Stites, eds. *Russia in the Era of NEP: Explorations in Soviet Society and Culture.* Bloomington, Ind., 1991.

Gorsuch, Anne E. *Youth in Revolutionary Russia: Enthusiasts, Bohemians, Delinquents.* Bloomington, Ind., 2000.

Lenoe, Matthew. *Closer to the Masses: Stalinist Culture, Social Revolution, and Soviet Newspapers.* Cambridge, Mass., 2004.

Read, Christopher. *Culture and Power in Revolutionary Russia: The Intelligentsia and the Transition from Tsarism to Communism.* New York, 1990.

MATTHEW LENOE

NEW LEFT. The *New Left* is a term that describes a varied set of social movements in Europe from the 1950s to the 1980s. What they had in common was a rejection of the capitalist system, the Cold War, and Soviet Marxism. Their politics were confrontational, and entailed a public and theatrical element in which they performed their rejection of the generation in power from 1940 to 1960. Youth politics and student politics emerged as forces in their own right, at times hostile to and at other times braided together with working-class militancy. The New Left emerged as a threat to the forces of order in Germany, France, and Italy in the spring of 1968. Thereafter, radical groups continued to oppose Western imperialism and to press for changes in the educational system and in factory work and discipline. Their aim was a kind of self-management or workers' control that would decentralize power and give ordinary people a greater say in determining the conditions of their daily lives.

By the early 1970s, the force of these social movements was largely spent. Some groups spun off into terrorism. Factions emerged to carry on the armed struggle through kidnappings, robberies, and assassinations, in particular in Germany and Italy. They were ruthlessly suppressed. Other groups took the vision of 1968 and reoriented it toward the struggle for human rights and civil rights. Radical dissent continued in the Soviet bloc until the collapse of communism in 1989. In Western Europe, it contributed to the broad movements supporting a new human rights regime and European integration.

The New Left began as a dissident Marxist faction in the 1950s. Starting in 1953, when dissenters were crushed in East Berlin, and reaching a peak in the period after Khrushchev's denunciation of Stalin's crimes and the Soviet invasion of Hungary in 1956, groups of Marxists either left the Communist Party or worked for its reform from within. The moribund nature of European communism was exposed fully in the Russian invasion of Czechoslovakia in August 1968. From then on, the "old left" meant, first and foremost, Communist parties still tied to the Soviet Union.

There was another sense in which the old left was rejected in this period. It was a term meant to convey the consensus politics of social democratic parties. In Britain, the Labour Party had lost its direction after the years of reconstruction between 1945 and 1950. To radicals, it was a trade union party dedicated to making the capitalist system work more efficiently. In Germany, the Social Democrats were partners in the economic miracle, which seemed to be the limit of their expectations. French and Italian socialists were similarly imbricated in the post-1945 order. The New Left, in contrast, wanted to depart from the field of political horse trading and forge bridges with workers

equally dissatisfied with their conservative trade union leadership.

The New Left was also categorically opposed to the foreign policy of European governments that either supported or acquiesced to American objectives. This opposition took two primary forms. The first was the rejection of the nuclear stalemate and its underlying theory of mutually assured destruction. The second was the championing of anti-American forces from Cuba to Vietnam.

In Britain, the Campaign for Nuclear Disarmament drew together many ex-communists and liberals in a loose alliance opposing the nuclear politics of Britain and the United States. Ending the deployment of nuclear weapons in Britain was one of their aims, which would lead, they hoped, to step-by-step nuclear disarmament. Similar demonstrations were held in Germany, bringing together clergymen, trade unionists, and students.

A second dimension to the anti-American character of the European New Left was its championing of radical causes challenging the United States as the free world's hegemonic power. The first of these struggles was the war for national liberation in Vietnam. Once the French had given up the fight in 1954, the Americans took over the defense of its client state, South Vietnam. As the war intensified in the mid- to late 1960s, the New Left coalesced around opposition to the war and support for Ho Chi Minh and the communist cause. On 17 March 1968, a major demonstration took place in front of the American Embassy in London's Grosvenor Square. There was a violent confrontation with police of a kind that occurred in many European cities. The politics of the streets over Vietnam took up where similar demonstrations against the French war in Algeria had left off earlier in the 1960s. Young radicals who joined the New Left offered vocal and visible solidarity with the cause of the Cuban revolution and the Palestinian resistance to Israeli occupation after 1967. The death of Che Guevara in Bolivia was viewed as a heroic death in the ongoing war against American capitalism. Che's profile became an icon of the New Left.

Most of these currents flowed into a set of conflicts that reached a boiling point in May through August 1968. Rudi Dutschke, leader of the New Left organization SDS, was shot three times in April 1968 by a right-wing fanatic, leading to violent confrontations in Berlin between students and police. On 2 June 1967, a student was shot to death in Berlin by an undercover agent at a demonstration against the Shah of Iran's visit to the United States. In Paris, the flashpoint was again an anti-American demonstration over Vietnam at the University of Paris campus at Nanterre. The arrest of demonstrators there led to much wider demonstrations in the center of Paris, during which university buildings were occupied. The rector then shut the university down. Student revolt mixed with industrial militancy in May 1968, and factory occupations paralleled university sit-ins. This indeed suggested a very different kind of left politics from that of the staid Communist or Socialist Parties.

The events of 1968 produced one of the core experiments of the New Left. In France it was termed *autogestion*, or self-management. The set of ideas was not restricted to France. In Belgium, liberation theologians and priests were actively drawn to the idea and contributed to its elaboration. So were trade unionists in Tito's Yugoslavia well before the events of 1968. The leaders of the military coup that seized power in Peru in 1968 also declared their commitment to installing forms of self-government of a similar kind. And in its first few years, the leadership of free Algeria proclaimed their support for decentralized institutional life; that brief period of freedom came to an abrupt end by the late 1960s.

There were, therefore, many variants to and sources of this set of ideas. Within this multinational array, three constituent elements stand out. The first is a commitment to the decentralization of political and social life, so that the search for a new order takes place in civil society and not in parliament or in the factory. The second is a demand for local autonomy in all places of work and public service, and the third is a vision of the replacement of the capitalist organization of consumption by cooperative institutions.

At the core of this program is the belief in the need to escape from the central state as the arbiter of the public good, and to substitute for its *dirigisme* more pluralistic modes of organizing the productive and creative forces of society. In this context, *dirigisme* meant the mindlessness of Communist lock-step thinking or the conformism of Western capitalism, which offered meaningless choices to the public every few years. Thus, national elections were a sideshow to these militants, and so were the intricacies of trade union politics. Instead of acting primarily to win pay raises, workers of all kinds were urged—in the words of one poster—to "demonstrate that workers' management of the firm is the power to do better for everyone what the capitalists did scandalously for a few."

One key element in this movement was its dynamic quality. It worked to produce an environment in which men and women could perpetually renew their commitment to those with whom they lived. It represented therefore a new social contract, based on a moral vision incompatible with the capitalist order. Echoes of anarchist thinking may be found here, though there are traces of an escape from alienation, as outlined in Karl Marx's early philosophical writings.

The dynamic element in this movement also included aspects of personal and sexual freedom that appealed to many recruits to the New Left. Springing from the Nanterre disturbances in May 1968 were many grievances, among them the limitation on the right of students to have guests of the opposite sex visit their dormitories. During the time when effective contraception became readily available, young people were not prepared to accept their professors' or their parents' rules about personal or sexual comportment. Thus, hair styles, jeans, and music symbolized this generational revolt.

What became of it? The massive hopes and exuberance of the New Left in 1968 faded rapidly in the following decade. Some of its adherents retreated into underground warfare, particularly the Baader-Meinhof group in Germany or the Red Brigades in Italy. Others, especially in Eastern Europe, weathered the harsh repression of the early 1970s and emerged to lead dissident groups that ultimately came to power. Finally, men such as Daniel Cohn-Bendit, a leader of the New Left in Paris in May 1968, turned toward European unification and human rights as the embodiment of their beliefs. In this form, the New Left survived until the end of the century.

See also **May 1968; Student Movements.**

BIBLIOGRAPHY

Anderson, Perry, and Robin Blackburn, eds. *Towards Socialism*. Ithaca, N.Y.,1966.

Bahro, Rudolf. *From Red to Green: Interviews with New Left Review*. London, 1984.

Berman, Paul. *A Tale of Two Utopias. The Political Journey of the Generation of 1968*. New York, 1996.

Ehrenreich, Barbara, and John Ehrenreich. *Long March, Short Spring. The Student Uprising at Home and Abroad*. London, 1969.

Fraser, Ronald, et al. *1968. A Student Generation in Revolt*. London, 1988.

Teodori, Massimo, ed. *The New Left: A Documentary History*. Indianapolis, Ind., 1969.

JAY WINTER

NEW SOBRIETY. The term *New Sobriety* (*Neue Sachlichkeit*) arose in German artistic circles during the mid-1920s. An umbrella term embracing numerous developments in painting, the visual arts, and literature during the turbulent post–World War I Weimar era, the New Sobriety seemed an effective label for capturing the spirit of the times among artists seeking to reground their work in "objective" reality following the abstractions of cubism and the vitalism of expressionism. Emphasizing a rigorous return to figural art, strong lines and color, and themes drawn from the characters, landscapes, and tableaux of the modern city and modern experience generally, the art of the New Sobriety balanced objectivity with an interest in social and to some extent political themes.

When the German museum director Gustav F. Hartlaub gave the title "The New Sobriety" to an exhibition of 124 paintings held in mid-1925 at the Mannheim Kunsthalle, the phrase quickly took on wide significance. The term, like the work of the thirty-two artists chosen for the exhibition, distinguished a particular postexpressionist, postcubist, and postfuturist sensibility. Less a style or a formal school than a worldview and way of seeing, the New Sobriety—as represented by such diverse artists as Max Beckmann, Otto Dix, George Grosz, and Alexander Kanoldt—reemphasized the concept of the everyday, the here and now, and the stark or even harsh realities of modern urban life. The New Sobriety thus opposed the futurists' fiery

visions and sweeping predictions, the expressionists' emotional gestures or views of apocalypse, and the cubists' abstraction of objects and spaces. Opting for rationality and a hardened (if also dramatized) sense of objectivity, practitioners associated with the New Sobriety, as well as with the related movements of verism and magic realism, expressed a certain exhaustion with the tumult and convulsive changes wrought by World War I and its immediate aftermath. Although individual painters' and writers' works differed substantially from one another, the New Sobriety was distinguished in tone by a self-conscious, even forced emphasis on stark characterizations and individual object qualities; a sharp, unsentimental view of the world, which included an embrace of "ugly" or "grotesque" subject matter; compositions assembled out of isolated objects and details, seldom integrated into an organic or experiential whole; and a manner of depicting human subjects with the same dispassionate detachment that the artist devoted to the objects and the environment, creating a particular, banal, dry yet taut atmosphere in many scenes.

This *Sachlichkeit* was "new" precisely because it seemed to be a rediscovery of the objective world following the aesthetic, philosophical, and psychological excursions of Dada, surrealism, expressionism, and cubism. It was also "new" because *Sachlichkeit* had been one of the watchwords of the progressive prewar design association, the Deutscher Werkbund, and before it, of art critics such as Ferdinand Avenarius of Dresden. As early as 1888, Avenarius had called for a "party of realists" (*Partei der Sachlichen*) in his journal, *Der Kunstwart,* one of the mainstays of Germany's broad-based art education movement. Avenarius's writings called upon these "realists" to monitor national health by promoting a culture that sensibly adapted German traditions to the altered realities of modern industrial and urban life. More concerned with "life reform" (*Lebensreform*) through arts education, attention to the tasteful design of domestic environments, and consumer education, the *Sachlichkeit* of the pre–World War I era nonetheless resurfaced during the Weimar era. Its particular form is evident in painters' efforts to reground German art in matter-of-fact material under the significantly altered conditions of life in Weimar Germany. In this respect too, New

Sobriety sensibilities, and particularly a general post–World War I "call to order" (*rappel à l'ordre*), can be seen as related to such post–World War I movements as the purism of Amédée Ozenfant and Le Corbusier, the industrial objectivity of Fernand Léger, the figural works of the Bauhaus artists Oskar Schlemmer and Joost Schmidt, and, more broadly, to the rational architecture of the "New Building" (*Neues Bauen*) and the radical functionalism of the Dessau Bauhaus director Hannes Meyer. The popularity of the New Sobriety waned, however, by the late 1920s, as cool detachment and social observation gave way increasingly to art influenced by rising political mass movements, nationalism, and technical progress. Nevertheless, the diverse body of works associated with the New Sobriety provide compelling documentation of the turbulence and creative ferment characteristic of Weimar Germany before the Nazi seizure of power.

See also **Architecture.**

BIBLIOGRAPHY

Hartlaub, Gustav F. *Neue Sachlichkeit.* Mannheim, 1925. Published in conjunction with the exhibition at the Städtische Kunsthalle Mannheim.

Schmid, Wieland. "Neue Wirklichkeit—Surrealismus und Neue Sachlichkeit." In *Tendenzen der Zwanziger Jahre,* edited by Stephan Waetzoldt and Verena Haas, part 4, vol. 15, pp. 1–36. Berlin, 1977.

Willett, John. *Art and Politics in the Weimar Era: The New Sobriety, 1917–1933.* New York, 1978.

Zeller, Ursula. "Neue Sachlichkeit." In *The Grove Dictionary of Art. From Expressionism to Post-Modernism: Styles and Movements in Twentieth-Century Western Art,* edited by Jane Turner, 267–270. New York, 2000.

JOHN V. MACIUIKA

NEW ZEALAND. On 5 August 1914, fifteen thousand people in Parliament grounds in Wellington cheered the news that New Zealand, as a loyal part of the British Empire, was at war with Germany. The country was led by William Massey, an immigrant from Ulster, a former Orangeman and a farmer. In March 2003, New Zealand, led by a former university lecturer and feminist, Helen Clark, refused to join its erstwhile allies, the United Kingdom, the United States, and Australia, in the armed invasion of Iraq. New Zealand stood as an independent Pacific country. The journey between these two events marked a huge change in New Zealand identity.

"BETTER BRITISH"

In August 1914 New Zealand considered itself in all respects British—or even "better British." The population of just over one million was overwhelmingly either immigrants from the United Kingdom (29 percent were born overseas in 1911) or descended from immigrants. Ethnically, over half were of English background (largely the south), a quarter were from Scotland, and a fifth were from Ireland, but of the Irish, two-fifths were from the Protestant communities of the north. Only about 13 percent of the population was of Irish Catholic heritage. There were just over fifty thousand Maori (fewer than half the number at the time of European settlement). Although there were parts of the North Island backcountry where Maori language and culture was still strong, there had been concerted efforts to incorporate Maori into the British world, backed up by theories that Maori were Aryans by race—"honorary whites." In the nineteenth century several thousand Germans and Scandinavians had arrived, followed by a number of Dalmatians who came to dig kauri gum in Northland. But all were quickly assimilated. In 1919 a government minister declared New Zealand "98.12% British." Only several thousand Chinese and a few Indians were excluded.

Trade reinforced the British connection. In 1914 New Zealand sent 81 percent (by value) of its exports to Britain, largely wool, frozen meat, butter, and cheese. In return Britain supplied 51 percent of its imports, largely manufactured items. Ideas also flowed south—London was the byline for most overseas news stories, books came from Britain, and young New Zealanders grew up sharing a pride in British heroes. If New Zealand was British in ethnicity and heritage, it was also "better British." It strove to avoid the congested cities and the class inequalities of the old country. A strong state might ensure that through a system of industrial arbitration, the country would be free of class conflict, and through measures such as votes for women, pensions for the elderly, and dwellings for workers, citizens would be protected from Old World abuses. Internationally, the success of New Zealand soldiers in the South African (Boer) War, followed by the success of its footballers on their 1905 tour of England and Wales, established the view that New Zealand men were superior examples of Anglo-Saxon manhood who could serve the empire in war and compensate for the racial "deterioration" in Britain's cities.

WAR

The next forty years intensified this worldview. On two occasions New Zealand conscripted men to serve in Europe's wars. The cost was severe. Some eighteen thousand died in World War I (8 percent of the eligible males) and over eleven thousand in World War II. New Zealand soldiers won fame (at least in their own eyes) at Gallipoli in 1915 and on the western front in 1916–1918. The next generation gained plaudits in North Africa in 1942 and Italy in 1944. Both wars reinforced the sense of New Zealand's destiny within the empire. In 1943 the country chose to send its division to Italy to defend Europe rather than bring it back to the Pacific to defend the homeland against Japan (as did the Australians). Both wars saw a strengthening of state regulation—in the first there was the imposition of social discipline such as the closing of pubs at 6 P.M.; in the second the regulation of the economy reached such levels of detail that even the size of men's trouser cuffs was defined. Despite the legend that New Zealand identity was founded on the heights of Gallipoli, this assumed that national identity occurred within the empire. On war memorials, the word *empire* was more common than *New Zealand,* the Union Jack more frequent than the New Zealand ensign.

In the interwar years the state fostered a secure egalitarian society. In the 1920s, as more immigrants arrived from Britain, Massey's Reform Government helped through loans to fund the growth of suburbs—single-family Californian bungalows on quarter-acre sections; and in the 1930s, as the world depression exposed New Zealand's vulnerability to the international market, the Labour Government, elected in 1935 and re-elected by a wide margin three years later, expanded a beneficent welfare state with public works schemes and the provision of state unemployment benefits and a public health system. New Zealand became a model to the world of Fabian socialism in action.

MIDCENTURY UTOPIA

In many respects the 1950s and early 1960s were the fulfillment of earlier aspirations. With high world agricultural prices, the economy boomed. In the early 1950s it was widely believed that New Zealand had one of the highest standards of living in the world. Unemployment disappeared. Following a fierce 151-day industrial conflict on the waterfront in 1951, there was little social conflict. Maori from rural areas and immigrants from England and Scotland (and twenty thousand from the Netherlands) flooded into the expanding cities, where they found a family utopia in the mushrooming suburbs. The country basked in its sporting successes in rugby games and long-distance running, and felt pride when a favorite son, Edmund Hillary, "knocked the bastard off" in 1953 (the "bastard" was Mt. Everest). Six months later New Zealanders turned out in remarkable scenes of enthusiasm to welcome Queen Elizabeth II to the country. New Zealand presented itself as the most prosperous, egalitarian, and beautiful country in the empire, and the one with the best race relations. Only a few intellectuals dissented. Some, such as the poet James K. Baxter, adopted a Bohemian lifestyle, others, like the novelist Janet Frame, followed earlier New Zealand intellectuals such as Katherine Mansfield and Ernest Rutherford into expatriation. With rugby, the price of butterfat, and the challenges of laying concrete drives as the focus of conversation, there was little to hold them.

ROOTS OF CHANGE

In the mid-1960s cracks began to appear in the foundation of this very British utopia. In 1965 the Prime Minister, "Kiwi Keith" Holyoake, reluctantly committed a small number of New Zealand troops to the Vietnam War to retain faith with the ANZUS alliance (formed with the United States and Australia), which had been signed in 1951. Protestors began to articulate an independent foreign policy. By the early 1970s this evolved into a strong antinuclear stance. Individuals and then the Labour Government of 1972–1975 challenged French nuclear testing in the South Pacific. This

Infantrymen from New Zealand fight with British forces in Libya, 2 December 1941. ©Bettmann/Corbis

"Vietnam generation" won power with the Labour Government of 1984. In quick succession, New Zealand in effect walked out of the ANZUS alliance by refusing to accept nuclear-armed or -powered ships, the country found itself in a dispute with France, whose agents sank a Greenpeace ship in Auckland Harbour, and the charismatic young Prime Minister, David Lange, a reluctant antinuclear zealot, lectured the world on nuclear issues at the Oxford Union.

The antinuclear movement drew on a growing concern for the environment. A plan to raise the level of a beautiful bush-clad lake in the South Island, Lake Manapouri, spurred a massive public protest and a change in public attitudes that eventually ended the logging of native forests. There were also changes to the family. In the early 1950s there was a remarkably low number of married women in the paid workforce. In the 1960s the average number of children born to adult women dropped, and married women took up jobs. A highly visible feminist movement campaigned for equal pay and reproductive rights. Identity politics extended to gay people, and in 1986 homosexual acts by consenting adult males were decriminalized. In 2004 women held the three top positions in the country, Governor-General, Prime Minister, and Chief Justice, and a civil union bill was passed that gave state recognition to long-term gay relationships.

RACE AND CULTURE

There were also dramatic changes in racial ideas. The early 1970s saw a Maori protest movement expressed most visibly by a land march from the far north to Wellington and by annual protests on 6 February, the day set aside to commemorate the signing of the Treaty of Waitangi between the Crown and Maori in 1840. The result was the establishment of a Waitangi Tribunal in 1975 to hear breaches of the treaty and a major renaissance in Maori culture and language. By 2004 the Maori population was over half a million strong, and there were flourishing schools, preschools, and three *whare wananga* (tertiary institutions) that used the Maori language. In addition, young New Zealanders began to campaign against sporting contacts with apartheid South Africa. In 1975 Robert Muldoon was elected Prime Minister as the voice of "the ordinary bloke." He promised not to interfere in sport. International embarrassment followed when African countries boycotted the 1976 Montreal Olympics because of New Zealand's participation. When a South African rugby team visited in 1981, there was violence in the streets—but no deaths—as New Zealander fought New Zealander over the issue.

A new consciousness about race led to changes in immigration laws. From the late 1960s on there had been a steady migration of Pacific Islanders into New Zealand. Then in 1974 the free entry of people from the United Kingdom was halted, and criteria for admission were changed to qualifications, not race. The result, starting in the mid-1980s, was a steady increase in migrants from nontraditional countries—especially Asia, Africa, and the Middle East. By 2001 only 70 percent of the New Zealand population was exclusively European in ethnicity, and the population of both the Asian and Pacific Island communities was approaching a quarter of a million in a total population of four million.

Many of these changes in attitude followed the emergence of an urban culture. As more people migrated to the cities, into Auckland in particular, and as specialized urban jobs proliferated, a growing university-educated middle class appeared. In the 1950s immigrants arriving from England commented that New Zealand cities seemed "closed" on the weekends. By the turn of the century, however, with liberal licensing and shopping laws in place, there was a lively urban culture—of galleries, eating places, museums, plays. New Zealanders now read books written and published by their fellow countrymen and women, and there was a strong interest in local history. The past was no longer a foreign country. New Zealand was known as much for its filmmakers—especially the Oscar-winning Peter Jackson—as for its sporting successes.

ECONOMIC CHANGE

Cultural changes came against a backdrop of major economic transformations. In 1967 wool prices fell, six years later Great Britain entered the European Economic Community (EEC), and the terms of trade shifted strongly against New Zealand. The country could no longer rest easy as Britain's offshore farm. Unemployment rose along with inflation. Robert Muldoon followed the old prescriptions of state control of prices and subsidies to export industries, and his government sponsored "Think Big" energy projects. It did not work. The Labour Government elected in 1984 proceeded to effect an economic revolution called "Rogernomics" after the Minister of Finance, Roger Douglas. The dollar was floated; state enterprises were sold off. Subsidies and protective tariffs were removed. For a time unemployment continued to rise. Resources and trade were steadily redirected. By the turn of the century the old agricultural standbys, wool, butter, and cheese, which in 1965 earned half the country's exports by value, each constituted under 4 percent. Now New Zealanders were exporting kiwifruit, high-class wines, forestry products, and fish. The largest earner of foreign exchange was tourism. The direction of trade had moved. The United Kingdom now took under 5 percent of the exports, below the levels taken by Australia, the United States, Japan, and China.

The revolution in New Zealand values and behavior that occurred in the thirty years after 1970 was at times painful. There was much anger. New Zealanders found it difficult to live in a more diverse society. In 1993 the first-past-the-post system of government was replaced by a proportional system; this was in part an act of anger against politicians who had moved too far too fast. Yet by the turn of the twenty-first century, the country was reaching toward an independent Pacific identity with a distinct and creative culture. With "God defend New Zealand" sung in both English and Maori at public ceremonies instead of "God Save the Queen," with the Governors-General being local figures and not pensioned British aristocrats, with appeals to the Privy Council abolished and discussions ongoing about removing the Union Jack from the flag, "better Britain" was far in the past. *Aotearoa* (the Maori name for the country) was fast approaching.

See also **Australia; British Empire; British Empire, End of; United Kingdom.**

BIBLIOGRAPHY

Belich, James. *Paradise Reforged: A History of the New Zealanders from the 1880s to the Year 2000.* Auckland, 2001. A highly original interpretation of New Zealand in the twentieth century.

King, Michael. *Te Puea: A Biography.* Auckland, 1977. A fine biography of a major Maori leader.

———. *The Penguin History of New Zealand.* Auckland, 2003. Strong on Maori history in the twentieth century.

Phillips, Jock. *A Man's Country? The Image of the Pakeha Male: A History.* Auckland, 1987. A study of the important role that male mythology has played in New Zealand identity.

Sinclair, Keith. *Walter Nash.* Auckland, 1977. A comprehensive biography of a major figure in the Labour Government of 1935–1949.

JOCK PHILLIPS

NICE TREATY. The fall of the Berlin Wall at the end of 1989, together with the prospect of greatly enlarging the European Union (EU) to the east, led to a series of additions to the treaties that had founded the European Communities. The deeper goal of integrating European nations remained constant, yet reform of the various existing institutions proved problematic. While a consensual view held to the necessity of seriously modifying the decision-making process, divergence of national interests and visions continually postponed anticipated reforms. Successive accords—the Maastricht Treaty in 1991, the Amsterdam Treaty in 1997, and the Nice Treaty in 2000—all confirmed the failure of the proposed reforms while announcing the need for further revision.

The Intergovernmental Conference (IGC) that brought into being the Nice Treaty had as its almost exclusive goal postponing implementation of the 1997 Treaty of Amsterdam, which, in a "protocol on the institutions with the prospect of enlargement of the European Union" had announced plans to call for "a comprehensive review of the provisions of the treaties on the composition and functioning of the institutions." Consequently, at the opening of negotiations to discuss the prospects of membership for an initial group of countries in central and Western Europe, the Helsinki European Council Summit of 10–11 December 1999 had convened an IGC to review treaties on four key issues: size and composition of the European Commission, the weighting of votes in the Council, extending the use of voting by qualified majority, and reform of the rules governing enhanced cooperation.

DIFFICULT NEGOTIATIONS IN A TENSE ATMOSPHERE
Negotiations began on 14 February 2000 with a special effort at transparency and openness, in response to sharp criticisms after previous meetings of the IGC. They were to be relatively short, lasting under ten months, thanks to a specific agenda and familiarity with the institutional issues and the much-discussed intention of enlarging the union. But transparency and celerity concealed a less flattering reality. After some three hundred hours, negotiators could not agree on the principal items on the agenda. Most of the decisions were taken during the summit of the Nice European Council, the longest in its history, 7–11 December 2000. In addition, the treaty provided for a new IGC in 2004, to be charged with resolving the remaining unanswered questions, which included apportioning jurisdiction between the European Union and the individual nations, the status of the Charter of Fundamental Rights, simplification of treaties, and the role of national parliaments.

The negotiators' problems may be explained in great part by the nature of their mandate. Unlike their predecessors, they were not content to merely apply numbers to the decision-making process, or to modify the institutional balance. They debated the place of member states in the different institutions of the EU and for the first time had to modify the balance of power initially ratified by the Treaty of Rome in 1957. Negotiators were thus led to openly defend the positions of their home countries. In addition, the debate did not benefit, as previously, from pairs of allied states—indeed, France and Germany seemed like a married couple on the verge of divorce—nor from the skill of the successive presidents of the European Union. Overall, negotiations for the Nice Treaty were dominated by anguish vis-à-vis the enlargement of the EU and also by the negotiators' determination to "limit the damage" to their own nations.

MINIMAL REFORM OF INSTITUTIONS

According to the protocol on institutions annexed to the Treaty of Amsterdam, the Nice Treaty was to handle essentially institutional reforms. However, these reforms failed to fulfill the goals set for them.

Modification of the balance of power in the Council for adopting decisions by a qualified majority was the first objective. The voting system ratified by the Treaty of Rome in 1957 depended on elaborate calculations to set the number by which a blocking minority could succeed in voting down proposals and also on a subtle balance among "small," "medium," and "large" member states. This method was proportionately recalculated each time the EU was enlarged. With the prospect of numerous new countries, however, it became clear that this method would no longer be practical.

In consequence, negotiators first considered a system that required a double majority of both member states and populations, proposed by the commission. But deep disagreements returned the discussion to options closer to the existing system; in any event, the principle of a simple majority of member states was retained. Fiery debates took place around the importance of using demographic criteria in weighting votes. Agreement was reached only at the cost of great complexity that did not square with the idea of a clear mechanism for apportioning votes, and which included all sorts of compensations. The question of a threshold for the qualified majority—earlier fixed at 71 percent of the votes—also provoked angry discussion. One protocol planned to increase the threshold figure to 72.3 percent in a union of twenty-five members, then to 73.9 percent in a union with twenty-seven member states. In addition, representatives of the larger states obtained a "demographic net" by which a member state can request that the qualified majority represent at least 62 percent of the union's population.

The second objective of the IGC was to limit the size of the European Commission. Various propositions were presented, from a drastic reduction in the number of commissioners to retention of the status quo. Because of persistent disagreement, revision was minimal. The Nice Treaty planned that, beginning 1 January 2005, each member state would have only one representative on the European Commission (EC), the five larger states losing their second representative. The treaty also provided that when the number of member states reached twenty-seven the number of commissioners would be inferior to the number of member states, but it did not specify how such a change might be implemented.

Although the composition of the European Parliament was not on the IGC's agenda, a new arrangement had to be considered in view of the coming enlargement of the EU, but the process had to be purely technical. During the summit at Nice, however, the French presidency decided to extend the negotiations to the European Parliament in order to reach an agreement on national voting weights on the Council of the EU. The upshot did not reflect any kind of objective rule but only obscure transactions; some states—notably Greece, Portugal, and Belgium—obtained a number of votes superior to other more populous candidate states. Finally, the number of seats in the European Parliament, with 25 members, came to 732 in spite of the Treaty of Amsterdam's limit of 700. According to the membership treaty for new member states, institutional reforms to apply 1 January 2005, including the composition of the Commission and the rules concerning qualified majority vote, were officially put into force 1 November 2004.

Other reforms on the agenda were less problematic and less criticized. The Nice Treaty clearly facilitated recourse to rules of enhanced cooperation as established by the Treaty of Amsterdam. This would enable member countries seeking greater integration in specific areas but meeting resistance on the part of other members, to cooperate more narrowly within the framework of the Union. The Nice Treaty reduced to eight the required number of states that must be willing to cooperate and suppressed the veto power of the other member states, while increasing the number of areas concerned.

Negotiators also had to examine the possibility of extending the use of the qualified majority vote. The treaty extended it to about thirty new provisions; the progress was perceptible, but the list was heterogeneous and excluded important policies such as taxation, social policy, right of political asylum and immigration, and economic and social cohesion. The treaty also addressed reforms concerning issues not initially on the agenda, such as modifying the appointments procedure for the president of the European Commission and reinforcing his or her authority and leadership. The treaty also increased the power of the European Parliament, notably by extending the procedure of co-decision, and it also changed the sharing of jurisdiction between the Court of Justice and the Court of First Instance while allowing the creation of specialized judicial panels. Finally, it reinforced the defense and security policy.

A TREATY ABOUT TRANSITION?

Although it facilitated enlargement of the European Union, the Treaty of Nice was from the very beginning considered a preamble to more significant reform. The "Declaration on the Future of the Union," an appendix to the treaty, provided for a new ICG, to convene in 2004, that would seek solutions to a variety of outstanding issues. These included delimitation of power-sharing between the EU and member states, the status of the Charter of Fundamental Rights, simplification of the treaties, and the role of national parliaments in the wider European context. Specialists in European integration, journalists, and representatives of the institutions concerned—the European Commission and European Parliament, first among many—openly criticized the treaty's lack of breadth and particularly its inability to ensure adequate institutional functioning once the enlargement took place. Critics denounced in particular the reinforcement of interstate logic in the composition of the Commission and the European Parliament. They also deplored the negotiators' failure to provide the EU with a political system that was more efficient, democratic, and open.

The IGC in 2000 and the European Council of Nice symbolized the lack of direction and the crisis of European integration. The absence of clear objectives, narrow defense of national interests, and negotiators' inability to simplify the decision-making process were only several of many problems. There was also the tendency to put off

numerous decisions, sharp exchanges, and resurgence of old conflicts between nations, and organized media leaks, among other issues. The limited results of the IGC meeting in 2000, together with the deep divisions provoked there and in the open, had at least the virtue of persuading the representatives of member states to consider a revision of the revision process itself in order to draft a more ambitious text—indeed, a European constitution. These failures, far more than the numerous interventions on the part of the European Parliament or the federalist movements, prodded the national leaders to convene a "Convention on the Future of Europe" the task of which was to enable the constitutional debate to break out of its strictly intergovernmental framework. By 2006 the outcome was by no means clear.

See also **European Commission; European Constitution 2004–2005; European Parliament; European Union; Maastricht, Treaty of.**

BIBLIOGRAPHY

Dashwood, Alan. "The Constitution of the European Union after Nice: Law-Making Procedures." *European Law Review* 26 (2001): 215–238.

Galloway, David. *The Treaty of Nice and Beyond: Realities and Illusions of Power in the EU.* Sheffield, U.K., 2001.

Melissas, Dimitris. *Perspectives of the Nice Treaty and the Intergovernmental Conference in 2004: Center of European Constitutional Law, Athens 2001.* Baden-Baden, Germany, 2002.

Muñoz, Rodolphe, and Catherine Turner. "Revising the Judicial Architecture of the European Union." *Yearbook of European Law* 19 (2000): 1–93.

Pescatore, Pierre. "Nice—Aftermath." *Common Market Law Review* 38 (2001): 265–271.

Shaw, Jo. "The Treaty of Nice: Legal and Constitutional Implications." *European Public Law* 7 (2001): 195–215.

OLIVIER COSTA

NICHOLAS II (1868–1918), Russian tsar and emperor.

Contemporaries and historians alike have viewed the last tsar in divergent terms, ranging from the autocratic and repressive "Nicholas the Bloody" to a deeply religious figure whose life ended in tragic martyrdom. Many have blamed Nicholas II for the 1917 revolution and all that it produced for the world, pointing to his refusal to allow serious political and social reform. Others have dwelled on his inadequacy: a weak and witless ruler, more concerned with his family, and especially his hemophiliac son and heir, than with the fate of his nation and empire. He was ill-equipped, it is said, to guide Russia into the twentieth century.

Research since the 1990s has created a more nuanced picture of a ruler guided by strong principles and values. He valued order and discipline in his personal life and in his expectations of others. Not surprisingly, he loved all things associated with the military, which he admired not only as an important institution in Russian life but as a model for an ideal society and polity. Family love and family order were also values in his own life and a virtuous model for the larger society and polity. At the center of this moral vision stood religion. Nicholas found personal comfort in faith, which gave him what contemporaries described as "serenity." Some saw this as a flaw—a fatalistic certainty that, as Nicholas often said, everything that happened in the world was precisely God's will.

All of this, along with the Russian political history he loved to study, helped shape his philosophy of rule, which directly influenced his decisions during the period from 1914 to 1917. He shared conservative doubts that human reason can improve the world, for human beings are morally weak creatures. What is needed are order and guidance imposed by divinely inspired authority. Nicholas saw his own role as autocrat as blessed and inspired. A guiding ideal was that of the "tsar-father" (*tsar-batyushka*) linked to his subjects not through institutions of representation and law but by an almost mystical bond of love and devotion. Connected to this faith was an abiding distrust of intellectuals, with their false rationalism and foreign ideas, and of Jews, who were alien to the "true Russian" folk and thus a danger to the sacred bond between tsar and people.

When war broke out in August 1914, Nicholas appeared on the balcony of the Winter Palace and wept as the people crowding the square fell to their knees and sang "God Save the Tsar." A year later, faced with a disastrous situation at the front and certain that his personal presence would rally the

troops, he took command of the army (against the advice of his closest advisors but encouraged by an "interior voice" heard while standing in church before an icon of Christ). This decision associated him more closely with the failing war effort and isolated him from the capital and the affairs of the government, leaving, it was often said, the state in the hands of the German-born empress Alexandra and the scandalous religious healer and prophet Grigory Yefimovich Rasputin. Ministers were continually replaced. Most important, Nicholas's government showed open contempt for the elected legislature (Duma), which sought to play a larger role in the national emergency. Every proposal to create a government that would work more closely with representative civic institutions was rejected by a monarch convinced that only pure sacred autocracy could save Russia. This political stalemate, an ineffective war effort, and an economy on the verge of breakdown combined with distrust of Alexandra and disgust with Rasputin, steadily undermined the authority of Nicholas's rule.

When strikes and demonstrations for bread, peace, and a responsible government brought the capital to a standstill in late February 1917, Nicholas ordered the commander of the garrison to "stop the disorders," which resulted in a mutiny. Military commanders and prominent politicians persuaded the tsar, for the sake of order and the war effort, to abdicate on 2 March (15 March, New Style) in favor of his brother Mikhail, who refused the throne. In early March the new Provisional Government placed Nicholas and his family under house arrest at a palace outside Petrograd. In August 1917 the Romanovs were evacuated to Tobolsk in the Urals, allegedly to protect them from the rising tide of revolution. After the Bolsheviks came to power in October 1917, the conditions of their imprisonment grew stricter and talk of putting Nicholas on trial grew more frequent. As the counterrevolutionary White movement gathered force, leading to full-scale civil war by the summer, the Romanovs were moved, during April and May 1918, to Yekaterinburg, a militant Bolshevik stronghold. During the night of 16–17 July, Nicholas, Alexandra, their children, their physician, and three servants were taken into the basement and executed. Whether this was on direct orders from Vladimir Lenin in Moscow (as many believe, though there is no hard evidence), or an option approved in Moscow should White troops approach Yekaterinburg, or at the initiative of local Bolsheviks remains in dispute, as does whether the order (if there was an order) was for the execution of Nicholas alone or the entire family. In 1998 their remains, long hidden in a mine shaft, were brought to St. Petersburg and interred in the church where other Russian emperors lie. In August 2000 the Orthodox Church in Russia canonized Nicholas and his family and servants as martyrs.

See also **Rasputin, Grigory; Russia; Russian Revolutions of 1917.**

BIBLIOGRAPHY

Primary Sources

Nicholas II, emperor of Russia. *The Complete Wartime Correspondence of Tsar Nicholas II and the Empress Alexandra, April 1914–March 1917.* Edited by Joseph T. Fuhrmann. Westport, Conn., and London, 1999.

Secondary Sources

Lieven, Dominic. *Nicholas II: Emperor of All the Russias.* London, 1993.

Steinberg, Mark D., and Vladimir M. Khrustalev. *Fall of the Romanovs: Political Dreams and Personal Struggles in a Time of Revolution.* New Haven, Conn., 1995.

MARK D. STEINBERG

1968. The year 1968 constitutes a milestone in European history. It would be more precise to speak of "the years of 1968" because the events of that year have been expressed in so many different ways and given rise to so many interpretations. In terms of ruptures in the social, cultural, and political fields (the emergence of new players and sociopolitical hopes, new relations to knowledge, and so on) 1968 was diverse. But it was also unified and more than its premature diagnosis as a "cultural crisis"; it was a movement supported by an intellectual discourse and carried out by young people who had become historical actors on a global level. The continued resonance of 1968 in the collective imagination highlights the exceptional character of that year.

THE EVENTS OF 1968

Attempts to explain the origins of 1968 have ranged from those that argue that the protests of 1968 were the genuine and inevitable result of the international transformations of the 1960s to others that treat the events as an unexpected thunderclap in a clear European sky. What did the diverse protest movements have in common? What were the national specifics of each?

The origins of 1968 also could be traced back to a university system ill equipped to handle the arrival of the baby-boom generation, along with the democratization of education and improvements in living standards (in France, there were 128,000 students in 1950 and 500,000 in 1968). Moreover, the social status of the students had changed: the majority of students no longer came from the upper classes but from the middle classes, and their parents could not afford to support them if they failed. European society, especially in the west, finally had to take into account changes that had taken place over two decades—such as an unprecedented prosperity that was now founded upon consumerism and the development of the service sector—and the kind of knowledge offered at the universities became a key to personal and social success. In fact, students, especially those who specialized in certain new, rapidly developing fields of study (such as the human sciences) without being assured of jobs, felt threatened by societal decline. Another factor was the war in Vietnam (1954–1975), the first conflict of which images were widely disseminated. During the Cold War, to defend the Vietnamese people or to support Fidel Castro in Cuba, Mao's Chinese Cultural Revolution, or Che Guevara's guerrilla activities was to reject American "imperialism." Awareness of the contrast between wealthy societies and the exploited third world became the motivation that allowed a university uprising to be transformed into a protest against capitalist society.

The protests in each European nation were also unique to that nation's history. In the Federal Republic of Germany at the end of the 1960s, tensions between young and old were exacerbated by the presence of American troops and the postwar generation's questioning of their parents' generation of wartime "perpetrators" (*Täter*). The trigger for unrest was the adoption of a plan, proposed in 1966 and hatched by the Grand Coalition

A poster of Mao Zedong hangs in the courtyard of the Sorbonne, Paris, May 1968.
©BETTMANN/CORBIS

between the Social Democrats (SDP) and the Christian Democratic Union (CDU), for special legislation allowing civil rights to be limited in a state of emergency. This legislation was required by the Western Allies in order to guarantee the safety of their troops stationed in Germany. The extraparliamentary opposition met in the German Socialist Student Union (SDS), a youth movement of dissidents from the SDP. The earliest protests took place in Frankfurt and at the Freie Universität in Berlin, which became the focal point for protests in 1967. Having a head start on movements in neighboring countries, West German protests culminated on 11 May 1968 with a giant demonstration in Bonn.

In France, the increasing politicization of students after the Algerian War (1954–1962), the influential role of their unions (the National Union of French Students), and the excessive personalization of government by an aging Charles de Gaulle (1890–1970) led to protests that expanded in concentric circles. First France faced a university crisis with massive student protests (the events of May 1968), then a social crisis with eight million on strike, and finally a political crisis that irrevocably shook the foundations of "your father's France."

The protests in Italy had similar causes, but they differed in the duration of the student uprisings, which began in Trento in 1966 and spread widely through several university centers (Pisa, Milan, Turin, Rome), continuing throughout 1968 and after ("the creeping May").

In some cases, the national context overshadowed international influences. Such was the case in

Spain where continuing student opposition to Francisco Franco's government merged with the workers' movement. But this was also the case with the Czech and Polish movements, where the watchword at every social level was the democratization of the countries' communist regimes. The demands of the Czech students were aligned with the hope for a "socialism with a human face"—the aim of the Communist Party under Alexander Dubček. Thus the students did not resort to violence because those in power seemed to them to be allies, at least during the three phases of the "Prague Spring," which lasted from the resignation of the all-powerful Antonin Novotny from the post of first secretary of the party in January 1968 to the invasion of the Soviets on 20–21 August.

However much these movements may have been determined by their particular national logics, they were nonetheless in resonance with one another. Demonstrations ranged from those supporting the African American fight for civil rights in the United States to those against the assassination attempt on the German student leader Rudi Dutschke. Thus Daniel Cohn-Bendit was able to declare retrospectively that the generation of baby boomers was "the first to live globally, across a tide of sounds and images, both physically and every day" (Cohn-Bendit, p. 10; translated from the French).

In spite of the clearly intellectual origins and orientation of these movements, intellectuals participated less on the scene than as points of reference. It could even be said that in 1968 intellectuals ceased to take on the role of "spiritual advisors." Of course, the student movement was inspired by Karl Marx and Sigmund Freud, Jürgen Habermas and the Frankfurt School, but often only in order to critique them and even to reject them. Country by country, there were different engagements: Jean-Paul Sartre was with the students; André Malraux and Raymond Aron were advisors or spokespersons for the government. Perhaps only Herbert Marcuse remained continuously "present" with his critique of alienation in capitalist society and in the Soviet regime. Intellectuals also exerted a mobilizing influence in Eastern Europe, but the figures there—such as Ludvik Vaculik, Milan Kundera, or Radovan Richta in Czechoslovakia—were more national.

In each country, the attitude of the workers' movements had a great influence on the way in which the protests developed for the students and intellectuals. The radicalization of their struggles since the mid-1960s and the influence of "leftist" movements gave the workers' demands a particular character: they were now situated outside the framework of the traditional union system, and they mixed old demands (for cost-of-living raises, for good working conditions) with new ones (against the underemployment of licensed professionals, for a less hierarchical model of management including self-management). The strikes mobilized new categories of workers who were younger, better trained, and not necessarily under the control of the unions. However, true engagements between students and workers never really came off, except in France and Italy. In France, student and worker movements came together in May 1968. But the attitude of the French Communist Party and the workers' union, mistrustful of the "*gauchiste* adventure" and anxious to maintain their monopoly on protest, was an obstacle to any real merger between students and workers. In Italy, however, the Communist Party and the union, less oriented toward the workers and more active in social causes, as well as a leftist faction outside of the traditional trade unions all favored the formation of a more durable alliance. In Czechoslovakia, it was the intervention of the Warsaw Pact forces that transformed the movement for democratization into a shared symbol of national independence. In 1968 the absence of a transformation of this apparent convergence into a true unification of the different protest movements revealed the new role of the working classes in wealthy societies: by refusing the "children of consumer culture" the right to threaten their dearly bought social integration, the working class ceased to be a historical agent for revolution and became instead a conservative social force. In this way, in the words of Habermas, "for the first time in the history of West Germany, students played a political role that had to be taken seriously."

RUPTURES AND TRANSFORMATIONS OF 1968
Alongside the traditional critique of systems of power and references to the revolutionary tradition of the workers movement, three new characteristics defined the movements of 1968.

Policemen charge student antiwar protestors, Rome, April 1968. ©BETTMANN/CORBIS

First was the "emergence of a new political repertoire." This essentially involved the radical critique of industrial democratic societies; the questioning of the traditional wielders of authority (fathers, teachers, and bosses); an extension of a Marxist-Leninist reading to the struggle between the classes on a global scale, transforming it into a struggle between the "proletarian" third world and the "imperialist" nations; and the rejection of the repressive bureaucratic regimes of the Eastern bloc. The values that were extolled were self-management, direct democracy, and the spontaneous dimension of collective action, all of which recalled the keywords of the Situationist International of the years 1957–1972. For that movement, society was the locus of individual alienation, where reified individuals are reduced to the role of puppets in their respective social groups. This new repertoire

was put into action in public statements, violent confrontations (occupations, riots approaching guerrilla warfare, barricades), but also in the liberation of transgressive speech ("Don't say, 'Professor, may I?'; say 'pig,' 'bitch'"; "under the pavement lies the beach"). Henceforth, the city and urban life became the primary scene for protests, with increasingly larger gatherings and the involvement of suburban areas.

Second was a "mistrust of the delegation of power" that was founded upon the rejection of status of a designated leader and upon the students' simple differentiation between leadership groups and the "base." Paradoxically, the fact that suppression and the media were more powerful than the tactics of collective action (publication of pamphlets, the ability to speak in public, familiarity with ideological discourses) led to the emergence of spokespersons: Rudi Dutschke for the SDS, and his subsequent radicalization of the movement ("Rudi the Red"), and the French-German student Daniel Cohn-Bendit, "Dany."

Third was the predominance of the extreme Left. Within the various student movements, there were anarchists (the black flag appeared at demonstrations, and there was an exaltation of spontaneity, and a call for the formation of communes); the Trotskyites, who were firmly entrenched in the student movements and repeatedly took up a discussion of the "bureaucratic degeneracy of the communist parties" and of Stalinism; the influence of Maoism and its anti-imperialist discourse, which greatly profited from positive perceptions of the cultural revolution as an alternative to the Soviet model that could be imported into the industrialist nations of Europe.

In the midst of all these frequently contradictory forces, there developed a new, strongly libertarian political sensibility. It was reflected in academia (the rejection of lecture courses and stuffy professors), in the liberalization of morals (critique of "sexual normality," the widespread consumption of drugs), in social relations (devaluing of the "bourgeois couple," the formation of communes), and in the status of women (equality in the workplace, and the feminist movement).

The year 1968 was also a time of tremendous cultural renewal, even if the connections between the protest movements and new forms of artistic expression were not always obvious. The counterculture, imported from the United States, nevertheless forged connections between marginality and protest, and between cultural and political protest, by which it combated the official culture, which was imposed by the dominant class through various means (political, sexual, spiritual, or fashionable) in order to reinforce the social order for its own profit. Thus starting in 1967, the Anti-University in London and the Critical University in Berlin proposed teaching of a political nature on such subjects as Cuba or the revolution and on other "underground" subjects (such as the organization of alternative structures and improvisation). The United Kingdom, the Netherlands with their "Provos" (a nonviolent anarchist movement that dissolved in 1967 after two years, but whose

influence was felt in France and Germany, notably through their proposals for alternative social and ecological projects), and Germany, with the experiments of the Kommune I and Kommune II, were the principal sites of the counterculture.

In France, Italy, and Spain, however, the students encountered only the fringes of the counterculture and then only as an effect, rather than a cause, of the events of 1968. Yet this does not mean that a cultural dimension to those events was totally lacking in these countries: the France of 1968 saw the occupation of the Odeon Theatre in Paris and the creation of revolutionary committees for cultural agitation and for new forms of art for the purpose of "transmitting culture to the people." Thus there coexisted mechanisms for alternative cultural productions (such as "happenings") and the phenomena of standardization through the diffusion of an "underground" culture, primarily musical (pop music, Bob Dylan's protest songs, or those of the less controversial Beatles).

In the Eastern bloc countries that were mobilized, the window of opportunity for freedom was too quickly closed and that prevented the emergence of an enduring artistic movement outside of the pockets of resistance. Even so, they did experience an unprecedented intellectual ferment, especially in Czechoslovakia, which saw the resumption of the literary magazine *Literani Listy*. In June 1968, this magazine published "Two thousand words addressed to workers, farmers, scientists, artists, and to everyone," a manifesto calling for liberalization, written by the playwright Václav Havel and designed by the artist Jaroslav Vozniak.

This cultural emergence was accompanied by a general critique of the media, both official (for example, television, the symbol of consumer society) and traditional (the press). Confronted with media that were largely hostile to them and that organized disinformation campaigns (inspiring the slogan, "The police speak to you every night at 8:00" in reference to French television), the protesters of 1968 attempted to set up their own information networks including meetings and general assemblies, publication of journals (such as *The Student*, published in Czechoslovakia starting in 1966), massive distribution of pamphlets and posters such as those from the Beaux-Arts workshop that incorporated graffiti and invited public debate.

In contrast, the events of May benefited from sympathetic coverage from private radio stations that broadcast information directly.

THE AFTERMATH OF 1968

The year 1968 affected countries differently according to the reaction of the authorities in place and the degrees of acculturation between the demands of the protesters and the aspirations of their societies as a whole.

The immediate effects In France, the victories were important. The universities were reformed according to principles of self-administration, inter-disciplinarity, and participation (the Faure law). Workers' salaries were adjusted in accordance with the Grenelle accords. There was also an expansion of the rights of trade unions. Despite the overwhelming victory of the Gaullists in the legislative elections of June 1968, the force of May 1968 dealt a mortal blow to the authority of the president of the republic, who resigned after the failure of a referendum in 1969. Without a doubt, given the attitude of the French Communist Party, these events led to a recalibration of influence within the Left to the advantage of the Socialist Party, which was able to harness hopes for social change with the candidacy of François Mitterrand and the joint platform in 1974.

In Italy, even though the links between the two phenomena were not direct, the events of 1968 degenerated into acts of extreme right-wing terrorism in 1969. The extreme Left responded with terrorist violence that they justified as a struggle against fascism. Thus the 1970s were marked by the kidnappings of several business and political leaders, by the emergence of the Red Brigades, and by their attacks on Rome and Milan. But the Italians also gained, after a referendum in 1974, the right to divorce and subsequently the right to have abortions. In addition, more familiar forms of speech in public—deriving from the protesters' feelings of comradeship—reflected a more general liberalization of Italian society.

The same evolution occurred in Germany. The immediate aftermath of 1968 witnessed the emergence of far-left terrorism but, again, with no clear relation to the protest movements. The Red Army Faction (the Baader-Meinhof Gang) committed a series of attacks against banking establishments and

Two men run from the wreckage of a burning car in the streets of Prague, 26 August 1968. ©KPA/ZUMA/CORBIS

American bases. But these troubled years also saw the emergence of alternative groups, such as the Greens, as well as open discussion of Germany's Nazi past. This time period also paved the way for the Social Democratic Party to come to power. Gustav Heinemann was elected president of West Germany in March of 1969, and a coalition government was led for the first time by a member of the SPD, Willy Brandt.

In nondemocratic countries, the positive effects of 1968 are more difficult to assess, as they did not attain expression as clearly within repressive societies. In fact, attempts to disrupt these regimes had only reinforced their control over society. After Russian tanks rolled into Czechoslovakia, followed by 250,000 troops, the government of Dubček was forced to accept the Moscow Protocols. This signified the "normalization" before the purges of 1969 forcibly smothered even the smallest hope for reform. In Spain, Franco declared a state of emergency in 1969 and arrested many of the protesters.

The legacy of 1968 The crucial year of 1968 is perceived differently in different countries. But for Europe as a whole, it is now viewed less as a founding event than as a revelation of the discrepancy between systems of authority inherited from the nineteenth century and the growth of a modern Europe. It seems to have acted as a catalyst for the emergence of new behaviors and a heightening of consciousness and as an accelerator for developments whose legacy and "spirit" are still felt today.

Despite its spectacular and explosive aspects, 1968 was not a revolution and perhaps not even a social uprising. But it is difficult not to see it at least as a social restructuring that historians must account for. As evidence, there is the emergence and even the acceptance of "youth" as a specific, though somewhat elastic, category, but also the plainly visible dynamics of the generations. For there was not just one but several generations of 1968: those born between 1940 and 1945 provided a number of the leaders of the protest movements; the rock-and-roll generation were the ones who marched in the streets; and the subsequent generation came to political consciousness in a world shaped by the events of 1968. Such a lineage would explain in part an ongoing nostalgia for 1968 that endures to this day (as symbolized by the election of Václav Havel as president of the Czech Republic in 1989).

At the level of restructuring, 1968 can be understood, a bit paradoxically, as an important step both in the process of modernization and in the march toward an exaggerated individualism—unless one sees in it, as some do, the last spasm of a twentieth century in complete disarray searching for solutions in the utopian visions of the nineteenth.

See also **May 1968; Prague Spring; Situationism; Student Movements.**

BIBLIOGRAPHY

Primary Sources

Cohn-Bendit, Daniel. *Nous l'avons tant aimée, la révolution*. Paris, 1986.

Dubcek, Alexander, with Andras Sugar. *Dubcek Speaks*. London and New York, 1990.

Marcuse, Herbert. *Eros and Civilization: A Philosophical Inquiry into Freud*. Boston, 1955.

———. *One Dimensional Man: Studies in the Ideology of Advanced Industrial Society*. Boston, 1964.

Morin, Edgar, Claude Lefort, and Jean-Marc Coudray. *Mai 68: la brèche*. Paris, 1968.

Secondary Sources

Caute, David. *The Year of the Barricades: A Journey through 1968*. New York: Harper and Row, 1988.

Fink, Carole, Philipp Gassert, and Detlef Junker. *1968: The World Transformed*. Cambridge, U.K., and New York, 1998.

Fraser, Ronald. *1968: A Student Generation in Revolt*. London, 1988.

Katsiaficas, George N. *The Imagination of the New Left: A Global Analysis of 1968*. Boston, 1987.

Kurlansky, Mark. *1968: The Year that Rocked the World*. New York, 2005.

FABIEN THÉOFILAKIS

1989. Despite having suffered terrible human and material devastation, the Soviet Union emerged from World War II as a victorious superpower, widely respected throughout the world. Paranoid by nature and mistrustful of the intentions of his wartime allies, Joseph Stalin began building a security buffer zone along the western borders of the country. As mutual suspicions and misunderstandings generated ever increasing hostility between the West and the Soviet Union, the countries of Central and Eastern Europe, just liberated from Nazi rule by the Red Army, were sovietized. Between 1945 and 1948, Poland, Czechoslovakia, Hungary, a newly created German Democratic Republic, Romania, Bulgaria, Yugoslavia, and Albania became parts of a Soviet bloc, introducing one-party, nonparliamentary political regimes and nonmarket, centrally planned economic systems on the Soviet model. In 1949 and 1955 the Council of Mutual Economic Aid and the Warsaw Pact, respectively, forged a Soviet-run economic and military alliance.

Several countries soon revolted against Soviet domination. Yugoslavia, under the leadership of President Josip Broz Tito, took an independent line and split with Stalin in 1948. Both Poland and Hungary revolted in October 1956; the

Hungarian Revolution became a war of independence against the Soviet superpower and was mercilessly crushed. In 1968 the reformist communist leadership in Czechoslovakia attempted to introduce "socialism with a human face," a more democratic variant of socialism, but was crushed as well by military force. After 1956 Poland freed the Catholic Church and stopped collectivizing agriculture, while Hungary, in spite of its military defeat and the bloody reprisals that followed, gradually abolished central planning and introduced a consumer- and market-oriented economic reform process. Poland became a land of permanent resistance, with spontaneous student revolts and workers' uprisings taking place in 1968, 1970, and 1976, leading to the Gdańsk revolt of 1980, which resulted in the foundation of the independent Solidarity movement, formally a union but in reality a political party. These episodes of protest deeply undermined the stability of the regimes and damaged what legitimacy they had achieved. The Stalinist restrictions that turned these countries into closed societies were eroded: both Poland and Hungary achieved certain "small" freedoms, freedom of travel fostered the spread of information, and opposition emerged.

ECONOMIC CRISIS AFTER 1973

The oil crises of 1973 and 1980 increased oil prices tenfold and signaled the transformation of the world economy. A new economic phenomenon, "stagflation," which combined stagnation and inflation, put an end to postwar prosperity. Unemployment hit even the advanced countries and shattered the less developed "peripheral" economies, including those of Central and Eastern Europe. The previously rapid economic growth of 3.9 percent per annum slowed down in the Soviet bloc to 1.9 percent, but soon Poland even experienced a decline of 1 percent, while Yugoslavia's economy shrank by 10 percent. Inflation became uncontrollable and manifested itself in these two countries as a hyperinflation of several hundred percent, reaching 1,000 percent per year, destroying economic stability. Export prices declined much faster and more steeply than import prices and generated a 30 percent increase in the trade deficit of state-socialist countries, such that they had to export one-third more goods for the same amount of imports. The economic benefits provided by the state-socialist regimes—

rapid growth, full employment, a slowly increasing standard of living—evaporated. The countries of Central and Eastern Europe rapidly accumulated debt amounting to roughly 100 billion dollars. Servicing that debt consumed a huge part of the national income, and repayment became more and more difficult. Yugoslavia, Poland, and Bulgaria soon asked for rescheduling.

The state-socialist countries did not find an exit from the downward spiral. The regimes' elite lost its self-confidence and all hope for a return to normalcy. The population became deeply dissatisfied and demanded change, and the opposition gained ground. The devastating economic crisis generated an unsolvable political crisis: the stage was set for collapse.

COLLAPSE IN POLAND AND HUNGARY

The widespread dissatisfaction of the Polish population led to the Gdańsk workers' uprising on 14 August 1980, with the shipyard electrician Lech Wałęsa at its head. Within a few days, the workers of 156 firms and shipyards participated and were joined by dissident intellectuals. The government sent a delegation and signed an agreement at the end of the month. Solidarity emerged as the authentic representative of the working class, and eventually as a political party. In the space of a few months, three million people joined the movement, and the independent and powerful Catholic Church lent its support. As a result, the monolithic political structures were broken down. Under strong Soviet political pressure and permanent military threat, the Polish Communist Party prepared a military coup. In February 1981 General Wojciech Jaruzelski, minister of defense, was appointed prime minister and, a few months later, secretary general of the Communist Party. On 13 December 1981 the communist-led army took over and proceeded to arrest the entire leadership of Solidarity and put the media, local governments, and industries under military leadership.

From behind the shield of martial law, the Jaruzelski government aimed to introduce radical economic reforms, solve the political and economic crises, and improve the situation of the population. It failed because it lacked popular legitimacy, suffered from a boycott by Western countries, and made severe mistakes. A wage-price spiral generated an inflation of 100 percent in 1982. The visits of the new Polish pope, John Paul II, mobilized millions of Poles and strengthened popular resistance. Strikes paralyzed the country.

In 1985 Mikhail Gorbachev became the head of the Soviet Communist Party and state and initiated his policies of glasnost (transparency) and perestroika (restructuring), aimed at achieving a democratic modernization of the country. He withdrew the Soviet troops from Afghanistan and changed the oppressive policy toward the satellite countries. The Soviet threat, which had been the only source of "legitimization" for the party-military regime of Jaruzelski, disappeared.

The Polish Communist Party looked for a compromise to save the regime: it granted partial and then general amnesties in 1984 and 1986, freed Solidarity leaders, and soon began secret talks. The Communist Party sought to share power in order to preserve some part of it, and the reemerging Solidarity, uncertain about possible Soviet actions, was ready for compromise. On 6 February 1989 roundtable negotiations began, and an agreement was reached by 5 April, stating that partially free elections would be held in June. One-third of the decision-making Sejm, the Polish parliament, and the entire newly established second chamber, the Senate (with one hundred seats), would be elected in free multiparty elections. Two-thirds of the Sejm would remain unchanged. The posts of president, prime minister, and ministers of defense and interior, the key positions in the government, would remain in the hands of the Communist Party. The government believed that it was a "good bargain." Wałęsa, however, pointed out the revolutionary significance of the new system, predicting that "the time of political and social monopoly of one party over the people was coming to an end" (*Radio Free Europe*, 3 March 1989, pp. 3–5).

His prophecy was fulfilled. The Communist Party was unable to gain a single seat from the freely elected parliamentary and senate seats: Solidarity had a landslide victory. President Jaruzelski could not form a government merely by monopolizing key positions. Committed to the democratic process, he at last accepted Solidarity's candidate, the Catholic opposition politician Tadeusz Mazowiecki, who on 24 August 1989 became the first anti-communist prime minister in the entire Soviet bloc

since 1948. A total takeover by Solidarity soon followed, and Wałęsa became the president of Poland. A totally free election in 1991 crowned the transformation.

In parallel with the peaceful Polish revolution, Hungary experienced a radical transformation, although taking a different path to revolution. The point of departure here was the 1956 revolution. In spite of reprisals, Hungary could not return to Soviet-type socialism. The reestablished communist regime had to make concessions to the population. János Kádár, the new party boss and prime minister, gradually turned toward economic reforms, which proved successful. The compulsory delivery system in the agrarian sector was abolished, and in 1968 the New Economic Mechanism was introduced. Compulsory planning was eliminated, and market prices and profit motivation for firms were gradually reintroduced. The shortage economy, so typical in Eastern bloc countries, disappeared, and the regime began to promote a strong consumer orientation, which came to be known as "goulash communism." From 1962 citizens could freely travel to the West. Starting in the early 1980s, private entrepreneurship was introduced by means of a partial privatization of the economy. State-owned companies were sold and rented out to private bidders. During the 1980s 60 percent of services, 33 percent of agricultural output, and 80 percent of construction work was produced by private firms. The share of the private sector in industry remained low, at 15 percent. Commercial banking and a Western type of taxation were also reestablished during the 1980s. Foreign direct investment became possible, and giant multinational companies, among others General Motors and General Electric, established subsidiaries in the country.

During the decades of reform, a great part of Hungarian intellectuals and reformers gradually undermined the regime, stopping short of revolt. Opposition remained relatively limited but had an important moral influence. The engine of transformation, however, came from within the party as a push for "social-democratization." The reformers demanded a radical shift toward the practice and ideology of the Western welfare states, including the pluralization of the political system. Since the aging and overcautious János Kádár was unable to push further, a coup within the party led to an extraordinary party conference in May 1988, which practically eliminated the old party leadership and led to a gradual takeover by the reform wing. Consequently, prior to the roundtable agreement in Poland and without any major turbulence in the streets, the Central Committee of the Hungarian Communist Party decided in February 1989 to hold free multiparty elections within a year. In October 1989 an extraordinary party congress dissolved the party itself, and two parties were established in its wake: the reform wing formed the Hungarian Socialist Party, which boasted a Western-type social democratic program, while another small party kept the old name and the character of a successor party. The reformist socialists (often called reform communists) naturally did not want to step aside; they wanted to lead the unavoidable transformation and were confident in their ability to win free elections. This did not happen. In March 1990 the reform socialists gained only 10 percent of the votes, while the newly founded right-of-center Hungarian Democratic Forum won a landslide victory and formed a coalition government with smaller opposition parties. The regime collapsed peacefully.

THE DOMINO EFFECT
In the summer of 1989 communism practically collapsed in Poland and Hungary, without opposition from the Gorbachev-led Soviet Union. When Nicolae Ceaușescu, the Romanian communist dictator, turned to Moscow suggesting that military intervention be used to stop Solidarity in Poland, he was turned down. Moreover, when the new Polish prime minister, Tadeusz Mazowiecki, made his first state visit to the Kremlin, Gorbachev said at the official banquet: "It might surprise some people, that I wish you success" (*Radio Free Europe*, 15 December 1989, pp. 14–15).

A door had been opened in the wall dividing East and West. The wall needed a real, physical opening, however, and this took place in the spring and summer of that year. The Hungarian reform-communist government of Miklós Németh announced in May 1989 the destruction of the Iron Curtain, the fortifications erected in the 1950s and 1960s along the old Hungarian-Austrian borders. Watchtowers and barbed wire fences were dismantled and even sold in small

pieces as souvenirs. This action had only a symbolic meaning because the Hungarians had passports and traveled freely, but it nevertheless gained tremendous practical historical importance. Thousands of East German tourists, who spent their vacation in Soviet bloc countries because they were prohibited from traveling to the West, recognized the opportunity and walked through the opened border to freedom. In the early summer months six thousand East Germans crossed the Hungarian border illegally via Austria to West Germany. Several thousand more waited in hurriedly built refugee camps on the Hungarian side of the border. Hungary had a valid agreement from 1969 that mandated it to stop German citizens from leaving Hungary for a third country without a visa, but the government decided to ignore it. After thorough negotiations, the border was officially opened on 11 September and was crossed by twenty thousand East Germans within a few hours. The entire world watched the dramatic crossing on television. It had shocking consequences: German tourists in Czechoslovakia jumped over the fences of the Bundesrepublik's embassy, and 2,500 gained asylum and free departure for West Germany. When the train whose path crossed through East Germany passed through Dresden, thousands of East Germans tried to stop it and climb aboard. They were attacked by the police, but the avalanche became unstoppable. Over three weeks in late October, 1.3 million East Germans participated in two hundred agitated demonstrations in Berlin, Dresden, and Leipzig.

The end came swiftly. On 7 October the ailing hard-line communist leader of the German Democratic Republic, Erich Honecker, gave a speech on the historical success of the GDR at a mass celebration of the fortieth anniversary of its foundation. Within a month, the police state had disintegrated. Personnel changes in the top leadership were made in a frantic attempt to calm the political storm: Honecker resigned on 18 October and was replaced by Egon Krenz, the former security chief. It was too late and too little. On 4 November one million people demonstrated in Berlin, and a few days later demonstrators began attacking and destroying the infamous Berlin Wall, symbol of the division of Germany and Europe. The regime had run out of options, and on 9 November the

Jubilant East German citizens cross the Hungarian border into Austria, September 1989. ©Time Life Pictures/
Getty Images

communist government announced the opening of the wall and "allowed" free travel to the West. A real exodus began: in a single week, five million East Germans visited West Berlin, and fifty to sixty thousand people left every month to resettle in West Germany. The hard-line East German communist regime collapsed, and the ordinary people virtually united the two Germanys.

An apathetic, hesitant Czech population, withdrawn from politics for two decades after the Soviet bloc invasion of Czechoslovakia in the summer of 1968, observed the collapse of the Polish, Hungarian, and German regimes next-door without reacting. However, on 17 November, following the collapse of the Berlin Wall, fifteen thousand young people, mostly students, gathered in Prague to celebrate the anniversary of the death of a student who had been murdered by the Nazis. The demonstration had been authorized to take place outside the city center, but the increasing number of students, already thirty to fifty thousand, marched toward Wenceslas Square in the heart of the city. Riot police attacked them, arresting a hundred and injuring more than five hundred people. All of a sudden, strike committees were founded, and on 20 November a crowd of two hundred thousand engulfed the streets. Václav Havel, a playwright and a famous dissident who had been arrested three times, addressed the protestors from a balcony in Wenceslas Square. The next day another hundred thousand demonstrators flooded Prague. Two days later three hundred thousand people participated in a mass demonstration organized by the opposition party Civic Forum in Prague. Simultaneously, a hundred thousand demonstrators occupied the streets of Bratislava, the Slovak capital city, and hundreds of thousands gathered to hear Alexander Dubček, the hero of the Prague Spring of 1968. A general strike was called for 27 November.

The neo-Stalinist government did not stand a chance. It reacted slowly and desperately: on

24 November a hardly known party official was appointed first secretary of the party, and on the 26th the old members of the Politburo were replaced by reformists. On 9 December Gustav Husák resigned from the state presidency. At that time the party tried stabilizing its position by forming a coalition government with leading opposition representatives Jan Čarnogursky and Jiří Dienstbier and technocrats such as Václav Klaus. These desperate attempts failed. At the end of the year Václav Havel was elected president, and announced in his New Year's message of 1990, "People, your government has returned to you" (Havel, pp. 395–396). The Czechoslovak "Velvet Revolution" did not meet with serious resistance.

This was not the case in Romania. After the collapse of the Berlin Wall, the paranoid dictator Nicolae Ceauşescu triumphantly presided at the Fourteenth Party Congress in Bucharest and masterminded the election of six members of his family to the leading bodies of the Communist Party. A longtime favorite of the West, he felt so sure of himself that in December he went on a state visit to Iran and, upon his return, called a mass gathering on Republican Square in Bucharest on 21 December to condemn the already explosive unrest in Timisoara, a border city of mixed Romanian and Hungarian population. He thought that he could rally the population to traditional nationalism and labeled the unrest an "anti-Romanian conspiracy." However, he had to retreat from the balcony of the Central Committee building when the officially gathered, pro-government demonstration turned against him. The square was cleared by the riot police, but the events became unstoppable. A state of emergency was declared and the army ordered to act, but the military leaders refused and several army units joined the uprising. The crowd attacked official buildings. The infamous elite Securitate army of seventy-five thousand remained loyal to Ceauşescu, and the streets of central Bucharest became a battlefield, resulting in the death of about one thousand people. Unlike other Communist parties in the region, the Romanian Communist Party, ruled with an iron fist by the Ceauşescu family, refrained from making spectacular personnel changes and refused to give up armed resistance. Its obstinacy provoked the bloodiest revolution in 1989.

A National Salvation Front rapidly emerged in the political vacuum, led by former officials of the regime who had been removed by the dictator, such as the retired general Nicolae Militaru, Petre Roman, Ion Iliescu, and Silviu Brucan. The crowd attacked the Central Committee building, and the bloody Christmas Revolution came to a grotesque conclusion: the dictator, his wife, and some of his closest aids escaped by helicopter from the roof of this building, landed on a field, and entered a waiting car. At the end of a car chase worthy of action movies, the dictator and his wife were taken to a military base, where a televised "trial" was hastily organized. The death sentence was immediately executed by a firing squad. The people of the country looked at the dead bodies of the couple on the screen. The popular revolt destroyed Romanian national Stalinism.

The regime also collapsed in Bulgaria, where the old and corrupt Todor Zhivkov leadership successfully suppressed any kind of reform orientation and opposition until 1989. In November of that year, nevertheless, a coup within the top inner circle of the party, organized by a reform-oriented group led by Petur Mladenov, replaced the old leadership. As everywhere else, they could not control the pace of change: free elections were held in the summer of 1990, and the regime collapsed peacefully.

Similar transformations began in multinational Yugoslavia but soon turned in the direction of a bloody civil war. Reforms to introduce a free market and democracy took a backseat to demands for national independence, and the first free elections strengthened nationalist lines and aspirations. After 1991 not only the communist regime but also Yugoslavia ceased to exist.

The domino effect hit Albania in 1991. Finally, the Soviet Union, cradle of the communist revolution, also abolished state socialism and disintegrated as a multinational state in 1991. In Europe 1989 became the year of miracles, "annus mirabilis."

See also **Albania; Berlin Wall; Ceauşescu, Nicolae; Cold War; Commonwealth of Independent States; Communism; Eastern Bloc; Germany; Gorbachev, Mikhail; Havel, Václav; Honecker, Erich; Hungary; Iron Curtain; Jaruzelski, Wojciech; Kádár, János; Poland; Romania.**

BIBLIOGRAPHY

Ash, Timothy Garton. *The Polish Revolution: Solidarity.* 3rd ed. New Haven, Conn., 2002.

Banac, Ivo, ed. *Eastern Europe in Revolution.* Ithaca, N.Y., 1992.

Berend, Ivan T. *Central and Eastern Europe 1944–1993: Detour from the Periphery to the Periphery.* Cambridge, U.K., 1996.

Brown, J. F. *Surge to Freedom: The End of Communist Rule in Eastern Europe.* Durham, N.C., and London, 1991.

Cohen, Lenard J. *Regime Transition in a Disintegrating Yugoslavia: The Law-of-Rule vs. the Rule-of-Law.* Pittsburgh, 1992.

Frankland, Mark. *The Patriots' Revolution: How East Europe Won Its Freedom.* London, 1990.

Gati, Charles. *The Bloc that Failed: Soviet–East European Relations in Transition.* Bloomington, Ind., 1990.

Glenny, Misha. *The Rebirth of History: Eastern Europe in the Age of Democracy.* 2nd ed. Harmondsworth, U.K., 1993.

Havel, Václav. *Open Letter: Selected Writings 1964–1990.* New York, 1991.

Radio Free Europe 14, no. 9 (3 March 1989).

——— 14, no. 50 (15 December 1989).

IVAN T. BEREND

NOBEL PRIZE. The first Nobel Prizes were awarded on 10 December 1901. The first laureate to step down from the podium at the Royal Swedish Academy of Music and receive a diploma from the hand of the crown prince of Sweden was Wilhelm Conrad Röntgen (1845–1923), laureate in physics. He was followed by the laureate in chemistry, Jacobus Henricus van't Hoff (1852–1911); the laureate in medicine, Emil Adolf von Behring (1854–1917); and the laureate in literature, Sully Prudhomme (1839–1907). The names of the laureates had not been announced in advance—a policy that was changed after a few years. In the first years of the Nobel Prize, there was no award for the recipients of the Peace Prize. On the tenth of December, Norway's parliament, the Storting, reached its decision as to who would receive the Peace Prize. The decision was announced the same day, and the new laureates were informed by letter. The first recipients of the Peace Prize were Jean Henri Dunant (1828–1910) and Frédéric Passy (1822–1912).

ALFRED NOBEL'S WILL

The whole of my remaining realizable estate shall be dealt with in the following way: the capital, invested in safe securities by my executors, shall constitute a fund, the interest on which shall be annually distributed in the form of prizes to those who, during the preceding year, shall have conferred the greatest benefit on mankind. The said interest shall be divided into five equal parts, which shall be apportioned as follows: one part to the person who shall have made the most important discovery or invention within the field of physics; one part to the person who shall have made the most important chemical discovery or improvement; one part to the person who shall have made the most important discovery within the domain of physiology or medicine; one part to the person who shall have produced in the field of literature the most outstanding work in an ideal direction; and one part to the person who shall have done the most or the best work for fraternity between nations, for the abolition or reduction of standing armies and for the holding and promotion of peace congresses. The prizes for physics and chemistry shall be awarded by the Swedish Academy of Sciences; that for physiology or medical works by the Karolinska Institute in Stockholm; that for literature by the Academy in Stockholm, and that for champions of peace by a committee of five persons to be elected by the Norwegian Storting. It is my express wish that in awarding the prizes no consideration be given to the nationality of the candidates, but that the most worthy shall receive the prize, whether he be Scandinavian or not.

FORMING THE NOBEL FOUNDATION

To understand the origin of the prizes, one must consider the life of the chemical magnate Alfred Nobel (1833–1896), who died on 10 December 1896 in San Remo, Italy. After a few days, it was learned that Nobel had left a will at a bank in Stockholm. The provisions of this will sparked great public interest. The executors of the will were Ragnar Sohlman and Rudolf Liljequist. Sohlman, then only twenty-six years old, had been Nobel's assistant, and Liljequist had worked with some of Nobel's industrial projects. In actuality, it was Sohlman, assisted by a lawyer named Carl Lindhagen (1860–1946), who realized Alfred Nobel's assets and established the Nobel Foundation to administer the capital that would provide the basis for the prizes.

Sohlman's task proved to be an extremely complicated one. The first problem he faced was to determine Alfred Nobel's legal place of residence. Nobel had lived in Sweden for only part of his childhood and a few years during the mid-1860s. However, he had owned a munitions factory at Bofors, Sweden, since 1893. This fact made it possible to transfer Nobel's assets to Sweden and establish the foundation there. Sohlman himself, armed with a revolver, carried out the transport of most of Nobel's financial papers and instruments from Paris to London and then to Stockholm. Finally, the entire legal process surrounding Nobel's will and testament was pursued at the district court in Karlskoga, the court of law that lay closest to the town of Bofors.

Just four months after Nobel's death, the Norwegian Storting accepted the task of selecting Peace Prize laureates and established a committee to begin this work. To select recipients of the other prizes, Nobel had named three academies in Sweden: the Royal Swedish Academy of Sciences, the Karolinska Institute, and the Swedish Academy. These organizations were more hesitant, and the negotiations with them took longer. In June 1898 agreements were reached regarding the principal arrangements for realizing the vision set forth in Nobel's will. Each of the three academies appointed members who continued discussing the statutes for the new Nobel Foundation. On 29 June 1900 the statutes were signed into effect by the King of Sweden and Norway, Oscar II (r. 1872–1907). The king, however, was doubtful about the prizes, which he viewed as insufficiently patriotic. The Swedish royal house found it difficult to accept the idea that laureates would be selected without regard to nationality. The awarding of Nobel Prizes in both Norway and Sweden was also a sensitive issue. Due to a strong Norwegian opposition movement, the long-standing union between Sweden and Norway was in decay. For these reasons, the king himself did not participate in the first Nobel ceremony, and had Crown Prince Gustaf represent the royal family.

The prizes are distributed in the order in which they are named in Alfred Nobel's will (see sidebar). For this reason, Röntgen was the first person to receive a Nobel Prize. The statutes adopted in 1900 establish that the funds may also be used in the selection process, as well as for the establishment of Nobel Institutes, the purpose of which was to contribute to the work of evaluating potential prize recipients. In 1905, when the union between Sweden and Norway was dissolved, special regulations were established for the distribution of the peace prize by the Norwegian Storting's Nobel Committee (officially known since 1977 as the Norwegian Nobel Committee).

SELECTING A NOBEL LAUREATE

The Nobel Foundation is not in any way involved in the selection of laureates. The Foundation is a private, independent organization that protects the interests of the committees involved and administers the capital that provides the basis for the prizes. The only official involvement by the government of Sweden is to appoint an auditor. This auditor also serves as chairperson for the Foundation's various auditors. In the same way, the prize-awarding organizations are independent, not only of the government, but also of the Nobel Foundation. This guarantees the objectivity and quality of the decisions made within the various organizations.

The selection of Nobel laureates is a lengthy and complicated process. For each prize, there is a Nobel Committee consisting of five members and a secretary. The committee has the right to appoint additional adjunct members. The standard procedures are the same for all of the scientific prizes. In September, the Nobel Committees on physics, chemistry, and physiology or medicine send out nomination forms to around three thousand persons, including previous Nobel laureates, professors at various universities around the world, members of the Royal Swedish Academy of Sciences, and the Nobel Assembly at Karolinska Institute. Nominations must be received before the last day of January. Normally, the nomination process results in the names of around three hundred candidates in each category. Following this, each committee consults numerous experts throughout the world to evaluate the work of the nominees. From June through August the committee writes its reports, which are submitted to the Royal Swedish Academy of Sciences and to the Nobel Assembly at Karolinska Institute and discussed at two meetings. In the beginning of October a vote is taken and a prize recipient for that committee is selected by simple majority. The decision cannot be appealed. Voting rights for the selection of laureates in physics and chemistry are held by members of the Royal Swedish Academy of Sciences (about 350 members). Voting rights for the selection of laureates in physiology or medicine are held by the members of the Karolinska Institute's Nobel Assembly (fifty members). Following the final vote the winners are informed and their names are made public.

The selection procedures for the Literature and Peace Prizes follow the same basic pattern as those for the scientific prizes. The Nobel Committee on Literature may be smaller than the committees for the scientific prizes, and fewer nomination forms are sent out. Nominations for the Literature Prize may be made by the members of the Swedish Academy, as well as members of other similar national academies, previous laureates, professors of literature and linguistics, and the chairpersons of national authors' associations. Generally, around 150 names are received. Through elimination, the list is reduced to fifteen to twenty names, which the committee continues to study and further reduces to a list of five names. Reports on the five candidates are compiled and discussed within the Academy. In October the eighteen members of the Swedish Academy go to their final vote. The winning candidate must receive more than half of the votes.

The Peace Prize differs from the other prizes on one important point: the Nobel committee appointed by the Norwegian Storting not only makes the nominations but also makes the final selection of the prizewinners. The Peace Prize Committee is also relatively small, with five members and a secretary. As with the other prizes, invitations to make nominations are sent out in September to members of parliament and governments around the world; members of international courts of law; university presidents; professors of history, philosophy, sociology, law and theology; directors of peace institutes; previous Peace Prize recipients; and previous members of the Norwegian Nobel Committee. The resulting list of candidates usually contains about 100 to 150 names. One rule common to all the prizes is that no one may nominate him- or herself.

Today, the scientific prizes and the Peace Prize are often shared. Until 1968 a Nobel Prize could in principle be shared by a large group of persons, if, for example, they had conducted a large scientific research project together. In 1968 the statutes were changed so that a prize cannot be shared by more than three recipients. These recipients may have cooperated or they could have been working on a maximum of two completely different projects. The Peace Prize is often awarded to organizations rather than individuals. The Literature Prize has been shared only four times (in 1904, 1917, 1966, and 1974).

THE VALUE OF THE PRIZE

The cash value of the prizes has varied greatly over the years. The 1901 winners received 150,000 Swedish crowns—a very large amount equivalent to about twenty times the annual salary for a university professor at that time. However, the Nobel Foundation was forced by the terms of the Nobel will to be extremely conservative in its investment strategies, and the return achieved on the capital was poor. In addition, the Foundation was not tax-exempt, and was for many years the largest single taxpayer in the city of Stockholm. In 1923 the prize amount reached its lowest level, 114,935 Swedish crowns. The actual value of this amount was less than a third of the original prize amounts. In 1946 the Nobel Foundation was granted tax-exempt status and undertook a thorough reform of its economic administration. In 1953 the Foundation's investment policies were updated so that its capital could be invested more aggressively. In 1991 the Nobel Prizes again reached their original value, in nominal terms six million Swedish crowns each. In 2005 the five Nobel Prizes were worth ten million crowns each.

When the Bank of Sweden celebrated its three-hundredth anniversary in 1968 its leaders decided to make a donation to the Nobel Foundation. The bank also instituted a new Prize in Economic Sciences in memory of Alfred Nobel. The Royal Swedish Academy of Sciences selects a recipient according to the same rules for the prizes in physics and chemistry. Since 1969 this prize has been awarded along with the Nobel Prizes. The Bank of Sweden donates the prize amount each year. Following the creation of the prize in economics the Nobel Foundation ruled that no additional prizes could be added to the Nobel roster.

THE NOBEL PRIZE IN THE EARLY TWENTY-FIRST CENTURY

The Nobel Prizes are among the most prestigious honors in the world. In monetary terms they are no longer the largest such prizes but their reputation has grown successively with the list of laureates. There are of course a few names that most people think should have been included on the long list of laureates (783 in 2005), but despite this, the careful selection process has guaranteed the quality of the choices made. The number of women laureates (a total of only thirty-three as of 2005) is far too low and there is an overrepresentation of Scandinavians, whereas laureates from regions other than Europe and North America are underrepresented. Nonetheless, in the history of the prizes, one hopes these disparities should be corrected with time.

The committees have not avoided controversial selections, especially in the cases of the Peace and Literature Prizes. When the journalist and peace activist Carl von Ossietsky (1889–1938) was awarded the 1935 Peace Prize Adolf Hitler (1889–1945) forbade all Germans to accept any Nobel Prize. Despite this fact, German laureates were selected in 1938 and 1939 (Richard Kuhn [1900–1967], chemistry, 1938; Adolf Friechrich Johann Butenandt [1903–1995], chemistry, 1939; and Gerhard Domagk [1895–1964], medicine, 1939). These laureates were allowed to accept their diplomas and medals after the war. According to the statutes, the monetary awards could not be paid out. In the same way, the Russian author Boris Pasternak (1890–1960) was forced by the Soviet government to decline his Literature Prize. The Burmese politician Aung San Suu Kyi (b. 1945) was not allowed to accept her 1991 Peace Prize and was held in house arrest by her country's government. On a number of occasions, the Literature Prize has been awarded to politically controversial writers, as, for example, in 2005, when it went to the British dramatist Harold Pinter (b. 1930).

In some years certain of the Nobel Prizes have not been awarded. In some cases the respective committee has been unable to agree upon a prize-winner, and postponed its decision until the next year. For example, Albert Einstein (1879–1955) was awarded the 1921 Nobel Prize in Physics in 1922, the same year that Niels Bohr (1885–1962) received the 1922 Physics Prize. On other occasions, war hindered the committee's work. For several years during both World War I and World War II, no Nobel Prizes were granted.

In the early twenty-first century, the awarding of the Nobel Prizes is a national holiday in both Sweden and Norway. Award ceremonies take place in the Stockholm Concert Hall and at the Oslo City Hall. The stately Nobel Banquet is held at the Stockholm City Hall, serves 1,300 guests, and is broadcast on television around the world. In the early years of the prizes, it was a gentlemen's dinner held at the Grand Hotel in Stockholm. The Nobel banquet held in Oslo is somewhat more modest, serving around 250 guests at the Oslo Grand Hotel. There are also sizable public Nobel organizations, such as the Nobel Peace Center in Oslo and the Nobel Museum in Stockholm. The Nobel Foundation also runs its own Web site, nobelprize.org, that makes information about the prizes available on the Internet.

See also **Science; Sweden.**

BIBLIOGRAPHY

Crawford, Elisabeth. *The Beginnings of the Nobel Institution: The Science Prizes, 1901–1915.* Cambridge, U.K., New York, and Paris, 1984.

Friedman, Marc Robert. *The Politics of Excellence: Behind the Nobel Prize in Science.* New York, 2001.

Larsson, Ulf, ed. *Cultures of Creativity: The Centennial Exhibition of the Nobel Prize.* Canton, Mass., 2001.

Nobel Foundation and W. Odelberg., eds. *Nobel: The Man and His Prizes.* 3rd rev. and enl. ed. New York, 1972.

Solman, Ragnar. *The Legacy of Alfred Nobel: The Story Behind the Nobel Prizes.* London, 1983.

OLOV AMELIN

NORTHERN IRELAND. Northern Ireland, consisting of six of the nine counties of Ulster, became a devolved administration within the United Kingdom under the 1920 Government of Ireland Act. Its creation was designed to remove Ulster unionist opposition to Irish home rule. The six-county state was the largest area with an ensured unionist majority. Two-thirds of the population were Protestant, and unionists won forty of the fifty-two seats in the new parliament; but there were significant areas with a nationalist majority along the western and southern fringes and in west Belfast. The establishment of a separate administration for Northern Ireland reflected Britain's wish to disengage from Ireland. The parliament was responsible for agriculture, education, local government, security, health, and welfare, but it had limited taxation powers; 90 percent of tax revenue went to the British exchequer. Northern Ireland continued to send members of Parliament (MPs) to Westminster, but Westminster did not concern itself with programs controlled by the local parliament.

EARLY STATEHOOD

The new state had a violent birth; between June 1920 and June 1922, 428 people were killed and 1,766 injured and many houses and businesses were destroyed. This violence was part of the guerrilla war that the Irish Republican Army (IRA) launched against the Crown forces in Ireland in its efforts to secure an Irish republic. A truce in July 1921 was followed by a treaty in December 1921, giving Ireland Dominion status. Northern Ireland, not a signatory to the treaty, had the right to opt out of the Dominion; if it did so, the boundaries of each state would be determined by a commission. The outbreak of civil war in southern Ireland in the summer of 1922 diverted republicans away from Northern Ireland and made it easier for the new state to survive. However, from the beginning the Northern Ireland government regarded Catholics as a disloyal minority that must be contained; a draconian Special Powers Act providing for internment and flogging was directed exclusively at the Catholic community. Most Catholics believed that the Boundary Commission would so reduce the territory of Northern Ireland as to make its survival impossible and refused to engage with the new state. In 1925, when it became evident that the Commission was proposing only minor boundary changes, the British and Irish governments agreed to suppress the report.

Although nationalist MPs took their seats in parliament in 1926, Northern Ireland continued to be racked by insecurity and defensiveness. The 1920 Act provided for proportional representation in all elections, in order to protect minorities, but legislation passed in 1926 and 1929 removed proportional representation in local and parliamentary elections. Ward boundaries in local authorities with a nationalist majority, such as Londonderry, were carefully manipulated to secure unionist control. The abolition of proportional representation was not directed exclusively against nationalists. The Northern Ireland prime minister James Craig (later Lord Craigavon, 1871–1940) feared that the emergence of a Labour movement or the fragmenting of the unionist vote might enable nationalists to gain control. This was never a realistic possibility. However, during the Depression of the 1930s, Catholics and Protestants protested together at cuts in unemployment relief. Sectarian divisions proved more powerful than class interest, and the alliance was short-lived. Although the Ulster Unionist Party held office continually from 1921 until the parliament was dissolved in 1973, Craig and his successors went to considerable effort to woo the Protestant electorate by a judicious combination of patronage in the form of jobs and public spending and the encouragement of fears that Northern Ireland was under threat from a disloyal nationalist minority or irredentist claims from Dublin. Dublin governments, preoccupied with maximizing independence from Britain, initially showed little interest in Northern Ireland. However Article 2 in the 1937 Constitution claimed jurisdiction over the entire island.

World War II was an important period for Northern Ireland's relationship with Britain. The Depression of the 1930s was more deep-seated in Northern Ireland than it was elsewhere in the United Kingdom, but the economy gradually revived under the stimulus of armament and clothing contracts and the presence of U.S. bases. Conscription was not introduced because of fears of nationalist opposition, and the numbers who enlisted in the forces remained low. In 1941 German bombs claimed 1,100 lives in Belfast, proportionately one of the heaviest casualties in the United Kingdom; the high death toll reflected inadequate air-raid precautions. The war exposed the limitations of the aging and complacent Unionist leadership; in 1940 Craig was succeeded as prime minister by veteran unionist John Andrews (1871–1956). In 1943 Andrews had to give way to a younger and more dynamic Sir Basil Brooke (Viscount Brookeborough, 1888–1973).

Northern Ireland's contribution to the Allied war effort was duly acknowledged by successive British governments. The 1920 Act required Northern Ireland to contribute toward the cost of imperial services. Although these payments were waived when economic conditions deteriorated, public services lagged seriously behind those in the United Kingdom. In 1946 however, Britain conceded parity of social services with the rest of the United Kingdom, and Northern Ireland participated fully in the postwar expansion of health, welfare, and educational services. Many Ulster unionists were uncomfortable with such heavy reliance on the state. Further reward for wartime service came when Westminster responded to the declaration of an Irish Republic by passing the 1949 Ireland Act, which gave the Northern Ireland parliament the right to determine whether it would remain part of the United Kingdom.

ESCALATING TENSIONS

Nationalists saw no hope of securing influence within Northern Ireland. An Anti-Partition League launched in 1945 was designed to unite Sinn Féin and the more moderate, church-controlled Irish nationalist party; in 1947 the campaign secured all-party support in Dublin. But efforts to bring international pressure to bear on Britain to end partition were fruitless. The 1949 Ireland Act strengthened partition by giving ultimate control to the Northern Ireland parliament. A desultory guerrilla warfare campaign began in 1954, and in December 1956 the IRA launched Operation Harvest—an anti-partition offensive consisting of raids on border custom posts, army barracks, and police stations. Northern Ireland Catholics gave the campaign only limited support, and the Dublin and Belfast governments interned suspected IRA members. In 1962 the IRA declared a ceasefire and shifted its attention to the socioeconomic issues in the Republic. With twelve IRA and six police deaths, the casualties were tiny compared

to those sustained on both sides in the later "Troubles."

Although Northern Ireland had the lowest standard of living in the United Kingdom it was significantly higher than that of the Irish Republic, and the population was rising. Between 1945 and 1963 investment in new industries created fifty thousand jobs, mainly in U.S. and U.K. firms attracted by generous tax concessions. By the early 1960s, however, a worldwide recession in shipbuilding and the aircraft and textile industries created a major economic crisis. Unemployment had traditionally been much higher among Catholics, who accounted for a disproportionate number of unskilled workers and were more likely to live in the less-developed areas in west Ulster. Catholic emigration counteracted the higher Catholic birthrate and stabilized the sectarian balance. But the job losses in traditional Ulster industries affected skilled workers, who were the backbone of Ulster unionism, and many reacted by voting for the Northern Ireland Labour Party. The Northern Ireland prime minister Lord Brookeborough was forced to resign. His successor, Terence O'Neill (1914–1990), sought to secure the future of Ulster unionism by instituting a program of economic planning that would bring material benefits to all citizens while anchoring Northern Ireland more firmly in the United Kingdom; he was also keen to promote better relations with the Catholic community and the Dublin government. But public gestures, such as meeting Irish prime minister Seán Lemass (1899–1971)—the first such meeting since 1922—and the first visit to a Catholic school by a prime minister of Northern Ireland prompted fears among unionists without delivering material benefits to the Catholic minority. A planned new town, a new university, and a motorway—key elements in his development program—were all located in predominantly Protestant areas, reinforcing Catholic beliefs that new-style unionism was only a modern version of the old partisan regime.

The 1963 election of a Labour government in Britain eroded the convention that the parliament of the United Kingdom did not discuss matters that were controlled by the Northern Ireland government. The Campaign for Social Justice (1964), a group of middle-class Catholics, linked up with Labour MPs to highlight discrimination in housing and employment. In 1967 these causes were taken up by the Northern Ireland Civil Rights Association, a coalition of liberal Protestants and Catholics whose title and modus operandi were modeled on the U.S. civil rights movement. Since the mid-nineteenth century, political marches in Northern Ireland had been used as a means of asserting control over territory, and marches frequently ended in intercommunal violence. When a march in Derry in October 1968 to highlight local housing discrimination was attacked by baton-wielding policemen, the pictures were carried on televisions throughout the world. The British prime minister, Harold Wilson (1916–1995), summoned O'Neill to London and pressed him to announce a series of reforms: an ombudsman, the abolition of Londonderry Corporation and other local authority reforms, needs-based allocation of public housing, and changes to the Special Powers Act. The fact that these concessions were made following mass protest, and under pressure from Britain, further weakened O'Neill's credibility within the Ulster Unionist Party (UUP). In February 1969 he called a general election and appealed for Catholic votes to shore up his mandate for reform. But the outcome was growing support for O'Neill's opponents within the UUP, and for Ian Paisley's (b. 1926) uncompromising Protestant Unionists (later the Democratic Unionist Party, DUP), and no evidence of Catholic support for O'Neill. He resigned some weeks later.

THE TROUBLES

August 1969 is generally regarded as the start of the Troubles. A traditional unionist march in Derry ended in riots, which spread to Belfast, resulting in seven deaths and the destruction of 179 properties (83 percent of which had been occupied by Catholics). The Northern premier James Chichester-Clark (1923–2002) called in the British army to restore peace, but overall responsibility for security remained with the Northern Ireland government. Catholics initially welcomed the British army as protection from Protestant attacks, but within months the army was under attack in Catholic areas. Although some members of the IRA had joined the civil rights movement, the IRA only became a significant fighting force after December 1969, when the Provisional IRA split away to launch a campaign against the British

army and the Northern Ireland government. Violence increased, particularly after the introduction of internment in August 1971, which was directed solely against nationalists, despite considerable evidence of unionist paramilitary activity. When an illegal anti-internment march in Derry on 30 January 1972 ended with thirteen marchers shot dead by British soldiers, Britain was forced to take control of security, and the Northern Ireland government resigned. The parliament was prorogued and direct rule from Westminster was introduced on 24 March 1972.

Direct rule was regarded as a temporary arrangement, pending the establishment of a government that would have the support of both the nationalist and unionist communities. By 1972 Britain was conscious that any lasting settlement had to secure the support of the Dublin government. The Sunningdale Agreement, signed in December 1973 by the British and Irish governments and leaders of the main constitutional parties in Northern Ireland, opened the way for a return to devolved government, with power shared between the UUP, the nationalist Social Democratic and Labour Party (SDLP) (which had emerged in 1971 as the voice of moderate nationalists), and the cross-denominational Alliance Party. Sunningdale provided for a Council of Ireland (a proposal contained in the 1920 Act) with equal membership from the Belfast and Dublin governments. Initially a consultative forum, the Council could evolve into an all-Ireland executive.

The combination of power-sharing with a Council of Ireland proved too much for Ulster unionists, and IRA and Protestant violence continued. In February 1974 anti-Sunningdale candidates took eleven of the twelve seats in the Westminster general election. A general strike by the Ulster Workers' Council in May 1974 brought Northern Ireland to a halt. The executive collapsed and direct rule was restored.

The years after 1974 were marked by cycles of violence and multiple efforts to achieve a political solution. Although the Troubles were seen as the recurrence of an age-old Irish struggle, they had much more in common with late-twentieth and early-twenty-first century intercommunal violence and terrorism: high-profile bombings and assassinations designed to gain media attention as well as "ethnic cleansing" of mixed communities in Belfast, Protestant families from border areas and Derry City, and Catholic families from Carrickfergus. Catholics who worked for the security services were targeted, as were couples of mixed religion; tit-for-tat atrocities were common. Manufacturing employment fell by 40 percent during the 1980s; the public sector became the dominant employer and fiscal transfers from Britain accounted for up to one-quarter of GNP. The IRA's objective, as in Ireland in 1920, was to put pressure on Britain to withdraw from Northern Ireland; Ulster unionists sought peace and continuing union with Britain.

NEGOTIATING PEACE

In November 1985 the British and Irish governments signed the Anglo-Irish Agreement, which created a mechanism for the Irish government to express its views on Northern Ireland policy. An Irish government secretariat opened in Belfast and provided nationalist input into policy in Northern Ireland. This strengthened the hand of the SDLP and enabled the party to withstand for a time the drift of nationalist voters to Sinn Féin. Unionists protested the agreement to little effect. The emergence of Sinn Féin as a significant electoral force can be dated to 1982, when IRA prisoners went on hunger strike to protest at losing political prisoner status. Bobby Sands (1954–1981), the first hunger striker, won a Westminster by-election for Sinn Féin, and although he died shortly thereafter, his candidacy and election confirmed the merits of combining politics with military action, described by the Sinn Féin leader Danny Morrison (b. 1953), who was also interned, as "the Armalite [rifle] in this hand and the ballot paper in this hand." But the British and Irish governments refused to engage in formal talks with Sinn Féin until the IRA declared a cease-fire.

The Joint Declaration for Peace (1993), also known as the Downing Street Declaration, was designed to reassure Sinn Féin and Ulster unionists. The British prime minister John Major (b. 1943) declared that Britain had no "selfish strategic or economic interest in Northern Ireland" and the Irish prime minister Albert Reynolds (b. 1932) declared that a united Ireland would only come with the consent of the majority in Northern

Ireland. This paved the way for an IRA cease-fire in August 1994, and ultimately, with significant involvement by U.S. president Bill Clinton, for the 1998 Belfast Agreement, also known as the Good Friday Agreement. The agreement restored devolved government to Northern Ireland, elected by a complex system of proportional representation, with an executive drawn from all the major parties. A north-south council consisting of ministers from both Irish governments could make decisions by agreement on matters of common interest, and a consultative British-Irish council would bring together ministers from all political assemblies in Britain and Ireland. The Irish government undertook to repeal Articles 2 and 3 of the 1937 Constitution, replacing them with an article affirming the entitlement of every person born on the island of Ireland to be part of the Irish nation.

The Belfast Agreement was endorsed by 71 percent of the Northern Ireland electorate. Catholic support was almost unanimous, whereas unionists were equally divided on the agreement. However the power-sharing executive that took office in December 1999 proved a fragile entity. The IRA's failure to disarm meant that first minister and UUP leader David Trimble (b. 1944) was repeatedly threatened by anti-agreement unionists. In October 2002 the Assembly was suspended and direct rule was restored. Northern Ireland remains a deeply disturbed society: many working-class communities are "policed" by republican and loyalist paramilitaries rather than by the new Police Service of Northern Ireland; paramilitaries are active in drug-running and other lucrative crimes; and although the economy has recovered, it remains dependent on financial transfers from Westminster. The DUP and Sinn Féin have displaced the more moderate UUP and SDLP as leaders of the Protestant and Catholic communities, and there is little evidence of any significant cross-religious vote, although multidenominational schools are flourishing. The political alignment means that it will be extremely difficult to establish a stable, power-sharing government. The DUP is committed to union with Britain and is not prepared to acknowledge any form of all-Ireland institutions, while Sinn Féin's goal remains an all-Ireland republic by 2016, centenary of the 1916 Rising.

See also **Catholicism; Crime and Justice; IRA; Ireland; Labor Movements; Paisley, Ian; Terrorism; United Kingdom.**

BIBLIOGRAPHY

Arthur, Paul. *Special Relationships: Britain, Ireland and the Northern Ireland Problem.* Belfast, 2000.

Buckland, Patrick. *The Factory of Grievances: Devolved Government in Northern Ireland, 1921–39.* Dublin, 1979.

Cox, Michael, Adrian Guelke, and Fiona Stephen, eds. *A Farewell to Arms? From "Long War" to Long Peace in Northern Ireland.* Manchester, U.K., 2000.

Elliott, Marianne. *The Catholics of Ulster: A History.* London, 2000.

Hennessy, Thomas. *A History of Northern Ireland, 1920–1996.* New York, 1997.

Hill, J. R., ed. *A New History of Ireland.* Vol. 7: *Ireland, 1921–1994.* Oxford, U.K., 2003.

Jackson, Alvin. *Ireland, 1798–1998: Politics and War.* Oxford, U.K., and Malden, Mass., 1999.

Mulholland, Marc. *Northern Ireland at the Crossroads: Ulster Unionism in the O'Neill Years, 1960–9.* New York, 2000.

MARY E. DALY

NORTHERN LEAGUE. Lega Nord (Northern League) is a political movement and party founded in November 1989 by the charismatic Umberto Bossi (b. 1941) and the theoretician Gianfranco Miglio (1918–2001). The League, which has its own newspaper, the *Padania*, takes as its symbol Alberto da Giussano who led the cities of the Lombard League to victory over Frederick Barbarossa (1122–1190) in 1176. The Northern League united the many alliances that arose in Northern Italy (the Lombard League, the League of Venice, the Piedmontese Union, the Piedmont Autonomists, and movements in Friuli, Trentino, and Liguria) in opposition to the traditional Italian parties, particularly those in charge of the government. The phenomenon of the leagues developed in the wake of a tendency that appeared in the 1980s, when various local and regional groups emerged in the agricultural zones of the Veneto and in the valleys of the Bergamo and Varese provinces. Territorial patriotism was the primary factor binding the league activists, who were recruited from all social strata, although most of the early members were industrial and agricultural workers. At first the political parties of Italy underestimated the phenomenon, dismissing it as a manifestation of the wealthy Northern society's dissatisfaction with the national government; nor did they feel threatened by the new political issue of autonomy, expressed in the slogan coined by Bossi: "Lombardy for the Lombards." The league phenomenon was also characterized by rude and violent polemical attacks against Southerners, who were considered parasites of the North. When in the mid-1980s the influx of migrants into Italy began to swell, racist elements aimed at immigrants were added to the polemic.

From 1985 on, with the growing crisis in the parties, the protest against "thieving Rome" (another slogan of Bossi's) became ever stronger and the leagues spread into cities as well, recruiting initiates from the middle class, merchants, small entrepreneurs, privately employed persons, and white-collar workers; in brief, they drew from that vast pool of traditionally moderate citizens who in the past had aligned themselves with the ruling parties and in particular with the Christian Democrats.

The effectiveness of Bossi's federalist message and the separatist sentiments of the Northern countryside exerted a strong attraction and raised doubts about the nationalization of the Italian masses after less than 150 years of national unity. In the 1989 elections for the European Parliament, the striking success of the League could no longer be ignored: in Lombardy it became the fourth party with 8.1 percent of the votes. Bossi, who had already been elected to the Senate in 1987, received significant support in the 1990 regional elections: almost 1.2 million Lombards voted the party ticket of the *carroccio*, the League's symbol depicting a medieval ox-drawn war chariot. The League vote in Lombardy reached 18.9 percent, attaining 13 percent even in Milan where Bettino Craxi (1934–2000) had in vain taken it upon himself to defend personally the power of the PSI (Italian Socialist Party), which had been undermined by the League's battle with the Milanese City Council led by Paolo Pillitteri (b. 1940),

Craxi's brother-in-law, who was later involved in the investigations for *tangenti* (bribe-taking).

In his protest against the centralized government, which he accused of penalizing the North in favor of other regions, Umberto Bossi waved the banner of a constitutional revision that would end the unitary experience and give rise to a federative government. The success achieved in Lombardy was repeated in the political elections of 5–6 April 1992, in which the League exceeded 8 percent of the votes at the national level and 20 percent in Lombardy, thus becoming an important political partner for any ally. In 1994 Bossi brought the League out of its isolation when he accepted the proposal of Silvio Berlusconi (b. 1936), who had just founded the Forza Italia party (FI), to enter into a joint electoral pact. Two alliances were thus formed, the "Freedom Pole" in the North (FI and Lega Nord) and the "Good Government Pole" in the South (FI and Gianfranco Fini's [b. 1952] Alleanza Nazionale). The two coalitions won the elections (27 March 1994) with the League attaining 8.4 percent of the votes. As soon as Bossi realized that he had allied himself with a leader, Berlusconi, whose media empire could swallow up the League votes, he attacked first Fini, whom he accused of backing southern statists, and then Berlusconi himself because of his old friendship with Craxi. The League then left the parliamentary majority, causing the collapse of the first Berlusconi government in December 1994. For the elections of 13 May 2001 the League once more allied itself with Berlusconi in the "Casa della Libertà" coalition (House of liberty), and as of early 2006 was still a ruling party in the government. A promise to institute federalism assured the loyalty of Bossi, who was appointed minister for Reforms and Devolution (the assignment to the regions of matters relating to health, education, and public security), a post that he resigned after he suffered a stroke in March 2004, at sixty-three years of age; he was replaced in July 2004 by Roberto Calderoli (b. 1956), who had until then been vice-president of the Senate.

See also **Berlusconi, Silvio; Craxi, Bettino; Italy.**

BIBLIOGRAPHY

Cento Bull, Anna, and Mark Gilbert. *The Lega Nord and the Northern Question in Italian Politics.* Basingstoke, U.K., 2001.

Diamanti, Ilvo. *La Lega: geografia, storia e sociologia diun soggetto politico.* 2nd ed. Rome, 1995.

Miglio, Gianfranco. *Io, Bossi e la Lega. Diario segreto dei miei quattro anni sul Carroccio.* Milan, 1994.

Tambini, Damian. *Nationalism in Italian Politics: The Stories of the Northern League, 1980–2000.* London and New York, 2001.

MARIA TERESA GIUSTI

NORWAY. The industrialization and the technical modernization that had begun in Norway in the nineteenth century continued rapidly after the turn of the century. The industrial growth was based on the immense resources of waterpower, often owned by foreign companies. In order to protect Norway's national resources from international financial interest the liberal party Venstre and the Norwegian Labor Party (DNA) demanded effective legislation. The concession law of 1909 was one of the most hotly debated political issues in Norway in the beginning of the century. Universal suffrage was established during this period—for men in 1898 and for women in 1913—and also different forms of social legislation.

At the outbreak of World War I Norway declared its neutrality. The economy, supported by mining, shipping, and the fishing industry, prospered during the war, but the merchant fleet was severely damaged by German submarine warfare. Mines and torpedos killed more than two thousand Norwegian seamen. Shortages of commodities and the increase in prices led to growing class conflicts and to the radicalization of the labor movement. In contrast to the majority of social democratic parties in Western Europe the DNA joined the Comintern in 1919. The centralization and the strong control by the Soviet Communist Party in Moscow forced the DNA to leave the Comintern in 1923, but during the 1920s the party maintained most of its radical policy.

Various liberal and conservative governments tried to solve the economic problems in the 1920s by liberal measures, but the deflation strategy hit the workers and the farmers especially hard, resulting in strikes and confrontations between workers and the military. The unemployment figure reached 33 percent in 1933. The DNA gained growing support, and in 1935 the party made an emergency agreement with the Agrarian Party. Government subsidies for farms and an ambitious social program were introduced, financed by increases in taxation. The economic situation was improved but unemployment remained high during the rest of the decade. The formation of a one-party labor government in 1935 marked a new epoch in Norwegian history. For three decades the party would dominate Norwegian politics. Besides the social conflicts also cultural differences were important; moral demands on temperance and Christian values created political tensions. Prohibition of the sale of liquor was initiated, largely due to support of this measure in the traditional western part of the country, but abolished after a referendum in 1927.

NORWAY DURING OCCUPATION

In World War II Norway again declared its neutrality, but this time the country was involved in the warfare. In April 1940 Great Britain laid mines in the Norwegian waters. On April 9 German troops invaded Norway and occupied the major cities. The German attack, operation *Weserübung,* also included the occupation of Denmark the same day. After a month of combat, mostly around Narvik in the north where an Anglo-French expeditionary force supported the Norwegian Army, Norway had to capitulate. The court and the government fled to London where a government-in-exile was established. The Norwegian merchant fleet (4.8 million tonnage in 1939) was only outnumbered by the British and American fleets. Thanks to the government's control of the merchant fleet, Norway could make an important contribution to the Allied cause in the war. However, the price was high. Half of the fleet was lost during the war.

In a radio broadcast the leader of the pro-Nazi National Unity (Nasjonal Samling or NS) Party, Vidkun Quisling (1887–1945), with the support of Adolf Hitler (1889–1945), proclaimed himself head of a "national government." After a couple of days the Germans changed their minds. However, the reichkommissar Josef Terboven (1898–1945) failed to gain support for other forms of collaborationist governments, and Quisling was

reinstated as "minister president" in 1942. Despite this imposing title and the nominally independent government, Quisling and his NS ministers were totally under the control of Terboven. The Nazification process was met by strong opposition from church leaders, teachers, universities, and various civic organizations. Although the German rule in Norway was milder than in other parts of Europe, many people were tortured or executed. At times innocent civilians were killed as retaliation for resistance actions. An illegal press and small groups of armed resistance were built up by the home front ("hjemmefronten"), in close cooperation with the government in London.

In 1944 Soviet troops occupied an area in the north of Norway. The rest of the country was liberated when the German troops capitulated to the home front in May 1945. A widespread settlement with the collaborationists took place. Eighteen thousand of them were sentenced to imprisonment and twenty-five executed, among them Quisling and two of his former ministers. After the liberation a coalition government was formed, but after the election in 1945 it was replaced by a Labor government with Einar Gerhardsen (1897–1987) as prime minister.

THE POSTWAR ERA

The tragic experiences of World War II influenced Norwegian security policy in the postwar era. Norway took part in the negotiations on a neutral Nordic defense union in 1948, although without much enthusiasm. Instead Norway in 1949 participated in the foundation of the North Atlantic Treaty Organization (NATO). However, NATO military bases and nuclear weapons were not allowed on Norwegian territory. A broad majority of the parties accepted the membership in NATO, but the country's security policy is sometimes the subject of intense debate.

The rebuilding of the country after the war was implemented with widespread consensus. Also the liberal, conservative, and Christian parties accepted rationings of provisions and fuel, import control, and government regulations regarding prices and investments. However, when the DNA in the 1950s tried to make these measures permanent and extend them, the opposition protested and a compromise was reached. This resulted in lessening state control of the economy. Reforms of housing, social security, and education were carried through, mostly by agreement. In 1967 a general insurance system with state pensions was introduced and later extended to unemployment insurance and health insurance. Due to the historically rooted decentralized character of Norwegian society, regional policy has become very extensive.

The overall costs of welfare arrangements have sharply increased, but because of income from the oil industry Norway has been able to maintain a high standard for social services and quality of life. The average lifespan is among the highest in the world. Criticism of the welfare state increased in the 1970s. The Conservative Party was in possession of the premiership from 1981 to 1986. The populist Progress Party (Fremskrittspartiet) more strongly attacked the costly welfare system. Nowadays the party more often criticizes the government for not using oil revenue to fund social programs. The Progress Party is also the most pronounced opponent of Norway's immigration policy. In the 1990s many refugees from Vietnam, Pakistan, and the former Yugoslavia arrived in Norway.

Not until 1965 was the DNA's power really challenged. The four center and right-wing parties formed a coalition government. Since then labor and liberal-conservative governments have alternated. The party conflicts are not based solely on the traditional left/right scale. Moral and religious values are also important. On two occasions, in 1972 and 1994, the Norwegian people have rejected, via referenda, membership in the European Union (EU). On both occasions, the majority of the parties and the established organizations have argued for membership. The fear of decreasing national independence and a worsening economic situation in the rural districts, combined with the historical memories—or myths—of humiliating unions with Denmark and Sweden, have been too strong to allow EU boosters to sway the opinions of Norwegian citizens. Social critics, the radical Left, the Center Party (former Agrarian Party), and agrarian and fishing organizations have formed a front against membership in the European Union. However, as a member of the now-diminished European Free Trade Organization (EFTA) and the European Economic Space (EES),

Norway is fully economically integrated in the European markets.

THE OIL ECONOMY

During the last decades the Norwegian economy has achieved a higher rise in GNP than has been experienced by most other countries. Norway is one of the richest nations in the world, largely because of the extraction of petroleum and gas resources from the Norwegian parts of the North Sea. The discovery of great supplies of petroleum and gas in 1969, and continuing exploration for more fields, have deeply affected the economy. The Norwegian state has kept a considerable share of the revenues generated by its offshore energy reserves. However, the new industry also has created problems for other parts of the economy—substantial price rises and higher wage levels. Fluctuations in the world petroleum market have profound effects on the country's economy.

At the centenary of the dissolution of the Swedish-Norwegian union in 1905, which gave the country total independence, Norway is a prosperous and respected country. In many cases Norwegian authorities, or individual citizens, have served as successful negotiators in several international crises: for example, in the Middle East (the Oslo-Agreement, 1993) and in Sri Lanka. A Norwegian, Trygve Lie (1896–1968) was the general secretary of the United Nations from 1946 to 1953.

See also **NATO; Quisling, Vidkun; World War II.**

BIBLIOGRAPHY

Derry, T. K. *A History of Modern Norway, 1814–1972.* Oxford, U.K., 1973.

Heidar, Knut. *Norway: Elites on Trial.* Boulder, Colo., 2001.

Hodne, Fritz. *An Economic History of Norway, 1815–1970.* Trondheim, Norway, 1975.

Shaffer, William R. *Politics, Parties and Parliaments: Political Change in Norway.* Columbus, Ohio, 1998.

TORBJÖRN NILSSON

NUCLEAR WEAPONS. On the morning of 6 August 1945, an American bomber dropped

"Little Boy" on the Japanese city of Hiroshima, killing tens of thousands of people and demonstrating to the world the awesome power of a new kind of weapon. Little Boy was an atomic bomb, the product of a secret U.S.-British-Canadian wartime effort known as the Manhattan Project. Over the years that followed, nuclear weapons transformed thinking about war and international politics. They were one of the central facts of the Cold War (1945–1989), shaping the conflict between the superpowers and sparking major crises. Their incredible destructive power threatened to destroy humanity but, simultaneously, formed the basis of international stability and peace.

ORIGINS AND THE MANHATTAN PROJECT

The roots of the Manhattan Project lay in the scientific achievements of the interwar period. In 1932 John Douglas Cockcroft (1897–1967) and Ernest Thompson Sinton Walton (1903–1995) of Cambridge University split an atom of lithium, proving that an atom's nucleus could be broken apart, releasing energy in the process. Building on Cockroft and Walton's work, the Italian physicist Enrico Fermi (1901–1954) showed that the atoms of almost every element could be split via neutron bombardment. This discovery, for which he won the Nobel Prize in 1938, raised the possibility of large-scale nuclear fission. According to this idea, one could start a chain reaction by splitting a few atoms of a radioactive substance (such as uranium), which would release both energy and neutrons, which in turn would split surrounding atoms, releasing still more energy and more neutrons. The result would be a huge amount of energy. Like many other European physicists in the 1930s, Fermi emigrated to the United States in order to escape the rising tide of fascism and anti-Semitism in Europe. Arriving in New York in 1939, and then moving to the University of Chicago, he produced the first controlled nuclear chain reaction in late 1942. The achievement was of major significance to the Manhattan Project, then already under way for more than a year.

In the late 1930s, a number of European émigré scientists worried that the Germans were trying to build an atomic bomb. If this happened, the consequences would be dire. On the basis of these concerns, Albert Einstein (1879–1955)—himself a German-Jewish refugee—wrote to President Franklin Delano Roosevelt (1882–1945) in August 1939, urging him to establish a program to accelerate the research already being done in American universities. Roosevelt agreed. The American government began to award grants for work on nuclear fission. The experiments that resulted formed the core of what became the Manhattan Project, which the president formally established in October 1941 by authorizing the development of atomic weapons.

Although Army General Leslie Richard Groves (1896–1970) was put in charge of the project, the American physicist Julius Robert Oppenheimer (1904–1967) was responsible for its scientific work. Oppenheimer established the project's headquarters at Los Alamos, New Mexico, and assembled a group of top scientists—many of whom had fled Europe—to collaborate on the research. Among those who worked on the project were Fermi, the German Hans Albrecht Bethe (1906–2005), the Hungarian Edward Teller (1908–2003), and the Austrian Victor Weisskopf (1908–2002), all leading experts on nuclear physics. One of the key problems facing the team was how to produce enough uranium-235, the element's fissionable isotope, and plutonium to build a bomb. To accomplish this task, enormous factories were built in Oak Ridge, Tennessee, and Richland, Washington, to extract uranium-235 from uranium ore and produce plutonium by bombarding uranium-238 with protons.

Once Fermi had established that a self-sustaining nuclear chain reaction was in fact possible, the only major obstacle left was how to turn the fissile material into a useful weapon. Two different kinds of bombs were built, one using uranium-235 and the other plutonium. In July 1945, two months after the German surrender, the first test of an atomic bomb took place in the New Mexican desert. Codenamed "Trinity," it produced an even bigger explosion than predicted. Less than a month later, the first atomic weapons used in war were dropped on Hiroshima and Nagasaki.

THE SOVIET BOMB

The American monopoly lasted scarcely four years. Even though the Soviets had been wartime allies, and even though the British and Canadians had been both allies and close collaborators on the Manhattan Project, the U.S. government asserted strict unilateral control over the manufacture of nuclear weapons after the war. Prior to 1945, there had been good reasons not to share any information with the Soviets. Though a partner in the fight against Nazi Germany, the Soviet Union had had an antagonistic relationship with the United States and Western Europe during the interwar period. During the war itself, it was doubtful whether the Soviets would withstand the German invasion. In these circumstances, it would have been foolish to share sensitive information with Moscow, because it could easily have ended up in Nazi hands. After the war, rising U.S.-Soviet tensions gave Washington cause to reconsider any thought of divulging its atomic secrets.

The Soviets made every effort to steal the Manhattan Project's secrets. Thanks to both the high quality of their espionage and sympathy for their cause among certain Western scientists, they were startlingly successful. Their most valuable spy in Los Alamos was Klaus Emil Julius Fuchs (1911–1988), a German-born physicist, devout communist, and longtime Soviet informer. So successful was he that none of his colleagues were aware of his covert activities. His work for Moscow was not discovered until 1950.

The information that he and others passed to the Soviets was of great use in both strategic and scientific terms. At the 1945 Potsdam Conference, the U.S. president Harry S. Truman (1884–1972) informed the Soviet leader Joseph Stalin (1879–1953) that the United States had built a "powerful new weapon." Long aware of the Manhattan Project thanks to the steady stream of information from Los Alamos, the Soviet leader feigned indifference, but was secretly concerned. There is some debate concerning whether Truman attempted—in what is called "atomic diplomacy"—to use the American nuclear monopoly to cow Stalin into concessions regarding eastern Europe. Regardless of whether this was Truman's intention, the Soviets certainly believed that the Americans were trying to frighten them, and they were determined to resist. Rejecting the Baruch Plan, an American proposal to bring atomic weapons under international control, Stalin ordered his scientists to build their own bomb as quickly as possible, and gave them all the resources and intellectual freedom necessary to do so.

They succeeded within four years. In August 1949 the Soviet Union conducted its first nuclear test. The intelligence that the Soviet spies had gathered certainly accelerated the development of the Soviet bomb, but it was by no means essential. The scientists working on the project, led by the physicist Igor Kurchatov (1903–1960) and overseen by Lavrenty Beria (1899–1953), the former head of the NKVD (People's Commissariat of Internal Affairs), were among the world's best and, in all likelihood, they would eventually have succeeded in building the bomb on their own. The infiltration of the Manhattan Project, as dramatic as it was, only saved the Soviets a few years of work. Nevertheless, the 1949 test was a huge surprise to the United States, which had expected to enjoy its monopoly until at least the early 1950s.

THE HYDROGEN BOMB

President Truman responded by ordering the construction of a hydrogen bomb, a fusion weapon that would be several hundred times more powerful than the fission bombs dropped on Japan. The decision was a controversial one among American scientists, many of whom, including Oppenheimer, opposed any further research on such devastating weapons. A hydrogen bomb would be so powerful, they argued, that it could only be used against civilian populations and was therefore inherently a tool of genocide. However, a number of equally eminent scientists supported Truman, including Edward Teller. Teller insisted that the Soviets would build a fusion bomb regardless of what the Americans did. The United States could not afford to be intimidated by the Soviet Union, leaving it no choice but to build a bomb of its own. Along with the hydrogen bomb came the counterintuitive idea that the weapon could be the cornerstone of international peace. If each side could threaten the other with total destruction, then neither would be willing to risk all-out war. This was the kernel of nuclear deterrence, the principle at the heart of Western and Soviet strategy for the duration of the Cold War.

By the time Truman approved the project in January 1950, the Soviets had already made good progress toward their own hydrogen bomb. Unlike their atomic bomb, which was largely based on American plans, Soviet scientists designed this weapon without outside help. Working under the guidance of the brilliant and young Andrei Sakharov (1921–1989), they scored a notable victory, detonating a deliverable bomb in August 1953, more than two years before the Americans. It is noteworthy that the Soviet government never wrestled with the same moral concerns about the hydrogen bomb that the Americans did, because from Moscow's point of view there was little qualitative difference between fission and fusion weapons. The American hydrogen bomb team, with Teller at its head, had tested a hydrogen device ahead of the Soviets, in November 1952 at Eniwetok Atoll in the Pacific. However, this device was so large and unwieldy—weighing more than eighty tons and requiring an enormous refrigerator—that it was of no military use. The test proved that it was possible to build a fusion device, but it took another three years for the Americans to build a usable bomb.

BRITISH AND FRENCH NUCLEAR WEAPONS

By the early 1950s, major changes in both American and Soviet strategy were under way. Nuclear and thermonuclear weapons were so powerful that it was difficult to consider their use in anything but all-out war. But in order to deter one's opponents from even low-level aggression, it was essential to convince them that one was willing to respond with all one's might. This logic undergirded President Dwight Eisenhower's (1890–1969) doctrine of massive retaliation, announced in 1954. One of the key problems with the strategy, however, was persuading American allies of its wisdom.

Right from the end of the Second World War, the United States refused to share either its nuclear research or the weapons themselves with its NATO (North Atlantic Treaty Organization) allies. Washington had pledged to defend these countries against Soviet attack, but insisted on retaining the final say over if and when nuclear weapons would be used. The Western Europeans grew increasingly uncomfortable with this arrangement and disliked their outright reliance on a potentially unreliable ally on such a fundamental issue as national defense. As a result, the British and French insisted

on developing their own independent nuclear deterrents.

British scientists had played a major role in the Manhattan Project but lacked access to crucial parts of the bombs' design. More work was needed. There was little debate within the new Labour government of Clement Richard Attlee (1883–1967) about whether it was worthwhile. Foreign Secretary Ernest Bevin (1881–1951), an adamant anticommunist, insisted that, as a great power with a large empire to govern, Britain needed its own nuclear arsenal. However, there was more to the question than just prestige. Wartime bombardment proved how vulnerable the country was to aerial attack, and nuclear weapons were the best way to deter any potential Soviet aggression. For these reasons, in January 1947 the government approved plans to build the bomb. In October 1952, shortly before the Americans tested their first hydrogen device, the British detonated an atomic bomb off the coast of Western Australia.

It took France rather longer to build an A-bomb. In the immediate aftermath of the Second World War, Charles de Gaulle (1890–1970) believed the country needed its own nuclear weapons, but France had fallen so far behind its allies in science and industry during the Nazi occupation that huge obstacles lay in its path. Strong domestic opposition from the Left meant that there was little political will behind the idea. However, after the 1954 defeat at Dien Bien Phu, the French government was determined to rebuild national prestige. The design and production of nuclear weapons was one way to achieve this goal, and the government of Pierre Mendès-France (1907–1982) approved the project. When de Gaulle returned to power in 1958, he gave the idea his full support. France conducted its first successful test in February 1960.

The logic behind the independent French nuclear arsenal, known as the *force de frappe,* was clear. De Gaulle was adamant that France had to remain a great power. In this light, it was unacceptable to rely on a foreign country—in this case, the United States—on a matter that went to the very heart of national pride. He also shared many of London's fears about the American commitment to his country's defense and believed that, for reasons of both security and prestige, France needed to maintain a certain distance from the United

States and NATO on military matters. There was no way to guarantee Washington's full support in the event of Soviet aggression, so France had to be ready to defend itself. Although these were reasonable concerns in theory, they did not hold up well in practice. The *force de frappe* came into being, but it was an open secret that it would never have been possible without a significant amount of American support. Just as Britain had to abandon its independent nuclear program in 1960 in order to cut costs, France still had to rely on the United States.

MUTUALLY ASSURED DESTRUCTION AND THE CUBAN MISSILE CRISIS

In nuclear weapons' first decade, they existed only in the form of bombs to be dropped from the air. The advances of the 1950s brought new ways to wage nuclear war. Alongside its nuclear research, the Soviet Union had been working on rocket technology with a view to building rockets that could be sent into space. It reached its target in 1957, when it launched a small satellite named *Sputnik* into orbit. Sputnik itself was not of great strategic value, but the rocket that propelled it was. If the Soviets could send a rocket into space, it followed that they could also hit any point in the world with that same rocket. They now had the ability to strike in the United States with a nuclear-armed missile.

The advent of Inter-Continental Ballistic Missiles (ICBMs) changed the Cold War's nuclear calculus. Prior to 1957, much of the continental United States was safe from atomic attack because it was out of range of even the best Soviet bombers. Sputnik destroyed this immunity. The result was panic in both the United States and Western Europe, and the start of a crash program to develop American missiles. A year later—with the help of German scientists such as Wernher von Braun (1912–1977), who had previously worked for the Nazis—the Americans succeeded, sending their own satellite into orbit. Nevertheless, there were widespread fears in Washington of a "missile gap" between the United States and the USSR, spurred on by the characteristically folksy boast of Nikita Khrushchev (1894–1971) that his country was producing missiles as quickly as it did sausages. Through U-2 surveillance flights over the Soviet Union, the Americans soon learned that the advantage in missile production was in fact theirs.

Regardless, the combination of ICBMs and hydrogen bombs meant that the stakes of the nuclear standoff were as high as they could possibly be. Before the development of the H-bomb, there remained the possibility that nuclear war, however horrible, could remain limited. Now, however, a full-scale war waged with thermonuclear missiles would almost certainly destroy entire countries and might even make the planet uninhabitable. On this basis arose the principle of mutually assured destruction, appropriately known as MAD. Neither the United States nor the USSR stood a chance of surviving, let alone winning, a nuclear war. In theory, this certainty would guarantee peace, because neither side could afford even the smallest risk of hostilities.

The theory came under severe strain during the Cuban missile crisis. The crisis was the single most dangerous moment of the Cold War and proved the risks of the nuclear arms race to both superpowers. The Soviet Union began sending nuclear missiles to Cuba after the Bay of Pigs, a failed American attempt in 1961 to overthrow the island's new socialist leader, Fidel Castro (b. 1926). Khrushchev was eager to support the young Cuban leaders, who reminded him of his own revolutionary past. Moreover, Cuba was an ideal site for the USSR's intermediate-range missiles and a beachhead for spreading communism to Latin America. Khrushchev believed he had the perfect opportunity to retaliate against the recent deployment of intermediate-range American missiles in Turkey and to restore some semblance of a strategic balance between East and West, especially given the USSR's relative lack of ICBMs.

When a U-2 flight discovered the Cuban missiles in October 1962, the American government faced a crisis. It could not tolerate hostile nuclear missiles so close to home, but how could it remove them? The administration of John Fitzgerald Kennedy (1917–1963) considered a number of options, including a full-scale invasion of Cuba, air strikes against the launch sites, and a naval blockade to prevent further missile shipments from getting through. The slightest provocation could trigger a nuclear attack on the United States, which would spark full retaliation and end only in mutual annihilation. Kennedy opted for the blockade. The first Soviet ship to encounter the blockade turned around, opening the door to a settlement. After secret negotiations, Khrushchev agreed to pull the missiles out of Cuba if the United States would remove its missiles from Turkey. Kennedy agreed, and the crisis came to an end.

ARMS CONTROL EFFORTS

The Cuban missile crisis was the clearest indication yet of how easy it would be to tumble into a catastrophic nuclear war. Some kind of arms control was necessary to reduce this danger. The first step in this direction came the year after the crisis, with the signing of the Limited Test Ban Treaty (LTBT). According to its provisions, signatories pledged to stop atmospheric tests of nuclear weapons in order to restrict their development and end the provocations that typically followed each test. All future tests had to happen underground.

The agreement was a modest but signal step, the first attempt to contain the use of nuclear weapons. In August 1963, the Americans, Soviets, and British signed the treaty. Insisting as ever on its independence, the only other nuclear power, France, refused to join them. Two months later, the superpowers also agreed to ban nuclear weapons from space.

Further progress was made in the late 1960s and into the 1970s, an era of calm and stability compared with the early Cold War years. Following the LTBT, the next major milestone was the Nonproliferation Treaty (NPT), concluded in 1968. Despite another French refusal to participate, the Americans, Soviets, and British brought the negotiations to a successful conclusion. The treaty committed them to prevent the spread of nuclear weapons to other countries. The higher the number of states that had nuclear weapons, the reasoning went, the greater the danger of their use in a conflict. Prestige was also on the line, since if the nuclear club could be kept small, the value of membership would remain commensurately high. Indeed, the three signatories gave no serious thought to reducing their stockpiles. It was enough to prevent others from building their own.

Into the 1970s, the superpowers refused to cut back the numbers of their missiles and weapons. They instead agreed to restrict their growth. SALT—the Strategic Arms Limitation Talks—was the result. Starry-eyed idealism motivated neither superpower. Each had pragmatic goals: the Russians some relief from the arms race at a time of economic trouble and the Americans a strategic advantage and fodder for President Richard Nixon's (1913–1994) reelection campaign. Negotiated both by arms control experts in Helsinki and Vienna and between the U.S. national security advisor Henry Kissinger (b. 1923) and the Soviet ambassador Anatoly Dobrynin—the so-called backchannel—the SALT agreements placed limits on antiballistic missile defenses and froze the construction of missile launchers for five years. These results were not overwhelming, but both sides were optimistic that they had built a solid foundation for future progress.

Nixon's successor, Gerald Ford (b. 1913), attempted to maintain the momentum that SALT had generated. In 1974 he and Leonid Brezhnev (1906–1982) agreed on a set of guidelines for the next round of arms control talks, known as SALT II. The goal was to pick up where the first agreement had left off, but the United States refused to discuss its nuclear forces in Europe, a key area of interest for the Soviets. Brezhnev, determined not to let the talks collapse, pressured his domestic critics—especially within the military—to accept the American terms. He succeeded, and negotiators agreed to a maximum of 2,250 missile launchers each. But Ford's successor, Jimmy Carter (b. 1924), insisted on cuts that were even more radical and less acceptable to the skeptics within the Soviet government. Brezhnev and the Soviet military were furious. It took until 1979 to repair the damage and reach a new agreement.

Although a deal was reached, it was never implemented. The United States Senate insisted that the agreement was unverifiable because there was no way to ensure that the Soviets would hold up their end of the bargain. Moreover, the broader process of détente collapsed in the wake of the Soviet invasion of Afghanistan in 1979 and the election of Ronald Reagan (1911–2004) in 1980. Hopes for arms control fell apart as Cold War tensions returned to levels unseen since the early 1960s.

ABLE ARCHER, GORBACHEV, AND THE END OF THE COLD WAR

Reagan came into office on a strong anticommunist platform. Rejecting any further arms control talks, he massively increased the American military budget. Part of this renewed toughness was the deployment of new nuclear missiles—Cruise and Pershing 2—in Western Europe as a response to the Soviets' recent installation of the new SS-20 missiles. Protestors organized massive rallies to oppose the move, but failed to stop it.

In this context of heightened tension, NATO staged a war game, dubbed "Able Archer," in late 1983. The Soviet military detected the exercises but, already on edge because of Reagan's bellicose rhetoric, mistook them for the prelude to a Western attack. Moscow put its forces on alert, ready to respond with nuclear weapons if necessary. The danger was not as acute as it had been during the Cuban missile crises, but both sides still approached the brink of nuclear war without ever intending to. The episode reminded Washington and Moscow of the wisdom of returning to the negotiating table.

The rise to power in 1985 of Mikhail Gorbachev (b. 1931) provided the opportunity for new arms control talks. In 1986 Gorbachev publicly proposed a plan to eliminate all nuclear weapons by the year 2000. The proposal was bold and unprecedented, and it caught the Reagan administration's attention. When the two leaders met at Reykjavik later that year, Gorbachev renewed his offer, and Reagan responded enthusiastically. However, the Soviet leader insisted that the Americans would have to abandon their Strategic Defense Initiative—a research program, popularly known as "star wars," to build a shield against ballistic missiles—before any deal could be reached. Reagan refused. The summit ended without agreement.

This was only a temporary setback. Both sides were now considering massive cuts to their nuclear arsenals, a situation that could not even have been contemplated five years earlier. They renewed their efforts, and reached a deal at the Washington summit in December 1987, agreeing to eliminate their nuclear weapons stationed in Europe. The Intermediate-Range Nuclear Forces (INF) treaty came into force in June 1988. This was the beginning of the end of the nuclear standoff that had lasted almost forty years.

The next major milestone came after the fall of the Berlin Wall in 1989. In July 1991 the United States and the USSR signed the Strategic Arms Reduction Treaty (START), the culmination of negotiations that had begun while Reagan was still in office. The first major commitment to reduce nuclear stockpiles since the invention of the atomic bomb, it required both sides to cut their arsenals by almost a third. It was a major accomplishment and proof that the Cold War was effectively over. The USSR itself collapsed in December, devolving the treaty's obligations onto its successor states. President George Herbert Walker Bush (b. 1924) and his Russian counterpart Boris Yeltsin (b. 1931) signed START II in January 1993. The treaty expanded on START I, radically restricting the possession of nuclear weapons and delivery systems to between three thousand and thirty-five hundred on each side. After ratification by the U.S. Senate in 1996 and the Russian Duma in 2000, it was superseded by the 2002 Strategic Offensive Reduction Treaty (SORT), which capped each side's nuclear arsenal between seventeen hundred and twenty-two hundred warheads.

Nuclear weapons continue to be a major issue in international politics, but the focus has shifted away from the major powers. There is increasing concern, particularly in the West, about the proliferation of nuclear weapons both to smaller states and to nonstate actors, especially terrorist networks. The Indian subcontinent has been relatively stable since the surprise Indian and Pakistani nuclear tests of 1998, but in the early twenty-first century there have been worries that North Korea and Iran were developing weapons of their own. In a similar vein, the American government cited Iraq's alleged nuclear weapons as a justification for the invasion of that country in 2003. Given the number of weapons in existence worldwide—and the availability of so-called suitcase bombs—it is impossible to stop the spread of nuclear technology completely. The threat of nuclear proliferation is one of the severest tests facing the international system in the early twenty-first century. Deterrence provided the basis for stability during the Cold War, but it remains to be seen whether any similar idea can be found to avert the use of nuclear weapons in years to come.

See also **Cold War; Cuban Missile Crisis; Disarmament; Potsdam Conference.**

BIBLIOGRAPHY

Beach, Sir Hugh, and Nadine Gurr. *Flattering the Passions; or, The Bomb and Britain's Bid for a World Role.* London, 1999.

Carlisle, Rodney, ed. *Encyclopedia of the Atomic Age.* New York, 2001.

Craig, Campbell. *Destroying the Village: Eisenhower and Thermonuclear War.* New York, 1998.

Fursenko, Aleksandr, and Timothy Naftali. *One Hell of a Gamble: Khrushchev, Castro, and Kennedy, 1958–1964.* New York, 1997.

Holloway, David. *Stalin and the Bomb: The Soviet Union and Atomic Energy, 1939–1956.* New Haven, Conn., 1994.

Rhodes, Richard. *The Making of the Atomic Bomb.* New York, 1986.

MICHAEL D. J. MORGAN

NUREMBERG LAWS. The Nuremberg Laws were the culmination of the Nazi Party's strategy to remove Jewish citizens from German public life. The Nazi regime wanted to create a legal system in which citizenship was to be granted on the basis of racial identity. In order to fulfill the Nazi aspiration of a state based on racial purity it was essential to separate different groups to prevent what the Nazi regime referred to as "racial mixing." The Nuremberg Laws were intended to reverse the assimilation of the Jewish individuals in German society and to this end legalized their segregation and persecution. These pieces of legislation were so-called because they were passed at the annual Nazi Party rally in Nuremberg in September 1935. Adolf Hitler had convened a special meeting of the Reichstag at the end of the annual Nazi Party congress at the Hall of the Nuremberg Cultural Association with the specific aim of ratifying three laws, two of which, the Reich Citizenship Law and the Law for the Protection of German Blood and German Honor, provided the legal basis for exclusion of Jews from German society, depriving them of the normal rights accorded to citizens. These two laws are often referred to together as the "Nuremberg racial laws." The third law passed at Nuremberg, the Reich Flag Law, ordained that black, white, and red were to be the national colors and the swastika was to become the national flag. The Reich Flag Law came about at a time when Hitler was beginning a grand rearmament. He wanted his new army to be a National Socialist one. To this extent the first step on the road to such an army was to be symbolic. The old imperial black, white, and red flag was to be abandoned in favor of the swastika.

The Reich Citizenship Law (*Reichsburgergesetz*) classified Jews as citizens of lesser value and stripped them of all political rights. Jews were to be officially placed in the category of alien subject (*Staatsangehorige*), a category of individual who belonged to the state but who did not enjoy any political rights. Those deemed to be of "German or related blood" were accorded full political rights and were accorded full citizenship of the *Reich*. In order to be recognized as a "full German" citizen, individuals would have to possess a Certificate of Descent or "Aryan Certificate" (*Arieernachweis*). These full *Reich* citizens (*Reichsburger*) were the only class of citizen to enjoy the full range of civil and political rights. Interestingly these so-called political and civil rights were not defined specifically. In fact, in practice, individual rights no longer existed in Nazi Germany, regardless of one's citizenship status. The Reich Citizenship Law created a notion of citizenship premised on racial characteristics. Thus unlike liberal concepts of individual rights this law promulgated a notion of inherent inequality based on one's ethnic background rather than recognizing the inherent equality of all citizens regardless of race, class, or religion.

The Law for the Protection of the German Blood and German Honor (Gesetz zum Schutze des deutschen Blutes und der deutschen Ehre) prohibited marriages and sexual relations between Jews (*Staatsangehorige*) and Germans (*Reichsburger*). It also outlawed the employment of German females under forty-five in Jewish households, declared null and void marriages contracted between Jews and "full Germans" in Germany or abroad, and prohibited Jews from raising the German flag. The punishment for breach of this law included imprisonment with hard labor.

Both the Reich Citizenship Law and the Law for the Protection of the German Blood and German Honor did not, however, define who a Jew was for the purposes of this policy. The regime moved to fill this legal void by preparing a complicated and contradictory classification system to determine who could be accorded "full German" citizenship. On the basis of Article III of the Reich Citizenship Law, a First Supplementary Decree was issued on 14 November 1935. This decree set out a classificatory system to distinguish Jews from "full" German citizens in accordance with the Nazi racialist ideology. The decree defined a "full" Jew as anyone descended from at least three Jewish grandparents. Two categories were created for those who were not "full" Jews but who were of mixed origins. These were referred to as *Mischlinge* (mixed race) "of the first and second degree." *Mischlinge* of the first degree were defined as those people with two Jewish grandparents, who were not married to a Jewish person and who did not belong to the Jewish religious community. However, *Mischlinge* of the first degree could be defined as "full" Jews for the purposes of the Nuremberg Laws if they were either members of the Jewish religious community when the Nuremberg Laws were promulgated on 15 September 1935 or who joined after this date; were married to a Jew, or were the offspring of a marriage with a Jew that took place after 15 September 1935; or were born as the result of an extramarital relationship with a Jew after 31 July 1936. *Mischlinge* of the second degree were defined as persons with one Jewish grandparent.

Mischlinge of the first degree required official consent to marry a "full German" or a *Mischling* of the second degree. They were permitted to marry another *Mischling* of the first degree or a "full Jew." However, if they married a full Jew they too would be defined as a full Jew for the purposes of the Nuremberg Laws. *Mischlinge* of the second degree did not require official permission to marry a German but were prohibited from marrying a full Jew or another *Mischling* of the second degree and required special dispensation to marry a *Mischling* of the first degree. Both categories of *Mischlinge* were prohibited from holding positions in the civil service and the Nazi party and were allowed to serve in the army only as private soldiers but not as officers. Full German citizens were not defined formally in the Nuremberg Laws except in the negative sense of not having any Jewish grandparents.

These labyrinthine and ludicrous classifications were intended to prevent what the Nazis called "racial mixing." The Nuremberg Laws created a category of crime called *Rassenschande*, literally "racial disgrace" but known colloquially as either "race defilement" or "racial pollution." Courts interpreted the laws very broadly often interpreting *Rassenschande* to mean any contact whatsoever, not just physical contact, with people classified as Jews by the Nuremberg Laws. In practice, courts saw *Rassenschande* as tantamount to high treason and meted out severe punishments to those accused of this crime. In the immediate period following the introduction of the Nuremberg Laws the average sentence for those found guilty of this crime was five years. In practice Jewish men accused of *Rassenschande* were given longer sentences than full German men accused of the same act. During the Second World War, those accused of such acts under the law were not even sent for trial but were either summarily executed or sent directly to concentration camps.

The Nuremberg Laws, although primarily directed against the Jewish population, were also employed against other groups deemed "inferior" by the Nazi regime. Thus, Wilhelm Frick, the *Reich* Minister for the Interior who had responsibility for the enforcement of the Nuremberg Laws, declared that the laws would be equally applicable to other groups defined as being of "alien blood" (*Artfremd*). He cited the examples of "Gypsies and Negroes."

The Nuremberg Laws led to the treatment of members of the Jewish community as socially excluded aliens. Members of the Nazi Party and civil servants were not allowed to visit or do business with Jewish-owned firms. The Nuremberg Laws were followed by a large variety of decrees, regulations, and laws that led to the purging of those classified as Jews from all jobs in education, local and national government, the arts, and the media. The Nuremberg Laws also prompted a large number of discriminatory regulations at the local and regional level. For example, ordinances at the municipal level prevented Jews from attending cinemas and from using public parks and other public facilities. Ultimately the distinction between "full Jew" and "full German" in the Nuremberg

Laws laid the legal groundwork for the implementation of the Nazi genocide of the Jewish population.

See also **Germany; Hitler, Adolf; Nazism.**

BIBLIOGRAPHY

Burleigh, Michael, and Wolfgang Wippermann. *The Racial State: Germany 1933–1945.* Cambridge, U.K., and New York, 1991.

Dawidowicz, Lucy S. *The War against the Jews 1933–45.* Reprint, London, 1990.

Friedländer, Saul. *Nazi Germany and the Jews.* Vol. 1: *The Years of Persecution, 1933–1939.* New York, 1997.

Gellately, Robert. *The Gestapo and German Society: Enforcing Racial Policy, 1933–1945.* Oxford, U.K., and New York, 1990.

Hilberg, Raoul. *The Destruction of the European Jews.* New York, 1985.

Kaplan, Marion. *Between Dignity and Despair: Jewish Life in Nazi Germany.* New York, 1998.

Kershaw, Ian. *The Hitler Myth: Image and Reality in the Third Reich.* New York, 1987.

Levin, Nora. *The Holocaust: The Destruction of European Jewry, 1933–1945.* New York, 1973.

Müller, Ingo. *Hitler's Justice: The Courts of the Third Reich.* Translated by Deborah Lucas Schneider. Cambridge, Mass., 1991.

Schleunes, Karl. *The Twisted Road to Auschwitz: Nazi Policy toward German Jews, 1933–1939.* Urbana, Ill., 1970.

Wollenberg, Jorg, ed. *The German Public and the Persecution of the Jews, 1933–1945: "No One Participated, No One Knew."* Atlantic Highlands, N.J., 1996.

PATRICK HANAFIN

NUREMBERG WAR CRIMES TRIALS. The trials of major Nazi leaders at Nuremberg, Germany, which dramatically changed international law and politics and introduced the criminal liability of political leaders for their atrocious acts, came close to not happening. The Nuremberg principle of arraigning state leaders for crimes against peace and humanity was unprecedented, and the British Foreign Office argued as early as 1942 that the crimes were so grave that ordinary judicial proceedings were unable to deal with the guilt.

The U.S. war department was the keenest supporter of setting up the tribunal as a way of demonstrating the superiority of the rule of law. Support for the use of judicial proceedings came unexpectedly from Joseph Stalin, the head of the Soviet Union. The Moscow trials of the 1930s had persuaded the Russian jurists that justice should be public and popular, while ensuring that the outcome would be certain convictions and executions. At the Yalta meeting of the leaders of United States, the United Kingdom, and the Soviet Union in 1944, Winston Churchill still favored the summary execution of war criminals. But the American-Soviet alliance won the argument, and the San Francisco summit meeting of May 1945 agreed to set up a military tribunal to try Nazi leaders. Under the London charter establishing the tribunal, eight judges were appointed, two each from the United States, the United Kingdom, the Soviet Union, and France.

The assistant U.S. Supreme Court justice Robert Jackson (1892–1954) was appointed chief American prosecutor by President Harry Truman. Jackson and the Americans became the driving force of the tribunal, smoothing the differences among the British, Soviet, and French lawyers. The trials were a first in every way, and legal arguments broke out in relation both to the list of defendants and the charges to be brought. Eventually twenty-two Nazis were prosecuted. Six were major leaders, such as Hermann Goering, Rudolf Hess, and Joachim von Ribbentrop, while others were chosen to represent different parts of the Nazi state. The framing of the indictment was equally difficult. The charge of war crimes existed in prewar international law and was the easiest to prosecute. But the crime of waging an aggressive war had no proper legal definition and could not cover atrocities against the German people or the elimination of civilians on grounds of race. The first problem was dealt with by the legal device of prosecuting the defendants for conspiracy to wage war. The latter was dealt with through the creation of the novel legal category of crimes against humanity. The conspiracy charge allowed the prosecution of a number of Nazi organizations and weakened the defendants' argument that the crimes did not exist at the time of their commission.

U.S. prosecutor Robert Jackson (left) and Soviet assistant prosecutor Colonel Yuri Pokrovsky listen to a speech during the Nuremberg war crimes trials, October 1946. ©BETTMANN/CORBIS

The trials started on 20 November 1945. The prosecution gave detailed evidence in relation to the charges, called witnesses, and cross-examined the defendants. The defense attacked the exceptional character of the trials, arguing that they were an example of victors' justice. The defendants challenged the jurisdiction of the tribunal, except in relation to war crimes. The defendants also challenged the retroactive application of criminal law, arguing that the novel category of crimes against humanity meant that the defendants could not have known the principles they were allegedly violating.

The court relied on prewar treaties banning wars of aggression and rejected the objection about the retroactive character of the criminal prosecutions. Trying to stay within the bounds of prewar legal concepts, the tribunal restricted the examination of crimes against humanity to those committed in the context of a war of aggression and excluded from the indictment acts committed before the invasion of Poland. The defense objections were often rejected by means of weak legal arguments, but the tribunal made it clear that the trials were creating a new type of postwar world order based on the rule of law.

The trials were concluded on 30 September 1946. Twelve defendants, including Goering and Ribbentropp, were sentenced to death. Hess was sentenced to life imprisonment, six defendants to various prison terms, and three were acquitted.

Those sentenced to death were hanged on 16 October 1946. By then Goering had committed suicide by poison smuggled into his prison cell.

The Nuremberg trials were a turning point in international law. The tribunal revitalized the ancient theory of natural law, which had been abandoned in the positivist dominance of the twentieth century. According to this theory, certain acts are prohibited by a universal law that stands higher than the law of the state. Those committing them cannot be excused by invoking the laws of their domestic legal system. The human rights revolution of the second half of the twentieth century owes much of its moral force to the arguments put forward at Nuremberg. By inaugurating the individual criminal liability of political leaders, the trials paved the legal way for the weakening of state sovereignty in cases of grave violations of human rights and the creation of a universal jurisdiction to deal with such crimes. The International Criminal Court that came into operation in 2002 is the direct descendant of the Nuremberg trials. Later experience indicates that the law and criminal responsibility cannot prevent atrocities on their own. But the aspiration is honorable, and the concept of crimes against humanity has created a universal standard that no government or politician should be able to violate with impunity.

See also **Concentration Camps; Goering, Hermann; Hess, Rudolf; Holocaust; Human Rights; War Crimes.**

BIBLIOGRAPHY

Primary Sources

Collected Recordings from the Nuremberg Trial of Major German War Criminals. Vincent Voice Library, Michigan State University. VVL-01-0001. Available at http://vvl.lib.msu.edu/showfindingaid.cfm?findaidid= Nuremberg.

Secondary Sources

Conot, Robert. *Justice at Nuremberg.* New York, 1983.

Douglas, Lawrence. *The Memory of Judgment: Making Law and History in the Trials of the Holocaust.* New Haven, Conn., 2001.

Marrus, Michael R., comp. *The Nuremberg War Crimes Trial, 1945–46: A Documentary History.* Boston, 1997.

Sands, Philippe, ed. *From Nuremberg to the Hague: The Future of International Criminal Justice.* Cambridge, U.K., 2003.

Smith, Bradley. *Reaching Judgment at Nuremberg.* New York, 1977.

Taylor, Telford. *The Anatomy of the Nuremberg Trials: A Personal Memoir.* New York, 1992.

COSTAS DOUZINAS

OCCUPATION, MILITARY.

OCCUPATION, MILITARY. While military occupation, the seizure and domination of foreign territory, is an ancient phenomenon, the twentieth century saw a rise in new, ideologically charged occupations. These differed greatly from the customs of *ancien régime* Europe, when territories were annexed or transferred from one dynastic state to another without reference to ethnicity or broader political justification (when Frederick II, king of Prussia [r. 1740–1786], seized Silesia from Austria in 1740, ancestral claims were a mere afterthought). While beliefs certainly played a role in prior wars, and while brutal realpolitik continued into the new century, the emphasis on ideological claims concerning politics and social organization was new in its intensity. Soviet dictator Joseph Stalin (1879–1953) declared during World War II that "this war is not as in the past; whoever occupies a territory also imposes his own social system. Everyone imposes his own system as far as his armies can reach. It cannot be otherwise."

TYPES OF OCCUPATION

Types of occupations can be distinguished in terms of the explanations advanced for them by the occupiers. In the first place, thinking about modern military occupations within Europe was affected by the experience of European imperialist powers overseas and their annexation of vast territories around the globe in the late nineteenth century. The political philosopher Hannah Arendt (1906–1975) intuited a connection between imperialism and the rise of modern totalitarian ideologies with vast appetites for conquest, and observed that the Nazis acted like foreign rulers in their own country before expanding their realm. Yet within Europe, ideological justification for military occupation was often couched in terms of popular legitimacy or democraticization, as liberation. With the occupation of defeated Germany in 1945, democratization and denazification were stated Allied aims, even as they were pursued differently in East and West. Stalin's imposition of communist rule on six Eastern European countries after World War II (Poland, Hungary, Czechoslovakia, Romania, Bulgaria, and East Germany), and Soviet annexation of the Baltic States (Lithuania, Latvia, and Estonia) with the introduction of political, economic, and educational systems modeled on the Soviet Union, were presented as a perfection of "people's democracy." Not all ideological justifications embraced the rhetoric of democracy. In the Nazi case, SS leader Heinrich Himmler (1900–1945) observed that the aim of their policies in the East was no longer Germanization of native populations, as in the past, but resettlement by pure Germans.

A further criterion for types of occupation involves the intended future goals for the territory, including whether the occupation is to be temporary or permanent, with the territory made over fundamentally, as a new order. Nazi racial resettlement plans for eastern Europe aimed to provide "living space" for a Germanic master race through expulsions and mass murder. After World War II, Soviet policies of Russification in the Baltic states continued over decades. Other military occupations have been rationalized by security needs. The planned fifteen-year Allied occupation of the Rhineland area after Germany's defeat in World War I was to give France added security against a revival of German aggression. In other cases, economic necessity is an element. When French and Belgian forces occupied the Ruhr valley region of Germany in January 1923, they aimed to extract reparations they were owed. Soviet dismantling of factories and confiscation of raw materials from eastern Germany from 1945 on was likewise an explicitly economic motivation. More recently, military occupations have claimed humanitarian motivations. NATO forces entered the Kosovo area of the former Yugoslavia on 12 June 1999 (under a United Nations mandate) to stave off mass ethnic cleansing by Serbian forces against the region's Albanian majority.

RULES OF BEHAVIOR

Depending on the stated aim of an occupation, occupiers can show a range of behaviors, from the mild to the murderous. German soldiers in France and Denmark, conquered in 1940, were ordered to be friendly and considerate of the civilian populations, to win them over. By contrast, in Belgium and northern France in 1914, exaggerated fears of guerrilla resistance led German forces to brutal reprisals in which they executed at least 6,400 civilians, in a policy of deliberate terrorization. The Soviet occupation of the Baltic states in 1940 was followed by targeted deportations of civilians to Siberia, to break local resistance. With the Nazi invasion of Poland in September 1939, a murder campaign called Operation Tannenberg ran in tandem with the establishment of the occupation, aiming to destroy Polish elites (by December 1939, up to 50,000 Poles had been killed). Historians argue that in eastern Europe during World War II, superiors tacitly tolerated German soldiers' abuses of the civilian population as a safety valve for the intense discipline the soldiers were under. In Belarus, more than 2 million civilians and POWs were murdered during World War II. In a cycle of revenge, Soviet forces moving onto German territory in 1944 and 1945 engaged in pillage, mass rapes, and brutalization of civilians (though instances of kindness and forbearance were also recorded).

Paradoxically, the same occupier can act in radically different ways in different occupied areas at the same time, for ideological reasons: Nazi occupation of eastern European countries was incomparably harsher than their rule in western and northern Europe, since Slavs and other non-German eastern Europeans had less racial value in the Nazi worldview.

INTERNATIONAL LAW

International law has not been able to regulate occupations effectively in an age of total war. This is evidenced by the fact that while up to 10 percent of deaths in World War I were civilian, this ratio rose to an estimated 50 percent in World War II. Yet the very fact of repeated attempts to legislate restraint testifies both to the brutality and breaking of custom, as well as the durable will to limit the destructiveness of occupations.

Conventions have sought to define legal and illegal combatants, rights to resist invasion, abolition of hostage taking and collective punishments (holding localities responsible for acts committed in their vicinity), security of private property, and other protections for civilians. They also underlined the occupying power's responsibility for the maintenance of civil order. Before World War I, the 1907 Hague Convention (IV) Respecting the Laws and Customs of War on Land represented a major attempt in this direction, but was interpreted differently and violated in the war. The 1929 Geneva Convention Relative to the Treatment of Prisoners of War did not settle questions about the treatment and status of civilians in occupied areas. Given added impulse by the atrocities of World War II, the four Geneva Conventions of 12 August 1949 built on earlier efforts (the Geneva Convention of 1864 and the Hague Conventions). Among these, the Convention for the Protection of Civilian Persons in Times of War also defined a right to civilian resistance against occupation, not only invasion. The Geneva Conventions were further elaborated in the controversial 1977 Additional Protocols to apply to guerrilla wars and civil wars. These international legal constraints, however, were and are often broken in practice.

LEGAL STRUCTURES

Occupiers impose new legal structures and institutions in their exercise of control. Drawing on the experience of European imperialism overseas, many occupiers recognized the benefits of indirect rule, as perfected in the British Empire, stressing cooptation of local elites and delegation of responsibility. Thus, many occupations also retain structures of the earlier authority. Hitler preferred cooptation of established national elites in conquered countries over patronage for local imitators of the Nazis, who were often marginal socially and politically. After its conquest in April 1940, the Nazis treated conquered Denmark as a "model protectorate," retaining its king, parliament, and civil administration. In occupied Soviet areas, from 1941, the Nazis initially retained the Soviet structure of collective farms, in spite of their condemnation of Bolshevism, because these farms were useful for centralizing control of the food supply. Legal structures also have charted the breakdown of relations between former allies in occupation, as the creation of two independent German states in 1949 under Western and Soviet patronage made clear. Finally, the formal outlining of legal structures is not a perfect description of real power relations in occupation, as in practice these legal strictures can be negotiated, violated, or subverted. Occupying powers also often use their authority to extract economic resources and labor. German occupiers used forced labor in both world wars. Under Nazi occupation, France was obliged to pay the costs of its own occupation, ultimately contributing some 40 percent of all foreign resources directed to the German war effort. Requisitioning of food without regard to the needs of the civilian population led to an estimated 300,000 Greeks starving to death under Nazi occupation.

SOCIAL LIFE UNDER OCCUPATION

It is a general truth that a military occupation is always a relationship, however brutal or enlightened that regime might be in real, day-to-day practice. An occupation also involves more than just two monolithic and opposed parties, the occupiers and the occupied: rather, distinct divisions and groupings can exist on each side and their mutual relations contribute to the dynamics of life under occupation. An important factor in shaping an occupation is whether there is a prior history of conflict or interaction between the parties, shaping preconceptions and prejudices. The Germans and French held traditional concepts of each other as hereditary enemies,

while American military occupation of a zone in western Germany after 1945 saw the emergence of newer stereotypes, less rooted in a distant shared past. Also, in the establishment of an occupation, first impressions seem crucial, with initial experiences conditioning the regime. In the German occupation of territories in eastern Europe in World War I, the encounter with unfamiliar lands and peoples and the devastation of Russian scorched-earth policies shaped the occupiers' perspective.

Social life under an occupation is determined by often radical status reversals. Earlier pre-invasion hierarchies are recoded, often in traumatic ways. Most obviously, the outside military forces demand deference and are atop the new social order. In the French occupation of the German Rhineland after World War I, French African colonial troops from Morocco and Senegal were among the occupying forces. German nationalists denounced this as a special humiliation, reversing the subordination of non-European peoples to Europeans. For its part, the occupying power can seek to co-opt groups within the subject population, in a policy of "divide and conquer." In both world wars, German authorities sought to encourage Flemish separatism in Belgium, with little success. In tandem with the occupation of the Rhineland after World War I, the French supported attempts to set up an independent Rhenish state. In Nazi-occupied Poland, a *Volksliste* or ethnic list of privileged persons of German ancestry was drawn up, including some two million Poles registered as Germans. Nazi occupiers also sought to scapegoat the Jewish minority within occupied populations, as a focus for displaced resentments.

Occupations also feature an altered demography of the subject population, especially in terms of gender. Fewer men of military age remain (killed, taken prisoner, or withdrawn in retreat), and the populace is disproportionately made up of the young, the old, and women, confronting a mostly male enemy military. Rapes have often accompanied military occupations, even when formally proscribed by military regulations. The Soviet army's mass rapes of German women in the years following 1944 did much to undermine the authority of the Soviet occupation and later the East German state. Less brutally, occupations are also often marked by fraternization (even when this is also forbidden), the interaction of the civilian population with the foreign military, and the emergence of personal relationships, whether based on prostitution or sincere emotion. Such fraternization is often condemned as "horizontal collaboration" by those unreconciled to the occupation. In World War I, an estimated 10,000 births resulted from German soldiers and French mothers in the occupied area, and in World War II, the result of occupation was 50,000 to 70,000 Franco-German babies (other estimates run far higher). In Nazi-occupied Norway, Germans fathered over 8,000 "war children." Such children often faced discrimination and shame after the occupation.

Frequently neglected in the historical narrative, occupations are also especially harsh on the mentally ill or disabled, who may find it even more difficult to adjust to the changed order and new rules of behavior and subordination, with dangerous consequences in emergency situations like checkpoints or searches.

RESISTANCE AND COLLABORATION

The social and political life of occupation opens up intense and complicated moral questions of how the occupied should react. Choices to resist or collaborate can change over time, often determined by perceptions of likely future prospects. It is also crucial to note that both resistance and collaboration are usually not all-or-nothing categories, but rather represent a spectrum of possible actions. One question brings some dilemmas into focus: under occupation, is doing business as usual a form of resistance or collaboration?

Resistance can come in forms large and small, ranging from armed attacks, sabotage, and spying on the enemy to more discreet reactions: reading underground literature, listening to foreign radio broadcasts, muttering sly jokes, or even simply maintaining a cold silence toward the occupier, avoiding eye contact. Active resistance tends to be rarer (it is estimated that only 2 percent of the French population were involved in active resistance against the Nazis), because of the extraordinarily high cost it can exact, not only personally for the resister if caught, but also in reprisals against relatives or hostages from the community at large, often undercutting popular support for the resistance. However, resistance tends to grow in proportion to calculation of likelihood of defeat, so

that resistance to the Nazis grew across occupied Europe after their defeat at Stalingrad in 1943, seen as a turning point in the war. Yet even resistance is not monolithic, as there are many cases of rival resistance movements fighting internal civil wars in tandem with their opposition to occupation. Resistance can also last very long: the guerrilla war of the "Forest Brothers" against Soviet occupation in the Baltics lasted into the 1950s.

At the other pole of possible reactions is collaboration, cooperation with the occupier, out of a variety of possible motives. The concept of "collaboration" was originally coined in France during World War II, and at first carried positive connotations of working together with the occupiers for the good of the defeated yet regenerated French nation, before acquiring its present negative aura. Though not under military rule, the Vichy French regime under the figurehead of Marshal Philippe Pétain (1856–1951), with the slogan of "Work, Family, and Country," enthusiastically sought a place in the "New Europe" of Hitler. Their anti-Semitic measures culminated in the rounding up and shipping of Jews from France to the Nazi death camps. A key criterion in whether collaboration is possible is whether the occupying forces see the subject population as capable or worthy of collaboration. The comparative scarcity of Polish collaboration with the Nazis during World War II, relative to elsewhere in occupied Europe, was due both to Polish patriotism and the Nazis' racial hatred. Collaboration could also be explicitly motivated by ideology. The craven attempts at collaboration of Norwegian Nazi leader Vidkun Quisling (1887–1945) made his name synonymous with treason (though paradoxically he was marginalized by Hitler's preference for cooperation with established elites). Committed anti-Semites from eastern European populations helped in the Nazis' genocide against the Jews. Occupying powers sometimes also seek to recruit auxiliaries or military forces to fight at their side. In World War I, Germany and Austria-Hungary declared a Kingdom of Poland on 5 November 1916, hoping to recruit a Polish volunteer army, but the results were utterly disappointing. Nazi rhetoric of a "New Europe" and a crusade against bolshevism inaugurated the creation of SS foreign legions in which an estimated 500,000 non-German Europeans served, though not all were volunteers. Finally, collaboration can also be motivated by simple opportunism. Denunciations of neighbors to the occupation authorities to settle private scores are key examples of the reversals of fortune and status that occupations bring.

The complexity of the issues of resistance and collaboration is further heightened in regions that experience successive occupations, like the Baltic states (Soviet occupation, 1940–1941; Nazi occupation, 1941–1944; Soviet reoccupation, 1944–1991). With each successive occupation, the labels of resister and collaborator can be suddenly reversed, with existential consequences.

AFTERMATH OF OCCUPATION

The impact of military occupation extends far beyond its establishment and consolidation, depending on whether it is eventually reversed, or whether it becomes permanent. Over time, military occupation can segue into civil administration and incorporation into the victor's territory. If an occupation is reversed by continued war or a peace settlement, the consequences are also far-ranging, as the reversal of hierarchies and subordination is again overturned. The result is not always a return to the status quo ante bellum. A vivid example is France after 1944, where liberation was accompanied by purges of alleged collaborators, in which at least 4,500 were executed immediately, with some 124,000 later put on trial. In what later would seem an asymmetrical verdict, French women accused of fraternization with Germans had their heads shaved and were paraded through the streets, while some prominent collaborators were not brought to justice. The French Fourth Republic was established to mark a break with the past. In Greece, frictions between different resistance movements erupted into a civil war. The overturning of Nazi rule in eastern Europe likewise led to acts of revenge against ethnic Germans in the region, who were expelled from their homes in the millions.

Liberated societies experience the need to deal with the traumatic collective memory of occupation, often replacing it with new public heroic narratives of united resistance, even as private memory retains the more complicated everyday realities. In international politics, the former occupier's acknowledgement of the occupation is an important factor. The famous scene of German

chancellor Willy Brandt (1913–1992) kneeling before a memorial to Jewish victims of the Nazis during his visit in December 1970 is emblematic of this. By contrast, more than a decade after the fall of the Soviet Union, the Russian government's official denial of the Soviet occupation of the Baltic states in 1940 continues to burden international relations and reconciliation between those neighboring states. The legacies of occupation are overcome only very slowly, if at all.

See also **Displaced Persons; Forced Labor; Holocaust; War Crimes; Warfare; World War I; World War II.**

BIBLIOGRAPHY

Bartov, Omer. *Hitler's Army: Soldiers, Nazis, and War in the Third Reich.* New York, 1991.

Cobb, Richard. *French and Germans, Germans and French: A Personal Interpretation of France under Two Occupations, 1914–1918/1940–1944.* Hanover, Germany, 1983.

Gildea, Robert. *Marianne in Chains: Daily Life in the Heart of France During the German Occupation.* London, 2002.

Glahn, Gerhard von. *The Occupation of Enemy Territory: A Commentary on the Law and Practice of Belligerent Occupation.* Minneapolis, Minn., 1957.

Höhn, Maria. *GIs and Fräuleins: The German-American Encounter in 1950s West Germany.* Chapel Hill, N.C., 2002.

Horne, John, and Alan Kramer. *German Atrocities 1914: A History of Denial.* New Haven, Conn., 2001.

Lagrou, Pieter. *The Legacy of Nazi Occupation: Patriotic Memory and National Recovery in Western Europe, 1945–1965.* Cambridge, U.K., 2000.

Liulevicius, Vejas Gabriel. *War Land on the Eastern Front: Culture, National Identity, and German Occupation in World War I.* Cambridge, U.K., 2000.

Lukacs, Richard C. *Forgotten Holocaust: The Poles under German Occupation 1939–1944.* 2nd rev. ed. New York, 1997.

Mazower, Mark. *Inside Hitler's Greece: The Experience of Occupation, 1941–44.* New Haven, Conn., 1993.

Naimark, Norman M. *The Russians in Germany: A History of the Soviet Zone of Occupation, 1945–1949.* Cambridge, Mass., 1995.

Prete, Roy A., and A. Hamish Ion, eds. *Armies of Occupation.* Waterloo, Ont., 1984.

VEJAS GABRIEL LIULEVICIUS

OLD AGE. "Old age" is the most diverse of all age categories, including people in their fifties through those past a hundred. It embraces some of the richest and the very poorest in all societies, the highly active and the severely decrepit. In the twentieth century this diversity expanded more than ever before. Survival to old age was more common in earlier centuries than is sometimes thought, but it was only during the twentieth century that most Europeans lived to old age and more people lived to be very old. In Britain at the beginning of the twentieth century an average of seventy-four people per year reached the age of one hundred; by the end of the century three thousand did so. Expectation of life at birth in 1901 was fifty-one years for men and fifty-eight for women; in 1991 it was seventy-six and eighty-one, respectively. In general, women outlived men. The pattern was similar elsewhere in Europe, though in Russia and some other former communist countries male life expectancy fell at the end of the century.

Longer life and fitness were due to unprecedented improvements in living standards, especially in income, diet, and hygiene, together with leaps in medical knowledge and techniques. Curiously, this achievement was widely received with concern about the "burden" of costs that growing numbers of older people would impose upon shrinking younger populations. This was partly because the rise in life expectancy in the first forty years of the century coincided with a general fall in the birthrate. Fears that populations were aging and declining led, particularly in Nazi Germany and fascist Italy, to attempts to bribe women to have more children and penalize the childless with bonuses and medals for mothers of numerous children and tax penalties for celibacy. Elsewhere, particularly in Britain and France, the response was panicky predictions of the decline of the western powers as they aged, while Asian and African countries retained high birthrates and youthful populations.

These fears retreated after World War II, when birthrates rose. They returned at the end of the century, however, as births again fell. In the 1980s doom-laden predictions of the adverse social and economic effects of the aging of populations were issued by such institutions as the World Bank.

Aging occurred at a different pace and with different effects in different countries. France experienced a low birthrate much earlier than other countries. As early as 1836, 9 percent of the French population was sixty or older; by 1976, this had reached 18 percent. Sweden's over-sixty population did not reach 9 percent until 1876, but its age structure changed faster and it reached 18 percent in 1962.

Some people ended their longer lives in physical and/or mental decline, though only a minority experienced long periods of dependency. The incidence of conditions such as Alzheimer's rose, partly because more people survived the diseases that had ravaged younger people in previous centuries, such as tuberculosis, to die of sicknesses of old age.

DEFINITIONS OF OLD AGE

A new language emerged for the stages of aging. A term coined in France, and widely used elsewhere in the later twentieth century, described the period of active old age as the "third age"; it followed the "first age" of childhood and youth and the "second age" of adult maturity. The later, less active and independent phase of life was the "fourth age."

Most older people throughout the century inhabited the third age. But the definition of the age boundaries and characteristics of old age changed. Subjective and everyday definitions of who was "old" and when old age began had long been variable and depended more on appearance and physical capacities than chronological age. Such subjective definitions increasingly collided with more-rigid bureaucratic boundaries, which were driven mainly by the introduction and spread of pensions. By the 1960s a pension was the normal expectation of older people throughout Europe. Pensions were most commonly payable starting at age sixty or sixty-five, sometimes fifty-five or seventy. The first state pensions were introduced in Germany in 1889 for workers, mainly male, at age seventy, or younger if they were permanently incapacitated. Denmark followed in 1892 with pensions targeted at the poorest people, mainly female, at age sixty. In 1908 they were introduced in Britain starting at age seventy; this age was lowered to sixty-five in 1925 and, for women only, to sixty in 1940. Increasingly, in noncommunist countries, the pension age became the normal age of retirement from paid work, and the prevailing pension age became, in popular as well as official discourse, the boundary between middle and old age. Yet no sooner were such usages established than they were rejected, by some, as defining older people negatively, as dependent on the state or on the young, for what they were not—no longer productive workers or citizens—rather than for their positive qualities. As a result of the search for more positive language, "senior citizen" became common usage in the United States and elsewhere, and "the elderly" gained acceptance in Britain, until the 1980s, when this also came to be seen as pejorative and was replaced by the ambiguous "older people." There were similar linguistic changes elsewhere in Europe.

Such changes were driven by perceptions of the dissonance between language that described people above a certain age as helpless and dependent and the visible reality that increasing numbers of them were not. Change was encouraged by articulate older people themselves as well as by professionals in the internationally growing field of gerontology, a creation of the mid-twentieth century, who were devoted to studying aging and old age and advocacy for older people when required.

WORK, RETIREMENT, AND PENSIONS

Retirement itself was new on a mass scale. At the beginning of the century those who could afford it chose when to retire. State officials and high-status employees in the private sector generally had secure pensions and a fixed retirement age, commonly sixty, sometimes fifty-five. Poor people worked for as long as they were able, sometimes to very late ages, generally at increasingly degraded tasks with diminishing incomes. In largely rural Finland, as in most other countries, old women worked as laundresses, cleaners, hawkers, laborers, or hod carriers on building sites. Old men took casual jobs as laborers on building sites or in road construction, work that disappeared during the long Finnish winter and that was seasonal everywhere. With unemployment normally came destitution.

If the poor old had surviving families (many did not given the high death rates of the early twentieth century), they were likely to also be too poor to give more than minimal support. Public welfare was minimal, and was generally stigmatizing. Better paid, mainly male, skilled workers often belonged to pension savings schemes. The

first state pensions were designed to diminish this degradation and to raise the status of people whose poverty was not their own fault. But pensions were rarely enough to enable old people to give up work, nor were they intended to be. They did (as was intended) assist children in supporting aging parents, or supplement personal saving.

In capitalist countries in the 1920s and 1930s, occupational and private pensions and retirement at around age sixty to sixty-five spread through the lower levels of "white-collar," mainly male, workers. Poorer manual workers also increasingly left permanent paid work at earlier ages than before because high unemployment left them unable to find other jobs once unemployed.

The Soviet Union, by contrast, was committed ideologically to the valorization of work and workers and to exhibiting the long-lived vitality that was possible in a workers' democracy. The country also needed maximum employment if it was to expand its economy, and it could not easily afford to pay large numbers of pensions. Hence it had a strong incentive to keep people at work until as late in life as possible. In 1935 Joseph Stalin proclaimed the importance of exploiting to the full the experience of older workers. In the Soviet Union, "pensioner" was a respectable identity, implying age and seniority rather than dependency. The social security system was designed to encourage people to work as long as possible; turning them into welfare dependents, it was said, would rob them of full participation in Soviet society. Instead, as they became unfit for their accustomed jobs, they were transferred to lighter employment. A skilled electrician might become a watchman, a carpenter, or a toilet attendant—as he might in the west, without the accompanying ideological rhetoric. A difference from the west, though, was that old people were officially represented as privileged citizens. Their lives were often very poor, though this was also true of younger Soviet workers. After World War II pensions improved somewhat for Soviet citizens who were too old to work, especially for professionals and those who were deemed to have given distinguished service to the USSR, but pressure on older people to keep working remained strong.

Soviet political leaders practiced what they preached, if in greater comfort. Stalin himself died in office in 1953 at the age of seventy-four, as did Leonid Brezhnev in 1982 at age seventy-six. Elsewhere, Winston Churchill had reached the state pension age of sixty-five in 1939 when World War II began, and he sustained a punishing workload as war leader for the next six years. He became prime minister again in 1951 at age seventy-seven, though by then he was in poor health; he retired, reluctantly, four years later. Charles de Gaulle became president of France in 1958 at age sixty-eight and remained in office for eleven years. Old men dominated the politics of many states in the mid-twentieth century, sometimes, especially the dictators, outstaying their capacities for the role, as did Francisco Franco, who in 1975 reluctantly gave up control of Spain when he was close to death at age eighty-three.

It was only after World War II, especially from the 1950s on, that improved pensions were introduced in all European countries (more quickly in some than others) and that retirement at age sixty or sixty-five became a normal phase of life for most people. However, simultaneously, many governments, including those of Britain and France, reversed their previous attitudes and argued that earlier retirement should be discouraged. It was believed that the shrinking numbers of younger workers, due to the low prewar birthrates, necessitated older people staying in the workforce to sustain the buoyant postwar international economy.

Nevertheless, retirement at sixty or sixty-five gradually became almost universal. Workers wanted a period of rest after long working lives, understandable because manual workers who were in their sixties in the 1950s might have been working since the age of twelve or thirteen. Nowhere did their pensions make retired workers rich, but they did enable them to survive without working, and, as living standards improved, more were helped by their children. But the sudden experience of limitless leisure late in life was not always easy. Many of this first generation of early retired manual workers expressed bewilderment, even depression, in the face of their newfound, unaccustomed leisure. Also, employers were not persuaded of the value of older workers except in traditional marginal jobs, and, increasingly, modern technology provided efficient alternatives to aging cleaners or frail watchmen. There was a shortage of younger workers due to low prewar birth rates and the increasing number of young people staying longer in education after the war. In expanding European economies employers compensated for the shortage of younger workers by employing women and immigrants rather than older people.

Through the second half of the twentieth century Europeans lived longer and were fit to later ages, but instead of working longer, they retired earlier than ever before. This process speeded up in the 1980s. By the 1990s almost one-third of Western European workers had retired permanently by the age of sixty. Some left willingly, on comfortable pensions, to enjoy relaxation, travel, and consumption. A new generation of WOOPIES (well-off older persons) was identified by advertisers, but they were a minority. Others gave up work more reluctantly.

It was sometimes argued that early retirement was the unavoidable consequence of changing technology: skills and knowledge became obsolescent ever faster, and older people could not keep pace. But the evidence pointed in the opposite direction. Older workers suffered from the belief of employers and others that they had declining abilities and low adaptability, but, whenever it was put to the test, older people, even those in their seventies or older, proved highly adaptable and capable of learning new skills. In fact, they were well adapted to the high-tech labor market of the late twentieth century, which required brain power rather than physical power. However, they were rejected from a shrinking labor market because they were more costly than younger people. But by the end of the century it was recognized that when they left the workplace, their experience and often greater reliability, compared with younger workers, departed as well. Also, enterprises and governments became concerned about the growing costs of pensions and the falling numbers of younger workers capable of paying the contributions required to fund the pensions of older people; accordingly, in the 1990s they sought to cut pensions. Both state and employer pensions were substantially cut in Britain and Denmark, though in France, Germany, and other Western European countries workers defended their pensions more successfully.

This alarm was due to the rising proportions of people sixty and older. In 1960, the percentages of these older people in the total population were 16 percent in France, 17.3 in Germany, 13.6 in Italy, 18 in Sweden, and 16.9 in the United Kingdom. By 1990, they were 19.1, 20.4, 20.2, 22.8, and 20.7, and they were projected to rise by 2020 to 26.1, 18.2, 30.3, 26.5, and 24, respectively, with corresponding reductions in the numbers of people aged fifteen to sixty, who were of actual or potential working age.

Workers, governments, and employers now had incentives to reverse the trend of the previous half-century by delaying retirement and extending the normal working life.

MEDICINE AND OLD AGE

Longer, active lives were partly due to changing medical knowledge. Only in the twentieth century did medicine achieve the capacity to diagnose and cure extensively, and only in the midcentury did medical services become easily and cheaply available to people of all ages in most countries. Many of these advances benefited younger people, enabling them to survive to later ages, but diagnosis and treatment of conditions common among older people, such as heart disease, hypertension, and cancers, improved, and they also gained from such new procedures as implantation of cardiac pacemakers and joint and organ replacements. Hormone replacement therapy was hailed as bringing the longed-for rejuvenation to post-menopausal women, though by the end of the century there were reports of adverse side effects. Modern technology could also be used to keep older people alive but with a poor quality of life, posing new ethical dilemmas for medicine.

In the beginning of the century a specialized medicine of old age, known as geriatrics, developed internationally. The term was coined in the United States in 1909 by an Austrian-born medical practitioner, Ignatz Nascher (1863–1944). Nascher believed that doctors paid insufficient attention to the ill health of older people: because they did not have long to live, it was not thought worthwhile to cure them. The persistence of this belief slowed acceptance of his work and ensured that geriatrics remained marginalized internationally. Nascher believed that the health of older people could be improved by better diet, exercise, and mental

stimulation and demonstrated its efficacy through experiments with older people in New York.

The desire to prolong active life, even to reveal the secret of rejuvenation, received stronger support in the Soviet Union, driven by the conviction that Bolshevism could revolutionize even the life span. Soviet gerontologists argued that humankind had the capacity to live much longer than the current norm, to age 120 and beyond, and that Soviet society could demonstrate its superiority by bringing this about. Statistics that demonstrated that theaverage Soviet life expectancy had improved since the Revolution of 1917 were invoked, though similar or greater gains were evident in non-communist countries. Experiments with hormones and glandular grafts from monkeys as a means to restore youthful vigor were encouraged. The Soviet press publicized feats of longevity that allegedly demonstrated that Soviet citizens were achieving exceptional life spans. A succession of Soviet medical researchers in the 1930s, 1950s, 1960s, and 1970s sought the secret of the apparently long life spans of Caucasian peasants, without success.

Geriatrics aroused more attention in non-communist countries as the numbers of older people, and the costs of their medical care, increased. By the 1930s large numbers of stroke patients were filling hospital beds because improvements in drug treatments kept them alive but did not restore their mobility. The increased use of physiotherapy and other forms of rehabilitation, pioneered in Britain, freed patients from hospitals in growing numbers. With the introduction in Britain in 1948 of a National Health Service that provided free health care for all citizens, and the establishment of similar systems throughout Europe, such practices became more widespread. Greater access to health care for poorer aging people revealed that attention to quite mundane but disabling conditions affecting their hearing, eyesight, teeth, and feet could greatly improve their lives. Conditions that had long been regarded as natural features of aging, to be endured, could be cured.

The outcome by the end of the century was the simultaneous survival of the largest numbers of fit people in their sixties and seventies ever known, and the largest numbers of chronically ill older people ever known. Many who recovered from acute conditions that would have killed them in earlier times succumbed to chronic disorders such as arthritis, diabetes, or Alzheimer's. But the majority of people surviving to their eighties and nineties at the end of the century did not suffer from acute illness and regarded themselves as in good health and capable of independent activity. For most people, even at very late ages, death was not preceded by a long period of serious dependency, though all of these experiences varied by age, class, and gender.

LIFESTYLES

More old people lived alone in the later twentieth century. This was often interpreted as meaning increasing loneliness, especially when linked to the falling birthrate, increased divorce, and increased geographical mobility. Some people were old, alone, and lonely. Many older people, however, preferred independence to dependence on their children. They were in frequent contact with family and friends even when they lived alone. Family size fell over the course of the century, but more older people than ever before had at least one surviving child following the decline in the high infant mortality rates that had been the norm throughout history. Children did not necessarily live close at hand, but improved communications enabled families to keep in ready contact by telephone or, later, e-mail, and to get together by fast means of transport. Separation was not initiated only by younger people. Increasingly, affluent older people in northern Europe moved to enjoy retirement in Spain or southern France, often returning close to their families as they entered the "fourth age."

Older, like younger, people changed their appearances. How they were represented and represented themselves changed as their styles of life became more varied. Older people in the later twentieth century tended to look younger than people of similar age in earlier times, not least because they were healthier and had their natural teeth rather than false teeth or none. Medical specialists suggested that seventy-five-year-olds in 2000 were physiologically similar to sixty- or sixty-five-year-olds in 1900.

The age-specific dress codes of earlier centuries disappeared, more gradually both in the countryside than in the towns and in poorer than in richer regions. It became easier for men and women to disguise the signs of aging, as cosmetics and hair dyes improved in range and quality and became cheaper and more readily available starting in the 1930s. Cosmetic surgery became more effective and cheaper and was increasingly used by the end of the century.

Some argued that a "cult of youth" forced older people to disguise their ages, denying them the possibility to "grow old gracefully" and "naturally." Others responded that there was nothing "graceful" about the "natural" aging of all too many old people in the past, and no obvious reason why at a certain age they should become less free to alter their appearance or be bound by more-rigid style conventions than the young. At the end of the century more older people had more freedoms than ever before and age boundaries were being destabilized.

See also **Childhood and Adolescence; Demography; Public Health; Social Insurance; Welfare State.**

BIBLIOGRAPHY

Falkingham, Jane, and Paul Johnson. *Ageing and Economic Welfare*. London, 1992.

Kirkwood, Tom. *The End of Age: Why Everything about Ageing Is Changing*. London, 2001.

Kohli, Martin, et al., eds. *Time for Retirement: Comparative Studies of Early Exit from the Labour Force*. Cambridge, U.K., 1991.

Lovell, Stephen. "Soviet Socialism and the Construction of Old Age." *Jahrbücher für Geschichte Osteuropas* 51 (2003): 564–585.

Pifer, Alan, and Lydia Bronte, eds. *Our Aging Society. Paradox and Promise*. New York, 1986.

Quine, Maria S. *Population Politics in Twentieth Century Europe*. London, 1996.

Rahikainen, Marjatta. "Ageing Men and Women in the Labour Market—Continuity and Change." *Scandinavian Journal of History* 26 (2001): 297–314.

Sauvy, Alfred. "Social and Economic Consequences of Ageing of Western Populations." *Population Studies* 2 (1948): 115–124.

Thane, Pat. "The Debate on the Declining Birth-rate in Britain: The 'Menace' of an Ageing Population, 1920s–1950s." *Continuity and Change* 5 (1990): 283–305.

———. "Geriatrics." In *Companion Encyclopedia of the History of Medicine*, vol. 2, edited by William F. Bynum and Roy Porter, 1092–1118. London, 1993.

———. *Old Age in English History. Past Experiences. Present Issues.* Oxford, U.K., 2000.

World Bank. *Averting the Old Age Crisis: Policies to Protect the Old and Promote Growth.* Oxford, U.K., 1994.

PAT THANE

OLYMPIC GAMES. The modern Olympic Games began in Athens in 1896 as a result of the enthusiasm of the Frenchman Baron Pierre de Coubertin. His vision, based on the sporting models of elite British and American schools and colleges, was of a peaceful sporting and artistic competition between nations. At the outset the games were closed to professional athletes and only amateurs could compete. This was a core principle at the heart of the Olympic movement that would not be changed until the early 1990s. The beginnings in Athens were small: 14 nations competed in 43 events. By 2004, when the Games returned to Athens, over 10,000 athletes representing 203 nations took part in 300 events. In the years preceding World War I, the Olympic Games struggled to establish themselves because they were linked to, and effectively overshadowed by, the World Expositions in Paris (1900) and Saint Louis (1904). By the time of the last pre–World War I Games, a level of stability had been found. In 1912 in Stockholm, 28 nations came together to compete in 102 events. The number of athletes had risen from 241 in Athens in 1896 to 2,407.

INTERWAR GAMES

World War I marked a period of change for the Olympic movement. Its administrative body, the International Olympic Committee (IOC), moved its headquarters from Paris to Lausanne, Switzerland, and the Games planned for Berlin in 1916 were abandoned. In the wake of the damage Europe suffered in the war, the 1920 Games were awarded to Antwerp to honor the suffering that had been inflicted on the Belgian people. The 1920 opening ceremony was notable for the introduction of the Olympic flag, the release of doves as a symbol of peace, and the presentation of the Athletes' Oath. The Olympic movement had, by virtue of staging the Antwerp Games, proved it had survived the war. The introduction of the flag, representing the unity of the five continents, and the symbolic release of doves also demonstrated that the Olympic movement considered itself a harbinger of peace and unity for the nations of the world. Such beliefs were, however, difficult to sustain. The more the Olympics grew in size and scale, the more readily were they used by nations in pursuit of their own ideological purposes.

In 1924 the Winter Olympics were introduced. These took place in Chamonix, France, and attracted sixteen countries competing in sixteen alpine events. The Winter Olympics have historically been dominated by European nations. Of the nineteen Winter Games that had been staged by 2002, only six had taken place outside of Europe. The medal winners for the winter sports have also been primarily European. Although the Japanese, Americans, and Canadians have performed well, it is the Nordic countries that have traditionally dominated.

In 1931 the Summer (Berlin) and Winter Games (Garmisch-Partenkirchen) were awarded to Germany. Although the German economy under the Weimar Republic lacked political stability, the other bidding city, Barcelona, was in an equally parlous state. The members of the IOC could not have foreseen the rise to power of the Nazi Party, and although there were debates about boycotting the Berlin Games, these were muted. The 1936 Berlin Games were dominated by the Nazi machine and every aspect was meticulously planned. Leni Riefenstahl's film *Olympia* recorded the event and her footage was transmitted live to a series of receivers across Berlin, creating the first televised Games. The Berlin Games have become associated in many people's minds with the African American athlete Jesse Owens. Against a background of Nazi efforts to use the Games to demonstrate the supremacy of "Aryan" athletes, Owens won four gold medals. The Berlin Games demonstrated how the Olympics could be harnessed for political purposes. Although no host nation would ever again go to such extremes, the Games' political potential had been illustrated for all to see.

POSTWAR GAMES

World War II resulted in the abandonment of the 1940 Games, set for Tokyo, and those planned for Helsinki in 1944. The first postwar Games were staged in London in 1948, when rationing was still

American athlete Jesse Owens runs the 200-meter race at the 1936 Olympic games in Berlin. Owens's outstanding performance at the games, where he broke two world records and won four gold medals, served as a direct refutation of the Hitler regime's insistence on the superiority of the so-called Aryan race. ©BETTMANN/CORBIS

in force and much of the city was still being cleared of bomb damage. Although attended by athletes from fifty-nine nations, the IOC banned Germany, Italy, and Japan for their part in the war. As the IOC's remit became increasingly global, the Summer Games were staged in various nations across the continents. Of the fourteen summer Olympics held between 1952 and 2008, only six were held in Europe. The IOC itself has remained in Lausanne, and its postwar presidents, with the exception of the American Avery Brundage, have all been European nationals. The growing commercial and political power of the IOC has meant that many international sporting organizations have also chosen Switzerland as their administrative

base. So although the Olympic Games are staged across the world, the IOC's location, elite personnel, and impact remain dominantly European.

Germany returned to the Olympic Games at Helsinki in 1952 and competed as a unified team until 1972, when it divided along political lines into two separate teams: the Federal Republic of Germany and the German Democratic Republic. The experience of Germany is indicative of one of the gravest problems for the Olympic Games in the years after 1945: the Cold War. Growing Cold War tensions produced an American-led boycott of the 1980 Moscow Summer Games (in opposition to the Soviet invasion of Afghanistan), and a reciprocal Eastern bloc boycott of the 1984 Los Angeles

Summer Games. The need for each of the major sporting nations to prove its athletic (and therefore ideological) supremacy also led to widespread use of intensive training methods and drug abuse, particularly by the German Democratic Republic in the 1980s. The 1972 Summer Games in Munich were also darkened by political activity when Palestinian terrorists kidnapped members of the Israeli wrestling team from the Olympic Village. The event culminated in a German attempt to free the hostages at Munich's Fuerstenfeldbruk airfield. The attempt failed and five of the eight Palestinians were killed, as were all of the Israeli hostages. IOC President Avery Brundage led a memorial service in the Olympic stadium and committed the Olympic movement to a policy of distancing itself from political events, stating "the Games must go on."

AFTER THE COLD WAR

The rapid collapse of the Soviet Union in the late 1980s meant that the Olympic movement had to adapt rapidly to a wide range of new nations. At the 1992 Albertville Winter Games in France, the last to be held in the same year as the Summer Games, the former Soviet states competed under the title of the Unified Team and under the flag of the Olympic movement. The changing geopolitics of that era were also reflected in the first unified German team since 1972, in separate teams for the Baltic states, and in the wake of the conflict in the former Yugoslavia in representation for Croatia and Slovenia.

In addition to dealing with the realities of post–Cold War politics, from the mid-1980s onward the Olympic movement also began adapting to the increasingly commercialized world of sport. Under the presidency of Juan Antonio Samaranch, the IOC underwent a series of radical changes. In 1992 it removed any vestiges of its earlier ban on professional athletes and from 1984 onward sold the commercial rights for the sponsorship of the Games and the use of the five-ringed Olympic logo. It also began selling exclusive television rights to the Winter and Summer Games for ever-increasing amounts of money. By 2004 the IOC's income was estimated at $2,236 million from television rights, $1,339 million from sponsorship, $608 million from ticket sales, and $81 million from product licensing.

By the time of the Athens Summer Games, the IOC was, without question, the single most powerful sporting organization in the world. It had successfully adapted de Coubertin's idea for an international sporting competition, charted its way through a plethora of complex political situations, adapted to new media technologies, adopted commercial models, and applied them to the selling of its sporting events.

See also **Cold War; Riefensthal, Leni.**

BIBLIOGRAPHY

Guttmann, Allen. *The Games Must Go On: Avery Brundage and the Olympic Movement.* New York, 1984.

———. *The Olympics: A History of the Modern Games.* Urbana, Ill., 1992.

Hill, Christopher. *Olympic Politics: From Athens to Atlanta.* Manchester, U.K., and New York, 1996.

MacAloon, John J. *This Great Symbol: Pierre de Coubertin and the Origins of the Modern Olympic Games.* Chicago, 1981.

Miller, David. *From Athens to Athens: The Official History of the Olympic Games and the IOC.* Edinburgh, 2003.

MIKE CRONIN

OPEC. The Organization of the Petroleum Exporting Countries (OPEC) is an international producers' cartel whose members' governments coordinate petroleum policies in order to receive the best possible price for the crude oil they export. OPEC nations regard such price coordination as the best means to safeguard their economic and political interests, both individually and collectively. The cartel's operation has had a profound impact on European economies since its founding in Baghdad in September 1960 by the governments of five developing, oil-producing countries: Kuwait, Iraq, Iran, Saudi Arabia, and Venezuela. Eight other developing countries joined later: Qatar (1961), Indonesia (1962), Libya (1962), United Arab Emirates (1967), Algeria (1969), Nigeria (1971), Ecuador (1973), and Gabon (1975). (Ecuador and Gabon left the cartel in 1992 and 1994 respectively.) OPEC's connections to Europe have been important to the organization. OPEC's secretariat (headquarters) has always been located in nonaligned European countries, first in Geneva, Switzerland (from September 1960 to September 1965), and then in Vienna, Austria (from September 1965), but OPEC was also founded to serve as a counterweight to the economic dominance of the United States, the United Kingdom, and the Netherlands in the global petroleum industry.

ORIGINS AND OBJECTIVES

In Western Europe, fuel oil replaced coal as the main source of industrial energy between 1945 and 1974, and gasoline usage increased with the spread of automobiles. Western Europe came to rely on petroleum products in ways it had not before World War II and, with few indigenous oil fields (the North Sea fields of Great Britain and Norway are the exceptions), it relied on imported oil to meet its major energy needs. Low crude oil prices, large-capacity supertankers, and the structure of the international oil market encouraged European dependency on imported oil. In 1960 the international oil market was dominated by the purchasing power and oil-field ownership rights of the "Seven Sisters," transnational oil corporations located in the United States (Exxon, Mobil, Texaco, Gulf, and Chevron) and Western Europe (British Petroleum and Royal Dutch Shell), who tried to keep crude oil prices low. OPEC formed in response to this situation and, worried by the fall of the value of the dollar in the early 1970s (all international oil exports were and still are priced in U.S. dollars), which lowered the value of their already low-priced oil exports, OPEC nations fought for more favorable terms of trade for the raw material they exported.

OPEC rose to international prominence in the 1970s and 1980s as some members (e.g., Iraq, Libya, and Saudi Arabia) nationalized their oil industries, and OPEC used its cartel power to raise the price of crude oil on the world market. Most notably, OPEC cut production and refused to sell oil to countries that had supported Israel in its 1973 war with Egypt and Syria, that is, the United States and its allies in Western Europe, especially the Netherlands. This producer embargo caused a fourfold increase in the price of oil from October 1973 to March 1974 and seriously disrupted the developed economies of Europe and North America and the developing economies of

non–oil producing countries in South America, Asia, and Africa. Of the nine members of the European Economic Community (EEC), only the Dutch faced a complete embargo because of support for the United States and Israel, while the United Kingdom and France received almost uninterrupted supplies, and the other members experienced only partial cutbacks.

The rise in oil prices had a much greater impact in Europe than the embargo itself. Not only was the traditional flow of capital reversed when massive amounts of "Petrodollars" now moved from the industrial nations of Europe and North America to Saudi Arabia, Kuwait, Iran, and the other oil-producing countries, but OPEC countries began exporting capital back to Europe and the United States. Petrodollars funded much of the United States, French, and British national debt and led to OPEC nations' investment in European firms, urban real estate, and vacation homes. A striking example of this new relationship was the Iranian state's purchase of 25 percent of the stock of the German steel firm Krupp for $75 million in 1974.

The aftershocks of the 1973 oil crisis rocked the world's economy, as high inflation and a series of recessions (dubbed "stagflation") persisted until the early 1980s. High oil prices continued until 1986, when they fell back to pre-1973 levels only to rise again slowly thereafter. The era of cheap energy was over, and the cost of living rose 32 percent to 46 percent for Europeans between 1968 and 1975. Unemployment reemerged as a problem in European economies for the first time since World War II (6.9 percent of the workforce in early 1978). The oil crisis brought an end to thirty years of high economic growth in the EEC and ushered in an era of high unemployment and economic stagnation. By 1980 stagflation was a major factor in the breakdown of the postwar "social contract" between business and labor and the rise of Thatcherism in the United Kingdom, while in Germany the "oil shock" helped catapult the Green Party, with its emphasis on energy conservation, into national prominence. However, as a measure of oil dependency (that is, the ratio between a country's oil imports and its total oil consumption) of the world's top oil consumers, France and Germany rank third and fourth worldwide, well ahead of the world's largest consumer, the United States, in sixth place.

EUROPEAN PRODUCERS AND OPEC

The role of European oil producers vis-à-vis OPEC is varied. The major European oil producing nations (United Kingdom, Norway, Azerbaijan, Russia, and Romania) are not members of OPEC and have occasionally used their production power to undercut OPEC prices and production quotas and maintain some energy independence. The United Kingdom follows the most independent policy and tends to use its high-grade reserves to mitigate OPEC-orchestrated price increases on the British economy. Russia was the world's largest oil producer until production collapsed in 1992, and it is striving to achieve that status again. Since 1997 Russia has attended numerous OPEC meetings and has made a number of commitments to reduce production and/or exports in coordination with OPEC, but these have had little effect. Norway is the world's third-largest oil-exporting country and generally does not participate in OPEC meetings but it has adjusted oil production with OPEC three times since 1998.

Nevertheless, OPEC continues to be a very powerful cartel. OPEC's oil exports represent about 55 percent of the oil traded internationally, and at the end of 2004, OPEC had proven oil reserves of 896,659 million barrels of crude oil, representing 78.4 percent of the world total of proven oil reserves. Most non-OPEC oil-producing countries are net importers of oil (Russia, Norway, and the United Kingdom are major exceptions), so OPEC still has a strong influence on the European oil market, especially if it decides to reduce or increase its level of production.

See also **Inflation; Recession of 1970s.**

BIBLIOGRAPHY

Blinder, Alan S. *Economic Policy and the Great Stagflation.* New York, 1979.

Yeomans, Matthew. *Oil: Anatomy of an Industry.* New York, 2004.

Yergin, Daniel. *The Prize: The Epic Quest for Oil, Money, and Power.* New York, 1991.

ALEXANDER M. ZUKAS

OPERA. In the immediate aftermath of the First World War, the prospects for opera as a viable twentieth-century art form looked bleak. The climate of sweeping political and cultural change brought about by the desire for postwar renewal and reassessment looked set to consign opera to Europe's imperial and monarchist past. Opera's spectacular combination of media (theater, music, dance) had always equipped it to mirror the status and ambitions of the European centers of power. Privileged as one of the pillars of official culture in the nineteenth century, opera evolved into ever grander proportions, partly in response to the growing prestige of the cities and nations in which it was performed. This excessive cultural artifact, together with the grandiose theaters built to present it, stood as a monument to a now discredited past. Opera, in short, was tainted by its political legacy.

There were other ominous signs for opera. How could Europe's wrecked postwar economies afford this most lavish of cultural traditions? And how would this multimedia art form compete against the emerging technology of cinema, which, in its "silent" era, closely resembled opera by combining dramatic narrative with live music? The message from commentators, historians, critics, and practitioners seemed clear: the era of opera, which had begun in a spirit of theatrical experimentation in the Italian courts of the early seventeenth century, had come to an end. When in the 1920s the theatrical director and reformer Bertolt Brecht singled out opera as synonymous with the old order, he arguably spoke for many.

Powerful factors, however, would weigh against this predicted decline. Among them was a creative tradition, rooted in prewar culture, which did not lightly discard its inheritance. For composers and directors who had learned their craft at the turn of the century, opera represented one of the pinnacles of personal achievement: an opera premiere in Paris or Berlin was a highly public and widely publicized event with the potential to establish or seal a reputation. Another factor was the institutional legacy of opera. Too much had been invested in the operatic infrastructure (theaters, management, publishing) to allow it to disappear meekly from the scene, while opera audiences included a core of loyal devotees. That these audiences often represented the most powerful and wealthy elements of European society meant that opera could depend on a degree of financial support even in the absence of sufficient government funding or wider public interest. And finally, technology, far from sealing opera's fate, would soon make it available to an audience unimaginable in the nineteenth century. Through sound recording and later video, opera freed itself from its dependency on the theaters of the large metropolitan centers and became a mass-media phenomenon. The century that should have witnessed the demise of opera actually gave it new life.

THE OLD AND THE NEW

If any event symbolized the transition from the old to the new order in opera, it was the premiere of Giacomo Puccini's *Turandot* at Milan's Teatro alla Scala on 25 April 1926. Puccini had died before completing the final act, leaving the relatively unknown Franco Alfano to set the final scene to music. The La Scala production was to feature Alfano's completion, but the conductor, Arturo Toscanini, planned a special gesture for the opening night. When the performance reached the end of Puccini's music, Toscanini put down his baton, bringing the performance to an abrupt end. It was a mark of respect from a longtime colleague and a moment of supreme theater in its own right. It also seemed to signal, nostalgically, the end of an era, leaving only a reverent silence in its wake.

Yet something new had also been heard, for Puccini's score pointed to a musical language that had not been heard in his earlier work. The soaring lyrical lines audiences associated with Puccini were still to be heard—the tenor aria "Nessun dorma" proved an immediate success—but this traditional Puccini sound was supplemented by echoes of a more dissonant and fractured music reminiscent of contemporaries such as Igor Stravinsky and Béla Bartók. In *Turandot* a composer of the operatic mainstream had embraced, if only guardedly, the sounds of modernism. Other composers went much further, challenging traditionally conservative opera audiences with new musical idioms and hitherto unthinkable dramatic material. In the Russian composer Dmitri Shostakovich's *Lady Macbeth of Mtsensk* (1934) and the Austrian composer Alban

Berg's *Lulu* (1937), sex and death, long staples of the operatic stage, seemed more graphically represented than ever, while the music shocked early audiences.

FINDING AN AUDIENCE

The real creative shift of the interwar years, however, is not to be found in the rise of the modernist avant-garde. Radical operas attracted headlines but did little to persuade opera audiences to forgo their established diet of Mozart and Verdi. Premieres were one thing, repeat performances quite another. A more influential trend can be seen in subtle shifts toward the new by creative figures who, like Puccini, could appeal to the opera houses of Europe and North America. Richard Strauss, whose *Salome* (1905) and *Elektra* (1909) had scandalized prewar audiences with lurid subject matter and gargantuan orchestral forces, now turned toward a more restrained, often neoclassical musical language and more intimate themes. *Ariadne auf Naxos* (1912; revised 1916) summoned the spirit and language of the eighteenth century, while the comedy *Intermezzo* (1924) offered a tongue-in-cheek self-portrait of the composer's domestic life. Strauss's new sphere formed part of a broader shift away from the grand musical forces and epic subject matter of nineteenth-century opera. The neoclassicism of *Ariadne* returns as a theme in much of the new repertoire of the 1920s and 1930s, notably in Paul Hindemith's *Cardillac* (1926) and Stravinsky's *Oedipus rex* (1927). Equally, the celebration of the everyday in *Intermezzo* returns in a variety of forms, most famously in the so-called *Zeitoper* (opera of the times), in which modern urban life found musical expression in the sounds of the city, contemporary dance music, and jazz. Although the embrace of popular music is often superficial and even condescending, operas such as *Jonny spielt auf* (1927; words and music by Ernst Krenek) gave the impression that the gap between opera and contemporary life had all but collapsed.

More genuinely infused with popular culture is the work of Kurt Weill, whose collaborations with Brecht challenged many of the traditions and assumptions of opera. With its popular-style songs written for singing actors rather than opera singers, *The Threepenny Opera* (1928) represents a kind of antiopera. But, like the more intimate theatrical

Helga Pilarczyk, in the title role, with Peter-Roth Ehrang in a 1962 production of Alban Berg's *Lulu* in Hamburg. GETTY IMAGES

works of prominent composers such as Stravinsky and Arnold Schoenberg, it is also a gesture toward a new kind of music theater that would ultimately extend the idea of opera in the latter half of the century. What the interwar decades showed was that the term *opera* was more flexible than had been imagined. Alongside the new intimacy, grand opera survived: the French composer Darius Milhaud's *Christophe Colomb* (1930) is a multimedia epic that requires film projection and simultaneous staging on separate platforms. And while contemporary life was a popular theme in opera of the period, the mythical and fantastic proved an enduring fascination, one that opera's resources seemed tailored to explore. Sergei Prokofiev's *The Love of Three Oranges* (1921) presents a vivid fairytale world brought to life in part by a musical language of extraordinary energy and color. The combination of the mundane and unreal can even be found clashing within individual works. In Leoš Janáček's *The Cunning Little Vixen* (1924), the animals of the forest are given operatic voice with

a vocal style that accentuates the patterns of earthy everyday speech in the composer's beloved Czech language.

If developments in repertoire shaped opera's reputation, so too did the phonograph. Although complete operas were available, the 78 rpm record required no fewer than fifteen disks (with thirty sides) for a two-hour opera, while the multimedia dimension of opera was reduced to sound alone. Excerpts suited the gramophone record better, and a market emerged for individual arias sung by the most celebrated singers. The reputations of the singers Enrico Caruso, Geraldine Farrar, Beniamino Gigli, Richard Tauber, and Tita Ruffo were greatly enhanced by, if not dependent on, the dissemination and commodification of their recorded voices. It was a market that would survive into the era of the compact disk, when these early-twentieth-century singers would be joined by Luciano Pavarotti, Placido Domingo, Maria Callas, and Jessye Norman. Whatever else opera has been about in the twentieth century, it has always been about the voice.

A PARTING OF THE WAYS

That all of these singers strenuously resisted twentieth-century music only serves to highlight the tension in opera between the popular demand for established classics and the development of new repertoire. By the 1950s it was becoming increasingly obvious that the generation of twentieth-century composers whose work could still find at least some favor with opera audiences was dying. In its place came a generation whose musical education had been less steeped in opera and who were determined to distinguish themselves sharply from their predecessors. Tellingly, some of the most important premieres of the decade—Stravinsky's *The Rake's Progress* (1951), Schoenberg's *Moses und Aron* (1957), Francis Poulenc's *Dialogues of the Carmelites* (1957)—introduced work by composers whose reputations had been formed largely or wholly in the interwar years. There were exceptions, of course. The decade marked the emergence of Benjamin Britten, Michael Tippett, and Hans Werner Henze, composers whose creative energies were heavily, and successfully, devoted to opera.

But more than ever opera was characterized by a split between conservative audiences and a modernist creative agenda that found its most extreme form in the composer Pierre Boulez's polemical call to burn the opera houses to the ground. While many of the leading figures of postwar music were drawn to the idea of musical drama, their work did not take a form that opera audiences tended to welcome. Composers and their collaborators took their cue, rather, from the antiopera of Brecht/Weill and the music theater of Schoenberg and Stravinsky. The 1960s, in particular, saw the emergence of radical ideas that seemed set to reshape the very notion of music for the theater. For his *Aventures* and *Nouvelles aventures* (1966), the Hungarian composer György Ligeti developed a "language" of affective vocal utterances that attempted to bypass traditional language barriers while maintaining a semantic ambiguity not unlike music itself. Presented in combination with Ligeti's vivid music and a carefully choreographed set of gestures, the works successfully construct a narrative that lacks specific content but remains nevertheless meaningful and theatrically effective.

The British composer Peter Maxwell Davies offered another kind of experiment in his *Eight Songs for a Mad King* (1969). Here the language is English, but the singer/actor is required to deliver the text (a poetic arrangement of the words of King George III of England during his bout of mental illness) with a range of advanced vocal techniques. The result is a disturbing theatrical exploration of insanity. As late as the 1970s it seemed that music theater of this kind might form a viable alternative tradition in musical drama, but, as with the most uncompromising operas of the interwar years, sustained public support failed to materialize, and its subsequent decline seems in retrospect inevitable. That music theater often took opera as its subject— *Opera* (1970), by the Italian composer Luciano Berio, and the set of five *Europeras* (1985–1991) by the American experimental musician John Cage, dismantle the tradition from within—served to confirm its status as the outsider looking in.

The decline of music theater needs to be viewed, however, in the context of a broader shift in contemporary music. The radical polemics of the 1950s and 1960s gave way to a more conciliatory approach. Alienating dissonance and rhythmic fragmentation tended to give way to more familiar and comprehensible sounds, a trend best illustrated by the rise of a musical language with American roots: minimalism, as the term implies, plays with the repetition and subtle manipulation of brief melodic and rhythmic ideas. Two of its most successful practitioners, the American composers Philip Glass and John Adams, have demonstrated that a mediation can be found between the opera house and the contemporary composer. Glass's *Einstein on the Beach* (1976) and Adams's *Nixon in China* (1987) marked the beginning of each composer's ongoing commitment to opera. While they do not quite challenge the place of *Carmen* or *La traviata* in the operatic repertoire, minimalist operas have been embraced with some enthusiasm by European audiences: in 2004 alone Glass's operas were staged in five European cities.

Even a number of the composers associated with radical music theater have maintained links with opera. Karlheinz Stockhausen, one of the leaders of the postwar avant-garde, has invested much of his career in the mammoth *Licht* cycle of seven operas (1977–2004), while Maxwell Davies,

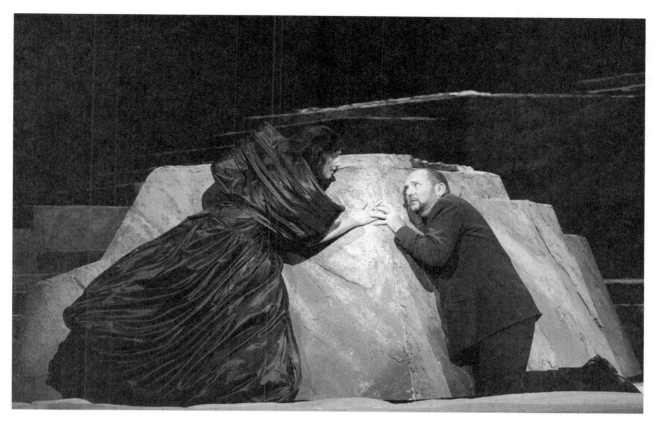

Nancy Maultsby and Robert Swensen in a production of Igor Stravinsky's *Oedipus Rex*, **Naples, January 2001.**
©Eric Robert/Corbis/Sygma

Ligeti, and Berio have all written more traditionally conceived operas. Even Boulez has ultimately spent a great deal of time conducting opera in the very institutions he once condemned. In part, the once angry young men of music have simply responded to shifting ideas about culture and experimentation. The more conciliatory path of the last decades of the century was in part a reaction against the perceived excesses of postwar radicalism. But there was something else that brought contemporary composers back into the opera house.

OPERA AS THEATER

For all the enthusiasm twentieth-century composers demonstrated toward the most radical developments in theater, the conservative tastes of opera audiences and administrators tended to stifle the introduction of new ideas about direction and staging. The demands of singing had always imposed limitations on directorial choice, leading to an

approach best captured by the phrase "stand and deliver." It would be misleading to tar all of opera with this brush (clearly there have always been singers who are also talented actors), but the ability of directors to impose a particular theatrical vision on a production has often been hindered by the star status of lead singers, who see no reason why their performance (with all its mannerisms) should be subject to interference. The problem was made acute in the twentieth century by the celebrity that leading opera singers enjoyed thanks to the medium of recorded sound, and tales abound of divas storming out of rehearsal when asked to alter their gestures or timing.

What is telling in accounts of early-twentieth-century productions is that the one figure deemed capable of competing with the singer's authority is the conductor. Director and designer were comparatively low in the pecking order, suggesting that the performance was construed in large part as a musical, rather than theatrical, event. Set designs adhered to naturalistic and pictorial principles: locales tended to be represented in a literal fashion, with often clichéd imagery painted on flats, perspective effects achieved through light and paint, and foliage and decoration in abundance. Signs of change were slow in coming, especially in relation to developments in spoken theater. The carefully considered, eclectic vision of the Austrian director and impresario Max Reinhardt was instrumental in establishing a stronger role for director and designer in opera. Reinhardt drew in part on the theories of the Swiss theorist Adolphe Appia, who proposed new approaches to the staging of the operas of that towering figure of nineteenth-century opera, Richard Wagner. In place of the detailed naturalism espoused by Wagner and adhered to by his successors at the Wagner festival in Bayreuth, Appia imagined abstract spaces in which light, rather than props and backdrops, would summon an atmospheric and dreamlike space in keeping with Wagner's spacious and moody music. Yet the approach was emphatically rejected by Wagner traditionalists, who insisted that Wagner's own detailed directions and descriptions should be observed almost literally.

It was only after the war that broader change became apparent, and it was the Bayreuth festival, oddly enough, that served as a catalyst. Wagner's grandsons had now taken charge and introduced sweeping reforms of the staging of Wagner's work. Wieland and Wolfgang Wagner argued that Wagner's stage directions were essentially historical relics that no longer bore any relevance to the meaning of the music. In place of these directions they offered an abstract vision of the psychological, rather than pictorial, truth of Wagnerian drama.

A quite different vision emerged from the work of Walter Felsenstein at the Komische Oper in Berlin beginning in the late 1940s. Emphasizing the actor's rigorous immersion in the psychological state of the character and the need to avoid allowing the act of singing to detract from the gestural communication of the actor's body, he established a new theatrical intensity and focus in operatic staging. His East German successors—figures such as Götz Friedrich and Harry Kupfer—would fuse these ideas with the acute contemporary social and political awareness foregrounded in Brecht's theater. The results were not always coherent or convincing, but the impact of these ideas and practices on the staging of opera in Europe is difficult to overestimate. Direction and design were increasingly being taken seriously in the opera house, and directors such as Patrice Chéreau, Alfred Kirchner, David Pountney, and Peter Sellars began to attract the sort of attention previously granted only to singers and conductors.

So complete was the transformation that a backlash was inevitable. Critics and audiences who viewed the operatic score as an almost sacred text resented what they saw as directorial intrusion. In Germany the term "director's opera" was applied to the new trend, implying that directors had taken possession of opera at the expense of composer, librettist, or musicians. The charge was not completely unfounded: there was often an indulgent aspect to the productions of the 1980s, as though directors viewed the opera as a vehicle for their own ideological message, regardless of its own connotations. But "director's opera" matured. Directors are now more subtle in their interpretation and realization, and only the most hardened traditionalists would deny that their work has revitalized opera. Perhaps attracted by opera's considerable resources and its fertile recent history, directors and designers from stage, film, and the visual arts now regularly accept invitations to work in the opera houses of Europe.

A NEW SYNTHESIS?

It is this new creative vitality that has opened the door for contemporary composers to return to the opera house. The core repertoire is as limited and old as ever, but it is interpreted with thoroughly contemporary theatrical means and it is now occasionally supplemented by new work in which contemporary musicians and theater practitioners join forces. In a way the story of twentieth-century opera comes full circle in a production of *Turandot* at the Salzburg Festival in August 2002. Featuring an imaginative production team including the director David Pountney and the Russian conductor Valery Gergiev conducting the Vienna Philharmonic Orchestra, this was the sort of collaboration of equals that now characterizes the best opera productions. Not least, the production was released on DVD, a technology that, with its multilingual subtitles and high-quality image and sound, seems tailor-made for opera. But there was a place here, too, for the contemporary composer. Luciano Berio had been invited to replace Alfano's completion of the opera with one of his own.

Consulting the original sketches, he promised a completion that would incorporate Puccini's plans, but, importantly, he did not erase his own compositional voice in the process. Rather than complete the score as though he were Puccini, he allowed his own soundworld to come through, thus acknowledging the historical and cultural gap separating the two composers. The juxtaposition, though unsettling, is a vivid symbol of the journey opera had taken in the twentieth century and a reminder of its double existence as historical artifact and living tradition.

See also **Bayreuth; Britten, Benjamin; Callas, Maria; Orff, Carl; Salzburg Festival; Schoenberg, Arnold.**

BIBLIOGRAPHY

Abbate, Carolyn. *In Search of Opera*. Princeton, N.J., 2001.

Dellamora, Richard, and Daniel Fischlin, eds. *The Work of Opera: Genre, Nationhood, and Sexual Difference*. New York, 1997.

Dolar, Mladen, and Slavoj Žižek. *Opera's Second Death*. New York and London, 2002.

Gilliam, Bryan, ed. *Music and Performance during the Weimar Republic*. Cambridge, U.K., 1994.

Sadie, Stanley, ed. *The New Grove Dictionary of Opera*. London, 1992.

Spotts, Frederic. *Bayreuth: A History of the Wagner Festival*. New Haven, Conn., 1994.

Sutcliffe, Tom. *Believing in Opera*. London, 1996.

Tomlinson, Gary. *Metaphysical Song: An Essay on Opera*. Princeton, N.J., 1999.

CHRISTOPHER MORRIS

OPERATION BARBAROSSA. The code name for the German attack on the Soviet Union in 1941, *Operation Barbarossa* refers to the surname of the Holy Roman Emperor Frederick I (r. 1152–1190), who during the Middle Ages organized a crusade in the east. The idea of a war against Russia was not new in history, as the invasions by Sweden under Charles XII in 1709 and by France under Napoleon I in 1812 show. In 1918 the German imperial army, which since 1915 had controlled parts of Poland and the Baltic states, for a short time occupied large parts of southern Russia, and German irregular forces were involved in the civil war (1918–1920) that followed the Russian Revolution. Against this background, Adolf Hitler (1889–1945) formulated around 1924/25 a plan intended to redirect German colonial drive away from Africa toward a Lebensraum (living space) in eastern Europe, envisaging total economic exploitation and a certain degree of German settlement in the region. Hitler consistently upheld that goal, despite political moves in other directions and a pro-Soviet orientation among the conservative elites of the German Reich. Already during the war against France in June 1940, while he was still in alliance with the Soviet leader Joseph Stalin (1879–1953), Hitler proposed a campaign against the Soviet Union. On 30 July 1940 he entrusted the army high command with military planning, which the latter had already started independently in June. In autumn 1940 this was still just one strategic alternative, since a campaign against Great Britain was high on the agenda. But in November 1940, after the failed attempt to occupy the British Isles, Hitler turned fully against the Soviet Union and on 18 December 1940 issued his Order (Weisung) No. 21 to prepare an attack against the Soviets, scheduled for 15 May 1941.

A THREEFOLD PLAN
The plan was threefold: first the military would carry out a blitzkrieg (lightning war), in which tank forces would cut deep into the Red Army and encircle its major forces. This action was expected to be completed in about eight to ten weeks. Second, the Germans would plunder the Soviet economy. The intention was to feed the German army entirely on Soviet agriculture, so as not to drain the food supply of the Reich. This would be accomplished by intercepting supplies from the southern regions of the Soviet Union that were intended for Russia and the larger cities. Millions of inhabitants were expected to die. This correlated to the third aspect of planning, ideological warfare. The German army would allow SS (Schutzstaffel) and police units to act independently in the rear areas and kill all alleged enemies there, while the army units themselves would murder the political functionaries of the Red Army. For every real or alleged act of resistance, utmost brutality would be applied in retaliation. Criminal behavior against the local population was to be prosecuted only in exceptional cases such as individual plundering or rape.

On 22 June 1941 the German army and its allies, especially Finnish, Romanian, Hungarian, and Italian troops, but also units from Croatia, Slovakia, and elsewhere, all together numbering 3.7 million men, attacked the Soviet Union. By comparison, the Red Army was materially superior, but there is no conclusive evidence that Stalin was prepared to stage an attack at that time against Germany. Thus, the so-called preventive war was an invention of the German propaganda machine. The Wehrmacht (regular army) soon advanced rapidly, especially Army Group North in the direction of Leningrad and Army Group Center toward Moscow; Army Group South lagged behind. But the schedule was already out of control by the end of July, a result of fierce Soviet resistance and supply problems. Indeed, the strategic value of the Red Army had been grossly underestimated.

In August, debates inside the German military leadership revolved around future steps; Hitler overruled most of his generals by directing the offensive to the south in order to occupy the agricultural areas of Ukraine, while most of the latter had preferred a frontal attack against Moscow. Nevertheless the German army, as expected, encircled large parts of the Red Army, especially around Kiev in September and in the Vyazma-Bryansk battle in October. On 2 October the Wehrmacht reinforced the center of the front and tried to attack Moscow in two waves. But the second of these had already slowed down in November, and the Red Army undertook a counteroffensive on 5 December 1941 that forced the German army to retreat some hundreds of miles in the center and in the south. Operation Barbarossa had failed; after the winter the German army retook the initiative in Operation Blau during summer 1942.

ADVANCE AND OCCUPATION

The German advance and occupation were accompanied by an unprecedented war of annihilation, as dictated by the second and third parts of the plan. During the first weeks, the occupied territories were put under military administration. Then, with the advance of the Wehrmacht eastward, approximately half of the territory was transferred to a civil administration, run by the so-called Reichsminister für die besetzten Ostgebiete (Minister for the eastern occupied territories), Alfred Rosenberg (1893–1946). He installed two administrative units, the Reichskommissariat Ostland, comprising the Baltics and western Belorussia, and the Reichskommissariat Ukraine, comprising most of Ukraine approximately up to the Dnieper and parts of southern Belarus. Romania received its own occupation zone, called *Transnistria,* situated from Odessa to the north. The German military occupation was divided between the armies near the frontline and army group areas in the rear. A wide net of German rule was put over the local population, reinforced by tens of thousands of auxiliaries, who worked for the occupation force.

The major political aim of the campaign consisted of economic exploitation. Industry was almost completely demolished either by the retreating Soviets or the advancing Germans; all food was requisitioned for the army. Official guidelines foresaw nutrition support only for those urban locals who worked in the German interest. As a consequence, hunger spread, especially in the cities, predominantly in the Leningrad area, in the Donets basin, northeastern Ukraine, and on the Crimea. Already by the end of 1941 mass death by starvation had occurred there, especially in the city of Kharkov.

Soviet prisoners of war (POWs) fared even worse. Approximately 3.4 million Red Army soldiers (including tens of thousands of women, but also civilians interned in POW camps) were in German captivity by the end of 1941. Tens of thousands were shot during the foot marches westward or died during railway transportation; the POWs were brought into improvised camps, often without any barracks or infrastructure at all. At the end of October 1941 the German POW administration lowered the food rations for those POWs who were weakened and not fully able to work. As a consequence, mass starvation spread; in most camps one hundred POWs died every day between October 1941 and May 1942. By the latter date, almost two million POWs had been killed by malnutrition, winter cold, and lack of medical support.

Only a minority of the POWs had been put to work by 1941; until October of that year, transports for work inside the Reich had generally been blocked by Hitler, who feared Bolshevik infiltration inside Germany. Nevertheless almost three hundred thousand men did enter Germany before that date.

For some months during 1941, POWs of specific non-Russian ethnicity, especially ethnic Germans, Balts, and Ukrainians, were released from captivity, most of them in order to join German services.

While the majority of the German frontline divisions started to kill alleged political functionaries right after captivity, most of the direct murders of POWs occurred in or nearby the camps. Certain groups of POWs were segregated—alleged political officers, Jews, and in the first months even men with an Asian appearance. They were either transferred to the security police or shot by the Wehrmacht units themselves. It has been estimated that more than 140,000 POWs died that way before 1944.

TREATMENT OF CIVILIANS

German propaganda claimed that this war served liberation from bolshevism. And indeed, especially in the western areas, Germans were often greeted as liberators. However, not only did the occupiers fail to dissolve the collective farms but they also brought with them a terror regime even more murderous than the Stalinist one. The crimes against civilians can be divided according to three groups of victims: Jews, political functionaries, and so-called suspects in connection with resistance.

The Jews were the main targets of German extermination policy. During the first weeks of the campaign, Jewish men were shot by SS and police; others fell victim to the pogroms of June–July 1941, which had been instigated by German police and local nationalist underground groups. From mid-August, SS and police units started to kill Jewish women and children, too, and by mid-September complete Jewish communities were annihilated, right after the occupation of each city. Thus by the end of 1941 at least five hundred thousand Jews had been killed, half of them in the Ukraine. The military administration supplied infrastructural support for the crimes; army commanders issued ideological orders to legitimate the genocide. In some cases Wehrmacht units shot Jews. Romanian occupation authorities started their own policy of annihilation against the Jews of the Odessa area. But most Jews soon lived under civil administration. Thus, in the western areas of the occupied territories the majority of Jews were still alive at the beginning of 1942.

Most functionaries of the Soviet party and state had been evacuated. Those apprehended were killed, unless they were considered indispensable for the economy. From the first day of the war, German units enacted excessive reprisal killings in response to alleged or real sniper attacks. This kind of reprisal was soon directed against Jewish or ethnic Russian civilians. In order to prevent the development of a partisan movement, orders were issued to kill all stragglers from the Red Army who did not present themselves to the German authorities, as well as persons on the move without permits. Those apprehended were either shot on the spot or put in internment camps. In July 1941 sporadic attacks by partisans started in Belarus, then also at the Latvian-Russian border, in the Bryansk area, and on the Crimea. German units killed tens of thousands of civilians as "partisan suspects" even before a bigger partisan movement was set up in 1942. Only a tiny minority of those killed had been armed.

By spring 1942, almost two million Soviet POWs had died and approximately six hundred thousand civilians had been killed outside of military action, not counting deaths by hunger. The German army lost around 460,000 dead, the Red Army at least 1.3 million, according to official statistics, which probably are not complete. Operation Barbarossa can be considered one of the most violent military campaigns in modern history, similar in dimension only to the Japanese occupation of China in 1937. The war against the Soviet Union constituted the central part of the National Socialist dictatorship, first as the ultimate aim of Hitler's policy, then as the most radical form of National Socialist rule, and finally of course, as the campaign that decided the fate of the Third Reich.

See also **Concentration Camps; Einsatzgruppen; Holocaust; Occupation, Military; Partisan Warfare; Pogroms; Prisoners of War; Resistance; Soviet Union; World War II.**

BIBLIOGRAPHY

Boog, Horst, et al., eds. *The Attack on the Soviet Union.* Volume 4 of *Germany and the Second World War,* edited by the Militärgeschichtliches Forschungsamt (Research Institute for Military History). Oxford, U.K., 1998.

Glantz, David M., and Jonathan M. House. *When Titans Clashed: How the Red Army Stopped Hitler.* Lawrence, Kans., 1995.

Hillgruber, Andreas. *Hitlers Strategie: Politik und Kriegführung, 1940–1941.* Frankfurt am Main, 1965.

Megargee, Geoffrey P. *War of Annihilation: Combat and Genocide on the Eastern Front, 1941.* Landam, Md., 2006.

Reinhardt, Klaus. *Moscow—The Turning Point: The Failure of Hitler's Strategy in the Winter of 1941–42.* Oxford, U.K., 1992.

Verbrechen der Wehrmacht: Dimensionen des Vernichtungskrieges, 1941–1944. Ausstellungskatalog. Edited by the Hamburger Institut für Sozialforschung. Hamburg, Germany, 2002. Also on DVD.

Weinberg, Gerhard L. *A World at Arms: A Global History of World War II.* Cambridge, U.K., 1994.

DIETER POHL

OPHÜLS, MARCEL (b. 1927), German-born filmmaker.

Marcel Ophüls was born in 1927 in Frankfurt, Germany, the only son of the filmmaker Max Ophüls (1902–1957). His father had achieved considerable renown in Germany before the family, which was Jewish, had to flee the rise of National Socialism; Marcel Ophüls has recalled that his father's film *Liebelei* (1932) was playing in Berlin when they left the city in 1933 for Paris, shortly after the Reichstag burned. The Ophülses eventually fled France as well and emigrated to the United States, where the elder Ophüls continued his career in Hollywood before returning to Europe after the end of the war. Marcel Ophüls attended Hollywood High School and the University of California at Berkeley, then the Sorbonne in Paris, where he met the filmmaker François Truffaut (1932–1984), among others.

Marcel Ophüls's drive to expose the truth of World War II and of the Holocaust was no doubt inflected by his early life experience. Ophüls worked with his father only once, as third assistant director on Max Ophüls's last film, *Lola Montès* (1955). Marcel began his own career as a director in France during the early 1960s, experimenting in various genres (biographical short, anthology, light comedy). But Ophüls did not find his own genre and voice until he directed an extensive documentary for French television in 1967 on the 1938 Munich crisis.

FILMOGRAPHY

Matisse (1960; short)
Love at Twenty (1962; West German segment)
Banana Peel (1963)
Make Your Bets, Ladies (1965; also known as *Fire at Will*)
Munich, or Peace in Our Time (1967; TV)
The Sorrow and the Pity: Chronicle of a French City under Siege (1969)
The Harvest of My Lai (1970; TV)
Clavigo (1970; TV)
Zwei ganze Tage (1970; TV)
America Revisited (1971; TV)
A Sense of Loss (1972)
The Memory of Justice (1976)
Kortner Geschichte (1980; TV)
Yorktown: Le sens d'une victoire (1982; TV)
Hotel Terminus: The Life and Times of Klaus Barbie (1988)
November Days (1991)
The Troubles We've Seen: A History of Journalism in Wartime (1994)

He realized that he could use the gravitas and length of documentaries as a way of telling truths about how important historical moments unfold and accumulate; this approach or ethos would deeply influence Claude Lanzmann (b. 1925) and other documentarians to follow. Ophüls also made certain to include his presence self-reflexively in his films, consistently including his voice as questioner (rather than splicing together a string of answers by interviewees to make it appear a more continuous narrative) and sometimes actually including himself in the shot. This reflexivity can be compared to the strategy of U.S. documentary filmmaker Errol Morris (b. 1948), whose voice is rarely heard and who is virtually never seen on camera.

Ophüls's first feature film is often considered his magnum opus: *The Sorrow and the Pity* (1969) is a 262-minute portrait of the French provincial town of Clermont-Ferrand during the Nazi occupation, as drawn retrospectively by participants and witnesses. It took Ophüls three full years to

A scene from Marcel Ophüls's documentary film about French collaboration with Nazis, *The Sorrow and the Pity*, 1970. NORDDEUTSCHER RUNDFUNK/THE KOBAL COLLECTION

amass the enormous quantity of interview footage that he eventually selected and cut down. It is a testament to his virtuosity that the viewer is left with the feeling that, for all the viewer has seen in four and a half hours, the story is even more complex and inexhaustible than the medium of film can capture, exhausted as one may be from watching. *The Sorrow and the Pity* is populated with all-too-human characters, from whom several insistent questions emerge: How is it that the Nazis came to occupy France so easily and fully? Does the desire to survive equal complicity? What does heroism look like, and what motivates it?

These questions were so expansive and important that Ophüls continued to ask them in different historical contexts throughout his career: *A Sense of Loss* (1972), for example, addresses the political and religious conflict in

Northern Ireland; and *November Days* (1991) is an examination of East Germans as they adjust to the end of socialism. With such volatile subject matter, Ophüls inevitably came under fire over the years, from within as well as without. In 1973 Ophüls took on an ambitious project titled *The Memory of Justice*, in which he set out to compare the behavior of French troops in Algeria and American soldiers in Vietnam to Nazi troops of the Third Reich. But when he refused to draw links between American GIs and the Nazis because he had not found any proof to back the claim, infighting ensued, and the final editing was assigned to another director as a result.

Ophüls was so demoralized by the experience that he vowed never to make films again, but after several years teaching at universities in the United States and working as a producer for American television newsmagazines, he returned once more to the subject of World War II and the Nazi occupation of France; his *Hotel Terminus* (1988) won an Academy Award. Instead of telling the story of one town, Ophüls tells the story of one man, Klaus Barbie. Barbie was the SS (Schutzstaffel) officer in charge of the Gestapo in Lyons, France, from November 1942 to August 1944. He was finally tried and convicted in 1987 for his personal involvement in torture, rape, deportations, and killings during World War II.

Ophüls once again interviewed everyone from French Resistance leaders and collaborators to the maids in the hotel Barbie occupied in Lyons (the Hotel Terminus), and his neighbors in Bolivia, where he fled after the war. Once again, Ophüls's distinctive cinematographic style is evident: his interviews are long, as are the shots that capture them. He does not distract viewers from the speakers by moving his camera obtrusively or cutting continuously back and forth between speakers. He also includes footage of the surrounding landscape between interviews, establishing a firm sense of *place*, which is reinforced by the title, *Hotel Terminus.*

Ophüls continued to press basic questions about history, justice, and moral responsibility. He again foregrounded the messenger's reflexivity in 1994, when he made a film called *The Troubles We've Seen*, which scrutinizes war reporting in Bosnia. As internecine wars become ever more labyrinthine in origin and persistence, Ophüls may find his vision of history vindicated.

See also **Cinema; Film (Documentary).**

BIBLIOGRAPHY

Ophüls, Marcel. *The Sorrow and the Pity: A Film.* New York, 1972.

———. *Hotel Terminus: The Life and Times of Klaus Barbie.* New York, 2004.

Porton, Richard, and Lee Ellickson. "The Troubles He's Seen: An Interview with Marcel Ophuls." *Cineaste* 21, no. 3 (1995): 8–11. Available as an e-document from Thomson Gale.

Thirard, Paul Louis. Review of *The Sorrow and the Pity.* In *Positif 50 Years: Selections from the French Film Journal,* edited by Michel Ciment and Laurence Kardish, 107–110. New York, 2002.

ANNE M. KERN

OPINION POLLS AND MASS-OBSERVATION.

It is no coincidence that Mass-Observation and the British Institute of Public Opinion (BIPO) were founded in the same year, 1937. Although equally underfunded in their early years, their coming into existence reflected a desire within the liberal democracies to measure what ordinary people believed in an increasingly complex modern world threatened by the spread of fascist and totalitarian regimes across Europe and beyond. Their initial marginality was confirmed by the status of their leaders. In the case of BIPO, Henry Durant was an unemployed doctoral student. Mass-Observation was begun by Tom Harrisson, an unorthodox amateur anthropologist and ornithologist; Charles Madge, a poet and later sociologist; and the surrealist artist and later film-maker, Humphrey Jennings. A further parallel was provided by a strong American influence. In 1935 George Horace Gallup had created the American Institute of Public Opinion, which was the model for its British equivalent. Mass-Observation owed much to the "Chicago School" of sociology, which had since the First World War pioneered the study of life-story writing of individuals in groups such as Polish peasants and other immigrant groups settling in America. In spite of these similarities, however, there were also profound differences in approach between BIPO and Mass-Observation as well as within the latter itself.

The founders of Mass-Observation were united in their desire to empower ordinary people "to speak for themselves" by producing an anthropology "of ourselves, for ourselves" (Calder and Sheridan). They believed that the modern mass media did not reflect the views of ordinary people and that as Europe was heading for a catastrophic civil war it was essential to connect people with each other and ensure that the government reflect the real views of its population. Nevertheless, there was tension between Harrisson, who believed that popular ethnographic fieldwork was the way to understand the "tribes of Britain," and Madge and Jennings, who were more interested in the collective subconscious of the British people as revealed in writing and everyday discourse. One of the shared errors of these remarkably precocious individuals (all were in their twenties and had no financial resources) was their claim to be scientific, a claim that many of their contemporaries, especially in the newly emerging discipline of sociology, utterly disputed.

By the outbreak of the Second World War, Jennings had already left Mass-Observation, and Madge was to do so shortly after, mainly in disagreement over Harrisson's decision to work for the government and its home intelligence unit to monitor public morale. Ironically, in terms of approach Harrisson had moved closer to the position of his cofounders and increasingly put emphasis on written material—war diaries and directives—and acknowledging that qualitative evidence was of much more importance than quantitative. Even when Mass-Observation did quantify its findings, it did so on material that was part of a far less structured approach than BIPO, which asked questions on a "yes/no" basis.

The Second World War was the point of the original Mass-Observation's greatest influence, and the methodology employed by Harrisson was vindicated by his successful prediction of a massive Labour Party landslide in the 1945 election. In contrast, BIPO and opinion polls remained marginal in the 1940s. While the approach of BIPO was ultimately to become dominant, and Mass-Observation was to fade away in the late 1940s (but to be revived successfully at the University of

Sussex in the 1980s, reviving diary, directive, and other life-story writing), it should not be assumed that the latter was an intellectual failure. In spite of its title, Mass-Observation increasingly believed in taking the *individual* seriously, and the huge archive it created revealed the complex and multi-layered responses and reactions of ordinary people in their everyday lives to the world around them. The Mass-Observation Archive remains the most intimate and powerful evocation of the public mood during the Second World War.

The contrast in approaches between Mass-Observation and BIPO came to a head in a public debate between Harrisson and Durant in 1942 at the British Psychology Society (and published in *Nature*, 9 May 1942). Durant stressed that "The history of science indicates that progress is most rapid when there is the most vigorous insistence upon exact statistical measurement" and that the social scientist had to be able to eliminate "subjective bias." In response, Harrisson argued that quantitative research was only useful as a "check, corrective and extension of the qualitative approach," and he rejected instant interviewing of large numbers of people, as carried out by BIPO and its successors, because it was done out of context and without any consideration of the relationship between interviewer and interviewee. In this respect, Mass-Observation was the precursor of the increasingly self-reflexive anthropology of the post-1945 era, the "thick description" urged by Clifford Geertz and the more tentative approach toward "truth" adopted by many postmodernists. At the time, however, Mass-Observation's influence was limited to sympathetic individual researchers on both sides of the Atlantic. The contemporary impact of Gallup's work in the United States was much greater, as is evidenced not only by BIPO but also the formation of the Institut Français d'Opinion Publique (IFOP) in 1938. The German occupation forced IFOP underground, but it was revived in 1944 after Liberation. The use of publicly accessible opinion polls was anathema to fascist regimes. Nevertheless, in both Nazi Germany and Vichy France, underground political resistance groups carried out informal polls, true to the democratic and antifascist objectives of those who pioneered the open gauging of public opinion.

See also **Postmodernism.**

BIBLIOGRAPHY

Primary Sources

Calder, Angus, and Dorothy Sheridan, eds. *Speak for Yourself: A Mass-Observation Anthology, 1937–1949.* London, 1984.

Madge, Charles, and Tom Harrisson. "Mass-Observation." *Nature* 149, no. 3784 (9 May 1942): 516–518.

Secondary Sources

Dorsey, John. "Public Opinion Research in France." *Public Opinion Quarterly* 16, no. 2 (summer 1952): 225–235.

Kushner, Tony. *We Europeans?: Mass-Observation, "Race," and British Identity in the Twentieth Century.* Aldershot, England, and Burlington, Vt., 2004.

Sheridan, Dorothy, Brian Street, and David Bloome. *Writing Ourselves: Mass-Observation and Literacy Practices.* Cresskill, N.J., 2000.

Worcester, Robert. *British Public Opinion: A Guide to the History and Methodology of Political Opinion Polling.* Oxford, U.K., 1991.

TONY KUSHNER

OPUS DEI. Opus Dei, the official name of which is the Priestly Society of the Holy Cross, is a Roman Catholic organization founded in Madrid in 1928 by José María Escrivá de Balaguer (1902–1975), who was made St. Josémaría in 2002. Although its first priest members were ordained in the early 1940s, only in 1947 did the Holy See begin to grant pontifical approval. The organization lived in a legal limbo until 1950 when Pope Pius XII granted definitive approval to Opus Dei. In 1982 Pope John Paul II granted to Opus Dei the status of personal prelature. By the early 2000s, the organization had approximately eighty-five thousand members, some fifteen hundred of them priests, in sixty countries, mostly in Western Europe and the Americas. The headquarters are now located in Rome. One of the most significant aspects of Opus Dei is that both the laity—men and women—and priests may join. (There are three different levels of membership for men and four for women.) The organization closely reflects the founder's socially conservative and hierarchical concept of society, as exposed in his writings, the best known being *Camino* (1939; *The Way*, 2002), a collection of 999 sayings and brief reflections.

Both the origins and evolution of Opus Dei are closely linked to Escrivá's own life and strong personality. In the early 1930s, he started a little center that recruited university students in Madrid. The sociological profile of the members was middle class and politically conservative, a sector being very much alienated by the policies carried out by the democratic Second Republic (1931–1939). When, in July 1936, the civil war broke out, Escrivá went into hiding to avoid being killed. He managed to escape to the Francoist zone, where he offered his services to the rebel authorities. At the end of the conflict, he returned to Madrid because the new political circumstances proved very favorable to Opus Dei. The crucial factor that initially propelled the organization was the support it found among some prominent Francoist politicians, especially Luis Carrero Blanco, Franco's right-hand man from 1941 until he was assassinated by the ETA (a Basque terrorist organization) in 1973. The dictatorship pursued a policy of purging Republican civil servants, professionals, and professors, which left numerous vacancies in those fields and opened the doors to many members of Opus Dei to rapidly advance in their careers. The Spanish Council for Scientific Research, several professorships, and high offices of the state were soon staffed with people related to the organization. The focus on the recruitment and training of competent professionals would prove a great asset in the future.

The height of public and political prominence for Opus Dei came in 1957, when the dictatorship finally decided to abandon autarky, the disastrous economic and social policies carried out by the successive governments since the end of the war. The ministries in charge of the newly adopted policy of economic modernization and liberalization were members of Opus Dei. The new policies enjoyed a resounding success that paved the way for the "miracle" of the Spanish economic recovery during the 1960s and early 1970s. This led to a more visible public presence for Opus Dei, and accusations by other Francoist sectors, especially the Falange, of hidden agendas. The democratic opposition also denounced the close links between Opus Dei and the dictatorship. Opus Dei always denied that the professional activities of its experts

or "technocrats" implied an official line adopted by the organization. The relationship between its leaders and those of the regime, however, was always fluid, and Escrivá himself accepted the title of Marquis of Peralta from the Francoist government. When democracy was restored in Spain in 1977, several ministers in the center and center-right governments that ruled from 1977 to 1982 and from 1996 to 2004 were members of Opus Dei.

The papacy of John Paul II, which began in 1978, opened a new period for Opus Dei after the not-always-fluid relationships with Pope John XXIII and, to a lesser degree, Pope Paul VI. Holding conservative moral ideas, the new pope believed that excesses and mistakes had been accepted in some sectors of the church after the Second Vatican Council, and he desired to correct some of these; in such endeavors, he found an excellent ally in Opus Dei. Its orthodox Catholicism and its material and human resources were put at the service of John Paul II's reorientation of the church. The reward came first in the granting of the long-sought personal prelature in 1982, which gave the organization complete independence from the local bishops, and later in 2002 with the unusually fast canonization of Escrivá, a move that was resented by many progressive Catholics and lay members in Spain for his links with the Francoist dictatorship.

See also **Catholicism; Franco, Francisco; John Paul II; Spain; Spanish Civil War.**

BIBLIOGRAPHY

Coverdale, John F. *Uncommon Faith: The Early Years of Opus Dei, 1928–1943.* Rev. ed. Princeton, N.J., 2002.

Escrivá de Balaguer, José María. *The Way.* Princeton, N.J., 2002.

Ynfante, Jesús. *El santo fundador del Opus Dei: Biografía completa de Josémaría Escrivá de Balaguer.* Barcelona, 2002.

ANTONIO CAZORLA-SANCHEZ

ORFF, CARL (1895–1982), primitivist musician.

Carl Orff was born in Munich on 10 July 1895. He studied at the Munich Academy and, beginning in 1920, with Heinrich Kaminski. His compositions established a type of primitivism associated with ancient practices such as ostinato (the persistent repetition of a musical figure at the same pitch throughout a composition) and raw emotional expression to produce works that have a pagan, sensual excitement. Orff scholars frequently mention the influence of Igor Stravinsky (especially Stravinsky's *The Wedding* and *Oedipus Rex*). Like Stravinsky and Olivier Messiaen among others, Orff regarded rhythm as the form-building element in music. His rhythm drew its strength from the simple patterns of folk tunes and peasant dances. He tended to avoid harmonic complexity and the intellectual attitudes inherent in contrapuntal writing. Most works, especially his most performed work, *Carmina burana* (1937), were designed as pageants for the stage. *Carmina* is the first part of a trilogy, the others being *Catulli carmina* (1943) and *Trionfo di Afrodite* (1953). Between 1925 and 1973, Orff composed approximately seventeen such dramatic works.

During the Nazi regime, many composers fled to the West or composed privately, knowing that their music would not be performed publicly. Orff composed in a style that was simple enough to please the Nazi authorities but still individual enough to succeed musically. His characteristic style first emerged full-blown in the dramatic cantata *Carmina burana,* a setting of secular, even ribald, medieval Latin and German songs. *Carmina* set a precedent: the textual declamation assumes the dominant role and syllabic settings are projected through elemental chantlike melodic figures, repeated incessantly to the percussive and sometime dramatic accompaniment of static triadic harmonies. Like Stravinsky before him, Orff frequently used ostinato patterns. *Carmina burana* creates a ritualistic incantation using a variety of forces, including a large orchestra and chorus and an impressive role for a baritone. A soprano soloist appears in part 3 and a countertenor has one solo. After completing *Carmina burana,* Orff instructed his publisher to destroy his previous works. Despite his desire to continue in a primitive, dramatic style, the second work in the triptych—*Catulli carmina*—is quite different musically, having a more reserved choral, almost renaissance style, though certainly some of the texts are more erotic than any in *Carmina burana.* Orff composed two operas based upon Grimms' fairy tales: *Der Mond* (1937–1938, revised

in 1941) and *Die Kluge* (1943). He also composed a trilogy of theater works based upon Greek subjects: *Antigonae* (1949), *Oedipus der Tyrann* (1959), and *Prometheus* (1966). The last work sets Aeschylus's original Greek. *Carmina burana* seems mild compared to the overpowering severity of the three "Greek" works. Orff's interest in limiting pitch content to an absolute minimum reached its extreme in the theater piece *Die Bernauerin* (1947), where spoken sections alternate with rhythmic settings of the text accompanied only by percussion instruments. Only twice are pitches employed at all, and even these are limited to a few notes, repeated over and over. Orff's style anticipates some of the techniques common to "minimalist" composers, for example, Steve Reich and John Adams. Orff is still of historical significance because he is the only German composer of his generation who remained in Germany during the Nazi regime and yet won widespread recognition abroad. His decision, like that of several other German composers of his time—Paul Hindemith, Ernst Pepping, and Kurt Weill—to ignore avant-garde musical techniques and compose music that would appeal to traditional audiences definitely proved successful for him.

Besides being a composer, Orff became a significant advocate for young children's musical education, even designing instruments for them to play. In 1924 he became familiar with the Émile Jaques-Dalcroze method of eurhythmics, a system that combined music and bodily movement. In 1942, with Dorothee Günther, he founded a school for gymnastics, music, and dance. He established what is now known as *Orff-Schulwerk,* a pedagogical system of music education devised to teach children with no prior formal music training to play and sing together and to improvise. In 1948 he began to adapt his ideas for children's radio programs. In the early twenty-first century, various centers worldwide certify music educators in the *Orff-Schulwerk* system, which is also noteworthy for its success with handicapped children. Orff's *Music for Children* (1950–1954) includes five collections of graded materials encompassing preliminary exercises, folk tunes, and dances. The Orff Center in Munich, under the auspices of the Bavarian State Ministry for Education, Culture, the Sciences and Arts, supervises the estate of Carl Orff and functions as a center for research on Orff.

See also **Messiaen, Olivier; Opera; Stravinsky, Igor; Weill, Kurt.**

BIBLIOGRAPHY

Böhm, Suse. *Spiele mit dem Orff-Schulwerk: Elementare Musik u. Bewegung f. Kinder.* Stuttgart, Germany, 1975.

Bitcon, Carol Hampton. *Alike and Different: The Clinical and Educational Use of Orff-Schulwerk.* Santa Ana, Calif., 1976.

Frazee, Jane. *Discovering Orff: A Curriculum for Music Teachers.* Mainz and London, 1987.

Glasgow, Robert G., and Dale G. Hamreus. *Study to Determine the Feasibility of Adapting the Carl Orff Approach to Elementary Schools in America.* Washington, D.C., 1968.

Günther, Dorothee. "Der Tanz als Bewegungsphanomenen." *Rohwolts Deutsche Enzyklopädie.* Number 1951/152. Hamburg, Germany, 1962.

Jans, Hans Jörg, and Verlay Hans Schneider, eds. *Welttheater—Carl Orff und sein Bühnenwerk.* Tutzing, 1996.

Keetman, Gunild. *Elementaria: First Acquaintance with Orff-Schulwerk.* Translated by Margaret Murray. London, 1974.

———. *Reminiscences of the Güntherschule.* American Orff-Schulwerk Association Supplement, no. 13 (spring 1978).

Keetman, Gunild, Hermann Regner, and Minna Ronnefeld, eds. *A Life Given to Music and Movement.* Edited by Hermann Regner and Minna Ronnefeld. Mainz, 2004. In German and English.

Landis, Beth, and Polly Carder. *The Eclectic Curriculum in American Music Education: Contributions of Dalcroze, Kodaly, and Orff.* Washington, D.C., 1972.

Liess, Andreas. *Carl Orff: Idee und Werk.* Edited by Hannelore Gassner. Zurich, 1977.

Orff, Carl. *The Schulwerk.* Translated by M. Murray. New York, 1978.

Orff, Carl, et al. *Carl Orff und sein Werk: Dokumentation.* 8 vols. Tutzing, Germany, 1975–1983.

The Orff Echo. Cleveland Heights, Ohio. The official bulletin of the American Orff Schulwerk Association. "Orff Zentrum" is available at http://www.orff-zentrum.de/forschung_biblio.asp. Contains more than 1,170 bibliographic entries.

Thomas, Werner. *Carl Orff, De temporum fine comoedia: Das spiel vom Ende d. Zeiten, Vigilia; Eine Interpretation.* Tutzing, Germany, 1973.

———. *Das Rad der Fortuna: Ausgewählte Aufsätze zu Werk und Wirkung Carl Orffs.* Mainz, Germany, 1990.

———. *Orffs Märchenstücke: Der Mond, Die Kluge.* Mainz, Germany, 1994.

Walter, A. "Carl Orff's Music for Children." *The Instrumentalist* 13 S (January 1959), 38–39.

Wheeler, Lawrence, and Luis Raebeck. *Orff and Kodaly Adapted for the Elementary School.* Dubuque, Iowa, 1977.

Wolfgart, Hans. *Orff-Schulwerk und Therapie: Therapeut. Komponenten in d. elementaren Musik- u. Bewegungserziehung.* Berlin, 1975.

Wuytack, Jos. *Musica Viva: An Introduction to Active Musical Education.* Paris, 1972.

LARRY PETERSON

ORGANISATION FOR EUROPEAN ECONOMIC COOPERATION (OEEC).

Established in 1948 by the recipients of Marshall Plan aid, the Organisation for European Economic Cooperation (OEEC) coordinated the efforts of its members to restore their national economies. A part of a network of national and international aid agencies, programs, and institutions, the OEEC provided the organizational framework to manage the post–World War II reconstruction of Western Europe. The OEEC represented the beneficiaries of the European Recovery Program (ERP) vis-à-vis the U.S. government. Having prepared the first ERP on the European side, the OEEC was later responsible for allocating ERP funds. After the end of the Marshall Plan, in 1952, the organization lost its importance, while it provided the basis for the subsequent and expanded development of the Organisation for Economic Cooperation and Development (OECD) in 1961.

On 5 June 1947, the U.S. secretary of state George C. Marshall, in a speech at Harvard University, introduced the idea of a U.S.-supported European recovery program. Rather than presenting a ready-made plan, Marshall emphasized that the Europeans needed to take the initiative. To receive American aid, Europeans were to cooperate and to formulate a joint economic program. The U.S. secretary of state's call was open to all European countries. To negotiate the proposed European recovery scheme, in July 1947, sixteen Western European states formed the Committee on European Economic Cooperation (CEEC). Intergovernmental negotiations with the United States started soon thereafter. On 16 April 1948, the CEEC set up the OEEC as a permanent organization to advance European economic cooperation. The founding members of the OEEC were Austria, Belgium, Denmark, France, Greece, Iceland, Ireland, Italy, Luxembourg, Netherlands, Norway, Portugal, Sweden, Switzerland, Turkey, and the United Kingdom. West Germany, originally represented by the Bizone (the combined American and British occupation zones) and the French occupation zone, officially entered the OEEC in June 1949, following the proclamation of the German constitution (Basic Law) in May 1949. Until returned to Italian sovereignty in 1954, the Anglo-American zone of the Free Territory of Trieste was also a participant in the OEEC. Spain joined the organization in 1959.

The headquarters of the OEEC was established in Paris. French official Robert Marjolin, previously involved in the preparation and implementation of the French plan to modernize France's industry (the Monnet Plan), became the organization's first secretary general. Marjolin was succeeded in 1955 by René Sergent, the former Assistant Secretary General for Economic and Financial Affairs at the North Atlantic Treaty Organization (NATO). The OEEC comprised a council that appointed an executive committee of seven members. The council's decisions required unanimity. The operational arm of the OEEC consisted of a complex structure of committees and working parties.

The OEEC was instrumental in assessing European requirements for U.S. aid and devising a system for regular consultation. Among the organization's functions were the preparation of an annual economic recovery program to distribute ERP aid and the allocation of scarce resources among the member states. Abolishing quantitative trade restrictions between its member states and fostering intra-European trade were further goals of the organization. A major achievement of the OEEC was the creation of a European Payments Union (1950). Set up for a limited period of four years (1948–1952) and operating through a counterpart fund, the ERP helped to contain inflation, revive trade, and restore production in Western Europe.

Managing the program on the U.S. side and acting as the OEEC's partner organization was the Economic Cooperation Administration (ECA), also founded in April 1948. The ECA promoted the unification of the European market through the OEEC as the basis for a stable Western Europe. For the Truman administration, the reconstruction of a democratic and capitalist (Western) Europe was essential in the fight against Soviet communism. The Marshall Plan was to provide both a successful economic tool to restore the European economies and a decisive U.S. foreign policy instrument. U.S. support for Western Europe proved politically significant in the early Cold War years. However, the economic impact of U.S. aid for European recovery has been challenged. As an international organization, the OEEC fell short of fulfilling American hopes of truly advancing European integration. The United Kingdom, in particular, was not prepared to compromise sovereignty to create a European customs union or a federation. With U.S. support and without British participation, European integration materialized in 1951 when the European Coal and Steel Community was established.

The OEEC's significance declined with the end of the ERP in 1952. In 1961, the OECD was established to succeed the OEEC. With the United States and Canada among its founding members, the new organization extended and transformed its European predecessor.

See also **European Coal and Steel Community (ECSC); European Union; Marshall Plan; NATO.**

BIBLIOGRAPHY

George C. Marshall Foundation. "The Marshall Plan: Selected Bibliography." Available at http://www. marshallfoundation.org/marshall_plan_bibliography.html. A concise annotated bibliography.

Hogan, Michael J. *The Marshall Plan: America, Britain, and the Reconstruction of Western Europe, 1947–1952.* New York, 1987. A comprehensive monograph on the Marshall Plan, encompassing the evolution of the OEEC.

OECD. *The European Reconstruction 1948–1961: Bibliography on the Marshall Plan and the Organisation for European Economic Co-operation (OEEC).* Paris, 1996. An annotated bibliography.

OECD. "Organization for European Economic Co-operation." Available at http://www.oecd.org/document/

48/0,2340,en_2649_34487_1876912_1_1_1_1,00.html.
A historical introduction to the OEEC.

BRIGITTE LEUCHT

———————————— ▪ ————————————

ORTEGA Y GASSET, JOSÉ (1883–1955),
Spanish philosopher and writer.

José Ortega y Gasset is regarded as Spain's greatest twentieth-century philosopher and one of the most influential ever to have emerged from the Iberian Peninsula. Having studied in Germany, Ortega was familiar with the German intellectual tradition, and his main reference points were the works of Edmund Husserl (1859–1938), Martin Heidegger (1889–1976), and Wilhelm Dilthey (1833–1911).

Ortega's philosophical thought is organized around three questions: Why do we do philosophy? What is truth? and What is reality? Seeking answers to these questions led Ortega to participate in a wide range of philosophical speculation, covering thinking about thinking (metaphysics), the nature of being (ontology), and the study of knowledge (epistemology). Ortega believed that the first third of the twentieth century constituted a period of crisis of a kind that only occurs once or twice every thousand years or so. Such periods are accompanied by fundamental rethinking of the nature of reality, carried out by exemplary philosophers—such as, by his own lights, Ortega himself.

Ortega's early view (1929–1933) that we (all) do philosophy because we are naturally inquiring beings gave way after his exposure to Dilthey's work to a historicizing of the philosophical act. This is the root of his disagreement with Heidegger, whom Ortega criticized for arguing that "surprise" is at the root of philosophizing. We are often surprised at the world, says Ortega, but we do not always respond by doing philosophy. In contrast, Ortega developed the idea that authentic philosophy is done at moments in which traditional beliefs come into question. One such moment was the period in the sixteenth century when revelation as a source of truth gave way to the methodology of doubt, exemplified in the work of René Descartes (1596–1650). Descartes's work gave rise to idealism and realism as competing ways of understanding what there is in the world. Ortega argued that neither of these schools of thought offers access to what he called "radical reality" (la realidad radical), defined by him as a reality that is suppositionless. Radical reality is reality prior to any thought about it, which is why Cartesian idealism cannot give a full account of reality. Ortega turns Descartes on his head, claiming that "I think because I exist" rather than "I think therefore I am." This leads Ortega to the conclusion that pure reason needs to be replaced by "reason from life's point of view" (la razón vital), with individual life as the radical reality through which all realities flow and from which reality is therefore best apprehended.

Individual life is so fundamental, indeed, that Ortega argued that even apparently self-evident truths such as 2 + 2 = 4 are only authentically true once they have been verified by the individual. Placing the individual life at the center of his intellectual project leads Ortega to offer a perspectivist account of the truth. Truth, for Ortega, is neither a matter of correspondence with some external reality nor of coherence in the sense of the internal consistency of a body of thought. Everyone, he says, has access to a portion of the truth. This does not mean, though, that Ortega is a relativist. He argues that some people have access to greater portions of the truth than others: some perspectives are broader and wider than others. The broadest and widest point of view is that which we get from life itself. Once again, pure reason is too partial a perspective to be able to provide the fullest account of the truth. The broadest perspective is possessed by the authentic individual who employs la razón vital to apprehend the world. This philosophical conclusion is crucial to the work for which Ortega is probably most famous—his sociology.

Ortega's best-known work, the *Revolt of the Masses,* is often misunderstood as a socially elitist diatribe against the irruption of the masses into political life. But for Ortega the mass is merely a collection of "average men"—aristocrats can betray the characteristics of the mass man, too. Ortega believed it essential that an elite take command once again—an elite characterized not so much by social class as by breadth of vision. This, Ortega argued, was the foundation stone of a truly modern politics. Ortega can be plausibly linked to the phenomenological and existentialist traditions that were central to European thought in the interwar and postwar years. His notions of authenticity, the centrality of the individual, and his discursive style, laced with everyday examples, are instantly recognizable as part of those traditions.

Ortega's intellectual reputation has suffered, perhaps, from his never collecting his thought in one book of philosophy through which he might have become better known—and from his being Spanish. Germany, France, and Britain were regarded as the powerhouses of philosophy of this period, and Ortega's reputation has been hard to establish in the face of northern European competition.

See also **Heidegger, Martin; Spain.**

BIBLIOGRAPHY

Primary Sources

Ortega y Gasset, José. *Qué es filosofía?* Madrid, 1958.

———. *Qué es conocimiento?* Madrid, 1984.

Secondary Sources

Dobson, Andrew. *An Introduction to the Politics and Philosophy of José Ortega y Gasset.* Cambridge, U.K., 1989. Comprehensive introduction to the context and content of Ortega's social, political, and philosophical thought.

ANDREW DOBSON

ORWELL, GEORGE (1903–1950), English author.

George Orwell was the wintry conscience not only of England but of much of the world through his two most influential books, *Animal Farm* (1945) and *Nineteen Eighty-Four* (1949). He was born Eric Arthur Blair in India, where his father was a civil servant with a position supervising the opium trade. In 1907 with his mother, who was of French descent from a family in the timber business in Burma, and his older sister, Marjorie, he came to England, where the family settled in Henley, joined by a younger sister, Avril. Orwell's father, except for leaves, remained in India for some further years. Orwell, with that social precision for which he became famous, characterized himself as a member of the "lower-upper middle class." They had that

position because of descent from a younger son of the aristocracy and from vicars, but not much cash to keep it up. As is the custom among his class, at the age of eight he was sent away to a boarding school, St. Cyprians, but he needed to be there on scholarship, which he resented. Years later he wrote powerfully, and not totally accurately, about his experiences there in "Such, Such Were the Joys." The power of his prose is such that the reader is convinced that the truth is being put forward. Orwell is much more of an artist than is generally allowed and is a creator of worlds through his prose. Hate the school as he did, it nevertheless gave him a good education and helped instill in him, in reaction, his particular sort of socialism, yet imbued him with love of country. His first two publications during World War I were highly patriotic poems in the Henley paper. He achieved the coveted position of being a king's scholar at Eton and was there from 1917 to 1921. He had an undistinguished career, and, quite unusually for a king's scholar, he neither went to university nor into a profession, but in a sense into the family business as a police officer in Burma from 1922 to 1927.

When he returned to England on leave he decided to abandon his job and dedicate himself to being a writer. The first five years of the attempt were extremely difficult, but he used his partially self-inflicted condition of poverty to provide the material for his first book, *Down and Out in Paris and London,* published in 1933. Partially not to embarrass his family and partially because he felt a need to distance himself from his past, he chose to write under a pseudonym, selecting that most English of first names, George, and the name of a river in Suffolk, near where his parents were then living. During the 1930s he became in terms of reputation a moderately successful novelist. His first novel, *Burmese Days* (1934), drew upon his experience as a policeman, as did two essays, "Shooting an Elephant" (1936) and "A Hanging" (1931), that have become among the most famous in the language. What was unusual in these writings was his pointing out the illegitimacy of imperialism without being at all sentimental—quite the contrary—about its victims. In rapid succession he wrote two further novels, *A Clergyman's Daughter* (1935) and *Keep the Aspidistra Flying* (1936). Both of these novels, of which he was not particularly proud, explored the effects of poverty upon members of the middle class. He himself was barely surviving financially. He came to the attention of Victor Gollancz, a prominent publisher and founder of the Left Book Club, who commissioned him to write a study of the effect of poverty in England. The result, *The Road to Wigan Pier* (1937), was a powerful account of the ravages of the Depression. Contrary to the wishes of the book club, the book also included an autobiographical essay combining a critique of the failures of middle-class socialists with a rather romantic vision of the warmth and values of working-class life.

As a reporter he went to Spain shortly after the outbreak of the Spanish civil war. The socialist world he found in Barcelona so inspired him that he joined the militia of the POUM, a semi-Trotskyite group. He was almost killed at the front when a bullet went through his neck. When he returned to Barcelona he was caught up in the fighting of the "May Days" in which the communists were trying to suppress those to the left of them. The experience of Spain made him committed to democratic socialism "as I understand it" as well as a dedicated anticommunist. His magnificent account of his time in Spain, *Homage to Catalonia* (1938), received scant attention and did not achieve much of a readership until it was reissued in 1952, when he was much better known and had become a useful document in the Cold War. On his return to England he published one more traditional novel, *Coming Up for Air* (1939), in which he contrasted the tawdry values of contemporary England with the quality of life earlier in the century.

His experience in Spain and his personal happiness in his marriage to Eileen O'Shaughnessy in 1936 ushered in the period in which he became a writer of his canonical essays and many shorter pieces. Although he never changed his name legally (remarking that he would then have to find another name to write under) he was known to those he met after Spain as "George Orwell." With great skill he now examined in sympathetic and insightful ways popular culture, such as his piece on boys' weeklies and comic postcards. He also became a guardian of the language (most famously in "Politics and the English Language," published in 1946). With the outbreak of World War II he committed himself to both patriotism and socialism, holding that England must change dramati-

Actor Edmond O'Brien poses beside a prop from the 1955 film version of George Orwell's novel *1984*. ©HULTON-DEUTSCH COLLECTION/CORBIS

cally politically while maintaining its traditional values. Both in terms of health and age he could not serve, other than in the Home Guard. He worked for the British Broadcasting Corporation on its Talks Service to India, and he became a regular columnist and literary editor for the socialist weekly *Tribune,* writing a very successful series of columns, "As I Please."

His ideas about how the communists betrayed the socialist revolution bore fruit in his fable *Animal Farm* (1945), which made him internationally famous. Four years later he published *Nineteen Eighty-Four* on the same theme. The central figure of the latter novel, Winston Smith, is employed to rewrite the past in order to make it conform to the ever-changing political position of Airstrip One (Britain), part of Oceania, one of the three great powers in the world. He made permanent contributions to the language—terms too easily used, as he would have hated, as clichés—such as "Big Brother," "Thought Police," "two plus two equals five," and indeed "Orwellian." He conceived the book as a warning rather than, as those on the right saw it, as a prophecy.

Of Orwell's traditional novels, *Burmese Days* is the best. All of his books of reportage are excellent, with *Homage to Catalonia* having great moral authority. *Animal Farm* is a gem. *Nineteen Eighty-Four*, though crude at times, has great power. He is one of the best essayists in the language, writing in the plain prose of the English tradition, being able to project both his personality and a sense of truth. Orwell died of tuberculosis in 1950.

See also **Anticommunism; Antifascism; Spanish Civil War; Totalitarianism.**

BIBLIOGRAPHY

Primary Sources

Orwell, George. *The Complete Works of George Orwell.* Edited by Peter Davidson. 20 vols. London, 1998.

Secondary Sources

Crick, Bernard R. *George Orwell.* Boston, 1980.

Sheldon, Michael. *Orwell.* New York, 1991.

Stansky, Peter, and William Abrahams. *The Unknown Orwell.* New York, 1972.

———. *Orwell: The Transformation.* New York, 1979.

Taylor, D. J. *Orwell: The Life.* New York, 2003.

PETER STANSKY

OUN/UPA. The Organization of Ukrainian Nationalists was an underground terrorist group founded in 1929 committed to the establishment of an independent Ukrainian state on lands regarded as ethnically Ukrainian. Its origins lie in the Ukrainian movement that emerged in Austrian eastern Galicia before 1914, where Ukrainian activists challenged the traditional dominance of Polish nobles. At the end of World War I, Ukrainians attempted to establish a West Ukrainian People's Republic with a capital in Lviv (Lvov). This attempt was defeated by superior Polish forces in 1919, and eastern Galicia was incorporated into Poland in 1923. Discontented Ukrainian veterans founded a Ukrainian Military Organization, which in 1929 merged with student groups to form the Organization of Ukrainian Nationalists (OUN).

OUN leaders were preoccupied with the failure of Ukrainians to create their own state in 1918. They blamed poor leadership, inadequate discipline, and (in central and eastern Ukraine) attachment to liberal or socialist ideals. Central and eastern Ukraine were incorporated by the Soviet Union, and nationalists failed to exert influence in Soviet Ukraine. Their main task in the 1930s was to gain the loyalty of Ukrainian youth in Poland. A decalogue, which the OUN inherited from a student organization, described the required sort of commitment. Ukrainian nationalists were expected, according to the OUN's "Decalogue," to "win a Ukrainian state or die in the battle for it" and to "aspire to expand the strength, riches, and size of the Ukrainian state even by way of enslaving foreigners." The Ukrainian nationalist thinker Dmytro Dontsov was influential within the OUN, but was not a member. The fascism of Italian dictator Benito Mussolini was the most appealing European model.

Within Poland the OUN had to compete with other Ukrainian parties. In Galicia socialist and democratic parties had greater public influence. In Volhynia, north of Galicia, it was outmatched by the Communist Party of West Ukraine. Where the OUN distinguished itself was in the practice of terror. After the regime of Józef Piłsudski tried to engage Ukrainian society, the OUN began a wave of robbery and arson in July 1930. This brought Polish pacifications. In August 1931 the OUN assassinated Tadeusz Hołówko, the leading Polish advocate of reconciliation with Ukrainians. In this way the OUN attempted to prevent Ukrainian accommodation to Polish rule. Polish diplomats negotiated non-aggression pacts with the Soviet Union (1932) and Nazi Germany (1934). This ended the hopes of many Ukrainians that Moscow or Berlin would help the Ukrainian cause and led to cooperation of legal parties with the Polish state. Seeing Germany as the power most likely to destroy Poland, leading members of the OUN cooperated with German military intelligence.

In 1938 a Soviet agent assassinated Ievhen Konovalets, leader of the OUN. The OUN split into two fractions, conventionally known as the OUN-M and the OUN-B after the names of their leaders, Andrii Melnyk and Stepan Bandera. Both fractions sought to exploit the opportunities they saw after September 1939, when the joint

German–Soviet invasion destroyed Poland. The OUN-M provided personnel for the Ukrainian social institutions the Germans permitted in occupied Poland. When Germany invaded the Soviet Union in June 1941, the invasion force included two battalions of Ukrainian nationalists. OUN-B activists in L'viv declared the existence of a Ukrainian state, but were arrested by the Germans. Both fractions supplied personnel for the German occupation authorities. Policemen collaborated in German occupation policies, including the murder of the Jews. As the war turned against Germany, the OUN-M accepted the German proposition to create a Waffen-SS division. Some OUN-B leaders, veterans of German service, decided to create their own Ukrainian Insurgent Army (UPA), mainly from former policemen. The UPA defended Ukrainians from German repressions and fought Soviet partisans. It also ethnically cleansed native Poles from western Ukraine in 1943 and 1944.

From 1944 the UPA fought against returning Soviet forces and the emerging communist regime in Poland. In 1947 Polish communist authorities used the pretext of UPA activity to ethnically cleanse Ukrainians from southeastern Poland. A few thousand Ukrainian nationalists, largely veterans of the Waffen-SS Division Galizien, managed to reach Italy in 1945. They were airlifted to Great Britain, whence some of them apparently took part in British or American missions inside the Soviet Union. Despite continuing factionalism, nationalists managed for several decades to dominate Ukrainian cultural life in western emigration, especially in Canada. In the independent Ukraine that emerged in 1991, the OUN played a visible but unsubstantial part in public life. By the time of the Orange Revolution of 2004, the OUN had redefined its own achievement, in Ukraine at least, as the preservation of Ukrainian language and culture.

See also **Ukraine.**

BIBLIOGRAPHY

Armstrong, John A. *Ukrainian Nationalism*. Englewood, N.J., 1990.

Motyl, Alexander J. *The Turn to the Right: The Ideological Origins and Development of Ukrainian Nationalism, 1919–1929*. Boulder, Colo., 1980.

Snyder, Timothy. "The Causes of Ukrainian-Polish Ethnic Cleansing, 1943." *Past and Present* 179 (2003): 197–234.

TIMOTHY SNYDER

OWEN, WILFRED (1893–1918), English war poet.

Wilfred Owen was a war poet of World War I, whose verse has become an iconic element in the language of remembrance of the 1914–1918 conflict. Owen was born in 1893 in the west of England. A staunchly Christian upbringing led him to serve as lay assistant to the vicar of an Oxfordshire parish. There he began to write poetry. Failing the entrance examination to the University of London, he went to Bordeaux, France, to teach English at a Berlitz school.

In 1915 he volunteered for military service, training at an officer's school in Essex, England, in March 1916 before joining the Manchester Regiment. His application to join the Royal Flying Corps was rejected, and on 12 January 1917 he arrived on the western front, on the Somme in northern France, near Beaumont Hamel, the site of murderous fighting the previous summer. He endured heavy artillery barrages, intense cold, and concussion in the following weeks. In May 1917 he was diagnosed as having shell shock and sent back to Britain.

He was treated in Craiglockhart War Hospital near Edinburgh. There he was able to rest and to write. He edited a soldier's journal or informal newspaper there entitled *The Hydra*, in which he published some of his finest poems. These were written in the company of another inmate, Siegfried Sassoon, who criticized and improved his verse. Owen's "Anthem for Doomed Youth" emerged at this time, with its exhortation that young men not repeat the "old lie" that it is noble and fitting to die for one's country. Here was a liminal message: the writings of a soldier pacifist, a man who chose to take up arms and would return to the front, but without the lies and delusions of armchair patriots. He took the same message from Henri Barbusse's trench novel *Under Fire,* and in later 1917 and early 1918 continued to write the verse that made him the carrier of the message of the pity of war.

Dulce et Decorum Est

Bent double, like old beggars under sacks,
Knock-kneed, coughing like hags, we cursed
    through sludge,
Till on the haunting flares we turned our backs
And towards our distant rest began to trudge.
Men marched asleep. Many had lost their boots
But limped on, blood-shod. All went lame; all
    blind;
Drunk with fatigue; deaf even to the hoots
Of gas shells dropping softly behind.

GAS! Gas! Quick, boys!—An ecstasy of
    fumbling,
Fitting the clumsy helmets just in time;
But someone still was yelling out and
    stumbling,
And flound'ring like a man in fire or lime . . .
Dim, through the misty panes and thick green
    light
As under a green sea, I see him drowning.

In all my dreams, before my helpless sight,
He plunges at me, guttering, choking, drowning.

If in some smothering dreams you too could
    pace
Behind the wagon that we flung him in,
And watch the white eyes writhing in his face,
His hanging face, like a devil's sick of sin;
If you could hear, at every jolt, the blood
Come gargling from the froth-corrupted lungs,
Obscene as cancer, bitter as the cud
Of vile, incurable sores in innocent tongues, —
My friend, you would not tell with such high zest
To children ardent for some desperate glory,
The old Lie: "Dulce et decorum est
Pro patria mori."

Owen returned to the front in September 1918, this time as company commander. He was awarded the Military Cross for leading his company against a machine-gun position on the Beaurevoi-Fonsomme line. In later October and early November he was with British units pushing back the German army along the Oise-Sambre Canal. On 4 November 1918 he was killed while attempting to cross the canal.

His family received the news of his death on the day of the Armistice (11 November 1918). In the following years a number of collections of his poems were published. Their rhythms and tones have molded British understanding of the Great War ever since. Owen had the music of the King James Version of the Bible in his ears but could not reconcile its majesty with the ugliness of artillery fire, gas warfare, and the brutality of trench fighting. He did not reject the sacred; he reconfigured it in his poetry as the language of pity and suffering for men who died like cattle. For this reason, he was condemned by some critics, including W. B. Yeats, on the ground that passive suffering was not a fit subject for poetry. Others saw his work as so antiwar that it could not possibly stand as the voice of the British army that withstood fifty months of combat and won the war. But these are minority views, which have faded over the years. Instead Owen has become the voice of the British army, and through it the British nation, enduring the torture of the Great War. All schoolchildren in Britain read Owen's poems as part of the required curriculum for the study of the English language. Because he died in the war, his verse has carried a particularly enduring stamp. He never lived to see the shabbiness of the interwar years or the return of war in the late 1930s and after. He captured the pose of the six million British men in uniform who entered the twentieth century and its brutality without intending to do so in 1914. Owen speaks for them still.

See also **Sassoon, Siegfried; World War I.**

BIBLIOGRAPHY

Bäckman, Sven. *Tradition Transformed: Studies in the Poetry of Wilfred Owen.* Lund, Sweden, 1979.

Hibberd, Dominic. *Wilfred Owen: The Last Year, 1917–1918.* London, 1992.

———. *Wilfred Owen: A New Biography.* London, 2002.

Kerr, Douglas. *Wilfred Owen's Voices: Language and Community.* Oxford, U.K., 1993.

McPhail, Helen, and Philip Guest. *Wilfred Owen.* London, 1998.

Stallworthy, John. *Wilfred Owen.* London, 1974.

JAY WINTER

PABST, GEORG WILHELM (1885–1967), Austrian film director.

Georg Wilhelm Pabst began his career in theater in Zurich and Germany in 1905, and from 1910 to 1914 he worked as an actor in New York. Returning to Europe at the outbreak of the First World War, he was interned in Brest, France, for the duration of the conflict. After the Armistice, he directed plays in Prague before beginning his film career in Vienna.

EARLY FILM CAREER

His first effort as a director was *Der Schatz* (1923; *The Treasure*), shot in a style not unlike the then-popular expressionism. Pabst gained renown with *Die Freudlose Gasse* (1925; *The Joyless Street*), with Werner Krauss; Asta Nielsen, a Danish actress and former star of German cinema; and a young new-comer named Greta Garbo. To describe the disastrous postwar social and economic conditions in Austria and Germany, Pabst emphasized the harsh impoverishment of middle-class life, comparing it with the life of the nouveaux riches, speculators, and black marketeers. The movie is based on the parallel lives and antagonisms of characters who belong to distinct social classes. As in some other contemporary productions, the street became a symbolic scenographic space, a place of encounter as well as separation and discrimination. The success of *Die Freudlose Gasse* brought Pabst international fame.

In revolt against the bourgeois order, Pabst approached sexuality with a Freudian perspective in *Loulou* (1929) released in the United States as *Pandora's Box,* an adaptation of two plays by the German dramatist Frank Wedekind (1864–1918). The American actress Louise Brooks plays a dancer in the title role. With her pageboy haircut and slender sensuality, she would come to embody feminine subversion and the archetype of the modern, liberated woman. With her intelligence and sexuality, free from conformist values, Loulou seeks to destroy masculine integrity and to defeat the social and moral constraints of the bourgeoisie. In a decadent and corrupt world, her only defense is her sublime and innocent beauty, to be used against men who wish to possess her. At a time when such behavior was considered scandalous and perverse, the film provoked the critics and received more virulent notices than had the play, and it was censored in parts and mutilated by cuts.

With the beginning of the sound era, Pabst, who was one of the founders of the Volksverband für Filmkunst (Popular Association for the Art Film) propounded his pacifism and internationalist ideas in two major films, *Westfront 1918* (1930) and *Kameradschaft* (1931; *Comradeship*), each released in a single, bilingual version, rare at a time when most films were released in multiple-language versions. Both films exposed the failings of capitalism, which like war has no victim other than the people. An adaptation of a short story written by Ernst Johannsen, *Westfront* tells the story of a group of German soldiers at the front. It was totally different from previous films with the same subject because it denounced the absurdity of the war—the ravages of which had been as much evident behind the lines as at the front—and because it treated its theme in an extremely realistic style. Pabst conveys his messages less through dialogue than through sophisticated visual effects such as the oppressive atmosphere created by long shots and lighting that accentuates contrasts. Censored under pressure from the Nazi Party, the movie was well received in France, especially by veterans, where it improved the image of Germany, much hated after the war.

The second film, *Kameradschaft,* was inspired by the 1906 mining catastrophe in Courrières, during which German miners helped to rescue their French comrades. Partly shot in 1920 around the coal mines of the Sarre, the movie glorifies working-class solidarity, praises Franco-German reconciliation, and exalts the idea of peace with restrained appeal to the memories of wartime (in one powerful scene, a dying miner thinks he is under gas attack in the trenches). It resembles an objective documentary, with its spare direction and the absence of aesthetic devices or music. The mine's passageways, meticulously reproduced in a studio in Berlin by Erno Metzner, seem quite as real as the exteriors that were shot on location. The same striving for realism caused Pabst to choose relatively unknown German and French actors who speak in their own language. Émile Vuillermoz, a critic for *Le Temps,* was deeply impressed by the movie and wrote: "The creation of this work marks an important date in the history of the Western European cinema." Indeed, Pabst was for his time a most politically engaged director.

LATER CAREER
Although his social and political views and ideology won him the sobriquet "Pabst the Red," he made some questionable dramatic and aesthetic compromises in some of his films. The best example is his 1931 adaptation of *Die 3groschenoper* (*The Threepenny Opera*). Although he collaborated on the script, Bertolt Brecht (1898–1956) thought that the film did not respect his play's sharp edge of social criticism. Believing that the "social thesis" of the original work had been betrayed, he sued. According to Brecht, artistic integrity demanded that the film, like the theatrical production, should

have "attacked bourgeois ideology" and demanded that Nero Films destroy the prints. He accused Pabst of being incapable of preserving the original intent of the piece when turning it into film, allowing commercial considerations to destroy Brecht's original vision. Brecht lost his lawsuit, but his long polemic, *The Threepenny Lawsuit,* an original discussion of the adaptation, caused a stir.

Shortly before Adolf Hitler's ascension to power, Pabst settled in France and spent time in Hollywood, where he directed *A Modern Hero* (1934); but he found himself in Germany at the beginning of World War II. Although he refused to submit to the injunctions of Nazi propaganda, he decided to continue making movies. He was later reproached for this decision, which was quite out of character with his long-held political views. His subsequent work lacked the demanding aesthetic and ideological character of earlier films and tended to lose visual effectiveness. Pabst's last movies, from *Der Prozess* (1948; *The Trial*) to *Durch die Wälder, durch die Auen* (1956; *Through the Forests, Through the Trees*) found him working at some remove from any formal preoccupation with using film to intensify and enhance reality. That aim had characterized the realist current in German cinema between the two world wars, represented by Joe May, Leo Mittler, and Piel Jutzi. But Pabst was the standard-bearer and leading light.

See also **Brecht, Bertolt; Cinema.**

BIBLIOGRAPHY
Amengual, Barthelemy. *G. W. Pabst.* Paris, 1966.

LAURENT VERAY

PACIFISM. At the end of the twentieth century Europeans could applaud themselves for the state of peaceful coexistence in which most among them lived out their lives. This sense of peace and security, however, was a novelty in a century marked by hostility, antagonism, and outright war. From World War I to World War II, from the wars of decolonization to the Cold War, Europeans engaged in a relentless series of violent clashes between competing states and ideologies.

A peace march in England, September 1924. ©Hulton-Deutsch Collection

This unyielding cycle of warfare destroyed millions of lives and reshaped countless others. It also led hundreds of thousands, if not millions, of Europeans to renounce armed conflict as a reasonable means of solving national differences and to adopt pacifism as a personal and political creed.

Those men and women who called themselves pacifists did not necessarily share the same beliefs. Some were absolute (or integral) pacifists, rejecting all wars under any circumstances. Others were conditional pacifists of various sorts. Socialist pacifists, for example, often rejected wars between capitalist nations but accepted the idea of violent struggle as a necessary means to achieving economic equality. Many other pacifists rejected wars of aggression but continued to maintain a belief in the necessity of national defense. European pacifists—like their counterparts on other continents—also disagreed over how to best translate their beliefs into action. For some, pacifism was essentially a personal commitment, and conscientious objection was the primary means of withdrawing support for war. For many others, collaborative and proactive protest against militaristic policies was the foremost priority. Pacifists, broadly speaking, were those individuals who believed warfare to be an unnecessary evil and who actively and methodically sought to eliminate it from the arena of international affairs.

THE PEACE MOVEMENT BEFORE 1914

At the turn of the twentieth century Europeans already had a long history of pacifism from which to draw. As early as the 1700s Anabaptists established a religious basis for pacifism, rejecting the authority of both the Catholic Church and secular governments. Instead, they withdrew into their own independent societies and refused to collaborate with state authorities, including in times of war. The Anabaptist precedent was followed by members of other Protestant religious sects,

Protestors opposed to U.S. president George Bush's plans to invade Iraq march in the streets of Bilbao, Spain, 15 March 2003. ©Reuters/Corbis

particularly the Religious Society of Friends (Quakers) in England, who also found inspiration for the rejection of war in Christian doctrine. Much later, in Russia, the novelist Leo Tolstoy (1828–1910) was also inspired by Christianity when he challenged humankind to rebel against evil by repudiating violence and refusing to compromise with an aggressive state.

By the 1800s Europeans began to organize in larger numbers in order to prevent the return of violent conflict. The London Society for the Promotion of Permanent and Universal Peace, the first major peace organization in Europe, was formed largely under Quaker auspices in 1816. Although members of dissenting sects remained important to the peace movement, in the nineteenth century some "friends of peace" also drew from secular sources of inspiration. Enlightenment ideas of rationality and progress led to reasoned critiques of warfare as economically unsound, politically ineffective, and socially destructive. Later in the nineteenth century members of Europe's

socialist movements also denounced international war as the inevitable product of capitalist society. Although few socialists rejected violent struggle outright, they did condemn wars between capitalist nations and sought to convince members of the working class that their governments viewed them as expendable cannon fodder.

In the 1890s these scattered voices for peace in the various nations of Europe began to come together into a veritable international movement. Although individuals such as Albert Skarvan, a Slovak doctor who went to prison in 1895 rather than serve in the Austro-Hungarian army, continued to act alone, most peace activists joined in groups in order to promote arbitration, international law, and disarmament as the surest paths to lasting peace. Twenty-five years later, on the eve of World War I, nearly two hundred European peace societies could be found stretching from Sweden down to Italy and from Portugal across to the Russian Empire. At the international level, pacifists regularly came together at annual Universal Peace Congresses;

their representatives met together regularly as an Interparliamentary Union, and their leaders had established a permanent International Peace Bureau in Switzerland. In 1901 the Frenchman Émile Arnaud (1864–1921), president of the International League for Peace and Liberty, gave the movement a new word to describe the ideals for which it stood: pacifism.

Women became an important force within the European peace movement in these decades. Indeed, it was a woman—the novelist Bertha von Suttner (1843–1914) of Austria—who was most responsible for arousing popular pacifist sentiment in Europe at the turn of the twentieth century. In 1889 von Suttner published *Lay Down Your Arms*, a novel that portrayed all the ills of modern warfare and was seen by her readers as a scathing indictment of militarism. The book became an instantaneous bestseller and was rapidly translated throughout Europe. Tolstoy was an early admirer, telling von Suttner that he thought her novel had the potential to galvanize opponents of war the way Harriet Beecher Stowe's (1811–1896) novel *Uncle Tom's Cabin* had advanced the cause of abolitionism in the United States. Von Suttner subsequently became one of the universally recognized leaders of the peace movement in Europe. In 1905 she became the first woman to be awarded the Nobel Peace Prize.

In the early 1900s European pacifists faced an uncertain future. The major European states entered the twentieth century nominally at peace, but enduring antagonisms between the major states, a heated arms race on land and sea, and competition for colonies abroad all were working to undermine international stability. Politicians and the press both freely fanned the flames of nationalism to advance their own agendas. Europe was indeed a powder keg. The spark that set it alight came 28 June 1914, with the murder of the heir to the Habsburg throne, Archduke Francis Ferdinand (1863–1914), by a Serbian nationalist. By the end of the summer, Europe was engulfed in what would become known as World War I, a conflict far more horrible than anything von Suttner or her fellow pacifists had ever imagined and which they proved utterly unable or unwilling to prevent. How can their failure be explained?

WORLD WAR I, CONSCIENTIOUS OBJECTION, AND WARTIME PACIFISM

The simplest answer to this question is that in 1914 pacifism was a minority movement. Those Europeans who did consider themselves pacifists, moreover, widely believed their governments were asking them to participate in a just war. Central Europeans lost their most persuasive voice for peace just when they needed her most; Bertha von Suttner died in her sleep just one week before the archduke's assassination. Throughout July 1914 moderate pacifists in France and Belgium actively sought to convince their governments to arbitrate the dispute between Austria and Serbia, and French antimilitarists from within the socialist and anarchist camps frantically demonstrated against the mounting war hysteria and campaigned for a general strike. Despite these efforts, the diplomatic situation deteriorated rapidly, as Germany, Russia, and France all mobilized for war. With Germany's invasion of neutral Belgium in August 1914, most pacifists in Western Europe rallied to their governments' calls for national defense. In Central Europe, where pacifism had never been as strong, the Habsburg and German governments quickly silenced the peace societies, and the most prominent pacifist leaders went into exile.

From 1914 to 1918, in both the west and the east, Europe became a battleground and a graveyard. With tanks and submarines, machine guns and heavy artillery, flamethrowers and poison gas, the armies of Europe attacked each other relentlessly, and the death toll continued to rise. By the time World War I was over between nine and ten million Europeans had lost their lives due to the direct consequences of fighting; millions of others lived on, mere shadows of the men and women they had once been.

Although they proved incapable of preventing the war, pacifists did not simply accept the bloodbath as it transpired. Some absolute pacifists refused to take up arms. For men from the continental belligerent countries, such action generally led to imprisonment, hard labor, and sometimes confinement in lunatic asylums. Neither republican France nor the empires of Germany, Austria-Hungary, and Russia recognized the right to conscientious objection.

In Britain the long history of pacifist commitment among dissenting sects made the question of conscientious objection more urgent. In 1914 Britain still depended on a volunteer army, and the initial challenge for pacifists was to prevent the institution of universal conscription. Both religious and socialist pacifists joined together in creating the No-Conscription Fellowship, the most important pacifist group in wartime Britain. When the British government introduced conscription in March 1916 the Fellowship transformed itself into a support organization for conscientious objectors, championing their cause in public while providing moral and material support to them and their families.

During World War I in Britain more than sixteen thousand men declared themselves conscientious objectors, a status formally recognized by the Military Service Acts of 1916. The fate of any individual objector was determined by a Local Tribunal, which was instructed to judge the sincerity of the man's convictions and to determine the terms of his release from military service. Most objectors agreed to perform some form of alternative noncombatant service or civilian work of national importance. Some served in the Friends' Ambulance Unit, founded by Quakers in 1914. Only absolutist objectors—who refused any service on the ground that it facilitated the war effort—faced prison terms. Among them was the philosopher and lifelong peace activist Bertrand Russell (1872–1970), whose eloquence and notoriety helped gain attention for the cause.

Conscientious objectors may have been few in number, but as World War I dragged on and the death toll mounted, antimilitarism germinated in new circles. Ultimately, World War I reinvigorated the pacifist movement in Europe, as witnesses to and participants in the debacle swore the Great War that had engulfed them would be the "last of the last."

Soldiers who had experienced all the horrors of the trenches became some of the most outspoken critics of modern warfare, despite the fact that they could and did face the firing squad for disobeying orders. On an individual level, an unknown number of men deliberately maimed themselves in order to escape further combat. Others revolted on a broader scale. For example, hundreds of soldiers from the French Fifth Division mutinied in June 1917, refusing orders to return to the front lines and demanding their leaders seek a negotiated peace. That same year, on the eastern front, mutinous troops joined with revolutionaries at home in demanding Russia's immediate withdrawal from the war.

World War I was the first war to be fought by soldiers with a high degree of literacy, and some began to wield their pens for the cause of peace. While home on leave in Britain, Second Lieutenant Wilfred Owen (1893–1918) wrote bitter, devastating poetry that decried the "old lie": how sweet and noble it is to die for the fatherland. Owen's fellow countryman and poet Siegfried Sassoon (1886–1967) also became a critic of the war. In July 1917 he published his "Soldier's Declaration," which condemned "the political errors and insincerities for which the fighting men are being sacrificed" (Ceadel, p. 56). These antiwar appeals temporarily landed both Owen and Sassoon in a psychiatric ward. The French soldier and author Henri Barbusse (1873–1939) fared better. In 1916 he published a socialist antiwar novel, *Le feu* (*Under Fire,* 1917), which became an instant bestseller in France and was awarded the prestigious Goncourt Prize for literature. The novel was rapidly translated for other European audiences and became one of the best-known antiwar novels of its day. Although author-soldiers like Owen, Sassoon, and Barbusse did not take an absolute pacifist position, they did help create a new aesthetic for war literature, one that replaced romantic heroism with cold realism and challenged Europeans to begin to confront the full horror of the war that raged around them.

The threat of military discipline undoubtedly prevented many other men from expressing fully their revulsion toward war, but the same threat could not be used to silence women. Throughout the war years women helped sustain the pacifist movement by stepping into leadership roles as their male counterparts were called to arms or imprisoned. Theodora Wilson Wilson edited and financed the *New Crusader,* a British Christian-socialist paper, after its founder was sent to prison as an absolutist objector. Similarly Hélène Brion, an outspoken French socialist and feminist, as well as a nursery schoolteacher, took over as president of the revolutionary National Federation of Teachers' Unions in 1916. Although it was not a pacifist organization per se, the Federation actively campaigned against war hysteria and for an immediate negotiated peace. In November 1917 Brion was arrested for alleged "defeatism." Her subsequent trial became front-page news, allowing Brion an unparalleled platform for her feminist-pacifist views. "I am an enemy of war because I am a feminist," she told the court. "War is the triumph of brutal force; feminism can only triumph by moral force and intellectual worth. There is absolute antipathy between the two" (Siegel, p. 47).

Feminists were also at the forefront of one of the first overtly antiwar conferences to be staged in Europe after the outbreak of hostilities. The conference was convened by Dr. Aletta Jacobs (1854–1929), president of the Dutch suffrage movement, who, in the face of mounting chauvinism, stubbornly insisted that women could remain united. Jacobs proceeded to coordinate the International Congress of Women, which opened at The Hague in April 1915 under the presidency of the American social reformer Jane Addams (1860–1935). Representatives of England, Belgium, Germany, and Austria were among the 1,136 delegates who met to discuss the grounds for preparing a permanent peace. The attendees insisted on the need for neutral mediation of the conflict, and they formed two delegations to meet with world leaders to press this agenda. They also insisted on women's enfranchisement as a necessary prerequisite to sustainable peace in Europe. Finally, they formed a permanent organization, later named the Women's International League for Peace and Freedom (WILPF), the oldest feminist peace organization still active today.

World War I thus reshaped and expanded the pacifist movement in Europe in multiple ways. It provided a precedent for the recognition of conscientious objection. Equally important, it popularized antiwar sentiment by vividly illustrating the devastating nature of modern warfare. Many of those who had once believed in the positive, transformative power of war lost faith, and interwar European culture reflected a new obsession with death and violence.

PACIFISM BETWEEN THE WARS

War veterans often found themselves haunted by jarring memories of their battle experiences, and in the interwar decades European art and literature reflected their obsessions and antimilitarist sentiments. The German veteran and artist Otto Dix (1891–1969) transferred his nightmares to canvas in paintings that portrayed the barren, decomposing landscapes of the western front as well as the ongoing agony and isolation of "crippled" veterans. Dix's compatriot Erich Maria Remarque (1898–1970) used the novel to similar effect. *Im Westen nichts Neues* (*All Quiet on the Western Front*), Remarque's 1929 bestseller, depicted the brutality of modern warfare and the disillusionment of the "lost generation" of men who survived the conflict but who never escaped from under its shadow. The antimilitarism of Remarque and Dix was not shared universally among German veterans, but it captured the imaginations and sentiments of a sizable minority whose voices are too easily forgotten amid the Nazis' mounting war cries.

In France, war veterans were among the most outspoken and organized critics of war in the 1920s and 1930s. Many French veterans rejected both nationalism and militarism and their associations were firm champions of the League of Nations and efforts at international reconciliation. War veterans also insisted that commemorative ceremonies in France remain funereal and civic. They asked the nation to remember their fellow soldiers' sacrifice rather than their victory. World War I, as they portrayed it, was a nightmare and a bloodbath. Drawing on the authority of their frontline experience, pacifist war veterans in France, as in other parts of Europe, demanded that their fellow citizens confront the full brutality of modern war.

Women continued to play a central role in pacifist organizations in the interwar decades. Many of them in fact laid claim to peace as a woman's issue. They framed their arguments in explicitly gendered terms, speaking as women and mothers whose sensitivity and maternal instinct dictated their revulsion to war. The peace activist Helene Stöcker (1869–1943) of Germany argued that antimilitarism was a particularly female responsibility because she considered war to be "an abuse of motherhood, a distortion of the duty to be the guardian of life" (Braker, p. 81). Similarly, the French socialist-pacifist Madeleine Vernet (1878–1949) sketched a moving portrait of the "Unknown Mother of the Unknown Soldier" to convince her female compatriots to turn their maternal grief into a force for peace.

The WILPF drew upon such sentiments in the 1920s and 1930s and established national sections throughout much of Europe and beyond. WILPF members engaged in a variety of activities designed to help foster international reconciliation and world peace. The German section, for example, raised money to plant trees in the devastated regions of Northern France, while the British section protested its government's treatment of Ireland. The WILPF also offered summer peace camps for children, and it advocated on behalf of disarmament and the League of Nations.

Franco-German reconciliation, collective security, mutual disarmament, peace education: all of these projects were cornerstones of moderate European pacifism in the interwar years. The French Association de la Paix par le Droit (Association of Peace through Law) and the Deutsch Friedensgesellschaft (German Peace Society) were among the important groups that advocated for peace through increased international cooperation and strengthening international institutions. Peace education was a particular concern of the French National Teachers' Union, which embraced pacifism by the 1920s and actively sought to remove all nationalistic and militaristic materials from that nation's schools. French and German teachers and historians also launched a project in the interwar years to strip history textbooks of their chauvinism and turn the discipline of history into a tool for reconciliation and peace.

In the hopeful diplomatic environment of the late 1920s enthusiasm for such cooperative paths to peace ran high. By the 1930s, however, the growing strength of fascism and the outbreak of war in China, Ethiopia, and Spain led some European pacifists to call for more radical measures. In Britain, the WILPF member Maude Royden (1876–1956) led a movement to found a Peace Army. Inspired by Mohandas Gandhi's (1869–1948) nonviolent campaign against imperialism, Royden sought unarmed volunteers willing to go to Asia and form a human barrier between

the Japanese and the Chinese. At the same time, in France, Victor Méric (1876–1933) founded the anarchist-leaning Ligue International des Combattants pour la Paix (International League of Peace Fighters) which rejected the slow, juridical path to peace and called for an open war against war by whatever means necessary.

For absolute pacifists, conscientious objection and the personal renunciation of war remained the most important forms of peace activism, and in the interwar years new organizations like the German War Resisters' League and the British No More War Movement advanced this agenda. In the early 1920s these two national bodies joined with groups from Holland and Austria in creating the War Resisters' International (WRI). Alongside the more overtly religious Fellowship of Reconciliation, the WRI diligently promoted conscientious objection throughout Europe, and it sought to convince European states to recognize objector status. In neither goal was the WRI particularly effective. After World War I the Scandinavian countries and Holland did establish civilian service schemes, but throughout most of continental Europe, compulsory military service remained law. In the new countries of Central Europe, military service was often seen as a near-sacred duty. In Joseph Stalin's (1879–1953) Soviet Union, conscientious objection was theoretically a possibility; in reality, it led to imprisonment or worse.

Pacifists in Great Britain continued to promote individual renunciation of war much more so than did their compatriots on the Continent, and the idea of "pledging" to refuse military service captured the nation's attention at two different times in the 1930s. The first incident occurred in February 1933, when the Oxford Union Society passed a resolution stating "that this House will in no circumstances fight for its King and Country" (Ceadel, p. 127). The pledge, coming ten days after Adolf Hitler's (1889–1945) rise to power, evoked considerable controversy, but ultimately most of its supporters were not absolute pacifists and backed collective security measures as the best means of ensuring peace.

The second movement was forwarded by Canon Dick Sheppard (1880–1937), a magnetic figure within radical religious circles and a vocal proponent of peace activism since the late 1920s. At the end of 1934 Sheppard published an open letter asking all British men to take the pledge: "We renounce war and never again, directly or indirectly, will we sanction or support another" (Ceadel, p. 177). Some fifty thousand men answered his call, and the enthusiastic response led Sheppard to found the Peace Pledge Union (PPU). With more than 130,000 members at its apogee, the PPU became the largest peace organization in Britain between the wars. Distinguished intellectuals, including Bertrand Russell, Aldous Huxley (1894–1963), and Vera Brittain (1893–1970), all lent the organization their support. Ultimately the PPU never developed a cohesive program beyond the pledge itself. Sheppard died in 1937 and the group supported the government's policy of appeasement in the face of Hitler's expansionist demands.

THE FASCIST CHALLENGE AND WORLD WAR II

The advent and spread of fascism in Europe proved to be the most difficult and, in the end, insurmountable challenge facing pacifists in the interwar decades. As early as 1933 Hitler's ascension to power caused some pacifists to rethink their convictions. Albert Einstein (1879–1955) is a prominent early example. In the 1920s Einstein had used his celebrity to support pacifism and conscientious objection. In 1933 he wrote to the king of Belgium that "in the present circumstances, I, if I were a Belgian, should not refuse military service, but accept it with my whole conscience, knowing that I was contributing toward the salvation of European civilization" (Ceadel, p. 125).

Italy's invasion of Ethiopia in 1935 and the outbreak of civil war in Spain the following year posed even more serious challenges. The inability of the League of Nations to impose any effective sanction against Italy began to undermine some pacifists' faith in collective security as the best means of preventing war. At the same time, the war in Spain galvanized leftists in Europe, many of whom readily applauded the Spanish republicans for their heroic struggle against international fascism.

Ultimately Hitler's oppressive regime in Germany and his aggressive incursions into Central Europe destroyed the interwar pacifist movement. Most members of pacifist organizations like the PPU and the Ligue International des Combattants de la Paix were outspoken antifascists; yet, throughout most of the 1930s, they also maintained that opposition to fascism did not imply support for war. In 1938, when Hitler demanded the right to annex the Czech Sudetenland to Germany, all of these organizations demanded their governments pursue a diplomatic solution, as did large sectors of the French and British populations. Yet when Hitler failed to live up to the terms of the Munich agreement and ordered his armies further into Central Europe in 1939 the vast majority of pacifists prepared for war.

Hitler's blitzkrieg across Europe made the question of pacifism all but irrelevant on the Continent. In France a few notable interwar pacifists, such as Professor Léon Émery, collaborated with the German occupiers, but most male pacifists took up arms in 1940, and many other pacifists, men and women, ultimately joined the Resistance. Among the European countries, only Great Britain had a sizable population of conscientious objectors—approximately sixty thousand—during World War II. As in World War I most performed some sort of alternative service as farm laborers, hospital porters, or ambulance drivers; some contributed to Britain's civil defense. For many, this war against fascism and authoritarianism aroused very different feelings than the seemingly pointless World War I. It also took far more lives. By the time of Japan's surrender in 1945 approximately sixty million people had died during the conflict.

World War II left the populations of Europe decimated and exhausted. Defeat and then occupation at the hand of the Nazis discredited pacifism in many circles. The rapid onset of the Cold War also stymied the peace movement, as some pacifists accepted the idea that Stalinism could only effectively be countered by arms. The explosion of the atomic bombs at Hiroshima and Nagasaki, however, provided a new purpose and momentum for the peace movement.

THE POSTWAR PEACE MOVEMENT AND NUCLEAR DISARMAMENT

In the second half of the twentieth century nuclear disarmament became the single most important focal point for the European pacifism. Granted, not all antinuclear activists were pacifists in any strict sense; many continued to accept the need for national defense with conventional weapons. After 1945, however, many Europeans believed nuclear disarmament to be the surest path to preventing mutual self-destruction in a now-imaginable apocalyptic war.

Immediately after World War II scientists in both the United States and Europe tried to derail a budding arms race by arguing that the U.S. government should turn over control of nuclear knowledge and technology to an international body. Their warnings were ignored. In 1949 the Soviets exploded an atomic bomb and both Britain and France began to develop their own nuclear programs. The French Atomic Energy Commission faced its first political crisis in 1950 when its founder, the nuclear physicist and Communist Party member Frédéric Joliot-Curie (1900–1958), declared he would never help build a bomb because its use would precipitate another world war. Under American pressure, Joliot-Curie was dismissed, and the Commission continued to pursue military research alongside the quest for nuclear energy. Throughout the 1960s, with the exception of the Communists, a broad consensus in France supported nuclear deterrence.

In Britain, by contrast, the quest for nuclear disarmament began to attract a larger following. In a chilling 1954 Christmas broadcast on the BBC, "Man's Peril," Bertrand Russell appealed to his compatriots to reject nuclear weapons, asking if humankind had become "so destitute of wisdom, so incapable of impartial love, so blind even to the simple dictates of self-preservation, that the last proof of its silly cleverness is to be the extermination of all life on our planet" (Brandon, p. 32). The explosion of Britain's first H-bomb in 1957 sent Russell and others into the streets in protest, and they formed a central organization to press their agenda: the Campaign for Nuclear Disarmament (CND). Throughout the early 1960s the CND repeatedly mobilized thousands of protesters and engaged in acts of civil disobedience. Following the CND's lead, the antinuclear movement began to spread to other parts of Europe—particularly in West Germany—as well as to the United States. The Partial Test Ban Treaty of 1963, however, calmed people's fears of nuclear contamination and stymied pacifists' organizing efforts.

NATO's 1979 decision to update Western Europe's nuclear missiles revived the British nuclear disarmament movement and helped awaken a broad-based antinuclear coalition on the Continent. In Britain CND membership skyrocketed and other peace groups began to command public attention. Among them was the Greenham Common Peace Camp, established by feminist-pacifist women in 1983 to oppose the installation of ground-based Cruise missiles. A constant presence throughout the 1980s, the Greenham women wove together radical feminism and pacifism in their protest. The British nuclear disarmament movement also gained a prominent new spokesperson: the peace activist and former history professor Edward Palmer Thompson (1924–1993), who argued passionately for a united and nuclear-free Europe.

The 1980s witnessed the revitalization of the antinuclear and pacifist movement on the Continent, particularly in West Germany. Already in the late 1950s the decision to equip the German army with tactical missiles capable of carrying nuclear warheads had led to a mass "Campaign against Atomic Death," which brought more than three hundred thousand West Germans into the streets in protest. From 1960 onward West German pacifists helped stage regular Easter Marches against nuclear arms. The emergence in 1980 of the German Green Party, with its overtly pacifist and antinuclear party platform, helped give new structure and legitimacy to the campaign for nuclear disarmament. By 1985 the annual German Easter March attracted nearly five hundred thousand people. In Belgium that same year more than 150,000 people flooded into Brussels to oppose the installation of Cruise missiles. In France, a heterogeneous Committee for the Nuclear Disarmament of Europe also staged public protests, even as the Socialist President François Mitterrand (1918–1996) insisted that "the nuclear warhead... remains, whether one likes it or not, the guarantee of peace" (Vaïsse, p. 336).

EUROPEAN UNIFICATION AND PEACE AT THE TURN OF THE TWENTY-FIRST CENTURY

The end of the Cold War in 1989 and the subsequent dissolution of the Soviet Union largely defused the nuclear disarmament movement in Europe. By the end of the twentieth century many of the major ideological divisions that had torn the Continent apart in prior decades no longer threatened the peace. With the creation of the European Union (EU) in 1992 and with the admission of eight Eastern European countries, plus Malta and Cypress, into the EU in 2004, Europeans sought to reinforce peace through economic and political integration. The European Union's Charter of Fundamental Rights, moreover, recognized the right of conscientious objection in all member states.

The opposition generated by the American invasion of Iraq in March 2003 demonstrated just how ideologically unified Europeans had become by the turn of the twenty-first century. The governments of France and Germany led the opposition to the war at the United Nations, while hundreds of thousands of antiwar protesters took to the streets in Stockholm, Athens, and a dozen capitals in between. Even in the United Kingdom, Spain, and Poland, where the governments in power supported the American invasion, a strong majority of the population was against the war. To the administration of the U.S. president George W. Bush, this outpouring of antiwar sentiment was a clear sign of European cowardice and decadence. To many Europeans who had survived the horrors of the war-torn twentieth century, however, "pacifist" was no longer a shameful epithet, and opposition to the Iraq war appeared a moral imperative.

See also **Atomic Bomb; Conscription; Disarmament; Dix, Otto; Owen, Wilfred; Russell, Bertrand; Sassoon, Siegfried; World War I; World War II.**

BIBLIOGRAPHY

Primary Sources

Barbusse, Henri. *Under Fire.* Translated by Robin Buss. Introduction by Jay Winter. New York, 2004.

Remarque, Erich Maria. *All Quiet on the Western Front.* Translated by A. W. Wheen. Boston, 1929.

Skarvan, Albert. *Life in an Austro-Hungarian Military Prison: The Slovak Tolstoyan Dr. Albert Skarvan's Story.* Translated and edited by Peter Brock. Syracuse, N.Y., 2002.

Von Suttner, Bertha. *Lay Down Your Arms: The Autobiography of Martha von Tilling.* Translated by T. Holmes. New York, 1972.

Secondary Sources

Braker, Regina. "Helene Stöcker's Pacifism in the Weimar Republic: Between Ideal and Reality." *Journal of Women's History* 13, no. 3 (2001): 70–97.

Brandon, Ruth. *The Burning Question: The Anti-Nuclear Movement since 1945.* London, 1987.

Brock, Peter, and Nigel Young. *Pacifism in the Twentieth Century.* Syracuse, N.Y., 1999.

Bussey, Gertrude, and Margaret Tims. *Pioneers for Peace: Women's International League for Peace and Freedom, 1915–1965.* 2nd ed. London, 1980.

Ceadel, Martin. *Pacifism in Britain, 1914–1945: The Defining of a Faith.* Oxford, U.K., and New York, 1980.

Cooper, Alice Holmes. *Paradoxes of Peace: German Peace Movements since 1945.* Ann Arbor, Mich., 1996.

Cooper, Sandi. *Patriotic Pacifism: Waging War on War in Europe, 1815–1914.* New York, 1991.

Hamann, Brigitte. *Bertha Von Suttner: A Life for Peace.* Syracuse, N.Y., 1996.

Hynes, Samuel. *A War Imagined: The First World War and English Culture.* New York, 1990.

Ingram, Norman. *The Politics of Dissent: Pacifism in France, 1919–1939.* Oxford, U.K., and New York, 1991.

Oppenheimer, Andrew. "West German Pacifism and the Ambivalence of Human Solidarity, 1945–1968." *Peace and Change* 29, no. 3–4 (2004): 353–389.

Prost, Antoine. *In the Wake of War: Les Anciens Combattants and French Society.* Translated by Helen McPhail. Providence, R.I., 1992.

Siegel, Mona. *The Moral Disarmament of France: Education, Patriotism, and Pacifism, 1914–1940.* Cambridge, U.K., and New York, 2004.

Vaïsse, Maurice. "A Certain Idea of Peace in France from 1945 to the Present Day." *French History* 18, no. 3 (2004): 331–337.

MONA L. SIEGEL

PAINTING, AVANT-GARDE. During the 1910s several European painters ventured independently of one another into abstract painting. Along with modern artists' use of found, industrially made materials, this was one of the most radical and important developments in twentieth-century art. Whether this new movement was propagated as nonobjective or as concrete art, as a new realism or as neoplasticism, the colors and forms on the canvas were no longer meant to bear a resemblance to the material world.

INFLUENCES AND JUSTIFICATIONS

The rationales and results of the artists differed greatly, as did their degree of success, but they all shared certain characteristics. They had been deeply impressed by French art since about 1880, by post-impressionism, by the early work of Henri Matisse (1869–1954), or by cubism. Painters such as Paul Gauguin, Vincent van Gogh (1853–1890), and, most radically, Matisse, had replaced local with nonlocal color, that is, they had represented objects in colors that did not correspond to the objects' colors in the world. Van Gogh, along with Paul Cézanne and Georges Seurat, had isolated marks on the canvas—as lines, patches, and dots respectively—disconnected from any descriptive value. In their cubist paintings and collages, Pablo Picasso (1881–1973) and Georges Braque (1882–1963) had revealed the language of Western pictorial representation to be entirely arbitrary and dependent for its meaning on semiotic context, opening the door for experimentation with other arbitrary signs. And all these painters stressed, to varying degrees, the essential flatness of the picture plane and no longer sought to create illusionist, perspectival spaces.

Yet most of these pioneering abstract artists initially hesitated in making the step toward complete abstraction because they worried that they would produce arbitrary, meaningless forms or merely decorative patterns. In combative manifestos and other written texts, they sought ways to justify their choices: they drew analogies to music, the most abstract among the arts; claimed they were representing immaterial realms such as emotions, the spiritual, the cosmos, the absolute, or utopia; argued they were reducing the painterly medium to its essential, indispensable elements; said they were playing with viewers' perceptual faculties; or asserted they were basing decisions purely on chance operations. Often, these justifications served to turn their abstract works into "trace representations," destabilizing the very definition of abstraction.

THE FIRST ABSTRACT PAINTINGS

The Czech artist František Kupka (1871–1957) is most frequently credited with creating the first abstract paintings in the history of modern art. His interest in representations of the cosmos and of music inspired him, beginning in about 1909, gradually to dissolve observed motifs into either vertical schemes or spirals. In about 1912, with paintings such as *Amorpha: Fugue in Two Colors* and *Vertical Schemes,* he arrived at an art devoid of recognizable elements. Kupka was loosely associated with orphism, a short-lived Parisian art movement that came to the fore in 1913 and united artists interested in pure color, the representation of light, and analogies between the visual arts and music. Its prominent member and spokesman, the French painter Robert Delaunay (1885–1941), in collaboration with his Russian artist wife, Sonia Delaunay-Terk (1885–1979), systematically pursued the study of color, especially the theory of simultaneous color contrast as advanced by the nineteenth-century chemist Michel-Eugène Chevreul. Like Kupka, Robert Delaunay made his first purely abstract painting following a series of paintings that increasingly abstracted specific representational motifs, in his case the Eiffel Tower, the sun, and a window. Thus, like Kupka's representations of music or the cosmos, the concentric circles with the most intense colors at the center in Delaunay's *Simultaneous Disk: Punch* (1913) still represent, in a sense, the radiating beams of the sun. Nevertheless, the painting qualifies as the most radically abstract painting made up to that point.

One finds the same trace representations in the art of Wassily Kandinsky, born in Russia in 1866 but based largely in Germany and France from 1898 until his death in 1944. In 1911 Kandinsky and Franz Marc founded Der Blaue Reiter, an association of German expressionist artists with whom Kandinsky pursued the visualization of immaterial and spiritual realms through gesturally applied, amorphously shaped, and intensely colored configurations. Kandinsky gradually embraced abstraction during the 1910s. At the beginning of that decade, the artist began to veil his representational imagery such as mountains, churches, and cows, painting them in nonlocal colors like the postimpressionists and embedding them in purely abstract shapes. The artist conspicuously inscribed the work known as the *First Abstract Watercolor* with the year 1910, but it was likely made only in 1913, when Kandinsky also began to talk about abstract painting in his writings. In any case, Kandinsky grew increasingly confident

Untitled (First Abstract Watercolor). By Wassily Kandinsky, 1910. Bridgeman Art Library

about abstraction, leaving behind worries about expressionless ornament, lifeless stylization, and arbitrary experimentation. Instead, he pursued what he called the spiritual in art. Defined, however vaguely, in his seminal written work, *Über das Geistige in der Kunst,* published in 1911, that term captured both an internal necessity of the work of art and a search for the absolute and thus encapsulated Kandinsky's ways of justifying his abstract art. Colors and forms, Kandinsky argued, have certain inherent meanings: for example, he frequently paired blue and yellow, illustrating his belief that blue is associated with the male sex, connoting severity, depth, and spirituality, while yellow is associated with the female, connoting gentleness, happiness, and sensuality. While often considered a pioneer abstract painter, Kandinsky thus remained deeply committed to representation in art, in

particular to a representation of the spiritual, of emotions, and of music. Likewise, Kandinsky retained allusions to landscapes—black arch elements reminiscent of mountains, for example, or shadings, superimpositions, and scale shifts that all give a sense of depth and space—until about 1922.

THE BAUHAUS

From then on, Kandinsky taught color theory and wall painting at the influential German art school the Bauhaus, and his abstract painting became increasingly geometric, even diagrammatic. Because of the school's focus on design and architecture, abstract painting was never central to the Bauhaus, though some of its most important teachers were abstract painters. Aside from Kandinsky, these included the German Josef Albers

(1888–1976), the Swiss Paul Klee (1879–1940), and the Hungarian László Moholy-Nagy (1895–1946). Albers, though he taught the preliminary course in the later Bauhaus years, was most influential as a teacher at Black Mountain College and Yale University following his emigration to the United States, and he is best known for his painting series *Homage to the Square* made there from 1950 on, in which he uses nested squares to explore optical relations and illusions of juxtaposed colors. Klee, an associate of Kandinsky's at Der Blaue Reiter, taught elementary design at the Bauhaus and subsequently took over the weaving workshop. As an abstract painter, he was particularly prolific in the medium of watercolor, making works informed by myths and mysticism as much as by his interest in the decorative. Moholy-Nagy, who taught the Bauhaus preliminary course during the 1920s and was head of the metal workshop, explored impersonal techniques in his paintings: he used airbrushes and spray guns, and even put in a telephone order to an enamel factory for the serial production of the same painting in three different sizes.

MALEVICH AND LISSITZKY

Kazimir Malevich, born in Russia in 1878 and active there until his death in 1935, exhibited what is usually considered his first abstract painting, the *Black Square*, in 1915. Perhaps unintentionally, he targeted the very ambiguity about what constitutes pure abstraction. The painting originated in a sequence of stage sets the artist had designed for the 1913 performance of the futurist opera *Victory over the Sun*, which tells the story of humankind's battle to transcend the present and the visible. The sets show the gradual eclipse of the sun, with a black area increasingly encroaching on a white square. Black forms take a variety of shapes throughout the sequence, which concludes with a black triangle covering half of the square, thus implying a black square as a result. Malevich exhibited the first of three paintings derived from this last stage set at the *0.10* exhibition in St. Petersburg in 1915, placed prominently in a high corner of the room, the traditional place for Russian icons. Whether it represents the eclipse of the sun or an abstract world beyond the visible is left open-ended. Similarly, Malevich plays with the question of what constitutes realism in a painting of a red square on

a white ground wittily entitled *Red Square: Painterly Realism of a Peasant Woman in Two Dimensions*, also of 1915. In his booklet *From Cubism and Futurism to Suprematism*, published on the occasion of the *0.10* exhibition, Malevich coined the term *suprematism* to assert the supremacy of his own art. But it also describes the utopian goals of his abstract paintings: to develop a supreme sense awareness in his viewers, to create a supreme space of infinity beyond human measure, and to reach a supreme or zero point of painting where the medium is reduced to its essential elements.

His *Suprematist Composition: White on White* (1918) exemplifies these goals. Viewers are forced to fine-tune their vision and spend time in order to see the different tones of white, aided by the different textures. The white monochrome gives a sense of lightness, immateriality, and infinity, and painting is reduced to its minimum: white paint on a white ground, a square derived from a square canvas. Malevich's impact is hard to overestimate. His students included the Poles Wladyslaw Strzeminski and Katarina Kobro, who further reduced art to its essence (Strzeminski worked with paint, Kobro with sculpture), as well as the Russian El Lissitzky (1890–1941), who developed Malevich's work in a more overtly political direction.

After studying architecture and engineering in Germany and becoming a prolific producer of book illustrations, in 1919 Lissitzky began his series of paintings and prints titled *Proun*, an acronym for the Russian equivalent of "Project for the Affirmation of the New." The *Proun*s worked against habitual ways of looking at and thinking about the world and instead fostered active ways of seeing and a heightened consciousness in their postrevolutionary audience. Keeping to a restrained palette of whites, grays, blacks, and only occasional color, and making use of a variety of textures, the *Proun*s feature painted and sometimes collaged geometric configurations projected isometrically, often axonometrically. Unlike perspectival projections, these force viewers to readjust constantly to the flip-flopping of space and volume, and allow the paintings to be viewed from different angles, so that one's perception of them changes even further. Lissitzky sometimes encouraged such turning by signing his *Proun*s on more than one side or by painting configurations suggesting a turning motion, often involving circles and spheres.

The political dimension of the *Proun*s was less overt, some say more sophisticated, than Lissitzky's work in graphic design, typography, photography, photomontage, and exhibition design. In 1921 Lissitzky essentially gave up painting in favor of these other media. His decision paralleled the sweeping, programmatic rejection of easel painting by the Russian constructivists, an artists' group formed in Moscow that year and committed to politically or socially useful material studies and designs. *Last Painting: Blue, Red, Yellow,* by the leading constructivist Alexander Rodchenko, is a landmark in that regard, announcing the end of the most important medium of Western art, once it had been reduced to its essential elements: monochrome panels painted in the primary colors. Unlike most of the constructivists and as a result in part of his training in Germany, Lissitzky cultivated relations and collaborations with an international range of artists and institutions such as Hans (Jean) Arp and the Bauhaus. His *Abstract Cabinet* for the Provinzialmuseum Hannover, now reconstructed at the Sprengel Museum Hannover, was an innovative design of sliding panels and changing wall surfaces for the exhibition of abstract paintings by him, Moholy-Nagy, Piet Mondrian, and others.

MONDRIAN, DE STIJL, AND SURREALISM
Mondrian, born in the Netherlands in 1872 but active primarily in Paris and later in New York City, where he died in 1944, made his first abstract painting several years after Kupka, Delaunay, Kandinsky, and Malevich. In a series of sketches and paintings depicting a pier running into the ocean, he gradually abstracted the motif and eventually arrived at *Composition with Lines* (1917), a white square canvas featuring a circular cluster of short black and white lines. Still, it would be three more years before his abstract painting reached its mature, iconic phase, which the artist called *neoplasticism*. That term encapsulated a new building, or composition, of painterly elements in such a way so as to create a perfect equilibrium or equivalence of its most essential opposites: of lines and planes, of color (the primaries) and noncolor (black

and white), of vertical and horizontal lines, of expansion and limitation (the illusion of forms moving outward or inward), and of the canvas as surface and the canvas as object. No one element was ever to take over; Mondrian composed each painting intuitively to come as close as possible to harmony, unity, and perfection, to create a sense of the universal through the particulars of painting. Unlike Kandinsky, Mondrian early on rejected theosophical theories—the occult aspects of painting and the implied possibility of representing the spiritual—and was committed instead to a Hegelian idealism, which was the origin of his commitment to a dialectical system.

The year 1932 was of central importance to Mondrian: he began the destruction of neoplasticism and everything he had worked for over the previous twelve years, introducing two adjacent black lines in his painting *Composition with Double Line and Yellow and Gray.* This seemingly simple gesture destroyed the balance of line and plane because the white space between the lines turned into a line, while the surrounding white areas remained planes. Mondrian's lines quickly multiplied over the course of the decade until, in 1941, with his painting *New York City,* he created a labyrinthine braiding and optical flicker of lines in which one's gaze becomes lost. During the last years of his life, Mondrian also experimented with moving painting into the realm of architecture, installing colored and white panels across the walls of his studio in New York City. Previously, he had been worried about this step, contending that it was too early to merge painting with the surrounding world, that architecture was too utilitarian and incapable of true equilibrium.

Mondrian disagreed on this point with most of his peers in De Stijl, a Dutch group of artists and architects founded in about 1917 by Theo van Doesburg. A central example of Van Doesburg's practice of abstract wall painting and interior design was his 1926–1928 collaboration with the German-French Hans (Jean) Arp (1886–1966) and Arp's Swiss wife, Sophie Taeuber-Arp (1889–1943), on the Café Aubette, a ten-room entertainment complex located in the center of Strasbourg. Their abstract wall paintings, some accentuating and others counteracting the preexisting historical structure, were complemented with the artists' designs for stained glass windows, furniture, and other decorative objects. In conceptually collapsing abstract painting and design, the entertainment complex forms an important breaking point with other pioneering abstract painters' anxieties. Indeed, Arp and Taeuber-Arp's abstract art from early on had directly confronted the dominant fears of their peers about arbitrariness and the decorative. Beginning in about 1915 they made abstract pictures that were woven or stitched—not surprising given Taeuber-Arp's training in textile design and weaving—and between 1916 and 1918 they made abstract collages, often in collaboration, in which the location of pieces of torn or cut papers was left to the laws of chance.

These procedures reappeared in the work of the Spaniard Joan Miró (1893–1983), the most important of the few abstract painters associated with surrealism—Arp too developed relations with the surrealists, but he was at that point active mainly as a sculptor. Miró would frequently drop pieces of torn paper and paint the resulting configurations; he would also draw and paint undirected doodles, leaving the decisions to chance and the unconscious. Combined with his use of intensely saturated colors, thin lines, and small scaled shapes crowded into large formats, Miró's paintings, as well as those of Taeuber-Arp, exude a sense of humor and playfulness rare in abstract painting during the first half of the twentieth century.

DEGENERATE ART AND THE AMERICAN ONSLAUGHT

Abstract painting, at least its public practice and exhibition, came to an abrupt end in Europe with the National Socialists' rise to power and the beginning of World War II. It was a showcase for what the Nazis declared forbidden and degenerate. In their minds, abstract painting such as that of Kandinsky and Mondrian, both included with more than one hundred artists in the 1937 exhibition *Entartete Kunst* (Degenerate art), not only revealed a lack of artistic skill but also insulted the German sensibility and destroyed natural form. Much abstract painting, like much modern art in general, was confiscated and destroyed (the complete Café Aubette, for example). Most abstract painters, like other modern artists, went into internal exile or emigrated to the United States.

This exodus, along with the war's destruction across Europe, played a major role in New York's stealing of the idea of modern art, as art historians commonly sum up the state of Western art after 1945. Surrealist and other European artists strongly influenced the American-made, large-scale, abstract gestural painting of the late 1940s and 1950s known as abstract expressionism. In turn, paintings by artists such as Jackson Pollock or Willem de Kooning multiplied in exhibitions throughout Cold War Europe as an expression of individual freedom. A new generation of primarily French, German, and Spanish abstract painters, who came to be known under labels such as *Informel, Tachisme,* or *Un art autre,* felt threatened by what they perceived to be an American onslaught. These young European painters—Wols (*Wolfgang Otto Schulze, 1913–1951*), Georges Mathieu (b. 1921), Hans Hartung (1904–1989), K. O. Götz (b. 1914), and Antoni Tàpies (b. 1923), for example—were painting abstract gestures like their American peers, but they were frequently perceived as derivative, especially by the now dominant American art market. This perception was partially the result of their much smaller, less assertive formats, which seemed like illustrations by comparison, but was also attributable to the artificial and decorative impression their techniques tend to convey. Mathieu, Hartung, and Götz's gestures appear staged, isolated, overblown, and contrived. Not surprisingly, Mathieu staged public performances of himself painting; Hartung's gestural strokes were copied from smaller sketches onto larger canvases and bore a striking resemblance to mid-twentieth-century furniture and interior design; and Götz marketed some of his earliest scraped, high-contrast paintings as advertisements for the chocolate maker Sprengel. In hindsight, however, this may be the redeeming quality and historical truth of the best of *Informel* painting: the way its gestures strove for an expression of emotional struggles and even freedom but ultimately revealed that expression to be always already mediated and false. That was fitting during an age when freedom from National Socialist brutality was immediately overshadowed by the massive consumption that defined postwar economic recovery and reconstruction.

MONOCHROMES

Informel painting, along with American abstract expressionism, dominated the European art world into the 1950s. Many young artists felt limited by or critical of its status quo, particularly its premise of subjective expression. The majority of postwar artists abandoned painting altogether, considering it a traditional medium, and turned instead to collage, sculpture, installation art, performance, photography, video, and other new media. A few stuck with abstract painting but often tested and expanded the boundaries of what constitutes the medium. The monochrome, a canvas covered evenly with only one color, was an alternative proposed by a group of loosely connected, at times collaborating painters across Europe: Yves Klein (1928–1962) in France, Lucio Fontana (1899–1968) and Piero Manzoni (1933–1963) in Italy, and Heinz Mack (b. 1931), Otto Piene (b. 1928), and Günther Uecker (b. 1930) in Germany. For all of them, the monochrome was a means of reducing painting to its most essential elements—a canvas on a stretcher and the application of one type of paint—and a way of either aspiring to or mocking notions of immateriality, infinity, and spirituality. Given the rupture of World War II, few of them knew initially about prewar precedents such as Malevich's suprematist white monochromes or Rodchenko's *Last Painting*.

Whether serious or ironic, Klein in particular claimed for himself the invention of the monochrome. Along the same lines, he also patented what he called *IKB*, or International Klein Blue, an ultramarine blue prepared with a binder made of ether and petroleum extracts that preserved the intensity and powdery appearance of the raw pigment. In 1955 Klein began making his signature blue monochromes, which emphasize the objectness and materiality of the picture by several means: matte heavy textures created by the pigment powder (or later by added materials such as sponges), rounded corners, paint that wraps around the edges, and occasional displays on poles or brackets to extend the works out from the wall. His 1957 exhibition *L'Epoca Blu* at the Galleria Apollinaire in Milan featured eleven identically sized and painted canvases that were marked with and sold at different prices. In the following year, Klein painted the walls of the Iris Clert Gallery in Paris white and exhibited the empty, monochrome room as *Le vide* (The void). Klein thus consistently undermined or mocked his own spiritual claims by stressing the

objectlike character of his monochromes, by claiming the real value of his paintings to be beyond the visible, and by making the invisible literal, visible, and exhibitable.

The monochrome also became a signature for Fontana, whose major bodies of work, the *buchi* begun in 1949 and the *tagli* begun in 1958, consist of punctures and cuts, respectively, into canvases painted monochrome, often in white but sometimes in garish colors such as orange or pink. The ambivalence found in Klein's work operates in Fontana's as well. On the one hand, the rhetoric of infinite space pervades the artist's writings, and he was at pains to make the space behind his cuts and holes look infinite by taping black gauze behind them. On the other hand, Fontana's colors, bordering on kitsch, and his physical violations of these formerly pure surfaces stress their materiality (the canvas fabric often bends inward) and introduce real, three-dimensional space into painting. By the same token, Fontana's slicing and puncturing gestures replicate and further isolate the heroic gestures of the *Informel* painters, while at the same time dismissing them with their literally destructive force.

Manzoni's attitude, by contrast, is unambiguously scoffing. His white monochromes called *Achromes,* made from 1957 on—part of a larger conceptually driven body of work that includes witty works such as cans titled *Merde d'artista* and perhaps actually filled with the artist's excrement, sold by the gram for the price of gold, and a simple pedestal inscribed upside down *Socle du Monde* (Base of the world)—employ a true variety of materials. Some are simply made of gesso or sewn fabric, others push beyond the limits of painting in the strict sense by using polystyrene, cotton balls, fiberglass, eggs, bread rolls, straw, rabbit skin, or other materials.

The usually white monochrome paintings made from the late 1950s into the early 1960s by Mack, Piene, and Uecker also dealt with immateriality and spirituality. The three formed the core of the artists' group Zero, which was also the name of their journal and alludes to their interests in infinity and a fresh start following World War II. In particular, they tried to capture the effects of light and shadow on their pictorial surfaces by covering these with patterns, textures, and, in the case of Uecker, nails. Their work with painting and reliefs merely constituted a prelude to subsequent work with kinetic sculptures and environments whose technological idealism and spectacular feel mirrored the optimistic, progressive spirit of the contemporary economic miracle in Germany.

CAPITALIST REALISM

The stress on materiality seen in Klein, Fontana, and Manzoni's painting and their turn against the existentialist premises of *Informel* were pushed even further in the work of a young group of German Pop artists: Gerhard Richter (b. 1932), Konrad Lueg (1939–1996), Sigmar Polke (b. 1941)—these three came to be known under the label "capitalist realism"—and Blinky Palermo (pseudonym of Peter Heisterkamp, 1943–1977). Their abstract painting of the 1960s and 1970s was steeped in the banalities of commodity culture and interior design. Lueg, who soon gave up his career as an artist to become an important art dealer, painted abstract paintings copied from designs of towels, washcloths, and wallpaper and made canvases of a sort from patterned or monochrome plastic sheeting, which, like most of Manzoni's achromes, were not painted at all. Polke's few but important abstract paintings consisted of patterns painted onto found, patterned, stretched fabrics or of isolated abstract pictorial elements, featuring ironic titles such as *Modern Art* or *Higher Beings Command: Paint Upper Right Corner Black*. In the last decades of the twentieth century, Richter, whom many regard as the most important European artist after World War II, made three series of abstract paintings apart from his more well-known blur paintings: copies of commercial color charts; stunningly bland gray monochromes with more or less visible brushwork; and heavily gestural paintings that nevertheless betray a sense of artifice by their garish palette, stilted strokes, and slick, seemingly airbrushed backgrounds. For these three artists, abstraction ran parallel to representations of banal objects and motifs in drawing and painting.

Their peer Palermo, by contrast, was an exclusively abstract painter and thus assumes a central place in the context of postwar European abstract painting. Two bodies of work, his so-called cloth pictures and his wall paintings, are closely related to the work of the capitalist realists. The cloth pictures intertwine pure abstract painting with commodity culture. They are not painted per se but made of pre-dyed monochrome cotton cloth bought in the department store and then sewn and stretched together in block stripes. The wall paintings, which combine abstract painting and design, employ a decorative vocabulary painted directly on the walls of exhibition spaces. For both the capitalist realists and Palermo, abstract painting was not removed from the world but was a means of commenting on it, indulging in it, or criticizing it more directly than ever before.

GRAV, BMPT, AND OP ART

Two groups of French abstract painters of the 1960s also continued the turn against *Informel* painting, specifically seeking to overcome subjective, arbitrary intuition and genius inspiration, which for long stood at the origin of art. The Groupe de Recherche d'Art Visuel (GRAV), founded in 1960, developed strategies of collective, anonymous, or conceptual making. François Morellet (b. 1926), for example, a founding member of the group, experimented with the minimum number of decisions needed to make an abstract painting. His answer was *16 Squares* (1953), a canvas with lines forming a modular grid based on a mere eleven decisions. He also developed the notion of chance procedures, as in *Random Distribution of 40,000 Squares Using the Odd and Even Numbers of a Telephone Directory* (1960). A second group, BMPT—founded in 1967 and consisting of the French Daniel Buren (b. 1938), the Swiss Olivier Mosset (b. 1944), Daniel Parmentier (b. 1927), and the Swiss Niele Toroni (b. 1937)—joined together to exhibit a type of conceptual painting, often staging painting events in public. Each artist chose a different configuration to paint his canvases and stuck with it: Buren vertical stripes, Mosset a central black circle, Parmentier horizontal bands slightly thicker than Buren's, and Toroni a regular pattern of same-sized brushstrokes. Buren especially went on to exhibit his stripes (soon made of commercial striped fabric on which Buren painted one printed white stripe with white paint) in various public, nonartistic settings, ranging from subway stops and buses to building facades and flags, thus questioning, among other things, the institutional definition of art.

The works of some of the members of GRAV were received together with what in the 1960s came to be known as Op Art. The movement was made famous by the popular 1965 exhibition *The Responsive Eye.* Although held at the Museum of Modern Art in New York, it featured primarily European artists. Op Art triggered in the beholder optical effects of movement, flicker, and distortions and tested the limits of human vision. Although there were also sculptures and reliefs at the exhibition, the popular image of Op Art was defined by the British painter Bridget Riley and her black and white canvases of rhythmically repeating and subtly distorting lines and patterns.

After the 1970s, abstract painting was increasingly relegated to the sidelines. Many artists returned to figurative painting, but in the early twenty-first century the majority work in other media such as sculpture, installation, video, and photography, where avant-garde art is alive and well.

See also **Bauhaus; Braque, Georges; Cubism; De Stijl; Degenerate Art Exhibit; Kandinsky, Wassily; Lissitzky, El; Malevich, Kazimir; Miró, Joan; Moholy-Nagy, László; Mondrian, Piet; Picasso, Pablo; Surrealism.**

BIBLIOGRAPHY

Andersen, Troels. *Malevich.* Exh. cat. Amsterdam, 1970.

Anger, Jenny. *Paul Klee and the Decorative in Modern Art.* Cambridge, U.K., 2004.

Battino, Freddy, and Luca Palozzoli. *Piero Manzoni: Catalogue raisonné.* Milan, 1991.

Bois, Yve-Alain. *Painting as Model.* Cambridge, Mass., 1990.

Bois, Yve-Alain, et al. *Piet Mondrian, 1872—1944.* Exh. cat. The Hague, 1994.

Buchloh, Benjamin H. D. *Neo-avantgarde and Culture Industry: Essays on European and American Art from 1955 to 1975.* Cambridge, Mass., 2000.

Cohen, Arthur A., ed. *The New Art of Color: The Writings of Robert and Sonia Delaunay.* Translated by David Shapiro and Arthur A. Cohen. New York, 1978.

Fer, Briony. *On Abstract Art.* London, 1997.

Fontana, catalogo generale. Milan, 1986.

Frantisek Kupka, 1871–1957: A Retrospective. Exh. cat. New York, 1975.

Gerhard Richter. 3 vols. Bonn, Germany, 1993.

Jean Miró: Escritos y conversaciones, edited by Margit Rowell. Valencia, Spain, 2002.

Kandinsky, Wassily. *Über das Geistige in der Kunst, insbesondere in der Malerei.* Munich, 1912.

Khan-Magomedov, Selim O. *Rodchenko: The Complete Work.* Cambridge, Mass., 1986.

Krauss, Rosalind E., and Margit Rowell. *Joan Miró: Magnetic Fields.* New York, 1972.

Lee, Pamela M. "Bridget Riley's Eye/Body Problem." In her *Chronophobia: On Time in the Art of the 1960's.* Cambridge, Mass., 2004.

Lissitzky-Küppers, Sophie, ed. *El Lissitzky: Life, Letters, Texts.* Translated by Helene Aldwinckle and Mary Whittall. Greenwich, N.Y., 1968.

Mehring, Christine. "Abstraction and Decoration in Blinky Palermo's Wall Paintings." *Grey Room* 18 (winter 2004): 82–104.

———. "Hans Hartung, Mid-Century Modern." In *Hans Hartung: 10 Perspectives,* edited by Anne Pontegnie. Milan, 2006.

Motte, Manfred de la, ed. *Dokumente zum deutschen Informel.* Exh. cat. Bonn, Germany, 1976.

Nationalsozialistische Deutsche Arbeiter-Partei Reichspropagandaleitung Hauptculturamt. *Führer durch die Ausstellung Entartete Kunst.* Exh. cat. Berlin, 1937.

Piene, Otto, and Heinz Mack, eds. *Zero.* Translated by Howard Beckman. Cambridge, Mass., 1973.

Richter, Gerhard. *Texte: Schriften und Interviews.* Edited by Hans-Ulrich Obrist. Frankfurt am Main, 1993.

Röthel, Hans K., and Jean K. Benjamin. *Kandinsky, Catalogue Raisonné of the Oil-Paintings.* Ithaca, N.Y., 1982–1984.

Rowell, Margit. *La peinture, le geste, l'action, l'existentialisme en peinture.* Paris, 1972.

Seitz, William C. *The Responsive Eye.* Exh. cat. New York, 1965.

Spate, Virginia. *Orphism: The Evolution of Non-figurative Painting in Paris, 1910–1914.* New York, 1979.

Troy, Nancy J. *The De Stijl Environment.* Cambridge, Mass., 1983.

White, Anthony. "Lucio Fontana: Between Utopia and Kitsch." *Grey Room* 5 (fall 2001): 54–77.

Yves Klein 1928–1962: A Retrospective. Exh. cat. Essays by Nan Rosenthal et al. Houston, 1982.

CHRISTINE MEHRING

PAISLEY, IAN (b. 1926), influential Protestant unionist minister in Northern Ireland.

The Reverend Ian Richard Kyle Paisley was born in the ancient ecclesiastical capital of Ireland, the City of Armagh, on 6 April 1926. His father, Kyle, was a Baptist minister who had been a member of the Ulster Volunteer Force that had opposed Home Rule before World War I. The family moved to Ballymena, County Antrim, in 1928 when Paisley's father became minister to a larger congregation. In 1942 Paisley spent a year in the Barry School of Evangelism in South Wales, returning to Belfast in 1943 where for three years he was a part-time student at a theological college run by the small Protestant sect, the Reformed Presbyterian Church of Ireland. Paisley's brand of evangelical Protestantism was deeply influenced by the literalist and separatist doctrines of American fundamentalism, and he developed close links with Dr. Bob Jones (1883–1968) of the Bob Jones University in South Carolina, which awarded him an honorary degree in 1966. In 1951, Paisley established his own Free Presbyterian Church in the Ravenhill area of Belfast, where he later erected the large Martyrs Memorial Church.

From the late 1940s, Paisley was involved on the fringes of unionist politics. He was a member of the Orange Order, although he resigned from it in 1962 and joined the dissident Independent Orange Order. He linked himself to an "independent unionist" tradition that combined religious fundamentalism with a populist critique of the unionist establishment for allegedly betraying working class Protestants and appeasing Catholics and nationalists. The original support for his organizations Ulster Protestant Action and the Protestant Unionist Party came from disaffected working class Protestants in Belfast. His political breakthrough occurred when a new unionist prime minister, Captain Terence O'Neill (1914–1990; prime minister 1963–1969), moved gingerly to address some of the grievances of Ulster's Catholic minority. Paisley identified O'Neill with the "appeasers" in the mainstream Protestant churches who supported the ecumenical movement in response to the Second Vatican Council (1962–1965).

Paisley's vivid revivalist preaching style, combined with a sharp wit and fierce caricatures of his religious and political opponents, allowed him to tap into reservoirs of class and ethnic resentments and insecurities in the Protestant community. His willingness to take his supporters onto the streets produced heightened inter-community tensions. In 1966 he was imprisoned for a protest outside the Presbyterian General Assembly. However, Paisley's support continued to grow as O'Neill faced the onset of the civil rights movement and its marches and street protests. Paisley put himself at the head of those ultra-loyalists who took to the streets to oppose the marches.

As the crisis of the unionist state deepened, Paisley emerged as the most strident voice of the Right. He claimed responsibility for O'Neill's resignation and harried O'Neill's successors as they introduced reforms under pressure from the British government. In April 1970, Paisley won a by-election for O'Neill's Bannside constituency at Stormont, and in the June 1970 general election he won the North Antrim seat at Westminster. By this time the civil rights movement had given way to the armed struggle of the IRA, and the conditions of violence and insecurity intensified the appeal of the Right within the Protestant community. In October 1971, the Protestant Unionist Party was transformed into the Democratic Unionist Party (DUP) as Paisley attempted to widen the appeal to disaffected unionists who had reservations about the influence of Protestant fundamentalism on his party. The suspension of the Stormont Parliament in 1972 was a major blow to the Unionist Party, but the DUP failed to exploit it because of Paisley's temporary support for the idea of the total integration of Northern Ireland within the United Kingdom. He was also faced with the emergence of an alternative leadership of the right in the person of the former unionist cabinet minister, Bill Craig (b. 1924), and his Ulster Vanguard movement.

In the elections for a new Northern Ireland Assembly in 1973, the DUP won 10 percent of the vote to the Ulster Unionists' 29 percent. Paisley joined with Craig and the right wing of the Ulster Unionist Party (UUP) to oppose the Sunningdale Agreement in December 1973 that established an executive based on power sharing between unionists and nationalists. He supported the Ulster Workers' Council strike when a combination of industrial action and intimidation by Protestant paramilitary groups brought the province to a standstill and forced the resignation of the executive in May 1974.

In the aftermath of the strike, the DUP's support expanded significantly as Craig isolated himself by his support for an "emergency coalition" with nationalists. At the same time, the Ulster Unionist Party was suffering from weak leadership and internal divisions. The DUP could rely on the single-minded commitment of members of the Free Presbyterian Church to present a united and hard-line image that appealed in a period of acute uncertainty. In the first elections to the European Parliament in 1979, Paisley topped the poll with almost 30 percent of the vote. In 1981 the DUP first inched ahead of the Ulster Unionist Party in the local government elections. However, this victory proved short-term and it was not until the elections for a Northern Ireland Assembly in October 2003 that the DUP would again surpass the UUP.

This reflected the unease in sections of the Protestant community with the religious extremism of many party members and activists, and also with Paisley's continued identification with militancy on the streets through events like the failed United Unionist Action Council Strike in 1977 and a DUP-sponsored vigilante organization, the "Third Force," set up in 1981. The party also suffered from its inability to shift Margaret Thatcher's commitment to the Anglo-Irish Agreement of 1985. By the 1990s, while Paisley continued to win massive votes in European elections, the DUP seemed to be confirmed in its position of second place to the UUP. However, the IRA cease-fire and the Good Friday Agreement of 1998 convulsed unionist politics in a way that benefited the DUP.

Paisley had opposed the agreement as a "sellout" to the IRA. Key aspects of the agreement, like the early release of paramilitary prisoners and police reform, were intensely unpopular among grassroots Unionists. As the UUP leader, David Trimble (b. 1944), accepted republicans in government and the IRA prevaricated on the decommissioning of its weapons, support for the UUP slumped and Paisley and his party benefited. However, given the continued strength of fundamentalism in the DUP, doubts remained that, even if his failing health would allow it, Paisley would crown his political career by becoming first minister of Northern Ireland.

See also **IRA; Northern Ireland; United Kingdom.**

BIBLIOGRAPHY

Bruce, Steve. *God Save Ulster: The Religion and Politics of Paisleyism.* Oxford, U.K., 1986.

Mitchell, Patrick. *Evangelicalism and National Identity in Ulster, 1921–1998.* Oxford, U.K., 2003.

Moloney, Ed, and Andy Pollak. *Paisley.* Dublin, 1986.

Smyth, Clifford. *Ian Paisley Voice of Protestant Ulster.* Edinburgh, 1987.

HENRY PATTERSON

PAKISTAN. It is an irony of history that Pakistan was a state demanded neither by its founding father, Mohammed Ali Jinnah (1876–1948), nor by the peoples of the territories that came to comprise the new country in 1947. The creation of Pakistan came at the cost of the partition of British India, approximately a million deaths, and the uprooting of some seventeen million people. Its two most populous provinces of Punjab and Bengal—both divided—sustained the largest share of these losses. Not only were regional solidarities violently rent, but Punjab was divested of its rich eastern districts and eastern Bengal of its industrial heart of Calcutta. For the remaining provinces of Pakistan—Baluchistan, the North Western Frontier Province, and Sind—the new territorial dispensation meant the corset-strings of a Punjabi-dominated center constraining their provincial autonomy. The Muslims from provinces in undivided India where they formed minorities might be supposed to have been its greatest beneficiaries. However, of the ninety-five million Muslims of pre-1947 India, almost a third remained in the Hindu-majority state either by choice or force of circumstance. Of those who moved to Pakistan, many have remained unassimilated, dubbed *Muhajirs* (migrants), within the homeland ostensibly created for them.

FOUNDING THE STATE

The founding of Pakistan is often traced to the reformer Syed Ahmed Khan's (1817–1898) articulation of the "two nation" theory in the 1880s. However, situating Syed Ahmed Khan in his times reveals that his concerns were more with securing the flagging fortunes of elite Muslims in north India than with advancing any separatist ideas. This required reconciling Muslims with British rule, Islamic ideas with Western modernity, and eschewing the Indian National Congress's anticolonial politics. Describing Muslims as a discrete community that Congress could not represent, Syed Ahmed Khan presumed greater unity among his co-religionists than empirical reality justified. But this was a perception reinforced by colonial censuses that had counted Indians into a Hindu "majority" and a Muslim "minority" community. In projecting Muslims and Hindus as two nations, Khan did not oppose the idea of an Indian nation as much as he sought to trump the majoritarianism he saw embedded in the Hindu-dominated Congress's nationalism that threatened to treat Muslims as a perpetual "minority."

Imperial systems of control through a balance between communities also lent support to the idea that Muslim interests needed separate representation. In October 1906, some Muslim leaders, with colonial encouragement, demanded separate electorates (granted by the 1909 Indian Councils Act) and in December 1906 established the All India Muslim League as a party that purportedly spoke for all Indian Muslims. While regional, linguistic, class, and sectarian divergences militated against a unitary conception of the Muslim community, this construction of the political category of "Indian Muslim" encouraged emphasis on religious identity to make demands from the colonial state.

This was the backdrop to Jinnah's revival of the two-nation theory in the late 1930s. In elections held in 1937 to create fully Indian ministries in the eleven provinces of British India, the Congress had won majorities in eight and the League in none. Beginning his political career in the Congress, Jinnah had little personal interest in the politics of religion. But the League's electoral debacle sent him in search of some way to unite the interests of Muslims in Hindu-majority provinces, where separate electorates had ensured the League's only victories, with those in provinces where they formed majorities but where cross-communal regional parties held sway. Religion provided a

common thread, and claiming that Muslim India constituted a "nation" offered a viable strategy to argue for equal representation with "Hindu India" in any central government institutions. At no point did Jinnah view "Pakistan" so defined as incompatible with a federal or confederal state structure encompassing a united India. It was only by raising the specter of a future Congress-dominated postcolonial state that Jinnah persuaded Muslim-majority provinces wedded to their autonomy to accept the League as their "sole spokesman" in all-India negotiations. In the end, the Congress's rejection of the British Cabinet Mission's proposals of 1946, which protected Muslim interests through powerful provinces that could discipline the center, extinguished the last hopes for an undivided independent India. The British transferred power to Pakistan on 14 August 1947 and to India a day later.

POSTCOLONIAL CONTINUITY

That, despite the upheavals of partition, the state did not collapse in either Pakistan or India is a testimony to the robustness of the colonial structures that survived in both countries after independence. Unlike India, however, which had inherited the mantle of the British Raj, Pakistan was defined as a seceding state and had to fashion its international identity anew, asking cap in hand for admission into the comity of nations. More importantly, it had to carve out a new political center and have its authority acknowledged by provincial politicians fiercely protective of their regional power. This task was rendered both more urgent by the outbreak of hostilities with India over Kashmir and harder by the fact that the only national party, the Muslim League, had little or no organizational structure in the areas that came to form Pakistan. Its main constituency had always been drawn from among Muslims in Hindu majority provinces now in India. The result was the early reliance by weak central politicians on the two main non-elected institutions, the civil bureaucracy and the army, put in place by the colonial state. This explains in large measure why, beginning with the same colonial legacy in 1947, whereas India was able to sustain more or less stable traditions of formal democracy, Pakistan's fifty-seven-year-old history has been dominated by military rule in collusion with the

Mohammad Ali Jinnah (on dais at left) is sworn in as governor-general of Pakistan, 17 August 1947. GETTY IMAGES

mighty civil service. Although federal in form, the Pakistani state emerged, like its colonial predecessor, as highly centralized in practice and reliant on the administrative fiat of the bureaucracy and a disciplined army.

THE CREATION OF BANGLADESH

The difficulties of national integration and the inadequacy of Islam as a force capable of overriding regional particularisms were forcefully illustrated by the secession in 1971 of East Pakistan. Separated by 1,000 miles of Indian territory from the western wing, East Bengal comprised over half Pakistan's population. Yet, despite this demographic edge, Bengalis were denied their due share in governance. Indeed, the fear of Bengali dominance led Punjabi politicians to collude with bureaucrats and the army to postpone democratic elections. Politically marginalized, the Bengalis were also severely underrepresented in the powerful bureaucracy and military. And economically, Bengali revenues from the export of primary goods such as jute were used to finance the development of the western wing, producing accusations of an "inner colonialism." Moreover, the center's imposition of Urdu and repression of the Bengali language and literature lent a cultural dimension to political and economic discontent. These various resentments fueled a campaign for provincial autonomy led by Mujibur Rahman (1920–1975) and his Awami League; in 1970, in the first national elections held in Pakistan, the party swept the polls in East Bengal. The Pakistani center ordered a military crackdown in March 1971, precipitating the dismemberment of the country as a Bengali Liberation Army, assisted by the Indian military, fought a war of independence that ended with the creation of Bangladesh.

ISLAM AND ISLAMIZATION

In the 1970 elections, the Pakistan People's Party of Zulfikar Ali Bhutto (1928–1979) won most seats in West Pakistan. Bhutto had campaigned on a platform of land reforms and state control of financial and economic institutions. His populism failed because of his inability to keep together the broad coalition of his supporters—economic and social groups with divergent interests linked only by a common opposition to twelve years of martial rule. Charges of corruption, nepotism, and authoritarianism against the Bhutto regime were used by the army to reassert control in 1977 against a backdrop of widespread social unrest. General Mohammad Zia-ul-Haq (1924–1988), who dismissed this first ever democratically elected government and hanged Bhutto in 1979, had to seek political legitimacy from Islamic groups and other similar constituencies that were in the forefront of opposition to Bhutto.

In Jinnah's vision of a democratic Pakistan, as enunciated in his speech to the Constituent Assembly on 11 August 1947, religion was to be a personal matter that had "nothing to do with the business of the state." Yet this perspective sat uneasily with the founding rationale of the state as a homeland for Indian Muslims. Islam as state ideology has played an ambivalent role in Pakistan. Religious groups such as the Jamat-i-Islami, founded by Syed Abul Ala Maududi (1903–1979), while opposing the demand for Pakistan as an expression of a godless nationalism, became among the most vocal advocates of an "Islamic state" after partition. However, while religious leaders have been kept on the periphery of state power, it was the periodic resort to Islam by temporal authorities to fortify weak secular legitimacies that opened the door to fundamentalist forces. This trend was accelerated under Zia-ul-Haq, whose regime (1977–1988) rested on the two supports of militarism and Islam. Yet even his Islamization program was selectively targeted at politically safe constituencies. Leaving the economy out of the purview of reform, his Islamic commitment was expressed through a series of purportedly religious ordinances in 1979 discriminating against women—effacing the distinction between rape and adultery and reducing the evidence of a woman to half that of a man. The genie of religious conservatism once out was difficult to re-bottle, as was demonstrated by the inability of Prime Minister Benazir Bhutto (b. 1953, prime minister 1988–1990 and 1993–1996), the first woman leader of an Islamic state, to repeal these laws. Political expediency assumed priority given her tenuous majority in parliament and the vociferous opposition to her assuming office from the orthodox Islamic lobby.

Another enduring legacy of the Zia-ul-Haq years was the rise in Shia-Sunni sectarian violence. The Iranian Revolution of 1979 had encouraged political activism among Pakistan's Shia minority (15 to 25 percent of the population), many of whom also opposed Zia-ul-Haq's Islamization as promoting a narrow Sunni vision incompatible with Shia interpretations. In response, the central government, with the help of the army and its intelligence wing and funding from Saudi Arabia and other countries in the Persian Gulf, bolstered a variety of Islamic institutions, especially *madrasas* (seminaries) propagating a particularly militant form of Sunni orthodoxy. Careering out of control in more recent times, sectarian violence claimed almost 1,300 lives in urban Pakistan alone between 1990 and 2002. And while, in the mid 1990s, the government made efforts to curb Sunni extremism at home, it was exported to Kashmir and Afghanistan.

ALLIANCE WITH THE UNITED STATES

Zia-ul-Haq's purely homegrown program of Islamization was queered by the American policy of organizing Muslim *mujahidin* (religious warriors) against the Soviet occupation of Afghanistan. As a result, generous funds and arms became available from the United States, Saudi Arabia, and the United Arab Emirates to underpin Zia-ul-Haq's support for Islamic groups in Pakistan. This was not the first time that the Pakistani state, through the instrumentality of its army, became subsumed into U.S. strategic planning. As early as in the 1950s, Pakistan had been enlisted as a valuable ally in the Cold War. Toward this end, Washington buttressed the Pakistani bureaucracy and the army as more reliable safeguards against communism than the unpredictable world of democratic institutions. Indeed, many observers suggest that the first military coup of General Mohammad Ayub Khan (1907–1974) in 1958 had tacit American support. Whether or not they were themselves concerned with "rolling back communism," both Generals Ayub and Zia-ul-Haq were grateful beneficiaries of the financial and military aid this alignment brought.

While U.S.-Pakistani relations have seen periods of cooling off, such as happened after the latter's nuclear tests in 1998, military and security ties were never broken and were reinvigorated in the aftermath of the 11 September 2001 attacks. In fact, while the United States had joined other parts of the world in condemning the coup of General Pervez Musharraf (b. 1943) in October 1999, more recently such criticism has been muted. President Musharraf, in turn, has deftly made an about-face from full-fledged support of the Taliban in Afghanistan to cooperation with the United States in dealing with Islamist forces in the region. Notwithstanding occasional doubts expressed in Washington about the Musharraf regime's sincerity in weeding out Islamic fundamentalists, the administration of George W. Bush (b. 1946) has been unstinting in praising Pakistan as a frontline ally in the "war against terror."

See also **Al Qaeda; British Empire; British Empire, End of; India; Islam; Islamic Terrorism.**

BIBLIOGRAPHY

Hardy, Peter. *The Muslims of British India.* Cambridge, U.K., 1972.

Jaffrelot, Christophe, ed. *Pakistan: Nationalism Without a Nation?* London, 2002.

Jahan, Rounaq. *Pakistan: Failure in National Integration.* New York, 1972.

Jalal, Ayesha. *The Sole Spokesman: Jinnah, the Muslim League and the Demand for Pakistan.* Cambridge, U.K., 1985.

————. *The State of Martial Rule: The Origins of Pakistan's Political Economy of Defence.* Cambridge, U.K., 1990.

Nasr, S. V. R. *The Vanguard of Islamic Revolution: The Jama'at-i Islami of Pakistan.* Berkeley, Calif., 1994.

Talbot, Ian. *Pakistan: A Modern History.* London, 1998.

Ziring, Lawrence. *Pakistan in the Twentieth Century: A Political History.* Karachi, 1997.

MRIDU RAI

PALESTINE. In 1516 Palestine, a geographic area that includes both present-day Israel and Jordan, was absorbed into the vast Ottoman Empire that at its pinnacle stretched across Europe and Asia. From this time until the end of the First World War, Palestine did not exist as a unified geopolitical entity. It was divided between the Ottoman province of Beirut in the north and the district of Jerusalem in the south. The Muslim inhabitants of Palestine, the vast majority of the population, were subjects of the Ottoman sultan-caliph, the religious and temporal head of the Islamic world, and local governors were appointed by the Ottoman court in Constantinople. There had been a dwindling Jewish presence in Palestine since biblical times, when this area comprised a Jewish state. By 1914, primarily a result of immigration from eastern Europe, Palestine's Jewish community (commonly known as the Yishuv), numbered seventy to eighty-five thousand, about 12 percent of the total population.

1914–1917: OTTOMAN PALESTINE

Since its formal establishment in the 1890s, the Zionist Organization, the Jewish national movement seeking the return of the Jews to their ancient homeland in Palestine, had attempted to gain Ottoman support for this ambitious goal. Following the Ottoman decision to enter the First World War on the side of Germany in November 1914, the Zionists looked to Great Britain, the leading anti-Ottoman power in the Middle East, for political support.

In November 1917 the British government issued the Balfour Declaration. Named after Lord Balfour (Arthur James Balfour; 1848–1930), Britain's foreign minister, it was issued in the form of a letter to Lord Rothschild (Lionel Walter Rothschild; 1868–1937), the leading figure in British Jewry. The Balfour Declaration called for the "establishment in Palestine of a national home for the Jewish people" and pledged that Great Britain would "use their best endeavours to facilitate the achievement of this object, it being clearly understood that nothing shall be done which may prejudice the civil and religious rights of existing non-Jewish communities in Palestine."

The following month the British army under the command of General Sir Edmund Allenby captured the holy city of Jerusalem. This constituted a grave setback to Ottoman prestige, heralded the ultimate defeat and dismemberment of the Ottoman Empire, and marked the beginning of almost three decades of British rule in Palestine.

1920–1948: BRITISH PALESTINE

British rule in Palestine was formalized when the League of Nations approved a British mandate for this former Ottoman possession in July 1922. The key clauses of the Balfour Declaration were incorporated into the mandate. This allowed the Yishuv to develop extensive educational and welfare services and to acquire large parcels of land from Arab landowners, absentee landlords, and peasants. Landmark institutions, such as the Hebrew University of Jerusalem, were opened and the Histadrut, the General Federation of Hebrew Workers in Palestine, was established. This body played a central role in rapidly developing the construction, industrial, and agricultural sectors in a period of rising Jewish immigration. A 1922 census estimated the total population of Palestine at 752,048, of which Muslims numbered 589,177 (78 percent of the population) and Jews numbered 83,790 (11 percent of the population). By 1947 the Jews comprised 31 percent of a total population of over 1.7 million.

This rise in the Jewish population was largely a result of an influx of Jews escaping Nazi persecution in Europe. However, Palestine's Arabs viewed Jewish immigration into Palestine as a political rather than a humanitarian issue. In 1921, 1930, and 1936 Palestinian Arab delegations visited London to express opposition to Zionism and continued immigration. There were also riots in 1920 and 1921 and a violent attack on Hebron's Jewish residents in 1929.

Haj Amin (Amin al-Husayni; 1893–1974), a member of a leading Palestinian Arab family, dominated Palestinian Arab politics during this period. Appointed grand mufti (expounder of Muslim law) by the British in 1921, he also headed the Arab higher committee, the de facto Arab leadership in Palestine. He played a key role in the Arab revolt against British rule that began in 1936. He also led Arab opposition to the July 1937 recommendation of the royal commission on Palestine (the Peel Commission) that called for the abrogation of the mandate and the partition of Palestine into Jewish and Arab states with a permanent mandate for Jerusalem.

In November 1938 the Woodhead Commission, set up to examine the feasibility of partition, rejected the Peel proposals as unworkable. In May 1939 the British government introduced the Palestine White Paper. This document severely restricted Jewish immigration into Palestine to a maximum of seventy-five thousand between April 1939 and 1944, after which time "no further Jewish immigration will be permitted unless the Arabs of Palestine are prepared to acquiesce in it."

Following the outbreak of the Second World War in 1939, the Palestinian Arab community showed little interest in opposing the Nazi menace and the mufti's position as Arab Palestine's most popular political leader was not diminished by his cooperation with Nazi Germany during the war. The Yishuv contributed greatly to the struggle against Nazism, but the war years saw a severe breakdown in relations between the Zionists and the British government over the White Paper policy, which was viewed as a subversion of the Jewish national revival in Palestine and the abandonment of European Jewry to their Nazi persecutor.

As such, in May 1942 the mainstream Zionist leadership for the first time officially endorsed the call for the creation of a Jewish state in Palestine, as opposed to a Jewish national home. At the same time extremist Jewish groups like the Irgun Zvai Leumi and the Stern Gang increased their attacks against British targets in Palestine, the most notorious of which was the 1946 bombing of the British military headquarters at the King David Hotel in Jerusalem that killed ninety-one people.

In 1947, in the face of Jewish insurgency and Arab hostility, Britain turned the Palestine problem over to the United Nations. On 29 November 1947 the United Nations approved (by 33 votes to 13 with 10 abstentions) a plan calling for the partition of Palestine into two independent states—one Jewish, the other Arab—linked in an economic union, with Jerusalem placed under an international regime.

1948–1967: THE WEST BANK UNDER JORDANIAN RULE

On 15 May 1948, less than twenty-four hours after the end of the British mandate and the proclamation of the establishment of the State of Israel, the combined armies of Egypt, Iraq, Lebanon, Transjordan (which in 1949 adopted the name Jordan), and Syria invaded the nascent Jewish state.

Displaced Jews gathered in Milan protest delays in permitting their emigration to Palestine, June 1946.
©BETTMANN/CORBIS

Israel was victorious in the ensuing war, and by the summer of 1949 it was in possession of far more territory than had been originally envisaged under the United Nations' partition plan. However, Jordan captured east Jerusalem and the west bank of the Jordan River. Jerusalem was divided into a Jordanian sector and an Israeli sector with a small no-man's-land and a demilitarized zone separating both sides. This meant that King Abdullah (Abd Allah ibn al-Husayn; 1882–1951), the founder of the Hashemite Kingdom of Jordan now ruled both banks of the Jordan River, as during the 1920s the British had placed the area of Palestine to the east of the river under Hashemite control.

By the time hostilities ceased in 1949, large numbers of Palestinian Arabs from the main urban centers of Jerusalem, Jaffa, and Haifa and from villages along the coastal plane of Palestine had fled their homes. The actual number of Palestinians who became refugees at this time is unknown.

Israel estimates the figure at 538,000, the UN estimate is 720,000, and Palestinian sources believe it to be 850,000. An emotive academic debate rages between scholars who argue that Israel expelled the refugees and those who claim that the Palestinian Arabs left of their own volition, intent on returning once Israel had been defeated.

In April 1950 King Abdullah annexed east Jerusalem and the West Bank into his kingdom. Unlike Palestinian refugees in other Arab countries, those under Jordanian jurisdiction gained automatic Jordanian citizenship and were integrated into the nation's economic, social, and political life.

However, Jordanian investment in the West Bank's infrastructure, industry, and social services was minimal, resulting in 200,000 West Bank residents moving to the East Bank and about 300,000 others emigrating abroad between 1949 and 1967. Many of those Palestinians who remained lived in refugee camps and were reluctant to integrate into Jordanian society. King Hussein, who succeeded his father King Talal I (r. 1951–1952) in 1953, faced growing economic and political pressure from this large and disaffected constituency. This situation deteriorated when the Palestine Liberation Organization (PLO), established in 1964, challenged Jordanian sovereignty over the West Bank and attempted to overthrow the Hashemite monarchy.

1967–2004: THE WEST BANK UNDER ISRAELI RULE

In the early morning of 5 June 1967, and in response to relentless threats from its Arab neighbors, Israel launched a surprise military attack on Egypt, Jordan, and Syria. By the time the UN Security Council–sponsored ceasefire had come into effect on 10 June, Israel had captured east Jerusalem and the West Bank from Jordan. Jerusalem was reunited under Israeli sovereignty and the West Bank was placed under administration.

In the wake of the war the PLO quickly evolved into the diplomatic and military representative of a Palestinian people who felt betrayed by the Arab world. In 1968 the PLO formulated its national covenant that declared the existence of the state of Israel to be null and void. In 1969 Yasser Arafat became head of the PLO, and his championing of the twin policy of international terror and diplomacy gained widespread support in the international community at a time of growing sympathy for anticolonial causes. In November 1974 Arafat had the distinction of becoming the first non–head of state to address the General Assembly of the United Nations.

The overwhelming majority of ordinary Palestinians in the West Bank opposed the occupation, but they did not participate in the armed struggle. Rather, they used their access to the larger and more developed Israeli economy to improve their standard of living, something their own primarily agricultural economy could not offer.

The number of Palestinians working in Israel rose from zero in 1967 to sixty-six thousand in 1975. During the 1970s the West Bank was the fourth fastest-growing economy in the world. This period also saw a significant fall in infant mortality and illiteracy rates, as well as a dramatic increase in life expectancy and attendance at schools and universities. All this influenced the social, economic, and political development of the West Bank, as the traditional pro-Jordanian elite was eclipsed by a younger generation of educated Palestinian nationalists in both urban and rural areas.

Between 1977 and 1991, the number of Jewish settlers in the West Bank grew from 20,000 to over 100,000. This became the major Palestinian grievance against Israel, and in December 1987 the *intifada*, a mass uprising against the Israeli occupation, began. The *intifada* highlighted the existence of a local Palestinian leadership capable of challenging the dominance of the PLO, which had been based in far-away Tunis since being driven out of Lebanon by Israel in 1982. The PLO's influence was further weakened by the growing appeal of Islamist groups like Hamas—the Palestinian branch of the Muslim Brothers, which came to prominence during the *intifada*—and by the collapse of its longtime patron the Soviet Union following the end of the Cold War.

At the Madrid Peace Conference of October 1991, and in subsequent bilateral political discussions with Israel, the Palestinians were represented by a joint Palestinian-Jordanian delegation, as Israel refused to negotiate with the PLO. However, secret talks between Israeli and PLO officials in Oslo, Norway, over the same period resulted in a peace agreement. On 13 September 1993, in a historic ceremony in the garden of the White House, Israeli and PLO leaders signed a Declaration of Principles on Interim Self-Government Arrangements (also known as DOP, or Oslo 1), which set out a framework for Palestinian self-rule in occupied territories prior to a final settlement.

Subsequent agreements in 1994, 1995, 1997, and 1998 extended Palestinian autonomy and provided for a gradual Israeli military redeployment and cooperation on security issues. The international community provided significant support for the economic, political, and social development of the West Bank following the signing of the Oslo Accords. The World Bank has estimated that annual donor assistance averaged one billion U.S. dollars per annum in these years.

Nevertheless, this massive investment did not result in ordinary Palestinians experiencing a noticeable rise in their living standards. This was because of widespread corruption and gross inefficiency within the Palestinian Authority, the governing body of the self-rule areas; as well as Israel's repeated closure of its borders to Palestinian goods and workers in response to a wave of Palestinian terrorism between 1994 and 1996.

By 1999, according to World Bank figures, the West Bank had recovered from the economic decline of previous years. However, the failure of Israel and the Palestinian Authority to reach a permanent settlement resulted in the breakdown of the Oslo process and the outbreak of the al-Aqsa *intifada* in September 2000. Israelis and Palestinians then experienced a period of violence and despair unprecedented even by the appalling standards of this tragic conflict. The death in November 2004 of the longtime Palestinian leader Yasser Arafat, a man whom many held responsible for the failure of Oslo, and the decision of the Israeli government to withdraw unilaterally and remove all settlements from the Gaza Strip presented a new opportunity for peace. But by the mid-2000s, creating the circumstances that would result in the establishment of a viable, sovereign Palestinian state in the West Bank still posed a significant challenge to Israel and the Palestinian Authority.

See also **British Empire; Israel; Zionism.**

BIBLIOGRAPHY

Primary Sources

Cmd. 5479, *Report of the Palestine Royal Commission.* London, July 1937.

Cmd. 6019, *Palestine: A Statement of Policy.* London, May 1939.

Secondary Sources

Friedman, Isaiah. *The Question of Palestine: British-Jewish-Arab Relations, 1914–1918.* New Brunswick, N.J., and London, 1992. A scholarly and intricate analysis of Britain's Palestine policy and its negotiations with Arabs and Jews during the First World War.

Karsh, Efraim. *The Arab-Israeli Conflict: The Palestine War 1948.* Oxford, U.K., 2002. A succinct and reader-friendly account of the 1948 war that examines the factors that led to the fighting and analyzes the war's impact on Israeli-Arab relations, Palestinian society, and the international community.

Morris, Benny. *The Birth of the Palestinian Refugee Problem Revisited.* Cambridge, U.K., 2004. A leading scholar argues that Israel was responsible for expelling Palestine's Arab population during the 1948 war.

Rabinovich, Itamar. *Waging Peace: Israel and the Arabs, 1948–2003.* Princeton, N.J., 2004. A comprehensive and informed history of Israeli-Arab relations by a leading scholar who was also Israel's ambassador to the United States during the 1990s.

Ross, Dennis. *The Missing Peace: The Inside Story of the Fight for Middle East Peace.* New York, 2004. A hugely detailed narrative account of the Oslo peace process by the senior U.S. negotiator.

Sayigh, Yezid. *Armed Struggle and the Search for State: The Palestinian National Movement, 1949–1993.* Oxford, U.K., 1997. A definitive study of Palestinian society and the PLO's struggle against Israel from the time of the 1948 war until the Oslo peace process.

Shamir, Shimon, and Bruce Maddy-Weitzman, eds. *The Camp David Summit—What Went Wrong?: Americans, Israelis, and Palestinians Analyze the Failure of the Boldest Attempt Ever to Resolve the Palestinian-Israeli Conflict.* Brighton, U.K., and Portland, Ore., 2005. A collection of easily accessible essays on why the Oslo peace process failed, written by academic experts and key Israeli, Palestinian, and American participants in the negotiations.

Sherman, A. J. *Mandate Days: British Lives in Palestine, 1918–1948.* London, 1997. An entertaining account of the British mandate based primarily on the diary entries and correspondence of British residents of Palestine during that period.

Shlaim, Avi. *The Iron Wall: Israel and the Arab World.* London, 2000. A critical examination of Zionism and Israel's responsibility for the Arab-Israeli conflict over the course of the twentieth century.

Watson, Geoffrey R. *The Oslo Accords: International Law and the Israeli-Palestinian Peace Agreements.* Oxford, U.K., 2000. A scholarly study from a legal perspective of the obligations imposed on both Israel and the Palestinians under the various Oslo peace agreements.

Vital, David. *Zionism: The Crucial Phase.* Oxford, U.K., 1987. The definitive scholarly account of both the Zionist movement and the Yishuv's evolution from the beginning of the First World War until the outbreak of the Second World War.

RORY MILLER

PALME, OLOF (1927–1986), prime minister of Sweden.

Sven Olof Joachim Palme, born to a well-established middle-class family, belonged to a postwar generation characterized by the polarized worldview of the Cold War. As a young student he was active in the splitting of the communist-dominated international student movement and participated in the creation of an alternative, pro-West organization. At the same time, international student activities gave him an early opportunity to travel in the Third World, and Palme's experiences there would have great significance for his future engagement with geopolitical issues.

A year at a university in the United States gave Palme insights into American society and its intellectual traditions. He maintained contacts with radical and liberal U.S. circles until the end of his life.

In 1953, at the age of twenty-six, Palme became political secretary to Tage Erlander, Sweden's Social Democratic prime minister (1946–1969). Palme quickly gained great importance for Erlander as a source of inspiration and as a partner in intellectual dialogue. During these years Palme had reason to occupy himself with a broad spectrum of issues and thus acquired a general education in politics that would stand him in good stead during his future political career.

Palme quickly acquired the image of a young man of the future. He was appointed minister (without a portfolio) in 1963. He was minister of communications from 1965 to 1967 and minister of education and culture in 1967. In 1969 he was elected chairman of the Social Democratic Party and simultaneously became prime minister.

During the 1960s Palme's name was increasingly linked to engagement in international affairs, above all because of his critical attitude toward the U.S. war in Vietnam. He delivered his sharpest critique in connection with the Christmas 1972 U.S. bombing of Hanoi, in a speech that compared the bombing with atrocities such as Guernica in Spain in 1937, Babi Yar and Treblinka during World War II, and Sharpeville in South Africa in 1960.

The Swedish Vietnam policy caused serious complications in Sweden's diplomatic relations with the United States. At the same time, Palme gained international attention. Palme had contact with many leading cultural figures, journalists, and radical politicians. During the 1970s he became an

Olof Palme (right) with the North Vietnamese ambassador to Sweden, Nguyen Tho Chan, at a reception in Stockholm, October 1969. ©BETTMANN/CORBIS

important partner in dialogue for leaders from the Third World. Through his work in the Socialist International, Palme made important contributions to the development of international social democracy in, among other places, Portugal.

Domestically Palme's first years as prime minister coincided with an era of social radicalization. During the first half of the 1970s Sweden went through its most comprehensive period of social reforms. Especially noted was Palme's engagement in the issue of equality between the sexes, and many of the reforms of the 1970s concerned family policies and women's labor market opportunities. At the same time, Palme showed political and tactical shrewdness. Social Democracy's electoral basis was steadily shrinking throughout the 1970s. Nonetheless, Palme managed to stay in power until 1976, when the Social Democrats were forced into opposition for the first time since the 1930s. The party returned to power in 1982, however, with Palme again as prime minister. By then, the radicalism of the 1960s and 1970s had been replaced by the neoliberalism of the 1980s, and Palme did not always feel altogether at home in the new political climate.

Palme continued to dedicate a significant portion of his political energies to international questions. He established the Palme Commission, an independent expert commission on issues of disarmament and security. Some of the commission's policy suggestions became irrelevant when the Cold War ended in the early 1990s. Palme was also appointed United Nations mediator in the conflict between Iran and Iraq, but his work did not lead to the hoped-for results.

On 28 February 1986, Olof Palme was shot dead on a street in Stockholm. The murder awakened strong passions and has, in retrospect, been characterized as a national trauma. Palme's death coincided with great changes in political and ideological values, which has led to its sometimes being seen as a symbol for the end of the Swedish Model. The investigation was badly mishandled and no one could be tied to the murder, which gave rise to extensive speculation and conspiracy theories.

Olof Palme was Sweden's leading postwar political personality. His strong political feelings and engagement were paired with extensive expertise, significant tactical skill, and great rhetorical talent. He also was controversial and provoked strong feelings. The political opposition presented him as a politician of confrontation, and in conservative circles one spoke of the existence of a palpable Palme-hatred, which has since abated. Although critics existed within the Social Democratic Party as well, the dominant tendency was to join together in personal support of Palme.

See also **Social Democracy; Sweden.**

BIBLIOGRAPHY

Åsard, Erik, ed. *Politikern Olof Palme.* Stockholm, 2002.

Elmbrant, Björn. *Palme.* Stockholm, 1996.

Fredriksson, Gunnar. *Olof Palme.* Translated by Roger Tanner. Stockholm, 1996.

Richard, Serge. *Le rendez-vouz suédois: Conversations avec Serge Richard.* Paris, 1976.

KJELL ÖSTBERG

PAPANDREOU, ANDREAS (1919–1996), Greek statesman.

The Greek statesman Andreas Papandreou was born on the island of Chios on 5 February 1919. He was the son of George Papandreou (1888–1968), a leading Liberal politician and prime minister. He studied at the University of Athens. As a student he was involved in a Trotskyite group, and during the Metaxas dictatorship he was arrested. In 1942 he enrolled at Harvard University, where he finished his dissertation in economics. During the 1950s he taught economics at several American universities. In 1959 he returned to Greece to head the Economic Research Center. When his father, who was the leader of the Centre Union Party, was prime minister in 1963–1965, Andreas was among his chief economic advisors. In 1964 Andreas Papandreou was elected a deputy with the Centre Union and was appointed deputy minister of Coordination. His radical views caused the reaction not only of the Conservative Party but also of the more moderate elements in his own party. He was accused of organizing a conspiracy group of leftist officers in the army and that was the beginning of a protracted crisis between King Constantine II (r. 1964–1973) and the government that led to the fall of the George Papandreou cabinet in July 1965.

When the Greek colonels seized power on 21 April 1967 Andreas Papandreou was arrested. In January 1968 he received the permission to leave the country. The same year he established the Panhellenic Liberation Movement (PAK) in Stockholm, and he set out to organize an underground group within Greece. During the military junta (1967–1974) he lived mostly in Sweden and Canada and was involved in a series of campaigns and meetings against the regime in Greece.

In 1974 he returned to Greece and founded the Panhellenic Socialist Movement (PASOK). The program of the party was quite radical and was a combination of nationalism, populism, and socialism. The influence of PASOK and of its charismatic leader grew spectacularly in the 1970s at the expense of the Center and the Left. In 1974 PASOK received 13.5 percent of the votes but in the next elections after three years it nearly doubled its votes (25 percent). In 1981 PASOK with 48 percent won a landslide victory over the right-wing New Democracy, and Papandreou became the first socialist prime minister in Greek history.

The outstanding achievement of PASOK was a result of the mass mobilization in hundreds of grassroots organizations and of Papandreou's personal charisma. The main slogan of PASOK in the 1981 elections was one word: "change." It reflected the drive of Greek society to overcome the legacy of discriminations against the Left that the Greek Civil War had inherited and the need for social justice and political reform. Yet the vagueness of the term *change* denoted the populist tendencies of Papandreou's rhetoric. The first term of the socialist government (1981–1985) was marked by measures of redistribution of the national income in favor of the lower classes, expansion of the role of the state in the economy, and the introduction of political and social reforms long overdue. In foreign relations Papandreou steered a middle course between the United States and the Soviet Union and developed good relations with Arab and Balkan countries, save Turkey. PASOK easily won the 1985 election with 46 percent of the vote, but in the second term (1985–1989) the socialist government moved to a more liberal direction. Due to the poor performance of the Greek economy the Socialist government initiated a program of stabilization that broke the cross-class alliance that had brought the Socialist Party to power. The government worked toward a closer cooperation with the European Community while Papandreou after a moment when the tension in Greek-Turkish relations reached its climax (1987) initiated the rapprochement with Turkey. However, many PASOK supporters were disillusioned by its economic policy and a series of corruption scandals, involving Papandreou himself, while his personal life attracted public criticism. PASOK lost the 1989 election, and after new elections and a bitter polarization the New Democracy came to power in 1990.

Papandreou was cleared of all charges and led PASOK to its second term in power. In 1993 PASOK won the election with 47 percent of the votes. Despite the socialist rhetoric, he followed a policy of liberalization and austerity that showed that the differences between the two major parties had largely disappeared. The priority was convergence of the Greek economy with the other European economies, and the objective was the inclusion of Greece in the European Monetary Union. His fragile health, however, would undermine his ability to govern, and in January 1996 he resigned and Kostas Simitis (b. 1936) became the new leader of PASOK. Andreas Papandreou died on 23 June 1996. His son, George Papandreou, minister of foreign affairs in Simitis's government, became the new leader of PASOK in 2004.

See also **Greece; Socialism; Turkey.**

BIBLIOGRAPHY

Clogg, Richard, ed. *Greece 1981–1989: The Populist Decade.* New York and Basingstoke, U.K., 1993.

Sotiropoulos, Dimitrios A. *Populism and Bureaucracy: The Case of Greece under PASOK, 1981–1989.* Notre Dame, Ind., and London, 1996.

Spourdalakis, Michalis. *The Rise of the Greek Socialist Party.* London, 1988.

POLYMERIS VOGLIS

PAPON, MAURICE (b. 1910), French Vichy government official.

Maurice Papon served as general secretary of the Gironde prefecture from 1942 until the Liberation of France in August 1944. On 2 April 1998, convicted of complicity in crimes against humanity, he was sentenced to ten years in prison and deprived of his civic rights in criminal court. As a former official of the wartime Vichy government who subsequently enjoyed a brilliant administrative career in the highest echelons of government, Papon's conviction came more than fifty years after his participation in the arrest and deportation of some 1,560 Jews during the German occupation.

EARLY CAREER

Papon was the son of a notary. After studies in law, literature, politics, and economics, he undertook, at age twenty-one, a career in public administration, first in the aviation ministry, then moving onto other government posts. Although in 1936 he supported the left-wing Popular Front, four years later Papon rallied to the National

Revolution led by Philippe Pétain. In 1941 he was appointed director of the cabinet of the general secretary in the Ministry of Interior, which was headed by Maurice Sabatier; he followed the latter to the occupied zone when the prime minister, Pierre Laval, appointed Sabatier to head the prefecture of the Gironde region in Bordeaux. In June 1942 Papon's appointment as secretary general of the Gironde placed him in charge of law enforcement and Jewish issues. Rigorous and diligent, Papon promptly organized roundups of Jews, who were sent to the transit camp at Drancy before being deported to Auschwitz.

As the end of the Nazi occupation drew near, Papon put himself at the disposal of Gaston Cusin, who had been named regional commissioner of the French Republic in Bordeaux. Cusin, in search of high-ranking civil servants who belonged to the noncommunist resistance, named Papon to become prefect, or administrative head, of the Landes region. Although the Committee of Liberation raised objections, Papon's nomination was confirmed by a commission in charge of purging the administration of collaborators.

POSTWAR CAREER

In the postwar period, Papon embarked on what became a brilliant career in the highest levels of government. In 1945 he served in the ministry of interior and two years later was appointed prefect of Corse. Four years later he was transferred to the administration in Constantine, Algeria, where he served as prefect; and in 1951 he became secretary general of the prefecture of police in Paris. In 1954 he was appointed to Morocco, then a French protectorate, before returning to Algeria in May 1956. Meanwhile, he had been made a Chevalier of the Legion of Honor in 1948 and was later elevated to the rank of Officier.

In March 1958 Papon was appointed prefect of the Paris police district, a post that he would occupy until 1967. Under his authority the Parisian police brutally suppressed a peaceful demonstration for Algerian independence organized by the Front de Libération National (National Liberation Front, FLN) on 17 October 1961. The number of Algerians killed has never been determined with accuracy, but estimates range from forty, as reported by the government, up to as high as four hundred.

Papon was forced to resign in 1967 in the wake of the Ben Barka affair, in which the French police were revealed to be complicit in kidnapping the leader of the Moroccan resistance movement. Briefly, Papon served as president of the aircraft manufacturing company Sud-Aviation. But in 1968 he returned to government when he was elected to the national assembly and subsequently appointed to preside over its budget commission; later he served as finance minister (1978–1981) in two successive governments led by Raymond Barre.

THE RETURN OF THE PAST

Papon certainly had little reason to expect his past in the Vichy administration would return to haunt him. But on 6 May 1981 the newspaper *Le canard enchaîné* published an article revealing Papon's role in the deportation of Jews from Bordeaux. At Papon's initiative, a panel composed of former fighters in the French Resistance met on 15 December 1981 and agreed that Papon had belonged to the movement, a claim subsequently corroborated by a card identifying him as a volunteer, which Papon had managed to obtain in the late 1950s. However, the panel argued that Papon should have resigned from his post at the head of the administration of the Gironde in July 1942.

Nevertheless, on 19 January 1983 some victims pressed charges, and Papon was indicted as complicit in crimes against humanity. A long period of judicial wrangling ensued, lasting over a decade. The trial, which finally started 8 October 1997, lasted about six months. It aroused great interest in the media, which at times spotlighted Papon, alert despite his age—he was eighty-seven—who was determined to defend his image as a former resistance fighter, and sometimes focused on the question of government complicity in the deportation of French Jews.

After his conviction in 1998, and the denial of his appeal in October 1999, Papon attempted to escape custody but was apprehended in Switzerland and returned to prison in Fresnes, near Paris. On 18 September 2002, he was freed on grounds of ill health by the Paris Court of Appeals, which was applying a new French law (4 March 2002) that ordered release of prisoners for whom incarceration put their life in danger. Papon's judicial saga did not end there, however, but continued to play out like the trial, as the condemnation of a man and the wartime French administration alike.

Seeking to rehabilitate his good name, Papon addressed the European Court of Human Rights. He obtained a preliminary victory on 2 July 2002 when the court in Strasbourg decided that the French courts had prevented Papon from receiving a fair trial. The European court said that the French appeals court had erred on 21 October 1999, when it denied his appeal on the grounds that he had not surrendered to authorities. Encouraged, Papon now did appeal his sentence, but it was denied on 11 June 2004. Papon was also fined 2,500 euros on 14 October 2004 for illegally wearing the medal of the Legion of Honor.

The French state's responsibility for the acts committed under the Vichy regime was affirmed by the Conseil d'État, the high administrative court, which stipulated that the facts for which Papon had been sentenced were not only the result of his misconduct but also the fault of the French government, in whose name he acted. The state, in a judgment handed down on 12 April 2002, was to be held responsible for half the court-awarded damages Papon owed as a result of the civil action against him.

By the way it played out, a media frenzy with extensive use of historians as expert witnesses, the trial of Maurice Papon, more than any other similar proceeding up to the present, ended by bringing to light ambiguities in the relationship of justice to both the memory and the history of Vichy France.

See also **Collaboration; War Crimes; World War II.**

BIBLIOGRAPHY

Conan, Éric. *Le procès Papon : Un journal d'audience*. Paris, 1998.

Jean, Jean-Paul, and Denis Salas. *Barbie, Touvier, Papon: Des procès pour la mémoire*. Paris, 2002.

RENÉE POZNANSKI

PARIS. Twentieth-century Paris was born in the 1860s, when Napoleon III (r. 1852–1871) put Georges-Eugène Haussmann (1809–1891) in charge of creating a capital worthy of France. This remodeling of an old city involved annexing the communities situated between the enclosures of the *fermiers généraux* (enclosures constructed between 1784 and 1787 for the purposes of levying a tax on merchandise entering Paris) and the fortifications erected by Prime Minister Louis-Adolphe Thiers in 1841. Paris would be served by a network of streets and boulevards able to accommodate the subsequent arrival of motorized transportation; it would possess a modern sewage system and water supply, as well as parks such as found in London. A geographical cleavage between poorer eastern and wealthier western parts of Paris during the first half of the nineteenth century, according to Maurice Agulhon, was marked symbolically by the "national-military imperial triangle" (composed of the Place Vendôme, l'Etoile, and Invalides) and "the liberal-secular-republican couple" (the Pantheon and Place de la Bastille). The Second Empire preferred to play up the economic power and associated values of the new France, represented by the new aesthetic of the railroad stations, such as the ornate restaurant at the Gare de Lyon, or the grand hotels and the Opéra Garnier, all to affirm the city's cosmopolitan character. One consequence was to reinforce—though perhaps less than once thought—the east-west division and the social cleavage between the older center of Paris and newer, wealthier sections of the city.

CITYSCAPE

Governing powers in the nascent Third Republic in the late nineteenth century, and successive presidents of the current Fifth Republic, have all attempted to leave their imprint on the cityscape of Paris, the symbolic center of French government, finance, and cultural life. The Third Republic continued and completed the work of Haussmann without significant modification apart from the state's financial disengagement. The regime's pedagogic character and mania for erecting statues, which dominated the city until the turn of the century, prompted republicans to engrave their own values in the architecture of the schools and the *mairies* of the various *arrondissements*. Two statues in particular, each of which symbolizes the Republic, were erected at Place de la République and Place de la Nation, reaffirming the east-west division.

The World's Fairs of 1889 and 1900 were occasions for lasting edifices of another kind. The Eiffel Tower, opened in 1889, became for all the symbol both of the city and of a triumphant modernity, offering the world a new image of France. The Paris subway, inaugurated with the 1900 exposition, promoted a distinctive image of the "city of light." The city thus transformed was allowed to play host to dramatic spectacles that showed off France's new national identity—such as the funeral of the novelist Victor Hugo in 1885, when his body was transferred to the Pantheon, restored for the occasion as a civic temple. Similarly, the new *Fêtes de la Fédération* was an annual banquet for the mayors of France.

Such a profusion of construction erupted in Paris that it was soon saturated by buildings. Beginning in the 1920s, many existing structures were put to new uses, conferred with new symbolism. Indeed, the unknown soldier's entombment beneath the Arc de Triomphe was one example; another would be the transfer of the remains of the socialist politician Jean Jaurès (1859–1914) to the Pantheon in 1924. Construction of new monuments diminished for several decades prior to the 1960s, when urban planners in Paris created a project that might be dubbed *New Haussmanism*. This plan, inspired by radical designs for renovation presented by Le Corbusier (Charles-Édouard Jeanneret; 1887–1965) in 1925 attempted to resolve the conflict between what was required to make Paris a great business center while still bearing the imprint of history and overall design. With legislation in 1962 (the Loi Malraux), the plan called for restoring historical monuments and full renovation of the decrepit peripheral neighborhoods that were annexed by Paris in the 1860s. The historic hub of food distribution in Paris, Les Halles, was transferred to Rungis, and the old Baltard pavilions were torn down to make way for the Forum des Halles, a shopping center inspired by the malls in the United States. Some new buildings markedly broke with the surrounding architecture, such the Tour Montparnasse. Whole neighborhoods were reconstructed from the ground up without regard for the original buildings or of the urban topography; this was the case at Front de Seine, La Défense, and Les Olympiades. Some buildings followed an international architectural style associated with the Fifth Republic, such as the Palais des Congrès and the Maison de la Radio. President Georges Pompidou (1911–1974) radicalized this modernization program, intending to "adapt Paris to the automobile and to renounce a certain aestheticism." He undertook construction of the *voie sur berge* by the Seine and the National Museum of Modern Art at Beaubourg. This architectural policy deeply affected the social fabric of the capital, which was losing small merchants, working-class jobs, and inexpensive lodgings, and declining in population.

This "second massacre of Paris," in the words of Louis Chevalier (1967), provoked a protest movement due to the conjunction of several factors, including studies that showed the importance of the nineteenth-century urban patrimony, the accession of Valéry Giscard d'Estaing (b. 1926) to the presidency, and, most important, an economic upturn in 1973. The plan for urban renewal soon was revised with greater concern for coherence of the cityscape, and renewed respect for the older lines of the city and for the overall fit of new construction within the existing neighborhoods. As one consequence, such projects as an express highway on the Left Bank and along the Canal St. Martin, more towers, and the "Vercingetorix" project behind Montparnasse were abandoned. The notion of historic monuments, broadened to include contemporary structures, preserved the Gare d'Orsay from demolition as well as the *Cité Fleurie*, the studios of the painters Paul Gauguin (1848–1903) and Amedeo Modigliani (1884–1920), and many others. When he came to office in 1981, President François Mitterrand (1916–1996) set about creating an architectural program that was sometimes described as "Pharaoh-noiac." The new Parc de la Villette and the project known as the "Grand Louvre," which involved transferring the Ministry of the Economy and Budget to Bercy, were part of the *grand travaux;* so was construction of the gigantic arch at La Défense, the new Opéra Bastille, and the much-discussed Tres Grande Bibliothèque. This was done with the intention of permanently reorienting Paris by constructing prestigious buildings in a way that would overcome the older tendency to develop the city to the west, with marked effects on its political, cultural, and everyday life.

POLITICS AND ADMINISTRATION
The state's stranglehold on Paris has not been accomplished exclusively or even principally through architecture. The domination has long been administrative and political.

Parisians gathered for a celebration of their liberation by Allied forces are threatened by sniper fire in the Place d'Étoile, August 1944. ©Hulton-Deutsch Collection/Corbis

For nearly a century, Paris was able to make and unmake political regimes, but this role diminished after the defeat of the Commune in 1871 and the rebirth of universal manhood suffrage in 1875. The law of 14 April 1871, passed with a majority of provincial representatives, restricted the role of Paris as much as possible and forbade its municipal council any political incursions into the nation's life. This legislation held with passage of the municipal law in 1884 after republicans were victorious. Paris, excluded by the law of 1884, remained without an elected mayor until 1973, when statutory modification brought it back under common law, permitting Jacques Chirac (b. 1932) to be elected to City Hall; Paris remains to this day formally under the supervision of the prefect of police.

Until 1909 Paris was politically Radical while the French government was obediently opportunistic and moderate. The municipal majority became right wing and remained that way even when the left wing took power nationally. However, the city recovered its role of opposition when Jacques Chirac was mayor of Paris and François Mitterrand became president of the Republic. Paris repeated the same pattern, passing power to the Socialist Party, at the time elsewhere in disarray, when electing a mayor in 2002 as the country chose Chirac the right-winger as president.

Its exceptionalism has long retarded the expression of a municipal identity that is distinctively Parisian. Putting to one side the city's motto, the capital has only with difficulty striven to acquire symbolic expressions; one example would be the equestrian statue of Etienne Marcel, provost of the Paris merchants of the fourteenth century, erected in the gardens of City Hall in 1888, though to little effect. Although a commemorative stela can be found in every commune in France, the honor of hosting the Arc de Triomphe with the tomb of the Unknown Soldier, which symbolizes all the war dead of France, exempted Paris from erecting a monument of its own. Municipal efforts to impose itself politically have been unusual because of a war that forced the national government to flee the capital in 1914.

FUNCTION AND IDENTITY

Extending over some nineteen thousand acres, Paris is considerably smaller than either London or Berlin. The prevailing population density is somewhat greater, with about five hundred inhabitants per acre. In the mid-nineteenth century the city was clearly more multifunctional compared to London, which early became associated with the service sector, or to Berlin, a mainly industrial city. So Paris remains. Before World War I, the old trades and professions that long occupied the center of Paris began to give way to upscale value-added industries. Industry moved from the center to the periphery of Paris, to factories in places such as Quai de Javel or Ile Seguin, which remained operational until not long ago, when they closed to make way for new construction. This phenomenon continued during and after the war. The automobile took over and remodeled the space of the city. The Salon de l'Automobile became an annual event; with 1933 came the lighted Citroën sign on the Eiffel Tower, and the metalworker, popularly called a *Metallo,* became another symbol of Paris.

The growth of industry brought employment to the secondary sector of manufacturing, which predominated until the economic crisis of the 1930s. When it began, deindustrialization was limited to Paris, but later it spread to include the entire region. An economic downturn during the 1970s only amplified this tendency. Half of all headquarters of companies that employed more than five hundred employees represented an unparalleled concentration of large companies, both French and foreign, as Paris and its surrounding region came to occupy a strategic place in the world economy. This "global city" forms part of a transnational economy as one of the four or five major centers of international business; it ranks fourth in the world in terms of production, third in productivity. Diversification, long ahead of London, has

lost steam, and deindustrialization is more intense than in the provinces; by 2006 Paris had just 850,000 jobs in industry, compared to 1,800,000 in 1975. As a consequence, Paris, long a working-class city, has become a city of executives and service workers. Where in 1975 the latter outnumbered factory workers by two to one, in 2006 that proportion was five to one.

These demographic shifts have effected the organization of the urban space and influenced politics—whether it is a question of luxury office buildings around La Défense, laws and regulations for preserving the city's historic center, or concern over the environment. They have sometimes affected political theater, such as the bicentennial parade organized by the graphic artist Jean-Paul Goude on Bastille Day in 1989, or various cultural celebrations and festivals, often playing to foreign visitors as much as to Parisians themselves and contributing to the exponential growth of tourism. The city runs a risk of turning into a museum and creating a nostalgic image of itself; in less than twenty years the city has added some seventy thousand square meters of museum space.

From a demographic standpoint, Paris has never ceased to expand as a region in terms of employment. With some 1.7 million inhabitants in 1861, Paris grew rapidly, less because of a rising birthrate than because of its status as a migratory magnet for the rural population. Until World War II, most newcomers to Paris came from the provinces, fewer from the surrounding countries; to this should be added the cosmopolitan influx of intellectuals and artists. By the end of the twentieth century, inflow from the provinces had ceded place to immigration from abroad; 14.5 percent of the Parisian population in 1999 consisted of foreigners. By 2006 immigration in Paris was more visible than in the past, whether in terms of politics or culture. It created neighborhoods of high visibility that remained nevertheless the space of more micro-local cohabitation than was found in other capitals.

This demographic growth, first confined to the twenty arrondissements (metropolitan boroughs) of Paris proper (2.9 million inhabitants in 1921 and 2.2 million in 2006) early on extended to the small, medium, and large suburbs, the constituents of what in 1976 became the region known as the

Île-de-France (nearly 12 million inhabitants in 2006). The lack of working-class housing (43 percent of the population in overcrowded or unhealthy housing in Paris in 1926), the price of available land, the need for housing and new infrastructure to absorb additional industry (water mains in the first place), and hygienic concerns all rapidly brought about the development of industrial and living sites outside the city limits. This phenomenon, which started in the 1890s, only grew more prominent in the 1920s without any special official policy or regulation. The suburbs nearest the city, collectively known as *La Petite Couronne,* grew up in an anarchic manner and resulted in widespread substandard housing. Laws designed to remedy the situation were adopted but had no chance of being implemented before the economic crisis of the 1930s. There was also the problem of public transportation, with the subways only serving Paris proper, unable to meet the needs of a growing commuter population.

Gradual destruction of the city fortifications started in 1919, and the municipal customs barriers, which came down in 1930, did not create a single municipality, as in London or Berlin. The "Prost Plan" for the region, developed in 1934, was not approved until 1939, on the eve of World War II. But legislation passed under the Vichy regime and after the war created a state-run urban zone. A conception expressed by Jean-François Gravier in his *Paris et le desert français* (1947) helped to guide a policy of decentralization that contributed to reduced industrial employment in the region (loi de 1955) and to the plan for urban redevelopment of the Paris region (PADOG), adopted in August 1960. The Fifth Republic's ambitious aims, however, soon rendered the program obsolete. A new plan, created in June 1965, envisaged construction of an entire region around eight new towns that would be served by a vast network of highways and a railroad system, to be known as the RER. It was only approved in 1976, just when the economic conditions prevailing at the time of its conception had disappeared. From 1954 the government also attempted to deal with the housing crisis that worsened with the baby boom and economic growth. Beginning in 1964 it undertook construction of mammoth housing projects in various locations in the suburbs, though

within a decade they were being severely criticized. The creation of these projects and its consequences were said to be a new urban disease known as "Sarcellitis" (after the first project, at Sarcelles, just north of Paris). The suburbs were largely unequipped to deal with the presence of these projects, either in terms of their construction or their inhabitants. Their massive development around Paris, together with the *péripherique,* the circular highway that separated the suburbs from the city proper, seemed to more clearly mark the frontier, preserving the sense of a fortified city, turned inward toward its center. Paris alone was created as a department in 1964.

The common law status accorded both city and region, together with the "general orientation" law passed in 1991, permitted improved financial arrangements and regional solidarity—limited, however, by new ways in which the city was developing. The influence of Paris as a "world city" continued to extend in ways that favored the networks, at the risk of new tensions between the city thus reconstituted and the abandoned interstitial spaces, as Marcel Roncayalo said in a 1994 article in *Le Debat* "that we know only are to be labeled negatively."

The Parisian population owes to its history and to all these various factors its diversity of cultures. The suburbs support various ethnic groups while individual neighborhoods in Paris continue to possess distinct identities such as can be found in Belleville, Ménilmontant, Montmartre, and Montparnasse. Paris is filled with professional and social groups of all provenance and kind. The population, taken as a whole, has so long been blended and mixed as to create a singular people defined by a way of life and thought. Lively urban spaces, from the Faubourg St.-Antoine to Belleville, Billancourt, Montparnasse, and Bastille all express the city's essence. This culture is not confined to Paris proper but, as Louis Chevalier suggests, can also be found in the surrounding *banlieues* (suburbs). Paris understood in this way has long meant a mix of professional, social, cultural, and ethnic categories that make for porous interaction among various groups. These powerful social mediators allowed for rich social relationships, attested to by the nature of family and social networks and the possibility of social advancement, which was easier in Paris than elsewhere.

Paris c. 1991. The Seine River is in the center; the Eiffel Tower can be seen in the distance on the left. ©PETER TURNLEY/CORBIS

From diversity arises the fluidity that has permitted this scattered aggregation to become a *people*—a single word representing the social complexity by which Paris grew unified and became whole. The special fabric of traditional neighborhoods and homes, more *populaire* than working class, has been part and parcel of the same process. Such neighborhoods have long constituted a powerful social apparatus for absorbing migrants of all origins; they are places through which they pass, not points of segregation. The working-class neighborhoods of Paris have mixed populations; they are open to a city of a modest size in comparison with London or Berlin, facilitating appropriation. One can walk and wander; quite unlike London, the cafés are open meeting places. Though tourists or the upscale public may rarely venture into the working-class districts—at least before the recent gentrification—the inhabitants of those neighborhoods move about as they like. In this sense, Paris creates social spaces and events that facilitate the circulation of people and ideas, and a mix of cultures friendly to creativity.

The loosely defined efflorescence of painting sometimes called the School of Paris, as one example, invented new images of the city and other modern works, some of which were influenced by Parisian street life. In another vein, occupation of the same social spaces and events helps explain French manifestations of social rejection and xenophobia, which were always less prominent in Paris than in the provinces. This is still true in the early twenty-first century, as indicated by the small number of voters for the political Far Right within Paris proper. The capital's history can periodically bring back to life all the various myths of the people and the city, something that constitutes an additional unifying factor. Images of workers at the barricades, evoked around Belleville and in the suburban "red belt," or *le peuple* of France as a whole, are evidence of an uncommon political identity.

Thanks to its history-laden streets, cafés, and boulevards, Paris constitutes an unparalleled politicized space. Its specifics are expressed in atypical ways, in its role, for example, during the Boulangist crisis of the 1890s and in the early stages of the emergence of the extreme right-wing patriotic leagues, which played a major role in French politics until their dissolution. Paris became the site of robust and frequent political interventions and street demonstrations that targeted elected representatives. It has ceased to be the place where regimes were created and undone and no longer represents France as a whole. That high-profile demonstrations in Paris in 1997, in support of the illegal immigrants known as the *sans-papiers*, were actually larger than 1995 manifestations in defense of social security indicated still more recently the existence of a "moral-minded people" as distinct from the "social-minded" people elsewhere.

Demonstrations in Paris can create important moments in the life of the nation; two examples are the battles between groups on the extreme right and the antifascists in February 1934 and the events of May–June 1968. Political centralization and the repercussions of events in the capital helped Paris remain influential in determining which issues acquired a national dimension and the point of reference for public opinion. In May 1968 *la France profonde,* its "silent majority," managed to make its voice heard only after the Gaullists organized a powerful demonstration on 30 May, at the same time that the dissolution of the National Assembly was announced. The riots taking place in "sensitive" neighborhoods only became a national problem once they reached the outskirts of the capital. This is the way that the rhythms of Parisian history and those of the nation continue to blend together.

See also **Bicentennial of the French Revolution; France; Le Corbusier; Riots in France; School of Paris.**

BIBLIOGRAPHY

Bastié, Jean. *Nouvelle histoire de Paris: Paris de 1945 à 2000.* Paris, 2001.

Chevalier, Louis. *Les parisiens.* Paris, 1967.

DANIELLE TARTAKOWSKY

PARIS, SCHOOL OF. *See* School of Paris

PARLIAMENTARY DEMOCRACY.

Parliamentary democracy is a political system in which legislative power and a genuine control of the executive power rest with a representative body, constituted through elections in which a broad majority of the population of a nation is expected to participate in a free and equal way.

For parliamentary democracy defined as such, Europe's twentieth century has been a period ridden with paradox. The thorough democratization of nineteenth-century parliamentary regimes—and therefore the birth of parliamentary democracy in the true sense of the word—after World War I was faced from the very start by alternative, antiparliamentary models of democratization, which made an end to parliamentary government, and to democracy, in large parts of Europe between the 1920s and the 1940s. Parliamentary democracy gained prominence again after World War II in Western Europe, in the 1970s in southern Europe, and after 1989 in Russia and Eastern Europe. Nonetheless, if these parliamentary regimes of the second half of the twentieth century were more democratic than their nineteenth-century predecessors, they were at the same time less parliamentary. The role of elected bodies in the political system was overshadowed by that of corporative groups, political parties, and the executive power.

1914–1945: RISE AND FALL

The political democratization that had characterized the last decades of the nineteenth century and the first decades of the twentieth was accelerated by the experience of World War I. In both the victorious and the defeated countries—and in the new nations that emerged out of the Habsburg Empire—new electoral systems came into being, based on male universal suffrage. Female suffrage, until World War I achieved only in Finland (1906), Norway (1913), and Denmark (1915), was introduced shortly after it in various countries at the national legislative level (Germany and Austria, 1918; the Netherlands, 1919; Hungary, 1920; the United Kingdom, partially in 1918 and fully in 1928). Moreover, many countries replaced the old majority rule with some form of proportional representation, considered to guarantee a more genuine reflection of the population in parliament. The most radical settlement was reached in the Netherlands in 1917, where the introduction of proportional representation went hand in hand with the creation of a single electoral district covering the whole country. In Germany, where universal male suffrage had existed since 1867, it was not only extended to include women and refined through the introduction of proportional representation, it also became a truly democratic instrument through the introduction of the principle of ministerial responsibility. The transformation of the Wilhelmine empire into the Weimar Republic therefore appeared as the most striking evidence for the triumph of parliamentary democracy.

And yet this victory of parliamentary democracy was only apparent, because the strident antiparliamentarism of the late nineteenth century was not laid to rest by World War I. On the contrary, the enhanced democratic consciousness of large groups of the population was directed against the elitism and the complacency of the parliamentary ruling classes. Moreover, the sudden extension of the suffrage—and therefore the arrival of large groups of inexperienced parliamentarians—seemed to strengthen the preexisting image of parliaments as impotent "debating clubs."

Only in Russia, a nonparliamentary, Soviet model of democratization was followed with success, but the attraction of this communist alternative was evident throughout the Continent. Nonetheless, the integration of most social democratic parties into the parliamentary system rendered the left-wing antiparliamentarism rather marginal. A much more palpable threat to parliamentary democracy came from right-wing alternatives, preaching a corporative organization of society, a strong leadership, and a homogenization of the nation. The first real implementation of this right-wing alternative to parliamentary democracy was the Fascist experience in Italy, where male general suffrage had been introduced in 1919. After the March on Rome in 1922, the Fascist leader Benito Mussolini gradually turned parliament into an impotent and undemocratic organism, before abolishing it altogether in 1938 and replacing it with an Assembly of Corporations.

Between 1920 and 1939, parliamentary institutions underwent a similar evolution in fourteen other states, mostly in central, eastern, and southern Europe—those parts of the Continent where parliamentary traditions had only recently been installed. In most of these countries, parliamentary democracy was not replaced by a modern, mass-based fascism, but rather by reactionary forms of authoritarianism. Strikingly, in some of these countries, the newly created parliamentary institutions deliberately marginalized themselves. This was the case, for example, in Hungary, where the first democratically elected unicameral parliament consisted mainly of counterrevolutionary forces. It immediately reinstalled the Hungarian monarchy and gave the temporary regent Miklos Horthy the right fully to overrule the parliament (1920). Under most of these authoritarian regimes, representative institutions were not abolished but were rather overshadowed by more powerful authoritarian and/or corporative structures. A striking example was offered by Romania, where in 1938 King Carol II reduced the parliamentary institution to a merely decorative body, deprived of all its legislative and controlling functions. A similar fate befell the Cortes of Spain after Francisco Franco came to power in 1938.

The most radical dismissal of parliamentary institutions occurred in Germany, where the National Socialist Party seized power in January 1933. Even if democratic appearances were upheld during this seizure of power, the parliamentary institutions were set aside from the very start of the Nazi regime. After the burning of the Reichstag—secretly inflicted by the Nazi leaders themselves—all non-Nazi members of parliament were expelled, and no new legislative elections were held in Germany until the end of the Nazi regime.

If the parliamentary institutions were fully maintained in the countries of northern and western Europe, they did not go unchallenged by the threat of antiparliamentary sentiments. During the whole of the 1930s, pleas for a strengthening of the executive power were uttered both by influential elites and by broad sections of public opinion. If structural measures in that direction were not taken in any of those countries, in practice governments did strengthen their position by exacting temporary unlimited powers from the parliament (as in Belgium in 1934) or resorting to a technocratic, nonpartisan style of reigning.

Parliaments in northern and western Europe lost power not only to executive bodies but also to newly created corporative organs, to which the socioeconomic organization of society was increasingly entrusted. The evolution in the direction of a planned economy, as propagated most of all by socialist leaders (Henri de Man in Belgium, Gunnar Myrdal and Per Albin Hansson in Sweden, Léon Blum in France), implied a structural weakening of parliamentary institutions.

As a response to these evolutions, parliaments in western and northern Europe tried to transform themselves in an attempt to enhance their political efficiency. Measures were taken to limit the length of parliamentary speeches, the parliamentary rules were made more severe (especially after some violent confrontations that occurred during the 1930s in several of these countries), and the plenary sessions lost their importance more and more to the work of specialized commissions, as they were created in several countries after World War I. Moreover, the existence of enduring parliamentary groups or factions, each of them representing political parties, became officially (though only gradually) recognized during this period, and members of parliament increasingly adhered to the directives of their parties. Through all these evolutions, parliaments became ever more removed from their nineteenth-century liberal roots, according to which they were deemed to be autonomous institutions in which independent representatives freely deliberated in order to promote the public good. If these measures were intended to adapt the parliamentary institutions to an age of mass democracy, they were not able to dispel the antiparliamentary sentiments within public opinion. On the contrary, the growing influence of political parties—an evolution that had already been well under way at the end of the nineteenth century—was one more reason to reject the parliamentary institutions.

1945–1975: A PARTIAL AND DECEPTIVE TRIUMPH

During World War II, parliamentary institutions were abolished in all countries occupied by the armies of the Axis Powers, so that they survived only in the United Kingdom, Ireland, Switzerland, Sweden, and Iceland (along with the powerless parliaments of authoritarian Spain and Portugal).

If parliamentarism in Western Europe crumbled therefore as a consequence of external military pressure, the relatively smooth way in which this happened betrayed the profound discredit into which parliamentary institutions had fallen. Even in countries with deep-rooted parliamentary traditions, broad segments of public opinion welcomed the disappearance of parliamentary institutions as an opportunity for national regeneration, while retaining a certain distance from Nazi Germany. This sentiment allowed for the success of Pétainism in France and of the Dutch Union (Nederlandse Unie) and Queen Wilhelmina in the Netherlands, as well as for the broad sympathy that King Leopold III of Belgium aroused in his conflict with the democratic government that had decided to continue the struggle at the side of the Allied Powers. Only during the second half of World War II—when the final defeat of the Axis Powers came in sight—did a positive appreciation of parliamentary institutions become generalized all over Europe.

After World War II, the prewar institutions were restored nearly intact in Western European countries, with their prewar political personnel. Attempts fundamentally to reform these institutions by strengthening the power of the executive and weakening that of the political parties (for example, the attempts by General de Gaulle in France, by Winston Churchill in the United Kingdom, and by the Nederlandse Volksbeweging in the Netherlands) failed. Only in West Germany, where the experience of the Weimar Republic served as a negative example, were constitutional innovations introduced in 1949 in order to prevent parliamentary instability from discrediting democratic institutions. Governments were to be overthrown only when alternative coalitions could be created (the constructive motion of distrust), and the position of the chancellor was strengthened. With the strong figure of Konrad Adenauer embodying this constitutional system, West Germany evolved rapidly into a stable democracy. The difference from the other main country with a fascist heritage, Italy, was important. According to the Italian constitution of 1948, presidents were elected by the parliament, which remained the most crucial political institution of the country. Italy would remain notorious for its political instability well into the 1990s. In the other Western European country long famous for its political instability, France, the role of parliament was firmly reduced in 1958, when de Gaulle succeeded in passing his new constitution, which gave birth to the Fifth Republic.

The antifascist consensus after World War II not only guaranteed the further existence of parliamentary institutions, it also contributed to their rapid democratization. Most notable in that regard was the extension of the vote to women in some countries with strong parliamentary traditions (France, 1944; Belgium, 1948). In the United Kingdom, moreover, the ancient principle of multiple voting for certain categories (graduates from Oxford and Cambridge, for example, got to vote for both a geographical representative and a representative of their university) was abolished in 1948. Another way of democratizing parliamentary institutions, the abolition of the aristocratic "First Chambers" (Senate, House of Lords), was advocated in many countries but carried through only in very few (Denmark, 1953; Greece since 1830). Bicameralism remained the norm.

In the countries that were liberated by the Soviet Union, the hope to found parliamentary institutions on a radically democratic basis was manifest in the years immediately after the war, when "people's democracies" were installed, in which communist leaders appeared to accept electoral procedures. From late 1946 onward, however, the totalitarian Stalinist model was imposed on these countries, leaving no room whatsoever for genuinely functioning representative institutions. In these Cold War circumstances, parliamentary institutions became more than ever symbols of the freedom of the capitalist world.

This symbolism notwithstanding, parliamentary democracy moved further away from its liberal bases in the decades after World War II. All over western and northern Europe, the prevention and management of social conflict were handed over to bilateral deliberations between the social partners (syndicates of laborers and of patrons), thus strengthening the corporative basis of the welfare state and reducing the role of parliaments. The grip of political parties and interest groups on parliamentary life grew stronger, turning liberal democracy into what has been called "consociational

democracy," where political conflicts are settled less through majority voting than through extraparliamentary deliberations between the political elites of different ideological groups. Moreover, the prestige of the national parliaments suffered from the loss of sovereignty of the nation-states, on the one hand to regional entities, on the other hand to new transnational constructions. These evolutions did not, however, fundamentally discredit the parliamentary model as such. In the construction of these subnational and transnational entities, the creation of directly elected representative bodies turned out to be crucial and highly symbolic moments. Significantly, these new parliaments (e.g., Europe, 1979; Catalonia, 1980; Flanders, Brussels, and Wallonia, 1994; Scotland, 1998) all opted from the start for universal suffrage and for unicameralism. But unlike the subnational parliaments, the European Parliament experienced difficulties from the start in legitimizing itself in the eyes of public opinion. This seems to indicate that parliaments can hardly fulfill their representational function in a context where no national sense of community exists.

1975–2004: A GENERAL BUT HALFHEARTED TRIUMPH

In spite of their structural loss of political influence, the symbolic power of parliaments remained important. That was proved in the 1970s, when the two remaining right-wing dictatorships of the prewar period were replaced with a constitutional monarchy (Spain) and a democratic republic (Portugal). In both of them, a freely elected parliament (bicameral in Spain, unicameral in Portugal) functioned as the central legislative and representative institution. In Greece, too, the end of the regime of the colonels in 1975 heralded the restart of parliamentary democracy, with a unicameral parliament as the cornerstone.

The end of the Cold War in the early 1990s seemed to seal the final triumph of parliamentary democracy. Indeed, in nearly all the formerly communist countries, regimes were installed that responded to the formal criteria of parliamentary democracies (moreover in Finland, the presidential "emergency system" was abandoned in 2000 in favor of a more truly parliamentary regime after the Soviet threat had disappeared). Their actual functioning, however, remained far removed from the nineteenth- and early-twentieth-century ideal of parliamentary democracy. This ideal appeared to be threatened less by the specter of dictatorship (although the presidential regimes in Russia and Belarus come very close to it) than by the lack of enthusiasm of the electorate. Indeed, time and again, the turnouts at elections in these new democracies proved to be disappointing. The repeated failure to reach the quorum necessary for valid presidential elections in Serbia between 2002 and 2004 can be seen as the most extreme illustration of this more general feature.

The Eastern European experience of the 1990s thus seems to reveal in a very significant and condensed way the central paradox that characterized the history of parliamentary democracy in Europe throughout the twentieth century. On the one hand, parliamentary institutions with a broad democratic basis have always been seen as necessary bulwarks against tyranny and (civil) war, which has rendered their existence ever more undisputed—even extreme right-wing parties at the end of the twentieth century spoke out in favor of parliamentary institutions. On the other hand, the consciousness that parliamentary institutions are unsatisfactory tools to cope with the complexity of modern society has only increased. The disbelief in the effectiveness of parliamentary politics, the continuing suspicion about the complacency of the political elites, and the growing autonomy of voters in respect to their parties have caused low turnouts in nearly all European countries. The responses to this evolution by the political elites have been various. Compulsory voting as a strategy to enhance citizens' participation in political life has been hotly debated but only rarely introduced. While Greece adopted this system in its 1975 constitution, the Netherlands and Austria repealed their long-standing tradition of compulsory voting. In Belgium and Luxembourg, where the vote was made compulsory in 1919, the system still exists but is severely under attack. According to its opponents, it does guarantee high turnouts at elections, but it does not necessarily imply political consciousness. On the contrary, these opponents consider compulsory voting to be one of the causes of the tremendous success of right-wing populism in the Dutch-speaking part of Belgium, because it would lend a political voice to antipolitical feelings.

The introduction of referendums as legislative tools is another strategy that has been advocated by many, mainly liberal, political actors and commentators who wanted to enhance citizens' involvement with politics. Apart from Switzerland, however, truly binding forms of referendum have nowhere been constitutionally consecrated so far. The resistance against it has been inspired by the fear that direct and binding consultation of the people would fundamentally undermine the foundations of representative democracy and would open the door for populist manipulation of the people. In this context, Charles de Gaulle's use of plebiscites—although itself not based on binding referendums—was often invoked as an excess to be avoided. In spite of these objections, however, the organization of nonbinding referendums at a national level became a relatively common practice in several countries. In the Netherlands, for example, the nonbinding, corrective referendum (a referendum on the validity of laws voted in parliament) became a legal tool of national politics in 2002. Even where popular consultations did not enter into the legal or constitutional framework, citizens gained ever more means to express their opinion on specific political topics through public opinion polls in the media. While engaging citizens' political awareness, this evolution further reduced the autonomy of national parliaments. Even less than at the beginning of the twentieth century are national parliaments in the early twenty-first century the center of gravity of political life in Europe. Insofar as European democracies still deserve the adjective *parliamentary*, it is mostly at a nominal and symbolic level.

See also **Citizenship; European Parliament.**

BIBLIOGRAPHY

Best, Heinrich, and Maurizio Cotta. *Parliamentary Representatives in Europe 1848–2000: Legislative Recruitment and Careers in Eleven European Countries.* Oxford, U.K., 2000.

Dunn, John, ed. *Democracy: The Unfinished Journey, 508 B.C. to A.D. 1993.* 2nd ed. Oxford, U.K., 1994.

Eley, Geoff. *Forging Democracy: The History of the Left in Europe, 1950–2000.* Oxford, U.K., 2002.

Held, David. *Models of Democracy.* 2nd ed. Cambridge, U.K., 1996.

Hobsbawm, Eric. *The Age of Extremes: A History of the World, 1914–1991.* New York, 1994.

Norton, Philip. *Parliaments in Contemporary Western Europe.* 3 vols. London, 1998–2002.

MARNIX BEYEN

PARTISAN WARFARE. *Partisan warfare* refers to organized military activities of groups not incorporated in regular armies; it is also called irregular warfare. The term is derived from the word *party* or *party follower,* and is used predominantly in central and eastern Europe. In southern Europe and overseas the term *guerrilla* is preferably applied, derived from "small war" in the Spanish language. Some historians distinguish between partisans as a more organized form of armed resistance with clear political goals, and guerrillas as predominantly individual fighters in small groups.

Partisan warfare was not a new phenomenon of the twentieth century. It came rather as a by-product of the establishment of standing armies during the eighteenth century. Partisan warfare turned up during the Silesian wars from 1740 and especially during the revolutionary American War of Independence. The most famous case remains the systematic guerrilla war against Napoleon's occupation of Spain from 1809.

In the twentieth century, partisan warfare evolved either in the context of modern regular warfare in general or as insurrectionary movements in peacetime. The fourth Hague convention on rules of land warfare (1907) provided a limited legal basis for partisan warfare, the right of citizens to form armed groups in case of warfare in their area. These should be protected by international law as long as they have a responsible leadership, are marked by specific signs or uniforms as combatants, and carry their weapons visibly in the open.

During World War I, partisan warfare appeared only on a small scale. Nevertheless German occupation troops in Belgium and northern France, influenced by the experience of the franc-tireur movement during the Franco-Prussian War of 1870, developed a specific guerrilla hysteria. For alleged acts of resistance they killed more than six thousand civilians in 1914–1915. In German-occupied Lithuania, organized groups attacked German institutions. Both the Triple Entente (France, Great Britain, and Russia) and the middle powers tried to initialize insurrections in the rear area of their enemy. The most famous cases are represented by the revolts organized by Lawrence of Arabia (Thomas Lawrence; 1888–1935) or the Easter Uprising (1916) in Ireland. The latter did not immediately lead to a partisan war, but the Irish war of independence (1919–1921) showed patterns of such. Albanians applied guerrilla tactics in their conflict with the Serbs in 1919.

The Russian civil war, which started in 1918, was both a regular and a partisan war. At least four groups can be identified: the communists, who propagated their fighting as a "people's war"; the "Whites," or counterrevolutionary forces; the nationalists, like the army of the Ukrainian directorate; and predominantly the "Greens," a loose conglomerate of peasant insurgencies especially in southern Ukraine, the lower Volga area, and western Siberia. Most famous was the partisan army of Nestor Makhno (1889–1934) in southeastern Ukraine, which over the years fought on different sides. The Russian civil war was characterized by utmost violence, killings of ideological enemies, excessive reprisals, and the murder of POWs (prisoners of war). It generated among the prevailing communist forces a tradition of partisan warfare, which was systematized by the military theoretician Mikhail Frunze (1885–1925) and laid down in the "Instruction on Partisan Warfare" from 1933. But during the 1930s, when the Soviet doctrine of the offensive took over, partisan warfare was no longer considered a model for the Red Army.

Between the world wars all over Europe a debate was going on about the war of the future. While some authors focused on the significance of strategic aerial bombing or fast offensives with tank forces, the majority of the military experts predicted a total war, involving the civilian population in warfare. Several authors considered the necessity of a "people's war" in the case of occupation of home territory. And even the British military, which generally did not fear occupation, developed future operational schemes in their 1939 "Principles of Guerilla Warfare."

Actually, partisan warfare did not play a significant role in armed conflict between 1921 and 1939 in Europe. The Spanish civil war (1936–1939), which at first glance showed all preconditions for a partisan war, was fought for the most part by regular armies. On the other hand, the European colonial powers were faced with insurrectionary warfare abroad—especially the Spanish and French armies in Morocco after the revolt in the Rif from 1921, Italy during the Second Sanusi War in Libya from 1923, and also the Netherlands to a certain extent during the communist uprising in the Netherlands East Indies (now Indonesia) from 1926/27.

WORLD WAR II

Twenty-first-century images of partisan warfare are to a large extent shaped by the experience of anti-Nazi, predominantly communist, armed resistance during the Second World War. But the historical picture is more diverse. The first armed attacks on German occupation power occurred in spring 1940, by remnant groups of the Polish army. But these remained isolated instances. The largest resistance group in Poland, the Polish Underground State—centered around the Home Army (Armia Krajowa) and supported by the government-in-exile—preferred a strategy of unarmed resistance until the time was ripe for general uprisings in the cities (Operation "Burza," or Storm), not for widespread partisan warfare. The second-largest movement, the right-wing National Armed Forces (Narodowe Sily Zbrojne) followed the same strategy. The small communist underground in Poland, which was established in 1942 and was largely controlled by the Soviet Union, at an early point set up the People's Guard (Gwardia Ludowa), which attacked not only German institutions but also other resistance groups. Only in 1944 did intensive partisan warfare start in Poland, predominantly during the uprisings in the cities, first in eastern Poland, from August 1944, culminating in the Warsaw uprising.

After the German attack on the Soviet Union, Stalin on 3 July 1941 called for the establishment of a partisan movement in the occupied Soviet territories, later even for a general people's war (*vsenarodnaya borba*). Preparations for partisan warfare had been stopped during the mid-1930s because it was not expected that Soviet territory would be a battlefield; so it took some

time to raise a considerable partisan force. Early groups in 1941 consisted of Red Army stragglers. The Soviet secret police, the NKVD (Narodnyi Komissariat Vnutrennikh Del, or People's Commissariat for the Interior), started to install larger partisan units, as the regional Communist Party organizations prepared for underground work on impending occupation. Attacks on occupation institutions started in August 1941 in Byelorussia, then extended to the Bryansk area and the eastern frontier of Latvia. The German occupation power—Wehrmacht (German army), SS (Schutzstaffel), and police—from the outset used extreme violence to terrorize the population and deter from partisan activity or support. The Germans succeeded in destroying partisan units in eastern Ukraine and on the Crimean Peninsula until the turn of the year 1941/42.

The year 1942 saw the establishment of an integrated partisan movement with a central staff. The movement constantly attacked rear lines and units of the army group center, especially in Byelorussia and central Russia, and from autumn 1942 also in northeastern Ukraine. German forces, in southern Russia together with Hungarian units, organized combined antipartisan raids, encircling partisan areas. These operations were accompanied by extreme violence against locals—whole villages were burned, and inhabitants murdered or deported. The antipartisan raids were only partly successful in the military sense. The Soviet partisan movement continued to expand; statistics on its personnel strength vary considerably, as German veterans and Soviet historians tended to inflate the numbers. Reasonable estimates are at 100,000 active partisans in 1942, and a maximum of 280,000 in summer of 1944. All in all, between 400,000 and 500,000 citizens supposedly fought against the occupation, not counting a "partisan reserve" supporting the armed fighters. In Byelorussia, the center of Soviet partisan warfare, Germans lost 6,000–7,000 dead, while they exterminated 300,000–350,000 inhabitants and partisans. The partisans themselves were only partly affected by German raids after 1941. It is estimated that only 20 percent of the partisans in Byelorussia died during the war. In sum, several tens of thousands of soldiers of the German army and their indigenous auxiliaries were killed by partisans, while almost half a million civilians died during antipartisan warfare.

The historical image of the Soviet partisan movement has changed considerably since the collapse of the Soviet Union. Its military effectiveness is considered as of limited value, restricted to the "rail war," the two major combined attacks against railways in the German rear during the summers of 1943 and 1944. The Soviet partisans were more effective in keeping up Stalinist rule in the areas under German occupation. Until the end of 1942, partisans killed thousands of real or alleged collaborators, often including their families. They stripped the local population of all agricultural goods and endangered them by provoking German reprisals. A large part of the Soviet partisan units were integrated into the Red Army or NKVD troops in 1944. The anticommunist groups in the territories annexed by the Soviet Union in 1939–1940 represent a specific case of partisans. Parts of these, in the Baltics and in western Ukraine, chose a tactical alliance with the German occupation in 1941–1942, but most of them turned against the Germans in 1943–1944 after realizing that the new occupier did not intend to create independent states in these areas. Especially in Latvia, Lithuania, and in western Ukraine, those groups fought both German occupation and the Soviet underground, despite some limited tactical negotiations with German authorities in 1944.

The archetype of partisan movements, as portrayed in public memory, is represented by the Yugoslav communist partisans under Josip Broz Tito (1892–1980). The Yugoslav communists after the German occupation in April 1941 did not take action before they were ordered to do so by the Komintern (Communist International) in July 1941. Already during autumn 1941 they were able to control a part of southern Serbia. Even earlier, remnants of the Yugoslav army took up resistance against the occupier. These scattered groups were loosely merged under the name Četniks, led by Drazha Mikhailovich (1893–1946). They pursued a greater Serbian policy and were supported by the government-in-exile and the British. German military and police reacted with unrestrained terror, they took reprisals for partisan attacks as a pretext to shoot all male Jews in Serbia. In 1942 partisan warfare moved to Bosnia, Croatia, and Slovenia,

thus more and more also directed against Italian and to some extent Hungarian occupation troops. Its expansion led to the enforcement of occupation military; in autumn 1943, 230,000 Germans and 220,000 Italians were present in Yugoslavia; the Germans lost approximately 14,000, the Italians 16,000 men in antipartisan warfare, most of them in 1943–1944. Tito's partisans, finally some four hundred thousand men and women, were able to liberate their country and Albania from occupation without the Red Army, albeit with Soviet support. At the same time the partisans took horrible revenge. They fought the Četniks, numbering between twelve and fifteen thousand, which had been abandoned by the British government in 1943, and in 1945 committed mass killings of real or alleged collaborators, including large parts of the German minority.

In western and southern Europe partisan movements developed at a later stage. In France the communist underground started to attack the German occupation from the summer of 1941 on. The French Resistance consisted of politically diverse groups. Nevertheless all armed organizations in February 1944 officially united as French Internal Forces (Forces Françaises de l'Interieur), which remained more in a waiting position. However, in 1943 an actual warfare of the so-called Maquis (French for *bushes*), rather independent groups, started to unfold in certain regions like the Jura, predominantly as a reaction to recruitment for forced labor, and intensifying after the allied landing in June 1944. The Germans resorted only at a comparatively late point to extreme violence. Killings of hostages intensified, as massacres occurred like the infamous crime at Oradour-sur-Glane. In Belgium similar armed resistance movements turned up, though much less active than the French one.

The Greek resistance, like the Yugoslav one, had to fight against three powers at the same time, German, Italian, and Bulgarian occupiers. The Communist National Liberation Front, ELAS (Ellinikos Laikos Apeleftherotikon Stratos), applied armed resistance from mid-1942 and controlled some of the mountain regions, while the anticommunist underground despite British support remained in a weaker position. From August 1943 on, Waffen-SS and Wehrmacht started an excessively violent retaliation policy in Greece, and then extended it

Female Četniks fighters with their male leader, Yugoslavia, May 1944. ©BETTMANN/CORBIS

to the regions that had been under Italian occupation. At least 25,000 civilians were killed, almost one million forcibly expelled from their homes.

The Italian resistance was activated by the German occupation of the country, which had been an Axis ally, in September 1943. As a result of widely differing political views, a common leadership for armed resistance was established only in June 1944, as the general command of the Corpo Volontari della Libertà (CVL; Voluntary Liberty Corps). Most of the resistance was active in central and northern Italy, especially in the mountain regions. Wehrmacht and Waffen-SS, especially in spring and summer 1944 reacted with massacres against the civil population, resulting in the murder of around ten thousand persons.

A very late case of armed resistance turned up in the Axis state of Slovakia, during the Slovak Uprising from August 1944, as German troops occupied the country. Parts of the former Slovak army now fought against the German occupiers, in cooperation with approximately 2,500 partisans. Until the liberation of the country almost 3,000 civilians were killed and another 30,000 deported to German camps.

FEATURES OF PARTISAN WARFARE

Partisan warfare during the Second World War showed some common features that were unique for this period: there were armed resistance groups all over Axis-occupied Europe. On the other hand, these resisters faced not only German repression, but also violence by Italian, Hungarian, Romanian, Bulgarian and, to a certain extent, Slovakian troops and police units. It goes without saying that the German Reich was primarily responsible for the crimes committed during antipartisan warfare. Only Germany in 1942–1943 installed a central institution for combating partisans, the Chef der Bandenkampfverbände (Chief of Antibanditry Units) of the SS, who directed operations in most Eastern European areas under civil occupation. The actual antipartisan warfare was taken over by Wehrmacht, especially security troops; by Waffen-SS; and by police units. All of them relied on hundreds of thousands of indigenous auxiliaries, who out of political beliefs, material incentives, or under coercion participated in the antipartisan actions.

In most countries a broad variety of political direction existed among the underground movement, only temporarily united against the Axis aggressors. In several cases, the underground units were not only fighting against occupiers but also among each other. The Allies provided a network for most of the major groups, initially the British Special Operations Executive, and during the second half of the war also the American Office of Strategic Services. The communist partisan warfare all over Europe was more and more directed by the Komintern in Moscow and after its dissolution in 1943 by other organs of the Soviet state, especially the Communist Party and the Secret Police NKVD. All of the Allies organized supply, trained personnel, and in many cases even parachuted personnel (mostly natives in exile) into the occupied countries. Several of the underground movements at the end of the war merged with regular armies (in Eastern Europe the newly created Soviet-based armies), and they provided a large part of the postwar elites.

Not only anti-Nazi and antifascist movements developed partisan organizations, even in Germany there was a long debate on the necessity of an irregular Volkskrieg (People's War) since the 1920s. Facing defeat in 1944, German SS and military started to issue plans for an underground warfare after allied advance, especially in Eastern Europe. The SS managed to build up small groups of foreign SS members or locals, especially in Latvia. Inside the Reich, plans for an underground army "Wehrwolf" (werewolves) under SS leadership were set up. Despite some spectacular actions under Allied occupation, only some small groups continued the fight, an overall organization never came into being.

EASTERN EUROPE FROM 1944

Partisan warfare in Europe was not over in 1945, but continued in Eastern Europe until the late 1940s. Noncommunist underground movements now fought against new Soviet occupations and indigenous communist attempts to take over the postwar states. The two main forces in the western Soviet Union were the so-called Forest Brothers in Estonia, Latvia, and Lithuania, and the Ukrainian Insurgent Army (UPA) in western Ukraine. They led a desperate war against internal troops of the NKVD (later MVD, Ministry of Interior). The latter already in 1940–1941 had established a department, from 1944 the Main Administration for the Combat against Banditism (Glavnoe Upravlenie po Borbe s Banditizmom, or GUBB). Soviet warfare against the anticommunist underground was especially ruthless and resulted in the killing of hundreds of thousands. According to Soviet statistics, until 1946, 70,000 partisans were killed and another 210,000 captured. In western Ukraine alone, until the early 1950s more than 150,000 civilians were murdered, not counting the higher figure of those Ukrainians deported from partisan areas.

A similar pattern is visible in postwar Poland, where parts of the Home Army continued to fight under the name Freedom and Independence (Wolność i Niepodległość, WiN), together with other noncommunist units. In Poland, NKVD troops together with the Polish new army and police tried to repress the underground, and killed tens of thousands. The Ukrainian minority in southeastern Poland in 1947 during "Vistula Action" was deported completely to western territories in order to dislocate them from the UPA. Minor armed anticommunist groups like the so-called Crusaders (Krizhari) were active in Yugoslavia. In Greece, the situation was almost the opposite. The communist ELAS continued its partisan activity, from 1946 under the name Democratic Army of Greece (Demokratikos Stratos Elados, or DDE), in order to install a communist government. It took the Greek National Army, with major assistance of the British, until October 1949 to overwhelm the communist guerrillas.

Most of the anticommunist underground groups in Eastern Europe were supported by the Western powers, especially by British intelligence.

Nevertheless, through espionage and infiltration the Soviet secret police was able to destroy them almost completely until the late 1940s. Remnants of these units, especially in the Baltics, fought against communist power until the early 1950s.

COLONIES

After 1947 Europe's involvement in partisan warfare again shifted to the colonies, which were seeking independence, often continuing the war that they had fought against the Axis powers until 1945. Now the Western Europeans were themselves fighting an antiguerrilla war. The British army fought the uprising of the Malayan Communist Party from 1948 until 1960, an episode called the Malayan Emergency. In East Africa they countered the Mau Mau uprising during the Kenyan Emergency from 1952 until 1960. Much more violent was the guerrilla war of the Netherlands against the Communist Party in Indonesia (1947–1948), at that time the Netherlands East Indies. France led the most intense guerrilla wars. Both the Indochina War of 1946–1954 and the Algerian War of 1954–1962 to a large extent were led as antiguerrilla campaigns, the latter with utmost violence. As the last colonial power, Portugal was also faced with uprisings, starting in Angola 1961.

The Geneva convention on POWs from 1949 envisaged a certain legal protection for irregular warfare, especially its amendment in 1977. After the 1960s, partisan or guerrilla warfare, unlike in Africa, Asia, and South America, ceased to play an important role in European military history. During the 1970s, some terrorist movements in Germany and Italy considered themselves "urban guerrillas," but showed completely different patterns. Also other ethnic terrorist groups claimed to fight for political aims and were responsible for assassinations, but did not resemble guerrilla movements. During the Cold War, East and West worked out insurgency plans in case of attack by the opponent. The North Atlantic Treaty Organization (NATO) secretly prepared the Gladio force, intended to continue resistance under a presumed Soviet occupation. But these projects became obsolete as communist regimes fell across Eastern Europe and the Soviet Union in the period from 1989 to 1991.

The Yugoslav Wars of 1991–1995 were accompanied by the return of partisan patterns. Militias and irregular forces played an important role during the conflict. Finally, partisan tactics have been applied by ethnic groups who sought to gain independence from the Russian Federation, as is visible in the Chechnyan Wars (1994–1996, and since 1999).

PRECONDITIONS OF PARTISAN WARFARE

Partisan warfare by and large originates in the establishment of regular armies and in the militarization of society. Partisan groups often consist of men (or women) who were not recruited, deserters, or soldiers who have lost contact with their armies. Most partisans are motivated either by political ideologies or suppressive acts of occupiers. Additionally partisans tend to recruit more personnel by coercion. Most partisan groups have a weaker hierarchy than regular forces, though at times more brutal discipline.

Partisan warfare requires certain strategies of legitimization for an activity, which is generally seen as irregular. During war the central legitimization is the combat against foreign occupiers and oppressors. The communist underground during the Second World War was also driven by ideological motives, especially the establishment of a new order and the dominance of the Soviet Union. In peacetimes national or ethnic independence seems to be the prevalent driving motive.

These legitimization strategies are not only important for the partisan group identity and the motivation to fight, but also in relationship to the population. Partisans are highly dependent on the local population, especially concerning personnel recruitment, logistical support, and communication. On the other hand, partisans not only control the locals but also often are able to establish a complete rule, especially in remote areas.

The natural environment is another precondition for partisan warfare. Since partisans often lack military strength, they are obliged to restrict their activities to areas, like forests or mountains, that are difficult to control using regular forces. That is one of the reasons why, for example, it was not possible to establish a partisan movement in most of Ukraine during the German occupation.

French resistance fighters known as Maquis march in the mountains in France, September 1944.
©Hulton-Deutsch Collection/Corbis

A general problem of partisan warfare is the lack of material. A majority of partisan groups have problems acquiring uniforms or even appropriate shoes for their members. Their armory consists primarily of low-tech weapons. Heavy weapons, which usually are not suitable for irregular warfare, are almost absent. Partisan groups either take over weapons of armies, or depend on foreign supply.

On the other hand, counterinsurgency warfare is much better equipped, but the military means have a limited effect, since partisans generally try to avoid direct military confrontation and restrict themselves to isolated attacks on infrastructure and enemy personnel. As a consequence, antipartisan warfare alters from general military tactics, acting either in small groups (sometimes disguised as partisans) or combing through areas with regular troops. Antipartisan warfare is dependent on disconnecting the local population from the partisans,

either by winning the "battle for the hearts and minds" by supporting the locals, or by delegitimizing the partisans, often officially called "bandits," by deterring the population through violence or by deporting or even exterminating the population. The latter was applied especially by the German occupation in the Soviet Union, Yugoslavia, and Poland, and to a certain extent by Soviet authorities in the annexed territories. In most cases antipartisan warfare is led in cooperation with indigenous auxiliaries, sometimes even by creating "defense villages."

Partisan warfare played an eminent role in war memory from the early 1950s. While West Germany and Austria only gradually recognized their resistance against the Nazi regime, most other countries based part of their identity on their history of armed resistance against the Axis occupiers. In Germany, however, the Eastern European partisans were demonized and held exclusively responsible for the radicalization of the occupation during the war. Only during the 1980s and 1990s did the perception shift. In the early twenty-first century it is obvious that the partisan movements represented only minor parts of the population, and that they had fought the war often with extreme violence. While the communist partisans now are considered as agents of Soviet rule or takeover, anticommunist armed resistance often serves as tradition for the new democracies in Eastern Europe. But the issue is still under debate.

CONCLUSION

Modern partisan warfare in Europe was discussed and planned already after the First World War, but had its high time between 1941 and 1948, with the spread of national socialist occupation and Soviet expansion thereafter. During the interwar period and after 1947–1948 antiguerrilla warfare in the colonies was high on the agenda until the early 1960s. Since then, partisan warfare lost its significance for European history, but remained important for the perception of the wartime period. After a rather heroic image during the first postwar decades, since 1990 a more sober picture has evolved, deconstructing the political myths surrounding the subject, showing the gruesome reality of partisan warfare and focusing on its victims.

See also **Colonialism; Occupation, Military; Warfare.**

BIBLIOGRAPHY

Asprey, Robert B. *War in the Shadows: The Guerrilla in History.* Rev. ed. New York, 1994.

Beckett, Ian F. W. *Encyclopedia of Guerrilla Warfare.* Santa Barbara, Calif, c. 1999.

———. *Modern Insurgencies and Counter-Insurgencies: Guerrillas and Their Opponents since 1750.* London, 2001.

Joes, Anthony James. *Guerrilla Warfare: A Historical, Biographical, and Bibliographical Sourcebook.* Westport, Conn., 1996.

Haestrup, Jørgen. *European Resistance Movements, 1939–1945: A Complete History.* Westport, Conn., 1981.

Laqueur, Walter. *Guerrilla Warfare: A Historical and Critical Study.* New ed. New Brunswick, N.J., 1997.

DIETER POHL

PASOLINI, PIER PAOLO (1922–1975), Italian writer and filmmaker.

Pier Paolo Pasolini was born in 1922 in Bologna, Italy. His father was a military officer allied to the Fascist government, so the family moved around Italy as Pasolini's father transferred from post to post. His mother was trained as a schoolteacher and passed on her love of books to her son. Pasolini remained devoted to her throughout his life. Pasolini was an intense artist from an early age, moving easily between writing, drawing, painting, and ultimately filmmaking. He was a published poet at nineteen (1942): *The Ashes of Gramsci* (1957) remains his most famous collection of poetry. *Boys of Life,* the first of several novels that depict the *borgate* (Roman slum neighborhoods) in which he lived at the time, was published in 1955.

Pasolini's first feature-length film, *Accatone* (1961), also took the youth of the *borgate* as its subject. Pasolini's early films are in black and white and use nonprofessional actors on location, thus adhering in some respects to the aesthetic of his neorealist forebears. Yet his use of classical music as an insistent presence on the sound track (e.g., when Bach suffuses a violent street fight) belies a highly complex, constructed quality that becomes more evident in later films. In *Mamma Roma* (1962), Pasolini pairs young nonprofessional actors with one of Italy's most celebrated actresses, Anna Magnani (1908–1973), who plays the mother of a doomed youth, Ettore. In the closing sequence, the camera films Ettore from the bottom of his feet as he lies dead on a bare slab, a clear reference to Andrea Mantegna's famous painting *Dead Christ* (c. 1466). Pasolini uses a flat pictorial style that would come to define his filmmaking, enhancing the viewer's sense that he is writing or painting on the film frame.

Pasolini's evocation of profane Christ figures throughout his early work—from Accatone and Ettore to the gluttonous actor who dies of indigestion while playing Christ in *RoGoPaG* (1963)—incited outrage on the part of authorities. He was briefly jailed in 1963 because his contribution to *RoGoPaG,* "La Ricotta," was deemed blasphemous. Concurrent with his filmmaking, Pasolini continued his literary and artistic pursuits, writing plays, doing translations, and producing social, literary, and

The Last Supper scene from Pier Paolo Pasolini's *Gospel according to St. Matthew*, 1964. Arco/Lux/The Kobal Collection

cinematic criticism. His regular articles in the Italian newspaper *Corriere della sera* and in the French *Le monde* made him one of the most influential intellectuals in Europe. In the mid-1960s, Pasolini described himself as a "mythic realist" and his cinematic process a "cinema of poetry": that is, he called for filmmaking that literally wrote with images of reality (in lieu of a more naturalistic "unfolding" of reality before a camera lens).

Pasolini made his meditation on Christ figures even more explicit in *The Gospel according to St. Matthew* (1964). He began using a 300-mm lens, further flattening the visual plane, in an effort to reproduce Renaissance perspective as it was developed in painting. Pasolini's Matthew is a political and religious radical, more Marxist than Christian ideologically, and yet the film was praised by

Catholic groups as a brilliantly humanizing depiction of the apostle. *Hawks and Sparrows* (1966; starring Totò, Italy's equivalent of Charlie Chaplin) also allegorizes the intersection between Marxism and Christianity, but with a much harder satirical edge.

By 1967 Pasolini had turned to a much more abstract and conceptual filmmaking. This phase comprises two adaptations from Greek mythology: *Oedipus Rex* (1967) and *Medea* (1969), starring the opera singer Maria Callas (1925–1977) in the title role. With *Teorema* (1968; Theorem), and *Pigpen* (1969), Pasolini pursued a broader inquiry into preindustrial mythology, militating against its loss in an increasingly commodified Western culture.

In his three subsequent films, Pasolini attempted to reach a wider, less strictly intellectual audience. Known as the *Trilogy of Life,* they are adaptations of popular canonical works of literature: *The Decameron* (1971), *The Canterbury Tales* (1972), and *Arabian Nights* (1974). But in place of a more conventional retelling, this trilogy is very focused on the eroticized body—the mud, the messiness of life. Pasolini eventually renounced all three films, having found his experiment to reach "the people" a failure, but at the same time said that he considered this trilogy the most ideological of all his films for its expression of the "precommercial" human body, a body free of the repressive forces of late capitalism.

His final film, *Salò, or The 120 Days of Sodom* (1976), constitutes a violent rejection of the *Trilogy of Life:* the film is a nightmarish story set in the northern Italian state of Salò in 1944, in which beautiful young adolescents are taken to a palace by Nazis and forced to undergo various humiliations, culminating in their execution. These shocking scenes are intertwined with stories by authors ranging from Dante to the Marquis de Sade. Because Pasolini was murdered just after finishing *Salò*, the world never had a chance to find out what—if anything—could follow such an inferno.

See also **Cinema; Italy.**

BIBLIOGRAPHY

Baranski, Zygmunt G., ed. *Pasolini Old and New: Surveys and Studies.* Dublin, 1999.

Pasolini, Pier Paolo. *A Violent Life.* Translated by William Weaver. Manchester, 1996. Paperback edition of Pasolini's second novel, originally published in 1958.

Rohdie, Sam. *The Passion of Pier Paolo Pasolini.* Bloomington, Ind., 1995.

Schwartz, Barth David. *Pasolini Requiem.* New York, 1992. Detailed biography.

Steimatsky, Noa. "Pasolini on *Terra Sancta*: Towards a Theology of Film." *Yale Journal of Criticism* 11, no. 1 (spring 1998): 239–258.

ANNE M. KERN

PASTERNAK, BORIS (1890–1960), Russian poet and writer.

Boris Pasternak was born in Moscow to a highly educated family, a son of the famous Jewish painter and professor Leonid Pasternak.

He studied music and law, but graduated from Moscow University with a degree in philosophy (1913). In 1912 he studied at Marburg University in Germany, and his exposure to Europe during this time significantly influenced him. Pasternak wrote his first poems in 1909–1913, participated in the literary avant-garde, and began publishing in 1913. In 1914 his first volume of poetry, *Twin in the Stormclouds,* came out. He also met with Vladimir Mayakovsky (1893–1930), whose urban and futurist poetry had a great impact on him. In late 1916 Pasternak published his second book of poems, *Over the Barriers.*

Initially sympathetic to the revolution, Pasternak welcomed the fall of the tsarist regime in 1917, and perhaps not accidentally, one of his most famous books of poetry, *My Sister Life* (published in 1922), bore the subtitle "Summer of the Year 1917," indicating when most of its poems were written. But the civil war with its hardships and atrocities drove Pasternak to an increasingly critical assessment of the revolution, as did the continuing reprisals and the growing Bolshevik pressure on writers and poets to glorify the new order. Despite his disenchantment, Pasternak stayed in Soviet Russia, even as his parents emigrated.

During the 1920s, he wrote several epic poems on revolutionary themes, such as *Lieutenant Schmidt* (1926) and *The Year Nineteen Five* (1927). In the Soviet press, he was often criticized for his intellectualism, "decadence," and pessimism, and was habitually regarded with suspicion. Yet, unlike many other turn-of-the-twentieth-century poets, Pasternak was allowed a certain autonomy in his work, retaining his predilection for lyric poetry and generally staying away from socialist realism. In 1928 he published *High Malady;* in 1931 his novel in verse, *Spektorsky,* appeared; and in the same year his autobiography, *Safe Conduct,* came out (it was banned shortly thereafter).

Pasternak was involved in the formation of the Union of Soviet Writers and spoke at its first congress in 1934. Appalled by the Great Terror of 1937–1938, he nonetheless showed courage, refusing to sign a writers' petition for the execution of Marshal Mikhail Tukhachevsky (1893–1937). Still, from 1936 on he spent ever more time in his country house near Moscow. After the Terror, he increasingly retreated from writing poetry and concentrated on translations, notably of Shakespeare, a work he performed brilliantly.

During World War II, Pasternak published two books of poetry, *On Early Trains* (1943) and *Earth's Vastness* (1945), which came closer to socialist realism than his other work. But it was after the war that he set upon what he regarded as his life's work—*Doctor Zhivago*. Written between 1945 and 1955, the novel represented a major reassessment of Russia's historical experience of the revolution and civil war. Having tried and failed to publish the novel in the Soviet Union, in 1956 Pasternak handed the manuscript over to the Italian publisher Giangiacomo Feltrinelli, who published the book in Italy in 1957. *Doctor Zhivago* immediately became a tremendous success in the West; numerous editions were published in the late 1950s alone.

In 1958 Pasternak was awarded the Nobel Prize in literature, not just for the novel but for his cumulative literary achievement. The prize provoked a fury among the Soviet leadership, both because Pasternak did not have official permission to publish in the West and because many viewed his novel as an attack on the revolution. Remarkably, when excerpts from *Doctor Zhivago* were published in the Soviet press in 1958, many readers, especially the elderly, reacted in the same negative way, apparently without orchestration. With its unprecedented freedom of humanistic and historical thought, *Doctor Zhivago* was duly appreciated in Russia only decades later (it was published there in 1988).

The target of a furious media campaign and pressure, Pasternak had to renounce the Nobel Prize. His health declined, and on 30 May 1960 he died at his home. Pasternak's funeral was attended by several thousand people, and students read his poems at his gravestone till sunset.

One of the most prominent literary figures in twentieth-century Russia, Boris Pasternak was also one of the few surviving poets of his generation who not only went together with the country through the cataclysms of revolution, war, and terror but also managed to retain an independence of mind, a certain dignity and aloofness from officialdom, and considerable freedom in writing and

in life. For many young poets of the post-Stalin decades, he and his verses represented a living link between the present and Russia's prerevolutionary literary culture, which increasingly many came to honor during the late Soviet years. In the twenty-first century Pasternak is admired and read in his own country, where he has long become a cultural legend.

See also **Russia; Samizdat; Solzhenitsyn, Alexander; Soviet Union.**

BIBLIOGRAPHY

Primary Sources

Afiani, V. Iu., and N. G. Tomilina, eds. *A za mnoiu shum pogoni: Boris Pasternak i vlast': Dokumenty 1956–1972.* Moscow, 2001.

Secondary Sources

Barnes, Christopher. *Boris Pasternak: A Literary Biography.* 2 vols. Cambridge, U.K., 1989–1998.

Fleishman, Lazar. *Boris Pasternak: The Poet and His Politics.* Cambridge, Mass., 1990.

Mallac, Guy de. *Boris Pasternak, His Life and Art.* Norman, Okla., 1981.

Pasternak, Evgeny. *Boris Pasternak: The Tragic Years, 1930–60.* Translated by Michael Duncan. Poetry of Boris Pasternak translated by Ann Pasternak Slater and Craig Raine. London, 1990.

DENIS KOZLOV

PAUL VI (1897–1978), pope from 1963 to 1978.

Giovanni Battista Montini, cardinal of Milan, was elected pope on 21 June 1963 in the midst of the uncompleted Second Vatican Council (Vatican II) called by his predecessor, John XXIII. Taking the name Paul VI, the new pope faced a growing divide in the council deliberations between conservative and liberal prelates. His approach to the remaining two council sessions was to support the progressive majority while at the same time ensuring that the rights of the conservative minority were respected. Thus Paul championed collegiality and established the synod of bishops; he mediated the issue of religious liberty in favor of the progressives and launched the practical methods to realize John XXIII's ecumenical dream. At the same time, he angered liberals by his unwavering support for the primacy of the pope and clerical celibacy, his condemnation of birth control, and his unilateral establishment of Mary as "Mother of the Church."

In certain ways Paul's entire papacy was a grand and precarious effort to lead the church in a time of great change and turmoil without permanently alienating either conservative or liberal Catholics. His five encyclicals echoed this approach, ranging from the call for renewal and dialogue within the church (*Ecclesiam suam,* 1964) to his reinforcement of traditional teachings on the Eucharist (*Mysterium fidei,* 1965) and celibacy (*Sacerdotalis caelibatus,* 1967). In *Populorum progressio* (1967), Paul focused on human development and criticized the divide between the rich and poor nations. He pointed out the shortcomings of the free market as a cure for poverty and called for "global solidarity." In *Humanae vitae* (1968), the pope's eloquent defense of human life was reduced by the world's media into a simplistic condemnation of artificial birth control. The negative reaction that it evoked among the liberal and secular press so stunned the pope that he never again, in the ten remaining years of his papacy, issued another encyclical.

Nonetheless, Paul never wavered in his support for "the preferential option for the poor" reflected in his worldview and social policy. His historic speech at the United Nations on 4 October 1965 condemned war and called upon cooperation between communist and capitalist nations. His *Ostpolitik* initiative toward Eastern Europe's communist bloc sought better diplomatic relations in order to improve the lot of Catholics in these countries. Ahead of his time, he was convinced that communist domination of Europe was a passing phenomenon and that the church must prepare for the future of free, democratic Eastern European states. At the time, however, conservatives saw his policy as a "sell out" to communist tyrants. The pope used the concessions that *Ostpolitik* brought him from Eastern bloc nations to appoint like-minded bishops, such as Karol Wojtyla (the future Pope John Paul II), who would eventually play a significant role in the fall of communism in Europe.

The pope's travels often took him to the Third World, where his focus on justice and peace and social reform was generally well received. In 1968 Paul's appearance in Medellín, Colombia, at the Latin American bishops' conference reinforced the church's option for the poor. Paul's support and elevation of key "liberation theology" bishops, such as Helder Câmara, Aloísio Lorscheider, and Paolo Evaristo Arns, gave impetus to a "third way" of development in Latin America, led by the church, between communism and capitalism, much criticized by conservative elements of society. His launching of the World Peace Day project on 1 January 1968, with the support of the United Nations, and his brokering of the Vietnam peace talks underscored his sustained and vocal opposition to war.

In the United States and Europe, Paul filled episcopal vacancies with pastoral priests who would support the implementation of the council's decrees. He also sought to "internationalize" the curia and the College of Cardinals, putting a mandatory retirement age on cardinals eligible to vote in a papal election. But his message of peace and social justice was often overwhelmed in the First World by controversies surrounding the flight from religious life, the new Mass, women in the church, and birth control.

In the latter years of Montini's papacy, Catholicism seemed wracked by fissures between right and left, conservative and liberal. Paul, however, stayed the course that he chose when he ascended the papal throne in 1963. He never wavered in implementing the social, theological, and liturgical reforms of Vatican II, but he never went beyond them either. In effect, he supported the progressive majority within Catholicism and ensured the rights of the conservative minority. In this, he was truly Catholicism's bridge to the modern world.

See also **Catholicism; Vatican II.**

BIBLIOGRAPHY

Primary Sources

John XXIII, Pope. *Giovanni e Paolo, due papi: Saggio di corrispondenza (1925–1962).* Edited by Loris Capovilla. Brescia, Italy, 1983.

Montini, Giovanni Battista. *Discorsi e scritti sul Concilio (1959–1963).* Brescia and Rome, 1983.

Secondary Sources

Hebblethwaite, Peter. *Paul VI: The First Modern Pope.* New York, 1993.

O'Reilly, Sean, ed. *Our Name Is Peter: An Anthology of Key Teachings of Pope Paul VI.* Chicago, 1977.

RICHARD J. WOLFF

PAVELIĆ, ANTE (1889–1959), Croatian politician and dictator.

The Croatian politician Ante Pavelić was born on 14 July 1889 in Bradina, Bosnia-Herzegovina, and died in 1959 in Madrid, Spain. Pavelić was the son of a railroad foreman of Croatian extraction who worked in Bosnia. In 1910, as a student in the Croatian capital of Zagreb, Pavelić joined the Croat Party of Rights, which invoked the model of Ante Starčević (1823–1896), "Father of the Croat Fatherland," in calling for a Croatian state and struggling against both Austrian domination and the Yugoslav project. He was briefly detained by the Austrians in 1912.

Yugoslavia was created in 1918. As a lawyer in Zagreb, Pavelić actively opposed the new state, which was dominated by Serbs. Stjepan Radić's (1871–1928) Croat Peasant Party, supported by the vast majority of Croat voters, defended the same cause but was committed to peaceful methods and ready to make compromises. Pavelić adopted a far more radical posture. In 1927 he became a member of the Yugoslavian parliament representing Zagreb. At this time he established contacts with Fascist Italy and, as a lawyer, defended terrorists of the Internal Macedonian Revolutionary Organization, who had mounted violent attacks against Serbian rule in Macedonia.

After the assassination of Radić and two other Croatian deputies on the floor of the Yugoslavian parliament in Belgrade and the institution on 6 January 1919 of "royal dictatorship" under Alexander Karadjordjević (r. 1921–1929 and 1929–1934), Pavelić abandoned legal political activity and took refuge abroad, first in Austria and then in Italy, where he settled. He received support from the Italian and Hungarian governments. He declared that he intended to fight against the Yugoslavian regime "by all possible means" and publicly espoused fascism. He created the Ustaše ("insurgent") movement, committed to clandestine terrorist struggle. Ustaše militants, who numbered no more a few hundred, received military training in camps in Italy and Hungary. In 1934 the Ustaše movement, on Pavelić's orders, organized the assassination in Marseille of King Alexander; the act was carried out by a Macedonian terrorist supported by a group of Croatians. Pavelić was condemned to death in absentia by a French court, but Mussolini refused to extradite him, merely imprisoning him for two years and placing constraints on Ustaše activity.

When the Germans invaded Yugoslavia on 6 April 1941 they would have preferred to entrust power in Croatia to the very popular Vladko Macek (1879–1964), head of the Croatian Peasant Party, but he declined. As early as 10 April 1941, the very day that the German forces entered Zagreb, the Ustaše leader Slavko Kvaternik (1878–1947) announced the creation of an Independent State of Croatia (NDH), to be led by a *poglavnik* or führer, namely Pavelić, who returned immediately from exile with his small group of expatriates.

The new state was independent in name only. It was subordinate from the outset to the German—and until 1943 the Italian—occupiers. Pavelić was thus obliged to cede parts of Dalmatia to Italy and he submitted completely to the wishes of Germany, sending Croatian troops to fight on the Russian front.

His domestic policies were a textbook application of fascist principles. Unbridled power was exercised by a single leader, Pavelić himself, and his orders were executed by a single party, the Ustaše movement, whose membership nevertheless remained quite small. The state was supposed to belong to the Croat nation, which, according to the official doctrine, was confined to Catholics and Muslims. All other groups—Orthodox Serbs, Jews, Gypsies—were massacred on a vast scale from the very first days of the new regime. The Serbs, who represented 30 percent of the population, had no choice but to rebel by joining one of the two movements of armed resistance: either the Četniks (Serbian nationalists) or the Partisans (communists).

The Croatian population overall at first welcomed the creation of an independent state as a liberation. But before long total subjection to the Germans—the arbitrariness of the regime, with its racist policies, arrests, and massacres—combined to create an ever-more-powerful opposition. More and more Croats joined the partisans, who eventually came to control a large portion of Croatia.

In 1944, anticipating the German defeat, two Croatian ministers, Mladen Lorković and Ante Vokić, wanted to approach the Western Allies and propose that Croatia change sides. When they brought this idea up with Pavelić, however, he had them arrested and later executed.

In May 1945, with the partisans at the gates of Zagreb, Pavelić organized the evacuation of thousands of Croatians, both soldiers and civilians, to Austria, where they could surrender to the British. In the event, the British handed them over to the partisans, who killed a great number of them. Pavelić himself separated from the group and managed to hide in Austria.

With the assistance of underground networks of Catholic priests, he later reached Italy and then Argentina. There he sought to organize the Croatian émigrés on a political basis. He even negotiated in 1954 with a former Yugoslavian prime minister, the Serb Milan Stojadinović (1888–1961), about how to set up a united exile front against Josip Broz Tito (1892–1980) that would bring together Serbs and Croats, though no agreement could be reached.

In 1957, in Buenos Aires, Pavelić was wounded in an assassination attempt. He left Argentina for Chile, and later moved to Spain, where he died as a result of his wounds in 1959.

See also **Bosnia-Herzegovina; Croatia; Tito (Josip Broz); World War I; World War II; Yugoslavia.**

BIBLIOGRAPHY

Hory, Ladislaus, and Martin Broszat. *Der kroatische Ustascha-Staat 1941–45.* Stuttgart, 1964. Emphasizes foreign policies and the persecution of minorities.

Tanner, Marcus. *Croatia: A Nation Forged in War.* New Haven, Conn., and London, 1997. Includes an excellent chapter on the Ustaše regime.

Tomasevich, Jozo. *War and Revolution in Yugoslavia, 1941–1945: Occupation and Collaboration.* Stanford, Calif., 2001. The most thoroughgoing and up-to-date study of Croatia in World War II.

PAUL GARDE

PEACE MOVEMENTS. *See* **Pacifism.**

PENICILLIN. In the second half of the twentieth century penicillin was the best known of a new class of drugs—antibiotics—that revolutionized the treatment of communicable diseases and allowed doctors to rapidly cure a large number of bacterial infections. Beyond its role as a specific therapy, penicillin, often referred to as the "Wonder Drug," initiated a transformation in the pharmaceutical industry and was the principal symbol of medical progress for a generation.

The word *penicillin* was coined by the Scots scientist Alexander Fleming (1881–1955) in 1929 for the substance produced by the mold *Penicillium* that he found to be active against certain disease-causing bacteria. Fleming, like other before him, notably C. G. Paine (1905–?) in Sheffield, England, tried to use the substance therapeutically but had little success and did not pursue the possibility. However, its potential was explored again in the late 1930s by Howard Florey (1898–1968) and Ernst Chain (1906–1979) at Oxford, who were researching naturally occurring antibacterial substances. With the help of Norman Heatley (1911–2004), they improved the purity and hence the activity of extracts from the mold. Penicillin was first tested successfully on mice in the May 1940.

The Oxford group treated their first patient on 12 February 1941, a policeman who was close to death due to an infection. His condition improved while he was being administered penicillin, but he died when supplies ran out. However, other successful cases followed and from the summer of 1941 the Oxford group began working with British companies to develop large-scale production. At this point in World War II, with British industry stretched and suffering regular bombing

Alexander Fleming photographed in his laboratory at St. Mary's Hospital in London c. 1929. ©BETTMANN/CORBIS

raids, such opportunities were limited, so Florey approached the United States government for assistance in production. He was referred to the U.S. Department of Agriculture and in turn to the Northern Regional Research Laboratory at Peoria, Illinois. Scientists there had the necessary expertise in fungal fermentation and introduced a number of crucial process innovations that enabled high-volume, high-quality production of pure penicillin. This enabled further clinical trials, all of which showed that penicillin had great advantages over the limited number of existing antibacterial drugs, being less toxic and curing a wider range of infections.

Penicillin was soon being trumpeted as a major boon to the war effort, helping save the lives of combatants and civilians, especially those with wound infections and burns, and as yet another

example of the contribution of science to social progress. In 1943 the U.S. government increased the priority given to penicillin, so by the end of the war it was being produced by many companies across the United States and to a lesser extent in Britain. Fleming became something of a celebrity and for a while the role played by Florey, Chain, Heatley, and the Peoria scientists who were all still actively at work on penicillin was eclipsed; however, in 1945 Florey, Chain, and Fleming were jointly awarded the Nobel Prize for Medicine.

In the late 1940s and early 1950s penicillin continued to enjoy a reputation as the "Wonder Drug," with demand outstripping supply. Penicillin had a major impact in saving lives and reducing suffering, and it transformed the image of the doctor from someone who helped patients manage their illnesses to someone who could cure disease. It also reduced the length of stay of surgical and infectious disease patients in hospitals, as secondary infections could be better controlled, although its use in general practice was limited by the fact that administration was by injection. While penicillin enjoyed an almost wholly positive public image, doctors and pharmaceutical companies were aware of two problems: first, penicillin-resistant bacteria, and, second, allergic reactions to the drug. The former had been known about since 1942, but the numbers of bacteria with this property increased with the rapid diffusion of penicillin and were common in hospitals in the 1950s. This led doctors to return to more traditional antiseptic and aseptic techniques and to look to new antibiotics being produced by the pharmaceutical industry. Allergies to penicillin can cause death and were more common in the 1950s, when high doses were used, than they are in the early twenty-first century. Although deaths were relatively rare, they often received wide publicity and, along with greater awareness of bacterial resistance, led to growing anxieties that penicillin might not be that wonderful after all. On balance, public confidence in the drug was not dented, as it was the experience of both patients and doctors that the benefits easily outweighed the risks. Indeed, it seems that penicillin was overused, with many doctors prescribing it for all infections, including viral infections (against which it is ineffective), on the grounds that it might prevent secondary bacterial infections. Another factor is that doctors were under pressure from patients who were unaware of the limitations and problems of the "Wonder Drug."

In the postwar period the huge market for penicillin and the problems with bacterial resistance led pharmaceutical companies to search for other naturally occurring antibiotics. The most important of these was streptomycin, introduced in 1946 as a treatment for tuberculosis, the most serious bacterial infection against which penicillin was ineffective. Scientists also found new penicillins produced by the various species of the Penicillium mold. Research in the 1950s concentrated on refining dosage recommendations and improving methods of administration—the first oral penicillins were introduced in 1954. In the late 1950s, research and development focused on semisynthetic and synthetic penicillins, with scientists offering improvements in administration and effectiveness. The range of new penicillins enabled doctors to keep ahead of bacterial resistance to antibiotics, but this has proved something of a treadmill and over time other drugs have replaced penicillins in the fight against resistant bacteria. However, for many common bacterial infections penicillin-based antibiotics remain the drug of choice at the start of the twenty-first century and continue to be a potent symbol of medical advance.

See also **Public Health; Science.**

BIBLIOGRAPHY

Masters, David. *Miracle Drug: The Inner History of Penicillin.* London, 1946. The first detailed account of the development of penicillin.

Wainwright, Milton. *Miracle Cure: The Story of Penicillin and the Golden Age of Antibiotics.* Oxford, U.K., 1990. A detailed study of the development of penicillin and the issues around its development.

Weatherall, Miles. *In Search of a Cure: A History of Pharmaceutical Discovery.* Oxford, U.K., 1990. Places the history of penicillin in the context of wider developments in pharmaceuticals.

MICHAEL WORBOYS

PERESTROIKA. Perestroika (restructuring) was one of the most profound processes of change in history. Intended at first only to reform the Soviet order, it ultimately led to the dissolution of the political system and the disintegration of the country, the Union of Soviet Socialist Republics (USSR). The law of unintended consequences operated with a vengeance, and yet there remains a fundamental debate about whether the changes inaugurated by Mikhail Gorbachev when he came to power in 1985 were a success or a failure. His administration managed to transform the moribund and repressive country ruled by the stultifying hand of the Communist Party of the Soviet Union (CPSU) into one firmly set on the road to democracy and was able to transcend the Cold War confrontation with the Western capitalist powers. However, in the process Gorbachev and his team managed to lose the country that was intended to be the subject of the reform process, and by the time that Gorbachev formally resigned from power on 25 December 1991, the USSR had disintegrated into its fifteen component republics.

COMING TO POWER

The Communist Party had ruled the country since Vladimir Ilyich Lenin seized power in October 1917. Despite five major changes of rulers, the political system remained remarkably similar right up to 1985, characterized above all by the dominance of the Communist Party. In March 1985 Gorbachev was selected by the Central Committee as general secretary of the CPSU, despite the misgivings of a large group of conservatives in the Politburo (the supreme body in the CPSU). One reason for Gorbachev's selection was an understanding that the country could no longer be allowed to drift. The economy had lost dynamism and was falling ever further behind the West, and society was increasingly immersed in alcoholism and other pathologies. There was a gaping gulf between the tenets of the core communist ideology, committed to equality and human emancipation, and the tawdry operating ideology that justified the privileges of the elite and the rule of the communist *nomenklatura* (the class of officialdom). Although the Soviet Union had achieved strategic nuclear parity with the United States in the mid-1970s, it was clear that the quality of Soviet military equipment was falling behind that of the West. The country was bogged down in a bitter war in Afghanistan, and its communist allies in Eastern Europe were restive.

Against this background the need for change was palpable, and thus Gorbachev was the beneficiary of broad popular and elite support in his early years as he sought to revitalize the Soviet Union. By starting a "revolution within the revolution" Gorbachev hoped to save the essentials of the system, above all the leading role of the party and the planned economy, and to transcend the increasingly pointless confrontation with the West. Gorbachev was the last exponent of "reform communism," the program of communist revival that had been attempted twenty years earlier by Alexander Dubček in Czechoslovakia under the slogan "socialism with a human face." The "Prague Spring" of 1968 was crushed by Soviet tanks in August of that year, and now Gorbachev sought to achieve what the Soviet Union itself had destroyed some twenty years earlier.

ASPECTS OF PERESTROIKA

There had been sporadic attempts earlier to reform the Soviet system, notably in the 1920s during the New Economic Policy (NEP) and under Nikita Khrushchev (1953–1964) following the death of Joseph Stalin. Perestroika was the third and greatest attempt at communist reform. Within months of coming to power Gorbachev launched the program that he called perestroika, which became ever more radical. Once changes began they could not be constrained by regime-led reform, and by 1991 pressure for a radical change of the system became overwhelming. The attempt in August 1991 by conservatives to hold back the tide of change precipitated the result that they sought to avert: the conclusive dissolution of the communist system of government and, by the end of the year, the disintegration of the USSR. Perestroika was characterized by the following features.

"Acceleration" and economic reform In the first phase some of the themes of Yuri Andropov's authoritarian reform program were revived. In the few months (November 1982–February 1984) of his brief rule following the death of Leonid Brezhnev, Andropov sought to impose labor and social discipline. To this program Gorbachev added the notion of *uskorenie* (acceleration), seeking to rejuvenate the existing economic system by the vigorous application of old remedies. The government led by Nikolai Ryzhkov launched an intensive investment program in an attempt to kick-start the economy. Major programs were announced, such as the promise that by the year 2000 all Soviet citizens would have an apartment of their own. Through acceleration the government sought both to reform the economy and increase output, contradictory demands that failed to achieve either. The misconceived antialcohol campaign launched at this time led to the increased production of bootleg liquor (*samogon*) and severe revenue losses. Gorbachev soon came to understand that more radical measures were required.

Although economic growth rates did initially rise, the period of acceleration in 1985 and 1986 failed to achieve genuine economic reform, and by 1990 the country was sinking into an ever deeper recession. In June 1987 a Central Committee plenum adopted a halfhearted plan for the economic transformation of the country that focused on greater autonomy for enterprises and increased rights for workers to elect their own managers. The legalization of cooperatives at this time served only to promote the criminalization of the economy. Reform plan followed reform plan, but none were consistently implemented. Inflation rose to catastrophic proportions as goods disappeared from the shops. The country became increasingly ungovernable as Ryzhkov's relatively conservative government was unable to implement its own version of reform, in part because of Gorbachev's lack of support, while more radical alternatives were equally unacceptable. Miners' strikes from June 1989 signaled that the regime was dangerously isolated, having lost the support of the workers, the class that it claimed to represent. The turning point was Gorbachev's failure in September 1990 to support the plan proposed by the team led by Stanislav Shatalin, Grigory Yavlinsky, and Yegor Gaidar proposing a rapid transition to the market in "five hundred days." The plan called for an end to price controls, fiscal and monetary discipline to contain inflation, and rapid privatization. The USSR was to be converted into an economic union with only loose political ties between the constituent republics. With the rejection of the plan, Russia launched its own economic reforms in November 1990.

Glasnost (openness) Censorship had been the hallmark of the Soviet system. Now under Gorbachev the veil of secrecy began to be lifted. At first Gorbachev sought to use glasnost in an instrumental way, as a means of using public opinion to exert pressure on recalcitrant officials to accept his reforms. Some limited debate was allowed about the Soviet past, in particular over the horrors of the Stalinist system, but the aim at first was certainly not the pursuit of truth or the achievement of freedom of speech. These only came gradually as the pressure for more open debate eventually created a genuinely free public sphere. A landmark in the development of this openness was the explosion in reactor number 4 at the Chernobyl nuclear plant on 26 April 1986. It was only when monitors in Sweden and other countries picked up the existence of a nuclear cloud

that the scale of the explosion became public. In the meantime, lives were placed at risk in the May Day march in neighboring Kiev. Finally Gorbachev made a public broadcast that recognized the scale of the disaster. The limits on glasnost were pushed back, and ever more became known about the crimes of the past, above all those committed by Stalin and his entourage. Some of the boldest commentators even began to criticize the founding father of the system, Lenin, despite Gorbachev's attempts to present the late Lenin of the NEP years as the precursor of perestroika. There were ever more critical commentaries on the inadequacies of the present, including poor health services, overcrowded schools, the special shops for the *nomenklatura* elite, and above all the widespread shortages of goods in the shops. These revelations could not but undermine the legitimacy of the Soviet order.

Development of civil society Meanwhile numerous "informal" (*neformaly*) groups of social activists began to form, known as informals because they operated in the gray area of official tolerance and their status was not recognized by Soviet law. These groups soon reflected every aspect of political life, with nationalists jostling against communist revivalists all the way through to semifascist groupings such as the Pamyat (memory) organization. This outburst of civil society demonstrated the energy that was latent in the Soviet system. The country had been industrialized and urbanized in the 1930s, accompanied by the massive development of the educational system. Perestroika now gave the hugely expanded intelligentsia the opportunity for inclusion in the political system based on equality and right rather than on conformity and arbitrariness. Intellectuals provided the motive force for perestroika. The informal groups provided the basis later for the emergence of a multiparty system. The emergence of an independent working-class movement, above all in the coal-mining industry, marked the point at which Gorbachev's strategy of reform from above was transformed into a revolution from below.

Demokratizatsiya (*democratization*) The January 1987 plenum of the Central Committee marked a watershed in the move away from authoritarian and toward democratic reform. The plenum called for the extension of competitive elections in the workplace, the soviets (councils), and in the party itself. The Nineteenth Party Conference in June–July 1988 marked the transition to the deepening of democratization. Attempts were made to formulate a grand strategy of political reform to modernize the entire system within the framework of one-party democracy and one-party parliamentarianism. Gorbachev's strategy was based on the CPSU retaining a predominant role; but the party was now to guide rather than lead. The principle aim was to create a "socialist legal state" with the separation of powers and a revived legislature.

Constitutional amendments in late 1988 created a three-chamber Congress of People's Deputies (CPD). The full Congress was to meet twice a year, while current parliamentary business was to be conducted by a smaller Supreme Soviet drawn from the CPD. This strange parliamentary model was to cause endless problems for the Soviet Union and later in Russia, where a similar model was adopted. The semifree elections of March 1989 for the new assembly saw the defeat of many communist officials and the return of some democrats. The CPD's first convocation in May 1989 was the scene of vigorous debates, televised live to an enthralled nation, and appeared to mark the onset of effective parliamentary politics. The CPD and its Supreme Soviet passed a significant body of reformist legislation, with new laws on freedom of conscience and religious belief and freedom of the press. The first steps were taken toward creating a law-governed state (*Rechtsstaat*), if not a democracy, something that distinguished perestroika from the rest of Soviet history. However, the Congress was unwieldy and lacked the necessary committee structure to set a coherent legislative agenda or to establish the routines for effective legislative activity or oversight over the executive.

The end of the Cold War Foreign policy was undoubtedly the sphere in which Gorbachev met with the greatest personal success. Although his reforms were initially greeted with scepticism, Gorbachev gradually won over the major Western leaders. Above all, U.S. president Ronald Reagan and Gorbachev found a common language in the pursuit of strategic arms reductions. At the base of his foreign policy was Gorbachev's view that the fundamental ideological principles on which the Cold War was fought had become anachronistic. The world in Gorbachev's view had become interdependent, and confrontation with Western imperialism did not inevitably have to take the form of armed confrontation. There would still be competition with the capitalist West, but this would no longer be the rivalry entrenched in Khrushchev's theory of peaceful coexistence. A new type of cooperative coexistence could be established in which the West and reformed Soviet Union lived peacefully together. This was the logic that led to the announcement of massive troop reductions in December 1988, the withdrawal of Soviet troops from Afghanistan in March 1989, the announcement of a "common European home" in 1989, and acceptance of the popular revolts against communism in the fall of that year. However, conservatives in the USSR insisted that Gorbachev was betraying Soviet national interests by giving away more than the country received, and this view still has considerable resonance.

The end of Communist rule Article 6 of the 1977 Soviet constitution talked of the CPSU's "leading role," and as long as the party's power remained constitutionally entrenched, the political system remained recognizably communist. However, there was a growing divergence between reform of the communist system and the development of a democratic form of Soviet power. This divergence was brought to the fore by the collapse of the communist systems in the East European "satellite" states in late 1989, symbolized above all by the fall of the Berlin Wall on 9 November. It became increasingly clear that Gorbachev's attempt to reconcile representative democracy with a leading role for the CPSU was untenable. One-party democracy was a contradiction in terms, and the attempt to achieve what Gorbachev called the "socialist pluralism of opinions" was challenged by the growth of genuine political pluralism in society. On 13 March 1990, under pressure from massive demonstrations that echoed the slogans seen in Eastern Europe earlier, the CPD modified the constitution to remove reference to the party's "leading role." The era of one-party rule, which had in effect lasted since October 1917, came to an end: free elections were introduced and the half-truths of glasnost gave way to genuine freedom of speech. Gorbachev's definition of perestroika as a party-led program of reform had now outgrown its creator.

DISSOLUTION AND DISINTEGRATION

To compensate for the erosion of party dominance, Gorbachev sought to strengthen the institutions of the Soviet state. Local soviets were given greater powers to manage their affairs, while in the center the institution of an executive presidency was established. On 14 March 1990, the day after the modification of Article 6, Gorbachev was elected president of the USSR by the CPD. His failure to engage in a national election weakened his legitimacy and allowed those who had a popular mandate to challenge his power. Party perestroika gave way to presidential perestroika. The transformation of the political system at last allowed liberalization to give way to genuine democratization.

Gorbachev had been able to consolidate his power faster than any previous Soviet leader, yet he still faced formidable opposition. By 1990 it was clear that the reform coalition was disintegrating and Gorbachev's own brand of communist reformism was losing support. Political life was becoming increasingly polarized, and Gorbachev's centrism was eroded from both sides. Conservatives warned that Gorbachev's policies were leading to the betrayal of socialism and the destruction of the country. The growing democratic movement also now diverged from perestroika's communist reformism and sought to introduce the basic features of a modern democratic system. The representative of this trend was Boris Yeltsin, who in 1986 had been appointed to head the Moscow party organization. He was the first top party leader openly to condemn the privileges of the party elite, and his stress on social justice earned him massive popularity. Elections to the Russian CPD in March 1990 saw a strong showing for democratic forces, organized in the movement "Democratic Russia," and in May 1990 Yeltsin was elected chair of the Russian parliament. The Russian declaration of state sovereignty on 12 June 1990 marked the moment when political control slipped out of Gorbachev's hands toward the individual republics. The winter of 1990–1991 saw Gorbachev isolated from the radical democrats and fearing the hard-line reactionaries.

The existence of the USSR was increasingly challenged by a number of republics. The three Baltic states (Estonia, Latvia, and Lithuania) had never reconciled themselves to incorporation into the Soviet Union in 1940 as part of the deal between Stalin and Hitler in August 1939, and now frustration with perestroika encouraged them to think of secession. Moldova had also been a victim of the Nazi-Soviet pact, while the Caucasian republics of Armenia and Georgia still hankered after the independence that they had lost as a result of Soviet invasions in 1921. Gorbachev only slowly reacted to the nationalist challenge, but ultimately sought to find a way of keeping the union together in a reforged Union Treaty. As far as the republics were concerned, this was too little too late, and in 1990 Lithuania led the way in declaring independence. The storming of the Lithuanian TV building in Vilnius on 13 January 1991, in which fifteen people were killed, provided vivid warning of the bloodshed that could attend the disintegration of the USSR.

Yeltsin rallied to the support of the Baltic republics, representing the repudiation of Moscow's traditional empire-building role and creating the conditions for the relatively peaceful disintegration of the Soviet "empire." Gorbachev's attempt to legitimize the authority of the Soviet Union in the following months by renegotiating the federation included a referendum on 17 March 1991 in which the great majority supported a renewed union, although the vote was held in only nine republics. In the "nine-plus-one" agreement of 23 April at his dacha at Novo-Ogarevo, Gorbachev conceded extensive powers to the republics and an accelerated transition to a market economy. The new Union Treaty would be one built from the bottom up, founded on the sovereignty of the republics and relegating Gorbachev and the central government to a secondary role. The treaty was formalized on 23 July 1991 and was to have been signed by some of the republics on 20 August. However, on 19 August 1991 the conservatives struck and tried to seize power in a coup that was as farcical as it was dangerous. Three days later the coup attempt collapsed, but the country could never be the same again. The attempt to hold the country together accelerated its disintegration. One after another the republics declared their independence, leaving Russia as the continuer state of the USSR.

CONCLUSION

Despite the revolutionary language, Gorbachev began as a reformer, but he became increasingly radical as he met opposition and the promise of his early reforms was not fulfilled. His tragic fate was to act as the destroyer rather than the builder. The more that he tinkered with the system, the deeper the crisis. His reform communism only exacerbated the problems of what was already a system in crisis and worsened the legacy facing the postcommunist governments. However, Gorbachev demonstrated that the Soviet system could be reformed, although the communist component would have to be removed. Failure to deal adequately with the economy and national aspirations provoked disintegration. It fell to Gorbachev's successors in Russia and the other republics to rebuild economies and to nourish the fragile shoots of democracy that perestroika had encouraged.

See also **Chernobyl; Gorbachev, Mikhail; 1989; Soviet Union; Yeltsin, Boris.**

BIBLIOGRAPHY

Brown, Archie. *The Gorbachev Factor.* Oxford, U.K., 1996.

English, Robert D. *Russia and the Idea of the West: Gorbachev, Intellectuals, and the End of the Cold War.* New York, 2000.

Gorbachev, Mikhail S. *Perestroika: New Thinking for Our Country and the World.* London, 1987.

Hahn, Gordon M. *Russia's Revolution from Above, 1985–2000: Reform, Transition, and Revolution in the Fall of the Soviet Communist Regime.* New Brunswick, N.J., 2002.

Harris, Jonathan. *Subverting the System: Gorbachev's Reform of the Party Apparat, 1986–1991.* Lanham, Md., 2003.

Hough, Jerry F. *Democratization and Revolution in the USSR, 1985–1991.* Washington, D.C., 1997.

Sakwa, Richard. *Gorbachev and His Reforms, 1985–90.* New York and London, 1990.

White, Stephen. *After Gorbachev.* 4th ed. Cambridge, U.K., 1992.

RICHARD SAKWA

PESSOA, FERNANDO (1888–1935), Portuguese poet.

Fernando António Nogueira Pessoa, one of Europe's great poets, was born in Lisbon, Portugal, on 13 June 1888, and died in the same city on 30 November 1935. Except for a few weeks at the University of Lisbon in 1906, he received his formal education in Durban, South Africa, where his stepfather served as Portuguese consul.

Pessoa's main concern and his true occupation was always his writing. He supported himself (barely) by handling English and French correspondence for several commercial houses in Lisbon. When he broke up with his lover, Ofélia Queiroz, the reason he gave was that his commitment was to his writing.

Bilingual and bicultural, Pessoa hoped at first to establish himself as an English poet. In his teens he tried but failed to place poems in English magazines such as *Punch* and had no better luck placing stories in journals such as *Cassell's*. In 1917 he submitted *The Mad Fiddler*, a book of poems, to the London publisher Constable. It was turned down. A year later, from Lisbon, he issued *Antinous* and *35 Sonnets*, chapbooks that were distributed in the British Isles to a lukewarm reception. His only publication in England came in 1920 when *The Athenaeum* published "Meantime," a short lyric poem. Encouraged, perhaps, by this modest success, he reissued *Antinous* in 1921, along with *Epithalamium* under the titles *English Poems I–II* and *English Poems III*, only to be disappointed by their reception. Only one other book would appear during his lifetime. *Mensagem* (*Message*), an arrangement of elegiac and prophetic lyrics on historical themes, was published in 1934.

Pessoa frequently contributed poetry and prose to journals and newspapers, beginning in 1912 with two remarkable essays on the present state of Portuguese poetry and its prospects. These appeared in *A Águia*, the organ for the so-called Nova Renascença (New renaissance) movement led by the poet Teixeira de Pascoaes, the prime advocate of *saudosismo*—an ethos characterized by nostalgia for the nation's heroic past. In addition to defining the nature and properties of modern Portuguese poetry, Pessoa prophesied the

EUROPE SINCE 1914

2005

imminent emergence of a "supra-Camões," a poet destined to supplant the sixteenth-century Luis Vaz de Camões as Portugal's national poet. Pessoa's career as a major Portuguese-language poet can be said to have begun on 8 March 1914. On that date, as Pessoa recalled twenty-one years later, he began suddenly to write poetry in different voices (he called them *heteronyms*—fictional personalities, each one the author of a distinctive body of writing) to which he gave discrete personalities and names. In this way, at that one sitting, he wrote the more than three dozen poems comprising *O Guardador de Rebanhos* (*The Keeper of Sheep*) by "Alberto Caeiro," followed immediately by *Chuva Oblíqua* (*Oblique Rain*), poems he attributed to himself, and then *Ode Triunfal* (*Triumphal Ode*) by "Álvaro de Campos." These heteronyms were joined by "Ricardo Reis," who had been devised by Pessoa in 1913 but whose poetry had not yet been written and would not be published for more than a decade. Thus, in 1914 began what Pessoa, rejecting the outward drama of action or plot, called his *drama-en-gente* (plays within persons).

In 1915 Pessoa was instrumental in founding *Orpheu,* an avant-garde journal. There he first published poetry under his own name (*Chuva Obliqua*) as well as major odes by Campos. In its two issues *Orpheu* set the course for twentieth-century modernist Portuguese writing.

In 1926 the young editors of the Coimbra-based journal *Presença* hailed Pessoa as Portugal's greatest living poet. In ensuing years this journal became a major outlet for his poetry. In its pages he published some of his most important work. Besides Campos's *Anniversario* (*Birthday*) and *Tabacaria* (*Tobacco Shop*)—a strikingly modern poem—Pessoa chose *Presença* for *Autopsicografia* (*Autopsychography*), a poetic statement of an *ars poetica*. In this poem, in accordance with his anti-romantic commitment to depersonalization, Pessoa reveals that the poet forges his work, that is, he "fakes" his feelings and sentient thoughts so as to "remake" them as he incorporates them into his poems.

Although Pessoa had published many of his major poems and essays in periodicals and newspapers, he left for posterity a trunkful of manuscripts, notes, and other unpublished material. His first editors soon embarked on a "collected works" project that by 2006 had not yet exhausted his literary remains. Remarkably, not until 1982 was *Livro do Desassossego* (*The Book of Disquiet*) compiled from Pessoa's scattered notes and jottings. Attributed to an assistant bookkeeper he named Bernardo Soares, this "anatomy" of deeply felt, trenchant meditations, these striking instances of self-examination, are considered by many to be among the great literary achievements of the twentieth century.

See also **Portugal.**

BIBLIOGRAPHY

Primary Sources

Pessoa, Fernando. *Poems I–II.* Lisbon, 1921.

———. *English Poems III.* Lisbon. 1921.

———. *Mensagem, Poemas esotéricos.* Edited by José Augusto Seabra. Nanterre, France, 1993.

———. *Fernando Pessoa & Co.: Selected Poems.* Edited and translated by Richard Zenith. New York, 1998.

———. *The Selected Prose of Fernando Pessoa.* Edited and translated by Richard Zenith. New York, 2001.

———. *The Book of Disquiet.* Edited and translated by Richard Zenith. New York, 2003.

Secondary Sources

Monteiro, George. *Fernando Pessoa and Nineteenth-Century Anglo-American Literature.* Lexington, Ky., 2000. Influences and affinities.

Sadlier, Darlene J. *An Introduction to Fernando Pessoa: Modernism and the Paradoxes of Authorship.* Gainesville, Fla., 1998. The complexities of Pessoa's multiple authorial identities.

Santos, Irene Ramalho. *Atlantic Poets: Fernando Pessoa's Turn in Anglo-American Modernism.* Hanover, N.H., 2003. Pessoa in the context of American poets such as Wallace Stevens, Hart Crane, and others.

GEORGE MONTEIRO

PÉTAIN, PHILIPPE (1856–1951), French soldier and politician.

Had Marshal Philippe Pétain died honorably in 1939, on the eve of World War II, at the age of eighty-three, some prestigious Parisian boulevard would today bear his name. He would have a secure place in history as the hero of Verdun, the battle most closely identified with the terrible violence of World War I and the suffering of the men and women who fought in it. By the time he was appointed commander-in-chief of the French army in May 1917, battles had become so deadly that soldiers began to mutiny. Pétain reestablished discipline that was strict but humane, concerned by the soldiers' fate. During the war Pétain developed a clear preference for a defensive rather than offensive strategy, and his great popularity was in part due to his image as the commander who shared the hardships with his troops.

After the victory that won him the supreme rank of marshal, Pétain became one of the most influential military chiefs in French history, advising right-wing and left-wing governments alike. After putting down riots in Morocco in 1925 and 1926, he continued to play a major role in military policy, and he served briefly in 1934 as minister of war. He had a major role in devising a strategy to fortify France's northern and eastern borders. The Maginot Line was thought to be inviolable; but the Germans, when they invaded France in 1940, merely took care to circumvent it.

Pétain was serving as the first ambassador to Spain after General Francisco Franco's victory in the civil war when he was recalled urgently to return from Madrid on 18 May 1940. With the German offensive under way, Pétain was appointed vice premier. A month later, the French army suffered total defeat. The wartime fate of the country was sealed in Nazi hands, and so was Pétain's. Succeeding Paul Reynaud—who wanted to pursue the fight against the Germans from North Africa—Pétain, as head of the government, signed an armistice with Germany. The Nazis occupied the larger part of the country that included Paris, the western coast, and industrial regions in the north and east. German authorities left the southern half of the country free of troops, leaving putative sovereignty there to the Vichy government (so named because its headquarters were situated in the small spa town of Vichy). But about one and a half million French prisoners of war remained in German captivity, and the French government paid the Reich huge sums for the daily cost of occupation.

On 10 July 1940 the National Assembly granted Pétain all powers—executive, legislative, judicial, and constitutional. He made immediate

Marshall Philippe Pétain speaks at the dedication of a World War I memorial c. 1940. AP/WIDE WORLD PHOTOS

use of them by abolishing the Third Republic and establishing a dictatorial regime. Suspending parliament, he arrogated to himself the right to make law. Several months later, in October, he launched a formal policy of collaboration with Germany and set out his program for "regeneration," known as the "National Revolution," a movement that combined the reactionary traditionalism of the far-right Action Française with the social conservatism associated with the Catholic Church and well-placed individuals known as *notables*. These partners planned a third path that was neither capitalist nor socialist, which became the basis for a major social program from the summer of 1940 to the spring of 1942. Essentially, apart from a few social reforms such as a campaign against alcoholism and pension reform, the program was antidemocratic and antirepublican, suspended civil liberties, segregated foreigners, and excluded Jews.

The Vichy social program won wide acceptance among the French, who were suffering a crisis of identity in the wake of their demoralizing defeat at the hands of the Germans. With the help of propaganda, Pétain was perceived as the father of the nation, an old man who had come out of a quiet retirement to save his country yet again. The obscure Charles de Gaulle's calls for resistance were sometimes heard but rarely avidly followed, and Pétain could occasionally be an energetic leader. He had the help of Pierre Laval, a politician of the Third Republic embittered after he was forced to resign from the government in 1936; later came Admiral François Darlan, a serious Anglophobe whose plan for France's recovery was to make of it essentially a German protectorate.

Collaboration with Germany quickly developed into a one-sided affair. The Nazis took the opportunity to loot the country while subduing the Resistance, which grew in strength after 1941 with support of the communists, and became a real power in 1943 after its reorganization by de Gaulle's delegate, former prefect Jean Moulin. The mass arrests and deportation of French Jews gave no relief, whether in terms of food supplies or the return of prisoners or war. Pétain continued his policy of collaboration even after the allies landed in North Africa, and the Vichy government was enfeebled by Nazi occupation in the south in November 1942. The Vichy government had no army or naval force, no colonial empire or unoccupied territory to call its own, yet Pétain continued to lend his name and declining legitimacy to the worst sorts of activities. Under the authority of Laval, to whom Pétain delegated all power, Joseph Darnand's pro-Nazi militia (*milice*) hunted French resistants, many of them being men who were trying to escape forced labor in Germany, and Pétain supported the Nazis and the *milice* in their increasingly brutal fight against the Resistance.

After the Allied landing at Normandy on 6 June 1944 and in southern France on 15 August, the Germans in their disorderly retreat brought Pétain out of France. After the final defeat of Germany, he met with the new French authorities in April 1945 to stand trial, which began on 23 July 1945. Found guilty of treason, his death sentence was commuted to life in prison by General de Gaulle. He spent the rest of his life in the jail on the island of Yeu, off the Brittany coast, where he died in July 1951. Since his death, his supporters and defenders of the fantastic thesis of the blade (de Gaulle) and the shield (Pétain) have continually requested that his ashes be transferred to Verdun,

where in 1916 he helped secure victory. The government, in spite of some ambiguity under the presidency of François Mitterrand, who had worked for the Vichy regime before becoming active in the Resistance, remained opposed to such a move, in consideration of the moral stain that Pétain's leadership from 1940 to 1944 had inflicted upon the country, never to be forgiven.

See also **Collaboration; Gaulle, Charles de; Laval, Pierre; Maginot Line; Mitterrand, François.**

BIBLIOGRAPHY

Burrin, Philippe. *France under the Germans: Collaboration and Compromise.* Translated by Janet Lloyd. New York, 1996.

Griffiths, Richard. *Marshal Pétain.* London, 1970. Reprint, London, 1994.

Miller, Gérard. *Les pousse-au-jouir du maréchal Pétain.* Paris, 1975. Reprint, Paris, 2004.

Paxton, Robert O. *Vichy France: Old Guard and New Order, 1940–1944.* New York, 1972. Reprint, with new introduction, New York, 2001.

MARC OLIVIER BARUCH

PHENOMENOLOGY.

The term *phenomenology* signifies in its Greek sense the study or science of phenomena as they appear to human subjectivity. As systematically formulated by the founder of the twentieth-century phenomenology movement, the German philosophy professor Edmund Husserl (1859–1938), it implies a return to a theory of perception, language, and knowledge that describes the various ways in which the world and its objects appear to human subjectivity as an agent of truth.

CLASSIC PHENOMENOLOGY

Husserl, first trained as a mathematician in Austria, turns to the philosophical justification of ideal mathematical and logical objects in his self-ascribed "breakthrough" work, the two-volume *Logical Investigations* (1900–1901). In these investigations, Husserl is concerned to safeguard the ideality of mathematical, logical, linguistic, and perceptual meanings and the transcendent objects to which they refer. In doing so, he argues against the common nineteenth-century psychological reduction of mental acts that intend ideal logical and mathematical theorems to mere immanent psychic phenomena.

The foundational principle of phenomenology is the notion of intentionality, a conception of the structure of the mind's presentations of the world according to which every act of consciousness, be it perception, expression, knowledge, imagining, or memory, is always a consciousness of something beyond itself. In the influential sixth Logical Investigation, Husserl goes beyond the prevailing Kantian restriction on the role of unconceptualized intuition as noncognitive and argues for the ability of the mind to intuit not just simple objects but also relations between objects or states of affairs. So, for example, one perceives relations of "a is next to b" or that "S is p" and what is thereby disclosed in the self-evidence of consciousness is being itself. The phenomenological conception of truth is then articulated not as correctness or accuracy of judgments but as the disclosure of objects and states of affairs in their being to and for the mind that intends them.

If intentionality and its disclosure of the primordial manifestation of truth is Husserl's legacy to the following generations of phenomenologists, his later "transcendental turn" remains the principal subject of contention in continental philosophy in the early twenty-first century. In his *Ideas Pertaining to a Pure Phenomenology* (1913), Husserl proposes the method of reduction, or bracketing, of our naive beliefs in the transcendent existence of worldly objects. This is considered necessary to reveal the nonempirical, or theoretical, capacity of the transcendental ego to constitute the sense of objects to appear as they do according to strict laws of correlation between intentional acts that, for example, perceive an object, and the object is perceived.

Husserl's most famous student and successor to his academic chair in Freiburg, Germany, was Martin Heidegger (1889–1976). Heidegger reconceives intentionality as a fundamentally practical directedness toward the world in our existential projects. In his landmark *Being and Time* (1927), he lays the groundwork for many subsequent existentialist themes by arguing that the primordial phenomena as encountered by the self manifest themselves in our authentic or inauthentic attitudes toward nontheoretical situations into which we are "thrown." These attitudes toward our existential projects must be adopted within the contexts of emotion, temporality, language, and in particular death. Throughout his writings, Heidegger rediscovers the Greek roots of the question of metaphysics as the question of the distinction between ordinary beings and their mode of being, or, as he puts it, as the question of the Being of beings.

EXISTENTIALIST PHENOMENOLOGY

In the immediate wake of Husserl and Heidegger, two French thinkers appropriated these phenomenological themes and set them more firmly into an existentialist context, where what is at stake is not so much the cognitive aspects of intentionality but our concrete embodied and meaningful human experiences. Maurice Merleau-Ponty (1908–1961) attempts to reconcile idealist and empiricist approaches to perception in his masterwork, *Phenomenology of Perception* (1945). Having intensively studied the late Husserl's texts on perception and embodiment, Merleau-Ponty brought to bear the findings of early twentieth-century Gestalt psychology in his argument against the dominant empiricist notion of perception. Fundamental to his work is the insight that the perception of a Gestalt figure characterizes the capacities of the embodied perceptual subject as much as, or even more significantly than, the simple passive response to external stimuli. Particularly influential on Merleau-Ponty was Christian von Ehrenfels (1859–1932), who introduced the term *Gestalt* in his groundbreaking 1890 study, "On Gestalt Qualities." The key principle of Gestalt psychology, which resonates with Husserl's notion of an intuitive grasp of holistic relations, is that a perceived whole, whether an event, a relation, or a complex and structured figure, cannot be reduced to the influence of atomistic sense stimuli. One might think here of the changing aspects of a familiar figure-ground image, in which one alternately sees two faces looking at each other or a candelabra, on the basis of the exact same sense data. Merleau-Ponty's appropriation of Gestalt psychology leads to his notion that it is only through a foreground and a background, the bodily horizons which are forever changing as the body moves in space and time, that perception as an existential phenomenon can be understood.

Although Jean-Paul Sartre (1905–1980) is perhaps best known for his 1938 existentialist novel *La nausée* and his monumental 1943 *Being and Nothingness*, he spent a good part of the 1930s studying the works of Husserl and Heidegger in Berlin. His earliest works focus on applying intentionality to emotional and imaginary experiences, although he disagreed vehemently with Husserl's conception of a transcendental ego beyond an empirical self. His early concern with nontheoretical meaningfulness in a seemingly meaningless world led him to his celebrated 1946 manifesto, "Existentialism and Humanism," a clarion call to those shattered by the ruins of World War II to fill the apparent void of objective meaning with one's own radical freedom. At this point Sartre's earlier existentialist phenomenology departs from the roots of classical phenomenology in its abandonment of the descriptive approach to phenomena that disclose themselves as meaningful in themselves.

The lasting significance of phenomenology after World War II is visible particularly in France. Thinkers such as Jacques Derrida (1930–2004), Emmanuel Levinas (1906–1995), and Jean-Luc Marion (b. 1946) have each in their own way refashioned the original notions of intentionality and descriptive phenomenology in literary, ethical, and religious directions. Throughout the twentieth century, the phenomenological movement in Continental philosophy has distinguished itself from Anglo-American analytic philosophy in widening the scope of description of meaningful phenomena beyond the linguistic and logical analysis of arguments. Its lasting significance is in its ever-developing holistic and nonreductionist approach to a wide range of human experiences that are capable of patient description of how things appear to us from themselves in manifold ways.

See also **Existentialism; Gestalt Psychology; Heidegger, Martin; Merleau-Ponty, Maurice; Sartre, Jean-Paul.**

BIBLIOGRAPHY

Primary Sources

Ehrenfels, Christian von. "On 'Gestalt Qualities.'" In *Foundations of Gestalt Theory,* edited by Barry Smith. Munich, 1988. Translation of "Über Gestaltqualitäten" (1890).

Heidegger, Martin. *Being and Time*. Translated by John Macquarrie and Edward Robinson. New York, 1962. Translation of *Sein und Zeit* (1926).

Husserl, Edmund. *Logical Investigations*. Vols. 1 and 2. Edited by Dermot Moran. Translated by J. N. Findlay. New York, 2001. Translation of *Logische Untersuchungen* (1900–1901).

Merleau-Ponty, Maurice. *Phenomenology of Perception*. Translated by Colin Smith. New York, 2002. Translation of *Phénoménologie de la perception* (1945).

Secondary Sources

Moran, Dermot. *Introduction to Phenomenology*. New York, 2000.

Polt, Richard. *Heidegger: An Introduction*. Ithaca, N.Y., 1999.

Sokolowski, Robert. *Introduction to Phenomenology*. Cambridge, U.K., 2000.

DANIEL J. DWYER

PHONOGRAPH. During the last half of the nineteenth century the idea of recording sound waves began to develop on both sides of the Atlantic. In France on 25 March 1857 Edouard-Leon Scott de Martinville (1817–1879) received a French patent for the "phonautograph," which made a visual image of sound waves on a cylinder, but did not play or reproduce any sounds. On 30 April 1877 another Frenchman, Charles M. Cros (1842–1888), deposited with the Academy of Sciences in Paris a description of a process for mechanically reproducing spoken words. On 24 December 1877 the American inventor Thomas Alva Edison (1847–1931) patented in the United States a machine that actually reproduced sound. Edison thus won the battle with Cros by inventing and then commercializing an actual "talking machine" that used cylinders. He was convinced that neither abstract ideas nor patent law alone would assure to inventors the fruits of their work. As a result, he and other American inventors quickly moved from invention to manufacturing and marketing.

From an early date Europeans made major contributions to recorded musical styles, provided influential recording artists, eagerly purchased recorded-sound products, patented and marketed their own inventions, and made financial investments that helped to create manufacturing plants in their countries. For example, Emile Berliner (1851–1929), a German inventor who emigrated to Washington, D.C., developed the microphone, the flat recording disc, and the gramophone player. His flat-disc recordings eventually replaced the more fragile and unwieldy Edison cylinders. In 1898 Berliner created the Deutsche Grammophon Gesellschaft, a company that pressed discs in Hanover, Germany, for the European market. He also organized the Berliner Gramophone Company of London, which marketed spring-driven playback machines in Britain and on the Continent.

American recording engineer/talent scouts such as Fred Gaisberg (1873–1951), who worked for Berliner, crisscrossed Europe recording such great opera singers as Enrico Caruso (1873–1921) and Nellie Melba (1861–1931). In this way and others, American inventors/entrepreneurs of recorded music vastly expanded their business, first through their affiliate companies and then through multinational conglomerates. As early as 1888 Edison marketed a phonograph through his Edison Phonograph Co. of the British Isles; the same organization re-exported them to Europe.

In the 1880s and 1890s the three leading American companies that came to control most of the important patents—Edison's National Phonograph Company, the Victor Talking Machine Company, and the Columbia Graphophone Company—set up affiliates in London, Paris, Hanover, St. Petersburg, Vienna, and Madrid. The Big Three, as they were known, dominated the recorded music business through their European affiliates until World War I seriously disrupted business. Nevertheless, from an early date, the influential French firm les Phonographes Pathé, founded in Paris in 1894 to demonstrate and market Edison products, subsequently manufactured its own cylinders, records, and playback machines. Pathé's records and machines were successful throughout Europe. It established offices from St. Petersburg to Madrid and New York City during the years between 1912 and 1929. So too, the German Carl Lindstrom Company established factories in Germany, France, Spain, Italy, Russia, Poland, Britain, Argentina, and Brazil.

The ingenuity and business acumen of American phonograph/record companies played a central role in bringing the Jazz Age to France on 78-rpm discs during the 1920s. Many French people who would never have heard jazz in a nightclub or dance hall purchased imported jazz records for enjoyment at home. Jazz recordings became a key staple in left-bank bohemian circles, and Charles Delaunay (1911–1988), son of the famous modernist painters Robert (1885–1941) and Sonia Delaunay (1885–1979), compiled the first jazz record discography.

The commercialization of radio in the 1920s, the growing economic crisis of the 1930s, and the outbreak of World War II again created serious setbacks for recorded-sound industries, especially in France. The factories of Pathé Frères, for example, had been turned to the war effort so that the company was unable to adopt the new technology of electrical recording; its diminishing markets exposed it to absorption in 1931 into the British conglomerate EMI (Electric and Musical Industries) the first of the global music corporations.

The triumph of the Allies in World War II, as well as the defeat of Germany, set in motion an intense period of growing American cultural influence in Europe, one that became particularly controversial among some intellectuals in France. American technology introduced the long-playing, $33\frac{1}{3}$-rpm record in France in 1951; the twelve-inch disc with micro-grooves provided running times six times longer than the old 78-rpm records and at half the price. As in the 1920s jazz was once again the major style preferred by French purchasers of American records. In the 1950s Edouard Ruault (1921–2005), a jazz pianist, changed his name to Eddie Barclay and founded Barclay Records, issuing both American and French albums that made his company the top music-production enterprise in France during the 1950s and 1960s. The "electrophone" and imported American LPs (*les disques noirs*) of the Vogue and Barclay labels became major consumer items of the postwar French Baby Boomer generation, who preferred them to the automobile, motor scooter, radio, and television set.

THE PHONOGRAPH AND ANTI-AMERICANISM

Claims by some left-wing French intellectuals, particularly communists, that post–World War II

Customers in a London store listen to records in phonograph booths, 1955.
©HULTON-DEUTSCH COLLECTION/CORBIS

American media expansion amounted to cultural imperialism have been disputed by historians on both sides of the Atlantic who see the phonograph as one of several different elements in a broader process of modernization of French life, a movement that included urbanization, new patterns of industrialization, technology, media, and consumer society. Moreover, the phonograph and recordings have often been lumped into anti-American generalizations actually focused on the film industry. In fact, the export business of recorded sound was not in itself an overwhelming economic force and relied upon radio play to increase its sales. Moreover, compared to Hollywood films, records and record players were far less obviously American since conglomerates recorded French, American, French-influenced American, and American-influenced French music on nationally ambiguous labels such as Vogue.

The 12-inch vinyl 33⅓-rpm LP record enjoyed twenty-five years of astounding growth in Europe before declining markedly in 1978 when it first encountered competition from the cassette tape. The compact disc, or CD, invented in the United States in 1982, arrived in Europe one year later, soon triumphing over the cassette. Like the LP before it, the CD then enjoyed soaring sales from 1983 to the turn of the twenty-first century, when the downloading of digital music files to computers, a revolutionary new technology for listening to recorded music, presently used by eight million French citizens, and their transfer to digital audio players, most using the MP3 format, began to take hold.

As the number of multinational conglomerates in the business of recorded music has fallen, the number of independent recording companies has risen in Western countries, and they have taken over the recording of specialized tastes in music. The biggest companies now tend to market only the most famous popular artists. As of 2006, recorded music in Europe and the United States struggles with complex issues of copyright law in a period of rapid technological change.

See also **Computer Revolution; Jazz; Leisure; Popular Culture; Technology; Television.**

BIBLIOGRAPHY

Grnow, Pekka. "The Record Industry: The Growth of a Mass Media." *Popular Music* 3 (1983): 53–75.

Lefeuvre, Gildas. *Le Producteur de Disques.* Paris, 1994.

Millard, Andre. *America on Record: A History of Recorded Sound.* Cambridge, U.K., and New York, 1995.

Tournes, Ludovic. "L'Americanisation de la Culture Francaise, ou la recontre d'un Model culturel conquer-ant et d'un Pays au Seuil de la Modernite." *Historiens et Geographes* (juillet/aout 1997): 65–79.

———. "Jalons Pour une Histoire Internationale de l'industrie du Disque: Expansion, Declin et Absorption de la Branche Phonographique de Pathe (1894–1936)." In *Histoire des Industries/Culturelles,* edited by Jacques Marseille and Patrick Eveno. Paris, 2002.

WILLIAM KENNEY

Edith Piaf, 1955. Portraits of the singer often emphasized the persona of a passionate and troubled woman. ©BETTMANN/CORBIS

PIAF, EDITH (born Edith Giovanna Gassion; 1915–1963), French singer.

Edith Piaf, writer and performer, is one of the best-known representatives of the tradition of the French chanson. Although she occupies a place in the lineage forged by Maryse Damia, Fréhel, and Marie Dubas, Piaf was also one of the female sing-ers who created a more international style of chan-son by making greater use of the microphone, recording technology, and the personal notoriety bestowed upon her by the press.

In many ways Edith Piaf was a child of the streets. She was born in the rue de Belleville, in the heart of working-class Paris. Her mother was a singer and her father a circus acrobat, but she was raised by her Berber grandmother, who lived in the neighbor-hood of Barbès, and by her other grandmother, who ran a brothel in the Normandy village of Bernay,

where by the age of thirteen Piaf would sing with her father as a way of earning their daily bread. At fifteen she began to sing with her "adopted" sister Simone Berteaut, before forming a trio with Camille and Suzanne Ribon that performed in the garrisons of Paris. She became a mother herself very young, but at twenty lost her young daughter, Marcelle, who died when she was two.

In the early 1930s Piaf left the streets to go onstage. Louis Leplée had her sing in his cabaret Le Gerny's on the Champs Elysées and came up with her stage name "la môme Piaf," or "little sparrow" (*piaf* is the Parisian slang term for *sparrow*). She recorded her first songs in December 1935 for Polydor Records ("Les mômes de la cloche," "La java de Cézigue," "L'étranger," "Mon apéro") and was interviewed on the radio. When Leplée was murdered the following year, Piaf was a suspect for a short while but was eventually cleared of any wrongdoing and went on to find new engagements through Jacques Canetti and Raymond Asso. She began to sing "Mon amant de la coloniale" and met the composer Marguerite Monnot, who would write melodies for her for the rest of her career. Jean Cocteau offered her a role in his play *Le bel indifferent* alongside Paul Meurisse, her lover at the time. Thanks to her public persona and the success of her records, she dominated the Alhambra stage of the European and the Bobino. Her private life completed the picture—the succession of lovers she appeared with throughout her life meant she frequently appeared in tabloid magazines. In 1937 she sang "Mon legionnaire" on ABC Radio, and recorded Michel Elmer's "L'accordéoniste" in 1940. During World War II she recorded for SACEM and met Yves Montand, whose career she launched by appearing onstage with him.

The postwar era ushered in a new stage in Edith's career, this time on the international celebrity circuit, a status she attained following a series of solo concerts in the United States in 1946 and while performing with the Compagnons de la Chanson in 1947. She fell passionately in love with the boxing champion Marcel Cerdan, whose tragic death in 1949 led her to write her "L'hymne à l'amour" the following year. In the early 1950s she entered a difficult period of alcohol and drug abuse. Also beginning to take shape at this time was her legend as a woman devoted to love and giving everything she had to her emotional songs and life—a legend projected by the press, her song lyrics, and her impressive stage presence. In 1952 she married Jacques Pills, whom she would divorce three years later. She appeared in several films designed essentially as vehicles for her songs, including *Si Versailles m'était conté* by Sacha Guitry in 1953 and *French Cancan* by Jean Renoir in 1954. With English-language pop and rock music beginning to displace the French chanson, Edith sang the French version of a rock and roll hit called "L'homme à la moto," Jean Drèjac's adaptation of Jerry Leiber and Mike Stoller's "Black Denim Trousers." Her greatest hits at the end of the 1950s catapulted her fame to its zenith: "La foule," "Milord" (by Georges Moustaki and Marguerite Monnot), "Mon manège à moi" (by Jean Constantin and Norbert Glanzberg), "Mon

Dieu," "Les mots d'amour," and "Non, je ne regrette rien." She multiplied her recitals at the Olympia in Paris and toured all over northern Europe. In her final recordings she made greater use of full orchestras, choruses, and echo chambers. In 1962 she married Théo Sarapo and performed with him as well. When she died in 1963 she was denied the rites of the Catholic Church, but for millions she remained unique, extraordinarily and lastingly popular.

See also **Cabaret; France; Theater.**

BIBLIOGRAPHY

Bret, David. *The Piaf Legend*. London, 1988.

Crosland, Margaret. *Piaf*. Rev ed. London, 2000.

Piaf, Edith. *My Life*. Translated by Margaret Crosland. London, 1990.

———. *The Wheel of Fortune*. Translated by Nina Rootes and Andrée Masoin de Virton. London, 2004.

SOPHIE A. LETERRIER

PICASSO, PABLO (1881–1973), Spanish artist.

Pablo Ruiz y Picasso was born in Málaga, Spain, and died in Mougins, France. Regarded as the most influential twentieth-century artist in Western Europe and North America, he worked with a broad range of media and was central to two radical manifestations of modern art: cubism and surrealism. Cubism, which established a shift in paradigms of visual representation (including the introduction of collage), was the product of a subcultural bohemian community indebted to Charles Baudelaire's mid-nineteenth-century concepts of modernity and the "painter of modern life." Surrealism, which aimed to combine the ideas of Karl Marx and Sigmund Freud to overthrow bourgeois values and social structures, was the product of a diverse community united in admiration of Picasso's work. This was still the case after a major political division in surrealism in 1929, represented by André Breton's *Second Manifesto of Surrealism* on one side and Georges Bataille's journal *Documents* on the other. The third issue of *Documents* (1930) was titled "Hommage à Picasso" and the first issue of *Minotaure* (1933), supported by Breton, had a cover designed by

Picasso. It also included an article by Breton on "Picasso in His Element" with sixty photographs by Brassaï (Jules Halasz) of Picasso's recent sculpture and studio.

Cubism and surrealism were developed in Paris, which was Picasso's base for most of his working life. His commitment to the city as a cultural and political symbol was a reason to remain as an act of resistance to Nazi occupation during World War II. Steeped in the leftist debates of the 1930s, Picasso supported the Republican cause against General Francisco Franco's fascists throughout the Spanish civil war, most publicly represented by *Guernica*, commissioned for the Spanish Pavilion at the 1937 Paris World's Fair, and his satirical etchings *Dream and Lie of Franco I* and *II* (1937). He was familiar with the ideological split, at the outbreak of the Spanish civil war, between his close friend Paul Éluard and Breton. Éluard could no longer adhere to Breton's disapproval of poems linked to specific events. For him, the pressing realities of fascism and the Popular Front's struggle for workers' rights meant that Breton's insistence on the purity of surrealism's ideals of Trotskyism was unsustainable. Picasso's sympathy with Éluard's position is evidenced by *Guernica;* his active support of the French Communist Party (PCF) in the years after the liberation of Paris in 1944; and his *Massacre in Korea*, which Picasso dated 18 January 1951. The latter was perceived in France and the United States as critical of U.S. military intervention (under the banner of the United Nations) to support anticommunists in the Korean War. The PCF attacked both President Harry S. Truman's decision in 1950 to send U.S. troops to Korea and the contemporary French war in Indochina as colonialist aggression.

Picasso's politics so troubled U.S. authorities that he appears in FBI files from the 1940s onward. In 1990 Herbert Mitgang ("When Picasso Spooked the F.B.I.," *New York Times,* 11 November) revealed some of these Cold War additions to the politics of representation. For example, Picasso's written contract in 1912 with the entrepreneurial art dealer Daniel-Henry Kahnweiler (and those of Georges Braque, André Derain, Juan Gris, Fernand Léger, and Maurice de Vlaminck between 1912 and 1913) was a landmark in the paradoxical history of avant-garde artists receiving regular payment for artworks that were critical of capitalist values of productive labor. A second example is his PCF membership card after 1944. Picasso, Léger, and other artists joined the PCF even though they were critical of the party's adherence to socialist realism with the beginning of the Cominform (Communist Information Bureau) in September 1947. Such sources have been the bases for diverse interpretations of Picasso's work and actions.

In the first two decades of the twentieth century Picasso and Braque saw themselves in a joint artistic project that led them to draw pioneering analogies with Orville and Wilbur Wright. Although there were other cubist groups with a variety of cultural and political agendas, the works of Picasso and Braque became focal points for critics and collectors. For example, Picasso's *Les demoiselles d'Avignon* (1907) achieved mythic status despite being rarely exhibited until purchased in 1939 by the Museum of Modern Art (MoMA) in New York City. Alfred H. Barr Jr., who was appointed MoMA's first director of painting and sculpture in 1929, enshrined the painting as a key moment in the museum's hegemonic convention of white-walled formalist display based on a particular narrative of artistic development in modern art. The painting also became central to Barr's paradigmatic accounts of modern art published as catalogs to MoMA's exhibitions such as *Cubism and Abstract Art* (1936) and *Picasso: Forty Years of His Art* (1939). Characteristics of *Les demoiselles d'Avignon*, however, are resistant to such limits. The painting was first described as "the philosophical brothel" by Picasso's intimate friends (probably by Guillaume Apollinaire), indicating sources in the erotic and sexual trade of prostitution (related to the red-light district of Barcelona, where Picasso lived between 1895 and 1900) and the transformation of ideas in the early years of the twentieth century, from theories of relativity and the fourth dimension to concepts of experience, duration, and identity. The painting therefore has been interpreted in terms of a range of discourses and concepts, including colonialism and "primitivism"; gender, sexuality, and venereal disease; male gaze and the objectified body; "Oriental" stereotypes in high art and popular culture; and history painting and academic representations of Vénus Anadyomène.

Similarly, Picasso's shift from so-called analytic to synthetic cubism has been interpreted in different ways. Many of his paintings and collages from 1909

The Charnel House. Painting by Pablo Picasso, 1945. DIGITAL IMAGE © THE MUSEUM OF MODERN ART/LICENSED BY SCALA/ART RESOURCE, NY

to 1913 are central to accounts of, on the one hand, the development of abstract art and, on the other, avant-garde explorations of visual representations as sign systems. The former connects the writings of Barr at MoMA and Clement Greenberg, the most influential U.S. art critic in the immediate post-1945 period. The latter is rooted in contemporary parallels such as the radical poetry, including experimental typography, of Stéphane Mallarmé and Apollonaire and the shift in the approach to language and linguistics in theorists such as Ferdinand de Saussure and Roman Jakobson. Both Jakobson and Picasso's dealer Kahnweiler discussed cubism as an art practice exploring the relationships among sign, signifier, and signified.

For some art historians, such as Rosalind Krauss and Yves-Alain Bois, the meanings of this exploration are fixed and ahistorical (like the lexical meanings of words) because for them Picasso was concerned with a systematic exploration of the conditions of representability entailed by the sign _solely within pictorial art_. For others, such as Patricia Leighten and Christine Poggi, these meanings are variable and contingent on specific social and historical conditions. They analyze Picasso's use of ephemeral materials from everyday culture in his papiers collés (pasted papers), or collages: newspaper cuttings, labels, advertisements, and wallpaper. Words, letters, and typefaces in these works are also scrutinized for their literal and metaphorical meanings, including Picasso's fascination with punning possibilities. For example, his still life of collaged elements (newspaper cuttings, bottle label, wallpaper, colored papers with gouache and charcoal) titled *La Suze* (1912) can be decoded as a representation of "modern life," specifically, café debates on contemporary politics, accompanied by a glass and bottle of Suze apéritif à la gentiane. Envisaged viewers, firstly Picasso's immediate group, familiar with visual sign systems and the spatial-temporal flux of modern life, were expected to be active "readers" (both literally and metaphorically) of such works. Here Picasso glued contrasting newspaper clippings from *Le Journal,* dated 18 November 1912, to create a dialogue. He cut and pasted pieces from three front-page reports on the current Balkan War with some inverted, an anarchist strategy of representing the world of capitalism and imperialism as "upside down." These are in dialogue with another account (from page 2 of *Le Journal*)—which is pasted the right way up for reading and specifically identified by a charcoal-drawn "arrow" that doubles as the rim and side of an aperitif glass—on an antiwar demonstration by forty to fifty thousand pacifists, syndicalists, trade unionists and socialists, which took place on 17 November in a working-class community near Belleville, Paris. In the middle of the work Picasso placed, as part of his "sign" for bottle, a label from an actual bottle of Suze, which is based on the herb gentian, named after Gentius, a pre-Christian Illyrian king. Illyria was an area that, at the time of Picasso's collage, made up the Balkan League, which was at war with Turkey in 1912–1913.

Picasso did not explore the radical implications of collages for modernist art practice, which ranged from the development of photomontage (for example, Hannah Höch's critiques of the social construction of femininity in Weimar Germany and John Heartfield's critiques of Nazism) to innovative graphic and typographic imagery in the Soviet Union during the 1920s. He focused on painting, printmaking, and sculpture and a broad range of subject matter from portraits of intimate friends and lovers to mythological themes with contemporary significance. These produced fresh areas for representation and interpretation, which made his work particularly important for surrealism's emphases on the unexpected and the uncanny.

Picasso's *Guernica* reveals both his cubist and surrealist allegiances in a representation of the bombing of the ancient Basque capital by the Condor Legion of Nazi Germany, which supported Franco's attack on the elected Republican government of Spain. The painting was both praised for its power of allusion and metaphor and attacked for its lack of realistic comprehensibility and effectiveness. Franco was so concerned by the international status of the painting and its antifascist message that he commissioned a Nationalist reply in 1943 on a claimed Republican atrocity of the Civil War: *Los fusilamientos de Paracuellos* by Mariano Izquierdo y Vivas (1893–1974). *Guernica* became a symbol of Spanish resistance during Franco's long dictatorship and had a major influence on U.S. artists such as Jackson Pollock. Picasso requested that the painting remain on display at MoMA until Spain returned to democracy. While at MoMA, *Guernica* had a further life as a symbol of Vietnam War protest. When news of the My Lai massacre of civilians by U.S. troops in Vietnam (March 1968) became public knowledge (November 1969), protesters used *Guernica* to signify that the United States was responsible for its own war crime: its Guernica at My Lai.

See also **Avant-Garde; Breton, André; Cubism; Éluard, Paul; Guernica; Painting, Avant-Garde; Surrealism.**

BIBLIOGRAPHY

Antliff, Mark, and Patricia Leighten. *Cubism and Culture.* New York, 2001.

Baldassari, Anne. *Picasso and Photography: The Dark Mirror.* Translated by Deke Dusinberre. Paris and New York, 1997.

Chipp, Herschel, B. *Picasso's Guernica: History, Transformations, Meanings.* Berkeley and Los Angeles, 1988.

Daix, Pierre. *Picasso: Life and Art.* Translated by Olivia Emmet. New York, 1993. Translation of *Picasso Créateur.*

Frascina, Francis. "Realism and Ideology: An Introduction to Semiotics and Cubism." In Charles Harrison, Francis Frascina, and Gill Perry, *Primitivism, Cubism, Abstraction: The Early Twentieth Century,* 86–183. New Haven, Conn., and London, 1993.

———. "Picasso, Surrealism and Politics in 1937." In *Surrealism: Surrealist Visuality,* edited by Silvano Levy, 125–147. New York, 1997.

Krauss, Rosalind E. *The Picasso Papers.* New York, 1998.

Leighten, Patricia. *Re-ordering the Universe: Picasso and Anarchism, 1897–1914.* Princeton, N.J., 1989.

Rubin, William, ed. *Pablo Picasso: A Retrospective.* New York, 1980.

Rubin, William, Hélène Seckel, and Judith Cousins. *Les demoiselles d'Avignon*. New York, 1994.

Utley, Gertje R. *Picasso: The Communist Years*. New Haven, Conn., 2000.

FRANCIS FRASCINA

PIŁSUDSKI, JÓZEF (1867–1935), the most important Polish statesman of his era.

Józef Klemens Piłsudski was born in historical Lithuania, in the Russian Empire, to a Polish noble family. He attended Russian high school in Vilnius, taking part in conspiratorial reading circles that transmitted Polish ideas such as Romanticism and positivism. In the Polish context, the former meant an attachment to the old, easterly, noble Poland before its partition in the eighteenth century as well as a belief in the special mission of individuals in the salvation of Poland and of Poland to the future of Europe. Positivism emphasized the importance of legal work to create a literate and active society. Piłsudski later spoke of a "Romanticism of plans" combined with a "positivism of means." The circles also transmitted new political ideas—socialism and nationalism—from Europe and Russia. Piłsudski, like others of his generation, tried to find some way to reconcile these two versions of mass politics.

In 1887 Piłsudski played a limited and unknowing role in a plot to assassinate Tsar Alexander III and was sentenced to five years of exile in Siberia. There he met Russian and Polish revolutionaries and intellectuals, including exiles of 1863. Upon his return to Vilnius, Piłsudski returned to illegal political work. In 1893 he joined the new Polish Socialist Party, which promulgated both socialism and national independence. He quickly became one of its leaders and published its organ, *Robotnik* (The worker). Arrested in 1900, Piłsudski escaped Russian prison by feigning madness. He settled in Kraków, Austrian Galicia, in 1902. In 1904, after the outbreak of the Russo-Japanese war, he traveled to Tokyo to negotiate with the Japanese. During the Revolution of 1905 Piłsudski wished to prepare a Polish uprising, while comrades expected the revolution itself to liberate their country.

After 1905 Piłsudski built a Polish paramilitary in anticipation of the next European war.

When World War I came in 1914, his Union of Riflemen formed the core of Polish legions incorporated by the army of Austria-Hungary. Piłsudski resigned from Austrian collaboration in 1916, then joined a German-sponsored national council. After refusing to swear loyalty to the Central Powers, he was imprisoned by the Germans in 1917. The defeat of Austria and Germany liberated Piłsudski, and the Entente victory opened the way to Polish independence. Piłsudski assumed the role of head of state and commander in chief, defining Poland's frontiers in a series of wars, including the Polish-Bolshevik War. He led the counterattack that defeated the Red Army in August 1920. He held power through 1922, when he resigned after judging that the powers of the president were too limited. He was also disappointed by the popularity of his rivals, the National Democrats.

Piłsudski's "retirement" was active, involving much speaking and writing, including a history of the Polish-Bolshevik War. He maintained influence within the foreign and defense ministries. Piłsudski returned to power by military coup in 1926. He complained of the corruption of parliamentarians but had no clear alternative to parliamentary democracy. In 1928 he created a "non-party bloc" to control parliament and in 1930 arrested leading opposition politicians. After serving as prime minister in 1926–1927, he contented himself with the positions of minister of war and general inspector of the armed forces. He governed by way of trusted men in important positions, concerned with restraining the National Democrats on the right as well as the communists and other radicals on the left. In this his regime succeeded, although at the cost of corrupting democracy. In foreign affairs Piłsudski steered a middle course between the Soviet Union and Nazi Germany, signing nonaggression pacts with each.

Piłsudski's governments announced a policy of toleration to national minorities, more than a third of the population. Jews were granted equal civil rights. Ukrainians, the largest national minority, were offered concessions in Volhynia. In Galicia, Piłsudski answered terrorism by Ukrainian nationalists with pacification. Belarusian organizations connected to the Far Left were banned. On the national question, his regime left a mixed record but no taint of chauvinism. Piłsudski died in 1935, leaving behind an authoritarian constitution designed for him personally. The collective dictatorship that followed embraced Polish nationalism. It was discredited by the defeat of 1939. The communists who ruled postwar Poland portrayed Piłsudski as a fascist. Two of his ideas informed elements of the Polish opposition to communism: that in domestic affairs loyalty to the state is a higher value than feeling for the nation; and that in foreign affairs the just treatment of the peoples between Poland and Russia was the key to security.

See also **Poland.**

BIBLIOGRAPHY

Garlicki, Andrzej. *Józef Piłsudski 1867–1935.* Edited and translated by John Coutouvidis. Brookfield, Vt., 1995.

Jędrzejewicz, Wacław. *Piłsudski: A Life for Poland.* New York, 1982.

Rothschild, Joseph. *Piłsudski's Coup d'Etat.* New York, 1966.

Snyder, Timothy. *Sketches from a Secret War: A Polish Artist's Mission to Liberate Soviet Ukraine.* New Haven, Conn., 2005.

TIMOTHY SNYDER

POGROMS. In the literal sense of the word, a *pogrom* connotes in Russian an attack perpetrated by one population group against another, accompanied by murders, pillage, rape, destruction, and/or various forms of extortion. In modern historical terms the word alternatively has been (1) restricted to refer specifically to massacres perpetrated against the Jews in Russia between 1881 and 1921 and (2) extended to designate all criminal acts carried out by one population group against another, aided by the neutrality, often supportive and complicit, of military and civilian authorities. Pogroms, which should be formally distinguished from the massacres and, even more so, from the genocides that have left such a lasting mark on the twentieth century, may nonetheless be their precursors.

RUSSIAN POGROMS

The pogrom must first be situated in the context of turn-of-the-century Russia, whose many political and social crises, protests, and popular uprisings regularly left the Jews at the mercy of the masses. Historians usually refer to three great waves of pogroms, each corresponding to a specific crisis phase leading up to the Bolshevik Revolution. The final tally is telling as concerns the scale of the phenomenon itself: historians agree there were about 887 "major" pogroms and 349 "minor" ones, together totaling some 60,000 victims.

The first wave of pogroms occurred from 1881 to 1884, when the country was convulsed by the crisis stemming from Tsar Alexander II's assassination by members of a revolutionary group on 13 March 1881. The government immediately portrayed the Jews as the ones primarily responsible for the popular unrest. Numerous race riots ensued throughout southern Russia, with the first attack occurring in the Ukrainian village of Yelizavetgrad in April 1881, buttressed by the support of a portion of the revolutionary groups seeking to promote any mass uprising likely to weaken the regime. Other pogroms quickly spread from this first village to others in the region and neighboring provinces, with Kiev being most affected in May. Given the indifference of the local authorities and police, the attacks continued throughout the summer. In this first phase, the pogroms were largely characterized by destruction of property, rapes, and beatings, but few deaths. (Ukraine was a region with a long tradition of anti-Jewish riots stretching back to at least the seventeenth century, when the massacre perpetrated by Bohdan Khmelnytsky's Cossacks took place.) Other attacks occurred in Warsaw during Christmas of 1881 and the following Easter.

In Belarus and Lithuania attacks against individuals and families increased. The new tsar, Alexander III, ordered commissions of enquiry into the riots, which explained them as being caused by "Jewish profiteering," thereby blaming their victims. Ultimately the actions taken by those in power were aimed more toward bending these events to domestic-politics ends than toward genuinely stopping them. Unable to curb the popular unrest that was the root cause of the anti-Jewish attacks, the government opted for a policy of systematic discrimination against them. It passed a *numerus clausus* (numeric restriction on admittance) for high schools and universities and initiated the administrative steps necessary to

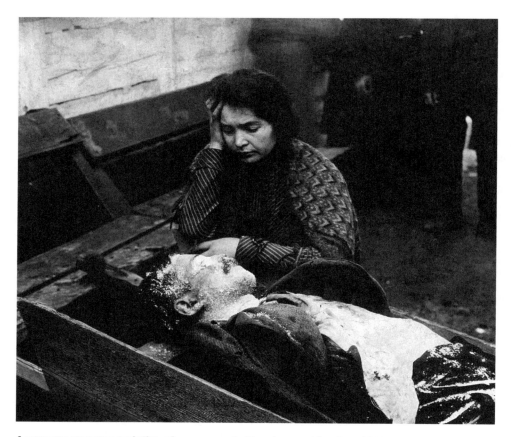

A woman mourns a victim of a pogrom in Proskurov, Ukraine, 1919. ©HULTON-DEUTSCH
COLLECTION/CORBIS

obtaining the expulsion of the Jews from the city of Moscow in 1891.

This first wave of pogroms lasted until June 1884 and would have incalculable consequences, constituting a radical caesura in Jewish history. It provoked a profound crisis of conscience about the impasse reached by Jewish life in the Russian Empire, resulting in unprecedented emigration. Nearly three million Jews left Russia between 1881 and 1917, convinced by the violence against them and the indifference of the authorities that their presence in the territory had become impossible. The pogroms of 1881 also had a decisive effect upon Jewish political thought, insofar as they were one of the main factors explaining the appearance of Zionism and Jewish socialism. The year 1881 may be viewed as the moment when Jewish history, from a chronological perspective, truly entered the twentieth century.

The second phase of pogroms lasting from 1903 to 1906 was linked to the period's revolutionary agitations. Tsar Nicholas II used anti-Jewish hatred, and the pogroms themselves, as a means of dividing and conquering the revolutionary groups. He openly encouraged attacks against Jews in order to divert the masses from their dissatisfaction and to identify the Jewish minority as the primary agitators. The Kishinev pogrom (Easter 1903) was typical of this second wave, leaving forty-five people dead, several hundred wounded, and fifteen hundred Jewish homes and business destroyed. From this date forward the pogrom became a constitutive element of Russian politics: the armed forces made common cause with the rioters, going so far as to defend them against Jewish attempts at self-defense. International public opinion was stirred by the events at Kishinev, and domestically the Jewish community realized the need to fend for itself, with young people swelling the ranks of Zionist and socialist circles. The wave of violent anti-Semitic attacks would remain strong until 1906. Government circles were responsible for fueling the second phase of pogroms, insofar as local authorities received instructions to let the rioters run their own course (meaning to support them) and to prevent as much as possible the forces of order from intervening. The tsar's own secret police printed pamphlets calling for the massacre of the Jews, including the hate-filled and virulent fraud *The Protocols of the Elders of Zion,* which was written, edited, and distributed by them with the aim of justifying the anti-Jewish activities by accusing Jews of having worldwide hegemonic goals.

The wave of pogroms that took place from 1917 to 1921 far surpassed its predecessors in the scale of the massacres it engendered and was directly linked to the October Revolution and ensuing civil war. The riots erupted at the end of 1917, and the rioters were initially soldiers demobilized from the tsarist army. The first geographical zone to be affected was Ukraine, which became independent in 1918 and experienced a long period of anarchy. The most violent attacks occurred in the cities of Berdichev and Zhitomir, but the most murderous was the Proskurov massacre in 1919, where seventeen hundred Jews were killed in the space of just a few hours. Simon Petlyura, Ukraine's prime minister at the time, presided over the inquiry, which primarily reinforced official complacency. He would be assassinated in 1926 by a young Jew named Shalom Schwarzbard, who had lost his family in the Ukraine pogroms and was acquitted at his trial due to extenuating circumstances.

During the civil war the Jews were victimized by the revolutionary troops, the uncontrolled peasantry, and the Whites. The latter group in particular viewed Jews as enemies needing to be eradicated in their entirety and proceeded to commit numerous massacres in the zones they occupied. The return of revolutionary troops to Ukraine may be portrayed therefore as having saved the region's Jews from much larger losses, or perhaps even total extermination. The actions of the Whites pushed large numbers of Jews into supporting bolshevism and Zionism. The pogroms of this third wave left tens of thousands dead and hundreds of thousands wounded.

The pogroms had a profound and lasting influence on the internal political, ideological, and cultural composition of the Jewish world. The proto-Zionist movement Hibbat Zion was formed immediately following the first attacks in 1881, at the same time as Leon Pinsker was writing *Self-Emancipation* (1882), a text that reaffirmed the pressing need for Jewish political thought to change course and which is considered the founding work of political Zionism. Following the second and third waves of violence Zionism definitively acquired its status as the main political current in Russian Judaism.

Jewish socialism was also born of these tragic events. A growing awareness of the danger in tsarist Russia largely explains the rise to power of the Bund (General Union of Jewish Workers) and the wide-scale participation of young Jews in the revolutionary and social-democratic organizations.

The pogroms also left a strong imprint on literary works by Jewish authors of the day, including both those writing in Hebrew (Hayyim Nahman Bialik, Saul Tchernichowsky) and in Yiddish (Shalom Aleichem, Sholom Asch, Isaac Leib Peretz). As it came to occupy a primary place in the Jewish minority's collective psyche, the pogrom became an incontrovertible point of reference for individual and communal reflection.

KRISTALLNACHT, OR THE NOVEMBER POGROM

Born in the Russian Empire and forever largely identified with it, the pogrom would nonetheless be taken to new heights by Nazism. An action that was unthinkable in the constitutional democracies of central and western Europe, it became a vital tool in the anti-Jewish policies of the new leaders of Germany. The logic at work in the events that shook the territories of the Reich on 9 November 1938, called *Kristallnacht,* the Night of Broken Glass, involved terror and scapegoating. The Nazi regime exploited the assassination of a German diplomat in Paris to unleash a massive pogrom throughout its territory, depicted as a spontaneous popular uprising. On the nights of 9 and 10 November, the anniversary of Adolf Hitler's 1923 failed putsch attempt in Munich, the Nazis let loose their men on Jewish synagogues and businesses. The final tally from the night of riots was unprecedented in Germany, although, in view of what was to come, it was trifling: 36 people killed, 36 others heavily wounded, 30,000 Jews arrested and shipped to concentration camps, 815 businesses destroyed, and 191 synagogues burned. The racial anti-Semitism of the Nazi regime, which would after 1940 engage in systematic and industrialized extermination, used the pogrom in this initial period as an instrument that went hand in hand with its policies aimed at discriminating against Jews and stripping them of their civil rights and freedoms. Still undecided at this stage concerning the question of the ultimate fate to be reserved for the Jews, the Nazis aimed to force them out en masse, thereby attaining as quickly as possible their ideal of a *"Judenrein"* ("cleansed of Jews") territory. The hurried departures also aided them in the rapid advancement of the "Aryanization" of the economy, another primary goal of the regime. These two goals were largely attained, and 9 November 1938 constituted a definitive turning point in the history of German Jewry.

POGROM AND GENOCIDE

Alongside the systematic and industrialized extermination of Europe's Jews, the Nazis made recourse to the pogrom in the territories that fell under their control after June 1941. The massive massacres perpetrated by the Einsatzgruppen were augmented by pogroms carried out by civilian volunteers in collaboration with the Nazis. In the Baltic states, Ukraine, and Byelorussia they were a means of ensuring the obedience and cooperation of the occupied populations and quelling their discontent. By redistributing Jewish goods among the assailants as a kind of wage, the occupying forces reinforced German power and the subjection of the administrative territories. Therefore the pogrom—a kind of homegrown massacre fueled by a traditional hatred of the Jews rather than the racial and redemptive anti-Semitism of the Nazis—did not entirely lose its raison d'être, even under the radically altered conditions generated by the war.

POGROMS AFTER NAZISM: THE MASSACRE OF THE SURVIVORS AT KIELCE

The pogrom as a mode of political action did not definitively disappear from Europe after the Holocaust. Although the vast majority of Jews had disappeared from Poland, several pogroms carried out against the survivors occurred in the immediate postwar period. The most egregious was in the village of Kielce on 4 July 1946.

When its two hundred or so survivors sought to reconstruct their former community, a violent anti-Semitic campaign ensued, unleashed by Polish nationalists with Communist support, culminating in the deaths of forty-two people, dozens more wounded, and the pillaging of Jewish goods. This pogrom led to the wide-scale departure of the remaining survivors in Poland. Kielce was the final pogrom to be perpetrated on the European continent.

The Holocaust profoundly transformed the way the pogrom is perceived. The unprecedented scale of the Nazi exterminations reduced it to being a kind of "second-rate" massacre. It is important to keep in mind however that the pogrom represents the phase in eastern and central European history when weak and crisis-stricken powers turned to the age-old hatred of the Jews as a political tool, using their sizable Jewish communities as scapegoats. The wide diffusion of traditional anti-Semitism was a gauge of the success these policies enjoyed, which were consistently redoubled as the level of the crises of state increased. The tolerance authorities displayed for the public disorder and heightened violence that accompanied the pogroms is only explicable in light of their belief that they served as effective diversions from popular dissatisfaction and discontent.

The anti-Semitism of the Nazi regime, given the nature of its syncretism, used the pogrom when it seemed to work in conjunction with its own interests; but deep down the pogrom was in its view highly inefficient with respect to the plans for extermination it pursued during the war. The pogrom was artisanal murder and violence; the Holocaust was an assembly line of death.

See also **Anti-Semitism; Holocaust.**

BIBLIOGRAPHY

Brass, Paul R. *Riots and Pogroms.* New York, 1996.

The Crystal Night Pogrom. Introduction by John Mendelsohn. New York, 1982.

Hoffmann, Christhard, Werner Bergmann, and Helmut Walser Smith, eds. *Exclusionary Violence: Antisemitic Riots in Modern German History.* Ann Arbor, Mich., 2002.

Kielce—July 4, 1946: Background, Context, and Events. A Collective Work. Toronto and Chicago, 1996.

Klier, John D., and Shlomo Lambroza, eds. *Pogroms: Anti-Jewish Violence in Modern Russian History.* Cambridge, U.K., and New York, 1992.

JACQUES EHRENFREUND

POINCARÉ, RAYMOND (1860–1934), French politician.

Raymond Poincaré was one of the most visible political figures in the Third Republic in the first decades of the twentieth century. A deputy at age twenty-seven, minister at thirty-three, in 1912 he was appointed prime minister. He served as president of France from 1913 to 1920 and, before illness forced him to leave office, he was twice more appointed prime minister, from January 1922 to March 1924, and again from July 1926 to July 1929.

For all that, only at the end of his life did Poincaré enjoy real popularity. Unlike his adversary Georges Clemenceau (1841–1929), Poincaré was tagged with disparaging nicknames such as "Poincaré-la-guerre" when a campaign in the 1920s accused him of being responsible for the First World War, and "L'homme-qui-rit-dans-les-cimetières" (the man who laughs in the cemeteries) after a snapshot showed him blinking from the sunlight as he entered a military cemetery. The cap he wore during visits to the front made him look like a cab driver, and that was another motive for mockery. Despite singular intelligence and eloquence—he was a rigorous jurist and a well-known lawyer—his cold exterior and punctilious personality prevented him from becoming genuinely popular.

EARLY CAREER

Poincaré was born in Bar-le-Duc and as a young boy witnessed the disastrous Franco-Prussian War of 1870–1871 that ended with the French losing Alsace and North Lorraine to Germany. He grew up to become a faithful patriot and also a convinced republican, which placed him close to the left wing in French politics. During the Dreyfus affair, Poincaré was a moderate "Dreyfusard" who opposed the trial but kept out of the fray and away from the affair's turmoil and from the Radical Party founded in its wake. Moderation would be the key characteristic of Poincaré's domestic political agenda. Apart from a brief position as finance minister in 1906, from 1896 to 1912 he held no cabinet posts. It is no surprise that from 1903 on he preferred a seat in the senate, a more conservative body than the chamber of deputies.

Although a specialist in matters of the budget, Poincaré preferred foreign policy. Appointed prime minister in 1912, he chose himself as foreign affairs chief, intending to pursue a firm policy with Germany and to shore up France's relations with its allies, particularly with Russia. During a visit to St. Petersburg in August 1912, Poincaré learned about secret treaties signed, with Russian involvement, by Balkan countries that aimed to evict the Turks from Europe. He was unhappy about the matter but decided to downplay the issue so as to maintain strong ties with Russia. This crucial decision encouraged Russian foreign policy makers in their conviction that they need not be preoccupied by French diplomatic opinion, even while jeopardizing peace in Europe.

Poincaré was elected president of France in 1913, winning against the radical republican Jules Pams, thanks to support he received from the Right. He was prepared, while remaining within the constitutional framework, to return the presidency to its former level of influence, which had slipped in recent years. Poincaré pursued foreign affairs while firmly supporting the policy of three years' obligatory military service, which was voted to be renewed that year.

WORLD WAR I

Poincaré was surprised by the crisis of July 1914 in the wake of the assassination of Archduke Francis Ferdinand, which he learned about on the return trip from one of his regular visits to Russia. At sea for most of the time with his prime minister René Viviani, and at the mercy of poor telegraphic communication, he was unable to play an important role. He had been accused before his departure of conspiring with Russia to make war; there exists no proof of this, and it is more likely that Russia acted without even considering the French position. Circumstances conspired to make Poincaré a war president.

Poincaré wrote some ten volumes of memoirs of the period of the First World War, entitled *Au service de la France* (1926–1933; In the service of

France). A final, eleventh volume was published posthumously a half century later. He also coined the famous slogan *L'union sacrée* (the sacred union) in a speech to parliament on 4 August 1914. His major role in French politics effectively ended in November 1917, when he decided he was obliged to appoint his rival Georges Clemenceau prime minister. Not only through war's end but throughout the debates around the Treaty of Versailles at the Paris Peace Conference (January–June 1919), Clemenceau kept Poincaré at a distance. The legislative chambers unanimously proclaimed on 11 November 1918 that Clemenceau and Marshal Ferdinand Foch had earned the "merit of the Nation"; but Poincaré had to wait until January 1920 to receive the same homage.

POSTWAR CAREER

After his presidency ended in 1920, Poincaré decided he still had an active role to play in politics and stood for reelection as senator from the Meuse region. He was reappointed prime minister in 1922 and again took charge of foreign affairs. He was then faced with applying the strictures of the Versailles Treaty, because Germany evinced reluctance to pay reparations. In addition, both Poincaré and Marshal Foch advocated a strong French presence in the Rhineland, in disagreement with Clemenceau, who initially wished to separate the Rhine's left bank from Germany. But the situation was favorable for Poincaré's policy and in 1923, after Germany failed to make scheduled reparations payments, he ordered the occupation of the Ruhr. While it caused great difficulties for Germany, the expensive troop deployment also marked the beginning of serious financial problems for France; moreover, the United States and England were strongly opposed to it. To pay for the occupation, Poincaré had to levy a considerable tax increase, which became one of the reasons he was defeated in the 1924 elections by a reunited coalition of left-wing parties. However, two years later the country's catastrophic financial situation brought him back to power. He turned over foreign affairs to Aristide Briand, who managed a conciliatory policy with Germany, while he took charge of finances.

Poincaré's rigorous economic policy bore fruit. The war had been financed principally by loans, and in 1928—after a serious devaluation of the

franc had reduced it to about one-fifth of its 1914 value—the economic situation improved. The creation of the Franc-Poincaré remained a symbol of France's financial recovery, supported by a clear economic upturn. When Poincaré retired for health reasons, France seemed to have recovered a measure of stability. By the time he died in 1934 at age seventy-four, however, the country was suffering from the effects of the worldwide economic crisis.

See also **Briand, Aristide; Clemenceau, Georges; Reparations; World War I.**

BIBLIOGRAPHY

Primary Sources

Poincaré, Raymond. *The Memoirs of R. Poincaré, 1915.* Translated and adapted by Sir George Arthur. London, 1930.

———. *Au service de la France: Neuf années de souvenirs.* 11 vols. Paris, 1926–1974.

Secondary Sources

Becker, Jean-Jacques. *1914: Comment les français sont entrés dans la guerre.* Paris, 1977.

Becker, Jean-Jacques, and Serge Berstein. *Victoire et frustrations: 1914–1929.* Paris, 1990.

Keiger, John F. V. *Raymond Poincaré.* New York, 1997.

JEAN-JACQUES BECKER

POLAND. Formed in the tenth century, Poland saw periods of national glory and independence as well as of foreign domination. Located at the center of Europe, it experienced all major events of the twentieth century: World War II, the tyrannies of Nazism and communism, the cataclysm of the Holocaust, and the collapse of socialist utopia.

During the sixteenth century the Polish-Lithuanian commonwealth was one of the most powerful states on the Continent. However, destructive wars against Russia, Sweden, and Turkey in the seventeenth century, coupled with a lack of political and socioeconomic reforms, led to the country's decay. In 1795, upon being partitioned by its three neighbors, Russia, Austria, and Prussia, Poland ceased to exist for 123 years. Throughout the nineteenth century the Poles repeatedly revolted against the partitioning powers, but without success. The advance of modern nationalism into Polish lands in the late nineteenth century nurtured two rival ideological currents advancing a national cause: the National Democrats and the Polish Socialist Party (Polska Partia Socjalistyczna; PPS).

Despite foreign dominance, Polish culture produced astonishing works of art. Among the greatest Polish contributors to European culture and science in the period of partitions were the composer Fryderyk (Frédéric) Chopin, the poet Adam Mickiewicz, the writers Bolesław Prus, Henryk Sienkiewicz, Władysław Reymont (the latter two recipients of the Nobel Prize for Literature), and Joseph Conrad (a Polish expatriate whose real name was Józef Teodor Konrad Korzeniowski), the great modernist playwright and painter Stanisław Wyspiański, the philosopher and art critic Stanisław Przybyszewski, and the scientist and two-time Nobel laureate Maria Skłodowska-Curie (Marie Curie).

1900–1918

At the turn of the century, Polish lands were still largely agricultural and industrially backward territories. The three imperial state administrations displayed conflicting approaches toward their Polish subjects, ranging from highly oppressive rule in Russian and German parts to cultural and political autonomy in the Austrian partition. The period prior to World War I saw the crystallization of political attitudes toward independence and the partitioning powers. Under the leadership of Józef Piłsudski, the PPS subordinated Marxist ideology to the struggle for independence, launching terrorist warfare and labor unrest against tsarist rule from 1905 to 1907. The National Democrats led by Roman Dmowski pursued ethnocentric nationalism and a pro–middle class socioeconomic agenda, opting for limited cooperation with Russia. In the Austrian partition, the powerful Polish aristocrats remained staunchly loyal toward the Habsburgs, while the mushrooming populist movement, under the command of Wincenty Witos, struggled for the material and cultural advancement of the peasantry.

During World War I, Piłsudski formed the Polish legions, military units fighting under the Austrian command against Russia, while Dmowski allied his followers first with the Russian Empire and subsequently with the Entente camp. In 1916 Germany and Austria-Hungary set up the Polish Kingdom, a German-Austrian protectorate carved from the territories captured from Russia. However, following the increasing domination of Germany over the Habsburg Monarchy and military stalemate on the fronts, Piłsudski terminated his support for the Central Powers and created a secret military organization. He was arrested in 1917 and interned in Magdeburg, Germany, until the end of the war. Meanwhile, the collapse of the tsarist empire paved the way for the recognition of an independent Poland by England, France, and the United States. Located in the West, Dmowski's National Committee gradually became the official representative of a future Polish state while facilitating the creation of the Polish army in France and preparing itself for participation in a peace conference. As the Bolshevik Revolution knocked Russia out of the war and military defeats forced the Central Powers to sue for armistice, Poland could finally regain its independence. On 11 November 1918 Piłsudski returned to Warsaw and took control of the Polish governmenton the next day. The eleventh of November 1918, the date the armistice was signed ending World War I, is commonly recognized as the rebirth of Polish statehood.

1919–1939

The Second Republic that emerged in the wake of World War I acquired its borders through the Paris Peace Conference, the anti-German revolts in the Great Poland region and in Silesia, and, overall, the victorious war against the Bolsheviks fought in 1919–1920. The conflict started as Polish and Soviet armies began moving into the territories evacuated by the Germans. In 1920 Piłsudski's plans for building the Poland-led federation to counterbalance the Bolshevik state prompted the Polish leader to conclude a military alliance with the Ukrainian Republic based in Kiev. However, by August 1920 the Soviet counteroffensive had brought the Red Army to the gates of Warsaw. Although the Poles defeated the invaders and chased them eastward, the 1921 Peace of Riga constituted a decisive blow to Piłsudski's federal concepts. Influenced by Dmowski's polonocentric attitudes, the Polish delegation won significant

Young refugee girl in Warsaw, Poland, during World War I. ©CORBIS

territorial concessions but tacitly ignored the Ukrainians' demands for independence.

Together with Czechoslovakia, Yugoslavia, and Romania, Poland was one of the major beneficiaries of post–World War I settlement in Europe. However, bitter border disputes as well as territorial claims advanced by Germany and other revisionist powers demonstrated the precariousness of the newly created states in the eastern part of the continent. All three countries were multiethnic states, with their minorities seeking either substantial autonomy or displaying strong irredentism. In Poland, minority groups, mostly Ukrainians, Jews, Byelorussians, and Germans, constituted one-third of the overall population. The successive governments were highly unsuccessful in handling ethnic minorities, wavering between forced assimilation, outright oppression, and increasing exclusion from the rest of society. To a similar extent, the Second Republic failed to implement a decisive land reform plan that might have solved many of the problems faced by the overpopulated, desperately poor, and backward countryside.

Politically the country steered toward authoritarianism. The 1921 constitution defined the lower chamber of parliament, the Sejm, as the strongest institution responsible for the construction of the cabinet. However, the principle of proportional representation coupled with a plethora of political parties resulted in frequent elections and unstable ruling coalitions. After a period of inefficient parliamentary democracy, Piłsudski staged a military coup in 1926 that led to a semidictatorial rule of his followers, commonly known as the *sanacja* (purification) regime. Political pluralism and direct elections were retained, but the 1935 constitution increased the powers of the executive government while reducing those of parliament.

Following Piłsudski's death in 1935, the military took over the government, showing increasingly authoritarian and nationalist traits. The shift from democratic politics to etatism, corporatism, and right-wing authoritarianism to regain political and economic stability was a widespread phenomenon in Eastern and central Europe. In Poland, Piłsudski's heirs also tried to outbid their staunchly nationalist and anti-Semitic opponents from Dmowski's National Democratic Party. Yet the Second Republic proved immune to the totalitarian currents of nazism and communism. The minuscule Communist Party of Poland, widely perceived as an antipatriotic and Jewish-dominated agent of Moscow, was liquidated by Joseph Stalin during the Great Purges in 1938. On the other hand, despite the existence of a strong nationalist Right, the regime's proto-fascist inclinations, and popular anti-Semitism, Poland did not develop a mass fascist movement comparable to those in Hungary and Romania.

Under its foreign minister Colonel Józef Beck, Poland moved away from being part of the French alliance system in Eastern Europe toward the independent tactic of balancing its relations with Nazi Germany, Western powers, and the Soviet Union. However, such a strategy was futile and short-lived. In the absence of a European collective security system, which could benefit small and medium-size states, there was little room for maneuver for Eastern European powers trapped between Nazi Germany and the Soviet Union. Having participated in the partition of Czechoslovakia in 1938, by the spring of 1939 Poland found itself the next target of German territorial claims. After Hitler's demands were spurned, war was inevitable. British and French security guarantees to Poland offered in March and April 1939 did not mitigate this threat as both states had little means to fight a successful military campaign. In addition, the summer of 1939 saw the failure of the tripartite negotiations among England, France, and the Soviet Union to create an anti-German collective security arrangement in Eastern Europe. The fate of the Second Republic was sealed by the Nazi-Soviet Pact of August 1939 which foresaw the partition of Poland between Germany and the Soviet Union. Still, in September 1939 Poland was the first country to offer armed resistance to Hitler.

Despite all of its failures, the Second Republic registered significant successes in culture and science. The Polish literary scene showed particular creativity. While the Skamander group, dominated by such figures as Julian Tuwim, Jarosław Iwaszkiewicz, and Jan Lechoń, practiced neoclassicist poetry, the younger generation of writers including Czesław Miłosz, Józef Czechowicz, and Aleksander Wat successfully cultivated the spirit of the avant-garde. Perhaps the most individualistic literary figures in prewar Poland were Stanisław Ignacy Witkiewicz, Bruno Schultz, and the young Witold Gombrowicz, whose works contested and revolutionized the genres of theater and prose. Witkiewicz is also counted among the greatest Polish painters of this period, alongside such figures as Jan Cybis, who expanded the notion of colorism. An art nouveau veteran, Xavery Dunikowski, whose talent exploded in the 1920s and 1930s, is still considered to be the greatest twentieth-century Polish sculptor. A long musical tradition was continued by Karol Szymanowski. In academia, Stefan Banach and Alfred Tarski were the towering figures of the Polish school of mathematics and logic. While Marceli Handelsman and Franciszek Bujak introduced modern historiography to Poland, Józef Chałasiński, Florian Znaniecki, Ludwik Krzywicki, and Stanisław Ossowski contributed importantly to the world of sociology.

1939–1945

Nazi Germany invaded Poland on 1 September 1939 and Soviet troops invaded from the east on 17 September. After Britain and France declared war on Germany on 3 September, the Polish-German war turned into World War II, even though Poland's Western allies had not yet launched a major offensive. The Poles resisted gallantly, but German units quickly overran the outnumbered and poorly equipped Polish army. The brutality of the Nazi onslaught was evidenced by numerous massacres of Polish civilians and prisoners of war and ferocious bombings by the Luftwaffe. The Polish government fled on 17 September to Romania, where it was interned. The mass Soviet invasion hastened the destruction of the Polish army. After a murderous siege Warsaw fell to the Germans on 27 September. The last Polish units capitulated in early October. On 28 September 1939 a new German-Soviet agreement partitioned Poland between the two powers.

In both zones the occupiers ruled ruthlessly. While Nazis massacred the Polish intelligentsia and ghettoized the Jewish population, the Soviets deported hundreds of thousands to the east and executed twenty thousand Polish officers, policemen, and government officials. The largest Soviet massacre took place in the forest of Katyń, east of Smolensk, in April 1940. Altogether six million Polish citizens perished in the war. The Nazis exterminated the country's three-million-large Jewish minority and, with the establishment of death camps such as Auschwitz, turned Poland into the major site of the Holocaust. Although condemned by the government-in-exile and main resistance organizations, the elimination of the Jews met with sympathetic reception among some anti-Semitic Poles who perceived it as an opportunity for social mobility and ethnic homogenization of the country.

Polish statehood continued in the form of the government-in-exile, headed by General Władysław Sikorski and grouping together former opposition politicians. Following France's defeat in 1940, the government moved to London. Those troops that escaped the September catastrophe formed the bulk of the Polish army that fought under Western command in Africa and Western Europe. Following the 1941 Nazi attack on the Soviet Union and the Polish-Soviet friendship treaty signed in the same year, a new army was formed in Russia. Evacuated to the Middle East in 1942, these units later fought in Italy, contributing to the Allied victory in Monte Cassino in May 1944.

The resistance movement was led by the Home Army (Armia Krajowa; AK), the largest partisan force in Nazi-occupied Europe, loyal to the government-in-exile. The Polish underground established its own courts, secret education institutions, clandestine press, publishing houses, and a network of couriers traversing Europe. Among the greatest Polish contributions to the Allied war effort were the breaking of the German Enigma code, the discovery of the German missile V-1, and detailed intelligence reports from Nazi Germany.

The Communist resistance movement consisted of the Polish Workers' Party (Polska Partia Robotnicza; PPR). Established in 1942, the PPR did not recognize the government-in-exile, running its own small military force. Following the

German discovery of Polish officers' mass graves in Katyń in 1943 and the Polish government's request to investigate the massacre, Stalin broke relations with the London Poles, set up the Union of Polish Patriots, and created the Polish army under Soviet command. After the Red Army advanced into Polish lands, the Soviets formed a Communist-dominated provisional government, taking administrative control over liberated territories. In an attempt to prevent a Communist takeover, the Home Army launched a series of strikes against the Germans while revealing its civilian and military structures to the Soviets as legitimate authorities. The biggest military offensive took place in Warsaw in August 1944. The Nazis crushed the Warsaw Uprising with utmost brutality, killing up to two hundred thousand people and burning the city to the ground, while the Soviets refused to assist the rebels. Moscow's refusal to render aid was partly based on military considerations. Romania's switch of sides in August 1944 prompted the Red Army to divert some of its forces to the Balkans. In addition, having recovered from the initial shock of defeats during the Soviet summer offensive, the Germans regrouped their forces in Poland and launched counterattacks. However, it was political factors that were of paramount importance. By September 1944 the Red Army had seized Warsaw's districts located on the Vistula's eastern bank and established bridgeheads west of the city. Yet the destruction of the noncommunist Home Army was to Stalin's advantage. The failure of the revolt paved the way for Soviet domination of Poland. The noncommunist intelligentsia was decimated and the government-in-exile lost any influence in the country. Those AK units that escaped the Warsaw debacle were hunted down by Soviet and Communist forces and massacred or deported to labor camps in the Soviet Union. At the Yalta Conference in February 1945, Allied leaders decided to move Polish borders westward, agreed on the creation of a coalition government dominated by the Communists, and called for free elections. By the end of the war in Europe in May 1945 Poland had been placed in the Soviet sphere of influence.

1945–1956
The immediate postwar period saw a limited political pluralism. The provisions of the Yalta

Two Polish women sit outside their ruined home in Warsaw, 1946. ©Bettmann/Corbis

agreement, which mandated free and unfettered elections, enabled the reemergence of several political parties, including the Polish Socialist Party, the Labor Party, and the agrarian Polish Peasant Party (Polskie Stronnictwo Ludowe; PSL), led by the former prime minister of the government-in-exile, Stanisław Mikołajczyk. Soon the agrarians became the major obstacle to Communist acquisition of absolute power. The bulk of anticommunist partisans who resisted Communist and Soviet security forces were destroyed by 1947, though in some areas skirmishes continued until the 1950s. Intimidated, harassed, and infiltrated, political opposition gradually succumbed to Communist pressure. Following the 1947 rigged elections and the merger of the Communists with the Socialists into the Polish United Workers' Party (Polska Zjednoczona Partia Robotnicza; PZPR) in December 1948, the Communist takeover of Poland was complete. In their march to absolute power, the Communists also benefited from the exhaustion of the war-worn population, the acceleration of demands for radical socioeconomic changes (strongly articulated by the Socialists, peasants, and parts of the intelligentsia) as well as the genuine enthusiasm among society to rebuild the devastated country.

The new regime quickly began copying the Soviet system by nationalizing banks and industry, launching giant industrialization, exercising near total control over society through ideology and coercion, and establishing a command economy. Polish foreign policy was subordinated to that of the Soviet Union. In 1955 the country joined the Warsaw Treaty Organization. However, the Communists never succeeded in conquering two enclaves of civil society: the Roman Catholic Church and private farmers. As a result of border shifts, population transfers, and the extermination of Jews, Poland became an ethnically homogenous country with a predominantly Catholic population. Led by the charismatic Cardinal Stefan Wyszyński, the church constituted an autonomous spiritual community and a repository of traditional values. Despite Wyszyński's arrest in 1953, Catholicism continued to play an important role, especially as the new industrial labor force, recruited mostly from peasants, cultivated strong religiosity. The fiasco of collectivizing agriculture stemmed from the internal divisions within the Communist Party. Władysław Gomułka, a Communist leader who spent the war in occupied Poland while leading the party during the first two postwar years, intended to build socialism in Poland by taking into account national specificities, social structures, political traditions, and cultural predispositions. He was expelled from the party leadership in 1948 and later arrested, but unlike other East European Communist leaders purged under Stalinism, Gomułka was never tried and executed. Too weak to afford bloody purges and show trials like those in Czechoslovakia and Hungary, the Polish party pursued a milder Stalinist course.

This relative ideological moderation (moderate compared to other Soviet satellites), coupled with the incompleteness of sovietization and the survival of Gomułka, contributed to the rapid collapse of Stalinism in Poland. Following Stalin's death in 1953 and a more relaxed political atmosphere in the Soviet Union, the PZPR began implementing economic and political reforms. However, Nikita Khrushchev's denunciation of Stalin's crimes at the Twentieth Congress of the Communist Party of the Soviet Union, commonly known as the "secret speech," put the Polish party in a deep legitimacy crisis. As reform Communists, intellectuals, and workers pushed for more reforms, the government freed political prisoners, liberalized censorship, and revived parliament. June 1956 saw a workers' uprising in Poznań. Although bloodily suppressed, the revolt accelerated the pace of change. In October 1956, acting against the objections of Soviet leaders and local hard-liners, the party decided to reinstate Gomułka as its leader. Despite the looming threat of military confrontation, dramatic negotiations with Khrushchev in Warsaw sealed Gomułka's return to power.

1956–1970

Gomułka's reappointment marked the culmination of the post-Stalinist political thaw in Poland. The new government halted collectivization, reestablished working relations with the church, and passed economic reforms that improved the standard of living and availability of consumer goods. After the reign of the doctrine of socialist realism, the late 1950s saw an explosion of intense cultural production. Films of Andrzej Wajda, Andrzej Munk, Wojciech Has, and Jerzy Kawalerowicz—to name only a few members of the Polish school—raised Polish cinema to international prominence. The younger generation of acclaimed filmmakers, including Roman Polański and Jerzy Skolimowski, debuted in the 1960s. In the sphere of fine arts, Jerzy Tomaszewski, Jan Lebenstein, and Józef Szajna gained worldwide acclaim for their role in the revival of graphics, poster designing, and painting. Polish theater became recognized thanks to plays of Tadeusz Różewicz, Sławomir Mrożek, and Tadeusz Kantor. Among the most notable literary figures were the older writers Jarosław Iwaszkiewicz and Jerzy Andrzejewski and representatives of the younger generation Tadeusz Konwicki and Marek Hłasko. Yet perhaps the most extraordinary works of Polish literature came from exile. Founded in Paris by Jerzy Giedroyc, the review *Kultura* and the Literary Institute actively promoted and publicized such figures as Witold Gombrowicz, Czesław Miłosz, Andrzej Bobkowski, and Gustaw Herling-Grudziński. Within Poland, Polish jazz left the catacombs and instantly won international recognition. Music of Krzysztof Komeda-Trzciński, Zbigniew Namysłowski, and Tomasz Stańko revolutionized European jazz.

However, by the mid-1960s the political atmosphere in Poland became more oppressive as the Gomułka regime grew increasingly authoritarian, conservative, and economically incompetent. Having tightened censorship, Gomułka antagonized the liberal intelligentsia, while a head-on competition between the party and the church over the 1966 Millennium celebrations of Polish statehood and the coming of Christianity to Poland alienated him from the clergy. In an attempt to legitimize its flagging rule, the regime embraced aggressive nationalism. It used anti-Semitism and Germanophobia to single out internal and external enemies: party liberals and young intellectuals, some of them of Jewish origin, as well as advocates of the Polish-German reconciliation. This "nationalization" of Polish communism culminated in the 1967–1968 anti-Semitic campaign. The brutal suppression of the pro-democratic student protests in March 1968, combined with the anti-Jewish witch hunt (which led to the forced emigration of thirteen thousand Polish Jews) and Polish participation in the Soviet-led invasion of Czechoslovakia in August 1968, discredited communism in Poland on ideological and moral levels. In December 1970, following the massacre of workers protesting food price increases on the Baltic Sea coast, the Polish party politburo sacked Gomułka, replacing him with Edward Gierek.

1970–1980

Gierek pacified labor unrest by withdrawing unpopular price increases and raising wages. A pragmatist and longtime member of the Belgian and French Communist Parties, Gierek believed that the regime should soften its ideological stance and coercion. In his mind-set, economic prosperity alone could guarantee social compliance.

Gierek started under promising auspices. He used cheap loans from the Soviet Union and the Western banks to launch rapid industrial modernization. As a result, wages soared and the availability of consumer goods greatly improved. However, by the mid-1970s economic growth rates began to drop. The misguided policy of investing in technically obsolete industrial projects failed to produce exportable goods that could be used to pay back loans. While rampant corruption rivaled the incompetent management of party officials, the regime conducted self-laudatory propaganda. The dissonance between Gierek's public message and the actual conditions in Poland resulted in widespread apathy, moral disillusionment, and opportunism, brilliantly portrayed in works of the young filmmakers Agnieszka Holland, Krzysztof Kieślowski, and Marceli Łoziński. Their biting critique of society in crisis was aptly dubbed the "cinema of moral concern."

In 1976 Gierek resorted to the very solution advanced by Gomułka six years earlier—a general food-price increase. As labor unrest engulfed Poland, in the city of Radom local party headquarters were besieged and burned. Despite government suppression of the riots in the form of brutal arrests, beatings, and the sacking of hundreds of workers, the government soon rescinded the price increases.

The pacification of protests had a mobilizing effect on dissident intellectuals who, in September 1976, formed the Committee for the Defense of Workers (Komitet Obrony Robotników; KOR). The KOR, among other things, offered legal advice and financial support to the prosecuted workers and their families. The group included former reform Communists, veterans of the 1968 student protests, and members of the prewar Socialist Party as well as several cultural figures and a clergyman. The KOR soon expanded its activities into the defense of human and citizen rights, underground publishing, the establishment of independent trade unions, and the overall promotion of a civil society. In comparison to dissidents in other Communist states, KOR members, though repeatedly harassed by police, enjoyed relatively lenient treatment. As the Polish government signed the Helsinki peace, security, and civil rights accords and tried to secure more loans, it chose not to antagonize Western leaders by brutalizing the opposition. By the end of the decade Poland boasted several opposition groups of different political persuasions.

The dialogue between intellectuals and workers promoted by KOR encompassed only a tiny fraction of the Polish society. However, the late 1970s saw the rapprochement between opposition intellectuals and the strongest autonomous institution in Poland, the Roman Catholic Church, whose leaders had become increasingly outspoken about human rights. The major boost to this trend was the naming of Cardinal Karol Wojtyła of Kraków as Pope John Paul II in 1978. During his 1979 trip to Poland the pope's sermons attracted millions of laypeople and paved the way for a spiritual revolution and political upheaval in 1980.

1980–1989

In the summer of 1980, a rising foreign-trade deficit, hidden inflation, and mounting national debt led to the government's decision to radically adjust prices and cut domestic food supplies. Strikes and work stoppages paralyzed the entire country. In the coastal city of Gdansk, workers of the Lenin Shipyard went on strike on 14 August 1980. Under the energetic leadership of the young free trade union activist Lech Wałęsa and coached by members of the democratic opposition, the strikers combined economic postulates with political demands. They soon established the Interfactory Strike Committee in the Baltic region. In addition to economic concessions, the committee's demands included the creation of independent trade unions with the right to strike, the release of political prisoners, and freedom of expression. The action sparked a wave of political strikes across Poland. By the end of August the government yielded to this pressure and signed a series of agreements allowing the establishment of independent and autonomous labor unions. These accords toppled the Gierek regime and paved the way for the creation of the Independent Self-Governing Trade Union "Solidarity" in September 1980.

The first autonomous labor organization in the Soviet bloc, Solidarity soon evolved into a nationwide movement that by the year's end claimed nine million members and in the following year ten million. During the sixteen months of its legal existence, the union sparked an unparalleled wave of social activism, patriotic euphoria, and national unity. By radicalizing its initial nonpolitical, self-limiting agenda, Solidarity sought a semipluralist system in which citizens would share with the Communist Party responsibilities for ruling the state. The realization of this program would essentially end communism in Poland. Subjected to Soviet pressure and eager to reinstate the Communist Party's rule, the government of General Wojciech Jaruzelski decided to destroy Solidarity by force. With the declaration of martial law on 13 December 1981, military and police units sealed off the country, arrested thousands of Solidarity activists, and introduced a draconic penal code. In 1982 Solidarity was officially banished.

Despite repression, Solidarity continued its struggle underground. It organized political protests, work stoppages, and established a massive network of clandestine institutions. By the mid-1980s Jaruzelski's government softened its stance and began implementing moderate social, economic, and political reforms. When Mikhail Gorbachev launched his perestroika reforms in the Soviet Union, Jaruzelski became his leading follower in the Eastern bloc, hoping to pacify society and reform the economy while retaining the political power of the Communist Party. However, the goals of liberalizing the political system and introducing market mechanisms without legalizing Solidarity proved contradictory. In 1988 the government's plans to implement austerity measures provoked a giant wave of Solidarity-led strikes. Conducted from February to April 1989, the Roundtable Talks between Solidarity and the government led to the legalization of the union and secured its participation in parliamentary elections. On 4 June 1989, in the first partially free elections conducted in Eastern Europe since Communist takeovers, Solidarity won an overwhelming victory, taking 99 of 100 seats in the Senate and all of the 169 seats it was allowed to contest in the lower chamber of parliament, the Sejm. In August 1989 Tadeusz Mazowiecki formed the Solidarity-led coalition cabinet, the first noncommunist government in the Soviet bloc.

1989–2005

Following Solidarity's victory, the Mazowiecki government implemented sweeping reforms. In 1990 it implemented economic "shock therapy," commonly known as the Balcerowicz plan (named after Deputy Prime Minister Leszek Balcerowicz), beginning a transformation to a market economy. However, with the collapse of communism in Eastern Europe, the political solutions reached by the Roundtable Talks became increasingly anachronistic. The year 1990 saw the division of Solidarity into numerous factions, disunited in their attitudes toward market reforms, de-communization, and Lech Wałęsa's presidential ambitions. In the presidential elections of 1990 Wałęsa defeated Mazowiecki, while the 1991 general vote produced a fragmented parliament. Rising unemployment, cuts in welfare spending, and an overall sense of insecurity in society resulted in the electoral victory of the ex-communist Alliance of Democratic Left (SLD) in 1993. Presidential elections two years later saw the leader of the alliance, Aleksander Kwaśniewski, defeat Wałęsa. Kwaśniewski went on to win a second term in 2000.

Despite these frequent changes, Poland nevertheless has become a fully fledged democracy and a market economy. The transition did not occur without serious difficulties, however. The country continues to battle high unemployment, low incomes, and a crumbling public infrastructure. Its oversize farming sector is costly and inefficient. Economic inefficiency coupled with corruption brought down the SLD government in 1997 and later its right-center successor, the Electoral Action "Solidarity" (AWS) cabinet in 2001. The SLD government of Leszek Miller, which ruled the country from 2001 to 2004, advanced political cronyism and corruption even further. Following Miller's resignation in 2004, the country was ruled by the minority government of Marek Belka. The general elections of September 2005 produced the defeat of the SLD and the victory of the national conservative Law and Justice Party (PiS) and Civic Platform (PO), another center-right party. Between them, the two parties took over 50 percent of the vote. However, the outcome of negotiations on forming a coalition government collapsed after Lech Kaczyński of PiS defeated Donald Tusk of PO in presidential elections in October 2005. In 2006, Poland had a minority government dominated by the Law and Justice Party. Kazimierz Marcinkiewicz of PiS served as prime minister.

Admittedly, most Polish political leaders, regardless of their political affiliations, contributed to Poland's integration with international institutions. In 1998 the country joined NATO and in May 2004 the European Union. A major U.S. ally in Europe, Poland participated in the U.S.-led invasion of Iraq; since 2003 Poland has led an international peacekeeping force of 9,000 troops, including 2,500 from Poland, in south-central Iraq.

In staunch contrast to the prewar period, Poland does not have any border disputes and protects its minorities according to international legal and ethical standards. After 1989 Polish diplomacy treated Soviet republics as full subjects of international law and ardently supported national movements in Belarus, Lithuania, and Ukraine. In December 1991 Poland was the first country to officially recognize independent Ukraine and played an important role in the peaceful resolution of the Ukrainian political crisis of 2005.

See also **Auschwitz-Birkenau; Eastern Bloc; Gomułka, Władysław; Jaruzelski, Wojciech; John Paul II; Katyń Forest Massacre; Miłosz, Czesław; Minority Rights; Occupation, Military; Piłsudski, Józef; Resistance; Solidarity; Ukraine; Wajda, Andrzej; Wałęsa, Lech; Warsaw; Warsaw Ghetto; Warsaw Pact; Warsaw Uprising; World War II.**

BIBLIOGRAPHY

Blobaum, Robert. *Rewolucja: Russian Poland, 1904–1907.* Ithaca, N.Y., 1995.

Davies, Norman. *God's Playground: A History of Poland.* 2 vols. New York, 1982.

Garton Ash, Timothy. *The Polish Revolution: Solidarity 1980–1982.* London, 1983.

Kersten, Krystyna. *The Establishment of Communist Rule in Poland, 1943–1948.* Translated and annotated by John Micgiel and Michael H. Bernhard. Berkeley, Calif., 1981.

Korboński, Stefan. *The Polish Underground State.* New York, 1981.

Michalek, Bolesław, and Frank Turaj. *The Modern Cinema of Poland.* Bloomington, Ind., 1988.

Miłosz, Czesław. *The History of Polish Literature.* 2nd ed. Berkeley, Calif., 1983.

Paczkowski, Andrzej. *The Spring Will Be Ours: Poland and the Poles from Occupation to Freedom.* University Park, Pa., 2003.

Polonsky, Antony. *Politics in Independent Poland 1921–1939.* Oxford, U.K., 1972.

Porter, Brian. *When Nationalism Began to Hate: Imagining Modern Politics in Nineteenth-Century Poland.* New York, 2000.

Snyder, Timothy. *The Reconstruction of Nations: Poland, Ukraine, Lithuania, Belarus, 1569–1999.* New Haven, Conn., 2003.

Wandycz, Piotr S. *The Lands of Partitioned Poland, 1795–1918.* Seattle, Wash., 1974.

MIKOŁAJ KUNICKI

POLICE AND POLICING.

At the beginning of the twentieth century, police institutions in Europe liked to think of themselves as deploying scientific and technological solutions to their tasks. But policing was largely an unskilled job. The daily duty for most police agents generally involved patrolling, usually on foot, in towns or cities. As the century progressed there was greater use of scientific and technological developments. Patrolling became increasingly mechanized; the gender balance and the ethnic complexion of many forces changed. Police institutions, by the very nature of their role, were also caught up in the darker side of European politics.

TECHNOLOGY AND POLITICS

Police responsibility for public safety and the good order of the highways necessitated a police response to the enormous growth of the motor vehicle as a means of both freight and personal transport. In the United Kingdom, where police regulation had rarely involved the bobby having to confront the respectable middle class, the development of the motorcar and accompanying regulations noticeably led to a souring of relations between the police and the respectable classes. Across the Continent in the aftermath of World War I some progressive police chiefs urged the deployment of forensic science and of nonlethal crowd control technology such as plastic bullets and water cannon. There were also experiments with radio technology, though often this was hampered by poor coordination between local forces in, for example, the use of wave bands.

Wilhelm Abegg (1876–1951), as head of the Police Section of the Prussian Interior Ministry in Weimar Germany, was a key figure in the determination to harness new technologies and to press the notion of the police as technocrats and defenders and helpers of the public at large. Abegg's attempts to portray the police as modern and to break with the autocratic past were subsequently hijacked by the Nazis. In 1934, the year after coming to power, the Nazis set aside a day for celebrating the police and building up their relationship with the public. The Day of the Police (*Polizeitag*), with charity collections by the police, bands, and parades, all designed to promote the police as the friend and helper of the public, proved so popular that in 1937 it became a weeklong event.

Not all German police officers were Nazis or became such overnight. Party membership, however, enhanced an individual's career prospects. Moreover, the free hand and encouragement that the party gave the police was popular with the rank and file. Fairly rapidly the detective police responsible for the pursuit of criminal offenders, the Kriminalpolizei, or Kripo, began to use methods similar to those of the secret state police, the Geheime Staatspolizei, or Gestapo. The most obvious example of this was when officers arrested those who they suspected *might* commit a crime. The Italian police institutions benefited similarly under Benito Mussolini, though membership of the Fascist Party was never a prerequisite for joining or serving in the police. The military police, the Carabinieri, appear also to have considered that their loyalty was to the king first rather than to Mussolini.

THE IMPACT OF WAR

The pressures of world war enabled governments to push through changes in police institutions that had long been considered. For example, in both the United Kingdom and France—under very different regimes—World War II provided the opportunity for centralization. In the former this meant the long-desired amalgamation of many of the smallest forces with their larger neighbors; in Vichy France it meant complete nationalization.

Occupation and dictatorial regimes across much of continental Europe created pressures on, and problems for, individual police officers, most notably the extent to which they should compromise with a new regime, resist, or rebel. In Spain during the civil war (1936–1939) most of the military police, the Guardia Civil, backed the Fascist rebels. In some countries occupied by Nazi Germany and its allies some police officers obeyed orders and arrested Jews, communists, and opponents of the regime. Except for the new racial policies, French police officers could console themselves that the pursuit of Bolsheviks, of other opponents of the regime, and of ordinary criminals was essentially what they had been expected to do under the Third Republic. In France, and in other occupied countries, a few resisted in varying

degrees and in various ways, though only in Denmark were the Nazi authorities compelled to dismiss the entire police institution and replace it with officers from the SS. In September 1944 nearly two thousand Danish police officers were transported to Buchenwald.

The postwar situation did not bring an end to political problems within the police forces. Only in the Soviet zone of Germany was a police force reestablished with a completely new workforce; no one who had served under the previous regime was allowed back into the service. In what became West Germany and in Italy, however, many police officers continued in their prewar and wartime posts, though in their respective zones of occupation American, British, and French police were deployed to restructure the German system using their own "democratic" models. The purge of police officers in Italy in the aftermath of World War II led to the dismissal of many of the anti-Fascist partisans who had been recruited as police (*polizia partigiana*). The postwar Italian police were portrayed as politically neutral, but nevertheless they infiltrated labor unions and political parties and some dabbled in right-wing plots.

Policing in Nazi Germany had focused on racial and social enemies of the national community, the *Volksgemeinschaft*. In what became the German Democratic Republic, as elsewhere in the Soviet Union's postwar empire, policing was directed against class enemies. Defeat in 1945 meant an end to the Gestapo, but in April 1950 the GDR developed an even more extensive and intrusive system of political surveillance through the Ministerium für Staatssicherheit (Ministry for State Security) or Stasi. At its peak the Stasi had some ninety thousand uniformed and plainclothes agents; but it also had possibly as many as one in sixty of the total population working in some way as informants.

ISSUES IN POSTWAR POLICING

The end of World War II heralded both the end of the European empires and also a considerable influx of peoples from those empires to the former metropoles. Prejudice and different cultural perspectives often fostered stigmatization. The aspirations of most of the European states to some form of multiculturalism eventually encouraged attempts, most notably in the Netherlands and the United Kingdom, to recruit members of these ethnic minorities into their police. The problem was rather different in France where the political culture denied any political significance to the personal identities, and hence ethnicity, of citizens and hence tended to militate against such action.

The growth of the women's movement also brought significant changes in police institutions and possibly also, as a result, in the nature of policing. Women officers had begun to be appointed to many forces early in the twentieth century, but their role was largely restricted to dealing with women, children, and welfare issues. Demands for equality at the workplace, particularly starting in the 1960s, meant that women were increasingly incorporated into roles identical to those of their male counterparts. Even at the turn of the millennium, however, some police institutions, particularly the military bodies in Italy and Spain, had responded to these pressures with much less alacrity than others.

In the second half of the century most of the major states of Western Europe experienced a significant growth in their crime statistics. These increases put pressure on the police. In Britain the growth of crime and, particularly, the spread of turf wars between drug gangs, led to the growing deployment of officers carrying firearms. Everywhere, police faith in, and use of, new technology addressed only some of the problems. Computerized record keeping and DNA technology were deployed with considerable publicity and expectation. So too, a few years earlier, was the extended use of motorized patrolling. Unfortunately the latter, while important given the public's use of motor vehicles and the enormous expansion of many towns and cities, served in many respects to separate the police further from the public. Beginning in the late 1980s new programs were established to increase trust and cooperation between the police and the public. In the United Kingdom many of these programs went under the heading of "community policing," while in France the term *police de proximité* was employed.

The turn of the millennium saw the police forces of Europe compelled to confront a series of issues emanating from new political structures and new global situations. The evolution of the European Union (EU) meant the bringing down of national barriers. But the development of international organized crime, particularly the drug trade—which contributed to the growth of crime and gang warfare in individual countries—people smuggling, and terrorism, encouraged new levels of, and systems for, international cooperation. The Schengen Agreement of 1985 and its various updates reduced border controls, harmonized provisions relating to entry to member states, and sought to foster cooperation on judicial matters. During the 1990s the European Police Office (Europol) was established to provide a bridge for mutual assistance and information sharing among police forces in the member states of the EU. These links involved cooperation with other agencies—customs and excise, drugs enforcement, immigration—not always perceived as being police though clearly involved with policing. As Europe's frontiers came down, so new barriers, checks, and policing structures needed to be developed.

See also **Crime and Justice.**

BIBLIOGRAPHY

Berlière, Jean-Marc. *Le monde des polices en France: XIXe et XXe siècles.* Brussels, 1996.

Emsley, Clive. *The English Police: A Political and Social History.* 2nd ed. London, 1996.

Fijnaut, Cyrille, ed. *The Impact of World War II on Policing in North-West Europe.* Louvain, Belgium, 2004.

Oram, Gerard, ed. *Conflict and Legality: Policing Mid-Twentieth-Century Europe.* London, 2003.

CLIVE EMSLEY

POLITICAL PRISONERS. The term *political prisoner* has had a wide currency since the early twentieth century without commanding an accepted definition. Individuals opposed to the policies of a particular state who have voiced or acted on their opposition have often found themselves subject to the criminal laws of sedition or treason, even though their objections may well have been based on ideological or moral grounds. It would be wrong to exclude all such people from being political prisoners, but a more viable distinction is to highlight those people who have been imprisoned primarily for their opposition to a particular regime or ruling party, even if they have been convicted under the criminal law of the country concerned and accused of crimes against the state. Although the concept of the political prisoner is usually associated with the autocratic regimes of the early twentieth century and the dictatorships of Joseph Stalin, Adolf Hitler, and Benito Mussolini, most states have found it necessary to imprison political opponents whose extremist ideologies or actions were perceived as inherently dangerous.

SOVIET UNION AND THE EASTERN BLOC

The tsarist regime in Russia had used both imprisonment and exile extensively to deal with political opponents and presumed subversives in the years before 1914. For example, most of the Bolshevik leaders suffered imprisonment for their beliefs at some point. After the Revolution of 1917, they instituted concentration camps for political opponents from mid-1918 onward close to major centers of population. The number of these camps was reduced from sixty-five in 1922 to twenty-three in 1923. At the same time, a new form of special concentration camp (SLON) was established on the Solovetsky Islands in Archangel Province. This was specifically designed to house counterrevolutionaries including White Guardists, reactionary clergy, and "hostile class elements." This system of corrective labor camps and corrective labor colonies in remote locations was expanded by the OGPU (security police) in the later 1920s to deal with the class struggle against the kulaks (wealthy peasants) through the creation of "special settlements." Estimates suggest 1.8 million people were exiled in the years 1930 and 1931 alone. On 15 February 1931 the OGPU also created a main administration for its camps, the Glavnoe Upravlenie Lagerei (GULag, now commonly rendered as *gulag*). Although directed primarily toward political and class enemies of the regime, the gulag system became increasingly intertwined with the Soviet need for labor in remote regions to drive forward industrialization. The victimization of the kulaks was followed by a law of 7 August 1932 on the theft of state property under which sentences of life imprisonment or even death could be levied for the most minor infractions. This brought 55,000 arrests in less than six months and 127,000 in four years.

The use of terror against political opponents and Soviet citizens in general became ever more pronounced through the 1930s. The murder of Leningrad Party leader and Politburo member Kirov in 1934 was used as an excuse to arrest those suspected of disloyalty inside the Communist Party. The Great Purge of 1936–1938 included the show trials of leaders such as Gregory Zinoviev, Lev Kamenev, and Nikolai Bukharin but also involved the mass arrests and deaths or imprisonment of huge numbers of party functionaries and state officials, including 70 percent of Central Committee members and 50 percent of Party Congress delegates. In addition, 35,000 Red Army officers, including 80 percent of colonels and 90 percent of generals, also became victims of the system. Estimates of the numbers who died in captivity vary enormously, but the total of political prisoners executed or worked to death runs into millions. Although the purges were abandoned in 1938, the system of internal exile, imprisonment, and incarceration in labor camps for political crimes was continued during the remainder of the Stalinist era and beyond. The gulag system reached its peak in the summer of 1950 when the camps, colonies, and prisons contained 2.8 million inmates. At that time the number of fresh admissions was between 600,000 and 700,000 per year, and it has been estimated that anywhere between 20 and 28 million people passed through or died in the system between the 1920s and 1950s, a large proportion of them for supposedly political offenses. However, the nature of the records and the categorization of prisoners make any precise estimation of true numbers impossible. Outside knowledge of the Soviet system came from Alexander Solzhenitsyn, whose books *One Day in the Life of Ivan Denisovich* (1962) and *Gulag Archipelago* (1973) were based on his personal experiences of imprisonment between 1945 and 1957.

The regimes in Eastern bloc countries of Europe under Soviet domination after 1945 also used harassment, arrest, and imprisonment of political, intellectual, and perceived class opponents. Thus, for example, Vaclav Havel, the playwright later to become president of the Czech Republic, spent many years in prison or under house arrest

Leonid Ramzin, center, confesses to being the head of the antigovernment Industrial Party during his trial, December 1930. Ramzin and eight other Russian scientists were convicted of acts of sabotage in a renowned Stalinist-era show trial. Several were sentenced to death, but their sentences were later commuted and they were eventually released from prison. ©HULTON-DEUTSCH COLLECTION/CORBIS

during the communist era. The German Democratic Republic (East Germany) also used imprisonment to deal with perceived class enemies and dissident intellectuals. In spite of releasing 21,187 political prisoners in the first ten months of 1956, East German jails still contained 23,674 people held for political reasons. Even in the 1970s there were between 4,000 and 6,000 political detainees held by the regime. These included dissident functionaries of the Sozialistische Einheitspartei Deutschlands (SED; German Unity Party) such as Rudolf Bahro, who was sentenced to eight years' imprisonment for his publication *The Alternative in Eastern Europe* (1977). In post-1945 Hungary, arrests for political reasons were commonplace in the later 1940s and early 1950s. Amnesties in 1953 and 1956 were followed by further mass arrests after

the Soviet suppression of reformism in the latter year. Thousands were subsequently condemned to imprisonment and forced labor, including the former premier Imre Nagy, who was arrested and shot by the KGB.

NAZI GERMANY AND FASCIST ITALY

Like tsarist Russia, imperial Germany had become increasingly worried about internal subversion by social democrats (SPD) in the years leading up to 1914 and had established a political police department in Prussia in 1912. In spite of plans embodied in the so-called Gebsattel Memorandum for martial law and military control of the factories to ensure production in the event of war, there was little real opposition to the war of 1914 except from the extreme left of the SPD, some of whose members were imprisoned for fomenting opposition to the war. During the Weimar Republic, political prisoners were a rarity, although *putschists* from both left and right, including Adolf Hitler, served jail terms for insurrection.

From its inception in 1933 the Nazi regime in Germany imprisoned vast numbers of political opponents in concentration camps. Nazi activists abducted and imprisoned their political opponents almost from the moment that Hitler became chancellor on 30 January. Thus the first "camps" were in the basements of buildings or other easily guarded locations. This illegal terror was regularized by the so-called Reichstag Fire Decree on 28 February that suspended personal liberties for the individual. Permanent sites at Dachau, Buchenwald, and Sachsenhausen soon replaced these "wild" camps. Administered initially by the SA (the Stürmabteilung, or "brownshirts"), control of the camps soon passed to the SS (the Schutzstaffel) under the police and security apparatus run by Heinrich Himmler. The camps were designed to run in parallel with the normal judicial and penal system but to dispense National Socialist justice. Initially, like the camps in the Soviet Union, they were supposed to rehabilitate inmates and turn them into useful members of society, but later the system became a means of provoking fear among the population at large and providing a source of labor. A criminal finishing a sentence might be rearrested and sent to a concentration camp for a period of protective custody (*Schutzhaft*) if the Nazis considered the original sentence too lenient.

Camp inmates were categorized under four headings: political opponents, "racial" opponents, criminals, and "asocials." The first victims of this system were the Communists who were thought capable of mounting a counterrevolution to the Nazis but whose organization was rapidly broken up and its members exiled or imprisoned. To them were added Social Democrats, trade unionists, and members of other parties who spoke out against the regime, as well as Catholics, Protestants, and Jehovah's Witnesses. One such was Pastor Martin Niemöller, founder of the Pastors' Emergency League, who was imprisoned in 1938 for "underhand attacks" against the state and then rearrested and committed to a concentration camp until

1945. The political prisoners in the camps were often the longest-serving inmates and often formed the internal administration of the camps as barracks leaders. Jews also became victims of the system of arrest without trial or appeal, with 30,000 being held in the aftermath of the November 1938 Kristallnacht pogrom. The system was enlarged in the prewar period with new camps built across Germany, and it is estimated that 200,000 people passed through the system between 1934 and 1939 with around 50,000 still being imprisoned at the outbreak of war.

As the regime broadened its the definitions of political "crimes"—from anti-Hitler or anti-Nazi sentiments, spreading rumors, or listening to illegal radio broadcasts to criminalizing any behavior with an oppositional aspect to it—so the numbers of political prisoners inevitably increased, although many were now being prosecuted under the criminal code. The concentration camps also took in large numbers of arrestees after the war against the Soviet Union began in June 1941 and again at the end of that year, when dissidents from occupied territories, the so-called night and fog (*Nacht und Nebel*) prisoners, were transferred to the Reich. By mid-August 1944 the concentration camp system held 524,286 people, but by this stage it included all manner of "opponents" of many different nationalities, not all of whom could be classed as political.

Germany's Axis partner, the Italian Fascist regime under Mussolini, also imprisoned political opponents and ultimately members of its own movement as well. Its most famous prisoner was Antonio Gramsci, the Italian Communist politician, journalist, and Marxist ideologue, who was arrested and tried before a special tribunal in November 1926 and then spent eleven years in jail, until shortly before his death in 1937. Although the Fascist regime allowed many political opponents to leave Italy, it also used exile to remote locations as a policy to deal with those regarded as politically unreliable.

SPAIN: CIVIL WAR AND THE FRANCO REGIME

Arrests for political reasons were commonplace in Spain before and during the 1930s. Large numbers of anarchists were arrested in 1933 and 1934 for

Political prisoners dig irrigation ditches in a labor camp in the Emsland region of Germany, 1935. LIBRARY OF CONGRESS

opposition to the center-right government of the Second Republic. During the Spanish civil war both sides interned supporters of their opponents, occasionally for their own protection against popular hatred. In this conflict many political prisoners were used as hostages and were subject to summary justice from political groups working within the Republican or Nationalist coalitions. Toward the war's end, in February 1939 the victorious Francisco Franco regime passed the Law on Political Responsibilities and took steps to arrest and incarcerate those in Spain who were thought to hold Republican sympathies. This included not only the politically active but also many people whose only "crime" had been nonattendance at Mass. Prisons and camps were packed to overflowing and the prisoners were subject to summary justice, with perhaps 200,000 being executed in the years during and after 1939. Estimates suggest that there were still 250,000 in prisons at the end of 1940, but this had been reduced to around 28,000 by 1944.

In spite of this mass killing, many thousands remained prisoners for decades, and the regime continued to use imprisonment against opponents. For example, in 1969 there were 1,101 political cases brought before the Spanish courts. The system ended only when Franco died and was replaced by King Juan Carlos in 1975. Thereafter most political detainees were freed. During the later years of the Franco regime in Spain, Basque nationalists and their paramilitary force Euskadi Ta Askatasuna (ETA) were subject to repression, arrests, and torture.

WESTERN EUROPEAN DEMOCRACIES

The major Western European democracies traditionally had constitutional guarantees to prevent the imprisonment of political opponents. The exceptions occurred in time of war or emergency. Thus, many Irish nationalists were imprisoned during the nineteenth and early twentieth centuries for their political beliefs. During World War I, Britain also used its emergency powers under the 1915 Defence of the Realm Act (DORA) to arrest Irish nationalist sympathizers, but these measures were often frustrated by Irish juries' refusal to convict those charged, even when the case involved criminal charges. After the Easter Rising in 1916, Regulation 14B was used to arrest a total of 3,509 people and then have them brought before military courts-martial. This resulted in numerous death sentences, fourteen of which were carried out.

At the outbreak of war in Europe in September 1939, the French Third Republic used the war and the Nazi-Soviet nonaggression treaty as an excuse to arrest large numbers of French Communists, but in general the liberal states of Western Europe had no plans to deal with pro-Nazi elements, and at the beginning of January 1940 there were only 49 detainees in Britain. The preference was for identification and surveillance of both potential enemy subversives and traitors, but this changed as the tide of war turned against the Anglo-French alliance. The British moved to arrest and intern German sympathizers and members of the British Union of Fascists, including its leader, Oswald Mosley. In total, around 2,000 British nationals were incarcerated under Regulation 18B and some remained in jail until the war ended in 1945. These relatively limited numbers of political prisoners were swamped by the internment of enemy nationals from May 1940, in spite of the fact that many were anti-Nazi or racial refugees from the Hitler regime. Mass internment of German and Italian nationals totaled 29,000 by the summer of 1940. Some were deported to the dominions and the rest held on the Isle of Man. Gradual releases took place as the threat to the United Kingdom receded, and by 1945 only 1,200 remained in captivity.

At the end of World War II many states occupied by the Axis Powers interned those who had joined indigenous national socialist or fascist parties and those who had collaborated with the occupying powers. Since then the numbers of political prisoners in democratic Western Europe have been small. All European states have ratified the 1950 European Convention for the Protection of Human Rights and Fundamental Freedoms, and most have also agreed to the 1987 European Convention for the Prevention of Torture and Inhuman or Degrading Treatment or Punishment. Those who might have been deemed political prisoners have been largely confined to regional independence movements such as the Basque separatists or Irish Republicans and to extremist political groups such as the Red Brigades in Italy and the Baader-Meinhof Group, or Red Army Faction, in Germany. For example, in the mid-1970s, in response to increasing levels of terrorism, the Italian government began arresting activists from the extraparliamentary Left, and their numbers peaked at around 4,000 in the early 1980s. Democracy after 1975 in Spain brought extensive autonomy for the Basque region, but the terrorism continued. After attempts at reconciliation with ETA failed, the Spanish government began to take a harder line, giving seven-year prison sentences in 1997 to the entire twenty-three-member leadership of Herri Batasuna, ETA's political wing, for collaboration with the armed group. They joined an estimated 500 to 700 imprisoned ETA activists.

The outbreak of sectarian violence in Northern Ireland in 1968 led to the government using internment at the Long Kesh/Maze prison as a device to remove both Catholic and loyalist paramilitary leaders from circulation. Reportedly subject to interrogations and torture in the early days of internment, their "political" status was removed in 1976, but internment remained a major weapon for the British government. It was reinforced by the use of Diplock courts, in which judges try criminal cases without a jury, ostensibly to remove the possibility of jury intimidation in criminal trials but also as a means of obtaining easier convictions for criminal offenses. The Good Friday Agreement of 1998 ended the process, and internees, as well as many paramilitaries convicted of criminal offenses, were released.

Since the 1960s the plight of political prisoners across the world has been given a higher profile through the activities of Amnesty International, a charity that seeks to protect the interests of those imprisoned on political grounds. It also publishes an annual international survey of imprisoned persons and assessments of the legislation and extralegal measures used to detain them.

See also **Concentration Camps; Crime and Justice; Gulag; Purges; Terror.**

BIBLIOGRAPHY

Appelbaum, Anne. *Gulag: A History of the Soviet Camps.* London, 2003.

Ivanova, G. M. *Labor Camp Socialism: The Gulag in the Soviet Totalitarian System.* Translated by Carol Flath and edited by Donald J. Raleigh. Armonk, N.Y., and London, 2000.

Krausnick, Helmut, et al., eds. *Anatomy of the SS State.* St. Albans, 1970.

Ruggiero, Vincenzo, et al., eds. *Western European Penal Systems: A Critical Anatomy.* London, 1995.

ROBERT MOORE

POP ART. In 1996 the *New York Times* art critic happily claimed that the renovated and glittering Times Square was indistinguishable from an art installation. American Pop Art, whose most celebrated artists had emerged from the commercial advertising sector, seemed to have reached its inherent telos in the gigantic billboards featuring models without affect, corporate signs in screaming colors, larger-than-life television screens, and the three-tier electronic stock ticker tape display towering over Broadway and Forty-second Street.

Confusion between art and advertising, image and object in our media-saturated culture is indeed a real possibility. But rather than collapse the difference, Pop Art first sharpened the senses for discerning this constellation by exploring the boundary between images and objects of art and images and objects of commerce. Pop was attacked by cultural conservatives in Europe, for whom all American culture was "catastrophic" (Martin Heidegger), by American formalists, who saw the canon of high modernism challenged by Pop's mass cultural contents (Clement Greenberg), and by leftists of all shades who saw only commodification and consumerist triumphalism in Pop's promiscuous imagery.

Pop Art celebrated something not easily compatible with notions of high art—a look at objects of everyday life or, more precisely, a look at media representations of objects of everyday life. But those objects were not the urban or domestic detritus recycled in Dada collages, in Robert Rauschenberg's *Combines,* or in French *décollage* art of the 1950s, which worked with anonymously defaced billboard advertising found in urban space. They were rather images of mass-marketed consumer goods at a time, the early 1960s, when consumerism, marketing, and advertising in the United States had reached a heretofore unknown state of frenzy. In Roland Barthes's words, Pop staged an object that was neither the thing nor its meaning, but its signifier. But this staging did not take on an existentialist, angst-ridden, or moralizing accusatory cast. American Pop did not rebel against middle-class society. It lacked the aggressive, often doctrinaire assault on aesthetic convention that had characterized an earlier European avant-garde and that resurfaced in the factional fights of the post-1945 neo-avant-gardes, culminating with the Situationist International (1957–1972), a Paris-based group of avant-garde artists who waged a political attack on the culture of spectacle in the 1960s. American Pop refused any pedagogical mission, that of debunking the media cliché as the product and producer of false consciousness, for example. Its preferred look at consumer objects was cool and aloof, self-conscious deadpan tinged with parody. The images were banal, taken from advertising, newspapers, comics, and other forms of mass culture, but often so garish, so magnified beyond natural proportions and "in your face" that they inevitably intensified and altered perception. Pop images were neither pure representation (referring the spectator to the consumer object) nor pure simulacra (referring merely to other images). In their apparent celebration of Americana as both at once, they coolly registered a dimension of anxiety, melancholy, and loss that has perhaps become more visible with the passing of time.

Important for an overall assessment of Pop as a critically innovative project is the broader cultural and artistic context of the 1960s. Pop Art contributed significantly to a cultural transformation that

As Is When: Wittgenstein in New York. Lithograph by Edward Paolozzi, 1965. Paolozzi was one of the originators of Pop Art in Britain, and his *As Is When* series, inspired by the life of philosopher Ludwig Wittgenstein, is widely viewed as one of the movement's masterworks. BRIDGEMAN ART LIBRARY

was later designated by the name *postmodern*. Central to this transformation was a shift in emphasis from production to consumption, from artist as producer to artist as agent (Andy Warhol's Factory), from creator to spectator, from artwork to text, from meaning to signifying, from originality to repetition, from high culture to mass culture. Pop Art crucially articulated many of the major terms of this transformation. It eradicated the boundaries between art and the everyday, not by reversing the hierarchy of high and popular, but by offering new ways of imaging their relationship.

The cultural politics of Pop is not exhausted by such formal and conceptual considerations. The notion that Pop Art harbored a hidden social critique of consumer culture behind its bland facade was always more prevalent in some European countries than in the United States, where Pop remained a more isolated phenomenon of the New York art culture and its galleries. In West Germany, by contrast, a wave of Pop enthusiasm swept the country after its first introduction at the 1964 documenta, an exhibition of modern and contemporary art. The conservative cultural critics, who were peddling Christian values, pastoralism, and, at best, the latest vintage of worn-out abstraction, denounced Pop Art as nonart, supermarket art, and kitsch, lamenting the Coca-Colonization of western Europe in apocalyptic tones. Between 1964 and 1968, the notion of Pop that almost magically attracted people did not refer only to the new art by Warhol, Jasper Johns, Roy Lichtenstein, James Rosenquist, Tom Wesselmann, and Claes Oldenburg. It also stood for beat and rock music, poster art, the flower child cult, and an emerging youth culture, indeed for any manifestation of what was then mistakenly called "the underground." In short, Pop became the synonym for the new lifestyles of a younger generation in rebellion against their parents and the conservative and repressive culture of the 1950s. Against the politically apologetic uses of the German high cultural tradition, this whole grab bag of Americana supported the new rebellious attitude and satisfied a generational desire for lifting the dead weight of a tradition whose collusion with Nazism had become all too obvious. Pop combined the cool detached look with a new intensity in perception, which resonated with a certain sensibility among the young. It challenged the European privilege given to indigenous high culture, with its traditions of anti-Americanism. Pop, American to the core, accelerated the decline of cultural nationalism in Germany—and not only there.

With the rise of the international protest movement against the Vietnam War and the radicalization of the student movement in 1968, however, the initial enthusiasm about things American turned sour. The battle cry against American cultural imperialism was now heard more often from the Left than from the Right. The Vietnam War, considered the logical outcome of Cold War ideology, complicated "America" for liberals and leftists. The rediscovery of Western Marxism (György Lukács, Karl Korsch, Antonio Gramsci, Ernst Bloch, Herbert Marcuse, Theodor Adorno, Max Horkheimer, Walter Benjamin) merged with a very German tradition of *Kulturkritik* and its ingrained cultural anti-Americanism to reveal Pop Art as the logical outcome of advertising and the culture industry: art as commodity and spectacle through and through. Thus the 1968 protest movements' call for the end of traditional art, for the merging of art and life, and for cultural revolution: *l'imagination au pouvoir* (power to the imagination). Pop Art had fallen from grace. Adorno in Germany, Guy Debord, Jean Baudrillard, and the situationists in France, provided the death knell.

The year 1968 marked a leftist cultural Europeanism combined with legitimate outrage at American military imperialism in Vietnam. That outrage blocked a more appropriate assessment of the ambiguity of Pop Art in critical terms: Pop as an art that did not just reproduce commodities, thus contributing to what Debord indicted as the culture of the spectacle, but that practiced an American version of situationist *détournement* (i.e., diversion or critical estrangement, defamiliarization) by reproducing reproducibility and thus getting to the very heart of capitalist commodity culture in the age of visual media. But it reproduced reproducibility with a difference. This difference remains a bone of contention. Umberto Eco once suggested that it is no longer clear whether we are listening to a criticism of consumer language, whether we are consuming consumer language, or whether we are consuming critical languages as consumer languages. Indeed, it is not clear. And perhaps we are doing all at the same time. But would we know that without Pop?

See also **Christo; Hamilton, Richard.**

BIBLIOGRAPHY

Buchloh, Benjamin H. D. "Villeglé: From Fragment to Detail." In his *Neo-Avantgarde and Culture Industry: Essays on European and American Art from 1955 to 1975,* 443–460. Cambridge, Mass., 2000.

Crow, Thomas E. *The Rise of the Sixties: American and European Art in the Era of Dissent.* New York, 1996.

Hermand, Jost. *Pop International. Eine kritische Analyse.* Frankfurt am Main, 1971.

Huyssen, Andreas. "The Cultural Politics of Pop." In his *After the Great Divide: Modernism, Mass Culture, Postmodernism,* 141–159. Bloomington, Ind., 1986.

Kimmelman, Michael. "That Flashing Crazy Quilt of Signs? It's Art." *New York Times,* 31 December 1996, A1.

Knabb, Ken, ed. and trans. *Situationist International Anthology.* Berkeley, Calif., 1981.

Madoff, Steven Henry, ed. *Pop Art: A Critical History.* Berkeley, Calif., 1997.

Mamiya, Christin J. *Pop Art and Consumer Culture: American Super Market.* Austin, Tex., 1992.

Wollen, Peter. "The Situationist International: On the Passage of a Few People through a Rather Brief Passage of Time." In his *Raiding the Icebox: Reflections on Twentieth-Century Culture,* 120–157. Bloomington, Ind., 1993.

ANDREAS HUYSSEN

POPULAR CULTURE.

Popular culture in twentieth-century Europe is the culture of mass appeal. In contrast to earlier periods when "popular" described essentially non-literary, folkloric, often local forms of culture, culture is seen as popular in the twentieth century primarily "when it is created to respond to the experiences and values of the majority, when it is produced in such a way that the majority have easy access to it, and when it can be understood and interpreted by that majority without aid of special knowledge or experience" (Bell, 1982, p. 443).

This modern idea of popular culture was linked to the rise of the mass media that dominated public life in the twentieth century. The popular press, the cinema, the gramophone, and its successors, radio, television, and the Internet, all addressed the mass public that came to characterize modern, industrialized Europe. Its rise had begun in the last decades of the nineteenth century, brought about by a number of interlinked economic and social factors, among them increased primary education, a rise in disposable income, the effects of urbanization, new means of transport and communication, increasing leisure time, and the commercialization of this leisure time with the rise of new forms of tourism, recreation, and entertainment.

SPECTATOR SPORT AND THE POPULAR PRESS

Spectator sport, one of the most popular forms of twentieth-century mass entertainment, was part of the commercialization of leisure that began in the late nineteenth century. Of the many forms of sport that became an integral part of popular culture in modern European societies, none has been more influential than football. Its professionalization was signaled by the foundation of associations (in England in 1863, in the Netherlands and Denmark in 1889, in Switzerland and Belgium in 1895, in Italy in 1898, and in Germany in 1900) that regulated rules, competitions, and leagues. As early as 1888 the first professional league was established, the English Football League. The Fédération Internationale de Football (FIFA), founded in Paris in 1904 as an amalgamation of national football associations, signaled the European-wide success of spectator sport.

The new mass-circulating newspapers of the late nineteenth century, and all other important media of popular culture after it, discovered and cultivated sport as a prime arena of entertainment. Indeed, the merging of sport, entertainment, and mass media became one of the driving forces of popular culture in the twentieth century. There were already clear signs for this before 1914. A prominent example was the *Gazzetta dello Sport,* one of the most popular twentieth-century Italian newspapers. Founded as a weekly in April 1896 but published daily from 1913 on, it organized mass sporting events as much as it disseminated them. The title page of its first issue announced a regional cycling race hosted by the newspaper; in 1909 the *Gazzetta* organized the first Giro d'Italia, the nationwide cycling contest.

In merging media and sports, the *Gazzetta* provided an early model for twentieth-century popular culture. Its deliberate distance from established politics and its direct participation in mass culture can be seen as paradigmatic for the popular press that expanded rapidly in most European countries toward the end of the nineteenth century. Innovations in printing technology were a contributing factor, but decisive for the rise of mass-circulating newspapers was the fact that they combined commercial success with popular appeal. Their economy relied primarily on advertising revenue rather than on the income from news vendors; they ensured mass circulation through a comparably low selling price, new forms of distribution, and new styles of journalism. Instead of politics and international affairs, the popular press focused on entertainment, sports, sensation, and practical advice. In Britain, the *Daily Mail* was the pioneer. Started by Alfred Harmsworth, later Lord Northcliffe, in 1896, it was the first British morning paper to sell for a halfpenny. It began with a circulation of 200,000 issues a day, rising to 400,000 in 1898 and 989,000 in 1900. The *Mail*'s success was soon imitated: the *Daily Express* was founded in 1900 and the *Daily Mirror* in 1903. From 1911 onward the *Mirror* topped the *Mail*'s circulation and was the first British "tabloid" (the word was coined in 1900 by Harmsworth) to reach a million copies.

It was in France, however, that Europe's biggest-selling popular newspaper was produced. With 1.5 million copies by 1914, *Le Petit Parisien* was the most widely read of the four popular papers that dominated the French market from the turn of the century (*Le Petit Journal*, *Le Matin*, and *Le Journal* being the other three). Together, they enjoyed a combined circulation of 4.5 million before World War I. In Germany, the *Berliner Illustrierte Zeitung* was the first to reach a circulation of one million. By 1914, the popular press was an established factor all over Europe, not only in the large urban centers, but also in smaller cities and their hinterlands. Kraków, Poland, with a population of approximately 120,000 people, had two hugely successful popular dailies by the outbreak of World War I. As elsewhere, their titles indicated a new readership and a new style of journalism: *Nowiny dla wszystkich* (News for everyone) and *Ilustrowany Kuryer Codzienny* (The illustrated daily courier).

CINEMA AND THE GRAMOPHONE

The second important agent of twentieth-century popular culture that was already well established by 1914 was the cinema. The Grand Café in Boulevard des Capucines, Paris, has a reasonable claim to being the location of its birth. It was here,

in December 1895, that Louis Lumière introduced his "cinematograph" to a public audience. In the two decades between then and World War I, Europe experienced a breathtaking expansion of the new medium. From the turn of the century, cinemas became a common feature of cities and smaller towns. By 1914, the number of registered cinemas in large European cities had reached hundreds, typically seating between two hundred and eight hundred guests. Rapidly expanding to regional and rural areas, the cinematograph overtook earlier popular art forms such as the music hall. By the outbreak of World War I, the cinema was firmly established as "the most popular form of amusement of the day," as an early historian of the cinema observed (Steer, 1913, pp. 11–12).

As with most other new forms of mass media after it, the rise of the cinema triggered debates about morality, education, and "the masses." Politicians, intellectuals, and self-acclaimed moral authorities, many of them associated with the "reform movement" that accompanied the cinema in its early days, advocated a range of restrictions for the new medium. Their moral concerns were not only about the content of films but also about the unregulated public space and the "semi-darkness" of the cinema, which they saw as encouraging loose morals. The cinema channeled anxieties about "the masses" and "the crowd," perceived as a threat by many intellectuals. The German novelist Alfred Döblin described the spectators in cinemas as "a monster of an audience, a mass cast out by that white, staring eye." For this crowd, entertainment was "necessary like bread." With a "reflex-like lust," the consuming crowd satisfied its "hunger for sensation." Advocates of the cinema, in contrast, stressed the educational and artistic potential of the new medium. The stage was set for future debates about the influence of popular culture on moral and cultural values.

In parallel to the cinema rose the gramophone. First demonstrated by the American inventor Emile Berliner in 1888, this was a device that could reproduce the sound stored in acoustically generated, laterally cut grooves in the surface of a rotating disc. Different formats and technologies coexisted during the decades before World War I, but the gramophone increasingly won over the "phonograph" developed earlier by Thomas Edison.

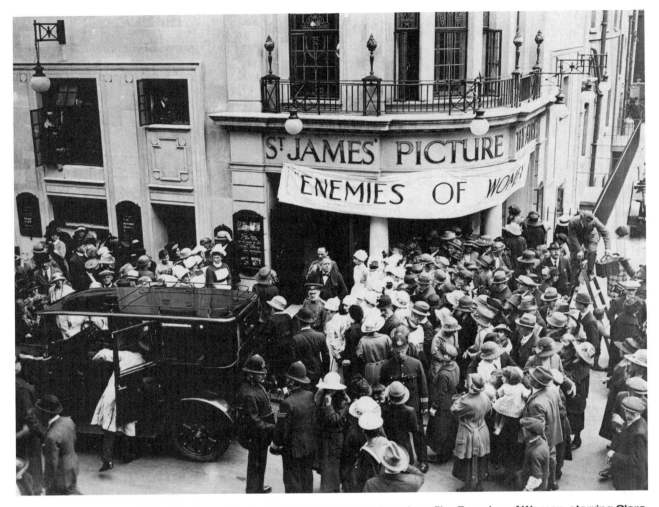

Londoners wait outside the St. James Picture Theater to see the American film *Enemies of Women*, starring Clara Bow, July 1923. By the outbreak of World War I, cinema had become an enormously popular form of amusement for Europeans. ©HULTON-DEUTSCH COLLECTION/CORBIS

There were to be many changes in the way music was recorded and reproduced during the twentieth century, from the shellac disc to the vinyl plastic record, the magnetic tape to the compact disc, but the underlying model introduced by the gramophone changed very little until the 1990s: music was stored on a record that was then mass-produced and sold. There was a mass market of music consumption in Europe as early as 1904 when the Italian tenor Enrico Caruso had his first million-selling record.

WAR AND ENTERTAINMENT

The year 1914 marked a new era in the development of popular culture. Although governments had attempted to influence and manipulate popular culture before the war, its use for propaganda purposes was only fully explored during World War I. A number of important developments, among them the consolidation of national film, media, and entertainment companies, were the result. This went perhaps the furthest in Germany, where the founding of the Universum Film AG, or Ufa, in December 1917, brought the most important production and distribution companies into one government-owned holding that was to play a major part in the expansion of mass culture in Germany in the first half of the twentieth century. Yet, the relationship between popular culture and war was about more than propaganda and censorship, power and manipulation. World War I was the first of the major European conflicts that was experienced and made sense of through mass entertainment. The cinematograph and the gramophone made it possible for even remote audiences to participate in as well as seek diversion from the war. It was during World War I that the aesthetic strategies by which popular culture approached and represented war in the twentieth century were first experimented with. This could be seen in the novelty of violence, killing, and death represented in film and in the nostalgic and romantic framing of the radically challenging effects of modern warfare—themes that were taken up with new intensity during World War II, when the radio offered an additional medium of popular culture.

RADIO

There were other important pioneers, such as Eduard Branly in France, Augusto Righi in Italy, and Alexander Popov in Russia, but Guglielmo Marconi is usually credited with the invention of the radio in 1895, harnessing the achievements of earlier innovators such as James Clerk Maxwell, Heinrich Hertz, and Oliver Lodge. Having failed to win support in his native Italy, Marconi brought the technology to Britain, where he demonstrated the potential of radio waves as a means of telegraphic communication. In 1914 he succeeded in transmitting speech over the radio, and in 1920 Marconi invited opera star Dame Nellie Melba to perform at his works in Chelmsford, demonstrating the potential of the "wireless" for entertainment. Whether state-controlled or industry-run, there were initially only a very few nationwide stations in European countries. The Netherlands led the way in regular broadcasting, putting out programs from The Hague in November 1919 through a station set up by the Netherlandse Radio-Industrie. In France the first radio station to broadcast was Radio Tour Eiffel, established in 1921 as a state station. In Britain, initial experimental stations were followed by the formation of the British Broadcasting Company, which began its daily schedule in 1922.

The radio soon reached much larger audiences than any other contemporary medium. By the late 1930s, roughly three out of every four households in both Great Britain and National Socialist Germany had a radio. In the context of popular culture, two aspects were particularly significant. First, these were simultaneous audiences. Programs could be heard at the same time by millions of listeners who did not have to be in the same location. Second, these were increasingly international audiences. The Geneva Plan for European wavelengths, drawn up in 1926, signaled that the new medium transcended national boundaries, a phenomenon that became a defining feature of popular culture in the twentieth century. While it offered a new experience of simultaneity, the radio did not make other agents of popular culture redundant. On the contrary, gramophone records, spectator sports, the cinema, and popular newspapers continued to flourish in the "age of radio."

During World War II the line between entertainment and propaganda was indistinguishable, in radio as in cinema and other arenas of popular culture. Indeed, forms of entertainment that were less directly political often proved to be more efficient in the mobilization of consent both in National Socialist Germany and in the Allied countries. The radio was the most important medium, in particular because it did not stop at boundaries and check points. To talk "live" to audiences all over Europe that could be reached simultaneously was a technological innovation that propagandists and politicians made use of in all countries. Charles de Gaulle's appeal on 18 June 1940, in which he coined the phrase "France has lost a battle; but France has not lost the war," became the most famous instance. Talking on "Radio London" over the airwaves of the British Broadcasting Corporation (BBC), he rejected capitulation to Germany and appealed to French listeners in Britain and on the Continent to join him in the resistance movement.

TELEVISION

It was not until after World War II that the most important medium of twentieth-century popular culture began its rapid rise. The technological foundations of television had been set in the first half of the twentieth century through experiments and inventions by William Crookes, Paul Nipkow, Karl Ferdinand Braun, and Boris Rosing. Drawing on their achievements, the Scottish inventor John Logie Baird demonstrated a workable system in the 1920s, holding the first public display of television at the department store Selfridges in London in

1925. In 1936 the BBC began to broadcast experimental television programs using Baird's system. However, the age of television actually began only in the 1950s when it became possible in large parts of Europe to receive images transmitted as electrical signals. Just as in the 1920s, when radio broadcasting had begun as a mostly state-controlled medium, publicly controlled institutions were given the license to transmit television programs: the BBC in Britain, RTÉ (Radio Telefís Éireann) in Ireland, RAI (Radio Audizioni Italiane) in Italy, TVE (Televisión Española) in Spain, ARD (Arbeitsgemeinschaft der öffentlich-rechtlichen Rundfunkanstalten Deutschlands), a consortium of public broadcasting services, in West Germany. In the 1980s and 1990s European countries began to "deregulate" and "liberalize" television, resulting in a competition between "public" and "private" channels and in the rise of new formats and programs of televised entertainment.

The number of households owning television sets increased steadily during the second half of the twentieth century. In 1955, only three out of one thousand inhabitants owned a television set in France, five out of one thousand in West Germany, and ninety-five out of one thousand in Britain. By 1972 there was roughly one television set per four inhabitants in these countries. Twenty years later the number had doubled. There was now one television set per two inhabitants in most countries of the European Union. Outside the European Union the picture was more diverse. According to the United Nations Educational, Scientific and Cultural Organization (UNESCO) estimates for 2000, San Marino was, with 849 television sets per 1,000 people, the European country with the highest and Bosnia and Herzegovina, with 111 sets per 1,000 inhabitants, the country with the lowest density of television receivers. The Europe-wide success of television did not necessarily result in the decline of other media of popular culture. Indeed, the average amount of time per day spent listening to the radio by European adults in 1989–1990 (174 minutes in Switzerland, 159 in Britain, 131 in France, 154 in Germany, 90 in Portugal, and 73 in Spain) represented an increase on the figures for 1950, when there had been very little competition from the television.

THE CRITIQUE OF POPULAR CULTURE

Of the many intellectual critics of popular culture in twentieth-century Europe, the sociologists and philosophers of the "Frankfurt School" have perhaps been the most influential. Theodor W. Adorno and Max Horkheimer provided a deeply pessimistic assessment of what they called the *Kulturindustrie*, the "culture industry," in their *Dialectic of Enlightenment* (*Dialektik der Aufklärung*, 1947). They saw popular culture as primarily driven by economic interest. This "commercial imperative," resulting in the commodification of culture, had deeply negative effects. Because they were produced according to economic considerations, advertising, television, film, and popular music encouraged a standardized and mechanical consumption of culture. Audiences were manipulated into becoming uncritical consumers of mass entertainment. The resulting conformity of society suited the economically powerful and ruling classes. Ultimately, the culture industry made mass audiences willing subjects in a repressive system of thought and organization.

Jürgen Habermas, the key representative of the generation of the Frankfurt School after Adorno and Horkheimer, offered a similarly pessimistic, but more historically based interpretation in *The Structural Transformation of the Public Sphere* (*Strukturwandel der Öffentlichkeit*, 1961). His model centered on the change from an eighteenth-century public in which a "rational-critical discourse" was cultivated, mostly by educated and propertied men supported by individual printers and publishers, to the modern public sphere in which mass consumption and the domination of a few capitalist enterprises, primarily interested in the generation of profit, resulted in the degeneration of critical discourse. This model did not go unchallenged, and Habermas accepted some of the objections in the foreword to the 1990 edition of *Strukturwandel*, acknowledging that his interpretation had suffered from too stark a contrast between an idealized depiction of the eighteenth-century and a pessimistically painted twentieth-century public sphere.

The various forms of "cultural studies" that blossomed at universities in the 1970s contributed significantly to the revision of models such as those by Adorno and Horkheimer as well as Habermas.

The Centre for Contemporary Cultural Studies at the University of Birmingham in Britain, founded in 1964, was one of the pioneering institutions developing the interdisciplinary study of popular culture. While many authors associated with the cultural studies approach saw the Frankfurt School as founding fathers of their enquiry into the relationship between society and culture, the new academic discipline produced important revisions of earlier, predominantly pessimistic, approaches to popular culture. Thus Stuart Hall and Tony Jefferson (*Resistance through Rituals,* 1976) still saw popular culture as shaped by hegemonic forces, yet simultaneously as a territory in which people could genuinely resist manipulation and conformity. Toward the end of the century popular culture became increasingly conceptualized as a space in which power and values were contested and negotiated. John Fiske (*Understanding Popular Culture,* 1989; *Reading the Popular,* 1989) was influential in emphasizing the capacity of popular culture to articulate the contradictory values of diverse audiences. Popular culture became interpreted much less as a form of coercion or as effecting a "cultural decline." Writers instead focused on the way in which popular media and cultural forms could be seen as a process of struggle and negotiation, the outcome of which was open-ended and continuously reevaluated.

INTERNET, CONVERGENCE, AND FRAGMENTATION

The experience of the last new mass medium of the twentieth century, the Internet, perhaps contributed to a less monolithic and pessimistic interpretation of popular culture. The Internet, a worldwide network of computer networks, developed out of a government initiative in the United States in the 1970s, under the direction of the Department of Defense, which aimed to connect computers in military and research establishments throughout the United States and overseas. European universities and research institutions joined this network in the mid-1980s. While its technology originated in a government initiative, the Internet had no central governing body or authority that regulated it. With the growth in the ownership of personal computers, the network expanded dramatically in the 1990s and became mostly used in the form of the World Wide Web. Technically speaking, the

"web" was the entirety of all computers linked to the Internet and storing documents that are mutually accessible through the use of a standard protocol. The computer scientist Tim Berners-Lee, credited with the creation of the World Wide Web, defined it as "the universe of network-accessible information, an embodiment of human knowledge." In September 2004, the Geneva-based International Telecommunications Union, an organization representing the telecommunications industry, estimated that there were 230,886,000 Internet users in Europe, an increase from 2000 of 124 percent. In countries such as Denmark, Germany, Finland, Netherlands, and the United Kingdom, roughly half the population used the new medium regularly. Within the European Union, Sweden had the highest Internet penetration with 74.5 percent and Greece the lowest with 15.3 percent. Outside the European Union the divergence was even stronger: while only 1 percent of Albanians used the Internet, 66 percent of Icelanders were "online."

By the end of the twentieth century, the extraordinary growth of the Internet had begun to transform many established practices and forms of popular culture. Convergence and fragmentation were two key words in the interpretation of these changes. The first was not necessarily a new phenomenon: the gramophone and the radio had "converged" just as much in the 1920s as television and Internet seemed to at the beginning of the twenty-first century. The second, however, reflected a trend that was suited to transform popular culture more profoundly. It had arguably begun in the 1980s when the success of the video cassette recorder (VCR) had brought about a change in viewers' relationship with television schedules. For the first time, patterns of individual demand could be accommodated: no longer did viewers have to conform to television schedules, they could store and view programs at their chosen time. The phenomenon of empty streets during the broadcasting of popular dramas or comedies, a visible sign for the simultaneous audiences and shared experience of popular culture, became increasingly rare. A number of new digital recording devices introduced in the 1990s accelerated this effect, as did the arrival of satellite, digital, and online transmission. The numbers of

Two young men with punk-influenced hairstyles and clothing on the subway, London, England, 1997. ©Gideon Mendel/Corbis

subscribers to these new services varied naturally greatly across Europe, but the United Nations Economic Commission for Europe (UNECE) estimated in 2003 that on average 73 out of 1,000 inhabitants in the European Union owned a satellite dish and that 162 out of 1,000 subscribed to cable television. By 2004, governments in a number of European countries expected digital television to supersede analog television during the first decade of the twenty-first century. Whether available via satellite, cable, or terrestrial aerials, new forms of television allowed for not only an unprecedented multitude of channels to be received, but also the selling of programs and films "on demand." As a result, a television program was no longer a singular event, but a commodity that could be selected, stored, and repeated at the consumer's choice.

The technological availability and changing formats of mass entertainment that came with the Internet pushed this process further, especially with the increasing success of "broadband" services.

This was a transmission technique that used a wide range of frequencies, allowing for higher volumes of data and several channels to be communicated simultaneously, even when using existing networks such as telephone circuits. According to media analysts, fifty-four million people in the European Union used broadband access to the Internet in 2004, twenty million more than in the previous year. This meant that consumers could browse Internet pages at high speed, download music or films as files, and play online games. Market researchers found that, as a result, Europeans changed what they did in their spare time. A quarter of broadband Internet users in Europe said in 2004 that they spent less time watching television and more time using the World Wide Web. The development of mobile phones and other portable devices capable of downloading Internet items of popular culture almost without any geographic restriction contributed further to the challenge of the television as the dominant medium and to a process that critics interpreted as the fragmentation or individualization of popular culture. Yet, while there was evidence that audiences did become more fragmented, the opposite continued to characterize the entertainment and media industry. Popular culture at the beginning of the twenty-first century continued to be dominated by a comparably small number of international companies that exercised a far-reaching influence by shaping and channeling tastes and fashions, issues and debates. Their power and its regulation remained at the heart of public debates about popular culture.

See also **Cinema; Football (Soccer); Leisure; Television; Tourism.**

BIBLIOGRAPHY

Adorno, Theodor W. *The Culture Industry: Selected Essays on Mass Culture.* London, 1991.

Adorno, Theodor W., and Max Horkheimer. *Dialectic of Enlightenment.* Translated by John Cumming. London, 1972. Translation of *Dialektik der Aufklärung* (1947).

Anderson, Patricia. *The Printed Image and the Transformation of Popular Culture.* Oxford, U.K., 1991.

Barthes, Roland. *Mythologies.* Translated by Annette Lavers. London, 1972. Translation of *Mythologies* (1957).

Bell, Michael. "The Study of Popular Culture." In *Concise Histories of American Popular Culture,* edited by M. Thomas Inge. Westport, Conn., 1982.

Benjamin, Walter. "The Work of Art in the Age of Mechanical Reproduction." In *Illuminations,* edited by Hannah Arendt, 219–253. Translated by Harry Zohn. New York, 1968. Translation of *Das Kunstwerk im Zeitalter seiner technischen Reproduzierbarkeit* (1936).

Berners-Lee, Tim, with Mark Fischetti. *Weaving the Web: The Original Design and Ultimate Destiny of the World Wide Web by Its Inventor.* San Francisco, 1999.

Bigsby, C. W. E., ed. *Approaches to Popular Culture.* London, 1976.

Bourdieu, Pierre. *On Television.* Translated by Priscilla Pankhurst Ferguson. New York, 1998. Translation of *Sur la television* (1996).

Briggs, Asa. *The Birth of Broadcasting.* Oxford, U.K., 1961.

———. *The Golden Age of Wireless.* Oxford, U.K., 1995.

Briggs, Asa, and Peter Burke. *A Social History of the Media: From Gutenberg to the Internet.* Cambridge, U.K., 2002.

Calhoun, Craig, ed. *Habermas and the Public Sphere.* Cambridge, Mass., 1992.

Carey, James W. *Communication as Culture: Essays on Media and Society.* Boston, Mass., 1989.

Chanan, Michael. *Repeated Takes: A Short History of Recording and Its Effects on Music.* London, 1995.

Charney, Leo, and Vanessa R. Schwartz, eds. *Cinema and the Invention of Modern Life.* Berkeley, Calif., 1995.

Charon, Jean M., ed. *L'État des médias.* Paris, 1991.

Debord, Guy. *Society of the Spectacle.* Detroit, 1970. Translation of *La société du spectacle* (1967).

Döblin, Alfred. "Das Theater der kleinen Leute." *Das Theater* 1, 1909.

Fiske, John. *Reading the Popular.* Boston, Mass., 1989.

———. *Understanding Popular Culture.* London, 1989.

Habermas, Jürgen. *The Structural Transformation of the Public Sphere.* Translated by Thomas Burger. Cambridge, Mass., 1989. Translation of *Strukturwandel der Öffentlichkeit. Untersuchungen zu einer Kategorie der bürgerlichen Gesellschaft* (1961).

Hall, Stuart, and Tony Jefferson, eds. *Resistance through Rituals.* London, 1976.

Lee, Alan J. *The Origins of the Popular Press.* London, 1976.

Marvin, Carolyn. *When Old Technologies Were New: Thinking about Electric Communication in the Late Nineteenth Century.* New York, 1988.

Postman, Neil. *Amusing Ourselves to Death: Public Discourse in the Age of Show Business.* New York, 1985.

Rowe, David. *Popular Cultures: Rock Music, Sport and the Politics of Pleasure.* London, 1995.

Steer, Valentia. *The Romance of the Cinema: A Short Record of the Development of the Most Popular Form of Amusement of the Day.* London, 1913.

Williams, Raymond. *Communications.* 3rd ed. London, 1976.

Winston, Brian. *Technologies of Seeing: Photography, Cinema and Television.* London, 1996.

JAN RÜGER

POPULAR FRONT.

In France, the name Popular Front (Front Populaire) refers to three different things: a political strategy, a mass movement, and an experiment in government. Owing to the unprecedented links among them, these elements generated a new political culture that had a lasting influence.

In July 1934 the French Communist Party (PCF; Parti Communiste Français) and the French Socialist Party (SFIO; Section Française de l'Internationale Ouvrière) ratified a pact of unity of action to combat fascism. In October, Maurice Thorez, secretary-general of the PCF, became worried about the Right's advances and the "fascist threat" and proposed extending this pact to the Radicals, in the form of a "popular front for freedom, labor, and peace." The Socialists and the Radicals were initially reluctant but agreed to the pact after the municipal elections of May 1935. A national committee of the Rassemblement Populaire (Popular Assembly; this official title never supplanted the earlier name) was constituted just after a powerful mass demonstration on 14 July 1935. The Socialists, Communists, and Radicals agreed on the principle of reciprocal withdrawals from the upcoming legislative elections. These withdrawals were conditional upon a common program, which was also ratified by the labor unions (reunited in March as the Confédération Générale du Travail, or CGT) and numerous associations (the Human Rights League, the Vigilance Committee of Antifascist Intellectuals, and so on). This was in all respects a first. The Comintern, initially hostile, upheld this strategy as a model during its Seventh Congress (July 1935)—although this did not bring about its widespread acceptance. In fact, this strategy was only viable in combination with the mass movement that had preceded it and that it helped amplify and modify.

That movement was embodied in the antifascist reaction to the antiparliamentarian offensive of 6 February 1934. It then grew in response to the crisis (demonstrations against government decrees) and the paramilitary leagues and changed in nature with the demonstration of 14 July 1935, in which "the folds of the red flag and the tricolor, the strains of *La Marseillaise* and the *Internationale*" were mingled all over France. This description was not gratuitous. At work was a symbiosis among antifascist, republican, and class cultures that allowed for the emergence of a completely new kind of political and popular culture. This nascent culture was also expressed in the working-class municipalities that were gained or preserved in 1935, which became laboratories of the avant-garde in the cultural, political, and social order. Their modern management style was an argument in favor of the accession of the Popular Front to head the country.

A 1936 pamphlet proclaims that the Popular Front opposes misery, fascism, and war, and offers bread, peace, and liberty. BRIDGEMAN ART LIBRARY

This dynamic obviously influenced the results of the legislative elections on 26 April 1936, as the economic crisis raged on. During the first ballot, a slight leftward shift of votes from the Right resulted in victory for the Popular Front. The Socialists outpaced the Radicals, strengthening their status as France's foremost party. The French Communist Party, ranked third within the coalition, made the most progress of all. In the second ballot the electoral system magnified the victory. The Popular Front won with a gain of some forty seats: 149 Socialists, 111 Radicals, and 72 Communists were elected. This shift in the balance of power, both unprecedented and unexpected, put Léon Blum, leader of the majority party within the victorious coalition, at the head of the government, although his party, since after World War I, had objected to the principle of "participation" in a bourgeois government. Because the Communists had opted for support without participation, the government was made up of Socialists and Radicals. Twenty-five of its members had never held positions of ministerial responsibility, and some were very young. For the first time, three undersecretariats were given to women (although the Popular Front's program had not retained the idea of giving them the right to vote). A Ministry of the National Economy was created to allow for the state to intervene more effectively in "all problems of an economic nature." The state further extended its sphere of influence by creating an undersecretariat for Sports and Leisure (prohibited, however, from any reductive subjugation of culture to politics). All of these were instruments of a new government culture. However, it soon became necessary to make compromises in light of an unprecedented situation.

The popular movement that had hastened the victory and helped delineate the new balance of power, far from disappearing with the victory, instead expanded and changed in nature. Léon Blum, immediately charged with constituting the new government, chose to wait for the expiration of the mandate of the Chamber of Deputies on 2 June to obtain his investiture in parliament. An unprecedented "social explosion" occurred in the interim. Between the two electoral ballots, employers fired workers for participating in a work shutdown on 1 May. Immediately after the victory, strikes broke out demanding that the workers be rehired. The strikes began on 11 May in the Breguet aeronautics factories in Le Havre, and from 14 to 20 May spread to various other aeronautics and metallurgical companies, with workers demanding salary increases, the institution of worker delegates, and protection of the right to strike. On 26 May the traditional homage to fallen Communards swelled to unprecedented proportions and became a catalyst. The strikes spread to other industries until only the public sector and the banks were spared—all without any directive from the labor unions beforehand.

On the eve of his parliamentary investiture Blum had obtained assurances that employers were prepared to make significant concessions to end the conflict. On 4 June he was invested by 384 votes against 209. On 7 June he brought representatives of the employers' federation, the Confédération Générale de la Production Française (CGPF), and the CGT together at Matignon. The agreement that was ratified represented a first in the history of social relations in France. It guaranteed a significant increase in salaries, union freedoms, and the institution of shop delegates in establishments with more than ten workers. Collective agreements by branch were to be established. A few days later the parliament adopted the law mandating the forty-hour work week and paid vacation time. It extended compulsory education by one year. But the strikes went on, spreading to additional companies, many of which had no union members, and peaking on 11 June.

The theory of Communist "double dealing" has fizzled out. But the fact that the labor unions were not necessarily behind each of the strikes, and that there was only a weak correlation between unionization and the decision to strike—the railway workers, 22 percent of them unionized, did not strike, while metalworkers, 4 percent of them unionized, spearheaded the strike and made up the largest contingent of strikers—is not enough to prove the opposite hypothesis of the strikes' "spontaneity." The postwar Taylorization of French industry and the resulting de-skilling and intensified pace of production were no doubt the root cause of the strikes, as is evident from their epicenter: the big, rationalized factories that were the anchor points of the general workers' union, the Confédération Générale du Travail Unitaire (CGTU), and which had felt the effects of the union's initiatives in the major conflicts of the 1920s. Employers' response to the crisis, in the form of increased production and, as a corollary, a rise in fatal accidents, intensified the malaise but did not generate a reaction. The electoral victory, and the hopes that it raised and the fears that it dissipated (relating to intervention of the forces of law and order) were the necessary detonator. The working class, fearful of being deprived of the fruits of the victory, did not wait. The strikes, experienced as a kind of liberation, became an affirmation of restored dignity. They ended only with the signing of collective agreements, some of which came in July or early August. This brought the risk of conflicts of interest with the middle classes involved in the alliance.

Léon Blum's economic choices were inspired by Franklin D. Roosevelt's New Deal. His intent was to "prime the pump" by boosting consumer spending and implementing a program of large-scale public works. The strikes, which forced him to act quickly and under pressure, at least led to the adoption of measures consistent with his initial aims in that they generated a tangible rise in purchasing power (the bankruptcy rate soon took a downturn). The few structural reforms included in the program were adopted along with the other measures: reform of the status of the Bank of France for increased state control, a National Wheat Office guaranteeing farm revenues, and nationalization of the armaments industry to bring it out from under the control of the arms dealers. The electrification of rural areas and the construction of roads, schools, and stadiums were supposed to expand the market, respond to new social needs, and modernize the economy. The essential part of the program was carried out in eighty days. Devaluation of the franc, although not included in the program, was meant to boost exports.

The beginnings of a recovery in the autumn were soon quelled by a counteroffensive on the part of employers. Small-scale employers, repudiating their negotiators, put on a show of strength around the question of the forty-hour work week. Further conflicts ensued, and tensions increased. The law on conciliation and arbitration, passed in 1937, was not enough to reverse the trend.

In July 1936 General Francisco Franco's military rebellion and the Spanish civil war increased the tensions: antifascism and pacifism, which had previously seemed to reinforce or be identified with one another, entered into a conflict of interests. Partisans and opponents of nonintervention clashed. On the nonintervention side were the Radicals, on the other the Communists, and between them was a line of demarcation sundering the CGT and the SFIO. Blum, worried about cutting off the country from Great Britain, decided in favor of nonintervention. This did not prevent the Radical senators from repudiating his government, which fell in June 1937. The Popular Front for a time tried to outlast Blum, then disappeared in April 1938 with the constitution of Édouard Daladier's government, which expanded toward the Right and took up the offensive against the forty-hour week, a symbol of the "ray of sunshine." The failure of the strike of November 1938 led to the liquidation of the remaining social gains, except for paid holidays. Just a few months later, Marshall Philippe Pétain blamed the defeat on the "spirit of enjoyment" to which the Popular Front had given free rein.

According to some studies, there was truth to this accusation. The victory of the Popular Front, perceived at the time as putting a brake on the rise of fascism in Europe, eventually created the conditions for a reaction. Young people, women, and immigrants, excluded from universal suffrage but transformed during these months into actors in a new mode of political life, and the world of labor, strong in its restored dignity, were the pivotal elements in the Resistance against the Vichy regime and the Nazi occupation in World War II.

What is more, the Popular Front occasioned a cultural revolution that profoundly transformed ways of experiencing and participating in French society. In this sense it was far more than a "ray of sunshine." In the political order, it meant that the French Left thereafter defined itself in relation to a twofold heritage of class and democracy, in the sometimes complex but henceforth indissociable relations between them. The ongoing interrelationship between collective mobilization and parliamentary action redefined politics. Individualism in politics declined. Organizations of all kinds, parties of the Left and the Right, unions and associations, all grew larger. The idea that "it pays to fight" became permanently entrenched in the collective consciousness and helped strengthen this culture of struggle.

In the cultural order, an active "cultural policy" in advance of its time allowed for democratic access to culture, which in all its forms—scientific and artistic, popular and scholarly, classic and avant-garde—received government support. The relationships that intellectuals and artists established with the world of labor generated renewed forms of expression, mainly in mass culture, with photography, song, and cinema at the forefront.

These forms were neither proletarian nor official but popular, in the image of the experience that gave rise to them.

But "culture" must also be understood in a broader sense. Here, change was expressed in the dignity that was restored to work and, by extension, to the body, its former appendage, through access to free time and the new forms of socialization in this freed time. Workers' relationship to history and to national (and international) consciousness was transformed. The experience permanently marked the collective consciousness. It enabled the union of the Left to maintain a vista of expectations until 1981, and it shaped an image that long served to perpetuate the view of the general strike as the ultimate expression of positive collective action.

See also Communism; Labor Movements; Socialism; Strikes; Trade Unions.

BIBLIOGRAPHY

Lefranc, Georges. Histoire du Front populaire. Paris, 1964.

Margairaz, Michel, and Danielle Tartakowsky. L'Avenir nous appartient. Une histoire du Front populaire. Larousse, France, 2006.

Prost, Antoine. Autour du Front populaire. Aspects de mouvement social au vigtième siecle. Le Seuil, France, 2006.

DANIÈLLE TARTAKOWSKY

PORTUGAL. One of Europe's oldest nation-states, Portugal by 1914 was a third- or fourth-ranked continental power, long past its brief time in the sun as a leading imperial and world power (a time that began in the 1470s and ended in 1580). If its size and location were marginal, its strategically located Atlantic islands (the Azores and Madeira, which were considered strategic during both world wars and the Cold War) and imperial possessions in Africa and Asia, as well as its tungsten mines, lent the small Iberian state more influence in world affairs during wartime than its military weakness warranted. Clinging sometimes desperately to its large overseas empire and constantly reminding its citizens of the country's central role in Europe's discoveries, Portugal was conditioned as well by other historic legacies, including continuing migration of its workers to richer countries; an Atlantic, maritime orientation; and dependence for defense of its metropolitan and imperial sovereignty on the Anglo-Portuguese alliance, world diplomacy's oldest connection.

THE FIRST REPUBLIC

In the twentieth century, Portugal experienced four different political systems: the twilight of the waning constitutional monarchy (1900–1910); the First Republic (1910–1926); a dictatorship with two constitutional phases: military dictatorship (1926–1933) and the Estado Novo (New State; 1933–1974), Europe's longest surviving authoritarian system; and democratic Portugal (established in 1974). For a period just before World War I, Portugal adopted a republican form of government (Europe's third republic) and appeared to be more advanced politically than other southern European states. The illusion died quickly: Portugal's novice parliamentary republic became the most unstable government in twentieth-century Western European history.

The republic compiled an unenviable record of civil strife, public violence, chaos, and instability. Forty-five governments held power in fifteen-and-a-half years, for an average lifespan of four months per government. American humorist Will Rogers quipped some years later that in Portugal a premier hardly had time to unpack his bags before he was out on the street; 1920s France coined a new verb, portugaliser, meaning "to bring political chaos to a situation." To excessive political instability was added legislative and executive instability and lack of administrative continuity. "Revolutions," or, more properly, military and civil insurrections to overthrow besieged governments, were frequent. As many as five thousand people died in civil strife in these incidents and in ephemeral civil wars; only one president served out his full four-year term (Antonio de Almeida, r. 1919–1923) and that was at great risk to his life and at the cost of his health.

The builders of the ill-fated republic included some talented leaders who had noble dreams and plans for modernizing Portugal but they confronted daunting conditions and complex problems. From the monarchy, the republic had inherited deadly legacies of poverty, 75 percent illiteracy, and heavy debt, and new republican policies sparked bitter opposition and raised the expectations of many groups—expectations the new system could not satisfy.

The republic began on 5 October 1910, when after several days of fighting in Lisbon a civilian and military conspiracy overthrew the monarchy and Portugal's last reigning king, Dom Manuel II of Braganza, fled into exile in England. From the beginning, the republic's political process was held hostage to repeated military interventions. Republican ideology was based on the belief that Portugal's backwardness was due largely to domination by a reactionary Catholic Church and an incompetent, profligate monarchy. In their efforts to modernize the country, republicans carried out a sweeping anticlerical policy, which by the spring of 1911 included separation of church and state; secularization of education, public holidays, and overseas missionary work at all levels; state confiscation of all church property, including church buildings; the legalization of divorce; and the expulsion of religious orders. To address what republicans perceived as a tradition of monarchical abuse of executive powers, the Constitution of 1911 also featured a prominent legislature and a weak executive, which was composed of a prime minister and a president elected by the two legislative chambers rather than directly by the people; fearing opposition from conservative rural classes as well as much of the career army, the republicans greatly limited the franchise and during many elections employed fraud and intimidation. In terms of the franchise, the republic, with the exception of one brief period, was less democratic than the final phases of the constitutional monarchy.

Heavy migration from Atlantic Island and northern Portugal had begun in the middle of the nineteenth century and the republic's instability, violence, economic problems, as well as its anticlerical policies, created a massive wave of emigration to the traditional destinations of these earlier migrants, Brazil and North America; this exodus reached a peak in 1912 and served as a kind of national social barometer. Table 1 indicates the pattern of Portuguese emigration during much of the twentieth century.

TABLE 1

Portuguese emigration, 1910–1988

1910	39,000
1912	88,000 (75,000 of this to Brazil)
1930	c. 30,000 (the Depression)
1940	c. 8,000 (World War II)
1950	41,000
1960	67,000
1965	131,000 (African colonial wars)
1970	255,000 (African colonial wars)
1974	80,859
1980	25,173
1988	13,332

Note: Figures do not include illegal emigration.

SOURCES: Douglas L. Wheeler. *Historical Dictionary of Portugal*, 2nd ed. Lanham, Md., 2002, pp. xxxvi–xxxvii; Maria Ioannis B. Baganha, "As correntes emigratorias portuguesas no seculo XX e o seu impacto na economia national," *Analise Social* 128, no. 39, (1994): pp. 959–980.

MILITARY DICTATORSHIP

What popular support the republic enjoyed in the early years was dissipated in a series of crises: a disputed anticlerical policy; an economy riven by unprecedented inflation, currency depreciation, capital flight, and heavy foreign and domestic debt; and the negative consequences of Portugal's participation on the Allied side in World War I. One political party, the Portuguese Republican Party, nicknamed the Democrats, dominated most elections and the congress, yet it lacked sustained popular support and alienated a wide range of many groups, including businesspeople, unions, employers, and the career military. By 1925, despite some useful reforms in education and society, the political system had reached a dead end. Although the military had tried to take power previously, it remained disunited until a grievance regarding contested privileges of an officer militia gave military conspirators the temporary unity necessary to organize a coup d'état. On 28 May 1926, in a bloodless coup, the professional military overthrew the republic and brought in a military dictatorship.

The military dictatorship established by "young lieutenants" found itself unable to solve the economic and political crisis or find effective leaders in the subsequent chaos of what a French writer aptly described as "barracks parliamentarism." In April 1928, military leaders asked an academic expert in finance to take charge of the ministry of finance and this extraordinary figure, Antonio de Oliveira Salazar (1889–1970), an economics professor at Coimbra University, soon dominated government, initiated reforms, and worked himself into the position of dictator. The reclusive, crafty Salazar was named prime minister in July 1932 and served in that post until he was felled by a stroke in September 1968. After 1930, the political system he had created labeled itself the New State and based itself on the varied ideologies of the ruling coalition, which included Catholics, monarchists, nationalists, conservative republicans, pseudofascists, fascists, and corporatists. Although for a period (1936–1944) the regime embraced the symbols, trappings, and selected ideas of fascism and from then on was consistently characterized by its opponents on the left as fascist, its inspiration was more strongly Catholic, nationalist, conservative, and corporatist than fascist. It maintained power for as long as it did for a number of reasons: its effective repressive machinery, dominated by a political police force; the complicity and support of the career military leadership, the Catholic Church, and the wealthier classes; the divided nature of the opposition; and a largely apolitical population. Regime domination of the media combined with press censorship to create the illusion of political peace and popular support, but in fact the only period when the regime had a measure of genuine popularity came before 1945. After World War II, political opposition became more intense and the regime confronted a series of unexpected crises.

When it came to power, the New State promised to overcome the economic crisis, balance budgets, stabilize politics, restore a depleted national pride, and deliver competent governance to a country still reeling from the experience of what some critics called "the nightmare republic." But authoritarian Portugal experienced a series of foreign policy, economic, and imperial crises that tested the talents of the ruling group. Stabilizing the empire's debt-ridden economy was a slow process, but the New State could claim at least some success by the mid-1930s. Two major back-to-back foreign policy crises, the Spanish civil war (1936–1939) and World War II (1939–1945) challenged Salazar as an interim foreign minister, and many

domestic reforms had to be postponed. Portugal's stalwart support for General Francisco Franco's Nationalists in the Spanish civil war was an important if little known factor in Franco's eventual victory over the Spanish Republicans in 1939. Portugal remained neutral in World War II but made important economic gains from wartime mineral (especially wolfram or tungsten ore for hardening steel) and food exports to the Allies once the Axis began to lose the war and once the Allies put pressure on Lisbon to assist their war effort. A major turning point came in October 1943, when Portugal granted the British (and later the Americans) lease rights for military bases in the Azores Islands, which proved to be an important precedent later in 1949, when Portugal was a founding member of NATO.

As large crowds of flag-waving Portuguese celebrated VE (Victory in Europe) Day on 8 May 1945 in Lisbon's streets, few could have imagined that their odd dictator would still be in office twenty-three years later. Portugal's ruling group faced a postwar economic downturn and after 1950 new anticolonial pressures. Portugal refused to decolonize its territories in India when Indian passive resistance marchers entered its enclaves in 1954 and 1955. It declared to the United Nations, when it was admitted as a member along with Spain in late 1955, that its territories in Africa, Asia, and Oceania were not colonies but "overseas provinces." Portugal confronted a Goa crisis after India won independence in 1947. In 1961, when insurgents rose in northern Angola, African colonial wars presented a new, unprecedented challenge to the armed forces, which (except for some volunteers who fought in the Spanish civil war) had not experienced combat since World War I. Another blow to both the regime and the empire was India's conquest of Portugal's Indian territories in only two days during December 1961.

Although by 1960 economic growth and development were steady, the colonial crisis that began in early 1961 presented a double challenge to the ruling group. The political fallout of the insurgencies in Angola was quickly repressed, and the slaughter of several hundred Portuguese settlers brought a surge of at least temporary popular support for the regime and weakened the already

A man suspected of being a member of the Portuguese secret police is arrested by soldiers of the Movimento das Forcas Armadas (MFA) following the overthrow of the Caetano government, April 1974. ©HENRI BUREAU/CORBIS SYGMA

divided opposition. The regime enjoyed a new, brief lease on life, but its aging leadership was forced to devote unaccustomed attention and resources to saving Angola and other African colonies from what it claimed were communist-inspired attacks and to convincing the world that although the other imperial powers had retired, Portugal, a NATO member, would take a stand in its empire.

REVOLUTION AND ITS AFTERMATH

Following a stroke in September 1968, the ailing Salazar was replaced by Marcello Caetano, a professor of law at Lisbon University who, although younger than Salazar by seventeen years, was one of the key architects of the New State and had served in many top posts. Although Caetano promised change within the system, he confronted a political system without a real future and a military crisis without a military solution. For several years,

Caetano was successful in bringing about minor reforms and reinforcing Portugal's forces in its three colonial wars, but by 1970 his political honeymoon was over. Internal opposition grew, as did massive emigration pressures, the human and financial costs of three simultaneous and widely dispersed colonial wars, and the restiveness of the career military. In 1973 the crisis deepened as career military officers entered into a conspiracy to overthrow the government. As had happened in 1926, an initial military grievance regarding the officers' privileges became the rallying cry that temporarily united career military personnel and galvanized them. They overturned a regime that during a thirteen-year war in Africa had been unable to end the conflict and had blamed the military for its failure. The regime had also been unable to deal effectively with a severe economic crisis that was due to an Arab oil boycott and an international recession, a confrontation between the police and the military in Africa, and defections among the regime's waning coalition of supporters.

On 25 April 1974, an organization of career military personnel, the Armed Forces Movement, an unusual military coalition led by a group called the captains, who had spent years fighting in the colonial wars, overthrew the New State in a bloodless coup d'état based in Lisbon. The group's initial program was threefold: to restore democracy and end the dictatorship; to end the empire; and to bring sustained economic development to a society hamstrung by poverty and great economic inequalities. Many of the captains were heavily influenced by Marxist-Leninist ideology and anticolonialism, but their presumed leader, the conservative war hero and senior general Antonio Spinola, was against rapid decolonization and favored a slow transition to a Portuguese-dominated federation of former colonies. Although he was initially appointed president of the republic, General Spinola resigned under fire from the more radical captains and led a failed coup to restore a more conservative government. For eighteen months, Portugal experienced a unique post-coup revolution during which 60 percent of the economy was nationalized; many workers went on strike (strikes had been banned under the New State) and occupied factories, housing, and farmlands; and the radical Constitution of 1976 was approved, decreeing a transition to socialism and the triumph of the proletariat. A severe economic crisis followed, along with rapid decolonization (except for East Timor and Macau), and the unexpected arrival in Portugal of at least 500,000 Portuguese and African *retornados* (returned ones), adding new social, economic, and political pressures to the revolutionary atmosphere. Moderate career military officers ousted the radical military elements on 25 November 1975 and began the process of the stabilization and normalization of the movement toward full democracy.

Since 1974 Portugal has maintained a stable democracy. Unlike the First Republic, this Third Republic (the New State is counted as the Second Republic) had a number of advantages that made possible its stability, wide freedoms, broad franchise, economic development, integration into the

TABLE 2

Numbers of Portuguese migrants overseas	
Brazil	1,000,000
France	630,000
South Africa	570,000
United States	520,000
Canada	420,000
Venezuela	400,000
Western Europe (besides France and Germany)	175,000
Germany	125,000
United Kingdom	70,000
Lusophone Africa	50,000
Australia	50,000
Total	4,010,000

SOURCE: Douglas L. Wheeler, *Historical Dictionary of Portugal*, 2nd ed., Lanham, Md., 2002, p. xxxvii.

European and world communities, and policies that sought to achieve economic equality, women's rights, the safeguarding of the environment, and a functioning multiparty democracy. Although in the early years the country experienced an economic crisis and recession, which lasted at least until the early 1980s, sustained growth and some prosperity followed. Post-1974 democratic Portugal has not directly confronted a war of its own overseas (it sent token contingents to theaters of war in the Balkans, Afghanistan, the Persian Gulf, and Iraq). It has a much lower emigration rate than in the past and has enjoyed a greater degree of political and social peace, with a modicum of economic prosperity for a larger number of citizens,

Portugal's long tradition of migration abroad has continued but at a much lower rate. According to *Overseas Portuguese Communities Population Figures by Country of Residence,* just over ten million people lived in continental and Atlantic Island Portugal in 2002, and another four million Portuguese citizens, amounting to about 40 percent of the nation's population, lived abroad as resident workers, although many regularly revisited Portugal. As Table 2 shows, the largest portion of the overseas Portuguese communities resided in Brazil, France, and North America, but Portuguese migrants are found in many other countries as well.

Portugal is poorer and less industrialized than Spain but considerable economic and social progress has been made since the troubled 1970s and early 1980s. The new Portugal enjoys wide democratic freedoms, a functioning multiparty system dominated by two parties, the Social Democrats and the Socialists, a more racially and religiously diverse population, greater literacy, and an improved (if still challenged) educational system. A major factor in the modernization of the country has been its membership in the European Union, which it joined in 1986. Loans and grants from the European Union, as well as the adoption of the euro, have helped transform the economy and infrastructure. Portugal's 1998 Expo, a kind of Lisbon World's Fair, demonstrated anew that the Portuguese have adapted to changes and yet have preserved their historic patrimony while at the same time attempting to safeguard another legacy, an environment under that is threat. Portugal, like so many other small Western European countries, seeks to preserve its unique identity and its best traditions at the same time that it faces a challenging future both as a nation and as a member of an expanding European Union.

See also **Fascism; Portuguese Empire; Salazar, Antonio; Spanish Civil War.**

BIBLIOGRAPHY

Costa Pinto, Antonio, ed. *Modern Portugal.* Palo Alto, Calif., 1998.

Ferreira, Hugo Gil, and Michael W. Marshall. *Portugal's Revolution: Ten Years On.* Cambridge, U.K., 1986.

Graham, Lawrence W., and Douglas L. Wheeler, eds. *In Search of Modern Portugal: The Revolution and Its Consequences.* Madison, Wis., 1983.

Mailer, Philip. *Portugal: The Impossible Revolution?* London, 1977.

Martins, Herminio. "Portugal." In *European Fascism,* edited by S. J. Woolf. New York, 1969.

Maxwell, Kenneth. *The Making of Portuguese Democracy.* Cambridge, U.K., 1995.

Wheeler, Douglas L. *Republican Portugal: A Political History, 1910–1926.* Madison, Wis., 1978.

———. "Antonio de Oliveira Salazar (1889–1970)." In *Research Guide to European Historical Biography.* Vol. 3. Washington, D.C., 1992.

———. *Historical Dictionary of Portugal.* 2nd ed. Lanham, Md., and Oxford, U.K., 2002.

DOUGLAS L. WHEELER

PORTUGUESE EMPIRE.

At of the end of World War I, Portugal held the world's fourth most extensive empire, smaller only than those of Britain, France, and Belgium. In the fifteenth century, Portugal had been the first European state to expand overseas and as of 1975, the year Portugal decolonized most of its remaining empire, it possessed the longest-surviving overseas domain. This empire was long distinguished by a high rate of miscegenation, a high proportion of native workers who migrated to adjacent colonies for better lives, and a lack of control of local trade in many colonies—the exceptions being Angola and some island colonies. Portugal was the poorest, least developed, and most sparsely populated of the imperial European states, but to a degree Portugal's economic motives for empire resembled those of the wealthier Britain and France, which sought new markets overseas and foreign exchange.

THE EMPIRE UNDER THE REPUBLIC

The final argument in any Portuguese debate over the empire was always a nationalist one: keeping this large empire—an empire more than thirty times the size of the home country—should not be seen as a luxury poverty-stricken Portugal could ill afford but as the factor that allowed the country once again to count for something in Europe and to survive as an independent state against its former nemesis, Spain. That the ruling group within Portugal, whether monarchist, republican, or authoritarian, believed this questionable notion is indisputable. In 1909 one patriot argued that empire was responsible for Portugal's "autonomous existence." Several regimes and generations later, in 1969, Portugal's former foreign minister, in a talk to a foreign audience, justified remaining in Africa after the other colonial powers had withdrawn by arguing that Portugal was the only country in Western Europe with only one landward neighbor.

As of 1914, Portugal's Third Empire (the first extends from 1415 to 1640; the second from 1640 to 1822; and the third from 1822 to 1975) was scattered, diverse, and underdeveloped, with inland tribes still unconquered. It consisted of disparate territories in Africa, Asia, and Oceania: in Africa, the Cape Verde Islands, Guinea-Bissau, Sao Tome, the Principe Islands, Angola, and Mozambique; in western India, Goa, Damao, and Diu; on the south China coast, the tiny colony of Macau; in Oceania, East Timor.

Military conquest had largely been completed by 1914 and Portugal's leaders looked forward to an imperial revival and consolidation. Portugal's first parliamentary republic (1910–1926) sought to conquer the final pockets of African and Asian resistance. Special attention was devoted to developing the largest colony, Angola, which also had the greatest mineral, energy, and agrarian resources. The republic promoted European settlement there and made unprecedented investment in roads, ports, railroads, and mining. It also made efforts to civilianize a militarized administration and to decentralize colonial administration.

At best, the unstable republic's colonial record was mixed. On the one hand, by 1919 Portugal's armed forces had completed the conquest of the main African colonies' hinterlands. Important initial investment had been made by largely foreign companies in railroads, roads, communications, and mining. In Portuguese East Africa, foreign-controlled chartered companies ruled significant chunks of the colony. On the other hand, the republic's European settlement schemes failed for the most part. By 1926 Angola was deeply mired in debt as well as in settler unrest and scandals regarding corruption, financial fraud, and African forced labor. The republic's policy of allowing greater freedom for foreign investment as well as colonial autonomy and decentralization had been badly discredited. Scandals concerning African forced labor and debt had aroused international media attention and League of Nations investigations, and Lisbon feared the loss of Portuguese sovereignty in Angola and Mozambique. To these mounting fears was added the wretched reputations of the foreign-controlled chartered companies in Mozambique. Following the military's overthrow of the first republic and the establishment first of a military dictatorship (1926–1933) and then of the New State dictatorship (1933–1974), a new colonial policy was implemented. The Colonial Act (1930) recentralized colonial administration, diminished colonial autonomy, increased restrictions on foreign investment to protect Portuguese investment

TABLE 1

Portuguese population in Angola, 1920–1974

1914	c. 14,000
1920	c. 20,000
1940	44,083
1950	78,000
1960	172,000
1974	330,000

SOURCE: Douglas L. Wheeler and René Pélissier, *Angola*, Westport, Conn., 1971, p. 138; Gerald J. Bender, *Angola under the Portuguese*, Berkeley, Calif., 1978, p. 228.

in the empire, and phased out the chartered companies in Mozambique. Stringent fiscal control by Lisbon reduced spending and balanced budgets. A significant imperial element featured heavily in this new authoritarian system. The scandals in Angola convinced the new government that Portugal's hold both there and in Mozambique was gravely imperiled. Britain, South Africa, and perhaps Germany might conspire to take control of all or part of these rich colonies, possibly in the guise of a League of Nations mandate. The new dictatorship, managed now by Antonio de Oliveira Salazar, had at the top of its agenda safeguarding the tottering empire and developing its largely untapped resources.

THE EMPIRE UNDER SALAZAR

The dictatorship's record of colonial rule was also mixed, but this repressive, efficient, and enduring regime had advantages over the hapless republic. It had more time to implement its policies, a greater measure of domestic and foreign investment for development (especially after World War II and even more intensively after 1961, when the African colonial wars began), a larger European settler population, and periods of greater prosperity and enforced political peace.

The New State sought to build up a pervasive colonial mystique in both propaganda and policy. One such ideology was Luso-tropicalism, which was designed to justify empire as well as flatter a certain national image among both foreign and domestic audiences. According to this idea, Portugal was a more effective colonial ruler than other European powers since the Portuguese lacked racial prejudice and adapted better to tropical conditions and cultures. This idea was actively debated after 1950, when anticolonial resistance and unrest were generated by nationalism in Africa.

One key belief of the ruling group was that increased white settlement in Angola and Mozambique would strengthen Portugal's hold over its colonies. Such migration would also serve several other purposes: finding employment for Portugal's unemployed; making Angola more Portuguese than other colonies, where local trade was often dominated by foreign traders; advancing an assimilation policy; and diverting to Africa Portuguese migrants who traditionally preferred Brazil or the United States. Until after World War II, this white settlement policy failed, but beginning in the early 1950s larger numbers of primarily rural Portuguese settled in Angola and Mozambique.

Table 1 indicates the growth of the Portuguese population in Angola from 1920 to 1974.

Based on precedents set under the republic and on French colonial practice, Portugal instituted a Native Statute featuring an assimilation policy and classification of the colonial population according to its degree of "civilization." Portuguese were classified as "civilized" and the mass of Africans in the three Native Statute colonies (Angola, Mozambique, and Guinea-Bissau) as "uncivilized." Africans could qualify as "civilized" if they became *assimilados* (assimilated ones), learning to read and write Portuguese, dressing and living like Europeans, holding a job in the wage economy, and in some instances possessing a Catholic birth or baptismal certificate. This entitled them to European rights. This practice began in the late 1920s and was further codified in the early 1950s, but it showed few practical results. By 1960 less than 2 percent of the African population in these colonies were *assimilados*.

After World War II, the economic and social conditions of the African masses improved to some extent, but poverty, poor health, illiteracy, and political, and racial repression continued to prevail. The assimilation policy moved at a glacial pace and the influx of Portuguese settlers in Angola, and Mozambique took jobs and housing from Africans, making matters worse. Until it was

Portuguese troops uncover a land mine planted by the Mozambique Liberation Front in the Tete region, September 1973. ©Bettmann/Corbis

abolished in 1961 and 1962, a key feature of the colonial economy was widespread African forced labor in public works, contract labor shipped to Sao Tome and the Principe Islands, and in the private sector. By 1947 forced labor had been abolished by the other colonial powers in Africa, but its continuation in Portuguese-controlled areas constituted a key grievance among African nationalists for another half generation.

Beginning in 1951, to deflect international criticism, Portugal decreed that its empire was composed not of colonies but of "overseas provinces." The change, however, was strictly semantic.

REBELLION

From January to March 1961 insurgencies in northern Angola sparked the first of Portugal's three African wars, ending one colonial era and beginning another. Yet another blow came in December 1961, when the Indian Army invaded Portuguese India and in two days conquered the enclaves of Goa, Damao, and Diu. Portugal was also saddled with two other colonial wars, guerrilla insurgencies that broke out in Guinea-Bissau in 1963 and in Mozambique in 1964. At first, the African rebels were poorly armed and trained, scattered and uncoordinated. Portuguese forces were able to confine the insurgencies to remote, largely frontier regions and urban terrorism did not develop. After 1966, however, the insurgencies spread widely in rural areas and Portugal was obliged to import more troops from the home country.

These colonial wars lasted from 1961 to 1974 and were the longest in African history, challenging Portugal's military preparations, which were initially modest, and generating the largest military mobilization in the country's history. Social, economic, and educational reforms followed, and forced labor and the assimilation policy were abolished. In theory, all adults, whatever their race or degree of "civilization," were now counted as Portuguese.

By 1974 insurgents in Guinea-Bissau, which was not a settler colony like Angola or Mozambique, held more than half the territory but were unable to capture the capital. In Angola the insurgency was limited to remote, rural areas but the largest portion of Portugal's armed forces was engaged there. In Mozambique, nationalist forces in the north and center began to attack more heavily populated areas and Portugal had to send reinforcements from Angola. After thirteen years, no end to the conflicts was in sight. Most of Portugal's chief military leaders were convinced that they could not be won militarily and that only negotiation and political solutions could end them. Portugal itself was increasingly pressed by economic, financial, political, and demographic pressures (heavy emigration from Portugal to escape the draft led to a labor shortage). However Premier Marcello Caetano, who succeeded Salazar, declined to negotiate with the African nationalists until it was too late.

On 25 April 1974, a military coup led by career officers in Lisbon overthrew the dictatorship and initiated both decolonization and the building of a democracy. By the end of 1975, more than 500,000 *retornados* (returned ones) had fled the former colonies, a good portion of them returning to Portugal.

The pace of decolonization was as follows: Guinea-Bissau, September 1974; Cape Verde Islands, June 1975; Sao Tome and Principe Islands, July 1975; Mozambique, July 1975; Angola, November 1975. East Timor was moving only slowly toward decolonization when in December 1975, after claiming a threat to national security, Indonesia invaded and annexed it. In 1999, after intense international pressure and a popular referendum that favored independence, Indonesia withdrew from East Timor and in 2001, with United Nations assistance, it achieved full independence. In 1999, Macau, Portugal's last colony, was handed over to the People's Republic of China.

See also **Colonialism; Decolonization; Portugal; Salazar, Antonio.**

BIBLIOGRAPHY

Bender, Gerald J. *Angola under the Portuguese: The Myth and the Reality.* Berkeley, Calif., 1978.

Clarence-Smith, Gervase. *The Third Portuguese Empire, 1822–1975: A Study in Economic Imperialism.* Manchester, U.K., and Dover, N.H., 1985.

Duffy, James. *Portugal in Africa.* Cambridge, Mass, 1962.

Newitt, Malyn. *Portugal in Africa: The Last Hundred Years.* London, 1981.

Vail, Leroy. "Mozambique's Chartered Companies: The Rule of the Feeble." *Journal of African History* 17 (1976): 389–416.

Wheeler, Douglas L. "Portugal in Angola: A Living Colonialism?" In *Southern Africa in Perspective: Essays in Regional Politics,* edited by Christian P. Potholm and Richard Dale. New York, 1972.

Wheeler, Douglas L., and René Pélissier. *Angola.* Westport, Conn., 1978.

DOUGLAS L. WHEELER

POSTMODERNISM. Since the late 1960s, when literary critics brought the term into circulation, *postmodernism* has been employed in what appears at first sight to be rather different contexts. Initially referring to a loosely defined set of innovations in practically all artistic disciplines, including architecture, it later came to include a new perspective on language, knowledge, even the idea of reality itself. In hindsight, we can see that the postmodern impulse first surfaced in the 1950s, well before American literary and cultural critics such as Ihab Hassan and Susan Sontag began to identify it as such. In the United States we find it in, for instance, the collages of Robert Rauschenberg (b. 1925), the ironic borrowings from popular art in the work of Roy Liechtenstein (1923–1997), the musical experiments of John Cage (1912–1992), the "happenings" of the late 1950s, and other developments that remind of us the continental European avant-gardes of the early decades of the twentieth century. We find echoes of Dada, but without its deliberately offensive political edge, and of surrealism, but without surrealism's belief in the role Sigmund Freud assigned to the "unconscious."

AMERICAN AND FRENCH VERSIONS

In its earliest phase, this American version of post-modernism was a mostly playful revolt against the solemnities, anxieties, and hierarchies of the 1950s and against the high seriousness and lofty moral purposes of much of its art. We find the same appreciation of playfulness and popular art forms in Robert Venturi's early 1960s reappraisal of the architecture of the Las Vegas Strip. In France we find a similar turning away from the concerns of an earlier generation, strongly marked in this case by the still recent experience of Nazi totalitarianism. Initially limited to literature, the postmodern reaction to the insistent moral seriousness of Jean-Paul Sartre, Albert Camus, and others was one of formal experiment and of self-reflexivity, as in the novels of Alain Robbe-Grillet (b. 1922), in which character, theme, and so on are secondary to an exploration of the formal possibilities that the novel as an art form offers.

This is not to say that we do not find playfulness in French postmodernism or that its American counterpart does not go in for formal experiment and self-reflexivity. In fact, as postmodernism developed and became resolutely international, playfulness, formal experiment, and the intense consciousness that accompanies self-reflexivity became virtually inseparable, as in the following questionnaire that the unsuspecting reader suddenly encounters in Donald Barthelme's *Snow White* (1967):

1. Do you like the story so far? Yes ( ) No ( )
2. Does Snow White resemble the Snow White you remember? Yes ( ) No ( )
3. Have you understood, in reading to this point, that Paul is the prince figure? Yes ( ) No ( )
4. That Jane is the wicked stepmother-figure? Yes ( ) No ( )
5. In the further development of the story, would you like more emotion ( ) or less emotion ( )?

A DEVELOPING SERIOUSNESS

By the 1970s postmodernism had developed its own seriousness. While in postmodernism's early stages this seriousness was less than obvious, partly because of its apparently willful superficiality, partly because of its interest in formal display, it now was pervasively present in novels such as Thomas Pynchon's *Gravity's Rainbow* (1973) or Robert Coover's *The Public Burning* (1977), providing a moral framework for their wild improbabilities, displays of self-reflexivity, unsettling asides to the reader, and general authorial zaniness.

It would, in fact, be fair to say that postmodern art, in one way or another, has been serious all along. Its borrowings from popular culture, its array of anti-interpretive strategies (disruptions, intentional incoherence, refusal to provide closure, apparent lack of artistic control, deliberate shallowness), its self-reflexivity, its confusing hybridity (as in landscape art or installations) and mixing of styles (as in postmodern architecture), serve an ultimately political purpose. Such typically postmodern features question the politics—based on a specific view of art, the artist, and art's social function—that dominated the postwar art world and its institutions. They reject the ideals of coherence (dominant in modernist literary criticism) and of purity (central to our understanding of modernism in the visual arts and to the modernist architecture of Bauhaus and its followers). They also call into question the uniqueness of the artistic object, the artist as hero, and the transcendence of art itself, that is, its status as the refuge of eternal aesthetic values in a commercialized world.

Postmodern art is thoroughly skeptical, first of all about art, but also about the role of the institutions, such as museums, that embody such ideals, and even about deeply entrenched humanist convictions concerning the uniqueness and autonomy of the individual. In the course of the 1970s, that skepticism, influenced by postmodern theory, was extended to all social structures, including gender roles, class and race relations, even capitalism itself. To put this differently, since its emergence in the 1950s postmodern art has of course, like all art, drawn our attention to itself, but also to an ever-widening social context. It has tried to make us ask questions such as: What is art? Who decides the answer—and why? Who is excluded by this definition? Who controls art's institutions? How are they funded?

LANGUAGE AND POWER RELATIONS

Postmodern theory, which in the later 1970s began to exert enormous influence, especially in the humanities, has its basis in France. It is best seen as an amalgam, the exact mixture depending on the theorist in question, of ideas and arguments derived from the writings of the Marxist sociologist Louis Althusser (1918–1990), the philosophers Jacques Derrida (1930–2004) and Jean-François Lyotard (1925–1998), the historian Michel Foucault (1926–1984), and the literary critic Roland Barthes (1815–1980). In all of its many versions, however, it is resolutely antihumanist and sees everything as inevitably partaking in relations of power. What distinguishes postmodern theory from other antihumanist perspectives that claim to have a sharp eye for the workings of power—such as Marxism—is its focus on language and on the way language constructs the world we (think we) live in.

For Derrida, language is inherently elusive and unstable. It is a centerless system of ultimately arbitrary signs that is never unequivocally anchored in reality and that never allows stable meaning—that is, truth—to emerge. As a result, language facilitates the emergence of false truths and a false order through oppositions (white versus black, masculine versus feminine, rational versus irrational, Western versus Oriental) in which one pole is routinely "privileged," that is, accorded superiority. For Foucault, language creates order through what he calls "discourses": networks of interlocking statements that have evolved over time

and that determine what counts as relevant and even true within the fields they control. Foucault discusses a limited number of discourses—medical, legal, sexological—but obviously there is a discourse for every imaginable field. It is these discourses, seemingly without origin and belonging to nobody, that effectively constitute reality as we know it and that embody and perpetuate power and confer it on those who can participate in them. To be outside discourses—where women and non-whites have found themselves over much of Western history—means to go unheard and to be powerless.

Postmodern theory aims to bring to light how texts and other forms of communication—including works of (literary) art—try to establish truths by privileging certain positions. It then goes on to "deconstruct" them by exposing their ambiguities and internal contradictions. Alternatively, it may show how those positions derive from one or more discourses that have no authority apart from their own insistent claims. In both cases, postmodern theory seeks to demonstrate that language—or, for that matter, any sign system—cannot accurately represent the world. It shows that it is language that creates our world and it alerts us to the fact that we are constantly duped into accepting as given, as natural, what is in fact fundamentally ungrounded.

The postmodern attack on language and, more generally, on all our conceptual systems, leads inevitably toward skepticism and relativism. For postmodernists, there is no such thing as truth; there are only positions that can always be traced back to the metaphoric play of language. For radical postmodernists, even the claims of science derive their authority only from the discourse within which they are presented. Needless to say, such views are highly controversial. More generally, postmodernism's skepticism with regard to individual agency, its resolute antirealism, and its suspicion of reason—which it tends to see as a repressive force—have generated widespread criticism. It should be said that postmodern theory is indeed not characterized by intellectual rigor, an attitude that can partly be blamed on its suspicion of reason, partly on sheer mischief, and partly on the fact that it took form in a literary rather than a philosophical environment. In spite of that, it has played an enormously important role by insisting on the ubiquitousness of power and the inevitability of politics and by constantly trying to do justice to the historically marginalized. Without postmodernism's groundbreaking radical questioning, new fields of study such as postcolonial or queer studies would not have emerged. Even new forms of political activism such as identity politics and single-issue politics would not have taken the shape they have.

See also **Architecture; Derrida, Jacques; Foucault, Michel; Lyotard, Jean-François.**

BIBLIOGRAPHY

Bertens, Hans. *The Idea of the Postmodern: A History.* London, 1995.

Butler, Christopher. *Postmodernism: A Very Short Introduction.* Oxford, U.K., 2002.

Connor, Stephen. *Postmodernist Culture: An Introduction to Theories of the Contemporary.* 2nd ed. Oxford, U.K., 1997.

Hassan, Ihab. *The Postmodern Turn: Essays in Postmodern Theory and Culture.* Columbus, Ohio, 1987.

Jencks, Charles. *What Is Postmodernism?* Rev. ed. London, 1996.

HANS BERTENS

POTSDAM CONFERENCE. The final summit conference of World War II (codenamed "Terminal") was held in the Berlin suburb of Potsdam between 17 July and 2 August 1945. The principal issues were the treatment of occupied Germany and that country's eastern border with Poland. Looming over all the discussions was the end of the war with Japan and the use of the atomic bomb.

PHASE ONE—DEADLOCK

The conference sessions took place in the Cecilienhof, a mansion built for the crown prince of Germany before the First World War, designed in English "mock Tudor" style. The American, British, and Soviet delegations were housed in the nearby film colony of Babelsberg, Germany's equivalent of Hollywood. Potsdam was the first

opportunity for Winston Churchill (1874–1965), prime minister of Great Britain, and Joseph Stalin (1879–1953), the leader of the Soviet Union, to meet the new American president, Harry Truman (1884–1972). The conference followed the pattern of earlier summits such as Yalta, with plenary gatherings of the Big Three and their staffs alternating with meetings of the foreign ministers, who handled the details of policy and planning.

When the conference opened on 17 July, a contrast in styles was immediately apparent. Truman masked his lack of experience with a direct, businesslike manner, insisting that he wanted "something in the bag" each day. Churchill loved to make long speeches, his natural loquacity exacerbated by the fatigue of five grueling years as war leader. Stalin, as usual, listened closely and said little: his interventions were terse, often brusque. At times each leader got on the others' nerves, their frustration intensified by the delays as comments were translated into either English or Russian.

The central issue was the postwar fate of Germany. The country had been divided into four zones of military occupation, under the Americans, British, French, and Soviets. On 18 July, the conference quickly accepted Truman's outline proposals for further progress. In each zone, the Allies would eliminate all relics of Nazism, bring war criminals to justice, and establish democratic government at the local level. For the time being, no central German government would be created.

But the Allies could not agree on the question of reparations. At Yalta they had accepted as a basis for discussion a figure of twenty million dollars, half of which would go to the Soviets, who had suffered most from Nazi depredations. But the Red Army had already systematically looted its zone in the east, and the British and Americans feared that if their zones also had to be stripped bare, they would end up subsidizing western Germany to keep its people alive. In effect, they would be making reparations to Germany, so that the Germans could pay the Soviet Union.

A related issue was the Polish border. It had already been agreed at Yalta that the Soviet Union would recover former tsarist territories in Ukraine, which Poland had controlled between the world wars. In turn, the Poles would gain former German territory in Prussia and Silesia, effectively moving Poland westward, but no conclusion on the western border had been reached at Yalta. Where to draw it was a very sensitive issue. The decision would determine the size of the Soviet zone of occupation in Germany and its capacity to extract reparations. As Churchill warned, it could also cause intense friction between Poland and the new Germany, as had happened after 1919.

Even more acrimonious were the debates about whether to recognize the new governments in some of the defeated Axis powers. The Americans and British wanted Italy admitted immediately into the United Nations. But they refused recognition to Eastern European countries such as Romania and Bulgaria, until their Soviet-imposed governments had been replaced. Stalin attacked this as unequal treatment. Churchill gave a long and effusive speech about Italy being a democracy, whereas the others were not. "Fiction," exclaimed Stalin. The exchanges became heated and no progress was made.

PHASE TWO—SOLUTIONS, OF A SORT

On 25 July the conference adjourned so Churchill could return to London for the result of the British general election. Still confident of victory; he expected to come back in a few days; his doctor even left half his luggage at Potsdam. Instead, Churchill's Conservatives suffered a humiliating defeat, and the Labour Party formed a new government. When the conference resumed on July 28, Clement Attlee (1883–1967) took Churchill's seat as Britain's prime minister. The former labor leader Ernest Bevin (1881–1951) was foreign secretary.

Churchill had been assertive; Attlee was much less so, and it was Bevin who championed British interests in a Churchillian manner. But the dramatic change of personnel weakened the British position, and in any case their power was now far less than that of the emerging "superpowers," the United States and the Soviet Union. One British diplomat wrote privately that it was not so much a meeting of "the Big Three" as of "the Big 2½." Truman was anxious to break the deadlock, and his secretary of state, James F. Byrnes (1882–1972), was a veteran political fixer. He offered Vyacheslav

Molotov (1890–1986), his Soviet counterpart, a deal whereby the Americans would give ground on the Polish border and the Russians would reduce their demands for reparations.

During 30–31 July this was fleshed out into a three-part package. The Americans conceded a Polish-German border along the Oder and Western Neisse Rivers—the extremity of Polish demands. To placate Bevin, this was billed as a temporary settlement, pending a final decision at a future peace conference. In return, the Soviets accepted that no cash totals for reparations would be established, but they were free to take what they wished from their own zone. After haggling over exact figures, it was also agreed that 10 percent of all industrial equipment in the three western zones that was "unnecessary for the German peacetime economy" would be given to the Soviets. A further 15 percent would be transferred in exchange for food, coal, and raw materials from the Soviet zone. The third element of the deal was agreement that the new council of foreign ministers, set up by the conference, would give priority to drafting a peace treaty with Italy, so that this country could be admitted to the United Nations. Treaties for Bulgaria, Romania, Hungary, and Finland would then be drawn up.

Relieved at this breakthrough on 31 July, the leaders dealt rapidly with a series of issues so that the conference could close on 1 August. One of the most significant was a quick and uncontroversial decision that German nationals living in Poland, Czechoslovakia, and Hungary should be transferred to Germany. Their expulsion was a fundamental demand of the new governments in these countries—tit for tat after years of Nazi repression—but it resulted in one of the biggest population movements of modern European history, involving twelve or thirteen million people. Although the Potsdam protocol stated that the transfer should take place "in an orderly and humane manner," the reality was very different, and estimates of German deaths run to one or two million.

Potsdam was intended only as a provisional settlement of German questions, pending a full-scale peace conference. But, as the Cold War deepened, the provisional became permanent. Although the

Allies had reaffirmed that Germany should be treated as "a single economic unit," as the British predicted, the agreements on zonal reparations accelerated the division of Germany.

THE ATOMIC BOMB

On 16 July the Americans conducted an atomic test at Alamogordo, in the desert of New Mexico. By 21 July, it was clear that this had been a resounding success, and the news buoyed up Truman and the American delegation. It also had an effect on their strategy. The Soviets had promised to enter the war against Japan in the middle of August, and U.S. army commanders, fearful of heavy losses when they invaded the Japanese home islands, still regarded this commitment as militarily vital. But Byrnes, in particular, thought that the bomb could enable the Americans to end the Pacific war without Soviet help; he even hoped it might make Stalin more tractable in Europe. On 24 July Truman told Stalin, with studied casualness, that the Americans had a new weapon of unusual destructive power. Stalin, equally casually, said he hoped they would make good use of it against Japan. Possibly Stalin was dissimulating; more likely, although aware of the U.S. project from Soviet agents, he did not appreciate its full significance until after the bomb was dropped on Japan.

Truman gave fuller details to Churchill: the British were collaborators in the bomb project, albeit now very much as junior partners. The two leaders agreed to issue an oblique final warning to Japan and the so-called Potsdam Proclamation of 26 July threatened the Japanese with "prompt and utter destruction" if their government did not immediately order "the unconditional surrender of all Japanese armed forces." When the Japanese prime minister announced four days later that there was "nothing important or interesting in the Allied declaration," Truman confirmed his order to use the atomic bomb, which was dropped on Hiroshima on 6 August.

See also **Japan and the Two World Wars; Nuclear Weapons; Warfare; World War II.**

BIBLIOGRAPHY

Primary Sources

Butler, Rohan, and M. E. Pelly, eds. *Documents on British Policy Overseas.* Series 1, vol. 1: *The Conference at Potsdam, July–August 1945.* London, 1984.

United States Department of State Historical Office. *Foreign Relations of the United States: The Conference of Berlin: The Potsdam Conference, 1945.* 2 vols. Washington D.C., 1960.

Secondary Sources

Chronos-Film. *Schloss Cecilienhof und die Potsdamer Konferenz, 1945.* Berlin, 1995. Illustrated companion volume to the Chronos video about the conference.

Feis, Herbert. *Between War and Peace: The Potsdam Conference.* Princeton, N.J., 1960.

Mee, Charles L. *Meeting at Potsdam.* London, 1975.

DAVID REYNOLDS

POULENC, FRANCIS (1899–1963), French composer.

A friend of Francis Poulenc once declared, "there is some of the monk and some of the rascal in him." Indeed, Poulenc may be the most delightful paradox in twentieth-century music. His enormous oeuvre spans from the sacred to the risque, but each piece speaks with the same engaging voice. Unlike many peers, Poulenc performed constantly, which kept him in contact with concertgoers, and never felt compelled to reinvent himself or adopt fashionable methods like serialism. Instead, he preferred to create, evolve, and just be who he was. Thus Poulenc became one of the world's most esteemed composers when art music often seemed indifferent to its audience.

The foundation for Poulenc's unique style formed early. His father, a devout Catholic from southern France who directed the Rhône-Poulenc pharmaceutical company, loved orchestral music and opera, especially that of the French composers Hector Berlioz and Jules Massenet. His mother, whose family was Parisian, played the music of Wolfgang Mozart and Frédéric Chopin at the piano and exposed her son to art, ballet, literature, and music, instilling passions sustained throughout his life. At fourteen, Poulenc began piano studies with Ricardo Viñes, who introduced him to the latest French, Spanish, and Russian music and encouraged his efforts at composition. By 1917 Poulenc's parents had died, but an inheritance enabled him to pursue music. Failing to enter the Paris Conservatoire that year, Poulenc was drafted to defend France, but his distinctive music already had begun to gain attention. As World War I ended, Poulenc became acquainted with the writer Jean Cocteau, whose collaboration with Erik Satie, Pablo Picasso, and the Ballets Russes on the ballet *Parade* (1917) had attracted many young musicians. Their aesthetic rejected Romanticism, Wagnerism, and impressionism, emphasizing instead simplicity, clarity, and "French sensibilities." During the euphoric, exhilarating postwar period in Paris, six of these *Nouveaux Jeunes* (new youth, young upstarts)—Darius Milhaud, Louis Durey, Georges Auric, Arthur Honegger, Francis Poulenc, and Germaine Tailleferre—were highlighted in 1920 by the journalist Henri Collet, who called them *Les Six,* comparing them to *Les Cinq Russes* (The Five Russians). As composers, *Les Six* had different styles, but their friendship and interest in artistic movements like cubism, surrealism, and fauvism fostered mutual encouragement and attracted publicity. Self-taught as a composer, Poulenc studied with fellow composer Charles Koechlin from 1921 to 1925 to improve his technique, even as his fame grew. From these influences and circumstances, Poulenc developed a style that was energetic, lyrical, and colorful, as well as spontaneous, humorous, and provocative, but above all personal and expressive.

Poulenc gained early fame with solo piano works, but collaborative genres seemed to inspire him more. His chamber music includes sonatas for violin (1943), cello (1948), flute (1957), clarinet (1962), and oboe (1962), plus works for diverse combinations of instruments and/or voices. With 137 *mélodies,* many written for his friend and frequent collaborator, the baritone Pierre Bernac, Poulenc's contribution to the intimate French vocal genre is rivaled in the twentieth century only by that of Gabriel Fauré. Yet Poulenc's creativity also could be extroverted, as concertos for harpsichord (1928), two pianos (1932), organ (1938), and piano (1949) demonstrate. The bawdy *Chansons galliardes* (1926; Ribald songs) as well

as the charming *L'histoire de Babar* (1945; Story of Babar) represent other aspects of his outgoing nature.

Poulenc's works for the stage may be his most important achievements. The early ballet *Les biches* (1923; The hinds) solidified his reputation as an innovative provacateur. In opera, his comic farce *Les mamelles de Tirésias* (1944; The breasts of Tirésias), the historical drama *Dialogues des Carmélites* (1957; Dialogues of the Carmelites), and a tragedy, *La voix humaine* (1958; The human voice), rank among the twentieth century's dramatic landmarks. Yet Poulenc may have been proudest of his sacred music. His *Litanies à la Vierge Noire* (1936; Litanies to the Black Virgin), *Mass* (1937), and *Stabat mater* (1950; Sorrowful mother) represent strikingly original yet heartfelt contributions to the Catholic choral literature.

During his last fifteen years Poulenc often visited the United States for concerts of his own music and was both touched and invigorated by the welcome he received. His *Gloria* (1959), commissioned by the Koussevitzky Foundation and premiered by the Boston Symphony, plus his *Sept répons des ténèbres* (1962; Seven responses for tenebrae), commissioned by the New York Philharmonic to celebrate the opening of Lincoln Center, attest to a warm, mutual affection. Poulenc once said, "Above all, do not analyze my music—love it" (Bernac, p. 13). It seems clear that Americans, as well as the French, and indeed music lovers around the world, have embraced his art as he wished.

See also **France.**

BIBLIOGRAPHY

Bernac, Pierre. *Francis Poulenc: The Man and His Songs.* Translated by Winifred Radford. New York, 1977. Brief biography and in-depth discussion of the composer's 137 *mélodies* by the singer who was his longtime friend and frequent collaborator.

Buckland, Sidney, and Myriam Chimènes. *Francis Poulenc: Music, Art, and Literature.* Aldershot, U.K., 1999. A collection of essays that offers a broad, contemporary survey of the composer's art.

Hell, Henri. *Francis Poulenc.* Translated by Edward Lockspeiser. New York, 1959. A brief, yet valuable portrait of Poulenc, written by a friend of the composer.

Poulenc, Francis. *Diary of My Songs*. Translated by Winifred Radford. London, 1985. A personal view of Poulenc's *mélodies* that reveals their artistic and aesthetic spirit.

Schmidt, Carl B. *Entrancing Muse: A Documented Biography of Francis Poulenc*. Hillsdale, N.Y., 2001. A thorough, in-depth biography of Poulenc, based on systematic research involving original documents.

JAMES WILLIAM SOBASKIE

POUND, EZRA (1885–1972), American poet.

Ezra Pound was born in Hailey, Idaho, but moved with his family at the age of two to Wyncote, Pennsylvania, a Philadelphia suburb. He completed his B.A. and an M.A. in Romance philology at the University of Pennsylvania. Then, after teaching briefly in Indiana, he left for Europe. He spent a few months in Venice, then moved to London in 1908, where he was soon frequenting the salon of Olivia Shakespear, a close friend of William Butler Yeats, for Pound the greatest living poet. During the winter months in the period from 1913 to 1915, he would serve as a reader and amanuensis for Yeats, and the two developed a lifelong friendship, despite their very different aesthetic preferences.

In 1912 Pound founded imagism, a poetic movement that emphasized precision and conciseness. In earlier accounts of modernism, imagism was hailed as a major breakthrough that paved the way for the early writings of T. S. Eliot and James Joyce. More recent critics have tempered these claims, stressing that Eliot and Joyce developed their aesthetics without reference to imagism and noting the extent to which imagism responded to futurism, yet did so in ways that evaded futurism's most challenging dimensions, such as its call for an aesthetics grounded in a systematic reading of social and economic modernity. Only two years later Pound joined with the painter Wyndham Lewis in founding vorticism, a more coherent and provocative movement, albeit one still indebted to futurism, as contemporaries immediately noted.

By 1915 Pound's interest was turning to Chinese poetry. Stimulated by the manuscripts of the Sinologist Ernest Fenollosa, he published *Cathay*, a book of translations that "created" Chinese poetry for English-speaking readers for the rest of the twentieth century. A year later he published *Certain Noble Plays of Japan,* an edited selection and reworking of Fenollosa's translations of Noh plays, and in 1918 he published "The Chinese Written Character as a Medium of Poetry," a meditation by Fenollosa that helped Pound to articulate his own aesthetics of juxtaposition.

During the decade from 1912 to 1921, Pound was a tireless editor and cultural impresario. He was foreign editor for the journal *Poetry* from 1912 to 1914, literary advisor to *The Egoist* from 1914 to 1917, editor of an independent section within *The Little Review* from 1917 to 1919, and then foreign correspondent and talent scout for *The Dial* from 1920 to 1921. In these positions he championed the writings of Eliot, Joyce, and Wyndham Lewis. As a cultural impresario he linked together extant journals, potential patrons, and innovative authors, creating institutional venues open to avant-garde writing. To the extent that Anglo-American literary modernism was a viable institution as well as an ensemble of specific texts, it was largely Pound's creation.

In 1920 Pound published *Hugh Swelwyn Mauberley,* a long poetic sequence that has become a modern classic. That same year he moved from London to Paris, where he would reside until late 1924, his residence punctuated by increasingly frequent journeys to Italy. From now on his energies would be devoted to *The Cantos,* an epic poem that consumed the rest of his life. While in Paris in early 1922, he edited Eliot's *The Waste Land,* deleting more than two hundred lines and transforming it into the published poem. A year later, in January 1923, while traveling in Italy, he had his first experiences with Italian Fascists, and he soon counted himself an admirer of Benito Mussolini.

In late 1924 he moved to Rapallo, Italy. His commitments to Mussolini and fascism deepened in subsequent years, and during the 1930s they were wedded to increasingly virulent anti-Semitism. Both make their presence felt in the portions of *The Cantos* that he published during the 1930s. During World War II Pound made a series of radio broadcasts sponsored by the Italian state, and for these he was indicted for treason by the United States. At the war's end he was arrested and incarcerated in a prison camp for U.S. army criminals located near Pisa, and there he wrote the *Pisan Cantos,* another installment of *The Cantos,* published to acclaim and controversy in 1948. Pound, meanwhile, had been flown to Washington, D.C., to stand trial, but was declared mentally unfit and committed to St. Elizabeths Hospital for the Insane, where he stayed until 1958. After his release, he returned to Venice, where he passed his last years. He continued to publish more installments of *The Cantos* during these years, but only the final volume, *Drafts and Fragments,* has found a warm reception from critics and readers.

In the afterlife of critical discussion, Pound has been as controversial as he was during his lifetime. He left a divided legacy, one in which real achievement is mixed with tedious self-indulgence, and genuine generosity is counterbalanced by ugly anti-Semitism.

See also **Fascism; Lewis, Wyndham; Modernism.**

BIBLIOGRAPHY

Kenner, Hugh. *The Pound Era.* Berkeley, Calif., 1971.

Pound, Ezra. *The Cantos of Ezra Pound.* New York, 1986.

———. *Personae: The Shorter Poems of Ezra Pound.* Edited by Lea Baechlerk and A. Walton Litz. Rev. ed. New York, 1990.

LAWRENCE RAINEY

POWELL, ENOCH (1912–1998), British politician and writer.

Enoch Powell was born in Stechford, Birmingham, to two teachers, Albert Enoch Powell and Ellen Mary Breese. His upbringing was lower middle class, disciplined, and dominated by scholarly pursuits. At seventeen, Powell won the highest award in the country for classical study, a scholarship to Trinity College, Cambridge. Always the bookish loner, Powell excelled there under the influence of the poet and classicist A. E. Housman. Upon graduation, in recognition for the brilliance of his dissertation on Thucydides, he was named a fellow of Trinity College. There he remained until 1937, publishing the first of what came to be four collections of poetry in that year. At twenty-five, Powell accepted a chair of Greek at the University of Sydney in Australia, thereby becoming the youngest professor in the Commonwealth. While there, he gained a reputation for his aggressive atheism, misogyny, and strict textual criticism.

In 1939 Powell returned to England to join the Royal Warwickshire Regiment. Over the next seven years, Powell rose from private to brigadier in the British army, working in intelligence in North Africa and India. It was in the army that he became, he said later in life, "deeply bound up with India." At the war's end, Powell decided that the best way to save the British Raj was in the House of Commons. Entering politics was the first step, he imagined, toward his ambition to become the viceroy of India.

The day Powell landed off a transport plane from India in 1946, he telephoned the Conservative Central Office. There began his dramatic forty-one-year career in politics. Powell took the seat of member of Parliament (MP) for Wolverhampton South West in 1950, a position he held until 1974. He embraced Anglicanism and, through that, developed a thoroughgoing belief in good and evil, the saved and the unsaved, which later became a crucial component of his vision of the British nation. In these early years of his political career, he joined the One Nation Group, writing pamphlets and books in support of free-market forces over state planning, such as *One Nation* (1950) and *Change Is Our Ally* (1954). Later, as the British Empire collapsed before him, he spoke out in public and in Parliament against the Commonwealth as a "gigantic farce," a product of Britain's inability to see beyond the now inappropriate "myth" of empire.

In 1958 Powell resigned from his position as financial secretary to the treasury when Harold Macmillan failed to endorse a monetarist agenda to contain inflation. Macmillan, despite this disagreement, appointed Powell minister of health. There he promoted an ambitious ten-year program to modernize the National Health Service. However, after just three years in office, Powell would again leave the government in opposition to the appointment in 1963 of a lord, Sir Alec Douglas-Home, to the leadership of the Conservative Party. Two years later he served as shadow minister of defense under Edward Heath, only to be dismissed after his infamous "Rivers of Blood" speech in 1968 against "New Commonwealth" immigration and the Race

Supporters of Enoch Powell protest immigration, London, September 1972. ©HULTON-DEUTSCH COLLECTION

Relations Bill of that year. More controversy was to follow in 1974, when Powell declined to seek reelection in Wolverhampton in opposition to the Conservative Party's pro-Europe stance, instead advising his supporters to vote Labour. He returned to Parliament, but never again as a Conservative Party member. Instead, that same year, he became an Ulster Unionist MP for South Down, where he remained until his defeat in the general election of 1987.

Enoch Powell remains one of the most controversial political figures in twentieth-century British history. To his supporters, Powell's troublesome career in politics reveals a man who put principles before loyalty to his party. To many, Powell was the "high priest of High Toryism." To most, he is remembered still for his outspoken, racist opposition to nonwhite immigration into Britain in the late 1960s. Nonetheless, his career may be read as a product of a crucial postwar transformation in the Conservative Party. His uncompromising monetarism and faith in the free market worked against the postwar political consensus and were clear antecedents to the direction of the Conservative Party under Margaret Thatcher. His Euroskepticism, support for Ulster, and attacks on immigration were representative of a Conservative vision of the post-imperial nation. Britain, Powell insisted, had to wake up to the "morning after the imperial night before." At the same time, he believed that only history legitimated national sovereignty and social order. If Britain, therefore, did not reclaim its stable and historical nationhood as a white, Christian island in the North Atlantic, Enoch Powell could see nothing but racial violence and national disintegration.

See also **Immigration and Internal Migration; Racism; United Kingdom.**

BIBLIOGRAPHY

Primary Sources

Powell, J. Enoch. *Freedom and Reality.* Edited by John Wood. London, 1969. A useful work on Powell's political philosophies regarding myth, statesmanship, and the nation.

———. *A Nation or No Nation?: Six Years in British Politics.* Edited by Richard Ritchie. London, 1978. Powell discusses national sovereignty and Britain's entry into the European Community.

———. *Reflections of a Statesman: The Writings and Speeches of Enoch Powell.* Edited by Rex Collins. London, 1991. A well-chosen collection of Powell's important broadcasts, speeches, and articles.

Secondary Sources

Heffer, Simon. *Like the Roman: The Life of Enoch Powell.* London, 1998. A thorough (thousand-plus-page) and sympathetic account of Powell's public and private life.

Shepherd, Robert. *Enoch Powell.* London, 1997. A nonpartisan biography of Powell.

MILLA SCHOFIELD

PRAGUE. For many centuries the metropolis of the kingdom of Bohemia, Prague (in Czech, Praha) became the capital of the Czechoslovak (now Czech) Republic on 28 October 1918. In 2005 the city had 1.2 million inhabitants living in an area of 192 square miles on both sides of the

Vltava River, spanned by eighteen bridges. Prague has an ancient historical core, but it is also a robust industrial agglomeration that produces nearly 12 percent of the entire output of the Czech Republic (heavy machinery and tools, steel and cars, chemicals, paper, and textile and leather goods) and continues to assert itself as the center of the Czech publishing and film industries. Prague is the seat of the central Czech institutions of higher learning, including Charles University, founded in 1348, the Technical University, the Academies of Arts and Sciences, and the National Library. In the early twenty-first century it has become a powerful magnet to international tourists (about three million each year) attracted to its profusion of Romanesque, gothic, Renaissance, baroque, and modern architecture and art, relatively untouched by the devastations of World War II.

GROWTH, MODERNIZATION, ARCHITECTURE

At the end of the nineteenth century Prague was a city in the Habsburg provinces with 167,178 inhabitants, but their number more than tripled by 1921 (676,178) and, by the incorporation of suburban communes and villages, rapidly increased to 962,200 (1938). World War II caused tragic losses of Jewish and Czech lives, and after the expulsion of most Germans in 1945, the number of citizens decreased to 931,525 (1950). Through intensive industrialization planned by the state during the communist period, Prague reached the one million mark in 1961 and went beyond that later. In 2005 numbers are stagnant, though informed estimates suggest the presence of tens of thousands of undocumented workers from Ukraine and other former Soviet republics. The presence of perhaps fifteen thousand Americans in the "Paris of the Nineties" has been reduced, by an official count, to three thousand. The acute problem of affordable living space for the younger Czech generation, at least in the central districts, has not been solved. The birthrate is falling and the population is aging, the average age being 42.5 years. The technological and architectural modernization of the city was launched with the demolition, beginning in 1895, of the fortifications and the impoverished medieval ghetto, which most Jewish inhabitants had left long before. In the early years of the century, Prague architecture, close to the Vienna Secession, was dominated by art nouveau (Jan Kotěra, František Bílek, and the famous 1911 Municipal House by Karel Osvald Polívka and Antonín Balšánek, with some interior decorations by Alphonse Mucha). Not much later, cubist buildings were constructed in the city center, including the House of the Black Madonna (Josef Gocǎr, 1912) and Josef Chochol's surprising apartment houses. Modernist steel-and-glass palaces were built on Wenceslas Square (the Bat'a House and the Hotel Juliš, 1931), and the Slovene Josip Plecnik, much liked by the Czechoslovak president, Tomáš Garrigue Masaryk, remodeled some parts of Prague Castle and built the modernist Church of the Sacred Heart (1933) in Vinohrady. The communist city planners, eager to make Prague the bastion of the "working masses," made the quick construction of mass housing their prime concern and by 1957 began to use the Soviet method of building with prefabricated panels; from 1961 to 1971 nearly sixty thousand small apartments were built in entire satellite towns to be reached by new subway lines (the housing units were called *paneláky* by the people but more often termed *králíkárny*, or rabbit warrens). After 1989 it was the first task of the building industry to rescue and to gentrify the deteriorating older buildings in the city core, but it was the American architect Frank O. Gehry's ultramodern National Dutch Insurance Company Building, popularly called the "Dancing House" (or "Fred and Ginger"), on the Vltava embankment that demonstrated the city's unbroken capability to seek rejuvenation once again.

CAPITAL OF THE FIRST REPUBLIC (1918–1938)

Inevitably, Prague as the capital of the First Republic had to cope with the problems of its different ethnicities and their political expectations. In the earlier nineteenth century, German speakers predominated, but industrialization and immigration from the Czech countryside changed the proportions of ethnicities and classes. In 1861 the Germans lost control of the city council, and while the number of Czech speakers doubled, the number of German-speaking citizens (mostly middle-class, and often Jewish) dwindled to thirty-two thousand, or 7.3 percent (1910). Prague German speakers were divided in their political allegiance between the activists, meaning those who were willing to be full-fledged citizens of the liberal republic, and the nationalists, who rejected republican institutions and in the 1930s turned to the Sudeten Party and Adolf Hitler. In the 1927 Prague municipal elections the German activists still mobilized twelve thousand votes (the nationalists four thousand), but the elections of 1938 demonstrated a catastrophic change (4,849 activist votes versus 15,423 for the nationalists).

GERMAN OCCUPATION AND FATE OF THE JEWISH COMMUNITY

Preparing his expansion eastward, Hitler ordered his Wehrmacht to occupy Bohemia and Moravia on 15 March 1939. Hitler himself did not stay overnight and left the newly established "protectorate" to the military and Konstanin von Neurath, a conservative diplomat of international experience who settled at the Palais Czernin, while the Gestapo, acting independently, resided at Bredovská Street. Prague citizens spontaneously demonstrated against the occupiers on 28 October 1939, commemorating the birthday of the republic, and after students rallied in the Prague streets in mid-November to participate in the burial of their colleague Jan Opletal, fatally wounded in October, all institutions of higher learning were closed by order from Berlin, many student functionaries were shot without trial, and twelve hundred students were transported to concentration camps. After Germany's attack on the Soviet Union, acts of resistance and sabotage continued to increase, and Hitler replaced the diplomat von Neurath with Reinhard Heydrich, SS chief of the Reich Security Office, who arrived in Prague on 21 September 1940. He immediately declared martial law. Within two months four hundred people, mostly of the intelligentsia, were executed; transport of Prague and Bohemian Jews to Terezín (Theresienstadt) and farther east was initiated; and workers in the factories were systematically wooed with better food rations, extra shoes, and an increase in wages. Heydrich was ambushed on a Prague suburban road on 27 May 1941 by a Czechoslovak commando unit flown in from England and died on 4 June. His death triggered new waves of terror in Prague and the entire country (including the destruction of Lidice and Ležáky). The commandos and their helpers were, through an informer's tip, discovered in the cellar of the Orthodox church in the center of Prague, where they all perished.

In the later years of the occupation, power rested with K. H. Frank (once propaganda chief of the Sudeten Party) who continued to rely on Czech collaborators and to favor the working people at a time when the Allies drew nearer and Soviet, Slovak, and Czech partisans fought in the mountains and forests. On 5 May the citizens of Prague, guided by a National Council, rose up against the occupiers. Initially they were successful, but strong SS regiments made their way into the city and fierce fighting on the barricades erupted. For a short while Russian soldiers under General Andrei Vlasov, who had originally joined the Germans to fight the Soviets, switched sides and attacked the SS, but the National Council told them that their help was not wanted (they left for the west) and the hard-pressed Czechs had to fight alone. On the morning of 9 May 1945 the first Soviet tanks appeared to liberate the jubilant city, precisely according to the agreement between Generals Dwight D. Eisenhower and Alexei Antonov that reserved the liberation of Prague for Soviet troops. The Jewish population of Prague numbered more than 55,000 when the city was occupied (the original number had increased due to refugees from Germany, Austria, and, after Munich, from the Sudeten region), and the Prague Palestine Office succeeded in sending 19,000 Jews to Israel before it was too late. Transports to Terezín/Theresienstadt began in the fall of 1941 and continued until mid-March 1945, with 45,067 Jews deported from Prague alone. Oddly, Nazi ideologues during the war had wanted to establish a "Central Museum" of the Jewish race, with the result that collected ritual objects and entire libraries in dozens of Prague warehouses and synagogues were saved from destruction. When the war ended only 4,986 of the Prague deportees returned, and on the wall of the Pinkas synagogue the names of 77,297 Bohemian and Moravian Jews who perished in the Shoah are inscribed. In 2005 the Jewish community of Prague consisted of approximately 1,600 people, including a few young Czechs who converted for ethical reasons.

THE REPUBLIC RENEWED, THE COMMUNISTS, AND THE VELVET REVOLUTION

In May 1945 President Eduard Beneš returned to Prague Castle, unfortunately via Moscow, to an uneven conflict with the Communist Party and its new mass organizations. He accepted a new government of Communists and fellow travelers on 25 February 1948 and resigned on 6 June, making way for Klement Gottwald, longtime chairman of the Communist Party. The new regime, late-Stalinist in orientation, radically changed the shape of Prague life; all private enterprises, even small barbershops, were collectivized, and many members of the former middle classes were "relocated" to the countryside. In 1951 the party turned against itself, and in a series of show trials accused Rudolf Slánský and thirteen other leading functionaries (most of them of Jewish origins) of an "imperialist and Zionist" conspiracy against the people. Eleven of the accused, including Slánský, were executed on 2 December 1952. Destalinization was slower than in Poland and elsewhere, but over time new clubs and organizations formed, such as those of the wrongly arrested and the Club of Committed Non-Party Members; Ludvík Vaculík's courageous reform manifesto *Two Thousand Words* (1968) was published; and the Slovak Alexander Dubček, as newly named first secretary of the party, became the figurehead of the "Prague Spring" (winter to summer 1968). The Soviet Union and the communist neighbors of the Czechoslovak Socialist Republic, as it was called after 1960, did not tolerate efficient reform, however, and the members of the Warsaw Pact occupied not only Prague but the entire country, sending in troops and tanks and destroying what was called "socialism with a human face." The student Jan Palach protested by public self-immolation, and the state imposed a "normalization" of political and cultural life which was but a neo-Stalinist regime without Stalin. A new wave of emigration began (for example, the writer Milan Kundera and the critic and Franz Kafka defender Eduard Goldstücker). The "normalization" deprived many citizens of their jobs, and it was increasingly difficult to silence the dissidents and the opposition. On 1 January 1977 a Charter was signed by hundreds of citizens declaring "a free, informal, and open civic community," which (relying on the Helsinki Accords) insisted on its right peacefully to discuss political change with the authorities. Ultimately the fall of the Berlin Wall in 1989 set in motion radical transformations in Prague, and within a few weeks a "velvet" revolution ended the forty-one-year-long communist

monopoly of power. A student demonstration on 17 November 1989, commemorating events in Prague fifty years before, was answered by police brutality in the streets; opposition and dissident groups resolved to work together, and on 19 November students and actors went on a university and theater strike in preparation for a general strike later. On 20 November and the days that followed, hundred of thousands of Prague citizens demonstrated in Wenceslas Square against the government. The Forum of Citizens decided to guide the mass protests, and the playwright Václav Havel, once a political prisoner and now chairman of the Forum, discussed political change with members of the communist government. In late December he was elected president of the republic, and when, on 8–9 June 1990, elections to the National Assembly were held, nearly 50 percent voted for the Forum, while the Communist Party polled 13 percent. In the Prague municipal elections of 1994, the Citizens' Democratic Party polled 40.89 percent of the votes, the Social Democrats 8.34 percent, and the Communist Party 7.26 percent.

REPUBLICAN LITERARY LIFE AND THE AVANT-GARDE

At the turn of the twentieth century Prague, with its many newspapers, theaters, and literary cafés, (among them the *Slavia*, the *Unionka*, and the *Deminka*) was the principal scene of Czech writing, though many "ruralist" authors preferred the quiet provinces. The founding of the *Moderni Revue* (1895) signaled the emergence of intellectuals of neoromantic vision (Julius Zeyer, Jiří Karásek ze Lvovic) and a "decadent" view of human relationships, often imported from European fin-de-siècle literature. Within ten years, however, younger writers (among them Stanislav Kostka Neumann and Fráňa Šrámek) felt far more attracted by the collective demands of anarchism or communism than by erotic refinements. Jaroslav Hašek, one of the most famous Prague writers of the twentieth century, invented the character of Švejk, the (seemingly) dumb soldier eager to survive, in 1912. During World War I, Hašek served in Russia as a Czech legionnaire and Bolshevik commissar, and after returning to Prague he expanded his character's exploits into *Osudy dobrého vojáka Švejka za světové války* (1920; The adventures of the good

A student climbs on a Soviet tank during a protest against the Soviet crackdown in Prague, August 1968.
©BETTMANN/CORBIS

soldier Švejk), the first of four satirical Švejk novels. The writers that were to represent the spirit of the independent republic published a literary *Almanach for the Year 1914* as early as 1914, and in the conflicts of the 1920s and 1930s they did not hide their indifference to empty aestheticism and the rigid demands of class warfare. Karel Čapek published translations of new French poetry (to be used by the Czech avant-garde), plays about the future fate of mankind, including *R.U.R.* (1920), and many charming books about animals, gardens, and travels in Europe. His brother Josef, an eminent artist who died in a concentration camp, published a book of philosophical ruminations; František Langer, after his return from Russia, wrote plays about his World War I experiences and about picaresque characters in the Prague suburbs; and Karel Poláček, who died in Terezín, liked to portray "little people" in small towns. Shortly after the founding of the republic, poets, artists,

and musicians of the Czech avant-garde formed the group Devětsil (The Magic Root) in 1920, their hectic admiration moving between the Soviet revolution and the powers of art. Vítzěslav Nezval, in his rich and melodious poems and his ideas about "poetism," celebrated the magic and seductive life of big cities (*Pražský chodec,* 1938; Walking in Prague). Vladislav Vančura, originally a member of the avant-garde, turned to a stringent prose exploring the Czech past, as in his *Obrazy z dějin národa českého* (1939–1940; Pictures from the history of the Czech nation). He was executed in Prague in 1942. The musical avant-garde of Prague, occasionally in close proximity to Devětsil, developed its own factions. Alois Hába, in charge of his own composition class at the conservatory since 1923, wrote atonal and microtonal music, while others, including Bohuslav Martinů and Erwin Schulhoff, a German-Jewish contemporary of Kafka, experimented with fusions of classical music and jazz (Schulhoff later turned to agitprop music). Jaroslav Ježek, in-house composer of the Jan Werich and Jiři Voskovec theater (originally close to the Devětsil group) became the true genius of Czech jazz in the 1930s and died in exile (New York, 1942).

PRAGUE WRITING IN GERMAN (1900–1945)

In the first years of the century and during the First Republic, Prague produced world-famous writers in German including Rainer Maria Rilke (who left Prague early), Franz Kafka, and Franz Werfel. Many of these writers came from Jewish families (who earlier in the nineteenth century had used Yiddish), sympathized with the Czech struggle for independence, and often translated Czech literature (Rudolf Fuchs, Pavel Eisner). The poet, novelist, and critic Max Brod liked to gather his writing colleagues around himself to organize their lives and publications; in his early novels (e.g., *Ein tschechisches Dienstmädchen,* 1909; A Czech servant girl) he finely probed what was called the Czech-German erotic symbiosis, but his later novels tend to be of a philosophical if not didactic kind. His closest friend was Franz Kafka, who worked in insurance offices most of his life and wrote long letters to women he loved, among them his first translator, Milena Jesenská. His stories and novels, such as *Die Verwandlung* (1915; The metamorphosis), *Der Prozess* (1925; The trial), and *Das Schloss* (1926; The castle), have attracted generations of dedicated readers trying to unravel their political, metaphysical, and existential meanings. Franz Werfel published exemplary expressionist poems (*Der Weltfreund,* 1911), wrote a famous novel, *Das Lied von Bernadette* (1941; The song of Bernadette), and lived with his wife, Alma Mahler, in Hollywood. Other Prague writers include Egon Erwin Kisch, untiring reporter in the service of the Communist International; Paul Leppin, charmed if not obsessed with the red-light corners of the old city; and Gustav Meyrink (not a native), who wrote the famous *Der Golem* (1915), repeatedly made into movies. It was the German occupation that dispersed, imprisoned, or killed the Prague German writers; among the few survivors were the novelist and sociologist H. G. Adler (who later died in England), Franz Wurm (now at Ascona), and the writer Lenka Reinerová, who, as of 2005, continued to live in Prague.

VICISSITUDES OF POSTWAR PRAGUE WRITING

Republican Prague, in spite of the later economic and political crises, was productive in literature and the arts, and while men dominated the poetic genres, women (such as Marie Majerová or Marie Pujmanová) importantly contributed to the development of the social and psychological novel. Modern poetry constitutes one of the glorious secrets of Czech literature. Josef Hora looked to Romantic tradition; František Halas forced language to articulate his tragic vision of life; Vladimír Holan, alone in the midst of Prague, cultivated the most difficult forms; and Jaroslav Seifert, in the days of Munich, published moving verse recited by old and young and, to the consternation of the communist functionaries, received the Nobel Prize for poetry in 1984. After the change of government in 1948 the communists used many sticks and a few carrots to keep the writers (many of them old party members) in line, but the official prescription for a Soviet type of socialist realism was embraced by few, and dogmatic critics like Ladislav Štoll ruled without mercy. Yet in the late 1950s and 1960s, concurrent with the stirring of the thaw, ironic and imaginative writing strongly reemerged: J. V. Škvorecký's *Zbabělci* (1958, written in 1949; The cowards) celebrates jazz and mocks heroic slogans; Bohumil Hrabal enlisted the many virtues of a surrealist Czech idiom, and Milan Kundera, in his first (and best) novel, *Žert* (1967; The joke), wrote with grim melancholy about love, revenge, and the changes of political life. As early as 1963 Kafka was publicly discussed by scholars and critics, and small theaters produced many plays, called "absurd," by little-known playwrights like Václav Havel (*Zahradní Slavnost,* 1963; The garden party). However, the "normalization" was unable totally to suppress the independent writing that was published in clandestine samizdat editions, and after the Velvet Revolution, continuities of writing—as in the prose of Philip Roth's Prague friend and ally Ivan Klíma or of Daniela Hodrová, Kafka's true Prague heiress—were as important as the new books by Michal Ajvaz, Jáchym Topol, Michal Viewegh, and Edgar Dutka.

See also **Beneš, Eduard; Charter 77; Czech Republic; Czechoslovakia; Destalinization; Dubček, Alexander; Havel, Václav; Prague Spring; Slánský Trial; Velvet Revolution.**

BIBLIOGRAPHY

Czech Modernism: 1900–1945. Boston and Toronto, 1989. Exhibition curated by Jaroslav Anděl et al. with contributions by Peter C. Marzio, Jiří Kotalík, et al.

Demetz, Peter. *Prague in Black and Gold: Scenes from the Life of a European City.* New York, 1997. A history, from the first Slavic settlements to T. G. Masaryk, considering the creative presence of Czechs, Jews, Germans, and Italians.

Eggers, Wilma. *Women of Prague: Ethnic Diversity and Social Change from the 18th Century to the Present.* Providence, R. I., 1995.

Eyal, Gil. *Origins of Postcommunist Elites: From "Prague Spring" to the Break-Up of Czechoslovakia.* Minneapolis, Minn., 2003.

Lützow, Count Francis. *The Story of Prague.* Illustrated by Nelly Erichsen. London, 1902. Much read in earlier generations.

Mamatey, Victor S., and Luža Radomír, eds. *A History of the Czechoslovak Republic, 1918–1948.* Princeton, N.J., 1973. Inclusive and precise.

Novák, Arne. *Czech Literature.* Translated by Peter Kussi and edited with a supplement (1946–1974) by William E. Harkins. Ann Arbor, Mich., 1976. A classic, though a little on the conservative side.

Rothkirchen, Livia. *The Jews of Bohemia and Moravia: Facing the Holocaust.* Lincoln, Neb., and Jerusalem, 2005. Inclusive and precise.

Sayer, Derek. *The Coasts of Bohemia: A Czech History.* Princeton, N.J., 1998. The best book about the modern Prague arts.

PETER DEMETZ

PRAGUE SPRING. In January 1968 the leader of the Communist Party of Czechoslovakia (CPCz), Antonín Novotný, was replaced by a little-known Slovak member of the party's ruling presidium, Alexander Dubček. In the ensuing months, a vigorous program of liberal-democratic reform emerged from within the party itself. It quickly found resonance among the rank and file of the party and throughout society, and touched off a rebirth of democratic politics.

The party's new course quickly won a level and quality of popular support unprecedented in the Soviet bloc. Yet as the popular movement developed, the leaderships of Czechoslovakia's allies grew increasingly alarmed. During the ensuing months of intensifying crisis the Czechoslovak leadership walked a tightrope, striving to appease its allies without alienating popular support. The "Prague Spring" was interrupted by the Soviet-led invasion of Czechoslovakia on 21 August 1968.

ROOTS

The sudden blossoming of democratic reform in Czechoslovakia surprised many observers. Until 1963 Czechoslovakia had presented an image of internal stability and unquestioning imitation of the Soviet practices. However, the Prague Spring had been long incubating. The CPCz was a mass-based party with strong national and democratic traditions. Paradoxically, it is precisely these strong democratic and national roots that help to explain the harshness of the regime that developed after 1948. Suppressing the democratic traditions of the CPCz and transforming it into a tightly disciplined Soviet satellite was a formidable task, the success of which was not deeply rooted.

In 1963 the tide began to turn. Tendencies long articulating beneath the surface began to have greater and more visible effect. The main impulses for change came from crisis in the national economy, desire for greater national autonomy in Slovakia, and developments in the international communist arena. The leadership, facing a wide range of acute problems, finally began to experiment with reforms. Forces of opposition and pluralization began to crystallize, which the regime was never after able to bring under control. Although implementation of reforms was inconsistent and incomplete, the trend toward liberal reform was never reversed.

By 1967 the leadership's policy of partial and vacillating reform had reached a dead end. The regime's authority had eroded severely because of increasing frustration with its failure to solve the accumulation of pressing problems facing the country. The atmosphere of fear that had provided the regime with stability had dissipated and turned to contempt. During this period elements in the party and society were able to articulate their ideas and gain increasing influence within the power structure. By midyear, the leadership had realized that they would either have to undertake widespread repressive measures or tolerate developments that were rapidly undermining its power

Czech students confront soldiers who have entered Prague to restore Soviet control, August 1968.
©BETTMANN/CORBIS

base. Halfhearted attempts at repression only aggravated the situation. The Congress of the Czechoslovak Writers' Union in June, which saw the most bitter criticism to date of party policies, was followed by a series of repressive measures against the writers and their organization. By fall, discontent in Slovakia with the party's centralistic policies became acute. This discontent was reflected by Slovak members in the party leadership. Novotný alienated them by attacking them as bourgeois nationalists. Finally, overall morale throughout the country had reached an alarming low point, and the economy was again on the brink of disaster.

The leadership was seriously split. The conviction was gaining ground within the higher party echelons that the crisis could not be resolved as long as so much power remained concentrated in Novotný's hands. As Novotný's weakness became increasingly apparent, even many of his former supporters deserted him. Novotný appealed to the Soviet party general secretary Leonid Brezhnev to intervene. Brezhnev flew to Prague and met with members of the Czechoslovak leadership. In leaving, Brezhnev told his hosts that the leadership question was their own business. In the end, Novotný voluntarily resigned the party leadership and himself proposed Dubček as his successor, while remaining for the time being as president of the republic.

Dubček did not come to power as a dedicated reformist with a clear program. His initial moves, though suggestive of reform, were cautious. Yet it had become clear that attempts to contain reform within neo-Stalinist institutional and ideological strictures were not viable. The new leadership faced a staggering challenge. Having inherited a party and society in crisis, it had to struggle on at least two fronts: to win the confidence of the population and of progressives within the party, by demonstrating commitment to change, and to overcome the influence of entrenched conservatives within the country's power structure.

In February, steps were taken to separate the jurisdictional domains of the government and the party *aparat* (bureaucracy), and to ensure that policy was made by elected bodies rather than by the *aparat*. The Czechoslovak writers were again allowed to publish a weekly newspaper. In February and March, the first personnel changes were made. The party presidium took steps to curtail censorship. And it promised to improve the system by which lower party bodies were informed about party affairs. Members of the presidium also attended a total of sixty-seven district and regional party conferences, explaining the leadership's new policies. Among other things, the revival of party life was emphasized, and elections by secret ballot promised.

SPRING

Involvement in the political process was at first hesitant. Not everyone believed that the change in party leadership meant real change. By March, however, a nationwide discussion had begun to gain momentum. It concerned domestic and foreign politics, the nature of socialism, and the country's precommunist past. The reform process acquired its own momentum, never being entirely under the control of the party. The leadership sought to reassert its influence by demonstrating that the party was the force most capable of leading the reform process.

On 5 April a draft program of liberal reform, *The Action Program of the Communist Party of Czechoslovakia,* was approved by a plenary session of the central committee. The rapidity with which this document emerged indicates that its contents had been prepared before the change of leadership. What was particularly new and significant about it was its unqualified endorsement of a consistently reformist program. For the first time, the party explicitly accepted a connection between economic and political reform. It addressed the demands of Slovaks for greater autonomy by proposing a new federal constitution. The constitution would also provide for a strict division of powers: The National Assembly, not the Communist Party, would be in control of the government. Courts

would be independent and would act as arbiters between the legislative and executive branches. Civil rights and liberties would be guaranteed, and those whose rights had been violated in the past would be fully rehabilitated. A radically new concept of the Communist Party and its "leading role" in society was outlined. Internal party democracy was to be maximized to the point where even minorities would be guaranteed the right to their own opinions. The party's "leading role" was to be based on the voluntary support of the people, earned by the party, rather than imposed by force. Dubček characterized the party's new course as "socialism with a human face."

RESPONSE OF WARSAW PACT ALLIES

The emergence of such a thoroughgoing, openly publicized program of liberal-democratic reform in a context of spontaneous, unmanaged political activity further alarmed the leaderships of Czechoslovakia's Warsaw Pact allies. Problems, tendencies, and pressures similar to those in Czechoslovakia existed in all these countries, including the Soviet Union itself. All had long been cautiously striving to repair the dysfunctional aspects of the political and economic system that had developed under Joseph Stalin. Yet all were also concerned about the subversive effects of reform on the monopoly of power that undergirded their authority. All were following the various efforts of their allies to address this dilemma. Czechoslovakia's emergent example of comprehensive reform based on genuine popular support, not fully managed by the party, increasingly frightened the allies. Dubček's epithet of "socialism with a human face" implicitly raised questions about the character of their own regimes.

The East German and Polish leaders, Walter Ulbricht and Władysław Gomułka, were particularly alarmed. Both faced imminent crises of authority and were already hard-pressed in containing intense pressures for change. Neighboring on Czechoslovakia, they were directly exposed to developments there. Ulbricht and Gomułka strove to impress on the Soviet leadership the danger represented by the Prague Spring. They were the most militant advocates of force to quash it. The Hungarian leadership under János Kádár tended to be supportive of the Czechoslovak reform movement. In contrast to Ulbricht and Gomułka, Kádár had long been cautiously pushing reform to the limits of Soviet tolerance. From Kádár's perspective, success of the Czechoslovak reformists would strengthen his position, while Soviet rejection of the Prague Spring would be detrimental to reform in Hungary. Although similar tendencies and ideas were also developing in Bulgaria and in the Soviet Union itself, both regimes were still firmly entrenched, so that they were not directly threatened with infection by the Prague Spring. It was mainly East Germany (GDR) and Poland that were threatened with a collapse of regime authority.

Throughout the Prague Spring, the Czechoslovak leadership stressed its loyalty to the Warsaw Pact and friendship with the Soviet Union and its other allies. This theme was articulated in the leaders' public speeches and embodied in all programmatic statements of the Czechoslovak party. It was affirmed at all meetings with Soviet and allied representatives. Nevertheless, by July it had become clear to the allies that developments in Czechoslovakia were unacceptable. Relations between Czechoslovakia and its allies had reached a point of acute crisis.

In early July, the Communist parties of the USSR, Poland, the GDR, Hungary, and Bulgaria invited the presidium of the CPCz to a conference to be held in Warsaw to discuss the situation. The Czechoslovak leadership, unwilling to be forced into the role of the accused, rejected the invitation. It proposed instead to discuss the situation in bilateral negotiations on Czechoslovak territory. The Warsaw conclave was held on 15–16 July without Czechoslovak participation. It resulted in the dispatch of an ultimatum-like letter to the Czechoslovak leadership. The response of the CPCz presidium, though moderate in tone, was firm in substance. It rejected the accusations, stressing that the CPCz relied on the voluntary support of the people. It would not reinforce its authority with repressive measures. It declared that Czechoslovakia had loyally fulfilled its obligations under the Warsaw Pact, and would continue to do so. It stressed that Czechoslovak socialism should accord with the country's conditions and traditions.

During the period of crisis touched off by the Warsaw Letter, a national unity almost without precedent anywhere was forged in Czechoslovakia. The CPCz spontaneously became the carrier of that unity. The Warsaw Letter marked a radical turning point in the internal political situation in Czechoslovakia. Up to this point, there had been considerable differentiation of political views in Czechoslovakia. Many believed that the leadership was not going far enough or fast enough with reform. Thousands of resolutions of support poured into party headquarters and more than a million people lined up in the streets to sign an appeal to the party presidium to maintain its position.

After protracted, tortuous private and public exchanges, the Czechoslovak and Soviet leaderships reached agreement on a bilateral meeting of their leaderships. The Soviets proposed that the meeting be held in the Soviet Union. But the Czech leadership held out for a meeting on Czechoslovak territory. The meeting finally took place from 29 July to 1 August in the Slovak border town, Čierna nad Tisou. The Soviets arrived in an intransigent mood, hoping to split the Czechoslovak delegation. When this failed, they adopted a conciliatory attitude. The negotiations ended with a communiqué that said virtually nothing except that a multilateral meeting would be held on 4 August in the Slovak capital of Bratislava between representatives of Czechoslovakia and the signatories of the Warsaw Letter. An agreement was signed at the Bratislava meeting. The communiqué released after the meeting was couched in orthodox communist phraseology. Nevertheless, it was seen as putting the seal on a Czechoslovak victory and an end to the period of crisis.

During the night of 20–21 August 1968, without warning, Czechoslovakia was occupied. Despite claims of the occupying powers that "leading Czechoslovak Party and state officials" had requested their assistance, no such officials ever came forward. A movement of peaceful, coordinated resistance emerged spontaneously. It protested the invasion, demanding the return to power of the arrested reformist leaders and proclaiming determination to continue the post-January course of the CPCz. The occupying forces were unprepared for such a response. After the failure of ad hoc attempts to establish a new authority, the Soviet leadership returned to power the very same leaders arrested on 21 August. The denouement was complex. Many important aspects of the reform movement that had disturbed the Soviet leadership continued to thrive and even evolve further, almost as if there had been no military intervention. Only after Dubček was forced to resign in April 1969, did the ice age return. The warmth of the Prague Spring, its cultural and political dynamism and effervescence, was over.

See also **Czech Republic; Czechoslovakia; Dubček, Alexander; Havel, Václav; Warsaw Pact.**

BIBLIOGRAPHY

Eidlin, Fred. "January, August, and After: Czechoslovakia's Triumph and Tragedy." *Radio Free Europe Research Czechoslovakia* 21 (1969), 34pp.

———. *The Logic of "Normalization": The Warsaw Pact Intervention in Czechoslovakia of 21 August 1968 and the Czechoslovak Response.* Boulder, Colo., and New York, 1980.

Golan, Galia. *The Czechoslovak Reform Movement: Communism in Crisis, 1962–1968.* Cambridge, U.K., 1971.

———. *Reform Rule in Czechoslovakia: The Dubček Era, 1968–1969.* Cambridge, U.K., 1973.

Hamsik, Dusan. *Writers against Rulers.* Translated by D. Orpington. London, 1971.

Hejzlar, Zdenek, and Vladimir V. Kusin. *Czechoslovakia, 1968–1969: Chronology, Bibliography, Annotation.* New York, 1975.

Journalist "M." *A Year Is Eight Months.* Garden City, N.Y., 1970.

Kusin, Vladimir V. *The Intellectual Origins of the Prague Spring: The Development of Reformist Ideas in Czechoslovakia, 1956–1967.* Cambridge, U.K., 1971.

Littell, Robert, ed. *The Czech Black Book.* New York, 1969.

Mlynar, Zdenek. *Night Frost in Prague: The End of Humane Socialism.* London, 1986.

Skilling, H. Gordon. *Czechoslovakia's Interrupted Revolution.* Princeton, N.J., 1976.

FRED EIDLIN

PRESS AND NEWSPAPERS. The newspaper, an industrial product that has spread to all corners of the world, is an invention born of Enlightenment Europe. As eighteenth-century Europe coalesced into the modern world, philosophy and commerce grew together with a new kind of journalism. Merchants and intellectuals found the power of reason to be a compelling force opposed to the autocracy of monarchy. The clash of the next century found its public sphere in the press. This idea of a public sphere, as described by the German sociologist Jürgen Habermas, became a necessary place for a growing industrial class to exchange ideas in the open to build the marketplace of modern European society.

The challenges creators of a modern European press faced in building the journalistic marketplace of ideas grew into the commercialized journalism of the twentieth century. News in Western Europe became an industrial commodity collected and distributed for profit. Government press controls were finally eliminated in France, Britain, Scandinavia, Holland, Belgium, and Switzerland. The press became somewhat free in other Western European countries, including Germany. Newspapers had grown from small entrepreneurial operations to industrial operations of sometimes huge magnitude. *Le petit Parisien* (The little Parisian) of Paris, in 1914 the world's largest, published 1.5 million papers a day, the crest of an unchallenged communications revolution representing power and influence. In much of Europe, newspapers had become closely entwined with their countries' political power. Most of France's lawmakers engaged in both journalism and politics. In Britain institutions like the London *Times,* nicknamed "the Thunderer," could make or break government ministries. Other countries may not have seen such close ties between journalism and politics. In Germany, particularly, politicians distrusted journalists. But in all of Europe the press by the eve of World War I served as the intermediary between political and economic power and a growing middle class. By the end of the century that influence had been reduced. In 2004 Europe's press remained powerful. But it was no longer a Power.

THE FIRST WORLD WAR
The war that changed everything offered a stage for European journalists to shine or to shame. Unfortunately many newspapers managed only the latter. That crisis of credibility soiled press

integrity over much of the Continent. The Great War burst upon a Europe shocked, yet militarily prepared, preparations that included plans for press censorship. In Britain the Defence of the Realm Act of August 1914 set up an explicit system of press control. Successive laws strengthened the act to allow authorities to seize papers publishing news that could alarm the public or undermine confidence in the government. In the first flush of wartime enthusiasm, publishers happily complied. They soon realized the government was not going to give up easily its power of censorship, and complaints mounted.

Britain's press control did not reach nearly as far as the comprehensive operation in France. No military leader during this war had a scrap of respect for journalists, in France in particular. France's leaders opted to bring back the Law of 1849 to create a mighty operation that grew to a spiderweb of censors controlling every publication in the country. Offending material could literally be scraped from the presses, leaving gaping blanks. The *union sacrée* ("sacred union," a promise to drop prewar squabbles) went only so far, as French editors saw capricious and draconian hatchet-work applied to their pages, but tight control remained throughout the war.

German newspapers before 1914 had not established the kind of close ties between journalism and politics familiar to the French and British. Nor had German journalists attained the kind of independence seen elsewhere in Europe. During the war a divided German civilian and military government squabbled over press freedom, the chancellor allowing publications and the general staff objecting. Still, German territory was not occupied as it was in France. Censorship remained somewhat less harsh and protests somewhat more restrained. German newspapers acquiesced to government decrees, an exception being the socialist *Vorwärts*.

Neutral Holland, Norway, and Sweden retained their strong tradition of press freedom throughout this war, while Switzerland's journalists split between German-speaking Swiss who strongly supported Germany and those who strongly supported France. The government responded by censoring potentially divisive polemic. Austria-Hungary controlled its press as tightly as its German ally, while

occupied Belgium could only respond to German censorship by developing an important network of underground newspapers.

Italy's newspapers, like those of Spain and Portugal, had not become the daily bread of existence as they had in the newspaper-saturated society of northern Europe. Spanish and Italians were among the lowest per capita newspaper readers of Western Europe. In northern Italy, important voices of the press gained political significance. Luigi Albertini, proprietor of Italy's most important daily, *Corriere della sera* (Evening mail) of Milan, hoped to make his newspaper the "*Times* of Italy." The anglophile publisher called for opposition to his country's treaty with the Central Powers. Rome declined to enter the war in August 1914. Finally the government weighed in on the side of the Allies, and now a senator, Albertini had his newspaper self-censor news of Italy's military unpreparedness until the country's disastrous loss at Caporetto.

Of the major western belligerent nations, Britain and France showed most evidence of the close prewar ties between press and government by promoting publishers into positions of wartime power. In Britain Lord Northcliffe (Alfred Harmsworth) had become the country's most important press baron, building a newspaper group on the influence of his popular *Daily Mail*. As the *Mail*'s low cost and mass appeal changed the face of the formerly staid London press, Northcliffe was able to finance acquisitions right up to "the institution" itself—the *Times*, London's power broker. Northcliffe enjoyed public support for his sensational attack against what he perceived as the war minister Lord (Horatio) Kitchener's wrongheaded munitions decisions, and in 1918 the critic joined the government as director of propaganda. ("Director of Lies," the German press called him.) The strongly anti-German Northcliffe worked within the administration by continuing to cooperate with the government's eager censorship. His *Times* emulated French and German newspapers in concealing the hideous cost of the war in men and money.

In France a newspaper launched one publisher-politician to the top of the wartime government. Georges Clemenceau too played a risky hand at discrediting authorities through press critique, in

Newspaper magnate Alfred Harmsworth, Lord Northcliffe (right) with journalist Willian Stead, London, 1921.
GETTY IMAGES

this case attacking government troop sanitation in his political daily *L'homme libre*. Censors responded with suspensions, but Clemenceau's long influence in government—he had been prime minister in 1907–1908—saved his newspaper from becoming another wartime fatality. By the end of 1917 the "tiger" who stared down the censor had again become prime minister. Would he abolish censorship? "I'm not an idiot," he responded. "Censors are my best police."

Twinned to pervasive censorship during this period was Western Europe's first formal campaign of propaganda in a century. In fact, some of Napoleon's principles became part of what now was called a "scientific" campaign to maintain morale at home while promoting a version of war aimed at influencing neutral nations. France ended the war with perhaps Europe's most comprehensive propaganda operation radiating from a six-

floor Paris town house. But Britain is often credited with most effectively directing the kind of material designed to snare the biggest neutral prize: the United States.

THE INTERWAR PERIOD

Four-and-a-half years of the most brutal slaughter the world had ever seen left much of Europe's press in financial ruin and with shredded credibility. In Britain, Northcliffe lost his health and finally his sanity and had to be locked out of the *Times* office before his death in 1922. A combined dip in circulation, advertising, and buying power left the *Times* open to purchase by an American, John J. Astor.

Postwar French newspapers found their situation even more dire. The country's press always had been more fragile than Britain's, squeezed by traditionally weak advertising and powerful monopolies controlling publicity and distribution. The Havas agency, the world's oldest news bureau, beat all competitors to establish control of nearly all newspaper advertising in France. After the war it propped up its money-losing news bureau by pushing up ad rates. Advertisers had never enthusiastically supported French newspapers, preferring publicity by billboard and handbill. Hachette, the second monopoly, controlled 2,250 newspaper points of sale in Paris and 50,000 in the rest of the country.

French newspapers suffered even more than British from their indiscriminate translation of *union sacrée* into fantastically unrealistic wartime journalism. The soldiers themselves labeled it *bourrage de crâne* (eyewash) in their lively trench newspapers, which developed into an extensive network challenging commercial journalism. As the soldiers returned after the Armistice, the awareness that the press had held back the truth led an already skeptical public to become even more so. Perhaps French newspapers were not entirely to blame, as heavily censored as they were, but they suffered the consequences. Adding to the difficulties was an economic malaise that hit the industry with inflationary expenses. While the interwar press saw strong growth in Britain, in France newspaper readers abandoned their press by the hundreds of thousands. In 1939 Britain sold 360 copies per 1,000 people, compared to 261 in France. The huge *Petit Parisien* dropped from 1.45 million in 1932 to 900,000 in 1939. While the country did not see the formation of newspaper chains familiar in Britain and Germany during this time, many French dailies in financial peril fell under control of large financiers, industrialists, and political extremists. Of eighty Paris dailies in 1914, by the eve of the Second World War thirty-one remained. Still, those titles provided among the world's most varied journalism, from the communist *L'humanité* to the fascist *Je suis partout* (I am everywhere).

In Britain inflation and economic challenges could be met by attracting a healthy dose of advertising. Press groups continued to acquire titles until most of the country's newspapers were held by four chains. London newspapers dominated, unlike those of Paris, which battled with a strengthening provincial press. A Canadian, Lord Beaverbrook (Max Aitken), challenged Northcliffe's *Daily Mail* with his *Daily Express,* also built on the popular formula offering the sensationalistic mix of crime, sex, and celebrity that Americans nicknamed "jazz journalism." This stood in stark contrast to that of the sober London dailies and established a distinctive dichotomy, popular press versus quality press, that still marked the character of London journalism at the beginning of the twenty-first century. London newspaper subscriber campaigns of the 1930s grew so generously that a reader could get a wide variety of free gifts, even life insurance, simply by subscribing. The popular-oriented *Daily Herald* became notorious for its gimmicks and for leading the pack in offering sensationalist "tabloid journalism" to attract more and more readers and more and more ads. Criticism had surfaced after the First World War that Europe's hyper-capitalist-driven press fed diversion and entertainment but left readers ignorant of critical political developments, and it surfaced again in the Second, with London's *Daily Herald* a frequently cited example.

Germany's newspapers had jumped to the *union sacrée* as enthusiastically as those of its adversaries and suffered similar loss of prestige after the 1918 Armistice. The financial crisis of hyperinflation in a weak economy challenged publishers. Many old titles fell into a large trust built by Alfred Hugenberg, who in the course of twenty years gathered together one of Europe's most powerful media groups. Hugenberg's papers offered considerable encouragement to fascist political groups, to the point where historians have suggested that the chain gave significant credibility and national exposure to the National Socialist (Nazi) Party. The Nazis enjoyed their own brand of popular journalism, however. In contrast to the traditionally sober German press, the Nazis launched sensationalist titles unmatched in their racist and violent rhetoric, the very definition of "gutter journalism." Joseph Goebbels, later Hitler's propaganda minister, himself published *Der Angriff* (The attack). By 1932 the Nazis controlled 120 newspapers. A year later the party would control them all—or what was left of them. Hitler's first victims were the socialist and communist newspapers, banned 28 February 1933. Goebbels demonstrated Nazi logic by defining journalists as public officials responsible to the state. A year later more than fifteen hundred papers had been closed. By the eve of war the press had become Goebbels's "disciplined orchestra."

The orchestra metaphor had not been a German invention. Nearly a decade before, another fascist established similar techniques based on propaganda ideas collected from wartime Britain and even inspired by Napoleon. Benito Mussolini in Italy reflected a general belief during this period that propaganda, properly administered, could control public sentiment. This was the "bullet theory" of press influence. Early academic research on the press had presented the argument that, like a silver bullet, any message presented correctly could sway the masses. More advanced media research after the Second World War generally discredited the bullet theory, but the press during earlier periods influenced a population less educated and with few options outside printed media.

Mussolini established his own noisy daily newspaper as a beginning on this road to propagandist control of the country. Introducing the idea of journalism as critical propaganda tool, Mussolini's *Popolo d'Italia* (Italian people) irritated the Italian government during the First World War. In 1922 Fascist influence had grown to sweep Mussolini into the premier's chair. Three years later he turned Italy into a dictatorship and dealt with the nonfascist press the way his party dealt with all opposition. Newspaper offices were smashed, editors beaten, journalists bullied, and publications confiscated. By 1926 Mussolini's government had closed two-thirds of the country's dailies. Mussolini gloated, "I consider fascist journalism as my orchestra." But one paper wouldn't play. *L'osservatore romano,* the independent Vatican's daily, continued to offer news unfiltered by Fascist propaganda. The Fascists found it difficult to control but did try to harass newsagents who sold it. Newsagents responded by selling it wrapped inside a Fascist daily, provided to buyers after an affirmative answer to the question "With or without?"

THE SECOND WORLD WAR

By 1940 Nazis controlled the press in countries with long-standing free-press traditions, including Norway, Denmark, Holland, and Belgium. Faced with the threat of German invasion, Sweden's newspapers maintained careful voluntary censorship. Switzerland maintained a tortured neutrality faced with its traditional dependency on the German economy. Spain's free press had already

been snuffed in one of the century's most horrific civil wars: Francisco Franco's Fascists maintained censors in every Spanish newsroom. Austria's short free-press era ended with a right-wing dictatorship, then Nazi occupation.

Censorship returned to France in 1939. With the German invasion of June 1940, nearly all Paris newspapers fled to Bordeaux. Major newspapers that chose to continue under occupation reappeared in non-occupied Vichy France, in principle not under German control but in reality closely censored by the puppet Vichy government. While the Second World War marked the final blow to what little credibility most French journalism had left, a network of underground newspapers played a key role in uniting French resistance against a brutal occupying force. Charles de Gaulle's call to resistance was reflected in Albert Camus's *Combat.* After the war the Resistance press would be called on to reinvent French journalism. Throughout occupied Europe these courageous clandestine newspapers managed to establish a tiny but important raft of resistance in a sea of tightly controlled propaganda.

In Britain newspapers did not suffer the harsh censorship of the First World War. In fact, politicians such as the sometime journalist Winston Churchill learned a lesson different from that of the dictators. Propaganda during World War I had misled the public. This time British war correspondents would be allowed on the fronts wherever they might be, and might even be able to criticize the government using their own good judgment. This self-censorship worked as well in Britain as it did in the United States during this war, producing coverage more complete and accurate than that of the last world war. Centralized operations on Fleet Street made the newspapers easy military targets, however. London bombings blew out two floors of the *Times* building and seriously damaged operations of other plants.

While the end of the First World War had left many of Europe's newspapers in a crisis of economics and credibility, the end of the Second World War left many of them out of business for good. In France, Germany, Austria, and Italy, practically none survived. Of the major belligerents, only Britain managed to salvage most of its prewar titles, yet even these were holding on to a precarious future in which, after three centuries, they no longer would enjoy a media monopoly. De Gaulle's newly liberated French government took Europe's most dramatic step to reinvent the country's journalism. Capitalist newspapers, it was maintained, had lost their mission to educate citizens and offer intellectually important writing. Solution? Elimination. This planned tabula rasa (clean slate) meant that every publication produced in occupied France had to go. Presses were given to the clandestine journalists who had risked death to inform readers during the war. As for *Le temps,* the prestige daily of Paris, de Gaulle had a particular plan. His government brought in a journalist respected for his intellectual rigor, Hubert Beuve-Méry, to direct a new paper designed to reflect the purity of journalistic excellence. *Le monde* operated on the presses of *Le temps,* with a special mandate and government subsidies. *Le monde* bowed to none of the supposed frivolity of popular journalism: no pictures, no entertainment, long, thoughtful articles, and highly restrained design. However, by 1950 many of the more doctrinaire former Resistance titles were gone. *Le monde* limped close to bankruptcy despite government subventions. Capitalist control inched back onto the tabula rasa as French publishers realized success meant attracting readers, and readers perhaps admired, but did not buy, intellectual rigor.

Allied occupiers in Germany concluded that Nazism had been nurtured by a sympathetic press, and so in both Germany and Austria they eliminated titles and journalists that had appeared during the war. The commanders of each sector, United States, Britain, France, and the Soviet Union, required German publishers to obtain a license, permission seldom available to former collaborationist journalists. Particularly vigilant were U.S. authorities, who hoped to eliminate the party-dominated press that they believed helped to violently politicize the Weimar Republic. Germany's old prestige titles were gone. But British authorities set up a new one, *Die Welt* of Hamburg (later moved to Bonn) in 1946, based on journalistic ideals of the *Times.* By 1948 it was banned from the Soviet zone, which maintained censorship while other sectors dismantled press controls. *Die Welt*'s 1949 circulation of more than one million dropped to only 300,000 a year later as new

The Paris offices of *Le monde*, 1969. GETTY IMAGES

competition bled readership. It remained, however, the prestige newspaper of Germany. In Hamburg a young publisher named Axel Springer bought *Die Welt,* beginning a press empire that by the end of the century dominated German media and expanded its network as far away as the United States. German readers in the early 1950s also were introduced to a concept new to the Continent, British-style sensationalism. *Bild* copied the British tabloid press to become as successful as titles like the *Sun* and *Daily Mirror* in London.

CHALLENGE OF POSTWAR CHANGE

After the war the British remained Europe's most avid newspaper readers. Circulation and advertising trickled back. Yet it was not enough to overcome the crosscurrents of a postwar Europe that served to accelerate a long-term trend driving titles out of business and concentrating ownership. Publishing a newspaper became ever more expensive and competitive. The members of the aggressive London press not only competed with each other but with a growing provincial journalism and expensive demands of unionized labor. The country's largest dailies had clearly lost the kind of political influence they had had before World War I. The new media of radio and television threatened to siphon off advertising. Some newspapers closed. Others were purchased by new press barons, beginning with Roy Thomson of Canada, who aimed at media concentration on a scale beyond that of the 1920s. British intellectuals and politicians worried about loss of voices in the marketplace of ideas and set up press commissions to study the merger threat. But unlike the efforts of the French government to nourish diversity through government subvention, free-market tradition in Britain worked against a parliamentary response.

Postwar Italian occupation authorities shut down newspapers that by 1945 were in effect Nazi propaganda sheets. Instead of simply eliminating the old titles, newspapers were able to restart with the word "new" attached, such as *Nuova corriere della sera.* Following a short postwar readership jump, however, Italy returned to its tradition of low newspaper consumption; circulation took a dramatic drop after 1955. By 1980 many Italian newspapers struggled: only one in ten Italians were buying a newspaper, the lowest rate in Europe.

Other Western European countries mirrored trends of falling circulation and concentration of titles. While Sweden's newspapers enjoyed the second-highest readership in Europe, consolidation left Swedes with fewer papers to read. Danish newspapers scrambled to explain their collaboration during the war but were not eliminated as in France and Germany. In Norway quisling collaborationists were barred from journalism. Both Norway's and Belgium's wartime clandestine presses had issued persistent resistance to German occupiers. Holland's Resistance press copied that of France, taking over former collaborationist titles, but also like France, many could not compete in a postwar free-market world. Austrian newspapers rekindled after the war experienced generally weak advertising in a country that for forty years had run a delicate course as crossroads between east and west. Swiss newspapers enjoyed a strong postwar

economy and a long tradition of press freedom. As for press control, except for a few instances in de Gaulle's France, only Spain's mostly unread journalism remained tightly censored by a fascist government that lasted until 1975, when freedom returned.

The waning of the twentieth century generally saw a continuation of trends that had begun nearly a century before: press concentration, economic difficulty, technological challenge, and loss of political clout. The press baron Rupert Murdoch reinvented the London *Sun* as a tabloid reaching a new extreme of the "three s's": sex, sports, and scandal. Including a daily topless "page three girl" brought its circulation to five million while the quality dailies struggled. In 1981 Murdoch shocked some of Britain's traditionalists by buying the ever-ailing *Times* from the Thomson chain. A strike had left Britain without the *Times* for a year in the late 1970s. Murdoch pulled the entire operation out of Fleet Street to a new plant, breaking the power of the unions and leading other London newspapers in an exodus from their traditional city-center concentration.

In Paris the prestigious *Le monde* faced four near financial collapses in two decades before finally succumbing to marketplace demands. It modernized its layout so that between 1994 and 2001 circulation grew from 354,000 to 415,000. In 2000 it was acquired by the Midi Libre group. Competing with *Le monde* as the century waned was a handful of dailies led by *Le Figaro,* which survived the postwar purge to become France's oldest Paris title. Its conservatism tended to attract stronger advertising. Generally, however, France's newspaper advertising has continued to be among Europe's weakest.

Germany's newspapers also struggled in competition with other media, concentration of titles, stagnating circulation, and the falloff in advertising revenue familiar throughout Europe. In the late 1970s two major Springer titles, *Die Welt* and *Berliner Morgenpost,* merged. The German press has responded to technological revolutions in its highly computerized offices and printing plants. At the end of the century, *Regioblick* (http://www. regioblick.de) was launched, the country's first newspaper produced entirely on the Internet. By 2004 all major European newspapers provided a

A man reads a British newspaper with advertisements and headlines only during a strike by journalists, London, November 1974. ©HULTON-DEUTSCH COLLECTION/CORBIS

companion website. Many of them, such as *Le Figaro,* also provided "push" web technology, offering free daily news briefings by email. Many media researchers believed advertising and circulation of traditional paper-based newspapers stagnated as the Internet carved away readers. Preliminary research did seem to indicate more news consumers were beginning to rely entirely on the Internet, a concern for broadcasting as well as ink-based journalism. Publishers began to include web-based numbers in circulation figures. Newspapers tried to find ways to make their websites pay, but by 2004 a formula for assured success using web-based advertising was still elusive. For most newspapers at the beginning of the new millennium, their paper product continued to generate most of their profits.

A new print-media challenge to the traditional press at the beginning of the century was the growth of free-distribution news dailies. A phenomenon of large urban centers, these giveaways were aimed at young readers. *Metro* and *20 Minutes* in Paris by 2002 had a combined circulation of eight hundred thousand. It was perhaps ironic that the key to the newspaper revolution of a century ago—offering nearly free newspapers filled with lively content to interest a younger generation—had been resurrected with some apparent success. As papers such as the *Times* discovered, newspapers that become institutions also become behemoths sometimes unwilling, perhaps unable, to change with their society. But throughout Western Europe, and indeed throughout the entire capitalist world, time and again publishers have found that to succeed in journalism they must give consumers what they want to consume. The key for each generation is determining what that is and how to do it.

See also **Computer Revolution; Propaganda; Television.**

BIBLIOGRAPHY

Albert, Pierre, and Fernand Terrou. *Histoire de la presse.* Paris, 1988.

Bainbridge, Cyril, ed. *One Hundred Years of Journalism: Social Aspects of the Press.* London, 1984.

Boyce, George, James Curran, and Pauline Wingate, eds. *Newspaper History from the Seventeenth Century to the Present Day.* London, 1978.

Charle, Christophe. *Le siècle de la presse, 1830–1939.* Paris, 2004.

Herd, Harold. *The March of Journalism: The Story of the British Press from 1622 to the Present Day.* London, 1952.

Marr, Andrew. *My Trade: A Short History of British Journalism.* London, 2004.

Olson, Kenneth E. *The History Makers: The Press of Europe from Its Beginnings through 1965.* Baton Rouge, La., 1966.

Walker, Martin. *Powers of the Press: Twelve of the World's Influential Newspapers.* New York, 1982.

Weill, Georges. *Le journal: Origines, evolution et rôle de la presse périodique.* Paris, 1934.

Wilke, Jürgen. "The History and Culture of the Newsroom in Germany." *Journalism Studies* 4, no. 4 (2003): 465–477.

Williams, Francis. *The Right to Know: The Rise of the World Press.* London and Harlow, U.K., 1969.

ROSS F. COLLINS

PRIMO DE RIVERA, MIGUEL (1870–1930), Spanish general and dictator.

Miguel Primo de Rivera was born in the Andalusian town of Jerez de la Frontera to an aristocratic family with landholding and military antecedents. In 1884 he followed his father and uncle into the military, enrolling in the General Military Academy. During the 1890s he experienced combat in Spanish North Africa, Cuba, and the Philippines. By 1908 he attained the rank of colonel and volunteered for duty in Spanish North Africa, where his battlefield accomplishments and family connections earned him rapid promotions. In 1915 he transferred back to Spain, being appointed military governor of Cadiz. This began his direct participation in domestic politics, which included serving in the Spanish Senate. In 1919 he was promoted to lieutenant general and selected as captain general of the important army garrisons of Valencia, Madrid, and Barcelona. In Barcelona he witnessed violent social and labor conflicts, political paralysis and electoral manipulation, regional separatism, and the impact of the army's 1921 colonial defeat in Spanish Morocco, which cost approximately ten thousand Spanish lives.

In the summer of 1923 the government's failure to resolve the ongoing conflict in Spanish Morocco and the parliament's pursuit of a "responsibilities" investigation against the army for the colonial debacle triggered a conspiracy of senior army officers to impose a military solution to Spain's political, social, economic, and colonial problems. Although Primo de Rivera was an unlikely candidate to lead this movement, given his anticolonial views, his prestige as a senior army general, his political and social conservatism, and the support he enjoyed among the Catalan elites and middle classes made his candidacy acceptable to the conspirators and to Alfonso XIII, king of Spain. On 13 September 1923 he issued a manifesto "to the country and the army" promising to restore order, discipline, and responsible government and bring a "rapid, dignified, and sensible" solution to the colonial war. On 15 September 1923 Alfonso XIII handed him political power as Spain's first military dictator. In one of his early public statements he indicated that his Military Directory would be a "brief parenthesis" of only ninety days in the country's political life in order to start its renovation.

Primo de Rivera's timetable was overly optimistic but consistent with his confident, pragmatic, and naive personality. Nevertheless, by suspending constitutional guarantees and imposing press censorship and martial law, he was able to bring rapid social and labor tranquility. His government's ongoing repression of the anarchosyndicalists, the Spanish Communist Party, and the regional separatists and its co-opting of the Socialist General Workers' Union ensured relative social and labor peace for most of his regime. Further, his disparagement of parliamentary politicians, the closing of parliament, the replacement of civil governors with military officers, and the imposition of military oversight over local government basically destroyed the liberal parliamentary system.

By the end of 1923 it was apparent that Primo de Rivera would need more time to regenerate Spain. As such, he institutionalized the Military Directory, which continued to govern Spain until 4 December 1925, when it was replaced by a civilian ministry. And in 1924 the dictator's supporters organized a government party, the Patriotic Union (UP), which espoused a vague program of nationalism, conservative Catholicism, authoritarianism, and corporatist economic and social programs. While not a true fascist party, some have seen it as a precursor to the radical Right during the Second Republic and Spanish fascism.

The years 1925 to 1927 saw the regime's apotheosis with a military victory in Spanish Morocco, economic expansion stimulated by high import tariffs, the encouragement of industrial concentration and basic infrastructure improvements, and extensive public works projects. After 1927 the dictatorship entered a period of decline as both the political and economic climate turned against it. A failed effort was made to institutionalize the regime through constitutional reform by establishing a nonelective National Assembly in October 1927. Its charge was to develop an alternative to the liberal 1876 constitution. The resulting draft constitution reflected rightist, mild authoritarian, and corporatist concepts and was roundly condemned by both monarchist liberals and the growing republican and leftist movements. As the economy took a downturn in 1929 and the government experienced large deficits and a collapsing peseta, antiregime discontent became more pronounced, even among the military. In January 1930, when Primo de Rivera canvassed the captain generals to gauge their support for his regime, he found little backing. Tired and sick with diabetes, he resigned on 28 January 1930, exiled himself to France, and died in Paris on 16 March 1930. He was buried in Jerez de la Frontera.

See also **Falange; Fascism; Spain; Spanish Civil War.**

BIBLIOGRAPHY

Ben-Ami, Shlomo. *Fascism from Above: The Dictatorship of Primo de Rivera in Spain, 1923–1930.* Oxford, U.K., 1983.

González Calleja, Eduardo. *La España de Primo de Rivera: La modernización autoritaria 1923–1930.* Madrid, 2005.

Rial, James H. *Revolution from Above: The Primo de Rivera Dictatorship in Spain, 1923–1930.* Fairfax, Va., 1986.

Sueiro Seoane, Susana. *España en el Mediterráneo: Primo de Rivera y la "cuestión marroquí," 1923–1930.* Madrid, 1992.

Tamanes, Ramón, and Xavier Casals. *Miguel Primo de Rivera.* Barcelona, 2004

SHANNON E. FLEMING

PRISONERS OF WAR. The phenomenon of prisoners of war (POWs) is thoroughly part of the twentieth century, an era of wars and prison camps. In Europe, some six to eight million prisoners were held captive during the First World War, and some eighteen million during the Second World War. The extent of captivity reflects the mass character of total war, which led to the instrumentalization of the captive. At the same time there arose a body of law pertaining to the prisoner's legal status. Nevertheless, POWs have long remained occluded in history. Imprisonment of captured soldiers bears the stamp of defeat, and societies at war have a hard time acknowledging those of their own who were defeated. This helps account for substantial variation in the way that prisoners have been treated by democratic and totalitarian regimes.

THE PRISONER OF WAR: A FACT OF MODERN WARFARE

Until 1899, despite the Lieber Code on the treatment of prisoners of war, written in 1863 during the U.S. Civil War, and the 1880 Oxford manual, *The Laws of War on Land,* soldiers captured in battle had no legal status, and their treatment at the hands of the enemy could be arbitrary. In reaction to European conflicts such as the bloody Battle of Solferino in 1859, the Franco-Prussian War in 1870–1871, and the Boer War, which began in 1899, an International Peace Conference took place at The Hague in the same year, initially defining captivity in war as a state of those soldiers who are protected once they agree not to take up arms against their captors. Another conference at The Hague in 1907 proposed a new version of these early regulations. From now on, prisoners of war had to be treated with humanity; they were to receive the same housing and food rations as the troops of the captor; they could be released in exchange for a promise not to further participate in the conflict; in addition, noncommissioned officers and soldiers could be put to work provided it were unrelated to the actual conflict. POWs were also to be freed as soon as practicable after cessation of hostilities. However, it should be noted that these regulations applied only if all belligerents officially adhered to the treaty.

The First World War marked a turning point in the history of prisoners of war. Seventy million soldiers bore arms in a conflict that lasted four years, in a mobilization of such magnitude that it effaced traditional boundaries such as the front and the rear, even the distinction between soldier and civilian. In this totalized conflict, POWs were forced to work, enabling their captors to exploit their economic value. Utilization of this workforce was justified, moreover, as a legitimate reprisal for violations first committed by the enemy. The same logic also justified minimal rations and various disciplinary measures. France, for example, aligned rations for its German prisoners with those accorded French POWs in German hands, while punishments included withholding mail, restriction of food, or imprisonment.

The magnitude of the conflict took the military by surprise, and soon there was a lack of adequate housing, poor hygiene, and deficient medical care. In Germany, some four thousand POWs had died by the spring of 1915. Bilateral agreements between governments underscored the limitations of the Hague treaties conventions, which had envisaged only a brief war. In July 1917, for example, a German-British agreement stipulated norms for housing prisoners. Another dealt with enforcement of discipline and the framework of prisoner exchanges.

Conditions of detention were affected by ideas about race or benefits that might accrue to the detaining power. For example, in Russia authorities ran separate camps. There were relatively privileged "first circle" camps reserved for POWs of Slavic origin—the future supporters of pan-Slavism—and a second category of camps in Siberia for German POWs. Liberation and repatriation were

TABLE 1

Prisoners of war: First World War

| Detaining power | Number of prisoners estimated held in: | | | | 1918 |
| | 1915 (1 February) | | | | |
	Germans	British	French	Russians	
Britain	15,000				328,000
France	50,000				350,000
Russia					2,250,000
Germany		18,000	245,000	350,000	2,400,000
Austria (Austria-Hungary for 1918)				250,000	916,000
United States					43,000
Total					6,637,000

Source: R. B. Speed, *Prisoners, Diplomats, and the Great War.* Westport, Conn., 1990.

conceived along similar lines. Control over German POWs in French hands was used to exert pressure on Germany to sign the Treaty of Versailles (1919). The increasing mobilization of various countries and the ferocity of the conflict lay behind different mortality rates among prisoners of war. In Germany, for example, the death rate among British POWs was 3.5 percent, for Russians, 5.4–6.5 percent, but for the Romanian soldiers, 29 percent.

All these issues made it clear that some of the rules devised at the 1907 Hague Convention needed revision. Advances emerged from the Geneva Conference of 27 July 1929. One new convention provided rules for the treatment of POWs, an addition to the 1907 Hague regulation, which forbade reprisals and stated that prisoners must be kept away from battle. The conditions of camps were to be improved; the intellectual and religious needs of POWs had to be met; prisoners also had to have the right to send and receive letters and packages. The convention specified regulation of prisoner's work, and indicated appropriate punishments, especially after escape attempts. Information bureaus were to be established in each country together with a Central Agency of Information. Finally, the clause that stipulated all belligerents must be party to the treaty was abandoned.

The Second World War was a major challenge to these attempts at humanizing imprisonment in

TABLE 2

Prisoners of war: Second World War

Estimated number of prisoners during the Second World War (European and African theaters)

Detaining power	During the conflict						1945 (Germans)
	Belgians	Hungarians	Americans	French	British	Soviets	
Britain							3,635,000
France							937,000
Soviet Union							3,060,000
Germany	215,000	130,000	102,000	1,850,000	130,000	5,000,000	
United States							3,097,000
Total							10,729,000

SOURCE: Y. Durand, *Histoire générale de la Seconde Guerre mondiale, 1939–1945*. Paris, 1989.

wartime. Although on the western front captivity during the Second World War continued along the lines that had characterized the earlier conflict, this war turned out to be longer and deployed even more troops. Some German POWs, for example, endured six years of conflict and then ten years of incarceration in the Soviet Union. Blitzkrieg warfare enabled Nazi authorities to imprison a very high number of captives in record time: 1.8 million French taken prisoner during May–June 1940; 5.16 million Soviets during Operation Barbarossa in the summer of 1941. These statistics help explain why living conditions for many prisoners of war were barely human. Millions would later face problems of repatriation long after the war was over.

The Second World War aggravated issues that had plagued prisoners during the 1914–1918 conflict. The "total war" launched by the Nazis obliged them to create a workforce composed of prisoners, first Western Europeans, then Eastern Europeans, primarily Slavs. They thus muddied the distinction between captive soldiers and other groups such as civilian prisoners and forced labor; together, by 1945, prisoners comprised one-third of the labor force in Germany.

In spite of the numbers, the conventions of POW captivity at times functioned better in this war than in the 1914–1918 conflict. The International Red Cross made more than eleven thousand visits to camps; and it was, for example, thanks to their military status that French and British Jewish soldiers were saved from extermination. This paradox derived from the Nazis' racial interpretation of the conventions. While POW status was by and large applied, the Nazis brutally mistreated prisoners belonging to the so-called inferior races. They refused to apply the POW conventions to Polish prisoners (whose country they declared had ceased to exist) or to countries that had not ratified the 1929 accords, such as Romania; thus, some 63.7 percent of Romanian POWs died in captivity. Soviet prisoners of war were systematically starved to death by the hundreds of thousands; some estimates put these deaths in the millions. These were violations of international law that the tribunal at Nuremberg in 1946 would incorporate as one of the four central elements in the war crimes indictment.

The end of the Second World War marked the start of the third and last mass captivity in Europe; these prisoners of war were almost exclusively German, though Italian prisoners were scattered throughout Eastern Europe too. Detaining powers were the former enemies of the Nazi regime, most of which had endured a devastating German occupation. This postwar captivity was marked by a sense of righteous vengeance, inflicting on German troops the same treatment and humiliations suffered by those they had occupied.

Postwar imprisonment began in the same poor and improvised conditions from which civilian populations also suffered. German POWs were designated as the "Disarmed Enemy Force" by the U.S. Army and "Surrendered Enemy Personnel" by the British. This distinction enabled those countries to avoid strict application of the 1929 Geneva Convention; there were fifty-six thousand deaths recorded in U.S. captivity, most of them detained in six *Rheinwiesenlager* (Rhine meadow camps). French authorities were not able to properly feed and house their German POWs. They justified detention by using German POWs for reconstruction, stretching to the limits rules of using prisoners as laborers. In the Soviet Union, German POWs worked to rebuild the socialist fatherland, especially in the gulag, where a quarter of them died.

In 1949 a third Geneva Convention took into account lessons learned from the war. It completed the earlier 1929 conventions and acknowledged the impossibility of distinguishing between civilians and combatants. From now on prisoners of war were defined as "all who have fallen into the power of the enemy." This convention extends the range of the humanitarian law and determines the roles and responsibilities of the detaining power. The latest additional protocols, added in 1977, attempted to update and adapt the conventions to new kinds of conflicts such as civil wars and guerrilla insurgencies. It considerably extended the categories of individuals having the right to POW status.

The recent European conflict in former Yugoslavia (1990–1995) pushed the convention to its limit and tested conventional wisdom and practice. The number of POWs was indeed limited; according to the U.S. Central Intelligence Agency (CIA), Serbs detained from 35,000 to 70,000 individuals in 135 camps in January 1993. But the ambiguous nature of the conflict—civil war or a war between nations—the "logic of criminalization," and the policy of ethnic cleansing led to a situation in which an entire nation's population was held hostage. Respect for the Geneva Conventions was hard to enforce. This war presented a backward step in the regulation of captives during wartime, a return to the premodern era.

Law governing prisoners of war developed slowly, and only in some cases did practice and codes of behavior coincide. But this has led to a paradoxical situation in which POWs get more protection than civilian detainees. In the cautious legal formulations of the conventions, military imperatives take into account the interests of captives, but the conventions do not resolve the legal and moral issue of whether it is fair to feed detainees while civilian populations starve. The evolution

TABLE 3

Number of German POWs after World War II

Captured by		Transferred to		Total number of prisoners by sectors
Soviet Union	3,155,000	Soviet Union	3,060,000	
		Czechoslovakia	25,000	East: 3,349,000
		Poland	7,000	
Yugoslavia	194,000			
United States	3,800,000	United States and/or American camps in Europe	3,097,000	
		France	667,000	West: 7,745,000
		Belgium	31,000	
		Luxembourg	5,000	
United Kingdom	3,700,000	United Kingdom	3,635,000	
		France	25,100	
		Belgium	33,000	
		Netherlands	7,000	
Total				11,094,000

SOURCE: W. Ratza, *Zusammenfassung*, vol. 15, Maschke, cited in Cochet, *Soldats sans armes*.

of the law has favored a principle of reciprocity in the absence of inspections and sanctions. It generated either a dynamic of escalation and retaliation leading to reprisals, as with the Soviet Union, or a dynamic of neutrality such as existed between Germany and the United States. This mechanism tends to consider POWs not from a military perspective as disarmed fighters but, rather, only as representatives of the enemy nation, thus becoming part of the enemy garrison to be defeated.

DEFINING A CULTURE OF CAPTIVITY

Captivity may be said to take place in four stages:

Capture, during conflict or after surrender. The seizure of weapons and personal items helped to define the status of victors and vanquished.

Arrival in transit camps. Prisoners were then transferred to base camps that held tens of thousands of prisoners, then finally to smaller camps. There followed enrollment and distribution of clothing distinctively marked in order to make the captive immediately recognizable. The camp was an enclosure whose space is limited by barbed wire and by its guards. Prisoners were affected by the military character of the camp (roll calls, searches, coexistence of national directorate and POW executive). Acculturation to this environment was all the more difficult in that POWs often changed camps.

Labor. Between 70 and 95 percent of European POWs during the two world wars were drafted into forced labor commandos. In theory, conditions of work for prisoners were to be identical to civilian labor of a similar kind, seeking to avoid competition with indigenous workers. POWs' attitude toward work ranged from the "River Kwai syndrome" that pushed prisoners to the limit, to the method of "slow in the morning and not too fast at night." POWs worked in all sectors, from agriculture to industry to mine-clearance. Exceptionally, a POW might become a free civilian worker, a procedure initiated by the Vichy government in wartime France in the 1940s. Although POW productivity was inferior, the prisoners represented an irreplaceable labor force and productive resource.

Liberation and demobilization. These ended both the experience of military service and of captivity, which from the beginning had an uncertain outcome.

The social side of POW life, an exclusively masculine environment in the twentieth century, was organized around principles of solidarity and exclusion. Comradeship in captivity was not an extension of the comradeship of war. It was based on utilitarian solidarity (protection against theft, acquisition of supplies) and organized in concentric circles (of acquaintances, persons from the same village or the same region) or by barracks, reinforced by discussion, nourished by rumors (about rations, escape, imminent liberation, and so on). Over time there developed a "language of the camps" (for example, in post-1945 POW camps in France, "Franzmann" for French or *nixcompris* = not understood).

To kill time, POWs enjoyed simple pastimes (cards and simple crafts), more elaborate activities (sports, orchestras, theater), and even religious observance. However, not all POWs succeeded in overcoming the *Stacheldrahtkrankheit* (barbed wire disease) that could and did culminate in despair and at times suicide.

Daily life in camps and on detachment details was organized around basic preoccupations:

Nourishment and strategies for maximizing it (using tobacco as a form of exchange).

Mail and the maintenance of links with the home front. Prisoners receiving packages could overcome feelings of alienation and abandonment. However, it did not fulfill the need for kindness and affection among the prisoners. The absence of any feminine presence at times fostered homoerotic or homosexual ties.

Escape. This occupied a special place in the culture of captivity. It showed the prisoner's attachment to his patriotic cause and a willful desire to end captivity. In the Second World War, there were thirty-five thousand successful escapes among English and American prisoners of war from German camps.

RETURN

A prisoner's welcome upon returning home rarely matched his hopes. The nation's recognition of his sacrifice was not extended to combatants whose status remained ambiguous and who had appeared at times as traitors. To obtain their rights, soldiers organized associations, such as the Volksbund zum Schutz der deutschen Kriegs und Zivilgefangenen in Germany in 1918. In France, only in 1922 was the honor "died for France" accorded POWs.

In the early twenty-first century, veterans associations welcome former POWs, who foster remembrance of both war and captivity. French and German POWs have worked on a rapprochement through sister cities arrangements and associations. Despite this institutional framework, it is unclear whether former POWs intend or are able to transmit their memories to succeeding generations. And it is uncertain to what extent prisoners of the wars of the twentieth century will in future remain a group apart from their comrades who avoided captivity.

See also **Concentration Camps; Forced Labor; Hague Convention; Nuremberg War Crimes Trials; Occupation, Military; Operation Barbarossa; Red Cross; War Crimes.**

BIBLIOGRAPHY

Cochet, François. *Soldats sans armes: La captivité de guerre: Une approche culturelle.* Brussels and Paris, 1998.

Djurovic, Gradimir. *The Central Tracing Agency of the International Committee of the Red Cross.* Geneva, 1986.

Fishman, Sarah. *We Will Wait: Wives of French Prisoners of War, 1940–1945.* New Haven, Conn., 1991.

Gammon, Victor F. *Not All Glory!: True Accounts of RAF Airmen Taken Prisoner in Europe, 1939–1945.* London, 1996.

Jackson, Robert. *The Prisoners, 1914–18.* New York, 1989.

Lindstrom, Hildegard Schmidt. *Child Prisoner of War.* As told to Hazel Proctor. Ann Arbor, Mich., 1998.

Maschke, Erich, ed. *Zur Geschichte der deutschen Kriegsgefangenen des Zweiten Weltkrieges.* 22 vols. Munich, 1962–1974.

Moore, Bob, and Kent Federowich, eds. *Prisoners of War and Their Captors in World War II.* Washington, D.C., 1996.

Overmans, Rüdiger. *In der Hand des Feindes. Kriegsgefangenschaft bon Antike bis zum Zweiten Weltkrieg.* Cologne, Weimar, and Vienna, 1999.

Rachamimov, Alon. *POWs and the Great War: Captivity on the Eastern Front.* Oxford, U.K., 2002.

Speed, Richard B. *Prisoners, Diplomats, and the Great War: A Study in the Diplomacy of Captivity.* New York, 1990.

Vance, Jonathan F., ed. *Encyclopedia of Prisoners of War and Internment.* Santa Barbara, Calif., 2000.

Vourkoutiotis, Vasilis. *Prisoners of War and the German High Command: The British and American Experience.* Houndmills, U.K., 2003.

FABIEN THÉOFILAKIS

PRODI, ROMANO (b. 1939), economist, industrial manager, politician, prime minister of Italy.

After Romano Prodi completed his law degree in Italy and some specialized postgraduate studies at the London School of Economics, he became a professor of economics and industrial politics with appointments to Trento (1973), Harvard (1974), the universities of Bologna (1975), and again Bologna (1989). He was cofounder of Prometeia, a center for economic research; chairman of Il Mulino publishing company (1974–1978); and between 1978 and 1979 minister of industry in the fourth government of Giulio Andreotti. He also chaired the scientific committee of Nomisma, a society for economic studies that he founded in 1981.

Although his 1978 ministerial stint lasted only a few months, it permitted Prodi to link his name to procedures for appointing special commissioners and rescuing industrial groups in crisis, and it served as the springboard for his 1982 appointment as chair of the state-owned Istituto per la Ricostruzione Industriale (IRI, Institute for Industrial Reconstruction), which was founded in 1933 to reform and reorganize the Italian financial system after the 1929 crisis and was the largest industrial holding company in the country.

During his seven years as chair of IRI (1982–1989), Prodi succeeded in making the company profitable: it went from a loss of 3,056 billion lire (about 3 million dollars) at the time he assumed leadership to a profit of 1,263 billion lire (about 1.2 million dollars) in 1989. Both Prodi and Franco Reviglio, who was appointed to lead the Ente Nazionale Idrocarburi (National Hydrocarbon Corporation), demonstrated their abilities and even a certain admirable independence from the political parties to which they owed their positions, the Christian Democrats (Prodi was close to its Catholic left wing) and the Socialist Party. Prodi initiated a rationalization process in IRI, which was a prelude to the massive privatization that began in the 1990s and met with resistance from political forces and from an administrative bureaucracy determined to defend its power.

Prodi privatized Alfasud, an Alfa Romeo car factory built in the south of Italy; however, the Craxi government blocked the sale of the Società Meridionale di Elettricità (Sme, Southern Electric Company, which had acquired some important food industries) to Carlo De Benedetti, then owner of Buitoni, a food product company.

Prodi completed his first term at IRI in 1989, when what has been called the era of the professors came to an end. After he left IRI he turned his attention to the university and to Nomisma, but he was not long absent from the public scene: in 1993 Carlo Azeglio Ciampi's government (28 April 1993–16 April 1994) asked him to replace the outgoing Franco Nobili as chair of IRI.

His tenure in office lasted only one year, during which he revived the privatization program: IRI ceded first the Credito Italiano (The Italian bank), then the Banca Commerciale (Commercial bank), and finally began the process of privatizing the agricultural and food sectors (Sme) and the iron and steel industries.

After the victory of the Freedom Pole and the Good Government Pole Coalitions in the April 1994 elections, Prodi submitted his resignation to the new prime minister, Silvio Berlusconi, leaving the chairmanship of IRI to Michele Tedeschi. His political activity dates from that moment. Mentioned many times as a possible secretary of the Partito Popolare Italiano (PPI; People's Party) and as a candidate for prime minister, Prodi promoted the center-left electoral coalition Ulivo (Olive Tree Coalition); on 2 February 1995 he was chosen as its leader. Traveling by bus, he began a long electoral campaign that led to the victory of the center-left coalition and to his appointment as head of the government in April 1996.

Many parties participated in his center-left government, which took office on 17 May 1996: the Partito Democratico della Sinistra (Democratic Party of the Left); the PPI; the Verdi (Green Party Federation); the Unione Democratica (Democratic Union), founded by Antonio Maccanico; the Rinnovamento Italiano (Italian Renewal); and Lista Dini (Dini Ticket), in addition to three experienced politicians, among whom were Carlo Azeglio Ciampi and Antonio Di Pietro. The Partito Rifondazione Comunista (PRC, Communist Refoundation Party) provided outside support for the government. Prodi remained as prime minister until 9 October 1998, when the leader of the PRC, Fausto Bertinotti, withdrew its support over the financial bill and budget estimate for the following year.

The following year, Prodi was appointed president of the European Commission, a post that reflected positively on Italy's image within the European Community. On 10 July 1999 he introduced his administration; among the European commissioners was Mario Monti, who was given the competition portfolio. As president of the European Commission, Prodi was the target of a series of criminal acts in Bologna in December 2003: two trash cans exploded near his residence; the shop window displaying his latest book in the Feltrinelli Bookstore was damaged; and a letter bomb concealed in a book sent to his home exploded when Prodi opened it, but he was not seriously injured.

His mandate to the European Commission expired on 31 October 2004, but Prodi remained in office for another two weeks when his Portuguese successor, José Manuel Durao Barroso, had difficulty getting his cabinet ministers ratified. Upon his return to Italy, Prodi was named leader of the Olive Tree Coalition for the 2006 elections and was elected prime minister in April 2006 by a narrow margin.

See also **Andreotti, Giulio; Berlusconi, Silvio; European Commission; Italy.**

BIBLIOGRAPHY

Primary Sources

Prodi, Romano. *Europe as I See It.* Translated by Allan Cameron. Cambridge, U.K., 2000.

Secondary Sources

Di Raimondo, Antonio, ed. *Prodi.* Rome, 1995.

Grandi, Roberto. *Prodi: una campagna lunga un anno.* Milan, Italy, 1996.

MARIA TERESA GIUSTI

PROKOFIEV, SERGEI (1891–1953), Russian and Soviet composer.

Born in tsarist Russia on 23 April 1891 (11 April, old style), Sergei Prokofiev lived and worked under the Soviet regime for the twenty years preceding his death in Moscow on 5 March 1953. Before that he had spent almost twenty years traveling and performing around the globe while remaining a loyal Russian and Soviet citizen.

This biographical trend of east to west to east, together with his generational position between the prerevolutionary Russian nationalistic classical culture and post–Bolshevik Revolution class-conscious internationalist arts made him a unique figure in European and Soviet music. Like Dmitri Shostakovich (1906–1975) his work included operas, ballets, symphonies, chamber music, cantatas, songs, and romances. Unlike Shostakovich, until his final return to the Soviet Union in 1933

Prokofiev did not experience the effects of out-right government censorship. Even then his operas and ballets were not banned or ostracized, although unfortunately the stage life of some of them was not as spectacular as the composer's talent warranted.

Prokofiev strove to be contemporary in content, and in the later part of his life more traditional in form, evading current fads and fashions. In the early part of his life before he moved to the West he was interested in Russian turn-of-the-century Silver Age poetry, historical subjects, and the classical literary heritage. In the second part of his life (in the West) until his return to the Soviet Union in 1933 he embraced the achievements of Western expressionist musical theater with its industrial themes. This reflected a certain ideological conformism on the part of the composer, which explains his quick and ardent acceptance of the Stalinist agenda in the arts and culture after returning to his home country.

Visiting France and England before the outbreak of World War I, he met the founder of the Ballet Russes, Sergei Diaghilev, who had also patronized Igor Stravinsky, and ultimately wrote three ballets for Diaghilev's company. His *Classical Symphony* (1917) was a modern reincarnation of Joseph Haydn's work. His opera *Love for Three Oranges* (1919) was commissioned by the Chicago Opera Association. He traveled for the next decade and a half, but ultimately, not feeling at home in the West (unlike Stravinsky), he returned to Moscow in 1933. The Soviet government gave him a luxurious apartment and Soviet premier Vyacheslav Molotov specifically instructed his minister for arts affairs not to interfere in Prokofiev's work.

Back in the USSR he wrote propagandistic works: *Cantata for the Twentieth Anniversary of the October Revolution* (1937; text selected from the works of Marx, Lenin, and Stalin, first performed thirty years later without Stalin's quotes); *Zdravitsa* (Hail) to commemorate Joseph Stalin's sixtieth birthday (1939); *Tale of a Boy Who Remained Unknown* (1944); and *On Guard for Peace* (1950). The titles of his choral works underscore the composer's outward submission to the dogmas of socialist realism that required showing life in romantic terms, keeping in mind the future optimistic and glorious resolution of all possible conflicts and present-day hardships. Though music by nature was less subject to censorship and government dictates, the verbal part of it (texts, lyrics, librettos, even the titles of symphonic movements) were subject to Communist Party and state scrutiny.

Prokofiev's opera *Semyon Kotko* (1939) dealt with the civil war in Ukraine and was shelved following the signing of the German-Soviet Nonaggression Pact. His epic opera *War and Peace* (1941–1952), with scenes based on Leo Tolstoy's novel of the same name, resurrected the heroic Russian past, but did not fit Stalin's design for the grandiose post–World War II nationalistic renaissance. The socialist realist opera *Tale of a Real Man* (1947–1948) glorified the deeds of a Soviet pilot who after losing both legs returned to his duties. Its completion coincided with ideology tsar Andrei Zhdanov's crackdown in music and it was heavily criticized. However, Prokofiev's ballets and film music were welcomed by the State and brought him wider official and popular recognition.

His ballet *Romeo and Juliet* (1935–1936) was staged at the Moscow Bolshoi and Leningrad Kirov theaters and became a constant feature of government-sponsored concerts. The *Tale of a Stone Flower* (1948–1950) suited the resurgence of Russian nationalist content after the victory in World War II. Prokofiev's role during the golden age of the Soviet cinema cannot be underestimated either. He was a favorite composer of the filmmaker Sergei Eisenstein, and his music for the epic movies *Aleksandr Nevsky* (1938) and the two parts of *Ivan the Terrible* (1942, 1945) won him two Stalin Prizes. That did not prevent Stalin from banning the second part of *Ivan the Terrible* after sensing allusions to his own reign.

Prokofiev, though recognized as one of the top Soviet composers, was not integrated into the official hierarchy to the extent of Dmitri Shostakovich or the Soviet Armenian composer Aram Khachaturian (1903–1978). He won six Stalin Prizes but was never awarded the title of People's Artist of the Soviet Union. His death on 5 March 1953 did not get national attention, in part because it coincided with Stalin's death on the same day, but his music was played in the

Column Hall where Stalin lay in state. According to newly released archival sources Prokofiev was even denied a prestigious government pension before his death. This injustice was addressed post-humously during Nikita Khrushchev's Thaw, when Prokofiev was the first among Soviet composers to be granted the newly established prestigious Lenin Prize (which replaced the now-discredited and discontinued Stalin Prizes).

While Stravinsky remained an eminently Russian composer and at the same time a citizen of the world, and Shostakovich was a mostly Soviet composer with strong cosmopolitan tendencies, Prokofiev can be considered a Russian Soviet composer. His life and work created a symbolic bridge between Russian prerevolutionary culture and turbulent Soviet-era upheavals. He remained one of the most accomplished masters of the twentieth century, leaving a treasure of ballets, operas, symphonies, suites, overtures, concertos, chamber music, choral works, piano sonatas, songs, and film music, and the beloved symphonic children's tale *Peter and the Wolf* (1936).

See also **Shostakovich, Dmitri; Soviet Union; Stalin, Joseph; Stravinsky, Igor.**

BIBLIOGRAPHY

Hanson, Lawrence and Elisabeth. *Prokofiev, the Prodigal Son: An Introduction to His Life and Work in Three Movements.* London, 1964.

Nestyev, Israel V. *Prokofiev.* Translated by Florence Jonas; foreword by Nicolas Slonimsky. Stanford, Calif., 1960.

Prokofiev, Sergei. *Prokofiev by Prokofiev: A Composer's Memoir.* Edited by David H. Appel; translated by Guy Daniels. Garden City, N.Y., 1979.

———. *Soviet Diary 1927 and Other Writings.* Translated and edited by Oleg Prokofiev. London, 1991.

LEONID MAXIMENKOV

PROPAGANDA. Propaganda and European history are indivisible. The modern concept of propaganda—in essence, mass persuasion—sprang from Europe's religious conflicts in the early seventeenth century. The leaders of the Roman Catholic Church coined the word at the time of the Reformation to describe the act of spreading, or propagating, the faith to unbelievers. It is a testament to the cultural politics of Protestant northern Europe that the term should have swiftly acquired an enduring negative connotation: in popular usage, *propaganda* is to *communication* as *murder* is to *killing*. European history, however, suggests that propaganda is not the monopoly of any one ideology and—like any tool—it can be used for good or evil.

WORLD WAR I

The practice of propaganda reached new heights in Europe during World War I and in the ideological struggles that followed it its wake. Europe and the world were changed as a result.

In 1914, Europe was awash with propaganda. The ideology of nationalism could be found everywhere, from school curricula to commercially produced ephemera. It permeated the print culture of the popular press and bound Europeans to their colonies overseas with talk of duty and ethnic destiny. The architects of that propaganda—the leaders who had profited from the cohesion that national missions and common enemies brought to their population—were trapped within their world of stereotyped friends and enemies by the events of August 1914. When a Serb extremist murdered the heir to the Austrian throne, Austria's rulers felt compelled to mobilize against Serbia, while the tsarist regime in Russia had traded so heavily on the rhetoric of pan-Slavism that it could not but intervene on Serbia's side. The web of rivalries, alliances, and reputations that had to be defended swiftly engulfed the Continent and its overseas colonies in war.

The outbreak of World War I presented the combatant nations with a major challenge: how to raise the armies and enroll the civilian support necessary to prosecute war on an unprecedented scale. Propaganda provided the mechanism for this. Britain led the way, recruiting publicists, artists, and writers for the cause, although it had no formal ministry of information until 1918. In Germany, propaganda remained largely in unskilled military hands and suffered accordingly.

A characteristic element in propaganda on both sides was the atrocity story, depicting horrors allegedly committed by the enemy. Famous stories, later proven false, included the report that the

Germans had created a "corpse conversion" plant at Vimy Ridge in France to turn the war dead into industrial products. Other common themes in World War I propaganda included the claim that God was on one's side and the notion that one must fight to demonstrate masculinity. Common methods of propaganda included posters and the relatively new medium of film. States managed news coverage of the war through censorship and by managing the presence of war correspondents with the troops. Private enterprise also played its part as patriotic wartime themes emerged in postcards, songs, and plays across Europe.

Combatants deployed propaganda on the battlefield. Leaflets crafted to demoralize or appeal for surrender were dropped over enemy territory by aircraft, a technique pioneered by Italy in its colonial wars in Tunisia. The combatant powers also campaigned to win the sympathy of neutral nations, the most important of which was the United States. Peace activists operated on both sides throughout the war, sometimes funded by their nation's enemy.

THE INTERWAR PERIOD

In the aftermath of the war, propaganda provided a convenient explanation for such events as the collapse of morale in Austria and Germany. Apologists for the German defeat, including Adolf Hitler (1889–1945), exaggerated the impact of wartime propaganda. But Hitler then sought to make the weapon of propaganda his own. Other uses of propaganda in the immediate wake of the war included the French use of propaganda to rebuild the birthrate and propaganda in many nations in support of peace. Major initiatives to this end included the League of Nations Union and a succession of powerful antiwar novels, including Erich Maria Remarque's (1898–1970) *All Quiet on the Western Front* (1929).

European governments were not the only practitioners of propaganda during World War I. The international socialist movement had long since adopted the methods of mass communication, and radical class-based propaganda was a feature of politics across Europe. In Soviet Russia, the Bolshevik Party under Vladimir Lenin (1870–1924) developed a two-tier concept of propaganda, drawing a distinction—first made by Georgi Plekhanov (1857–1918)—between propaganda,

Soviet propaganda poster from 1920 reads "Peasants and Workers Unite against the Priests and Barons."
BRIDGEMAN ART LIBRARY

which he defined as giving many ideas to one person, and agitation, which he defined as giving one idea to many people. The Bolsheviks became masters of both. In October 1917 the Bolsheviks seized power. Communist propaganda now had the additional impetus of a nation-state behind it. In 1919 Lenin established the Communist International (Comintern) to ferment international revolution and in the following decades the Soviet Union pioneered a number of important propaganda techniques at home and abroad, including international radio broadcasting in 1927, with regular Radio Moscow services beginning in 1929, and elaborate propaganda films, the best known being those created by Sergei Eisenstein (1898–1948). Later Soviet techniques included disinformation—the spreading of rumors.

The rising leaders of interwar Europe hurried to deploy the ideological weapons of World War I. In Italy Benito Mussolini (1883–1945), a former newspaper editor who had once taken money to print French wartime propaganda, now led the fascist movement. Fascist propaganda looked back to the golden age of ancient Rome. The fascists used propaganda to make their members feel as though they were a part of a great movement. Uniforms, banners, and songs all played a part, with the image of the leader at the fore. In Germany Hitler used similar techniques and themes to energize his National Socialist Party. Hitler believed that without modern communications the Nazi party would not have come to power in 1933. Similar, although smaller, movements could be found across Europe, including Belgium's Rexists, Norway's Nasjonal Samlung, and Britain's British Union of Fascists. Many of these parties used Europe's well-established vein of anti-Semitism as a key element in their propaganda.

The dictatorships of Hitler and Mussolini and of Joseph Stalin (1879–1953) in the Soviet Union shared an approach to propaganda that included rigid censorship and direction of the mass media and education; a love of spectacle, whether as parade or monumental architecture; and a cult of the leader. Film propaganda in all three societies emphasized escapist fantasy musicals and romances rather than heavily ideological fare such as the famous Nazi film *Triumph of the Will* (1935). All three states were involved in major efforts to project their influence internationally through both political and cultural propaganda. Examples included an emphasis on international sporting events, most famously the Berlin Olympics of 1936.

The totalitarian propaganda effort overseas led to a countercampaign by the democratic nations to both consolidate their own empires and display their culture to others. France had been investing in the projection of its language and culture around the world through the Alliance Française, an organization of private citizens who taught the French language, since the 1880s. The French Foreign Ministry founded a cultural department in the early 1920s. Britain did nothing until the 1930s when, in 1932 it inaugurated the empire service of the British Broadcasting Corporation (BBC) and then created the British Council in 1934. Other major efforts included the launch of Radio Netherlands in 1927. Although noble in intent, such work could not stave off the coming of war in 1939.

WORLD WAR II

World War II saw a marked divergence in propaganda techniques between the totalitarian and democratic countries. Nazi propaganda, coordinated by the Reichministerium für Volksauflärung und Propaganda (State ministry for popular enlightenment and propaganda) under Joseph Goebbels (1897–1945) emphasized the dynamism of the regime and concealed its setbacks, whereas the British Ministry of Information, which eventually found stable leadership under Brendan Bracken (1901–1958) sought to work as far as possible with facts. The British government was so shy of ideology as to avoid defining its war aims until the summer of 1941. During the war, the BBC developed a reputation for telling the truth, whether the news was good or bad, and provided a platform for governments-in-exile to address their home countries.

As had happened in World War I, the combatants in World War II competed for American opinion. Although the Germans had the advantage of merely needing to sustain America's neutrality, Britain won the struggle for American opinion mainly by helping American journalists report the Blitz on London at first hand. Britain's prime minister, Winston Churchill (1874–1965) did much to capture the American imagination in the same way that he had earlier rallied his own population. Britain also coordinated propaganda from the European governments-in-exile through a United Nations Information Organization. On the battlefield, the Nazis used propaganda as a variation on the artillery barrage to soften up their enemies. The populations that folded before the Nazi onslaught in 1940 had seen German military might in newsreels and heard broadcasts from Berlin. They knew exactly what was coming. But propaganda also played a key role in the Allied counteroffensive after D-Day, with the successful use of appeals to surrender. The Allies learned that the most effective psychological warfare used truth and flattered its listeners that they had done enough to enable them to lay down their weapons without loss of honor.

POSTWAR EUROPE

In the aftermath of World War II, propaganda played a major part in the reconstruction of Europe, but the period also saw a new propaganda

Children's propaganda parade, Moscow, 1924. The parade was part of a gathering of children from all over the world organized by Communist leaders as a counterpart to the International Scout Jamboree held that year in England. The children carry placards denouncing greedy capitalists and anticommunist, or "white," Russians. ©BETTMANN/CORBIS

struggle as the wartime tensions between Stalin and the western Allies widened into the Cold War. To begin with, the Allied Powers worked on re-education in Germany and were much helped in this by a small army of returning exiles and memories of the liberal Weimar era of the 1920s. Key institutions of re-education included a string of newspapers such as *Die Welt* and *Neue Zeitung*, radio stations, and a special newsreel called *Welt im Film* (The world in film). The wider U.S. effort to rebuild Western Europe through the Marshall Plan (announced in 1947) also included a major propaganda component. Each national Marshall Plan office included an information bureau to publicize American investment in that country and promote associated ideas, from an awareness of U.S. products to a detailed understanding of American management techniques. Funding for this

came from the host nations, hence Europe has been said to have subsidized its own indoctrination.

The Soviet Union saw the Marshall Plan as part of an American plan for economic domination and insisted on the nations in its sphere remaining outside the plan, and it increased both Soviet propaganda and real political power within that sphere. A succession of rigged elections brought Communist governments to power in Poland and Hungary (both 1947), Czechoslovakia (1948), and elsewhere. In 1947 Moscow created Cominform, an umbrella organization for Communist Party propaganda around the world. Set-piece struggles between communist and capitalist propaganda early in the Cold War included the Italian election campaign of 1948. The U.S. government secretly subsidized the Christian Democratic Party, which won the election. Communist propaganda gambits included a powerful drive for peace at the time of the Korean War (1950–1953), which was undermined by the brutality of Soviet intervention in Hungary in 1956. In 1949 the nations of Western Europe joined the United States in the North Atlantic Treaty Organization (NATO), which included a small public relations section and regular talks to coordinate member states' propaganda policies.

Europe became a cultural battleground for the Cold War. Both the Soviets and the United States sought to draw intellectuals to their cause. Particular elements in the American agenda for Europe included greater political unification, although there was no shortage of Europeans campaigning for the same goal. European intellectuals from the noncommunist left benefited from U.S. Central Intelligence Agency money filtered through the Congress for Cultural Freedom, but America's commercial culture had much more impact. In both Western and Eastern Europe, American popular culture, and most especially films and music, spoke of a certain freedom. In contrast, Soviet culture produced under the deadening hand of state censorship seemed rigid and unattractive. France in particular attempted to place restraint on the penetration of American popular culture, restricting the number of American films that could be released and policing the entry of English words into the French language.

European nations continued to invest in cultural propaganda around the world. Germany created a new international cultural apparatus called the Goethe Institute and began new multilingual international radio broadcasts on *Deutsche Welle*. Austria excelled at the art of what advertising people later came to call re-branding, using tourist publicity to make the world think—as one U.S. observer put it—that Beethoven was Austrian and Hitler was German. France and Germany instituted a wide range of cultural exchanges that facilitated their unprecedented rapprochement. Belgium used the 1958 Brussels World's Fair to showcase its postwar recovery.

During these years, Europe decolonized. Its empires had rested on a great deal of propaganda, not least about white supremacy, and their demolition required ideologies of equal weight. Anticolonial propaganda mixed local influences with the appropriation of European nationalism and its trappings of anthems, banners, uniforms and ideologies. Anticolonial propagandists included Mohandas K. Gandhi (1869–1948) in India and the Caribbean-born Frantz Fanon (1925–1961) in North Africa. In places where the European exodus was marked by a local insurgency, the retreating imperial nations deployed the techniques of psychological warfare as part of their counterinsurgency tactics with varying degrees of success.

Postwar Western Europe was characterized, for the most part, by its free media. Exceptions included the right-wing dictatorships in Spain and Portugal, but these too had liberalized by the 1980s. Political movements flourished, including the women's movements; a lively antinuclear and peace movement (especially strong in Scandinavia); environmental movements; and movements both in support of and in opposition to the emerging presence of ethnic minorities within European populations. Each deployed propaganda. The movement for European integration moved forward with elite rather than mass support, although the accession of individual states first to the European Economic Community and then to the European Union, and later the adoption of the common European currency, saw a succession of referenda with attendant propaganda campaigns.

During the postwar period, television rapidly became the major medium of political communication, although for most Europeans television tended to be an alternative to rather than an energizing element in political realm. European television was marked by a strong state presence and much regulation in matters of content. European governments restricted the political use of television and attempted to limit political ownership of commercial channels, although the most obvious exception to this has been in Italy, where in the 1990s the media mogul Silvio Berlusconi (b. 1936) rose to the premiership. During the 1990s, the Internet became a major channel of propaganda on the Continent. Some political parties also experimented with the use of Short Message Service (SMS) text messages on mobile phones.

During the 1970s, the Cold War underwent a marked thaw and West Germany in particular pressed for reconciliation with the East. The thaw culminated in the Helsinki Accords of August

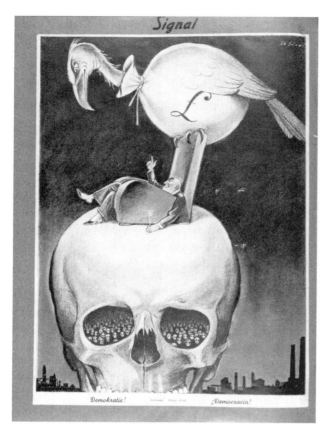

Democracy! A cartoon from the first issue of the German propaganda magazine *Signal* depicts European democracy as a vulture created by wealth and supported by the subjugation of the masses. BRIDGEMAN ART LIBRARY

1975, which included provisions for the free exchange of cultural materials. During the 1980s, old themes re-emerged and such figures as the British prime minister Margaret Thatcher (b. 1925) and the Polish-born Pope John Paul II (1920–2005) were relentless in their criticism of the Soviet empire. The deployment of American cruise missiles in Europe sparked a revival of the antinuclear movement and a fresh wave of propaganda for peace.

Propaganda played a key role in the dramatic political changes that swept across Eastern Europe in 1989. The populations of the East knew about the material and political benefits of Western European life from decades spent watching Western television and listening to Western radio. The bankruptcy of a communist system that feigned love for its people while repressing news

of events such as the Chernobyl accident of 1986 was not in doubt. As the Soviet Union lost its ability to repress its neighbors, the collapse of the communist system in Europe became inevitable. All it took was news of unpunished defiance in one country—East Germany—and people across the region pushed for change. The borders opened and the barriers fell. On the night of 9 November 1989, the citizens of Berlin began to demolish the wall that had divided their city since 1961. In some places, the mass media repeated stories that later proved to be untrue or exaggerated. In December 1989 reports of a massacre of ten thousand people in Timisoara, Romania, stoked revolution in that country, although in fact only ninety-seven had died. The collapse of communism brought the fragmentation of Yugoslavia into warring states. The conflict, which lasted through out the 1990s, included claims and counterclaims of atrocities. Both Serbs and Muslims alleged that the other side had fed their babies to zoo animals. Such stories helped fuel real atrocities.

Despite the triumph of democracy in postwar Europe, the political fringe has engaged in an undercurrent of political violence. Terrorism must be considered a form of propaganda in which the event is planned as much for its value as political communication as for its economic impact on bricks, mortar, blood, or bone. The anarchist Mikhail Bakunin (1814–1876) spoke of *"le propaganda par le fait"*—propaganda by means of action. Terrorism has been a particular feature of movements for regional autonomy in Europe, such as the campaigns for Irish and Basque independence. There have also been shorter-lived political campaigns, such as the extreme left terrorism of the Baader-Meinhof Gang in 1970s West Germany or Brigatte Rossi (Red Brigades) in 1980s Italy. At the start of the twenty-first century, the threat of Islamic terrorism loomed large across Europe. The debate over the correct response to Islamic terrorism, and specifically the U.S.-led invasion of Iraq in 2003, deeply divided European opinion, with much propaganda on both sides.

In the early twenty-first century European propaganda stood at a crossroads. Although the European Union already had many of the trappings of a super-state, it had seldom exercised a political voice on the world stage. In the absence of a

European international cultural program, Britain's British Council and Germany's Goethe Institute began a basic program of cooperation, sharing office locations in the former Soviet Union. It is a small beginning but one that would have been utterly unimaginable in 1914.

See also **Cinema; Communism; Nazism; 1989; Radio; Radio Free Europe; Television; World War I; World War II.**

BIBLIOGRAPHY

Cole, Robert. *Propaganda in Twentieth Century War and Politics: An Annotated Bibliography.* Lanham, Md., 1996.

Cull, Nicholas J., David Culbert, and David Welch. *Propaganda and Mass Persuasion: A Historical Encyclopedia, 1500 to the Present.* Santa Barbara, Calif., 2003. A single volume that acts as a guide to the subject and includes country-specific entries for most European nations.

Ellul, Jacques. *Propaganda: The Formation of Men's Attitudes.* Translated by Konrad Kellen and Jean Lerner. New York, 1965. A classic study of the rise of propaganda in twentieth-century life.

Taylor, Philip M. *Munitions of the Mind: A History of Propaganda from the Ancient World to the Present Era.* 3rd ed. Manchester, U.K., and New York, 2003. A concise overview of the subject of propaganda, with emphasis on its role in war.

Taylor, Richard. *Film Propaganda: Soviet Russia and Nazi Germany.* 2nd rev. ed. London, 1998. A valuable comparative treatment of the Nazi and Soviet use of a particularly powerful medium of propaganda.

Wagnleitner, Reinhold. *Coca-Colonization and the Cold War: The Cultural Mission of the United States in Austria after the Second World War.* Translated by Diana M. Wolf. Chapel Hill, N.C., 1994. A seminal study of U.S. cultural propaganda in postwar Austria.

Welch, David, *The Third Reich: Politics and Propaganda.* New York, 2002. A comprehensive introduction to Nazi propaganda.

NICHOLAS J. CULL

PROSTITUTION. In twentieth-century Europe, prostitution defied easy classification because its legal, ideological, and social history developed over the course of the century and varied between countries. The definition and treatment of prostitutes reflected diverse perceptions of sexuality, women's rights, morality, and the regulatory role of the state. Moreover, war and peace, demographic trends, scientific and medical developments, political ideologies, and the activism of individuals and groups influenced the changing attitudes toward prostitution as they called into question the social, cultural, and medical foundations of the sexual double standard that underlay prior definitions of prostitution.

In the late nineteenth century most European governments saw prostitution as a threat to morality, social order, public health, and gender roles and adopted a regulatory system—usually based on the French model that had emerged in the early nineteenth century following the ideas of Alexandre-Jean-Baptiste Parent-Duchâtelet (1790–1836)—that included compulsory registration, medical examinations, and licensed brothels. From Imperial Russia to Victorian England prostitution was illegal, yet it existed everywhere, usually declared to be a "necessary evil." Governments attempted to control and regulate prostitution, which was defined almost everywhere as an exclusively female phenomenon. Specific regulations were grounded in the work of medical, criminological, legal, and social scholars, and most reflected the sexual double standard of the day that posited that women were the carriers of disease, immorality, degeneracy, and vice and had to be controlled, while men were seen as victims of their uncontrollable sexual urges. Primarily, however, governments sought to regulate women's sexuality and enforce specific gender roles. Sodomy laws existed in most European countries, but male prostitutes were not regulated. By the end of the nineteenth century the existing regulatory systems came under increasing pressure from groups including women's rights activists, moral purity campaigners, sexologists, and the medical establishment. The most successful campaign against regulated female prostitution was the drive to abolish the Contagious Disease Acts in Great Britain, which culminated in their repeal in 1886. Though most states held on to their regulatory policies until 1914, it became increasingly clear that brothelized prostitution did not achieve its goals. The incidence of venereal disease continued to rise, public order could not be guaranteed as many prostitutes eluded the grasp of officials, and ideas of male and female sexuality were changing rapidly.

Prostitutes stand in windows to attract customers in a street in Germany, 1949. ©HULTON-DEUTSCH COLLECTION/CORBIS

WORLD WAR I THROUGH WORLD WAR II

During the First World War most belligerents, worried about unrestricted fraternization, venereal disease, and a decline in troop morale, renewed their faith in brothels. Strictly supervised by military administrations and with a main focus on disease prevention, a range of brothels set up along the front lines, reflecting the hierarchy of military men. This time, however, both men and women were subject to medical examinations, sending new and complex messages about the relationships among prostitution, female sexuality, and traditional gender roles. Fears of "unruly" and unfaithful women persisted as it became harder to control the sexual behavior of women on the fronts and home fronts during the war years.

After the war, views about sexuality and gender roles changed dramatically in many European countries and so did the legal status of prostitution. Women received the vote almost everywhere (France is a notable exception), and it proved difficult to maintain the sexual and moral double standard embodied in regulated prostitution. Moreover, criminological and medical views that had provided the ideological underpinning for regulationism lost scholarly credibility. Laws, rules, and activism surrounding prostitution focused increasingly, if not exclusively, on disease prevention as sanitary concerns triumphed over criminal and moral ones. In interwar Germany, for example, regulations for prostitutes were abandoned in 1927, when a new law designed to reduce the incidence of venereal disease subjected both men and women to primarily voluntary medical examinations, decriminalized female prostitution, and closed licensed brothels. In France many brothels closed down in favor of institutions that tended to separate the working and living quarters of the women, many of which had better hygienic conditions than ever before, thus removing prostitutes from the all-powerful control of brothel-keepers.

When National Socialists took power in Germany in 1933 and later occupied much of Europe during the Second World War, prostitution policies changed again, this time reflecting the racist and sexist ideologies of the Nazi regime. Women were to be primarily mothers and propagators of the race. Prostitution was recriminalized and brothels reintroduced. Mindful of Nazi racial ideology, there existed a multiplicity of brothels as German and foreign men were not allowed to visit the same establishments. Prostitutes in Nazi Germany were treated not only as criminals but also as social outcasts and deviants. In Germany, prostitutes were subject to ever stricter health regulations, stripped of their civil and legal rights, forcefully sterilized, and interned in prisons and concentration camps. Increased surveillance of soldier's wives reflected the fear of miscegenation and sexual behavior that defied acceptable gender roles.

During the war a network of brothels was organized and administered by Nazi authorities for German troops, often staffed by women arrested for prostitution at home. In occupied and Vichy France, officials were able to use existing brothels that had survived since the late nineteenth century. By 1942 a clearly structured and increasingly standardized hierarchy of brothels reflected the hierarchy of the military personnel and racist Nazi ideology. Brothels across Nazi-occupied Europe were designed to regulate the contact between German troops and local civilians but also to perform public health functions as medical experts claimed that strictly regulated prostitutes minimized the spread of venereal disease.

AFTER 1945

Since 1945 sexual norms, laws, and values in Western European societies have undergone a radical liberation as they shifted in emphasis from regulation of prostitution to its toleration. In most Western European countries, prostitution was again legalized in the postwar period, though most states initially retained regimes of medical supervision ranging from compulsory to voluntary. The postwar period also saw the end of the brothel structure as women everywhere abandoned the strictures of brothels for other environments such as strip clubs, sex shops and the streets, especially in the climate of the "sexual revolution" of the 1960s and 1970s, which gave rise to new morals and

sensibilities as well as sex industries. As women in general have demanded and experienced emancipation, so have prostitutes. As more and more sexual and moral taboos were broken, both the appearance and the demand for prostitutes continued to undergo changes. Additionally, the definition of prostitution expanded in the postwar period and came to include male prostitution.

New laws passed in many Western European states were concerned for the first time with protecting prostitutes from disease and exploitation, and activist groups advocating for the rights of sex workers have become increasingly organized, vocal, and successful. In communist Eastern Europe and in the Soviet Union, prostitution officially did not exist and was forced underground. Since the 1990s human trafficking in sex workers from these areas into Western Europe has increased dramatically.

The Federal Republic of Germany in 1953 introduced a law for the prevention of venereal disease, which legalized prostitution but still subjected women to medical examinations and hence defined and stigmatized prostitutes. Forced examinations ended in 1987, and in 2002 the now-unified Germany adopted a law designed to end the stigmatization of prostitutes by explicitly tolerating and categorizing prostitution as an acceptable occupation in the service sector integrated into the welfare state.

The postwar period in France also saw the end of regulationism as laws focused on procurers rather than prostitutes, especially after 1960. Prostitution, however, continued to be stigmatized as a social scourge, and French police retained their repressive mentality. In an attempt to draw attention to the conditions in the prostitution milieu, end their social stigmatization, and participate in the welfare state, French prostitutes in 1975 rebelled against police repression by rioting, engaging in public relations campaigns, and occupying churches all across the country. Though they did not achieve their proposed changes, they succeeded in creating a new and more open discourse about the role of prostitution in modern French society.

Yet the atmosphere of liberalization and toleration of the late twentieth century produced ambivalent results. Although most European states now view prostitution as legal unless it is exploitative, international sex trafficking (mostly from non-European countries in Asia and Latin America), especially of young women and children, the exploitation of international sex workers, and sex tourism have become significant problems. New diseases, especially HIV/AIDS, have replaced syphilis and gonorrhea and brought old concerns about public health back into public discourse. Among other international organizations, the European Union has recently taken on the issue of prostitution and human trafficking in sex workers.

See also **AIDS; Feminism; Sexuality.**

BIBLIOGRAPHY

Barrett, D., with E. Barrett and N. Mullenger, eds. *Youth Prostitution in the New Europe: The Growth in Sex Work.* Dorset, U.K., 2000.

Corbin, Alain. *Women for Hire: Prostitution and Sexuality in France after 1850.* Translated by Alan Sheridan. Cambridge, Mass., 1990.

Elman, R. Amy. *Sexual Politics and the European Union: The New Feminist Challenge.* Providence, R.I., 1996.

Freund-Widder, Michaela. *Frauen unter Kontrolle: Prostitution und ihre staatliche Bekämpfung in Hamburg vom Ende des Kaiserreichs bis zu den Anfängen der Bundesrepublik.* Münster, Germany, 2003.

Hall, Lesley Ann. *Sex, Gender, and Social Change in Britain since 1880.* New York, 2000.

JULIA BRUGGEMANN

PSYCHIATRY. Psychiatry in Europe around the time of the First World War was torn between psychotherapeutic and biological approaches. It is important to locate these traditions in earlier developments. Psychiatry as a discipline had begun around the time of the French Revolution. It was centered in mental hospitals and emphasized the somatic, or physical, treatment of patients with such remedies as hydrotherapy and sedatives. European psychiatrists in the nineteenth century stressed the genetic sources of illness, with particular emphasis on "degeneration," meaning a worsening of illness from one generation to the next. Asylum psychiatrists attached particular importance to brain anatomy and believed that mental illness could be associated with lesions in the physical structure of the brain. Of course, psychiatric illness existed outside of the mental hospital, yet it was treated in the community not by psychiatrists but by neurologists or physiatrists, specialists in physical treatments who generally practiced in spas under the guise of treating "nervous," not mental illness.

Around 1880 this biological approach began to be challenged by psychiatrists who believed in the efficacy of psychotherapy, not hydrotherapy and sedatives. Prominent among these early psychotherapists were Hippolyte Bernheim at the University of Nancy, who in 1883 proposed nonhypnotic suggestion, in addition to hypnosis, as a way of treating lesser nervous illnesses. In 1902 Jules-Joseph Dejerine, a neurologist at the Salpêtrière Hospice in Paris, began sketching out a treatment of the psychoneuroses involving "isolation" of the patients and intensive psychotherapy. Two years later, in 1904, Paul Dubois, professor of neuropathology in Berne, argued that psychoneuroses could best be treated by a kind of "rational" talking therapy emphasizing give-and-take between doctor and patient. First at the Salpêtrière then at Sainte-Anne Mental Hospital, the psychiatrist Pierre Janet in the decade before the First World War continued his efforts to lay out a psychotherapy aimed at reducing "psychological tension" and thus relieving "obsessions and psychasthenia," the title of his 1903 opus. Thus there were numerous attempts in the years before the First World War to construct a psychotherapy that would serve "ambulatory" (nonhospitalized) patients living in the community.

Yet by 1904 these early efforts started to become overshadowed by the kind of psychotherapy that Sigmund Freud (1856–1939) in Vienna introduced, called "psychoanalysis." Beginning in the 1890s, Freud postulated conflicts in the "unconscious" mind as the source of psychoneurosis; he advocated treatment with psychotherapy involving free association (to determine where poorly remembered childhood sexual experiences and fantasized traumas lay) and the analysis of dreams. Among Freud's early publications were *Studies in Hysteria*, cowritten in 1895 with Vienna family doctor Josef Breuer, and *The Interpretation of Dreams* in 1899. By 1904 psychoanalysis was on the brink of becoming an international movement and would attain an amplitude that caused such figures as Bernheim, Dubois, and Dejerine to be almost completely forgotten.

Thus, psychiatry before the First World War was divided between a corps of asylum doctors practicing somatic treatments on patients with major illnesses such as schizophrenia and manic-depressive illness, and psychotherapeutically oriented neurologists and family doctors in private practice, who were just beginning to catch Freud's message and to start plumbing their patients' psyches about early childhood experiences and dreams.

FROM 1900 TO THE SECOND WORLD WAR

The asylums continued to grow in population, yet the main trends in psychiatry shifted to university hospitals and to private practice. In academic psychiatry, interest changed from the anatomical concerns of the late nineteenth century to diagnosis and "psychopathology," meaning the study of the patients' actual symptoms (rather than hypothetical "diseases" the patient might have). This was in particular a German story, yet it will be discussed here because of the great influence of German-speaking authorities on international developments. Throughout the second half of the nineteenth century, German authors had puzzled over the various psychiatric diseases and how to classify them.

Emil Kraepelin (1856–1926), professor of psychiatry in Heidelberg, then after 1903 in Munich, is the central figure in the nosology story. (*Nosology* means the classification of diagnoses.) As a young physician, in 1883 he had brought out a textbook of psychiatry, called simply *Psychiatry*. Yet ongoing experience made him modify his ideas, and in the fourth edition of the textbook in 1893 he revived the concept of his predecessor, the German physician Karl Kahlbaum (1828–1899), that the best way to classify psychiatric diseases was on the basis of clinical course rather than momentary symptom picture. In this edition, Kraepelin said that there was a special form of psychotic illness (psychotic meaning delusions and hallucinations) in which the patients' personalities and intellects deteriorated irreversibly, ending in "dementia." Kraepelin called it "dementia praecox," or premature dementia, seen often in young people. In the sixth edition of his textbook in 1899, Kraepelin said that there

was a second main form of illness, involving such mood disorders as mania and depression, in which the patients experienced a fluctuating course over their lives rather than deteriorating. He called this disease "manic-depressive illness," and the Kraepelinian firewall between dementia praecox and manic-depressive illness dominated psychiatric thinking for the next century. In 1908 the Zurich psychiatry professor Eugen Bleuler rebaptized dementia praecox as "schizophrenia."

The psychiatric clinic at Heidelberg University had proven an especially fruitful source of thought, and it was here that the young psychiatry trainee Karl Jaspers (1883–1969) in 1913 authored the most important book ever written about psychopathology, *General Psychopathology,* a work that influenced understanding of patients' experience of illness as profoundly as Kraepelin had influenced formal thinking about mental "diseases." The close study of patients' symptoms became a European specialty, and Jaspers's book was not even translated into English until 1963.

Kurt Schneider, a contemporary of Jaspers then in Cologne, stirred up the study of mood disorders in 1921 with his distinction between "vital" and reactive depression. (*Vital* meant serious depression, often called "endogenous.") In the 1920s Schneider also elaborated a series of diagnostic symptoms he believed characteristic of schizophrenia; today, these symptoms are referred to as "Schneiderian," or first-rank, criteria in diagnosing that illness.

German academic psychiatry also developed a strong interest in the inheritance of mental illness, or psychiatric genetics. Unlike earlier "degeneration" doctrines that relied heavily on anecdote, psychiatric genetics properly understood was a statistical discipline, based on studies of twins and family trees. (In a twin study, the difference between the presence of an illness in monozygotic [one-egg] twins and dizygotic [two-egg)] twins is a measure of the influence of the genes.) In 1928 Hans Luxenburger at the German Psychiatric Research Institute in Munich undertook the first twin study.

Yet the doctrine that swept much of academic and community psychiatry between the two world wars in Europe was psychoanalysis. In 1902 Freud founded his "Psychological Wednesday Society" in Vienna, out of which emerged the first psychoanalytic society. In 1908 the first international psychoanalytic congress convened in Salzburg (the second in Nuremberg in 1910, the third in Weimar in 1911). In 1920 the first psychoanalytic outpatient clinic was opened in Berlin. By the 1920s, psychoanalysis was being avidly discussed everywhere, and even though most psychiatrists did not become analysts, Freud's doctrines certainly became the basis of psychotherapy, remaining so until the 1970s.

The Nazi seizure of power in Germany in 1933, and the Anschluss (annexation) of Austria in 1938, spelled the provisional end of psychoanalysis as a European movement. Freud's books were banned, his Jewish collaborators chased into exile. In 1938 the Freud family fled Vienna for London, where Freud died the following year. Many well-known analysts ended up in the United States and Canada, giving psychoanalysis a new impetus in the New World.

A final important prewar development was the emergence of physical treatments of the brain and mind. These began in Vienna in 1917 as the psychiatry professor Julius Wagner von Jauregg (1857–1940) originated the malarial cure of neurosyphilis (spread of syphilis to the central nervous system; malaria raised the body temperature, thus arresting the growth of the organisms that cause syphilis; the malaria was then cured with quinine). In 1930 Manfred Sakel, a young Austrian physician practicing in a private psychiatric hospital in Berlin, revolutionized the treatment of psychosis ("schizophrenia") with his insulin cure: large doses of insulin put patients into hours-long comas; after a long series of these treatments they often recovered from their psychosis.

In 1935 Ladislaus von Meduna, a young Budapest psychiatrist, developed the first convulsive therapy: deliberately inducing convulsions with a substance such as camphor or pentylenetetrazol (Metrazol, Cardiazol) in order to relieve psychosis (and depression). Despite the unpleasant optics of the convulsions (which had few lasting side effects), the treatment was surprisingly effective, and convulsive therapy began its long trajectory that continues even today. In 1938 the Rome psychiatry professor Ugo Cerletti suggested inducing the

convulsions with electricity rather than chemically (patients disliked the latter approach because they felt terrified if the convulsions did not immediately begin after the injection; with electroconvulsive therapy, or ECT, unconsciousness was immediate; the patients had no recollection of the fit when they awoke, and were willing to have additional treatments).

FROM THE 1950S TO 2004

After the Second World War, the principal new development in psychiatry was psychopharmacology, the treatment of symptoms arising from mind and brain with drugs. There had been innovations in pharmacological treatments even before the war, such as the introduction in the 1930s of amphetamines for mild depression. A good deal of research into mental mechanisms was stimulated with the diffusion of lysergic acid diethylamide, "LSD-25," the mental effects of which were discovered in 1943 by the Swiss medicinal chemist Albert Hofmann at Sandoz Limited in Basel.

Yet the true revolution of psychopharmacology—for indeed it was revolutionary to shift the treatment of mental illness from psychotherapy for the mind to pharmacotherapy for the brain—commenced in 1952 with the discovery by several Parisian physicians that a phenothiazine-type antihistamine called chlorpromazine, made by the Rhône-Poulenc company, effectively improved the symptoms of psychotic illness. The success of chlorpromazine in chronic patients in the back wards of mental hospitals led to the synthesis in the 1950s and 1960s of a whole series of other phenothiazines. In 1958 the butyrophenone class of antipsychotics was initiated by the Janssen company in Belgium (haloperidol being the first); in 1958 as well the thioxanthene series of antipsychotics was launched by the Lundbeck company in Denmark (chlorprothixene the first). These drugs, called "antipsychotics" in North America, "neuroleptics" in Europe, had an incalculable impact on the treatment of schizophrenia and psychosis: it now became possible to discharge large numbers of patients from asylums to the community. The "institutional era" in the history of psychiatry started to end. This was entirely a European story.

Then came drugs for depression. In 1957 the Swiss psychiatrist Roland Kuhn discovered that a compound of the Geigy company in Basel called generically imipramine (trade name Tofranil) was helpful in the treatment of vital depression. It was the first antidepressant for serious, hospital depression. Imipramine spawned a whole series of tricyclic antidepressants (so called because of their ring structure). Simultaneously in the early 1950s, the usefulness of iproniazid, developed in Europe from Geman rocket fuel, and of reserpine, developed in India from a traditional medicinal plant (*Rauwolfia serpentina*), was being explored.

By the mid-1960s the entire range of serious psychiatric illnesses had become eminently treatable, either with ECT or with pharmacotherapy. Psychiatry started to swing from offering psychotherapy to the provision of medication. It was a great sea change.

DEVELOPMENTS COUNTRY BY COUNTRY

There are great differences from country to country in the level of scientific accomplishment in psychiatry. These differences give rise to reflection about the social and political conditions that make for or hinder progress.

Germany and Austria There is no doubt that before 1933 psychiatry was dominated by German and Austrian clinicians and scientists. Just as French was once said to be the language of diplomacy, German was the language of psychiatry. The German dominance of the international field commenced with the Berlin psychiatry professor Wilhelm Griesinger in the 1860s, who proposed the modern university psychiatric clinic, founded the premier international scientific journal, the *Archive for Psychiatry and Nervous Diseases,* and advocated a biological basis for psychiatric illness. By 1904 the German psychiatric tradition had become deeply organic, heavily dependent on autopsy findings, and preoccupied with nosology. The major centers were Heidelberg, Berlin, Munich, and Vienna. Psychoanalysis made only limited inroads into biological thinking at German universities.

A real turning of the page occurred with the Nazi seizure of power in 1933—1938 in Austria— as the Jewish scientists who had formed the backbone of excellence of the German system were driven out. This represented a blow from which German psychiatry never really recovered. Since the Second World War there have been few German contributions to psychopharmacology, psychopathology, or psychotherapy of international significance. In the 1960s a great passion for Freud's doctrines began to sweep German academic psychiatry that had only partly abated by the early 2000s.

In retrospect, between 1933 and 1945 in psychiatry, Germany and Austria went from sixty to zero, as it were, partly because of the loss of so many premier scientific figures from emigration and the Holocaust. A discipline cannot lose many figures such as Franz Kallmann, the Berlin psychiatric geneticist who ended up at Columbia University, without suffering grave harm. The loss of a hundred Kallmanns contributed to the end of the German predominance in psychiatry and to the rise of American predominance.

Switzerland The Swiss bridle at the notion that they are part of "Germany." There are three Swiss narratives in the psychiatry story. The first begins with the rise of the Zurich cantonal hospital and psychiatric clinic, the "Burghölzli," to world fame in the last quarter of the nineteenth century. In 1904 Eugen Bleuler, of "schizophrenia" fame, was the professor of psychiatry, and he and his son Manfred Bleuler made numerous important contributions, notably Eugen Bleuler's 1910 work on schizophrenia, in which he proposed a much milder version of the disease than Kraepelin's unremittingly downhill concept.

A second Swiss moment of excellence was research on the somatic therapies, such as insulin and Cardiazol, centered on Max Müller in the Münsingen mental hospital in the 1930s and 1940s. A third such moment was Swiss research on psychopharmacology, led by Paul Kielholz and other figures, in Basel and Zurich in the 1960s and after.

In the late 1930s, with the eclipse of Germany and Austria, Switzerland was probably the world's epicenter of research in psychiatry. Swiss clinicians were doubtless aided considerably by contact with the great pharmaceutical companies of Basel: Sandoz, Hoffmann-La Roche, Geigy, and Ciba, three of which by 2004 had merged into Novartis, leaving only Hoffmann-La Roche standing alone.

The United Kingdom England and Scotland rivaled Germany as a psychiatric great power during the nineteenth century. In 1923 the Maudsley Hospital in London, led by Edward Mapother, opened its doors; it was to become the major British training center for psychiatry. Aubrey Lewis, perhaps the greatest name in mid-twentieth-century English psychiatry, became clinical director of the Maudsley in 1936 (and professor of psychiatry in the University of London in 1946). Lewis and Michael Shepherd led the British charge toward social and community psychiatry between the 1940s and 1960s, which was possibly the most important English innovation in these years. (Social psychiatry emphasizes community care and social rehabilitation rather than individual psychotherapy or psychopharmacology.) Although there had been a lively interest in biological psychiatry ever since Joel Elkes had founded in 1951 the Department of Experimental Psychiatry in Birmingham, it was only in the 1970s that psychiatry as a whole began to shift toward psychopharmacology; in 1974, under the aegis of the Leeds psychiatrist Max Hamilton (creator of the Hamilton depression scale), the British Association of Psychopharmacology was founded.

In psychopharmaceuticals, Britain has always been an international leader. In 1995 Glaxo and Wellcome merged to form Glaxo Wellcome (becoming GlaxoSmithKline in 2000 in a union with the Philadelphia firm SmithKline & Beecham). In 1999 the Swedish firm Astra joined with the English company Zeneca to form a second British pharmaceutical giant, AstraZeneca.

France In the twentieth century, France lost its status as a center of psychiatric care and research. The land of such nineteenth-century giants as Philippe Pinel and Jean-Martin Charcot did not in the twentieth century produce any great psychiatric figures beyond the rather bizarre Parisian psychoanalyst Jacques Lacan and the circle around Jean Delay, professor of psychiatry in Paris from 1946 to 1970. It was Delay who supervised the clinical trials of chlorpromazine in 1952, aided by Pierre Deniker; Pierre Pichot, who introduced psychological testing to France, was Delay's other famous student. After the 1960s, as in Italy and Germany, French psychiatry became increasingly swept up in psychoanalysis and really vanished from the international stage except for its highly innovative

pharmaceutical firms such as Sanofi Synthélabo, formed by a merger in 1998.

Italy Italian contributions to the international story have really been limited to Ugo Cerletti's electroconvulsive therapy in 1938. In the 1960s, as elsewhere, Italy became caught up in the vogue for psychoanalysis. Simultaneously, psychiatry became highly politicized and various political parties including Democratic Psychiatry (Psichiatria Democratica) demanded the complete closing of all provincial mental hospitals, achieved in a 1978 law. Access to ECT also became highly restricted, indeed unavailable in most parts of Italy. By 2004 Italy had become a kind of psychiatric museum of the 1960s, idolizing countercultural politics, radical deinstitutionalization, and psychoanalysis.

Spain and Portugal There have been virtually no major contributions from Iberia to modern psychiatry. In 1950 Juan Jose Lopez Ibor, a member of the department of psychiatry of the University of Madrid and a student of the German psychopathological tradition, described "anxious thymopathy" as a distinctive illness, comparable to the "vital depression" of Kurt Schneider. In 1936 the Lisbon neurology professor Egas Moniz proposed the ablation of much of the frontal lobes of the brain as a remedy for psychosis (the procedure was called leukotomy, also lobotomy), a contribution for which he received a Nobel Prize in 1949. It is said that the Nobel Prize committee became subsequently so horrified at having misbestowed this honor that no further Nobel Prizes were conferred in psychiatry.

Denmark In proportion to its population, Danish contributions to the international narrative of psychiatry have been extraordinary, in the twentieth century beginning with August Wimmer, director of the provincial psychiatric hospital St. Hans in Roskilde, who in 1916 originated the diagnosis "reactive psychosis." In 1954 Mogens Schou at the Aarhus university clinic in Risskov undertook a randomized clinical trial, one of the first in psychiatry, to test the efficacy of lithium in mania, the beginning of Schou's lifelong work on lithium (which he also determined to be an effective maintenance treatment of depression). Erik Strömgren, from 1945 professor of psychiatry at Aarhus, was among the pioneers of the epidemiology of psychiatric genetics, and Ole Rafaelsen, in his Psychochemistry Institute in Copenhagen, trained a generation of Danish and international psychopharmacologists. The Lundbeck company, which around 1945 began targeting the central nervous system, has worked closely with such Danish clinicians as Jorgen Ravn in the development of the thioxanthenes and other drug classes. Danish clinicians were closely involved in the late 1960s and early 1970s with the psychopharmacology training programs of the Copenhagen office of the World Health Organization.

Sweden Another Nordic psychiatric great power, Swedish psychiatry in the twentieth century has focused around the Karolinska Institute in Stockholm, where in 1979 Marie Asberg, working with Stuart Montgomery in England, devised the "Montgomery-Asberg Rating Scale for Depression," or MADRS, used throughout the world in depression research. In 1957 pharmacologist Arvid Carlsson, then at the University of Lund (later at Gothenburg), discovered the role of dopamine as a neurotransmitter. For his dopamine research, Carlsson received a Nobel Prize in 2000. Working with Carlsson, in 1982 the Astra company introduced zimeldine, the first of the so-called selective serotonin reuptake inhibitors, or Prozac-style remedies that bear the catchy acronym "SSRIs."

Eastern Europe and the Soviet Union As for Eastern Europe and the Soviet Union, it would be unfortunate to let the political abuses to which psychiatric care was often subject overshadow the real contributions to the international story. Within the framework of conditioned reflexes set by the great Russian neurophysiologist Ivan Pavlov (1849–1936), a physiologically oriented psychiatry flourished in the Soviet Union. B. M. Teplov reviews this work in his book *Thirty Years of Soviet Psychology,* published in Russian in 1947. V. A. Gilyarovsky, author of a widely used psychiatry textbook, undertook EEG tracking of antropine-induced psychoses. In Hungary, psychiatrist Joseph Knoll, professor of pharmacology in Budapest, synthesized in 1961 the drug selegiline (marketed in the United States as Deprenyl), important in the treatment of Parkinson's disease and possibly useful in the treatment of depression and dementia and in staving off the effects of aging. In Prague, a team of clinicians and pharmacologists led by the psychiatrist Oldrich Vinar, and including the chemist M. Protiva, synthesized in 1962 the popular antidepressant drug dothiepin (Prothiaden in many markets) and generally spearheaded psychopharmacology in Eastern Europe. Numerous important Eastern European contributions to psychiatric drug discovery have remained widely unknown abroad.

CONCLUDING OBSERVATIONS

What makes for excellence in a crossnational context? Three factors emerge as salient. One is the existence of a university system based on the "Humboldtian" model of combining teaching and research, conceived by Wilhelm von Humboldt (1767–1835), the Prussian education minister in Berlin, in Napoleonic times. The Swiss and Scandinavian universities were very much constructed on this German-style model, in contrast to much of Mediterranean university life, where research is done at an often lackadaisical pace and teaching assigned to assistants. Second, international attainment in psychiatry since the Second World War has tracked psychoanalysis inversely: those countries where analysis became all the rage in the 1960s and after simply fell off the research map. Finally, progress in clinical psychiatry and the neurosciences has often occurred in connection with research-oriented pharmaceutical companies, especially in Switzerland, Denmark, and Sweden, that have sought out academics for collaborative research.

See also **Freud, Sigmund; Jaspers, Karl; Psychoanalysis; War Neuroses.**

BIBLIOGRAPHY

Angel, Katherine, Edgar Jones, and Michael Neve, eds. *European Psychiatry on the Eve of War: Aubrey Lewis, the Maudsley Hospital, and the Rockefeller Foundation in the 1930s.* London, 2003.

Ayd, Frank J., and Barry Blackwell, eds. *Discoveries in Biological Psychiatry.* Philadelphia, 1970.

Berrios, German. *The History of Mental Symptoms: Descriptive Psychopathology since the Nineteenth Century.* Cambridge, U.K., 1996.

Berrios, German, and Roy Porter, eds. *A History of Clinical Psychiatry: The Origin and History of Psychiatric Disorders.* London, 1995.

Healy, David. *The Psychopharmacologists: Interviews.* 3 vols. London, 1996–2000.

———. *Let Them Eat Prozac: The Unhealthy Relationship between the Pharmaceutical Industry and Depression.* New York, 2004.

Howells, John G., ed. *World History of Psychiatry.* New York, 1975.

Pichot, Pierre. *A Century of Psychiatry.* Paris, 1983.

Shorter, Edward. *A History of Psychiatry: From the Era of the Asylum to the Age of Prozac.* New York, 1997.

———. *A Historical Dictionary of Psychiatry.* New York, 2005.

EDWARD SHORTER

PSYCHOANALYSIS.

Europe—both east and west—gave birth to psychoanalysis, but psychoanalysis eventually traveled through the whole world, and much of its history was determined by events in the United States. European psychoanalysis does have its own history, however, one that was interrupted at least three times: by World War I, by World War II, and by the 1960s.

WORLD WAR I AND THE INTERWAR YEARS

To Sigmund Freud, the Austrian neurologist and founder of psychoanalysis, it appeared as if World War I might end the psychoanalytic movement. "What [Carl] Jung and [Alfred] Adler have left intact of the movement is now perishing in the strife among nations—science sleeps" he wrote Ernest Jones, a British associate (Paskauskas, 1993; letter of 25 December 1914). Yet, the war itself provided a great inspiration to psychoanalysis in the form of the shell shock crisis. Analysis—only a decade or so old when the war broke out, and riven by schisms in the years preceding the war—nonetheless appeared vastly superior to its neurologically based rivals; above all, it accepted the reality of shell shock and provided some means of treatment. In addition, the apparent irrationality of the war, the widespread sense that events were out of conscious control, gave a new encouragement to psychoanalysis. As a result, in the last years of the war it gained both public attention and internal strength.

In 1918 the first postwar analytic congress was held in Budapest, Hungary, at the invitation of Béla Kun's communist regime, which planned to build a clinic to treat war neuroses. The Budapest Congress adopted two resolutions that shaped the postwar history of analysis: first, to prepare for "mass," that is, publicly financed, therapy, and second, to require that every analyst be analyzed. Both resolutions arose from the crisis provoked by the war. The first was based on the idea that psychotherapy should be considered an entitlement, like health care in general. As the analytic congress passed a resolution to prepare for publicly financed therapy, Freud explained: "the poor man should have just as much right to assistance for his mind as he now has to the life-saving help offered by surgery . . . the neuroses threaten public health no less than tuberculosis" (Freud, vol. 17, p. 167). At the same time, analytically oriented outpatient clinics, such as the Tavistock in London and Bellevue in New York, which were aimed at patients unable to afford private fees, were being founded abroad.

As a result of the resolution on mass analysis, European analysis had a socially oriented cast throughout the 1920s and 1930s. February 1920 saw the opening of the Berlin outpatient Polyclinic on Potsdamerstrasse, financed by Max Eitingon, housed in a building renovated by Freud's son Ernst, and offering low-cost, government-supported psychotherapy. Mass analysis also meant that analysts would play an educative role as part of the social-democratic culture of the time. In England and Austria, for example, the term *applied analysis* described analytic work in nursery schools, child guidance clinics, teenage consultations, and social work.

In addition to endorsing public clinics, the Budapest Congress also endorsed the requirement of a training analysis for every analyst. The purpose of the resolution was to secure the independence of analysis by gaining control over training and licensing. It aimed to distinguish analysis both from popular techniques, for which no training was necessary, and from psychiatry, which required a medical degree. The prerequisites for becoming an analyst, according to Freud, were "psychological instruction and a free human outlook." Many analysts had no medical degree, including Oskar Pfister (minister); Hermine Hug-Hellmuth, Anna Freud, and Barbara Low (teachers); Lou Andreas-Salomé and Otto Rank (writers); Hans Sachs (lawyer); Ella Freeman Sharpe (literature professor); August Aichhorn and Siegfried Bernfeld (social workers); and Ernst Kris (art historian).

As the war ended, interest in psychoanalysis exploded. Before the war, psychoanalysis had been effectively a *Männerbund*, an all-male circle centered around a charismatic father figure. (The first female analyst, Margarete Hilferding, had been admitted in 1910.) After the war, the "psychoanalytic movement," a diverse collection of national societies all seeking to turn the circle around Freud into a discipline or profession, replaced the *Männerbund*. The size and diversity of the movement is suggested by the first postwar congress, held in The Hague in September 1920, a meeting with the character of a reunion. Participating were 112 individuals: 62 from Austria and Hungary, 16 from Holland, 15 from Britain, 11 from Germany, 7 from Switzerland, and 1 from Poland. Four years later, the International Psychoanalytic Association (IPA) had a total membership of 263.

Stymied in their efforts to win legitimacy from the university, and capitalizing on the popularity of analytic practice, postwar analysts created a separate profession, developing a core curriculum, standardized forms of practice, and regularized mechanisms of succession to replace the committee that had been formed around Freud before World War I. To this end, they established "institutes," all-purpose centers that combined a society, a clinic, and formal training through course work, supervised clinical practice, and didactic or "training" analyses. Although an inner circle centered on Freud persisted, it became increasingly peripheral to the main thrust toward professionalization. Substantial control passed to a new generation distinguished from the *Männerbund* in terms of age, gender, sexuality, and political orientation.

The age differences were dramatic. Whereas Freud had been born in 1856, Melanie Klein was born in 1882, Otto Rank and Helene Deutsch in 1884, Karen Horney in 1885, Franz Alexander in 1891, and Wilhelm Reich, a prodigy, in 1897. They were all still young in the 1920s and recognizably "modern" in their sensibilities and values. Freud, by contrast, had negative feelings about such exemplary products of modernity as the radio, the telephone, film, feminism, abstract art, and U.S. culture. The distinction between old and young inflected many debates of the period, including those over brief therapy, female sexuality,

and the place of the United States in the analytic movement.

The gender composition also shifted dramatically. The number of female analysts rose from two before World War I to approximately fifty in the immediate postwar period. By 1929 the majority of new trainees were women. Many had been teachers, and many were mothers. The changing gender composition of the movement encouraged a dramatic shift in its preoccupations to the mother–infant relationship, the mother–daughter relationship, and female sexuality.

The shift concerning sexuality is more difficult to trace, but two incidents of the immediate postwar period are revealing. In 1920 an openly homosexual doctor applied for membership in the Dutch Psychoanalytic Association. Its members turned to Jones for advice, and he counseled against admittance. Sachs, Karl Abraham, and Eitingon urged from Berlin that this was a matter for the individual society to determine, although they added, there should be a presumption that any homosexual was neurotic, unless analysis demonstrated otherwise. Even Sándor Ferenczi, long a champion of legalization of homosexuality, insisted that "these people are too abnormal" to be analysts. Freud, in contrast, recommended acceptance, but conceded that the matter was ultimately to be determined by the local society. In 1921, in another incident, Jones wrote Freud informing him that he was refusing psychoanalytic training to a homosexual. Freud again disagreed: "we cannot exclude such persons without other sufficient reasons, as we cannot agree with their legal persecution. . . . [A] decision in such cases should depend upon a thorough examination of the other qualities of the candidate" (Jones, p. 9).

Politically, the ethos of the analytic movement became more democratic. Whereas in 1910 Freud had argued for an elite "along the lines of Plato's republic," by the 1920s he advocated local autonomy, as just noted. After World War I, moreover, disagreements did not necessarily provoke schisms. Rank and Ferenczi left the analytic movement voluntarily, albeit amidst turmoil; they were not excluded. In 1927, when the International Training Commission tried to impose lay analysis on the New York Psychoanalytic Society, Anna

Freud led the opposition, calling it an obvious injustice.

Before the war, psychoanalysis had been mixed up with many other forms of psychotherapy, such as mind cure, Jungianism, Adlerianism, and mental hygiene, as psychiatry was increasingly called. The revisions sparked by the shell shock experience—the theory of the ego, the idea of the death instinct, a revised theory of anxiety, a new orientation to the mother—led to a sharp distinction between psychoanalysis and the rest. While there were many ways to characterize this distinction, Freud drew the line with his assertion that the ego was the locus of resistance. Deeply rooted in his thought, this idea became central to modernist culture, as well as to the practice of psychoanalysis itself. If, as is often said in the early twenty-first century, psychoanalysis is "pluralistic" or "polycentric," that it has no agreed-upon core theory, until the end of the 1960s, it did have a core theory: it was the theory of the analysis of the resistance or negative transference. No other therapy did this, at least not in a systematic fashion. This was why there was psychoanalysis at all, and not just psychotherapy.

After the rise of the Nazis, refugees took the analytic theories of the 1920s and 1930s—the so-called structural theory—to the United States where it was termed "ego psychology." But the true beginnings of ego psychology were in postwar Europe. There were several different centers, each with different variations.

Supported by government funds and recognized by the medical community, the Berlin Psychoanalytic Institute, run by Abraham, Eitingon, and Ernst Simmel, was the flagship for the entire movement. Benefiting both from proximity to and distance from Vienna, and sponsoring the influential Kinderseminar, the discussion group of younger analysts such as Otto Fenichel, Käte Friedländer, Edith Jacobson, and Georg Gerö, the institute pioneered in ego psychology. Berlin also housed the Verlag (the psychoanalytic publishing house) and the *Internationale Zeitschrift für Psychoanalyse* (*International Journal of Psychoanalysis*), edited by Sándor Radó.

Along with Berlin, international analytic politics took shape around the London and Vienna Societies. The British Psychoanalytic Society, with about fifty-five members, housed Jones, a central figure in the IPA who maintained close relations not only with Sigmund and Anna Freud, but also with the far-flung parts of the ex–British Empire, especially the United States. It benefited from a relatively democratic and woman-friendly environment and was also associated with a substantial publishing effort: Leonard and Virginia Woolf's Hogarth Press, which published the English edition of the *International Journal of Psychoanalysis,* the English translations of Freud, and the International Psychoanalytical Library. Reflecting its inaugural place in the history of psychoanalysis, Vienna produced ego psychology's definitive formulation, Anna Freud's *The Ego and the Mechanisms of Defense* (1936).

Alongside Berlin and Vienna three important variations of European ego psychology emerged in London, Paris, and Budapest. In London, Klein proposed an object-relational view of the ego. Developing an ethic of responsibility, rather than an ethic of justice, providing what some have called a feminine alternative to Freud, Klein's thought resonated with a new, middle-class orientation to the problem of building up and sustaining personal relations, as opposed to the problem of autonomy implicit in the theory of the Oedipus complex. In Paris, Jacques Lacan developed a second alternative to ego psychology in his famous "mirror stage" article. According to Freud, "where id was there shall be ego" defined analysis, but Lacan insisted (cf. *Ercits*) that the ego or "I" was a defensive response to the traumatic discovery of emptiness, an imaginary "crystallization or sedimentation of images of an individual's own body and of self-images reflected back to him or her by others." Finally, in Budapest, Ferenczi argued that the original state of the neonate was one of expecting to receive without having to give anything in return. Passive receptivity, not agency, was the driving force of development, and a "corrective emotional experience," not insight, was the means of cure.

The great debates over female psychology in the interwar years also were debates over the development of the ego. Ego psychology, beginning during World War I and marked especially by Otto Rank's *The Trauma of Birth* (1923), took psychology back before the Oedipus complex to the early relationship with the mother, what later came to be called the pre-Oedipal stage. This raised

A patient undergoes psychoanalysis, c. 1940. ©HULTON-DEUTSCH COLLECTION/CORBIS

the question of what difference the early mother–child relationship made to sexual development—especially to object choice—in both sexes. For the boy, it was clear that the early relationship to the mother generally preceded a female object choice. How, however, did the girl come to form a male object choice, given that her earliest relations were with the mother? All the debates over "penis envy," and over whether females followed an "autonomous" line of sexual development were efforts to answer this question. Autonomy—the goal of analytic ego psychology—also rested on the relationship to the mother.

WORLD WAR II AND THE IMMEDIATE POSTWAR YEARS

Psychoanalysis thrived in the interwar years until, in 1933, the rise of the Nazis destroyed its main society—in Berlin—and much of its self-confidence.

As fascism triumphed, psychoanalysis crumbled. The Paris Psychoanalytic Society was abolished when the Nazis entered Paris. Italian analysis was put out of business by the anti-Semitic laws of 1938. In the Soviet Union, Stalin had condemned analysis in 1927, but after the Nazi victory analysis was banned. Hungarian analysis passed into "non-Jewish" hands; meetings had to be reported to the police in advance. In the Netherlands, training continued in secret. Only in neutral Switzerland did analytic societies continue to operate openly.

Most poignant, certainly, were the experiences of analysts and analysands in concentration camps. Some struggled to maintain an analytic perspective even there, thus testifying to the ability of the analytically oriented to suspend consideration of the immediate environment. Many analysts perished. After the Germans invaded Hungary in 1944, Jószef Mihály Eisler (a member of the

Hungarian Psychoanalytic Society since 1919), Miklos Gimes, Zsigmond Pfeifer, and Geza Dukes died in the camps. The Yugoslav analyst Nikola Sugar, also a member of the Hungarian society, died at Theresienstadt. David Oppenheim, a classics teacher with whom Freud had cowritten his first piece on folklore and who left Freud over the Adler controversy, was murdered in a camp. Auguste Watermann had fled Hamburg in 1933, but was never fully accepted by the Dutch Psychoanalytic Association. After the Germans invaded Holland, he was arrested with his wife and child and deported to Vreemdelingen at Westerbork, then to Theresienstadt, then to Auschwitz, where all three were killed. Ernst Hoffman, a Jew from Vienna, had fled to Antwerp in 1933 and trained the future founders of the Belgian Psychoanalytic Society before he was deported in 1942 to a camp in Gurs, France, dying soon after. Sabina Spielrein was shot to death during a forced march, along with her two daughters, in a ravine outside Rostov. Fugitives from German occupation forces included Leo Eitinger in Norway and Hans Keilson in the Netherlands. Camp survivors included Eddy DeWind, Elie Cohen, and Viktor Frankl. Leopold Szondi, who coined the term *destiny analysis,* survived Belsen and lived until 1986. Raoul Wallenberg's intervention saved the Hungarian-Jewish analyst István Hollós. Gottfried R. Bloch, a Czech analyst, survived Auschwitz and later lived in Los Angeles. John Rittmeister, a communist psychoanalyst and member of the Resistance, executed by the Gestapo in Berlin in 1943, was remembered by East Germans as a hero and by West German analysts as a Bolshevik spy. Nevertheless, it should be said that while Nazism destroyed many analytic societies, its refugees also created new ones—in Palestine, South Africa, and Argentina and ultimately throughout Latin America.

World War II moved the center of gravity to the United States. Nevertheless, one European society had prospered during the 1930s and had survived the war: the British Psychoanalytic Society into which Klein introduced her pioneering innovations and to which Anna Freud and many other analysts had fled in 1938.

Klein was born in 1882 in Vienna, was analyzed by Ferenczi in Budapest, and studied with Abraham in Berlin. There she had been one of the first to practice analysis on children, whose "presenting symptoms" were typically problems at school. Viewing early learning as directed at the mother, she interpreted inhibitions on learning as resulting from the child's fear of retaliation for what the child perceived as its hostile wishes. From this Klein concluded that the mother, not the father, was the original authority figure. In the late 1920s, Klein began developing an alternative to the Freudian paradigm.

Klein's key move was her insistence, contra Freud, that the superego originated in early representations of the mother, long prior to the Oedipus complex. This innovation had far-reaching implications. First, it implied that the conflicts that were formative for the individual were often very primitive, closely tied to biological survival. This represented a major departure from Freud, for whom material frustrations became meaningful only later, after they had been reconfigured as moral imperatives.

Second, Klein's view of the inner object world was strikingly different from Freud's. In Freud's, there was always a third term—the superego—that stood apart from the ego and judged it. For Klein, in contrast, all relations were saturated with ethical and moral content, but there was no independent or impersonal viewpoint. Rather, the Kleinian inner world was a complex, three-dimensional, differentiated landscape of gratifying and frustrating, rivalrous and supportive, "part" and "whole" objects. The result, Klein claimed, would be "a new understanding of the unconscious and of internal relationships as they have never been understood before apart from the poets."

Finally, Klein's view implied a different diagnosis of the fundamental problem facing modern men and women. For Freud, the key problem had been to strengthen the ego so as to give the individual some freedom from the superego, from the demands of the id, and from society. For Klein, in contrast, the problem was to build up an internal world of whole objects, that is, to forge and sustain personal connections.

The predominance of the U.S. analysts after 1945, and the intolerance with which they treated Klein, meant that her thought remained isolated for a long time. After World War II, the Americans sponsored a revival of analysis in Europe, more or less as part of the Marshall Plan. Ego psychology, now understood as an American innovation, returned to Europe—an example of what has been termed the "pizza effect," the invention of some item or idea in Europe, its export to the United States, and its return to Europe as if it were American. The new or rebuilt European societies often followed the American lead, although there were many exceptions. In Germany, the real successor to psychoanalysis was the Frankfurt School critical theorists, especially Alexander Mitscherlich, whose *The Inability to Mourn* (with Margarete Mitscherlich; 1967) applied analysis to Nazism and German nationalism. The most important exception, however, was Lacan, who emerged with Sacha Nacht and Daniel Lagache as one of a troika that ran the reconstituted Paris Psychoanalytic Society and who found a way to make Freud a major figure in French thought.

Freud had described the ego as a psychical agency, originating in the systems of perception and consciousness, and serving the drives toward self-preservation and sexual release. Beginning with his famous "mirror stage" lecture, delivered to the IPA's Marienbad Congress in 1936, Lacan rejected Freud's characterization of the ego as an agent. Psychical development, Lacan argued, began not with agency but with primal lack, terror, or the emptiness of nonexistence. The "ego of narcissism," as Lacan called the "I," was a defensive response to the traumatic discovery of this emptiness, an imaginary construction, a "crystallization of images." Having no basis in the organism's instinctual drives, it was better thought of as an object than an agent.

Deriving his basic orientation from surrealism, which characterized the unconscious in linguistic and imagistic rather than instinctual terms, Lacan described the ego of narcissism as born into discourses, meaning unconscious, multivoiced, streams of associations governed by their own rules of exclusion, prohibition, and privilege. Examples of discourse include the "name of the father," the "desire of the mother," and larger, social discourses such as those of religion, nationality, and politics. Seeking to rescue the unconscious from the prevailing "confused, unitary, naturalistic conception of man," Lacan defended Freud's death instinct hypothesis as a reminder that "in man, there's already a crack, a profound perturbation of the regulation of life."

In his 1953 "Rome Discourse," a private lecture given to friends and associates in the midst of an official analytic congress, Lacan contrasted his notion of an ego adrift in discourse to both American ego psychology and British object relations. Emigration to America and "the absence of the social 'resistances' in which the psychoanalytic group used to find reassurance," he argued, had led ego psychologists to repress the "living terms" of analytic experience; they had become obsessionally preoccupied with technique, "handed on in a cheerless manner." And while the Kleinians had opened up important new areas, such as "the function of the imaginary" (phantasy), object relations (existential phenomenology), and countertransference (the analyst's transference), the naturalistic British emphasis on dependency and maternal care also vitiated Freud's discovery.

THE CRISIS OF THE 1960S

After the two world wars, the 1960s represented the third great crisis in the history of European psychoanalysis. The cultural revolutions of the 1960s—the New Left, the women's movement, gay liberation—were really attempts to act out and to politicize many of the questions of sexuality and personal identity that psychoanalysis restricted to the consulting room. Many attempts were made to combine psychoanalysis with Marxism; others criticized psychoanalysis for its sexism, homophobia, and medicalizing authoritarianism; and a host of new psychotherapies arose that promised to replace psychoanalysis, often drawing on its theories.

Lacan was the main European figure to survive the upheavals of the 1960s. Preaching a "return to Freud" he rejected the U.S.-dominated analytic establishment arguing that "l'analyste ne s'autorise que de lui-même" (the analyst does not authorize himself). One result was *le champ freudien*, the freeing of psychoanalysis from medicine, and its integration into the social, cultural, and lifestyle changes that characterized the 1960s. Claiming to replace René Descartes's *cogito*, or "I think," with *ça parle*, where *ça* meant language, Lacanianism articulated the growing sense that it was through media images and discourse, rather than the workplace, that social domination was secured; in other words, Lacan believed that language determined human actions, and not the reverse. By 1974, there were three important French analytic groups, each with its own journal: the official Société Psychanalytique de Paris (the aforementioned Paris Psychoanalytic Society; publisher of *Études freudiennes*), with nearly five hundred members, among the largest analytic societies in the world; Lacan's École freudienne (publisher of *Scilicet*); and the French Association for Psychoanalysis centered around Jean LaPlanche and Jean-Bertrand Pontalis (publisher of the *Nouvelle revue de psychanalyse*). New thinkers, such as Didier Anzieu, Piera Aulagnier, Janine Chasseguet-Smirgel, and André Green, expanded the parameters of both analysis and philosophy. In 1994, when official membership in the IPA was less than nine thousand, about three thousand of whom were North Americans, France boasted about five thousand non-IPA analysts, four-fifths of them Lacanian. Much of Lacan's influence was in the Catholic world—such as Italy, Spain, and Portugal—where the clerical establishment had successfully resisted the influence of analysis earlier.

The British Psychoanalytic Society also survived the 1960s but with nothing like the influence of the French. At the end of the war, the members had mooted their differences by forming three training paths taught by associates respectively of Klein (Group A), Anna Freud (Group B), and a Middle or Independent Group, which included such figures as D. W. Winnicott, Michael Balint, and W. R. D. Fairbairn. Often touted as a triumph of English rationality, moderation, and compromise, the solution had the effect of further marginalizing Klein's thought. The same centripetal tendencies that brought the society's members into a powerful but short-lived alliance during the war propelled them into disparate, centrifugal orbits afterward, its leading members turning to criminology, ethology, psychiatry, and the writing of memoirs. By the end of the century the still-vital British society had 405 members out of a population of 60 million: one of the thinnest ratios in the developed world.

The 1960s also produced a kind of normalization of the Jewish origins of and influence on psychoanalysis. For one thing, Jewish analysts had always refused to allow the IPA to meet in Germany. In 1985 they relented. An exhibit

illustrating the history of the Göring Institute dominated the meeting, held at Hamburg. A German analyst remarked, "Thank God that you have been willing to come; for forty years we have been living alone with our shame." Even so, the Jewish question remained symptomatic for some. Thus the English/Punjabi analyst Masud Khan's 1988 autobiography, *The Long Wait*, describes Khan exulting at throwing off his "Yiddish shackles," and complaining that the "Judaic-Yiddish-Jewish bias of psychoanalysis" had always cramped his "personal ethnic style."

Normalization progressed in other senses as well. In 1979 the profession founded an internal historical organization led by Alain de Mijolla, even as its larger history was being written by outsiders, such as Paul Roazen, Henri Ellenberger, Peter Gay, Michael Molnar, Elisabeth Roudinesco, Frank Sulloway, Alexander Etkind, and Carl Schorske. New journals, notably *Psychoanalysis and History* (first published in 1988), replaced hagiography with established methods of historical research. The British, French, and German societies built major research collections.

But what, actually, is meant by normalization? Perhaps more than many other histories, the history of psychoanalysis is punctuated by traumas: that is, by catastrophes that remain "actively vital and yet incapable of resolution." These include personal violations, misshapen lives, wasted years, destroyed documents, secret archives, forgotten lapses, and ruptures. Normalization has not unfolded smoothly. The most explosive example of this has been the attempt to understand the weak response of analysts to the Nazis and, indeed, to the Holocaust itself.

Prior to the 1960s, acceptance by the IPA had been taken as proof of a "place among the persecuted" for German analysts, thus allowing them "to escape from the burden of [their] national past." When activists of the late 1960s became analysts, however, that cover became subject to critical scrutiny. In 1980, at a conference at Bamberg, Germany the younger analysts exploded: "Who was your analyst?," "What were you doing?," "From what has come this feeling of mysteries, lies, the pathology of the reality sense?" Helmut Dahmer, Regine Lockot, Geoffrey Cocks, and others unearthed the history of the Göring Institute and the exclusion of Reich. In 1997 a leading German analyst, Werner Bohleber, explained the absence of important theoretical developments in post-1960s German psychoanalysis by the fact that German analysts remained so utterly preoccupied with their past.

The samizdat and other anticommunist movements that triumphed in 1989 allowed another broken cord of analytic history to be picked up. In the Soviet Union in 1979 Aron Belkin drew on analysis to explain the national malaise, suggesting that "identification with the Supreme Guide [Stalin] had crushed the family father figure, forced the individual to regard as diabolical any alternative . . . and eventually caused the death of thought." Eugen Kogan described "the obsessive identification with the father who had disappeared, the feeling of shame towards the father who had been deported or eliminated as an enemy of the people, and the solitude and wanderings of the son." Under Mikhail Gorbachev's program of glasnost (openness) starting in the mid-1980s, Freud's works were published in Russian for the first time since the early 1930s. Andrei Zagdansky's 1989 film *The Interpretation of Dreams* celebrated the event by counterposing readings from Freud's texts with archival film from Soviet history.

In its great days, European psychoanalysis had stood at the confluence of two distinct currents. One was scientific. Its most important point of reference was the Darwinian vision of the human being as an organism driven by internal needs that it sought to satisfy in specific environmental settings. This current expressed itself in the close relations between psychoanalysis and neurophysiology, for example, in the idea that the instincts were on the "border" between the soma and the psyche, or in the idea that the mind discharged tension or acted reflexively in ways that were similar to the nervous system. It also led to the view that such characteristics of the psyche as the developmental stages of sexuality, or the functions of the ego, were the product of a long evolutionary history, the continual adaptation of inner and outer realities.

The other stream was humanistic. Its most important expression had been the analytic focus on the moral struggle of the human being, a struggle that arose in relation to the parents and that ended in the confrontation with death. This stream drew on literary sources such as the Hebrew Bible and the Greek tragedians, on William Shakespeare, Johann Wolfgang von Goethe, and Fyodor Dostoyevsky, and on modernist literature and philosophy, even when psychoanalysis disavowed them; and it also responded to the need for an everyday or "folk" understanding of psychological life. Freud fused these two currents into an extraordinary new synthesis, neither wholly scientific nor wholly humanistic. What made this synthesis both coherent and compelling was the discovery of a new object: the idiosyncratic, meaning-saturated, morally inflected psychical life of the human being.

Always embattled, the psychoanalytic conception of the human subject had been drastically weakened during the 1960s. That project had drawn its strength from its ability to integrate its scientific and its humanistic currents. In the 1970s these currents parted ways. Psychoanalysis divided into two divergent projects, a quasi-medical therapeutic practice aimed at treating mental and emotional disorders and a set of new approaches to the study of culture. The two new projects—the "therapeutic" and the "hermeneutic"—underwent separate development. The scientific lineage of psychoanalysis gave way to neuroscience, brain research, and psychopharmacology, at first in the United States and then, more slowly, elsewhere. The humanistic and literary lineage gave way to cultural studies, feminist theory, "queer" theory, and to the study of identity, narrative, and representation. The ethic of self-reflection fell away entirely, as new versions of mind-cure "empowerment" triumphed. At the beginning of the twenty-first century, the future of analysis remained in doubt.

See also **Freud, Sigmund; War Neuroses.**

BIBLIOGRAPHY

Brecht, Karen, Volker Friedrich, Ludger M. Hermanns, Isidor J. Kaminer, and Dierk H. Juelich. *"Here Life Goes on in a Most Peculiar Way": Psychoanalysis Before and After 1933.* Hamburg, Germany, n.d.

Cocks, Geoffrey. *Psychotherapy in the Third Reich: The Göring Institute.* 2nd ed. New Brunswick, N.J., 1997.

Etkind, Alexander. *Eros of the Impossible: The History of Psychoanalysis in Russia.* Translated by Noah and Maria Rubins. Boulder, Colo., 1997.

Freud, Sigmund. *The Standard Edition of the Complete Psychological Works of Sigmund Freud.* Translated from the German under the general editorship of James

Strachey in collaboration with Anna Freud. 24 vols. London, 1953–1974.

Gay, Peter. *Freud: A Life for Our Time*. New York, 1988.

Grosskurth, Phyllis. *Melanie Klein: Her World and Her Work*. New York, 1986.

Jones, Ernest. *Body Politic*. Toronto, 1977.

King, Pearl, and Riccardo Steiner, eds. *The Freud–Klein Controversies, 1941–1945*. London, 1991.

Lacan, Jacques. *Ecrits*. Translated by Alan Sheridan. London, 2001.

Lieberman, E. James. *Acts of Will: The Life and Work of Otto Rank*. New York, 1985.

Paskauskas, Andrew R., ed. *The Complete Correspondence of Sigmund Freud and Ernest Jones, 1908–1939*. Cambridge, Mass., 1993.

Roudinesco, Elisabeth. *Histoire de la psychanalyse en France*. 2 vols. Rev. ed. Paris, 1994.

Sharaf, Myron. *Fury on Earth: A Biography of Wilhelm Reich*. New York, 1983.

Young-Bruehl, Elisabeth. *Anna Freud: A Biography*. New York, 1988.

ELI ZARETSKY

PUBLIC HEALTH. Public health refers to the science and practice of protecting and improving the health of a community through a variety of means, including preventive medicine, health education, control of communicable diseases, application of sanitary measures, and monitoring of the environment.

Although the sanitary movement of the mid-nineteenth century helped to lower death rates from enteric diseases, particularly cholera, epidemic disease remained commonplace throughout an increasingly industrialized Europe. Scholars therefore trace the modern era of public health in Europe to the late-nineteenth-century "bacteriological revolution" and to broader contemporary health programs initiated by state governments as they took shape during the last quarter of the nineteenth century. At the root of these programs was the realization among state leaders that proper maintenance of public health could help ensure social stability, prosperity, and order. Indeed, better public health could help to make healthier and therefore more productive citizens. The tension that existed in this rationale—namely the exercise of government authority to achieve community health, on the one hand, and the restriction of individual rights, on the other hand—is a recurring theme in the history of modern European public health programs, and it informs issues of public health in early-twenty-first-century Europe.

THE "BACTERIOLOGICAL REVOLUTION"
Led by the research of two scientific rivals—Louis Pasteur (1822–1895) in France and Robert Koch (1843–1910) in Germany—the emerging sciences of microbiology and immunology paved the way to substantial changes in thinking about the cause and transmission of disease.

Until the 1880s, the miasma theory of disease prevailed in scientific circles. This theory held that diseases such as cholera were caused by a noxious form of miasma, a term meaning "bad air," derived from the Greek word for "pollution." Through the therapeutic research of Pasteur and the bacteriological research of Koch, the germ theory of disease took shape, advancing the claim that microorganisms may be the cause of disease. Further breakthroughs by Koch, by his assistants Friedrich Loeffler (1852–1915) and Georg Gaffky (1850–1918), and by others who used Koch's methods of cultivating and isolating bacteria yielded identification of the bacteria responsible for diphtheria, typhoid, tetanus, and cholera. Such efforts, combined with further scientific and technical advancements, led to the introduction of the first generation of vaccines for use in humans, including those for rabies (1885), plague (1897), diphtheria (1923), pertussis (1926), tuberculosis (1927), tetanus (1927), and yellow fever (1935). Bacteriology also opened the door to better disease control among infected populations. State public health policies had long implemented quarantines and isolation to control the spread of disease. But with the advent of greater knowledge of disease-causing bacteria, authorities could exact a more targeted response to a disease outbreak, whether among travelers in rural areas or populations in dense urban centers.

The "bacteriological revolution" yielded a reaction that became integral to the further development of public health in Europe through the first two decades of the twentieth century. Even as deaths from infectious disease declined, deplorable health conditions remained for the working classes and urban poor. Contemporary commentators found the germ theory by itself to be insufficient in the promotion of better public health. Increasingly, socialists and radical physicians questioned the value of leaving community health to scientific thinking alone. Greater social measures, they claimed, such as improved diet, safe and hygienic living and working conditions, and health education, would prove equally if not more beneficial to improving community health. Across Europe, state governments and local municipalities reacted by initiating a variety of public health measures that sought not only to improve public welfare but also to protect and enhance government authority. Reform-minded voluntary health agencies joined the effort by reacting to the perceived failure of public leaders to address deplorable conditions among the working classes. As responsibility for the health of the public shifted from the individual to the government, such responsibility became a matter of politics and, therefore, an entitlement of citizenship.

THE RISE OF SOCIAL MEDICINE

The period from 1914 to 1918 and the decades following the "war to end all wars" mark complex chapters in the history of public health in Europe. Although social medicine was already under way before the war as a means to ameliorate various causes of poor health—or, in some cases, the *perceived* causes of poor health—it grew significantly from wartime experience and yielded uneven results across nations. Among the many conditions addressed in a variety of ways were infant mortality and maternal welfare, venereal disease and prostitution, and poor working conditions.

During the first two decades of the twentieth century, ubiquitous rates of infant mortality became major threats to public health. Child and maternal health programs therefore emphasized nutrition to counterbalance malnourishment, health education and inspection to correct parental ignorance and school environments, and hygiene to eliminate contaminated food. The pronatalist campaign emerged in France, while across Britain voluntary and local government sanitary societies taught hygiene to children. In Germany, Czechoslovakia, Russia, and Italy schoolteachers

taught children games, drills, and gymnastic exercises as means to stay healthy. Significantly, German concerns about the broader implications of child and maternal health, and no less reproductive hygiene, took on new meaning during the 1930s as Adolf Hitler radicalized what had earlier been a relatively moderate national eugenics movement. In Nazi hands, positive eugenics became a means to achieve a "pure" German race. "Racial hygiene" programs of the Third Reich included awards to "Aryan" women who had large numbers of children. These programs also involved impregnation of "racially pure" single women by members of the Schutzstaffel (SS), which formed the basis of the Nazi police state and was the major instrument of racial terror in the concentration camps and occupied Europe.

The interwar period also saw negative eugenics become a means to address concerns about child and maternal health and no less the health of the nation. Following its establishment in 1922, Sweden's National Institute for Race Biology sponsored research in social engineering that ultimately led to the forced sterilization of an estimated sixty thousand "unfit" men and women between 1936 and 1976. While Nazi eugenics programs offered rewards to certain people, they also involved forced sterilization of hundreds of thousands of men and women who were viewed as mentally and physically "unfit," compulsory "euthanasia" programs that killed tens of thousands of institutionalized individuals with disabilities, and the systematic killing during the Holocaust of millions of "undesirable" Europeans including Jews, Gypsies, and homosexuals. Such programs existed alongside extensive experimentation on live human beings to test Nazi genetic theories, ranging from simple measurement of physical characteristics to horrific experiments carried out in concentration camps.

Contemporaries also understood that venereal disease and prostitution threatened public health, especially during World War I. From 1914 through the demobilizations that extended into the early 1920s, military authorities of the major combatant nations used education and official entertainment as means to keep their soldiers away from liquor and local prostitutes, and therefore fit for service. In Britain, voluntary-aid organizations such as the YMCA and Salvation Army assisted in this effort by establishing distinctive "rest huts" on the home front and overseas where soldiers could enjoy hot drinks, hearty meals, and the company of "motherly" women volunteers. Based in part on prewar efforts to ameliorate living conditions of the urban poor, these "homes away from home" were intended to help preserve men not only for battle but also for postwar life as husbands and fathers. After the war, such efforts to promote abstinence gave way to a pragmatic acceptance that distributing condoms was a more effective means of controlling venereal disease.

Following World War I, poor working conditions and the poor health of laborers were also identified as threats to public health. This concern was perhaps most evident in the establishment of the International Labour Organization (ILO) in 1919 through the negotiations of the Treaty of Versailles. Adopted by the Paris Peace Conference in April 1919, the constitution of the ILO stated plainly that "conditions of labour exist involving such injustice hardship and privation to large numbers of people as to produce unrest so great that the peace and harmony of the world are imperiled." Politics and economy certainly drove the mission of the ILO, but so too did health and welfare. "The solemn obligation of the International Labour Organization," as its constitution concluded, was to "further among the nations of the world programmes which will achieve . . . adequate protection for the life and health of workers in all occupations; provision for child welfare and maternity protection; . . . [and] the provision of adequate nutrition, housing and facilities for recreation and culture."

POSTWAR EUROPE

Across Europe after World War II, spending on all aspects of public health increased in real terms as government leaders held that economic growth could emerge through welfare state programs that made citizens healthier and better educated. West Germany's welfare model took shape from roots in the late-nineteenth-century Bismarck Era, while France's social security system emerged from conservative politics and Britain's National Health Service did so from the Labour government and its minister of health from 1945 to 1951, Aneurin

Bevan. The hopes of the future did not come to pass, however. Even as the rates of infectious diseases and infant and child mortality in Europe reached unprecedented lows, economic growth slowed, making public health and medical programs more difficult to finance. Poverty, unemployment, and a host of new conditions placed increasing demands on welfare states. By the late 1960s, the purview of public health in Europe, and no less in industrialized nations around the world, had expanded to encompass chronic diseases (such as heart disease and cancer) and their causes (such as smoking), aging populations, disparities in health (because of race, ethnicity, gender, and occupation), obesity, and domestic violence. European state intervention in public health grew through the mid-1970s when economic crises of that decade required unprecedented cuts in public spending. Critics of the welfare state at this time claimed that its attempt to "provide for all" revealed a substantial failure to discriminate in favor of those in greatest need. This failure, critics argued further, had created a culture of dependency.

NEW CHALLENGES

In 2000 the European Commission issued the first coherent and coordinated strategy for a Europe-wide public health strategy. Adopted formally by the European Union in 2002, the program indicated three priority objectives: to improve information and knowledge for the development of public health; to enhance the capability of responding rapidly and in a coordinated fashion to threats to health; and to promote health and prevent disease by addressing health determinants across all policies and activities.

The commission's strategy, alongside those of individual European nations, helps illuminate the variety of public health priorities facing Europe in the twenty-first century. The foremost among these is how best to recalibrate the welfare state commensurate with promises of freedom and security, with economic and political constraints driven by European unification and interdependence, with the market forces unleashed by globalization, and, to be sure, with new, emerging, and changing threats to public health such as influenza, severe acute respiratory syndrome (SARS), West

Nile virus, and human immunodeficiency virus/ acquired immunodeficiency syndrome (HIV/ AIDS).

RECENT SCHOLARLY INTERPRETATIONS AND DEBATES

First published in 1958 and updated and expanded in 1993, George Rosen's *A History of Public Health* documents health regulation in Western societies from ancient Greece to the modern United States. It is a standard text that should be read by anyone who wishes to know more about the history of public health and understand recent scholarly interpretations and debates. Rosen's story is a chronological account of social progress arising chiefly from the technological advance of science and medicine in combating endemic and epidemic diseases. The growth of public health, Rosen argued, paralleled the rise of centralized government and was the result of scientific and medical knowledge triumphing over ignorance.

In the 1970s and 1980s, however, scholars substantially challenged the heroic interpretation of public health progress held by Rosen and his contemporaries. In his book *The Modern Rise of Population* (1976), Thomas McKeown agreed that modern medicine and public health had relieved suffering, but he argued that the decline of epidemic diseases, and especially those that affected children and young adults, stemmed not from the outcome of triumphant state medicine and public health programs but rather from better immunity resulting from better nutrition. In his book *The Great War and the British People,* first published in 1986 and revised in 2003, J. M. Winter advanced the paradox that while World War I and the mobilization of British society brought with it unprecedented slaughter, it was an occasion of substantial improvement in the life of the civilian population of Britain. Munitions canteens made food easily available to the nearly one million workers in munitions factories, rates of infant mortality declined, and rationing resulted in the healthy developments of scarcer alcohol; weaker beer; less consumption of sugar, butter, and meat; and more of consumption of bread and potatoes. Winter's book is a landmark study that deserves attention by anyone interested in wartime health, regardless of time period.

The 1980s and 1990s saw further challenges to and modifications of Rosen's interpretation. These new arguments were based largely on views of public health programs as instruments of social control through which elite society protected its power rather than emancipated the underprivileged classes from conditions that caused disease, famine, and poverty. Michel Foucault, for example, identified repressive discipline emerging from the centralized state and its clinics and hospitals. Other scholars of this period, including David Armstrong and Bryan S. Turner, recognized more broadly the inevitable tension that arises in the power of the expanding regulatory state, between individual civil liberties, on the one hand, and the collective needs of the community, on the other hand. Recent scholarship in the field, including work by Daniel Kevles, Paul Weindling, and others, has explored this tension in a variety of contexts, including eugenics, a case in which they show how rational and comprehensive public health planning can yield murderous public policy rather than freedom from disease and suffering.

Other scholars have revealed further complexities in the history of public health that depart substantially from Rosen's view. For example, no longer do historians see public health programs as being emblematic of or the result of centralized industrial government. In Germany, France, and elsewhere, local governments have at times exerted substantial local autonomy in matters of public health. Local studies, therefore, have been integral to recent scholarship, but so too have been projects that examine global public health, such as the new, emerging, and changing threats described above, and international agencies, such as the World Health Organization, that have attempted to work both within and across nations to achieve for all peoples the highest possible levels of physical, mental, and social well-being.

See also **Bevan, Aneurin; Eugenics; Welfare State.**

BIBLIOGRAPHY

Armstrong, David. *Political Anatomy of the Body: Medical Knowledge in Britain in the Twentieth Century.* Cambridge, U.K., 1983.

Brown, Theodore M., Marcos Cueto, and Elizabeth Fee. "The World Health Organization and the Transition from 'International' to 'Global' Public Health."

American Journal of Public Health 96, no. 1 (2006): 62–72.

Brunton, Deborah, ed. *Medicine Transformed: Health, Disease, and Society in Europe, 1800–1930.* Manchester, U.K., 2004.

Foucault, Michel. *The Birth of the Clinic: An Archaeology of Medical Perception.* Translated by A. M. Sheridan Smith. New York, 1973. Reprint, New York, 1994.

McKeown, Thomas. *The Modern Rise of Population.* London, 1976.

Porter, Dorothy. *Health, Civilization, and the State: A History of Public Health from Ancient to Modern Times.* London, 1999.

Porter, Dorothy, ed. *The History of Public Health and the Modern State.* Amsterdam, 1994.

Rosen, George. *A History of Public Health.* Expanded ed. Baltimore, 1993.

Sigerist, Henry. *Landmarks in the History of Hygiene.* London, 1956.

Turner, Bryan S., with Colin Samson. *Medical Power and Social Knowledge.* 2nd ed. London, 1995.

Weindling, Paul. *Health, Race, and German Politics between National Unification and Nazism, 1870–1945.* Cambridge, U.K., 1989.

Winter, J. M. *The Great War and the British People.* 2nd ed. Houndmills, Basingstoke, U.K., 2003.

JEFFREY S. REZNICK

PUBLIC TRANSPORT.

Urbanization and the attendant increase in population density in the confined space of cities, especially historic cities never designed for rapid transport, created ever more daunting challenges from the nineteenth century onward. City life and public transport had long been at odds: ancient Rome was already famous for its traffic jams. In the early twentieth century the issue of "traffic" was highlighted by the spokespeople of the modernist International Congresses of Modern Architecture (CIAM), who argued that the city met four main needs: living, working, self-cultivation, and transit. The expansion of cities was inseparable from the need for transport to carry a working population dwelling in ever more distant suburbs into and out of the center.

The growth of suburbs in the twentieth century produced a vast increase in commuter shuttling between central business districts and dormitory communities. European cities, however, afforded far less room for transit needs than their American counterparts (the Los Angeles model, for example). The Americans devoted roughly four times more urban space to transportation than the Europeans. The average European, whatever the mode of transport, traveled from two to four times daily. The highly mobile Americans moved about far more frequently. Mobility was naturally a function of many factors, not only socioprofessional considerations (senior managers traveled more than wage workers, the working population more than the nonworking) but also the size and geography of urban areas. Statistics show, however, that over time mobility related to work and to the organization of the workday increased less than mobility associated with leisure activities and social life. The level of dependence on the private automobile continued to rise throughout the century, while the increasing average speed (until congestion intervened) of both private and public transport made it practical for people to travel farther and farther from city centers. In the Paris region, annual family travel after World War II averaged 4,500 kilometers by private car, 800 kilometers on two-wheeled vehicles, and 800 kilometers by public transport. The average European daily travel time was approximately one hour a day. Unfortunately, travel was subjected to uniform time constraints, giving rise to immense rush-hour overloads that could ultimately be relieved only by a staggering of work hours. In consequence, cities and their transit systems were vulnerable to paralysis at certain times of day or in the case of exceptional events such as demonstrations, power failures, and storms.

THE RANGE OF CHOICES

Public transport alternatives to the dominance of the private car took several forms during the twentieth century.

Streetcars and buses The electric tram or streetcar emerged at the end of the nineteenth century as a means of decongesting town centers. After the First World War streetcars and various kinds of trolleybuses began, albeit very gradually, to give way to buses, which could maneuver their way through automobile traffic. The changeover was

Workers dig new tunnels for the expansion of the London underground railway, November 1937. ©HULTON-DEUTSCH COLLECTION/CORBIS

very slow, for there was little difference in running costs between the two transit systems in densely populated neighborhoods. The dismantling of tram and trolleybus networks accelerated in the 1950s.

Metropolitan railways The construction of underground metropolitan railways (which did not in fact run always or exclusively underground) in order to speed up mass transit and reduce street congestion began in large and medium-sized European cities before the close of the nineteenth century. These networks could transport between five and ten thousand people per hour. Their extension beyond city limits was not always a simple matter, however, and the Paris metro, for instance, was not extended into the suburbs until the years

between the two world wars. The cost was of course onerous, and generally only cities with a population of a million or more were able to undertake such a project. The greater the population density, the greater the expense for infrastructural work (often giving the advantage to the bus and sometimes to the tramway option). As a cost-saving measure, entirely automated trains became more and more common in the later twentieth century, while the number of service workers in stations was often drastically reduced in the interest of productivity. Closed-circuit television made it possible for engineers to monitor passengers getting on and off trains. Critics charged, however, that security was being given short shrift, and cited such incidents as the fire that caused thirty-one fatalities at the King's Cross station in London in 1987.

A musician plays in a Paris subway station, 1975. ©Owen Franken/Corbis

Suburban rail Peri-urbanization and its effects were a marked feature of the twentieth century. Public transportation systems effectively addressed the periphery/center axis, but travel between one suburb and another was by and large left to the automobile. Trains were the preferred way of getting to and from the city center. As suburbs spread outward, the traffic on such lines increased accordingly. The electrification of commuter networks helped make the trains more comfortable, but in many instances complementary systems were called for. In the Paris region, for example, older railroad lines were converted and new ones were constructed under the metro tracks in order to create a Regional Express Network (RER), opened in the 1960s, which speeded travel to and from suburban stations and the airports. It thus became possible for some three hundred thousand commuters to reach central Paris without changing trains.

THE REVERSAL OF THE 1970S

In most European countries, awareness of the deleterious impact of the automobile on urban space dawned around 1970. Hitherto cars had benefited from purchase prices that tended in relative terms to decline, from cheap gasoline, and from a very low level of public consciousness about environmental issues. Signs of crisis had nevertheless been visible for some time, as street-level public transport, essentially buses, began to suffer the effects of continual traffic jams and lose passengers. During the 1970s most European cities reacted with measures designed to encourage the further development of public transport.

The policy change of the 1970s was associated with the crisis of values reflected in the political events of the late 1960s, after which it was common to stress the limits of growth and the risks it held for healthy living conditions. The assumption that the automobile was king came under fire. By this time, in fact, a large proportion of journeys by car were no more than a few kilometers long, and the majority of them were unrelated to work. The economic crisis that followed the first "oil shock" in 1973 made the need for policy change seem

Passengers board an electric tram train in Gothenburg, Sweden, 2004. GETTY IMAGES

even more urgent. A shift in favor of public transport took place with strong government involvement. It was now viewed as essential that mass transit become more comfortable and more efficient in terms of service speed.

The solutions adopted varied from country to country. They included the building of metro systems, the reintroduction of streetcars, various extrafiscal ways of subsidizing commuter travel, and restrictions on automobile use. By the end of the century a good many cities had new streetcar systems that were quieter and more reliable than their predecessors. In Manchester trams made their reappearance in 1992, although the new network might as easily be described as a metro, because in some districts the cars run underground, as they also do in Brussels. Several French cities, among them Nantes, Grenoble, Bordeaux, and even Paris, chose streetcars over new underground railway lines on grounds of cost. These new tramways were of modern conception, however: they drew electric power from beneath, for example, thus eliminating

dangerous and unsightly overhead cables. Technological progress made it possible to improve not only the performance but also the image of hallowed forms of public transit. Several places, notably in Scandinavian countries, experimented with buses powered by liquefied natural gas (LNG), considered less polluting than diesel. Electric buses were also tried—small vehicles well suited to the narrow streets of the historic cities of Italy and elsewhere. But electric vehicles still had drawbacks, notably lack of independence and excessive weight. Meanwhile completely automated metro trains continued to evolve. Wireless communications networks could be expected to provide instant information to passengers waiting, say, at a bus stop. Monitoring of incidents or rush-hour dispatch management could be streamlined by means of GPS-type technology. Various kinds of "bimodal" trolleybuses and articulated buses might also be mentioned. The introduction of dedicated bus lanes on main thoroughfares did much to improve schedule speed.

The effects of the policy shift of the 1970s were felt over the long term. Bus ridership increased greatly, for example, and service speed picked up somewhat. The expanding urban periphery made cars ever more necessary for suburbanites, especially for intersuburban travel, yet measures taken in favor of public transport, such as the simplification of fare structures, bore much fruit.

SIGNIFICANT COSTS

The modernization of public transport and its diversification in response to new needs inevitably entailed considerable expense. Municipal governments devoted a large part of their budgets (often as much as 25 to 30 percent) to transport. In view of the financial outlays involved, local authorities rarely took direct responsibility for management; instead they delegated the organization of urban and peri-urban mass transit to private enterprise (under a variety of legal arrangements). As a result, large international transport concerns gradually emerged, operating across Europe and even beyond; the Connex group was a case in point, operating at once in Scandinavia, Great Britain, and France. At the same time, because of the massive scale of the infrastructure involved, the state frequently intervened in this structurally unprofitable sector, where, generally speaking, commercial receipts represented only a quarter of outlays, subsidies a further third, and private capital investment the remainder. In the 1980s Great Britain abandoned this model: the state gradually withdrew and left the field of mass transportation in the hands of the private sector. Other possible revenue sources were considered, from tolls on cars entering the city to taxes on drivers to support mass transit.

In the simplest terms, reducing the cost of public transportation depended far less on conserving energy than on economizing on labor. But more complex calculations were in order. The overall social cost of each particular mode of transport needed to be taken into account, for any reduction in automobile traffic meant a reduction in noise levels, air pollution, congestion, energy consumption, and security risks. The issue of air pollution due to motor vehicle emissions became more and more crucial as awareness grew of the danger of greenhouse gases. Once fully sensitized to the hazards of high concentrations of car-generated pollution, Europeans were receptive to such restrictions on automobile use in urban centers as park-and-ride plans for commuters, high tolls (London), pedestrianization in historic districts (Florence), or the establishment of bus-only lanes (Paris). The introduction of parking meters in the 1970s was an early attempt to discourage motorists from driving into city centers or staying there long; meters quickly spread to provincial towns. In France, Besançon was one of the first places to set up pedestrian zones.

Individual and collective awareness of the necessity of rationalizing the development of mass transit caused European governments to commit themselves politically and financially. There was a notable return to planning with respect to mass transit, a tendency endorsed by a largely urbanized population eager to remedy air pollution and improve the quality of life. By the end of the twentieth century it was apparent that public transport policy must not be allowed to trail behind urban development; on the contrary, the one had to be conceived in parallel to the other. The quality of transport systems became a public-relations priority for European cities.

See also **Automobiles; Railways.**

BIBLIOGRAPHY

Bairoch, Paul, and E. J. Hobsbawm, eds. *L'età contemporanea: Secoli XIX–XX.* Vol. 5 of *Storia d'Europa.* Torino, Italy, 1996.

Barker, T. C., and Dorian Gerhold. *The Rise and Rise of Road Transport, 1700–1990.* London, 1993.

CERTU. *Collectivités territoriales et transports publics urbains dans les États de l'Union Européenne.* Lyons, 1996.

Les chemins de fer en temps de concurrence (choix du XIXè siècle et débats actuels). Revue d'histoire des chemins de fer 16/17 (1997).

Gaillard, Marc. *Du Madeleine-Bastille à Météor: Histoire des transports parisiens.* Amiens, 1991.

Garbutt, Paul E. *London Transport and the Politicians.* London, 1985.

Giannopoulos, G., and A. Gillespie, eds. *Transport and Communications Innovation in Europe.* London, 1993.

Hughes, Murray. *Rail 300: The World High Speed Train Race.* London, 1988.

Merger, Michèle, Albert Carreras, and Andrea Giuntini. *Les réseaux européens transnationaux XIX-XXè siècles: Quels enjeux?* Nantes, 1995.

Mitchell, B. R. *International Historical Statistics: Europe, 1750–1993.* 4th ed. London, 1998.

Muscolino, Piero. *I trasporti pubblici di Roma: Notizie ed immagini dal 1845 ai nostri giorni.* Rome, 1987.

Schulze, Max-Stephan, ed. *Western Europe: Economic and Social Change since 1945.* London, 1999.

ALAIN BELTRAN

PURGES.

The term *purge* has a peculiarly ominous tone because it has been intimately associated with the terror in communist countries. In fact, historically it denotes two distinct political operations in the Soviet Union. One was a process whereby institutions such as the state bureaucracies and the Communist Party sought to expel (purge) those functionaries suspected of political deviation and professional incompetence: leftovers from the old regime, former members of non-Bolshevik political parties, political oppositionists, and others deemed politically unreliable or professionally incompetent. The other was political repression and terror, a purge of society in general from "enemies."

PURGE AS ROUTINE CLEANSING

The first process was not necessarily free from terror, but it was not meant to be a terror operation. It was most famously associated with the repeated "cleansing" operations within the Communist Party. Not dissimilar in kind from the exclusion of Nazi members from state institutions in postwar Germany or, in postcommunist Eastern Europe, of those associated with the secret police and political terror, the cleansings were meant to keep the party free from opportunists and other undesirable elements. Two specific factors made purges of the party inevitable. One is that whereas the party needed a broad mass political base and wished to broaden its membership, as it did first in 1917 when the party emerged from underground and expanded rapidly, it also had to maintain its political purity as a communist avant-garde party. The other is that the absence of pluralism and the system of one-party dictatorship necessitated purges.

Since those who sought political activity, even those who disagreed with the Communist Party, had nowhere else to go and therefore sought to channel the Communist Party from within in the direction they desired, the party appeared constantly diluted by subversives who had to be removed. Scholars of "totalitarianism" have developed an elaborate theory on the need for a "permanent purge" for maintaining the party's revolutionary élan by eliminating the corrupt and the deviant.

The constant purge process did not appear adequate to the party leaders when they decided on sudden and radical policy changes. Therefore the Communist Party resorted periodically to party-wide purge campaigns. Some early cases had already occurred in 1918–1919 when the party was deeply involved in the civil war against the counterrevolutionaries. The first major party-wide purge campaign took place in 1921–1922, when the party was forced by economic necessity to retreat from revolutionary war to peaceful economic reconstruction (the New Economic Policy or NEP) through a partial reintroduction of market relations. This purge reduced the membership by nearly a quarter. The purge was followed by a rapid expansion of party ranks in the mid-1920s, particularly after the death of Vladimir Lenin, the leader of the party, through special recruitment campaigns of workers. Toward the end of the 1920s Joseph Stalin emerged as the victor in the struggle for power among the party elite and, ending NEP, turned to enact his "revolution from above" (rapid industrialization and wholesale collectivization). This inaugurated another party-wide purge carried out purportedly to strengthen the party's "fighting capacity." This purge was enacted simultaneously with recruitment campaigns to further "proletarianize." Yet by 1933, when Stalin's "revolution from above" had confronted a grave crisis owing to widespread famine, recruitment was terminated and another party-wide purge was executed. The party leadership found that many formerly trustworthy functionaries were not in sympathy with the harsh economic and political measures taken to cope with the famine crisis. As a result, a very large number of party members fell victim to the purge. The 1933 purge still failed to satisfy the party leaders, who continued membership inspection in various forms for the next several years.

This process merged with the second kind of purge, terror and repression, in the mid- to late 1930s against the backdrop of the increasing threat of war. From 1933 to 1938 the Communist Party membership thus declined by more than 40 percent, from 3.5 million to 1.9 million (Rigby, p. 52).

The purge of the 1930s created a host of problems, starting with the chaos of bookkeeping and ending with the destruction of the lives of numerous loyal party members. So traumatic was the experience that Stalin, addressing the Eighteenth Party Congress in 1939, declared that although the purge campaign strengthened the party by expelling the politically unreliable, grave mistakes had been committed during the campaigns and that the party would have no need to resort to further mass cleansings. Indeed, such mass operations were officially abolished and were never to be repeated.

This did not mean that routine purges disappeared. They continued. Moreover, localized purges also took place in various areas of the country, for example, in those areas of the Soviet Union occupied during World War II (including the newly incorporated union republics such as the Baltic states), in order to purge the party of those members suspected of desertion, collaboration with enemy forces, and other crimes.

PURGE AS TERROR

Purge as political terror began immediately after the October Revolution. The new revolutionary government created a secret police (Cheka) soon after the revolution to fight the counterrevolutionary forces. During the civil war that followed (1918–1921), as many as 150,000 death sentences were given in the country. Even this figure is probably underestimated. During the relatively peaceful NEP (1921–1927), approximately 10,000 people ("political criminals") were sentenced to death by the secret police (from 1923, the OGPU). Stalin's "revolution from above," which marked a sharp turn from NEP and met resistance both from within the party and the government and from Soviet society in general, led to a sharp increase in the number of political death sentences meted out. In the four years from 1928 to 1931 more than 30,000 were sentenced to death in the country for political crimes (all data on terror here and later come from Popov, p. 28).

These numbers are merely the tip of the iceberg. During the four years of Stalin's "revolution from above" almost half a million people were arrested for alleged political and economic crimes (such as "economic wrecking"), most of whom were sentenced to prison terms or exile. It was at this time that the infamous gulag (soviet labor camps) expanded rapidly. In collectivizing the countryside, the party purged it of the kulaks (rich peasants), branded as "class enemies" (rural bourgeois), and their supporters. This dekulakization operation dispossessed probably more than three million peasants. In addition, in 1928–1932 more than ten million people fled the countryside to the city, a large number of whom did so involuntarily.

When the immediate goals of Stalin's "revolution from above" were achieved, the purge operation declined to a degree, as far as the number of death sentences were concerned—about seven thousand much lower than the previous few years. The number of arrests remained very high, however, amounting to close to half a million. This reflected the fact that Stalin used political purges as terror widely during the famine of 1932–1933 (which itself claimed several million lives). The famine crisis and the terror used to cope with it marked a new stage in the history of Soviet purge. Up until then, the main target of the purge was the "class enemy," but during the famine crisis the target began to shift subtly from the "class enemy" to the "enemy of the people." This new, class-neutral image of enemy encompassed virtually anyone, including tried and tested party members. The famous Soviet prosecutor Andrei Vyshinsky under Stalin noted in 1933 that having lost the battle, the enemy now resorted to "methods known as quiet sapping" rather than direct frontal attack and sought to conceal its wrecking acts with all sorts of "objective reasons," "defects," and the contention that the incidents did "not seem to be caused by malicious human intent." Therefore, Vyshinsky emphasized, the enemy "becomes less detectable and hence it becomes less possible to isolate him" (Kuromiya, 1988, p. 318).

This meant that mass purges were inevitable in order to capture hidden enemies, even at the cost of the innocent. Indeed, it was then, 1932–1934, that even Communist Party members began to be arrested in great numbers and even executed as enemies. It was then that, against the background of international threat from the east (Japan) and the west (Germany), foreigners, foreign-born Soviet citizens, and those associated with them came under suspicion and were purged in significant numbers. Thus, many individuals born in Harbin, Warsaw, Riga, Bucharest, and elsewhere were purged (executed) for their alleged foreign connections. Even party members who hailed from abroad (Koreans, Bulgarians, Poles, Ukrainians, Russians, and others) were subjected to the same fate. Numerous people (Poles, Ukrainians, and others) were arrested and executed for their alleged membership in "nationalist" organizations or in foreign (German, Japanese, Polish) "spy networks" (almost all of these accusations were fabricated by the secret police). The government began to collect data on all "suspect" national groups (such as ethnic Germans) in the country. All this paled, however, in comparison with what came to be known as the Great Purge (or Great Terror).

THE GREAT PURGES

There is no universally accepted consensus on exactly when Stalin started the Great Purge. Many concerned with Ukraine, which was hard hit by the famine and the purge in 1932–1933, contend that it began at that time. Some assert that it began with the murder of Sergei Kirov, the head of the Leningrad party organization, in December 1934. Some suggest that Stalin launched it with the first Moscow show trial in August 1936. Yet others attribute it to the summer of 1937 when indisputably mass terror operations began. Most scholars tend to agree, however, that the Great Purge virtually came to a halt by the autumn of 1938, when Stalin's chief executioner, the secret police chief Nikolai Yezhov, was removed from his post. In the four years from 1935 through 1938, nearly 2 million (in 1937 and 1938 alone more than 1.3 million) people were arrested. Of them, nearly 700,000 were sentenced to death (Popov, p. 28; Wheatcroft, pp. 129–135). Although these data are almost certainly incomplete, the two years of 1937 and 1938 account for 99 percent of these death sentences. The execution rate of the arrested was 44 percent in 1937 and 59 percent in 1938, whereas it was less than 1 percent in 1935 and 1936.

Who was purged? It used to be believed that the main victims of the purge were the Soviet elite. Most famously, the three Moscow show trials (held in 1936, 1937, and 1938) highlighted prominent Bolsheviks (such as Grigory Zinoviev, Lev Kamenev, Georgy Pyatakov, and Nikolai Bukharin), most of whom were executed immediately after their trials. While it is likely that the elite suffered disproportionately because of their visibility and their positions of responsibility, in fact "little people"—workers, peasants, and other "ordinary" Soviet citizens—accounted numerically for the majority of the victims, as became clear after the opening up of previously closed Soviet archives in the 1990s. Formerly repressed kulaks, criminals, ministers of religion, and other politically "undesirable" elements were specifically targeted by a special mass operation in 1937–1938 (the so-called kulak operation). Many others, such as the unemployed and the elderly, regarded as socially "unproductive" and dependent were purged along with other target groups. In some cases, even those already incarcerated were executed as if imprisonment were not enough. Similarly, specific national groups (particularly "diaspora nations" in the Soviet Union such as ethnic Germans, Poles, Greeks, Latvians, Koreans, and Chinese) were targeted for purge in special mass operations ("national operations") in 1937–1938. Many people who were associated in one way or another with those targeted groups of people were also purged. Although these mass operations initially had concrete numerical goals for arrest and execution, in the course of their implementation a competition-like frenzy by the secret police operatives, which in turn was sanctioned by Stalin, resulted in numbers that far exceeded the original goals.

The Great Purge represents the most violent aspect of the Soviet Union. Naturally it has been represented in various artistic forms, most notably in literature. Arthur Koestler, in his famous novel *Darkness at Noon* (1940), modeled his hero after Bukharin (an old Bolshevik who was executed in 1938), describing his capitulation to Stalin's bloody carnival as deriving from his own revolutionary ideology: his erstwhile fight against Stalin and refusal to totally capitulate were grave political crimes in the face of the dire threat to the very survival of the regime posed by foreign enemies

The funeral of Sergei Kirov, Moscow, December 1934. Acting as pallbearers are (from right): Joseph Stalin, Kliment Voroshilov, Vyacheslav Molotov, Lazar Kaganovich, and Andrei Zhdanov. Stalin used the murder of Leningrad party leader Kirov, which he may in fact have orchestrated, as one pretext for subsequent purges. ©BETTMANN/CORBIS

such as Germany and Japan. The poet Anna Akhmatova, whose family was destroyed by the Great Purge, wrote about it in a famous series of poems, *Requiem*. The poems were inspired by a nameless woman who, like Akhmatova, stood countless hours in the lines outside a prison in Leningrad. The woman "recognized" the famous poet and whispered ("everyone spoke in whispers there") into her ears: "Can you describe this?" Akhmatova answered, "I can." The vast majority of those purged in these years (and, for that matter, before and after under Stalin) have been rehabilitated since as innocent victims of Stalin's terror. Why did the Great Purge take place at all? There is much scholarly debate on this and there is no consensus. Some influential older theories, which explain certain aspects of the Great Purge well,

have proved inadequate to explain its extent: that Stalin wanted to remove all former oppositionists, particularly the old Bolsheviks who possessed a degree of independence of mind, or that Stalin wanted to replace old elite cadres with young ones. One new theory is that the Great Purge was part of a gigantic social engineering attempt. However, this fails to explain the concentration of the killings in just two years (1937 and 1938) and the necessity of killing rather than incarceration, let alone the implementation of the "national operations." Another theory is that Stalin indeed faced a growing internal threat in the country, especially from the "dekulakized" peasants and other repressed elements. Yet this interpretation has so far not shown whether the threat indeed existed or whether the threat had increased so much that

Stalin suddenly felt compelled to initiate mass purge operations. Yet another theory, which is not entirely new, claims that it was a preemptive strike against all real and imagined enemies who might pose a grave political threat from within in case of war from without. This, according to critics, fails to explain the social engineering aspects of the purge. So the debate continues.

It is noteworthy that Stalin and his henchmen such as Vyacheslav Molotov and Lazar Kaganovich never failed to defend the Great Purge as an absolute necessity even though some mistakes were made and innocent people suffered. Their justification was that without the Great Purge the country would have lost to Nazi Germany because the internal "enemies of the people" would have risen up against the Soviet government. It was the Great Purge that made it possible to secure the rear for war. Such a justification has been equally passionately disputed by many who claim that the country won the war against Nazi Germany not thanks to the Great Purges or Stalin's leadership but in spite of the Purge and in spite of Stalin.

How Soviet society reacted to the Great Purge is another difficult issue. Some appeared to support the terror against the "enemies of the people" without question, while others merely toed the official line. Many upwardly mobile individuals benefited from the purges, but there were also people who did question what appeared to be madness. Still, there were very, very few cases of open dissent, because even those Soviet citizens who did not believe in the actions of the government were intimidated or frightened and generally could not, or did not, try to understand what was happening.

AFTER THE GREAT PURGE

Purges did not cease with the end of the Great Purge. At reduced levels, they continued. The areas newly incorporated into the Soviet Union in 1939–1940 were thoroughly purged of "bourgeois" and other suspect elements. The war against Nazi Germany intensified the hunt for suspected spies, defeatists, deserters, and others, and after the war many people suspected of collaboration were purged. During and after the war Stalin questioned the political loyalty of certain ethnic groups (Chechens, Crimean Tatars, and others) and resorted to brutal ethnic cleansings by removing

them entirely from their native lands. All the Soviet POWs and civilian laborers repatriated from Germany after the war were carefully screened and many were purged. In western borderlands such as western Ukraine, where nationalist forces continued to fight a civil war against the Soviet forces into the 1950s, the purge operations were extraordinarily brutal. However, the Great Purge was not repeated. Even most of those Soviet citizens who took arms against the Red Army managed to survive in the gulag. Thus it was in 1950 that the gulag population reached its peak under Stalin.

In sum, whereas the purges devastated the entire nation, they served the political leadership well by removing suspect members from the Communist Party, the government, and Soviet society in general. The necessity for purges, which were conducted routinely and sometimes violently, stemmed in large part from the system of one-party dictatorship and the lack of political pluralism. Stalin's obsession with "enemies" made the purges an integral part of Soviet politics. The purges terrorized the entire country, both the elite and the ordinary people, affecting, in one way or another, nearly every family in the Soviet Union under Stalin. Although the purges were not necessarily unpopular, the majority of the population had no choice but to accept them and live on the terms dictated by the regime.

See also **Akhmatova, Anna; Bolshevism; Gulag; Soviet Union; Stalin, Joseph; Terror.**

BIBLIOGRAPHY

Primary Sources

Akhmatova, Anna. *The Complete Poems of Anna Akhmatova.* Translated by Judith Hemschemeyer and edited by Roberta Reeder. Updated and expanded ed. Boston, 1994.

Chuev, Felix Ivanovich. *Molotov Remembers: Inside Kremlin Politics: Conversations with Felix Chuev.* Edited by Albert Resis. Chicago, Ill., 1993. Very interesting memoir by a close associate of Stalin's.

Davies, R. W., Oleg V. Khlevniuk, and E. A. Rees, eds. *The Stalin-Kaganovich Correspondence 1931–1936.* Documents translated by Steven Shabad. New Haven, Conn., 2003. Collection of top-secret correspondence between Stalin and his close colleague Kaganovich, 1931–1936.

Getty, J. Arch, and Oleg V. Naumov. *The Road to Terror: Stalin and the Self-Destruction of the Bolsheviks,*

1932–1939. New Haven, Conn., 1999. A collection of important documents related to purges and terror.

Ginzburg, Lidiia. *Zapisnye knizhki. Vospominannia. Esse.* St. Petersburg, 2002.

Lih, Lars T., Oleg V. Naumov, and Oleg V. Khlevniuk, eds. *Stalin's Letters to Molotov, 1925–1936.* Translated by Catherine A. Fitzpatrick. New Haven, Conn., 1995. Collection of top-secret correspondence between Stalin and his close associate Molotov, 1925–1936.

Popov, V. P. "Gosudarstvennyi terror v sovetskoi Rossii, 1923–1953 gg. (istochniki i ikh interpretatsiia)." *Otechestvennye arkhivy* 2 (1992): 20–31. Contains and discusses very useful and important data on the statistics of terror.

Secondary Sources

Binner, Rolf, and Marc Jung. "Wie der Terror 'Groß' wurde: Massenmord und Lagerhaft nach Befehl 00447." *Cahiers du monde russe* 42, nos. 2–4 (2001): 557–613.

Brzezinski, Zbigniew K. *The Permanent Purge: Politics in Soviet Totalitarianism.* Cambridge, Mass., 1956. A classic totalitarian interpretation of purges.

Conquest, Robert. *The Great Terror: Stalin's Purge of the Thirties.* New York, 1968. One of the earliest and most exhaustive studies of the Great Purge.

Fitzpatrick, Sheila. "Stalin and the Making of a New Elite, 1928–1939." *Slavic Review* 38, no. 3 (September 1979): 377–402.

Getty, J. Arch. *Origins of the Great Purges: The Soviet Communist Party Reconsidered, 1933–1938.* New York, 1985.

———. "'Excesses Are Not Permitted': Mass Terror and Stalinist Governance in the Late 1930s." *Russian Review* 61, no. 1 (2002): 113–138.

Holquist, Peter. *Making War, Forging Revolution.* Cambridge, Mass., 2002.

Khlevniuk, Oleg. "The Objectives of the Great Terror, 1937–1938." In *Soviet History, 1917–53: Essays in Honour of R. W. Davies,* edited by Julian Cooper, Maureen Perrie, and E. A. Rees, 158–176. London, 1995.

Kuromiya, Hiroaki. *Stalin's Industrial Revolution: Politics and Workers, 1928–1932.* New York, 1988.

———. "Accounting for the Great Terror." *Jahrbücher für Geschichte Osteuropas* 53, no. 1 (2005): 86–101.

Martin, Terry. *The Affirmative Action Empire: Nations and Nationalism in the Soviet Union, 1923–1939.* Ithaca, N.Y., 2001.

Merridale, Catherine. *Ivan's War: The Red Army 1939–45.* London: Faber and Faber, 2005.

Naimark, Norman M. *Fires of Hatred: Ethnic Cleansing in Twentieth-Century Europe.* Cambridge, Mass., 2001.

Rigby, T. H. *Communist Party Membership in the U.S.S.R., 1917–1967.* Princeton, N.J., 1968.

Weiner, Amir. *Making Sense of War: The Second World War and the Fate of the Bolshevik Revolution.* Princeton, N.J., 2001.

Wheatcroft, S. G. "Towards Explaining the Changing Levels of Stalinist Repression in the 1930s: Mass Killings." In *Challenging Traditional Views of Russian History,* edited by Stephen Wheatcroft, 112–146. New York, 2002.

HIROAKI KUROMIYA

PUTIN, VLADIMIR (b. 1952), president of Russia.

Vladimir Vladimirovich Putin's rise to power was aided by little except his own talent and abilities, although his assumption of the presidency was facilitated by the attempt by his predecessor, Boris Yeltsin, to find a way of ensuring the continuation of reforms and his personal security. Putin was born into a family of workers in Leningrad (renamed St. Petersburg in 1991) and spent his early years in a communal apartment. Brought up as a street urchin, the young Vladimir displayed leadership qualities from an early age. At school he took a particular interest in history and literature. In sixth grade in 1965 Putin entered the Pioneers, quickly becoming leader of the class group, and entered the Komsomol organization two years later. Having unexpectedly chosen to enter a chemistry secondary school, he completed the last two years and left secondary school in 1970.

After an unsuccessful experiment with boxing, when his nose was broken, Putin took up the martial arts in the late 1960s. In 1973 he became a master at sambo and in 1975 in judo, becoming in 1976 the city champion. Putin traveled throughout the country as part of his team. As he has noted, "It was sport that took me off the street." Putin was a typical product of the Soviet Union of that era, no longer inspired by the ideals of communism but deeply patriotic. The Brezhnev era gradually turned into stagnation, and for Putin the idea of joining the security service (the KGB) appeared a way of serving the country while gaining a profession. Putin was never a dissident, although he was well aware of the failings of the system. He recounts how when in ninth grade (age sixteen) in 1968 he turned up at the reception office of the Leningrad KGB and was told that it did not accept volunteers but took only those who had done military service or graduated from college. It was a rather romantic representation of the work of the security organs that led Putin to the KGB, and even his parents had no idea about the visit.

In 1970 at the age of seventeen Putin managed to win a place in the highly competitive Law Faculty of Leningrad State University. In his fourth year at university the KGB invited Putin "to work in the agencies." He joined the KGB in the summer of 1975, training for a year before joining the First Department, monitoring foreigners and consular officials in Leningrad. As a KGB operative he also had to join the Communist Party (CPSU). In 1983 Putin married Lyudmila Shkrebneva, born in Kaliningrad in 1958. The Putins' two daughters, Maria (b. 1985) and Yekaterina (b. 1986), were named after their grandmothers. In August 1985 Putin was posted to the KGB office in Dresden. He had an undistinguished career in East Germany, working in "political intelligence" to recruit agents to be trained in "wireless communications," although Putin has insisted that his post involved political work rather than technical intelligence gathering. Mikhail Gorbachev's reforms in the USSR exposed Erich Honecker's hard-line regime in East Germany and the USSR stood by as Honecker fell in November 1989.

Putin returned to the Soviet Union in February 1990 faced with serious choices about his life path. He planned to study international law at Leningrad State University, but after a brief period there he joined the administration of the Leningrad mayor, Anatoly Sobchak (a former law professor), as head of the city committee for foreign economic relations. Putin resigned from the KGB with the rank of lieutenant colonel on 20 August 1991, the second day of the attempted coup launched against Gorbachev's reform communism by hard-line conservatives. During the coup Putin managed to reach an agreement with the Leningrad KGB that they would maintain their neutrality, and as a reward Sobchak subsequently appointed him one of three mayoral deputies. With the dissolution of the old order Putin's membership in the CPSU simply lapsed. Revealing strong administrative talents and loyalty he rose rapidly, and from March 1994 to 1996 he was first deputy mayor overseeing the law enforcement agencies and the media. Putin loyally stood by Sobchak as the latter revealed an inability to build consensus and was voted out of office in 1996.

Again Putin was faced with a career choice. He resigned from the city administration and entered the St. Petersburg Mining Institute, where he wrote a candidate dissertation. In June 1996 he entered the presidential administration in Moscow, at first as head of the general affairs department but thereafter rising rapidly: on 26 March 1997 he was appointed a deputy to the head of the presidential administration and head of the Main Control Administration (GKU). On 25 May 1998 he was appointed first deputy chief of staff responsible for relations with the regions, where he became acquainted with the situation in the country and headed the presidential commission drafting treaties on the division of responsibilities between the center and the regions. On 25 July 1998 he returned to the FSB (the Federal Security Service, successor to the KGB) as head, a job that he took on reluctantly. On 29 March of the following year he was given the additional post of secretary to the Security Council and thus became one of the most powerful men in Russia.

Meanwhile Yeltsin had been looking for an appropriate successor, and after a number of false starts he decided on Putin, observing his character traits, notably loyalty and single-mindedness. On 9 August 1999 Putin was appointed prime minister, only to be engulfed by a new crisis: the Chechen invasions of Dagestan and the apartment block bombings in Moscow and elsewhere. By the time that he assumed the presidency in late December he had gained considerable administrative, educational, and personal experience. On 26 March 2000 he won the presidency in the first round, and on 14 March 2004 he gained a second term following years of extraordinary popularity.

As leader Putin was a marked contrast to Yeltsin, fit and healthy, with a careful approach to policy making. His leadership was overshadowed by the second Chechen war, launched as a response to the invasions of Dagestan. The occupation of the republic was marked by atrocities on both sides, and Putin's attempt to "Chechenize" the conflict by appointing a former insurgent, Akhmad Kadyrov, as president was derailed by the latter's death in a bomb blast on 9 May 2004. Putin's second term was dominated by the problem of terrorism. He also clipped the wings of the oligarchs, insisting that business leaders should not stray onto the field of politics. As for the regions, Putin sought to reestablish the authority of the federal center through a reform of the Federation Council and ensuring regional compliance with federal laws and norms. In the economy Putin continued Yeltsin's push toward a market economy and international economic integration, above all by joining the World Trade Organization (WTO). However, to achieve this Putin reduced political pluralism and through a variety of administrative measures ensured a State Duma compliant to his will. Too often it appeared that Putin sought to achieve post-Soviet goals through neo-Soviet methods. In foreign policy Putin pursued a strongly pro-Western and Europe-centered policy. Putin was the first world leader to send a message of condolence and support to President George W. Bush following the 11 September 2001 terrorist attacks on the United States and made Russia part of the "coalition of the willing" in the war against terrorism. Relations with the European Union and individual European states became closer than ever before. Russia under Putin made a decisive civilizational choice in favor of Western-style modernization, but the technocratic-bureaucratic style in which this was achieved undermined the pluralism and democracy that has been characteristic of the West.

See also **Chechnya; Gorbachev, Mikhail; Russia; Soviet Union; Yeltsin, Boris.**

BIBLIOGRAPHY

Primary Sources

Putin, Vladimir. *First Person: An Astonishingly Frank Self-Portrait by Russia's President Vladimir Putin.* London, 2000.

Secondary Sources

Black, J. L. *Vladimir Putin and the New World Order: Looking East, Looking West?* Lanham, Md., 2003.

Herspring, Dale R., ed. *Putin's Russia: Past Imperfect, Future Uncertain.* Boulder, Colo., 2003.

Jack, Andrew. *Inside Putin's Russia.* London, 2004.

Kuchins, Andrew, ed. *Russia after the Fall.* Washington, D.C., 2002.

Lo, Bobo. *Vladimir Putin and the Evolution of Russian Foreign Policy.* Oxford, U.K., 2003.

Sakwa, Richard. *Putin: Russia's Choice.* London and New York, 2004.

Shevtsova, Lilia. *Putin's Russia.* Washington, D.C., 2003.

Truscott, Peter. *Putin's Progress.* London, 2004.

RICHARD SAKWA

QUANTUM MECHANICS. Quantum mechanics, which is primarily concerned with the structures and activities of subatomic, atomic, and molecular entities, had a European provenance, and its story is in some ways as strange as the ideas it espouses. Although the German physicist Max Planck (1858–1947) is often credited with originating quantum theory, and although this theory's fundamental constant, which ushered in the disjunction between macroscopic and quantum realms, is named in his honor, it was the German Swiss physicist Albert Einstein (1879–1955) who really grasped the revolutionary consequences of Planck's quantum as a discrete quantity of electromagnetic radiation (later named the photon). Ironically, Einstein would later distance himself from the mainstream interpretation of quantum mechanics.

The Danish physicist Niels Bohr (1885–1962), by combining the nuclear model of the atom with quantum ideas, developed an enlightening explanation of the radiative regularities of the simple hydrogen atom, but the paradoxes of his theory (for example, nonradiating electron orbits) and its failure to make sense of more complex atoms led to a new quantum theory, which, in its first form of matrix mechanics, was the work of the German physicist Werner Heisenberg (1901–1976), whose arrays of numbers (matrices) represented observable properties of atomic constituents. Heisenberg's matrix model was highly mathematical, unlike the visualizable models favored by many scientists.

However, in 1926 the Austrian physicist Erwin Schrödinger (1887–1961), basing his theory on a wave interpretation of the electron developed by the French physicist Louis de Broglie (1892–1987), proposed a wave mechanics in which he treated the electron in an atom not as a particle but by means of a wave function. Within a short time physicists proved that both matrix and wave mechanics gave equivalent quantum mechanical answers to basic questions about the atom.

Quantum mechanics proved extremely successful in providing physicists with detailed knowledge, confirmed by many experiments, of all the atoms in the periodic table, and it also enabled chemists to understand how atoms bond together in simple and complex compounds. Despite its successes quantum mechanics provoked controversial interpretations and philosophical conundrums. Such quantum physicists as Max Born (1882–1970) rejected the strict causality underlying Newtonian science and gave a probabilistic interpretation of Schrödinger's wave equation. Then, in 1927, Heisenberg introduced his uncertainty principle, which stated that an electron's position and velocity could not be precisely determined simultaneously. Impressed by Heisenberg's proposal, Bohr, in Copenhagen, developed an interpretation of quantum mechanics that became standard for several decades. This "Copenhagen interpretation," even though for some it was more a philosophical proposal than a scientific explanation, garnered the support of such physicists as Heisenberg, Born, and Wolfgang Pauli (1900–1958). But its unification of objects, observers, and measuring devices; its acceptance of discontinuous action; and its rejection of classical causality were unacceptable to such scientists as Einstein, Planck, and Schrödinger. To emphasize the absurdity of the Copenhagen interpretation, Schrödinger proposed a thought experiment involving a cat in a covered box containing a radioactive isotope with a fifty-fifty chance of decaying and thereby triggering the release of a poison gas. For Copenhagen interpreters, "Schrödinger's cat" remains in limbo between life and death until an observer uncovers the box; for Copenhagen critics, the idea of a cat who is somehow both alive and dead is ridiculous.

This and other quantum quandaries led some physicists to propose other interpretations of quantum mechanics. For example, David Bohm (1917–1992), an American physicist who worked in England in the period of American anticommunist hysteria associated with Senator Joseph McCarthy (1908–1957), proposed that Schrödinger's wave function described a real wave "piloting" a particle, and that the paradoxes of quantum mechanics could be explained in terms of "hidden variables" that would preserve causality. Einstein, who had been critical of the Copenhagen interpretation since its founding (he stated that "God does not play dice," and a mouse cannot change the world simply by observing it), proposed, with two collaborators, a thought experiment in which distantly separated particles could, if the Copenhagen interpretation were true, instantaneously communicate with each other when an attribute of one of them is measured. Einstein would have been surprised when, much later, this experiment was actually done and resulted in quantum nonlocal communication being verified. The paradoxes of this instantaneous "entanglement" have become largely accepted by both physicists and philosophers.

After the early achievements of quantum mechanics it was natural for physicists to attempt to unify it with the other great modern theory of physics, relativity. In the late 1920s the Swiss-born English physicist Paul Dirac (1902–1984) developed a relativistic wave equation whose significance some scholars compared to the discoveries of Newton and Einstein. The Dirac equation was not only elegant but it also successfully predicted the positive electron. Even though Dirac declared

that the general theory of quantum mechanics was "almost complete," the full union of quantum mechanics and general relativity had not been achieved. Einstein spent the final decades of his life searching for a way to unify his general theory of relativity and Scottish physicist James Clerk Maxwell's (1831–1879) theory of electromagnetism, and many theoreticians after Einstein have proposed ideas attempting to join together quantum mechanics, a very successful theory of the atomic world, and general relativity, a very successful theory of the cosmic world. Superstring theory is one of these "theories of everything," and its assertion that everything, from gigantic galaxies to infinitesimal quarks, can be explained by the vibrations of minuscule lines and loops of energy in ten dimensions has generated enthusiastic supporters as well as ardent critics, who maintain that the theory, though elegant, is unverifiable and unfalsifiable (and hence not even a scientific theory).

The British cosmologist Stephen Hawking (b. 1942) has brought his interpretation of quantum physics and general relativity together to deepen astronomers' understanding of black holes, regions of spacetime in which gravitational forces are so strong that not even photons can escape. Some optimists claim that the unification of quantum mechanics and general relativity has already been achieved in superstring theory, whereas pessimists claim that this quest is really attempting to reconcile the irreconcilable. As Wolfgang Pauli, Einstein's colleague at the Institute for Advanced Study, once said of his friend's search for a unified field theory: "What God has put asunder, let no man join together."

See also **Bohr, Niels; Einstein, Albert; Science.**

BIBLIOGRAPHY

Al-Khalili, Jim. *Quantum.* London, 2003. There have been many popularizations of quantum theory, and this illustrated vade mecum by an English physicist is a good example of the genre.

Mehra, Jagdish, and Helmut Rechenberg. *The Historical Development of Quantum Theory.* 6 vols. New York, 1982. Some historians of science, wary of the authors' uncritical approach, have expressed reservations about the nine books of this set (some volumes have two parts), but the massive amount of scientific, historical, and biographical material collected by the authors can be helpful if used judiciously.

Penrose, Roger. *The Road to Reality: A Complete Guide to the Laws of the Universe*. New York, 2005. In this comprehensive mathematical and historical account of scientists' search for the basic laws underlying the universe, an important theme is the exploration of the compatibility of relativity and quantum mechanics.

ROBERT J. PARADOWSKI

Vidkun Quisling (center, holding coat) talks with investigators beside a mass grave where Norwegian victims of Gestapo executions are buried. ©BETTMANN/CORBIS

QUISLING, VIDKUN (1887–1945), Norwegian "minister president" (1942–1945) during the German occupation.

Vidkun Quisling was born in an isolated area of Telemark in southeast Norway. His father was a well-read parson interested in old Norwegian history, a subject that greatly inspired Vidkun. He was deeply affected by nationalist feelings in 1905, when the Swedish-Norwegian union was dissolved, and became an officer with the highest marks ever from the military academy. As an aspirant in the general staff from 1911, he worked with Russian affairs. After missions as a military attaché, he was engaged in relief work in Russia with the Arctic explorer and national hero Fridtjof Nansen. At that time Quisling admired the Bolshevik Revolution. He offered both the still-revolutionary Norwegian Labor Party and the Communist Party his help in creating the Red Guards.

However, back in Norway in 1929, he had swung to the right. In an article commemorating the death of Nansen in 1930, Quisling declared his sympathies for corporative arrangements, religious norms, and elitist rule. He also paid tribute to "the Nordic race." In 1930 the Nordic Folk Awakening was founded, a tiny organization that can be seen as a forerunner to Nasjonal Samling (NS). Well-known landowners, lawyers, academicians, and the president of the Industrial League became members. Quisling was empowered to act as an executive committee on his own. The fascist principle of having a "führer" was thus adopted for the first time in Norway.

As defense minister in the Farmer's Party government (1931–1933), Quisling spent most of his time combating the labor movement. Harsh measures were taken against strikers, and he accused the Labor Party of treason and of collaboration with the Soviet Union. After the tumultuous years in government Quisling had become a well-known politician. He founded the NS in 1933, but its support in the election—2.2 percent—was a disappointment. The following year the fascist character of NS was strengthened: brown uniforms, the Nazi salute, a pro-German foreign policy, Quisling's unrestricted power, and anti-Semitism. The 1,700 Jews in Norway were described as a threat to the Nordic race. But Quisling failed this time also, with the local elections in 1934 and the parliament elections in 1936 being clear setbacks. While the main enemy, the Labor Party, formed a coalition government with the Farmer's Party in 1935, NS went into the political wilderness. Many leading figures left the party. Right up to the German occupation in 1940, Quisling was an isolated extremist with an insignificant group of followers.

Quisling's most important allies in Berlin were the Nazi ideologist Alfred Rosenberg and the head of the navy, Erich Raeder. Not before 1939 did Hitler pay any real attention to him. When they met in December 1939, Hitler was influenced by Quisling's firm belief that Norway would not uphold its neutrality against Great Britain. Quisling wanted to gain support for a coup d'état in Norway, but he was not informed of Operation Weserübung, the German invasion of Norway and Denmark on 9 April 1940. After the invasion Quisling proclaimed himself head of the government but was soon removed by the Germans. However, in February 1942 Quisling was appointed "minister president" by the real man in power, the Reich commissioner Josef Terboven.

Quisling's efforts to Nazify Norwegian society were strongly resisted by the church, the teachers, and other professional and industrial organizations. Later on sabotage and the shooting of collaborators also occurred. The membership of NS rose to 43,000 in 1943, far from the proclaimed goal of 100,000. Quisling was totally dependent on Terboven, and he contributed to the recruitment of young Norwegians to the eastern front and to the deportation of Norwegian Jews. Quisling was so alienated from public opinion that he thought he would be allowed to negotiate with the resistance after the German capitulation in May 1945.

Instead, he was arrested as a common criminal and tried, accused of treason in accordance with civil and military law. His lawyer asserted that Quisling had aimed to rescue the country from warfare while the king and the government had left their duties, but Quisling was sentenced to death and executed in the old fortress Akershus in Oslo on 24 October 1945.

The term *quisling* as a synonym for *traitor* was introduced by a Swedish journalist in April 1940. As an insult the term has gained worldwide currency. However, in Norway the historical person Quisling is still a living memory, and therefore *quisling* usually means a Norwegian collaborator during the war or refers to Quisling himself.

See also **Collaboration; Norway; Occupation, Military; World War II.**

BIBLIOGRAPHY

Dahl, Hans Fredrik. *Quisling: A Study in Treachery.* Cambridge, U.K., 1999.

Hoidal, Oddvar K. *Quisling: A Study in Treason.* Oxford, U.K., 1989.

TORBJÖRN NILSSON

RACIAL THEORIES. Racial theories are attempts at defining social collectivities (classes, political groups, nations, conglomerates of nations) by linking them, through hereditary principles, to their origins. Even if these hereditary principles may be interpreted in "spiritual" terms, the concept of race does imply at least an implicit reference to biological notions. From biologism racial theories borrow their essentialist overtones, although some of them may stress the importance of environmental factors in the genesis and evolution of races. Because they do not necessarily impose hierarchies on these biologically defined collectivities, racial theories are not by definition racist. Conversely, many forms of racism are based on racial stereotypes rather than on racial theories. Finally, the use of the word *race* is not an indispensable condition for racial theories. All the elements implied in the definition above can also be present alternatively in concepts such as folk (*Volk*), ethnicity, or even culture.

NINETEENTH-CENTURY ORIGINS

In their modern form, racial theories originate in the nineteenth century, as the result of a conflation of the positivist urge to apply the methods of the natural sciences to the study of humankind, and the Romantic urge to stress the differences between (groups of) peoples against the universalistic claims of Enlightenment. As such, racial theories offered a modern legitimization to mostly premodern forms of inequality and difference. Particularly the newly

created science of physical anthropology provided the criteria and the tools "objectively" to subdivide humans into biological groups (cephalic indexes, skin pigmentation, and eye colors). More often than not, these physical measurements turned out to confirm preexisting linguistic, religious, or cultural differences. Nonetheless, by the last decades of the nineteenth century, nearly all human, behavioral, and biomedical sciences adopted race as a primary explanatory concept.

If a "scientific" approach to the concept of race was first of all used to legitimize social differences (Joseph-Arthur de Gobineau; 1816–1882) or differences between political tendencies (Augustin Thierry; 1795–1856), after the Franco-Prussian War (1870–1871) it was predominantly used to define entire nations and to harden the boundaries between them. From that same period onward, linguistic, cultural, and/or religious markers of "European" identity became racialized, which also made older stereotypes of "non-European" peoples into scientific "facts." The racialization of the primarily linguistic concept of the Aryans (those peoples speaking Indo-European languages and who were now deemed to descend from some Caucasian people) was crucial to the rise of modern, biological anti-Semitism. In the description of the colonized peoples, too, inherently universalistic discourses of the European civilizing mission gave way to racial categorizations.

Next to a tool for the demarcation of nations, race also became one for their homogenization. The idea that each nation had to rest on a racial core automatically entailed the idea that this core had to remain strong and pure and therefore had to be defended against "degeneration." An important line of thought within the late-nineteenth-century science of eugenics stressed that the mixing of races was at least one of the causes of degeneration and therefore had to be prevented.

EVOLUTIONS OF RACIAL SCIENCE, 1914–1950

By the first decades of the twentieth century, race as a scientific concept seemed to be at its retreat. One-time defenders of the concept now came to the conclusion that the search for biological origins was more complex than expected and did very little to explain social or political differences. Rather than to the total demise of the concept, however, this evolution contributed to its transformation into a cultural or even metaphysical category—as in the case of Ludwig Gumplowicz (1838–1909) and Houston Stewart Chamberlain (1855–1927)—and to a greater allowance for environmental determinants. Even those who explicitly rejected the concept of race—such as the American anthropologist Franz Boas (1858–1942), the British biologist Julian Huxley (1887–1975), or the German Catholic eugenicist Hermann Muckermann (1877–1962)—could not free themselves from its essentialist substrate. If the concept of race within western European academic circles was no longer generally accepted as a primary key to the understanding of humankind, the idea that nations or ethnic groups rested at least partly on a biological substratum remained widely accepted within scientific and intellectual discourses. The late-nineteenth-century subdivision of the European population into three subspecies of the Caucasian race (Nordic or Teutonic, Celtic-Alpine, and Mediterranean—with the Dinaric race most often considered to be a variant of the last) remained a part of the European self-understanding until well into the twentieth century. Within every nation, specific variations on this general theme existed, whereas in some of them, alternative racial theories were elaborated—for instance in the "non-Aryan" countries Hungary and Finland, where racial affinities with either the Turks or the Mongols were construed. Ethnic categories continued to play an important part in sciences such as "national psychology," folklore studies, art history, and literary history.

Only in countries where the autonomous evolution of science was impeded by authoritarian and nationalistic state policies, the concept of race was reinstalled as a key-concept in the human sciences. More overtly than nineteenth-century racial science, the official racial ideologies of twentieth-century totalitarian regimes were aimed at legitimizing national unity and superiority. In Nazi Germany, Hans Günther's *Rassenkunde des deutschen Volkes* (1922; Ethnology of the German people) provided the basic text underpinning the thesis that the Germans represented the purest breed of the superior Nordic race. An even more striking example of the political malleability of racial science is offered by Fascist Italy. If racial theories had played a marginal role in that country during the 1920s, the national-socialist idea of Nordic superiority was adopted after 1933, until Benito Mussolini (1883–1945) switched, in 1939, to the theory that the Italians predominantly belonged to the Mediterranean stock. The alliance with Nazi Germany compelled him, however, to return to a spiritual "Nordicism," whose main theorist was Julius Evola (1898–1974).

THE POLITICAL IMPLICATIONS OF RACIAL THEORIES, 1914–1950

In spite of their scientific claims, racial theories during the twentieth century served nearly inevitably as legitimizations of political causes. Most of all, they underpinned the general idea that the boundaries of the state had to coincide with those of an ethnically defined nation. This premise had important consequences both on international European politics and on the internal politics of many European states.

At the level of international politics, racial theories strengthened the claims for a geopolitical reorganization of Europe on an ethnic basis, as a necessary antidote against the Great Power imperialism that had led to the First World War. The principle of national autodetermination, which lay at the basis of the Paris Peace Treaties (1919–1920) implied that ethnolinguistic criteria were recurred to in order to redraw the map of Europe. This same concept—with an often implicit racial foundation—could however also be used as a justification for irredentist claims endangering the tenuous equilibrium of those same Paris Treaties. Although many of these irredentist claims remained primarily founded on historical and linguistic claims,

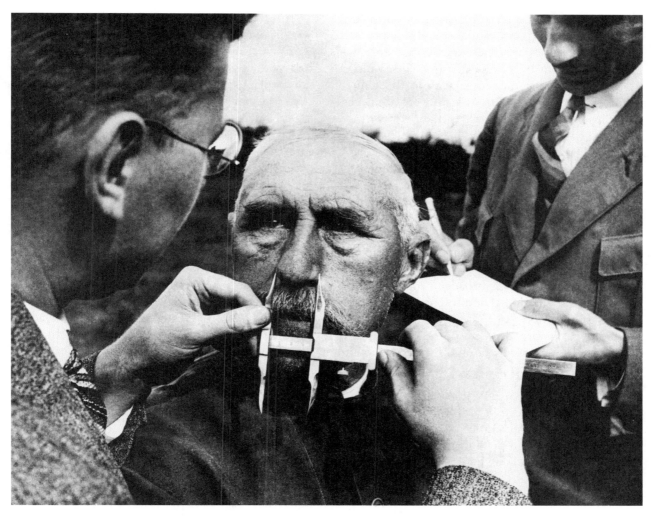

Nazi officials take facial measurements to determine a man's racial descent c. 1941. ©Hulton-Deutsch Collection

they were now strengthened and, to some degree, altered by racial theories. The reference to biological origins and "ethnographic" affinities made it possible to stretch a nation's ambitions to territories to which it did not have clear linguistic or historical connections. This was, for example, the case with the Greater Serb imperialism (whose ethnic legitimization was provided first and foremost by the geographer Jovan Cvijic), as well as with the claims Bulgarian nationalists laid on Macedonia (whereas the Greek claims on that same territory were based on religious and historical arguments). The best illustration of this evolution is, however, provided by the history of German annexationist ideas. Nineteenth-century pan-Germanism had primarily been a Romantic movement aspiring to close political ties between linguistically kindred nations. After the First World War, on the contrary, a large-scale scientific quest was being set up in Germany to legitimize a revision of the Treaty of Versailles by laying bare archaeological, toponymical, prehistorical, ethnological, and anthropological evidence of the Germanic elements across the boundaries of Germany. From the late 1920s this evolved into a very broad project of *Ostforschung* and *Westforschung*, studying the "ethnic history" of large parts of eastern and western Europe. Although this was certainly not the explicit intention of all scientists involved, these projects evidently helped to legitimize Nazi annexationism during the Second World War.

At the level of internal politics, the urge to create ethnically homogeneous nation-states could result in very different measures. The role of racial theories in the elaboration of stringent nationality and immigration laws was certainly important, though rarely explicit. The eugenic measures that were taken in many northern European countries (inspired by similar measures taken in the United States) from the late 1920s onward were not necessarily inspired by racial ideas. In the Swedish case, though, racial motives did play a role (it was because the so-called Tattare were allegedly a degenerate race of Swedish-Gypsy miscegenates that they were subjected to eugenic measures). It was, however, in Germany above all that eugenics was considered, already since the Weimar years, from the viewpoint of "racial hygiene." The Nuremberg Law of September 1935, prohibiting the intermarriage between Aryans and Jews, was but one part of a much broader program of purification of the nation that also entailed the compulsory sterilization (1933) and medical killing of all those that were deemed to be unfit for the German race. The collaboration of the medical professions to this program was overwhelming.

As such, eugenics policies could turn into a defense of ethnic cleansing, although this word is generally used to refer to the systematic removal of an entire people—and of all its traces—from a concrete territory. That this could be considered, in the wake of the Paris Treaties, as a nearly legitimate procedure of nation-building, was again due to the racial and essentialist logic behind it, even if it was most often legitimized by linguistic or historical arguments. In a racialist scheme, the assimilation of minority groups appears as an impossibility. Not surprisingly, it was the Swiss anthropologist Georges Montandon (1879–1944) who, in 1915, proposed massive resettlements of populations as the solution to the "nationality problem." Montandon would later become one of the driving forces behind the anti-Semite politics of the Vichy regime.

The same racial logic stands necessarily behind genocide, the ultimate form—and often the logical outcome—of ethnic cleansing. Thus, the mass murder of the Armenians by the Turks in 1915 found its ultimate rationale in the racially based pan-Turanic myth of the latter, just as the judeocide of the Second World War can only be explained by the Nazis' dream of an Aryanized Europe.

In the war policy of the German National Socialists, the consequences of racial thought both on international and on internal politics were carried to their extremes. Nazi imperialism cannot be fully explained with reference to irredentist motives or to Machiavellian great power politics but was the logical outcome of National Socialism's racist and social Darwinist premises and its intent to restructure the map of Europe along ethnic lines. The occupation policies that were followed in the conquered territories highly differed according to the racial qualities that were attributed to their populations (colonization and enslavement of the Slavonic, military occupation of Romanized Celtic, direct Nazification of Germanic territories), whereas the whole of Europe had to be systematically freed from all non-Aryan elements (Jews and Gypsies), and the racial qualities of the Germanic peoples themselves had to be enhanced through active eugenics and population politics. The internal differences that existed between different Nazi-ideologues concerning the question of race seemed to alter little to the broad consensus on this simple scheme.

AFTER THE SECOND WORLD WAR: RACE TRANSFORMED INTO CULTURE

The war effort of the Allies was only marginally motivated by antiracist concerns, and in the postwar trials a clear difference was made between the scientists directly involved in genocide and those racial theorists who had provided its scientific backgrounds. Most of the latter continued their professional careers in postwar Germany but diverted their focus from the study of races to either that of cultures (in the human sciences) or that of human genetics and population policies (in the biomedical sciences). After the discovery of the death camps, indeed, the previously existing critiques of the concept of race were bolstered, causing the concept to lose its credibility in the European scientific discourse. Nonetheless, the essentialist notions implied in the concept of race seem to have been largely transmitted to more "idealist" notions of culture and ethnicity. These gained a central position in the cultural relativism defended by anthropologists such as Ruth Benedict (1887–1948) and Claude Lévi-Strauss (b. 1908), but also in the interpretative framework of postwar prehistorians, archaeologists, and ethnologists.

That the logic of racial thinking did not immediately disappear after the end of the war became clear from the fact that during the 1940s ethnic cleansing remained a respectable way of dealing with political problems, both in central Europe and in the Soviet Union. The beginning of the Cold War, however, would highly diminish the need for national self-assertion and therefore also the political functionality of racial theories. Not surprisingly, the end of the Cold War witnessed a return of racial theories both at the scientific and the political level. Western Europe, with its relatively stable nation-states and its highly regulated class-relations, seems to be reticent to lift the taboo on explicit racial theories, as can be concluded from the hostile reception of American research on the relationship between race, intelligence, and behavior (most notably Richard Herrnstein and Charles Murray's *The Bell Curve,* 1994). Nonetheless, the more restrictive immigration politics in most Western European countries during the 1990s have been accompanied by growing research into the relationship between ethnicity and unaccepted behavior. In the Balkans, the resurgence of ethnic nationalism entailed a resurfacing of older ethnopsychological theories such as those by Jovan Cvijic and Dinko Tomasic explaining the differences between the Yugoslav peoples as differences between Dinaric "highlanders" and non-Dinaric "lowlanders." Even if these differences are explained in geographical and historical rather than in biological terms (whereas for the demarcation between the Greeks and the Albanians cephalic indexes are being recurred to), in their essentialism they owe much to the history of racial thought.

See also **Anti-Semitism; Eugenics; Fascism; Nazism.**

BIBLIOGRAPHY

Beyen, Marnix, and Geert Vanpaemel, eds. *Rasechte wetenschap?: Het rasbegrip tussen wetenschap en politiek vóór de Tweede Wereldoorlog.* Leuven, Belgium, 1998.

Bošković, Aleksandar. "Distinguishing "Self" and "Other": Anthropology and National Identity in Former Yugoslavia." *Anthropology Today* 21, no. 2 (April 2005): 8–13.

Broberg, Gunnar, and Nils Roll-Hansen, eds. *Eugenics and the Welfare State: Sterilization Politics in Norway, Sweden, Denmark, and Finland.* East Lansing, Mich., 1996. 2nd ed., 2005.

Carmichael, Cathie. *Ethnic Cleansing in the Balkans: Nationalism and the Destruction of Tradition.* London and New York, 2002.

Colander, David, Robert E. Prasch, and Falguni A. Sheth, eds. *Race, Liberalism, and Economics.* Ann Arbor, Mich., 2004.

Eickhoff, Martijn, Barbara Henkes, and Frank van Vree, eds. *Volkseigen: Ras, cultuur, en wetenschap in Nederland, 1900–1950.* Zutphen, Netherlands, 2000.

Ernst, Waltraud, and Bernard Harris, eds. *Race, Science, and Medicine, 1700–1960.* London and New York, 1999.

Gillette, Aaron. *Racial Theories in Fascist Italy.* London, 2002.

Hannaford, Ivan. *Race: The History of an Idea in the West.* Baltimore, Md., and London, 1996.

Kohn, Marek. *The Race Gallery: The Return of Racial Science.* London, 1995.

Malik, Kenan. *The Meaning of Race: Race, History, and Culture in Western Society.* London, 1996.

Mosse, George. *Towards the Final Solution: A History of European Racism.* London, 1978.

Naimark, Norman M. *Fires of Hatred: Ethnic Cleansing in Twentieth-Century Europe.* Cambridge, Mass., and London, 2001.

Stone, Dan. "Race in British Eugenics." *European History Quarterly* 31 (2001): 397–425.

Turda, Marius. "Fantasies of Degeneration: Some Remarks on Racial Antisemitism in Interwar Rumania." *Tr@nsit: Europäische Revue,* 2003. Available at http://www.iwm.at.

———. *The Idea of National Superiority in Central Europe, 1880–1918.* Lewiston, N.Y, 2005.

———. "Small States, Big Ambitions: Debating Nation and Irredentism in the Balkans, 1890–1920." In *Statehood before and beyond Ethnicity,* edited by Linas Eriksonas and Leos Müller, 275–301. New York, 2006.

Weindling, Paul. *Health, Race, and German Politics between National Unification and Nazism, 1870–1945.* Cambridge, U.K., 1989.

MARNIX BEYEN

RACISM. Racism is an ideology that holds the human species is composed of discrete subpopulations or "races" whose distinctive traits are attributable to common ancestry, and that so-called races are characterized by different and unequal physical and mental endowments; racism can also refer to related exclusionary and discriminatory practices, and their effects. While the term *racism* dates to the anti-Nazi struggles of the 1930s, racist ideology and practice emerged earlier in the context of European colonialism and slavery. While race may appear to be an undeniable characteristic of individual persons, scholars have demonstrated that racial categories themselves are cultural products rather than accurate reflections of biology. Racism finds multiple expressions, from individual talk and thought to political mobilization to government intervention. Because it views biology and culture as inextricably linked, racist ideology invokes an idealized nation and makes appeals to the state. Finally, as a theory of history, a prescription for relations between races, and an agenda for the future, racism as ideology and practice must be understood in the context of political and economic competition. The history of racism in Europe since 1914 clearly demonstrates that: (1) racial classification is a contested and variable process, (2) racist thought and action takes many forms, (3) racism and nationalism are closely linked and that the most forceful racist movements rely on state power, and (4) racism is a means and by-product of domination and conflict.

UNIVERSALITY OF RACE AND RACISM IN THE EARLY TWENTIETH CENTURY

Race was a term used quite loosely in the early twentieth century. The term could refer to the major divisions (black, brown, red, yellow, white) of the species identified by Johann Friedrich Blumenbach in the late eighteenth century, to regional subpopulations, or even to nationalities, linguistic families, coreligionists, or economic classes. Various physical features and even psychological dispositions, assumed to be ancient and unchanging, were identified as racial traits. While some maintained that pure races still existed, most scholars described contemporary populations as composed of a mixture of racial elements. Europeans, for example, were commonly said to represent a mixture of long-headed, fair-haired Nordics; round-headed Alpines; and long-headed, brunette Mediterraneans.

Racist hierarchies generally accompanied racial classification. In an age in which Europeans dominated the globe, science promised to reveal the laws of nature, and political and economic might

were viewed as evidence of evolutionary fitness, the physical and mental superiority of whites over non-whites, and of rich over poor, was widely accepted as indisputable fact. While there was broad agreement that culture and heredity were linked, opinion differed as to the nature of the connection. Those who saw environment shaping human potential argued that education could exercise a beneficial effect on the less fortunate. For those who maintained that biology was destiny, the intrinsic superiority of whites justified colonialism and the appropriation by force of others' labor, resources, and territories. The constraints imposed by nature meant that nonwhites should not experience the same opportunities for education and self-governance enjoyed by whites. Advocates of Nordic supremacy likewise attributed the noblest elements of European civilization to ancient warriors and claimed special privileges for their descendants. A similar line of argument held that within European society workers and minorities were destined to serve the upper classes, who ruled by virtue of superior blood.

This line of reasoning found scientific expression in the eugenics movement. The goal of eugenics, a term coined by Francis Galton in 1883, was the improvement of the human species through selective breeding. Galton claimed that mental ability was a fixed, measurable entity, and that heredity shaped behavior in a simple and direct fashion. The key to improving the English population therefore lay in promoting beneficial traits by encouraging childbirth among the more able and in suppressing deleterious traits by preventing childbirth among the less able. According to Galton, Christian charity and government assistance for the poor, handicapped, and mentally ill were misguided because they stifled the competition that defined evolutionary success.

Eugenics quickly gained institutional recognition and, in the United States and Germany especially, political support. The rediscovery in 1900 of Gregor Mendel's research on genetics appeared to validate Galton's claims, as did August Weismann's theory of an immutable "germ plasm" of hereditary material. The first International Eugenics Conference was held in 1912, and for the next thirty years eugenicists figured prominently in genetic research and intelligence testing, and they

Nordamerikas Kulturträger an der Westfront

Unter den Gefangenen der ersten Tage der deutschen Offensive im Westen
befanden sich auch zahlreiche Neger

PK-Aufn. Scheck   66732   Presse-Hoffmann

German propaganda poster c. 1944. The poster shows captured black American troops and reads "Among the prisoners of the first day of the German offensive in the west, humiliated negroes." ©CORBIS

proposed social engineering schemes, including sterilization of the "unfit." While eugenicists ranged across the political spectrum, they believed the scientific management of human populations would result in progress. For its advocates, eugenics offered a hard but scientific perspective into intense competition among countries and the social turmoil associated with industrialism and urbanization. European eugenicists took white superiority for granted, but their focus lay in improving national stock. The English were especially concerned with correcting the perceived defects of the working class. Prominent German scientists sought to identify and promote "superior" traits through the practice of "racial hygiene," the German variant of eugenics established by Alfred Ploetz in the early twentieth century.

RACISM IN NAZI GERMANY

The Weimar years (1918–1933) were characterized by social turmoil, political violence, and economic depression. Vocal anti-Semites blamed the German defeat in World War I on Jews, and there were calls for a renewed German nation under the firm command of a strong leader. Scientists increasingly sought biological causes for social phenomenon. Publications sang the praises of ancient Nordics and their German descendants. The nationalist publisher J. F. Lehmann brought out a series of very popular books promoting racial theories of history. Hans Gunther's *Racial Studies of the German People* (1923) claimed mixing was bad and that the Nordic race was pure and superior to others. *Human Heredity and Racial Hygiene* (1923), written by leading scientists Erwin Baur,

Eugen Fischer, and Fritz Lenz, argued for the creation of an improved German nation through selective breeding. Advocates of racial hygiene, drawing inspiration from the political success of eugenicists in the United States, proposed limiting childbirth among the "unfit."

Adolf Hitler, the leader of the Nazi Party, promised to restore German honor through racial purification. For Hitler, race explained the past, established a plan of action for the present, and promised a glorious destiny. According to Hitler, Aryans, as brave warriors and creators of true culture, were superior to other races. While he had read the works of Gunther, Fischer, and others, Hitler eschewed their scientific terminology in favor of talk of "blood." He argued that Aryan blood had been polluted by intermarriage with inferiors; only with racial purification could Aryans attain their true destiny. As evil incarnate, Jews schemed to destroy Aryans through intermarriage, communism, and finance capitalism. The role of the state, declared Hitler, was to secure Aryan supremacy by purging the German nation of its bad blood and by destroying enemies, especially the implacable Jews, within Germany and beyond its borders.

With the seizure of military and political power in 1933, the Nazis commanded the resources and prestige of the scientific and medical establishment. Vocal anti-Semites and advocates of Nordic supremacy received promotions, while those who doubted the superiority or the existence of the Aryan race or who saw Jews as merely different were forced out or compelled to adopt Nazi policy. Anthropologists, geneticists, psychiatrists, and physicians celebrated Nordic superiority, dismissed non-Aryan colleagues, established guidelines for the evaluation of "worthy" and "less valuable" races, trained SS doctors, participated in genetic courts, issued certificates of racial status, aided forced sterilization programs, lent racial expertise to resettlement plans for the occupied east, and helped to plan and execute mass murder. Represented as rigorously scientific, the Nazi racial project was in fact characterized by flawed assumptions, suspect methods, flimsy evidence, and political expediency.

In their radical effort to reshape society in accordance with racist theory, the Nazis sought to take control of sexuality, reproduction, and life itself. The Germanic or Aryan elements of the population were identified and promoted through loans and other subsidies for young couples, honors for mothers of many children, certificates to marry, and other measures. Abortion, homosexuality, and sexual relations or marriage with a Jew were defined as race treason. At school and in ubiquitous youth organizations, children and young adults learned that the ideal man was vigorous and pitiless, the ideal woman a faithful wife and fecund mother. The elite SS prided itself on extensive background checks guaranteeing racial purity, and observed elaborate rituals for marriage and childbirth.

The Nazis immediately set out to purge what they regarded as impurities within the German population. The biracial children of African French occupation troops and German mothers, much maligned as "Rhineland bastards," were tracked down and sterilized. Institutionalized mentally ill and handicapped persons were subjected to forced sterilization and harsh conditions. From 1933 to 1939 another three hundred thousand men and women were forcibly sterilized on the grounds that they carried "hereditary diseases" such as "feeblemindedness," schizophrenia, blindness, physical deformities, and alcoholism. The Nazis also imprisoned, terrorized, and sometimes sterilized those they denigrated as "asocial." This vaguely defined category included women who changed partners regularly, vagrants, criminals, communists, unionists, prostitutes, and anyone who failed to demonstrate adherence to Nazi ideology. "Gypsies" (Sinti and Roma) were hounded into special camps and kept under observation. Jews, identified as the racial enemy of the German people, were subjected to systematic discrimination and dispossession. Laws in 1933 and 1935 barred Jews (and their spouses) from government jobs, professions, and other occupations; restricted their access to education; forbade marriage and sexual relations with non-Jews; and reduced Jews to second-class citizens. Increasing violence and discrimination, especially after 1938, stripped Jews of their possessions and compelled many to emigrate.

With the invasion of Poland in 1939, the Nazi racist project became increasingly brutal and

ART AND ARCHITECTURE

The Promenade. Painting by Marc Chagall, 1917. Chagall's introduction of elements of fantasy into his paintings distinguished him as an exemplar of French expressionism. Scala/Art Resource, NY/© 2006 Artists Rights Society (ARS), New York/ADAGP, Paris

RIGHT: *Twilight.* From the cycle "Ecce Homo" by George Grosz, 1922. Profoundly disillusioned by the events of World War I, George Grosz, along with other German expressionist artists such as Max Beckmann and Otto Dix, developed a satirical style of painting. Grosz here creates caricatures of typical Berlin citizens. Bildarchiv Preussicher Kulturbesitz/Art Resource, NY/ © 2006 VAGA

BELOW: *White Zig-Zags.* Painting by Wassily Kandinsky, 1922. Kandinsky was the founder of abstract expressionism, seeking to convey emotion through color and suggestive, though not representational, forms. Cameraphoto Arte, Venice/Art Resource, NY

LEFT: *Elephant of the Celebes.* Painting by Max Ernst, 1921. Ernst was pivotal in the development of the Dada movement and later became associated with the surrealists. This early work manifests the dadaist technique of adapting found imagery, in this case a piece of farm equipment, to create startling new images. TATE GALLERY, LONDON/ART RESOURCE, NY/© 2006 ARTISTS RIGHTS SOCIETY (ARS), NEW YORK/ADAGP, PARIS

BELOW: *Partial Hallucination: Six Images of Lenin on a Piano.* Painting by Salvador Dalí, 1931. Dalí presented dream imagery in a realistic and detailed manner to create some of the most renowned paintings of the surrealist movement. CNAC/ MNAM/DIST. RÉUNION DES MUSÉES NATIONAUX/ART RESOURCE, NY/© 2006 SALVADOR DALÍ, GALA-SALVADOR DALÍ FOUNDATION/ARTISTS RIGHTS SOCIETY (ARS), NEW YORK

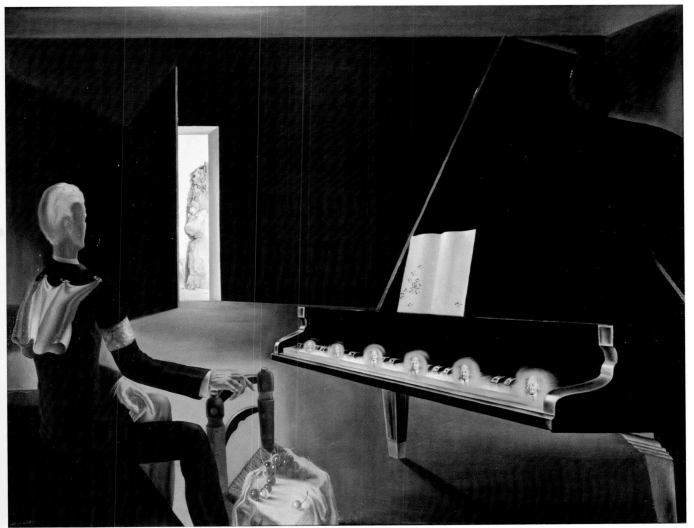

LEFT: *They Are Writing about Us in Pravda.* Painting by Alexei Vasilev, 1951. Vasilev's works are examples of socialist realism, the state-sanctioned style of art and literature during much of the Soviet period in Eastern Europe. Socialist realist artists sought to further the aims of the Soviet state by presenting an idealized view of communist life. SPRINGVILLE MUSEUM OF ART, SPRINGVILLE, UTAH/BRIDGEMAN ART LIBRARY

BELOW: *Night Fishing at Antibes.* Painting by Pablo Picasso, 1939. Picasso continued to explore the possibilities of his cubist technique throughout much of the twentieth century, recreating here a fishing scene drawn from his stay in the French coastal town of Antibes. This painting is often seen as a reflection of Picasso's unease over increasing violence in Europe, the act of fishing symbolizing the possibility of sudden, unforeseen death. DIGITAL IMAGE © THE MUSEUM OF MODERN ART/LICENSED BY SCALA/ART RESOURCE, NY/© 2006 ESTATE OF PABLO PICASSO/ARTISTS RIGHTS SOCIETY (ARS), NEW YORK

OPPOSITE PAGE: *Sack-O-Sauce.* Collage by Eduardo Paolozzi, 1948. The Pop Art movement in Europe was inaugurated by artist Eduardo Paolozzi in a 1952 lecture at the London Institute of Contemporary Arts titled "BUNK," in which he presented a series of collages created from comic books, postcards and magazines. Paolozzi drew upon the stylistic legacy of Dada and surrealism to create an ironic view of contemporary culture. TATE GALLERY, LONDON/ART RESOURCE, NY/© 2006 ARTISTS RIGHTS SOCIETY (ARS), NEW YORK/DACS, LONDON

OPPOSITE PAGE, TOP: The Bauhaus archive and museum, Berlin. Designed by Walter Gropius, 1964 (built 1979). Gropius is noted for his innovative use of modern technologies and materials, including concrete on steel-frame construction and glass brick. © ANGELO HORNAK/CORBIS

OPPOSITE PAGE, BOTTOM: Notre Dame du Haut, Ronchamp, France. Chapel designed by Le Corbusier, 1950. This later design by one of the most noted European architects of the twentieth century departs from his earlier works in its more rounded forms, a response to the building's hilltop setting. © ARCHIVE ICONOGRAFICO, S.A./ CORBIS

TOP RIGHT: The interior of the Educatorium at Utrecht University, Netherlands. Designed by Rem Koolhaas, 1993–1997. Koolhaas, winner of the Pritzker Architecture Prize in 2000, has created a markedly contemporary style in his works, which attempt to restore a human scale to public buildings. AP/WIDE WORLD PHOTOS

BOTTOM RIGHT: Guggenheim Museum, Bilbao, Spain. Designed by Frank O. Gehry, 1997. Gehry's free-form expressionistic building was created to reflect as well as house the museum's collection of modern art. © TIBOR BOGNÁR/CORBIS

BELOW: Mixed media work by Dieter Roth, 1972. Roth's oeuvre reflects several of the major features of European art of the later twentieth century: experimentation with radically different forms and materials, exploration of the very nature of art, and disillusionment with life in modern society. HAMBURGER KUNSTHALLE, HAMBURG, GERMANY/BRIDGEMAN ART LIBRARY /COURTESY OF THE ESTATE OF DIETER ROTH

TOP RIGHT: *192 Colours.* By Gerhard Richter, 1966. German artist Richter absorbed many of the avant-garde influences of the mid-twentieth century, a fact which is reflected in his wide-ranging oeuvre. Richter diverged from the dominant trend toward performance-based works, however, to focus on painting. His *192 Colours* is an example of his early interest in pure abstraction. BRIDGEMAN ART LIBRARY

BOTTOM RIGHT: *The Man who Flew into Space from His Apartment.* Installation in the series "Ten Characters" by Ilya Kabakov, 1988. Artists' experiments with form eventually led to the creation of works called installations, large-scale pieces designed to increase viewer interaction. Kabakov's version shown here creates a powerful indictment of life in the Soviet Union. CNAC/MNAM/DIST. RÉUNION DES MUSÉES NATIONAUX/ART RESOURCE, NY/©2006 ARTISTS RIGHTS SOCIETY (ARS), NEW YORK, VG BILD-KUNST, BONN

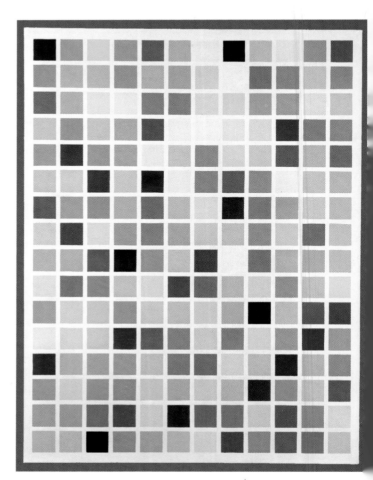

systematic. Mobile death squads of the SS rampaged, murdering communists, intellectuals, political opponents, and whole Jewish communities. Nazi scientists sorted the conquered by racial type. Children judged to have Aryan blood were taken from their families and shipped to special SS residential centers within Germany. Slavs were forced to work in Poland, and millions were sent to Germany as slave labor. Within months 1.5 million Jews from Germany, Poland, and Austria were herded into ghettos in occupied Poland. Under cover of war, the Nazis also began a "euthanasia" program known as T4, killing some seventy thousand terminally ill and "incurably feebleminded" individuals from 1940 until the program was terminated the following year amid popular protest. Following the advancing army into the Soviet Union in 1941, SS units again murdered political opponents and Jews; within the first six months of the campaign the SS alone had slaughtered some seven hundred thousand. For Hitler, control of the Soviet Union would secure the space and resources required for lasting Aryan supremacy. As racial inferiors, Slavic peoples would serve the master race; as race enemies, Jews would be forced out or eliminated. In 1942 the Nazis began to implement the Final Solution, drawing on the personnel responsible for and techniques from the T4 program. Jews from the occupied areas were transported to five massive death camps, where they were murdered in gas chambers or worked to death alongside "Gypsies," Soviet prisoners of war, and "asocials." The death toll from the death and work camps was without precedent, and included 5 million to 6 million Jews, half of the 5.5 million Soviet prisoners of war, and most of the Sinti and Roma populations.

REPUDIATION OF RACISM AND DEMISE OF THE RACE CONCEPT

The virulent racism of the 1920s and 1930s did not go unchallenged. In a series of books published in the early 1930s the British biologist Lancelot Hogben criticized the class bias and simplistic biological determinism of eugenics. His studies demonstrated the complexity of heredity, the reciprocal effect of environment and genes, and the complexity of behaviors such as intelligence. At the same time many anthropologists in Britain and the United States were abandoning the

construction of racial typologies based on the measurements of the head and other body parts; developing the methods of ethnography, or long-term residential research, they instead accounted for cultural diversity in terms of social and environmental factors.

But it was the Nazi eugenic project and the specter of a bellicose Germany that galvanized the antiracist critique. In Britain, Julian Huxley and Alfred Haddon's *We Europeans* (1935) exposed the fallacy of pure races, pointed out the arbitrary divisions of racial classifications, dismissed the idea of a Jewish race as a conflation of religion and biology, and rebutted the claims of Nordic or Aryan supremacy. In the United States, Franz Boas, a German-born Jew and leading figure in anthropology, organized students and colleagues in the battle against racism. In *The Mind of Primitive Man* (1911; expanded and updated in 1938), he showed how supposedly stable features such as head form changed, called for the analytic distinction between race, culture, and language, and argued for the primacy of environment in the development of behavior and mental capacities. He delighted in describing the long history of migration and intermingling of populations within Europe, and stressed the creativity born of such heterogeneity. The Nazis ordered his book burned.

Racism lost scientific and political legitimacy with the revelation of Nazi atrocities. In the postwar period, European governments espoused egalitarian principles and eventually criminalized anti-Semitism, Holocaust denial, and other forms of racism. Ashley Montagu, a former student of Boas and also an immigrant to the United States, assembled an international cast of scientists and in 1950 and 1952 oversaw the composition of statements on race by the United Nations Educational, Scientific and Cultural Organization (UNESCO). According to these statements, while humanity may be classified into major groups, no pure races exist nor have they ever existed; populations constantly change because of migration and the mechanisms of genetic transmission; race mixing presents no biological danger, and there are no proven differences in intelligence between races; because heredity has no necessary connection to language, geographical area, or nationality, it is

A boy wears a racist slogan on his forehead during an anti-immigration protest in England, 1980. ©HULTON-DEUTSCH COLLECTION/CORBIS

incorrect and misleading to describe such populations as races.

Drawing on the "new synthesis" of Mendelian genetics and Darwinian natural selection pioneered by biologists before the war, C. Loring Brace, Frank Livingstone, and others joined Montagu's attack on the race concept in the 1950s and 1960s. They argued that racial typologies poorly describe human diversity because classification hinges on one or a few traits and because traits such as skin color or blood types do not come in neat packages corresponding to traditional racial categories but are instead distributed along a cline or continuum. Rather than merely grouping populations on the basis of a few traits, students of human biology and natural history now sought to understand how and why genetic frequencies changed within and across populations. After initial resistance, most physical anthropologists turned away from the study of race and embraced population genetics. Social scientists also engaged in the

postwar reevaluation of race. Studies traced the career of the race concept in the context of colonialism, slavery, and anti-Semitism, and demonstrated the presence and effects of racism in popular culture and institutions.

NEW FORMS OF RACISM

If racism in Europe was directed primarily at Jews, Slavs, and minority populations before and during World War II, immigrants became the principal targets later. The postwar rebuilding effort and subsequent economic boom required massive inputs of labor, and governments and business interests across Western Europe sought additional workers in (former) colonial possessions and the Mediterranean basin. While most governments imposed restrictions after 1973, the foreign-born population has continued to rise because of family unification, asylum seekers, unauthorized entry, and the transformation of former countries of emigration such as Italy, Spain, and Greece into immigrant destinations. Amid great diversity in legal status, occupational profile, and ethnic origins, many immigrants confront substandard, often segregated housing, limited opportunities for advancement, and negative stereotypes. Children of African and Asian ancestry in particular experience the legacy of old racial hierarchies in subtle and overt forms; they worry that their skin color disqualifies them from full participation in European society even as they struggle to articulate their experience in a political context in which racism does not officially exist.

Anti-immigrant political mobilization and violence have gathered momentum since the 1980s. Because espousing openly racist ideology in a public forum is considered immoral if not illegal in most European countries, anti-immigrant political entrepreneurs denounce racism, distance themselves from neo-Nazis and other violent extremists, and avoid the language of race. Instead, they claim that foreigners constitute an economic burden, provoke social discord, and threaten national culture with their non-European customs; uncaring elites more interested in money than their own citizens have, they say, betrayed national culture. While the first examples of this attack on immigrants appeared in Britain in debates that led to restrictions on Commonwealth immigration, the most able and influential anti-immigrant politician has been Jean-Marie Le Pen. Le Pen describes immigrants as the ruin of France and has been repeatedly convicted of inciting racial hatred for his characterization of the Holocaust as a "detail" of World War II. He long served in the European Parliament and has garnered significant electoral support in his perennial bids for the French presidency. His Front National has served as a model for later populist-nationalist parties across the European Union. This ideology may be regarded as a new form of racism in that culture has replaced former racial terms. Like traditional racism, this view represents social groupings as unchanging entities, places peoples implicitly or explicitly in a hierarchy, condones and encourages popular expressions of intolerance, and calls for exclusionary policy. Such ideologies commonly gloss over class and other divisions to portray the nation simplistically as the enduring, homogeneous legacy of a people.

Several strands of racism and antiracism were evident in Europe in the final years of the twentieth century and the first years of the twenty-first. Under the euphemism "ethnic cleansing," Serbian forces committed mass murder and systematic rape against other nationalities in the former Yugoslavia in the 1990s. To the west, neo-Nazis continued to assault Jews, Roma, and people of non-European ancestry. Populist-nationalist parties enjoyed success at the polls in virtually every Western European state, and terrorist attacks by Muslim fundamentalists heightened anxiety about the integration of the Continent's large and growing Muslim population. At the same time immigrants and their descendants continued to contribute to a vibrant multicultural Europe, while scholars and organizations investigated racism in everyday culture, public discourse, and institutions, and the European Union and its member states monitored racism and upheld antidiscrimination laws.

See also **Ethnic Cleansing; Eugenics; Holocaust; Immigration and Internal Migration; Minority Rights; Nazism; Riots in France.**

BIBLIOGRAPHY

Barkan, Elazar. *The Retreat of Scientific Racism: Changing Concepts of Race in Britain and the United States between the World Wars.* Cambridge, U.K., 1992.

Burleigh, Michael, and Wolfgang Wippermann. *The Racial State: Germany, 1933–1945.* Cambridge, U.K., 1991.

Cole, Jeffrey. *The New Racism in Europe: A Sicilian Ethnography.* Cambridge, U.K., 1997.

Dijk, Teun A. van. *Elite Discourse and Racism.* Newbury Park, Calif., 1993.

Essed, Philomena. *Understanding Everyday Racism: An Interdisciplinary Theory.* Newbury Park, Calif., 1991.

European Monitoring Centre on Racism and Xenophobia. Available at http://eumc.eu.int.

Lentin, Alana. *Racism and Anti-Racism in Europe.* London and Ann Arbor, Mich., 2004.

Miles, Robert, and Malcolm Brown. *Racism.* 2nd ed. London, 2003.

Montagu, Ashley. *Man's Most Dangerous Myth: The Fallacy of Race.* 6th ed. Walnut Creek, Calif., 1997.

Stepan, Nancy. *The Idea of Race in Science: Great Britain, 1800–1960.* Hamden, Conn., 1982.

Stocking, George W., Jr. *Bones, Bodies, Behavior: Essays in Biological Anthropology.* Madison, Wis., 1988.

Wrench, John, and John Solomos. *Racism and Migration in Western Europe.* Oxford, U.K., 1993.

JEFFREY E. COLE

RADAR. Radar is a device that detects reflected radio signals to provide an electronic means of measuring distance and location of an object. The term *radar* originated in the United States during World War II as an acronym for *ra*dio *d*etection *a*nd *r*anging.

The phenomenon of radio reflection was first observed in 1887–1888 by the German physicist Heinrich Hertz. This aspect of Hertz's experiments was largely forgotten by the end of the nineteenth century, when attention shifted to very long-wave radio waves, which Guglielmo Marconi had demonstrated could be used for radio.

Radio reflection was rediscovered in the early 1920s by radio hams using shortwave radio. In November 1923 American amateurs established two-way radio contact with a French ham operator in Nice. Although the cause of this phenomenon was not understood until 1925, these long ranges were made possible by the shortwave radio signals being reflected by the ionosphere, a previously little understood layer of the upper atmosphere. This discovery sparked immediate interest in short and ultrashort—also known as ultrahigh frequency (UHF)—wavelengths. In the late 1920s and early 1930s, a variety of new high-power shortwave receiver and transmitter radio valves, antenna systems, and related devices were introduced. Particularly important was the perfection by 1930 of a cathode ray tube (CRT), which could graphically display received signals.

As radio researchers turned their attention to shorter wavelengths, they began again to observe the reflective properties of these signals. The initial applications of radio reflection were in the measurement of distances. By early 1925 scientists used this phenomenon to demonstrate the existence of the ionosphere. Radio reflection was also utilized in devices used for geodetic surveying and in aircraft altimeters.

In the early 1930s scientists began observing interference to radio signals caused by passing aircraft. In 1930 radar research began at the United States Naval Research Laboratory. In 1933 Dr. Rudolph Kühnold, chief of the German navy's Signals Research division, began work on a radar system. Tests on radio location devices began in France in January 1934 and in the Soviet Union in July of that same year.

In January 1935 Robert Watson Watt proposed to the British government the development of a radio location system to detect and track approaching bombers. Watson Watt was authorized by the Air Ministry to assemble a team of radio researchers at the Bawdsey research laboratory. By the end of 1938 the Bawdsey researchers had developed the Chain Home radar system, providing early warning of a bomber attack at ranges up to sixty miles. At the same time, Air Marshal Sir Hugh Dowding, commander in chief of Fighter Command, and Sir Henry Tizard, who chaired the Committee for the Scientific Survey of Air Defence, directed a series of experiments that integrated information from the Chain radar stations into a comprehensive air defense system. During the summer of 1940, in the Battle of Britain, this air defense system made it possible for the Royal Air Force to defeat the Luftwaffe's efforts to win air superiority over Great Britain.

Prior to the war a group of Bawdsey scientists led by E. G. Bowen developed much smaller radar sets for use on aircraft and ships. Early airborne sets were hampered by the comparatively long wavelengths available. In February 1940, at the University of Birmingham, John Randall and Harry Boot produced the cavity magnetron, a revolutionary radio valve that could generate sufficient quantities of microwave radiation. By the end of 1941 the first microwave radar, the Royal Navy's Type 271, was introduced into service. The Type 271 soon proved instrumental in allowing escorts to detect German U-boats during Battle of the Atlantic.

In the summer and autumn of 1941, Tizard headed the British Technical Mission to North America. The mission resulted in a full Anglo-American exchange of information on radar, including the magnetron. This led to the establishment of the Radiation Laboratory at the Massachusetts Institute of Technology. Effectively mobilized, Allied scientists developed an extensive array of radar and radar countermeasures that proved decisive in campaigns as diverse as the Battle of the Atlantic and the strategic bomber offensives against both Germany and Japan.

Germany also developed a highly effective radar-based air defense system, which inflicted massive casualties on Allied bombers. The system only failed in early 1944 when American long-range escort fighters annihilated the German fighter force. None of the Axis powers emulated the Allies' use of microwave radar.

After the war radar was used to dramatically improve marine and air navigation and control systems. Direct postwar spin-offs of radar included medical imaging, microcircuitry, radar mapping, and radio astronomy.

See also **Aviation; Britain, Battle of; Warfare.**

BIBLIOGRAPHY

Brown, Louis. *A Radar History of World War II.* Bristol, U.K., and Philadelphia, 1999.

Buderi, Robert. *The Invention That Changed the World.* New York, 1996.

Pritchard, David. *The Radar War: Germany's Pioneering Achievement, 1904–45.* Wellingborough, U.K., 1989.

Swords, Seán S. *A Technical History of the Beginnings of Radar.* London, 1994.

Zimmerman, David. *The Great Naval Battle of Ottawa.* Toronto, 1989.

———. *Top Secret Exchange: The Tizard Mission and the Scientific War.* Montreal and Stroud, U.K., 1996.

———. *Britain's Shield: Radar and the Defeat of the Luftwaffe.* Stroud, U.K., 2001.

DAVID ZIMMERMAN

RADIO. A medium of mass communication with great immediacy, radio proved a major catalyst of social and political change in twentieth-century Europe. Radio grew from research pioneered by many European scientists, including the Scotsman James Clerk Maxwell (1831–1879), the German Heinrich Rudolph Hertz (1857–1894), the Russian Alexander Stepanovich Popov (1859–1906), and the Italian Guglielmo Marconi (1874–1937), who patented a wireless telegraphy device in 1900. Rival claims to be the inventor of radio had some propaganda significance later in the century. The device was initially used for maritime communication. Experimental audio transmissions included a series of weekly live concerts broadcast from the Belgian royal palace at Laeken from March to 20 August 1914, over what was then known as TSF (*télégraphie sans fil*, or wireless telegraphy). A new medium was taking shape, only to be interrupted by the coming of World War I.

During the early 1920s entrepreneurs in many European countries founded radio stations. The first major station was that of the Nederlandse Radio Industrie, founded in Holland in 1919, a year before the Westinghouse station KDKA began broadcasting in Pittsburgh, Pennsylvania. The Dutch company Philips also played a leading role in the mass production of radio equipment. Danmarks Radio began in Denmark in 1920 and had a monopoly from 1926. November 1922 brought inaugural broadcasts by both Radiola (later Radio Paris) in France and the British Broadcasting Company (later Corporation) from London. The first regular Czechoslovakian broadcasts began in May 1923, and Germany's first official radio station, Radiostunde Berlin (later Funkstunde Berlin), began broadcasting in October 1923. Belgian commercial broadcasts also began that year. In the mid to late 1920s many European countries founded state-run corporations to regulate and direct the new medium. Examples included the Yleisradio (General Broadcaster) in Finland in 1926 and the BBC in 1927. The Belgian government founded a public radio station in 1930.

In March 1927 Radio Netherlands began short-wave broadcasts to the Dutch East Indies and ushered in European external services. Major services included Radio Moscow and Deutscher Kurzwellensender (from Zeesen, near Berlin), both founded in 1929; Vatican Radio, founded in 1931; and BBC Empire Service in 1932. Swiss Radio International began in 1935 and Radio Prague's external services began in 1936. Some international services were purely commercial, such as the English-language broadcasts by Radio Normandy (1926–1939) or the multilingual Radio Luxembourg, launched in 1933.

Radio had an immense social impact on interwar Europe, providing the cultural glue to cement national consciousness and bringing the outside world closer as never before. The medium soon acquired a political significance as the ideal platform for the demagogic leaders of the era, most notoriously Benito Mussolini in Italy and Adolf Hitler in Germany. Hitler, who much preferred speaking to live audiences, once remarked that without radio and other modern methods of communication there would have been "no victory for National Socialism." Following the Nazi conquest of Europe, the great radio stations of the region became channels of Nazi propaganda, while the BBC in London provided a home from which governments in exile could broadcast to their occupied countries. For most of the war the British government took care to avoid inciting armed rebellion that would merely lead to the futile loss of life. The British Political Warfare Executive created a number of "black" propaganda radio stations, including one that purported to be a station run by German soldiers hostile to Hitler, designed to sow division within the Nazi state.

During the postwar years radio was both a medium of Americanization within Western Europe and a route to challenge the Soviet domination of Eastern Europe. The United States government broadcast to all of Europe over the Voice of

British Broadcasting Company sound effects staff working on a 1951 radio broadcast of H. G. Wells's *War of the Worlds.* ©HULTON-DEUTSCH COLLECTION/CORBIS

America, and sponsored politicized broadcasts to Eastern Europe over Radio Free Europe (founded in 1950) and its sister station aimed at Russia, Radio Liberty. In Berlin the Americans operated a station called Radio in the American Sector, and in Austria they established Radio Rot Weiss Rot (Red White Red). No less significantly, Europeans could tune in to hear American pop music on the stations of the Armed Forces Network, created to serve American servicemen garrisoned in Europe. European stations also played their role in the radio cold war, with Deutsche Welle (relaunched in 1953) and the BBC World Service attracting substantial audiences in the Eastern bloc. It is significant that the first target for Polish anticommunist rioters in 1956 was the government station that jammed Western broadcasts; however, the Hungarian rising of 1956 underlined the danger of encouraging open rebellion, as Radio Free Europe had done.

European state broadcasters, bound by regulations designed to protect live music from competition from recording, were slow to respond to audience interest in American and American-inspired music. This created a niche for pirate radio stations such as Radio Mercur, which broadcast from international waters off Denmark and Sweden from 1958 to 1962, or Radio Caroline, which broadcast from the North Sea to Britain from 1964 to 1967. In the 1960s many European countries modernized their domestic broadcasting to include more music but also to protect cultural and spoken-word programming. In 1965 the three French radio stations France I, II, and III rebranded as France Inter, France Musique, and France Culture, while in 1967 in Britain the BBC created its first pop music station, Radio One, and rebranded its light program, third program, and home service as Radios Two, Three, and Four. In 1981 the victorious candidate for the presidency of France, François Mitterrand, made the deregulation of French broadcasting a major campaign promise and swiftly delivered reform.

In the 1980s radio played a major role in the political changes between East and West, with Western radios challenging the communist control of the media and ensuring that each country in the region knew about the march of reform in its neighbors. The process reached its climax in 1989. Radio remained significant as Yugoslavia fragmented. Station RTS Belgrade became a mouthpiece for the nationalist dictator Slobodan Milosevic, while a youth-oriented rock music station founded in 1989 called B92 opposed the regime. B92 weathered intimidation and various bids to close it down, and in 2000 the station played a major role in rallying opposition to Milosevic in the election.

See also **Cinema; Radio Free Europe; Television.**

BIBLIOGRAPHY

Briggs, Asa. *The BBC: The First Fifty Years.* Oxford, U.K., 1985. A concise history of the British Broadcasting Corporation.

Collin, Matthew. *This Is Serbia Calling: Rock' n' Roll Radio and Belgrade's Underground Resistance.* 2nd ed. London, 2004. A case study of radio in Yugoslavia.

Historical Journal of Film, Radio and Television (1981–)

Journal of Radio Studies (1992–).

Wagnleitner, Reinhold. *Coca-Colonization and the Cold War: The Cultural Mission of the United States in Austria after the Second World War.* Translated by Diana M. Wolf. Chapel Hill, N.C., 1994. A seminal study of American cultural propaganda in postwar Austria.

NICHOLAS J. CULL

RADIO FREE EUROPE.

Radio Free Europe (RFE), established in 1949, and Radio Liberty (RL), established in 1951, were the most successful propaganda vehicles of American psychological warfare during the four decades of the Cold War. The radio stations run by the United States government contributed to a great extent to the survival of democratic values and desire for freedom among the people of the Soviet bloc countries.

RFE/RL MISSION

Soon after the end of World War II, numerous signs indicated that the Soviet leaders intended to ignore the agreements reached between the Allies at the Yalta Conference and tighten their grasp over Eastern Europe, and in the longer run they aspired to dominate the western part of the Continent as well. During the war the Soviet regime accumulated a remarkable reputation in Europe. The Soviet Union tried to counterbalance its economic vulnerability by aggressive propaganda intended to construct an image of the moral and political superiority of the Soviet system. The Americans believed that despite their military and economic advantage, they could not stop Soviet expansion if they failed to place maximum strain on the Soviet imperial zone from inside. They feared the potential brainwashing impact of the totalitarian communist propaganda machinery. The task was to hamper consolidation of Soviet control over satellite countries, keep aspirations for national independence alive, and alter the view that the Soviets were on a track of successful expansion.

In June 1948 the National Security Council adopted George Kennan's proposal and created a new department within the CIA, the Office of Policy Coordination (OPC), for conducting covert operations. Kennan's draft stated that these operations should include propaganda, economic warfare, subversion, and assistance to underground resistance movements and refugee liberation groups. The actions had to be so planned and executed that the U.S. government could plausibly disclaim any responsibility for them. In a memorandum on 29 October 1948, Frank G. Wisner, the first head of the OPC, outlined four functional groups of the office, the first of which was in charge of "psychological warfare," including the use of the press and radio.

The communist takeover throughout the Eastern European region in 1948 accelerated the organizational work. The National Committee for a Free Europe (NCFE), created in early 1949, assembled prominent Eastern European émigré politicians and intellectuals and established a publishing division, Free Europe Press, and two broadcasting divisions. RFE targeted the Soviet satellites in Eastern and Central Europe. RL broadcast in Russian and in the languages of the republics of the Soviet Union. The recruitment of the editorial and research staff started in 1949.

Both the NCFE and RFE/RL, like Crusade for Freedom, their ostensible fund-raising organization, pretended to be civil initiatives without direct involvement of the U.S. government. RFE/RL had a unique ambition. Unlike traditional foreign radio services, the national desks of RFE/RL intended to become "domestic" radio stations of the target countries. Their mission was not limited to the promotion of American political and cultural values. Besides breaking the information monopoly of communist propaganda, RFE/RL also wanted to facilitate the liberation of the "captive nations." In order to achieve this task, RFE/RL employed émigré journalists and experts. To provide well-established inside information from the Soviet bloc, the research staff monitored the official communist press and national radios as well as Western media sources. In addition, RFE/RL worked with the CIA to set up "field offices" near the largest refugee camps around the Soviet bloc. RFE/RL agents interviewed refugees in order to collect intelligence data and unmanipulated information on the everyday reality of the communist orbit. By using this information in their programs, the stations were able to make the impression that they were indeed present in the everyday life of these countries. Moreover, as "nongovernmental" institutions representing Eastern European émigrés, RFE/RL programs and rhetoric could go beyond official American foreign policy claims.

The CIA involvement in the RFE/RL operations remains a debated and sensitive issue. Although Crusade for Freedom pursued a spectacular campaign among the American public, in fact RFE/RL received funds from the budget of the CIA until 1971, when RFE/RL funding and oversight responsibilities were transferred to the Board for International Broadcasting. The CIA used the information amassed by the radio and research staff as well as their expertise in evaluating the situation in the Soviet bloc. The State Department regularly issued policy guidelines for assuring that the broadcasts fit the framework of the American strategy. Although American supervisors at the stations worked under State Department/CIA mandate, accounts of RFE/RL history usually assert that direct political control or preliminary censorship of the programs was not exercised. RFE/RL also resisted attempts to use radio programs to convey coded messages to secret agents working in the region.

American Cold War policy had to face several dilemmas that also made an impact on RFE/RL programs. The programs had to follow a narrow path of maintaining the ideological and political pressure but not provoking "premature upheavals," as the subsequent National Security Council directives and RFE policy guidelines repeatedly stressed. A related issue was whether they should encourage splits within the communist parties and between Moscow and the satellites, thus promoting the "evolutional" disintegration of these regimes, or rather bet on the anticommunist resistance. The second option partially contradicted the first one. Finally, national sentiments were among the core elements of potential anti-Soviet resistance in the satellites, but RFE/RL had to avoid several pitfalls in exploiting those sentiments. The revival of extreme-right nationalism might have blocked the future democratic development of these societies. In addition, RFE/RL editorial desks represented nations that harbored traditional distrust and hostility toward each other. The handling of minority issues, therefore, required extreme caution. RFE/RL programs must not give the impression that American foreign policy was biased or bound to any of the particular national aspirations concerning the change of the existing borders.

COMMUNIST RESPONSE
The communist authorities always regarded RFE/RL as the most dangerous "enemy" stations and responded to the programs, above all, by jamming—transmitting noise or other electronic sounds on the same frequencies. Because shortwave broadcasts could not be jammed directly from the target area, jamming required a common effort from the Soviet bloc countries. The intensity of the jamming varied from time to time and from country to country. The Soviet Union jammed broadcasts from 1953 to 1988.

The communist authorities also tried to intimidate the audience at home and the RFE/RL staff abroad. Listening to RFE/RL broadcasts was a criminal offense in most Soviet bloc countries, especially in the 1950s. Communist secret services repeatedly made criminal attempts against the

American actor Gregory Peck broadcasts an appeal for donations to support Radio Free Europe, Munich, Germany, October 1953. ©BETTMANN/CORBIS

stations. The most serious assault took place in February 1981, when a bomb exploded at the RFE/RL building in Munich.

THE EARLY COLD WAR YEARS

The headquarters of RFE/RL was set up in Munich, in Englishcher Garten. The initial broadcasts started in July 1950, by shortwave transmitters at Lampertheim and Holzkirchen. On 1 May 1951, 11.5 hours of daily programming to Czechoslovakia marked the official inauguration of RFE. Later that year, regular programs to Romania, Hungary, Poland, and Bulgaria also aired. Radio Liberty started its services on 1 March 1953, a few days before Joseph Stalin's death.

In the first half of the 1950s, American policymakers did not envision a decades-long commitment to defeat Soviet communism, and "rollback" strategy prevailed. RFE/RL programs and operations reflected the aims of this policy. The tone of the broadcasts was aggressive, highly emotional, and ideological. Numerous programs not only targeted the system and communist political practice in general but conveyed threatening and discrediting messages to individual members of the party and governmental apparatus. After Stalin's death in March 1953, the pressure increased. A major contribution to the programs came from the highest-ranked defector of those times, Josef Swiatlo, a former top commander of the Polish security forces. RFE programs were also supplemented by a joint operation with Free Europe Press. In Operation Prospero, Veto, and Focus, thousands of balloons dropped leaflets, booklets, and other propaganda materials (among them the early translations of George Orwell's *Animal Farm*) in order to increase the will to resist among the public in Czechoslovakia, Poland, and Hungary. Some leaflets carried messages in the name of "national resistance movements" that did not exist on ground.

The suppression of the Berlin uprising in 1953 and the events in Poland and Hungary in 1956 dispelled the illusion that the communist regimes would soon collapse. Many critics held RFE programs and operations responsible for the tragedies and human sacrifice in Eastern Europe between 1953 and 1956. In fact, none of the RFE programs called for upheavals or promised American military intervention either in 1953 or in 1956. However, RFE broadcasts and operations did give the impression that the United States was ready to help the "captive nations" liberate themselves. Therefore these tragedies gave credit to the concerns that the Eastern European nations might easily misinterpret the liberation rhetoric of the American government. After 1956, RFE/RL broadcasting policy had to be accommodated to a long-term cohabitation with Soviet rule in Eastern Europe.

DÉTENTE AND THE COLLAPSE OF COMMUNISM

After the 1956 Hungarian revolution, President Eisenhower immediately stopped the balloon projects. An investigation into RFE programs discovered grave mistakes in the broadcasting policy. Some of the directors and editorial staff were removed. Throughout the years of détente, changes were implemented in the programs. Although the programs never overlooked the final goal and RFE remained critical, aggressive anticommunist propaganda became muted. Emphasis shifted to the promotion of internal evolution and gradual liberalization of the communist regimes. RFE gave moderate support to "liberals" and "autonomists" and encouraged political and economic reforms. In these years critics of RFE raised opposite objections than in the 1950s: it had become too "soft" and "compromising" toward the communists.

From the second half of the 1970s, the economic and political crisis became more serious all over the Soviet bloc. The Soviet intervention in Afghanistan and the emergence of the independent Polish trade union Solidarity indicated that the international environment had changed. Dissident movements and circles that opposed the regimes on the basis of human rights started to proliferate in the Soviet Union and its satellites, partly inspired by the human-rights provisions of the international Helsinki Accords of 1975. Samizdat (underground publishing) activities began to flourish. From January 1981 the new Reagan administration took a firmer stand against the Soviet Union. These developments brought changes in RFE/RL management and brodcasting policy as well. RFE/RL became an important disseminator of samizdat in the Soviet bloc. They ran regular programs on dissident activities and put on air the works of prominent dissident politicians and thinkers. With the help of RFE/RL, the samizdat publications could reach a much wider audience in their homelands. The programs provided publicity, which gave a limited protection for dissident figures. Thus RFE/RL indeed contributed to the peaceful democratic transition that took place from 1989 onward in the former Soviet bloc.

During the first half of the 1990s the structure and mission of RFE/RL was reshaped. The headquarters was moved from Munich to Prague in 1995. RFE/RL continues to broadcast to the areas of the former Soviet Union, the Balkans, and critical areas of central Asia and the Middle East. In the meantime, the corporate records and the radio archives from the Cold War were transferred to the Hoover Institution at Stanford University. The Cold War archives of the former research units in Munich were deposited in the Open Society Archives at Central European University, Budapest, Hungary.

See also **Cold War; Dissidence; Eastern Bloc; Radio; Samizdat; Television.**

BIBLIOGRAPHY

Etzold, Thomas H., and John Lewis Gaddis, eds. *Containment: Documents on American Policy and Strategy, 1945–1950.* New York, 1978.

Grose, Peter. *Operation Rollback: America's Secret War behind the Iron Curtain.* Boston, 2000.

Mickelson, Sig. *America's Other Voice: The Story of Radio Free Europe and Radio Liberty.* New York, 1983.

Mitrovich, Gregory. *Undermining the Kremlin: America's Strategy to Subvert the Soviet Bloc, 1947–1956.* Ithaca, N.Y., 2000.

Nelson, Michael. *War of the Black Heavens: The Battles of Western Broadcasting in the Cold War.* Syracuse, N.Y., 1997.

Puddington, Arch. *Broadcasting Freedom: The Cold War Triumph of Radio Free Europe and Radio Liberty.* Lexington, Ky., 2000.

Urban, George. *Radio Free Europe and the Pursuit of Democracy.* New Haven, Conn., 1997.

Warner, Michael, ed. *The CIA under Harry Truman: CIA History Staff, Center for the Study of Intelligence.* Washington, D.C., 1994.

ANDRAS MINK

RAILWAYS. Railroad construction was a prime factor in European growth and national unification in the nineteenth century. The great rail networks the twentieth century inherited consequently varied a good deal in density and form, depending on the country concerned. Even before 1900, two great competitors to rail transport had made their appearance, namely the automobile and the airplane. Indeed, the railways of the twentieth century had to face several serious challenges: ever more lively competition from other means of transport, the need to maintain the profitability of existing infrastructure, and the persistent problem of the private or public ownership of the railroads.

The first response of the industry was of a technological kind, as steam locomotion gave way to diesel power and especially to electricity, allowing for significant increases in speed. It was during the interwar period (1918–1939) that the European railroads achieved their maximum expansion. Even at the time, the growing threat of road transport provoked pessimistic assessments: "Parliaments must resolve," said the leading

TABLE 1

Railroad track in use, by country (kilometers)				
	1914	1930	1960	1993
France	37,400	42,400	39,000	32,557
Italy	19,125	22,119	21,277	19,465
Spain	15,533	17,278	18,033	13,060
Sweden	14,360	16,523	15,399	10,884
United Kingdom	32,623	32,632	29,562	16,536

SOURCE: Mitchell, pp. 676–681.

French civil engineer, Raoul Dautry, in 1933, "to declare certain rail lines devoid of public interest and initiate a national program of closings." The financial losses of the railroads became legendary as a more and more significant proportion of freight was hauled by road, not to mention the ever increasing numbers of automobile travelers (although, for the moment at least, the institution of the family car was no more than an idea). The extension of paid holidays for workers did not create the windfalls for the railroads that had been anticipated. In the 1930s some attempts at diversification were made, as in Great Britain, where three railroad companies launched Railway Air Services in order to compete with the airlines, or in France, where road-haulage concerns subsidiary to the railroads were set up. The idea of an integrated transportation system was proposed in several European countries, though a long-term solution along these lines was never found.

In the immediate wake of the Second World War, rail was practically the only available way of hauling freight. As European reconstruction proceeded, growing competition from road transport was buttressed by the fact that it offered greater flexibility, as, to a lesser degree, did air freighting. As a technical matter, trucks could transport more goods more quickly than railroads, and this capacity increased along with the improvement of the highway system and above all with the advent of superhighways.

The railroad industry reacted by abandoning less profitable sectors (notably short-haul lines). And as the total low-profit track miles dropped, so did the number of railroad workers (by between 15 and 60 percent across Europe in the years 1950–1980). This decline gave rise to much social tension in the form of railroad strikes and protests in rural areas concerning reduced passenger service. Diversification in the design of railroad cars, the

automation of signal systems, and the elimination of small stations were among changes designed to counter this decline, which in fact paralleled that of the railroads' main client, heavy industry in general. In a Europe where speed and competitiveness were ever more important, truck hauling offered a solution free of the interruptions caused in rail transport by frequent unloading and reloading.

NATIONAL VARIATIONS

The issue of control over the railroads was a continual preoccupation in European countries, which made very varied choices in the matter, although certain overall tendencies may be identified. In Spain, for instance, a period of nationalization extended from 1913 to 1941. Even before the First World War, the Spanish were prone to speak of a "railroad problem," meaning that their system did not work well and needed replacing. In 1920 the state was obliged to advance large sums of money to the railroad companies and, beginning in 1923 and especially during the Primo de Rivera dictatorship (1923–1930), such subsidies continued to grow. After the Spanish civil war (1936–1939) the head of state, Francisco Franco, nationalized the railroads, creating the Spanish National Railway Network, or RENFE. The French experience was similar, and in 1937 a national system was established, a joint enterprise with majority public ownership known as the Société Nationale des Chemins de Fer (National Railroad Company), or SNCF. In the United Kingdom, the state assumed control of the private railroad companies during the First World War but restored their private status when peace returned. The companies were then "grouped" by the Railways Act of 1921 into four large concerns, namely the Great Western Railway, the London, Midland and Scottish Railway, the London and North Eastern Railway, and the Southern Railway.

Whereas the first half of the twentieth century was thus characterized by nationalizations, spurred by the fact that the reconstruction of European economies tended to increase the influence of the state, the emphasis shifted in the 1970s and especially in the 1980s. It appeared now that the state was unable to support free competition, having become entangled in management-union politics to the point where it could not make the right

The Duchess of Gloucester, a steam locomotive built for express service between London and Scotland, departs from Euston Station, London, c. 1937.
©HULTON-DEUTSCH COLLECTION/CORBIS

TABLE 2

Freight hauled, by country (billions of tonne-kilometers)						
	Rail		Road		Air	
	1955	1985	1955	1985	1955	1985
France	46.9	55.8	18.6	89.1	0.07	2.9
Germany	78.1	124	25	105	–	2.5
Italy	14.7	18	29.5	144	–	0.8
United Kingdom	34.9	15.4	31.9	99.1	0.07	2.3

SOURCE: Armstrong, p. 214.

policy decisions at the right moment. A debate began, notably in Brussels, between free-market liberals on the one hand and the defenders of the public sector on the other. It emerged clearly that the state had not performed badly with respect to railroads—the most striking evidence being France's achievements with high-speed trains— but the outcome nevertheless favored the partisans of free-market laissez-faire. The Italian rail system, run directly by the state since 1905, underwent a long and arduous privatization between 1985 and 1995. Most countries separated infrastructural from commercial management. Regulatory authorities (as in the case of other "utilities") were responsible for maintaining properly competitive conditions. This weakening of the state's position was often to be explained as much by high budget deficits (to which the railroads frequently contributed) as by ideological pressures. The Italian Ferrovie dello Stato became a limited liability company not entirely emancipated from its public-

service role. The British railroads, nationalized in 1948, began running at a loss as early as the 1950s, despite modernization plans. The British experience with privatization is widely viewed as emblematic. British Rail was broken up into 125 private companies, beginning in 1994; the last British Rail train ran in Scotland in 1997. Several new entities were created (including Railtrack Track, the Office of Passenger Rail Franchising [OPRAF], and the Office of the Rail Regulator) in the context of franchising different parts of the network and encouraging competition. It is still too early to draw conclusions about the British experience. Delays, high accident rates, and lethargic modernization are much in evidence, but such shortcomings may be seen as the legacy of an exhausted state system.

SPEED

These changes in the legal status of the railroads occurred against a backdrop of dramatic technological change. In face of the challenge from road transport, the railroads naturally made the most of their traditional strengths in the public mind, namely security and reliability. But increased speed was undoubtedly the most powerful response to the expanding market share of both trucks and planes. The early success of the Shinkansen bullet train, introduced in Japan in 1964, was proof positive that high-speed links between major cities drew passengers. The Germans had already set out to develop magnetic levitation (maglev) trains that resolved the problem of friction. In theory such trains could achieve speeds in excess of 400 kilometers per hour. The French, for their part, founded their TGV (Train à Grande Vitesse) high-speed system on the basis of traditional technology developed to near perfection. The construction of new dedicated lines for these trains

TABLE 3

Rail passengers carried, by country (billions of passenger-kilometers)			
	1950	1970	1988
Belgium	7	8.3	7
France	26.4	41	62.6
West Germany	30.3	38.1	46.4
Italy	23.6	34.8	48.3
Spain	7.1	13.3	16.3
United Kingdom	32.5	30.4	31.7

SOURCE: Armstrong, p. 220.

generally allowed distances themselves to be shortened. The TGV trains beat speed records: in 1955 the SNCF had established a new world speed record of 331 kph in somewhat risky fashion with an electric locomotive, a record surpassed only in 1981, when the first French TGV achieved 380 kph. More importantly, however, the TGV was a great hit with the public. The first, Southeastern, line was made even more profitable because its construction involved no great engineering feats. In 1990 the TGV train Atlantique achieved a speed of 515 kph. This kind of performance meant that rail transport for distances under eight hundred kilometers could once more compete with its rivals. Good marketing and pricing policies by the SNCF made France's main lines profitable.

Other countries could not match France's success. While French rail passengers could travel from Paris to Lyon in two hours by the beginning of the 1980s (on a TGV with an average speed of 213 kph), it still took six hours to get from Rome to Milan—longer than in 1939—at an average speed of 100 kph. In a Europe by now determined to think globally, such zones of backwardness could not be allowed to subsist within an increasingly internationalized network. Consequently, the Italians and the Spanish proceeded to develop tilting trains, the best known being the Pendolino on the Florence-to-Rome route (la Direttissima). The British had less success in the 1970s with their Advanced Passenger Train, which suffered from low investment in the rail sector. TGV lines later made their appearance in Spain, Germany, and Italy. At first, however, such broad support for the high-speed option did not mean that the technology was standardized: The French TGVs went through several generations (Southeastern,

Atlantic, North), Germany's Intercity Express trains likewise went through ICE and ICE-M versions, while Spain developed its own AVE and Italy its ETR 500 high-speed systems. Little by little, though, standardization began to win out over national technological and industrial traditions.

THE CHANNEL TUNNEL

This grand project has a very long history indeed. In 1750 the Academy of Amiens held a contest for the best proposal on how to create a permanent link across the English Channel. After Napoleon conceived the idea of invading England with his Grand Army, there was never any shortage of thinkers and visionaries eager to address this challenge. A good case in point is Aimé Thomé de Gamond, who produced numerous projects for bridges and both submerged and excavated tunnels. Inspired by Saint-Simonism—the system of socialism conceived by Claude Henri de Saint-Simon—and the Manchester school of nineteenth-century liberalism, a group met in 1872 and established the Channel Tunnel Company. At the time, the British were interested in a faster route to India, while the French wanted their country to become an obligatory trade crossroads. Two kilometers of tunnel were dug in 1875. But the British aborted the project for fear of invasion, the favorable position of Queen Victoria notwithstanding. Overland links (the Alpine tunnels of Simplon, Mont-Cenis, Saint-Gothard, and Lötschberg) subsequently came into their own, and the port of Antwerp, notably, handled a great part of Asian trade. Tunnel enthusiasts rallied once again in the 1920s, arguing that direct rail connections between the two main colonial powers in the world would be of strategic importance. The Second World War and reconstruction put the project back on the shelf. Later, however, when the SNCF initiated its high-speed explorations in the 1960s, the idea of a direct line via tunnel to London emerged spontaneously. In 1975 the British Labour government backed off from the project on the grounds of the cost of a new London-to-Dover rail line (this time, only 500 meters of tunneling had been done). The French then fell back on their Southeastern TGV line, inaugurated in 1981. The great success of that line, coupled with the ever growing need to connect Great Britain to Europe and the Lille region's

TABLE 4

Average speed of passenger trains in kilometers per hour				
	1950	1960	1970	1982
France	96	109	125	144
West Germany	78	103	114	131
GB	96	105	110	121
Spain	101	103	107	113
Switzerland	102	104	106	110
Austria	81	99	105	110
Italy	84	98	104	97

SOURCE: *Corriere della Sera*, 1984.

aspiration to become a transport hub, eventually created conditions that made the old "Chunnel" plan seem both necessary and feasible. In 1982 the British prime minister Margaret Thatcher and the French president François Mitterrand lent their decisive support, and on 29 July 1987 a Franco-British agreement was finally ratified authorizing the construction and exploitation of a tunnel under the English Channel. The French could henceforth look forward confidently to rail links not only with London but also with Cologne and Amsterdam via Brussels. The modernization of the rail network of southeastern England (which resembled a commuter-rail system) was also needed, but this was tackled only gradually; the second portion of a dedicated high-speed line from central London to the Channel Tunnel is scheduled to open in 2007, at which point the London–Paris run should take about two-and-a-half hours.

From the technical point of view, the Channel Tunnel was a triumph, but difficulties were encountered over contractual, security, and financial issues. The tunnel was opened on 6 May 1994. Within a few years talk of high-speed lines or links gave way to talk of a high-speed network, and Western Europe's high-speed rail lines became one of its defining spatial components.

By the end of the twentieth century, high-speed trains were handling 12 percent of all rail passenger traffic in a group of seventeen countries, an impressive proportion in view of the number of lines yet to be built. Debate among experts continued, however, an important unanswered question being whether high-speed rail should serve major cities alone or whether entire regions could

benefit from its expansion. Was there not a danger that high-speed intercity service might create a tiering of regions within states, with some regions being well served while others were left out? The prospect at the close of the twentieth century was continual growth in trans-European trade and ever more apparent signs of dangerous overdevelopment. A new sensitivity to problems of security, environmental protection, and energy savings might be expected to favor the sort of collective transportation solutions that rail offered. In practice, however, the railroads continued to be penalized by policies sharply biased toward road transport, which by the turn of the century was garnering 72 percent of freight haulage and 88 percent of passenger traffic, as compared with 15 and 6 percent respectively for the railroads. The continuing construction of a unified Europe cannot bypass the question of the environmental planning of the whole territory and the need to restore a reasonable balance among regions. In this context rail transport must necessarily play a structuring role, as it did in the nineteenth century, when towns that declined rail service experienced slower growth. By the end of the 1990s, many different approaches to the question of the European railroads presupposed the advent of global policies based on a thorough comparative study of the direct and indirect costs of the transportation alternatives. Rail was indisputably the most appropriate choice from the standpoint of sustainable development (as witness, for example, the clear superiority of rail freight in view of the excessive growth of heavy-truck traffic). A transport policy that challenges the hegemony of laissez-faire economics, however, has yet to be framed.

See also **Automobiles; Public Transport.**

BIBLIOGRAPHY

Armstrong, John. "Transport and Communications." In *Western Europe: Economic and Social Change since 1945,* edited by Max-Stephan Schulze, 212–233. London, 1999.

Bairoch, Paul, and E. J. Hobsbawm, eds. *L'età contemporanea: Secoli XIX–XX.* Vol. 5 of *Storia d'Europa.* Torino, 1996.

Barker, T. C., and Dorian Gerhold. *The Rise and Rise of Road Transport, 1700–1990.* London, 1993.

CERTU. *Collectivités territoriales et transports publics urbains dans les États de l'Union Européenne.* Lyons, 1996.

Les chemins de fer en temps de concurrence (choix du XIXè siècle et débats actuels). Revue d'histoire des chemins de fer 16/17 (1997).

Gaillard, Marc. *Du Madeleine-Bastille à Météor: Histoire des transports parisiens.* Amiens, 1991.

Garbutt, Paul E. *London Transport and the Politicians.* London, 1985.

Giannopoulos, G., and A. Gillespie, eds. *Transport and Communications Innovation in Europe.* London, 1993.

Hughes, Murray. *Rail 300: The World High Speed Train Race.* London, 1988.

Merger, Michèle, Albert Carreras, and Andrea Giuntini. *Les réseaux européens transnationaux XIX-XXè siècles: Quels enjeux?* Nantes, 1995.

Mitchell, B. R. *International Historical Statistics: Europe, 1750–1993.* 4th ed. London, 1998.

Muscolino, Piero. *I trasporti pubblici di Roma: Notizie ed immagini dal 1845 ai nostri giorni.* Rome, 1987.

ALAIN BELTRAN

RASPUTIN, GRIGORY (1869 or 1872–1916), Russian mystic and court favorite.

With good reason it has been argued that Grigory Yefimovich Rasputin, an unordained Russian mystic and holy man, helped discredit the tsarist government, leading to the fall of the Romanov dynasty in 1917. Contemporary opinions variously saw Rasputin as a saintly mystic, visionary, healer, and prophet, or as a debauched religious charlatan. Historians can find evidence for both views, but also much uncertainty: accounts of his life have often been based on dubious memoirs, hearsay, and legend.

Rasputin was born in the western Siberian village of Pokrovskoye in either 1869 or 1872. A pilgrimage to a monastery in 1885, as penance for theft, and a reported vision of the Mother of God on his return, turned him toward the life of a religious mystic and wanderer. He also evidently came into contact with the banned Christian sect known as the khlysty (flagellants), whose impassioned services ending in physical exhaustion led to rumors that religious and sexual ecstasy were combined in their rituals. Suspicions, generally not accepted by historians, that Rasputin was a khlyst—how else to explain the notorious sexual life of this "holy man"?—threatened his reputation to the end of his life. As Rasputin's renown grew, he attracted the attentions of critics who accused him of using religion to mask his desire for sex, money, and power. Still, many people, from clergy to society ladies to members of the imperial court, were drawn to Rasputin's magnetic personality, spiritual passion, and simple words of wisdom.

In 1905, amidst the upheavals of revolution, Nicholas II and his family "came to know a man of God, Grigory, from Tobolsk Province" (Nicholas II's diary, 1 November 1905). Rasputin would remain, until his death in 1916, a trusted friend and confidant of the imperial family and a growing force in the life of the state and the church. For Nicholas, the peasant and holy man Rasputin was what the tsar urgently needed in these years of crisis: a voice of the common people loyal to the sacred principle of autocracy; a man whose reputation as a seer could help the tsar hear God's voice; and a healer whose prayers visibly relieved the agonizing pain from hemophiliac bleeding of Alexei, the tsar's young son and heir. Contemporaries and historians have variously attributed Rasputin's effect on Alexei to hypnotism, autosuggestion, traditional Russian healing practices, and an authentic power to heal through prayer. Between 1905 and 1916, a series of investigations revealed Rasputin's debauchery, but the tsar dismissed these reports.

Like many spiritually minded Russians, Rasputin spoke of salvation as depending less on the clergy and the church than on seeking the spirit of God within. He also maintained that sin and repentance were interdependent and necessary to salvation. Thus, he claimed, yielding to temptation (for him personally, this meant sex and alcohol), even to humiliation (to dispel the sin of vanity), was a necessary step on the road to repentance and salvation. Rasputin was deeply opposed to war, both from a moral point of view and as likely to lead to political catastrophe. During World War I, Rasputin's increasing drunkenness, sexual promiscuity, willingness to accept bribes in return for helping petitioners who flocked to his apartment, and efforts to have his critics dismissed from their posts made him appear increasingly cynical.

Rasputin exercised considerable political influence, especially during the war, through his friendship with Nicholas and Alexandra, the tsaritsa, and his cultivation of a network of high-placed allies in state and church. There is no evidence that he directly shaped policy, but he did influence appointments of officials, and many of these officials then became part of the "Rasputin clique." Nicholas did not always accept Rasputin's advice, however, and he reminded his wife in 1916 that "Our Friend's opinions of people are sometimes very strange." In the notorious "ministerial leapfrog" of these years, marked by a flurry of high-level dismissals and appointments, Rasputin's nominees were often successful, though public rumors of his influence (as well as of intimate relationships with the empress and perhaps her children) exaggerated his power.

To end this scandal, a group of conservatives—a prince, a right-wing member of the Duma (parliament), and a grand duke—murdered Rasputin on the night of 29–30 December (16–17 December, old style) 1916. He was poisoned, shot when the poison proved ineffective, and dumped in the river; an autopsy found that Rasputin had drowned. When the Romanov family was executed by the Bolsheviks less than two years later, the daughters were discovered to be wearing amulets containing portraits of Rasputin.

See also **Nicholas II; Russia; Russian Revolutions of 1917.**

BIBLIOGRAPHY

Fuhrmann, Joseph T. *Rasputin: A Life.* New York, 1990.

Radzinsky, Edvard. *Rasputin: The Last Word.* Translated by Judson Rosengrant. London, 2000.

MARK D. STEINBERG

RATHENAU, WALTHER (1867–1922),
German-Jewish industrialist and political leader.

Walther Rathenau led a varied life, as an industrialist, intellectual, wartime administrator, and politician, before he was assassinated by extreme right-wing terrorists in June 1922. Rathenau's career embodied the challenges of coming to terms with the transformations in politics and business that took place between the 1890s and the 1920s. Born into a Jewish family, he moved among the elites of Wilhelmine Germany. He was educated at the universities of Strasbourg and Berlin, received a doctorate in physics, served in the army for one year, and then entered AEG (German General Electric), the company his father had set up, following the collapse of his first business venture.

By the outbreak of war he was one of the leading industrial figures in Germany. Nonetheless he was critical of what he, like many contemporaries, saw as the materialism of his age and the conditions of the workers. In a series of publications, including *Zur Kritik der Zeit* (1912; Criticism of the age) and *Die neue Gesellschaft* (1919; The new society), he suggested that economic growth would, in the long run, enable workers to devote more time to their intellectual development. However, many of his books were utopian and received a mixed reception. At a more practical level, he was involved in negotiating the Stinnes-Legien pact between employers and workers in 1918, which guaranteed the eight-hour day and gave the workers a greater stake in the running of companies.

He was also an advocate of greater state involvement in economic matters, a view not shared by most other German industrialists. During the First World War, he set up the Raw Materials Office in the Prussian Ministry of War, after warning in early August 1914 that Germany would run short of munitions. The state distributed raw materials to those firms that were best able to exploit them. While Rathenau did not undermine the principles of property ownership, he sought to limit free competition by allowing the state to direct economic activity. At the same time as he advocated greater state involvement in the economy, he also urged that the industrial and professional middle classes should have a greater say in political affairs. German power was no longer based on the officer corps or aristocracy, though he admired their past achievements, but on its economic growth. Before and during the war he advocated reform of the Prussian electoral system and the constitutional position of the Reichstag. This would create domestic harmony and strengthen Germany abroad. Yet by the end of the war he was pessimistic about Germany's future, criticizing the lack of political maturity.

Rathenau, following official visits to German colonies in 1907 and 1908, had argued that

Germans lacked the political nous and governing ability of the British. His notes during these trips reveal him to be a skeptic of the value of colonies; nonetheless, Germany could not withdraw, especially after the atrocities committed in colonial wars between 1904 and 1907. Despite showing some sympathy for the plight of Africans, Rathenau had been imbued with the racism of his age and considered the Africans to be indolent and in need of Western support.

In terms of foreign policy, Rathenau was far more interested in Germany's position in Europe than its imperialist expansion. Before World War I he had tried to avert the Second Moroccan Crisis in 1911 by negotiating a deal between German and French companies in Morocco. He consistently argued for collaboration between Germany and France. During the war he rejected the more extreme war aims of large territorial annexations. Instead he argued that a customs union with Austria, Italy, the Netherlands, and Belgium, with France possibly joining later, would preserve Germany's place in Europe. He also saw a customs union as an effective means of countering the growth of U.S. economic power. His ideas anticipated those of Aristide Briand in the late 1920s. After the war Rathenau was initially on the margins of German politics. However, in 1920 and 1921 he began to play a role in the attempts to revise the Treaty of Versailles. At Wiesbaden in June 1921, as minister for reconstruction, he met the French minister, Louis Loucheur. They worked out an agreement for German aid to reconstruct northern France. However, both were hampered by domestic political opposition, and the agreement never materialized. He became foreign minister in January 1922. Frustrated by France, he turned to Britain and then later to Soviet Russia. In April 1922 he signed the Treaty of Rapallo with the Soviet Union in an effort to stave off German isolation. On 24 June 1922 he was murdered, a victim of the antirepublican and anti-Semitic terrorist group Organisation Consul.

See also **Germany; Versailles, Treaty of.**

BIBLIOGRAPHY

Primary Sources

Rathenau, Walther. *Walther Rathenau: Industrialist, Banker, Intellectual, and Politician. Notes and Diaries, 1907–1922.* Edited by Hartmut Pogge von Strandmann. Rev. and extended ed. Oxford, U.K., 1985.

Secondary Sources

Felix, David. *Walther Rathenau and the Weimar Republic: The Politics of Reparations.* Baltimore and London, 1971.

Williamson, D. G. "Walther Rathenau: Realist, Pedagogue, and Prophet, November 1918–May 1921." *European Studies Review* 6 (1976).

WILLIAM MULLIGAN

RATIONING. Assisted by the development of state bureaucracies and technologies of mass communication, rationing enabled governments to plan, control, and restrict the allocation of scarce resources. It was commonly used during periods of war, famine, and other emergencies to ensure equitable distribution of food, fuel, and consumer goods. In order to keep prices affordable for the lowest paid, rationing was usually accompanied by price fixing and compulsory savings schemes. All the major European combatant nations implemented some form of rationing during World Wars I and II, as normal peacetime production of essentials declined and each side attempted to strangle the other's supplies of food and raw materials. Rationing was also continued by some nations after 1918 and 1945 to cope with postwar shortages. As well as being a familiar part of military life, rationing was central to governments' attempts to maintain wartime civilian morale, persuading their public that hardships were being shared equally across class and other boundaries.

WORLD WAR I, 1914–1918

The scope and allocation of rationed items during World War I depended on the phase of the conflict and the state of supplies in a particular country at a given time. Germany, for example, introduced clothes rationing and restrictions on the use of soap. France put limits on the number of lightbulbs that could be used to illuminate people's homes. But food was the principal focus of rationing. In Germany, where food shortages threatened widespread starvation, bread rationing began in 1915 and was followed by a general scheme in 1916,

Residents of Berlin collect their ration of potatoes, October 1947. The collapse of the German economy combined with poor harvests to create severe food shortages in the postwar period, forcing Allied occupation officials to impose harsh rationing restrictions. ©BETTMANN/CORBIS

coordinated by the newly created War Food Office. A combination of Allied blockade and the diversion of resources away from agriculture meant that food rations in Germany fell below subsistence levels. Consumption of cereals, meat, and fats dropped sharply and a black market flourished; perhaps as much as 50 percent of all food in Germany was bought illegally after general rationing began. As elsewhere in Europe, food shortages were most acute in urban areas; the rural population could supplement rations with their own "self supplies," and governments found it difficult to monitor rations in the countryside. When a poor harvest in 1917 brought a food crisis to German cities such as Berlin and Leipzig, the resulting strikes and massive "bread and peace" demonstrations

undermined the German war effort. There were similar problems in Austria, where more than six hundred thousand workers went on strike in January 1918 after the flour ration was cut.

In contrast, Britain's food supplies were largely undisturbed before 1917, despite the fact that the country was more dependent on imported food than any of its European neighbors. Britain experimented with "voluntary rationing" in February 1917, by which the authorities issued guidelines on what people should eat and hoped that individuals would adjust their diets accordingly. When the success of the U-boat blockade produced a food crisis in late 1917, the government issued ration cards as part of a general scheme the following January. As was the case in France, where ration cards were made compulsory in June 1918, the controlled distribution of food and accompanying price controls were aimed more at defusing worker discontent than at preventing starvation. Britain and France had both seen how food shortages in the cities had contributed to military collapse and revolution in their wartime ally Russia. In Italy, where prewar living standards were relatively low, the wartime drop of 10 percent in agricultural production meant real hardship for millions, particularly in the northern cities. Both Turin and Milan saw unrest in 1917 after a poor harvest. Ration cards were made obligatory in Italy in 1917, first for bread and later for other foodstuffs. Along with Britain, where sugar, fats, and meat were rationed until 1920, Italy continued to use ration cards until 1921.

WORLD WAR II, 1939–1945

Lessons learned about rationing in 1914–1918 guided state policies during World War II. Again, however, black markets thrived. Most countries, including neutrals such as Switzerland, introduced general rationing schemes at an early stage of this conflict. In Germany, where the Nazis were determined to avoid the starvation diets that broke popular support for the Kaiser's war effort, rationing was introduced in August 1939. By plundering supplies in occupied territories, German food rations remained among the highest in Europe until the latter part of the war. At the other end of the scale, rationing in the Soviet Union did little more than ensure that malnutrition was spread equitably across the population. Millions of Soviet citizens had relied on food rations during the 1930s. After the German invasion of 1941, the average Soviet worker's diet consisted of one pound of bread per day plus a few scraps of fat and meat. Miners and metalworkers were entitled to a greater allowance because they did heavy physical work, but such was the shortage of food that the full ration was not always met. Only by growing vegetables in every patch of garden available did the Soviet people avoid starvation. In France, the Vichy government administered a system of ration cards from September 1940 onward. Food allocation was dependent on age—each consumer was placed into one of six age bands—and there were extra allowances for heavy laborers and pregnant women. By 1941 virtually everything that could be bought in French shops was rationed. Britain rationed butter, bacon, and sugar from January 1940; in March, meat and other items were added to this list. In 1941 the government introduced a "points" system of rationing for clothes; this was extended to tinned foods and then other foodstuffs in 1942. Under this scheme, consumers received points in the form of coupons and could choose how to spend their allocation. The point value of particular items was adjusted in line with domestic production, shipping losses, and seasonal preferences.

POSTWAR EUROPE

Wartime rationing was relatively popular in Britain, where it was regarded as an egalitarian feature of the "people's war." By forcing people to eat a more nutritious diet, it also produced health benefits. It was much less popular in the postwar years, not least because food rations in 1947 fell below their wartime level. Most countries phased out rationing in the late 1940s, including the Soviet Union, which scrapped restrictions in December 1947. Britain maintained rationing in some form until 1954, and briefly reintroduced petrol rationing during the 1956 Suez crisis. The Netherlands rationed fuel in the oil crisis of 1973. In Nicolae Ceausescu's Romania, where food exports were increased to meet the country's crippling foreign debt, strict rationing of food was maintained from 1982 until the regime's downfall in 1989.

See also **Agriculture; Marshall Plan; Reconstruction.**

BIBLIOGRAPHY

Hardach, Gerd. *The First World War, 1914–1918.* Translated by Peter and Betty Ross. London, 1977.

Kroener, Bernhard. *Germany and the Second World War.* Vol. 5: *Organisation and Mobilisation of the German Sphere of Power.* Part 2: *Wartime Administration, Economy, and Manpower Resources, 1942–1944/5.* Translated by Derry Cook-Radmore. Oxford, U.K., 2003.

Milward, Alan S. *War, Economy, and Society: 1939–1945.* London, 1977.

Osokina, Elina. *Our Daily Bread: Socialist Distribution and the Art of Survival in Stalin's Russia, 1927–1941.* Translated by Kate Transchel and Greta Bucher. London, 2000.

Williams, John. *The Home Fronts: Britain, France, and Germany, 1914–1918.* London, 1972.

Zweiniger-Bargielowska, Ina. *Austerity in Britain: Rationing, Controls and Consumption, 1939–1955*. Oxford, U.K., 2000.

Mark Donnelly

RECESSION OF 1970S.

Strictly defined, there were two economic recessions in the 1970s, one dominating the years 1974–1975 and another the years 1979–1982. They are linked by being each initiated by increases in oil export prices imposed by the Organization of the Petroleum Exporting Countries (OPEC). In 1973–1974 OPEC quadrupled the price of oil exports and over the period 1978 to May 1980 doubled the existing price. These moves were intended to impose OPEC's own desired prices on the major transnational oil companies, who had themselves fixed the lower sales prices from the earliest years of exploration. In western eyes the increases were a threat to the West's vital strategic resources. In the producers' eyes they were the righting of an international injustice. Adjustment to such steep increases was very difficult, leading to shortages of gasoline and a heavy burden on consumers, particularly in countries such as the United States, where gasoline consumption was especially high.

The two recessionary episodes are linked also by their close succession. Countries that suffered the most in the first recession also suffered the most in the second because the recovery from the first was more difficult and in many cases not completed before the second episode began. Above all, however, they are linked by marking the definitive end of the great boom that began in 1945. The period 1974–1982 seemed a return to the economic difficulties of the years between the two world wars. It made it evident that governments had not, as they had begun to think, discovered a science of economic policy management that had banished severe depressions and unemployment forever. In both recessions unemployment and inflation moved sharply upward together, dispelling the idea that the management of the economy could rest on the belief that there was a trade-off between these two phenomena.

In retrospect, two other aspects of the oil-price quarrel seem more important than OPEC's decisions. One is the weakness of a prolonged period of prosperity that had come to depend increasingly on oil as the main source of energy. The other is the extent of common interest between the developed West and the relatively undeveloped oil-producing countries. Rich though they were, oil producers such as Saudi Arabia and Libya, the two initiators of the first oil-price shock, and Iran, the initiator of the second, needed their customers to provide the financial services that would lead to the reinvestment of their oil profits in domestic economic development. Most OPEC countries had little else to export other than oil. Thus, the common interest could only be endangered if prices drove those oil consumers depending mainly on imports toward investing in other forms of energy.

Delays in reaching a common understanding were attributable to lack of agreement over foreign policy issues between consumers and suppliers and to the character of domestic politics in the OPEC countries. Saudi Arabia was a deeply conservative supporter of American foreign policy. Libya, however, was seen as a troublesome and unpredictable international revolutionary state. Iran, the initiator

TABLE 1

	1970	1971	1972	1973	1974	1975	1976	1977	1978	1979	1980	1981	1982
Percentage year on year growth of Real Gross Domestic Product at market prices													
USA	-0.3	3.1	5.4	5.5	-0.6	-0.7	4.9	5.2	4.7	2.4	-0.2	3.0	-2.3
Germany (Federal Republic)	5.1	3.1	4.2	4.6	0.5	-1.7	5.5	3.1	3.1	4.2	1.8	-0.1	-1.0
France	5.7	5.4	5.9	5.4	3.2	0.2	5.2	3.1	3.8	3.3	1.1	0.3	1.6
UK	2.2	2.6	2.1	7.6	-0.9	-0.9	3.7	1.2	3.5	2.0	-2.6	-1.3	2.3
Italy	5.3	1.6	3.2	7.0	4.1	-3.6	5.9	1.9	2.7	4.9	3.9	0.1	-0.3
Japan	9.8	4.6	8.8	8.8	-1.0	2.3	5.3	5.3	5.0	5.1	4.9	4.2	3.0
OECD	3.5	3.7	5.3	6.1	0.8	-0.3	4.8	3.7	3.9	3.2	1.3	1.8	-0.3

SOURCE: OECD, *Historical Statistics, 1960–1982* (Paris, 1984), 44.

of the second price increase, was strongly asserting its national identity and its independence from the United States. None of the Arab large-scale oil producers—Iraq, Kuwait, Libya, Quatar, and Saudi Arabia—could be readily recognized as a democracy. Neither could Iran. This was not an encouraging framework for negotiations, and the recycling of oil-producers' profits by the developed Western world at first went ahead only slowly.

WEAKNESSES IN DEVELOPED ECONOMIES

Economic weaknesses in the developed countries played at least as big a part in the recessions as the increases in oil prices. Oil was not the commodity whose price rose the most over the decade 1972–1983. Food prices rose more, and this was attributable to the economic policies of the developed countries. Trade liberalization was not intended to extend to trade in agricultural products as ambitiously as it did to manufactures. The European Community's common market and its Common Agricultural Policy were based on the maintenance of Community preference in trade in its own agricultural products. The Community's trade with underdeveloped countries was protective of European farmers, closing the door on the import of any agricultural product covered by the Common Agricultural Policy, except when in Europe that product was out of season. The usual array of veterinary and horticultural safety rules were more rigorously imposed on exporters from developing countries than they were within Europe itself. For example, the share of agricultural exports from Africa as a proportion of the Community's total agricultural imports fell in every decade from 1960 to 2000. The United States replicated much of the European pattern of protectionism. Both Europe and North America subsidized their indigenous food producers and also their food exports to the underdeveloped world. That food prices in the developed world were a prime promoter of inflation was one consequence, a certain slowness of growth in the demand for manufactured exports from the developed world another.

Manufacturing industry was also experiencing in that decade a persistent change in its nature. What was at the time referred to as "deindustrialization" was the beginning of a sweeping change in the employment structure of manufacturing, whose output came to depend increasingly on what would previously have been classed as service-sector employment, such as design and marketing, and less on the physical labor of manufacturing. Responses to the two recessions were closely linked to this change. The remarkable volatility of the Italian economy was linked to its successes in the service-sector aspects of manufacturing. The successful record of the German economy in the 1970s, in contrast, hid its failure to invest more in the service-sector aspects of manufacturing. Traditional German engineering and chemical exports did not decline so much as in other developed countries. The dismal performance of the British manufacturing sector at the same time diverted attention from its early shift toward industrial service-sector employment. In part, therefore, the recessions of the 1970s were caused by restructuring in the nature of manufacturing employment, which in turn was restructuring the pattern of international trade.

LESSONS

From this troubled decade simple, but important, lessons can be drawn. A boom of unprecedented length had changed the composition of

TABLE 2

Unemployment as a percentage of total labor force													
	1970	1971	1972	1973	1974	1975	1976	1977	1978	1979	1980	1981	1982
OECD	3.3	3.8	3.9	3.5	3.9	5.4	5.6	5.5	5.4	5.4	6.1	7.1	8.5
USA	4.8	5.8	5.5	4.8	5.5	8.3	7.6	6.9	6.0	5.8	7.0	7.5	9.5
Germany (Federal Republic)	0.6	0.7	0.9	1.0	2.1	4.0	4.0	3.9	3.7	3.3	3.3	4.6	6.7
France	2.4	2.6	2.7	2.6	2.8	4.1	4.4	4.7	5.2	5.9	6.3	7.3	8.0
UK	2.2	2.8	3.1	2.2	2.1	3.2	4.8	5.2	5.1	4.6	5.6	9.0	10.4
Italy	5.3	5.3	6.3	6.2	5.3	5.8	6.6	7.0	7.1	7.5	7.4	8.3	8.9
Japan	1.1	1.2	1.4	1.3	1.4	1.9	2.0	2.0	2.2	2.1	2.0	2.2	2.4

SOURCE: OECD, *Historical Statistics, 1960–1982* (Paris, 1984), 39.

international trade in such ways that contemporaries could not predict the trading future. Most commentary on the recession of the 1970s correctly identifies Japan and Germany as the countries that escaped with the least damage to their economies. They were, however, by the end of the 1980s experiencing a stagnation of their exports relative to the growing strength of exports from, for example, the United Kingdom, which in the 1970s had been the least competitive of the major exporters. There is much evidence that it was the severity of the recessions that accelerated the shift in the commodity composition of British exports and in the pattern of employment.

Ability to overcome the problems of the 1970s was closely related to management-labor relations and to the encouragement of flexibility in working hours. This in turn meant heavy pressures on labor unions to conform to new patterns. Germany was the country where this posed the greatest difficulty. The impact of these changes on politics and on society in the West was varied among countries. The United Kingdom had perhaps the least to preserve from that period because it was then the most slowly growing of the industrial powers. France, Germany, and Japan had, in this context, the strongest reasons for conservatism. The United States, which grew only slowly in the 1950s but did much better in the 1960s was sharply divided over possible responses to 1970s conditions.

The weaknesses ascribable to the treatment of the underdeveloped world by the developed are ascribable to all the developed economies. OPEC did no more than draw attention to their existence. One verdict on the 1970s recessions might be that exceptionally long periods of high economic growth can leave developed economies at risk from the less sophisticated. Another would be that cooperation between them was the wiser way forward. Arab oil earnings, kept in European banks and invested in approved international development projects proved one way out of the recessions.

See also **Common Agricultural Policy; OPEC.**

BIBLIOGRAPHY

Blackaby, Frank, ed. *De-industrialisation*. London, 1979.

International Labour Office. *World Recession and Global Interdependence: Effects on Employment, Poverty, and Policy Formation in Developing Countries*. Geneva, 1987.

Organisation of Economic Co-operation and Development. *OECD Economic Surveys: The United States*. Paris, 1974, 1976.

Alan S. Milward

RECONSTRUCTION. Nine million soldiers died in World War I, and some fifty-five million people perished in World War II, many of them civilians. Millions received physical and mental wounds that left permanent marks. The total wars of the twentieth century caused human suffering on an unprecedented scale, particularly in Europe. Reconstruction thus had to go far beyond repairing material damage; it had to encompass the societal fabric itself. This task could not be left to individuals alone. States had to accept new responsibilities as welfare states. International cooperation was to be the key to success.

While new countries were taking shape in Eastern Europe amid civil war and conflicts over borders and minority rights, reconstruction in Britain, France, and Germany after 1918 took place within a comparatively stable framework that rested on the cooperation of organized interests, among them the previously excluded trade unions. Their governments faced entirely new challenges as millions of returning soldiers had to find jobs; disabled veterans, war widows, and orphans needed financial support; and the debts that state budgets had incurred over the course of the war had to be brought under control. Absent functioning international cooperation, reconstruction ultimately remained shaky at best. After 1945 reconstruction took place against the backdrop of the emerging Cold War. Germany, heavily destroyed, politically powerless, and morally devastated, became the main site of the conflict between Western-style democracy and Soviet communism. As Europe west of the Iron Curtain, aided by the United States, developed much more successful mechanisms of economic growth and cooperation than its eastern counterpart, it entered an unprecedented era of stability and prosperity.

RECONSTRUCTION AFTER WORLD WAR I
Reintegrating the soldiers into the economy proceeded remarkably smoothly in Britain, France, and

Germany. Within only half a year, six million German soldiers were back home and at work again. The disintegration of the German army in fall 1918 sped up the process, and employers were eager to provide returning soldiers with their previous jobs. The employers also accepted the new eight-hour day that created the demand for additional jobs, as did the expansion of the public sector. Preventing an overthrow of the newly established republic by a Bolshevik revolution was given priority over making profits. A staggered system of demobilization, in which older workers with special skills were demobilized first and younger ones were kept under military discipline longer, helped streamline the process and defuse radicalism in Britain. In France, the huge agricultural sector absorbed many returning soldiers and reduced the burden on industry. Demobilization's swift success was only possible, however, because most women left, more or less voluntarily, the factory jobs they had taken over after the outbreak of the war in 1914. This should not be construed, however, as rollback of an alleged emancipation during the war, as some scholars have argued. Recent studies have shown that, while the long-term trend of giving women more access to clerical and administrative jobs was, if anything, sped up by the war, women remained cast, during and after it, primarily as wives and mothers whose skills and virtues were different from and complementary to those of men.

More than half a million German women lost their husbands and 1.2 million children lost their fathers in the war. About 1.5 million German soldiers returned home with permanent disabilities; this was more than a tenth of all males drafted. The figures for Britain and France were similar. Because private charities alone could not provide the needed financial support, governments had to step in and shoulder a substantial burden for the foreseeable future. From the mid-1920s to the early 1930s, a fifth of Germany's national budget went into war pensions—far more than was spent on unemployment relief. However, recipients in all countries, particularly the disabled, regarded their benefits as insufficient. In Germany, where disability was determined as reduction of average earning capacity, special protection in the labor market was granted to the severely disabled and payments were higher than in the other two countries, but even

those payments barely reached subsistence level. British legislation focused on the degree of disablement with little regard for previous occupation and social status but offered vocational training. These courses, however, were cut back substantially when the government drastically reduced its expenditures in 1921–1922. France, in line with its republican tradition, privileged disabled veterans politically by recognizing every wound received during the war without further examination but did not establish any protection in the labor market before 1923.

Under these circumstances, reducing public debts turned out to be a difficult task that was to have harsh social consequences. As governments had been forced to issue bonds and to use the printing press to cover unprecedented war expenses, inflation was rampant at the end of the war, but it eased the transition to a peacetime economy. In Britain, it fueled a speculative postwar boom that came to an abrupt end in 1920, with prices peaking at two and a half times their prewar levels. The return to the gold standard in 1925 kept inflation at bay, but, by overvaluing the pound sterling, it also held British exports down. Although newer industrial sectors such as the electrical supply and motor vehicle industries showed remarkable growth and put Britain in a better position overall than France and Germany, unemployment doubled compared to the prewar level.

France saw its budget particularly burdened by the need for material reconstruction in the areas that had been occupied by Germany and destroyed by fighting. French industrial production was down to only 60 percent of its prewar level when war ended; in the north, 220,000 houses as well as seventeen thousand miles of roads and railroad tracks had to be rebuilt. To speed up reconstruction, the French government borrowed more money from its citizens after 1918 than during the war. As a result, the franc kept tumbling. By 1926 it had fallen to less than one-tenth of its prewar value; at that point the government sharply raised taxes and drastically cut down its expenditures.

The Treaty of Versailles stipulated that Germany pay reparations to the victors for the costs of the war. This has often been described as the major reason why inflation in Germany, in contrast to Britain and France, ended in complete disaster. Moreover, it has been argued that reparations placed a huge economic and political burden on the German reconstruction effort that eventually resulted in the failure of the Weimar democracy. Historical research since the mid-1980s has cast doubt on this deterministic interpretation, however. While it is true that the Treaty of Versailles provided nationalist propaganda with a prime tool with which to discredit the republic, it did not prevent Germany from rising to the status of a major power again, as became painfully clear over the course of the 1930s. Employment and investments were held aloft until 1923 by an "inflationary consensus" that encompassed big business, labor, and the government. Due to differences among the Allies and German delaying tactics, a total was set on German reparations only in the spring of 1921.

When at an Allied conference in London it was finally announced that Germany had to pay 132 billion gold marks in annual installments of about three billion marks, the value of the currency began to decrease rapidly, falling to less than 1 percent of its prewar dollar value until the summer of 1922. The German government took steps to fulfill its obligations, only to state that full compliance was in fact impossible. Whether that was true remains an open question, but there is no doubt that making a sustained effort would have required the government to drastically raise taxes and cut public expenditures, thereby further undermining the shaky new republic. Such measures could no longer be avoided, however, after the collapse of the mark and German economy in the hyperinflation of 1923. This had come in the wake of Germany's announcement that it was suspending reparation payments, France's retaliatory occupation of the economically vital Ruhr region, and German resistance against that occupation.

The government reached a new agreement on reparations, drafted by a committee led by American expert Charles G. Dawes, that stipulated lower annual payments and provided Germany with an international loan of 800 million marks to get the economy started again. Although, in contrast to a widespread popular view, the German inflation did not wipe out the middle classes, since the inflationary effects on mortgages and bonds in many cases canceled each other out, its final stage left traumatic memories of a world turned upside down. That the consolidation of reparations should occur under American auspices demonstrated how dependent Germany as well as Britain and France had become on the United States as a result of the huge debts they had incurred during the war. This consolidation rested on shaky ground, however, as it was based on many short-term loans that flowed into Germany after 1924, comprising a large share of its foreign debt. When they were withdrawn in the wake of the "Black Friday" of 1929, it became apparent that economic reconstruction after World War I had been a hollow success.

Much less is known about how returning soldiers, their families, and the survivors of the fallen came to terms with the psychological turmoil of the war than about postwar social and economic policy. Fears that veterans would infect societies with violence proved, on the whole, to be unfounded. In Britain, violent crime actually declined after the war. Widespread violence was a feature of postwar politics in Germany and Italy, but those engaging in it made up only a minority of all veterans. Veterans' organizations, which attracted large followings in France and Germany, lobbied for higher pensions and broader political aims, but they may also have served as meeting grounds where veterans could converse about their war experiences and thereby cope with them more easily. Literature and movies about the war, regardless of their ideological messages, provided another medium for coming to terms with individual experiences, especially from the late 1920s on. The construction of thousands of war memorials in Britain, France, and Germany showed the need for public sites to mourn the dead and remember the war. Memorials in the two victorious countries emphasized the defensive aspects of their participation in the war, whereas German memorials often struck an aggressive posture. The inability of German politicians to agree on one concept for a national memorial demonstrated how deeply split Germans were over the meaning they should attribute to a war that had ended in defeat.

RECONSTRUCTION AFTER WORLD WAR II

In contrast to its hesitation after 1918, the United States took the lead in reconstructing Europe after 1945. During the final phase of the war it helped establish international agreements and agencies to

The East Berlin State Opera House during reconstruction, March 1955. ©BETTMANN/CORBIS

guarantee the success of the reconstruction process and the stability of the international order. While the United Nations was to solve international political crises, the Bretton Woods agreement, along with the International Monetary Fund and the World Bank, was to create an international economic order based on free trade, with the U.S. dollar as leading currency. The underlying assumptions were that the Soviet Union as well as Britain and France would be cooperative and that international trade would pick up quickly after the end of the war. Within two years, however, it became clear that these assumptions had been too optimistic.

The United States responded in June 1947 by offering the European Recovery Program. This package of material and financial aid was proposed for countries in both Western and Eastern Europe, but those in the east were forced by Joseph Stalin to reject the offer. Devised and announced by U.S. secretary of state George C. Marshall, it came soon to be known as the Marshall Plan and has been the subject of considerable discussion. Until the 1980s the prevailing view was that the Marshall

Plan saved a Western Europe on the brink of total collapse and put it on a path of steady growth, thereby consolidating a benign American hegemony that had been emerging since 1944–1945. Subsequent research has substantially modified this interpretation, however. It has shown that Europe—west *and* east—experienced strong domestic growth as early as in 1947. Imports to Western Europe, however, were severely hampered by the lack of dollars, and it was here, in averting a dangerous monetary crisis, that the Marshall Plan had its greatest economic impact. Equally important was its psychological impact, reassuring Western Europeans of U.S. support and giving them confidence in the future. Research since the mid-1980s has also demonstrated that Britain and France pursued nationalist agendas of European economic cooperation reminiscent of those after 1918. This cooperation eventually came in the form of agreements between a small number of states, beginning with France and Germany. The two countries approached each other and established a joint control body for coal and steel production in 1951 after French attempts to gain control over Germany's heavy industry had been met with stiff American and British resistance. Hence, contrary to American objectives, state planning, not the free market, became the founding principle of what would develop into the European Community over the next decade.

Inflation was again a problem in the immediate postwar years, particularly for France and even more so for Germany, but its negative effects were soon superseded by the unprecedented growth rates of the 1950s—around 4 percent annually—that paved the way for full employment and mass consumption at the end of the decade. In 1948 West Germany had introduced the new "Deutsche Mark," which was to become the symbol of its postwar prosperity. Reparations did not become a major political issue after 1945, nor did they slow down economic recovery for an extended period. They widened the economic gap, however, between West Germany and East Germany. Whereas West Germany was allowed to terminate its payments to the western Allies in 1952, East Germany had to provide reparations equal to a much higher share of its GDP (roughly 25 percent) to the Soviet Union until 1954. Economic reconstruction was furthermore facilitated by the fact that the aerial war had done less damage than it seemed. It had mainly affected housing and infrastructure but had left three-quarters of Germany's production capacity intact.

Immediately after the war, Europeans widely agreed that unfettered prewar capitalism had been a catastrophic failure and should be replaced by a combination of state ownership of key industries, central economic planning, and a comprehensive welfare system. As the oppressive consequences of the Soviet grip on Eastern Europe became apparent and the economic recovery attributed to the Marshall Plan began to show its luster, Western Europeans turned to conservative leaders, while remaining committed to the expansion of state functions. This was most notable in Britain, where Winston Churchill, after his return to power in 1951, kept key legislation enacted by the previous Labour government such as the nationalization of the coal mines and the tax-financed National Health Service. In France, which emerged from a four-year-long German occupation with a worn-down production apparatus, the state took control of 20 percent of the economy and used central planning to modernize the steel industry as well as electricity and the railroads. The social policy of Christian conservative Konrad Adenauer in West Germany started with housing construction, family allowances, and payments for the eight million expellees and refugees from the east; it was ambitiously expanded in 1957, when old age pensions were raised substantially and were tied to the rise of wages and salaries.

The reconstruction of European political systems began with the punishment of those deemed key figures, supporters, and collaborators of the Nazi regime. More brutal and pervasive in the east, where they turned into purges of all opponents of the newly emerging Communist order, these measures treated societal elites rather leniently in the west, sparing many civil servants, most notably the police. In West Germany, where particularly comprehensive efforts at denazification were made in the American zone of occupation, top members of the Nazi party were successfully excluded from further political influence, yet many less prominent

figures escaped punishment. While this made it easier to integrate former Nazi supporters in the new democracy, it postponed a thorough reckoning with the crimes of the Nazi regime.

All over Western Europe parliamentary democracy was now successfully revived. Coalition building overcame the bitter cleavages between Left and Right that had torn apart countries in the interwar period, as the Cold War drew Social Democrats and their allies in the trade unions steadily away from the communists. France's Fourth Republic, shaky from the start, did not survive the turmoil of decolonization and gave way to a presidential system tailored to General Charles de Gaulle at the end of the 1950s. In West Germany, the three Allies supervised the creation of a viable democratic system that deviated from the Weimar Republic in crucial respects. It shifted power to the parliament and joined political Catholicism with conservative Protestantism and free market liberalism in the new and moderate Christian Democratic Union, which was to become the leading party on the right.

The mental wounds that World War II inflicted were much more diverse than those of World War I. In addition to the experiences of the returning soldiers there were those of the survivors of the death and the concentration camps, the former slave laborers, the civilians who had survived the bombardment of their cities, the expellees and refugees, and the many women who had been raped by enemy soldiers, particularly in eastern Germany. One reaction to this multitude of horrors was silence and the attempt to move on. World War II did not spawn a new generation of war memorials, writers did not produce literary accounts as powerful as the ones published after 1918, and veterans' organizations did not become a prominent feature of the postwar public sphere. Another reaction was the construction of national memories of the war that portrayed the nation as a community in suffering and resistance, thereby neglecting the extent of collaboration and active participation in the crimes of the Nazi regime. In particular, this reconstruction of national communities in many countries failed to explicitly include the Jews. Moreover, the Holocaust became the subject of public debate only after more than a decade of silence.

CONCLUSION

The collapse of the Soviet empire in the late 1980s enabled Eastern Europeans to eventually revive parliamentary democracy themselves and, by entering the European Union, take the creation of a supranational Europe a crucial step further. But the end of the Cold War also spawned a new violent conflict in the former Yugoslavia. Atrocities against civilians in this war made postwar reconstruction a difficult endeavor that required tight international supervision akin to that imposed on Germany after 1945. In 2005, reconstruction was still an ongoing process there. Also, in the 1990s, Europeans began debating World War II and the Holocaust with renewed intensity, focusing on issues that immediately after the war had been treated either with silence or in a self-serving way. While Germans engaged in controversial discussions about the conduct of the Wehrmacht, slave labor, the air war, and a Holocaust memorial, in other countries collaboration with the Nazi regime and its share of responsibility for the Holocaust became the subjects of heated debates. Almost two generations after a successful material reconstruction, healing the mental wounds of World War II remained a painful and open-ended undertaking.

See also **Marshall Plan; Versailles, Treaty of; World War I; World War II.**

BIBLIOGRAPHY

Primary Sources

Keynes, John Maynard. *The Economic Consequences of the Peace.* 1920. With a new introduction by David Felix. New Brunswick, N.J., 2003. Highly influential critique of the Treaty of Versailles, especially of reparations, by one of the key economic theorists of the twentieth century.

Secondary Sources

Bessel, Richard. *Germany after the First World War.* Oxford, U.K., 1993. Comprehensive account of demobilization and its social and cultural ramifications.

Bessel, Richard, and Dirk Schumann, eds. *Life after Death: Approaches to a Cultural and Social History of Europe During the 1940s and 1950s.* Cambridge, U.K., 2003.

Bourke, Joanna. *Dismembering the Male. Men's Bodies, Britain, and the Great War.* Chicago, 1996. Original study of masculinity and gender relations during and after the war.

Cohen, Deborah. *The War Come Home: Disabled Veterans in Britain and Germany, 1914–1939.* Berkeley, Calif., 2001.

Downs, Laura Lee. *Manufacturing Inequality: Gender Division in the French and British Metalworking Industries, 1914–1939.* Ithaca, N.Y., 1995.

Ellwood, David W. *Rebuilding Europe: Western Europe, America, and Postwar Reconstruction.* London, 1992. Overview of reconstruction after 1945 with particular focus on economic issues.

Feldman, Gerald D. *The Great Disorder: Politics, Economics, and Society in the German Inflation, 1914–1924.* New York, 1993. Magisterial and detailed account of the German inflation, centered on the decision-making among the political and economic elites.

Geppert, Dominik, ed. *The Postwar Challenge: Cultural, Social, and Political Change in Western Europe, 1945–58.* Oxford, U.K., 2003.

Grayzel, Susan. *Women's Identities at War: Gender, Motherhood, and Politics in Britain and France During the First World War.* Chapel Hill, N.C., 1999. Shows the continuity between wartime and postwar debates.

Kuisel, Richard F. *Seducing the French: The Dilemma of Americanization.* Berkeley, Calif., 1996. On economy and society after World War II.

Lagrou, Pieter. *The Legacy of Nazi Occupation: Patriotic Memory and National Recovery in Western Europe, 1945–1965.* Cambridge, U.K., 2000.

Maier, Charles S. *Recasting Bourgeois Europe: Stabilization in France, Germany, and Italy in the Decade after World War I.* Princeton, N.J., 1975. Describes "corporatist" reconstruction based on agreements between state, capital, and labor.

Moeller, Robert G., ed. *West Germany under Construction: Politics, Society, and Culture in the Adenauer Era.* Ann Arbor, Mich., 1997.

Pedersen, Susan. *Family, Dependence, and the Origins of the Welfare State: Britain and France, 1914–1945.* Cambridge, U.K., 1993.

Roberts, Marie-Louise. *Civilization without Sexes: Reconstructing Gender in Postwar France, 1917–1927.* Chicago, 1994. Analyzes the fears of national decline attributed to women's emancipation.

Winter, Jay. *Sites of Memory, Sites of Mourning: The Great War in European Cultural History.* Cambridge, U.K., 1995.

Wirsching, Andreas, and Dirk Schumann, eds. *Violence and Society after the First World War.* Munich, 2003. First issue of *Journal of Modern European History*. Compares key countries in Western and Eastern Europe.

DIRK SCHUMANN

RED ARMY FACTION. Active in West Germany from 1970 until its disbandment in 1998, the Red Army Faction (RAF; in German, Rote Armee Fraktion) was one of the archetypal politically violent revolutionary leftist groups. Like its ideologically similar contemporaries, such as the Red Brigades in Italy and the Weathermen in the United States, the RAF grew out of the climate of radical student protest and left-wing dissent common in the late 1960s. The revolutionary violence of the RAF did not aim to overthrow the state directly through force of arms. Rather, it was somewhat more symbolic: as well as attacking representatives of "imperialism" (such as the U.S. military presence in West Germany, NATO, and industrial and commercial interests), the group apparently hoped to provoke the state into a massive overreaction against the RAF and the broader radical Left, with the purpose of exposing to the masses what the group saw as the coercive, oppressive, and still fascist nature of the state.

Although the name *Red Army Faction* was not formally used until 1971, the existence of the group is often dated from the May 1970 freeing of Andreas Baader from custody by a group including Gudrun Ensslin and Ulrike Meinhof. These three would become the nucleus of what became popularly known as the "Baader-Meinhof group."

The first communiqué to use the term *Red Army Faction* was "The Concept of the Urban Guerrilla," released in April 1971. In it, the group says that urban guerrilla warfare represents "the only revolutionary method of intervention available to what are on the whole weak revolutionary forces" and "the urban guerrilla's aim is to attack the state's apparatus of control at certain points and put them out of action, to destroy the myth of the system's omnipresence and invulnerability."

After the deaths in prison of the RAF's so-called historical leadership, the center of power in the RAF leadership shifted to those outside the prisons, and the emphasis of the "second generation" (led by Brigitte Mohnhaupt and Christian Klar) moved away from attempts to secure prisoner releases back toward what they saw as the main anti-imperialist struggle. After a period of reorganization, the RAF's next high-profile attack was the nearly successful attempted assassination of NATO commander Alexander Haig in Belgium in June 1979. There were no high-profile attacks after that until August 1981, when a car bomb exploded at a U.S. Air Force base. In September, an attempt was made to kill the U.S. army's European commander, General Frederick Kroesen, in a rocket attack. This was the last attack carried out under the second generation of the RAF leadership, who were arrested in November 1982.

The third-generation leadership did not make its presence felt until December 1984, with the attempted car bombing of a U.S. base. During the 1980s and early 1990s, the RAF engaged in assassinations or attempted assassinations of industrialists and government officials, another bombing of a U.S. base (in conjunction with the French group Action Direct), and a machine-gun attack on the U.S. embassy in Bonn. The joint operation with Action Direct was the first collaboration between two European left-wing terrorist groups. A joint communiqué stated: "The revolutionary movement in Western Europe must today move its fight into a new phase by intensifying the discussion and organization of its offensive against the imperialist apparatus with all its political, economic, and military ramifications on all levels." It continued: "Each strategic, anti-imperialist operation and offensive changes the entire balance of power in favor of the revolution and contributes to the on-going disintegration of the imperialist system of states."

In 1992, however, following the collapse of the Eastern bloc and the reunification of Germany, the RAF declared a cessation of violence against representatives of business and the state. Despite this, in 1993 the RAF destroyed a newly built prison with 600 pounds of commercial explosives and retaliated with several small firebombs for the death of one of its members in a shootout with police. Thereafter, the organization was inactive.

In April 1998 the RAF announced its official disbandment, saying "almost 28 years ago, on 14 May 1970, the RAF was born from an act of liberation: today we are ending this project. The urban guerrilla in the form of the RAF is now history." And in a piece of philosophical introspection, they added that revolutionaries desire a world in which nobody has the right to decide whether another person lives or dies, and that attacking people in their capacity as functionaries of the state is "a contradiction to the thoughts and feelings of all revolutionaries in the world—it contradicts their notion of liberation."

See also **Al Qaeda; Islamic Terrorism; Terrorism.**

BIBLIOGRAPHY

Alexander, Yonah, and Dennis A. Pluchinsky. "Red Army Faction." Chap. 3 in their *Europe's Red Terrorists: The Fighting Communist Organizations.* London, 1992. Detailed overview, incorporating the text of some RAF communiqués.

Aust, Stefan. *The Baader-Meinhof Group: The Inside Story of a Phenomenon.* Translated by Anthea Bell. London, 1987. Exhaustive account of the origins of the RAF and its activities until the deaths of the first-generation leadership.

Pluchinsky, Dennis A. "An Organizational and Operational Analysis of Germany's Red Army Faction Terrorist Group (1972–91)." Chap. 2 in *European Terrorism Today and Tomorrow,* edited by Yonah Alexander and Dennis A. Pluchinsky, 43–92. Washington, D.C., 1992. Very detailed overview of the RAF's organizational structure and activities.

Varon, Jeremy. *Bringing the War Home: The Weather Underground, the Red Army Faction, and Revolutionary Violence in the Sixties and Seventies.* Berkeley, Calif., and Los Angeles, 2004. See especially chapters 5 and 6 and pages 30–35, 38–44, 62–73, and 301–311.

GARRETT O'BOYLE

RED BRIGADES. The Red Brigades (Brigate Rosse), were a clandestine terrorist group that arose in 1969 from the extreme fringe of the Movimento Studentesco (Student Movement) of 1968. Disappointed with the failure of youth protests to bring about a revolution, on 20 October 1970 the Red Brigades announced their formation as "autonomous workers' organizations ... prepared to do battle with the employers on their own ground" (Ginsborg, p. 487). This meant, in practice, a decision to emphasize armed struggle. Like other terrorist groups before them, the Red Brigades hoped to accelerate the course of history.

Their impatience grew as they saw the early 1970s pass without the revolution drawing closer. They determined that the extensive and, for the most part, legal struggle that they had previously engaged in was a dead end and that results could be achieved only by violent and illegal action that would exacerbate the contradictions in Italian capitalism and make a conflict between exploiters and the exploited inevitable.

ORIGINS OF THE RED BRIGADES

The founders of the Red Brigades came from diverse ideological and social backgrounds. Some, like Renato Curcio and Mara Cagol, had studied at the University of Trent and had belonged to Maoist groups; others such as Alberto Franceschini and his comrades from Reggio Emilia, a city near Bologna, had been members of the Federazione Giovanile Comunisti Italiani (Italian Communist Youth Association). Many came from strong Catholic backgrounds and had passed from the religious idealism of adolescence to revolutionary groups, mostly Potere Operaio (Workers' Power) and Lotta Continua (Continuous Struggle), finally ending up in terrorist bands; still others were from working-class families or the lower middle class.

The primary model of the radical terrorists was the South American urban guerrilla. Two books on the Tupamaros, published by the Feltrinelli publishing house, became a kind of do-it-yourself manual for the early Red Brigades. Another fundamental point of reference was the Italian partisan movement of 1943 to 1945; the terrorists interpreted the Resistance movement as the most conspicuous example of a youthful minority using violent means to achieve just ends. The question of the influence that social movements and revolutionary groups had on the spread of terrorism after 1968 will be debated for a long time. The widespread justification of proletarian and revolutionary violence, however, was without doubt fertile soil for the growth of terrorism. Moreover, continual clashes in cities such as Milan between police, revolutionaries, and neofascist groups accustomed many activists to violence, facilitating their association with terrorist brigades.

The difference between the revolutionary movement and the terrorist bands was greatest with respect to their affinities. The revolutionary groups understood that in order to change Italian society they needed to form a mass movement that would profoundly affect the core of civil society itself and change its conscience. The terrorists chose clandestine life and violent action, isolating themselves from reality and society. The communiqués they issued reflected an abstract ideology whose slogans masked the absence of any social analysis. They were incapable of measuring the effects of their actions and of evaluating the resulting consequences: not only did they kill in cold blood, but they contributed to the destruction of the movement that wanted to change Italian society.

FROM PROPAGANDA TO ARMED STRUGGLE

The first actions of the Red Brigades dated from 1970 and were limited mainly to Milan and Turin; they were characterized by a virulent propaganda campaign directed against any proposals for reform, which they viewed as giving in to the bourgeois state. Later, however, in 1972 and 1973, the struggle became more physical and more violent, with attacks on and sabotage of factories in order to destroy certain production facilities emblematic of the capitalist economic system. Then the brigades began striking not only at institutions but also individuals. Their early targets were right-wing trade unionists, administrators, and foremen, especially in the Milanese factories of Pirelli, Sit-Siemens, and Fiat. The first kidnapping organized by the Red Brigades occurred in March 1972, when a manager of Sit-Siemens was abducted but released twenty minutes later with a placard around his neck that read, "Idalgo Macchiarini, fascist manager of Sit-Siemens, brought to justice by the Red Brigades. The proletariat has taken up arms; for the *padroni* it is the beginning of the end" (Ginsborg, p. 489). Early in 1974 the brigades changed their methods and ushered in the most violent phase of their activity. Often financed with money from robberies and kidnappings, they chose magistrates, police officials, journalists, and political or labor activists as their principal targets.

On 18 April 1974 the Red Brigades abducted and held for thirty-five days the Genoa judge Mario Sossi. The kidnapping propelled them to national notoriety. Although the government refused the brigades' request to free certain political prisoners of the 22 October terrorist group, Sossi was nevertheless released unharmed.

FIRST STRIKES AGAINST THE RED BRIGADES

On 1 June 1974 the police superintendent Emilio Santillo was appointed to head the newly created office for combating terrorism. It was in that year that the brigades began to incur their first losses. On 8 June, Curcio and Franceschini were arrested, betrayed by "Brother Mitra," the alias of Silvano Girotto, a police informer who had infiltrated the terrorist group, or—according to a different version of the story—a genuine militant who had had a change of heart and decided to cooperate with the authorities. On 18 February 1975 Curcio escaped from prison, but he was arrested again on 18 January 1976. On 17 June 1974, in Padua, the brigades killed two militant neofascists in the headquarters of the Movimento Sociale Italiano, a fascist-leaning party. On 15 October 1974 the police discovered a brigades hideout near Milan. A policeman was killed in the operation.

Violence on the part of both the Red Brigades and fascist terrorists increased in 1975 and 1976. Initially they shot their victims in the legs and then they began to murder them. On 15 May 1975, in the first example of *gambizzato* (wounded in the legs)—a macabre neologism that has entered into common use—Massimo De Carolis, the group leader of the Christian Democratic Party (DC) in Milan, was wounded in the legs by Red Brigades commandos. On 4 August two Red Brigades members killed a police officer. On 8 June 1976 the state prosecutor, Francesco Coco, together with his bodyguards, died in an ambush, and on 1 September the deputy police superintendent of Biella, Francesco Cusano, was assassinated.

Between 1 and 3 June 1977, several persons were *gambizzati*: journalists Vittorio Bruno, the assistant editor of the Genoa daily *Secolo XIX;* Indro Montanelli; and Emilio Rossi, the manager of TG1, a television news program. Nino Ferrero, editor of the newspaper *Unità*, was shot by Revolutionary Action (an extreme left-wing group) commandos on 18 September; Carlo Casalegno, assistant editor of the Turin newspaper *La Stampa*, was killed on 16 November. The brigades proudly claimed responsibility for his assassination, calling

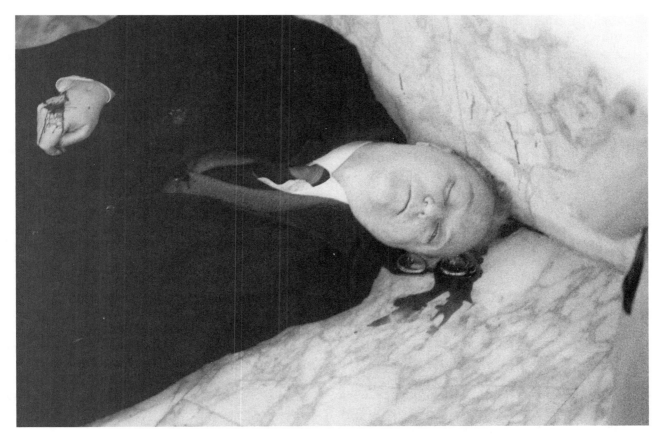

The body of law professor Vittorio Bachelet following his murder by the Red Brigade, Rome, Italy, February 1980. ©GIANNI GIANSANTI/SYGMA/CORBIS

him a "servant of the state." Industrial managers were also considered "servants of the imperialist state": Carlo Castellano, a manager of the Ansaldo Company and a member of the Italian Communist Party (PCI), was shot in the legs on 29 November.

THE KIDNAPPING OF ALDO MORO

As a result of their arrest in 1974, Curcio and Franceschini were tried beginning 9 March 1978 in a barracks in Turin; it concluded three months later with sentences of fifteen years imprisonment. On 10 March in Turin the brigades killed a police marshal.

The attacks and ambushes culminated on 16 March 1978 with the kidnapping in Rome's Via Fani of Aldo Moro, president of the DC's National Council, as he was going to the Palazzo Montecitorio for the debate on a vote of confidence in the fourth government of Giulio Andreotti—the first one to be supported by the PCI; his five bodyguards were murdered. On

20 April the Red Brigades announced in their seventh communiqué—characterized, like the others, by a five-pointed star logo—that they were willing to free Moro in exchange for "Communist prisoners." On 3 May Andreotti communicated the government's refusal to deal with the brigades. After undergoing a series of humiliating trials by the so-called People's Tribunal, Moro was murdered on 9 May. His body was found in the trunk of a red Renault 4 in Via Caetani in Rome, halfway between Via del Gesù (where the seat of the DC was located) and Via delle Botteghe Oscure (the headquarters of the PCI).

The Moro killing signaled a change in the Red Brigades' fortunes in many ways, especially in the fight against terrorism conducted both by the political forces and by the antiterrorist agencies of the state. On one hand, the attacks against people continued uninterrupted, carried out by the Red Brigades and by various other groups; on the other hand, the repression of terrorism was intensified thanks in part to the collaboration of some brigade members who dissociated themselves from the organization.

THE RESUMPTION OF TERRORISM AND THE NEW RED BRIGADES

After the abduction of the magistrate Giovanni d'Urso (kidnapped 12 December 1980, released 15 January 1981) and the highly publicized kidnapping in 1981 of U.S. General James Dozier (later freed by security forces), the Red Brigades entered a period of calm that lasted from 1982 to 1984. Nevertheless, the brigades' claims of responsibility for the murders of Ezio Tarantelli (an advisor to the Confederazione Italiana Sindacato Lavoratori, the Federation of Italian Trade Unions) in March 1985 and of DC Senator Roberto Ruffilli in April 1988 were evidence of continuing terrorist activity. The New Red Brigades took credit for the murder in Rome on 20 May 1999 of Massimo D'Antona, an advisor to Antonio Bassolino, minister of labor in the center-left government of Massimo D'Alema (21 October 1998–17 April 1998). They stated that D'Antona had been condemned to death because he was the author of the Employment and Development Pact and the head of the advisory committee on labor legislation. On 19 March 2002 in Bologna terrorists assassinated Marco Biagi, a specialist in labor problems and an advisor to the minister of welfare, Roberto Maroni, a member of Silvio Berlusconi's center-right government (2001–). In January Biagi had published an article that initiated the debate on the constitution's Article 18, which pertained to the dismissal of workers and the reform of labor.

See also **Communism; Italy; Moro, Aldo; Resistance; Terrorism.**

BIBLIOGRAPHY

Aglietta, Adelaide. *Diario di una giurata popolare al processo delle Brigate Rosse.* Milan, 1979.

Bobbio, N. *Storia di lotta continua.* Milan, 1988.

Bocca, Giorgio. *Noi terroristi: Dodici anni di lotta artmata ricostrituiti i discussi con i protagonisti.* Milan, 1985.

Caselli, Gian Carlo, and Donatella Della Porta. "La storia delle brigate rosse: strutture organizzative e strategie d'azione." In *Terrorismi in Italia,* edited by Donatella Della Porta and Gianfranco Pasquino. Bologna, 1984.

Catanzaro, Raimondo. *The Red Brigades and Left-Wing Terrorism in Italy.* New York, 1991.

Dalla Chiesa, Nando. "Del Sessantotto e del terrorismo: Cultura e politica tra continuità e rottura." *Il Mulino* no. 273 (1981): 53–94.

Fenzi, Enrico. *Armi e bagagli: Un diario dalle Brigate Rosse.* Genoa, Italy, 1986.

Galli, Giorgio. *Storia del partito armato, 1968–1982.* Milan, Italy, 1986.

Ginsborg, Paul. *Storia d'Italia dal dopoguerra a oggi: Società e politica, 1943–1988.* Turin, Italy, 1989.

Magone, G. G. "Il terrorismo che stabilizza." *L'Indice* no. 8 (1986): 4.

Meade, Robert C. *The Red Brigades: The Story of Italian Terrorism.* New York, 1990.

Papa, Emilio R. *Il processo alle Brigate Rosse: Brigate Rosse e difesa d'ufficio: Documenti.* Turin, Italy, 1979.

Pavone, Claudio. "Sparo dunque sono: Il nodo della violenza." *Il Manifesto,* 6 May 1982.

Sciascia, Leonardo. *The Moro Affair: And the Mystery of Majorana.* Translated by Sacha Rabinovitch. New York, 1987.

Tranfaglia, Nicola. "La crisi italiana e il problema storico del terrorismo." In *Labirinto italiano: Radici storiche e nuove contraddizioni,* edited by Nicola Tranfaglia. Turin, Italy, 1984.

MARIA TERESA GIUSTI

RED CROSS. Formally known in the early twenty-first century as the International of Red Cross and Red Crescent Movement, the Red Cross is the largest humanitarian network in the world, active in almost all countries. The movement is made up of the International Committee of the Red Cross (ICRC), the International Federation of Red Cross and Red Crescent Societies (formerly the League of Red Cross Societies), and the national Red Cross and Red Crescent societies. Several times component parts of the movement or one of its leading figures have won the Nobel Peace Prize: Henry Dunant in 1901; the ICRC in 1917 and 1944; and the ICRC and the League of Red Cross Societies in 1963.

The Red Cross Movement is guided by seven fundamental principles: humanity, impartiality, neutrality, independence, voluntary service, unity, and universality. These are designed to ensure the

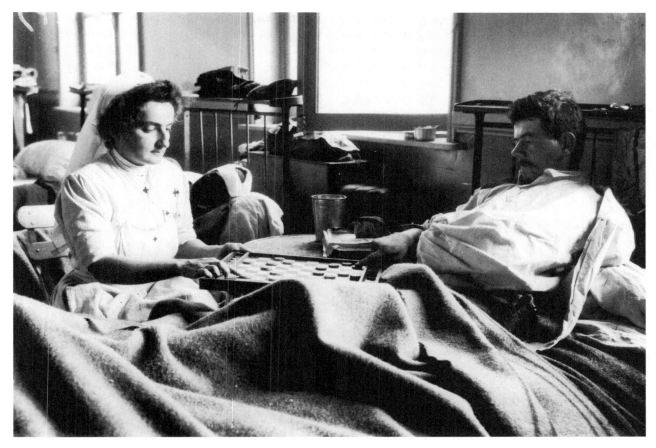

A Red Cross nurse plays checkers with a wounded soldier, France, 1914. Bridgeman Art Library

organization's cohesiveness and the permanence of its activities.

The movement uses two symbols as its distinguishing mark: a red cross or a red crescent on a white ground. National societies usually use one or the other according to their state's choice. There are some nations, however, who do not recognize themselves in either emblem, and for this reason in December 2005 the movement adopted an additional symbol, the red crystal.

To coordinate efforts and clarify the respective roles of the ICRC and the International Federation, an International Conference of the Red Cross and Red Crescent held regularly—in principle every four years—with the participation of the nations signatory to the Geneva Conventions. Precisely because of this participation, the decisions of the conference can have significant formative effects on international law. In the intervals between conferences, liaison among the component parts of the organization is maintained by the Standing Commission of the International Red Cross and Red Crescent.

ORIGINS OF THE RED CROSS

The idea of the Red Cross arose from the initiative of the Swiss Henry Dunant, who witnessed the terrible suffering of wounded soldiers at the battle of Solferino (Italy) in 1859. In the absence of any military medical services, Dunant called on local people for help and improvised aid to the injured men abandoned on the battlefield. Dunant recounted this experience in his book *Un souvenir de Solférino* (1862; *A Memory of Solferino*) and made two proposals as to how help might be furnished, without distinction, to all soldiers wounded in combat. First, he suggested that in peacetime, and in each country, national aid committees should be set up with the power to intervene during military conflicts; second, he urged nations to recognize and respect a number of principles governing the action of such committees. In February 1863, Dunant and four fellow Genevans—Louis Appia, Guillaume-Henri Dufour, Théodore Maunoir, and Gustave Moynier—took the first step in realizing these ideas by founding an "International Committee for Aid to Wounded Soldiers." In 1875 this committee would officially become the International Committee of the Red Cross (ICRC). Its headquarters is still in Geneva, and its members are still exclusively Swiss.

In August 1863 the committee convened an international conference in Geneva to consider how best to remedy the lack of official medical services for armies on campaign. This meeting produced ten resolutions that became the bedrock of the International Movement of the Red Cross.

After the 1863 conference the International Committee for Aid to Wounded Soldiers set itself two goals: the swift establishment of national societies for aid to war casualties and the concluding of an international treaty underwriting the neutrality of medical aid administered to the wounded in time of war. Accordingly, ten national societies were founded in June 1864, and in August of the same year, at the invitation of Switzerland, a diplomatic conference opened in Geneva with sixteen nations represented.

At the conclusion of this conference, on 22 August, representatives of twelve nations signed a "Convention for the Amelioration of the Condition of the Wounded and Sick in Armed Forces in the Field." This was the First Geneva Convention. It was quickly ratified by the signatories, and many other nations adhered to it later.

It should be emphasized that the First Geneva Convention constitutes the cornerstone of public international law, because it constitutes the first multilateral treaty concluded in peacetime, open to all nations. By establishing the wounded soldier's right to protection and assistance, the convention marked the birth of modern humanitarian law, specifically "Geneva law," which is concerned with the treatment of the victims of war.

The First Geneva Convention was revised and expanded in 1906, and modified once more in 1929, at which time another convention was adopted "relative to the treatment of prisoners of war." In 1949 all the Geneva Conventions, of which there were now three, were again revised, and a new,

Fourth Convention was signed "relative to the protection of civilian persons in time of war." In 1977 two new treaties were signed by many nations and added to the Geneva Conventions of 1949. These "additional protocols" concerned, respectively, "the protection of victims of international armed conflicts" and "the protection of victims of non-international armed conflicts."

INTERNATIONAL COMMITTEE OF THE RED CROSS (ICRC)

Ever since its founding, the ICRC has continued to further the Red Cross's action in the world by encouraging the creation of new national societies of the Red Cross and Red Crescent and by urging nations to sign the Geneva Conventions. It is a strictly neutral intermediary, its mandate being to protect and assist victims of conflict. It was on this basis that the ICRC sent its representatives to the scenes of the Prusso-Danish War (1864), the Austro-Prussian War (1866), and the Franco-Prussian War (1870–1871).

As part of its intervention during this last-mentioned conflict, the ICRC set up a tracing agency whose purpose was to allow soldiers, be they wounded, sick, or prisoners, to get news to their families. This kind of activity was undertaken once more in the wars that followed, including the last Russo-Turkish War (1877–1878), the Serbo-Bulgarian War (1885), the Balkan Wars (1912–1913), and World War I (1914–1918).

The duration and magnitude of World War I led the ICRC to undertake new kinds of action. Red Cross delegations were sent to prison camps to review the physical and material conditions of detention and call if need be for improvements therein. The ICRC also concerned itself with the fate of civilians in enemy hands, seeking to obtain treatment for them similar to that promised to prisoners of war. When hostilities ended, it organized the repatriation of hundreds of thousands of POWs and came to the aid of populations hit by famine and epidemic.

The impact of World War I also led the ICRC to work for the expansion of international humanitarian law, spurring the revision of the First Geneva Convention in 1929 and the framing at that time, as mentioned above, of the Third Convention on the treatment of prisoners of war. In the interwar years the ICRC conducted several major campaigns of protection and aid, most notably during the Italo-Ethiopian War of 1935–1936 and the Spanish civil war of 1936–1939.

World War II was especially onerous for the ICRC. It was of course confronted by immense demands on its services, and more than three thousand new workers had to be taken on. The organization strove to maintain delegations in all the belligerent countries, while about eleven thousand visits were made to prison camps, and an estimated thirty-six million care packages distributed.

The ICRC found it difficult to intervene in favor of some prisoners of war, especially in view of the fact that neither the Soviet Union nor Japan was bound by the Geneva Convention relative to the treatment of POWs. It attempted to apply the convention in a de facto manner, but met with only very partial success in this. German prisoners in Soviet hands and Soviet prisoners held by the Germans were simply not protected by the convention. The situation was little different in the Far East, where very few prison-camp visits were ever made.

As for civilians, the ICRC failed to gauge the massive scope either of the genocide of the Jews and Gypsies, or of the persecution of other minorities by the Nazis. Even though the humanitarian law of the time offered little recourse with respect to the protection of civilians, the ICRC could have exercised its right to intervene far more vigorously than it did. The organization envisaged a public denunciation of the genocide, but the proposal was rejected after intense discussions within its committee. This diplomatic silence during the Holocaust constitutes one of the gravest episodes in the ICRC's history.

The catastrophic balance-sheet of World War II, with its gigantic civilian toll, was the motivation for the new Geneva Convention concerning the protection of civilian populations in wartime and for the revision of those conventions already in effect. Four newly framed conventions were thus adopted on 12 August 1949.

Between 1946 and 1970, aside from tasks related to the aftermath of World War II

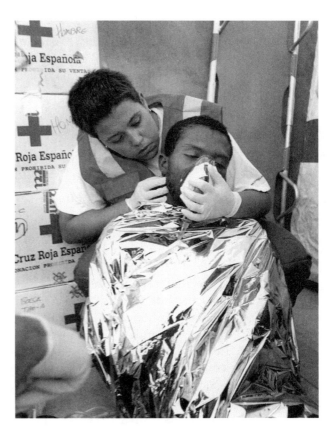

A Spanish Red Cross volunteer helps an African man who nearly drowned trying to reach the Spanish island of Fuerteventura in a small boat, July 2004. ©JUAN MENDIAN/REUTERS/CORBIS

(repatriation, search for the missing, family reunification), the ICRC launched protection and aid programs in several armed conflicts. It intervened in the Korean War (1950–1953); in the Hungarian uprising of 1956–1957; in military conflicts in the Near East (1948–1950, 1956, 1967, 1973); in anticolonial wars in Algeria (1955–1962) and the Congo (1960); and in the Nigerian civil war (1967–1970).

In the realm of international humanitarian law, the ICRC drafted the two protocols that were added to the Geneva Conventions in 1949. These two treaties, which took into account the new forms of conflict and set forth rules designed to protect civilians during hostilities, were adopted on 8 June 1977 by the diplomatic conference convened in Geneva between 1974 and 1977.

Between 1960 and 1990, the ICRC intervened ever more frequently in the Third World, as for instance in the conflict between India and Pakistan (1971–1975), in the wars in Indochina (Vietnam, Cambodia, and Laos), the Iran-Iraq War (1980–1988), and the first Gulf War (1991). It also acted in the upheavals and conflicts that shook Chile, El Salvador, Nicaragua, Angola, Ethiopia, and Sudan and was in the field in Poland in 1981–1984 and in Romania in 1989–1990. Between 1986 and 1990, the ICRC played a role in a total of eighty countries.

During the years from 1990 to 2000, the so-called humanitarian decade, as nongovernmental organizations (NGOs) mushroomed and the humanitarian efforts of the United Nations were boosted by the end of the Cold War, the ICRC's activity likewise expanded considerably. The organization was represented during all the main conflicts of the period—in Somalia, the former Yugoslavia, Kosovo, Rwanda, Chechnya, and Sudan. In the first years of the twenty-first century, too, the ICRC continued to deploy broadly alongside the United Nations (UN) and the NGOs.

NATIONAL RED CROSS AND RED CRESCENT SOCIETIES

Directly descended from the national relief societies for assisting the war wounded, the national societies of the Red Cross and Red Crescent total 183 as of 2006, with several million members and volunteers and some three hundred thousand employees in all. Each year these societies assist millions of people.

The main requirements for recognition as a national society are as follows: the society must be established within the frontiers of a country that subscribes to the Geneva Conventions; must be the sole such entity in that country and recognized by its government; must have an autonomous status; must use the emblem in conformity with movement regulations; must recruit members without distinction as to race, sex, social class, religion, or political opinion; and must pledge to respect the fundamental principles of the Red Cross.

During peacetime, the national societies are merely auxiliaries to their respective governments in the social sphere: they may establish and manage hospitals; train nursing staff; provide aid to the disadvantaged, the handicapped, or the elderly; deliver emergency care in the event of natural disaster; and so on. In this capacity they are subject to all national laws. In 2003, however, the need for a clearer definition of this auxiliary function vis-à-vis state authorities made itself felt, for the original conception of the mandate—the provision of aid to wounded and sick soldiers on the field of battle—had become so blurred that the universal calling of the national societies was not always apparent.

For the national societies have an international role: in collaboration with the International Federation or the ICRC, they serve the needs of victims of armed conflict or natural disaster everywhere. Each is therefore expected to support peer societies in other countries and bolster their preparedness for future eventualities.

INTERNATIONAL FEDERATION OF RED CROSS AND RED CRESCENT SOCIETIES

In the wake of the very considerable efforts of the national societies during World War I, it was decided that they should federate as an international organization. At the suggestion of the president of the American Red Cross War Committee, Henry P. Davison, the League of Red Cross Societies was founded on 5 May 1919 in Paris. Its purpose was to initiate and foster cooperation between the national societies in the work of improving health, preventing illness, and reducing suffering in the world.

This new organization at first sought to take over the leadership of the Red Cross Movement from the ICRC, even putting the latter's continued existence in jeopardy. The ICRC stood firm, however, and managed to maintain its position while proposing possible forms of coexistence with the league. In 1928, in order to define the respective responsibilities of the two organizations, the Red Cross for the first time in its history adopted a set of statutes.

In 1919–1920, the league conducted its first great relief campaign when it aided the victims of a typhus outbreak in Poland. A year later it assisted a famine-stricken Russia. In 1923, with the help of thirty-five national societies, it collected 277 million Swiss francs for earthquake victims in Tokyo. During the 1930s the league assisted refugees from the Spanish civil war (1936–1939) and from a Czechoslovakia under threat from the Third Reich (1938).

The league was also very active in the areas of health care and youth work. It ran training courses for health workers and mounted campaigns against a variety of epidemic diseases including tuberculosis, venereal disease, and malaria. As part of this activity, in 1922 the league founded the Youth Red Cross as a means of enlisting young people in the struggle for better understanding among peoples and enduring peace.

During World War II the league's activities were sharply reduced due to political divisions. The organization nevertheless continued to ensure communications among the various national societies, and otherwise concentrated on the expansion of those of them that were not directly affected by the war. Together with the ICRC, moreover, it set up a joint relief commission that carried out vast operations for the relief of civilian populations.

After the war, the league resumed its traditional activities, with the emphasis on the promotion of peace. Beginning in 1948, it promoted blood donation, pressing the national societies to organize blood drives.

Between 1948 and 1990 the league organized various relief actions for refugees and disaster victims. The league and a number of national societies provided relief to refugees of many nationalities: Palestinian (1948–1950), Hungarian (1956–1957), Algerian (1958–1962), and Vietnamese (1975–1985). The league also came to the aid of earthquake victims, as in Morocco and Chile in 1960, Turkey and Guatemala in 1976, Mexico in 1985, and Armenia in 1988; and it helped populations suffering the effects of tidal waves and cyclones in the Gulf of Bengal (1966–1973, 1977–1982).

See also **International Law; Prisoners of War; Refugees.**

BIBLIOGRAPHY

Boissier, Pierre. *From Solferino to Tsushima: History of the International Committee of the Red Cross.* Geneva, 1985.

Bugnion, François. *The International Committee of the Red Cross and the Protection of War Victims.* Oxford, U.K., and Geneva, 2003.

Durand, André. *From Sarajevo to Hiroshima: History of the International Committee of the Red Cross.* Geneva, 1984.

Haug, Hans. *Humanity for All: The International Red Cross and Red Crescent Movement.* In cooperation with Hans-Peter Gasser, Françoise Perret, and Jean-Pierre Robert-Tissot. Berne, Switzerland, 1993.

Pictet, Jean. *The Fundamental Principles of the Red Cross Proclaimed by the Twentieth International Conference of the Red Cross, Vienna, 1965: Commentary.* Geneva, 1979.

Reid, Daphne A., and Patrick F. Gilbo. *Beyond Conflict: The International Federation of Red Cross and Red Crescent Societies, 1919–1994.* Geneva, 1997.

ISABELLE VONÈCHE CARDIA

REFUGEES.

REFUGEES. Global conflicts, including the Cold War, and the collapse of empires and civil wars were the major impetus for the involuntary displacement of people in the twentieth century. The focus herein is on the key moments of crisis that led to the displacement of civilians in Europe, the role played by states in prompting flight or establishing the terms of resettlement, and the efforts that were made to manage crises and to relieve the conditions in which refugees found themselves.

WORLD WAR I

It was during World War I that the word *refugees* first became a familiar term in European public life. Following the German invasion of Belgium on 4 August 1914, tens of thousands of Belgian civilians crossed the English Channel to find refuge in the United Kingdom. Their arrival prompted a flurry of private charitable activity, including the War Refugees Committee launched by Flora Lugard (1852–1929), former colonial correspondent for the *Times* of London. By the time the war ended, in November 1918, 140,000 Belgian refugees were registered in the United Kingdom. Other refugees fled to the Netherlands where they were housed first in government-built camps and later on in cheap bungalows capable of being dismantled and quickly reassembled elsewhere. Camp life emphasized health, hygiene, and hard work making toys and household goods.

British officials acknowledged an obligation toward refugees, whose plight reflected the Allies' inability to stem the enemy onslaught that exposed the devout Catholic inhabitants of Belgium to "pagan" Germany. But in their anxiety about "undesirable aliens," government officials kept close track of the refugee population. Belgians complained, to no avail, about the Aliens Restriction Act (5 August 1914), which required them to notify the police of any journey they made of more than five miles and confined them to specific areas of the country. Plans were drawn up to resettle the refugees in Chile and in South Africa, but the Belgian authorities rebuffed these proposals on the grounds that refugees should contribute to national reconstruction. Most returned to Belgium by 1919. The relief effort was informed by a mixture of condescension and genuine concern for human suffering. The novelist Edith Wharton (1862–1937) wrote a short story titled "The Refugees" lampooning the rush by comfortable British families to adopt a refugee as a social adornment.

The Austrian invasions of Serbia in 1914 and 1915 produced a catastrophic displacement of soldiers and civilians, amounting to one-third of the prewar total. Half a million refugees made their way across the mountains into Albania. Many ended up in Corfu, Corsica, and Tunisia; perhaps 200,000 died en route. Other Serb refugees were incarcerated in Austrian camps and treated as forced labor. The Society of Friends (American and British Quakers) along with the American Red Cross lent their support to the relief of the refugees. The Serbian Relief Fund, created by the historian Robert Seton-Watson (1879–1951), brought some refugee children to the United Kingdom.

Events elsewhere also generated large numbers of refugees. In Austria-Hungary Jewish civilians, fearful of tsarist troops, fled from the empire's eastern territories of Galicia and Bukovina to the relative safety of Vienna where they came under the care of middle-class Jews. In the Ottoman Empire, Armenians were targeted by the Young Turks as "disloyal" and "subversive" elements. Hundreds of thousands of Armenians were disarmed, arrested, and sent east. Many were simply killed. A minority escaped to safety, either to Syria or to the Russian-controlled Transcaucasus. By the beginning of 1916 more than 100,000 ex-Ottoman Armenians sought refuge in Erivan (now Yerevan), then a small town. Philanthropic efforts mobilized Armenian society in the Russian Empire, where

relief agencies supplied food and medicine, looked after orphans, and provided basic schooling.

The Russian Empire itself was another site of population displacement. Civilians fled to the interior to escape the German and Austrian invasion. The Russian high command deported German, Jewish, Polish, and other subjects of the tsar. By the beginning of 1917 there were six million refugees and forced migrants, roughly equivalent to 5 percent of the total population. The war generated extensive voluntary as well as governmental intervention. Municipal authorities, diocesan committees, and private charities established schools and orphanages. Peasant communities and rural cooperatives harnessed their established mechanisms of self-help to the task of assisting the newcomers. Overall the war brought about an impressive relief effort. Humanitarian initiatives provided evidence of a newly emerging professional ethos in late imperial Russia, giving social workers, doctors, psychiatrists, statisticians, and lawyers practice in scrutinizing and managing the tsar's subjects.

Crucially, because resources were thinly stretched, the tsarist state also devolved some of the responsibility for refugee relief onto newly formed "national committees" (Polish, Jewish, Latvian, and Armenian—although not Russian or Ukrainian). These committees mobilized "national" opinion at home and abroad. Within an emerging patriotic intelligentsia, this aspect of refugeedom inspired a sense of calamity that gave rise to a vision of national solidarity. Deliberate action was needed, as one Latvian activist put it, to ensure that Latvians avoid "the lot of the Jews, to be scattered across the entire globe." Polish activists spoke of "preserving the refugee on behalf of the motherland." These patriotic elites engaged in a new national politics, instructing the refugee population in their rights and responsibilities.

World War I was thus significant in various senses. It created or legitimated a broad range of relief agencies and professional expertise. It trained patriotic leaders in the practice of government. The political scientist Hannah Arendt (1906–1971) famously suggested that the successor nation-states in eastern Europe were associated with a refugee-generating process. This is only part of the story. By giving patriotic elites direct access to a nascent national community and training them in

Refugees who fled the fighting in the town of Lublin, Poland, camped on a roadside, September 1915.
©BETTMANN/CORBIS

the art of government, refugeedom played a more fundamental role, helping to crystallize the new nation-state.

THE LEGACY OF WORLD WAR I

The Russian Revolution unleashed a bitter civil war between those who supported and those who opposed the Bolsheviks. Having failed to overthrow the new regime, anti-Bolshevik elements fled Russia. Most never returned, settling instead in "temporary" refugee camps in Turkey, Bulgaria, Yugoslavia, and Greece. By 1922 more than 27 percent of the total Russian refugee population had settled in Germany; some estimates put their number in Berlin alone at 360,000. A further 20 percent settled in Poland, 16 percent in the Balkan states, and 10 percent in France. Around 17 percent settled in the Far East, where conditions remained deplorable throughout the 1920s and 1930s, with the remaining 10 percent scattered elsewhere. Welfare organizations such as Zemgor (the Union of Towns and Cities, formed in 1915) provided basic material support. A handful

returned to Soviet Russia under an amnesty issued in September 1920.

What of those displaced earlier within the former Russian Empire? Many non-Russians were motivated to return by a desire to participate in the reconstruction of their newly independent "homeland." Between 1918 and 1924 around 130,000 people were repatriated to Latvia, and a further 215,000 to Lithuania. By 1925 the total number of Polish citizens who had been repatriated from the Soviet Union stood at 1.3 million. They endured appalling conditions; typhus was a major health hazard. Relief workers, such as the British Quaker Ruth Fry (1878–1962), encouraged these returnees to get back on their feet by lending seed, timber, and petty credit. Matters were not helped by the tendency of Polish, Latvian, and Lithuanian officials to portray the returnees as potential subversives. Border guards barred or delayed the return of nonnational refugees. Jews, in particular, suffered discrimination.

One legacy of the war was thus the promotion of a sense of exclusion that had pernicious consequences as new nation-states emerged from the wreckage of multinational empires. This was often accompanied by downward social mobility, as with Hungarian refugees who, under the terms of the Treaty of Trianon (4 June 1920), found themselves a beleaguered minority in newly independent Czechoslovakia, Romania, and Yugoslavia. Having forfeited the privileged position they enjoyed as landed gentry in the old Austro-Hungarian Empire, they fled to a truncated Hungarian state, forming the backbone of a reactionary and revanchist politics.

MANUFACTURING REFUGEES: THE GREEK-TURKISH POPULATION EXCHANGE

Another legacy of war was the exchange of population between Greece and Turkey as provided in the Lausanne Convention (30 January 1923) and endorsed by the Treaty of Lausanne (24 July 1923), whose purpose was "to bring to a final close the state of war which has existed in the East since 1914." The treaty followed the defeat of the Greek army in Anatolia and the sacking of Smyrna in the autumn of 1922, following which 900,000 Turkish nationals of the Greek Orthodox faith fled for Greece. Their hope of a speedy return at the end of hostilities was quickly dashed. Under the Lausanne Convention, 350,000 Muslims were uprooted from Greece and moved to Turkey. Some estimates suggest that up to half a million displaced persons remained unaccounted for following this exchange. The League of Nations established a Refugee Settlement Commission in Greece, but resources were badly stretched and most refugees lived in makeshift barracks.

The *Mikrasiates* (Asia Minor refugees) prided themselves on being more cosmopolitan and devout than their new neighbors. Local Greeks were portrayed as unsophisticated "shepherds"; they in turn poked fun at refugees as "stupid" and "baptized in yogurt." But the newcomers made a significant contribution to the Greek economy by developing new industries such as carpet weaving and tobacco production. (They also introduced the bouzouki, a stringed instrument, and *rebetika,* a type of urban folk music, to mainland Greece.) Politically the poorer refugees initially supported the Liberal Party led by Eleutherios Venizelos (1864–1936) but subsequently switched

allegiance to the Greek Communist Party, which, until it was banned in 1936, campaigned on behalf of "workers, peasants and refugees." Meanwhile the displaced Muslim refugees fared little better in Turkish society.

THE INTERNATIONAL REFUGEE REGIME AND EUROPE'S REFUGEES

The international refugee regime has its origins in the aftermath of World War I. In August 1921 the League of Nations created a High Commission for Refugees (HCR), led by the renowned Norwegian Arctic explorer Fridtjof Nansen (1861–1930). This was an initiative to support Russian and Armenian refugees. Many members of the league originally hoped that the refugee problem would be solved by repatriation. These hopes were soon dashed. Nansen supplied refugees with identity documents in order that they not be returned involuntarily to Soviet Russia. By 1923 thirty-nine governments recognized the right of holders of the "Nansen passport" to cross international boundaries, provided that they did not thereby adopt another nationality.

The League of Nations had no funds of its own to spend on the relief and resettlement of refugees; its agencies played a supporting and coordinating role instead, relying where possible on financial assistance from national governments and voluntary bodies. Armenian refugees settled in France, encouraged by the authorities who wished to address the shortage of labor following World War I. Many were housed in refugee camps such as Camp Oddo in Marseille, where they remained until 1927. Nansen wanted to settle others in South America, a destination later favored by the U.S. delegates to the Evian Conference on Refugees in July 1938.

In accepting the Nobel Peace Prize in 1938, the Nansen International Office for Refugees spoke of the "material benefits" that the prize would bring to the refugees under its care. It went on to "rejoice above all in the moral effect that the Nobel Committee's decision cannot fail to exert on world opinion by emphasizing the enormous importance of the refugee problem." The following years brought little evidence of such "moral effect" and multiplied the "refugee problem" many times over.

THE SPANISH CIVIL WAR AND THE RISE OF NAZISM

The Spanish civil war (1936–1939) produced massive internal and external displacement. As early as June 1936 some sixty thousand refugees entered France; by October 1937 five times that number had settled there, in the relatively friendly environment created by Léon Blum's Popular Front government. The mood did not last. Following General Francisco Franco's march on Barcelona, which fell to Nationalist forces in January 1939, an estimated 300,000 refugees gathered at the French border. Border officials turned them back. Conditions in the French refugee camps were rudimentary and refugees faced much local hostility, but they stayed put. Following the international recognition granted the Franco regime after World War II, they abandoned hope of returning to Spain.

Others ended up in the United Kingdom, having been sponsored by local fundraising groups and the Trades Union Congress. Some assistance was orchestrated by Katharine, Duchess of Atholl (1874–1960), known as the "Red Duchess," who achieved brief notoriety. The Basque Children's Committee subsequently published a journal that enabled refugees to keep in touch and to publish their memoirs; significantly, it was titled *Amistad*. Meanwhile the French arranged for around five thousand Spanish refugee orphans to be resettled in the Soviet Union. (Adult refugees were often deported to the gulag.)

In response to the growing numbers of Jewish refugees from Nazi Germany and Poland, the French government contemplated settling them in Madagascar, thereby avoiding the need to locate them in Palestine. The American Jewish Joint Distribution Committee supported this proposal, but it foundered because of colonial opposition. In a familiar refrain, the French government accused German refugees of being "spies and subversives" and accordingly imposed tough restrictions on entry.

In 1938 (the year of *Kristallnacht*) the situation worsened dramatically in Germany, Austria, Czechoslovakia, and Italy. Édouard Daladier (1884–1970), restored to power as French prime minister in April 1938 and resolutely opposed to the Popular Front, hurriedly introduced a decree on French residence, distinguishing the "new" from the "old" (i.e., Russian and Armenian) refugees and affirming that France had reached a "saturation point." Other distinctions were also drawn, notably between the "authentic" political refugees and the "undesirable" economic migrant, although this wholly arbitrary dividing line did not stop some politicians from advocating the import of cheap refugee labor.

The Geneva Convention on Refugees (4 July 1936 and 10 February 1938) provided relief to refugees from Nazi Germany. A key advocate was the British lawyer Norman Bentwich (1883–1971). The HCR, however, had no mandate to address the needs of refugees from Nazi-occupied Austria and elsewhere in Europe. The U.S. president Franklin D. Roosevelt convened the Evian Conference to attempt to resolve their plight, but it achieved little. French ministers reiterated their concerns that an "influx" of refugees would undermine domestic security. British delegates refused to allow any discussion of Palestine as a potential destination. The desperate refugees already in France found it increasingly difficult to secure even temporary residence permits.

WORLD WAR II AND ITS AFTERMATH

Population displacement in World War II, including compulsory deportation, was eerily reminiscent of World War I. The chief theater of displacement was Europe. One million Poles and Polish Jews left western Poland following the German invasion. From 1939 to 1941 Ukrainians fled westward to Germany from Soviet-occupied western Ukraine. The Soviet premier Joseph Stalin deported German settlers from the Volga region in 1941. Poles were expelled from Ukraine by nationalist forces in 1942. There were numerous involuntary movements of population elsewhere. Existing refugee groups were exposed to great risk. In France, for example, interned Spanish civil war refugees were exposed to the German onslaught in 1940.

As the tide of war turned, the retreat of the German army from the territories it occupied since 1938 was accompanied by a mass flight of five million ethnic Germans, who feared reprisals from partisans and the Soviet Red Army. Others were expelled "spontaneously" by local communities in Poland and Czechoslovakia. The Potsdam

Refugees fleeing Germany cross a partially destroyed railroad bridge over the Elbe River near the town of Tagemunde, May 1945. ©HULTON-DEUTSCH COLLECTION/CORBIS

Conference (17 July–2 August 1945) sanctioned these "transfers." By mid-1947 the Allies counted 10.5 million ethnic German refugees in the occupation zones. The settled population regarded these *Vertriebene* (exiles) with alarm, believing that they threatened the health and integrity of the German *Volk*. Meanwhile dedicated *Landsmannschaften* (homeland societies) gave the expellees a degree of collective identity and political leverage. The additional burden that they placed on resources was subsequently alleviated by the West German "economic miracle," which provided them with greater security without extinguishing hopes of a return to their former homes in Eastern Europe.

In May 1944, 200,000 Crimean Tatars, irrespective of occupation and Communist Party membership, were summarily transported to Uzbekistan on grounds of collective ethnic disloyalty. Little is known of the lives they lived or of the ways in which they may have sought to maintain a sense of collective identity. The Stalinist state also inflicted enormous harm on the so-called kulak-bandit population of the Baltic states and western Belorussia during the postwar collectivization drive. Between 1948 and 1952 farming households were forcibly transferred from the Baltic states to the Urals and Siberia. The impact of these deportations too remains virtually uncharted territory.

At the end of the war displaced persons (DP) camps sprang up throughout liberated Germany, Austria, and Italy, initially under the auspices of the United Nations Relief and Rehabilitation Administration and then the International Refugee Organization, which was responsible for resettling refugees. Over five hundred such camps were still in existence in 1948, housing 800,000 refugees.

The DP camp was by definition a place of incarceration, but it nevertheless provided an opportunity for a degree of self-administration. Camp authorities sponsored cooperative businesses, educational ventures, music and theater companies, and scout troops. DP camps also became a training ground for future political activists. Officials repatriated reluctant Ukrainian and other refugees to the Soviet Union. Relief workers spoke up for DPs who wished to move to North America and Australia, formulating their appeals with a "human interest" angle rather than concentrating on legal formulas. Around 400,000 DPs traveled to the United States under the Displaced Persons Act (25 June 1948).

Inevitably the schemes for resettling the DPs tended to favor the young and able-bodied workers. Under the European Voluntary Worker (EVW) program, the British government dispatched officials to the DP camps to identify "quality" workers, in order to satisfy the demand for labor in key occupations such as textiles and agriculture. Other EVWs were assigned to jobs in hospitals and sanatoria. The elderly or sick became known as the "hard core," stranded in the camps until they died or were rescued by charitable government officials. Thus the program to resettle refugees was governed primarily by economic considerations, not by the wish to save Baltic, Polish, or Ukrainian DPs from Soviet retribution.

Other episodes of displacement are less well known. The Italian-Yugoslav peace treaty in 1947 required defeated Italy to renounce Istria. Some 300,000 *profughi* (refugees), fearing retribution by Yugoslav partisans, left Istria between 1947 and 1954, settling first in refugee camps and then in shelters built by the Italian government in Trieste, itself a contested city. (Some camps survived until the 1960s.) Styling themselves *esuli* (exiles) rather than refugees, they recounted these momentous events in terms of "national" suffering, martyrdom, and (more recently) "ethnic cleansing," thereby sustaining contemporary irredentist claims and demands for compensation. Thus population displacement continues to reverberate in political and social life.

The aftermath of World War II witnessed the creation of a new international refugee regime in which the focus shifted from the group (as with Russian refugees) to the individual. Signatories to the 1951 Convention relating to the Status of Refugees acknowledged as a general principle that refugees could claim protection if they were subject as individuals to a "well-founded fear of persecution, on grounds of race, religion, nationality, membership of a particular social group or political opinion." Crucially, the convention applied only to refugees who had been displaced by events prior to 1 January 1951, and signatories could confine their obligations to refugees from events occurring in Europe alone. It also enshrined the principle that refugees could not be returned to the country that persecuted them. The convention came into force on 22 April 1954, by which time the Office of the United Nations High Commissioner for Refugees (UNHCR) had been in existence for three years. Given its limited budget, the UNHCR could do little more than resettle small numbers of displaced persons in conjunction with voluntary agencies.

THE COLD WAR AND EUROPE'S REFUGEES

Echoes of World War II—as a consequence of the Sovietization of Eastern Europe—can be detected in the displacement that followed the 1956 Hungarian uprising against Soviet domination. Hungarian refugees were embraced by the UNHCR, notwithstanding the 1951 convention, on the grounds that their "persecution" could be directly attributed to the postwar turmoil and the Sovietization of Eastern Europe. In the space of a few months around 200,000 Hungarian refugees, mostly from Budapest, crossed the border into Austria and Yugoslavia. Western governments addressed the refugee crisis at once, lest displaced Hungarians contribute to the "destabilization" of Austria, which had only recently said farewell to Soviet occupation forces. Hungarian refugees were welcomed in the United States, Canada, and Britain on the grounds that they were the living embodiment of communist persecution. They offered firsthand accounts of life behind the Iron Curtain to Western social scientists and intelligence agencies. Other Hungarian dissidents were simply deported to Soviet prison camps.

The UNHCR became the main agency responsible for assisting Hungarian refugees. Various nongovernmental organizations and private agencies also intervened, including the Red Cross. The

Bosnian refugees sit outside train carriages serving as temporary homes in a camp in Cakovec, Croatia, c. 1991–1995. ©HOWARD DAVIES/CORBIS

situation in Hungary was important for other reasons. It was the first occasion in which a refugee crisis reached a wider public audience through television coverage.

CRUCIBLES OF DISPLACEMENT

In 1974 Turks and Greeks once again experienced population displacement, this time as a consequence of the Turkish invasion of Cyprus, which took place against the background of deteriorating relations between Greek and Turkish Cypriots. Displaced Greek villagers resented being labeled *refugees,* a term that implied that they would not soon return to their homes. In response to refugee activists, the Cyprus government set aside houses abandoned by Turkish Cypriots or made affordable housing available to the refugees, and the UNHCR provided emergency funding to assist with resettlement programs. Women played the key role in

maintaining refugee households. Some refugees demonstrated resourcefulness in establishing new businesses that traded on their status: hence, "Refugee Kebabs" and "Refugee Taxis."

Twenty years later, the collapse of communism in Eastern Europe contributed to civil war in the rapidly fracturing state of Yugoslavia. In Bosnia and Herzegovina around 2.5 million people were displaced in the early 1990s, representing more than half the total prewar population. Most of them were Bosnian Muslims. Some 1.3 million were internally displaced, with the remainder split more or less equally between adjacent regions such as Croatia and Western Europe (especially Germany and Austria), where they had faced considerable obstacles to entry. Private initiatives, prompted in part by the constant media attention to the conflict, enabled many refugees to seek asylum in the

West or at least to deal with unsympathetic government officials. In Bosnia itself relief operations were coordinated by the UNHCR, but its officials ultimately lacked the wherewithal to prevent attacks on Muslim enclaves in the so-called safe havens. One result was the massacre of Bosnian Muslim refugees in Srebrenica. Following the Dayton Accords (December 1995), the process of repatriation commenced. According to the United Nations, more than a million people displaced by the war in Bosnia and Herzegovina in the early 1990s returned home from elsewhere in former Yugoslavia or from abroad. Half went back to areas where they remained ethnically in a minority. Their return posed enormous problems in restoring infrastructure, education, and health care; rebuilding homes; and simply finding jobs. Others remained in Western Europe (where they frequently faced an uncertain future) or traveled farther afield.

Intervention by the North Atlantic Treaty Organization (NATO) in the conflict in Kosovo during 1999 contributed to the murder or deportation of tens of thousands of Kosovar Albanians, who were trapped by the closure of the border with Macedonia. NATO's program of "military-humanitarian cooperation," designed to move people to a place of safety, ultimately created pockets of ethnically homogeneous populations. When Kosovar Albanians returned to their homes, they faced enormous difficulties in rebuilding their lives. Albanian militias wreaked revenge upon the Serb population of Kosovo by expelling them in turn.

The collapse of the Soviet Union prompted ethnic Russians to leave their homes in Central Asia where they had settled, in some cases for two or three generations. Many Russian families left what is termed the "near abroad" either under duress or because of fears of future disadvantage or violence. They have since become an important subgroup in post-Soviet society, whose relentless economic decline has put a great strain on the provision of dedicated welfare programs. Russia's displaced persons (most of whom reject the designation "refugee," unless they encounter direct persecution or violence) live in poor accommodations and have experienced downward social mobility, alleviated somewhat by various self-help strategies. The outbreak of conflicts, whether between newly independent states (such as Armenia and Azerbaijan) or within the Russian Federation (in particular, Chechnya), produced further displacement and hardship. Contemporary opinion makes much of earlier episodes of forced migration, an issue discussed in the final section.

CONTEMPORARY REPERCUSSIONS AND THE "REVENGE OF THE PAST"

The memory of displacement survives in cultural practices and in political activity. Anthropologists trace the persistence of a refugee identity among Greeks who were displaced from Anatolia in 1923 and who settled in Piraeus. Well into the 1970s their descendants readily referred to one another as *prosfiges* (refugees), affirming a sense of separate identity from "the locals" and underpinning claims for compensation from the Greek government. Italian exiles in Trieste continue to depict Istria and the surrounding region as a "pure" Italian land appropriated by Yugoslavia. Nevertheless, the formation of "collective memory" is invariably contentious and uneven. For some individuals, displacement and resettlement evoke more positive memories rather than corresponding to a sense of trauma.

Many of the displacements of population associated with World War II and its aftermath—the Stalinist deportations of national minorities and "class enemies," the expulsion of Germans from Poland and Czechoslovakia, the displacement of ethnic Italians from the Julian March—continued to reverberate in the later twentieth century and beyond. With the liberalization and final collapse of Soviet communism, deported nationalities such as the Crimean Tatars made their way back from Central Asia to the "homeland" they had been forced to abandon. Second- and third-generation activists have asserted their right to be heard and compensated.

CONCLUSIONS

Discussions of refugees typically center around two categories. The first category is that of the refugees, whose experience has often been depicted in terms of loss and victimization. While these characterizations correspond to aspects of reality, they by no means encompass the entirety of experience. Younger Italians from Istria spoke of the refugee camp as a place offering adventure and even

Muslim refugees in a camp in Turanje, Croatia, 1994.
©PETER TURNLEY/CORBIS

liberation. For others, such as some refugees from the Spanish civil war, the camp was a springboard to avenging past suffering by conducting acts of terror. This is neither to romanticize the refugee experience nor to exaggerate its transformative potential, but it does suggest that the experience was not one-dimensional or uniform.

The second category is that of the relief workers, typically belonging to nongovernmental organizations and with careers to make and budgets to manage. Many of the descriptions of refugee life that have become public have been generated not by refugees but by professional or semiprofessional relief workers who are normally bound by the conventions of the sponsoring agency. Relief workers and relief agencies have not simply responded to disasters, as represented in the modern mass media. They are actors in their own right, usually speaking on behalf of refugees rather than bringing them into the conversation.

Another conclusion is that the history of Europe's refugee population during the twentieth century was related to broader political changes. These include the replacement of multinational polities by nation-states as well as other changes of regime associated with revolutionary upheavals and civil conflict. The Bolshevik Revolution transformed the terms of the debate for generations to come, enabling unsympathetic states to label refugees as potential communist subversives, as happened in central Europe during the 1920s and France in the later 1930s. Hungarian refugees from communism served as ideological fodder during the Cold War. More broadly, Europe witnessed ruthless state practices, targeting populations for exclusion or excision. In the early twenty-first century such practices have called forth international action and thus eroded state sovereignty. Humanitarian intervention has undoubtedly saved the lives of many refugees, but whether or not this seismic political shift has improved the longer-term prospects of displaced persons is less certain.

See also **Ethnic Cleansing; Immigration and Internal Migration.**

BIBLIOGRAPHY

Ballinger, Pamela. *History in Exile: Memory and Identity at the Borders of the Balkans.* Princeton, N.J., 2002. Anthropological study of the Istrian peninsula in past and present.

Baron, Nick, and Peter Gatrell, eds. *Homelands: War, Population, and Statehood in Eastern Europe and Russia, 1918–1924.* London, 2004.

Cahalan, Peter. *Belgian Refugee Relief in England during the Great War.* New York, 1982. Now somewhat outdated, but the only full study available.

Caron, Vicki. *Uneasy Asylum: France and the Jewish Refugee Crisis, 1933–1942.* Stanford, Calif., 1999. Comprehensive account of policy and public opinion.

Gatrell, Peter. *A Whole Empire Walking: Refugees in Russia during World War I.* Bloomington, Ind., 1999.

Hirschon, Renée. *Heirs of the Greek Catastrophe: The Social Life of Asia Minor Refugees in Piraeus.* Oxford, U.K., 1989. Sensitively traces the legacy of the 1923 Greek-Turkish population exchange, based on fieldwork conducted in 1972.

Holborn, Louise W. *Refugees, a Problem of Our Time: The Work of the United Nations High Commissioner for*

Refugees, 1951–1972. 2 vols. Metuchen, N.J., 1975. Massive study of the UNHCR during its first quarter century.

Kulischer, Eugene M. *Europe on the Move: War and Population Changes, 1917–1947.* New York, 1948. Brilliant and pioneering study based on reading in a dozen languages.

Kushner, Tony, and Katharine Knox. *Refugees in an Age of Genocide: Global, National, and Local Perspectives during the Twentieth Century.* London, 1999. Informative study that focuses on the United Kingdom, using oral testimony where appropriate.

Loizos, Peter. *The Heart Grown Bitter: A Chronicle of Cypriot War Refugees.* Cambridge, U.K., 1981. Sensitive and personal account by a social anthropologist.

Marrus, Michael R. *The Unwanted: European Refugees in the Twentieth Century.* New York, 1985. 2nd ed. Philadelphia, 2002. Standard modern overview and a useful starting point for further research.

Pilkington, Hilary. *Migration, Displacement, and Identity in Post-Soviet Russia.* London, 1998.

Proudfoot, Malcolm. *European Refugees, 1939–1952: A Study of Forced Population Movements.* Evanston, Ill., 1956.

Simpson, John Hope. *The Refugee Problem: Report of a Survey.* London, 1939. Classic in-depth study of the interwar period.

Skran, Claudena M. *Refugees in Inter-war Europe: The Emergence of a Regime.* Oxford, U.K., 1995. Sober account based on the League of Nations archives.

Wyman, Mark. *DPs: Europe's Displaced Persons, 1945–1951.* Ithaca, N.Y., 1998.

PETER GATRELL

REINHARDT, MAX (1873–1943), Austro-German theater director.

Max Reinhardt is remembered in America chiefly for spectacular stage productions that included Karl Vollmoeller's *The Miracle,* Franz Werfel and Kurt Weill's *The Eternal Road,* and Shakespeare's *A Midsummer Night's Dream* (in both stage and film versions). Reinhardt's illustrious career assumes special significance because it coincides with a major shift in the evolution of modern Western theater: the rise of the director as the key figure in theatrical production. Reinhardt's reputation in theater studies is assured

by the decisive role he played in this transformation as well as by his charismatic artistry, innovative appropriation of new theater technology, and fruitful experimentation with theater spaces and locales.

Born Maximilian Goldmann into an impoverished lower-middle-class merchant family in Baden, near Vienna, Reinhardt (initially a stage name) started his career as a struggling actor in Vienna and Salzburg. In 1894 he was discovered by Otto Brahm, the director of Berlin's renowned Deutsches Theater, where the young actor soon gained critical acclaim for his persuasive portrayals of older characters. Eager to transcend the gloom-and-doom moralism of the prevailing naturalist style, Reinhardt in 1901 cofounded an avant-garde literary cabaret called Noise and Smoke (Schall und Rauch), which perceptively satirized current trends and theatrical practice and came to function as an experimental laboratory for the fledgling director. Renamed the Kleines (thereafter Neues) Theater, this house championed important new dramatic works, among them Maxim Gorky's *Lower Depths,* Oscar Wilde's *Salomé,* Hugo von Hofmannsthal's *Elektra,* and Frank Wedekind's *Erdgeist.* Reinhardt's reputation as a director was solidly established by 1905 with his stylish trendsetting production of Shakespeare's *A Midsummer Night's Dream,* a play that remained a personal favorite.

That same year Reinhardt was chosen to succeed Brahm as head of the Deutsches Theater, which Reinhardt soon bought and transformed into Germany's most renowned stage. He also opened an adjacent chamber theater (Kammerspiele) for more intimate domestic dramas. Exploiting the highly developed talents of his theater ensemble, he started an acting academy that for decades schooled many of what were to become Germany's leading actors and actresses in the refinements of modern stagecraft. In addition to his resident theaters, which were all privately financed, self-supporting ventures, Reinhardt also maintained a touring company that spread his fame and influence far beyond Germany's borders. In little more than a decade, this Viennese Jewish immigrant actor came to occupy a preeminent place in Wilhelmine Berlin's cultural ascendancy. As the Viennese writer Hermann Bahr once noted, the dynamism and daring of the young German capital presented an ideal complement to Reinhardt's own relentless impatience to create. During World War I the Reinhardt stages maintained a feverish theatrical pace, including ambitious Shakespeare and German play cycles as well as guest tours in neutral countries. The completion of the architect Hans Poelzig's modernist Grosses Schauspielhaus in 1919 allowed unrestrained expression to Reinhardt's instinct for mass theater and the monumental, particularly in classical Greek and Shakespearean productions.

Reinhardt's ongoing dramatic experiments, large and small, progressively dissolved existing static stage limitations and substituted a dynamic three-dimensional realism that conflated word, image, scenery, stage, actor, and audience into a new theater of shared participation. This consummate theater magician both psychologized external reality (the text) and externalized the psychic stream of consciousness underlying the text through seamless scene changes, novel lighting devices, sound effects and musical underpinning of the action, and much more. Reinhardt's ability to kaleidoscopically generate ever new, previously unimagined images betrays an aesthetic affinity with cinema, especially silent cinema, which is steeped in pantomime, dance, and gesture rather than words. In an underlying aesthetic sense, Reinhardt's verbal reductionism and image-enhanced "total" theater may well have influenced the directorial styles of F. W. Murnau and Ernst Lubitsch, both former Reinhardt actors, and perhaps even Fritz Lang, a longtime devotee. Reinhardt's exploitation of new potentialities for staging and scene design—organic crowd movements, chiaroscuro lighting techniques, the stage conceived as a poetic multimedia space—prefigured later cinematic developments. Many Reinhardt actors, moreover, made a successful transition to film work. Several personal cinematic attempts and many unrealized film plans notwithstanding, Reinhardt at bottom had an aversion to this canned medium with its assembly-line production techniques. His relation to expressionism is also ambiguous, since Reinhardt supported a "Young Germany" subscription series of expressionist productions early on, even before the end of the war, but refused to direct any of these himself and eventually came to eschew expressionism's subjective stylized vision as

inherently untheatrical. Reinhardt could more accurately be called a Viennese impressionist, an older term once ascribed to fin-de-siècle Viennese society and culture, referring to an ability to organize fleeting aspects of reality into an architectonic whole, to combine analytic detail and synthetic fusion into one (or more) compelling vision(s).

The social upheaval that accompanied Germany's defeat in 1918 deprived Reinhardt of much of his prewar prestige, funding, and upper-middle-class audience. After unsuccessfully trying to promote mass theater from a bourgeois (rather than a proletarian) perspective, which aroused critical hostility, Reinhardt abandoned cosmopolitan Berlin for provincial Salzburg. Jointly with the composer Richard Strauss and the writer Hugo von Hofmannsthal, Reinhardt instituted the Salzburg Festival in 1920, which reestablished ties with an earlier Austrian baroque folk theater tradition. The morality play *Everyman* (in Hofmannsthal's adaptation) performed on the steps of Salzburg Cathedral became a signature event of the festival. Also regularly performed were Calderon-Hofmannsthal's *The Salzburg Great Theater of the World* inside the splendid baroque Kollegienkirche and Goethe's *Faust* in the old summer riding academy transformed into a medieval village by the architect Clemens Holzmeister. From his château Leopoldskron, on whose period restoration he lavished great personal resources, Reinhardt reigned as international cultural ambassador throughout the 1920s and 1930s. Reinhardt's U.S. debut, financed by the legendary Otto Kahn, came in 1924—war in 1914 had precluded an earlier scheduled appearance—with Vollmoeller's *Miracle* pantomime, whose great success (299 New York performances and a five-year tour) led to a triumphant return engagement in 1927 that proffered German and European theater classics. Reinhardt also reestablished his reputation at home with noteworthy new productions of Carlo Goldoni's *A Servant of Two Masters* in the splendidly restored Theater in der Josefstadt in Vienna and the newly constructed art deco Komödie playhouse in Berlin.

Forced by the Nazi takeover to relinquish his German theaters in early 1933, Reinhardt became increasingly peripatetic, traveling initially to England, then to America the following year to direct *A Midsummer Night's Dream* at the Hollywood

Bowl and a subsequent film adaptation with an unrestricted budget for Warner Bros. Studios. He also mounted several lavish outdoor Shakespeare productions in Florence and Venice. Intermittently he returned to Salzburg to entertain the international set and maintain the festival as a beacon to Austrian independence. With Anschluss in 1938, Reinhardt's Austrian properties were confiscated, although he was permitted to retain some personal effects. He and second wife, the actress Helene Thimig, immigrated to the United States, where they divided their energies between East and West Coasts. Reinhardt became a naturalized U.S. citizen in 1940. Theatrical activities in America included a Hollywood workshop for stage and screen students, an unsuccessful California Festival on the Salzburg model, several film projects that never materialized, and the beginnings of an auspicious repertory theater in New York that promoted collaboration with young actors and new playwrights such as Thornton Wilder (*The Merchant of Yonkers*) and Irwin Shaw (*Sons and Soldiers*). Shortly after his seventieth birthday—he was engaged at the time in a production of the musical *Helen Goes to Troy,* based on the Melhac-Halévy-Offenbach operetta *La Belle Hélène*—Reinhardt died of a stroke at his residence in New York's Gladstone Hotel. A memorial concert at Carnegie Hall was conducted by Bruno Walter.

In the early twenty-first century Reinhardt's prestige rests largely on his transformation of the modern theater director's role from that of general manager to artistic coordinator of the entire production. His importance is further substantiated by the synergy he engendered among many of the leading actors, playwrights, designers, and musicians of his time. A self-made man with only minimal formal education, Reinhardt schooled himself in the theater arts and attracted talented artists, technicians, and literary advisors to help him execute his novel conceptions with style and intelligence. His memorable productions encompassed almost every style in dramatic literature, and at one time nothing and no one seems to have escaped his spell. Through lifelong artistic and technological experimentation, Reinhardt once again marshaled all arts in service to the theater, thereby reconfiguring traditional adversarial relationships between actors and audience toward a more "modern" theater of mutual association.

See also **Lang, Fritz; Murnau, Friedrich Wilhelm; Theater.**

BIBLIOGRAPHY

Fetting, Hugo, ed. *Max Reinhardt Schriften: Briefe, Reden, Aufsätze, Interviews, Gespräche, Auszüge aus Regiebüchern.* Berlin, 1974. Extensive primary sources as well as secondary material about Reinhardt.

Fuhrich-Leisler, Edda, and Gisela Prossnitz, eds. *Max Reinhardt: "Ein Theater, das den Menschen wieder Freude gibt …" Eine Dokumentation.* Munich, 1987. Text and photo documentation of Reinhardt's major productions and professional career.

Fuhrich, Edda, and Gisela Prossnitz, eds. *Max Reinhardt: The Magician's Dreams.* Translated by Sophie Kidd and Peter Waugh. Salzburg, Austria, 1993. Important primary source materials, including letters and interviews, intermixed with reflections by others.

Huesmann, Heinrich. *Welttheater Reinhardt: Bauten, Spielstätten, Inszenierungen. Mit einem Beitrag 'Max Reinhardts amerikanische Spielplaene' von Leonhard M. Fiedler.* Munich, 1983. Exhaustive reference guide to Reinhardt's complete theater productions.

Reinhardt, Gottfried. *The Genius: A Memoir of Max Reinhardt by His Son Gottfried Reinhardt.* New York, 1979. Reinhardt's life and career from his younger son's perspective.

Sayler, Oliver M., ed. *Max Reinhardt and His Theatre.* Translated by Mariele S. Gudernatsch and others. New York, 1924. Early but still pertinent reflections by Reinhardt and colleagues on fundamental aspects of his work and their significance.

Tollini, Frederick. *The Shakespeare Productions of Max Reinhardt.* Lewiston, N.Y., 2005. Reinhardt's Shakespeare productions treated as seminal texts for comprehending his dramaturgical development.

Wellwart, George E., and Alfred G. Brooks, eds. *Max Reinhardt, 1873–1973: A Centennial Festschrift of Memorial Essays and Interviews on the One Hundredth Anniversary of His Birth.* Binghamton, N.Y., 1973. Reflections by contemporaries.

Willett, John. *The Theatre of the Weimar Republic.* New York, 1988. Excellent discussion of twentieth-century German theater in historical perspective.

HERBERT POETZL

REMARQUE, ERICH MARIA (1898–1970), German writer.

Erich Maria Remarque, born Erich Paul Remark in Osnabrück, Germany, on 22 June 1898, was the son of a Catholic printer and was educated in the Catholic schools of Osnabrück. He was a gifted child, excelling in class and playing the piano with great distinction. At eighteen he was inducted into the army and posted to the eastern front, where he was severely wounded after seven weeks. His wounds ruled out the possibility of his following the career he had been envisaging as a concert pianist.

In the chaos of postwar Germany, Remarque worked variously as a street vendor, a tombstone engraver, an organist, and a teacher. Some of his experiences of this time supplied material for his fiction: thus a headstone-engraving workshop between the world wars is the setting for the novel *Der schwarze Obelisk* (1956; *The Black Obelisk*, 1957).

Remarque's decision to write was motivated both by passion and by the need to earn a living. He published an unsuccessful first novel, *Die Traumbude* (The dream room) in 1920, and he found work as a music, theater, and sports reporter. In 1925 he married Ilse Jutta Zambona, a union that turned out to be tumultuous. Remarque would later have romantic liaisons with the German-born actress Marlene Dietrich, the Swedish-born actress Greta Garbo, and the American actress Paulette Goddard, whom he eventually married in 1958.

Im Westen nichts Neues (*All Quiet on the Western Front*) was first published in 1929 and met with immediate worldwide success. The next year the novel was turned into a Hollywood film by the director Lewis Milestone. The film was also a great success, initiating Remarque's long-standing relationship with the cinema and with the American cinema in particular. As many as nineteen films or television films have been made in five countries on the basis of Remarque's work. *All Quiet* itself was adapted a second time in 1979. Appearing as it did at the end of the 1920s, Remarque's book marked the return to European and world consciousness of the repressed experience of the First World War, and it heralded a new wave of war literature of every persuasion in all the former belligerent countries.

Remarque's trademark was a realistic description of combat, of the suffering and death of soldiers, suffused by a measure of pathos. *All Quiet* and its author very soon became icons of

international pacifism, and this status was only reinforced when the film was banned in Germany in 1931, Remarque forced into exile, and his books burned immediately after the Nazis came to power in 1933. Remarque settled at first in Switzerland, where he had bought several properties with his royalties. In 1935 the prominent Nazi leader Hermann Goering (1893–1946) invited him back to Germany—in vain, for Remarque was an unwavering anti-Nazi. After 1939 he spent much of his exile in the United States, where he had many connections, especially in Hollywood. He was an active member of the exile community, as witness his participation in congresses of exiled and antifascist writers in Paris in June 1935 and in New York in May 1939.

The success of *All Quiet* was followed by that of *Der Weg zurück* (1931; *The Road Back*, 1931) and *Drei Kameraden* (1937; *Three Comrades*, 1938), novels that continued their predecessor by describing the upheavals of the postwar period in Germany. These works too were soon filmed in the United States, the first in 1937 by James Whale, and the second in 1938 by Frank Borzage.

In 1943 Remarque's sister Elfriede was executed by the Nazis. The next year, working for the Americans, he wrote a manual of political reeducation to be used in the rehabilitation of Germans after the war.

In *Arc de Triomphe* (1946; *Arch of Triumph*)—filmed in 1947 with Ingrid Bergman and Charles Boyer—and later in *Die Nacht von Lissabon* (1962; *The Night in Lisbon*, 1964), Remarque took the experience of exile as his theme. In 1947 his own exile status ended when he was naturalized as a United States citizen. *Der Funke Leben* (1952; *Spark of Life*) dealt with the concentration camps, while the action of *Zeit zu leben und Zeit zu sterben* (1954; *A Time to Love and a Time to Die*), filmed by Douglas Sirk in 1958, took place on the Russian front in the Second World War; once again, the subject was the tragedy of the individual swept up despite himself in the maelstrom of war. In 1955 Remarque cowrote the screenplay of *Der Letzte Akt* (*Ten Days to Die*), a West German film directed by Georg Wilhelm Pabst evoking the last ten days of the life of Adolf Hitler (1889–1945).

Remarque's literary activity as well as his cinema work continued unabated through the 1950s and 1960s. During these years many distinctions and honors were bestowed on him.

Erich Maria Remarque is too often looked on as a one-book author. *All Quiet on the Western Front* was indeed one of the first worldwide bestsellers. But if Remarque never surpassed this first great success, he produced many other best-selling novels. It is not unfair to say, however, that he was an author with but one main theme, namely war and the disruptions it entails.

See also **Cinema; Dietrich, Marlene; Pacifism; World War I.**

BIBLIOGRAPHY

Barker, Christine R., and Rex W. Last. *Erich Maria Remarque.* London, 1979.

"Erich Maria Remarque-Peace Center Osnabrück." Available at http://www.remarque.uos.de.

Owen, Claude R. *Erich Maria Remarque: A Critical Bio-Bibliography.* Amsterdam, 1984.

Schneider, Thomas. *Erich Maria Remarque: Ein Chronist des 20; Jahrhunderts, Eine Biographie in Bildern und Dokumenten.* Bramsche, Germany, 1991.

Westphalen, Tilman, ed. *Erich Maria Remarque: 1898–1970.* Bramsche, Germany, 1988.

NICOLAS BEAUPRÉ

RENAULT. In 1899 Louis Renault (1877–1944), son of drapery and button manufacturer Alfred Renault, and two of his four brothers established a business in a small workshop in a garden shed in Billancourt, a Paris suburb on the Seine River. A year with steam boiler maker Delaunay Belleville had proven Renault's brilliant engineering skills, and being an ambitious motorist, he decided to build a motorcar by himself. His first vehicle, finished in 1899, featured a De Dion-Bouton motorcycle engine with less than two horsepower, front-mounted with shaft drive to the rear axle via a three-speed gearbox, plus wheel steering—unusual enough in those days when belt or chain drive was common and only tiller steering was offered by other manufacturers.

Louis, Marcel, and Fernand Renault were persuaded by friends and business people to produce a series of that sturdy little vehicle called Type A, so by the end of 1899, they had finished seventy-one cars in the prototype pattern, with the help of sixty workers.

SUCCESSFUL RACING CAREER

Production grew rapidly, as new premises in Billancourt were built; new and bigger models followed the Type A. From 1902 on, Renault used engines of the company's own design. Racing became the most important means of advertising, so Louis and his brothers participated with specially prepared cars in all major events of the time, such as the 1902 Paris-Vienna town-to-town race, which Marcel won outright, defeating much more powerful competitors. One year later, however, Marcel Renault lost his life in a road accident after leading the Paris-Madrid race as far as Bordeaux. The race was stopped there, and Renault quit motor sports for a few years. Back on the scene in 1906, a 12.1 liter Renault driven by Hungarian driver François Szisz won the French Grand Prix, the very first Grand Prix event in history. In 1907 he competed in a similar car, but it was not until 1977 that Renault cars were back on the Grand Prix stage. And in 2005 the Spanish Formula One driver Fernando Alonso won, for the first time, the Grand Prix World Championship for Renault. Renault-powered cars had won the Formula One World Championship in 1992, 1993, 1996, and 1997 with the British Williams team and in 1995 with Benetton supplying cars, manpower, and organization. In 2005, however, both the engine and the car were purely Renault. Alonso, only twenty-four, was the youngest Grand Prix driver ever to become World Champion.

MASS PRODUCTION AND STATE-OF-THE-ART DESIGN

The famous "coal scuttle" hood and dashboard-mounted radiator became Renault features from 1904 to 1928. More than a dozen competitors copied this striking design. As production in Billancourt increased, so did the model range: Renault's aim was to satisfy every customer, so by 1905 the program consisted of fifteen different models with two- and four-cylinder engines up to 4.4 liters.

Design for the 1929 Renault Reinastella by Howard Darrin and Thomas L. Hibbard. ©BETTMAN/CORBIS

During the 1920s and 1930s, Renault became a market leader in France. Since 1907 Louis Renault had owned 97 percent of the company shares; in March 1922 the enterprise became incorporated. Small and medium-sized cars proved to be bestsellers, and only few eight-cylinders were built, like the mighty 40 CV 7.2 liter, a masterpiece of engineering. Main competitors were Peugeot and, beginning in 1919, Citroën, but Renault managed to maintain its engineering and marketing leadership. In the early 1930s, Renault set up Europe's most advanced car factory on the Isle de Segiun in the Seine River.

Aerodynamic bodies with one-piece windshields and sloping radiator grilles marked a new era in the early 1930s, and again Renault was among the first to feature the new design trend with headlamps set in the front wings. Renault sedans, coupes, convertibles, and limousines shared a reputation for being the best. Renault cars were the traditional transport for French presidents up to 1939.

POSTWAR PROSPERITY

In 1939 Louis Renault did not change to tank production as he had done in 1915 but continued producing cars as he thought the conflict would soon be over. But when the Germans took control of the factory in 1940, they forced Renault to produce military trucks for them. For "helping the enemy," Louis Renault was arrested in 1944, accused of collaboration; he died soon after. His company was nationalized by the French state in 1945, declared as "Régie Nationale des Usines Renault."

Under the leadership of Pierre Lefaucheux (1898–1955), the company again rose to prosperity and commercial success. Its main product was the popular little 4 CV car: 1.1 million were built up to 1962, thus dominating the small car market against Citroën's rustic 2 CV. Its successor, the Renault 4, was even more successful, with 8.5 million units produced between 1962 and 1992. It was the first Renault with front-wheel drive, a technology that Renault adopted after the rear-engine design was phased out in 1968.

With the streamlined, unitary-construction Dauphine, Renault started its prosperous export activities to the United States. Other internationally popular models were the 16 beginning in

1965, the 5 ("Le Car" in the United States) beginning in 1972, and the 20 beginning in 1975, not to forget the Clio (introduced 1990) and the Twingo (1995).

AMERICAN AND JAPANESE CONNECTIONS
Renault's first important business collaboration with a U.S. manufacturer was in 1963 when the French company started to produce the American Motors (AMC) Rambler in France under license, a link that resulted in Renault taking over a 46.9 percent stake in AMC in 1979. In the United States, Renault began competing strongly with Volkswagen by manufacturing its own cars in the country. When Chrysler acquired AMC in 1987, Renault's ties were phased out. As a replacement, Renault bought 36.8 percent of Nissan in 1999, paying $1.7 billion to become the fifth largest car manufacturer in the world. The stake rose to 44.4 percent in 2001. Nissan in turn took a 15 percent stake in Renault in 2002. Renault also bought Samsung Motors of Seoul (Renault Samsung Motors) and Dacia in Romania, a former Renault licensee. Technology transfer, engineering, sales, and marketing forces were combined to mutual benefit for Renault and Nissan. In 2000 Renault and Nissan had more than 350,000 dealer outlets around the globe.

In 1996 Renault was privatized under chief executive Louis Schweitzer (b. 1942), a successor to Georges Besse (1927–1986), who had been assassinated by leftist militants in November 1986. Only one year earlier, Renault had recovered from a severe slump. The worst year in a sequence of five, 1985 saw a number of strikes and a decline in productivity, which led to losses. Although its cars were successful both on the road and on the racetrack, Renault reported a loss of 12.5 billion francs in 1984. The government intervened and Besse was installed as chairman; he set about cutting costs dramatically, selling off many of Renault's non-core assets, withdrawing from motor sports, and laying off many employees. It took another year to re-establish stability.

Since 1947 strikes had not been a major threat to Renault because the labor unions—mainly communist controlled—always had a strong foothold. During the 1960s, paid holidays for Renault workers had been raised from two weeks to three, then

even four. The company was renowned in France for its social welfare programs and generous pension plans. After Besse came Raymond Lévy (b. 1927), who continued Besse's strategy, slimming down the company considerably with the result that by the end of 1987 Renault was financially stable again, also thanks to new and innovative car models.

COMMERCIAL VEHICLES
Renault's commercial vehicle production had always been strong as well. The company had built its first diesel engine truck as early as 1929, merged with Berliet in 1974, and, after a number of further acquisitions, set up Renault Véhicules Industriels (RVI) in 1979. The traditional American truck producer Mack joined forces with Renault in 1990, and in 2001 the RVI group was integrated into Volvo Trucks Holding with Renault securing a minority stake. Leading in modern design and innovative engineering, RVI revolutionized the European truck industry ahead of Scania, IVECO, MAN, and Mercedes-Benz. In the smaller range, Renault again made history with the Espace model line, a completely new kind of multipurpose van for the European markets launched in late 1985.

EXPANDING FURTHER
In 2004, 130,500 employees worldwide worked for Renault, and the financial year featured a turnover of 60 billion euros against 55 billion in the previous year. The government of France owned a mere 15.7 percent of the company. The passenger model range consisted of eleven basic models with more than fifty derivates and versions. Independent Renault factories were active in Argentina, Belgium, Brazil, Spain, and Turkey while assembly production took place in Colombia, Madagascar, Mexico, the Philippines, Portugal, and Venezuela. In many European countries, including Germany, Renault was the bestselling non-domestic make, leading Japanese imports by far. The well-loved slogan, always in French and not translated, was simply "Renault, créateur d'automobiles." In 2004 Renault became known for its car safety record: it was the car manufacturer with the largest number of models achieving the maximum five-star rating in the Euro New Car Assessment Program (NCAP) crash tests.

While Mégane, Laguna, and Clio continued to be bestsellers, there were also bizarre hybrids like the Avantime and the luxury sedan Vel Satis that sold poorly.

In 2004 Renault reported a 43 percent rise in net income, to 3.5 billion euros. The Group (Renault, Dacia, Renault Samsung Motors) posted a 4.2 percent increase in worldwide sales to a record 2,489,401 vehicles, representing a global market share of 4.1 percent and 40.7 billion euros in revenue. It is clear that Renault retained its position as the leading brand in Europe.

See also **Automobiles.**

BIBLIOGRAPHY

Boulogne, Jean. *La vie de Louis Renault.* Paris, 1931.

Dumont, Pierre. *Les Renaults de Louis Renault.* Paris, 1982.

Fridenson, Patrick. *Histoire des Usines Renault.* Paris, 1972.

Hatry, Gilbert. *Louis Renault, Patron absolu.* Paris, 1982.

Loubet, Jean-Louis. *Renault: Histoire d'une entreprise.* Paris, 2000.

Loubet, Jean-Louis, Alain Michel, and Nicolas Hatzfeld. *Ile Seguin: Des Renault et des hommes.* Paris, 2004.

Picard, Fernand. *L'épopée de Renault.* Paris, 1976.

Saint-Loup. *Renault de Billancourt.* Paris, 1955.

Seidler, Edouard. *The Renault Challenge.* Lausanne, France, 1973.

McLintock, J. Dewar. *Renault, the Cars with the Charisma.* Cambridge, U.K., 1983.

Tacet, Daniel, and Gérard Zenoni. *Renault secret d'Etat.* Paris, 1986.

Thévenet, Jean-Paul. *Louis Renault, Histoire d'une tragédie et d'une nationalisation.* Paris, 1985.

HALWART SCHRADER

RENOIR, JEAN (1894–1979), French filmmaker.

The second son of the painter Pierre-Auguste Renoir (1841–1919), Jean was born in Paris in 1894. He studied philosophy at the University of Aix-en-Provence, before joining the cavalry in 1913 as part of his compulsory military service. After war broke out in 1914, he served as an officer in the Alpine unit and as a pilot in the French Flying Corps. He was wounded by a bullet to his thigh and never lost a slight limp. The year of his father's death, 1919, was also the year of his marriage to the actress Andrée Heuchling, who worked under the stage name Catherine Hessling.

Fascinated by film during the war, Renoir set up a film production company in 1924 with the resources of his inheritance. His early work was in the silent film period, and many of his scripts were vehicles for Hessling. All his ventures were commercial failures. When talking films became the rule, he began to work with a film editor, Marguerite Mathieu, who became his working partner and lifelong companion.

Renoir's most creative period was the 1930s, when he created three films, each considered a masterpiece. *The Grand Illusion* (1937) is the most powerful war film made in this period—or in any other period—and shows everything about war without showing a single battle scene. Jean Gabin plays Maréchal, the French everyman in this film, who escapes from a German prisoner-of-war camp with his Jewish companion, Rosenthal, played by Marcel Dalio. Their escape is made possible by the choice of nation over class by a fellow French prisoner, de Boildieu (Pierre Fresnay), who rejects his social bond with the German commandant and social equal, von Rauffenstein (Erich von Stroheim), and goes to his death to enable his fellow Frenchmen, though social inferiors, to get away. En route to Switzerland, Maréchal and Rosenthal are cared for and protected by a German widow, played by Dita Parlo. Maréchal falls in love with her, and though impelled to leave to rejoin his unit, swears to come back and marry her after the war. Is that the "Grand Illusion," or is it that the decency of these men and women are about to be thrown away again, this time in an even more devastating war, which everyone in 1937 could see was just around the corner?

The Human Beast came the following year, 1938, and also starred Jean Gabin in an adaptation of Émile Zola's novel. It is a political work in which Gabin, as Jacques Lantier, plays a tragic figure. Renoir believed that "Jacques Lantier interests us as much as Oedipus Rex," and film had to include workers and give them "all the preoccupations which, in ancient literature, seemed reserved for

Advertising poster for Jean Renoir's film *La bête humaine,* based on the novel by Emile Zola, 1938.
BRIDGEMAN ART LIBRARY

single bourgeois and aristocratic individuals" (Sesonske, p. 123). That is why he adapted Zola's well-known tale of a railway disaster.

Renoir himself acted in his third masterpiece of the 1930s, *The Rules of the Game* (1939). In this film, shot in a château in the Loire, Renoir shows the absurdity of the rhythms and content of the lives of the privileged classes and of those who serve them. The technical virtuosity of his camera work, his mixing of foreground, background, and middle distance, influenced many later film directors. These techniques were effortlessly deployed by Renoir, whose respect for his actors enabled them to present the story seamlessly, humanely, movingly. No other film director married these technical and literary skills to such great and enduring visual effect. A famous shooting party scene in the film again suggests the mayhem and war looming just over the horizon, about to swallow up these terribly vulnerable and confused men and women.

In *The Rules of the Game,* as elsewhere, Renoir constructed the film as a collective piece of work. His actors formed part of the creative core of the enterprise, to a degree not matched until the German director Rainer Werner Fassbinder (1946–1982) and the Spanish director Pedro Almodóvar (b. 1949) resumed the practice fifty years later.

Renoir left France in 1941 during the German occupation and became an American citizen. He worked in Hollywood during World War II but never adapted to the studio focus of filmmaking in the United States. His later films all hovered between theater and cinema, but none reached the poetic and visual power of the trilogy of masterpieces completed in just three years between 1937 and 1939. Renoir died in 1979.

See also **Cinema.**

BIBLIOGRAPHY

Braudy, Leo. *Jean Renoir, the World of His Films.* Garden City, N.Y., 1972.

Curot, Frank, ed. *Nouvelles approches de l'oeuvre de Jean Renoir: Actes du colloque international de Montpellier, 17-18-19 septembre 1994.* Montpellier, France, 1995.

O'Shaughnessy, Martin. *Jean Renoir.* Manchester, U.K., 2000.

Serceau, Daniel, ed. *L'homme prisonnier des images: Étude de Partie de campagne de Jean Renoir.* Clermont-Ferrand, France, 1996.

Sesonske, Alexander. *Jean Renoir, the French films, 1924–1939.* Cambridge, Mass., 1980.

JAY WINTER

REPARATIONS. At the end of World War I, there was considerable support both in the French Chamber of Deputies and the British House of Commons in favor of punishing Germany and indemnifying the allies. Led by Woodrow Wilson (1856–1924), the U.S. delegation to the peace conference in Paris opposed the idea of punitive indemnity and favored compensation for actual damages.

THE TREATY OF VERSAILLES

The reparation clauses of the Treaty of Versailles stated Germany's responsibility for "all the loss and damage" to which the allies and the United States had been "subjected as a consequence of the war imposed on them by the aggression of Germany and her allies" (Article 231). Germany's financial responsibility was defined as damage done to civilians and their property (Article 232). To determine the sum of German payment, the treaty provided for a reparation commission composed of representatives of the principal recipients. To it was assigned the task of drawing up a thirty-year schedule of payments, and with doing so within two years (Article 233). Article 231 became known as "the war guilt clause." It reflected the belief of the allies that Germany and its allies were morally responsible for all the damage caused by their armed forces. Germans across the political spectrum were offended by the implication that the war was a result of German aggression and that Germany alone was responsible for it. Article 232 reflected the reality that Germany could not pay the entire costs of the entire war, and that Germany's actual financial obligations were to be defined more narrowly and specifically. The appointment of a reparation commission reflected the fact that it was not possible to total up allied reparation claims or to estimate German capacity to pay with any reasonable accuracy in 1919. There was no definitive reparation settlement in the Versailles treaty.

THE LONDON SCHEDULE

At a conference held in Spa in July 1920, the creditors apportioned prospective reparation receipts among themselves: For France 52 percent; 22 percent for Britain and the empire; 9.3 percent for Italy; 8 percent for Belgium; 5.9 percent for the Kingdom of Serbs, Croats, and Slovenes; 3 percent for the other nations. The reparation commission determined German's total debt to be 132 billion gold marks (33 billion dollars). As it was impossible to verify or reconcile the various national claims and because German capacity to pay was as yet unknown, the figure represented a political compromise among the creditors. The sum was divided into three series of bonds. The "A" and "B" series' totaled 50 billion marks, and Germany was liable for interest and principle over a period of thirty-six years. The annual payment was set at two billion gold marks plus a sum equal to 26 percent of the German exports. The "C" bonds of 82 billion bore no interest and were not to be issued until the "A" and "B" bonds were paid off. The schedule, had it been paid, would have amounted to a transfer of around 7 percent of German national income. Delivered to the Germans in May 1921, it became known as the London schedule.

Some scholars have argued that 7 percent of national income was not an insurmountable burden and that the London schedule was within Germany's economic capacity. What was lacking in Germany was the political determination to cut domestic consumption and raise taxes. Others have argued that the London schedule was not feasible. Transferring the annual payments would have required a significant trade surplus and thus a cut in imports and an increase in exports. They doubt that any of the weak coalition governments of the Weimar Republic could have accomplished the massive government intervention in the economy to have achieved this or that the victors of the war would have been willing to accept a flood of German exports in iron, steel, and textiles, which were already under considerable world pressure. In the payment of the London schedule, two large issues were at stake. How would the costs of the war be distributed? Could reparation be an instrument that France could use to prevent Germany from becoming the most powerful economy in Europe?

Over the next eighteen months German governments such as that of Joseph Wirth, instead of raising taxes to meet the London schedule, aimed to demonstrate that the London schedule was impossible to meet. And as part of that strategy they permitted price-wage inflation and currency depreciation. No French government, such as those of Aristide Briand and Raymond Poincaré, could allow Germany to avoid payment of the London schedule and preferred harsh sanctions—the occupation of the Ruhr Valley—if British cooperation could be won. British governments, such as that of David Lloyd George, regarded reparations as a burden on German, European, and British economic recovery, and they resisted sanctions as something that would damage the German economy without fulfilling the London schedule. American bankers refused to lend money to Germany to stabilize the mark without a long

Germany Is Crushed by the Treaty of Versailles. Political cartoon by E. Schilling, 1931. Schilling reflects the popular view that the burden of reparations was borne by workers, while wealthy bankers remained untouched. BRIDGEMAN ART LIBRARY

moratorium and a reduction in the London schedule. Moreover none of the principal countries involved conducted policies that were coherent or consistent.

Meeting at Cannes in January 1922, the reparation commission granted Germany a temporary reprieve in exchange for promises to increase taxes and balance the budget. In Berlin this proved to be politically impossible. By January 1923 Germany was in default not only on cash payments but also on payments-in-kind. French and Belgian engineers and troops occupied the Ruhr district to impose sanctions and to seize the coal there as reparation payment. German workers refused to work the mines and the trains, adopting a strategy of passive resistance. They were supported by payment from the government, and inflation now became astronomical. In September the newly appointed chancellor of Germany, Gustav Stresemann, was compelled to end passive resistance unilaterally. The occupation authority (Inter-Allied Control Commission for Factories

and Mines, or MICUM) then succeeded in concluding an agreement with Ruhr mine owners to deliver coal and be reimbursed by the government in Berlin, which would receive credit on the reparation account.

THE DAWES PLAN

Led by London, the reparation creditors took up a suggestion made earlier by the American secretary of state, Charles Evans Hughes, that an international commission of experts be convened to resolve the reparation question. It met in Paris in January–April 1924 and was composed of leading banking figures and financial experts from each of the major creditor powers and from the United States. It was chaired by Charles Gates Dawes, a prominent midwestern businessman and banker and director of the Federal Office of the Budget. Subsequently he was awarded the Nobel Peace Prize and served as vice president of the United States in the Coolidge administration. The second American expert was Owen D. Young, a lawyer from upstate New York and chairman of the board of directors of the General Electric Company and the Radio Corporation of America.

The scheme the committee devised was temporary by intention—a way of testing German capacity to pay with a graduated series of annuities beginning at one billion gold marks per year in 1924–1925 (approximately one-half of the London schedule) and increasing to 2.5 billion in 1928–1929. The latter was termed the standard Dawes annuity. These figures amounted to from 1.8 to 3.2 percent of German national income. German transportation, excise, and customs revenues were earmarked for the reparation account. An agent general for reparations was appointed who was to see that payment of the annuities would not weaken the economy and that the transfer abroad of large sums of currency would not threaten the stability of the mark. The post was filled by S. Parker Gilbert, a former undersecretary of the treasury, and future chairman of the board of Morgan Stanley. The technical details of the plan were worked out by Sir Joshua Stamp of Britain and Emile Francqui of Belgium. Winning the agreement of all the experts can be credited to Young's skills as a negotiator. The plan was adopted at a conference in London in July–

August 1924 attended by the creditors and Germany with American observers. There Édouard Herriot, the French premier, agreed that France would withdraw all troops from the Ruhr within one year and, at American and British insistence, not again impose sanctions against Germany unilaterally.

THE YOUNG PLAN

In September 1928 Gilbert persuaded the creditors and the Germans to agree to appoint another committee of financial experts to discuss a definitive and final reparation settlement. The French and British agreed among themselves to set the German payments high enough to indemnify France and Belgium and to cover their war debts to each other and to the United States. Germany would be rewarded, the British insisted and the French agreed, with the end of allied military occupation of the Rhineland, which was scheduled to continue until 1935. The Germans believed that because there would be American experts on the committee, annuities would be determined by German capacity to pay without borrowing, resulting in a sharp reduction in payments from the Dawes level.

The committee met in Paris from 11 February to 7 June 1929. It was chaired by Young. The second American expert was John Pierpont Morgan Jr. The Young plan divided German payments into two schedules. Germany would pay annuities averaging 2.05 billion marks for thirty-seven years. These payments were 20 percent below the standard Dawes annuity. Of that, 674 million were to be paid unconditionally and was subject to commercialization. Seventy-five to eighty percent of that portion went to France, offering to France the prospect of advanced receipts of German reparation. The remaining portion was conditional—subject to a two-year moratorium at Germany's request. Following the thirty-seven year period, Germany would pay annuities rising slightly from 1.567 billion to 1.684 billion for a period of twenty-one years—into the 1980s. The thirty-seven-year schedule covered indemnities, interallied war debts, and service on the Dawes loan. The twenty-one-year schedule covered war debts only. Young stated that the plan represented minimum creditor requirements.

The chief German delegate was Hjalmar Schacht, the president of the Reichsbank. He sought to limit the annuities to German capacity to pay without borrowing, which he stated to be 1.65 billion marks for thirty-seven years. His hope that a committee of independent experts with German membership and with American representation would reduce payments to this level proved to be illusory. Instead the plan was shaped by the demands of the creditors that their debts to the United States and to each other be covered by receipts from Germany—a matter of particular importance to France, the chief war-debt debtor and the United States, the chief war-debt creditor. The process by which the plan was formulated was not depoliticized; the committee was dominated by members of the boards of central banks and former officials of ministries of finance. They were experts and they also spoke for the interests of their nations.

At the Young conference Britain's portion of the annuity was diminished in favor of the other creditors. At the conference held to adopt the Young plan, which met at the Hague in August, Philip Snowden, the British chancellor of the exchequer, succeeded in restoring partially Britain's losses and secured for Britain a larger share of the unconditional annuity. The British agreed to end military occupation by December 1929 and the French by April 1930. In Germany the Nazis and nationalists collaborated and launched a campaign against the Young plan and demanded a national plebiscite on the issue. They were not successful in blocking the plan.

THE END OF REPARATIONS

To preserve payment of international commercial debts at the time of the Austro-German banking crisis in 1931, U.S. president Herbert Hoover (1874–1964) called for a one-year moratorium on all intergovernmental debts in June of that year. In the months that followed, the German government of Heinrich Brüning agitated for a complete abolition of reparations. The British also favored abolition. The American Congress strongly opposed any abolition of war debts, and the U.S. government rejected any linkage of war debts and reparations. The French sought political compensation for any concessions they might make. At the Lausanne conference in June 1932, reparations were ended;

the Young plan payments were abolished with a final lump sum payment of three billion marks. In all, the Germans paid 19.1 billion marks in reparation, nowhere near the 50 billion of the London schedule "A and B bonds." Less than one-third of it was in cash. The British and French both defaulted on their war-debt payments to the United States in 1933. In January 1934 Congress passed the Johnson Act prohibiting any further government lending to nations in default on their debts to the United States.

See also **Dawes Plan; Depression; Rhineland Occupation; World War I.**

BIBLIOGRAPHY

Feldman, Gerald D. *The Great Disorder: Politics, Economics, and Society in the German Inflation, 1914–1924.* New York, 1993.

Jacobson, Jon. "The Reparation Settlement of 1924." In *Konsequenzen der Inflation,* edited by Gerald D. Feldman, Carl-Ludwig Holtfrerich, Gerhard A. Ritter, and Peter-Christian Witt, 79–108. Berlin, 1989.

Kent, Bruce. *The Spoils of War: The Politics, Economics, and Diplomacy of Reparations, 1918–1932.* Oxford, U.K., 1989.

Marks, Sally. "The Myth of Reparations." *Central European History* 11 (1978): 231–255.

———. "'Smoke and Mirrors': In Smoke-Filled Rooms and the Galerie des Glaces." In *The Treaty of Versailles: A Reassessment after 75 Years,* edited by Manfred F. Boemeke, Gerald D. Feldman, and Elisabeth Glaser. Cambridge, U.K., 1998.

Steiner, Zara. *The Lights That Failed: European International History, 1919–1933.* New York, 2005. Chapters 1, 4, and 9.

Trachtenberg, Marc. *Reparation in World Politics: France and European Economic Diplomacy, 1916–1923.* New York, 1980.

JON JACOBSON

RESISTANCE.

"Resistance," as a category covering all forms of opposition against the new European order imposed by Nazi Germany, has no conceptual unity. It covers a variety of reactions against very different regimes imposed and different policies pursued in different countries and regions of Europe at different times of Nazi expansion, from 1938 until 1945. The form these reactions took—their means of action, their organization, their development, their political program, and even their ideology—were first of all dictated by the German aggression to which they were reacting and the intrusive policies of the occupier to transform their societies. Secondarily resistance was shaped by endogenous factors, such as the respective weight of radical political movements in the prewar political arena; traditions of insurrection and armed struggle, as well as of civil disobedience and distrust of state authority; the legitimacy of prewar political institutions; and social cohesion or the lack of it, because of social, political, or ethnic polarization. To clarify these matters, the marginal movements of dissent against national dictatorship in Germany or in Italy are not dealt with here, because they proceed from a very different dynamic and cannot be subsumed under the same analytical umbrella as the movements that emerged in the countries Germany and Italy occupied. It is not that resistance in Italy or Germany was of no importance; it is rather that the historical phenomenon that contemporaries understood as resistance was located in countries occupied by the Axis Powers.

The term *resistance* has been variously used to describe partisan attacks on German troop transports; military intelligence gathering for the Allied services; the killing of collaborationist "traitors"; the networks organizing the hiding and, sometimes, escape of Allied aircrew, Jews, and requisitioned workers; the printing and distribution of underground newspapers and pamphlets; the attitudes of the churches toward Nazi rule; and the preparation of postwar politics by political movements. Depending on the definition adopted, the term *resistance* refers to small nuclei of radicalized guerrillas; military professionals with technical expertise in intelligence gathering and transmission; large-scale networks involving the active participation of thousands of individuals and the complicity of tens if not hundreds of thousands; or even the mainstream of political opinion, including their traditional elites, in a given country during the last months of the occupation. Differences pertain both to the nature and the scale of the phenomenon, and each definition is also implicitly normative. Some more radical forms of resistance are condemned by part of the national opinion and postwar historiography as "terrorism." Other mainstream forms focused on the preparation of the postwar are similarly decried as *attentisme*—the tendency to wait and see—or cowardice. Measuring resistance in terms of military effectiveness is highly problematic. Defining it in terms of ideological coherence is similarly bound to failure. Not all antifascist movements were at all times anti-German, nor were all anti-German movements forcibly antifascist. The attitude of communist parties while the German-Soviet Nonaggression Pact lasted illustrated the first contradiction; the precocious radical action by ultranationalist authoritarian movements in occupied countries, in Ukraine, Poland, Serbia, or Belgium, exemplify the latter.

Nevertheless, it is the merger in some occupied countries of all these various strands of "resistance" into a "home front" in the months leading to liberation that has retrospectively created the image of a united and organized movement, equally involved in the struggle against the occupier and, drawing legitimacy from this combat, in the foundation of a new postwar order. Yet, both activities were often more dissociated than glorifying narratives admit. The turmoil of war also offered a unique opportunity for political revolutions, replacing prewar political elites, forcing through radical political agendas, benefiting from wartime polarization. In its mildest form, this involved the drafting of new constitutions or political platforms for reforms to be implemented after the liberation, such as the nationalization of certain economic sectors or the reinforcement of social rights. In its more radical forms, this involved the purging of political enemies who had chosen the occupier's side through imprisonment, expulsion, or execution and/or the expropriation and expulsion by legal or by violent means of ethnic minorities, seizing on the extreme violence unleashed by Nazi population policies to settle once and for all the unresolved minority questions of the nation-states born from or reshaped by World War I. The fault lines between collaboration and resistance are much less clear here than in cases in which concrete action against the occupier is involved, simply because domestic political agendas often occupied a much higher priority. The radical nature of wartime political revolutions depended on the degree of turmoil, the level of violence, and the destruction or delegitimization of prewar political structures. Two factors are therefore crucial in outlining a typology of the war experience and the reactions it triggered: space and time.

GEOGRAPHIC FACTORS

The spatial factor derives from the fundamentally and deliberately asymmetrical nature of Nazi rule in Europe. Between the two extreme ends of the timescale on which Nazi planners projected their program—the immediate strategic contingencies of battle and the ultimate ideological goals of transforming the European continent in an imperial order destined to last one thousand years—there was an almost infinite latitude for experimentation, provisional solutions, and a very peculiar management of priorities, of a military, economic, or ideological nature. Very schematically, one can distinguish three geographical areas.

Eastern Europe The war in eastern Europe occupied the most central place in the Nazi ideology, because this was where the Lebensraum, the vital space of colonization for the German race, was located—a space to be vacated by a war of annihilation (*Vernichtungskrieg*), wiping out local elites and overall decimating the indigenous population. This war of destruction was primarily waged in Poland, Ukraine, and Byelorussia and to a lesser extent in the Baltic countries. It was accompanied by large-scale murder, genocide, civil war, and ethnic cleansing. Collaboration was a desperate choice, devoid of any hope for an alternative political order, because the Nazi occupier never offered any other perspective than a brutal and planned policy of colonization, plunder, starvation, and deportation as outlined, for example, in the detailed and sinister *Generalplan Ost*.

The region was moreover the scene for multiple occupations and shifting front lines. The German–Soviet partition of Poland in September 1939 created waves of refugees, mostly eastward, but the anticipation of a better life in the Soviet zone was soon to be disappointed by harsh Stalinist policies. The German invasion of the USSR in June 1941 provoked new waves of evacuation and retaliatory killings. The loyalties of Poles, Ukrainians, Lithuanians, and Jews to either of the occupiers of prewar Poland inevitably caused civil war fault lines to run partly along ethnic lines. Anti-Soviet

Ukrainian nationalists similarly initially welcomed the German army as liberators, only to discover that, apart from the recruitment of auxiliary military and police personnel, the German occupier had no wish whatsoever to create a viable Ukrainian nation. By 1943, the security situation for Ukrainian auxiliaries in the German-controlled forces was such that they deserted in droves to the Soviet partisans or the Ukrainian nationalist partisans. After having actively participated in the elimination of the local Jewish population, from 1943 onward, Polish, Ukrainian, and Lithuanian nationalists would increasingly turn on each other, trying to carve out ethnically homogeneous areas in the anticipation of a postwar settlement. While both the Polish anticommunist Home Army and the Polish communist partisans waged a heroic battle for survival against the German occupier, the prospect of a united front was never an option, as the brutal events of the autumn of 1944 illustrate, when the Red Army patiently witnessed from the outskirts of Warsaw the elimination of the nationalist insurrection by the German Army.

Southeastern Europe Southeastern Europe, particularly the Balkans, form a second area with a distinct fate. The German invasion responded to the strategic imperative to occupy the northern shore of the Mediterranean in order to avoid a British landing rather than the implementation of any precise planning or ideological design. The winter famine in Greece in 1941 and 1942, for example, was the result of cynical neglect and contempt for the lives of the local population and not of any deliberate calculation. In Yugoslavia in particular, a country that had verged on civil war ever since its creation after World War I, extreme brutality against the civilian population combined with murderously divisive occupation policies, as practiced by the German, Italian, and Hungarian occupiers, exacerbating tensions among Serbs, Croats, Bosnian Muslims, Slovenes, ethnic Hungarians, ethnic Germans, Jews, and Gypsies, degenerated into generalized internecine killing. The creation of a Croat fascist—Ustaša—State and the annexation policies in other areas were particularly nefarious in this regard.

In this context of anarchy, the tiny prewar communist parties emerged as the most efficient and credible endogenous force. Partisan republics,

organizing the redistribution of land and capable of halting ethnic violence, both by offering an alternative political creed and by ruthlessly eliminating its nationalist adversaries, established the only homegrown communist regimes in Europe outside the Soviet Union, in Albania and Yugoslavia. In Greece only the intervention of twenty-two thousand British troops could avert a similar scenario. Unlike postwar France, Italy, or the German Democratic Republic, which would rhetorically proclaim to be political regimes born from resistance struggle, the Albanian and Yugoslav communist parties effectively transformed a clandestine underground apparatus into a new ruling elite, with all the problems this entailed. By 1957 Milovan Djilas, himself a partisan hero, would describe in *The New Class* how a regime built on this historical legitimacy was hermetically closed to the younger generations and fundamentally frozen in its evolution.

Western and central Europe Finally, there is the heterogeneous group of occupied countries from western and central Europe—Norway, Denmark, the Netherlands, Belgium, Luxembourg, France, and Czechoslovakia. Here the Nazi occupier proceeded to limited annexations of regions integrating the Reich—the Sudeten area, Alsace-Lorraine, the whole of Luxembourg, and the Eupen-et-Malmédy area ceded to Belgium in 1919—but mainly, the occupation policy was one of *Aufsichtsverwaltung,* a policy of economic exploitation at minimal cost, leaving the national administration largely intact.

The institutional setting in this third area was extremely heterogeneous. Czechoslovakia was dismembered between the annexed zone, the protectorate of Bohemia-Moravia, and the fascist clerical puppet state of Slovakia. Denmark, which had accepted the entry of German troops into its territory, was placed under the protection of a German governor, but was otherwise allowed to maintain its institutions, to the point that it even held free elections in March 1943—elections that did not even alter the internal political balance. In France, political events anticipated German decisions as to the fate of its institutions, as the national assembly of the Third Republic dissolved itself and elected a World War I hero, the elderly Philippe Pétain, as head of a new authoritarian state. Pétain's first

Danish resistance fighters on a rooftop c. 1945. ©CORBIS

decision was to offer an armistice and accept unconditionally the terms imposed by the German occupier, including the partitioning of the country into a southern zone, unoccupied until November 1942, a central zone under German military rule, and the "forbidden zone" of the coastal defense line. In Norway, the Netherlands, Luxembourg, and Belgium, the national governments and, with the exception of Belgium, heads of state, had fled to London before the French collapse, in the hope of continuing the war. In Norway, the Germans first instituted military rule and later installed the fascist government of Vidkun Quisling, a notoriously failed experiment in the exportation of their political model. In Belgium, they opted for military rule for the whole duration of the occupation, while in the Netherlands they imposed civilian Nazi rule under *Reichskommissar* Arthur Seyss-Inquart.

In spite of these very contrasting institutional settings, Nazi policies in this third area were both comparable and coordinated. National and local administrations were left in place, with an overall relatively prudent policy to replace recalcitrant civil servants with politically more obedient personnel. The central concern was to limit the German presence and avoid major disruptions. The army, procurement ministry, and the SS leadership had conflicting views on the priorities guiding occupation policy; these parties were concerned, respectively, with: military security by avoiding radical policies, maximal economic benefit or Nazification, and an all-out war against the ideological enemies of the Reich. The first two imperatives did dominate the occupation policy, with one brutal exception: the deportation of all Jews from these territories to the centers of mass death in eastern Europe, a quite disruptive policy, but one that was an unquestionable priority on the Nazi agenda. The mass deportation of Jews in the summer of 1942 was one example of an operation planned for the whole area in a concerted timetable. Another example is the deportation of workers for German industry, after a policy of voluntary recruitment, reaching a peak in the summer of 1943. Obviously, these coordinated policies provoked comparable reactions and delineated a common horizon of action for local resistance movements.

The view of the occupier The vantage point for an integrated analysis of these very heterogeneous situations, between the three groups and inside each of the groups described above, is of course the perspective of the German occupier. Even though the pursued goals were entirely different depending on the geographical reach, Nazi Germany also acquired considerable expertise in occupation management in general and in counterinsurgency in particular—an experience carefully studied by the U.S. military in particular after 1945. The science of occupation management started from an analysis of the precedent of World War I. The first occupation of Belgium had mobilized an inordinate number of military and administrative personnel, for a disappointing return on investment in economic terms, and a catastrophic impact on Germany's public relations, an error Nazi planners were determined to avoid in 1940. Nazi domination over half a dozen countries by the summer of 1941 offered a new sample for comparative analysis.

Extremely instructive in this regard is the report published by the occupation expert and SD (Sicherheitsdienst) man Werner Best concerning his study tour of occupied capitals in August 1941. At the height of the Nazi onslaught on the Soviet Union, Best tried to establish the elementary rules allowing the most efficient management of any given occupied territory, with a minimal input of German military and administrative personnel. After a stint as occupation expert in Paris in 1940 and 1941, Best would apply his conclusions as German governor of Denmark. Best, whose credentials as a first-hour Nazi and anti-Semite cannot be doubted, not only allowed the elections of March 1943, but he also organized or at the very least tacitly authorized the discreet evacuation of the tiny Danish Jewish community over the

Copenhagen Sound. The predictable disruption and polarization a manhunt in the streets of the capital would have caused were a price Best was not willing to pay for the sake of adding one thousand victims to a continental program killing several millions. Denmark continued to be the exemplary student in the classroom of occupied nations, to the point of causing genuine concern among the Danish elites about the postwar treatment of Denmark after an Allied victory. Best then proceeded to negotiate with the Danish "underground" on a mutually agreed program of "demonstrative *Sabotagetätigkeit*," a series of spectacular but harmless bomb attacks, sufficient to convince Allied capitals of the Danish resistance spirit, but not destructive enough to hinder German logistics, nor to force the occupier into retaliation and a spiral of terror and counterterror that would threaten the mutually beneficial *Aufsichtsverwaltung*. But the evacuation of the Copenhagen Jews did pass to posterity as one of the most heroic and humanitarian resistance acts in the whole of occupied Europe.

CHRONOLOGICAL FACTORS

A second parameter is chronology, and more particularly the duration and proximity of battle. On the eastern front, the military confrontation raged uninterruptedly from June 1941 through April 1945 and with it the spiral of radicalizing violence, among belligerents and against the civilian populations caught between the hammer and the anvil, with intense partisan activity behind the German lines. The awkward position of Italy in the geographical typology described above illustrates the pertinence of the chronological factor. Until September 1943, Italy was an occupation force and cobelligerent with the Wehrmacht on the eastern front. After the Italian surrender and until April 1945, the very slowly receding front line crossed the peninsula, with the polarizing effects of massive violence observed elsewhere. From the urban revolt in Naples to the guerrilla battles in the hills of Tuscany and Emilia-Romagna, the military confrontation spilled over into local civil wars, with over ten thousand civilians killed in massacres by German troops and the auxiliaries of the Salo Republic. No country better illustrates the difference between antifascism and resistance than Italy. By 1926, Benito Mussolini had effectively placed the political opposition against his regime out of harm's way. Antifascism was limited to the milieu of political exiles, and domestic public opinion was characterized by consent rather than widespread opposition and subversion. The Allied and, consequently, German invasions triggered very different reactions, and the sheer violence and displacement of the military confrontation mobilized a partisan movement both in size and strategy more akin to the Balkan situation than to that of the occupied countries of western Europe. One year later, the advance of the Red Army in south-central Europe would cause short but intensely violent confrontations in the Axis states of Hungary, Romania, and Slovakia. There are in this regard obvious difficulties in comparing the Hungarian "resistance" in April 1945 with the Norwegian resistance in April 1940.

In western Europe, resistance is foremost characterized by physical separation from the battlefield. In May and June 1940, the battle lasted for five days in the Netherlands, eighteen in Belgium, and forty days in France—too short to allow for any organized, nonmilitary resistance to emerge. Until the return of battle in June 1944, resistance was mainly limited to intelligence, escape lines, the underground press, or the preparation of popular militias for D-Day and H-Hour. Radical formations who engaged in bomb attacks or shooting of the German Army were condemned in most underground newspapers, which deemed such a strategy both useless from a military point of view and wasteful of civilian lives because of the draconian retaliation they provoked. The Allied landings opened a wholly new and very violent chapter, with the full-out engagement in battle of resistance troops and generalized guerrilla warfare. Large-scale massacres of civilians, such as in the French village of Oradour, where 642 civilians were killed, or in the Vercors, where a partisan uprising was massacred by retreating German troops, occurred only in the wake of the invasion, partly because of the emergency transfer of troops from the eastern front who imported their brutal methods of counterinsurgency. Similarly violent episodes occurred during the Battle of the Bulge in December 1944 and January 1945. The partisan warfare in western Europe is mostly a rural phenomenon, coinciding with the length of regular military engagement in a given locality. Major cities such as Paris and Brussels were spared from potentially murderous liberation battles.

A last important chronological distinction applies to the "end" of resistance. For Poland, Ukraine, and the Baltic countries, anti-Soviet partisan activity continued into the late 1940s. For parts of central and eastern Europe, particularly for the Balkans, including Greece, 1945 is not the end of the cycle of civil war, ethnic cleansing, expropriation, and political violence. The second half of the decade from 1938 to 1948 is in that regard often more fundamental than the five years up to 1943.

COMMON CHARACTERISTICS OF THE RESISTANCE MOVEMENTS

These fundamental differences serve as an elementary precaution to any generalizing overall interpretations of the phenomenon of resistance in Nazi-occupied Europe. With these reservations in mind, one can, however, outline a few common characteristics of the organized opposition to Nazi rule in Europe.

A first useful distinction applies to the forms of engagement. One should not confound "intentional" resistance of highly motivated "first movers" with the less political "functional" resistance of large networks. Intentional resistance involved patriots and nationalists, who rejected German occupation because it violated national sovereignty, and a broad alliance of antifascists, the most active and organized of which were the communist parties. Functional resistance involved individuals, groups, and institutions that occupied a particular place in society allowing them to give crucial support to an organized resistance movement. There are notoriously few intentional resisters among farmers and clerics, yet both social groups came to play a crucial role in the hiding and feeding of an ever increasing clandestine population, including resistance militants whose identity has been discovered by the enemy, Allied prisoners of war and recovered aircrew, Jews, and requisitioned workers. Farms, monasteries, orphanages, and boarding schools had the real estate, the means, and the advantage of not being suspected of subversion, which allowed them to play a pivotal rule in the "humanitarian" resistance all over

Europe. Policemen, as well as civil servants working in the labor administrations and the municipal registry offices, were faced with a very different choice. Their daily tasks involved often-considerable assistance to the occupation authorities in tracing the addresses and identities of wanted individuals or lending assistance to their arrest. Under the increasing pressure of the ever more intrusive policies of occupation, disobedience and/or resistance became an inevitable choice. Warning searched-for individuals or delivering forged papers was often a less dangerous approach than a blanket refusal to cooperate with the occupation authorities. The dynamic of engagement in resistance activities is thus very different for each of these groups.

This distinction between intentional and functional resistance also offers the possibility of reconstructing a chronology of resistance engagement different from the chronology of battle outlined above. Practical difficulties of logistics and organization are a major factor that occupies a central place in the first generation of historiography on resistance movements. Establishing contacts between exile governments in London and resistance movements on the Continent and, often only in a second stage, among resistance movements themselves, working in complete isolation, took one to two years. Facilitating these contacts through radio transmitters, rather than emissaries and "mailboxes," in southern France, Spain, Portugal, and Switzerland, took even longer. Charles de Gaulle's emissary, Jean Moulin, for example, was parachuted into the French Alps in January 1942, but only after a perilous return to London in February 1943 did he succeed, at the end of May 1943, in creating the Conseil National de la Résistance (National Resistance Committee), representing most movements, parties, and trade unions in occupied France. The Belgian government-in-exile set up a highly inventive system of financial support for workers in hiding to escape labor conscription in Germany, through guaranteed loans by Belgian banks, but the scheme started functioning only in April 1944. Conflicts between movements, emissaries, British services, and exile governments, the arrest of emissaries, and highly successful infiltration operations by the German counterintelligence, *Abwehr*, notoriously in the Netherlands in the so-

called *Englandspiel,* all made these efforts long and costly in terms of human lives.

Resistance was also intrinsically a bet on the future. The military and geopolitical prospects were therefore a crucial factor: the invasion of the Soviet Union in June 1941; the U.S. declaration of war in December of that year; the halting of the German offensive on the eastern and North African fronts; the first German defeats, especially at Stalingrad at the start of 1943; and the Allied landings in North Africa, Italy, Normandy, and the Provence all affected public opinion in the occupied countries and, by creating hope for a liberation from German presence, encouraged resistance. Even more decisive were the concrete policies pursued by Nazi Germany in the occupied regions. During the killing spree of the Einsatzgruppen on the eastern front in the summer of 1941, there was hardly any organized resistance, and the local Jewish population was completely taken by surprise by these indeed inconceivably brutal actions. It was only in the following months that the partisan movement organized its actions behind enemy lines. During the *razzias* (roundups) of the summer of 1942, the Jewish population of western Europe was similarly taken by surprise. The fact that the first three months of deportations represented two-thirds of the total number for the whole of the war shows the effectiveness of the various forms of resistance to the German policies that developed in the ensuing months. Among them, Jewish immigrant militants of the communist parties in both France and Belgium—the famous Francs tireurs et Partisans–Main d'Œuvre Immigrée—formed the most radical units of urban guerrillas in a fight for survival, targeting also the personnel organizing the deportations. One year later still, the labor draft took the form of massive roundup operations, but by the end of the summer of 1943, the yields of the German labor recruitment policies dropped dramatically, thereby fueling the resistance with tens of thousands of clandestines to hide, feed, and, for a minority among them, enroll in Maquis formations preparing for guerrilla warfare. The failure of the labor draft from the summer of 1943 onward was undoubtedly the main success of the resistance in western Europe and the main factor explaining its transformation from an active minority into a mass movement involving all sectors of the occupied society.

The combination of these factors helps to explain the early engagement of nationalists in the resistance, during the fall of 1939 in Poland; the summer of 1940 in Norway, the Netherlands, and Belgium; from April 1941 in Serbia and Greece; followed by the simultaneous entry of communist militants all over occupied Europe in June and July of 1941. A broadening of the basis occurred late in 1942 and in the course of 1943, particularly through the dynamic of "functional" resistance involving resisters with a very different profile. In late 1943 and during 1944, the expectation of a German retreat then created space either for a process of unification of a national resistance front anticipating the formation of a new postwar political coalition, such as in most western European countries, or a situation of civil war in the absence of prospects for coalition and power-sharing, such as in eastern and southern Europe. Resistance is thus a central category in understanding the war experience and postwar trajectory of European societies, but one whose impact has to be measured carefully in political, social, and even cultural terms depending on the geographical and chronological setting, and it is furthermore necessary to distinguish between the different forms of engagement in the struggle against it.

See also **Antifascism; Collaboration; Einsatzgruppen; Occupation, Military; Vlasov Armies; Warsaw Uprising; World War II.**

BIBLIOGRAPHY

Gerlach, Christian. *Kalkulierte Morde: Die deutsche Wirtschafts- und Vernichtungspolitik in Weissrusland, 1941 bis 1944.* Hamburg, Germany, 1999.

Gross, Jan Tomasz. *Polish Society under German Occupation: The Generalgouvernement, 1939–1944.* Princeton, N.J., 1979.

———. *Revolution from Abroad: The Soviet Conquest of Poland's Western Ukraine and Western Belorussia.* Rev. ed. Princeton, N.J., 2002.

Herbert, Ulrich. *Best: Biographische Studien über Radikalismus, Weltanschauung und Vernunft, 1903–1989.* Bonn, Germany, 1996.

Kedward, H. R. *In Search of the Maquis: Rural Resistance in Southern France, 1942–1944.* Oxford, U.K., 1993.

Mazower, Mark. *Inside Hitler's Greece: The Experience of Occupation, 1941–1944.* New Haven, Conn., 1993.

Moore, Bob, ed. *Resistance in Western Europe.* Oxford, U.K., 2000.

Snyder, Timothy. *The Reconstruction of Nations: Poland, Ukraine, Lithuania, Belarus, 1569–1999.* New Haven, Conn., 2003.

Tomasevich, Jozo. *War and Revolution in Yugoslavia, 1941–1945: Occupation and Collaboration.* Stanford, Calif., 2001.

Tönsmeyer, Tatjana. *Das Dritte Reich und die Slowakei, 1939–1945: Politische Alltag zwischen Kooperation und Eigensinn.* Paderborn, Germany, 2003.

PIETER LAGROU

REVOLUTION OF 1917. *See* **Russian Revolutions of 1917.**

REXIST MOVEMENT. Rex was the principal extreme-right political movement in francophone Belgium from the mid-1930s until its collapse at the end of the Second World War. It was led throughout its brief existence by a young Catholic journalist, Léon Degrelle, and its origins lay in the mood of dissatisfaction that developed in the early 1930s among supporters of the Catholic Party, which had been a major force in Belgian politics since the 1880s. Degrelle and his colleagues were predominantly young intellectuals, notably from the University of Louvain (Leuven), who had been inspired by the more militant rhetoric of a Catholic social and political order current among Catholic groups in Belgium during the 1920s. Their noisy denunciation of the corruption of some of the Catholic Party's leaders led to their expulsion from the party, and Degrelle decided to establish Rex (a label derived from *Christus Rex,* Christ the King) as an independent political movement to fight the parliamentary elections in May 1936.

The youthful dynamism of the Rexist election campaign, and the skills of Degrelle (aged only thirty) as a propagandist and orator, won support for its antipolitician message and vague promises of a new social and political order. In the elections Rex won 11 percent of the vote and had twenty-one deputies elected to parliament. Most of the Rexist votes appear to have been at the expense of the Catholic Party, notably in the southern provinces of Liège and Luxembourg, where Rex's attacks on the parliamentary regime matched more specific material grievances among small businessmen and farmers. The moment of Rexist success proved, however, to be short-lived. Trying to capitalize on the momentum created by their electoral success, Degrelle stood in a by-election in Brussels in April 1937 against the Catholic prime minister, Paul Van Zeeland. All of the other political parties called on their supporters to vote for Van Zeeland, and Degrelle was decisively defeated. In response, the Rexist leader adopted a more consciously fascist style and ideology and developed closer links with Fascist Italy and Nazi Germany. By the time of the parliamentary elections in April 1939, Rex had lost much of its credibility and won only 4 percent of the vote.

After the German invasion and subsequent occupation of Belgium in May 1940, the Rexists were one of many political forces that initially called for some form of "new order" in Belgium. Degrelle had narrowly escaped death in May 1940, when he had been arrested by the Belgian authorities as a suspected fifth columnist and subsequently transported to detention in France. On his return to Belgium in the summer of 1940, he was determined to seize the political opportunity. But the German military authorities showed little interest in Degrelle, preferring to work with elements of the prewar Belgian elite and the Flemish nationalists of the Vlaams Nationaal Verbond (Flemish National League). In an attempt to capture German attention, the Rexist leader adopted an explicitly collaborationist stance in January 1941. This radical evolution failed, however, to bring him Nazi patronage and prompted a wave of resignations from the already depleted Rexist movement.

Increasingly isolated within Belgium, Degrelle created a small military unit of predominantly Rexist volunteers, the Légion Wallonie, in the summer of 1941 to join the German campaign against the Soviet Union. Degrelle left Belgium with these troops in August 1941 and remained a serving soldier, and ultimately the commander of the Légion, on the eastern front until the end of the war. His military service and more especially his cultivation of an alliance with

the SS eventually brought him some rewards. Hitler received Degrelle in February 1944 and awarded him the Iron Cross, and he became a convenient propaganda figure for the Nazi regime in its efforts to portray the war in the east as a European crusade against bolshevism. There is, however, no evidence that Hitler supported Degrelle's ever more unrealistic dreams of re-creating the Burgundian Empire, incorporating Belgium and areas of France, in the western borderlands of the Third Reich. Degrelle's grandiose political ambitions were, moreover, sharply at odds with the increasingly beleaguered situation of the Rexists within Belgium. During the latter war years Rexists were appointed by the Germans to positions of authority, especially as *bourgmestres* (mayors) of towns in southern Belgium. Public hostility toward them deepened as the war progressed, and many Rexists were the targets of attacks by resistance groups. After the war many Rexist militants were tried by the Belgian authorities for collaboration with the German occupiers. Degrelle, however, was able to escape in May 1945 from the Third Reich to Spain, where the Spanish authorities allowed him to live in semi-hiding until his death in 1994.

See also **Action Française; Belgium; Fascism; Nazism.**

BIBLIOGRAPHY

Conway, Martin. *Collaboration in Belgium: Léon Degrelle and the Rexist Movement, 1940–1944.* New Haven, Conn., and London, 1993.

Stengers, Jean. "Belgium." In *The European Right: A Historical Profile,* edited by Hans Rogger and Eugen Weber, 133–156. London, 1965.

MARTIN CONWAY

RHINELAND OCCUPATION. Since the wars of Louis XIV (r. 1643–1715) and the French Revolution, control of the river Rhine had been a matter of dispute between France and the German states. The strategic, geopolitical, and economic importance of the Rhineland became even more important as it developed into the greatest industrial concentration in Europe with its coal mines and heavy industry.

A pregnant example of the "Black horror on the Rhine" campaign against the French employment of African troops on the Rhine can be found in one of the many brochures edited by the Deutsche Notbund gegen die Schwarze Schmach in Munich. The author, Bruno Stehle, quotes the Italian statesman Francesco Nitti, who gave an interview to the American United Press, organized by the Notbund:

An extract from Nitti's interview follows: "Assume, he says, that America had lost the war, and that Germany had brought its regiments to New York and Boston, and intended to keep them there for say fifteen to twenty years, until it had collected a contribution of 100 or 150 billion dollars, such a proceeding might have seemed unbearable to Americans. But if the Germans, to put the brand of contempt on all white Americans, had stacked regiments of negroes in the cities along the Atlantic coast, what a howl of impotent rage would then have gone forth. And remember," says Nitti, "that these African regiments are composed of savages for the most part untouched by any contact with civilization, and if the victorious Germans had then demanded after all this formal humiliation, that American women and American girls must in one form or the other be supplied to the carnal lust of these Africans, Africans barely removed from the practices of voodoo and cannibalism, all America would have resounded with horror at this barbarity and pollution."

Source: Dr. Bruno Stehle, *The Shame of France* (Munich, 1923), p. 14.

TERMS OF THE PEACE (1919)

When the German government sued for an armistice in October 1918, the French marshal Ferdinand Foch expressed the French view that security and hegemony were synonymous. He not only wanted the bridgeheads over the Rhine but also wanted to secure the Rhine as France's new eastern border. Article V of the armistice treaty of 11 November 1918 stipulated that the Allied armies should occupy the left bank of the Rhine, and this was completed five weeks later. The German authorities anticipated their arrival with anxiety, as revolutionary activity spread across the country. The British occupied the bridgehead at Cologne and surroundings with the Belgians on their northwest flank,

and the Americans occupied Koblenz. The French occupied Mainz and controlled by far the largest part of the Rhineland with a huge occupation army of 250,000 men at its peak in March 1920.

Before the opening of the peace conference on 18 January 1919, the French press and influential writers such as Maurice Barrès had stressed Franco-Rhenish affinity. The Rhenish population, because of its ethnic origins, culture, and religion, was in their view antagonistic to Germanic, Protestant, and authoritarian Prussia. Also the military and the industrialists pleaded for annexation or at least the creation of an independent Rhineland nation. These ambitions encountered insurmountable objections from the British and Americans, who saw it as an expression of French imperialism. Only after long negotiations was a compromise finally signed in Versailles on 28 June. As head of the French delegation, Georges Clemenceau had obtained a double guarantee of French security: military measures included demilitarization and a fifteen-year occupation of the Rhineland with its bridgeheads, as well as a formal extension of the wartime alliance.

THE OCCUPATION GOVERNMENT

The purpose of the Rhineland occupation was to ensure that the Germans paid reparations. All political, military, economic, social, and racial issues affecting postwar Europe interacted in a complex way in the Rhineland. During the peace negotiations there was increasing separatist agitation. All subsequent French governments supported this separatism through what they called "peaceful penetration" or cultural propaganda. The Rhineland Republic proclaimed by Dr. Hans Dorten on 1 June 1919 evaporated immediately because of a lack of real popular support, but in the latter months of 1919, Dorten altered his professed goal to one of Rhenish autonomy within a federal Reich. However, the greatest political force in the Rhineland was the Catholic Zentrumspartei (Center Party), which kept its distance from central government but did not support separatism, and its stance limited the appeal of such ideas. However, the mayor of Cologne, Konrad Adenauer, harbored private notions about a grand West German/Rhineland state taking its place beside Prussia and Bavaria within the Reich, but this was only likely if the Weimar Republic collapsed through inflation and internal crises. Attempts

A tank accompanies French troops entering a city in the Rhineland, 1923. ©Hulton-Deutsch Collection/Corbis

in 1923 to set up separatist governments in the Rhineland and the Palatinate under the protection of the French garrison, which to Germany seemed to threaten the very integrity of the state, also failed through a lack of support and suspicion of French motives. After February 1924 no more was heard of the separatist movement in the Rhineland.

The authority of the commander-in-chief of the occupying armies was considerably restricted by the inauguration of the Inter Allied Rhineland High Commission (IARHC) in January 1920. Based in Koblenz, it was composed of three high commissioners (British, French, and Belgian) under a president, the French commissioner Paul Tirard (1879–1945). (There was also a German co-opted member and an American representative who had observer status.) Against the tradition of military occupations and at the instigation of the British and Americans, who feared the influence of the

French military, the IARHC was a civil administration and acted independently from the governments it represented, although the Germans never stopped accusing the commission of being under strong French influence.

The ambiguities and complexities of French policy together with the Anglo-American unwillingness to continue wartime economic cooperation goes a long way in explaining the political crises of the 1920s. The rigor of French reparations policy depended in large part on an American willingness to subsidize the French recovery. The postponement of a world financial and economic peace settlement served only to weaken the new German Republic politically. On two occasions the occupation authorities intervened when Germany did not fulfill its reparations obligations. In March 1921 the big harbors of the Ruhr (Ruhrort, Düsseldorf, Duisburg) were occupied, and in January 1923

French and Belgian troops occupied the Ruhr after the reparations commission declared that Germany had not met its set quota of timber deliveries. Another recurring theme in the negotiations between the IARHC and the German government was the decommissioning of secret arms depots and the disbanding of the various paramilitary forces created after 1918. The activities of the German security police as a quasi-military formation also continued to irritate the Allied powers.

GERMAN RESISTANCE

From the beginning of the occupation, Berlin had decided that the occupying French army should be hindered as much as possible, while there should be full cooperation in the American and British areas. This policy was specifically designed to divide the English speaking contingents from their French ally. When the peace conditions became known in the spring of 1919, the animosity of the Rhenish population grew. It was fueled by the harsh measures of the French occupying forces: curfews, the proclamation of martial law, the hindering of communication with the unoccupied territories, postal censorship, and the duty of all German officials to salute French officers. The many French troops and the billeting of their officers in private houses led to shortages of food and of housing. French aims of ensuring military security and economic reparations were at odds with the idea of winning over the hearts and minds of the population in order to create a buffer state between France and Prussia. The German government successfully launched a policy of passive resistance during the Ruhr occupation of 1923. Apart from 188,000 people evicted from their houses, the 132 Germans killed, and the deaths of some French and Belgian soldiers, the oppressive measures left a legacy of bitterness that eventually became a further factor in the weakening of the Weimar Republic. Measures taken by the high commission against protests by right-wing extremist groups provoked fierce protests from Berlin, despite the fact that similar measures were taken elsewhere by the German authorities themselves.

Tirard's attempts at "peaceful penetration" were countered by the German government with a vehement propaganda campaign with which Berlin hoped to rally world opinion against France. In more than five hundred publications and

A racist German poster denounces the French use of black troops during their occupation of the Rhineland, 1924. ©MARY EVANS PICTURE LIBRARY/THE IMAGE WORKS

pamphlets, French occupation policy was vilified, for example, by using powerful images of starving German children. Already humiliated by the occupation itself, the Germans felt even more humiliated by the use of French colonial troops. Tens of thousands of "coal black savages from Africa" were accused of roaming out of control across the Rhineland, raping German women at will, infecting the population and "polluting" German blood. In reality, there were never more than five thousand black West African troops stationed in Germany, and all of them had been withdrawn by June 1920. The accusations of rape rarely proved to be true, and in general, the Rhenish population seems to have been less antagonistic to the French colonial troops than to their white counterparts. The overtly racist "Black horror on the Rhine" campaign that emanated primarily from Hamburg, Berlin, and Munich, and was intended to raise antipathy against France, nonetheless had a major international impact between 1920 and 1922.

The end of 1923 saw a stabilization of the German currency that paved the way for financial reform and the rescheduling of reparations through the Dawes Plan. French problems with the continued occupation of the Ruhr led to the withdrawal of their forces by August 1925, and this paved the way for a more comprehensive security treaty for the states of western Europe. The Locarno Treaty of October 1925 included the Rhineland Pact, in which France, Britain, Belgium, and Italy contracted to maintain the inviolability of both German and French borders, and the demilitarized zone in the Rhineland was accepted and guaranteed. American troops had already been withdrawn in February 1923. British troops were then transferred to the Koblenz bridgehead and had their headquarters at Wiesbaden. France, while linking evacuation closely with reparations payments in order to extract the greatest possible economic and political compensation, nevertheless became more interested in speeding up the process. Pressure from the German foreign minister Gustav Stresemann coupled with Anglo-French difficulties in maintaining the occupation, and the further rescheduling of reparations agreed to in the Young Plan ultimately led to a partial military withdrawal in 1929 and a complete evacuation in June 1930, some five years before the originally agreed-upon date. Ultimately, Allied Rhineland policy did little to serve the interests of German democracy or the security aspirations of the major western European powers.

See also Germany; Imperial Troops; Nazism; Occupation, Military; Racism.

BIBLIOGRAPHY

Primary Sources

Allen, Henry T. The Rhineland Occupation. Indianapolis, Ind., 1927.

Reismüller, Georg, and Josef Hofmann. Zehn Jahre Rheinlandbesetzung. Breslau, Poland, 1929.

Tirard, Paul. La France sur le Rhin: Douze années d'occupation rhénane (1919–1930). Paris, 1930.

Secondary Sources

Bariéty, Jacques. Les relations franco-allemandes après la première guerre mondiale, 10 novembre 1918–10 janvier 1925. Paris, 1977.

Edgerton, Robert. Hidden Heroism: Black Soldiers in America's Wars. Boulder, Co., 2002.

Edmonds, James Edward. The Occupation of the Rhineland, 1918–1929. London, 1944 (1987).

Hüttenberger, Peter, and Hansgeorg Molitor, eds. Franzosen und Deutsche am Rhein, 1789, 1918, 1945. Essen, Germany, 1989.

Wein, Franziska. Deutschlands Strom—Frankreichs Grenze: Geschichte und Propaganda am Rhein, 1919–1930. Essen, Germany, 1992.

Williamson, David G. The British in Germany, 1918–1930: The Reluctant Occupiers. New York, 1991.

DICK VAN GALEN LAST

RIEFENSTAHL, LENI (1902–2003), German dancer, movie actor, director, producer, photographer.

A woman of many talents and a controversial international figure, Leni Riefenstahl (born Berta Helene Amalie Riefenstahl on 22 August 1902 in Berlin, she died 8 September 2003 at Pöcking am Starmbergersee) was a student of painting and a successful dancer, art forms that were to influence her later work in film and photography. Her career in filmmaking began in the mid-1920s in a genre of popular German films known as "mountain films," largely under the direction of Dr. Arnold Fanck, with such revealing titles as Der heilige Berg (1926; The Holy Mountain), Der grosse Sprung (1927; The Great Leap), Das Schicksal derer von Hapsburg (1928; The Destiny of the Hapsburgs), directed by Rolf Raffé, Die weisse Hölle vom Piz Palü (1929; The White Hell of Pitz Palü), Stürme über dem Mont Blanc (1930; Storm over Mont Blanc/ Avalanche), Der weisse Rausch (1931; The White Ecstasy), and SOS Eisberg (1933). The films featured majestic (and realistic) location shots of mountains, clouds, sea, storms, and heroic, athletic characters who struggle valiantly to survive in a tempestuous natural environment.

Having learned cinematic techniques from acting in these films, Riefenstahl undertook to produce, direct, film, and star in her own mountain

A scene from Riefenstahl's *Olympia*, 1938. OLYMPIA-FILM/THE KOBAL COLLECTION

film, *Das blaue Licht* (1932; *The Blue Light*), revealing a predilection for the monumental, the heroic, for nature images that function as indicators of energy, beauty, and power (elements of the landscape, especially mountains, clouds, flowers, water), a ritualization of life, an eroticized vision of national and feminine perfection, a celebration of the human body, and a metamorphosis of every-day life into an aesthetic experience. These films have been said to show the "continuity of Weimar cinema (especially Fritz Lang) with Nazi cinema" in their "recurrent visual motifs" and "monument-alism" (Elsaesser, p. 187). Both these films and Riefenstahl's documentaries use visual images and sound to valorize instinct, emotion, ritualized action, and theatricality, and both mobilize cinema to alter, transform, and unsettle perceptions of the real, confusing fiction and life and rendering life as fiction.

The ongoing fascination with, censure of, and apologetics for Riefenstahl centers largely on the documentaries she directed in cooperation with the Nazi authorities in the 1930s. *Sieg des Glaubens* (1933, *Victory of Faith*), a short propaganda film for the National Socialist Party, creates on a smaller scale the motifs and techniques that characterize her longer and more expensive documentaries. Described as "the most powerful, influential pro-paganda film in nonfiction cinema" (Barsam, p. 128), *Triumph des Willens* (1935; *Triumph of the Will*), lavishly funded and with a crew of 120, including thirty cameras and twenty-nine newsreel camerapersons as backup, celebrated the 1934 Nuremberg Nazi Party Rally as spectacle, using ritualistic and ceremonial visual and sound images that deified Hitler, heroized his followers, and, through the shots of the architecture, joined the past grandeur of the German nation to the present promise of National Socialism. The film orchestrates images of clouds, mist, smoke, architecture, and party banners and standards, and choreographs the worshipful masses with a montage of sound that mixes Wagnerian music, folk songs, chants, and party anthems. It eroticizes the submission of the masses to the leader, objectifies and aestheticizes the male body, and glorifies the technology of war. An ordinary party rally is metamorphosed into a religious and erotic event that compels the spectator to rethink connections between politics and filmmaking.

Equally monumental and spectacular is *Olympische Spiele* (1938; *Olympia*), a two-part film comprising *Fest der Völker* (*Festival of the Nations*) and *Fest der Schönheit* (*Festival of Beauty*), Riefenstahl's documentary of the 1936 Olympics. Largely funded by the Nazi Propaganda Ministry and filmed by a camera crew of forty-eight individuals, including six cameramen and sixteen assistants, it focuses on the presence of Hitler, the beauty of the athletes' bodies, the theatricality of their performances, the grandeur of the classical setting, and the participation of the masses: the marathon and diving sequences are a "symphony of movement" (Hinton, p. 57). Through edited images of the sculpted and wholesome young male bodies, including that of the black athlete Jesse Owens, the film highlights their classical poses, their discipline and control, and their almost otherworldly solitariness against a background of clouds, fire, and water. *Olympia* is more than a record of the games; it is a dramatic sexualized experience of art as spectacle.

After the war, Riefenstahl was arrested several times by the Allies. Some of her property was confiscated, and she was blacklisted. She was finally "de-Nazified" in 1952. Her film *Tiefland* (Lowlands), begun in the 1940s, was finally released in 1954 but was poorly received. In the 1970s she went to Africa and, while she never realized a film documentary of the Nuba tribe, her photos were published in a volume, *The Last of the Nuba* (1973), in which, once again, the subjects' bodies are sexualized and aestheticized.

Her autobiography, *Sieve of Time* (1992), is not an apology for but a justification of her life and work in films. Her films and persona were the subject of a documentary film, *The Wonderful Horrible Life of Leni Riefenstahl* (1993). Her claim that she was creating art and not engaging in politics and her denial of responsibility have continued to trouble critics, but her work has led many to reexamine documentary representation and the role of the filmmaker in relation to fascism.

See also **Cinema; Film (Documentary); Hitler, Adolf; Nazism; Olympic Games; Propaganda.**

BIBLIOGRAPHY

Barsam, Richard Meran. *Film Guide to Triumph of the Will.* Bloomington, Ind., 1975.

Elsaesser, Thomas. "Leni Riefenstahl: The Body Beautiful, Art Cinema, and Fascist Aesthetics." In *Women and Film: A Sight and Sound Reader,* edited by Pam Cook and Philip Dodd, 186–197. Philadelphia, 1993.

Giesen, Rolf. *Nazi Propaganda Films: A History and Filmography.* Jefferson, N.C., 2003.

Graham, Cooper C. *Leni Riefenstahl and Olympia.* Metuchen, N.J., 1986.

Hake, Sabine. *German National Cinema.* London, 2002.

Hinton, David B. *The Films of Leni Riefenstahl.* Lanham, Md., 2000.

Riefenstahl, Leni. *The Last of the Nuba.* New York, 1973.

———. *The Sieve of Time: The Memoirs of Leni Riefenstahl.* London, 1992.

Schulte-Sasse, Linda. *Entertaining the Third Reich: Illusions of Wholeness in Nazi Cinema.* Durham, N.C., 1996.

Sontag, Susan. "Fascinating Fascism." In *Movies and Methods: An Anthology.* 2 vols. Edited by Bill Nichols, 1:31–44. Berkeley, 1976–1985.

The Wonderful Horrible Life of Leni Riefenstahl. Directed by Ray Müller. London, 1993.

MARCIA LANDY

RIOTS IN FRANCE. In October and November 2005, riots began in the northern suburbs of Paris, quickly extending to many other cities and towns. It was the worst such trouble in France since the spring of 1968. The precipitating event was the death of two adolescents, age fifteen and seventeen, on 27 October. They had fled when they believed that they were being chased by police in Clichy-sous-Bois. They tried to hide in an electric transformer and were electrocuted, with another boy seriously hurt. A town of 28,300 people, Clichy-sous-Bois is the sixth poorest commune in France. About 70 percent of the population of the notorious housing projects (*cités*) are Muslims, like the two boys. The incident and the events that followed must be seen in the context of the longstanding resentment of and resistance to the police among minority youth in the grim French suburbs. In all, during the two months, more than nine thousand vehicles were set ablaze, and three thousand people were arrested. Most of those rioting were young males of North African or West African extraction.

The troubles quickly spread to the suburbs of Lyon, Lille, Saint-Étienne, and Strasbourg, among other places where such reactions could be anticipated, but also, surprisingly enough, to Colmar, Clermont-Ferrand, Pau, Orléans, Dijon, and Brive-la-Gaillarde, among others. There were also incidents in Belgium and Germany. The forms of resistance in themselves were not new—the hurling of Molotov cocktails and burning of cars had marked New Year's Eve in Strasbourg for years. There had been riots on a much smaller scale in 1983, and in the town of Montbéliard in 2000. However, the geographic reach of the troubles, along with the fact that they lasted about two months, was unprecedented. In the 2005 riots, there was violence, to be sure, but it was far less random than it appeared.

Surprisingly, there was only one death—a man beaten to death while trying to put out a fire in a garbage container in Stains, a suburb of Paris—and only a few injuries. The army was never called in. Moreover, despite the fact that several attacks on schools, churches, buses, the Lyon *métro,* and even sporting facilities took place, damage was surprisingly limited, far less, for example, than the events of May 1968, or the riots in Los Angeles in 1992 following the acquittal of policemen who had been filmed beating a black man. Even the mindless arson attacks on buildings were done at night, so that buildings would be empty. The destruction of empty cars, however unfortunate, did not hurt people. Despite a generalized hatred of the police, not a single policeman was killed or even seriously

wounded, despite the fact that on some occasions rioters fired live rounds.

Resistance to the Compagnie Républicaine de Sécurité (CRS)—the militarized state security police who arrive on any scene in large, almost fortified vans—has traditionally been very strong. The government strategy of the criminalization of petty misdeeds—modeled after changes in policing in New York City ("no tolerance")—may have been counterproductive, by accentuating the enormous gulf between the young of the suburbs and French identity. The government of President Jacques Chirac had eliminated funds that had made possible "beat" policing, and thus the police became ever more isolated from such communities, particularly given increased reliance on the Brigade Anticriminalité (Anticrime Brigade, BAC). The government also had eliminated funds for a program that provided some jobs for minorities in the suburbs.

POLITICAL RESPONSES

The riots quickly took on a political dimension. Nicholas Sarkozy—the minister of interior with aspirations to become president of France and a rival of Dominique de Villepin, the prime minister, and himself the son of Hungarian immigrants—cynically manipulated the situation. He poured gasoline on the flames by referring to the rioters as "riff-raff," or even scum ("*racaille,*" which can, in current parlance, also refer to a "tough guy"), and suggested that the suburbs should be disinfected "to get rid of the scum." To many, this seemed a blatant attempt to win the support of voters who support the extreme right-wing and violently anti-immigrant Front National of Jean-Marie Le Pen, a strategy that one of Sarkozy's predecessors, Charles Pasqua, had attempted several years before. The football star Lillian Thuram denounced Sarkozy's remarks as "contemptuous and humiliating," serving to awaken "latent racism" in France. The Gaullist president Jacques Chirac vainly attempted to remain above the fray, having the 8 November declaration of a state of emergency (which imposed curfews and jail sentences and heavy fines for violators) read to journalists on his behalf. However, he appeared to be more and more ineffective, isolated, and virtually ignored.

On the right, attempts were made to blame religion for the troubles: Bernard Accoyer, parliamentary leader of the Gaullist party, the Union for a Popular Movement, claimed that polygamy among Muslims was one reason contributing to the sad situation of many families in the suburbs. Some journalists in other countries (such as the United States) also sought to place the riots in the context of fears of Islamic extremism, although religion had little to do with the events. At times, television coverage made the troubles seem worse than they were in some places.

CULTURAL AND ECONOMIC CONTEXTS

In view of the disadvantaged situation of minorities on the edge of French urban life, it is indeed surprising that such troubles did not come long before. Unlike suburbs in the United States, many French suburbs became the residence of the poor and marginalized. Large-scale immigration to France from Algeria, Morocco, and Tunisia, former French colonies in North Africa, and then from West Africa, began in the late 1960s. French employers, aided by the state, sought workers for expanding business. When the economic slowdown came in 1973–1974 and in subsequent years, the arrival of immigrants continued, but there were far fewer jobs awaiting them. The Muslim population of France by 2005 was estimated at about five million people. Many of them live in the suburbs, now populated by a third generation of under- or unemployed young people, a situation that has increased the inequality between two worlds.

Traditionally in France and in many other European countries suburbs had developed in the nineteenth and twentieth centuries as the residence of concentrations of poor workers on the margins of urban life, where costs were cheaper and factories were located. The tall apartment houses constructed in the late 1960s and 1970s (Habitations à Loyer Modéré, HLMs) have become identified with life in the suburbs, long after they were first applauded for providing small, basic apartments to people of modest means in such cités. Conditions in such housing projects have declined rapidly, with physical deterioration and considerable delinquency, including some drug-dealing. And because so many residents are poor, a great number of families require state assistance (generating

inevitable complaints about bureaucratic red-tape and probably generating apathy as well), adding to the stigmatization of the suburbs. Moreover, continued, aggressive police intervention makes even more apparent the inability of the state to improve economic conditions on the margins of French urban life.

In 2005 the rate of unemployment in France stood at about 10 percent (three million people), but among young people it was at least 23 percent and in the suburbs much higher than that, having risen from 28 percent to 40 percent between 1990 to 2000. The unemployment rate for foreigners and French with origins in non-European countries stood about 36 percent. In Clichy-sous-Bois at the time of the riots, 80 percent of the population lived in what are classified as *Zones urbaines sensibles* (Sensitive urban zones), and 35 percent in public housing. The unemployment rate for young people between age eighteen and twenty-five stood at 60 percent, and about 33 percent of the population as a whole. Even those minorities with advanced education or training face discrimination as they seek jobs. Many find only jobs paying the minimum wage, eight hundred euros per month, barely enough to survive. About two-thirds of minority youth in the suburbs live in a precarious economic situation. Many depend on an informal economy. Thus, as the French economy (along with Germany, Italy, and many other European states) has struggled with a high rate of unemployment, minority populations have fared far worse than the rest of the population. A man of Arab origin put it this way: "I raise my children hiding from them the fact that I no longer have any hope for them. But the real drama is that they understand all that. They grow up in this bloody chaos, and they suffer…there is no future for the children of immigrants here."

Many of their children and grandchildren face discrimination and have little or no sense of belonging to France—although most of them are French citizens—nor do they have much connection to the countries of their parents' or grandparents' origin. Minority families pay taxes, and young men had to serve in the armed forces before conscription ended. Minority youths grow up with a sense of fundamental inequality and many do not "feel French" because the are much more likely than a nonminority French person to be stopped by the police to have their identification papers checked, stopped or even arrested for no reason, or refused entrance into a nightclub because they are Muslim. The *cités* of the suburbs carry with them enormous stigmatization, perceived by many people of means to be crime-ridden and dangerous.

Such young people feel part of neither culture, individualized, while influenced by, for example, some aspects of American popular culture, such as the Americanization of rap music, stressing individualism, indeed emphasizing a macho culture and in some ways perhaps even violence ("I dream of putting a bullet in the head of a cop," goes one lyric). The multicultural reality of many French suburbs contributes to individualization, undercutting positive collective responses to an adverse situation. This stands in contrast to the ghettos that exploded in violence in the United States in the 1960s, where common ethnic identity and solidarity were considerable, and accompanied, as well, the hope and changes brought by the civil rights movement.

IMPLICATIONS

The failure of French republican socialization has been virtually complete. This could be seen in mounting problems in the schools of the suburbs, particularly the middle schools and lycées, where teachers were increasingly demoralized by indifference and even violence. Moreover, the recent law forbidding the wearing of religious symbols in schools increased the sense of exclusion felt by Muslims because it was clearly directed against the headscarves (foulards) worn by Muslim women.

Moreover, the French Republic has refused even to acknowledge the existence of ethnic groups, for example in censuses. Thus the state does not take into account racial and ethnic categorization, which makes it difficult for any kind of researchers to study minority populations. At the same time, the minority populations, particularly the young, manifested increasing intolerance of the discrimination they faced. In some ways, the failure of a succession of governments in France has come back to haunt them. The riots were thus both an expression of anger and a cry for respect and assistance.

The government's response was to talk about the necessity of "order," but there was little talk about equality. Ironically, the state of emergency that the government declared was based on the "state of siege" law that had been imposed during the Algerian War of Independence (1954–1962). This fact was not lost on Arab minorities, who recognized that they were being treated in 2005 as their grandparents had been fifty years earlier.

The riots made clear the breakdown of civil society in such suburbs. Voluntary associations struggled to remain alive. Indeed the government had recently withdrawn subventions for them. The Communist Party had for decades been a significant source of solidarity for workers in the suburbs (thus, the "red belt" around Paris in the 1920s and 1930s, and even the 1950s, when workers voted for Communist representatives, or deputies, and municipal governments), but the decline of the Communist Party has been precipitous. And the decline of factory production undercut class solidarity and indeed working-class culture—indeed a significant percentage of traditional French workers, who once supported the Left, came to blame immigrants for their loss of jobs and began to vote for the Front National. In any case, the unions have lost much influence in France, and particularly in places that have suffered deindustrialization. Many white workers, who lived in the same buildings as minority workers in the 1970s, began to move out in the 1980s, some taking advantage of a government program that helped them buy apartments, purchases very few minority families could afford. This is very unlike the riots in 1968, when students and workers had leaders who provided effective, vocal leadership. Thus, virtually no one spoke for the minority populations in the multicultural suburbs of Paris and other cities and towns. The influence of Harlem Désir, Socialist member of the European Parliament, is exceptional. Overall, the electoral process seemed to lead nowhere. Very few minorities had reached positions of authority or influence in government posts. No one seems to represent them.

By mid-November 2005, some state of normalcy had returned. The French government finally lifted the state of emergency in early January. The prime minister, Dominique de Villepin, restored one hundred million euros in credits that had been lopped off budgets for subventions, including to voluntary associations, and announced more job training programs, similar in some ways to those *emplois jeunes* (public jobs for young people) that had been implemented to provide temporary jobs to young people during the previous several years. Enormous problems remained. Funds do not exist to create enough jobs that could become permanent, and the high rate of unemployment and decades-old patterns of discrimination represent daunting challenges.

The allocation of funds to the disadvantaged suburbs will not necessarily bring about the structural changes necessary to bring hope to and integration of the excluded of the suburbs, particularly when combined with police determination to reestablish "order" at all costs. Increased penalization will only increase the sense of exclusion felt by minorities in the suburbs. Moreover, a few successes will not solve the larger problem of marginalization and the lack of acknowledgment in the public sphere of meaningful ethnic and cultural differences, and anger about the accompanying, racism, exclusion, and discrimination. Yet, for the moment, some of the people who had taken action in the suburbs even had the feeling that they had won by bringing more into public focus recognition of the problems they faced. France's lucrative tourist trade, however, hardly skipped a beat. Tourists, after all, never visit such suburbs, and the riots were far from the center of tourist Paris.

See also **Chirac, Jacques; France; Immigration and Internal Migration; Le Pen, Jean-Marie; Minority Rights.**

BIBLIOGRAPHY

Beaud, Stéphane, and Michel Pialoux. *Violences urbaines, violence sociale: Genèse des nouvelles classes dangereuses.* Paris, 2003.

Fourcault, Annie, ed. *Banlieue rouge, 1920–1960: Années Thorez, années Gabin; Archétype du populaire, banc d'essai des modernités.* Paris, 1992.

Merriman, John. *Aux marges de la ville: Faubourgs et banlieues en France, 1815–1870.* Translated by Jean-Pierre Bardos. Paris, 1994.

Wacquant, Loïc. "Red Belt, Black Belt: Racial Division, Class Inequality, and the State in the French Urban Periphery and the American Ghetto." In *Urban Poverty and the Underclass: A Reader,* edited by Enzo Mingione. Oxford, 1996.

———. *Parias urbains, ghetto, banlieue, état.* Paris, forthcoming.

JOHN MERRIMAN

ROLLAND, ROMAIN (1866–1944), French writer.

Romain Rolland was born 29 January 1866 and grew up in a middle-class, republican family in Clamecy (Nièvre) in Burgundy, France, where his father was a notary. In 1886 he matriculated at the École Normale Supérieure. There he embarked on studies in history, which were crowned by his success in the teaching certification examination (*agrégation*) of 1889. In the same year, he was awarded a scholarship that allowed him to spend the next two years at the École Française in Rome. There he met Malwida von Meysenburg, who influenced his view of Germany. In Rome he cultivated his taste for music and art and in 1895 earned his doctorate in musicology. He then became a lecturer at the Sorbonne; he also taught at the École Normale Supérieure. Meanwhile, he published plays and the biographies of several artists, the most famous of which is *Beethoven* (1903). From this point on, Romain Rolland was to some degree "Beethoven's high priest," in the words of Esteban Buch. And indeed, the figure of the Romantic musical genius plays a major role in his magnum opus, *Jean-Christophe,* a novel of artistic apprenticeship written between 1901 and 1914 and published in ten volumes. The work, which won the prize of the Académie Française in 1913, presents European civilization as a synthesis of German and French influences.

Rolland was living in Switzerland when World War I began in August 1914 and decided not to return to France. He thus became a voluntary exile from his country of origin and more generally from a Europe now at war. In 1914, while living in Geneva, he published a series of articles in the *Journal de Genève,* including the famous "Audessus de la mêlée" (Above the battle). Because of the position he took, he came under fire from both the Germans and the French. He was the target of German intellectuals such as Gerhart Hauptmann, whom he criticized for remaining loyal to a kaiser he scorned and from whom he demanded a firm and resolute condemnation of German atrocities committed in Belgium. During this time, admittedly, his criticisms of Germany were harsher than those he reserved for France, though he did warn France against employing colonial troops, whom he called "those savage hordes." That racist argument was current at the time, though more commonly voiced by the enemies of France, as in the *Aufruf an die Kulturwelt* (Appeal to the civilized world) by ninety-three German intellectuals and professors in 1914. But when he attacked political leaders, generals, churches, intellectuals, and the socialist elites who had exploited the idealism of young soldiers for their own ends, Rolland aimed his remarks at all the countries at war.

The major criticisms of Rolland came from his compatriots, however, who were familiar with the articles he had written despite their having been censored. He was considered a traitor to his country. The authorities shared this point of view and did not allow him to return to France until May 1919.

The slander he had faced, the Nobel Prize for Literature he received in 1915, his meetings in Switzerland with pacifists of all nationalities, and his involvement with the Red Cross all led him to an ever more radical form of pacifism. In 1916, together with Henri Guilbeaux, he founded the pacifist and internationalist review *Demain* (Tomorrow). He provides a fictionalized account of these years in his semi-autobiographical novel *Clérambault* (1920). From this time on, Romain Rolland became something of a cult figure for young intellectuals on the left, pacifists and Europeanists such as the poet Pierre-Jean Jouve, whom he met in Switzerland and who published the first biography of Rolland in 1919. On his return to France, Rolland became a living incarnation of left-wing pacifism, while remaining for many French people (especially those on the right of the political spectrum) a symbol of "defeatism." His pacifism, however, did not prevent him from engaging in polemics with the other tutelary figure of French pacifism, Henri Barbusse. Immediately after the war, the two intellectuals had come together to proclaim their allegiance to "independence of mind" by issuing manifesto after manifesto against the intellectual Right, which, under the aegis of Henri Massis, had proclaimed itself the

"party of intelligence." Between 1921 and 1923, the pacifist alliance between Barbusse and Rolland broke down. Rolland refused to join Barbusse's movement Clarté (Clarity) and criticized him for placing his pacifism and independence of mind at the service of the Communist Party. This did not prevent Rolland from being so drawn to the USSR a decade later that he became one of its loyal "fellow travelers." In 1933, for instance, he published the pro-Soviet novel *L'âme enchantée* (*The Soul Enchanted*). Only in 1939, with the German-Soviet Nonaggression Pact, did Rolland's procommunist convictions waver: he publicly reaffirmed his support for the cause of the democratic countries. But his political positions now elicited little interest. He retired to Vézelay in his native Burgundy and died there in 1944.

See also **Barbusse, Henri; Pacifism.**

BIBLIOGRAPHY

Becker, Jean-Jacques. "Au dessus de la mêlée." In *14–18, la très Grande Guerre*, edited by the Centre de Recherche de l'Historial de Péronne. Paris, 1994.

Fisher, David James. *Romain Rolland and the Politics of Intellectual Engagement*. Berkeley, Calif., 1988.

Jouve, Pierre-Jean. *Romain Rolland vivant, 1914–1919*. Paris, 1920.

Klepsch, Michael. *Romain Rolland im Ersten Weltkrieg: Ein intellektueller auf verlorenen Posten*. Stuttgart, Germany, 2000.

NICOLAS BEAUPRÉ

ROLLING STONES. The story of the Rolling Stones began in 1960 on a train when Mick Jagger met Keith Richards, who was carrying record albums by Chuck Berry and Muddy Waters, among other rhythm-and-blues artists. Both teenagers had been born in 1943 in Dartford, England. Jagger studied at the London School of Economics and was the son of a physical training teacher, while the rebellious Richards, who had dropped out of school, was the son of an electrical engineer. Joined first by troubled guitarist Brian Jones (1942–1969), and then by Charlie Watts (b. 1941) (who was strongly influenced by jazz) on drums, and finally by Bill Wyman (b. 1936) on bass guitar, the Stones began to play in London clubs, where

The Rolling Stones, 1967. From left: Charlie Watts, Bill Wyman, Mick Jagger, Keith Richard, and Brian Jones.
©HULTON-DEUTSCH COLLECTION/CORBIS

they first began to attract attention, in 1963. They signed on with Andrew Loog Oldham (b. 1944), who would help launch their careers as their producer and manager, quickly leading to their first record, "Come On," released that June.

A disastrous tour of the United States followed in 1964. In contrast to the frenetic reception accorded the Beatles, the Stones played to general indifference, mocked to their faces by Dean Martin (1917–1995) on the variety show *The Hollywood Palace* and denied an appearance by the most successful television presenter, Ed Sullivan (1902–1974). Their long hair seemed downright disorderly compared with that of the somewhat more proper and relatively clean-cut Beatles, who had

been greeted as conquering heroes on their arrival. In Omaha, Nebraska, a policeman pointed a pistol at Richards, believing he had put whisky in the Coke he was drinking. In the meantime, the Stones developed a loyal, passionate, and sometimes even hysterical following. More records and successful albums followed, some of their songs reflecting the influence of rhythm and blues. Concerts in The Hague and Paris ended in riots. A second U.S. tour in 1964 drew wildly enthusiastic crowds. The Stones played Carnegie Hall, and even Ed Sullivan finally invited them on his stage, insisting that they change the lyrics of "Let's Spend the Night Together" to "Let's Spend Some Time Together," which Jagger sang into the camera with rolling eyes and a sneer. Of the Stones, the mayor of Milwaukee said, "This concert is an immoral thing for teenagers to exhibit themselves at . . . such groups do not add to the community's culture or entertainment."

The Stones made an enormous impact in 1965 with the release of "(I Can't Get No) Satisfaction," which sold more than a million copies in the U.S. before being released in Britain. With Jagger doing the vocals in an incredibly energetic and provocative fashion, strutting and dancing, by the late 1960s the Stones had become rock-and-roll cult figures, releasing seminal, blues- and country-influenced albums such as *Beggars Banquet* (1968) and *Let It Bleed* (1969), and performing hits such as "Honky Tonk Women," "Jumping Jack Flash," "Ruby Tuesday," and "Street Fighting Man" in sold-out sports stadiums. In 1969, Jones quit the Stones and in July of that year was found dead in his swimming pool, a death in which drugs and drink played a role. Shortly thereafter, the Stones played in London's Hyde Park, commemorating Jones, who was replaced by Mick Taylor (b. 1948). A concert in Altamont, California, later that year turned ugly. Following several violent incidents as other groups played, when the Stones were onstage a member of the Hell's Angels motorcycle gang, which had unfortunately been given some responsibility for security, stabbed a man to death. Although the Stones could in no way be faulted for the violence, they maintained their reputation as the "Bad Boys of Rock." ("Would You Want Your Daughter to Marry a Rolling Stone?" memorably screamed British tabloid headlines.) They channeled the anger of young people in the late 1960s and early 1970s over the Vietnam War and racial prejudice into stormy and sometimes blatantly erotic music. When they sang "You can't always get what you want," they moved away from the softness of the Beatles, reflecting the harsher realities of a violent period on both sides of the Atlantic. The Stones helped fuse popular culture in Britain and the United States, and had a considerable influence in many other countries as well.

Sticky Fingers (1971) and *Exile on Main Street* (1972) became classic albums, and in 1975 guitarist Ron Wood (b. 1947), formerly of the Faces, joined the Stones, replacing Mick Taylor. In 1978, with Wood firmly entrenched in the band, the Stones released their fiery response to the punk and disco movements, *Some Girls*. The album was a huge success, both critically and artistically, and was highlighted by the multimillion-selling, disco-influenced "Miss You," the Stones' biggest single in years. Following the critical acclaim and popularity of 1981's *Tattoo You*, featuring "Start Me Up," subsequent albums in the 1980s and 1990s failed to generate the same enthusiasm. "We were sort of feeding a machine rather than controlling it," was the way Richards put it in retrospect. However, the Stones' worldwide tours set the standard for rock-and-roll spectaculars. Wyman left the Stones in 1993, but Jagger, Richards, Wood, and Watts rocked on, the passing of the years neither diminishing their energy nor their popularity, despite periodic rifts between Jagger, who wrote most of their lyrics, handled much of the business aspects and marketing for the group, and recorded several albums of his own, and Richards, who contributed most of the music (and also recorded on his own) and battled and eventually overcame problems with drugs. The phenomenally successful *Steel Wheels/Urban Jungle* tour (1989–1990) was followed by *Voodoo Lounge* (1994–1995) and *No Security* (1999) circuits, each of which were suspected of being the last one for the Stones.

Jagger, lead singer for what once seemed to its critics a scruffy, even threatening band, was knighted by the queen of England in 2002. Three years later, the Stones kicked off another so-called final world tour in the United States, each performance sold out, whether in a club, arena, or gigantic stadium, with scalped tickets going for incredible prices. In September 2005, the group released *A Bigger Bang*, their most well-received album since *Tattoo You*, yet another sign that rock's bad boys continue to defy age and time.

See also **Beatles; Leisure; Popular Culture.**

BIBLIOGRAPHY

Dalton, David, ed. *Rolling Stones*. New York, 1982.

Loewenstein, Dora, and Philip Dodd. *According to the Rolling Stones*. London, 2003.

Pascall, Jeremy. *The Rolling Stones*. London and New York, 1977.

Sanchez, Tony. *Up and Down with the Rolling Stones.* New York, 1979.

Tremlett, George. *Rolling Stones Story.* London, 1974.

JOHN M. MERRIMAN

ROMANIA. When World War I broke out, Romania, an independent kingdom since 1881, remained neutral until August 1916. It finally joined the allies in order to gain territory from Hungary, especially Transylvania. But the war went badly, and the government and army withdrew to Moldavia. The Russian Revolution of October 1917 cut Romania off from Allied support and forced the government to sign a separate peace with the Central Powers in May 1918. The collapse of the Austro-Hungarian Empire and Germany enabled Romania to reenter the war in November 1918 and to gain a victor's share of the rewards at the Paris Peace Conference (1919–1920).

Romania's territory and population more than doubled. Transylvania was added from Hungary, Bukovina from Austria, and Bessarabia from Russia. Greater Romania (113,000 sq. mi. with a population of about eighteen million, according to the census of 1930) fulfilled the aspirations of Romanian nationalists since the nineteenth century to encompass almost all Romanians within its borders. But now Romania had become a multinational state by incorporating substantial Hungarian, German, and Jewish minorities (7.2, 4.1, and 4.0 percent, respectively, in 1930). Romanian governments discouraged manifestations of self-determination and discriminated in particular against Jews, who were always the quintessential "other."

THE INTERWAR PERIOD

The fundamental political question between the world wars was the survival of democracy. Its prospects seemed bright in the 1920s. The Liberal Party, headed by the wartime prime minister Ionel Brătianu, the defender of middle-class social and economic interests, and the National Peasant Party, headed by Iuliu Maniu and representing the great mass of the population, supported parliamentary government. The Peasant Party's electoral victory in 1928 was the high point of the democratic cause.

Democracy was under constant threat in the 1930s. Carol II (r. 1930–1940), who came to the throne in 1930, was determined to rule Romania in his own, authoritarian way. The Great Depression struck largely agrarian Romania particularly hard, as agricultural prices collapsed and unemployment soared. The inability of elected governments to deal effectively with the crisis persuaded many to turn to extreme-right parties for quick solutions. The Iron Guard, founded by Corneliu Codreanu in 1927 (as the Legion of the Archangel Michael), gained popularity among all social classes with its appeals to nationalism, anti-Semitism, and Orthodox spirituality. But the Communist Party, outlawed in 1924, attracted little support, because most Romanians considered it an agent of the Soviet Union and were repelled by its lack of patriotism and disdain for the peasantry. Carol used the turmoil to proclaim a royal dictatorship in 1938 and abolished all political parties in favor of his Front for National Rebirth.

Romania's foreign policy between the wars was anchored to the international order created with the Treaty of Versailles (1919). Liberal and National Peasant leaders were staunch advocates of collective security. They promoted regional alliances such as the Little Entente in 1921 and the Balkan Entente in 1934 and supported international peace and disarmament initiatives. Above all, they put their faith in France and Britain to uphold the Versailles settlement and protect Greater Romania's frontiers. But such faith seemed ill-placed, as France and Britain did little to aid Romania during the Great Depression and stood by as Nazi Germany repeatedly violated the peace settlement. Relations with the Soviet Union were strained because of Bessarabia, and the establishment of diplomatic relations in 1934 brought little improvement. Carol II and rightist politicians turned to Germany, but the German-Soviet Nonaggression Pact (23 August 1939) caused alarm in Bucharest. The defeat of France in June 1940 deprived Romania of any great-power protection, and in the next three months the dismantling of Greater Romania took place. It lost a third of its territory: Bessarabia and northern Bukovina to the Soviet Union, northern Transylvania to Hungary, and southern Dobruja to Bulgaria. Carol II could not survive the disaster, and

Troops of the Iron Guard parade through the streets of Bucharest, Romania, October 1940. ©BETTMANN/CORBIS

on 6 September he abdicated in favor of his son, Michael I (r. 1927–1930; 1940–1947).

The Romanian economy achieved significant growth between the wars, but in many sectors underdevelopment persisted. Industry—particularly steel, coal, and oil—showed the most promise, and on the eve of World War II domestic producers could satisfy the country's needs for textiles and chemicals. But the advanced technology and machines required for further development still had to be imported. Agriculture, which accounted for the largest share of the gross national product and provided nearly 80 percent of the population with its main source of income, remained underdeveloped. Despite a massive land reform between 1918 and 1921, when some fifteen million acres were taken from large holdings and distributed to peasants, agriculture remained burdened by inefficient methods and primitive technology.

The state played a crucial role in economic development through its power to encourage favored industries by subsidies and tax advantages. The Liberals, the chief proponents of industrialization, insisted that the state alone could provide the

coordination necessary to bring the economy up to a European level. As economic nationalists they preferred to modernize Romania by themselves and avoid dependence on foreigners, but they were obliged to seek loans and investments on international financial markets as indispensable for their project.

The prewar structures of Romanian society remained largely in place in the 1920s and 1930s. Population continued to increase, but death rates as well as birthrates were the highest in Europe. Most Romanians lived in the countryside, as barely 20 percent were urban dwellers. Within the peasantry considerable class differentiation had occurred, because of growing capitalist relations, and a wide gap separated the well-off from the majority who lived in perpetual want. Illiteracy remained a serious problem—only 57 percent of Romanians in 1930 could read—but progress was being made. Perhaps the most significant social change was the rise of the middle class. The large landowning stratum had disappeared with land reform and was replaced by a small urban bourgeois elite that dominated economic and political life. Its rise was symptomatic of the urbanization of Romanian society, as the number and size of cities grew. Bucharest, the capital, with a population of 631,000 in 1930, was the largest city by far and the industrial, financial, and cultural center of the country.

The war and continued economic and social change made more acute the long-standing debate among intellectuals and politicians over national identity and paths of development. The "Europeanists," like the literary critic Eugen Lovinescu (1881–1943), were convinced that Romania was destined to follow the western European model of industrialization and urbanization. The "traditionalists," on the other hand, like the theologian and journalist Nichifor Crainic (1898–1972), argued that Romanians must remain faithful to themselves, that is, to their agrarian social and Eastern Orthodox spiritual heritage and avoid the "contamination" of western capitalism and rationalism. Advocates of a third way, between capitalism and collectivism, like the economist Virgil Madgearu (1887–1940), insisted that Romania could become modern and prosperous by cleaving to small-scale peasant agriculture, while at the same time learning from the West.

WORLD WAR II AND AFTERMATH

World War II was a crucial turning point for modern Romania. It suffered the consequences of having joined Germany's attack on the Soviet Union. General Ion Antonescu, who had forced Carol II to abdicate in September 1940 and ruled as a military dictator throughout the war, saw no alternative to an alliance with Germany. He formed an authoritarian National Legionary State with the Iron Guard, but the two partners proved incompatible. Antonescu demanded order and efficiency, but the Guard abhorred planning and programs, and in January 1941 Antonescu crushed the Guard, eliminating it as a significant political force.

Antonescu (and most Romanians) enthusiastically entered Germany's war against the Soviet Union in June 1941 in order to recover Bessarabia and northern Bukovina. But unlike Iuliu Maniu, who urged restraint after these initial objectives had been achieved, Antonescu sent the Romanian army deep into Soviet territory. By committing Romanian men and raw materials fully to

the German cause, he hoped to gain a favorable place in the Europe of Adolf Hitler (1889–1945) and to recover northern Transylvania. At home he geared the economy to the war effort and indulged in an anti-Semitism that resulted in the deaths of some 120,000 Jews. The German (and Romanian) defeat at Stalingrad in January 1943 jeopardized the very foundations on which modern Romania had been built.

Democratic politicians tried to arrange a surrender to the Allied Powers in 1944 in order to avoid an occupation by the Red Army. But the United States and Britain instructed the Romanians to deal directly with Soviet authorities. Nor could democratic forces persuade Antonescu to change course. Together with King Michael I they carried out a coup on 23 August 1944; they arrested Antonescu and proclaimed Romania's adherence to the Allied war effort against Germany. A week later the Red Army occupied Bucharest, signaling the beginning of a new era in Romanian history.

Between 1944 and 1947 a struggle for control of Romania took place between the revived National Peasant and Liberal parties and the Romanian Communist Party. The Communists, few in number at the beginning, enjoyed the full backing of Soviet occupation authorities, whereas Maniu and his followers could rely on the West only for moral and diplomatic support; the Red Army occupied the country, and the Allied Control Commission, which supervised Romanian affairs until a final peace treaty was signed, was dominated by the Soviet Union. In January 1945 the Soviet leader Joseph Stalin (1879–1953) approved a seizure of power by Romanian Communists and forced a reluctant king to appoint Petru Groza, a communist sympathizer, prime minister on 6 March 1945.

The pro-communist government used every means available to it to destroy the opposition. The Communist Party itself undertook a vigorous campaign to increase its membership and win support among the population, especially minorities, women, and the poor, while at the same time disrupting the activities of the democratic parties. Maniu and his associates sought aid from the West to counter Soviet pressure and prevent the absorption of Romania into the communist bloc,

Women ride on a Soviet tank, Bucharest, Romania, August 1944. The entry of Soviet troops into Romania in 1944 precipitated the overthrow of the Antonescu regime and the eventual surrender to Allied forces. ©YEVGENY KHALDEI

but the West offered little support beyond protests of communist tactics. In February 1946 the West gave up the one important lever it still possessed when it recognized the Groza government in return for a promise of early elections. But Groza put off elections until November because the Communists and their Soviet backers could not be certain of success. When voting finally took place on 19 November the official results gave the Communists and their allies an overwhelming victory. Evidence uncovered after 1989, however, proved that the opposite had happened—the National Peasants had scored a decisive victory.

The Communists' seizure of power now accelerated. The peace treaty with the allies signed in Paris in February 1947 freed them from any supervision by the Western powers. The formal return of northern Transylvania to Romania may have enhanced the regime's standing with the populace, but the Soviet Union's retention of Bessarabia

and northern Bukovina reinforced the sense of foreboding many Romanians had of an uncertain and dangerous future. The Communists relentlessly destroyed the remaining opposition, a campaign that culminated in the condemnation of Maniu to life imprisonment. They then eliminated the anomaly of a king in a communist state by forcing Michael I to abdicate on 30 December 1947, when they also proclaimed establishment of the Romanian People's Republic. The way was now open to quicken the pace of sovietization, which led to a separation from Western Europe more formidable than anything the Romanian principalities had known during the centuries of Ottoman domination.

THE COMMUNIST SYSTEM

In the late 1940s and 1950s the Romanian Communist Party imposed a regime that was totalitarian and collectivist. A new constitution, based on the Soviet model, provided the legal framework for the new political system. Henceforth, the Communist Party would be the sole source of power, while government institutions would serve as executors of its will. To enforce obedience the party created an elaborate security system manned by the secret police (Securitate) and reinforced by an extensive prison network, neither of which was constrained by elementary principles of justice. These were the main instruments of class war that the party used to destroy the bourgeoisie and the old political class and to subordinate intellectuals to its will. The party also discouraged competition. It abolished private organizations of all sorts and put in their place mass organizations, supervised by the party, whose purpose was to mobilize support for its policies. It gave special attention to churches. It persuaded the hierarchy of the Orthodox Church, to which the great majority of Romanians belonged, to accept the new order, and it abolished the Romanian Greek Catholic Church in 1948, when its bishops rejected "reunion" with the Orthodox Church. Within the party itself a long-running struggle for power ended in 1952 with the victory of the so-called native wing, consisting largely of ethnic Romanians and led by Gheorghe Gheorghiu-Dej, over the "Muscovites," those who had been based in Moscow in the interwar and war periods and were mostly of non-Romanian ethnic origins.

The Communists' restructuring of the economy followed similar arbitrary patterns. The party arrogated to itself the direction and planning of the economy and proceeded to nationalize all the means of production and distribution. It focused resources and investments on heavy industry in order to accelerate the building of socialism, and it neglected consumer goods. In agriculture, whose main function now was to provide raw materials for industry and cheap food for the growing urban working class, the party forcibly collectivized all productive land, a process completed in 1962.

In cultural life, the party demanded that writers and artists devote their talents to the achievement of both its immediate social and economic goals and its vision of the future. The tenets of socialist realism rather than the creative impulses of individuals became the criteria of "good" literature and art. Schools and universities were assigned the crucial task of educating coming generations, particularly the children of urban workers and peasants, who, the party decreed, would form a new intellectual elite committed to socialism. Characteristic of cultural life in the 1950s was sovietization and russification. The Soviet Union's accomplishments in all fields received fulsome praise, and the Russian language became an obligatory subject of study in schools. This cultural offensive was designed to turn the Romanians away from their traditional Western orientation, but it had the opposite effect of reinforcing their long-standing Russophobia.

Soviet dominance was a stark fact of life during the period. In international relations Romania became tightly bound to the Soviet Union. It joined the Council for Mutual Economic Assistance (Comecon), established by Stalin in 1949 to counteract the Marshall Plan and to coordinate economic activity within the bloc, and it joined the Warsaw Treaty Organization (the Warsaw Pact), the Soviet Union's response to the North Atlantic Treaty Organization (NATO), in 1955. Relations with the West reached their nadir in the mid-1950s. The Soviet Union's influence in the country's internal affairs was also paramount, as its "advisors" thoroughly infiltrated the party and state bureaucracies. The personality cult of Stalin knew no bounds, and even after his death and the denunciation of his crimes by Nikita Khrushchev (1894–1971) at the Soviet party's congress in 1956, the rigidities of Stalinism persisted. Yet, signs of a loosening of the Soviet grip were evident, notably the withdrawal of the Red Army of occupation in 1958.

The 1960s witnessed significant changes in the Romanian Communist Party's domestic policies and foreign relations. It gave more attention to consumer goods and housing construction and social services. A noticeable relaxation occurred in cultural life. The subjects and the means allowed writers and artists were broadened, and historians could approach aspects of the past that had been forbidden ground. The regime revived cultural contacts with the West and signed a cultural exchange agreement with the United States in 1960. But there was no political liberalization, even though a general amnesty was granted political prisoners in 1964, and there was no renunciation of rigid central planning and direction of the economy.

Romanians gather in the street to applaud the execution of Nicolae Ceauşescu, 25 December 1989.
©DAVID TURNLEY/CORBIS

A Romanian national communism emerged, which expressed itself in renewed expressions of national feeling and increased tension with the Soviet Union. Gheorghiu-Dej's policies embodied both tendencies. An inveterate Stalinist, he had no sympathy for Khrushchev's destalinization campaign out of fear that he might become one of its objects. He also resisted Khrushchev's attempts to use Comecon to relegate Romania to the role of a supplier of agricultural goods and raw materials within the bloc, thereby thwarting the Romanian party's efforts to industrialize and build a strong national economy. The growing friction culminated in Gheorghiu-Dej's April Declaration of 1964, in which he asserted the right of every communist state to achieve socialism in its own way without outside interference.

THE CEAUŞESCU REGIME

Nicolae Ceauşescu, who succeeded Gheorghiu-Dej as head of the party following the latter's death in

1965, carried on his predecessor's foreign policy. To reduce dependence on the Soviet Union he cultivated economic relations with the West, and to enhance support for the party at home he appealed to national feeling and cultivated hostility to the Soviet Union. This "independent" foreign policy culminated in his denunciation of the Soviet-led crushing of the Prague Spring in Czechoslovakia in 1968. But his concern was not the suppression of reform; rather, he feared that Soviet leaders might move in similar fashion against him. But the Soviet reaction was mild. Ceauşescu's challenge hardly seemed to warrant a military response, for Soviet leaders were reassured by his maintenance of the Communist Party's monopoly of power, his adherence to the Warsaw Pact, and his contempt for Western political and moral values.

Ceauşescu's courting of the West in the 1970s and early 1980s contrasted sharply with his domestic policies—the tightening of ideological discipline, the expansion of party controls over mass organizations, and unprecedented intrusions into the everyday lives of people. He initiated a stringent antiabortion campaign as a means of increasing the population, and he undertook a "village systematization" campaign designed to destroy the traditional peasantry and transform it into a rural proletariat. His "July Theses" of 1971, which enunciated the principles behind such behavior, set Romania on a course that was to lead to his own destruction. He persisted in adhering to the rigid economic model adopted in the 1950s, which had dire consequences for both agriculture and industry and brought on a declining standard of living for the majority of people. To bolster his popularity he indulged in a cult of personality unprecedented in Romanian history and promoted a brand of nationalism that reached absurd proportions in "protochronism," the doctrine that Romanians had been the first to achieve a whole series of intellectual and scientific breakthroughs. Minorities were further marginalized. Germans and Jews left the country whenever they could because they no longer saw a future for themselves in Romania, whereas Hungarians, despite cultural and social pressures, stayed in Transylvania because they regarded it as their home. Things went badly in foreign relations, too. The West, deterred by Ceauşescu's brutal domestic policies, cut off the financial support it had once offered him as a reward for his defiance of the Soviet Union. He had, reluctantly, to seek aid from the Soviet Union for his struggling economy, a move that was doubly abhorrent to him, because of the far-reaching reforms introduced after 1985 by Mikhail Gorbachev (b. 1931).

Ceauşescu had turned Romania into a police state and had subordinated all institutions, including the Communist Party, to his will by the late 1980s. He ruled, with his wife, Elena, mainly through the Securitate and was unmoved by the material hardship and moral desperation that gripped the population. His position seemed unassailable, but within a single week, 16–22 December 1989, he was brought down by a combination of spontaneous popular uprisings and a coup d'état carried out by disgruntled reform-minded Communists and members of the Securitate and army. Ceauşescu and his wife were arrested, hastily convicted of genocide, and executed on 25 December. The Communist Party simply disintegrated; no formal proclamation of dissolution was necessary.

POST-COMMUNIST ROMANIA

The forces opposed to Ceauşescu created the National Salvation Front (FNS), which undertook to guide the country through the transition from communism to democracy. Serious differences soon developed within the FNS over the pace and objectives of change, and those who wanted a complete break with the communist past and the rapid introduction of liberal and free-market institutions left the Front. Those who remained and dominated the organization were former Communists. In the elections of May 1990 the FNS won a solid victory; the opposition was poorly organized, and FNS leaders played on the fears of the public that the opposition intended to roll back the social benefits of the communist era and cause great hardship for ordinary people.

The FNS directed the country's fortunes until 1996 under Ion Iliescu, who was elected president in June 1990 and reelected in October 1992, when his party, the FNS, became the largest in parliament. He was a reformist Communist in the mold of Mikhail Gorbachev who favored a kind of guided democracy and was suspicious of the free market. Yet, his government eliminated the most blatant abuses of the Ceauşescu regime: it restored civil liberties, ended the village systematization program, restrained the security forces, loosened controls on the media, and allowed organizations such as the Greek Catholic Church to operate freely again.

The voters approved a new constitution in December 1991, which offered hope of stability by instituting a democratic republic and reserving extensive powers to the president, but myriad problems beset the new regime. The most persistent were economic. The loss of markets after the collapse of the Soviet Union in 1991 and the failure to find new ones in the West had disastrous consequences. When in 1992 Iliescu sought aid from international financial institutions and had to liberalize prices and make other economic concessions the results were uncontrolled inflation, a reduced standard of living, and widespread unrest. As a result, Iliescu's party, renamed the Party of Social

Democracy in Romania (PDSR) and then, in 2001, the Social Democratic Party (PSD), suffered defeat in the elections of 1996.

The new president was Emil Constantinescu, the candidate of the Democratic Convention of Romania (CDR), which, founded in 1992, brought together various center and moderate right parties. The new government tried to reinvigorate the economy by removing controls on food and energy, accelerating privatization, and reorganizing tax structures, but it had little success; inflation remained high, wages fell, and the economy continued to contract.

The populace became convinced that the CDR government was incapable of solving the country's economic and social problems. They turned again to the former Communists, who, they thought, could provide at least experience and efficiency, and in 2000 they elected Iliescu as president again. As a measure of the widespread frustration, many voters gave their support to the ultranationalist Greater Romania Party (PRM). Led by Corneliu Vadim Tudor, it won 19 percent of the vote on a platform promising an authoritarian government and strong measures against ethnic minorities, especially the Hungarians in Transylvania. Iliescu surmounted the challenge and governed as before with the aid of an oligarchy that combined political power with immense economic advantages, while the majority of the population struggled to subsist on inadequate incomes and rising living costs. But in international relations the country drew closer to the West. In April 2004 Romania joined NATO, and accession talks with the European Union, begun in 1999, had progressed to the point that admission was foreseen for 2007. In the 2004 elections the PSD was replaced by a center-right coalition promising genuine reform, with Traian Băsescu, of the Democratic Party and former mayor of Bucharest, as president.

See also **1989; Destalinization; Eastern Bloc; Warsaw Pact.**

BIBLIOGRAPHY

Fischer, Mary Ellen. *Nicolae Ceausescu: A Study in Political Leadership.* Boulder, Colo., 1989.

Gabanyi, Annele Ute. *The Ceausescu Cult: Propaganda and Power Policy in Communist Romania.* Bucharest, 2000.

Gallagher, Tom. *Modern Romania: The End of Communism, the Failure of Democratic Reform, and the Theft of a Nation.* New York, 2005.

Haynes, Rebecca. *Romanian Policy towards Germany, 1936–40.* New York, 2000.

Hitchins, Keith. *Rumania, 1866–1947.* Oxford, U.K., 1994.

————. *The Identity of Romania.* Bucharest, Romania, 2003.

Kligman, Gail. *The Politics of Duplicity: Controlling Reproduction in Ceausescu's Romania.* Berkeley, Calif., 1998.

Ornea, Z. *The Romanian Extreme Right: The Nineteen Thirties.* Translated by Eugenia Maria Popescu. Boulder, Colo., 1999.

Roberts, Henry L. *Rumania: Political Problems of an Agrarian State.* New Haven, Conn., 1951.

Shafir, Michael. *Romania: Politics, Economics, Society: Political Stagnation and Simulated Change.* London, 1985.

Verdery, Katherine. *National Ideology under Socialism: Identity and Cultural Politics in Ceausescu's Romania.* Berkeley, Calif., 1991.

KEITH HITCHINS

ROMANIES (GYPSIES).

While the major episode in Romani history during the nineteenth century was the abolition of slavery in Romania and the resulting massive out-migration from that part of Europe to the rest of the world, the twentieth century was marked by two main events: the Holocaust and the collapse of communism in Europe. It also saw the emergence of organized Romani political activity, which flourished following the end of the First World War in eastern Europe. In the Soviet Union however, all Romani activism was quickly suppressed by dictator Joseph Stalin (1879–1953), who later forbade speaking the Romani language.

The First World War saw no specific actions taken against Romanies, although they suffered considerable losses in combat. This was particularly so in the conflicts between Austria-Hungary and Serbia. Romanies fought loyally for Serbia, and a monument was later erected in Belgrade "in recognition of the Romani heroes who died or were killed during the 1914–1918 war."

INTERWAR PERIOD

The interwar experience of Romanies was characterized by antagonistic reception, a movement to develop Romani political organizations, and increasing persecution of Romanies by the Nazi government.

Reception in western and northern Europe In 1922 in Baden the German government began the process of fingerprinting and photographing all Romanies. In Switzerland in the following year, the Pro Juventute child welfare organization began the forced permanent removal of Romani children from their parents, a practice that lasted until 1984. In 1926 a law was passed in Bavaria to combat "Gypsy nomads."

In Prussia in 1927 Romanies were required to be photographed and fingerprinted and to carry identity cards, and in Bavaria none were allowed to travel in family groups or to own firearms. Those over sixteen were liable for incarceration in special work camps. A group of Romanies was tried for cannibalism in Slovakia, and a Norwegian law forbade the entry of Romanies into that country. A year later in Germany, Romanies were placed under permanent police surveillance, in direct violation of the constitution of the Weimar Republic. In 1929 the Munich municipal government jointly established the Division of Gypsy Affairs with the International Criminology Bureau (Interpol) in Vienna. Working together they imposed up to two years detention in "rehabilitation camps" for Romanies aged sixteen years and older.

Development of Romani political structures Meanwhile in Romania, the General Association of Gypsies of Romania was founded by Nicolae Gheorghe, who organized a conference in Bucharest called "United Gypsies of Europe." He sought to establish a national commemoration of the abolition of slavery each 23 December. His organization also envisioned a Romani hospital and university, and pushed for better communication and cooperation with Romani populations outside of Romania. It was at that conference that the official green and blue Romani flag was adopted.

The late 1920s also saw the emergence of a Romani "royal line" in Poland, dominated by members of the Kwiek family, descendants of slaves liberated in Romania seventy years before. A number of Kwieks had been able to establish a dynasty and be recognized as "kings" by local police and government officials, who even endorsed their elections. Michael Kwiek II, who succeeded his father King Gregory in 1930, held court regularly. In 1934 he announced his aim of creating a Romani state on the banks of the Ganges in India, the original Romani homeland. This far-reaching plan was terminated when he was forced to abdicate and leave Poland by his successor, Mathias Kwiek. Mathias made a number of proposals to the Polish government for civil and social reform for the nation's Romani population, but general anti-gypsyism, and tensions within the Romani community over competition for the throne, resulted in little being accomplished. Among those contending were Joseph Kwiek, who had his own plan for a Romani homeland in South Africa, and Basil Kwiek, who had helped to depose King Michael.

It was not until 1937 that Janusz Kwiek successfully petitioned the archbishop of Warsaw to recognize him as king of the Romani people in the country. As a consequence, invitations were sent to various European heads of state, and he was crowned Janos I on July 4 of that year. He approached the Italian Fascist government of Benito Mussolini (1883–1945) to ask that Romanies be allowed to settle in an area between Somalia and Abyssinia. The following year, however, Dr. Tobias Portschy, the Nazi provincial governor of Burgenland in Austria, recommended that the Romani population be eliminated, rather than simply removed from Europe, and sterilization measures were immediately stepped up. The establishment of a Romani colony in Africa never materialized. With the Nazi invasion of Poland and the policy of extermination of the Romanies, Romani unity was critically disrupted. Kwiek, as leader, was ordered to collaborate with the death squads, but refused, and was executed. Meanwhile, some members of the Kwiek family had moved to France, where their talent for stimulating Romani political activity later helped to establish a new organization, the World Romani Community.

Nazi persecution In 1920 Karl Binding and Alfred Hoche had published *On the Disposition of*

A memorial to Romani Holocaust victims stands near the site of the former concentration camp at Lety, now in the Czech Republic. GETTY IMAGES

Lives Unworthy of Life, employing in the title a phrase coined in 1863 by Richard Liebich to describe Romanies. The book appeared in Germany and recommended euthanizing those with "incurable hereditary diseases." On 26 May 1933 the new Nazi government introduced a law to legalize sterilization; on 14 July the cabinet of Adolf Hitler (1889–1945) passed a law against the propagation of "life unworthy of life," using Liebich's phrase. It was "the law for the prevention of hereditarily-diseased offspring," and operated against certain categories of people, "specifically Gypsies and most of the Germans of black color." Perceived "criminality" was interpreted as a genetic, that is, racial defect characterizing Romanies, and as such an incurable disease. In Nazi Germany from January 1934 onward, Romanies were selected for transfer to camps for processing, which included sterilization by injection and castration. Camps were established at Dachau, Dieselstrasse, Sachsenhausen,

Marzahn, and Vennhausen during the next three years. Starting on 15 September 1935, Romanies became subject to the restrictions of the Nuremberg Laws, which forbade intermarriage or sexual relations between "Aryan" and "non-Aryan" peoples. Romanies were no longer allowed to vote, and a policy statement issued by the Nazi Party stated: "In Europe generally, only Jews and Gypsies come under consideration as members of an alien people."

In March 1936, the first document referring to "the introduction of the total solution to the Gypsy problem on either a national or an international level" was drafted under the direction of State Secretary Hans Pfundtner of the Reich's Ministry of the Interior, and the main Nazi institution to deal with Romanies, the Racial Hygiene and Population Biology and Research Unit of the Ministry of Health, was established in Berlin. Its expressed purpose was to determine whether Romanies were "human" or "subhuman" (*Untermenschen*). Romanies were cleared off the streets of Berlin and put into a camp because of the upcoming Olympic Games. In 1937 a Nazi law was passed that stated that a person could be incarcerated for being inherently, as well as actually, a criminal.

The first Nazi documents to mention the "Final Solution of the Gypsy Question" were issued on 24 March and 8 December 1938, signed by the chief of the Gestapo, Heinrich Himmler. Between 12 and 18 June that year, "Gypsy Clean-Up Week" (*Zigeuner-aufraumungswoche*) was in effect, and hundreds of Romanies throughout Germany were rounded up and incarcerated. Hitler's chancellery received a report stating that "Gypsies place the purity of the blood of the German peasantry in peril." The following year, the Office of Racial Hygiene issued the statement that "All Gypsies should be treated as hereditarily sick; the only solution is elimination. The aim should therefore be the elimination without hesitation of this defective element in the population."

WORLD WAR II

In January or February 1940 the first mass murder of the Holocaust took place in the concentration camp at Buchenwald, when two hundred fifty

Romani children from Brno were used as guinea pigs to test Zyklon-B, later used in the gas chambers at Auschwitz-Birkenau. In Czechoslovakia, special camps for dispatching Romanies were built at Lety and Hodonín. On 31 July 1941 Reinhard Heydrich, head of the Reich main security office and the leading organizational architect of the Nazi's final solution, ordered the Einsatzkommandos "to kill all Jews, Gypsies and mental patients." In Slovakia, the "Decree on the Organization of the Living Conditions of the Gypsies" ordered that Romanies be physically separated from the rest of the population.

In Croatia in May 1942, the government and the Ustaša police jointly ordered the arrest of all Romanies for transportation to the extermination camp at Jasenovac. Their personal valuables were sent to the Vatican, where they evidently remain. On 31 July the Ministry of the Eastern Occupied Territories reaffirmed to the Wehrmacht (German regular army) that Romanies and Jews were to be dealt with identically. Justice Minister Otto Thierack stated, "Jews and Gypsies should be unconditionally exterminated." At this time the Nazis were beginning to compile data on Romani populations in Britain and elsewhere in anticipation of the eventual takeover of those countries. On 16 December, Himmler signed the order stating that "[a]ll Gypsies are to be deported to the Zigeunerlager at Auschwitz concentration camp regardless of their degree of racial admixture," marking the actual implementation of the final solution of the Gypsy question. On the night of 2–3 August 1944, twenty-nine hundred Romanies were gassed and cremated at Auschwitz-Birkenau, in an action remembered as *Zigeunernacht* (Night of the Gypsies).

POSTWAR PERIOD

At the Nuremberg War Crimes Tribunal in October 1945, the former SS general Otto Ohlendorf stated that in the killing campaigns "there was no difference between Gypsies and Jews," although no Romanies were called to testify on their own behalf. Current estimates now place Romani losses in the Holocaust as high as one and a half million. In 1950 the Wurttemburg Ministry of the Interior denied war crimes reparations claims by Romani survivors, stating "Gypsies were persecuted under the National Socialist regime not for any racial reason, but because of an antisocial criminal record." In 1980, a West German government spokesman, Gerold Tandler, called Romani demands for war crimes reparations "unreasonable" and "slander[ous]." The U.S. Holocaust Memorial Council was established in Washington, D.C., but no Romanies were invited to serve on it.

During the years following the war, the Romani population in Europe was numb. Political activity was minimal, and Romanies were reluctant even to identify their ethnicity publicly or to draw attention to it through group effort. No reparations had been forthcoming for the Nazi atrocities committed against them, and no organized attempts had been made by any national or international agency to reorient the survivors such as were being put into large-scale effect for survivors of other victimized groups; instead, prewar anti-Romani legislation continued to operate against them. In Germany, until as late as 1947, those who had come out of the camps had to keep well hidden or risk being incarcerated once again, this time in labor camps, if they could not produce documentation proving their German citizenship.

Developing Romani political structures This began to change in 1959, when Ionel Rotaru, a Romanian Romani living in France established the World Romani Community. His endeavors gained support from as far afield as Poland and Canada; he drew up elaborate, nationalistic plans for the Romanies, including the creation of an autonomous territory within France, and a homeland in Somalia. He sought schooling, the repeal of anti-Romani laws, the development of Romani-language literature, and war-crimes reparations from the German government. He founded the Romani Cultural Center in Brussels and went so far as to have Romani passports printed. His utopian ideals proved to be a threat to the government of Charles de Gaulle (1890–1970). Said to be embarrassed by Romani claims for war crimes reparations, that government in 1965 made the World Romani Community illegal. Rotaru continued to fight, however, and the notion of a geographical homeland, Romanestan, remained uppermost in his mind. It was important, he said, to have "a

A young Romani boy behind barbed wire at a camp for internally displaced persons near Pristina, Kosovo, 1999. Following the Balkan ethnic cleansing episodes of the 1990s, many thousands of Romani were confined in camps for those designated as internally displaced persons, or IDPs. ©HOWARD DAVIES/CORBIS

territory which would serve as a refuge in the event of persecution."

In that year also, and in response to de Gaulle, a new organization called the International Gypsy Committee was created to replace it. Its leader was the French Romani, Vanko Rouda (Jacques Dauvergne) whose more pragmatic approach concentrated on issues such as war crimes reparations rather than Romani passports. It stimulated the creation of affiliated bodies in other countries, such as the Romani Council in Britain and the Nordic Roma Council in Sweden. Within six years, twenty-three international organizations in twenty-two countries had been linked by the International Gypsy Committee. In 1971 it organized the first

World Romani Congress, an event funded in part by the World Council of Churches and the government of India and attended by representatives from India and some twenty other countries. At the congress, the green and blue flag from the 1933 conference, now embellished with the red, sixteen-spoked chakra was reaffirmed as the emblem of the Romani people, and the national anthem, *Dž>elem Dž>elem*, since sung at all congresses, was adopted. The International Gypsy Committee was renamed the International Rom Committee at the congress and became the permanent secretariat and executive authority presiding over the congress. From it, negotiations were successfully initiated with the Council of Europe (primarily in connection with anti-Romani legislation and free passage), and with the government of West Germany (in connection with war crimes reparations).

The second World Romani Congress took place in Geneva in April 1978, attended by sixty delegates and by observers from twenty-six countries. This time, the Indian links were more heavily emphasized and better represented: the prime minister of the Punjab, and his ministers of foreign affairs and of education, as well as a number of other dignitaries from India came, and were instrumental in urging the congress to apply for nongovernmental status within the United Nations. A petition was drawn up and in November 1979 was presented in person to the Nongovernmental Organizations (NGO) bureau of the United Nations in New York. Making the formal request for consultative status was a delegation led by the honorary president of the Romani Union, the actor Yul Brynner (1915–1985). By the following February, this request had been granted. An earlier petition seeking recognition of the Romanies had been sent to the Office of the United Nations High Commissioner for Human Rights by the International Rom Committee in 1968 but was unsuccessful.

At the Geneva congress, a committee called the International Romani Union—whose name has gradually come to stand for the International Rom Committee itself—had been created to plan the third World Romani Congress. That took place in Göttingen in 1981, with three hundred delegates from over twenty countries participating. In 1993 the United Nations approved elevation from

Observer to Special Consultative (Category II) status for the International Romani Union, which is now registered in the Economic and Social Council, the Department of Public Information, United Nations Children's Fund (UNICEF), and as a nongovernmental organization.

Between 4 and 13 April 1990, the fourth World Romani Congress took place at Serock on the outskirts of Warsaw, Poland, sponsored in part by United Nations Educational, Scientific, and Cultural Organization (UNESCO) and in July 2000 the fifth World Romani Congress was convened in Prague, in the Czech Republic. The sixth World Romani Congress took place in Italy in 2004, and elected the Polish Romani journalist Stanislaus Stankiewicz as its new president.

Continued persecution The overriding theme of the Geneva congress in 1978 had been the fate of Romanies in the Third Reich, but while numbers of survivors of the *Baro Porrajmos* (the Romani Holocaust) testified and the resolution was made that the issue of reparations be tackled head-on, the German governments still remained intractable in their position not to give full acknowledgment to Romani losses under the Nazis. Four years later, one German newspaper wrote that Romanies had "insulted the honor" of the memory of the Holocaust by wanting to be associated with it. In 1988 the East German government announced its resolution to pay $100 million in war crimes reparations to Holocaust survivors, but refused to include Romanies as recipients. Thousands of Romani refugees were expelled by the German government in 1992, which paid Romania $20,000 to take them back. In response to the rising tide of antigypsyism, the UN Commission for Human Rights passed a resolution that same year to protect Romanies. In Barcelona, Spain, Romanies were cleared from the streets by police and confined to El Campo de la Bota in preparation for the forthcoming Olympic Games.

In Bradford, England, laws were introduced in 1985 forbidding Romanies from entering that city's limits without a permit. In October the next year, the U.S. Congressional Caucus on Human Rights sent a petition to the government of Czechoslovakia protesting its policy of the coercive sterilization of Romani women and the forcible permanent removal of Romani children from their families. In Hungary, street gangs were reported as beating up Romanies, but "police [we]re giving violence against Gypsies low priority."

The fall of the Berlin Wall in 1989 brought major changes to Europe's six to eight million Romanies. The resulting rise of ethnic nationalism led in its extreme form to "ethnic cleansing," particularly in the Balkans. Romanies, with no country of their own in which to find refuge, suffered particularly harshly. Refugees from central Europe began seeking asylum in the West, particularly Canada and Britain, making headline news. Responses have included the creation in 1995 of an advisory council on Romanies by the Council of Europe and of the European Roma Rights Center in Budapest in 1996. A conference entitled The Prevention of Violence and Discrimination against Romanies was held in Romania in 1997. In 2001 a delegation of Romanies from many countries attended the World Conference against Racism, Racial Discrimination, Xenophobia, and Related Intolerance in Durban, South Africa, and delivered a petition to the United Nations asking that they be recognized as a nonterritorial nation with a permanent seat in the UN Assembly.

The situation did not seem to be improving at the beginning of the twenty-first century. *The Economist* was able to report that throughout Europe, Romanies were "at the bottom of every socio-economic indicator: the poorest, the most unemployed, the least educated, the shortest-lived, the most welfare dependent, the most imprisoned and the most segregated." A World Bank report dated 2003 stated, "Roma are the most prominent poverty risk group in many of the countries of Central and Eastern Europe. They are poorer than other groups, more likely to fall into poverty, and more likely to remain poor. In some cases poverty rates for Roma are more than 10 times that of non-Roma. A recent survey found that nearly 80 percent of Roma in Romania and Bulgaria were living on less than $4.30 per day. ... Even in Hungary, one of the most prosperous accession countries, 40 percent of Roma live below the poverty line."

See also **Ethnic Cleansing; Eugenics; Forced Labor; Holocaust; Refugees.**

BIBLIOGRAPHY

Acton, Thomas, ed. *Gypsy Politics and Traveller Identity.* Hatfield, U.K., 1997.

Crowe, David. *A History of the Gypsies of Eastern Europe and Russia.* New York, 1995.

Danbakli, Marielle, ed. *Roma, Gypsies: Texts Issued by International Institutions.* Paris, 2001.

Fings, Karola, Herbert Heuss, and Frank Sparing. *From "Race Science" to the Camps.* Vol. 1 of *The Gypsies during the Second World War.* Translated by Donald Kenrick. Hatfield, U.K., 1997.

Fraser, Angus. *The Gypsies.* Oxford, U.K., 1992.

Guy, Will, ed. *Between Past and Future: The Roma of Central and Eastern Europe.* Hatfield, U.K., 2001.

Hancock, Ian. *The Pariah Syndrome: An Account of Gypsy Slavery and Persecution.* Ann Arbor, Mich., 1987.

———. *We Are the Romani People.* Hatfield, U.K., 2002.

Kenrick, Donald, ed. *In the Shadow of the Swastika.* Hatfield, U.K., 1999.

Kenrick, Donald, and Grattan Puxton. *Gypsies under the Swastika.* Hertfordshire, U.K., 1995.

Szente, Veronika. *Racial Discrimination and Violence against Roma in Europe.* Budapest, 2001.

IAN HANCOCK

ROME. Rome's history in the twentieth century is tied to its unique legacy as the seat of ancient Rome and the center of western, Catholic Christianity. This dual legacy continues to shape the "third Rome"—that of the capital of modern Italy.

UNIFICATION TO WORLD WAR I
Following the disintegration of the Roman Empire, Italy was divided politically for centuries. Only in 1861 did Italy achieve political unification. Victor Emmanuel II, king of Sardinia, became Italy's first king (r. 1861–1878). Rome, the desired capital, remained under papal rule, protected by French troops. When the French withdrew during the Franco-Prussian War, Italian troops stormed into Rome on 20 September 1870. Rome became Italy's capital despite the protests of Pope Pius IX (r. 1846–1878), who refused to recognize the Italian state.

Rome rapidly grew in size and population. Between 1871 and 1911 the population increased from 212,000 to 518,000. The government constructed new public buildings, and developers built thousands of new dwelling units for residents of all classes. The city lacked heavy industry, relying principally on its role as the home of the national bureaucracy. Government employment and the building industry formed the economic foundation of the city.

Large new government buildings, such as the Palace of Justice, intentionally declared Rome's new political role in ways that both rivaled and defied the papacy. The first Protestant churches appeared soon after unification, as did monuments to Giuseppe Garibaldi (1807–1882), the national hero of unification, and to the philosopher Giordano Bruno, executed for heresy in 1600. To celebrate the fiftieth anniversary of unification in 1911, the government unveiled the huge, white marble monument of King Victor Emmanuel II on the Piazza Venezia, in the heart of the city.

WORLD WAR I
When Europe went to war in 1914, Italy remained neutral, but a movement began favoring Italian intervention. One of the interventionist leaders was Benito Mussolini, a radical socialist and editor of the Socialist Party newspaper *Avanti!* The Socialist Party opposed the war and so expelled Mussolini from the party and the paper. The interventionist cause prevailed. Italy entered the war in May 1915 as an ally of Britain, France, and Russia against Germany and Austria-Hungary.

The Italian army engaged the Austrians in the mountainous border area in northeast Italy. Although the Italian army suffered a devastating defeat at Caporetto in 1917, it recovered sufficiently to defeat the Austrians by November 1918 at the end of the war. Italy received the South Tyrol on the Italian side of the Alps, even though the population was overwhelmingly German-speaking.

Immediately after the war Italy experienced economic, social, and political distress. Nationalists believed Italy had not received sufficient new territory from the dismembered Austrian Empire and dubbed the peace agreements the "mutilated victory." Thousands of returning veterans could not find work. Workers went on strikes and occupied factories. Peasants tried to seize land. Some, inspired by the Russian example, advocated revolution.

In March 1919 Mussolini and a few hundred followers founded the Fascist movement. By the next year armed Fascist squads were using violence to attack Socialists and to defend rural property owners. The Fascists claimed that they were trying to restore law and order while preventing a Bolshevik-style revolution. The central government in Rome seemed weak and indecisive. Fascist squads took over a number of provincial towns and then threatened to march on Rome in October 1922. King Victor Emmanuel III (r. 1900–1946) decided against using the army to stop the Fascists and on 29 October 1922 asked Mussolini to become prime minister as head of a coalition government.

FASCIST ROME

Rome now became Mussolini's Rome, the heart and center of the so-called Fascist revolution. Mussolini moved his office to the Palazzo Venezia in the center of the historic city and adjacent to the Victor Emmanuel monument, which now included the tomb of the Unknown Soldier. Mussolini appeared on the balcony of the Palazzo Venezia to deliver his major speeches to thousands of people crowding the Piazza Venezia. He presided over frequent special ceremonies on the steps of the Victor Emmanuel monument. For twenty years the Rome of emperors, popes, and prime ministers became Mussolini's Fascist Rome.

Mussolini established a new governorship to administer the city. It was through this *Governatorato* that he set about rebuilding the city. As *duce* (leader), he declared that the Rome of the twentieth century had to confront the problems of "necessity and grandeur." The former constituted the needs of a modern city: housing, sanitation, streets, communications, and social services. The latter were the monumental aspects of Fascist Rome that had to be worthy of existing side by side with the monuments of ancient and Christian Rome such as the Colosseum, the Arch of Constantine, the Circus Maximus, and St. Peter's Basilica. The new Fascist Italy would define itself as the modern expression of *romanità* (Roman spirit), evoking ancient Roman greatness.

The Fascist regime accelerated the growth of Rome as the bureaucratic center of the national government. It built large new ministries for the navy, the air force, and the corporations, which were to bring about Italy's political and economic reorganization. The prospects of government employment or work in the building trades thus continued to draw thousands of Italians to Rome during the Fascist period. Between 1922 and 1941 the population doubled from 600,000 to 1.2 million.

The policy of rebuilding Rome for necessity and grandeur meant that the city became a vast construction site for twenty years. Mussolini regularly appeared at building projects to have his picture taken with workers and again on inaugural days when work was completed. The two most common dates for such events were 28 October and 21 April, the dates commemorating the Fascist March on Rome and the traditional date of Rome's birthday, respectively.

Mussolini declared that the transformation of Rome would clear away slums, provide clean new housing, improve traffic, and put people to work. The goal of increasing employment during the Great Depression through public works was not unique to Italy, as America's New Deal demonstrated, but in Rome's case it formed an integral part of Mussolini's hope to create a new Fascist society under his infallible leadership. As one slogan put it, "Mussolini is always right!"

Fascism sought to create a series of "cities" within Rome. It began with the historic core city that lay within the wall built during the reign of the Emperor Aurelian (r. 270–275). A series of projects transformed the area from the Piazza Venezia and the Victor Emmanuel monument to the Colosseum, on one side, and to the Circus Maximus on the other. The neighborhood between the monument and the Colosseum was demolished and a broad new street, the Via dell'Impero (Empire Street), opened on 28 October 1932 to celebrate the tenth anniversary of the March on Rome. It ran alongside the main Roman Forum and uncovered portions of the forums of Julius Caesar, Augustus, and Nerva.

The neighborhood on the other side of the Victor Emmanuel monument also disappeared to allow the construction of a wide street running to the Circus Maximus. This Via del Mare (Street

Opening festivities for the Via dell'Impero, November 1936. ©BETTMANN/CORBIS

to the Sea) would connect with streets built a few years later running out to the seaside town of Ostia, site of ancient Rome's port. The Circus Maximus itself was cleared of ramshackle buildings in 1934. This huge space, once the site of ancient Rome's chariot races, provided space for a series of large exhibitions in the 1930s, showcasing the achievements of Fascism.

The transformed historic center of Rome became the route for many parades and rallies staged by the regime. When Adolf Hitler visited Rome in 1938, he stood with Mussolini and the king on the reviewing stand next to the Arch of Constantine and the Colosseum as the long parade passed by and turned onto the Via dell'Impero.

Mussolini set out in the late 1920s to solve the "Roman Question," the unresolved tension between the Italian state and the Roman papacy. Negotiations led to the Lateran Treaty of 1929, which established a religious "city" within Rome. The Fascist government made a financial settlement with the church, recognized Vatican City as a sovereign state, and acknowledged the special place of the Catholic Church in Italy. Pope Pius XI (r. 1922–1939) thus gained an official status for the papacy and the church, while Mussolini received national and international acclaim for this political and diplomatic breakthrough. Several years later the regime demolished the neighborhood in front of St. Peter's to construct yet another wide new avenue, the Via della Conciliazione (Street of Reconciliation). Work was completed after World War II in time for the papal holy year of 1950.

The Fascist regime promised to produce a new generation of Italians to carry out the Fascist revolution, conceived as a hypernationalism, uniting Italians as never before and making Italy a major European and imperial power. Great emphasis was placed on youth groups, physical training, sports, and preparation for military service. Mussolini launched a project to create a major sports "city" for the leading boys' youth group, the Balilla. The Foro Mussolini, today the Foro Italico, arose on an open area facing the Tiber River north of the Vatican. It included two sports stadiums, an indoor swimming pool, tennis facilities, a building dedicated to fencing, and a youth hostel. The Stadium of Marbles, named for the athletic male figures surrounding it, seated twenty thousand and was used for athletic and military demonstrations and rallies.

To provide higher education for the new Fascist Italy, the regime built a "university city," opened in 1935. For the first time the University of Rome had a centralized campus with buildings designed by a group of Italy's leading architects.

The largest building project of the regime was a new "city" that arose several miles south of the historic center. It was scheduled to be the site of a Universal Exposition of Rome (Esposizione Universale di Roma, or EUR) in 1942 to celebrate the twentieth anniversary of the March on Rome. World War II caused the cancellation of the exposition, and building came to a halt. Development of the EUR section resumed in the 1950s and became part of the southwestern expansion of the city in the area of the new international airport, Leonardo da Vinci.

The most dramatic project Mussolini sponsored was the draining of the Pontine Marshes south of EUR and the city center. The newly acquired land provided farms for several thousand immigrants from northern Italy and the building of five new cities: Littoria (now Latina), Sabaudia, Pontinia, Aprilia, and Pomezia. The concept of land reclamation, *bonifica* in Italian, became a metaphor used by the regime to champion its moral and political redemption of the nation. This area also underwent significant growth after World War II.

Italy's conquest of Ethiopia in 1936 drew the condemnation of the League of Nations, but Hitler's Germany gave Italy diplomatic support. Consequently, Mussolini spoke of an emerging Rome-Berlin "Axis," and the two fascist powers gave military support to General Francisco Franco during the Spanish civil war from 1936 to 1939. In May 1939 Italy and Germany signed the Pact of Steel. Nevertheless, when Germany invaded Poland on 1 September 1939, Italy remained neutral.

In May 1940 German forces overran the Netherlands and Belgium and swept into France. By June it was clear that a German victory was inevitable. Mussolini made the fateful decision to enter the war and invade France. On 10 June 1940, he appeared on the balcony of the Palazzo Venezia to announce Italy's declaration of war.

Italian armed forces did poorly in the ensuing conflict. By mid-1943 an Italian army of 250,000 had been destroyed in the Soviet Union, and German and Italian forces surrendered to the Allies in North Africa. The Allies then conquered Sicily and prepared to invade mainland Italy. The first bombing raids on Rome inflicted considerable damage east of the city center in the area of the Basilica of San Lorenzo and the new university campus. These military reverses led to the dismissal of Mussolini by the king on the morning of 25 July 1943, following an all-night meeting of the Fascist Grand Council, which had taken a vote of no confidence in Mussolini.

The announcement of Mussolini's dismissal brought rejoicing in the streets of Rome. Italians believed that the war was over for them. The new Italian government negotiated an armistice with the Allies that it announced on 8 September, but the Germans quickly rushed in armed forces to confront the Allied troops that had invaded southern Italy. The Germans rescued Mussolini and set up a puppet Fascist government in northern Italy.

The Roman armed Resistance emerged in September 1943 and continued until the liberation of Rome by Allied troops on 4 June 1944. The first clashes took place on the 8th, 9th, and 10th of September when civilians joined Italian army units to fight German troops entering the city through the Aurelian Wall at the Gate of St. Paul. The overwhelming strength of the Germans, however, forced the Resistance underground.

The German occupation brought many hardships to Romans. In October 1943 the Gestapo entered the ghetto, rounded up over 1,000 Jews, and immediately shipped them to Auschwitz. Food was scarce, Nazi and Fascist army and police units combed the city, a curfew was imposed, and suspected Resistance members or sympathizers were jailed and tortured.

On 23 March 1944, the twenty-fifth anniversary of the founding of the Fascist movement, Resistance members set off a bomb in the heart of Rome that killed thirty-three members of a German police battalion. In retaliation, 335 Roman men and boys were executed south of the center in the Ardeatine Caves. A monument to these victims opened on the site in 1951.

Roberto Rossellini's 1945 film, *Rome, Open City,* commemorated the sufferings of the Romans during the Nazi occupation through the story of the collaboration of a Communist Party Resistance member and a Catholic priest. Rome, the center of Mussolini's Fascist Italy, now became the symbol of the anti-Fascist collaboration of Italians of all political persuasions that would form the foundation for a postwar society.

POSTWAR ROME

Italians voted in a national referendum in 1946 to abolish the monarchy. A new constitution establishing the Republic of Italy went into effect on 1 January 1948. The constitution provided a weak executive, a reaction to Mussolini's dictatorship, and a multiparty system based on proportional voting. The Christian Democratic Party became the largest vote getter, followed by the Communists, the Socialists, the Social Democrats, the Republicans, the Liberals, and the neofascist Italian Social Movement. On both the national and municipal levels, coalition governments were required as no one party had an absolute majority.

Rome abolished the Fascist *Governatorato* and restored a government with a mayor and a city council. Initially, the Christian Democrats and the Communists received the largest portion of votes, about 33 percent each, with the remaining one-third shared by half a dozen smaller parties. As with the national government, it took coalitions to elect a mayor and run the city government. Throughout the period of the Cold War (1945–1989), the Christian Democrats managed to form national governments that excluded the Communists, but that was not the case in Rome. Postwar mayors came from the Christian Democratic, Communist, and Socialist Parties. The first Communist mayor took office in 1976, and Communists filled the office until 1985.

The population continued to grow after the war, increasing from 1,650,000 in 1951 to a peak of 2,850,000 in 1981 before decreasing to 2,650,000 by 1997. The city also grew in area. The municipal government adopted a new master plan in 1962 to replace the Fascist one of 1931. The city faced a number of issues related to housing, transportation, social services, and developing areas. After the war large numbers of Italians, mostly from the poorer south, flooded Rome looking for jobs. Most of these poor immigrants lived in hastily built or illegal housing that sprang up on the periphery of the historic center. The beginnings of economic prosperity, Italy's so-called economic miracle of the 1950s and 1960s, along with Rome's master plan of 1962, brought some order to the city's growth and a general improvement in conditions.

Some political division marked the planning for the city's growth. The Left favored development to the east, whereas conservatives backed growth to the south. The Fascist origins of EUR lay behind the debate, and various compromises were reached that allowed growth in all directions. EUR did provide land for government and business buildings, including Rome's first skyscrapers. Mussolini's new cities to the south also attracted new business that fed the growth of Rome in that direction.

The historic center saw little population growth and experienced some decline by the end of the century. Neighborhoods once considered working class such as Trastevere and Testaccio underwent a measure of gentrification. Public housing grew in areas outside the center that continued a pattern established by Mussolini's regime. When the Fascists demolished neighborhoods in the 1930s, they moved the displaced Romans to inexpensive public housing well beyond the center, which allowed the government to maintain more firm control of its working-class population. Postwar growth followed a similar pattern, with major housing developments in the southern and southeastern sectors of the city.

Postwar Rome continued the practice of extending public park space in once aristocratic properties such as the Villa Ada, the Villa Doria Pamphili, and the Villa Borghese, the latter of which includes several museums and Rome's zoo. The Fascist regime had also created public spaces in the historic center such as the Circus Maximus; the Cestio Park, renamed for the Resistance after the war; the Park of Trajan, adjacent to the Colosseum; and the Park of Hadrian, surrounding the Castel Sant'Angelo. The large park on the Janiculum Hill overlooks the Trastevere neighborhood and includes the city's botanical gardens.

By the 1980s Rome had several modern supermarkets, but Romans continued to do most of their food shopping in open and covered markets, filled with stalls, and in small shops specializing in one product: fruit, vegetables, fish, cheese, meat. Retail clothing stores include the luxury, high-fashion shops below the Spanish Steps, several department stores, specialty shops, and open-air stalls selling less expensive clothing.

In the last twenty-five years of the century, Rome attracted large numbers of foreign immigrants. Initially, Filipinos and East, West, and North Africans were most conspicuous. Following the end of the Cold War and the collapse of the Soviet Union, large numbers of eastern Europeans joined the migration to Rome, and at the turn of the twenty-first century yet others came from South Asia and Latin America. Italy's declining birthrate increased the demand for workers to fill low-wage jobs. The new immigrants typically worked as domestics, as street vendors, and in other low-paying jobs unattractive to native Romans. About 20 percent of the newcomers were Muslims, leading to the construction of Rome's first mosque in 1995.

Rome is no longer an isolated city surrounded by empty countryside as it was in the early twentieth century. The enlarged city of the early twenty-first century is part of a metropolitan area that extends east to the Leonardo da Vinci Airport and Ostia on the sea and southeast to EUR and toward the Fascist new towns in the province of Latina. EUR contains a collection of government buildings, banking and business skyscrapers, museums, sports facilities, and upper-middle-class residential dwellings that make it second only to the historic core as an urban center. Overall, the contrast between a prosperous city center and a poor periphery of workers and immigrants has faded. Rome has become a more integrated city. The improved economy has led to better housing and social

services and more mixing of social groups in many neighborhoods.

Economic prosperity made it possible for middle- and working-class Italians to buy automobiles. Rome's 50,000 cars after the war grew to over 800,000 by the mid-1970s and to 1.6 million by 2000. Traffic jammed central Rome's streets, and every piazza and curbside became a parking lot. The construction of a ring road linked to the major highways helped with the flow in and out of the city. Certain areas of the historic center were declared off-limits to private automobiles. The bus system continued to provide reasonably cheap and efficient service throughout the city, but it often ran large deficits. The subway system, begun by the Fascists, opened its first line between the main train station and EUR in 1955. This Line B has since been expanded and joined by a Line A that intersects at the main train station. Traffic congestion also brings stress to historic monuments through street vibration and air pollution.

Italy experienced a wave of domestic terrorism in the 1970s fueled by both left- and right-wing extremists. Government officials were often the targets of assassins' bullets. In 1978 the Red Brigades abducted the Christian Democratic leader and former prime minister, Aldo Moro. The government refused to negotiate with the abductors. On 9 May 1978 Moro's body was found in the trunk of a car in downtown Rome, midway between the party headquarters of the Christian Democrats and the Communists. Public revulsion at the Moro murder and the subsequent capture of leading terrorists led to the end of this period of the "years of lead" by the mid-1980s.

TWENTY-FIRST-CENTURY ROME

By the early 1990s, with the end of the Cold War and the collapse of the system known as *partitocrazia* (rule of the parties), after the revelation of the long-standing bribes that funded the major political parties, a new set of political parties and coalitions emerged on the national level. Nevertheless, Rome continued as the political center of Italy. The political importance of Rome reinforced its role as a center for lobbyists, insurance, banking, retail and wholesale business, the media, and communications. Rome also became the national center for newer enterprises such as computer technology and pharmaceutical companies.

Rome also serves as a major cultural center for Italy. The city was both the location and the subject of many postwar films, such as Roberto Rosellini's *Rome, Open City* (1945); Vittorio De Sica's *Bicycle Thief* (1948) and *Umberto D.* (1952); Federico Fellini's *La dolce vita* (1960) and *Roma* (1972); and Pier Paolo Pasolini's *Mamma Roma* (1962). The Fascist-built Cinecittà (Cinema City) provided facilities for film and television productions. Late-twentieth and early-twenty-first-century Rome has also been a magnet for writers. Carlo Levi, Alberto Moravia and Elsa Morante have all written in and about Rome. Many of Italy's leading literary journals are based in Rome, as is its most prestigious annual literary award, the Strega Prize. Rome maintains a flourishing art community with its geographical center on the Via Margutta near the Spanish Steps.

Since 1300 the popes have declared holy years every twenty-five years that attract pilgrims from all over the world. Pius XII held one in 1950 and Paul VI in 1975. The Second Vatican Council, convened by John XXIII in 1962, also reinforced the role and image of Rome as the center of Roman Catholicism. John Paul II's Holy Year and Jubilee of 2000 was eagerly embraced by Major Francesco Rutelli, a member of the Democratic Party of the Left, the successor to the Italian Communist Party. The year 2000 thus embodied both Rome's historical legacy and its role as a modern city.

The city received a facelift in the several years leading to the Jubilee. Scores of churches, buildings, and tourist sites were cleaned and restored. Streets and parking facilities were improved. Romans had to cope with the resulting disruption of traffic and the sight of scaffolding throughout the city. The funds came from the church, the national and municipal governments, and businesses. Rome had hosted the Summer Olympic Games in 1960 and the World Cup soccer matches in 1990, but the Jubilee surpassed both of these major events in size and scope. It underscored the significance of tourism in Rome's economy in attracting millions of additional visitors. As Rome entered a new century and a new millennium it proudly displayed itself as the expression of its unique legacy as the Rome of antiquity, the Rome

of the papacy, and the Rome of the modern nation of Italy.

See also **Fascism; Italy; Mussolini, Benito.**

BIBLIOGRAPHY

Agnew, John A. *Rome*. Chichester, U.K., 1995.

———. *Place and Politics in Modern Italy*. Chicago, 2002.

Boardman, Jonathan. *Rome: A Cultural and Literary Companion*. New York, 2001.

Bondanella, Peter. *The Eternal City: Roman Images in the Modern World*. Chapel Hill, N.C., 1987.

Cannistraro, Philip V., ed. *Historical Dictionary of Fascist Italy*. Westport, Conn., 1982.

Fried, Robert C. *Planning the Eternal City: Roman Politics and Planning since World War II*. New Haven, Conn., 1973.

Ghirardo, Diane. "From Reality to Myth, Italian Fascist Architecture in Rome." *Modulus*, no. 21 (1991): 10–33.

Ginsborg, Paul. *A History of Contemporary Italy: Society and Politics, 1943–1988*. London, 1990.

———. *Italy and Its Discontents: Family, Civil Society, State, 1980–2001*. New York, 2003.

Hibbert, Christopher. *Rome: Biography of a City*. New York, 1985.

Katz, Robert. *The Battle for Rome: The Germans, the Allies, the Partisans, and the Pope, September 1943–June 1944*. New York, 2003.

Kostof, Spiro. *The Third Rome, 1870–1950: Traffic and Glory*. Berkeley, Calif., 1973.

Mack Smith, Denis. *Modern Italy: A Political History*. Ann Arbor, Mich., 1997.

Varriano, John. *A Literary Companion to Rome*. London, 1991.

BORDEN PAINTER

ROME, TREATY OF. From 1 to 3 June 1955 the foreign ministers of the six members (Belgium, Federal Republic of Germany, France, Italy, Luxembourg, the Netherlands) of the European Coal and Steel Community (ECSC) met in Messina and Taormina in Sicily, Italy. The result was the so-called Messina resolution, which was a careful blend of German, Italian, and especially Benelux (Belgium, Netherlands, and Luxembourg) memorandums. The resolution envisaged two main avenues for "relaunching" European integration: a sectoral approach and a more comprehensive economic integration approach. The more functional, sectoral approach, which was supported by Jean Monnet, who then headed the High Authority of the ECSC, and by the Belgian foreign minister Paul-Henri Spaak, originally encompassed both the communications and energy sectors, including civil atomic energy. Yet the report of the Intergovernmental Committee, which was organized after Messina, met in Brussels, and was headed by Spaak, recommended focusing sectoral integration on atomic energy. As for overall integration—an approach initially presented by the Dutch foreign minister Johan Willem Beyen at the Organization for European Economic Cooperation (OEEC) in 1952 and that then found its way, in modified form, into the ill-fated 1953 draft treaty for a European Political Community—the report favored the creation of a customs union with a common external tariff as opposed to the realization of a free trade area. By the end of 1955, the United Kingdom announced it would no longer participate in the Intergovernmental Committee. The "Spaak report" was issued on 21 April 1956 and was approved at the Venice Conference of Foreign Ministers on 29–30 May 1956 as a basis for treaty negotiations. The ensuing intergovernmental conference, again under the chairmanship of Spaak, led to the signature of the Treaties of Rome on 25 March 1957 and their subsequent ratification by the six founding members of the ECSC. Both treaties entered into force on 1 January 1958. Two new communities were created: the European Atomic Energy Community (Euratom) and the European Economic Community (EEC).

EURATOM

During the negotiations some key issues had to be addressed, which did much to reveal the stakes for the participants as well as for other countries. As far as Euratom was concerned, Louis Armand, the French mastermind behind the Euratom proposal, who was also a member of the board of the French Commissariat à l'Énergie Atomique, envisaged it as a pool of atomic resources, which would launch Europe on the road to energy independence. He expected to obtain U.S. help through the "Atoms for Peace" program announced by President Dwight Eisenhower in December 1953. Beyond

reducing European dependence on energy imports, Euratom was also seen by the advocates of the French military program as a way of having France's partners foot most of the bill for an isotopic separation plant (which would produce enriched uranium, a key ingredient in manufacturing atomic bombs) by mentioning the creation of this plant in the Euratom treaty. In addition, the French and the Americans hoped that Euratom could become a means of completing the unfinished business of controlling the German nuclear industry. Even though the Federal Republic of Germany (FRG) had temporarily renounced the manufacture of nuclear weapons during the Western European Union (WEU) negotiations, it had not renounced civil production, and there was no guarantee that it would not one day decide to go from peaceful uses of nuclear energy to military uses. But while the French initially advocated a centralized procurement and supply of fissile materials as well as control by Euratom, it soon became clear that if Euratom control stood in the way of the French nuclear program, the French National Assembly would never support the treaty. This was so even though Guy Mollet—the leader of the French Socialist Party—Monnet, and the German socialists initially envisaged Euratom as being exclusively limited to the peaceful uses of nuclear energy, notably to ensure that the Germans would participate in Euratom on a basis of equality with other member states. The French, including Mollet, accordingly ended up supporting a solution in which Euratom did not control the use of fissionable materials destined for military purposes: Euratom would keep ownership rights of the materials up to the point where its control of these materials passed to the Western European Union. Since the FRG had renounced the manufacture of nuclear weapons to the WEU, it now found its whole nuclear sector controlled, while the French could pursue the development of their own nuclear military program.

But France did not succeed in obtaining all of its priorities. The United States, intent on using Euratom not only to further European integration but also for nonproliferation purposes, insisted on the exclusive ownership by Euratom of all fissionable materials provided by the United States and other sources. It also deemed it contrary to U.S.

interests to help the six ECSC members build an uranium enrichment plant. Hence the announcement by Washington that it would guarantee an almost unlimited supply of enriched uranium to feed foreign nuclear power plants at a price that would be half or one-third that of European-produced uranium-235. Euratom would be given preferential treatment. Faced with such an offer, the six countries gradually abandoned the idea of building their own European enrichment plant. The Euratom treaty did not mention the construction of such a plant, which also considerably reduced the interest of Euratom for the French military nuclear program. Other difficulties during the Euratom negotiations included German insistence on private ownership of fissionable materials as opposed to Euratom ownership, the existence or the prospect of bilateral agreements for the sale of enriched uranium between the United States and some ECSC members, and competition from the British proposal of an OEEC cooperative plan on nuclear energy.

THE EUROPEAN ECONOMIC COMMUNITY
France's partners were mostly keen to have a European common market. The Benelux countries depended greatly on their export trade and anticipated substantial advantages from a lowering of trade barriers and increased competition within the EEC. The Germans, with the exception of Minister of Economic Affairs Ludwig Erhard, who preferred a European free trade area to a protectionist EEC, anticipated great benefits from a single market in industrial goods. But France's partners were much less supportive of Euratom than France was and insisted that the two treaties should be linked, so that there would be no Euratom if the EEC did not also come into existence. France was against linking the two treaties, as were the United States and Monnet, who feared that the EEC treaty would face ratification difficulties in France and might therefore doom Euratom. The French initially did not show much enthusiasm for the creation of a general common market, in which they feared competition from their neighbors, especially since their price levels were higher than some of their partners. Much of the French civil service preferred protecting French industry from German competition until it grew strong enough to withstand it. By contrast, Guy Mollet,

who became the French prime minister in February 1956, and his foreign minister, Christian Pineau, were more favorable to the EEC, which they saw as a means of modernizing the French economy by opening it to foreign competition.

To convince French public opinion to support both treaties, Mollet and Pineau tried to focus on the creation of Euratom first and on the EEC second, to allow for enough time to gather support for the latter. Mollet organized important debates in the French National Assembly: one on atomic energy in July 1956 and another on the EEC in January 1957. They were instrumental in gathering support from French deputies and in sending signals to France's partners on what would and would not "sell" in France to ensure ratification of the treaties. On the EEC, France insisted on the creation of a common agricultural policy, a key demand of the French National Assembly and French farmers. France also asked for a harmonization of social charges so that French employers would not be put at a disadvantage in the common market and to preserve its levels of social welfare. This proposal included a standardized working week of forty hours, standardized overtime payment rates to equal those of France, equal pay for both sexes, and a harmonization of paid holidays. In addition, France requested the association of its overseas possessions with the common market so that goods from these territories would receive the same treatment as French goods. In the end, the EEC treaty did mention the future creation of a supranational common agricultural policy, although details were to be filled in by future negotiations. The treaty also contained important social provisions, including equal pay for equal work for men and women, an equivalence of paid holidays, and the creation of a European Social Fund. It provided for close economic ties between the EEC and overseas countries and territories having special relations with its members and for an investment fund to promote economic and social development.

Institutionally, the Rome treaties were a careful compromise between the concerns of small countries, who feared being dominated by larger ones, and French aversion to and German support for supranational institutions. The result was a strengthening of the council, the progressive introduction of qualified majority voting, and a relative weakening of the Euratom and EEC Commissions as compared to the High Authority of the ECSC. All in all, the Rome treaties negotiations amounted to a challenging balancing act between the intergovernmental and the supranational dimensions in building the European Communities. The treaties were signed without limitation in time and with no possibility for withdrawal.

See also **European Coal and Steel Community (ECSC); Organisation for European Economic Cooperation (OEEC).**

BIBLIOGRAPHY

Boussuat, Gérard. *Faire l'Europe sans défaire la France, 60 ans de politique d'unité européene des gouvernements et des présedents de la République française (1943–2003).* Brussels, 2005.

Deighton, Anne, ed. *Building Postwar Europe: National Decision-Makers and European Institutions, 1948–1963.* New York, 1995.

Devuyst, Youri. *The European Union Transformed: Community Method and Institutional Evolution from the Schuman Plan to the Constitution of Europe.* Brussels, 2005.

Dinan, Desmond. *Ever Closer Union: An Introduction to European Integration.* 3rd ed. Boulder, Colo., 2005.

Küsters, Hans Jürgen. *Fondements de la Communauté Economique Européene.* Luxembourg, 1990.

Lundestad, Geir. *Empire by Integration: The United States and European Integration, 1945–1997.* Oxford, U.K., 1998.

Milward, Alan. *The European Rescue of the Nation State.* London, 1994.

Skogmar, Gunnar. *The United States and the Nuclear Dimension of European Integration.* New York, 2004.

Winand, Pascaline. *Eisenhower, Kennedy, and the United States of Europe.* New York, 1993.

———. "European Insiders Working inside Washington: Monnet's Network, Euratom, and the Eisenhower Administration." In *The United States and the European Alliance since 1945,* edited by Kathleen Burk and Melvyn Stokes, 207–238. Oxford, U.K., 1999.

PASCALINE WINAND

ROSENBERG, ALFRED (1893–1946),
German Nazi leader and writer.

In the eyes of posterity Alfred Rosenberg was the main theorist of National Socialism. His life is indeed an object lesson in the nature of Nazism as a historical phenomenon, as a belief system, and as a set of state policies.

Rosenberg was born in Reval (Tallinn), Estonia, into a well-to-do *Volksdeutsche* (ethnic German) family. He thus belonged to one of those German minorities dispersed throughout the Austro-Hungarian and Russian empires, whose destiny was a burning issue in the early part of the twentieth century. As a citizen of the Russian Empire, Rosenberg was not among the German populations deported at the beginning of World War I, and he completed his engineering and architectural studies in Moscow before fleeing the Russian Revolution of 1917. He witnessed the outbursts of virulent Germanophobia in Russian cities, notably in Petrograd and Moscow. In his flight he passed through France, as did many refugees from World War I and the Russian Revolution, and then made his way to Munich.

Nothing is known of Rosenberg's political radicalization or of his relationship to the German nation during the war, but it is certain that in 1918 he was embarked upon a militant career that would take him from the Thule Gesellschaft, a *völkische* (people's movement) and anti-Semitic group of activists, via the teachings of Dietrich Eckardt, a Munich journalist who was Hitler's mentor, to the Nazi Party (NSDAP) itself, which he had joined by 1920. There he was quickly assigned tasks relating to propaganda and theory, writing fervid anti-Semitic pamphlets and concocting a theory of Jewish-Masonic conspiracy. As a result of these efforts, Rosenberg inherited the mantle of Eckardt when the latter died while editor in chief of the NSDAP newspaper the *Völkischer Beobachter* (People's observer). Rosenberg later served as a stand-in for Hitler when the Nazi leader was imprisoned after the Munich Beer Hall Putsch of 9 November 1923, and formed a replacement organization for the banned NSDAP. He was also the founder of a Militant League for German Culture, an organization whose name underlined the continuity between Nazi themes and earlier rhetorics of justification for World War I. What the name did not signal, however, was the deep-seated racism that Rosenberg had internalized and that is

Alfred Rosenberg addresses a crowd c. 1925.
©HULTON-DEUTSCH COLLECTION/CORBIS

chief ideologist of the Third Reich, and he had much to do with unofficial policies abroad; while head of the NSDAP's foreign-policy department, for example, he worked closely with the clandestine networks of Nazified *Volksdeutsche* that constituted a kind of fifth column in central and eastern Europe.

Thus, while Rosenberg's main activity had to do with party dogma and its dissemination, his ethnic German roots and his familiarity with the Russian and Baltic worlds equipped him to affect internal developments in an eastern Europe destined to become the colonizable *Hinterland* of the developing Third Reich. It was the combination of these two supposed areas of competence that qualified Rosenberg for the post of minister of occupied eastern territories, which he took up in 1941. In this capacity he played a leading part in the Nazis' occupation policies. His activity was subject, however, to the proliferating tendencies so characteristic of Nazi institutions. He set up a civil administration to carry out the NSDAP's rapacious policies in Ukraine, Belarus, western Russia, and the Baltic states, yet he never managed to gain control over either the Polish territories governed by Hans Frank or the lands of southeastern Europe. Nor did he ever muster the means to challenge the overwhelming influence of the SS in those regions. After a vain attempt in the winter of 1941 to be put in charge of policy on the Jewish question, which was by now clearly genocidal in character, Rosenberg was gradually marginalized. But even as a Nazi philosopher whose books went unread and a minister with limited powers, he contributed decisively to a radicalization of occupation policies that cost millions of lives in the western territories of the Soviet empire.

It was on the basis of this dual role—as official ideologue of the Reich and predatory and genocidal administrator of its colonies—that Alfred Rosenberg was tried at Nuremberg, condemned to death, and executed on 16 October 1946.

See also **Fascism; Germany; Nazism; Occupation, Military.**

BIBLIOGRAPHY

Piper, Ernst. *Hitlers Cheideologe.* Munich, 2005.

discernible in all his writings, including his major work, *The Myth of the Twentieth Century* (1930), often considered the most important contribution to Nazi ideology after *Mein Kampf.* Though deemed obscure even by the Nazis themselves, Rosenberg's theoretical contribution hewed fast to the party's picture of history, focusing on the definition of *Aryan* and the circumstances of the decline of Aryan populations in India.

After becoming a parliamentary deputy representing the Rhineland in 1930, Rosenberg concentrated on theoretical issues and on the regulation of scientific research. From 1934 on he was responsible for the party's censorship of science, and in 1939 he founded an Institute for Research on the Jewish Question, under whose aegis, during World War II, he organized a campaign of meticulous cultural pillage, looting many eastern European libraries in order to build up the collections of this improbable research center. Rosenberg was the

Whisker, James B. *The Philosophy of Alfred Rosenberg: Origins of the National Socialist Myth.* Costa Mesa, Calif., 1990.

CHRISTIAN INGRAO

ROSSELLINI, ROBERTO (1906–1977), Italian filmmaker.

Roberto Rossellini was born into a well-educated, vivacious bourgeois family in Rome. His self-proclaimed "zest to understand" the world around him was first cultivated by a salon of artists, writers, and musicians who filled the Rossellini family home each Sunday during his childhood and early adolescence. Curiously, a similar atmosphere of passionate intellectual and political discussion was re-created amid the desperation and poverty of World War II Rome, when refugees and political dissidents in hiding whiled away the time talking. In both instances, Rossellini gleaned a crucial education in ideas of history, culture, and truth, all of which would emerge as obsessive themes in his filmmaking. Throughout his early life, Rossellini loved and was deeply influenced by the movies he saw from directors as varied as Charlie Chaplin, King Vidor, and F. W. Murnau.

Yet Rossellini was equally affected by the historical and political moment he lived in: while his father was a brazen antifascist, Rossellini was ambiguous about his allegiances before and during World War II. Many admirers of Rossellini's later films have tended to "forget" that one of Rossellini's first experiences on a film set was *Luciano Serra Pilota* (1938), supervised by Mussolini's son, Vittorio. Rossellini's own first features—*The White Ship* (1942), *The Pilot Returns* (1942), and *The Man with the Cross* (1943)—can all be interpreted, at least superficially, to be fascist propaganda, commissioned as they were by the Fascist-controlled government. But some critics have interpreted these initial films as compromises made "by any means necessary" during wartime and have argued that they nonetheless contain the seeds of a fierce individualism in the face of crumbling societal and political edifices, a vision that Rossellini explores more deeply in three films that followed the war and that catapulted him to international fame: *Rome, Open City* (1945), *Paisà* (1946), and *Germany Year Zero* (1948).

Rome, Open City tells the story of Italy's capital in 1944, toward the end of the war. *Open City's* depiction of the bit players experiencing major historical events—the partisan who decides to fight against the Nazi tide, the people who try to protect him, the children who suffer the daily deprivation and danger of living in an occupied city—was revolutionary in its ability to render the war close and intimate. When the soldiers rushing to round up the opposition pause to look up the skirts of the young girls above them on the stairwell, we feel as if we have become witness to life *as it happens* rather than life merely represented. Thus Rossellini became known as the "father of neorealism." He used nonprofessional actors on location (as opposed to re-creating scenes in the studio), but at the same time consistently experimented with different film stocks (depending on what he could find during the war) and available lighting. Perhaps most important, he displayed a strong inclination toward melodramatic narrative elements.

So what do we mean when we use the term *neorealism,* and why is Rossellini considered its "father"? The films that followed Rossellini's postwar trilogy may provide some insight. *Germany Year Zero* is the heartbreaking story of a little boy so overwhelmed by the aftereffects of war that he ends up poisoning his father and then killing himself. It was filmed amid the actual rubble of postwar Germany. After it was completed, Rossellini entered into a personal and professional relationship with the Swedish-born actress and Hollywood star Ingrid Bergman (1915–1982). Bergman and Rossellini's relationship caused an international scandal, since they were both married when they began seeing each other romantically. An unofficial boycott of their films ensued, which was ultimately detrimental to both their careers. They eventually married and had three children together, including the actress Isabella Rossellini, star of *Blue Velvet* (1986).

Bergman and Rossellini made a number of films together, including *Stromboli* (1949) and *Voyage in Italy* (1953). *Voyage* inspired the members of the French new wave to name Rossellini the "father of modern cinema," widening the scope of his supposed paternity. The new wave's adulation did not stem primarily from his direct reproduction

A scene from Rossellini's *Open City*, 1945. Pina, a pregnant widow with two children (played by Anna Magnani), has been shot and killed by German soldiers. EXCELSA/MAYER-BURSTYN/THE KOBAL COLLECTION

of reality (again, this is the common misconception about "neorealism"). Instead, the writers at *Cahiers du cinéma* admired his pioneering use of narrative "gaps and fragments," by which he told stories much closer to reality *as we experience it.*

Although Rossellini continued to make films and television programs until his death in 1977, none achieved the acclaim of the films from the late 1940s and early 1950s. Rossellini seemed despondent about the future of the modern cinema he was said to have spawned: in 1963 he called a press conference and very dramatically proclaimed cinema "dead." During the 1960s and 1970s, Rossellini worked primarily in television, creating historical programs with an educational aim. Some were re-creations of the remote past, such as *Acts of the Apostles* (1969), *Socrates* (1970), and *The Age of the Medici* (1973), while others were biographical features, such as *Year One* (1974), about Alcide de Gasperi (1881–1954), the Christian Democratic politician and first postwar Italian premier—another *pater patriae* of the postwar world.

See also Cinema; Italy.

BIBLIOGRAPHY

Bondanella, Peter. *Films of Roberto Rossellini.* Cambridge, U.K., 1993.

Brunette, Peter. *Roberto Rossellini.* New York, 1987.

Gallagher, Tag. *The Adventures of Roberto Rossellini.* New York, 1998. A comprehensive biography and filmography written by the noted film scholar.

Rossellini, Roberto. *My Method: Writing and Interviews.* Edited by Adriano Aprà. Translated by Annapaola Cancogni. New York, 1992.

ANNE M. KERN

Muslims protest Salman Rushdie's novel *The Satanic Verses*, London, 1990. ©ZEN ICKNOW/CORBIS

RUSHDIE, SALMAN (b. 1947), Anglo-Indian author.

Ahmed Salman Rushdie was born in Bombay, India, on 18 June 1947, eight weeks before Indian independence was declared. His was a prosperous Muslim family; his father had attended King's College, Cambridge, and brought up his family with a deep respect for British culture. Salman Rushdie's childhood was spent, in the words of the title of the 1981 novel that made his reputation, as one of "midnight's children," those born in the shadow of both freedom and the bloodshed attending partition of Hindu India and Muslim Pakistan. After attending the Cathedral School of Bombay, he continued his education at Rugby School in the British Midlands and at King's College, Cambridge, from which he graduated with a degree in history in 1968. By then his family had moved to Pakistan, to which Rushdie temporarily returned after Cambridge.

Rushdie had become, he said repeatedly, a non-Muslim Muslim, a British Asian, a non-

European European. The ambivalence of his approach to both British and South Asian society and politics dominates virtually all his writing. In *Shame* (1983), he exposed the corruption of the military and political elite of Pakistan, "that fantastic bird of a place, two wings without a body, sundered by the land-mass of its greatest foe, joined by nothing but God" (p. 194). In *Shame,* Rushdie presented a thinly disguised Benazir Bhutto, prime minister of Pakistan, in the form of the "Virgin Ironpants." In *Midnight's Children* he had conjured up the frightening figure of the "Black Widow," easily decipherable as Indira Gandhi during the State of Emergency she introduced in 1977. Awarded the prestigious Booker Prize for the best work of fiction in 1981, Rushdie had indeed arrived in English literary culture.

In 1988 he arrived as well in international politics. The casus belli between Rushdie and upholders of the Islamic faith was the publication in 1988 of *The Satanic Verses*. This rambling, complex mixture of satire and fantasy presents two entirely distinct stories. One concerns the degrading treatment nonwhite immigrants receive in British society. The other is a story based on the medieval legend that Satan insinuated some lines into the Koran by whispering them surreptitiously in Mohammed's ear. Rushdie added insult to injury: he named prostitutes after the twelve wives of Mohammed and called Mecca "Jahilia," or "ignorance" in Arabic. He gave Mohammed the name "Mahound" and thereby conjured up an older non-Muslim tradition in which "Mahound" the Prophet was a charlatan or madman. What more did devout Muslims need to hear before concluding that Rushdie aimed to discredit Islam itself?

British Muslims took to the streets. On 14 January 1989, copies of *The Satanic Verses* were burned publicly in Bradford, home to a large population of Muslims whose origins were in poor rural areas of Pakistan. Two weeks later thousands of Muslims demonstrated against Rushdie in London's Hyde Park. Overseas the book also became a cause célèbre. The book was banned in Bangladesh, Saudi Arabia, South Africa, and India. This is the background to the *fatwa,* or death sentence, on Rushdie promulgated by the Ayatollah Khomeini in 1989, after which Rushdie went into hiding. Police protection was provided in Britain. In Pakistan, six demonstrators were killed in Islamabad in mass protests over Rushdie's supposed vilification of Islam. Rushdie was barred from India. It was only on 7 September 1995, six years after the *fatwa* was issued, that Rushdie appeared in public, at Westminster City Hall in a debate on "writers against the state." In 1998 the Iranian authorities promised not to enforce the *fatwa,* but in 2005 Iran's Revolutionary Guards claimed that the *fatwa* still stood. Rushdie remains a marked man.

The Rushdie affair highlighted the vulnerability of the Muslim community in Britain. Faced by the temptations of Western culture, British Muslims from South Asia feared the loss of their children to secularism. Not having Arabic—the language of the Koran—as their native tongue, these Asian Muslims in Britain were even more vigilant in the defense of the Holy Text; they lacked the self-confidence simply to ignore a novel written by a Muslim-born writer who had ceased to believe in Islam. On the other side, the controversy brought into high relief the issue of Muslim assimilation of British "values" and anticipated later conflicts over Western military action in the Persian Gulf and Middle East.

Rushdie's later fiction is more eclectic, reflecting his decision to leave Britain for the United States. *The Moor's Last Sigh* (1995) is set in contemporary India, against the backdrop of Hindu terrorism against Muslims. *The Ground beneath Her Feet* (1999) deals with rock music, and *Fury* (2001) follows the life of a writer trying to start a new life in New York. *Shalimar the Clown* (2005) returns to Kashmir, and its destruction in the course of the Indo-Pakistani conflict over control of it. Here Rushdie speaks obliquely of terrorism, and more directly of this beautiful and troubled land where his most celebrated novel, *Midnight's Children,* began.

See also **Islamic Terrorism/Al Qaeda.**

BIBLIOGRAPHY

Appignanesi, Lisa, and Sarah Maitland, eds. *The Rushdie File.* Syracuse, N.Y., 1990.

Booker, M. Keith, ed. *Critical Essays on Salman Rushdie.* New York, 1999.

Easterman, Daniel. *New Jerusalems: Reflections on Islam, Fundamentalism, and the Rushdie Affair.* London, 1992.

La'Porte, Victoria. *An Attempt to Understand the Muslim Reaction to* The Satanic Verses. Lewiston, N.Y., 1999.

Lévy, Bernard-Henri. *Avec Salman Rushdie: Questions de princip.* 6. Paris, 1999.

Ruthven, Malise. *A Satanic Affair: Salman Rushdie and the Rage of Islam.* London, 1990.

Weatherby, William J. *Salman Rushdie, Sentenced to Death.* New York, 1990.

JAY WINTER

RUSSELL, BERTRAND (1872–1970),
English mathematician, philosopher, and peace activist.

Bertrand Arthur William Russell, 3rd Earl Russell, won the Nobel Prize for Literature in 1950. Born to an aristocratic family in 1872, he was orphaned at the age of two. Raised by his grandmother, he was educated by private tutors

Bertrand Russell and his wife with George Clark, a fellow member of the Committee of 100, during a break from Russell's trial for disturbing the peace, September 1961. ©HULTON-DEUTSCH COLLECTION/CORBIS

and studied mathematics and philosophy at Trinity College, Cambridge. A brilliant academic performance led to his election as a fellow of his college in 1895.

Russell was thoroughly immersed in European life and thought. In 1894 he served as attaché to the British embassy in Paris and spent considerable time in Germany studying social democracy. In 1900 he attended the Mathematical Congress at the Universal Exhibition in Paris. There he engaged in the study of mathematical logic, arising from the work of the Italian mathematician Giuseppe Peano. This led to his first major publication, entitled *The Principles of Mathematics* (1903), and to his celebrated work, jointly written with Alfred North Whitehead, *Principia Mathematica* (1910–1913). Among his fundamental claims was the view that all of mathematics could be deduced from a relatively small set of logical axioms. A popular version of this argument was published as *An Introduction to Mathematical Philosophy* in 1919. Russell was elected a fellow of the Royal Society in 1908.

After the outbreak of the World War I, Russell's politics did not sit well in the environment of Trinity College, where he was fellow and lecturer. Russell opposed the war, the extension in the powers of the state, and the harsh treatment of conscientious objectors who refused to serve in the army after the imposition of compulsory military service in 1916. He wrote indignantly about the fate of men who refused to fight and clearly offended many of his colleagues whose sons were in uniform or had already been killed in action. In 1916 Trinity College did not renew his lectureship. The following year, the British government denied him a passport to take up a post at Harvard University. Later in 1917 he wrote an article in an antiwar journal stating that U.S. troops coming to Europe were more likely to be used as strike-breakers than as combatants. That statement led to six months in prison. As the son of an earl, he was given relatively comfortable quarters, but he was a prisoner of conscience nonetheless. Both in and out of prison, he proceeded to develop his political outlook and took up guild socialism, a libertarian theory that emphasized the power of trade unions to organize social life at the point of production, so that the state and its coercive powers would not be necessary. Here was a set of ideas that pointed toward a decentralized social order at a moment when war had centralized virtually everything. Russell's suspicion of centralized authority was at the heart of his political thinking, as is evident in his 1918 lectures published as *Roads to Freedom*. Guild socialism faded away, but not the distrust of the state and the military that in Russell's mind lay behind it.

In 1920 he went on a political voyage first to Soviet Russia, to study bolshevism, and then to China. His distrust of the centralized state made the Bolshevik experiment appear dangerous to Russell. On his return, he turned his mind to educational experimentation. He and his second wife, Dora Black, opened a libertarian school in London. In 1927 he published one of his most celebrated and controversial essays, "Why I Am Not a Christian." In 1929 he wrote *Marriage and Morals*, a powerful attack on conventional sexual morality. His work as a philosopher gained increasing international recognition, though in 1940 his appointment to teach at City College of New York was blocked on the grounds that he did not believe in morality. The Barnes Foundation outside Philadelphia offered him an alternative five-year post, but after taking up this post in 1940, he was dismissed by Barnes himself three years later. In 1944 his old college, Trinity, reelected him as a fellow, righting a wrong of the previous war.

In 1945 Russell published his most widely read book, *A History of Western Philosophy,* taking the view that a proper understanding of philosophy could help resolve the disputes that had cost millions of lives in the two world wars. In the 1950s Russell was an outspoken opponent of the development and use of nuclear weapons. In the 1960s Russell was a leading figure in the movement against the Vietnam War, convening an unofficial war crimes tribunal in London. His standing as a political maverick in Britain was unique. The grandson of a prime minister and a peer of the realm, he represented the freethinking element of British intellectual life. His two-volume *Autobiography* (1967–1969) is one of the classics of the English language.

See also **Pacifism; Socialism; Vietnam War.**

BIBLIOGRAPHY

Ayer, A. J. *Bertrand Russell*. New York, 1972.

Griffin, Nicholas, ed. *The Cambridge Companion to Bertrand Russell*. Cambridge, U.K., 2003.

Klemke, E. D., ed. *Essays on Bertrand Russell*. Urbana, Ill., 1971.

Monk, Ray. *Bertrand Russell*. New York, 1999.

Ryan, Alan. *Bertrand Russell: A Political Life*. New York, 1993.

JAY WINTER

RUSSIA. The Russian Federation, or Russia, formally emerged from the ruins of the Soviet Union in December 1991, as a result of the Belaya Vezha agreement between the leaders of Russia, Belarus, and Ukraine. Many Soviet citizens and foreigners, however, viewed the Soviet Union itself as an extended Russia (Soviet Russia was a commonly used synonym). The Russian Federation inherited from the Soviet Union more than 75 percent of its territory and the distinction of being the largest nation in the world, 50 percent of its population, its nuclear weapons and foreign debt, and the long-standing ambivalence about the extent of its belonging to Europe. Russia was recognized by the international community as the USSR's main successor state, inheriting its seats in the United Nations Security Council and other international institutions, including the Conference on (since 1994, Organization for) Security and Cooperation in Europe (OSCE). Additionally, it was invited to join most major international institutions, including the Group of Seven, whose membership had been sought by the Soviet Union. Yet it was predictably frustrated in its hopes of the early 1990s to achieve a deep integration with the North Atlantic Treaty Organization (NATO) and the European Union (EU), which would have obliterated the entire history of Soviet conflict with the West. Instead, Russia found itself repeatedly at odds with NATO over the latter's eastward expansion and attack on Yugoslavia. It has had a more difficult record of relationships with multinational institutions, such as the OSCE, than with individual Western European nations, especially Germany, with whom it has built a robust economic and geostrategic partnership, as well as Italy and France. Russians' sense that the pro-Western ("Atlanticist") policies of their first post-Soviet leadership contributed to the incorporation of most of their former allies, satellites, or dependencies in Eastern Europe into the EU and NATO, while Russia itself was taken advantage of and left out in the cold, is widely shared across Russian society and has a deep impact on Russia's relations with the West.

IMPERIAL LEGACIES, MULTIETHNICITY, AND THE AMBIGUITIES OF IDENTITY

The prevalent post–Cold War view of historical Russia as an empire that dominated its non-Russian subjects against their will tells an important part of a much more complex story. Unlike countries of Western Europe with their well-defined geographic and ethnic boundaries, Russia's neighborhood—the East European plain and the southern steppe—historically consisted of underpopulated and unsecured frontiers shifting together with unformed and fluid national identities. Russia's political culture, with its preeminent concern with security, was shaped by recurrent threats of invasions from the east, the west, and the south. The vulnerability of Russia's agricultural and urban civilization, built against formidable odds on an infertile land and in a hostile climate, left its rulers continuously preoccupied with acquiring stable and defensible borders and securing access to naval trade routes of European commerce. This implied the need to establish and fortify Russia's presence in the Baltic, Black, and Caspian Seas and in the Caucasus Mountains. The resulting empire both oppressed its subjects, like any other, and generated a measure of stability and protection for some of the ethnicities whose alternative option was often to be controlled by a rival power, such as Poland (in the sixteenth and seventeenth centuries), Sweden (early eighteenth century), Turkey or Iran (sixteenth to nineteenth centuries), or Germany or the British Empire (late nineteenth and early twentieth centuries).

The multiethnic composition of the Russian Empire, together with spontaneous as well as government-engineered migration and intermixing of ethnicities, resulted in a long-standing uncertainty about the geographic and ethnic boundaries of Russia proper, and hence about the definition of Russian national identity. The internationally recognized borders of the Russian Federation of the early twenty-first century reflect Soviet-era administrative mapping, which was not planned with future sovereign states in mind and often cut across even clearly recognized ethnic and historical boundaries. Early-twenty-first-century Russia remains multiethnic and multiconfessional, albeit much less so than the Soviet Union or the Russian Empire had been. Ethnic Russians (*russkie,* in the narrow sense of this word) comprise 80 percent of its population. Most of them are nominally adhering to the Russian Orthodox Church, primarily as represented by its Moscow patriarchate. After seven decades of state-imposed atheism, the levels of actual observance or commitment to Orthodoxy remain fairly low, and official clergy are often seen as compromised by their excessive deference to Soviet and post-Soviet secular authorities; minor, autonomous branches of Russian Orthodoxy, including Old Believers and local parishes of the Russian Orthodox Church Abroad, continue to exist alongside the Moscow patriarchate, while the active presence of both historically established Western Christian denominations and churches as well as new charismatic movements and cults is often seen as dangerously subversive proselytizing. Meanwhile, more than twenty million ethnic Russians—between 15 and 20 percent of their total number—remain outside the Russian Federation's borders as a result of the Soviet collapse; their levels of ethnic and religious identification are often higher than among Russians living in the Russian Federation.

Ethnically non-Russian minorities and non-Orthodox confessions represent a much smaller share of the population than in the Soviet Union or the Russian Empire but have continued to play pivotal roles in the debate on Russian identity. Russia remains one of the most multiethnic nations in the world, with 140 nationalities listed in the

2002 population census. It is generally recognized, even among the groups usually defined as nationalist, that a purely ethnic definition of Russianness and ethnonationalism of an Eastern European type would be an undesirable break with the tradition of an inclusive and open national identity, however "imagined" this tradition may seem to outsiders. Hence the status accorded to principal minority groups. Alongside Christianity, Islam (with fifteen to twenty million faithful, according to various estimates), Buddhism, and Judaism (several hundred thousand each) are recognized as "traditional religions" by the 1997 law, although the rights of these and other minorities are not infrequently violated in practice, especially at local levels. Minorities are often included in the definition of *russkie* in the broader sense (as a "super-ethnos," to use a popular Russian term), as indicated, for example, by a recent debate on the specifically Russian (*russkii*) Islam. The term *rossiyane* implies "civic" allegiance to the common Russian statehood; it was widely used in the Yeltsin-era official parlance, but has become unpopular by association and is rarely employed.

FROM RUS TO THE RUSSIAN EMPIRE

Most international scholarship, as well as Russia's own historical tradition, trace the origins of the Russian nation to the state of Rus, an association of Slavic, Scandinavian, and Finnish tribes, with historical capitals in Novgorod (862–882), Kiev (882–1169), and Vladimir (1169–1320s). It is considered the common ancestor of Russians, Belarusians, and Ukrainians. (This view has been disputed, however, by Ukrainian nationalist scholars and their co-thinkers in the West claiming the Kievan Rus to be a Ukrainian state par excellence). The Rus, whose princes adopted Christianity in its Byzantine version in 988 and participated in European power plays and family relationships with French and German royal dynasties, was weakened by internal feuding and lost its independence to the devastating Mongol invasion of 1237 to 1240. This period, known in Russia as the Mongol-Tatar Yoke and involving struggle as well as cooperation and some degree of cultural rapprochement with the occupiers, was later blamed by Europeanized Russians of the nineteenth and twentieth centuries for Russia's loss of its original Europeanness and its cultural, as well as geopolitical, estrangement from the West. Other thinkers,

primarily of the Eurasianist school, saw the Mongol and Tatar influences, with the resulting internal diversity of Russia and its "otherness" vis-à-vis Europe as a source of Russia's unique civilizational characteristics of inclusiveness and breadth, in contrast to European nation-states, and as the basis for its special calling, to serve as a bridge between the East and the West. In another variation on this theme, many educated Russians believed that Russia's resistance had saved the rest of Europe from subjugation by exhausting the nomadic drive of the Mongols and thus fulfilled a historic mission that was duly appreciated by the West. This belief was epitomized in 1918 in Alexander Blok's classical work *The Scythians,* reflecting widespread disillusionment and a sense of betrayal that, some argue, contributed to the failure of Russia's pro-Western democratic revolution of February 1917 and paved the way for the Bolshevik coup.

In a more radical response, democratic and revolutionary thought in nineteenth- and twentieth-century Russia often took the shape of reaction against the perceived foreignness of the post-eighteenth-century ruling class with its military-bureaucratic establishment (e.g., Pavel Pestel, early Slavophiles, Mikhail Bakunin, and the Pan-Slavs). Other radical democrats, including Alexander Herzen and some of the early Marxists, as well as authoritarian revolutionaries such as Vladimir Lenin, held more ambiguous and complex views of Europe, recognizing the need to borrow its technological and cultural achievements in order to catch up with it on the path of modernization, but few among the generally antitsarist educated class, the intelligentsia, fully accepted western Europe as an unquestioned cultural or socioeconomic model (the major exceptions in the early twentieth century included the historian Pavel Milyukov, the founder and leader of Russia's liberal Constitutional Democratic Party, and Georgy Plekhanov, the founding father of Russian Marxism, who oscillated between democratic and authoritarian tendencies). Significantly, one of the ideological discussions of the early twentieth century that later contributed to the demise of Leon Trotsky as a potential successor to Lenin and the leader of the Russian Revolution was over the project of the "United States of Europe"—the ideological blueprint of the future European Union: Trotsky argued that the Bolsheviks should support the idea and that revolutionary Russia itself might become part of united Europe, whereas Lenin and Joseph Stalin dismissed the idea as unrealistic in view of the profound power inequalities and resulting divergences of interests within Europe, and argued that a Bolshevik Russia should play on these divisions rather than pursuing a remote pan-European utopia.

FROM IMPERIAL TO SOVIET RUSSIA

By 1914, after a suppressed democratic revolution of 1905 to 1907 and a program of reforms promoting capitalism in the countryside through the forced dissolution of peasant communes, Russia's economy was on the path of fast yet fragile growth. It was highly dependent on Western investment, loans, and technologies, and riven by social and cultural tensions—between the cities and the countryside, the rich and the poor, and the ethnically Russian and German elites and oppressed national minorities, such as Poles and Jews. Its high culture and the arts, combining deep Europeanization with commitment to their peasant roots, reached a historical peak of creativity known as the "Silver Age" and were among the driving forces of European modernism. Yet in politics, Russia's technological dependency on German industries and financial dependency primarily on French money led to its geopolitical oscillation between the German and the Franco-British military blocs. It joined the latter, the Entente Cordiale, but was the odd man out in this alliance because of Tsar Nicholas II's erratic diplomacy and autocratic policies at home. It was forced into World War I by Kaiser William II's resolve to push Russia out of the Balkans and its own loss of international prestige, which was eroding the domestic authority of tsarism. The allies tried to boost Russia's morale by a secret treaty providing for the acquisition of the Straits—a coveted slice in the future partition of Turkey. But the failure of political and military leadership, attempts at separate negotiations with Germany, and the resulting demoralization of the army and society at large led both Russia's liberal elite and Western allies to conclude that Nicholas II and his tiny ultraconservative entourage had become the main obstacle to the war effort.

The tsar was deposed with ease after several days of popular revolt in Petrograd. The new Provisional Government was a coalition led by pro-Western liberals committed to pursuing victory under the slogan of "revolutionary defense." But the revolution quickly went out of control, with the rise of the Petrograd Soviet increasingly challenging the Provisional Government, which itself became dominated by socialist parties and was frequently reshuffled from the inside. The failure of a renewed war effort and military retreat, the grassroots pressure for a radical agrarian reform blocked by the liberals in the Provisional Government, and, finally, the agitation of Lenin and his supporters for separate peace with Germany and their confrontation with the Provisional Government in July 1917 debilitated the government, discredited the principle of democratic coalition that lay behind it, and accelerated the search for a new, iron-willed leadership in all parts of the spectrum.

In November 1917 this role was unilaterally assumed by Lenin and his supporters in the Central Committee of the Bolshevik Party, who seized power in Petrograd with the help of military deserters and marines, and then tried to legitimize their one-party rule as revolution by the soviets. In the course of their struggle with other socialist parties and unions opposed to this scenario, the Bolsheviks managed to split their leading rival, the Socialist Revolutionary (SR) Party, and persuade the splinter Left SR Party to join them in a coalition, accepting for the time being its platform of the socialization (rather than nationalization) of the land. Although the Bolsheviks came to power promising to speed up the convocation of the democratically elected Constituent Assembly, after they lost this election to the SR majority, Lenin changed his mind and eventually dissolved the assembly by force. The assembly was in session for only one day, proclaiming the Russian Democratic Federal Republic, which never materialized. After its dispersal, the Congress of Soviets dominated by the Bolsheviks proclaimed the Russian Soviet Federal Socialist Republic, with a constitution disenfranchising the "exploitative classes," including, in practice, a large fraction of the peasant population of the country.

Meanwhile, as Germany gained decisive advantage on the battlefield, and the Russian army virtually disintegrated, Lenin secured support or acquiescence of his party, against the will of most of its other leaders and many in the rank and file, to an ignominious separate peace with Germany, the Treaty of Brest-Litovsk (March 1918), leading to huge territorial losses and vast German control

A steel worker sells cabbages from his motorcycle to earn extra money during a period of runaway inflation, Magnitogorsk, Russia, 1993. ©SHEPARD SHERBELL/CORBIS SABA

over the Russian economy. The Left SRs quit the government in disagreement and soon were provoked by Lenin's security forces into a rebellion in which they were crushed and eliminated from the stage. The one-party rule was effectively established and then cemented over the two years of resistance both to the White Guard, fighting in effect for the restoration of the monarchy, and to the military intervention of Western powers along Russia's coastal perimeter. While the bulk of the population in the overwhelmingly peasant Russia was not supportive of the Bolshevik policies, Russians often acquiesced to them as to the lesser evil. By 1922, all political parties, left and right, except for the Communists, had been eliminated by repression and expulsions from the country.

RUSSIA AND THE SOVIET UNION: AMBIGUOUS COEXISTENCE AND THE PARTING OF WAYS

In 1922, with the signing of the Union Treaty, the Russian Soviet Federal Socialist Republic (RSFSR)

formally became one of the four founding states of the Soviet Union, together with Ukraine, Byelorussia, and the Transcaucasian Federation. Over the next seventy years, the Soviet Union expanded to fifteen republics, some of them, such as the Baltic states and Moldova, annexed or taken over from previously sovereign entities, and others, such as Kazakhstan, carved out of the RSFSR's territory. Soviet official ideology oscillated between internationalist emphasis on "the friendship of the peoples" and "Soviet patriotism" (the prevalent rhetoric of the more liberal periods, such as the 1920s and 1960s) and calculated appeals to Russian national pride at the threatening junctures of World War II and the Cold War. There is no consensus on Russia's actual role in the Soviet Union: while nationalists in countries such as the Baltic states and Georgia see Russia as the prime oppressor under the guise of the Soviet Union, many Russian nationalists since the 1980s have argued that Russia was used by the communist regime as a donor for other republics that benefited from its economic might, natural resources, and human capital in the course of their modernization. Also, unlike other republics, the RSFSR before 1990 did not possess a fully developed administrative apparatus distinct from the institutions of the government of the Soviet Union, which became another source of nationalists' complaints. The unaccountable Soviet leadership, in spite of its large share of ethnic Russians, was widely seen as denationalized and having lost touch with the true interests of Russians as a people. Russian dissidents from the 1960s to the 1980s consistently took the side of national minorities and their organizations in the republics of the Soviet Union, providing international visibility to Ukrainian, Baltic, Georgian, and other human rights and opposition advocates.

Accordingly, Russian politicians, brought onto the public stage by Mikhail Gorbachev's democratization and glasnost, did not see Russia as having a major stake in the Soviet Union's common future and by and large did not see any potential dangers to Russia in the Soviet Union's demise until the latter became irreversible. Thus, most Russian democrats and, indeed, some nationalists encouraged the "parade of sovereignties" across the Soviet Union and even took an early lead in the process. Russia's famous nationalist writer Valentin Rasputin envisioned Russia's potential secession from the Soviet Union well before other republics began their drive for independence. On 12 June 1990 the RSFSR's Congress of People's Deputies, chaired by Boris Yeltsin, proclaimed Russia's sovereignty, becoming the first Soviet republic after the Baltic states to do so; the Russian parliament opposed the hardliners' attempts to suppress secessionist movements elsewhere, offering recognition to the Baltic states without any conditions with regard to Russia's strategic interests or the Russian population remaining in the area. In September 1990 Nobel Prize–winner Alexander Solzhenitsyn called for Russia's total disengagement from eleven republics, in the hope of potentially salvaging the union with Ukraine, Belarus, and Kazakhstan, but Russian democrats dismissed his proposal as overly conservative. The botched coup attempt of August 1991 under the slogan of preserving the Soviet Union (nowadays widely seen as an episode in the power struggle within the Soviet establishment) did not elicit any support in Russia: to the contrary, whatever public action in Russia did occur was directed against the coup and in support of Russia's Supreme Soviet, or the "White House" (so nicknamed because of the color of its

headquarters). After the coup, the Russian parliament further contributed to the Soviet Union's demise by supporting Yeltsin in his takeover of the Soviet Union's assets and institutions on Russian territory and approving the program of unilateral price decontrol that implied the abandoning of attempts to preserve a Soviet Union–wide economic community. The parliament also pursued the principled policy of noninterference in the centrifugal developments within Russia itself, and blocked the executive's attempt to suppress the revolution in its constituent republic of Chechnya in November 1991.

RUSSIA'S POST-SOVIET EXPERIENCE

The central role in the Soviet Union's demise and Russia's disengagement from other republics belonged to Yeltsin and his narrow circle of associates, whose overarching goal was to get rid of Gorbachev's supremacy. Yeltsin managed both to ride the wave of a vague protest movement and to secure support of key groups in the Soviet establishment displeased by Gorbachev and threatened by grassroots democratization. He had no ideological commitments and at various points used radical Russian nationalists, liberal intellectuals, and anti-Russian nationalists in the republics to strengthen his position against Gorbachev.

His biggest success, however, came from his opportunistic alliance with Russia's mass-based democratic organization, the Democratic Russia movement (DemRossiya), which mobilized street support for his policies at all the critical points, most importantly in August 1991. The movement had approximately three hundred thousand active supporters and won solid majorities in the councils of major industrial cities. Its social base consisted of the educated and westernized "middle class" largely unprepared for the transformative role in society that it could potentially assume: it was characterized by utopian naiveté, lack of a systemic vision of the problems of the country and the world, excessive idealizing of the West caused by decades of isolation behind the Iron Curtain, poor understanding of contradictions among social strata and conflicting geopolitical interests, and the inadequacy of its political leadership. Economically, it was entirely dependent on guaranteed government employment and unprepared for an abrupt abrogation of these guarantees and the collapse of real incomes caused by price liberalization and hyperinflation in 1992. This so-called shock therapy (even though this label is disputed by neoliberal economists) caused a fundamental and permanent change to the structure of Soviet society by dealing a blow to this "middle class" from which it never recovered as a stratum. Accordingly, DemRossiya quickly lost most of its volunteer activists to the struggle for economic survival, and the younger crop of actual and potential supporters to "brain drain" abroad, while its leadership split over the assessment of reforms. Since DemRossiya's split in 1992, the democratic movement in Russia never recouped its losses, and its previous mistakes left a bitter disenchantment with the very ideas of democracy and collective action. Yabloko, the only democratic party that managed to build some grassroots support and maintain a presence in the parliament from 1993 to 2003—only because of its relatively consistent critique of Yeltsin's policies and of the past democratic experience—still never reached DemRossiya's size and stature. And even it was eventually eliminated from the Duma by a combination of voter apathy and insecurity, concentration of financial and media resources in the hands of the Kremlin, and growing popular mistrust of "Western-inspired" solutions.

These internal developments, coupled with Russia's frustrated attempts at a high-speed integration with major European and Euro-Atlantic institutions, eventually led Russia's authoritarian and inward-looking legacies to reassert themselves. This trend was, however, denied by many observers as long as the policies of Russia's successive leaders offered domestic and foreign players exceptional opportunities for economic or geostrategic gain. Yeltsin used force to disband the democratically elected parliament that had brought him to power, changed the constitution of the country in a referendum whose legitimacy and outcome were questioned by many, and, in spite of his poor health, ruled Russia at his whim, hiring and firing several prime ministers and eventually passing the baton to his chosen successor who had never run for a public office before being elected president. The new constitution established a super-presidential system viewed at the time as instrumentally useful to liberal reformers but increasingly deplored by them ever since. Two military invasions in the rebellious constituent republic of Chechnya, in 1994 and 1999, cost thousands of Chechen and Russian lives and left

deep scars on the tissue of both societies. Economic reforms pursued in the early 1990s with varying degrees of intensity failed in their declared purpose of creating a private economy based on medium and small businesses, as the domestic market for industrial production remained limited by mass poverty, while Soviet-era or potential foreign markets were lost to geopolitical retrenchment. In the 1990s Russia's manufacturing and high-technology industries largely collapsed, except for the weapon production; its gross domestic product (GDP) shrank twofold; corruption flourished, while budgetary funding and government resources were channeled away from the public sector and the sphere of production into private hands and financial activities. The social costs of these policies for Russia's population were as high as the cost of a major war, if not higher: from 1992 to 2003, the number of Russians shrank by over 4 million people to 143 million total (in spite of the influx of 5.5 million labor migrants from other post-Soviet states), and male longevity declined from sixty-five to about fifty-eight years, because of the collapse of affordable health care, increasing cardiovascular diseases caused by stress, and rising violence.

By 1998, the government, led by "young reformers," gambled on attracting foreign capital by offering up to 100 percent yearly returns on government promissory notes (GKOs), which led to financial bankruptcy, debt default, and the devaluation of the ruble. The latter, coupled with rising commodity prices, helped Russia to several years of economic growth, at approximately 6 percent of GDP, enabling it to reestablish its solvency and accumulate large foreign reserves, which have been used to form the Stabilization Fund. The downside of this process was the exacerbation of Russia's reliance on commodity export at the expense of all other economic activities. Although President Vladimir Putin and Russia's elite have been boastful of the nation's role as a major energy power, failed attempts to translate this into geopolitical gains as, for example, in relations with Ukraine and Western powers, showed its limited utility in the absence of other resources. And given the concentration of economic assets in the hands of the government and corporate bureaucracies tied to the commodity sector, poverty and inequality have stayed high, and Russia's overall health and demographic outlook is increasingly bleak: according to one of the estimates done by the United Nations Population Division, if the current trend is not reversed, Russia may be expected to lose twenty-one million people between 2000 and 2025.

The structural constraints on the development of a truly autonomous capitalist class and the reassertion of authoritarian rule eventually led to the elimination of the few independent business empires built in the 1990s by the so-called oligarchs, at a relatively low political cost to the Kremlin. Three leading business tycoons who had played major political roles in the 1990s and then supported, to various extents, democratic opposition to Putin, have been stripped of their assets and either forced out of the country or, in the exceptional case of Mikhail Khodorkovsky, Russia's richest man and owner of the YUKOS oil empire, sentenced to labor camp.

Russia's economic recovery achieved since the late 1990s, however partial and one-sided, and the relative stabilization of its geopolitical standing, may eventually pave the way for the ascendancy of a more democratically minded group of leaders within the ruling stratum. An alternative scenario—continuing humiliation and retreat in the post-Soviet space, with or without an economic downturn—is likely to result in more authoritarianism, further alienation of Russia's educated youth from the West, increasing support for homegrown and foreign-born Islamic radicals in the impoverished North Caucasus, and prolonged turmoil in this region, with unpredictable consequences for the international community.

See also **Russian Civil War; Russian Revolutions of 1917; Soviet Union.**

BIBLIOGRAPHY

Arbatov, Alexei G., K. Kaiser, and R. Legvold, eds. *Russia and the West: The 21st Century Security Environment.* Armonk, N.Y., 1999.

Cohen, Stephen F. "Was the Soviet Union Reformable?" *Slavic Review* 63, no. 3 (2004): 459–488.

Hough, Jerry F. *Democratization and Revolution in the USSR, 1985–1991.* Washington, D.C., 1997.

Kingston-Mann, Esther. *In Search of the True West: Culture, Economics, and Problems of Russian Development.* Princeton, N.J., 1999.

Kotz, David M., and Fred Weir. *Revolution from Above: The Demise of the Soviet System.* London, 1997.

Lieven, Anatol. *Chechnya: Tombstone of Russian Power.* New Haven, Conn., 1998.

Poe, Marshall T. *The Russian Moment in World History.* Princeton, N.J., 2003.

Reddaway, Peter, and Dmitri Glinski. *The Tragedy of Russia's Reforms: Market Bolshevism against Democracy.* Washington, D.C., 2001.

Riasanovsky, Nicholas V., and Mark D. Steinberg. *A History of Russia.* 7th ed. New York, 2005.

Rieber, Alfred. "Struggle for the Borderlands." In *The Legacy of History in Russia and Post-Soviet States,* edited by S. Frederick Starr, 61–90. Armonk, N.Y., 1994.

D. GLINSKI

RUSSIAN CIVIL WAR. After the pressures of World War I brought about the collapse of imperial Russia's tsarist regime in March 1917, a weak Provisional Government proved unable to resolve the profound social and political divisions in Russian society. In November 1917 Vladimir Lenin's Bolshevik party capitalized on growing worker and soldier discontent and overthrew the Provisional Government. The Russian civil war was a bitter and devastating conflict to determine Russia's future after the Bolshevik takeover. In simplest terms, the civil war from 1918 to 1920 pitted the Reds (Lenin's communist Bolshevik party) against the Whites (those opposed to the Bolsheviks, particularly tsarist military officers). In reality, the war was a complex, many-sided struggle among political, social, and ethnic movements with roots extending before World War I and with fighting continuing into the early 1920s.

ORIGINS OF THE WAR

The tensions producing the Russian civil war date to the pre–World War I Russian Empire. Russian society was characterized not only by a deep divide between the tsar's regime and the population, but also by suspicion and misunderstanding between elite, educated society on one side, and workers and peasants on the other. After the fall of Tsar Nicholas II, the Provisional Government could not heal Russian society's deep fissures. Moderate and liberal parties, especially the Constitutional

Democrats (Kadets) initially dominating the new Provisional Government, were committed to democratic reform but not the socialist reorganization of society. Russian workers, peasants, and soldiers, on the other hand, grew increasingly radical over the course of 1917, and their support for more radical parties, particularly the Bolsheviks and the peasant-backed Socialist Revolutionaries (the SRs), grew accordingly.

Lenin's seizure of power in November 1917 only added to the tensions in Russia, creating conflict among Russia's socialist parties over whether the Bolsheviks would rule alone or, as many leftists hoped, as part of a multiparty left-wing coalition. In the immediate wake of the Bolshevik Revolution, efforts to broker a settlement between Lenin and other socialist parties, particularly by the influential Railway Workers' Union, went nowhere. Lenin's adamant refusal to share power, except for token collaboration with the left wing of the SR party (the Left SRs) made a political settlement impossible to achieve. At the same time, armed clashes began between the Bolsheviks and their right-wing opponents: the Bolshevik seizure of power in Moscow required several days of street fighting, and holding onto authority in Petrograd required a force of Red Guards, improvised worker militias, to hold off a desultory attempt to seize the city by Cossack troops under the command of General Peter Krasnov.

Impending elections to the Constituent Assembly, a constitutional convention to craft a new political order for Russia, prevented immediate civil war. The Bolsheviks' rivals, particularly the SRs, expected that the elections would prove their popular support. The SRs received a clear plurality of the vote, comfortably more than the Bolsheviks, and with allied parties would hold a clear majority in the Constituent Assembly over the Bolsheviks and their Left SR allies. For just that reason, Lenin permitted the assembly to meet only a single time on 5 January 1918 before forcibly shutting it down and eliminating the possibility of reconciliation with other socialists.

While the anti-Bolshevik socialist parties pinned their hopes on the Constituent Assembly, conservatives and tsarist army officers organized armed resistance. The old tsarist army disintegrated, and many officers and military cadets fled south to Cossack territory on the Don River to organize a counterrevolutionary movement, believing the Cossacks to be natural supporters of Russia's old order. Hastily organized Bolshevik forces under Vladimir Antonov-Ovseenko invaded the Don at the end of November 1917, seizing the region's major cities and driving a nascent anti-Bolshevik force of military officers and cadets, the Volunteer Army, south through the frozen steppe.

By February 1918, Lenin's political situation appeared to be secure. The Constituent Assembly had been shut down without incident, and Bolshevik troops were clearing the Don of counterrevolutionaries. Unfortunately for Lenin, Russia's unfinished war against Germany flared again in February 1918. Immediately after seizing power, Lenin had concluded a cease-fire with Germany. Negotiations for a final peace had gone nowhere, however, as German demands, particularly for an independent Ukraine under German domination, had proven unacceptable. After Leon Trotsky, veteran revolutionary and Lenin's negotiator, declared "no war, no peace" in response to a German ultimatum, the Germans decided to take by force what the Bolsheviks would not give them. As the German army rapidly seized huge stretches of Russian territory, Lenin had no forces capable of offering more than token resistance and was compelled to accept the draconian terms of the Treaty of Brest-Litovsk, signed 3 March 1918, ceding enormous territories in the Baltics, Byelorussia, and Ukraine. In addition to providing shelter for national separatist movements in the Baltics and Ukraine, this surrender generated enormous opposition from a substantial number within the Bolshevik party, and more from the Bolsheviks' Left SR allies, who withdrew from coalition with the Bolsheviks. In an attempt to restart the war with Germany, Left SRs assassinated the German ambassador in early July, and attempted to seize control of the city of Moscow. Bolshevik forces crushed this revolt, and the Menshevik and SR parties were expelled from Soviet organizations. After an assassination attempt on Lenin at the end of August 1918, the Bolsheviks unleashed a Red terror against all varieties of opposition, executing thousands of political enemies.

White Russian soldiers execute Bolshevik captives, January 1920. ©BETTMANN/CORBIS

In May and June 1918, Bolshevik power was further shaken by an ill-advised effort to disarm the Czech Legion. The Czech Legion was a military unit composed of Czech and Slovak prisoners of war, released in order to fight against the Central Powers. When Russia left the war, the Czechs began a long journey across Siberia to the Pacific to reach Western Europe and continue the fight. While the legion stretched along the Trans-Siberian Railroad, Trotsky's effort to disarm them instead provoked the Czechs to seize control of the railway, removing much of Russia east of the Volga River from Bolshevik control in a few weeks, and giving a vital boost to anti-Bolshevik movements.

Though political violence had been common since the fall of the tsar, anti-Bolshevik forces became far more organized and coherent in the late spring and summer of 1918, while the Bolsheviks turned decisively away from improvised

Red Guard forces, and began the construction of a new and strictly organized Red Army under Trotsky's skilled and charismatic leadership. In order to find experienced commanders for his new Red Army, Trotsky forcibly conscripted tens of thousands of tsarist officers, the military specialists, to command Bolshevik forces over the objections of many in his own party.

By the summer of 1918, the two sides in the civil war were increasingly clear and defined. The Red side essentially consisted of the Bolshevik party and those under Bolshevik rule. The Bolsheviks did govern in concert with the Left SRs until the summer of 1918, and even later than that worked efficiently with small revolutionary parties and individual sympathizers at the local level. Nonetheless, the Bolsheviks' lack of real partners gave them unity and hierarchy under Lenin's dominant but never unquestioned leadership. Their movement enjoyed a coherence that the Whites never had.

The Whites, by contrast, had little to tie them together besides opposition to bolshevism. Dispersed around the edges of the empire, several separate White governments operated with little coordination between. Their peripheral position provoked tensions with non-Russian ethnic groups, who found their national aspirations at odds with the Whites' commitment to a restored Russia. The SRs, claiming to represent Russia's peasantry and seeking a revolutionary transformation of the countryside, had little in common with the former tsarist officers who came to dominate the White movement.

The two sides were in many ways alike. In practical terms, they were attempting to build states and fight a war using a peasant population at best ambivalent toward their aims. Both sides were able to draw upon a militarized population, trained for violence by forty years of universal conscription and the experience of total war. The alienation of Russia's peasantry from both causes forced the Reds and Whites alike to conscript unwilling peasants into their armies, and produced massive levels of desertion. Both presided over economic disintegration, and turned to forcible requisition of grain from the peasantry to feed their cities and soldiers. Unwilling soldiers and hostile peasants meant that both employed mass violence and repression; White terror was retaliatory or the result of indiscipline, whereas Red terror was systematic and deliberate. Both sides emerged from the political culture of the Russian Empire and especially World War I: their instincts were authoritarian, centralizing, and committed to employing the state to control and transform Russian society and the Russian economy. In that sense, the Whites were not particularly conservative. Even leaving aside the large number of explicitly revolutionary parties and individuals in their heterogeneous movement, there was little sentiment among them for full restoration of the old regime, particularly the Romanov dynasty.

Amid growing chaos, increasing numbers of foreign troops intervened in Russia to back the Whites in their struggle against the Reds and in hopes of reopening a Russian front against the Germans and their immense occupied territory. Small contingents of Allied troops began landing in Russian ports in spring 1918 to secure war matériel accumulated from Allied deliveries over the course of the war. By late 1918, this had become a substantial Allied presence aimed at assisting the overthrow of the Bolsheviks, with British and American forces occupying Russia's northern ports, and American and Japanese in the Russian Far East.

Behind the Czech shield, and with increasing Allied aid, a host of governments sprang up in the Urals, Siberia, and Central Asia in 1918, united by nothing but opposition to the Bolsheviks. Several of the most significant met in Ufa in September 1918 to form a united Directory, with a capital at Omsk. Internecine tensions between revolutionary and conservative forces continued unabated, and in November 1918 a coup overthrew the Directory and installed Admiral Alexander Kolchak as dictator of a Siberian regime plagued throughout its brief existence by corruption, political intrigue, and incompetence.

THE CLIMAX OF THE CIVIL WAR

Through the fall of 1918, Red forces pushed east toward the Ural Mountains to regain territory lost to the Czech Legion, but their offensive stalled in October, and the front stabilized west of the Urals. By spring 1919, Kolchak had prepared an offensive, one that he vaguely hoped would lead to Bolshevik collapse or enable him to link up with other centers of White resistance, an idea utterly incompatible with the enormous distances separating the White centers of power. The thinly spread Bolshevik forces were, however, initially incapable of stopping Kolchak, and his troops approached the Volga River by the end of April. Kolchak's successes spurred further improvements in the discipline and training of the Red Army, despite the resentment that military order produced in lifelong revolutionaries. As Kolchak pushed west, however, his supply lines grew increasingly tenuous, his forces more stretched, and the inadequacy of his thinly populated base in Siberia more apparent. At the end of April 1919, a Red counteroffensive broke Kolchak's lines and sent his forces into rapid retreat toward the Urals. The end of any immediate danger from Kolchak triggered a dispute within the Bolshevik high command over whether Red forces should continue pursuing Kolchak or be diverted to the south to defend against General Anton Denikin's push north toward Moscow. The Red Army's commander-in-chief, Ioakim Vatsetis, supported by Trotsky, controversially argued for the turn south until he was finally replaced by Sergei Kamenev in June.

Kolchak's headlong flight and Bolshevik pursuit continued uninterrupted through the Urals into Siberia. With Kolchak's regime collapsing, Czech soldiers arrested him in Irkutsk in January 1920. He was executed by local Bolsheviks the next month. The Reds' triumphant march did not extend all the way to the Pacific. Japanese and American troops still occupied much of the Russian Far East. To prevent further conflict, the Bolsheviks engineered the creation in April 1920 of the Far Eastern Republic, a nominally independent buffer state. With final Japanese withdrawal from Siberia, the Far Eastern Republic was reabsorbed into Soviet Russia in 1922.

After the defeat of Kolchak's push from the east in spring 1919, the Bolsheviks faced their greatest White threat with an offensive from the south by the Volunteer Army, under the command of Denikin and incorporating the remnants of the Don Cossacks. In May 1919 Denikin began a drive north toward Moscow. Devoid of the human or material resources needed to sustain an offensive over that distance, Denikin's push was an enormous gamble. The skill and dedication of his officer-heavy army, however, let his troops get within 300 kilometers (190 miles) of Moscow by October 1919. Simultaneous with Denikin's final push to Moscow, a much smaller White force under Nikolai Yudenich attacked east from the Baltic states toward Petrograd.

The Bolsheviks benefited from their central location and unified command, enabling them to transfer troops to threatened sectors through the rail network centered on Moscow, and using Bolshevik soldiers as elite troops to stiffen half-hearted peasant conscripts. Denikin and Yudenich both stalled short of victory, and were forced into increasingly desperate retreat. Denikin's movement collapsed as the Allies who had been bankrolling it saw the Whites as a lost cause. Denikin was removed as head of the White movement in the south and replaced by Baron Peter Wrangel, who made a last stand in the Crimea. After a short respite provided by the Russo-Polish War in summer 1920, Wrangel's Crimean stronghold was finally overrun in November 1920.

Though Wrangel's defeat meant the end of organized White resistance, the Bolsheviks still faced a growing but fragmented peasant insurgency, provoked by conscription and particularly by ruthless seizures of peasant grain to feed Bolshevik cities and soldiers, which raged through 1921. This burgeoning Red-Green civil war was as brutal as the Red-White war; the Bolsheviks used poison gas on several occasions to clear forests of peasant insurgents. Only the advent of the peasant-friendly New Economic Policy in spring 1921, combined with massive military force, brought the large but uncoordinated peasant uprisings under control.

CIVIL WAR IN THE BORDERLANDS

The civil war in peripheral regions of the Russian Empire added ethnic and national issues to the social and political disputes raging within Russia proper. In Ukraine, for example, Ukrainian nationalists had established their own autonomous government, the Central Rada, in March 1917. This coexisted uneasily with the Provisional Government, as essential questions of central authority and regional autonomy remained unanswered, while social and economic disintegration accelerated. Two weeks after the Bolshevik Revolution, the Central Rada proclaimed a new Ukrainian National Republic—socialist, ostensibly multiethnic, and loosely federated with Russia. The Bolsheviks denounced this as completely unacceptable, and Bolsheviks in Ukraine formed a rival government based in Kharkov. Backed by a hastily assembled Red Army, Ukrainian Bolsheviks seized Kiev in February 1918, forcing the Central Rada to flee west. The Central Rada was saved by German patronage; the Treaty of Brest-Litovsk provided German protection to the Ukrainian National Republic and a temporary respite from Bolshevik pressure. The Central Rada regained Kiev with German aid, but the German masters proved impatient. In April 1918, the Germans overthrew the Central Rada and replaced it with a more tractable hetmanate under the nominal control of the former tsarist general Pavlo Skoropadsky.

Skoropadsky's acquiescence to German seizures of Ukrainian grain bred growing resistance. As a result of Germany's defeat in November 1918 and the withdrawal of German troops, a new government, the Directory, seized power from Skoropadsky in December 1918 and reestablished the Ukrainian National Republic. The Directory remained in Kiev only briefly, as an invasion from Russian territory led by Ukrainian Bolsheviks seized the city again in February 1919. In this political chaos, as the Ukrainian countryside descended into total anarchy, the Bolsheviks managed to hang on to power in the cities until August 1919, when Denikin's offensive from the south expelled them again. After Denikin's defeat, Bolshevik forces pushed south into Ukraine in late 1919 and 1920, ending civil war with the systematic imposition of Bolshevik control.

Imperial Russia's Baltic provinces followed a different pattern, but one still marked by civil conflict. Lithuanians under German occupation formed a National Council. In Latvia, partly occupied, the population grew increasingly polarized between nationalists and a growing number of Bolshevik sympathizers. In Estonia, the largely non-Estonian population of the cities grew increasingly radical over the course of 1917, sympathizing with the Bolsheviks. After Lenin's takeover, Baltic Bolsheviks proved too weak to consolidate control in the short months before German forces expelled them at the beginning of 1918. Nationalist assemblies in all three Baltic states declared independence, symbolic gestures at best given the reality of German domination.

As in Ukraine, Germany's defeat fundamentally altered the political balance. With German withdrawal, the Estonian and Latvian provisional governments scrambled to assemble armed forces to hold back an immediate Bolshevik invasion. Financial and material support from Britain and Finland to Estonia, and German military intervention in Latvia, enabled the expulsion of Bolshevik forces by spring 1919. In Lithuania, local forces did the same by late summer. All three established independent national republics.

In Central Asia, the pattern was quite different. Russian-dominated cities were surrounded by a nomadic and agrarian Muslim hinterland. The urban, industrial Russian population moved to support the Bolshevik takeover and established a Turkestan Soviet Republic centered in Tashkent. Contact with the Bolshevik heartland was, however, cut off for two years by the Orenburg

Cossacks north of the Caspian Sea. The Turkestan republic waged a desperate struggle for survival in isolation against inchoate Muslim opposition, as well as local Whites and Cossacks. In autumn 1919 Kolchak's defeat opened up a connection to Russia proper, and Red troops poured in to eradicate the local Cossack population and subordinate the Muslims to Soviet control.

The legacy of the civil war was enormous. Loss of life from combat, repression, starvation, and disease totaled perhaps seven to eight million, far more than Russia lost during World War I. Russian cities emptied, as recent immigrants from the countryside returned to their villages in search of food, and men were conscripted into the warring armies. Much of Russia's landowning and professional class simply fled the country to escape the Bolsheviks' new order. The Bolsheviks created a new government at the same time they fought a war, creating a centralized and authoritarian structure far removed from socialism's democratic ideals. Continuing Bolshevik mistrust of the peasantry and of the outside world marked the 1920s and 1930s, and aided Joseph Stalin's rise to power.

See also **Russian Revolutions of 1917; Trotsky, Leon.**

BIBLIOGRAPHY

Lincoln, W. Bruce. *Red Victory: A History of the Russian Civil War*. New York, 1989.

Mawdsley, Evan. *The Russian Civil War*. Boston, 1987.

Swain, Geoffrey. *The Origins of the Russian Civil War*. London, 1996.

DAVID R. STONE

RUSSIAN REVOLUTIONS OF 1917.

By 1917, Russia was ripe for revolution and change was in the air. Industrialization had created a growing industrial workforce that labored for low pay in often-terrible conditions and mostly lived in urban slums. The new middle class and "educated society" wanted greater legal rights and participation in affairs of state. The peasantry still hungered for that portion of the land they had not received in the emancipation from serfdom. Signs of restiveness could be detected among the half of the population who were not ethnic Russians. The Revolution of 1905 and the reforms that followed had failed to resolve the serious problems confronting the country. Revolutionary movements had waxed and waned since the 1860s, and new and better organized ones had emerged in the first two decades of the twentieth century. Russia's quasi-autocratic political system, and especially Nicholas II's clinging to the outdated notion of himself as god-given autocrat ruling over loyal subjects, was more and more an anachronism. To make matters worse, Nicholas was a far from capable ruler. The disasters of World War I, with its huge losses of men and dislocation of the economy, magnified all of Russia's problems. Whether revolution, especially one such as what followed, was inevitable remains a debatable issue, but clearly the conditions were present by the opening of 1917: incompetent government, a discredited and obstinate monarch, alienation of educated society, deteriorating economic conditions, a revival of social-economic tensions and industrial strikes, an extreme war-weariness, resentful soldiers, and a revival of activity by revolutionary parties. The sense that something had to break soon was widespread.

THE FEBRUARY REVOLUTION AND THE NEW POLITICAL SYSTEM

Among the many sources of discontent in Russian society as 1917 opened, the first stage of the Russian Revolution, the February Revolution, developed out of a wave of industrial strikes in Petrograd in January and February. (Petrograd, formerly St. Petersburg, was the capital at the time.) These turned toward actual revolution when, on 23 February, "Women's Day," female workers at a few factories, angered by food shortages on top of their already difficult economic situation and general discontent, marched out from their factories demanding "bread." They called on men at nearby factories to join them. The next two days more and more factories joined the demonstrations, until it included most of the industrial workforce in the capital. Students and broad sections of the urban lower and middle classes joined the antigovernment demonstrations on the twenty-fifth. Soldiers called out to help break up demonstrations acted with reluctance. On 26 February the government ordered troops to fire into the crowds. Dismayed by the shooting on the twenty-sixth, one detachment, when ordered to form up again on the morning of 27 February, revolted. This quickly spread to other regiments.

By midday the government lost control of the means of armed coercion and quickly collapsed.

To this point the revolution had been mainly a popular revolt, with little leadership beyond what came from factory-level activists and isolated individuals who emerged as organizers of factory demonstrations or leaders in attacks on police stations and other symbols of authority. The revolutionary parties, whose main leaders were in exile, had played little leadership role during the February demonstrations. Now, however, significant political leadership was necessary to consolidate the revolution that had taken place in the streets. Two groups stepped forward late on the 27 February to play this role. One was a group of mostly liberal and moderate conservative political leaders in the State Duma (a legislative assembly elected on a limited franchise based mainly on wealth). They were concerned about the uprising's implications for the war effort, but also realized that this might offer the opportunity to force Nicholas to reform the political system. During the evening of the twenty-seventh they proclaimed the formation of a "Temporary Committee of the State Duma," which would assume governmental responsibility in Petrograd. They undertook to secure the revolution as an opportunity to limit Nicholas's authority while containing the revolution's radicalism. At the same time, a multiparty group of socialist intellectuals met at the Duma building and led workers and soldiers in the formation of the Petrograd Soviet of Workers' and Soldiers' Deputies. This was a more avowedly revolutionary body, committed to turning the street revolt into a sweeping social and economic as well as political revolution.

The Duma Committee and the Petrograd Soviet leaders immediately, if warily, began to cooperate to consolidate the February Revolution and form a new government. On 1 March came news of support for the revolution in Moscow and other cities and increased demand for Nicholas's abdication. On 2 March the Duma and Soviet negotiators announced formation of a "Provisional Government" that would govern Russia until a new governmental system could be created by a Constituent Assembly, which was to be elected by universal franchise. The same day Nicholas II gave way to the reality of events and to the pressures from his army commanders, and abdicated.

1917г.
Дни революціи.
Автомобиль-Сани быв. царя Николая II.

Soldiers gather around the automobile owned by the former tsar, following his abdication, Petrograd, March 1917.
The expensive automobile clearly serves as a symbol of the perceived excesses of the imperial family. ©CORBIS

The new government was drawn primarily from the liberal political leadership of the country. Its head, as minister-president, was Prince Georgy Lvov, a well-known liberal. Politically it was dominated by the Constitutional Democratic Party (the Kadets), the main liberal party. An offer to the Petrograd Soviet to have well-known socialist Duma members join was turned down, but one, Alexander Kerensky, the popular hero of the February Revolution, joined anyway. He soon became the government's most prominent member. The Petrograd Soviet leaders promised to support the new government insofar as it pursued policies of which they approved. Although the Duma soon faded as an important political institution, the existence of the Petrograd Soviet alongside the Provisional Government robbed the latter of much of its actual authority, giving rise to what quickly was dubbed "dual power" (*dvoevlastie*). In this the government had the generally recognized official authority and responsibility but not the effective power, while the Soviet had the actual power and popular authority but not responsibility for governing. This was because the Soviet commanded the

primary loyalty of the industrial workers and garrison soldiers, the main bases of power in Petrograd. Moreover, a similar situation developed in the cities across the country, where new city governments, drawn primarily from liberal educated society, replaced the old government authorities, while alongside them local soviets of workers and soldiers deputies sprang up and wielded real power.

The new political structure was very unstable, but during March and April its contours became clearer as a fundamental political realignment took place. Central to this was the emergence of three broad political blocs that were in many ways more important than traditional parties: liberals (including almost all nonsocialists), moderate socialists, and radical left socialists. The liberals (most importantly the Kadets) dominated the Provisional Government at first and then shared power therein with the moderate socialists from May to October. The moderate socialists—the Menshevik and Socialist Revolutionary (SR) parties predominantly—controlled the Petrograd and most other soviets around the country and became increasingly influential in the government. The radical left—Bolsheviks, left-wing Mensheviks and SRs, and anarchists—were at first a small, minority voice, but soon grew as the liberals and moderate socialists failed to satisfy popular aspirations. Monarchist and truly conservative political parties, the old right wing of Russian politics, were largely swept away by the revolution and played little role in 1917.

Within this political realignment, the authority of the Soviet and the overwhelming popular identification with the socialist parties meant that the political future of the revolution hinged on the outcome of struggles for influence among the socialist parties and within the Soviet. Two political leaders returning from exile with fundamentally different programs of revolutionary action, Irakli Tsereteli and Vladimir Lenin, drove the political realignment among the socialists and the development of Soviet policies.

Tsereteli, a Georgian Menshevik, returned from Siberian exile on 20 March and headed a group that forged the Menshevik-SR led bloc of moderate socialists under the banner of "Revolutionary Defensism." The key to the Revolutionary Defensist bloc's identity and success was the peace issue. The revolution had released a pent-up demand for an end to the suffering of the war. The Revolutionary Defensists developed a program calling for vigorous efforts to end the war by negotiations among the warring powers on the basis of a "peace without annexations or indemnities," defense of the country *and the revolution* until then, and cooperation with the government to achieve this. This policy, which repudiated the previous policy of war to victory, spoke not only to the broad popular desire to end the war but also to the unwillingness to suffer a defeat and possible German domination. From April to September the Revolutionary Defensists dominated the Petrograd Soviet, and most local soviets in other cities until then or later. In May they entered the Provisional Government and supported "coalition government," that is, one based on a centrist alliance of moderate socialists and liberals, which formed the various cabinets of the Provisional Government from May until the October Revolution.

The radical left was ill defined, disorganized, and lacking strong leadership until the return of major political leaders, mostly from abroad. These included Lenin of the Bolsheviks as well as some prominent Mensheviks and SRs, who quickly formed radical left wings of those parties in opposition to the dominant moderate wings. Lenin in particular galvanized the radical left. On his return to Russia on 3 April, he electrified politics with his "April Theses." He denounced all cooperation with the Provisional Government, criticized the moderate socialist leaders of the Soviet, and called for rapid movement toward a new, more radical revolution. The radicals and Bolsheviks pressed for more rapid and more sweeping social and economic reforms, demanded more vigorous efforts to end the war, criticized the policies of the coalition government and Soviet leadership, and increasingly called for the Provisional Government's replacement by a socialist government based on the soviets. The Bolsheviks were the most strident, but the left SRs, left Mensheviks, anarchists, and others were a key part of the radical left bloc. Initially the radical left's extremism was out of keeping with the mood of optimism following the overthrow of the autocracy. Their opposition stance, however, positioned these parties and groups to become the beneficiary of any failures of the government and Soviet leadership to solve the many problems facing the country.

The first crisis of the new political system, the "April Crisis" (18–21 April), arose over the war. Pavel N. Milyukov, the Kadet leader and new foreign minister, took the position that Russia's national interests transcended the revolution and required that Russia continue the war to a complete victory. The socialists in the Soviet, however, attacked this policy, demanding that Russia find a way to end the war. Tsereteli's Revolutionary Defensism provided a seemingly viable, and very popular, way to do so. Milyukov's attempts to defend a policy of war to victory led to massive antigovernment street demonstrations. The April Crisis clearly showed the preponderant power of the Soviet and the need to restructure the government to reflect that. This took place on 5 May when Milyukov and some other liberals were replaced by several of the leading members of the Soviet in the first "coalition government" of liberals and moderate socialists.

POPULAR ASPIRATIONS AND THE DEMAND FOR "ALL POWER TO THE SOVIETS"

The formation of the coalition government heightened the expectations of the population that

A meeting of the Petrograd Soviet of Workers and Soldiers Deputies, April 1917. ©BETTMANN/CORBIS

the revolution would fulfill their aspirations. The February Revolution released the pent-up frustrations and aspirations of the population, which vigorously put forward what they expected from the revolution. The Provisional Government instituted important and far-reaching reforms, especially in civil rights and individual and group freedoms, but was confronted by long lists of popular demands that went far beyond those. These demands would be difficult to meet under the best of circumstances, which 1917 was not. The industrial workers, who had begun the revolution, demanded increased wages, an eight-hour day, better working conditions, dignity as individuals, an end to the war, and other aspirations. Soldiers demanded and implemented fundamental changes in the conditions of military service, and then became the most ardent opponents of continuing the war. Peasants laid claim to the land and greater control over their lives and villages. The educated middle classes looked forward to expanded civil rights and a society based on the rule of law. Women demonstrated for the right to vote and better access to education and professions. National minorities demanded expanded use of their language, respect for cultural practices, and political autonomy within a federal state. Hundreds of groups—soldiers' wives, medical assistants, apartment residents' associations, over-age soldiers, and other "groups" large and small—expected the government to address their needs and hopes. For all inhabitants of the Russian state, of whatever class, gender, ethnicity, occupation, or other attribute, the revolution stood for the opening of a new era and a better future, and they expected the new political leadership to deliver that.

Moreover, the people of the Russian Empire quickly organized to fulfill their aspirations. Within a few weeks they created a vast array of organizations for self-assertion: thousands of factory committees, army committees, village assemblies, Red Guards, unions, nationality-based parties, ethnic and religious organizations, cultural and educational clubs, women's and youth organizations, officers' and industrialists' associations, householders' associations, economic cooperatives, and others. These many organizations and the continuous meetings represented genuinely popular movements and gave form to the hopes and aspirations of the peoples of the empire. The interrelationship of the political parties and these many organizations, especially the more powerful ones such as factory and soldiers' committees, was a key issue of the revolution. Political leaders struggled to garner the popular support of these organizations, while the populace and their organizations, selecting from a rich buffet of political, social, economic, and cultural ideas, searched for leadership that could articulate and fulfill their aspirations. Unmet aspirations drove the revolution leftward throughout 1917 as the population sought new leaders—local and central—who would fulfill their goals. Recognizing the role of these aspirations and the activities and significance of the new organizations, and how those linked up to political movements, is essential to understanding the development of the revolution. Without them, the activities of "high politics" and leaders make little sense.

Popular aspirations and attitudes were reflected in the powerful language and symbolism that developed immediately after the February Revolution. Words such as *democracy* and *republic* were powerful positive terms, marking off political and social boundaries, whereas *the bourgeoisie* and *counterrevolutionary* had similar but negative force. The language of class was particularly powerful because it both defined important identities and united—or separated off—large groups and could be used to mobilize them politically. Streets, places, and objects were given revolutionary names to replace ones with tsarist connotations. Revolutionary songs accompanied most public activity in 1917. Visually, not only were tsarist emblems torn down and destroyed, but also new ones took their place. Red, the color of revolution since the nineteenth century in Europe, was omnipresent in banners, cockades, armbands, ribbons in buttonholes or pinned to garments, and elsewhere. Street demonstrations and marches became part of daily life. The new revolutionary vocabulary, ideas, symbols, and marches came together in the "festivals of freedom" that were so popular in the early months. Moreover, a universal meaning was assigned to the revolution. Almost the entire political spectrum held that the revolution was not merely a Russian event, but one that would exercise great influence across Europe and the globe, in the manner of the French Revolution of 1789. Lenin's belief that the revolution was the beginning of worldwide socialist revolution was only the most extreme form of a commonly held faith that the revolution would change both Russia and the world.

The liberal and Revolutionary Defensist (moderate socialists) political alliance that controlled the Provisional Government after April found it impossible to meet the many, often conflicting, aspirations of the population, and the general optimism of spring gave way to a summer of discontents. First and especially pressing, the coalition not only failed to find a way to end the war but also decided to launch a military offensive in June that was unpopular from the beginning and soon turned into a devastating defeat. War, worsening economic conditions, industrial conflict, rising crime and public disorders, rural discontent over land distribution, and unfulfilled aspirations fueled a demand for "All Power to the Soviets." On the surface this meant simply that an all-socialist government based on the Petrograd Soviet or a congress of soviets should replace the Provisional Government. Underlying it, however, was a demand for a government that unequivocally advanced the interests of the worker, peasant, and soldier masses against the "bourgeoisie" and privileged society, one that would rapidly carry out radical social and economic reforms and end the war. Workers, soldiers, and others turned toward arguments that stressed that they could achieve peace and fulfill their economic and other aspirations only through a new revolution that would produce a radically different government more attuned to their needs.

The demand for Soviet power and the underlying frustrations of the workers and soldiers burst loose with the tumultuous disorders usually called the "July Days" or the "July Uprising." Some units of the Petrograd garrison—which consisted primarily of troops training as replacements for the front—had become increasingly discontented with the policies of the government and bitterly opposed the new military offensive. Their discontent coincided with growing restiveness in nearby factories. The two sets of discontents interacted with each other and exploded the evening of 3 July. Soldiers and workers, encouraged by anarchist, Left SR, and Bolshevik factory activists, now undertook to force political change. In the early evening, workers from several factories and soldiers of the First Machine Gun Regiment took to the streets chanting "All Power to the Soviets" and other radical slogans. By midnight tens of thousands of workers and soldiers had assembled at Soviet headquarters, where they angrily demanded the transfer of all power to the Soviet. The Revolutionary Defensist leadership of the Soviet refused, and the demonstrations temporarily broke up between and three and four A.M. on 4 July.

The Bolshevik party leadership had not planned or authorized the demonstrations, contrary to an enduring myth that they did so as part of a calculated attempt to seize power. Lower-level Bolshevik activists, however, had been prominent among those radicals whipping up popular discontent and the demand for Soviet power. Finally, in the early morning hours of 4 July, faced with the fact of massive demonstrations and demands from their supporters for action, the Bolsheviks' Central Committee (without Lenin, who was vacationing in Finland) announced its willingness to support and lead "a peaceful demonstration" in support of an all-socialist government based on the Soviet. Hardly had it done so and Lenin returned, however, than the demonstrations floundered. The unwillingness of the Petrograd Soviet's Revolutionary Defensist leaders to take power, news that troops from the front were arriving to support the Soviet leaders and government, and a sensational release of documents purporting (falsely) to show that the Bolshevik leaders were German agents, combined to deflate the demonstrations. By 5 July they were over. There was a temporary reaction against the Bolsheviks and radical left. The government ordered the arrest of Lenin and some others, who fled into hiding, where Lenin stayed until the October Revolution.

A peculiar situation developed after the July Days in which the newspaper headlines and political leaders spoke of a conservative reaction, even a possible military dictator, whereas the events of daily life printed on the inside pages revealed a steady radicalization of the population. The latter was conveyed both in news articles about the radical left bloc's capture of one worker or soldier committee and organization after another in reelections, and in the general popular discontent revealed in other stories. The question of land distribution remained

a major source of dissatisfaction, among both peasants and soldiers, and rural violence continued. A general economic disintegration coupled with inflation made workers fear the loss of gains made thus far and fueled industrial conflict. Economic crisis brought hardship to everyone, especially the urban masses, as necessary goods became unavailable or prohibitively expensive. Fears grew about adequate food provisions for the cities and the army. On 10 August there was only enough bread reserve in Petrograd for two days, among other signs of shortages. Separatist movements in some of the national minority regions gained momentum. There was a dramatic increase in crime and public disorders. Society appeared to be disintegrating and life increasingly insecure. The government and the Revolutionary Defensist leaders of the Soviet seemed unable to meet people's basic needs, much less fulfill their aspirations for improvements.

Governmental instability and frequent reorganization added to these problems. The original cabinet of the Provisional Government had been replaced by the first "coalition" on 5 May, still under Prince Lvov. On 2 July this government resigned, and it took until 23 July to complete formation of a new one under Kerensky's leadership. Talk of this cabinet's replacement immediately filled the newspapers. Some conservatives began to look for a military man, "the Napoleon of the Russian Revolution," to accomplish a "restoration of order." Attention increasingly settled on General Lavr Kornilov, the newly appointed commander of the armies. Kornilov and Kerensky shared an apprehension about the growing signs of disintegration and the growing popularity of the radical left, and both agreed on the need for "order," including restructuring the government again and somehow reducing the influence of the Petrograd Soviet. The two did not trust each other, however, and Kerensky became convinced that Kornilov was planning a coup d'état against him and hastily dismissed Kornilov as army commander on 27 August. Kornilov, outraged, flung a small military force against Petrograd. His attack quickly collapsed, and with it the short-lived drive for "order." Kerensky's government also collapsed, ushering in nearly a month of renewed governmental crisis.

The Kornilov affair, with its threat of counterrevolution, crystallized all the discontents and fears of the mass of the population into an even more

A demonstration march in Petrograd, June 1917. As political leaders debated the nature of the new government, various groups of Russians organized to fulfill their aspirations. These protestors carry a banner reading "Long Live Education for the People." ©BETTMANN/CORBIS

insistent demand for Soviet power. The main beneficiaries of this were the radical parties, especially the Bolsheviks. They had been gaining influence and support in August as they criticized the government and Revolutionary Defensists leaders of the Soviet for their failure to end the war and meet other popular aspirations. The Kornilov fiasco catapulted a Bolshevik-led radical Left coalition into control of the Petrograd Soviet, the main bastion of revolutionary authority, and also into the leadership of the Moscow and many other city soviets and of workers' and soldiers' organizations. It is worth stressing that the Bolsheviks and their allies, primarily the Left SRs, won control of these soviets through elections, as moderate deputies either became radicalized and switched parties or were replaced by their factory and army electors with more radical spokesmen. This popular support was genuine and essential to the Bolshevik seizure

of power in October, a fact often lost sight of because of the later Bolshevik dictatorship.

By mid-September, the question was not whether the Provisional Government (now in its fourth incarnation) would be replaced again, but how and by whom and in what manner. Ever larger segments of the political elite as well as the general population believed that the time had come for some type of new, all-socialist, government. This came close to implementation by agreement among socialist party leaders in late September, but failed. The question, however, would not go away, and by October attention began to focus on the forthcoming Second All-Russia Congress of Soviets (a congress of delegates from soviets across the country) as the vehicle for creating such a government. Given the often-stated calls of the Bolsheviks and their allies for the soviets to take power, the question now was not so much would they attempt to replace the Provisional Government by the Congress of Soviets, but instead centered around the details. Exactly how would it happen? What would be the exact nature of the new government? To what extent and how successfully might Kerensky's government resist? Would this spark civil war?

THE OCTOBER REVOLUTION

"What are the Bolsheviks planning to do?" That was the question debated on street corners, in newspapers, and in public meetings during October. This question tormented Lenin as well. From his Finnish hiding place—an order for his arrest dating from the July Days still existed—Lenin feared that the Bolsheviks would do too little, too late. He already had turned away from any idea of cooperation with the moderate socialists in some kind of shared Soviet power. Ignoring the debates going on in Petrograd about what kind of broad socialist government to form, Lenin shifted to a strident call for an immediate armed seizure of power by the Bolsheviks. Lenin believed that the fall of 1917 offered a unique opportunity for a radical restructuring of political power and for a man such as himself.

Lenin's call divided the party leadership. A minority supported Lenin's call to arms. Another group, led by Grigory Zinoviev and Lev Kamenev, two of the most important Bolshevik leaders, urged caution and favored a broad coalition of socialists in a democratic left government, probably created at the

Constituent Assembly (elections having been scheduled for November). An intermediate position, increasingly identified with Leon Trotsky and probably representing a majority of the party's leadership, looked to the forthcoming Second All-Russia Congress of Soviets as the vehicle for the transfer of power. They expected that the Bolsheviks and other parties supporting Soviet power would have a majority at the congress, and the congress could then declare the transfer of power to itself. Although this itself would be a revolutionary move, they believed that Kerensky's government would be unable to resist. Despite Lenin's demands, therefore, the party's political efforts focused on the forthcoming Congress of Soviets and the selection of deputies to the congress who would support a transfer of power.

Frustrated and fearing that an irretrievable opportunity was slipping by, Lenin took the chance of moving from Finland to the outskirts of Petrograd. On 10 October he met, for the first time since July, with the Central Committee of the party. After an all-night debate the Central Committee seemingly gave in to Lenin's passionate demands for a seizure of power. It passed a resolution stating that an "armed uprising" was "the order of the day." This resolution later became central to the myth of a carefully planned seizure of power carried out under Lenin's direction. It was, in fact, something different and more complex than that. First of all, it did not set any timetable or plan for a seizure of power. Rather, the resolution was a formal reversion of Bolshevik party policy to the idea that an armed uprising was a revolutionary necessity, but did not commit the party to a seizure of power before the Congress of Soviets or at any other specific time or by any specific means. Nor did it start actual preparations for a seizure of power, as many within the Bolshevik leadership pointed out in discussions in the following days. Despite Lenin's bullying, the party leadership continued to focus on the Congress of Soviets as the time, place, and vehicle for the transfer of power. This would be the new "revolution" called for in the Bolshevik resolution of 10 October as well as in hundreds of local workers' and soldiers' resolutions for "All Power to the Soviets." The Bolsheviks' Left SR allies also were aiming at the congress to take power and form an all-socialist government.

At this point Lenin was the recipient of a series of unforeseeable lucky breaks that made possible the violent seizure of power that he wanted and gave rise to the durable myth of a secretly and well-planned Bolshevik coup d'état. First, on 18 October the moderate socialists decided to postpone the opening of the Congress of Soviets from the twentieth to the twenty-fifth. This was momentous, because the Bolsheviks were totally unprepared for and could not have attempted any seizure of power before the twentieth even if they wished. The five extra days changed everything; 20–24 October were days of furious public debate over numerous issues (preparation to send garrison troops to the front, the danger of a German invasion, moving the capital to Moscow, the severe economic and food crisis, factory closings, the instability of the government, etc.). These issues had Petrograd in turmoil. Moreover, because a declaration of the transfer of power at the Congress of Soviets, however much expected, would after all be an insurrectionary action that Kerensky presumably would resist, both sides undertook during these days to mobilize supporters. Bolsheviks and Left SRs worked successfully to secure the support of the volatile soldiers of the garrison for "Soviet power," thus destroying any ability of the government to use its soldiers against the seizure of power by the Congress of Soviets.

The October Revolution actually began in response neither to any plan of Lenin's nor to any act by the Congress of Soviets, but because of an action by Kerensky, which proved to be Lenin's second lucky break. The government, apprehensive over the rising demand for Soviet power and Bolshevik influence, decided on a minor strike against the Bolsheviks. During the predawn hours of 24 October, the government sent military cadets to close down two Bolshevik newspapers. The alarmed newspapermen ran to Soviet headquarters, where Soviet leaders declared that counterrevolution had again reared its head and called on soldiers and armed workers to defend the Soviet and the revolution and guarantee the opening of the Congress of Soviets the next day. Their posture was basically defensive. Throughout 24 October, pro-government and pro-Soviet forces engaged in a series of confused and uncoordinated confrontations for control of key buildings and the bridges over the rivers. The pro-Soviet forces had the greater numbers, morale, and determination—nobody wanted to die for the Provisional Government—and by midnight they controlled most of the city, with almost no shooting.

At this point the character of events changed. Lenin, who had been hiding the past few days on the edge of the city and was unable to have much influence on events, on hearing accounts of the events in the city made his way to the Soviet headquarters after midnight. Lenin now pressed the Soviet leaders to offensive action. Around midmorning on 25 October he wrote a proclamation declaring the Provisional Government overthrown, which was quickly printed and distributed through the city. Lenin had, against all odds and logic, achieved his goal of an armed seizure of power before the congress, but he got it because of Kerensky's ill-considered action, not because of the implementation of a Bolshevik plan for an armed seizure of power.

Attention now shifted to the Congress of Soviets, which opened at 10:40 the evening of 25 October. The congress, as expected, had a majority in favor of Soviet power. The Bolsheviks, although the largest party, were not a majority and had to rely on the Left SRs and others to form a majority. Everything was in place for creating a multiparty, all-socialist government, what "Soviet power" had meant throughout 1917, and the first motions and speeches pointed in that direction. Suddenly, at this point Lenin received yet another unpredictable stoke of good luck: the moderate socialist SRs and Mensheviks denounced the Bolsheviks and walked out. This left the Bolsheviks with an absolute majority and in full control of the congress, which proceeded to declare the Provisional Government overthrown and all power to rest in its own hands. Lenin had his full seizure of power and an all-Bolshevik government.

In recognizing the unpredictable strokes of luck, or opportunities if one prefers, that came Lenin's way during October, one should not draw the conclusion that this was all an accident. The October Revolution was a complex mixture of the actions of individuals, of powerful long-term political and social forces moving toward a radical government of some type, and of unpredictable events of the moment, which combined to shape its specific form and outcome. The nature of the October Revolution should serve as a reminder of the complexity of history, of the intermingling of long-term "causes," chance of the moment, and even personal will.

FROM SOVIET POWER TO BOLSHEVIK REGIME

The Russian Revolution did not end with the "October Revolution." Indeed, many in October 1917 saw it as merely another political crisis, punctuated with the usual street disorders, producing yet another "provisional" government (a term the new government in fact used at first). Instead, the dispersal of the Constituent Assembly on 6 January 1918 is a better point to take as the end of the revolution in the precise usage of the term and the transition to civil war. During the period from 25 October to 6 January, Lenin successfully turned a revolution for Soviet power into Bolshevik power, while pushing the country into civil war and the new regime toward dictatorship.

The immense popularity of the idea of Soviet power allowed the new Bolshevik government to consolidate its power during the following weeks. It was able to defeat an attempt by Kerensky to use troops from the front to regain power, it overcame a serious effort during the first week after the October Revolution to force it to share political power through formation of a broad multiparty socialist government, and it witnessed the successful spread of "Soviet power" across much of Russia as local soviets opted for support of the new Soviet regime. At the same time, Lenin and Trotsky worked to polarize political opinion and to strengthen the Bolshevik hold on power. They did this in part through swift movement to meet popular aspirations by a decree distributing land to the peasants, by an armistice with Germany, by extension of workers' authority in management of factories, and by other measures. They brought some Left SRs into the government as junior partners, thus broadening slightly their political base while retaining Bolshevik domination of the government. They also tightened control through press censorship, the formation of the Cheka (political police), repressive measures against the Kadet Party, and other actions to suppress opposition.

The final act in marking the end of the revolution and the onset of civil war was the dispersal of the Constituent Assembly. The elections to the Constituent Assembly and its forthcoming convocation kept alive not only the notion of a future broad multiparty socialist government, but also a sense that Lenin's government was only another temporary—provisional—government. This muted early opposition to the new government, but also presented Lenin and the radical left with a great dilemma. As predicted, the elections in November gave the SRs a majority that, however unstable, would control the Constituent Assembly when it opened on 5 January 1918. Any government coming out of the assembly would be a coalition, probably the broad socialist coalition that the slogan "All Power to the Soviets" originally was thought to mean. Accepting the authority of the elections and the Constituent Assembly meant yielding power, and this Lenin was unwilling to do. His unwillingness led the Bolsheviks and Left SRs to prepare action against the assembly. This came on 6 January when Lenin shut down the Constituent Assembly by force after only one meeting. Its dispersal was not essential for maintenance of a socialist government, or even "Soviet power," but it was necessary if Lenin and the Bolsheviks were to hold power and for such a radical government as they envisioned.

By closing the Constituent Assembly, Lenin ended the possibility of the Russian Revolution playing itself out in the political arena. With that closed, his opponents had no recourse but to arms, and civil war now replaced the political and social revolution of 1917. The decision also drove the Bolsheviks further down the road toward establishing a new dictatorship and destroyed the democratic hopes of the "radiant days of freedom," as one poet had described the optimistic early days of the revolution.

HISTORIOGRAPHY

Writing and interpreting the history of the revolution began almost immediately as part of the post-1917 struggles both within the Bolshevik Party and between it and its opponents, domestic and foreign. Ironically, among both Bolsheviks and anti-Bolsheviks, in both the Soviet Union and the West, an overarching interpretation quickly emerged focused on Lenin, the Bolshevik party, ideology, and high politics, largely divorced from the broader political and social context. Despite scattered scholarly works earlier, both a fundamental questioning of the original interpretation and a substantial body of scholarly writing on the revolution emerged only in the late 1960s. The initial new Western scholarship, while still mostly focused on political history, questioned some of the traditional portrayals of a monolithic Bolshevik party and the nature of revolutionary politics and the October Revolution. The historiography of the revolution then expanded rapidly in the 1970s and 1980s. Historians began to examine the revolution "from below," and a new "social history" replaced the former focus on ideology, high politics, and Lenin with a new emphasis on social groups and a deepening social polarization that shaped the outcome of the revolution. Scholars also began to produce studies on the provinces and nationality regions as well as more sophisticated histories of political parties. By the 1990s, some scholars began to apply cultural and linguistic approaches to the study of the revolution. In the Soviet Union, although the extreme control of the era of Joseph Stalin relaxed after his death in 1953, scholarship remained handicapped by the need to retain most of the standard interpretation and falsifications set down earlier. The collapse of the Soviet Union finally allowed scholars in Russia and other former Soviet areas to take up the same types and, increasingly, quality of scholarship that had become the norm in the West. At the opening of the twenty-first century, scholars, especially in the West, began to take an interest in placing the revolution within a longer Russian and/or a broader European context. A revived interest in political history, sometimes called "the new political history," situated politics more explicitly within the social and cultural context. The historiography of the Russian Revolution of 1917 remains a vibrant, exciting, but less ideological, field.

See also **Bolshevism; Kadets (Constitutional Democratic Party); Kerensky, Alexander; Lenin, Vladimir; Mensheviks; Nicholas II; Russian Civil War; Trotsky, Leon.**

BIBLIOGRAPHY

Abramson, Henry. *A Prayer for the Government: Ukrainians and Jews in Revolutionary Times, 1917–1920.*

Cambridge, Mass, 1999. Revolution and civil war in Ukraine with emphasis on the "Jewish Question."

Acton, Edward, Vladimir Iu. Cherniaev, and William G. Rosenberg, eds. *Critical Companion to the Russian Revolution, 1914–1921.* Bloomington, Ind., 1997. Outstanding collection of essays by prominent scholars.

Browder, Robert Paul, and Alexander F. Kerensky, eds. *The Russian Provisional Government, 1917: Documents.* 3 vols. Stanford, Calif., 1961. Excellent collection of documents on the Provisional Government and 1917.

Figes, Orlando. *A People's Tragedy: The Russian Revolution, 1891–1924.* New York, 1997. Provocative and readable study of the revolutionary period, with special focus on the people rather than political leaders.

Figes, Orlando, and Boris Kolonitskii. *Interpreting the Russian Revolution: The Language and Symbols of 1917.* New Haven, Conn., 1999. An intriguing look at the use of language and symbolism in the revolution, especially the cult of Kerensky.

Harding, Neil. *Leninism.* Durham, N.C., 1996. Stimulating look at Lenin's political thought and its relation to his political activities; compare with Service and White.

Hasegawa, Tsuyoshi. *The February Revolution: Petrograd, 1917.* Seattle, Wash., 1981. Best account of the February Revolution.

Hickey, Michael C. "Local Government and State Authority in the Provinces: Smolensk, February–June 1917." *Slavic Review* 55, no. 4 (1996): 863–881.

———. "The Rise and Fall of Smolensk's Moderate Socialists: The Politics of Class and the Rhetoric of Crisis in 1917." In *Provincial Landscapes: Local Dimension of Soviet Power, 1917–1953,* edited by Donald J. Raleigh, 14–35. Pittsburgh, Pa., 2001. Hickey's articles on a provincial city are very enlightening about the process of revolution.

Holquist, Peter. *Making War, Forging Revolution: Russia's Continuum of Crisis, 1914–1921.* Cambridge, Mass., 2002. Stimulating study of continuity and change through the broader upheaval, focusing on the Don Cossack lands.

Keep, John L. H. *The Russian Revolution: A Study in Mass Mobilization.* London, 1976. Looks especially at the role of various organizations (soviets, factory committees, etc.) and how the Bolsheviks were able use them to gain and then consolidate power in 1917 and early 1918.

Koenker, Diane. *Moscow Workers and the 1917 Revolution.* Princeton, N.J., 1981. Excellent study of the revolution in Moscow, focused on the industrial workers.

Koenker, Diane P., and William G. Rosenberg. *Strikes and Revolution in Russia, 1917.* Princeton, N.J., 1989. Outstanding work on strikes and their political and social impact.

Melancon, Michael. "The Syntax of Soviet Power: The Resolutions of Local Soviets and Other Institutions, March–October 1917." *Russian Review* 52, no. 4 (1993): 486–505. An account of the political struggles at the local level that raises important issues.

Rabinowitch, Alexander. *The Bolsheviks Come to Power: The Revolution of 1917 in Petrograd.* New York, 1976. Reprint, Chicago, 2004. Pathbreaking account of the Bolshevik Party and the events leading up to and including the October Revolution.

Radkey, Oliver H. *The Agrarian Foes of Bolshevism: Promise and Default of the Russian Socialist Revolutionaries, February to October 1917.* New York, 1958. Detailed account of the SR Party during 1917; a later book continues the story into early 1918.

Raleigh, Donald J. *Revolution on the Volga: 1917 in Saratov.* Ithaca, N.Y., 1986. Excellent study of the revolution through an in-depth examination of an important Russian city and province.

Read, Christopher. *From Tsar to Soviets: The Russian People and Their Revolution, 1917–21.* New York, 1996. Very good one-volume account of the revolution and civil war.

Rosenberg, William G. *Liberals in the Russian Revolution: The Constitutional Democratic Party, 1917–1921.* Princeton, N.J., 1974. The standard—and excellent—study of the Kadets in the revolution and civil war.

Sanders, Jonathan. *Russia, 1917: The Unpublished Revolution.* New York, 1989. The revolution in a fascinating collection of photographs.

Service, Robert. *Lenin: A Biography.* London, 2000. Very good; compare to Harding and White.

Smith, S. A. *Red Petrograd: Revolution in the Factories, 1917–1918.* Cambridge, U.K., 1983. Perhaps the best account of the revolution among the industrial workers of Petrograd.

Steinberg, Mark D. *Voices of Revolution, 1917.* New Haven, Conn., 2001. Letters and other documents from workers, soldiers, and peasants, with a stimulating introductory essay.

Suny, Ronald Grigor. *The Revenge of the Past: Nationalism, Revolution, and the Collapse of the Soviet Union.* Stanford, Calif., 1993. Outstanding account of the role of nationalism in the revolution and its impact on the end of the Soviet Union, yet brief and readable.

Wade, Rex A. *The Russian Search for Peace, February–October 1917.* Stanford, Calif., 1969. A study of the interaction of Russian revolutionary politics and World War I.

———. *The Russian Revolution, 1917.* Cambridge, U.K., 2000; 2nd ed., 2005. Stresses the interaction of social and political currents in producing the revolution's outcome.

Wade, Rex A., ed. *Revolutionary Russia: New Approaches.* London, 2004. Collection presenting the most recent approaches to writing the history of the revolution.

White, James D. *Lenin: The Practice and Theory of Revolution.* Houndmills, Basingstoke, U.K., 2001. Good shorter study of Lenin as revolutionary; compare to Harding and Service.

Wildman, Allan K. *The End of the Russian Imperial Army.* 2 vols. Princeton, N.J., 1980–1987. This two-volume set provides the best, and most detailed, account of the revolution in the army.

REX A. WADE

SAINT-EXUPÉRY, ANTOINE DE
(1900–1944), French writer and aviator.

Born in Lyons, France, into an aristocratic family in somewhat straitened circumstances and educated in Catholic institutions, Antoine-Marie-Roger de Saint-Exupéry lost his father when he was four years old and did not shine at school. Uncertain about a career, he learned to fly during his military service, having failed the naval academy's entrance examination. Subsequently he worked as a pilot, alongside such celebrated aviators as Jean Mermoz and Henri Guillaumet, for the commercial companies that in 1927 became Aéropostale. For a time he covered trans-Mediterranean routes (Toulouse, Casablanca, Dakar); later he pioneered the air link between Buenos Aires and Patagonia. It was in Argentina that he met Consuelo Suncín, with whom he had a passionate and chaotic relationship; the two were married in 1931, but this union did not bring Saint-Exupéry the stability for which he perhaps hoped.

His life was to be a combination of action and writing, turning him into a best-selling author and founder of a new fiction genre, the aerial adventure. His first book was *Courrier du Sud* (1929; *Southern Mail*), followed by *Vol de nuit* (1931; *Night Flight*) and *Terre des hommes* (1939; *Wind, Sand and Stars*). His novels transformed the distinctly accident-prone pilot Saint-Exupéry into a heroic, self-transcending figure, and the plane he flew and the hostile environment he braved likewise became a school of reflection and meditation. "The earth," he wrote in *Wind, Sand and Stars,*

"teaches us more about ourselves than all the books. Because it resists us. Man discovers himself when he measures himself against the obstacle. But for this he needs a tool" (*Terre des hommes,* p. 1; translated from the French). That tool was the airplane. For Saint-Exupéry the air postal service was in effect a kind of monastery where he learned austerity and self-sacrifice—but also brotherhood and solidarity.

His growing celebrity opened the door to journalism, and Saint-Exupéry made many visits as a reporter to Spain and Germany, where he became aware of the horrors of fascism. In 1939 he joined the air force and the following year arrived in the United States, where his books were best-sellers, especially *Wind, Sand and Stars,* and in some cases had been made into films, like *Night Flight* (1933) with John and Lionel Barrymore, Clark Gable, and Robert Montgomery. In 1942 the publication of *Flight to Arras* (*Pilote de guerre,* 1942) met with extraordinary success in the United States, where the novel topped the best-seller lists for six months. It was followed by *Lettre à un otage* (1943; *Letter to a Hostage*), dedicated to Saint-Exupéry's friend the Jewish novelist Léon Werth, who had stayed in France: "As French as you are, I feel that you are doubly in danger of death, first as a Frenchman, and secondly as a Jew." In exile, Saint-Exupéry proclaimed the necessity of continuing the struggle, despite France's defeat in 1940, and of defending human rights against the onslaught of Hitlerism; he placed all his hopes in an American intervention in the war in Europe. He supported the idea of a union of all the French exiles, but internecine conflicts, personal rivalries, and differences of perception ultimately made this an unattainable goal. Saint-Exupéry was sharply criticized by others in the exile group, notably by André Breton and Jacques Maritain, for his supposed failure to distance himself from the Vichy regime in France. With his romantic and aristocratic vision, Saint-Exupéry found disputes among the French intolerable, and he took refuge in an almost existentialist cult of action: "You reside in your act itself," he wrote. "Your act is you" (*Flight to Arras*).

Although he was by now overage, he was determined to return to war. He succeeded in this and made many reconnaissance flights over France. It was on one of these missions that he crashed off the French coast on 31 July 1944. His disappearance remained a mystery until his Lockheed Lightning was found in 2000. By the time Saint-Exupéry's last novel, *Citadell* (*Wisdom of the Sands*), was published posthumously in 1948, man and myth had become one. His renown would become immense and worldwide—driven, though not immediately, by his children's story *Le petite prince* (*The Little Prince*), which appeared in 1943 in both French and English and has since been translated into some two hundred languages. This story embodies all the power of Saint-Exupéry's humanism, tolerance, and desire to "restore spiritual meaning to humanity" (letter of June 1943). "One sees clearly only with the heart. Anything essential is invisible to the eyes"—such is the secret imparted by the fox to the little prince about how to become wise in face of the madness of men. In the end it was no doubt because he wore two hats, that of the pilot and that of the writer, that Antoine de Saint-Exupéry became the living embodiment of modern adventure.

See also **Aviation; France; Resistance.**

BIBLIOGRAPHY

Chadeau, Emmanuel. *Saint-Exupéry.* Paris, 2000.

Mehlman, Jeffrey. *Emigré New York: French Intellectuals in Wartime Manhattan, 1940–1944.* Baltimore, Md., 2000.

Schiff, Stacy. *Saint-Exupery: A Biography.* New York, 1994.

F. GUGELOT

SAKHAROV, ANDREI (1921–1989),

Soviet nuclear physicist and human rights advocate awarded the Nobel Peace Prize in 1975.

Andrei Dmitrievich Sakharov first received wide attention in July 1968, when his essay "Reflections on Progress, Peaceful Coexistence, and Intellectual Freedom" appeared in a Dutch newspaper and less than two weeks later on the front page of the *New York Times*. During the next decade Sakharov, a nuclear physicist by training, gained increasing notoriety as the most prominent representative of the community of human rights activists in the Soviet Union who came to be known as dissidents. But Sakharov had already exerted a considerable influence on international politics years earlier and was thus well known to the Kremlin leadership, even as his name remained a secret to the broader public. A designer of nuclear weapons, Sakharov came up with the key technical insight that earned him the title "father of the Soviet hydrogen bomb." His work assured that the United States would not hold a monopoly on this category of weapon, capable of explosive power many hundreds of times that of the bombs that destroyed Hiroshima and Nagasaki. For his efforts on behalf of defense of the Soviet Union, Sakharov received numerous state awards (including the Stalin Prize) and was elected a full member of the Soviet Academy of Sciences at the unprecedented age of thirty-two.

Sakharov's drive to influence Soviet policy for the public good predates his emergence as a dissident. His concern about the baneful influence of Trofim Lysenko on Soviet genetics contributed to his preoccupation with the health risks of nuclear radiation, caused by fallout from the enormous test explosions of thermonuclear devices he had designed. He took his campaign for a moratorium on nuclear tests to the highest levels of the Soviet nuclear establishment and more than once to the Soviet leader Nikita Khrushchev himself. As he wrote in his memoirs, "I had come to regard testing in the atmosphere as a crime against humanity, no different from secretly pouring disease-producing microbes into a city's water supply" (*Memoirs*, p. 206). Sakharov's concerns, bolstered by a worldwide peace movement, led to the Limited Nuclear Test Ban Treaty, signed in Moscow in August

Andrei Sakharov, photographed on the day he was notified of his Nobel Prize, 9 October 1975. ©BETTMANN/CORBIS

1963, banning atmospheric tests. Unfortunately, nuclear testing continued underground and at an accelerated pace, but at least without the scourge of radioactive poisoning of the air. In the late 1960s Sakharov promoted a mutual ban on antiballistic missile (ABM) systems, convinced, along with many U.S. and Soviet scientists, that a competition in defensive and offensive weapons would increase the risk of nuclear war. Their work contributed to the signing of the 1972 ABM Treaty.

Sakharov had worked in the weapons field from the time of his university days, when wartime evacuation from Moscow sent him and his fellow students to the east to finish their studies and then work in a munitions factory. He conducted nuclear weapons research from 1948 until the Soviet authorities revoked his security clearance two decades later in response to publication of his "Reflections" essay abroad.

The years 1968–1980 witnessed Sakharov's most active work on behalf of human rights in the Soviet Union. He was alarmed at the attempt by Leonid Brezhnev and other Soviet leaders to rehabilitate the reputation of Joseph Stalin, the Soviet dictator whose crimes had been denounced by Khrushchev in a short-lived "thaw" that brought a measure of political and cultural freedom to Soviet society. Sakharov pursued an approach popular with the so-called Helsinki movement to conduct political activity strictly in accordance with Soviet law and call upon the government to obey its laws as well—thus his efforts on behalf of freedoms of religion, of speech, and of movement, guaranteed by the Soviet constitution, and his frequent attendance at trials where political prisoners were sentenced on trumped-up charges. He was awarded the Nobel Peace Prize in 1975, much to the dismay of the Soviet leadership.

In 1980 the Soviet authorities sent Sakharov into internal exile in the closed city of Gorky, in retaliation for making public his opposition to the Soviet invasion of Afghanistan. Along with his wife, Elena Bonner (b. 1923), Sakharov conducted a number of hunger strikes in support of people seeking to emigrate or receive medical treatment abroad, and he also drafted his memoirs, under constant harassment by the secret police. In December 1986 the reformist leader Mikhail Gorbachev invited Sakharov to return to Moscow. There he pursued a brief but important career as a political figure during the perestroika era, serving as the moral compass of the democratic movement in the Congress of People's Deputies, to which he was elected by his constituency at the Academy of Sciences. In December 1989 a heart attack killed him in his sleep. Years later, his colleagues in the human rights movement continued to regret his untimely passing as they faced the challenges of an increasingly authoritarian regime under Vladimir Putin and a brutal war in Chechnya.

See also **Arms Control; Brezhnev, Leonid; Dissidence; Nuclear Weapons; Perestroika; Putin, Vladimir; Stalin, Joseph.**

BIBLIOGRAPHY

Primary Sources

Bonner, Elena. *Alone Together.* Translated by Alexander Cook. New York, 1986.

———. *Vol'nye zametki k rodoslovnoĭ Andreia Sakharova.* Moscow, 1996.

Sakharov, Andrei. *Progress, Coexistence, and Intellectual Freedom.* Translated by the *New York Times.* New York, 1968.

———. *Memoirs.* New York, 1990.

———. *Moscow and Beyond, 1986–1989.* Translated by Antonina Bouis. New York, 1991.

Secondary Sources

Altshuler, B. L., et al. *Andrei Sakharov: Facets of a Life.* Gif-sur-Yvette, France, 1991.

Evangelista, Matthew. *Unarmed Forces: The Transnational Movement to End the Cold War.* Ithaca, N.Y., 1999.

Gorelik, Gennadii. *Andrei Sakharov: Nauka i svoboda.* Moscow, 2000.

Holloway, David. *Stalin and the Bomb: The Soviet Union and Atomic Energy, 1939–1956.* New Haven, Conn., 1994.

Lourie, Richard. *Sakharov: A Biography.* Hanover, N.H., 2002.

MATTHEW EVANGELISTA

SALAZAR, ANTONIO (1889–1970), Portuguese politician.

The "Catholic dictator" of Portugal, Antonio de Oliveira Salazar led one of the longest dictatorships in twentieth-century Europe. In 1968 after he suffered a cardiovascular attack, he was removed from power. He died two years later.

The son of a modest rural family from Vimieiro, a village in central Portugal, Salazar had a traditional Catholic upbringing and completed most of his intellectual and political education before the First World War. He attended a seminary but abandoned the ecclesiastical path in order to study law at the University of Coimbra on the eve of the fall of the monarchy. A reserved and brilliant student, he led the best-known Catholic student organization in Coimbra, the Christian Democratic Academic Centre (Centro Académico de Democracia Cristã, or CADC). His friendship with the future cardinal patriarch of Lisbon, Manuel Cerejeira, dates from this period. He pursued a university career as a professor of economic law, and his only political activity during the liberal republic (1910–1926) took place within the strict limits of the social Catholic movement. He was one of the leaders of the Catholic Center Party (Centro

Católico, or CC) and was elected as a deputy for them in the elections of 1921. With the early dissolution of parliament in July 1921, Salazar left his position as deputy, and returned to his academic life and a more discreet involvement in Catholic political circles. Nevertheless, he did not lose any opportunity to reaffirm his position as the country's leading specialist in finances, which eventually resulted in his being invited to join the first cabinet formed following the 1926 military coup. However, after noting that the political situation remained highly unstable, Salazar declined the invitation. He was asked again two years later, and this time he accepted, but only on condition that he receive important powers over the other ministries in order to resolve the dictatorship's budgetary crisis.

Between 1928 and 1932, the year in which he became prime minister, Salazar, with support from the Catholic Church and important sections of the armed forces, came to dominate the military dictatorship. Benefiting from a new constitution, which was the product of a compromise between corporatism and liberalism that had been approved in a popular plebiscite in 1933, Salazar created a single party from above, designed to remain weak and elitist from the very outset. Its purpose was simply to ensure political control. It was used as a tool for the selection of members for the Chamber of Deputies and the local administration, as well as to provide some legitimacy in the regularly held "non-competitive elections."

Salazar was a master at manipulating this perverted rational-legal legitimacy, and he had little need to seek recourse in charismatic leadership in order to rise above the bureaucratic and governmental mediation between himself and the nation. The military origins of the regime ensured that his position remained linked to that of the president, General António Óscar de Fragoso Carmona (1869–1951), who had been elected in direct elections in 1928 and who retained the authority to dismiss any of his appointed officials, including Salazar.

The Portuguese New State became radicalized with the outbreak of the civil war in neighboring Spain in 1936. Some of the regime's organizations that had been inspired by the Fascists—for example, the paramilitary youth movement, Portuguese Youth (Mocidade Portuguesa, or MP), and the anticommunist militia, Portuguese Legion (Legião

Portuguesa, or LP)—introduced elements of the cult of the leader. Nevertheless, the more traditionalist conservatism continued to dominate the majority of the written press, which was closer to the paternalistic "prime ministerial" model of dictatorial leadership. The Catholic Church, both by its influence within official institutions and by its powerful nucleus of autonomous institutions, was transformed into a powerful and complementary instrument of ideological socialization. Nationalism and "providence" both completed and introduced elements of diversity into the official discourse.

With its declaration of neutrality in 1939, the Portuguese dictatorship was able to survive the Second World War thanks mainly to the concessions it made to the Allied Powers and to the rapid onset of the Cold War. The development that most concerned Salazar about the new international order after 1945 was decolonization. At the beginning of the 1960s, the African nationalist movements began their armed struggle, which led to the outbreak of colonial wars in Portuguese West Africa (Angola), Portuguese East Africa (Mozambique), and Portuguese Guinea (Guinea-Bissau). Salazar died in 1970, convinced that he was still Portugal's leader. His regime was overthrown by a military coup in 1974.

See also **Portugal; Spanish Civil War.**

BIBLIOGRAPHY

Cruz, Manuel Braga da. *As origens da democracia Cristã e o Salazarismo.* Lisbon, 1980.

Lucena, M. de. "Salazar." In *Dicionário de história de Portugal.* Vol. 9: *Suplemento.* Edited by António Barreto and Maria Filomena Mónica. Porto, 2000.

Pinto, António Costa. *Salazar's Dictatorship and European Fascism: Problems of Interpretation.* New York, 1995.

Salazar, Antonio de Oliveira. *Discursos e notas políticas.* Vol. 1. Coimbra, 1935.

ANTONIO COSTA PINTO

SALZBURG FESTIVAL.

The Salzburg Festival was founded in 1920 in the hope that it would make musical and theatrical classicism contemporary again, at least for some five weeks every summer in the small Austrian city of Salzburg. It has become one of the most prestigious music festivals and is one of the few that has managed over the years to bridge the gap between an international musical tradition unhampered by problems of linguistic translation and a national theatrical one in the native language. The Salzburg Festival's ability to weather the history of central Europe in the twentieth century stems from the flexibility of its original conception and the commercial acumen of its producers. The "Salzburg Idea" had its beginnings in the late nineteenth century, when a group of musicians founded the International Mozart Foundation in 1870 and decided its proper home was not Vienna, where Mozart had spent most of his creative life, but Salzburg, where he had been born in 1756 and from whose archbishop's service he had angrily and permanently resigned in 1781. The founders of the "Mozarteum," as it was soon known, envisioned Salzburg as an Austrian rival to Richard Wagner's Bayreuth. They intended Mozart to be the central but not sole composer whose work would be played, and they sought to re-create the Salzburg-Vienna nexus of Mozart's career.

Despite fund-raising efforts, nothing substantial developed until 1917, when a newly founded Salzburg Festival Society in Vienna approached the theater director Max Reinhardt (1873–1943), whose innovative productions had made him famous in German-speaking Europe. The Berlin-based Reinhardt was interested enough in the possibilities of Salzburg as an artistic center to buy the Schloss Leopoldskron, an eighteenth-century castle in Salzburg, and to begin to gather together fellow artists, including the librettist and playwright Hugo von Hofmannsthal and the composer Richard Strauss (1864–1949). The Salzburg Festival subsumed Mozart, particularly his operas, under Reinhardt's and Hofmannsthal's vision of aesthetic experience as something that created an ideal community in which rich and poor could come together and people's deepest spiritual needs could be met.

The first Salzburg Festival featured concerts of Mozart's orchestral music under the direction of Bernhard Paumgartner, along with Reinhardt's remarkable production of Hugo von Hofmannsthal's *Jedermann* (Everyman), in which Reinhardt used the city itself as the stage. The voice of Death came down from the Hohensalzburg, the city's landmark fortress, above the cathedral square, and actors mingled with the audience. Despite the quasi-mythical aura of this performance, the new festival had to respond to financial and artistic controversies during the 1920s. Paumgartner wanted the instrumental concerts of the festival to focus on the lesser known works of Mozart, thus providing an alternative to big city concerts, but he ran into the opposition of Richard Strauss, who saw mediocrity lurking in the call for diversity of programming. Once the festival began producing three Mozart operas a year, financial problems dominated. Politicians from the leading Austrian parties—the Christian Social Party, the Social Democratic Party, and the Nazi-linked German Nationalist Party—complained that ticket prices were beyond the means of ordinary citizens and that spending by the influx of foreign tourists enriched only a small minority of Salzburgers. Under the savvy leadership of Provincial Governor Franz Rehrl, the festival began to receive large subsidies from local and provincial governments, and from the Austrian state; nevertheless, the strong trend toward ever higher ticket prices and wealthy international audiences continued, as it does in the twenty-first century. Salzburg aficionados look back upon the 1930s, before the German annexation of Austria in 1938, as the most glorious period of the festival, a time when it attracted larger crowds than Bayreuth and, especially after 1933, made real the fragile dream of cultural brilliance associated with enlightenment and toleration. These were the years when the festival became a showplace for Arturo Toscanini's antifascist stance, but also when the glitz led it to be dubbed "Hollywood on the Salzach." After 1938 many of the luminaries of the interwar festival, including Reinhardt and Bruno Walter, fled, leaving it in the hands of sometimes brilliant musicians with dubious moral credentials, Wilhelm Fürtwängler and Richard Strauss among them. Ironically, Reinhardt's vision of a festival for the people probably came closest to being realized during the Nazi years because (as in Bayreuth, though to a more limited extent) the performance arenas were filled with state-subsidized ticket holders, whether workers in "Strength through Joy" programs or soldiers on leave.

With the sponsorship of the United States occupation authorities, the Salzburg Festival was revived after the war. After maneuvering through denazification difficulties, musical luminaries such as Fürtwängler, Elizabeth Schwarzkopf, and finally and most important, Herbert von Karajan guided the festival to its postwar glory. New buildings and new repertoires kept it vital, as did new generations of concertgoers. Franz Rehrl's motto, that culture equals business, was never truer than after the war, yet its defenders would argue that the spirit of Mozart and of musical humanism continues to shape its theatrical and musical offerings.

See also **Austria; Opera; Theater.**

BIBLIOGRAPHY

Gallup, Stephen. *A History of the Salzburg Festival*. London, 1987.

Steinberg, Michael P. *Austria as Theater and Ideology: The Meaning of the Salzburg Festival*. Ithaca, N.Y., 2000.

CELIA APPLEGATE

SAMIZDAT.

Samizdat (literally "self-published"), a Russian neologism dating from the 1950s, refers to a large and diverse body of unofficial texts that circulated outside state-censored publishing monopolies in the Soviet Union after the Second World War and, by the 1970s, in the Soviet bloc countries of Eastern Europe. Samizdat became the chief mode of communication within the so-called second or alternative cultures that developed in postwar socialist societies and served as a critical bridge between dissidents in those countries and the West.

Strict control over the printed word in the Soviet Union required that every work appear with the imprimatur of a state-owned publishing house such as the Gosudarstvennoe Izdatelstvo (State publisher, Gosizdat for short) or Politicheskoe Izdatelstvo (Political publisher, or Politizdat). Possession of duplicating and printing machines was tightly regulated. In 1953, faced with the impossibility of getting his poems approved by state censors, the Moscow poet Nikolai Glazkov created a series of typed, hand-sewn volumes on the title pages of which there appeared the words "Moscow—1953—Samsebyaizdat." The ironic final term, roughly "by myself publisher," was later shortened to "samizdat," which soon became the byword for an entire textual counterworld. To be sure, the practice of copying and circulating subversive homemade texts goes back centuries—it may be as old as censorship itself. But samizdat achieved a historically unparalleled range and degree of influence. While the word itself was diligently kept out of Soviet dictionaries, by the 1970s it had entered the lexicon of virtually every European language.

Samizdat was above all a distinctive mode of textual reproduction in which networks of writers and readers copied and circulated unsanctioned works in the privacy of their apartments. The primitive tools it employed—typewriter and carbon paper—led one writer to describe it as a return to the pre-Gutenberg era. Using a stack of a dozen or more alternating sheets of carbon and onionskin paper, an author would type (firmly!) multiple copies of a given work, typically single-spaced with no margins so as to economize on paper. Individual copies would then be distributed to close friends, who might be obliged to return the favor by typing another set of copies (again using carbon paper) and distributing them to their friends, or to return the original with additional copies to the author for further distribution. As with a chain letter, time limits were often imposed on these activities, producing frenzied periods of round-the-clock reading and/or typing.

Much of the initial postwar samizdat consisted of poetry by outstanding early twentieth-century figures such as Osip Mandelstam, Anna Akhmatova, and Marina Tsvetaeva. By the 1950s, however, circulating texts included much longer works of banned fiction by such writers as Andrei Platonov, Mikhail Zoshchenko, and Boris Pasternak, as well as translations into Russian of texts by Albert Camus, Arthur Koestler, George Orwell, and other foreign authors. Following Stalin's death in 1953, during the period known as the "thaw" (1953–1968), the volume and variety of samizdat grew dramatically as more Soviet citizens looked to homemade texts to explore topics and styles banished from official media. These included religious life, labor and concentration camps, and artistic genres other than the officially sanctioned socialist realism. More works appeared that had never been published

anywhere, such as the journal *Sintaxis* (1958–1960), Yevgenya Ginzburg's harrowing gulag memoirs *Journey into the Whirlwind,* and the transcript of the 1964 trial of the young Leningrad poet Joseph Brodsky. During the thaw, the circles of samizdat readers widened considerably, extending well beyond the main cities of Moscow and Leningrad. A typical samizdat text could find a readership of anywhere from several hundred to many thousands. In addition, a significant number of samizdat texts were smuggled out and published in the West (a technique later dubbed *tamizdat,* or "over-there publisher") or broadcast back to the Soviet Union via shortwave radio stations such as Radio Free Europe or the Voice of America (known as *radizdat,* or "radio publisher"). By the late 1960s Soviet samizdat had expanded to include the entire range of textual genres, from poetry and novels to petitions, historical documents, open letters, and periodicals. Among the latter were the *Chronicle of Current Events,* founded in 1968 as a kind of underground newsletter of the dissident movement as a whole (most issues included a bibliography of newly circulated samizdat works), as well as the *Ukrainian Herald,* the *Zionist Herald of Exodus,* the *Chronicle of the Lithuanian Catholic Church,* and the Russian nationalist journal *Assembly.* Except for the official Communist Party line, nearly every ideological viewpoint found expression in samizdat, including neo-Marxist, neofascist, monarchist, liberal, nationalist, anti-Semitic, religious, and anarchist.

Although samizdat as such was not technically illegal in the Soviet Union unless its content could be shown to be "anti-Soviet," the police and security services worked mightily to suppress its distribution, seizing samizdat texts during apartment searches and arresting their owners. But repression failed to crush what one writer called the "self-contained and singularly original sphere for the realization of society's spiritual and intellectual life." Devastating indictments of Soviet history such as Roy Medvedev's *Let History Judge* and Alexander Solzhenitsyn's *Gulag Archipelago* sent shock waves across the Soviet Union and beyond. By the 1970s, in fact, the samizdat phenomenon had spread to the Soviet satellite states in Eastern Europe (as well as China). Underground editions of the works of émigré writers such as Czesław

Miłosz and Witold Gombrowicz appeared in Poland; in Czechoslovakia the writer Ludvík Vaculík edited hundreds of samizdat texts in the series *Petlice* (Padlock).

Eastern European samizdat, which also drew on traditions of underground publishing dating from the period of Nazi occupation, tended to employ more advanced techniques of reproduction such as mimeographs and photocopying. With educated publics less favorably disposed toward their socialist rulers than in Soviet Russia, samizdat in Eastern Europe quickly developed an enormous audience. In Czechoslovakia, the human rights group Charter 77 circulated dozens of samizdat essays and documents indicting the regime's treatment of its citizens. In Poland, the emergence in the late 1970s of popular resistance among practicing Catholics, students, and especially workers transformed samizdat into a genuinely mass phenomenon. The periodical *Robotnik* (The worker) reached a peak production of seventy thousand copies in August 1980; in its pages the unofficial trade union Solidarność (Solidarity) made its platform known to the Polish public, the Polish government, and the world.

Poland offers the strongest example of samizdat's vital contribution, on both a moral and practical level, to the dismantling of Soviet-style socialism in Europe. In the Soviet Union, where the range of sentiments expressed in samizdat was considerably wider and its propagation more limited, samizdat texts contributed only indirectly to socialism's collapse. But Soviet samizdat nonetheless established the terms for the turbulent public conversation that followed the collapse and that continues into the early twenty-first century.

Beyond its political relevance, samizdat represents a distinctive phenomenon in the modern history of print culture. While contemporaries often considered it the cultural analog to the so-called second economy (the underground black market within state-run socialist economies), samizdat was in fact a system for circulating (textual) products entirely *outside* the force field of market relations, a remarkable approximation of the socialist ideal of nonprofit-driven exchange. In this sense, perhaps, it suggests less the pre-Gutenberg era than that quintessentially modern mode of free textual exchange, the Internet.

See also **Akhmatova, Anna; Charter 77; Dissidence; Havel, Václav; Mandelstam, Osip; Miłosz, Czesław; Pasternak, Boris; Radio Free Europe; Solzhenitsyn, Alexander; Soviet Union; Totalitarianism; Tsvetaeva, Marina.**

BIBLIOGRAPHY

Eichwede, Wolfgang, ed. *Samizdat: Alternative Kultur in Zentral- und Osteuropa: Die 60er bis 80er Jahre.* Bremen, Germany, 2000.

Feldbrugge, F. J. M. *Samizdat and Political Dissent in the Soviet Union.* Leiden, Netherlands, 1975.

Hopkins, Mark. *Russia's Underground Press: The Chronicle of Current Events.* New York, 1983.

Skilling, H. Gordon. *Samizdat and an Independent Society in Central and Eastern Europe.* London, 1989.

BENJAMIN NATHANS

SARAJEVO. The founding of Sarajevo, the early-twenty-first-century capital city of the sovereign state of Bosnia-Herzegovina, may be dated to 1462. In that year, Isa-beg Isaković, the Ottoman Turkish governor (*Saray*) of the newly conquered province of Bosnia, began building his residence and a mosque on the site of the modern city. The expansion of Ottoman dominion during the next two hundred years saw Sarajevo develop as the major center of commerce and culture in European Turkey. By 1660 the city numbered eighty to a hundred thousand inhabitants, and many foreign visitors came to marvel at the health and prosperity of the inhabitants. A contemporary Turkish traveler recorded 17,000 substantial houses, 170 mosques, 1,050 shops where artisans both made and sold their goods, and 110 fountains, testimony to the affluent and gracious lives of the citizens, both public and private. Native Bosnian Muslims, Christians, Jews, Turks, and Greeks rubbed shoulders in the famous marketplace (*Baščaršija*), the hub of gossip and commercial life. Sarajevo was at the summit of its power, second only to Istanbul in importance in the Balkans, and by this period was self-governing, choosing its own chief administrator. In earlier times, Bosnia was administered by officials (*kapetans*) appointed from Istanbul, but during the eighteenth century the native Bosnian Muslims made the office hereditary, displacing imperial authority. Sarajevo was their city, beyond the effective rule of the Sultan, whose vice-roys (*viziers*) chose to reside in Travnik after about 1690.

The sacking and burning of Sarajevo by Prince Eugene of Savoy in 1697 signaled the end of the city's golden age, although the effects of the long and gradual Ottoman decline did not bite hard until the nineteenth century. In 1807 the population still stood at around sixty thousand, helped by the city's growing trading links to the north. Nemesis came when rebellions in Serbia (1804) and Greece (1821) ushered in a century of Balkan national struggles for independence, fuelled by peasant revolts against intolerable economic exactions. The Sultan introduced measures to modernize the entire Ottoman system of rule, some of them intended to ameliorate the conditions of the Sultan's Christian subjects in Bosnia, and head off trouble there. The economic privileges and religious conservatism of the native Bosnian Muslim elite drove them into armed rebellion, led by the *kapetans*. Istanbul responded by sending an army into Bosnia in 1850. Sarajevo was occupied and plundered; the population decreased to only twenty thousand in 1851.

Years of fighting and unrest engulfed the region, and order had to be restored by the great powers. At the Treaty of Berlin (1878) control of Bosnia-Herzegovina passed into the hands of the rival Austro-Hungarian Empire, which administered the province as a protectorate on behalf of Turkey. The change represented a leap into modernity for Sarajevo. The physical character of the city was hitherto defined by the Old City. Now a "second" city grew up, enlarging the boundaries of Sarajevo for the first time since its Ottoman heyday. By 1914 sixty major new public buildings had been built in Central European style, situated on wide boulevards, along which the first trams ran. Energetic imperial administrators forced the pace of industrialization. State monopoly enterprises producing tobacco and textiles were founded, railways and roads grew apace, and small private businesses flourished. Signs of the new times were the first iron bridge across the city's river Miljačka, replacing the earlier wooden structures, and a modern underground sewerage system.

The social structure of the city was likewise radically altered. Officials and professional people came in from other parts of the Austro-Hungarian

Empire to staff the new schools and the municipal hospital. By 1910 the population of Sarajevo had climbed to fifty-one thousand, and was changing in ways that reflected its recent history. Religious confession, which in practice corresponded pretty exactly to ethnic allegiance, was used in compiling Austrian census returns. These statistics indicate that in 1910 Muslims made up one-third of the inhabitants, whereas in 1879 the proportion was two-thirds. Catholics accounted for another one-third (mainly imperial functionaries from outside Bosnia), compared with only 3 percent in 1879. Orthodox Christian believers (Serbs) made up 16 percent, a figure unchanged since 1879. The proportion of Jews in the city also remained constant throughout the period at about 10–12 percent.

In 1908 Austria-Hungary formally annexed Bosnia-Herzegovina, igniting Serbian nationalism. Muslims made up 32 percent of the total population of Bosnia in 1908, Orthodox (Serbs) 43 percent, and Catholics (Croats) 23 percent. Shorn of their dominant position under Ottoman rule, the Muslims adapted as best they could to their new masters, and managed to protect both their culture and their large estates, which were still worked by the sharecropping Christian peasantry, as in Ottoman times. The Croat peasants were relatively content with their prospects in a Catholic empire in which the kingdom of Croatia had a recognized if subordinate constitutional place. The Serb peasants, the largest ethnic group, had won neither land nor political recognition, and some looked for a solution in political violence. On 28 June 1914 Gavrilo Princip (1894–1918), a Bosnian Serb, fired the shots that killed the Austrian heir apparent, Archduke Francis Ferdinand (1863–1914), during an official visit to Sarajevo. A month later, Austria-Hungary declared war on Serbia, precipitating the cataclysmic Great War of 1914–1918. Turkey joined the war on the side of the Central Powers against the Allies, but defeat in 1918 ended with the dismemberment of both the Ottoman and Austro-Hungarian empires.

SARAJEVO IN YUGOSLAVIA, 1918–1992

The tide of war swept across the Balkans southeastward, leaving Bosnia in its rear. Sarajevo survived the fighting without major physical damage, but Austria-Hungary treated the Serbs on its territory as enemy

A street in Sarajevo, 1955. At the center of the photograph are three Muslim women on their way to the market. GETTY IMAGES

aliens and incited ethnic hatreds between Muslim and Serbs that tore Bosnia apart. The Serbs took revenge on their Muslim neighbors after the war, unleashing a campaign of terror in which landgrabbing and racial bigotry fed each other. When the Kingdom of the Serbs, Croats, and Slovenes (which would be renamed "Yugoslavia" in 1931) came into being at the Treaty of Versailles in 1921, Bosnia-Herzegovina did not appear on the map as a recognized geographical entity. The new state was organized politically along ethnic lines during the interwar years and the Muslims were not granted the status of a founding people. The population of Sarajevo was sixty-six thousand in 1921, rising to seventy-eight thousand in 1931. It was still a major city in a country that contained only three urban centers with a population of more than one hundred thousand, but Belgrade and Zagreb grew by two-thirds in the same period, to about two hundred

thousand inhabitants. Patterns of trade and commerce had shifted decisively northward. Even the main city of Slovenia, Ljubljana, although smaller than Sarajevo, far outstripped it in economic dynamism and civic independence.

Lacking the status of a regional administrative capital and isolated from the main flows of economic advance, Sarajevo became something of a backwater, but the bare statistics do not capture the essential life of the city. In 1931 Muslims made up 38 percent of the population, Catholics and Orthodox Christians about a quarter each. Remarkably, despite the interethnic violence that had so disfigured the very recent past, Sarajevans managed to preserve a sense of community that echoed the early centuries of Ottoman rule. In 1927 an American writer reflected on the mingling of the faiths in peaceful activity and mused on tolerance as the greatest of virtues as he watched an

Orthodox peasant give alms to a blind Muslim street musician. Sarajevans loved their city for its beauty and its glorious natural setting, for its café life, for its distinctive Turkish-influenced musical tradition, including the *sevdalinka*, romantic songs of love and yearning. One of them speaks of "Sarajevo, breath of my breath," and it is a quintessentially Bosnian sentiment—not Muslim, Serb, or Catholic. Sarajevans shared a centuries-old civic culture, and spoke a common language, a dialect of Serbo-Croatian not found in Croatia and Serbia. Sarajevo was also a city associated with liberal political currents aimed at reducing the sway of the Serbs within Yugoslavia. Intellectuals and public servants held two major national congresses in Sarajevo and Zagreb in 1922 to promote reform and introduce federal government and in 1929 Sarajevo became briefly the headquarters of Yugoslavia's main Croatian opposition party, until the introduction of royal dictatorship ended parliamentary politics in 1929.

The brief peace was blown away by the Nazi invasion of Yugoslavia in April 1941. A Croatian fascist (Ustaše) puppet state was created, the Independent State of Croatia, which administered most of Bosnia, but not Sarajevo, which was left in the German zone of occupation. The ancient community of Sephardic Jews in Sarajevo was an immediate casualty, together with their Ashkenazi brethren elsewhere. Between them, the Germans and the Ustaša regime slaughtered four out of five (fifty-seven thousand) of Yugoslavia's prewar Jewish population, and one-third (eighteen thousand) of the Gypsies (Roma). The Croatian fascists also set about the genocide of Serbs on their territory. More than a million Serbs perished in Bosnia-Herzegovina. Many Serbs fled to join Tito's communist partisans operating in Bosnia, and Sarajevo was virtually emptied of Serbs. They returned after 1945 to a city ruled by the iron hand of the Communist Party of Yugoslavia.

Bosnia-Herzegovina was established constitutionally as a constituent republic of a federal Yugoslavia under Tito (Josip Broz, 1892–1980), but power was in practice monopolized by the Communist Party. It was in its origins a harsh, Stalinist regime, but it did at least give Bosnia and its capital city forty-five years of peace, the longest period free from wars and invasion since 1878. The policy of forced industrialization, and of equalizing conditions in the six republics, worked to the benefit of Bosnia. Major investments in industry, including defense industries located in Bosnia for strategic reasons, brought rising standards of living and the movement of peasants to urban centers. The population of Sarajevo was 115,000 in 1945; by 1971 it had more than doubled, to 359,000; and by 1991 it stood at 527,000. The increase occurred mainly in the municipalities around the Old City, which drew in mainly ethnic Serbs from the countryside to work in the new factories, creating a new stratum of peasant-workers.

In keeping with Marxist doctrine, and mindful of the bloody history of Yugoslavia's peoples, the party stamped down hard on all signs of nationalist and religious deviations. The government of Sarajevo was entrusted to a republican party leadership that operated on a strict quota basis, with all the top jobs rotated in turn among Serbs, Muslims, and Croats. Bosnia was held up as a model of socialist "brotherhood and unity" (the party watchwords), and the 1981 census revealed Sarajevo as the most "Yugoslav" of cities. One in five Sarajevans chose to identify themselves as "Yugoslav," compared with about 5 percent nationally. As the gradual liberalization of Yugoslavia took hold, this sense of belonging to a community not defined by narrow ethnic ties bred an increasing cosmopolitanism in creative life. Sarajevo's intelligentsia was at the forefront of the flowering of the arts in Yugoslavia in the 1970s and 1980s that brought films, poetry, plays, and music to a national audience. Tourism opened a door to the wider world as well. The communists might anathematize religion, but they restored historic monuments in the quest for hard currency, and visitors from all over the world flocked to admire Sarajevo's unique cultural legacy. The growing status of Sarajevo as an international European city was confirmed in 1984 when the city was chosen to host the Winter Olympics.

The site where athletes competed before the world's cameras is derelict in the early twenty-first century. Changes in the international economy and security situation left Yugoslavia beggared within a few years, and nationalist conflicts destroyed Tito's Yugoslavia. In a final effort to retrieve its fortunes, the party called its Fourteenth Congress in January 1990 but the Croatian and Slovenian delegates walked out early in the proceedings. The chairman of the meeting called for a recess, from which the

Graffiti on a ruined building reflects the sentiments of Sarajevo residents during the siege of 1992–1995. ©HOWARD DAVIES/CORBIS

delegates never returned. The Communist Party of Yugoslavia disappeared during a coffee break.

THE SIEGE OF SARAJEVO AND AFTER, 1992–2005

There followed two years of political vacuum, at the end of which the European Union and the United States recognized Slovenia, Croatia, and Bosnia-Herzegovina as independent states (December 1991–April 1992). Sarajevans among all ethnic communities saw what was coming. They tried to assert the values of civilized society through mass demonstrations and avert war. In August 1991 one hundred thousand peace activists staged a rally in the city, and in September thousands formed a human chain linking places of worship of all the faiths—mosques, churches, and synagogues. Sadly, they failed in their efforts. The Bosnian Serbs, led by Radovan Karadžić (b. 1945), rejected the authority of the Sarajevo government, and proclaimed the Republika Srpska (Serb Republic) as an independent entity. A Bosnian Serb Army (BSA), fifty to eighty thousand strong, com-

manded by General Ratko Mladić (b. 1943), was formed out of purportedly Bosnian Serb personnel of the Yugoslav People's Army, and immediately laid siege to Sarajevo on 5 April 1992. The BSA inherited the immense firepower of the Yugoslav military machine, but lacked the manpower to take the city from its determined defenders, and the siege was not lifted until 29 February 1995.

From a strategic and military point of view Sarajevo had little significance for the Serbs compared with Banja Luka and Knin in northern Bosnia, but its symbolic and political importance was huge. By 2 May 1992 the noose had tightened around the city. Of the half-million or so inhabitants of Sarajevo, four hundred thousand were trapped, frequently near to starvation, and in constant fear of snipers. Queuing for water or going to market meant death for many. In two notorious incidents involving mortar-fire (5 February 1994 and 28 August 1995) 111 people were killed and hundreds injured. Artillery barrages from the heights surrounding Sarajevo also inflicted heavy casualties, although that was a random, impersonal danger. Shells rained down on the city at the rate of 329 for every day of the siege, with no other purpose than to destroy cultural monuments and civic infrastructure and so break the spirit of the city. Mosques were favored targets and the priceless treasures of the National Library went up in flames. By the time the siege was lifted, it is estimated that twelve thousand people had lost their lives, with another fifty thousand wounded, and thirty-five thousand buildings had been destroyed completely.

The first fourteen months were the worst. There was heavy fighting between ethnic factions within the city, as some Serbs tried to link up with the besiegers in the suburbs, and the sympathies of Western publics were not matched by the effective action of their governments. Matters improved after mid-1993, when the United Nations Protection Force (UNPROFOR) managed to open an overland supply route for humanitarian aid through Split, via Kupres and Vitez, and the United Nations contrived from time to time to secure the opening of the Sarajevo airport to airlifts. Crucially, engineers of the Army of the Republic of Bosnia-Herzegovina carried out the remarkable feat of digging a tunnel under the airport, with a light railway along which goods and people could be transported. Even so, the situation in Sarajevo remained dire. The plethora of memoirs and histories of the siege record all the range of human responses to extreme conditions. In the absence of a civil administration, gangsters carved up the city, and there were many instances of murder, rape, and looting as rival groups fought for supremacy. The gangsters had their uses, however: they helped to buy weapons through their criminal connections outside, while the Western embargo on arms to the Bosnian government was maintained. There are also many tales to tell of neighborliness, black humor, despair, and self-sacrifice—all of them stories of the sheer will to survive and to preserve the semblance of normal life. One witness recalls how crosses taken from the cemeteries were burnt for fuel in the bitter winter months; those so minded might find a pleasing symbolism here, connected with the reversal of the cycle of life and death.

During 1994–1995, military developments, and the greater activity of Western governments acting militarily through NATO, forced the Bosnian Serb Army back. The massacre of Bosnian Muslims at Srebrenica (July 1995) brought to a head steadily growing demands for the international community to put an end to the fighting, and the Dayton Accords, in December, finally allowed Bosnia-Herzegovina to sink into a sullen and exhausted peace. By this time the population of Sarajevo had been halved (250,000), but grew to an estimated 400,000 by 2002, as refugees poured back to their homes. In the Sarajevo canton (district), the biggest ethnic group by far (80 percent) in the early twenty-first century is the Bosniaks, the Bosnian Muslims, who have adopted this appellation as the distinctive name to express their ethnic identity, and in the Old City they account for virtually the entire population. The Serb presence in the canton is 11 percent, and Croats total 7 percent. Claims that 150,000 Serbs were the victims of ethnic cleansing are extremely improbable. They were allowed to leave by the Bosnian Serb Army at the beginning of the siege, and the most likely explanation is that they have chosen not to return, preferring to remain in Republika Srpska. Sarajevo is now a Bosniak city, its multiethnic past a memory.

Sarajevo is now the capital of an independent Bosnia-Herzegovina for the first time in its history, but sovereign power is limited by the overriding mandate of the United Nations' High Representative. Dayton created a federal Muslim-Croat entity in one half of the country, with the Republika Srpska comprising the other half. Taxation, defense, and internal security, the hallmarks of all state authority, are not under the control of the Sarajevo government, but divided in a complicated formula among three sources of authority. Bosnia is the poorest country in Europe, dependent on massive Western subventions, and only a quarter of Sarajevans have jobs. The physical damage to Sarajevo has been repaired as far as possible, but the problem of state-building is another matter altogether, and the future of the city is uncertain.

See also **Bosnia-Herzegovina; Karadžić, Radovan; Milošević, Slobodan; Mladić, Ratko; Tito (Josip Broz); World War I; Yugoslavia.**

BIBLIOGRAPHY

Benson, Leslie. *Yugoslavia: A Concise History.* Rev. and updated ed. Houndmills, Basingstoke, Hampshire, U.K., and New York, 2004.

Kapić, Suada. *The Siege of Sarajevo, 1992–1996.* Sarajevo, 2000.

Malcolm, Noel. *Bosnia: A Short History*. New York, 1994.

Nedzad, Kurto. *Sarajevo 1462–1992*. Sarajevo, 1997.

LESLIE BENSON

SARTRE, JEAN-PAUL (1905–1980), French philosopher.

Jean-Paul Sartre was born on 21 June 1905 in Paris and died on 19 April 1980 in Paris. A philosopher, novelist, dramatist, editor, polemicist, and political activist, Sartre came to public attention in 1938 with the publication of the novel *Nausea*. It was in the immediate postwar years, however, that intense public interest in his pessimistic philosophy of radical personal responsibility and political engagement—which came on the heels of publication of his 1943 philosophical work, *Being and Nothingness,* and was popularly known as existentialism—made him perhaps the most famous intellectual in the world.

Sartre was born into a comfortable Protestant and Catholic family. Upon the death in 1906 of his father, a naval officer who had taken part in colonial campaigns in Southeast Asia, Sartre moved with his mother to her parents' house outside of Paris. After studying at the prestigious lycées Henri IV and Louis-le-Grand in Paris, Sartre entered the competitive École Normale Supérieure, an institution of higher education that was designed to prepare teachers but also functioned as a training-ground for most of France's prominent intellectuals. Raymond Aron (1905–1983) and Paul Nizan (1905–1940) were classmates and friends, and another classmate, Simone de Beauvoir (1908–1986), placed second—behind only Sartre—on her *agrégation,* the graduating exam that entitled one to become a teacher. Sartre and Beauvoir met in 1929, the year of the exam. They developed a deliberately unconventional intellectual and amorous relationship that spanned fifty years.

During the 1930s Sartre taught philosophy at a high school in Le Havre. This period was characterized by intellectual exploration and political apathy. He was largely unaffected by witnessing the Nazi seizure of power in 1933 in Berlin, where he spent the year studying German philosophy, especially the phenomenology of Edmund Husserl (1859–1938). During this decade, Sartre published a number of minor works of philosophy, including *The Transcendence of the Ego* (1937). His career as a public figure was launched with the appearance of *Nausea,* whose pessimistic examination of the brute reality and meaninglessness of human existence caused a furor in Catholic-dominated France. Sartre's career was put on hold, however, at the beginning of World War II. He was mobilized in 1939 and captured in June 1940. While interned in a prisoner-of-war camp, he studied the philosophy of Martin Heidegger (1889–1976). In 1941 Sartre returned to Paris to teach high school. There he wrote the cryptically anti-Nazi play *The Flies* (1943) and took some small part in the intellectual resistance against German occupation.

It was also at this time that Sartre published his first great philosophical work, *Being and Nothingness.* The most important early influence on Sartre's philosophy had been Husserl, from whom Sartre took the idea that consciousness is always consciousness *of* something. Sartre adapted the idea to mean that consciousness is a practical activity that is always intentional in nature—that is, directed toward something that is not itself. From this idea, Sartre developed a philosophy of existence, or Being, that he divided into two categories: the for-itself (human consciousness) and the in-itself (inert matter). In his view, humans, unlike inanimate objects or animals, are conscious of themselves and of objects; they are constantly engaged in directed, intentional activity (although they are typically unaware of the most mundane of this activity). Moreover, he argued, this activity is radically free. Unlike the in-itself, which is completely present to itself and therefore cannot take a position either on itself or the world outside of it, the for-itself is pure spontaneity. Sartre claimed that consciousness is not a thing but rather as pure directed activity is a *nothingness,* and therefore no force other than its own can impinge upon it. The upshot of this description of the two regions of Being is that the radically free for-itself is always responsible for its actions, and to claim otherwise is to live in "bad faith."

Sartre's philosophical description of freedom and responsibility resonated strongly and immediately with the French public. After the war, *Being*

Jean-Paul Sartre, c. 1939. ©Hulton-Deutsch Collection/ Corbis

and Nothingness became a bestseller. Owing to the popularization of its ideas and to such plays as *No Exit* (1944), with its famed line, "Hell is other people," Sartre became one of the most well-known intellectuals in France and in the world, particularly in the Americas.

"Existentialism"—a word Sartre did not typically use to describe his own philosophy—became a cultural phenomenon, particularly among young people. Its basic tenet that existence precedes essence implies that all social rules, morality, and judgments about gender and race are social constructs and barriers to human freedom. His own unconventional lifestyle with Beauvoir in particular was cause for both fascination and moral censure. These attitudes increased when Beauvoir published *The Second Sex* (1949), a historical and phenomenological description of women as beings subordinate to men. Although Beauvoir considered

her own work to be derivative of Sartre's, there is considerable debate concerning her influence on the writing of *Being and Nothingness,* as well as Sartre's later turn toward limiting his notion of radically free subjectivity by examining the way that external circumstances do indeed constrain human choice.

During this period Sartre founded the most important French journal of the postwar era, *Les Temps Modernes* (Modern times), and he wrote the plays *The Respectful Prostitute* (1947), which took U.S.-style racism as its subject, and *Dirty Hands* (1948), which examined the moral dilemmas of communism. Increasingly interested in politics, Sartre announced a theory of intellectual engagement in his essay, "What Is Literature?" (1947), in which he argued that all literature must take as its object its era's most pressing concerns. With the beginning of colonial war in Indochina and the onset of the Cold War, the intellectual field became more polarized. Sartre gravitated toward socialism and remained critical of the oppressive and morally objectionable nature of communism. His reading of Georg Wilhelm Friedrich Hegel (1770–1831) and Karl Marx (1818–1883) during that time; his concern for supporting French workers, who were overwhelmingly communist; his abhorrence of the ongoing colonial war in Indochina; and his growing misgivings about the actions of the United States, particularly in Korea, led him to become a fellow traveler of the French Communist Party in 1952.

The 1956 Soviet intervention to put down the Hungarian revolution was the direct cause of Sartre's break with the Communist Party, as it was for many French intellectuals. By that year, a more important domestic event began to take center stage in Sartre's writing and activity: the Algerian war for independence, which began in 1954. In early 1956 Sartre sketched a critique of colonialism as a system whose primary objective was to produce a mass of subhuman beings who lacked political rights and economic power and thus could not contest their own exploitation. He would later argue in his preface to Frantz Fanon's (1925–1961) *The Wretched of the Earth* (1961) that the only means the Algerians had been given with which to contest this exploitation was violence—but a violence for which they were not responsible, as it was a "counterviolence" created by the violence of the system of exploitation itself.

The early 1960s marked an important turning point for Sartre. In 1960 he published the first volume of his second great philosophical work, *The Critique of Dialectical Reason*, which attempted to synthesize existentialism and Marxism and to provide an account of history in which the innumerable, random acts of individuals would lead to a single meaningful narrative. To do so, he introduced as his basic categories praxis and the practico-inert, arguing that human activity (praxis), though free, constantly creates structures (the practico-inert) in which praxis is embedded and that thus constrain that freedom. Also in this work, he devised a theory of revolutionary action that tried to account for the negative outcomes of revolution, such as Stalinism. The projected second volume, which was to complete the argument, was not published during Sartre's lifetime.

Sartre continued his involvement with Third World liberation movements by lending early support to Fidel Castro's (b. 1926 or 1927) regime (which he later criticized) in Cuba and advocating radical and sometimes violent means for gaining Algerian independence. As a result, a right-wing terrorist organization tried to assassinate him twice toward the end of the French-Algerian war by planting bombs in his apartment. In 1963 Sartre published his autobiographical work, *The Words*, and was awarded the Nobel Prize in 1964, but declined it. In the mid- to late-1960s Sartre became an activist for peace in Vietnam, presiding over the International War Crimes Tribunal initiated by Bertrand Russell (1872–1970) in 1967. In the closing speech to that body, Sartre argued that the United States' military tactics in Vietnam constituted genocide under its Geneva Convention definition. Sartre was recognized as a broad influence on and a supporter of the student revolutionaries of 1968.

In the 1970s Sartre became involved with young French Maoists who aimed, rather unsuccessfully, to organize French workers. His health failing, Sartre went blind in 1973. Yet he remained politically active, teaming up with Michel Foucault (1926–1984), Jean Genet (1910–1986), and other intellectuals to agitate against racial discrimination directed at non-European immigrants, and he continued his intellectual endeavors by publishing a massive, although unfinished, study of Gustave Flaubert (1821–1880). In 1980, the year of his death, Sartre published *Hope Now*, a controversial series of dialogues with Benny Lévy (1945–2003), his secretary at the *Temps modernes* and a young ex-Maoist who was rediscovering his Judaism. In this book Sartre appeared to renounce some of his earlier positions on the fundamental nature of conflict between individuals and on revolutionary violence. Sartre died shortly thereafter, and an estimated fifty thousand people attended his funeral.

See also **Aron, Raymond; Beauvoir, Simone de; Camus, Albert; Existentialism; France.**

BIBLIOGRAPHY

Primary Sources

Beauvoir, Simone de. *Force of Circumstance: The Autobiography of Simone de Beauvoir.* Translated by Richard Howard. New York, 1992.

Sartre, Jean-Paul. *Being and Nothingness: A Essay on Phenomenological Ontology.* Translated by Hazel E. Barnes. New York, 1956. Reprint, New York, 1984.

———. *The Critique of Dialectical Reason.* Vol. 1: *Theory of Practical Ensembles.* Translated by Alan Sheridan-Smith. London and Atlantic Highlands, N.J., 1976.

———. *Colonialism and Neocolonialism.* Translated by Azzedine Haddour, Steve Brewer, and Terry McWilliams. London and New York, 2001.

Secondary Sources

Aronson, Ronald. *Camus & Sartre: The Story of a Friendship and the Quarrel That Ended It.* Chicago, 2004.

Cohen-Solal, Annie. *Sartre: A Life.* Translated by Anna Cancogni. New York, 1987.

Murphy, Julien S., ed. *Feminist Interpretations of Jean-Paul Sartre.* University Park, Pa., 1999.

Poster, Mark. *Existential Marxism in Postwar France: From Sartre to Althusser.* Princeton, N.J., 1975.

Santoni, Ronald E. *Sartre on Violence—Curiously Ambivalent.* University Park, Pa., 2003.

Sorum, Paul Clay. *Intellectuals and Decolonization in France.* Chapel Hill, N.C., 1977.

PAIGE ARTHUR

SASSOON, SIEGFRIED (1886–1967), English poet.

Siegfried Lorraine Sassoon was one of those who, through poetry and memoir, fashioned the enduring image of the British soldier in the trenches of World War I. He was born in southeast England; his father, a Jew from a Sephardic family, died when the boy was nine, so he was raised by his mother, a Catholic. He developed a very un-Jewish taste for country life and hunting, and a more ecumenical flair for poetry. He passed through the finishing schools of the country gentry, Marlborough College and Clare College, Cambridge, where he matriculated in 1905 and left a year and a half later.

Sassoon volunteered for military service two days before the declaration of war in August 1914. He initially served in the Sussex Yeomanry, but later he was posted to the Royal Welch Fusiliers, where he met the poet and fellow junior officer Robert Graves. By 1916 the Sassoon family had lost one son. Siegfried's brother Hamo was mortally wounded at Gallipoli and buried at sea. A close friend, Tommy Thomas, was also killed. Sassoon took on increasingly dangerous missions on the western front in the aftermath of these losses. His nearly suicidal raids on German lines earned him the nickname "Mad Jack." He won the Military Cross for bringing back the wounded from no-man's-land. In the first week of the Battle of the Somme (July 1916), Sassoon approached a German trench on his own, threw four bombs into it, and was amazed to see fifty or sixty Germans fleeing in terror. Shortly thereafter he contracted enteric fever and was invalided home. He returned to France in February 1917 and was wounded in the shoulder.

It was at this time that Sassoon came to believe that the war was being continued for no reason at all. While on leave in London he met a number of pacifists, including the philosopher Bertrand Russell, and the circle of intellectuals and writers around Lady Ottoline Morrell. With their encouragement, he wrote his commanding officer to say he was not returning to the front and was prepared to face a court-martial in order to expose the insanity of the war. His letter appeared in the *Times* of London and was read into Hansard, the British parliamentary record, by Lady Ottoline's husband, Philip Morrell. The army was in a quandary. Sassoon was a decorated, brave officer. He could not be convicted of cowardice. Instead they decided that anyone who considered the war was insane must be insane himself. Rather than being court-martialed, Sassoon was sent for convalescence to Craiglockhart War Hospital just outside of Edinburgh.

There he met the physician W. H. R. Rivers, who saw right away that Sassoon did not suffer from shell shock but rather had an "antiwar complex." In extensive conversations, the two men shared their joint predicament. Rivers had to cure men of their illness in order to send them back to the place where they had become ill; Sassoon had to leave his men at the front in order to get them back from the front through protest and political pressure. Sassoon broke first. He could not stand the thought that anyone would construe cowardice in his decision not to go back to the front. So Rivers's patient was "cured" and returned to the men with whom he served, "in whose eyes I find forgiveness."

In his time at Craiglockhart, Sassoon befriended the fellow poet Wilfred Owen. They made an odd couple: Owen was about five feet tall; Sassoon more than six feet, six inches tall. But their poetry was very much on the same level. Together the two men produced some of the finest war poetry in English or in any other language. Owen was killed in the last week of the conflict, just before the Armistice on 11 November 1918. Sassoon was posted to Palestine and then back to France, where he was wounded again in July 1918. He survived the war.

In a way, Sassoon never left the trenches. His war poetry sold well and he became a literary figure in postwar England, befriending John Galsworthy, D. H. Lawrence, and Thomas Hardy, among others. He served as literary editor of the socialist newspaper the *Daily Herald* and then proceeded to put together the two volumes of his memoirs, which have become classics: *Memoirs of a Fox-Hunting Man* (1928) and *Memoirs of an Infantry Officer* (1930). These memoirs were presented jointly in the parody of John Bunyan's *Pilgrim's Progress* under the title *Sherston's Progress* (1936). He continued to write, but he never found a voice as powerful as that of the verse and prose that captured his trench experience. He did not serve in the Second World War and died in 1967.

See also **Owen, Wilfred; Russell, Bertrand; World War I.**

BIBLIOGRAPHY

Campbell, Patrick. *Siegfried Sassoon: A Study of the War Poetry*. London, 1999.

Moeyes, Paul. *Siegfried Sassoon, Scorched Glory: A Critical Study*. Basingstoke, U.K., 1999.

Quinn, Patrick J. *Missing Muse: The Early Writings of Robert Graves and Siegfried Sassoon*. Selinsgrove, Pa., 1994.

Thorpe, Michael. *Siegfried Sassoon: A Critical Study*. London, 1966.

Wilson, Jean Moorcroft. *Siegfried Sassoon: The Making of a War Poet*. London, 1999.

JAY WINTER

SAUSSURE, FERDINAND DE (1857–1913), Swiss linguist.

Ferdinand-Mongin de Saussure was born in Geneva, Switzerland, on 26 November 1857. He studied at the University of Geneva and subsequently at the University of Leipzig. In 1878, while still a student, he published *Mémoire sur le système primitif des voyelles dans les langues indo-européennes* (Memoir on the primitive system of vowels in the Indo-European languages). This work proposed a highly original solution to a complicated problem in comparative philology and gained him an early reputation among specialists in the field of language studies.

In 1880 he moved to Paris and for ten years taught at the École des Hautes Études. In 1891 he returned to Geneva on being appointed to a professorial post at the university. The lectures on general linguistics, on which Saussure's main claim to fame rests, were courses delivered to students in the years 1907–1911. They remained unedited at Saussure's death in 1913, but his students' notes were collated, amalgamated, and published as a single book three years later by two of Saussure's colleagues, Charles Bally and Albert Sechehaye. This was the celebrated *Cours de linguistique générale* (Course in general linguistics), which was to become for many scholars the authoritative statement of the theoretical basis of modern linguistics as an academic discipline.

Given the circumstances surrounding the posthumous publication, it is hardly surprising that questions have been raised about the extent of editorial intervention in the shaping and content of the text. The editors themselves queried whether Saussure would have approved. But in spite of misgivings, Saussure's name has remained firmly attached to the main doctrines set out in the text first published in 1916. These may be summarized as follows.

1. Autonomy of linguistics. Saussure was concerned to establish that linguistics, though closely connected to anthropology, sociology, psychology, and physiology, was nevertheless an independent discipline with its own aims and methods. The program of this independent discipline, according to Saussure, comprised (i) the description and history of all known languages, (ii) investigating the forces universally and permanently operative in all languages and establishing general laws that would explain all particular linguistic phenomena, and (iii) defining linguistics itself.

2. Primacy of speech. Saussure regarded linguistics as dealing essentially with human speech. Writing, for him, was not a linguistic phenomenon, but a different and subsidiary form of communication, having as its function the representation of speech.

3. *Langue* and *parole*. The disciplinary autonomy of linguistics was based on distinguishing clearly between *la langue*, the collective speech system of the community, and *la parole*, the practical use of this system by individuals. For Saussure, the former took priority over the latter. Although he promised his students lectures on *la parole*, these lectures were never given. What we have in the *Cours* is almost exclusively concerned with *la langue*.

4. Synchrony and diachrony. Saussure insisted on separating the study of the language system as existing at a given point in time (synchrony) with the study of changes that might intervene over a period of time (diachrony). He regarded the confusion of synchronic with diachronic facts as one of the main weaknesses of language studies in his day.

5. The linguistic sign. Saussurean linguistics recognized only two axioms. The first was the arbitrariness of the linguistic sign and the second was its linearity. What Saussure understood by "absolute arbitrariness" was the total lack of connection between the form (*signifiant*) of the sign

and its meaning (*signifié*), though he also recognized "relative arbitrariness" in cases where components of a sign are independently meaningful (as in *nineteen = nine + ten*). For Saussure, both *signifiant* and *signifié* were psychological in character. As regards linearity, Saussure assumed that every utterance consists of a single chain of sound in which all items are sequenced one by one in an arrangement of simple concatenation. Linearity is the basis of "syntagmatic" (as distinct from "associative") relations. Associative relations are based on similarity of form or meaning. Thus in *Fish swim, fish* and *swim* combine syntagmatically, while *fish* and, say, *herring,* are related associatively (in this instance, semantically). Both axioms are essential to Saussure's conception of linguistic analysis.

6. Semiology. Saussure envisaged linguistics as one part of a more comprehensive study of the life of signs in society, which he termed *sémiologie* (often misleadingly translated into English as "semiotics").

7. Structuralism. Although Saussure never used this term himself, his view of each *langue* as a homogeneous, self-contained whole, within which all units are defined solely by their mutual relations, was often called "structuralist." It became extremely influential after his death not only in linguistics but also in anthropology, literary studies, and other fields.

Later interpreters picked out particular elements in Saussure's teaching that suited their own agenda, while ignoring the rest. Literary and artistic theorists seized on the doctrine of arbitrariness and used it to validate forms of literature and visual art that would otherwise have been dismissed as worthless, even degenerate. Many of Pablo Picasso's paintings and James Joyce's "unreadable" novel *Finnegans Wake* (1939) are examples. As late as 1965, Joseph Kosuth used Saussurean underpinnings to present a controversial tripartite exhibit at the Museum of Modern Art in New York. It comprised a chair, a photograph of the chair, and a blown-up image of the text of a dictionary entry for the word *chair.* In psychoanalysis, Jacques Lacan (1901–1981) achieved notoriety by claiming that the unconscious was structured in the arbitrary manner of a language. This claim rescued Sigmund Freud (and others) from the necessity of explaining the

logic of the connection between patients' symptoms and the meanings attributed to them by the analyst. Perhaps the most striking use of Saussure was in the field of anthropology. There Claude Lévi-Strauss (b. 1908) invented a whole discipline ("structural anthropology") dedicated to the idea that a society's culture consists of many systems (kinship, costume, cuisine, myths, etc.), each of which is structured like a language and can be analyzed accordingly. Most of these applications would almost certainly have surprised and possibly dismayed Saussure.

See also **Barthes, Roland; Semiotics.**

BIBLIOGRAPHY

Primary Sources

Saussure, Ferdinand de. *Course in General Linguistics.* Edited by Charles Bally and Albert Sechehaye. Translated by Roy Harris. London, 1983. Translation of *Cours de linguistique générale,* 2nd ed. A critical edition of the French text, giving variants from the students' notes, was published by Rudolf Engler (Wiesbaden, Germany, 1968).

Secondary Sources

Culler, Jonathan. *Saussure.* 2nd ed. London, 1986.

Harris, Roy. *Saussure and His Interpreters.* 2nd ed. Edinburgh, 2003.

ROY HARRIS

SCHMIDT, HELMUT (b. 1918), German politician.

Helmut Heinrich Waldemar Schmidt was the fifth chancellor of the Federal Republic of Germany (West Germany) from 1974 to 1982. Born in Hamburg in 1918, he served in the Wehrmacht (German army) and attained a degree in economics in 1949. Schmidt's political career took off during the first postwar decade. Active in the Hamburg Social Democratic Party (Sozialdemokratische Partei Deutschlands, or SPD), he was elected to the Bundestag (federal parliament) in 1953. A leading member of the SPD's postwar generation, Schmidt established himself as an expert on finance and security questions during the 1950s and 1960s. During the chancellorships of Konrad Adenauer (1949–1963) and Ludwig Erhard

(1963–1966), he worked with Willy Brandt and other SPD leaders to edge the party away from socialist economic and anti-Western security policies toward an acceptance of market economics, NATO, and the European Community. With the culmination of this strategy came the formation of the Grand Coalition in 1966, a power-sharing arrangement that featured the Christian Democrat Kurt Georg Kiesinger as chancellor, Brandt as foreign minister, and Schmidt as leader of the SPD's parliamentary group.

After the 1969 elections, Brandt replaced Kiesinger as chancellor and formed a ruling coalition with the smaller liberal Free Democratic Party (Freie Demokratische Partei, or FDP). Schmidt assumed a series of important posts within the new government. As defense minister he supported Brandt's diplomatic opening to the East, the New Ostpolitik, while maintaining strong ties with Washington, London, and Paris. In 1972–1974, amid the country's growing economic difficulties, Schmidt took over as finance minister and economics minister. His popularity persisted through the first oil crisis (1973–1974) and a deepening economic recession, even as Brandt's suffered a precipitous decline. In the wake of revelations about an East German spy in his entourage Brandt resigned, leaving the chancellorship to Schmidt in May 1974. In 1976 Schmidt secured reelection by a small margin, beating back a challenge from the Christian Democratic candidate, Helmut Kohl (b. 1930).

As chancellor, Schmidt focused his energies on the Federal Republic's economic problems. At home he instituted a policy of fiscal austerity—a break with the previous government—and made the battle against inflation and for economic growth his main priority. This caused strains with Brandt, who had stayed on as SPD chairman, and with the party's left wing, but served as glue for the coalition with the Free Democrats, long supporters of a free-market orientation. Abroad, Schmidt and his foreign minister, the FDP chairman Hans-Dietrich Genscher (b. 1927), worked through multilateral channels to cope with international economic problems. In 1975 Schmidt and Valéry Giscard d'Estaing (b. 1926) of France organized the first of a series of annual meetings of leading industrialized countries—later known as the G-7 and G-8 summits—to discuss and coordinate macroeconomic policies. During the late 1970s, both men initiated the European Community's Exchange Rate Mechanism (ERM), a successful effort to foster economic convergence and inject new momentum into the flagging European integration process.

During the early 1980s a confluence of international and domestic policy problems overwhelmed Schmidt's chancellorship. Growing East-West tensions undermined his multilateral approach to foreign policy. Schmidt had always prided himself as a mediator between East and West, a strong supporter of the West open to dialogue and diplomacy with the East. This stance proved very popular through the 1970s and contributed to his 1980 reelection victory over Franz-Josef Strauss (1915–1988), leader of the Bavarian Christian Social Union (Christlich-Soziale Union, or CSU) and foreign-policy hawk. But the Soviet invasion of Afghanistan in 1979 and crackdown on Solidarity in Poland in 1981 combined with U.S. sanctions and arms buildup to undermine East–West détente. Schmidt's efforts to engage the Soviet leadership in continued dialogue aroused the suspicions within the administrations of Jimmy Carter (b. 1924) and Ronald Reagan (1911–2004). In late 1981 he managed to persuade Reagan to enter negotiations over intermediate-range nuclear forces (INF) in Europe. But despite Schmidt's best efforts to foster a compromise, no progress was made through the summer of 1982.

By that point Schmidt's domestic political position had unraveled. His popularity had remained high through the late 1970s, reinforced by the country's relatively strong economic performance and the success of his campaign against the terrorism of the radical Red Army Faction. But the second oil crisis of 1979 and subsequent recession undermined Schmidt's economic policies and political fortunes. After his 1980 victory over Strauss, a renewed emphasis on fiscal austerity drew sustained criticism from within the SPD. Brandt provided cover for a series of younger party leaders on the party left, who were upset about Schmidt's perceived cooperation with the INF policies of the Reagan administration and abandonment of the party's traditional strong support for the welfare state. SPD disunity and the FDP's eagerness to press ahead more forcefully with austerity measures brought the coalition to the breaking point. In October 1982 Genscher and the FDP abandoned

Schmidt and joined a CDU-led government under Kohl.

See also **European Union; G-8 Summit; Germany; Welfare State.**

BIBLIOGRAPHY

Primary Sources

Schmidt, Helmut. "A Policy of Reliable Partnership." *Foreign Affairs* (spring 1981).

————. *Men and Powers: A Political Retrospective.* Translated from the German by Ruth Hein. New York, 1989.

Secondary Sources

Carr, Jonathan. *Helmut Schmidt: Helmsman of Germany.* New York, 1985.

THOMAS BANCHOFF

SCHMITT, CARL (1888–1985), German legal theorist.

Carl Schmitt was among the most important and controversial legal theorists of twentieth-century Europe. Schmitt's work raised profound questions about sovereignty, legitimacy, and the viability of liberal parliamentarism, while his life raised profound questions about the appropriate relationship between philosophical thought and political action.

Schmitt was born in the Protestant Westphalian town of Plettenburg, into a family that was politically active and devoutly Catholic. Despite his family's limited means, Schmitt's brilliance earned him a scholarship to a good gymnasium, where he received a humanistic, liberal education. He studied jurisprudence in Strasbourg, Munich, and Berlin, completing his *Habilitationschrift* (second dissertation) in 1914.

Schmitt volunteered for the infantry at the beginning of World War I, but a back injury meant that he spent the war in Munich in the noncombat position of censor. After the war he took an academic position at Bonn, where he became an outspoken champion of the traditional Right. He advocated in the courts and in the journals for the Weimar constitution's emergency provision (Article 48) as a means of curbing the excesses of Communist and Nazi agitators. Among his influences at this time was Max Weber, and among his interlocutors was Leo Strauss. Schmitt joined the Nazi Party in May 1933. A prestigious teaching post in Berlin was his reward. Celebrated as the Nazi "crown jurist," he publicly supported Adolf Hitler's "Night of the Long Knives," though a close friend of Schmitt's was among its victims. When doubt was cast on his loyalty in 1936 and his own safety came into question, Schmitt quietly left the party. His writings of the time were incisive but emphatically anti-Semitic, characteristics reflected in his decidedly theological postwar notebooks.

After the war, Schmitt was arrested and brought to Nuremberg but never tried. Though banned from teaching, he remained a highly regarded figure among German legal scholars throughout the twentieth century. He was honored with Festschriften, collections of essays, on his seventieth and eightieth birthdays, which included articles by luminaries such as Reinhart Koselleck. Schmitt died at the age of ninety-six in Plettenburg, the town where he was born, just as the force of his work began to dawn on English-speaking scholars.

Schmitt's ideas revolve around an opposition between the value neutral, rule governed, and technical on one hand, and the decisive and political on the other. He opposes "the political" and "the sovereign" to what can be discussed scientifically or executed technologically. In *The Concept of the Political* (1932), Schmitt describes the political as a decision based on the criterion of friendship or enmity. By "enemy" Schmitt means one who poses a threat to a people's way of life. Deciding who the enemy is cannot rest on further criteria or norms. Liberalism's fault is precisely its incapacity to decide based on "political" criteria alone. Schmitt argues in *The Crisis of Parliamentary Democracy* (1923) that liberalism is instead characterized by ceaseless discussion and by the domination of private interests that depoliticize and hence dehumanize public life. Because law cannot rule on its own, legitimacy cannot rest on formal legal positivism or rational discussion. *Legality and Legitimacy* (1932) thus advocates a system where the *Reichspräsident* can act as a "commissarial dictator," a concept Schmitt first explored in *Dictatorship* (1921). The dictator must be able to defend the constitution unchecked by a parliament too neutral to outlaw parties (such as the Communists and Nazis) who explicitly aim to destroy it. Schmitt's preference for decisive and unitary action is also reflected in his definition of "sovereignty" in *Political Theology* (1922) as characteristic of he who "decides on the exception." The constant possibility of an unexpected crisis means someone must be above norms, able at any moment to decide who the enemy is and then to act decisively to destroy it.

Hannah Arendt, Franz Neumann, and Walter Benjamin are among those influenced by Schmitt's work, which took on a renewed importance across the political spectrum in the last two decades of the twentieth century. He is the Right's philosopher of unified leadership, of politics that leaves liberal fantasies for the comfort of the bourgeoisie. For the Left, he challenges liberal parliamentarism's illusory neutrality, its cooptation by private, class-based interests. Despite his popularity at the turn of the twenty-first century, the question remains whether Schmitt's ideas are separable from his political past. While his participation in Nazi politics does not, of itself, negate the value of his thought, the compatibility of his ideas with Nazism suggests that scholars should be cautious in drawing on his ideas without carefully considering their ramifications.

See also **Arendt, Hannah; Communism; Liberalism; Nazism.**

BIBLIOGRAPHY

Primary Sources

Schmitt, Carl. *The Concept of the Political.* Translated by George Schwab. New Brunswick, N.J., 1976.

————. *The Crisis of Parliamentary Democracy.* Translated by Ellen Kennedy. Cambridge, Mass., 1985.

————. *Political Theology: Four Chapters on the Concept of Sovereignty.* Translated by George Schwab. Cambridge, Mass., 1985.

————. *Legality and Legitimacy.* Translated by Jeffrey Seitzer. Durham, N.C., 2004.

Secondary Sources

Dyzenhaus, David. *Legality and Legitimacy: Carl Schmitt, Hans Kelsen, and Hermann Heller in Weimar.* Oxford, U.K., 1997.

McCormick, John P. *Carl Schmitt's Critique of Liberalism: Against Politics as Technology.* Cambridge, U.K., 1997.

Meier, Heinrich. *The Lesson of Carl Schmitt: Four Chapters on the Distinction between Political Theology and Political Philosophy.* Translated by Marcus Brainard. Chicago, 1998.

Schwab, George. *The Challenge of the Exception: An Introduction to the Political Ideas of Carl Schmitt between 1921 and 1936.* New York, 1986.

NOMI CLAIRE LAZAR

SCHOENBERG, ARNOLD (1874–1951), Austrian-born composer, teacher, and theorist.

Through both his music and writings, Arnold Schoenberg influenced the evolution of music in the first half of the twentieth-century more than any other composer. He was born in Vienna and spent much of his life there, with several periods in Berlin (1901–1903, 1911–1915, and 1925–1933); during the last of these periods he was Ferruccio Benvenuto Busoni's successor at the Prussian Academy of Arts. Nazi anti-Semitism led him to immigrate to the United States in 1933, where he settled in Los Angeles, teaching at the University of California. Even though his music was often attacked and never widely performed, his rejection of tonality before World War I and development of the twelve-tone method afterward profoundly influenced composers in both Europe and the United States.

Although his early works (1899–1906) follow in the Romantic tradition of Richard Wagner and Johannes Brahms, Schoenberg's contrapuntal and motivic complexity and increasing chromaticism led to expressionist or atonal works (1907–1916) that radically depart from the harmonic conventions of earlier European music. Schoenberg described atonality as the "emancipation of dissonance," and found that it required new harmonic procedures that later proved crucial to his twelve-tone method. Schoenberg's atonal pieces constantly vary and develop motivic material—he later termed this "developing variation"—and use phrase structures that are continuous and asymmetrical rather than periodic and balanced. Developing variation, coupled with freedom from tonality, produced motives and themes that seldom repeat and frequently use all twelve pitches of the chromatic scale. Simultaneously, asymmetrical phrase structures allowed Schoenberg to reconceive musical texture. No longer bound by traditional textures of theme and accompaniment, he explored new polyphonic textures, densely structured by multiple voices. His atonal style well suited the expressionist aesthetic shared by many Viennese at the time. Just as visual artists abandoned representation and conveyed emotions with abstract forms, Schoenberg rejected traditional forms and textures to create a contextual style with immediacy, spontaneity, intense expression, and—most important—brevity. (Examples are Three Piano Pieces, op. 11; *Erwartung* [Expectation], op. 17; and *Pierrot Lunaire,* op. 21.)

By 1916, Schoenberg apparently had exhausted the potential of atonality, for he published no new works for seven years. Later, he wrote that he used these years to systematize new harmonic procedures that could generate longer forms. In "Composition with Twelve Tones," Schoenberg explained that only after he conceived of musical space in "two-or-more dimensions" and learned to exploit all twelve chromatic pitches did he arrive at the basic principles of the twelve-tone method. These principles are quite simple: the pitch material of each piece is structured by a unique ordering of the twelve pitches of the chromatic scale (called a row or series). The series can appear in different forms (retrograde, inversion, and retrograde inversion), and all forms can be transposed. Crucially important, the order of the twelve pitches in the series must not vary in all its forms and transpositions. Because harmonic space has two or more dimensions and because the series determines the ordering of pitches but not their registers or durations, the series can unfold in many different configurations. In Schoenberg's view, the value of the twelve-tone method was that it could generate longer musical forms than could his atonal procedures.

From 1923 until 1933, Schoenberg published pieces that developed and consolidated the twelve-tone method. (See especially Suite for Piano, op. 25; Wind Quintet, op. 26; Suite [Septet], op. 29; String Quartet no. 3, op. 30.) While the new method further solidified his reputation as an innovator and revolutionary, his twelve-tone works are in a profound sense conservative. They re-create traditional forms (for example, sonata form, rondo form, and baroque dance forms) and use more traditional textures and phrase structure than his atonal works. Schoenberg's modernist aesthetic—in which the artist as revolutionary prods art along its evolutionary path—ironically rested on Hegelian ideas common among nineteenth-century Romantics. While art without innovation was inconceivable to him, Schoenberg believed its relentless evolution also had to be connected to the past. His new method of composing older forms fits well with these aesthetic beliefs.

Although his twelve-tone works had little success with the critics or the public, Schoenberg had extraordinary influence on European composers, partly through his writings and teaching. No composer before him wrote as extensively about compositional techniques. Most important was *Harmonielehre* (Theory of harmony), published in 1911, and later came studies of counterpoint, composition, and form. Schoenberg was one of the most recognized teachers of his day, counting among his students Anton Webern and Alban Berg, who both took his twelve-tone technique and developed it into their own distinctive styles.

The profound disillusionment of artists after World War II led many European composers to reject their cultural heritage, including the neoclassical style that dominated France and Germany before the war. Turning to Schoenberg's revolutionary new method, composers like Olivier Messiaen and his students Pierre Boulez and Karlheinz Stockhausen extended serial techniques to dynamics, rhythm, and articulation (referred to as *integral serialism*). While adopting Schoenberg's serial method, Boulez and Stockhausen took Webern's music as their primary model. They criticized Schoenberg for his timidity in returning to older textures and forms that failed to develop the true potential of the method. Other prominent serial composers in the early 1950s were Luigi Nono, Luciano Berio, Henri Pousseur, and Luigi Dallapiccola.

By the late 1950s, over-systemization of the smallest components of musical structure had led to lack of contrast, a sameness in sound, and a lack of formal direction. Composers such as Boulez and Stockhausen then began using serial procedures only for larger features of form, such as textural density, durations among sections, and registral transformations. These procedures depart from Schoenberg's, but derive from his twelve-tone method.

In the United States, Schoenberg's music was harshly reviewed and seldom played, but he had continued influence. Milton Babbitt was his principal disciple, extending Schoenberg's serial techniques in a direction different from the Europeans. Several of Schoenberg's American works engage religious and spiritual topics, exploring both Jewish issues and the repercussions of fascism (for example, *Ode to Napoleon Buonaparte*, op. 41; *A Survivor from Warsaw*, op. 46; his unfinished opera *Moses and Aron*). Several works composed close to his death return to nontraditional forms and recapture some of the expressive spontaneity of his atonal works (for example, String Trio, op. 45, and Violin Fantasy, op. 47). Immediately after Schoenberg's death in 1951, Igor Stravinsky (Schoenberg's fellow émigré in Los Angeles and archrival) dropped his popular neoclassical style and, until his death in 1972, adopted serial techniques (though quite unlike Schoenberg's). By the end of the twentieth century, serialism—and Schoenberg's influence—were still alive, but now only as one compositional method among many.

See also **Berg, Alban; Boulez, Pierre; Modernism; Stravinsky, Igor.**

BIBLIOGRAPHY

Primary Sources

Schoenberg, Arnold. *Letters.* Edited by Erwin Stein. Translated by Eithne Wilkins and Ernst Kaiser. London, 1964.

————. *Fundamentals of Musical Composition.* Edited by Gerald Strang. London, 1967.

————. *Theory of Harmony.* Translated by Roy E. Carter. Berkeley, Calif., 1983.

————. *Style and Idea: Selected Writings of Arnold Schoenberg.* Edited by Leonard Stein. Translated by Leo Black. New York, 1975. New expanded edition, Berkeley, Calif., 1984.

————. *Sämtliche Werke.* Edited by Josef Rufer and Rudolf Stephan. Mainz, Germany. 1966–2002.

Secondary Sources

Dahlhaus, Carl. *Schoenberg and the New Music.* Translated by Derrick Puffett and Alfred Clayton. Cambridge, U.K., 1987.

Hyde, Martha M. "Dodecaphony: Schoenberg." In *Models of Musical Analysis: Early Twentieth-Century Music,* edited by Jonathan Dunsby, 56–80. London, 1993.

Neighbour, Oliver W. "Arnold Schoenberg." In *The New Grove Second Viennese School,* edited by Stanley Sadie, 1–85. New York, 1983.

Schoenberg, Berg, and Webern: A Companion to the Second Viennese School. Edited by Bryan R. Simms. Westport, Conn., 1999.

Stuckenschmidt, Hans H. *Arnold Schoenberg: His Life, World, and Work.* Translated by Edith Temple Roberts and Humphrey Searle. London, 1977.

MARTHA M. HYDE

SCHOOL OF PARIS. The School of Paris is not a school in the strict sense of the term, as applied by Walter Adolph Gropius (1883–1969) to the Bauhaus, nor is it simply a group of artists working in Paris. Its more complex genesis is connected with social and political conditions and with modern artistic practices during the period 1910–1930 in Paris. Artists of different nationalities and various disciplines settled in Montmartre or Montparnasse before the First World War and thus formed a melting pot of foreign artists who had fled their countries of origin or were drawn to Paris as a cultural center. The most famous of these included Marc Chagall, Pablo Picasso, Tsuguharu Foujita, Amedeo Modigliani, Juan Gris, Moise Kisling, Jacques Lipchitz, and Ossip Zadkine. This cosmopolitan circle was mainly based in La Ruche—a pavilion that was still standing from the 1900 Exhibition—which housed some artists' studios. On this site, around one hundred forty artists, painters, and sculptors, both immigrants and French (including Henri Laurens, Alexander Archipenko, Fernand Léger, Moise Kogan, and Chaim Soutine) associated with writers and poets such as Guillaume Apollinaire or Blaise Cendrars. These particular conditions contributed to this dual production that was both literary (proliferating through publication in many New York journals) and artistic.

A COSMOPOLITAN SCHOOL

In addition to their precarious social situation (no status and little income), the foreign artists were confronted with the difficulties of exhibiting their work in the face of the "official" French artists.

The political, social, denominational, cultural, and linguistic differences of these artists revived the anti-Semitism and xenophobia that had been exacerbated by the context of the First World War. Then, the economic crisis of the 1930s was leaving marks of hatred throughout Europe and contributing to the rise of the extreme right. Confronted with this rise in racism and xenophobia characterized by an underlying reticence toward the artistic cosmopolitan circle, some Parisian critics sought to establish legitimacy for the innovative artists, in the awareness that the latter were helping to transform the Parisian art scene by simultaneously bringing their own artistic practice and personal experience to bear. In January 1925, in a series of articles in *Comœdia* and a book published in October 1925 entitled *Les berceaux de la jeune peinture: L'École de Paris* (The cradles of modern painting: The School of Paris), André Warnod coined the name *School of Paris* and championed a contemporary French independent art from the Academy against the official art. He wanted the foreign artists to be integrated alongside the French artists. He strongly accorded "recognition to the art of foreigners working in Paris" and emphasized the fact that "the School of Paris exists. Art historians of the future will be better placed than we are to define its nature and to study its constituent elements, but we can still assert its existence and its magnetic force, which is bringing us artists from all over the world.... The part played by the works of Picasso, Pascin, Foujita and so on in contemporary art is well known" and the foreign artists "also definitely assert the existence of the School of Paris." Warnod's recognition of this "school" marked the resurgence of Paris as an artistic center and gave legitimacy to the foreign artists living and working there since the beginning of the twentieth century and producing independent modern art. The School of Paris became a reflection both on artistic matters and on cultural acceptance. The production of a body of painting by national geniuses gave way to a cosmopolitan painting. It was not until the end of the 1920s that several exhibitions were held by the School of Paris. The sixteenth Venice Biennale in 1928 devoted a room to the School of Paris that was separate from the room in which French art was represented.

The different artistic practices formed a productive melting pot. In painting from 1911, the cubism of Georges Braque and Picasso, inspired by primitivism, was exhibited at the Salon des Indépendants. The movement was joined by Juan Gris, Alexander Archipenko, Diego Rivera, Jean Crotti, Alice Bailly, Gino Severini, and Leopold Survage. Sonia Delaunay, Marc Chagall, Amadeo de Souza-Cardoso, and Frantisek Kupka were sensitive to the chromatic contrasts of "Orphism." Piet Mondrian produced abstract paintings that resulted from a new interpretation of art, while other painters, such as Jules Pascin, Kisling, Eugene Zak, Chaim Soutine, Foujita, and Modigliani, continued with figurative art and portraiture. Constantin Brancusi's sculptural practices (he set off from Romania on foot in 1904 to reach Paris) presented reflections on the honing of the figure and on the plinth not only as a pedestal but also as an integral part of the art work. Joszef Csaky and Jacques Lipchitz transposed cubist explorations into three dimensions. Ossip Zadkine produced "primitive" sculptures with refined forms, while Foujita, Modigliani, and Archipenko pursued their pictorial reflections in sculpture.

From the 1920s, artistic activity in Paris also changed through the practice of photography. A group of independent foreign photographers such as Brassaï (Gyula Halász, who lived in Paris from 1924 and published *Paris after Dark* in 1933), Man Ray (who came from New York), André Kertész (a Hungarian artist like Brassaï), Paul Outerbridge, George Hoyningen-Huene, Berenice Abbott, Germaine Krull, Laure Albin-Guillot, and Madame D'Ora (most of the photographers in the School of Paris were women) produced mainly photographs combining Parisian elements with ones from their countries of origin. In May 1928 the first Salon Indépendant de la Photographie was opened.

The continuation of the School of Paris and its international impact from 1910 to 1920 were due to the support of foreign art dealers. Paris became the setting for meetings between artists, writers, poets, intellectuals, dealers, and collectors in the circle of the American writer Gertrude Stein (who settled in Paris in 1903), who played a fundamental role in the exchanges between Paris and the United States while giving huge support to the foreign artists working in Paris. The breakthrough of artists from the School of Paris became increasingly apparent in the 1920s and 1930s. The circulation of art works via the activity of foreign art dealers once again legitimized the name "School of Paris" and defined the French capital as a modern metropolis and forum of exchange until the outbreak of the Second World War, which encouraged artists to flee to the United States.

SECOND SCHOOL OF PARIS

From 1941, there was a revival of figurative painting that prepared the way for a second "School of Paris." After the Second World War, the abstract work of action painters such as Hans Hartung, Pierre Soulages, Gerard Schneider, and of *informel* artists such as Jean Dubuffet and Jean Fautrier, or again the artists of the Denise René gallery, gave rise to new explorations. The term *School of Paris* was used once again, thenceforth as an obsolete and clumsy reference to a Parisian scene that was at the center of artistic creative production at the beginning of the twentieth century. In 1947 the opening of the Jeu de Paume gallery and the Musée National d'Art Moderne in Paris testified to a desire for rapprochement between French cultural institutions and contemporary painting. The "elders" of the School of Paris were thenceforth consecrated there. It seems fitting to give the final words to Constantin Brancusi, who said in 1922: "In art, there are no foreigners."

See also **Avant-Garde; Braque, Georges; Chagall, Marc; Gropius, Walter; Picasso, Pablo; Stein, Gertrude.**

BIBLIOGRAPHY

Brassaï. *Paris after Dark.* Translated by Stuart Gilbert. New York, 1987.

Chapiro, Jacques. *La Ruche.* Paris, 1960.

Dorival, Bernard. *L'École de Paris au Musée national d'art moderne.* Paris, 1961.

L'École de Paris, 1904–1925: La part de l'autre: Musée d'Art Moderne de la Ville de Paris, 30 novembre 2000 au 11 mars 2001. Paris, 2000.

L'École de Paris? 1945–1964. Luxembourg, 1998.

Warnod, Jeanine. *L'École de Paris: Dans l'intimité de Chagall, Foujita, Pascin, Cendrars, Carco, Mac Orlan, à Montmartre et à Montparnasse.* Paris, 2004.

CAROLINE TRON-CARROZ

SCHRÖDER, GERHARD (b. 1944), German politician.

Gerhard Schröder became the seventh chancellor of the Federal Republic of Germany in 1998. Born in 1944 in Mossenberg, Schröder studied law in Göttingen and rose within the youth wing of the Social Democratic Party (Sozialdemokratische Partei Deutschlands, or SPD) in Lower Saxony. He belonged to a younger generation of SPD leaders that emerged out of the 1968 student movement and rose within the party ranks under the Federal Republic's first two SPD chancellors, Willy Brandt (1969–1974) and Helmut Schmidt (1974–1982). Schröder was elected to the Bundestag (federal parliament) in 1980. After a CDU-led government under Helmut Kohl succeeded Schmidt in 1982, he turned his attention to state-level politics and was elected to two terms as governor of Lower Saxony (1990–1998). In September 1998 Schröder bested Kohl in national elections and formed a coalition with the Green Party, which entered national government for the first time. The "red-green" coalition secured reelection in 2002.

Both as governor and as chancellor, Schröder's main field of interest and action has been economic policy. A protégé of Schmidt, he emerged as a prominent representative of the reform wing of the SPD, committed to economic modernization. As governor of Lower Saxony, Schröder implemented a series of measures designed to improve regional competitiveness, including a reform of the civil service, and became well-known for his high-profile, direct negotiations with industrial leaders. His overall record was mixed. Lower Saxony attracted increased levels of capital investment during his tenure, but its overall level of unemployment remained higher than the national average. Schröder's reputation as an economic manager contributed to his reelection in 1994 and again in 1998, shortly before he ran as his party's candidate for the chancellorship.

Schröder's main rival for SPD leadership during the 1990s was Oskar Lafontaine (b. 1943), governor of the Saarland and leader of the party's left wing. A proponent of a robust welfare state, Lafontaine replaced Rudolf Scharping as party leader after the latter lost to Kohl in the 1994 elections. Amid the country's economic downturn of the late 1990s, the result both of the financial burdens of reunification and of a slumping European and international economy, Schröder's reputation as an economic manager and strong campaigner helped to secure the nomination for 1998. After his victory over Kohl, Schröder brought Lafontaine into his government as finance minister. But a half year later differences over the extent and trajectory of economic and social reform sparked Lafontaine's resignation and Schröder's assumption of the position of party chairman. He then tried, with mixed success, to slow the growth of social spending, overhaul the pension system, and modernize Germany's system of higher education. The new immigration law of 2002, which simplified naturalization for foreigners living in the country, was one of the major legislative accomplishments of his first term in office.

In the field of foreign policy, Schröder and his foreign minister, Joschka Fischer of the Greens, pursued a pragmatic course. Schröder combined an Atlantic and pro–European Union (EU) orientation with economic support for and cooperation with Russia and East and Central Europe. In 1999 he overcame opposition within the pacifist wing of his own party and approved the deployment of German troops as part of NATO's multinational forces in the Balkans. The second half of Schröder's first term was overshadowed by the terrorist attacks of 11 September 2001 and the U.S.-led response. Schröder and Fischer supported U.S. intervention against the Taliban in Afghanistan late that year and sent a small contingent of German troops to join in the effort. But both men refused the entreaties of the administration of George W. Bush (b. 1946) to support military action against Iraq. Schröder's refusal to participate in an invasion—even under eventual UN auspices—proved popular with the German electorate and contributed to his electoral victory over Edmund Stoiber of the Bavarian Christian Social Union (Christlich-Soziale Union, or CSU) in September 2002.

Schröder's second term began under difficult circumstances. He worked, with limited success, to improve relations with the Bush administration after the March 2003 invasion of Iraq strained transatlantic relations. At the same time he successfully pressed for the accession of ten East and Central European countries to the EU in May 2004. On the domestic front, the combination of continued high unemployment and slow growth led to a precipitous drop in Schröder's popularity. In the wake of a string of SPD losses in state elections, he gave up the post of party chairman and redoubled the government's effort to reform Germany's social welfare and labor market policies in a more market-friendly direction. In 2003–2004 his reform efforts met resistance within the SPD and with the Greens even as they were impeded by the Christian Democratic majority in the Bundesrat, or federal chamber. The fate of those reforms was bound up with his own political fate—in the elections held in September 2005, Schröder lost to Angela Merkel, the leader of the conservative Christian Democratic Union (Christlich Demokratische Union Deutschlands, or CDU).

See also **Brandt, Willy; Germany; Schmidt, Helmut; Social Democracy.**

BIBLIOGRAPHY

Camerra-Rowe, Pamela. "Agenda 2010: Redefining German Social Democracy." *German Politics and Society* (March 2004).

Harlen, C. M. "Schröder's Economic Reforms: The End of Reformstau?" *German Politics* 11, no. 1 (2002): 61–80.

Patzelt, Werner. "Chancellor Schröder's Approach to Political and Legislative Leadership." *German Politics* 13, no. 2, (June 2004): 268–299.

Vinocur, John. "Downsizing German Politics: Gerhard Schroder, Man from the Plains." *Foreign Affairs* 77, no. 5 (September/October 1998).

THOMAS BANCHOFF

SCHUMAN, ROBERT (1886–1963), French politician.

Few politicians destined to play a leading role in Franco-German reconciliation and in European integration could have been better placed than Robert Schuman. Born in Luxembourg, he grew up in Metz, which since the Franco-Prussian War of 1870–1871 had been part of Germany. He attended university in Bonn (along with Konrad Adenauer) and Munich and took his law degree in 1912 from Humboldt University in Berlin. Having survived the war, he returned to Metz (now a French city once again) in 1918 and owing to influential contacts with steel magnates, was elected *député* for the Moselle *département* (county) in 1919. During the interwar years, he belonged to the Parti Républicain Populaire—a Christian Democrat formation—and devoted his energies to helping his region adapt to life as part of France.

His close friendship with the prime minister Paul Reynaud (1878–1966) saw him appointed in 1940 to the ministry for refugees, but his early ministerial career was short-lived. As a lifelong conservative, he sympathized with and briefly joined the Vichy regime of Philippe Pétain (1856–1951) but left to play a minor part in the Resistance, associating himself with the nascent Christian Democrat Republican Popular Movement (Mouvement Républicain Populaire, or MRP). Elected to the National Bureau of the MRP in 1945, Schuman soon achieved national prominence, notably after his return to parliament later that year for his old constituency of Moselle. The following year, he was appointed minister of finance, pursuing classical liberal policies designed to curb inflation and to strengthen the franc. But the instability of the French party system under a tripartite coalition of Communists, Socialists, and Christian Democrats could not withstand the onset of the Cold War (1945–1989). After the exclusion of the Communists from government in 1947, Schuman became prime minister from November to July 1948. In that position, he battled with Communist strikers and an ongoing financial crisis, only temporarily staved off by his negotiation of stop-gap aid from the United States pending the arrival of aid via the Marshall Plan.

Thereafter, he was appointed foreign minister, a post he was to dominate under ten successive administrations until January 1953, one of the rare instances of ministerial stability in the ill-fated Fourth Republic. It was in this post that he carried out most of the work that remains associated with his name. Schuman adopted a dual program: Atlanticism and Europeanism. Cultivating close links with the U.S. ambassador Jefferson Caffery, he was instrumental in supporting both the Marshall Plan and the creation of the North Atlantic Treaty Organization (NATO), whose ratification he ensured by an impassioned speech in parliament in July 1949. However, he had misgivings about U.S. policy in Korea.

But it was his contribution to European integration that secured him his place in history. As a child of both Germany and France, he more than anybody sensed that reconciliation was the only policy. It had been resistance to the ambient French desire to restrict German coal and steel production that had led to the fall of his own government in 1948. But Schuman understood politically what the French economist Jean Monnet (1888–1979) had devised pragmatically: that punitive measures against German production were detrimental to France and the whole of Europe. He therefore embraced Monnet's scheme for the pooling of coal and steel in the European Coal and Steel Community (ECSC) and put his own name behind the "Schuman Plan." In his speech launching the plan in May 1950, he said: "World peace cannot be safeguarded without the making of creative efforts proportionate to the dangers which threaten it. . . . The coming together of the nations of Europe requires the elimination of the age-old opposition of France and Germany." The pooling of coal and steel, he concluded, "will make it plain that any war between France and Germany becomes not merely unthinkable but materially impossible." The objective was primarily political; the method economic and industrial. There, in a nutshell, is the initial essence of the European integration project. Schuman went on to defend Jean Monnet's other brainchild, the (stillborn) European Defence Community, a position that eventually led to his departure from the French government. It was above all his devotion to a Catholic universalism and his belief in the value of West European civilization, which he saw as threatened by communism, that drove Schuman toward his Europeanist positions.

The volatility of political life under the Fourth Republic severely disrupted one of its most promising careers. Although Schuman briefly served as justice minister in 1956–1957, his political influence ended with the return to power of Charles de Gaulle (1890–1970) in 1958. However, fittingly, he was elected to be the first president of the European Parliament in 1958. He died in 1963.

The main square at the heart of the European Community institutions in Brussels, featuring the European Commission on one side and the European Council on the other, is named after Schuman. In 2004, in recognition of his devout

Catholicism, Pope John Paul II (r. 1978–2005) set in motion the process that could lead to his beatification.

See also **European Coal and Steel Community (ECSC); European Union; Monnet, Jean.**

BIBLIOGRAPHY

Primary Sources

Monnet, Jean. *Jean Monnet–Robert Schuman: Correspondance, 1947–1953.* Lausanne, France, 1986.

Secondary Sources

Lejeune, René. *Robert Schuman (1886–1963): Père de l'Europe.* Paris, 1988.

Meier, Barbara. *Robert Schuman.* London, 2004.

Poidevin, Raymond. *Robert Schuman.* Paris, 1988.

JOLYON HOWORTH

SCHUMPETER, JOSEPH (1883–1950), Austrian economist and sociological theorist.

Joseph Alois Schumpeter was in his lifetime an influential figure in economics. Now he is thought of more as a fertile sociological theorist. Born in the Austro-Hungarian Empire in the Czech province of Moravia, he was successively a practicing lawyer before the Mixed Tribunals in Egypt (1907–1908) representing the interests of foreign investors there, an instructor in law and economics in the Universities of Vienna and Czernowitz (Cernauçi, Romania; 1909–1911), and professor of economics at Graz University (1911–1918).

The defeat of the empire in 1918 and its dismemberment into separate national units, an event that he regarded as tragic, propelled him to political eminence as minister of finance of the rump state of "German Austria" (1919). He was forced to resign that post in the same year when the Social Democratic Party, seeking to nationalize a large steelworks, the Alpine-Montangesellschaft, exposed the less-than-transparent way in which he had thwarted them by selling the company's shares for foreign exchange to support the weakening Austrian currency on international exchange markets. He became president of the Biedermann Bank (1921–1924), but his financial help to a group of Hungarian nobles who staged in Austria a bungled

coup against the communist regime of Béla Kun (1886–1937) in Hungary forced his resignation.

There were few prospects of a return to academic life in Austria for a supporter of the restoration of the emperor who was also an opponent of any merger with the postwar German Republic, but it was, ironically, a German University, Bonn, that offered him a post as professor of public finance (1925). Soon, however, the Nazi movement, with its implicit threat to the independence of Austria, persuaded Schumpeter to emigrate further. After twice being visiting professor of economics at Harvard University he accepted a permanent post there in 1932. He served a spell as president of the American Economic Association, and it was in the United States that he wrote his later works and died.

Born in the same year as John Maynard Keynes (1883–1946), he was similarly influenced by the Great Depression of 1929. He interpreted such downward cyclical movements as "creative destruction," replacing outdated production methods by new technologies. Like Keynes, he argued that monetary and fiscal policies should be used to accelerate a return to equilibrium. He questioned, however, the value of economic equilibrium as a concept. Economic policy, he argued, had always to operate on an economy in perpetual movement and therefore in unique historical circumstances. Any state intervention in the economy beyond short-term relief was necessarily acting in ignorance.

Schumpeter's later works can be understood as an extended description and theoretical interpretation of a long-run process of economic development and social change, to much of which equilibrium was irrelevant. It could not, he argued, explain the movement of capital, of interest rates, or entrepreneurial initiative. He questioned the prevailing views that the competition of individuals generated uniquely advantageous conditions for economic growth and that rational expectations were a sound analytical basis for economic theory and policy. From such standpoints he constructed a dynamic analysis of economic development. The insertion of cultural factors into this description led to a vision of capitalism with some affinity to that of Karl Marx (1818–1883), of powerful forces working to destroy any existing equilibrium so that it might never again become attainable. All economies, he believed, would become "socialist," in the sense that entrepreneurs would no longer be dynamic individuals but, instead, major corporations. Nevertheless, innovation would remain the driving force in development and for this, investment, sound money, interest, and entrepreneurship remained essential. Because these depended on a society whose base was private property, Schumpeter came politically to one conclusion diametrically opposite to those of Marx; only in a capitalist society would economic development take permanent root.

His work led to attempts to formalize and categorize the particularities of societies that generated a higher proportion of entrepreneurial activities. Such work was far from mainstream economic theory, and historical research provided only contradictory answers. For their wide range of intellectual inquisitiveness, many of Schumpeter's publications remain, nevertheless, stimulating and relevant.

See also **Depression; Keynes, J. M.**

BIBLIOGRAPHY

Primary Sources

Schumpeter, J. A. *Business Cycles: A Theoretical, Historical, and Statistical Analysis of the Capitalist Process.* 2 vols. New York, 1939.

———. *Capitalism, Socialism, and Democracy.* 3rd enl. ed. New York, 1970.

Secondary Sources

Shionoya, Yuichi, and Mark Perlman, eds. *Schumpeter in the History of Ideas.* Ann Arbor, Mich., 1994.

Stolper, Walfgang F. *Joseph Alois Schumpeter: The Public Life of a Private Man.* Princeton, N.J., 1994.

Swedberg, Richard. *Joseph A. Schumpeter: His Life and Work.* Cambridge, U.K., 1991.

ALAN S. MILWARD

SCIENCE. In the sixteenth and seventeenth centuries Europe was the birthplace of the scientific revolution, and in the eighteenth and nineteenth centuries many of the greatest discoveries had been made by European scientists. In the twentieth century this situation changed, and while European scientists continued to dominate most fields of science in the decades before World War II, the United States became, in the second half of the century, the world's paramount scientific power. During the first half of the twentieth century many American physicists and chemists felt their educations were incomplete without doctoral and postdoctoral studies at European universities, but after World War II young European scientists flocked to American universities and industries. This "brain drain" from European countries was in part due to the sumptuous financial support they received for their research. Other evidence for this change in the geographical focus of scientific achievement is in the Nobel Prizes. Europeans won a preponderance of the Nobel Prizes in science during the first half-century of the awards, but in the next fifty years American scientists surpassed their European colleagues. For example, between 1980 and 2003 the United States had 154 science laureates compared to Europe's 68.

Europe has been and continues to be an important part of Western science, and in the period from World War I to the early years of the twenty-first century European science experienced changes that were characteristic of Western science. For example, scholars have studied the accelerative changes of Western science, and some have concluded that the exponential growth of scientific knowledge in Western countries during the twentieth century far surpassed, both quantitatively and qualitatively, all scientific developments in previous centuries. Derek J. de Solla Price, the father of scientometry, has taken a nuanced approach in his studies on the growth of numbers of scientists, their specialized fields, their journals and articles, and so on. For example, in his study of the output of scientific papers before, during, and after the upheavals of the twentieth century, he found that, while Great Britain's output remained substantially stable, such countries as France and Germany experienced decreases, whereas other European countries, which had previously been minor scientific contributors, experienced exceptional growth. The Soviet Union in particular, even though isolated by Cold War politics, multiplied its production of scientific papers in spectacular fashion due to the ability of members of the Soviet Academy of Sciences to take advantage of insecurities among political leaders and obtain immense financial support for scientific research.

Many Soviet scientists and those scientists in other European countries who worked for industries emphasized the applications of discoveries for practical purposes. Science for the sake of science, or pure science, flourished in Germany before and after the Nazi period. When Paul Forman, John Heilbron, and Spencer Weart did a study of physics at various academic institutions, they found that such European countries as Britain and Germany retained their prominence in pure science throughout the early decades of the twentieth century, but the United States, beginning in the 1930s, showed signs of achieving the world leadership that American physicists would consolidate in the second half of the twentieth century.

In both Europe and the United States, twentieth-century scientific changes were increasingly sophisticated and complex, with the multiplication of many disciplines and subdisciplines. Through his researches Derek J. de Solla Price has documented the growth of what he called "big science." The American Manhattan Project to build the atomic bomb, which profited from the help of many émigré European scientists, is a classic example of big science, but such international endeavors as CERN, the European Organization for Nuclear Research, which required thirty million dollars to construct and further millions in annual operating costs, illustrate that, though science on this scale was no longer financially feasible for individual European countries, collaboration could bring such results as basic discoveries in high-energy physics, even though these had little or no practical benefits. Besides expensive facilities, big science required large numbers of scientists and technicians. The need for ever larger research teams meant ever greater government support, and this had both good and bad consequences. These massive endeavors produced valuable discoveries that would not have been possible in the modest laboratories characteristic of "little science," but scientists often found that government money came with restrictions on their curiosity and creativity. For example, they experienced pressure to choose research projects with a greater likelihood for practical applications. The public also became concerned about the exorbitant price of making what some saw as esoteric and irrelevant discoveries, whereas other European citizens expressed alarm about certain discoveries in physics and biology that posed potential dangers to human life and the environment. Indeed, some scientists founded organizations to alert the public of these dangers and to campaign for their control or elimination.

THE EVOLUTION OF EUROPEAN SCIENCE (1914–2004)

Twentieth-century European achievements in the traditional and new sciences are too extensive to analyze in detail, but common themes and illustrative examples can provide a sense of the significant changes that occurred in European science during a tumultuous time. Such achievements as general relativity and quantum mechanics revolutionized the earlier accomplishments of Isaac Newton's gravitational theory and John Dalton's atomic theory. Other European discoveries were made in such new hybrid fields as biochemistry, geophysics, and molecular biology. Two world wars and the Cold War hindered Europeans in many areas of pure and applied science, particularly when compared to the United States, but despite these difficulties the range and depth of European contributions are impressive.

In physics the two most important modern theoretical discoveries were made by Europeans. During World War I, while working at the University of Berlin, Albert Einstein published his general theory of relativity, which interpreted gravitation as due to the curvature of space-time. In the 1920s the French physicist Louis de Broglie developed a wave theory of such subatomic particles as the electron, and this later helped the Austrian physicist Erwin Schrödinger formulate his wave mechanical model of the atom, which was shown to be equivalent to an earlier formulation of quantum mechanics that its German discoverer, Werner Heisenberg, called matrix mechanics. European physicists were also at the forefront in using X rays to determine the structures of many important crystals. The most fundamental discoveries in atomic and nuclear physics were also the work of Europeans. For example, in 1932 the English physicist James Chadwick discovered the neutron, a particle that played an important role in the 1938 discovery of nuclear fission by Otto Hahn and Fritz Strassmann (correctly interpreted by Otto Frisch and Lise Meitner as the splitting of the atomic nucleus). Leo Szilard, a Hungarian Jewish physicist who fled to the United States, realized that the fission of the uranium nucleus might produce a chain reaction, an idea that was the basis of both the nuclear reactor and the atomic bomb.

In the life sciences Europeans participated in momentous discoveries both before and after World War II. For example, the Scottish bacteriologist Alexander Fleming discovered the antibiotic penicillin in 1928, and the German biochemist Gerhard Domagk, while working for IG Farben, discovered the first of the antibacterial sulfa drugs. These and other drugs saved many lives both during and after World War II. However, according to many scholars, the most important discovery in the life sciences was the double helical structure of deoxyribonucleic acid (DNA) in 1953 by an American, James Watson, and an Englishman, Francis Crick, while working at the Cavendish Laboratory of Cambridge University. This discovery proved to have far-reaching consequences not only for biology but also for medicine and many other fields, including criminology.

SCIENCE AND POLITICS

Twentieth-century European governments influenced both the progress and retrogression of science in the decades from World War I to the start of the twenty-first century. Particularly in peacetime, several European governments provided financial support for scientific research through such institutions as the British Department of Scientific and Industrial Research (founded in 1916), the Consiglio Nazionale delle Ricerche in Italy (founded in 1923), and the Caisse Nationale des Sciences in France (founded in 1930). In Germany, the Kaiser Wilhelm Society (Kaiser Wilhelm Gesellschaft) founded many research institutes. When Einstein moved to Berlin from Switzerland he became the director of the Kaiser Wilhelm physics institute. Because of his enormous prestige, Einstein was able to keep his position even though he ardently opposed World War I. Max Planck, Einstein's friend and fellow physicist, initially signed the Manifesto of the Ninety-Three Intellectuals, written in support of the German invasion of Belgium, but he became the only signer to recant publicly. After the war Planck became president of the Kaiser Wilhelm Society and worked with the Weimar government to rebuild German science.

British biochemist Alexander Todd posing with a model of the DNA molecule, 1957. Todd won the Nobel Prize in Chemistry for his work in synthesizing nucleotides, compounds that form the structural units of DNA and RNA. LIBRARY OF CONGRESS

A much studied case of the influence of politics on science occurred in the Soviet Union during the 1930s and succeeding decades. Trofim Denisovich Lysenko, a Ukrainian biologist interested in genetics, came to believe that he could improve wheat strains by manipulating the environment. Lysenko was conducting his research during the massive forced collectivization of Soviet agriculture, which caused the starvation of millions of peasant farmers. Lysenko, whose views on the inheritance of environmentally acquired characteristics were repudiated by most biologists, provided Soviet politicians, especially Joseph Stalin, with a seemingly easy way out of the crisis and one that meshed with communist economic and philosophic theories. Lysenkoism, as Lysenko's pseudoscientific theory came to be called, turned out to have a devastating effect on Soviet agriculture and biology.

World War II strengthened government control of science in many European countries, especially Germany and the Soviet Union. Some scholars have called Nazism the first systematic antiscience movement that had sufficient political power to translate its ideology into what proved to be horrendous social policies. Adolf Hitler's ideologues developed an "Aryan science," one of whose policies was the destruction of the "Jewish physics" of Einstein. These policies forced not only Einstein but many other talented Jewish scientists to leave Germany for Britain and the United States. The racist ideology of Aryan science resulted in the deaths of millions of Jews, Gypsies, Poles, and others deemed to be subhuman. It also led to the horrific medical experiments by Josef Mengele in one of the Auschwitz concentration camps. In another sphere, Hitler shunted funds from an incipient atomic bomb project, headed by Werner Heisenberg, to the V-2 rocket project, headed by Wernher von Braun.

After World War II the British helped revivify German science by setting up the Max Planck Society (Max Planck Gesellschaft), which sought to maintain and expand the successes of the Kaiser Wilhelm Society by ridding it of the corruptions caused by previous Nazi control. By the end of the Nazi period the number of Kaiser Wilhelm institutes had declined to thirteen, but by 1990 the number of Max Planck institutes had grown to seventy-seven. The West German government also fostered close cooperation between these institutes and the educational system. Funding for scientific research increased not only in Germany but also in other European countries after the war. This funding helped slow the "brain drain" of European scientists to the United States.

Increased government involvement led to European developments in nuclear reactors and nuclear bombs. In contrast to the American emphasis on water-cooled reactors, Britain and France chose to develop gas-cooled systems. France, in particular, became more heavily reliant on nuclear power for its energy than any other European country. Politics played a primary role in the Soviet Union's development of the atomic bomb (first tested in 1949), as it did for the British and French atomic bombs. Because of lavish government support, the Soviet Union had, by the early 1980s, the world's largest community of scientists. Many of these scientists participated in such big-science projects as artificial satellites. The Soviet Union surprised the world by orbiting Sputnik in 1957, and this was followed by the first dog in space,

the first man in space, and the first images of the previously unseen side of the moon.

The scientific and technological successes of Nazi Germany and the Communist Soviet Union served to counter those scholars who claimed that only politically democratic societies could foster such achievements. The collapse of the Soviet Union in 1991 revealed how complex the interaction between politics and science can be. Although Russian scientists in the 1990s now had freedom, their productivity declined precipitously, mainly due to a financial crisis that caused research budgets to be drastically cut. Russian biologists were ideologically free to accept Mendelian genetics, but they lacked the funds to do significant DNA research.

The collapse of the Soviet Union and the federalization of the European Union helped to change the nature of European science. Scientists from Eastern and Western Europe were now free to move to whatever country offered them the best opportunity to pursue their research. After "brain drains" from Western Europe to the United States and from Eastern to Western Europe, several governments came to the realization that policies that encouraged private, industrial, and government support for research would help to stabilize what had been a debilitating loss of scientific talent.

SCIENCE AND TECHNOLOGY

During the eighteenth and nineteenth centuries, discoveries in various European countries had a significant influence on technology. The primary example, of course, is the industrial revolution, which occurred first in England in the eighteenth century and then spread to France and other countries. Many scientific discoveries in the twentieth century also led to new industries. For example, the detailed understanding of chemical structure developed by European chemists contributed to such successes as the German dye and drug industries. Some of Europe's largest dye companies diversified into pharmaceuticals, pesticides, and plastics. These companies also played a formative role in the development of industrial research laboratories, where chemists continued to invent new materials, some of which led to the formation of other industries.

Scientists in various European countries contributed to the creation and development of new technologies in both world wars. For example, the

German-Jewish chemist Fritz Haber was the moving force behind the development and use of poison gases in World War I, which initiated modern chemical warfare. Ernest Rutherford, the British discoverer of the atomic nucleus, helped to develop scientific techniques for discovering and destroying German U-boats. During the late 1930s and throughout World War II, scientists in Britain, Germany, and the United States invented increasingly sophisticated radar systems. The network of radar installations lining the British coast helped the English win the Battle of Britain. Also helpful in the British war effort were such code breakers as Alan Turing, a computer pioneer who used electronic machines to decode letter sequences produced by the German Enigma coding device. This important work provided the foundation for later information-based industries.

After the war, the United States, whose science-based industries escaped the conflicts unscathed, was able to out-compete European companies until the 1960s, when revived industries such as the German chemical and automobile makers were able to acquire significant global market shares. In the 1970s European countries began to coordinate their research and development. For example, the European Science and Technical Research Committee (CREST), with representatives from many countries, began in 1974 to examine various projects, with a particular emphasis on energy. Committee members had the power to commit their governments to such research projects as the Joint European Torus (JET), with the goal of producing a commercial thermonuclear device for generating vast amounts of energy.

SCIENCE AND ECONOMICS
The connections among science, technology, and economic growth are complex. With two world wars, the Great Depression, and several economic recessions and recoveries, the economic picture of twentieth-century Europe was also complex. Nevertheless, economists have noticed a rough correlation between a country's expenditures on research and development (compared to the gross national product) and its per capita income. Rich countries were able to spend a greater proportion of their national wealth on research and development than poor countries, and some evidence indicates that this investment contributed to the rich countries getting richer. However, the relationship between science and the economy is more cryptic than these generalizations indicate. For example, money poured into pure scientific projects often have no (and sometimes even a deleterious) effect on the economy. Furthermore, when scientific discoveries do have the potential to be developed into technologies that might have a beneficial impact, government or company officials have to decide which discoveries to choose.

Although economics is often described as a social science, it has not developed laws as predictive as the sciences of astronomy, physics, and chemistry. Moreover, the goals of scientists often differ from those of economists and politicians. After the devastation of World War II, many scientists, politicians, and economists recognized that science and technology would play a formative role in economic recovery, but it would be a slow process since new infrastructures would have to be built and new scientists and technicians educated. Eventually several European countries recovered their economic health. They then realized that a new era of global competition necessitated some type of collective management of science, technology, and industrialization. The Organization for Economic Cooperation and Development was founded to deal with these issues. Similarly, the European Research Council, with the power to act independently of its member nations, had the goal of fostering scientific research that would make Europe more competitive than its global rivals. However, some scientists have been critical of these organizations, pointing out that the research institutes that have been most successful were those run by scientists, not by bureaucrats or technocrats.

Throughout the history of twentieth-century Europe, it has been difficult to understand how to measure the costs and benefits of scientific research. Budgets and benefits differ between big and little science, academic and industrial research, and between various scientific disciplines and subdisciplines. In certain European countries some government-sponsored research has been criticized because of the unjustified dominance of prestigious professors at large universities (to the detriment of gifted scientists working at small universities). Other critics pointed to certain sciences that received the lion's share of government grants. For example, during the 1960s in Great Britain, half of the Science Research Council's budget went to nuclear physics and a quarter to space research, with only 25 percent for all other sciences.

Similar disparities occurred in the distribution of research and development funding to corporations. For example, aerospace industries received over a hundred times as much as railroad companies. Furthermore, as modern sciences and technologies have developed, the costs for equipment and personnel have also increased. Consequently, expenditures for science increased multiplicatively in the period after World War II in such countries as Great Britain, Germany, and the Soviet Union. Some scholars believe that this exponential growth of money for science cannot continue, and a saturation point will eventually be reached. However, others, basing their predictions on the law of accelerating growth exemplified in the computer industry (where computers have become exponentially more powerful and less expensive), believe that science is indeed an endless frontier where new discoveries will create powerful technologies that will fuel greater economic growth.

SCIENCE AND SOCIETY

Several scholars have divided their analysis of the influence of science on twentieth-century European society into the pre– and post–World War II periods. In the nineteenth century and the pre–World War I period science, according to these scholars, had only a modest influence on the lives of most people, even in such highly scientific countries as Germany and England. The most important impact of science on ordinary people was through such technologies as the electric light, telephone, and automobile.

In the interwar period European countries experienced a revulsion against the poison gases that had caused over a million casualties in World War I, including 91,000 deaths, and this led, in 1925, to the Geneva Protocol outlawing all use of chemical and biological weapons, which was ratified within a few years by France, Italy, Germany, and Britain (but not by the United States until 1975). An even stronger revulsion against nuclear weapons followed World War II, leading to the founding of various organizations whose goal was the elimination of nuclear weapons from Europe and the world. Other groups blamed scientists for inventing pesticides such as DDT, whose rediscovery by a Swiss chemist, Paul Müller, in 1939 led to its massive use during and after World War II. Public concern over the negative effects of this chemical on birds and humans led to its being banned in America and various European countries in the late 1960s and early 1970s. When the worst nuclear power plant accident in history happened at Chernobyl in Ukraine in 1986, a radioactive cloud spread westward across Europe, contaminating countries as far from the Soviet Union as Great Britain. This accident made several European countries, but not France, more hesitant to rely on nuclear power for their increasing energy needs.

Although these examples of the negative social consequences of science and technology could be multiplied, so, too, could the positive social consequences. For example, improved understanding of such infectious diseases as smallpox led to its eradication from Europe (and, by 1980, from the rest of the world). Improved diets, drugs, and medical procedures led to the lengthening of healthy lifespans in most European countries. Despite these examples, some scholars point out that it is actually difficult to analyze the influence of science on European societies, since this influence differed from country to country, from upper to lower economic classes within countries, and from government to military to industrial to academic and other institutions.

Some scientists, concerned about the negative social consequences of certain scientific discoveries, formed organizations such as the British Society for Social Responsibility in Science. Members of this organization hoped to heighten scientists' awareness of the social impact of their work and to make politicians and citizens cognizant of how decisions about scientific and technological research and development can have a good or bad effect on society. These organizations soon discovered that they were but one of many pressure groups seeking to influence government policies related to science and technology. For example, Eastern European countries have been plagued by severe pollution problems, but politicians have been reluctant to develop stringent regulations about pollutants because of their high costs in a weak economy.

Some sociologists of science have studied the factors that tended to inhibit the development of scientific research in various European countries after World War I. For example, Joseph Ben-David discovered that countries having universities with scientific institutes dominated by distinguished professors tended to be slow to introduce new disciplines or to effectively exploit new scientific discoveries. In another study, which compared academic and industrial research laboratories, scholars found that laboratories whose research teams and leaders took risks comparable with their human and technical resources tended to be more successful than laboratories whose leaders and researchers showed excessive deference to the officials who controlled their funding.

Besides influencing society through academia, industry, and government, scientists also influence society through the diffusion of scientific knowledge. As such issues as global warming, genetically modified food, nuclear wastes, and ozone-layer depletion illustrate, it is necessary for the public to be scientifically well informed in order that enlightened science policies be put into action. Surveys of the public in various European countries on this topic have generated some surprising results. For example, in Germany social scientists discovered that the degree of citizen interest in science-policy issues depended on how involved they were in general political issues. These studies also revealed a discrepancy between government and citizen priorities about which scientific issues were most important. Since most citizens learn about science from newspapers, magazines, and television rather than from scientific journals, scientists have attempted to bridge the gap between experts and laypeople by educating journalists through such organizations as the European Initiative for Communicators of Science. With the increasing complexity of scientific theories, popularization of modern science has not been easy, and one study found that the gulf between scientists and the European public actually widened during the second half of the twentieth century.

SCIENCE AND CULTURE

Because culture involves the totality of socially transmitted arts, beliefs, institutions, and many other products of human ingenuity, analyzing the impact of science on the cultures of a variety of European countries is a daunting task. Nevertheless, by isolating certain branches of culture, such as religion, philosophy, art, music, and literature, and certain countries, such as England and Germany, some sense of the breadth and depth of the interaction between science and culture can be achieved. In 1959 C. P. Snow, an English scientist and novelist, proposed in *The Two Cultures and the Scientific Revolution* that modern culture was becoming increasingly split between traditional humanistic culture and modern scientific and technological culture. Humanistic critics responded that only one culture existed, theirs, and later scholars argued that Snow had oversimplified complex cultures and subcultures with his polarization.

Although religious influence on various European countries lessened during the twentieth century, the interactions between science and religion have continued to interest scholars. Because there are so many different religions and fields of science, potential interactions among these in various countries can become mind-bogglingly complex. Nevertheless, some conclusions can be drawn. European scientists tend to be more atheistic or agnostic than the general public, and religious scientists, be they Christian, Muslim, or Jew, experience little problem in accepting scientific theories and the facts that they try to explain. In 1925 the British philosopher Alfred North Whitehead argued in *Science and the Modern World* that European religious developments in previous centuries actually prepared the way for twentieth-century science. Even traditional European conflicts between science and religion, as exhibited by the opposition between creationism and evolutionism, were mitigated in twentieth-century Europe, and Pope John Paul II expressed his (and his church's) acceptance of evolutionary theory, which he felt was compatible with a Christian teleological understanding of the world. Albert Einstein stated in 1940 that "science without religion is lame, religion without science is blind."

Important European scientific discoveries during the period from 1914 to 2004 also influenced philosophy. For example, Einstein's special theory of relativity forced philosophers to deepen their analyses of time, simultaneity, the spatial dimensions, matter, and energy. His general theory of relativity forced philosophers to rethink their views on the interactions between space and matter. Werner Heisenberg's uncertainty principle called classical determinism into question. Neo-Darwinism, a twentieth-century blending of Darwinian natural selection and Mendelian genetics, influenced both left-wing and right-wing philosophers. Social Darwinists of the Left emphasized cooperation in nature to bolster their socialistic political philosophies, whereas social Darwinists of the Right emphasized competition in nature to bolster political philosophies ranging from laissez-faire capitalism to Nazism. According to some scholars, science and philosophy after World War II became deeply divided, with most scientists believing that philosophy was totally irrelevant to what they were doing. Nevertheless, philosophers of science continued to analyze the conceptual basis of modern scientific theories.

Some humanists have questioned whether modern science has had a beneficial or deleterious effect on artistic creativity in twentieth-century Europe. Opinions vary about modern art, but agreement exists about the influence of science on particular artistic movements. For example, in *Einstein, Picasso: Space, Time, and the Beauty that Causes Havoc* (2001), Arthur I. Miller analyzed parallelisms between Einstein's relativity theory and Picasso's cubism, especially in their creation of new ideas of space and time. The scientific analysis of the persistence of vision influenced such artistic representations of motion as Marcel Duchamp's *Nude Descending a Staircase* (1912).

Science influenced twentieth-century European music by means of new instruments, methods, and compositions. With the improved scientific understanding of acoustics, electricity, and materials, inventors were able to create such new instruments as the theramin, synthesizers, and the electric guitar. Paul Hindemith's opera *Die Harmonie der Welt* (1957; The harmony of the world) was based on the life of the astronomer Johannes Kepler, who, like Hindemith, was trying to discover the secrets of the universe. Composers such as Iannis Xenakis and Edgar Varèse deliberately modeled their creative techniques on mathematics and the new physics. Xenakis used the Maxwell-Boltzmann law in composing *Pithoprakta* (1955–1956), game theory in composing *Duel* (1958), and group theory in composing *Nomos alpha* (1966). For Varèse, the scientist represented a creative

individual with access to the mysteries of nature, a theme he developed in his unfinished *L'astronome* (1928–1929). Varèse combined electronic and traditional instruments in creating compositions that were inspired by such scientific ideas as ionization, random Brownian motion, and quantum theory.

Scientists were the subjects of several important literary works in twentieth-century Europe, and science influenced the creation of new literary genres. In the three versions of Bertolt Brecht's *Leben des Galilei* (1943, 1947, and 1955; The life of Galileo), Brecht changed his interpretation of the scientist from the duplicitous hero of free inquiry to the social criminal who pursues scientific knowledge to the neglect of the well-being of humanity (the atomic bomb was the chief reason for Brecht's revisions). In the hands of such talented writers as Aldous Huxley and Stanisław Lem, European science fiction became much more than an escapist genre. In *Brave New World* (1932) Huxley revealed the dangers that a scientifically planned totalitarian society posed for human freedom. Lem, who has been called the only science fiction writer worthy of a Nobel Prize, probed the effects of radically different alien intelligences on human psychology in such novels as *Solaris* (1961). Other European writers, such as the Italian Umberto Eco, have used modern scientific ideas in such novels as *Il pendolo di Foucault* (1988; Foucault's pendulum).

THE FUTURE OF EUROPEAN SCIENCE

Futurology—the forecasting of the future development of science, technology, and society by extrapolations from contemporary trends—is a problematic discipline, but this has not prevented some analysts from attempting to envision what European science will be like in succeeding centuries. John Horgan, a science journalist, has expressed his pessimism about science's future in *The End of Science: Facing the Limits of Knowledge in the Twilight of the Scientific Age* (1996). After interviewing many scientists in Europe and America, he concluded that most of the fundamental theories concerning matter, life, and human beings have been made, and new theories will be so esoteric that they will be unable to be verified or falsified. By contrast, John Maddox, who edited *Nature* magazine for many years, is optimistic about science's future. In *What Remains to Be*

Discovered: Mapping the Secrets of the Universe, the Origins of Life, and the Future of the Human Race (1998) he argues that the best science is yet to come, when a "theory of everything" will be formulated and the problem of human consciousness will be solved.

Modern European science has helped solve many problems but created a plethora of others—moral, social, political, and environmental—and how successfully these problems are solved will determine the future of European civilization. Some scientific optimists believe that superintelligent computers will facilitate the solution of these problems, but others feel that the solutions will require more than science and technology—they will require enlightened, sensitive, and loving human beings.

See also **Academies of Science; Atomic Bomb; Atomic Energy; Curie, Marie; Einstein, Albert; Eugenics; Lysenko Affair; Penicillin; Quantum Mechanics; Sputnik.**

BIBLIOGRAPHY

Ben-David, Joseph. *The Scientist's Role in Society: A Comparative Study.* Englewood Cliffs, N.J., 1971. By comparing the development of institutional science in Germany, Britain, and America, Ben-David explores how social and political support were used to validate scientific programs.

Beyerchen, Alan D. *Scientists under Hitler: Politics and the Physics Community in the Third Reich.* New Haven, Conn., 1977. Analyzes how physicists were pressured to conform to Nazi ideology rather than to traditional scientific norms.

Haas, Ernst B., Mary Pat Williams, and Don Babai. *Scientists and World Order: The Uses of Technical Knowledge in International Organizations.* Berkeley, Calif., 1977. Studies the impact of science and scientists on international organizations, including those of twentieth-century Europe.

Graham, Loren R. *What Have We Learned about Science and Technology from the Russian Experiment?* Stanford, Calif., 1998. Argues that the interactions between science and politics in the Soviet Union reveal the strengths and weaknesses of social constructivism.

Heilbron, J. L., ed. *The Oxford Companion to the History of Modern Science.* New York, 2003.

Hermann, Armin, et al. *History of CERN.* 3 vols. Amsterdam, 1987–1996. The standard account of the origin, evolution, and accomplishments of the European Organization for Nuclear Research.

Krige, John, and Dominique Pestre, eds. *Science in the Twentieth Century.* London, 1997. Covers such topics as how politics has shaped the way science is practiced and how culture influences scientific modes of thought—in short, how science is subject to the dynamics of society.

Price, Derek J. de Solla. *Little Science, Big Science—and Beyond.* New York, 1986. A revised edition of the classic work on the exponential growth of modern science.

Taton, René. *Science in the Twentieth Century.* Translated by A. J. Pomerans. London, 1966. Analyzes the century's scientific achievements by disciplines.

Zimon, John. *The Force of Knowledge: The Scientific Dimension of Society.* Cambridge, U.K., 1976. This thematic analysis of the history of modern science emphasizes the social and institutional context of important discoveries and theories.

ROBERT J. PARADOWSKI

SCOTLAND.

SCOTLAND. In 1914, Scotland appeared to be a nation with a historic identity; a comfortable part of the United Kingdom, a powerful contributor to the British Empire; buttressed by an economy based on the production of raw materials and metal products. The Presbyterian churches were key institutions and their General Assemblies important forums. In politics, the general elections of 1910 had seen the endurance of a Liberal hegemony largely unbroken since 1832. By the end of the twentieth century, much of this had changed.

ECONOMY

Industrial strength hid latent weaknesses: superficially bolstered by World War I, recession struck in the interwar period. Problems were compounded by an antiquated structure and failure to develop new industries: the production of coal, metal, and textiles dominated. Although the coal and iron industries of the west of Scotland were closely integrated, the more important relationship between iron and steel was poorly developed, leading to endemic inefficiency in that sector. Closer links existed between Clydeside shipbuilding and the steel industry, but that proved problematic by the 1920s as the latter contracted.

Unemployment rose to unparalleled levels (27.7 percent in 1932), especially in areas of western and central Scotland where the bulk of these heavy industries were located. The bulk of Scottish output was destined for the export market, inducing extreme vulnerability to international economic fluctuations, but during the 1920s and 1930s the protection of home markets in Europe and the United States exacerbated this. The Scottish workforce, although containing a core of skilled workers, was poorly paid and unable to generate domestic demand for high-value products that would have aided economic diversification. Key sectors of the economy, such as the banks and insurance companies—so important to Edinburgh and the east of Scotland—and the indigenous railway companies were taken over by metropolitan concerns.

World War II further exposed these weaknesses with its demand for more sophisticated products, but they were also masked by the state intervention of that conflict and its aftermath. The program of nationalization undertaken by the Labour government elected in 1945 had a profound effect in Scotland where so much heavy industry remained, despite the vicissitudes of the interwar years. The influence of government profoundly affected the shape of the economy in the postwar years, through nationalization and the regional policies implemented from the mid-1960s to the 1980s.

The penetration of the Scottish economy by foreign multinational corporations, mostly in the electronics industry, has led to a swath of central Scotland being labeled "Silicon Glen." These enterprises have tended to conduct fairly low-level, branch-plant operations and have proved to be "footloose," as an early twenty-first-century rash of closures by firms such as Motorola has demonstrated. The sum total of these changes has been the alteration of an economy largely based on heavy industrial processes to one dominated by bureaucracy and services. There were nearly 750,000 workers in manufacturing in 1901, only around 350, 000 in the 1990s; services and administration employed just over 350,000 in 1901, but over 900,000 by the end of the century. A major change occurred in the late 1960s with the discovery of oil in the North Sea; this has had a particular impact on the regional economy of the northeast of Scotland, but indigenous enterprise has not fully

capitalized on this and critics argue that the revenues have been squandered by U.K. governments.

SOCIETY

Despite economic confidence, there were massive social problems in Scotland in the early part of the twentieth century, most obviously shocking housing conditions. The rapidity of urban expansion in the nineteenth century, combined with the feudal nature of Scots land law, created extreme densities of population and massive overcrowding in the traditional form of Scottish housing: the tenement block divided into multiple dwellings. Although the nascent Labour movement sought to publicize these issues, real attention was not given to the problem until a series of rent strikes during World War I. During the interwar years, both Conservative and Labour governments passed legislation to subsidize local authorities to build houses for rent and to clear slums. These initiatives saw the establishment of the vast public housing sector that, augmented by further building programs and attempts at urban renewal in the twenty years after World War II, was such a distinctive feature of Scottish society. In some areas of Scotland, 70 to 80 percent of the population lived in such houses. This was undermined in the 1980s as the Conservative government reduced support to local authorities and encouraged sitting tenants to purchase their houses at a discount.

At the other extreme of Scottish society, there has been a small landed elite: much Scottish land is of low value and agricultural potential and, partly because of this, huge estates were built up in the nineteenth century. Although the government intervened to become a large landowner in the 1920s, private land ownership has remained an important part of Scottish society and, concomitantly, anti-landlordism is a key feature of Scottish political rhetoric.

Oddly, for a society characterized by such extremes, a persistent aspect of Scotland's view of itself was that of a "democratic society" characterized by social progress, especially through the power of educational attainment. Repeated sociological investigations have found little evidence for this, but have exposed the foundation of the myth in nineteenth-century Presbyterian ideology and idealized views of the Scottish education system.

Coburg Street, Glasgow, October 1956. An apartment building in the notorious Gorbals slum district of Glasgow exemplifies poor housing conditions in overpopulated sections of Scottish cities. ©HULTON-DEUTSCH COLLECTION/CORBIS

Scottish demography has also been distinctive (as the table shows), with the key features being the massive emigration of the 1920s that resulted in a population decline in that decade, and the declining population, especially in western urban areas, since the early 1970s.

POLITICS

In 1999, a devolved parliament and executive was established with responsibility for most areas of Scottish domestic policy, with the exception of social welfare. A coalition of Labour and Liberal Democrat ministers has controlled the executive since 1999. Scottish political history over the course of the twentieth century, however, has not simply been a discussion of constitutional options, with most debate following a British agenda and focusing on the economy, social welfare, defense, and foreign policy.

Prior to World War I, the Liberals dominated; social change and shifts in the political agenda, notably over housing, led to a breakthrough by the Labour Party at the 1922 general election and the eclipse of the Liberal Party. From the 1920s to the 1960s, the Labour Party and the Scottish Unionist Party (as the Scottish Conservatives were known until 1965) dominated elections in Scotland. A notable result came in the 1955 general election when the Unionists polled just over 50 percent.

The Scottish political map became more diverse in the 1960s as the Liberals emerged from the doldrums and the Scottish National Party (SNP)

TABLE 1

Scottish population (in millions)	
1891	4.025
1901	4.472
1911	4.760
1921	4.882
1931	4.842
1939	5.006
1951	5.096
1961	5.179
1971	5.228
1981	5.130
1991	4.998
2001	5.062

won its first seat since 1945—at Hamilton in 1967. The excitement peaked in October 1974 when the SNP won over 31 percent of the vote and eleven seats. This prompted the Labour government to consider Scottish Home Rule, but legislation was stillborn after an inconclusive referendum in 1979 and the subsequent election of a Conservative government. During the 1980s and 1990s, nationalism waned and Scotland remained loyal to Labour as the Conservatives governed by virtue of their U.K. majority: this was perceived by some to constitute a "democratic deficit." With the return of a Labour government and a modest nationalist revival in 1997, the way was clear for the implementation of devolution.

IDENTITY AND CULTURE

Much writing about Scotland in the twentieth century has been pessimistic, with justification; but flickers of optimism can be discerned in the survival of Scottish identity and in cultural activity. An institutional identity based on the troika of the church, law, and education systems is no longer so powerful; neither, it seems, is an ethnic identity. But newer forms of identity, based on historical memory, sense of place, and cultural traditions are developing. Scotland is a nation of interlocking cultures revolving around the English, Gaelic, and Scots linguistic traditions enlivened by European and Asian immigration.

Literary culture evolved markedly over the twentieth century, from a parochial and moralizing "Kailyard" school of writers, such as Sir James Matthew Barrie, to the realism of such as James Kelman. Scottish writers have consistently experimented with language; none more so than Christopher Murray Grieve (Hugh MacDiarmid), the self-conscious publicist of the cultural "Renaissance" of the interwar years, poet and controversialist in English and Scots. Scottish Gaelic has produced the lyrical verse of Somhairle MacGill-eain.

Popular culture provides one of the areas where Scotland is most visible as an independent identity on the international stage at sporting occasions. This can be a unifying force, but also provides for intense local rivalries, such as that between Glasgow's two leading football teams, Rangers and Celtic, which is overlain with religious sectarianism.

See also **British Empire; Ireland; United Kingdom.**

BIBLIOGRAPHY

Bogdanor, Vernon. *Devolution in the United Kingdom.* Oxford, U.K., 1999.

Cameron, Ewen A. *Land for the People? The British Government and the Scottish Highlands, c. 1880–1925.* East Linton, U.K., 1996.

Campbell, R. H. *Scotland since 1707: The Rise of an Industrial Society.* 2nd ed. Edinburgh, 1985.

Cooke, Anthony, Ian Donnachie, Ann MacSween, and Christopher A. Whatley, eds. *Modern Scottish History, 1707 to the Present.* 5 vols. East Linton, U.K., 1998.

Craig, Cairns. *The Modern Scottish Novel: Narrative and the National Imagination.* Edinburgh, 1999.

Craig, Cairns, ed. *The History of Scottish Literature.* Vol. 4: *The Twentieth Century.* Aberdeen, U.K., 1990.

Daiches, David, ed. *The New Companion to Scottish Culture.* Revised and updated version. Edinburgh, 1993.

Devine, T. M. *The Scottish Nation: A History, 1700–2000.* London, 1999.

Devine, T. M., and Richard Finlay, eds. *Scotland in the Twentieth Century.* Edinburgh, 1996.

Dickson, A., and J. H. Treble, eds. *People and Society in Scotland.* Vol. 3: *1914–1990.* Edinburgh, 1992.

Finlay, Richard. *Modern Scotland: 1914–2000.* London, 2004.

Harvie, Christopher. *No Gods and Precious Few Heroes: Twentieth Century Scotland.* 3rd ed. Edinburgh, 1993.

———. *Fools' Gold: The Story of North Sea Oil.* London, 1994.

Houston, R. A., and W. W. J. Knox, eds. *The New Penguin History of Scotland: From the Earliest Times to the Present Day*. London, 2001.

Hutchison, I. G. C. *A Political History of Scotland, 1832–1924: Parties, Elections, and Issues*. Edinburgh, 1986.

———. *Scottish Politics in the Twentieth Century,* Basingstoke, U.K., 2001.

Knox, W. W. *Industrial Nation: Work, Culture and Society in Scotland, 1800–Present*. Edinburgh, 1999.

Lenman, Bruce. *An Economic History of Modern Scotland, 1660–1976*. London, 1977.

Lynch, Michael, ed. *The Oxford Companion to Scottish History*. Oxford, U.K., 2001.

Macdonald, Catriona M. M., and Elaine W. McFarland, eds. *Scotland and the Great War*. East Lothian, U.K., 1999.

McCrone, David. *Understanding Scotland: The Sociology of a Nation*. 2nd ed. London, 2001.

Mitchell, James. *Strategies for Self-Government: The Campaigns for a Scottish Parliament*. Edinburgh, 1996.

Scott, Paul H., ed. *Scotland: A Concise Cultural History*. Edinburgh, 1993.

Smout, T. C. *A Century of the Scottish People, 1830–1950*. New Haven, Conn., 1986.

Wightman, Andy. *Who Owns Scotland*. Edinburgh, 1996.

EWEN A. CAMERON

SEBALD, W. G. (1944–2001), German novelist.

When W. G. Sebald died in a car accident in December 2001, he was at the height of his literary career, having just published his last novel, *Austerlitz*, to international acclaim. He left behind three other works in prose—*Schwindel. Gefühle* (1990; *Vertigo*, 2000); *Die Ausgewanderten* (1992; *The Emigrants*, 1996); and *Die Ringe des Saturn: Eine englische Wallfahrt* (1995; *The Rings of Saturn*, 1998)—as well as several volumes of literary criticism and poetry. He was a professor of European literature at the University of East Anglia in Norwich, England, where he had lived on and off for more than three decades. Sebald's prose can be situated at the confluence of three traditions: first, nineteenth-century German realism, represented by such writers as Gottfried Keller and Adalbert Stifter and characterized by detailed descriptions of the natural world; second, literary modernism, represented by the work of Alfred Döblin, Franz Kafka, and Thomas Bernhard; and, third the German-Jewish literature of memory produced after the Holocaust by figures such as Paul Celan, Jean Améry, and Peter Weiss. Because Sebald is one of only a handful of German writers to confront the Holocaust and the burden of memory explicitly, his prose represents an important articulation of the possibilities and pitfalls of the German-Jewish interrelationship after World War II.

Sebald was born in the provincial Bavarian town of Wertach im Allgäu on 18 May 1944. He did not have any firsthand experience or knowledge of the catastrophes taking place in Europe during the last year of the war, but as he noted in *Luftkrieg und Literatur* (1999; *The Natural History of Destruction*, 2003), these unseen horrors formed the background of his life. It would not be an exaggeration to say that he spent his entire literary career struggling with what it meant to write literature after World War II and, perhaps even more urgently, responding—through the personalized medium of literature—to the dialectic of remembering and forgetting at the core of postwar German culture. Significantly, he examined this dialectic from England, writing all his major works from the vantage point of a German expatriate and consistently thematizing this perspective in his prose through his searching German narrators.

Although he is best known for those of his literary works that touch upon aspects of the Holocaust, Sebald probes many of the buried layers of Europe's violent past: the carving up of Africa by the colonial powers at the end of the nineteenth century; the ecological catastrophes caused by pollution and the exploitation of the natural world; and the history of modern warfare, particularly the firebombing of German cities, to mention just a few. In so doing, he dissects both the human and the natural history of destruction, illuminating them poignantly in his works through haunting topographies of memory. Sebald describes these topographies through labyrinthine narratives that fold back on themselves, creating precarious constellations of word and image, history and literature, biography and autobiography.

Breaking the taboo on speaking of German suffering, Sebald gave a set of polemical lectures in Zurich in 1997; they were subsequently published as *Luftkrieg und Literatur*. He accused German authors of repressing and strategically avoiding the trauma of the firebombing by uncritically identifying with the postwar ideology of the "economic miracle." Claiming that virtually every extant account of the firebombing was to some degree untrue, Sebald called for the creation of a synoptic and artificial view of the destruction. He used the techniques of literary modernism to describe the real firebombing of Hamburg in 1943, thereby indicating how literature could help people comprehend, work through, and even write catastrophic history.

This creation of a new, decidedly modernist space between literature and history is nowhere more apparent than in his last work. Hailed as his greatest achievement, one that placed him on a par with Franz Kafka and Marcel Proust, *Austerlitz* is a fictional story about the recovery and transmittal of memory based on real events. In it, a German narrator befriends a Jewish man named Austerlitz, who, as he discovers in the course of their meetings and journeys together, was sent by his parents to England on a *Kindertransport* (children's transport) before his family was murdered by the Nazis. But the story Sebald tells is far from simple: as a periscopic composite of text and images, it is a timely meditation on the possibility of remembering, representing, and transmitting the traumatic past in the uncertain spaces of the present.

See also **Germany; Holocaust.**

BIBLIOGRAPHY

Eshel, Amir. "Against the Power of Time: The Poetics of Suspension in W. G. Sebald's *Austerlitz.*" *New German Critique* 88 (winter 2003): 71–96.

Hell, Julia. "The Angel's Enigmatic Eyes; or, The Gothic Beauty of Catastrophic History in W. G. Sebald's *Air War and Literature.*" *Criticism* 46, no. 3 (summer 2004): 361–392.

Huyssen, Andreas. "Gray Zones of Remembrance." In *A New History of German Literature*, edited by David E. Wellbery, 970–975. Cambridge, Mass., 2004.

Long, J. J., and Anne Whitehead, eds. *W. G. Sebald: A Critical Companion.* Seattle, Wash., 2004.

Presner, Todd Samuel. "'What a Synoptic and Artificial View Reveals': Extreme History and the Modernism of W. G. Sebald's Realism." *Criticism* 46, no. 3 (summer 2004): 341–360.

TODD SAMUEL PRESNER

SECULARIZATION. Before the French Revolution the term *secularization* had a precise meaning in Catholic usage, where it denoted a change in status as a result of which a person or thing passed from the sacred to the profane. Only later was the word used—in a sense first acquired in North America—to designate a set of tendencies affecting relations between church, state, and society. Thereafter *secularization* and its French, Italian, and German cognates took on many connotations. Broadly speaking, *secularization* meant the "disenchantment of the world," to use Max Weber's expression. In other words, it embraced all those processes in the intellectual, social, political, legal, or ethical spheres that tended to create greater independence relative to religion by invoking modernity and relativizing the role of suprahuman or supernatural agency. It is important to note, however, that this does not mean that secularization was antireligious: rather, its spread resulted not in the eviction of religion from European history but merely in a change in its place.

RELIGION AND MODERNITY

Religion in no way disappeared at the beginning of the twentieth century in Europe. A first wave of secularization even made it clear that religion and modernity were not necessarily at odds. The German sociologist Max Weber (1864–1920), and later the German scholar Ernst Troeltsch (1865–1923), revealed the links between the Reformation, economic modernity, and social progress. Reform, far from cultivating the past or nostalgically embracing an unchanging tradition, was called on to transform the world. In parallel fashion, a movement developed within Catholic culture that sought to abandon intransigence toward modernity and embrace the nation-state, democracy, and liberalism. There was a strong feeling, in short, that Christianity, instead of resisting the modern world, could become an agent of it that was preferable to non-Christian alternatives such as materialism. It was thus possible, by the eve of the First World War, to discern secularizing movements within the Christian religion itself. In France, for instance, where in 1905 the state had detached itself from the churches and no longer recognized them formally, members of minority faiths—Protestants and Jews—tended to support the legislation. As for the Catholics, there was deep condemnation of the end of the Concordat, or agreement between church and state, by the Holy See and the clergy, but there were others who supported the Law of Separation of 1905, the foundation of the secular French system. These dissidents made two arguments: first, that this secularization of the state gave their church more freedom, and, secondly, that the institution's new place in society would inspire renewed militancy among the faithful.

Such considerations have led some historians to view secularization as a two-pronged movement: on the one hand, it implied a religious mutation in society, which is to say a change in a given society's relationship to religion; and on the other hand it meant that religions themselves were affected as they accepted the pressure to adapt to the secularization and modernization of society at large and even to undertake some measure of "internal secularization" (Rémond). In the 1980s, the French philosopher Marcel Gauchet offered a hypothesis, considered far-reaching by some and risky by others, according to which Christianity (meaning Roman Catholicism and Protestantism—the Orthodox Church, like Islam, being a separate issue) was itself a motor of the modern. One reason among others was that it embodied secularizing and transformative forces tending, precisely, to "disenchant the world." In Gauchet's account, history will eventually come to view Christianity as "the religion that pointed the way out of religion."

This approach has been at least partially thrown into doubt by reiterated claims that, if not religion per se, then at least religiousness enjoyed a renaissance in the late twentieth and early twenty-first century. Reviving an idea first mooted over a century ago by the French sociologist Émile Durkheim (1858–1917), sociologists and historians have evoked a permanent presence of religious phenomena in contemporary society, while at the same time stressing the difficulty of pinpointing them in view of secularization's dual impact—that on religious faiths and that on society in general. From this point of view religion

is said to have taken new forms, less visible, more highly diluted within the social body, and capable of colonizing realms seemingly far removed from religion, such as sports or the ecology movement. The idea is that once secularization has occurred, religion undergoes a series of metamorphoses, but continues to play its part in the social construction of everyday life and continues to render parts of life sacred.

Other authors, while dropping the claim that organized religion has a pivotal social function, have nonetheless stressed those features of religious belief systems that have survived two centuries of secularization. In some cases such features have succeeded in exercising great influence in the late twentieth or early twenty-first century; examples would be evangelical movements or the congregations of "churchless" believers. Evangelicals and devotees of television preachers reflect trends of American provenance initiated in Europe in the 1970s and 1980s. And—again as in the United States—Europe is experiencing a proliferation of philosophico-religious, existential, and charismatic groups promising adepts personal self-fulfillment.

Such groups do not always enjoy good relations with ensconced religious authorities. The same may be said, as well, for the various intransigent and fundamentalist versions of Catholicism, Protestantism, Eastern Orthodoxy, Judaism, and Islam. Within all these major faiths, dissident or radical tendencies have arisen that appeal to the double authority of tradition and scripture. Fundamentalisms built on such foundations demand that secularization be resisted, that the sole authority should be that of sacred texts, and that the state and society should likewise comply with their teachings. This is the basis, for example, of the French Catholic fundamentalism of Monseigneur Marcel Lefebvre (1905–1991), as it is of the Islamic fundamentalism of the Union of Islamic Organizations of France (UOIF), whose constituency is Belgian and Swiss as well as French.

FEATURES OF TWENTIETH-CENTURY SECULARIZATION

Such orientations, however, run counter to the historical progression of secularization in the twentieth century, the main features of which are worth recalling. First of all, with respect to the triangular relationship between state, church, and society, the twentieth century was characterized by a continual rearrangement of the links between states and the religious faiths practiced within their borders. The general tendency in Europe had two aspects. On the one hand, states gradually wrested law, customary practices, science, public offices, and the formal acts of private life from the control and regulation of religious institutions. On the other hand, again in a gradual way, they gave up intervening in internal church affairs. Exception must be made for the recent past of countries where the church is an established one (as in Great Britain) or a state institution (as in Prussia, Denmark, or Finland). In eastern Europe, the autocephalous Orthodox churches were long the creature of state power, used to assert national identity, and this has left traces still readily discernible at the beginning of the twenty-first century in Romania, Bulgaria, and Serbia. So far as social mores are concerned, secularization produced great changes, including the continual spread of civil marriage, divorce, secular schooling, the liberalization of common law, contraception, legal abortion, equitable treatment for different religious faiths, the emancipation of women, and the extension of marital rights to sexual minorities.

In parallel with such trends, the churches have come to accept freedom of choice in religious affiliation—a shift reflected, for example, by the Second Vatican Council. They have adopted similar positions on schooling, and considerably softened their attitudes toward the divorced and the unmarried. Meanwhile, though, they have received substantial guarantees of autonomy from the state, especially with respect to the management of their own affairs. In this last respect, the negative experience of totalitarian and authoritarian regimes continues to exert an influence.

The effects of secularization on the social realm are pointed up most strikingly in two ways. First, by the continuing decline in religious practice, especially among the young: in 2000, 70 percent of Germans under thirty stated that they had no religious affiliation. Second, by a dilution of religious beliefs within society as a whole: sociological studies at the end of the twentieth century found that in many European countries, with respect to such articles of faith as the devil, hell, angels, or purgatory, the position of believers, whether practicing Christians or not, and that of people stating no religious affiliation were tending to become indistinguishable; similarly, the values invoked by both groups in connection with their individual lives were very similar, and derived from religious traditions. One author has described this phenomenon as a "privatization of the Ten Commandments."

In response to the constitution proposed for the European Union in 2005, representatives of the Catholic, Protestant, and Orthodox churches, while supporting the idea in general, deplored the absence of any explicit reference to Christianity. They nevertheless acknowledged that the values espoused in the document's preamble and charter of rights bore the clear stamp of Christian values. Jewish or Muslim leaders could undoubtedly have made a similar claim. Secularization has thus led to a blunting of claims that Europe is a Christian project, while diffusing Judeo-Christian values throughout the Continent.

See also **Catholicism; Islam; Jews.**

BIBLIOGRAPHY

Chadwick, Owen. *The Secularization of the European Mind in the Nineteenth Century.* Cambridge, U.K., 1990.

Luckmann, Thomas. *The Invisible Religion: The Problem of Religion in Modern Society.* New York, 1967.

Rémond, René. *Religion et société en Europe: La sécularisation aux XIXe et XXe siècles, 1780–2000.* Paris, 2001.

Wilson, Bryan R. *Religion in Secular Society.* Harmondsworth, U.K., 1969.

BERNARD DELPAL

SEGHERS, ANNA (1900–1983), German novelist.

Anna Seghers became renowned in the United States when her novel, *Das siebte Kreuz* (*The Seventh Cross*)—about a prisoner in prewar Nazi Germany who escapes from a concentration camp—became a Book-of-the-Month Club selection in 1942 and in 1944 was made into a film starring Spencer Tracy. Seghers was born Netty Reiling on 19 November 1900 in Mainz, on the Rhine River, to well-off Jewish Orthodox parents. In 1924 she received a doctorate in art history after writing a thesis on Jews and Judaism in the works of Rembrandt. The same year her first story, "Die Toten auf der Insel Djal" (The dead on the Island Djal), a gothic tale, appeared under the pen name Antje Seghers. She married Hungarian-born László Radványi (1900–1978), who, as a teenager in Budapest, had belonged to the Budapest Sunday Circle of progressive Jewish intellectuals. Under the guidance of the philosopher György (Georg) Lukács, the group—which included the sociologist Karl Mannheim, the film critic Béla Balázs, and the art historian Arnold Hauser, among others—focused on questions of chiliasm and revolutionary messianism. At the end of World War I, again following Lukács's example, Radványi and other members of the circle turned to Marxism and communism. In 1928 Seghers herself joined the German Communist Party. That same year her short novel, *Aufstand der Fischer von St. Barbara* (*Revolt of the Fishermen of Santa Barbara*), brought her the prestigious Kleist Prize. The book, whose author was given as "Seghers" without a first name, was widely praised for its terse, "manly" prose. The label resurfaced in feminist debates of the 1980s and 1990s, both in Germany and in the United States, about gender and authorship. Anna Seghers—as she called herself after the publication of *The Revolt of the Fishermen*—was criticized for marginalizing women and depicting them as passive sufferers of history made by men. Seghers's defenders insisted that her female figures needed to be interpreted in their historical context and that a close reading revealed their independence and toughness. With her turn to Marxism, Seghers broke her ties to Judaism, though her work remained saturated with both Jewish and Christian imagery. This severing of ties to the Jewish community engendered criticism as well. In the 1990s, as interest in the Holocaust reached new heights, Seghers was reproached for not merely ignoring but even denying her Jewish roots. The counterargument held that communists in general—whether Jewish or Christian—tended to ignore their religious roots and that, to the extent that Jews were considered a "race," for communists, class issues overrode race issues. More specifically, a careful reading of Seghers's work, from her dissertation to the short novella "Der Ausflug der toten Mädchen" ("The Outing of the Dead Girls")—one of her masterpieces—to the late

Anna Seghers delivers a speech in Berlin, May 1942.
©BETTMAN/CORBIS

works revealed an intense, if often ambivalent, preoccupation with Jewish matters.

Seghers was among the first to leave Germany after the Nazis came to power in January 1933. Throughout her difficult life as an exile in Paris and later in Mexico City, taking care of her two young children and her husband (a political scientist), Anna Seghers continued to produce a large body of work, which eventually included nine major novels and more than sixty novellas, short stories, and fairy tales, as well as essays on aesthetic questions and the political issues of the day. In 1935 in Paris, she participated in a historical conference of antifascist writers, along with French novelists André Malraux and André Gide, German dramatist Bertolt Brecht, Austrian novelist Robert Musil, British novelist E. M. Forster, and Soviet writers Isaac Babel and Boris Pasternak, among others. Following *The Seventh Cross* she wrote *Transit* (1944), one of the key works of the exile period, about the desperate struggles of refugees trying to leave the French port city of Marseilles ahead of the advancing German army. In Mexico she befriended Diego Rivera and other muralists and created an international circle of friends that lasted for the rest of her life.

After returning from Mexico City to a devastated Germany in 1947, Seghers settled in communist East Berlin. Among East Germany's most celebrated writers, she received numerous awards and was elected president of the writers union in 1952. Brecht, Heiner Müller, and Volker Braun adapted her works for the stage. She had an equally profound influence on women writers, foremost among them Christa Wolf, and her works became the object of intense feminist inquiries. Seghers remained loyal to the communist regime, at times intervening on behalf of friends and fellow writers, at other times remaining quiet. The government never entirely trusted her and had her observed by the secret police. She came to rely more and more on her international circle of friends, among them the Brazilian novelist Jorge Amado, the Chilean poet Pablo Neruda, and the Soviet writer Ilya Ehrenburg. Many of her later works take place in the tropical climates of Mexico, the Caribbean, and Brazil, far from her increasingly inhospitable homeland. She died on 1 June 1983 in Berlin. By then her ostracism in West Germany during the Cold War was fading, and after German unification (1990) she came to be considered one of the major novelists of the twentieth century.

See also **Communism; Germany; Jews.**

BIBLIOGRAPHY

Primary Sources

Seghers, Anna. *Transit.* Translated by James A. Galston. Boston, 1944.

—. *Revolt of the Fishermen of Santa Barbara; A Price on His Head.* Edited by Valerie Stone. *Revolt of the Fishermen of Santa Barbara* translated by Jack Mitchell and Renate Mitchell. *A Price on His Head* translated by Eva Wulff. Berlin, 1960.

—. "The Outing of the Dead Girls." In *3 German Stories,* edited by Elisabeth Langgässer, Anna Seghers, Johannes Bobrowski; translated by Michael Bullock, 13–45. London, 1984.

—. *The Seventh Cross.* Translated by James A. Galston. New York, 1987.

Secondary Sources

Fehervary, Helen. *Anna Seghers: The Mythic Dimension.* Ann Arbor, Mich., 2001.

Romero, Christiane Zehl. *Anna Seghers. Eine Biographie.* 2 vols. Berlin, 2000–2003.

Wallace, Ian, ed. *Anna Seghers in Perspective.* Amsterdam, 1998.

ROBERT COHEN

SEMIOTICS. Semiotics studies the various ways meanings are expressed by and embodied in systems of signs and symbols. In its European as opposed to its American form it originally was known as "semiology." It grew out of the conception of Ferdinand de Saussure (1857–1913), formulated in his *Cours de linguistique générale* (1916; *Course in General Linguistics,* 1959), of a "semiology" as a general science of the life or circulation of signs in society. Using the "sign character of language" both as model and as standard for other sign systems, European semiotics extended its interests far beyond language to such domains as art, literature, myth, and religion, and even to advertising and fashion systems.

DEFINITIONS AND DISTINCTIONS

The linguistic *sign,* according to Saussure, is two-faced: it is the inseparable union of a "signifier" and a "signified." *Language* for Saussure was a system with a distinctive structure and was intrinsically social. It must be distinguished from *speech,* its realization in concrete instances. Any act of speech, like a move in a chess game, *selects* from a set of preexisting units and *combines* them in rule-governed or rule-creating ways. This distinction between the axis of selection and the axis of combination (the paradigmatic and the syntagmatic) is matched by another, perhaps more subtle and far-reaching distinction: that between form and substance. Language, Saussure claimed, is a system without positive terms. The linguistic sign gets its meaning from its relations to other signs, not from its positive characteristics or its relations to the world. Using the clue of the difference between a "significant" sound and a mere "material" sound, Saussure thought of language as a socially sanctioned system of correlations between sign units.

This idea of the sign, as defined by its relations to other signs, will be carried over to the whole cultural domain.

This set of distinctions led to a theoretical revolution in linguistics and in cultural theory that went under the name of structuralism. Structuralism attempted to discover the significant units in cultural systems quite generally and to set out the patterns of relation between them. Literary texts, for example, were shown by the Prague School to be complex acts of speech made possible by, and defined by, preexisting language-like systems without which they could not be created or understood. Texts stood in relation not just to previous texts but to all contemporaneous texts, too. Here are to be found the roots of the later notion of "intertextuality."

Early semiotics was faced with the serious problem of what seemed to be an irreconcilable opposition between semiotic systems and individual creativity, as manifested in the arts, both visual and literary. This theme was explored by such writers as the Russians Valentin Voloshinov (1895–1936) and Mikhail Bakhtin (1895–1975). They showed that texts, as utterances, transcend the individual-society dichotomy by being *situated,* but not predetermined, historically shaped and distinctively pitched rhetorical forms or "voices." Novel texts were seen as emergent forms of "verbal interaction," as shifting performances of meaning. But they are not mere repetitions of past meanings that were already present in the system.

The focus on a creative social-historical logic of discourse was balanced by the exploration of a semiotic logic of the deep, unchanging structures of myth by Claude Lévi-Strauss (b. 1908). Following Saussure's lead, Lévi-Strauss attempted to reduce the multiple forms of myth to variations on a few ultimate units and their systems of oppositions—raw/cooked, nature/culture, clean/unclean, endogamous/exogamous, and so forth.

Roland Barthes (1915–1980) further extended the language-based semiotic model to describe modern cultural myths and also the "rhetoric" of the image. Barthes was fascinated by the linguistic analogy and by not just the power of language but also the language of power embodied in the great mythic themes we live by and that enter into and define our individual and social identities. It was

Barthes, along with Jacques Lacan (1901–1981), who affirmed that even the psyche, that is, the self, is "structured like a language," as a coded system of oppositions, a realization of structures of signifiers, which one had no immediate access to or control over. The "self" became essentially a decentered "place" in the play of signs, a theme developed on the philosophical plane by Jacques Derrida (1930–2004).

OTHER DISCIPLINES

Semiotics, then, as a discipline has more than mere theoretical concerns to deal with. Semiotic analysis becomes a form of self-reflection, even of political opposition, since it makes visible the hidden systems of meaning that define the space of one's life. Whether these systems are "prison-houses" or "happy homes" cannot be settled by semiotics itself.

Semiotic concerns and orientations also entered into the work of psychology. Of special interest is the work of the German Karl Bühler (1879–1963), and of the Russian Lev Vygotsky (1896–1934). Foregrounding and generalizing the distinction between *significant* sounds and sounds as merely *physical* phenomena, Bühler explored how the apprehension of something as a sign depended on one's powers to abstract distinctive features in the sign complex as well as in things and objects in the world. This power of abstraction, clearly present in the perception of language, led Bühler to develop a semiotic model of human perceptual powers quite generally. Perception itself, he showed, was a multiform process of sign-reading. The perceptual field is filled with a plethora of symptoms, signals, and symbolic structures that must be "picked out" as significant from their non-significant surroundings. Vygotsky also explored the semiotic dimensions of the perceptual sphere, drawing extensive and fruitful parallels between signs and tools as essential, indeed, indispensable, supports for the development of consciousness. Vygotsky showed that semiotics has an unavoidable genetic dimension alongside its structural and historical dimensions, laying in this way the groundwork for a semiotically informed cultural psychology.

The ineluctable embodiment of perception in signs and sign systems had important consequences especially for a semiotically informed aesthetics. Consequently, the visual arts, with special focus on painting, sculpture, and architecture, have been subjected to semiotic analysis. What makes up sets of visual signifiers, however, is a serious problem for a specifically semiotic approach to visual art. The approach taken by European semiotics availed itself of the great phonological analogy: significance, or meaning, arises through difference, and the differences can be coded or uncoded. What, then, are the constitutive differences and oppositions in either the marked or carved surface (painting and sculpture) or a building? What makes some significant and others non-significant? These systems of differences and oppositions point to one another in intricate and not always obvious ways. They encompass both the formal and content poles of any meaning-bearing artifact, whether thematically exploited or working "behind the backs" of seemingly autonomous creators.

The production of meaning, semiotics holds, is always embedded in, and exploits, sets of conventions. And, strangely enough, novel artistic meanings can also emerge out of the system, although just how remains a perplexing problem. Art in all its forms, seen from the semiotic point of view, bears witness to the fact that there is no "pure" perception or innocent eye. A large semiotic literature has been devoted to these themes. Of primary importance is the work of Maurice Merleau-Ponty (1908–1961), who was perhaps the most important philosopher to first recognize the revolutionary role of Saussure's semiotic insights for philosophy and for aesthetics.

Roman Jakobson (1896–1982), the great Russian linguist, applied semiotic insights to literary and phonological theory, foregrounding especially the poetic function of language, which was marked by the "palpability" of signs. The notion of palpability is clearly not restricted to language signs but to artistic signs of all sorts. Émile Benveniste (1902–1976), a distinguished French linguist, also reflected on the extension of the linguistic analogy to other systems of signs, concluding that while language was the "interpreting system" par excellence, one may not deny that the realm of signs permeates the whole cultural world. This is precisely the enduring central thesis and theme of European semiotics.

See also **Barthes, Roland; Derrida, Jacques; Jakobson, Roman; Lacan, Jacques; Lévi-Strauss, Claude;** Merleau-Ponty, Maurice; Postmodernism; Saussure, Ferdinand de.

BIBLIOGRAPHY

Chandler, David. *Semiotics: The Basics.* New York, 2002.

Innis, Robert, ed. *Semiotics: An Introductory Anthology.* Bloomington, Ind., 1985.

Nöth, Winfried. *Handbook of Semiotics.* Bloomington, Ind., 1990.

ROBERT E. INNIS

SEMPRÚN, JORGE (b. 1923), Spanish writer and political activist.

The son of an ambassador from the Spanish Republic who in 1937, during the Spanish civil war (1936–1939), chose exile in France, Jorge Semprún joined the French Resistance while still a teenager and was deported to Buchenwald in 1943. On his return to France he joined the Communist underground struggle against the Spanish dictator Francisco Franco (1892–1975). After leaving the Communist Party in 1964, he produced a very rich literary oeuvre in which he analyzed his various combats. Five books retrace the experience of his deportation, in particular.

Jorge Semprún was born into one of Spain's great families on 10 December 1923 in Madrid. His father, Carlos Semprún y Gurrea, a jurist, diplomat, and liberal editorialist, sided with the Republic and became its chargé d'affaires at The Hague. As a result, Jorge followed his father into exile as a "Red Spaniard" at the fall of the Republic, to which he remained faithful ever after. Family contacts enabled him to avoid the Gurs deportation camp, in which a number of Spanish republicans in exile were imprisoned after Franco's victory; he studied in Paris at the Lycée Henri IV and then at the Sorbonne and was active in the movement surrounding the journal *Esprit*. He interrupted his studies in philosophy to join the Resistance, both as part of the British network headed by Maurice Buckmaster and as a member of the communist resistance groups Francs-Tireurs et Partisans (FTP) and Main d'Oeuvre Immigrée (MOI). At the age of twenty he was deported to Buchenwald.

Upon his release, stateless, he devoted himself to militant engagement in the Spanish Communist Party. Beginning in 1953 he coordinated underground resistance activities against the Franco regime on behalf of the Central Committee of the exiled Spanish Communist Party; he later joined the Central Committee and the politburo. From 1957 to 1963, he worked underground—at great danger (his successor was shot)—for the Communist Party in Franco's Spain, under the pseudonym Federico Sánchez.

After his expulsion from the not-yet-destalinized Communist Party in 1964 he turned toward his twofold vocation, as a screenwriter for two films by Alain Resnais, *La guerre est finie* (1966; *The War Is Over*) and *Stavisky* (1974), and above all as a writer. In his writing he returned to his experiences as an antifascist, resistant deportee, and as a militant communist. Twenty years after his deportation, writing at last made sense of his experience, and once he had begun he never stopped: he gave voice to the experience of the camp by writing a narrative that is also a novel, through the transformation of individual beings into other individuals, and through snatches of memory adapted to writing: "We have made this journey into fiction; I have thus obliterated my solitude in reality. What good does it do to write books, if one does not invent the truth? Or at least, what seems true."

The works *L'évanouissement* (1967; The blackout), *Le grand voyage* (1963; *The Long Voyage*, 1964), *Quel beau dimanche* (1980; *What a Beautiful Sunday!*, 1982), and *Le mort qu'il faut* (2001; The necessary dead man), together with *L'écriture ou la vie* (1994; *Literature or Life*, 1997), make up a coherent and fascinating collection of fictions, essays, and narratives. Jorge Semprún also collaborated on many television programs, including a dialogue with the writer and Holocaust survivor Elie Wiesel (b. 1928) that was published under the title *Se taire est impossible* (1995; To remain silent is impossible), in which Semprún states:

> And then, in this experience of Evil, the essential thing is that it will have been lived as an experience of death.... I say "experience" for a reason.... For death is not something that we might have brushed up against, or rubbed shoulders with, or escaped from, like an accident we emerged from unscathed. We lived it....We are not escapees, but ghosts....And this, of course, can only be said abstractly. Or while laughing with other ghosts....Because it's not believable, not

sharable, barely comprehensible....And yet, we shall have lived this experience of death as a collective experience, and what's more, a fraternal one, merging our being-together...as a *Mit-Sein-zum-Tode*. (Translated from the French)

In *Autobiographie de Federico Sanchez* (1978; *The Autobiography of Federico Sanchez and the Communist Underground in Spain*, 1979), Semprún does not shy away from self-criticism. As a member of the Communist Party, he had benefited from the protection of the *Prominente* (special prisoners) at Buchenwald. "Nowhere did I proclaim my innocence. I remained silent, sacrificing the truth on the altar of the absolute Spirit that, for us, was called the Spirit of the Party." Through writing, he tried to move beyond the contradictions of his experience.

When Spain again became democratic Semprún returned to politics, on the condition that it would be in the service of culture. He served as minister of culture from 1988 to 1991 in the Socialist government of Felipe Gonzales. He rose to great fame and received a series of prestigious European literary prizes.

See also **Holocaust; Resistance; Spain; Spanish Civil War.**

BIBLIOGRAPHY

Primary Sources

Semprún, Jorge. *The Autobiography of Federico Sanchez and the Communist Underground in Spain.* New York, 1979.

———. *Federico Sánchez vous salue bien: Roman.* Paris, 1993.

Semprún, Jorge, and Elie Wiesel. *Se taire est impossible.* Paris, 1995.

Secondary Sources

Suleiman, Susan. "Historical Trauma and Literary Testimony: Writing and Representation in the Buchenwald Memoirs of Jorge Semprún." *Journal of Romance Studies* 4, no. 2 (summer 2004).

ANNETTE BECKER

SENGHOR, LÉOPOLD SÉDAR (1906–2001), first president of Senegal and developer of negritude and African socialism.

Léopold Sédar Senghor was a man of politics and a man of culture who in both areas was devoted to

Léopold Sédar Senghor, photographed on the set of a French television show, Paris, 1977. ©SOPHIE BASSOULS/CORBIS SYGMA

finding a balance between Europe and Africa. Born in Joal, French West Africa (present-day Senegal), Senghor was the fifth of six children of Gnylane Bakhoum and the trader Basile Diogoye Senghor. Senghor's very name signified his dual influences. Sédar was Serer, the prominent ethnic group of Joal. Catholicism, a French export, inspired the name Léopold and Senghor's attendance of a school run by the Fathers of the Holy Spirit at Ngazobil in 1914.

As a schoolboy he was subjected to a peculiarity of colonialism that imposed the French curriculum upon Africans. Senghor struggled to become assimilated, a French boy with black skin, whose diligent studies and quick mind led him to Dakar, the capital of French West Africa. After briefly attending the Libermann Seminary, Senghor switched to the secondary school in Dakar. In 1928 he obtained the French high school degree with honors, and the Government General of French West Africa granted him a scholarship with which to pursue studies in France.

Senghor arrived in a Paris recently introduced to jazz by African Americans and in which African art and artifacts fascinated avant-garde intellectuals and artists. Yet Senghor's priority was his education, and he attended first the renowned Lycée Louis-le-Grand and then the Sorbonne, studying Latin and Greek and exploring French authors ranging from the poet Charles Baudelaire to the writer Maurice Barrès. In order to sit for the *agrégation,* the most prestigious teaching degree in France, Senghor had to be naturalized French. He was, in 1933, and passed the exam in grammar in 1935.

Starting in 1931, through his studies Senghor met those with whom he started deliberating negritude, an intellectual movement that focused upon culture to express the politics of black identity within the context of European colonialism. These men and women included the Martinicans Aimé Césaire and three of the seven Nardal sisters, Jane, Andrée, and Paulette, as well as the French Guianan Léon Damas.

Senghor also discovered the Harlem Renaissance writers and met René Maran, the first black man to win the celebrated Prix Goncourt for a novel, *Batouala* (1921). This constellation of black thinkers allowed Senghor to reevaluate his European education and African origins. In 1936 Senghor wrote "The Portrait," a poem that expressed affection for the region around Tours, where he was teaching classics and French, and that also was the work in which he first used the term *negritude*.

During World War II, Senghor was called upon to serve in a regiment of colonial infantry but was soon made a prisoner of war. After the war, Senghor was invited to help write a new constitution for France. Senghor's invitation to serve on the Monnerville Commission introduced him to politics and to the injustice of the continued political misrepresentation of colonies within the *métropole* (France proper). In 1945 Senghor returned to Senegal to complete his dissertation with research on Serer and Wolof poetry. While there he was persuaded to run for one of two seats Senegal had been given for the Constituent Assembly of the Fourth Republic and won as a socialist. He argued that Africans should assimilate the best of European culture, recognize a rich African tradition of culture and politics, and work on a political relationship with France which would resemble that between capitals and provinces.

An engaged intellectual, Senghor decided to commit to politics. He traveled around Senegal expressing interest in people's lives and started a newspaper, *La condition humaine* (The human condition), which provided cultural and political education for African readers. In 1948 Senghor broke away from the French Socialist Party and created the Senegalese Democratic Bloc. He advocated greater independence for Africans within the French Union, using ideas he had developed through negritude and African socialism. Negritude became a theory of group identity while African socialism, elaborated in the late 1950s, encouraged intercultural exchanges at the political and social levels between Africa and the West. Senghor believed African traditions, offset by the progressivism of Western socialism, would ensure a strong Africa.

In 1958 Senghor invited a number of parties to join the Senegalese Progressive Union. Careful not to seem ungrateful for France's role in West Africa,

he waited until December 1959 when Charles de Gaulle accepted Senegal as a nation and promised the French Fifth Republic's support. Senghor was elected president of an independent Senegal in January 1961 and led the country until 1980. After retiring he returned to his initial passion, working on committees at the French Academy, to which he was inducted in 1984, and continuing to write. Senghor died in Verson, France.

See also **Colonialism; French Empire; Negritude.**

BIBLIOGRAPHY

Primary Sources

Senghor, Léopold Sédar. *The Collected Poetry*. Translated by Melvin Dixon. Charlottesville, Va., 1991.

Secondary Sources

Hymans, Jacques Louis. *Léopold Sédar Senghor: An Intellectual Bibliography*. Edinburgh, 1971.

Vaillant, Janet G. *Black, French, and African: A Life of Léopold Sédar Senghor*. Cambridge, Mass., 1990.

JENNIFER ANNE BOITTIN

SERBIA. By the first months of 1914 the Kingdom of Serbia seemed the most successful of the independent states that had emerged across southeastern Europe during the nineteenth century. Its modernized army, mobilizing 350,000 men from a population of 2.9 million, won victories in both Balkan Wars of 1912–1913, first against the Ottoman Empire and then against neighboring Bulgaria. The region's one native monarch, King Peter Karadjordjević (1844–1921), ruled under constitutional restraints and a parliament elected by near universal male suffrage. The tariff war of 1906–1911 with Austria-Hungary had secured economic independence from Serbia's huge northern neighbor. Family holdings predominated among a peasantry accounting for more than 80 percent of the population. The cultural and intellectual life of Belgrade displayed the growing European ambiance of the region's other capital cities but enjoyed the advantage of greater press freedom.

The next ninety years were not kind to that apparent promise. Two world wars and the wars of Yugoslavia's dissolution in the 1990s are partly responsible. So, however, is political conflict within Serbia's changing borders and a problematic relation with the much larger territory, a large number of Serbs included, that became Yugoslavia after 1918 and again after 1945. Already by 1914, the First Balkan War had added Kosovo, the much-remembered site of the medieval Serbian state's defeat by Ottoman forces in 1389, and Vardar Macedonia to the territory of "inner Serbia." Total population swelled to 4.4 million but reduced the 90 percent Serb and Serbian Orthodox proportion before 1912 to less than 70 percent. The ethnic and religious majority in Kosovo had long since become Albanian and Muslim, in the Vardar region Slav Macedonian and Bulgarian Orthodox.

In July 1914 Austria-Hungary seized on the assassination in Sarajevo of the heir to its throne by a Bosnian Serb to declare war on Serbia. In World War I Serbia's suffering began with the costly repulse of two Austro-Hungarian offensives. There followed a deadly typhus epidemic; and a German-led offensive that forced its army, government, and accompanying civilians to retreat across Kosovo and Albania to the island of Corfu by the winter of 1915–1916. The death toll to that point alone approached half a million. Hard Austrian and harder Bulgarian occupations divided Serbia's 1914 territory until 1918. Then a Serbian army reconstituted with French-led forces on the Salonika Front broke through Bulgarian lines in October 1918 and quickly retook the lost territory.

Pressed by advancing Italian troops and the internal disorder of a disintegrating Austro-Hungarian army, a National Council of Slovenes, Croats, and Serbs hastily assembled in Zagreb and accepted Serbia's terms for the founding of the first Yugoslav or South Slav state on 1 December 1918. In return, Serbian troops stemmed the Italian advance and restored order in formerly Habsburg Croatia-Slavonia and Bosnia-Herzegovina. Yet it was not until 1921 that a constituent assembly, minus most Croat votes, could establish the Kingdom of Serbs, Croats, and Slovenes on unitarist terms under a Serbian King, Alexander Karadjordjević (1888–1934). Its thirty-three district administrations were made responsible to Belgrade's central ministries. They were subdivided

so that the two million Serbs outside of Serbia, where only 2.6 million survived the war, would have local majorities in some of Bosnia-Herzegovina, Croatia, the Vojvodina, and Macedonia, and all of Kosovo. The two latter territories were now called South Serbia and placed under semi-martial law well into the 1920s.

Several disadvantages stood in the way of the Serbian dominance of this first Yugoslav state, as assumed by its detractors and anticipated by prewar political leaders such as Nikola Pasić (1845–1926). Long head of the previously dominant Radical Party, Pasić could remain prime minister again until 1926, but only through a series of unstable coalition governments. Serbia's political spectrum had divided into five parties, while single parties represented not only the Slovenes, Croats, and Bosnian Muslims but also increasingly the Serbs from outside of Serbia. Other disadvantages were the greater war damage suffered by Serbian industry, the failure of its banking sector to attract much of the private capital now concentrating in Zagreb, and the retreat of the European capital market from the state loans so helpful to prewar Serbia. Culturally, some effort to make Belgrade the center of a single, new Yugoslav identity briefly attracted intellectuals and artists from other ethnic areas but failed to survive the 1920s. Projects to create a single educational system would not even get started until the 1930s.

By then, King Alexander had abolished both the parliament and the established political parties, while redividing the renamed Kingdom of Yugoslavia into only eight *banovine* (provinces). Their borders favored Serbs but not Serbia. From 1929 to 1931 his royal dictatorship was a reality, enforced by new powers for the Interior Ministry in Belgrade. His closest army advisors fought the pressures rising for relaxation from 1931 to 1934 but could not prevail after the king's assassination in 1934 at the hands of radical Croatian and Macedonian nationalists. A new prime minister, Milan Stojadinović (1888–1961), revived the economy, first through favorable trade arrangements with Nazi Germany and then with rearmament favoring Serbian industry. But he could not come to terms with either the Serbian Orthodox Church or the Croatian Peasant Party. By 1939 his successors had agreed to larger and largely Croatian

Serbian peasant women help soldiers move large guns during World War I, January 1915. ©Bettmann/Corbis

banovina that prompted rising Serbian demands for one of their own, including most of Bosnia.

The German invasion of April 1941 then intervened to dismember the first Yugoslavia and occupy Serbia. A military coup in Belgrade had just overthrown the Regent Paul's government for agreeing to join the Nazi's Tripartite Pact. The brutality of the Nazi occupation intensified as both the Yugoslav Communist Party under Tito (Josip Broz, 1892–1980) and remnants of the royal Yugoslav army under Dragoljub Mihajlović organized competing resistance movements. Kosovo became part of a Greater Albania under Italian occupation and a Kosovar Albanian administration that killed or expelled interwar Serb immigrants. War deaths there and in Serbia proper totaled 150,000, versus 300,000 Serbs killed elsewhere in Yugoslavia. Tito used his partisans' expulsion into Bosnia and Croatia to build multiethnic support

for the Communist Yugoslavia that took power quickly in 1945. The Chetniks' limited collaboration, more with the Italians than the Germans, allowed the larger Communist forces to join the Soviet army in sweeping them aside in Serbia.

The new Communist federation made Serbia a constituent republic within its pre-1912 borders. Neighboring Vojvodina became a province and Kosovo a region, promising subordination to Serbia given their respective Serb plurality and minority. And so at first they were, particularly in Kosovo under the hard-line Interior Minister Alexander Ranković (1909–1982). After he was deposed in 1966 and Kosovar Albanians rioted the following year, the region's own affairs, education and police powers included, passed increasingly out of Serbia's hands.

For the 60 percent of Yugoslavia's Serbs inside Serbia, their republic received little advantage from containing the capital city and having Serbs disproportionately represented in the Communist parties of Bosnia and Croatia. In the 1945 elections Serbia's noncommunist parties were the only ones to seriously dispute the Communist accession to power, their population the only one to abstain significantly, some 30 percent. The smallholding peasantry and the Serbian Orthodox Church survived Communist pressures by the early 1950s, but with reduced numbers and less influence. By 1965, Serbian Communist liberals were at the forefront of a proposal to introduce market-oriented economic reforms, reduce political influence in enterprise management, and retreat from any Serb-centered view of Yugoslavia. Their dismissal by Tito in 1971 along with Communist liberals in Croatia, Slovenia, and Macedonia as well, opened the way in the Serbian party for younger apparachiks, more opportunist than hard-line. Slobodan Milošević (1941–2006) moved ahead on just that basis. His chance would come after Tito's death in 1980.

Serbia's economy and society were by then struggling, like the rest of Yugoslavia, with increasing inflation, enterprises under decentralized but still political management, and now subdivided workers' councils. There were added problems for Serbia, increasingly portrayed by Belgrade's freer media after Tito's death as the result of discrimination from other republics. Its payments to the lower-income republics and Kosovo seemed a greater burden than for Croatia and Slovenia, with incomes respectively two and three times Serbia's (and Yugoslavia's) average. Belgrade's infrastructure and amenities were increasingly neglected in a confederal framework where the other republics could agree that the city that was also Serbia's capital should not be favored. What had been the most open, European, and multiethnic cultural and educational center in Yugoslavia began turning in on itself during the 1980s. Serbian nationalism emerged in theater, literature, and finally in politics.

As inflation accelerated, Yugoslavia's post-Tito political stalemate also frustrated economic reform. Milošević used added anxiety about the declining Serb population in Kosovo to take control of the Serbian party. After the other communist regimes in Eastern Europe collapsed in 1989 he sought to save party control of all but Slovenia and western

Croatia. He deployed a Serbianized Yugoslav army and paramilitary forces to challenge the secession of first Croatia in 1991 and Bosnia-Herzegovina in 1992. By 1996 the surviving Federal Republic of Yugoslavia consisted only of Serbia (10.6 million people including Vojvodina and Kosovo) and Montenegro. Blaming the immiseration of the Serbian economy and the social demoralization of Belgrade in particular on Western sanctions, Milošević's criminalized regime survived even after the NATO bombing campaign of 1999 and his agreement to withdraw Serbian forces from Kosovo. The bombing on top of the Serb refugee influx of the 1990s left the public with an enduring sense of victimization, rolling together all of Serbia's suffering in the wars of the twentieth century.

Within a year's time, however, Serbia's political culture rallied. Demonstrations spread from city to city, rejecting the falsification of votes in a hasty election that Milošević had called to maintain his position as president. He and his regime were forced to resign in October 2000. Since then, Serbia's return to its pre-1912 democratic promise has struggled to answer for the war crimes and criminality of the 1990s, to overcome the long legacy of the failed communist economy, and to avoid the crippling political divisions of the 1920s. For his courageous if compromised pursuit of that promise, Prime Minister Zoran Djindjić (1952–2003) was assassinated in 2003. But the struggle has continued.

See also **Belgrade; Kosovo; Milošević, Slobodan; Montenegro; Sarajevo; Tito (Josip Broz); World War I; World War II; Yugoslavia.**

BIBLIOGRAPHY

Cohen, Lenard J. *Serpent in the Bosom, The Rise and Fall of Slobodan Milošević.* Boulder, Colo., 2001.

Dragovic-Soso, Jasna. *Saviours of the Nation? Serbia's Intellectual Opposition and the Revival of Nationalism.* London, 2002.

Lampe, John R. *Yugoslavia as History: Twice There Was a Country.* 2nd ed. Cambridge, U.K., and New York, 2000.

Mitrovic, Andrej. *Serbia's Great War, 1914–1918.* London, 2006.

Pavlowitch, Stevan K. *Serbia: The History of an Idea.* New York, 2002.

Wachtel, Andrew. *Making a Nation, Breaking a Nation: Literature and Cultural Politics in Yugoslavia.* Stanford, Calif., 1998.

JOHN R. LAMPE

SEXUALITY. In the course of the twentieth century, sexuality became a site of increasing significance for a variety of historical reasons. One factor was the growing interest and success in controlling fertility, which had major consequences for women's experience of sexuality and for the relationships between men and women. Another factor was an intensifying preoccupation with questions of sexual orientation. Sexual orientation became an important target of both medicine and the law, formed the basis of political movements, and profoundly shaped the self-understandings of individuals. Over the course of the century, and at the same time that sexuality accrued ever greater personal significance, sexual matters also acquired increasing political salience. Sexuality became a prime arena of (often highly public) social and cultural conflict, a main motor of economic development, and a key locus of government-citizen negotiation. In a constantly reconfigured combination of stimulus and regulation, liberal and conservative impulses together have worked to make conflicts over sexual matters consequential for politics writ large.

CHANGING ATTITUDES BETWEEN THE WARS

In the wake of World War I, there was an increased emphasis on heterosexual mutuality and sexual compatibility within marriage in all European nations. This focus was attended by a notable decline in prostitution and a concomitant rise in premarital intercourse (for both men and women) with potential marriage partners. Within this context there also arose highly publicized campaigns for greater contraceptive access and abortion rights (often accompanied by backlashes led by the churches and conservative political parties). In addition, sex counseling centers were established in central and northern Europe, and sex advice literature written for popular audiences proliferated. The Dutch author Theodor Hendrick van de Velde's *The Ideal Marriage* (1926) became a

bestseller translated into many languages; in Britain, Marie Stopes's books *Married Love* (1918) and *Radiant Motherhood* (1920) were immensely popular. Sexological researchers, who had begun in the later nineteenth century by studying "perversion" and "deviant" forms of sexuality, turned their attention to explicating "normal" sexuality and attempting to alleviate dysfunctions and inhibitions.

Frequently, the advocates of heterosexual mutuality also justified their work by asserting its "eugenic" value. Eugenic attitudes were hardly the preserve of the political Right, but were often shared by feminists, socialists, and liberals, and by Jews as well as Christians. Belief that more pleasurable sex led to healthier babies and better parenting coexisted uneasily with overt racism and anxiety about declining European birthrates, as well as with normative ideas about what constituted proper sexual behavior.

In the interwar period, homosexual male and lesbian subcultures became more visible in many European cities, as did the further development of activism to decrease homophobia in the populace and to abolish laws that criminalized male homosexual acts. (Only in Austria and Sweden were lesbian acts criminalized as well.) In an intricate interaction between medical professionals and individuals who felt themselves to have nonnormative orientations, new theories of the etiology of homosexual object choice were formulated. Some insisted on a congenital basis for homosexuality, while others emphasized psychological and developmental factors. Homosexuality was variously theorized as a form of fetishism or narcissism, a deficit in heterosexual vigor or maturity, or (more traditionally) as an illness or a sin. The discovery of sex hormones in the late 1920s complicated these debates even further, and conflicts over the potential remediability of nonnormative orientations not only divided those who advocated decriminalization from those determined to maintain criminalization but also divided each side against itself.

WORLD WAR II AND ITS AFTERMATH

The rise of fascism in Italy and Spain and the rise of National Socialism in Germany and then Austria were accompanied by aggressive campaigns to raise birthrates not only through positive incentives but also by making access to contraception and abortion more difficult. Especially in Italy and Spain, the fascist parties were able to frame these campaigns as in keeping with Catholic Church teaching. In Nazi Germany and Austria, along with the many countries that came under Nazi rule and occupation during World War II, the concern with raising the quantity of births was coupled with a thoroughly racist form of eugenics. Jews, Sinti, and Roma, along with civilians in the occupied territories and foreign laborers imported to work within the Reich, as well as health-impaired individuals and the mentally disabled and enfeebled within Germany and Austria, were targeted for sterilization, involuntary abortion, and mass murder. Yet although the Nazi Party had initially come to power—and garnered substantial support from the Protestant and Catholic Churches—on a "family values" platform that promised to clean the streets of prostitution, the kiosks of pornography, and the cities of homosexual club life, within two to three years it was evident that Nazism decisively encouraged premarital and extramarital heterosexual sex, and not only for reproduction. The celebration of both nonmarital and marital heterosexuality as an "Aryan," "Germanic" prerogative coincided with a sharply radicalized and escalated prosecution of homosexuality and the murder of thousands of homosexual men. Ultimately, the majority of the populace did not experience the Third Reich as a sexually conservative time.

Although the immediate aftermath of the mass carnage of World War II was characterized in many nations by chaos and economic hardship and by what contemporaries described as an ongoing atmosphere of libertinism, by the early 1950s far more conservative mores were ascendant. In consistently democratic nations such as Britain, as well as in countries tainted either by collaboration with Nazism or by Nazism itself, the Christian churches reacquired considerable prestige and cultural and political influence. A redomesticated heterosexuality also became a widely held popular ideal, not least as a response to the many ways sexuality had escaped the familial framework during the war years. In a Cold War climate of heightened emphasis on the nuclear family, respectability, and intensified concern with gender difference, newly punitive attitudes toward premarital heterosexual

intercourse coincided with a refurbishing of homophobic attitudes and laws under Christian Democratic Party auspices. (Also in post-Vichy France, for example, Charles de Gaulle's government retained legislation developed during Nazi occupation that criminalized consensual homosexual acts between those over and those under eighteen years of age.)

The only exceptions to the larger conservative postwar pattern were the Scandinavian countries of Denmark and Sweden. Their Social Democratic governments maintained the rationalized concern with sexual health that had once, during the interwar era, been so prevalent also in other nations. Homosexuality and abortion had been decriminalized in these nations in the course of the 1930s and 1940s and remained so; contraceptives were legal and available. But in most European countries in the 1950s, contraceptives were difficult to obtain and abortion remained illegal, albeit widely practiced. By the end of the 1950s and the beginning of the 1960s, it was estimated that France and West Germany each were home to one million illegal abortions per year, and rates in Italy were thought to be even higher. Treatment of homosexuality was less punitive in most predominantly Catholic countries (including Belgium, Italy, Portugal, and Spain) than in most predominantly Protestant countries, although post-Nazi Austria continued to criminalize both male and female homosexuality. France in the 1950s, despite its regulation of youth homosexuality, also did not criminalize consensual adult homosexuality (and indeed had not done so since the late eighteenth century). But 1950s England and West Germany saw intensive prosecution of male homosexuality.

LIBERALIZATION
The early 1960s saw the first sustained efforts to undo the postwar culture of sexual conservatism. Increasing use of titillating images and narratives in advertising and journalism, and the indisputable popularity of a growing pornography market, exposed the gap between official norms and mainstream values. Liberal public intellectuals, politicians, artists, and students began openly to challenge the existing terms of debate. They argued that it was the difficulty in obtaining contraception that fueled epidemic proportions of reliance on illegal

abortion, declared that the criminalization of homosexuality was part and parcel of a larger hostility to sexuality, and advanced the values of consent and privacy. The birth control pill, developed in the early 1960s, made available to married women in the mid-1960s and also to the unmarried by the late 1960s, decisively separated intercourse from the possibility of procreation and created the opportunity for women to experiment more widely without fear of consequences. Across Western Europe, a combination of increasing public debate and progressive activism, both outside of and within parliaments, led over the course of the later 1960s and into the first half of the 1970s to significant legal changes. The advertising of contraception, for instance, was legalized in France in 1967, the same year that England decriminalized male homosexuality. Abortion was also legalized in England in 1967—not least under the impact of the scandal of birth defects caused by Thalidomide. Abortion was either partially or completely decriminalized in West Germany, France, and Austria in the mid-1970s, and decriminalized in Italy in 1978. Over the course of the 1960s and 1970s, the censorship of pornography ceased or was significantly curtailed in many nations.

Sex rights activist movements emerging within and around the New Left radically politicized sexuality. Whether inspired by the rediscovered Weimar-era work of Wilhelm Reich or by the 1960s writings and speeches of the Frankfurt school philosopher Herbert Marcuse, sex radicals criticized the ideals of monogamy and the nuclear family and advanced antiauthoritarian parenting styles. They celebrated what they saw as the (at once politically and personally) transformative power of sexual liberation. And pointing to the United States' brutal war in Vietnam, they challenged conservatives to explain how racism and killing could be considered morally acceptable, while sex was considered immoral. "Make Love Not War" became one of the premier slogans of the era.

No less crucial, however, were liberalizations going on within the Christian churches. In Britain, for instance, already in the more conservative era of the 1950s, Protestants had been strong advocates of greater sexual mutuality in marriage, and the Catholic Griffin Report of 1956 recommended—as did the British government's

Wolfenden Committee Report of 1957—that male homosexuality be decriminalized. In the 1960s and 1970s, both Protestant and Catholic theologians, clergymen, and laity actively worked to reformulate Christian mores with regard to sexuality. In France, there were Catholic priests among the advocates for homosexual rights, and self-identified Catholic doctors spoke out in favor of contraceptive use. In West Germany, an official commission of the Protestant Church deemed premarital intercourse acceptable for a couple intending to marry, while the Catholic bishops of West Germany departed from the Vatican's position to declare formally that they endorsed the use of the Pill. In Italy, Catholics worked together with socialists to formulate social-justice-based arguments in order to secure abortion rights for women. In adapting to the new more permissive climate, the churches were reaching out to their own rank and file.

REACTIONS

At the same time, militant political movements organized around issues of sexual desire and pleasure also contributed to the growing publicity surrounding sexuality. Thus, for example, in part growing out of the New Left's sex rights activism and in part reacting against it, new feminist and gay and lesbian movements challenged the often misogynist and/or heterosexist assumptions informing much of the mainstream sexual revolution. Feminists also criticized a culture that frequently trivialized rape and sexual harassment alike. The backlashes against feminism and "out" homosexuality were not far behind, and themselves spawned major public movements—joined by men and women—to reclaim traditional femininity and reassert heterosexuality as normative. These antifeminist and antihomosexual movements were complexly related to the late 1970s' dynamic of both spreading ongoing liberalization and a new weariness and growing anxiety over what were perceived to be the sexual revolution's downsides and excesses.

When the HIV/AIDS epidemic was first identified in the early 1980s, in short, there were already popular, media, and government tendencies toward greater conservatism once again apparent. The initial impulse among politicians and public health officials to label AIDS a "gay disease" was spurred both by homophobic disregard for gay lives and by deep-seated but not fully acknowledged ambivalence about the liberality of heterosexual mores. Much discussion also centered on drug users and immigrants. Governments were quick to propose quarantining those who had been infected but slow to sponsor research for treatment or cure, and also often slow to promote safer sex practices for fear of being seen as endorsing non-monogamous sexuality. Recommendations for fidelity or abstinence missed the point that it was the practices, not the number of partners, that either blocked or facilitated the spread of the disease. Massive mobilization and numerous local initiatives by queer communities ultimately succeeded in convincing public health officials to change their tactics and encouraged government spending on medical research. As of 1996, with the introduction of antiretroviral drugs, the disease, although not curable, became far more manageable within Europe. The crisis has moved to the more impoverished regions of the world in the early twenty-first century.

The 1990s saw a complex combination of liberalization and revived conservatism. Many European nations legalized same-sex unions. Out-of-wedlock births lost all stigma. Traditionally conservative Catholic countries such as Ireland and Austria saw major gains for homosexual rights, due not least to pressures to adopt the standards of the European Union. Gains were also made in Ireland in the areas of access to contraception and abortion, not least under the impact of sexual scandals within the Catholic Church, including clergy abuse of children. The 1990s also, however, saw a return to more traditional values among youth and a revitalized trend toward romance and fidelity among both hetero- and homosexuals. The growing minority of Muslims within Europe, along with the renewal of fundamentalist forms of Islam, with their especially restrictive treatment of female sexuality, have also tested Europeans' assumptions about their own liberality. Some liberals, for instance, have not hesitated to use racist anti-Muslim arguments to defend sex education in schools.

The turn from the twentieth to the twenty-first century has brought new developments that some scholars now bundle together under the rubric "neosexual revolution." This term is an attempt to capture a major reconfiguration in the very essence of what sexuality is and means under the impact of a number of trends: the mass marketing of sexual psychopharmacology in the form of Viagra and other drugs (with their ability to split the capacity to perform from the experience of desire); the exponential explosion of Internet and video pornography, phone sex, and cybersex (a situation in which it becomes increasingly unclear whether people are making love with a partner or more with the images crowding in their heads); a tendency to find the "ego trip" of narcissistic self-display at least as exciting as the physiological sensation of orgasm; and an attempt to optimize the time investment in sexual encounters so as to make them less disruptive of career advancement. Some are now calling the new state of affairs "the onanization of sexuality." In short, while sexuality, as the twentieth century knew it, has become ever more important in the media, it may once again be becoming less important in individual lives.

See also **AIDS; Body Culture; Demography; Homosexuality.**

BIBLIOGRAPHY

Bauer, Ingrid. " 'Austria's Prestige Dragged into the Dirt . . .'? The 'GI-Brides' and Postwar Austrian Society (1945–1955)." *Contemporary Austrian Studies* 6 (1998): 41–55.

Bunzl, Matti. *Symptoms of Modernity: Jews and Queers in Late-Twentieth-Century Vienna*. Berkeley, Calif., 2004.

Collins, Marcus. *Modern Love: An Intimate History of Men and Women in Twentieth-Century Britain*. London, 2003.

Cook, Hera. *The Long Sexual Revolution: English Women, Sex, and Contraception, 1800–1975*. Oxford, U.K., 2004.

Grossmann, Atina. *Reforming Sex: The German Movement for Birth Control and Abortion Reform, 1920–1950*. Oxford, U.K., 1995.

Herzog, Dagmar. *Sex after Fascism: Memory and Morality in Twentieth-Century Germany*. Princeton, N.J., 2005.

Herzog, Dagmar, ed. *Sexuality and German Fascism*. New York, 2005.

Martel, Frédéric. *The Pink and the Black: Homosexuals in France since 1968*. Translated by Jane Marie Todd. Stanford, Calif., 1999.

Marwick, Arthur. *The Sixties: Cultural Revolution in Britain, France, Italy, and the United States, c. 1958–c. 1974.* Oxford, U.K., 1998.

Mossuz-Lavau, Janine. *Les lois de l'amour.* Paris, 1991.

Pedersen, Susan. "National Bodies, Unspeakable Acts: The Sexual Politics of Colonial Policy-Making." *Journal of Modern History* 63 (December 1991): 647–680.

Rydström, Jens. *Sinners and Citizens: Bestiality and Homosexuality in Sweden, 1880–1950.* Chicago, 2003.

Sevegrand, Martine. *Les enfants du bon Dieu: Les catholiques français et la procréation au XX siècle.* Paris, 1995.

Søland, Birgitte. "A Queer Nation? The Passage of Gay and Lesbian Partnership Legislation in Denmark, 1989." *Social Politics* 5 (1998): 48–69.

Watney, Simon. *Policing Desire: Pornography, AIDS, and the Media.* 3rd ed. London, 1997.

DAGMAR HERZOG

SEYSS-INQUART, ARTHUR (1892–1946), Austrian politician.

Arthur Seyss-Inquart was born 22 July 1892 in the village of Stannern, Austria. He studied law and fought in the Austrian Tiroler Kaiserjäger during World War I on the eastern front and in Italy, finally reaching the rank of *Oberleutnant*. After the war he established himself as an attorney in Vienna. Devotedly Catholic and anti-Semitic, he believed the only hope for Austria was Anschluss (annexation) with Germany. He joined a secret pan-German organization, the German Brotherhood, and also became associated with the Austrian Nazi Party after 1932, although he was not included in the membership. As a result of German pressure, he became a Staatsrat (state councillor) on 17 June 1937. Hitler also coerced the Austrian chancellor Kurt von Schuschnigg (1897–1977) into aligning his government more closely with the Third Reich and insisted on the appointment of Seyss-Inquart as minister of security and interior, which happened on 16 February 1938. After a further German ultimatum, Schuschnigg resigned, and Seyss-Inquart succeeded him as chancellor on 11 March 1938. Under continued pressure from Berlin, he invited German troops into Austria and brought about the legalization of Anschluss on 13 March. The ambitious attorney was rewarded with the rank of SS Gruppenführer and was also nominated as Reichsstatthalter (governor) of the Ostmark until 30 April 1939. He then served in Hitler's cabinet as minister without portfolio until the Germans conquered Poland. In October 1939 he was appointed as deputy to Hans Frank, to assist with the creation of the so-called General Government in occupied Poland.

After the German invasion of the Netherlands on 10 May 1940, Seyss-Inquart was appointed by Hitler as Reich Commissioner for the Occupied Dutch Territories on 18 May 1940, and he took up his position on 29 May 1940. He was assisted by four Generalkommissare (commissioners general) who took charge of the Dutch administration, which, after the Dutch government had left for London, was in the hands of senior permanent civil servants. The Dutch civil administration was left intact, and Seyss-Inquart and his German-Austrian Generalkommissare limited themselves to outlining policy and overall supervision.

Seyss-Inquart saw his main task as preparing the Dutch, as a Germanic people, for future annexation to the Reich. Initially he hoped to win the Dutch over to the benefits of Nazism in a friendly manner, but within a year he was confronted with a degree of opposition that led to the realization that National Socialism was seen as profoundly alien to the Dutch mentality. Further ideological and economic demands on the country created an even greater sense of outrage against curbs on personal freedom and precipitated three major strikes in 1941, 1943, and 1944. Realizing that the German attempts at Nazification had failed, Seyss-Inquart took an increasingly hard line, such that the dynamics of repression and resistance led to the collapse of civil society in the last year of the occupation. Although not always directly involved, Seyss-Inquart was responsible for hundreds of executions (often as reprisals). On 5 September 1944 he proclaimed a state of siege and some weeks later imposed a collective punishment on the Dutch people by cutting off the supplies of food and fuel to the west, thus precipitating a famine and many civilian deaths in the severe last winter of occupation, 1944–1945. Seyss-Inquart failed in his attempts to win over the Dutch people ideologically and also failed to extract labor and resources from the country without encountering widespread opposition. His one major success was in relation to racial policy—75 percent of the Jews in the Netherlands were deported and nearly all of these perished in Polish concentration camps.

Proposed as foreign minister by Hitler during his last days as chancellor, Seyss-Inquart escaped from the Netherlands to North Germany, where he was subsequently arrested near Hamburg by advancing British troops on 4 May 1945. Put on trial at Nuremberg, he claimed to have served Dutch interests but was found guilty of war crimes and crimes against humanity. He was hanged on 16 October 1946 in Nuremberg prison.

See also **Austria; Germany; Nazism; Netherlands; World War II.**

BIBLIOGRAPHY

Primary Sources

Seyss-Inquart, Arthur. *Vier Jahre in den Niederlanden: Gesammelte Reden.* Berlin, 1944.

Secondary Sources

Davidson, Eugene. *The Trial of the Germans: An Account of the Twenty-two Defendants before the International Military Tribunal at Nuremberg.* Columbia, Mo., 1997.

Hirschfeld, Gerhard. *Nazi Rule and Dutch Collaboration: The Netherlands under German Occupation, 1940–1945.* Translated from the German by Louise Willmot. Oxford, U.K., 1988.

Neuman, Henk J. *Arthur Seyss-Inquart: Het leven van een Duits onderkoning in Nederland: met authentieke brieven tijdens zijn gevangenschap geschreven.* 2nd ed. Utrecht, Netherlands, 1989.

DICK VAN GALEN LAST

SHEVARDNADZE, EDUARD (b. 1928), Soviet foreign minister and president of Georgia.

Eduard Amvrosevich Shevardnadze was born in the village of Mamati in western Soviet Georgia. The young Eduard grew up with the knowledge that some of his family had suffered from the Stalinist regime. Yet after graduating from the state pedagogical institute in Kutaisi, he rose rapidly in the Komsomol (Communist Youth Union) and the Communist Party. In 1968 he was named minister of internal affairs in Georgia, and when the Soviet party chief Leonid Brezhnev launched a campaign to rid Georgia of corruption and favoritism, he elevated Shevardnadze to party leader of Georgia (1972). Four years later he became a member of the Central Committee of the Communist Party of the Soviet Union (CPSU).

In Georgia he was a vigorous campaigner against crime and corruption, though ultimately powerless before the country's "black" and "gray" markets and the system of kinship politics that made evasion from the law prevalent. Even though he fought against manifestations of Georgian nationalism, he developed a rapport with the public. In 1978, when Georgians publicly demanded restoration of Georgian as the official language of the republic, he defied Moscow's initial objections and made that concession. His reforms attracted the attention of a rising young Russian communist, Mikhail Gorbachev, who in a famous private conversation confided to Shevardnadze his conviction that the Soviet Union could not go on much longer without reform. When Gorbachev became general secretary of the CPSU in 1985 he surprised the world by bringing Shevardnadze to Moscow as a member of his Politburo and minister of foreign affairs.

The Gorbachev-Shevardnadze foreign policy, known as the "New Thinking," transformed the Soviet Union from a dedicated adversary of the West into a much more cooperative interlocutor. Concern for the interests of a generalized humanity replaced the idea of international class struggle between capitalist and socialist camps. Arms reduction, withdrawal of Soviet troops from Afghanistan, and a refusal to back militarily Soviet-style communist regimes in Eastern Europe all became part of a post–Cold War foreign policy. Identified with this radical shift in policy, Shevardnadze incurred the wrath of communist hardliners, and when Gorbachev appeared to turn way from reform, Shevardnadze resigned his position (December 1990). Only after the anti-Gorbachev coup of August 1991 did he return to the foreign ministry as the USSR disintegrated and Gorbachev's power withered.

When independent Georgia's first president, Zviad Gamsakhurdia, led his nation into civil and ethnic war, influential Georgians invited Shevardnadze back to reunify the country. His supporters defeated Gamsakhurdia, but Shevardnadze

Eduard Shevardnadze. Escorted by bodyguards, the former foreign minister arrives at the Russian parliament building during the coup attempt of August 1991. ©PETER TURNLEY/CORBIS

could not bring the whole country under his control. Georgians were driven out of Abkhazia and South Ossetia and Shevardnadze was forced to accept de facto Russian hegemony in those regions. To placate Russia he agreed to join the Commonwealth of Independent States (CIS), the primary tie left for former Soviet states.

Having established a degree of security for Georgia, and after surviving an assassination attempt, Shevardnadze was overwhelmingly elected president of Georgia in November 1995. He brought order to its streets, ridding the cities of the free-standing militias, but was unable to revive the economy or restrain the growing corruption. His popularity began to decline in the second half of the 1990s, at least within Georgia, though he maintained a respectable international reputation. But even his highly placed friends in Western capitals began to desert him in the early twenty-first century. Though reelected president in April 2000, it was widely recognized that the election had been marred by irregularities. By this time many saw the Shevardnadze as part of the

problem rather than a solution to the country's economic and political woes.

In November 2003 Shevardnadze and his allies overplayed their hand in an attempt to win the elections to the Georgian parliament. Popular outrage fed into a movement led by the charismatic Mikhail Saakashvili, a young politician earlier groomed by Shevardnadze himself. While the president was speaking to parliament, Saakashvili and his followers broke into the hall, and security men whisked a confused Shevardnadze to safety. Rather than use force, Shevardnadze decided to resign. His opponents agreed to allow him to remain in Georgia. This "Rose Revolution" effectively ended the political career of the man who had dominated Georgia for more than thirty years. His legacy in his homeland remains mixed, while his achievements in foreign policy contributed to the end of the Cold War.

See also **Brezhnev, Leonid; Cold War; Gorbachev, Mikhail.**

BIBLIOGRAPHY

Primary Sources

Shevardnadze, Eduard. *The Future Belongs to Freedom.* Translated by Catherine A. Fitzpatrick. New York, 1991.

Secondary Sources

Ekedahl, Carolyn M., and Melvin A. Goodman. *Wars of Eduard Shevardnadze.* State College, Pa., 1997.

Palazchenko, Pavel, and Don Oberdorfer. *My Years with Gorbachev and Shevardnadze: The Memoir of a Soviet Interpreter.* State College, Pa., 1997.

Suny, Ronald Grigor. *The Making of the Georgian Nation.* 2nd ed. Bloomington, Ind., 1994.

Suny, Ronald Grigor, ed. *Transcaucasia, Nationalism, and Social Change.* Rev. ed. Ann Arbor, Mich., 1996.

RONALD GRIGOR SUNY

SHOSTAKOVICH, DMITRI (1906–1975), Soviet composer.

Dmitri Shostakovich was born in St. Petersburg (Leningrad) on 25 September (12 September, old style) 1906, and died in Moscow on 9 August 1975. Chronologically his life and work coincided with the Bolshevik Revolution and the historical events that ensued in Russia and the Soviet Union: civil war, industrialization, collectivization of the peasantry, Stalin's great purge, World War II, destalinization, and the Cold War and nuclear arms race. These cataclysms left an indelible mark on the composer's life and on his work. Unlike his older contemporaries Igor Stravinsky (1882–1971) and Sergei Prokofiev (1891–1953), Shostakovich never emigrated or spent much time abroad. Living and creating inside Soviet Russia made him an eminently Soviet artist.

Shostakovich graduated from the Petrograd (later Leningrad) Conservatory in 1923 (piano) and 1925 (composition). His reputation was established with his *First Symphony* (1924–1925), performed in 1926. By the time of his death he had created fifteen symphonies, rivaling Beethoven and Mahler as one of the most prolific symphonic composers of all times. He had worked as a pianist at a movie theater as a student, and his fascination with the cinema influenced his successful work on film scores. His ventures into musical theater were less successful. His first opera, *The Nose* (first performed in 1930), was based on a satirical story by nineteenth-century writer Nikolai Gogol. It drew sharp criticism from the censors and proletarian zealots in art circles and the official press. His next opera, *Lady Macbeth of Mtsensk District* (*Katerina Izmaylova,* 1934) presented a gloomy picture of provincial tsarist Russia. It angered Stalin and was condemned in *Pravda.* Shortly afterward the ballet *Limpid Stream* (1935) was also withdrawn from the repertoire and banned.

The Soviet regime exerted a rigid control of the arts, and Shostakovich was forced to create music that the regime considered appropriate, namely film scores, grandiose symphonies, and programmatic cantatas and songs based the on lyrics of state-approved poets. He wrote music for the major blockbusters of the Stalinist era: *Trilogy about Maxim* (1934–1938; an epic about the making of a communist hero in prerevolutionary Russia); *The Great Citizen* (1938–1939; based on murdered Bolshevik Sergei Kirov's life and death); *The Young Guard* (1947–1948; about the young communist group's exploits under the Nazi occupation); *The Fall of Berlin* (1949; glorifying Stalin's command during World War II); and *Unforgettable Year 1919* (1951; depicting Stalin's genius during the civil war). After Stalin's death he wrote much less ideologically compromised film music (e.g., *Gadfly* [1955], *Hamlet* [1964], and *King Lear* [1971]).

The fulfillment of state orders for film scores gave the composer relative freedom in his symphonic, concerto, and chamber music works as well in song cycles. The official acceptance of his symphonies was uneven and reflected the ups and downs of the country's political life. The *Second* (*October*) (1927) and *Third* (*Labor Day*) (1929) symphonies, set to the lyrics of now-forgotten communist poets, were hailed. The *Fourth* (1935–1936) was withdrawn during rehearsal and not performed for thirty years. The *Fifth* (1937) was heralded as a triumph of socialist realism in music. The *Sixth* (1939) was silenced. The *Seventh* (1941), the famous *Leningrad Symphony,* was proclaimed a triumph of antiwar art and played around the world. The *Ninth* (1945) was briefly banned. The *Eleventh* (1957) bore the subtitle *The Year 1905:* the year of the revolution Vladimir Lenin called the great rehearsal for the 1917 Bolshevik triumph. The *Twelfth*

Symphony (1961) was dedicated to Lenin. The *Thirteenth* (1962) was written to the poetry of young nonconformist poet Yevgeny Yevtushenko. Its first part, "Babi Yar" (the name of a ravine in the Ukrainian capital, Kiev, where the Nazis massacred tens of thousands of Jews in World War II), infuriated the authorities, and Nikita Khrushchev personally attacked Yevtushenko. Only his last symphony, the *Fifteenth* (1971), a genuine farewell to life, was not manipulated by the authorities.

The Soviet regime's treatment of Shostakovich was typical of official suppression and control of the arts during the Stalinist period and in the years after Stalin's death. But the regime also made Shostakovich the most officially honored composer in modern history. He was the winner of five Stalin Prizes and of the Lenin and State Prizes, a Hero of Socialist Labor, and a People's Artist of the USSR. He was a longtime deputy to the Supreme Soviet (parliament) and for the last fifteen years of his life he was a member of the Communist Party and worked as a head of the Union of Composers of Russian Federation enjoying luxurious apartments, cottages, cars, and trips abroad.

The uniqueness of Shostakovich's standing lay in the fact that he was totally integrated into the political and artistic hierarchy and at the same time was revered around the world and especially in the West as one of the greatest composers of the century. In the context of the Cold War, the detente achieved on the Shostakovich front was unusual. It was challenged four years after his death in a book entitled *Testimony: The Memoirs of Dmitri Shostakovich as Related to and Edited by Solomon Volkov*, published in the United States. The book depicted the composer as an embittered and suffering man, at best an internal émigré within his own country, at worst a secret dissident, if not anticommunist and anti-Soviet. The book followed a tradition long established in the West after the Bolshevik Revolution, that of publishing explosive revelatory memoirs, letters, diaries, and testimony of famous and powerful Soviet personalities (e.g., the foreign minister Maxim Litvinov or the alleged British spy and colonel of military intelligence Oleg Penkovsky). What united these bestsellers was the fact that by the time of publication their "authors" were dead and in most cases the books appeared only in translation and the Russian original was not made public.

The case of *Testimony* looked equally suspect. In 1980 U.S. scholar Laurel Fay convincingly showed that the book was partly based on materials published in the Soviet press. Its anti-Soviet and anticommunist portions were made up largely of dissident oral history, stories, and legends that abounded in Russian intellectual circles in the second half of the twentieth century. The book's defenders were vehement in its support, sometimes confusing the notion of the veracity of a document with its authenticity, which was unequivocally and repeatedly denied by the composer's widow, Irina Shostakovich. The *Testimony* controversy foreshadowed a pattern of justifying and rehabilitating iconic Soviet personalities of the twentieth century that emerged in post-Soviet Russia. The stream of fashionable "internal suffering" revelations and confessions, revisionist in nature, became a trend and included many honored Soviet writers, musicians, ballerinas, painters, filmmakers, and actors who were well integrated in the Soviet hierarchies.

The Shostakovich controversy, far from being resolved, has helped to enhance the stature of the composer as one of the most enigmatic, prolific, and interpreted musicians of the past century. Together with his countrymen Stravinsky and Prokofiev, he became a musical ambassador of Russian culture on a worldwide scale.

See also **Prokofiev, Sergei; Soviet Union; Stravinsky, Igor.**

BIBLIOGRAPHY

Primary Sources

Shostakovich, Dmitri. *Dmitry Shostakovich: About Himself and His Times.* Compiled by L. Grigoryev and Ya. Platek. Translated from the Russian by Angus and Neilian Roxburgh. Moscow, 1981.

———. *Story of a Friendship: The Letters of Dmitry Shostakovich to Isaak Glikman, 1941–1975,* with a commentary by Isaak Glikman. Translated by Anthony Phillips. Ithaca, N.Y., 2001.

Secondary Sources

Blackstock, Paul W. *Agents of Deceit: Frauds, Forgeries, and Political Intrigue among Nations.* Appendix by George F. Kennan. Chicago, 1966.

Brown, Malcolm Hamrick, ed. *A Shostakovich Casebook.* Bloomington, Ind., 2004.

Fay, Laurel E. *Shostakovich: A Life.* New York, 2000.

Fay, Laurel E., ed. *Shostakovich and His World*. Princeton, N.J., 2004.

Ho, Allan B., and Dmitry Feofanov. *Shostakovich Reconsidered*. London, 1998.

Testimony: The Memoirs of Dmitri Shostakovich, as Related to and Edited by Solomon Volkov. Translated by Antonina W. Bouis. New York, 1979.

LEONID MAXIMENKOV

SIBELIUS, JEAN (1865–1957), Finnish composer.

Jean Christian Julius Sibelius was born on 8 December 1865 into a middle-class Swedish-speaking family in Hämeenlinna (Tavastehus), a provincial town north of Helsinki. At this time, Finland was a grand duchy of the Russian Empire. Sibelius's father died of typhoid in 1868, and his mother raised him. Their summers were spent at the Baltic seaport of Loviisa. Sibelius began violin lessons with the local bandmaster in Hämeenlinna in 1880, and his earliest surviving composition, a duet for violin and cello called *Vattendroppar* (Waterdrops) dates from around this time.

Sibelius enrolled at Helsinki University to read law in 1885, but swiftly abandoned his studies and took up a place at the Helsinki Music Institute, founded by Martin Wegelius (1846–1906) in 1881. Among the teachers on staff was the Italian-German pianist and composer Ferruccio Benvenuto Busoni (1866–1924). Sibelius graduated in 1889 and spent the next academic year in Berlin, studying counterpoint with Albert Becker (1834–1899). After returning to Finland, he traveled to Vienna in 1890 to study with Robert Fuchs (1847–1927) and Karl Goldmark (1830–1915). His year in Vienna made a deep musical impression on the young composer. He heard the Third Symphony of Anton Bruckner (1824–1896), and, inspired by reading the Finnish national epic the *Kalevala,* he began composing his first large-scale orchestral work, the highly original choral symphony *Kullervo*. On his return to Finland, he heard the rune singer Larin Paraske (1833–1904) and incorporated stylized musical figures based on her singing in parts of *Kullervo*. The work was premiered on 28 April 1892, the same year that Sibelius married Aino Järnefelt, daughter of a prominent upper-class family with strongly nationalist leanings.

Throughout the 1890s tensions had been growing between the Russian authorities and popular demands for an independent Finnish state. Many of Sibelius's works from this period were associated with the struggle for national identity and draw on themes or characters from the *Kalevala*. The First Symphony was premiered on 26 April 1899, followed by *Finlandia,* one of Sibelius's most popular compositions, on 4 November. The symphony was subsequently performed at the Universal Exposition in Paris in 1900, as Sibelius's musical horizons became increasingly international. The Second Symphony (1900–1901), often heard as a patriotic call for Finnish liberation, was actually written in Italy.

The Second Symphony received its first American performance in Chicago in 1904. Later that year, Sibelius moved out of Helsinki to a villa in the country, called Ainola. The change of scene coincided with a significant shift of aesthetic focus away from the rich Romanticism of the first two symphonies toward a leaner, more concentrated musical style. The Third Symphony of 1907 is strikingly compressed: the third movement combines the functions of scherzo and finale telescoped into a single unbroken musical span. The Fourth Symphony (1911) is even more epigrammatic and has since gained a reputation as being one of the most difficult and modernist of Sibelius's symphonic works.

Sibelius traveled to the United States in 1914, at the invitation of Carl Stoeckel (1858–1925), to conduct the premiere of his tone poem *The Oceanides* at the Norfolk Festival in Connecticut. The outbreak of World War I, however, isolated Sibelius from international musical markets, especially in Germany, and may have prompted a significant period of compositional reassessment that resulted in the first version of the Fifth Symphony (1915, rev. 1916–1919). During the Finnish Civil War of 1918, Sibelius's sympathies lay with the White Army led by Baron Carl Gustav Emil Von Mannerheim (1867–1951), rather than with the Communists. Sibelius's later diary entries, and often his music, are marked by an increasingly powerful mood of inwardness and withdrawal. James Hepokoski has argued that the final two symphonies (1923 and 1924, respectively) and the tone poem *Tapiola* (1926) can be heard as concentrated meditations upon aspects of the Nordic natural world. Though Sibelius worked on an Eighth Symphony in the 1930s, parts of which were professionally copied, he probably burned the manuscript, and no major new works appeared after the completion of *Tapiola* in 1926. Sibelius's reputation in the United Kingdom and North America was at its height, but he increasingly sought to withdraw from public view. Sibelius died on 20 September 1957.

Sibelius's critical reception has followed a cyclic trajectory through twentieth-century music. Initially celebrated in Finland as a national hero, his symphonies were later upheld as the model for a progressive post-Beethovenian modernism. His perceived right-wing political connections, and supposed association with the blood-and-soil ideology of Nazism, partly accounted for the decline in his reputation after World War II, principally at the hands of writers such as Theodor Adorno (1903–1969) and René Leibowitz (1913–1972). The end of the twentieth century, however, saw renewed interest in Sibelius and his innovative approach to musical texture and form from a broad range of scholars and composers, from members of the French spectral school such as Tristan Murail to leading lights of British contemporary music and American minimalists such as John Adams.

See also **Finland.**

BIBLIOGRAPHY

Abraham, Gerald, ed. *Sibelius: A Symposium*. London, 1948.

Goss, Glenda Dawn. *Sibelius: A Guide to Research*. New York, 1998.

Goss, Glenda Dawn, ed. *The Sibelius Companion*. Westport, Conn., 1996.

———, ed. *Jean Sibelius: The Hämeenlinna Letters*. Helsinki, 1997.

Grimley, Daniel M., ed. *The Cambridge Companion to Sibelius*. Cambridge, U.K., 2004.

Hepokoski, James. *Sibelius, Symphony no. 5*. Cambridge, U.K., 1993.

Jackson, Timothy L., and Veijo Murtomäki, eds. *Sibelius Studies*. Cambridge, U.K., 2001.

Layton, Robert. *Sibelius*. 4th ed. London, 1992.

Murtomäki, Veijo. *Symphonic Unity: The Development of Formal Thinking in the Symphonies of Sibelius*. Translated by Henry Bacon. Helsinki, 1993.

Parmet, Simon. *The Symphonies of Sibelius: A Study in Musical Appreciation*. Translated by Kingsley A. Hart. London, 1959.

Tawaststjerna, Erik. *Sibelius*. 3 vols. Edited and translated by Robert Layton. London, 1976–1997.

DANIEL M. GRIMLEY

SINN FÉIN. The Irish radical nationalist political movement and party, Sinn Féin, was founded around 1905. However, the present Sinn Féin party's claim to be the oldest political party in Ireland disguises profound changes in its ideology, tactics, and personnel over the course of the twentieth century. Translating as "Ourselves" and promoting the principle of Irish self-reliance, the Sinn Féin movement emerged from a number of political groups, including Cumann na nGaedheal (founded 1900) led by Arthur Griffith, the National Council (1903), and the Dungannon Clubs (1905) in Belfast. The Dungannon Clubs and Cumann na nGaedheal merged in April 1907 as the Sinn Féin League, becoming Sinn Féin in 1908. Although Sinn Féin contested many local elections and the 1908 North Leitrim by-election (which proved a crushing defeat), the movement was always more of a pressure group than merely a political party, providing a meeting ground for various disparate nationalists, feminists, pacifists, socialists, and Irish language enthusiasts, brought together by their rejection of Irish devolution (Home Rule) and using the radical nationalist press to convey its message. Griffith was the party's principle ideologue, despite his unwillingness to become involved in formal party politics. Griffith's two major works, *The Resurrection of Hungary* (1904) and *The Sinn Féin Policy* (1906), suggested that Ireland, under a system of dual monarchy with the English Crown, should become economically self-reliant and that Irish members of Parliament (MPs) would abstain from Westminster and create an Irish national assembly instead.

1916–1921

Prior to the 1916 Easter Rising in Ireland, Sinn Féin stood at the margins of Irish politics; in August 1909, the party could boast only 581 members, 211 of whom came from Dublin. But its importance lay in establishing the split between constitutional nationalists and separatists that would change Irish politics in 1917 and 1918. Following the Easter Rising (which was erroneously dubbed the "Sinn Féin Rebellion"), the British government's suppression of the party and its attempts to introduce conscription to Ireland during 1918 gave Sinn Féin a popularity undreamed of before World War I. During 1917 Sinn Féin gained four important by-election victories. A year later, its membership had risen to 112,080 members, and in the December 1918 election Sinn Féin gained 48 percent of the vote and 73 out of 105 parliamentary seats at Westminster, including the first woman to be elected as an MP, Constance Markievicz. Sinn Féin, however, did not take up these seats, instead establishing the first Dáil Éireann (Irish Parliament) that claimed to be the legitimate government of Ireland. Hostilities began shortly afterward between the British forces and the Irish paramilitaries (including the IRA), and as the Anglo-Irish conflict escalated, Sinn Féin became increasingly marginalized, seeing its share of the vote fall to 30 percent in the local elections of 1920. The Anglo-Irish Treaty that ended the war in 1921, despite being negotiated by Griffith and Michael Collins on the Irish side, was deeply contentious to many within the Sinn Féin movement, especially the continued connection between Ireland and Britain embodied in the Oath of Allegiance to the English Crown required of all members of the newly elected Irish assembly. Unable to reach consensus, the separatist republicans of the Sinn Féin movement, led by Eamonn de Valera, opposed the treaty, leading to the outbreak of civil war in Ireland.

1923–1970

Defeated in the Irish civil war, Sinn Féin emerged again in May 1923, recognizing the second Dáil (elected a year earlier) as the legitimate government of Ireland. By 1926, de Valera had become disillusioned with Sinn Féin's failure to acknowledge the political realities of Ireland and moved away from the party to form Fianna Fáil. Only a rump Sinn Féin party remained, and from 1926 onward it did not contest Irish Free State elections and became an increasingly irrelevant republican ghetto. The 1930s were notable only for the election of

Margaret Buckley as president of the party in 1936, the first female leader of an Irish party, and Sinn Féin's transferral of the second Dáil's powers as the legitimate government of Ireland to the army council of the Irish Republican Army (IRA) in 1938 on the commencement of its bombing campaign on mainland Britain. The IRA increased its hold over Sinn Féin, infiltrating the party in 1949.

THE 1970S AND 1980S

By the end of the 1960s, tensions in the party between socialists wanting electoral participation and militarists grew and resulted in a split in the republican movement at the end of 1969. The Provisional IRA took up the armed struggle against the British armed forces during the 1970s, with Provisional Sinn Féin continuing to be a support group for the IRA, as Gerry Adams, who emerged as the leader of Sinn Féin during the 1980s, later recalled doing little more than selling newspapers and raffle tickets.

With Adams, Martin McGuinness, and others coming to the fore in the party, the 1980s saw the beginnings of a coherent political strategy for Sinn Féin. At the height of the hunger strikes by republican prisoners in 1981, Sinn Féin decided to abandon decades of abstention from political activity and contest the Fermanagh-South Tyrone by-election. In April 1981 Bobby Sands, the leader of the hunger strikes, was duly elected MP. At that year's *Ard Fheis* (annual party conference), leading republican Danny Morrison summarized this strategy of militarism and electoralism as combining the ballot box with the Armalite (a light machine gun, popular with the IRA at this time). Politics began to complement, but not replace, armed struggle, and Sinn Féin became increasingly influential in the republican movement. By 1986 Sinn Féin had abandoned abstentionism and had recognized the southern Irish state, allowing Sinn Féin to take up their seats in the Irish Dáil.

SINN FÉIN AND THE PEACE PROCESS

The first signs that politics might one day replace armed struggle as Sinn Féin policy came at the end of the 1980s. Acknowledging the need to find agreement with the unionist majority in Northern Ireland, the 1987 Sinn Féin election manifesto, *A Scenario for Peace*, was an important policy

A British soldier cautiously approaches a car bearing campaign posters for Gerry Adams, Belfast, 1997. AP/ WIDE WORLD PHOTOS

statement that affirmed the necessity of a political route for the party. What became known as the peace process in Northern Ireland can be seen to have commenced shortly afterward in 1988 when John Hume (leader of the majority nationalist party in Northern Ireland, the Social Democratic and Labour Party [SDLP]) began secret talks with Gerry Adams. These discussions were initially fruitless, but marked the starting point of Sinn Féin's entry into the political mainstream.

Following the Hume-Adams document of April 1993 and the Downing Street Declaration of December 1993 between British Prime Minister John Major and the Irish Taoiseach Albert Reynolds, an IRA cease-fire began in 1994. Subsequently, Sinn Féin political progress was slow but assured during the 1990s. In the 1997 Irish elections, Caoimhghín ó Caoláin became the first Sinn Féin member to take his seat in the Dáil Éireann since 1922. The historic 1998 Belfast Agreement (called the Good Friday Agreement) admitted Sinn Féin to all-party talks, restored devolved government to Ireland, and established a North-South ministerial council. It was, in the historian Alvin Jackson's description, the Anglo-Irish Treaty of 1921 for slow-learning republicans. Seen by Sinn Féin as an interim measure on the road to an independent Ireland, the Belfast Agreement brought the party fully into the political mainstream, and in the 2001 general election, Sinn Féin surpassed the SDLP as the majority party among the Catholic nationalist community of Northern Ireland, winning 21 percent of the vote in the national and local elections.

See also **Ireland; Northern Ireland.**

BIBLIOGRAPHY

Davis, Richard P. *Arthur Griffith and Non-Violent Sinn Féin.* Dublin, 1974.

Feeney, Brian. *Sinn Féin: A Hundred Turbulent Years.* Dublin, 2002.

Jackson, Alvin. *Home Rule: An Irish History 1800–2000.* London, 2003.

Laffan, Michael. *The Resurrection of Ireland: The Sinn Féin Party, 1916–1923*. Cambridge, U.K., 1999.

O'Brien, Brendan. *The Long War: The IRA and Sinn Féin*. 2nd ed. Syracuse, N.Y., 1997.

Taylor, Peter. *Provos: The IRA and Sinn Féin*. Rev. ed. London, 1998.

D.A.J. MacPherson

SITUATIONISM.

SITUATIONISM. In the first issue of *Internationale situationniste,* published in 1958, *situationism* was defined as "a meaningless term derived from situationist. There is no such thing as situationism, which would mean a doctrine of interpretation of existing facts. The notion of situationism is obviously devised by anti-situationists" (*Internationale situationniste*, p. 13). This statement shows the uncompromising, oppositional quest for avant-garde purity that characterized this movement, founded in 1957 by seven intellectuals of various Western nationalities. The Situationist International placed itself within a subversive lineage that included surrealism and the lettrist movement of the Romanian poet and megalomaniac Isidore Isou, but its assault on culture, inextricably linked to political revolution, sought to overcome past "betrayals": the integration of surrealism into the art establishment and Isou's eschewal of communism.

The situationists waged war on what their dominant figure, Guy Debord (1931–1994), termed the "society of the spectacle," a society where individuals were passive consumers of art, leisure, education, and politics and were separated from the product of their labor. The spectacle was "diffuse" in the case of Western liberal democracy and "concentrated" in the authoritarian communism of the East. Debord and his comrades aimed to construct a "situation," defined as "a moment of life concretely and deliberately constructed by the collective organization of a unitary ambience and a game of events" (p. 13). The "situation" was a moment of intensity that broke with the drudgery and illusory pleasure of everyday life, a moment when the spectator became a subject of history and created what another situationist theorist, Raoul Vaneigem (b. 1934), called the "poetry of acts" rather than the "poetry of words."

Various techniques were used by the situationists: psychogeography, "the study of the specific effects of the geographical environment, consciously organized or not, on the emotions and behaviour of individuals," and, linked to this, the *dérive* (drift) or "technique of transient passage through varied ambiances" (p. 13). The aim was to redraw the map of an urban environment in the grip of the spectacle, to imagine utopia and make it come into being. The situationists' attitude toward art was also aggressive, entailing the *détournement* (hijacking) of existing aesthetic elements: Asger Jorn (1914–1973) painted over kitsch pictures found in flea markets; Debord made films that provoked the viewer out of passivity, and, most important, situationists created iconoclastic cartoon strips and graffiti.

About three hundred people passed through the Situationist International during its brief history, including the Scottish novelist Alexander Trocchi (1925–1984), the Dutch architect Constant (1920–2005), and the French critic (and Debord's first wife) Michèle Bernstein. Almost all were expelled for deviating from the group's principles, mainly at the behest of Debord. In the International, artistic creation was eclipsed by the revolutionary project. The events of May 1968 seemed to be the "situation" par excellence: an insurrection that took the establishment, both Gaullist and Communist, by surprise, one that challenged everyday life and in which slogans and propaganda techniques pioneered by the situationists were much in view. Revolution in the developed and prosperous societies of the West seemed possible and imminent.

The revolutionary tide ebbed, however, and the sudden popularity of situationist ideas gave rise to the unwelcome figure of the *pro-situ,* a passive consumer of badly digested "situationism." In the face of this, in 1972 Guy Debord dissolved the organization: at the time, there were only two members pure enough to remain. Debord embarked on an obscure period of wanderings; then, around the time of the collapse of communism in Eastern Europe, he returned to his theory of the spectacle. In his last writings, Debord noted the fusion of "diffuse" and "concentrated" spectacles into an "integrated" form: there was no longer any opposition to the dictatorship of a capitalist system now out of control; the much-vaunted "rights of man" meant those of "man as spectator." In November 1994 Debord, having been diagnosed with an incurable illness, shot himself through the heart: this suicide was interpreted by many as one last, desperate expression of revolt.

Apart from their seminal role in the intellectual climate of May 1968, situationist ideas have had a considerable cultural impact: on postmodernist philosophy, for example, notably that of Jean Baudrillard (b. 1929), and on British popular culture, embodied, notably, in the punk rock band the Sex Pistols. Since his death, Debord has become an icon, his image often stenciled on walls in bohemian areas of Paris. But this last detail may point to the limits of the situationist enterprise; Debord was a theorist of revolution who had an impact only in intellectual circles and not among the proletariat, which, in true Marxist fashion, he had theorized as revolutionary subject.

See also **Baudrillard, Jean; Consumption; 1968; Popular Culture.**

BIBLIOGRAPHY

Primary Sources

Blazwick, Iwona, ed. *An Endless Adventure—An Endless Passion—An Endless Banquet: A Situationist Scrapbook.* New York, 1989.

Debord, Guy. *Comments on the Society of the Spectacle.* New York, 1990.

———. *Society of the Spectacle.* New York, 1994.

Vaneigem, Raoul. *Revolution of Everyday Life.* Translated by John Fullerton and Paul Sieveking. 2nd ed. London, 1979.

Secondary Sources

Home, Stewart. *The Assault on Culture: Utopian Currents from Lettrisme to Class War.* Translated by Malcolm Imrie. London, 1988.

Hussey, Andrew. *The Game of War: The Life and Death of Guy Debord.* New York, 2001.

Internationale situationniste. Paris, 1997.

Jappe, Anselm. *Guy Debord.* Translated by Donald Nicholson-Smith. Berkeley, Calif., 1999.

Marcus, Greil. *Lipstick Traces: A Secret History of the Twentieth Century.* Cambridge, Mass., 1990.

GAVIN BOWD

ŠKODA. Pilsen Machinery Works, later Škoda, was founded in 1859 by Ernst Waldstein, who purchased an ironworks factory near Pilsen, in the Czech lands. In 1869 Waldstein sold the company to its director, a young engineer named Emil von Škoda, who transformed it into the most important engineering firm in the Austro-Hungarian Empire—which then governed the Czech lands—and, subsequently, its principal arms manufacturer. At first Škoda concentrated on the production and processing of steel. From 1886, however, when Škoda began experimenting with armor plating, military production became increasingly important. Civil production included steam engines, turbines, and equipment for sugar refineries, breweries, mines, and iron works. In 1899, Pilsen Machinery Works became a shareholding company, named Škoda Works (Škodovy Závody), with the majority of the shares in the hands of its owner. At the time of Škoda's death, in 1900, the company had forty-two hundred employees, and its products were sold the world over. With the First World War, production reached its peak: during the conflict, Škoda supplied the empire with more than 12,000 artillery pieces, and by 1917 it employed 30,000 people.

In 1918, with the collapse of the Austro-Hungarian Empire and the birth of Czechoslovakia, Škoda was nearly dismantled, lacking both the financial resources needed for reconversion and a market for its products. In addition, since Škoda was owned by an Austrian citizen (Emil von Škoda's son Karl) and by German banks, the Czechoslovak government applied the 1919 act of domestication of joint-stock companies, transferred the company's headquarters from Vienna to Prague and, after delicate negotiations, backed the acquisition of controlling interest in the company by the French company Schneider-Creusot. Relations between the Czechoslovak government and the company remained close, however. In these years, the government appears as a protector of Škoda interests, as a purchaser of its products, a channel for orders from other countries and a guarantor of its foreign credits, as well as rescuing it from financial difficulties. This ensured Škoda's almost uninterrupted growth from 1921 to 1938, as well as the establishment of a horizontal monopoly on the entire Czechoslovak engineering industry.

In 1925 Škoda acquired one of the leading Czechoslovak automobile makers, Laurin & Klement, thus tying its brand to the history of automobile manufacturing. Škoda-Auto (Akciová

Společnost pro Automobilový Průmysl), as the new shareholding company was named, modeled itself after the "American model of mass production," but it was able to tread the thin line between the technological and organizational modernity of Fordism and the realities of a limited market. In 1936 Škoda Auto was the domestic market leader with sales totals of three thousand vehicles, which increased the following year. In 1937, it employed over five thousand workers and produced more than eight thousand vehicles.

Following the new balance of power established in 1938 by the Treaty of Munich, Schneider sold its shares, leaving the company in the hands of German investors. On 15 March 1939, Czechoslovakia was occupied by German troops, and Škoda became part of the Reichswerke Hermann Göring A.G. After 1940 civilian production was limited, and the company's energies turned to supplying the military.

After the war, Škoda was nationalized on 7 March 1946, and broken up into several companies: Škoda Works was responsible for the production of machine tools, locomotives, electrotechnical materials, and arms. Škoda-Auto plant, renamed Automobiles National Plants (Automobilové Závody, Národní Podnik), became the center of Czechoslovak automobile production.

During the Cold War, the divergent destinies of Škoda-Auto and Škoda Works reflected the priorities of the Communist regime, which came to power in February 1948, and the growing international tension. With the First Five-Year Plan (1949–1953), most of the country's resources—raw materials and manpower—were directed to heavy industry. Škoda automobiles became less and less competitive because of poor investment, obsolescent plants, and a chronic shortage of raw materials and manpower. From the 1960s on, economic reforms and a new emphasis on consumer goods throughout the socialist bloc revitalized Škoda-Auto: a new plant was built and, though not without difficulty, new automobiles of good quality were produced (Octavia, Rapid, Favorit, 1000 MB) in consistently high volumes. In 1989, with the fall of the Berlin Wall, the company stipulated a joint venture with Volkswagen, which relaunched the Škoda brand on the global automobile market.

The communist takeover could not stop the growth of Škoda Works: by 1989 Škoda controlled more than twenty plants and was active in ninety-one different product groups; production included electric locomotives and trolleys, energy equipment and systems, heavy industrial machinery, rolled steel, forges, presses, castings, and other mechanical devices. Privatization of Škoda Works proved more complex: after the failure of talks about a joint venture with Siemens in 1992 and a long restructuring process, the firm in the early 2000s was controlled by an international investment group.

See also **Automobiles; Czechoslovakia; Volkswagen.**

BIBLIOGRAPHY

Fava, Valentina. "Tecnici, ingegneri, e fordismo: Škoda e Fiat nelle relazioni di viaggio in America." *Imprese e Storia* 22 (2000): 201–249.

Kožíšek, Petr, and Jan Králík. *L&K-Škoda. The Flight of the Winged Arrow.* Vols. 1 and 2. Prague, 1995.

Teichová, Alice. *An Economic Background to Munich: International Business in Czechoslovakia, 1918–1938.* Cambridge, U.K., 1974.

VALENTINA FAVA

SLÁNSKÝ TRIAL.

On the last day of July 1951, the veteran Czechoslovak communist leader Rudolf Slánský (1901–1952) celebrated his fiftieth birthday. Citizens from around the country sent congratulations to the Communist Party secretary general. Czechoslovak president Klement Gottwald bestowed Slánský with the "Order of Socialism" and had a factory named after him. Amid this wave of adoration, however, there was an ominous sign: Soviet leader Joseph Stalin failed to send a congratulatory note. Sixteen months later a Czechoslovak court sentenced the former secretary general to death together with ten other leading members of the country's Communist Party. Although a small fraction of the hundreds executed and thousands imprisoned by the Czechoslovak communist regime, the show trial of Slánský arguably represented the zenith of Stalinist terror in the country. For if the party's secretary general was not safe, then no one was.

The February 1948 communist coup d'état in Czechoslovakia was followed by a series of trials of noncommunist politicians, generals, and industrial leaders. After the split between Stalin and Yugoslav leader Tito (Josip Broz) in the spring of 1948, however, the Soviets, fearful that other satellites might follow Yugoslavia's lead, pressured East European communist regimes to seek out traitors within their own ranks. Leading figures used the opportunity to rid themselves of rivals, who were accused of being "Titoists" and Western spies. In Poland, the general secretary of the Communist Party, Władysław Gomułka, was purged. In Hungary, Interior Minister László Rajk was tried and executed. In Bulgaria the same fate was meted out to Traicho Kostov, secretary of the Central Committee.

Despite the purges raging in neighboring countries, the Czechoslovak Communist Party moved slowly to unmask alleged traitors within its own ranks. This reluctance to act most likely stemmed from the party's internal cohesion, a result of its successful coup d'état, executed without the direct support of Soviet forces. In the course of carrying out their own purge, however, the Hungarian secret police forced Noel Field, an American humanitarian who had been a double agent of the Soviets and Americans, to confess to contacts with alleged Western agents in the Czechoslovak Communist Party. The Hungarians passed on these names to Prague. Moscow generously offered to send Soviet advisors to help Czechoslovakia overcome its dissatisfactory inaction.

In response, the Czechoslovak secret police established a special unit to uncover antistate elements within the party. Headed by Karel Šváb, the unit arrested Otto Šling, a regional leader of the Communist Party. Šling fit the profile of later defendants: he had fought in the Spanish civil war, had spent World War II in London, and was "of Jewish origin." Under extended and repeated torture, Šling confessed to being a saboteur and named accomplices. According to the secret police, conspirators led by Šling intended to overthrow Slánský and replace him with Marie Švermová, the widow of a World War II communist resistance leader. With the arrest of several high-ranking communists, including the Slovak foreign minister, Vladimír Clementis, the Czechoslovak Communist Party's leaders were satisfied. Moscow, however, was not.

Research by Igor Lukes has demonstrated that the trial was not entirely a secret police creation

from behind the Iron Curtain. When Czechoslovak exiles in the West became aware that Slánský had fallen into Stalin's disfavor, they sought to encourage the communist leader to defect. If that failed and the plot was exposed, the exiles hoped that their attempt would nonetheless cause a crisis within the communist leadership. The plan was to contact Slánský through his alleged mistress, but the courier the exiles chose had already been uncovered and turned by the Czechoslovak secret police. As a result the letter, addressed to the "Great Sweeper" (i.e., purger), never reached its intended recipient. Instead, once the secret police figured out the true identity of the addressee, the letter became evidence in the fabricated plot against Slánský.

Although Gottwald initially resisted Stalin's demand to arrest Slánský, Soviet pressure and the Great Sweeper letter quickly wore the Czechoslovak leader down. At 1 A.M. on 24 November 1951 Slánský was arrested as he returned to his house from a dinner at the home of the country's premier, Antonín Zápotocký. After six months of torture and a failed suicide attempt, Slánský confessed. He admitted to being a Titoist, to working with the Freemasons, and to supporting Zionism. In the months before and after the secretary general's arrest, dozens of other leading communist officials were detained, tortured, and forced to confess to made-up crimes against the party and state.

On 20 November 1952 Slánský finally went on trial along with thirteen others. In addition to the former secretary general, the accused included the former foreign minister (Clementis), two former deputy foreign ministers (Vavro Hajdů and Artur London), two former deputy ministers of foreign trade (Evžen Löbl and Rudolf Margolius), the former deputy ministers of national security (Šváb), national defense (Bedřich Reicin), and finance (Otto Fischl), a former party deputy secretary general (Josef Frank), and several less prominent figures in the communist apparatus (Bedřich Geminder, Ludvík Frejka, André Simone, and Šling).

Slánský's fellow defendants shared several characteristics beyond personal and professional ties to the former party secretary general. First, a number had lived in or had contact with the West and thus were suspected by the Soviets of "foreign contagion." They had fought in the Spanish civil war, spent

World War II in London, and/or were connected in some way to the conduct of Czechoslovakia's foreign affairs after the war. Second, several of the defendants had held economic positions in the government and, thus, could be blamed for the difficulties that had resulted from collectivization and industrial mismanagement. Finally, eleven of the fourteen defendants, including Slánský, were described in the indictment as being "of Jewish origin." Stalin's growing anti-Semitism, which culminated in the 1953 Doctor's Plot, hit surprisingly fertile soil in Czechoslovakia. Although Czechoslovakia had been known as the region's most tolerant state in the interwar period, the trial unleashed a wave of anti-Semitic hatred in a country largely bereft of Jews. Clementis, the former foreign minister, also faced charges based on ethnicity: he stood accused of "bourgeois nationalism" for his alleged support of Slovak separatism.

The prosecutor charged the fourteen men with a litany of crimes and demanded the death penalty for all. According to the indictment: "The accused, as Trotskyite, Titoite, Zionist, and bourgeois-nationalist traitors created, in the service of the U.S. imperialists and under the direction of Western espionage agencies, an anti-state Conspiratorial Center, undermined the people's democratic regime, frustrated the building of socialism, damaged the national economy, carried out espionage activities, and weakened the unity of the Czechoslovak people and the Republic's defensive capability in order to tear it away from its close alliance and friendship with the Soviet Union, to liquidate the people's regime in Czechoslovakia, to restore capitalism, and to drag the Republic into the imperialist camp once again and destroy its national sovereignty and independence."

The trial was a rehearsed show, with hand-picked participants and a captive national audience. The defense attorneys were chosen by the secret police only one week before the trial began and had to submit their closing arguments for approval. All but three of the thirty-five witnesses were held in prison prior to the trial. As for the defendants, they were instructed that their fates depended on their performance. In the weeks before the trial interrogators repeatedly rehearsed the cross-examination with the defendants. These practice sessions were taped so that if one of the accused deviated from the script, state radio could immediately cut off the live broadcast and play the prerecorded version to the country. Ultimately, the beaten-down actors learned the script too well: twice the prosecutors skipped a question by mistake and a defendant gave the correct answer to the missing query.

After seven days, according to plan, the court sentenced eleven of the defendants to death and handed down life sentences to Hajdů, Löbl, and London. In response to this surprising "lenience," the public sent thousands of letters demanding capital punishment for all. After President Gottwald rejected their pleas for clemency, the eleven were executed by hanging before dawn on 3 December 1952. Their remains were cremated and discarded in an unknown location. (According to rumors, secret police officers cast the ashes onto a muddy road to help dislodge their truck.) In subsequent years the condemned were erased from the country's history books and public press.

Although Czechoslovakia experienced relatively weak destalinization following Khrushchev's rise to power in the Soviet Union, the country's communist leadership still felt obliged to investigate the show trials of the early 1950s. The commission they established, however, was little more than a whitewash that established that Slánský had been guilty of an "anti-state conspiracy." A later commission, set up in 1962, admitted that the conspiracy charge had been a fabrication but exonerated the communist leadership and blamed Slánský for other crimes. It took till the 1968 Prague Spring for a government commission to admit, privately at least, that the Slánský trial had been a lawless fabrication committed with the knowledge and even direction of the Communist Party's leadership. The report (Pelikán, 1971), however, was tabled and then suppressed after the Soviet invasion of August 1968 and only published abroad.

See also **Czechoslovakia; Prague Spring; Purges; Stalin, Joseph.**

BIBLIOGRAPHY

Primary Sources

London, Artur. *The Confession.* Translated by Alastair Hamilton. New York, 1970.

Pelikán, Jiří, ed. *The Czechoslovak Political Trials, 1950–1954: The Suppressed Report of the Dubček Government's Commission of Inquiry, 1968.* Stanford, Calif., 1971.

Secondary Sources

Kaplan, Karel. *Report on the Murder of the General Secretary.* Translated by Karel Kovanda. Columbus, Ohio, 1990.

Kovály, Heda Margolius. *Under a Cruel Star: A Life in Prague 1941–1968.* Translated by Franci Epstein and Helen Epstein with the author. Cambridge, Mass., 1986.

Lukes, Igor. "The Rudof Slánský Affair: New Evidence." *Slavic Review* 58, no. 1 (spring 1999): 160–187.

BENJAMIN FROMMER

SLOVAKIA. Prior to the outbreak of World War I, Slovakia was part of the Austro-Hungarian Empire and was considered part of Hungary. Following the end of World War I Czechs and Slovaks campaigned for the establishment of an independent state. In October 1918 Slovakia declared itself independent and joined the Czech provinces (Bohemia, Moravia, and Silesia) to form the new Republic of Czechoslovakia.

During the interwar period Czechoslovakia was eastern Europe's only functioning parliamentary democracy. However, there were issues that divided the Czechs and Slovaks. The Czech lands were more densely populated than Slovakia and more industrial. The Slovak population was also generally poorer and less educated and overwhelmingly Catholic. The Prague government attempted to address economic inequities by industrializing Slovakia in the 1920s but these efforts were cut short by the Great Depression. As a result Slovak resentments grew in the 1930s and a separatist movement emerged, led by Father Andrej Hlinka (1864–1938) and Jozef Tiso (1887–1947).

After the infamous Munich agreement of September 1938 dismembered Czechoslovakia, on 14 March 1939 Slovakia, led by Tiso, declared its independence and quickly became a German puppet. However, in August 1944 about sixty thousand Slovak troops rose up against the Tiso regime and its Nazi backers in the so-called Slovak National Uprising, which was quelled with much brutality. At the close of World War II Soviet troops overran all of Slovakia and much of Bohemia

After the war Czechoslovakia was reestablished and elections were held in 1946. Although the Democratic Party won the elections in Slovakia, the Czechoslovak Communist Party won in the Czech Republic and became the largest party across the Federation. Eventually the communists seized power in a coup in 1948.

Under the communists there were concerted efforts to industrialize Slovakia; these efforts were centered around heavy industry and processing of raw materials. Rapid economic development led to the emergence of an increasingly vibrant Slovak intelligentsia and greater influence by Slovaks in national politics. Ultimately, in 1968, this culminated in the ascension of Alexander Dubček (1921–1992), the head of the Slovak Communist Party, to the position of Czechoslovak Party leader. Dubček's program of creating "socialism with a human face" involved significant social, economic, and political reforms. However the "Prague Spring" quickly ended on 21 August 1968 when Soviet and Warsaw Pact troops invaded Czechoslovakia. Dubček was replaced by Gustav Husák (1913–1991), who was also Slovak. Under Husak social, political, and economic life stagnated.

The 1970s also witnessed the rise of an organized dissident movement, Charter 77. This movement became the leadership core of the Velvet Revolution that brought about the downfall of communist rule in Czechoslovakia on 17 November 1989. Subsequently, two movements emerged to guide the transition process, Civic Forum (OF) in the Czech half of the Federation and Public against Violence (VPN) in Slovakia. A transition government was formed in December 1989, and elections, held in June 1990, were won by OF and VPN. However these organizations quickly disintegrated and were replaced with a new spectrum of political parties.

Between 1990 and 1992 negotiations over a new federation constitution became bogged down over the issue of Slovak autonomy. Elections were held in June 1992 for the Czech and Slovak National (republic-level) councils and Vladimír Mečiar's (b. 1942) Movement for a Democratic Slovakia (HZDS) won the elections in Slovakia. Mečiar negotiated the agreement to divide Czechoslovakia. On 1 January 1993 an independent Slovakia was established. In the new state, Slovaks comprised about 85 percent of the population; other groups included Hungarians (more than 10 percent), Roma (Gypsies), and Czechs.

Mečiar's party ruled Slovakia for most of the first years after independence, except for a nine-month period in 1994. Mečiar established a semi-authoritarian government and used state pressures to bully opponents and suppress ethnic Hungarian dissidents. Finally, Mečiar's party was voted out of office in the parliamentary elections of 1998 by a coalition led by Mikuláš Dzurinda (b. 1955). The governing coalition again won the September 2002 parliamentary election, although with only a three-seat majority in the parliament. The coalition included Prime Minister Dzurinda's Slovak Democrat and Christian Union (SDKU), the Party of the Hungarian Coalition (SMK), Christian Democrat Union (KDH), and the Alliance of the New Citizen (ANO). The principal opposition included Mečiar's HZDS, SMER (led by Robert Fico [b. 1964]) and the Communist Party of Slovakia. The Dzurinda government has rigorously pursued democratic and free-market reforms that helped pave the way for both NATO and European Union membership. Slovakia joined NATO on 29 March 2004 and became a member of the European Union on 1 May 2004.

See also **Charter 77; Czechoslovakia; Dubček, Alexander; Munich Agreement; Prague; Prague Spring; Velvet Revolution.**

BIBLIOGRAPHY

Haughton, Timothy. "Vladimír Mečiar and his Role in the 1994–1998 Slovak Coalition Government." *Europe-Asia Studies* 54 (2002): 1319–1338.

Henderson, Karen. *Slovakia: The Escape from Invisibility.* New York, 2002.

Kirschbaum, Stanislav J. *A History of Slovakia: A Struggle for Survival.* New York, 1995.

Krause, Kevin Deegan. "Slovakia's Second Transition." *Journal of Democracy*, 14 (2003): 65–79.

Rothschild, Joseph. *East Central Europe between the Two World Wars.* Seattle, 1974.

JOHN ISHIYAMA

SLOVENIA. At the start of World War I (1914–1918), no country called Slovenia existed.

The people known as Slovenes—united by their South Slavic language, their Roman Catholic faith, and strong traditions of agricultural life, crafts, commerce, mining, and metallurgy—nearly all lived in a cluster of provinces in the southern part of the Habsburg Empire, which was multinational in the extreme. German-speakers (Austrians) and Hungarians together made up less than 50 percent of the population; other national groups in the empire included Czechs, Croats, Bosnians, Serbs, Romanians, Italians, Poles, Ruthenians, Jews, and Slovaks, as well as Slovenes. The Slovene lands—Carniola and its neighboring provinces—had been incorporated into the Habsburg royal domains in the fourteenth century.

SLOVENES UNDER THE EMPIRE

By the end of the nineteenth century, in addition to their traditional rural roles, Slovenes had begun playing a significant urban role, characterized by their presence in commerce, the professions, industry, and government; they had also developed a national program and a slate of political parties. Having saved their language from Germanization, Slovenes wanted their provinces to be united in a single administrative unit within the Habsburg Empire. They also generally supported Yugoslavism, the vaguely defined but powerful idea that Slovenes should cooperate politically and culturally with other nearby Slavic peoples such as Croats and Serbs. Nonetheless, Slovene clericals, liberals, and socialists differed on many political and economic issues. As a political force, Slovene nationalism had not originated with the new middle class, as it had in many parts of Europe. Instead these ideas of cultural unity and popular sovereignty were elaborated and introduced for the most part by scholars and writers, spreading by means of cultural societies, reading rooms, and economic cooperatives.

As happened elsewhere in Central Europe and the Balkans, literature was the most highly developed of the arts in the early twentieth century. Numerous Slovene poets and fiction writers experimented with general European trends in the arts and constituted the movement known as the *moderna*; they included Oton Župančič (1878–1949) and Lili Novy (1885–1958). The work of the two greatest writers of the period, the Yugoslav-oriented socialist Ivan Cankar (1876–1918) and the prophetic, surrealistic Srečko

Preseren Square in Ljubljana, Slovenia. The Tromostovje (Triple) Bridge, designed by noted Slovenian architect Joze Plecnik, is in the foreground. ©SIME/CORBIS

Kosovel (1904–1926), had important political ramifications. The journalists Zofka Kveder (1878–1926) and Louis Adamič (1898–1951) published significant works on the status of women and on Slovene national identity, respectively.

As subjects of the Habsburg Empire, Slovenes fought on the side of the Central Powers in World War I—a war that brought great hardship to the region, especially the bloody battles with Italy along the Isonzo (Soča) River in the Alps. The Austrian government cracked down hard on suspected nationalists, but the Habsburg Empire collapsed and Slovenia emerged from the war as a constituent element of the new multiethnic Kingdom of Serbs, Croats, and Slovenes, popularly known as Yugoslavia. Most Slovenes accepted the new Yugoslavia, but the country failed to meet most popular expectations, due to the heavy-handed rule of Serbian political and economic elites. At least 350,000 Slovenes remained in Italy and Austria, but Slovenes now formed 8.5 percent of the new Yugoslavia, enjoyed a high degree of territorial unity, were protected from Austrian and Italian revanchism, and played an important role on the political scene in the federal capital, Belgrade; by contrast, in the old Habsburg Empire they had formed only 2.6 percent of the population and possessed only diluted political power. Outstanding cultural features of this time include the prolific modernist architect Jože Plečnik (1872–1957).

WORLD WAR II AND THE COMMUNIST ERA

Yugoslavia was dismembered by Axis forces in April 1941. The Third Reich annexed a great deal of Slovene land and began depopulating it in order to create Lebensraum (living space) for Germans and Austrians. Slovenia was also torn apart by a civil war among resistance groups. The Communist Party of Slovenia, founded in 1937, organized various resistance groups into a Liberation Front on 27 April 1941 and led a bloody antifascist struggle.

Conservative political and religious groups formed the Slovene Alliance the next year; they fought the Axis less, due to their mistrust of the Communists, their belief in an eventual Allied victory, and their desire to restore the prewar social order. Small numbers of Slovenes, usually known as the Home Guards (*Domobranci*), engaged in bloody collaboration with the German and Italian occupiers, especially as the power of the Communists, or partisans, grew across the region. The partisans, whose overall commander was the half-Slovene Josip Broz Tito (1892–1980), emerged victorious at the end of the war and transformed Yugoslavia into a socialist state, albeit a maverick one that was free of Soviet domination after 1948.

The evolution of this second Yugoslav state was complex. Interwar Yugoslavia had lifted the Slovenes to a new level of unity and autonomy, and socialist Yugoslavia both continued these trends and provided the setting for Slovenia's industrialization and urbanization. Slovenia faced problems, including a lack of democratic political rights, even with the development of the relatively mild Yugoslav system by the early 1960s, and the recurring danger of assimilation or at least cultural restriction threatened by Communist unitarists in Belgrade. Still, Slovenia developed its industrial base, foreign trade, and tourism under League of Communists' rule; in 1945 it had been the most socioeconomically developed of the Yugoslav republics, due to tourism, trade, and industrial policy, and the gap between Slovenia and the rest of the country widened over the decades, indicating that Slovene society benefited materially from being part of Yugoslavia.

Most Slovene Communists developed a reputation as both savvy defenders of Slovenia's cultural uniqueness and pragmatic, moderate politicians. Even Edvard Kardelj (1910–1979) Tito's heir apparent, helped steer Yugoslavia on an experimental third path between Soviet-style socialism and the west, which stressed the importance of national rights and left many powers in the hands of local governments. Outstanding cultural figures from this period include the writer Edvard Kocbek (1904–1981), a Christian socialist who had fought alongside the Communists in the war but became a dissident in the 1950s. He was best known for his poetry but also wrote groundbreaking prose and intriguing essays on politics and art. Kocbek has been called the conscience of his nation.

After Tito's death in 1980, Yugoslavia lurched from crisis to crisis. By the time Serbian strongman Slobodan Milošević (1941–2006) effectively gutted the Yugoslav political system in the late 1980s, Slovene intellectuals and politicians, many writing in the journals *Nova Revija* and *Mladina,* were preparing for the radical possibilities of confederation or even independence. Slovene civil society was well developed, embracing pacifist, feminist, and environmental movements. A heady alternative scene had developed in music and art, exemplified by the collective Neue Slowenische Kunst (NSK) and the internationally famous industrial band Laibach. Broad sections of society were alarmed at the Serbian imposition of martial law in Kosovo and generally believed that the rule of law had to be respected by the government and that the political system needed to be pluralized; whether the solution lay in reform or a very loose asymmetrical confederation remained an open question during the political and economic crises of the breakup of Yugoslavia. After a referendum in late 1990, the Slovene parliament, along with Croatia, declared independence on 25 June 1991. A brief, successful war against the Serb-dominated Yugoslav army followed. Slovenia had no traditional Serb-populated areas as did Croatia and Bosnia-Herzegovina, which Milošević fought much harder to keep in Yugoslavia.

In the early twenty-first century, Slovenia is a country of two million with a parliamentary system of government; it joined both NATO and the European Union (EU) in 2004 and has pursued a gradual but successful process of economic transition to a market economy. The centrist Liberal Democratic Party has been the main political force, albeit in coalition, but in 2000 conservative movements began to gain strength. Milan Kučan, a moderate former Communist, was president for two terms; Janez Drnovšek, a Liberal Democrat who had served several terms as prime minister, replaced him in 2002.

Occupying one of the rotating seats on the UN Security Council in 1998 and 1999, membership in the EU and NATO, and chairing the Organization for Security and Cooperation in Europe in 2005 have increased Slovenia's international profile since independence. Olympic teams, a recovering tourist industry, and hosting the first meeting between the new presidents of the United States and Russia in June 2001 have also boosted the country's confidence. Relations with Italy and Austria, sometimes thorny because of property disputes and minority rights, have settled down; only economic and border issues with Croatia remain somewhat unpredictable. Companies and international organizations have increasingly come to value Slovenia's expertise on and proximity to areas of conflict in the Balkans.

Major social issues in Slovenia include investigations and commemorations of the postwar massacres carried out by partisans at Kočevski Rog, determining the status of a large group of stateless Yugoslav refugees known as the erased, clarifying official relations with the Catholic Church, and constructing a socially responsible version of capitalism. Outstanding cultural figures include Drago Jančar (b. 1948), whose prose and drama combine keen psychological insight with an intellectually demanding sense of historical memory; the iconoclastic scholar Slavoj Žižek, the poets Tomaž Šalamun and Aleš Debeljak, and the young fiction writer Jani Virk, who has a keen eye for national foibles.

See also **Bosnia-Herzegovina; Serbia; Tito (Josip Broz); Yugoslavia**

BIBLIOGRAPHY

Primary Sources

Cankar, Ivan. *Dream Visions and Other Selected Stories.* Translated by Anton Druzina. Willoughby Hills, Ohio, 1982. Hard-hitting sketches on political and social themes from the era of World War I.

Huttenbach, Henry, and Peter Vodopivec, eds. *Voices from the Slovene Nation.* Special issue of *Nationality Papers* 21, no. 1 (spring 1993). Captures Slovene debates on reform and independence.

Kardelj, Edvard. *Reminiscences. The Struggle for Recognition and Independence: The New Yugoslavia, 1944–1957.* London, 1982. A sample of views and activities from the life of Slovenia's longtime Communist viceroy.

Kocbek, Edvard. *Embers in the House of Night. Selected Poems.* Translated by Sonja Kravanja. Santa Fe, N. M., 1999. Important selection of poetry that is at once pastoral and intellectually demanding.

———. "Reflections on Spain." Translated by John K. Cox. *Slovene Studies* 25, nos. 1–2 (2005): 57–62. A thought-provoking essay on political and spiritual issues that reveals Slovenia's connections to the rest of Europe.

Milač, Metod. *Resistance, Imprisonment, and Forced Labor: A Slovene Student in World War II.* New York, 2002. An important memoir from World War II.

Secondary Sources

Cox, John K. *Slovenia: Evolving Loyalties.* New York, 2005. The most comprehensive history of Slovenia in English. Traces the growth of Slovene ideas of sovereignty and the development of a pluralist society.

Plut-Pregelj, Leopoldina, and Carole Rogel. *Historical Dictionary of Slovenia.* Lanham, Md., 1996. The best reference work ever written on Slovenia. Extremely detailed coverage through all periods of Slovene history by two veteran scholars.

JOHN K. COX

SOCCER (FOOTBALL). *See* **Football (Soccer).**

SOCIAL DEMOCRACY. Originally the term *social democracy* was interchangeable with that of *socialism*. In the last quarter of the nineteenth century the most influential European socialist party was the German Social Democratic Party, both Bolsheviks and Mensheviks were factions within the Russian Social Democratic Labor Party, and one of the most sectarian and radical organizations of the British Left at the time styled itself the British Social Democratic Federation (founded by H. M. Hyndman in 1881 as the Democratic Federation and renamed after 1884). It was only in the decades following the Second World War that the term *social democracy* came to acquire specific connotations including an abiding commitment to the rules of parliamentary democracy and the acceptance of capitalist relations of production albeit in a regulated form.

ORIGINS

The origins of such views can be traced to distinctive strands of late-nineteenth-century socialism such as Fabianism and the kind of revisionism propounded by the German writer and politician Eduard Bernstein in the 1890s. Most socialist parties, however, even before 1900, distinguished between an end goal—a socialist society where the means of production, distribution, and exchange would be held in common—and intermediate reforms that could take place within capitalism. The revisionists dispensed with the final goal.

The Fabian Society, a largely middle-class British organization founded in 1884, advocated gradual and peaceful social change and rejected the Marxist theory of class struggle. Its most prominent advocates were Sidney Webb and Beatrice Webb, the playwright George Bernard Shaw, and the novelist H. G. Wells. The society derived its main inspiration from the British radical utilitarian tradition and opposed the formation of an independent socialist party, though it eventually supported the creation of the Labour Party and became affiliated to it. The report the Fabians presented to the 1896 Congress of the International (drafted by George Bernard Shaw) sided explicitly with those Socialists who were prepared to support progressive "bourgeois" reforms. Like Eduard Bernstein (who was influenced by the Fabians and formulated his so-called revisionism while living in London between 1888 and 1901), they did not believe in any inevitable collapse of capitalism.

Bernstein, in a series of articles published between 1896 and 1898 in *Neue Zeit* (later published in English as *Evolutionary Socialism* in 1899), claimed that capitalism had reached a new stage—unforeseen by Karl Marx (1818–1883)—in which it had developed a self-regulating structure capable of avoiding crises while the development of parliamentary democracy enabled the working class to struggle against the bourgeoisie in conditions of legality and equality. Bernstein noted that even though there was a growth in large corporations, there was also a parallel expansion of small and medium-size firms everywhere in Western Europe and North America, contrary to what Marxist doctrine had assumed. Moreover, society, far from becoming sharply divided between an ever smaller group of wealthy capitalists and an ever larger army of dispossessed proletarians, produced a growing range of intermediate social groups. Bernstein's followers, then a minority within the movement, no longer believed that the final aim, the *Endziel*, could define the operating principles for current political practice. In a much-quoted phrase, Bernstein declared that he was not interested in the final goal of socialism but in social progress and the political and economic work necessary to bring it about.

Though this revisionism was formally rejected by socialist parties, most socialist politicians and trade unionists were more gradualist than their rhetoric indicated, though, like the French Socialist leader Jean Jaurès (1859–1914), they remained firmly of the opinion that the final goal of the movement had to be maintained as a symbolic commitment.

The advent of communism in Russia, where the "end goal" of a society without capitalism appeared to have been realized, forced many socialists to reexamine the ideology of the final goal, but it was only after the Second World War that a clearer redefinition of *social democracy* emerged.

In the interwar period, however, various socialist thinkers, such as G. D. H. Cole, examined the possibility for a radical socialist advance in nonrevolutionary situations. The New Fabian Research Bureau produced detailed studies on economic policy, emphasizing "social" control of industry as the distinguishing feature of socialism rather than abolition of private property. Others pointed out that some form of resistance would be expected not only from entrepreneurs but also from trade unionists. Evan Durbin, was well aware of this. In his *Politics of Democratic Socialism* (1940) he explains that trade union practices would constitute a problem for socialist planning. Yet, throughout Europe, particularly in France in the 1930s and Germany in the 1920s, trade unions were in favor of planning, while the main socialist parties were distinctly unenthusiastic.

AFTER 1945

The remarkable socialist electoral successes in Western Europe (except in Italy and France) following the end of the Second World War brought about a further development of social-democratic policies. The socialist parties in power, above all the British Labour Party, faced the question of managing capitalist economies. They had to deal with practical problems such as postwar reconstruction and welfare reforms. They had to ensure that there would be no return to the unemployment of the 1930s. They had to cajole the trade unions to contain their wage demands while ensuring economic growth and productivity increases. The end goal was not abandoned but put further into abeyance. The main thinkers behind the new social democracy were not socialists but liberals such as John Maynard Keynes (1883–1946), who explained how it was possible to use macroeconomic policies to avoid unemployment, and William Henry Beveridge (1879–1963), who had written the blueprint for a welfare state in which citizens would be looked after "from the cradle to the grave."

Such advances, far from leading to a period of electoral consolidation for Western European socialism, marked its high tide. By the end of the 1950s, with a few exceptions, socialists were still in power only in the Nordic countries. The Cold War played a part in the difficulties faced by the Left, since socialists had to distinguish themselves constantly from the negative model of Soviet communism. This effort was particularly marked among Social Democrats operating in countries aligned with the the United States under the umbrella of North Atlantic Treaty Organization (NATO). Indeed, some parties, notably the Labour Party in Britain and the socialist parties of Belgium, France, Norway, and Holland, had been among the initiators of the Atlantic alliance. Others, such as the German Social Democrats and the Italian Socialists, eventually abandoned their position of neutralism or equidistance and, as they advanced toward political power, joined the pro-Atlantic consensus.

The most important pressure toward social democratization, however, was not the Cold War but the real success of capitalism in the 1950s. Far from crumbling, or stagnating, as so many had wrongly forecast in the 1940s, the Western economies saw, in the years 1955–1964, their strongest economic performance to date. A "golden age" of capitalism appeared to have dawned. The sorry record of capitalism of the interwar years receded from collective memory. Not only did full employment become a reality almost everywhere, but also the consumer society, with all its material seductions, became a mass phenomenon. The bulk of the working class, far from becoming increasingly poor—as some, notably the French communists, still believed as late as the late 1950s—was beginning to share in the general prosperity. Making matters more difficult for the Left was the fact that much of this growth had

taken place under the aegis of governments of the Right, notably the Conservatives in Britain, the Gaullists in France, and the Christian Democrats in Germany and Italy, who had adopted social and welfare policies not dissimilar from those advocated by Social Democrats. Neoliberalism, at least in the 1950s and 1960s, was not the key to electoral victory.

Various thinkers, both in Europe and in North America, suggested that the era of socialism was over. Following, consciously or not, the ideas pioneered by Bernstein, they declared that capitalism had changed so remarkably that the old dogmas of the Left, such as central planning and nationalizations, should be jettisoned. The era of the "end of ideology," harbinger of the postindustrial society—the American social theorist Daniel Bell (b. 1919) had been the prescient exponent of such concepts—had arrived. The question was now how to manage the "affluent society"—a phrase coined by the American economist John Kenneth Galbraith (1908–2006)—and the contrast between private affluence and public squalor.

European intellectuals tried to integrate this type of thinking in a reinvigorated or modernized concept of socialism. In Britain the most influential text of the new revisionism was Anthony Crosland's *The Future of Socialism* (1956). This was a more systematic summa (comprehensive treatise) of arguments put forward by earlier Labour revisionists such as Douglas Jay and Hugh Gaitskell (party leader after 1955). Crosland decreed that capitalism had solved the problem of accumulation and that socialists should concentrate on ensuring an equitable social division of the fruits of growth. Wealth redistribution, not the abolition of capitalism, was the goal. This belief was increasingly shared by all socialist revisionists throughout Europe. In any case, they argued, nineteenth-century capitalists no longer existed. The owners of capital were no longer in charge. Control, and hence power, had shifted to the managers of large joint-stock companies. Such separation between owners and managers had been noted since the interwar years by Keynes, earlier revisionists such as the Belgian Labor Party leader Hendrick de Man, and writers such as the Americans Adolf Augustus Berle and Gardiner C. Means (*The Modern Corporation and Private Property*, 1932), and popularized by James Burnham, a former Trotskyist, in his influential *The Managerial Revolution* (1941), published in

France with a preface by the socialist leader Léon Blum.

Since Crosland saw socialism as something to be achieved incrementally, it was still an "end state," though one that could be reached only after a long process of molecular social and political change. Meanwhile socialist policies simply described a set of values, such as that every individual should have an equal chance. So long as there was a substantial private sector, declared Crosland, socialists must logically applaud the accumulation of private profits and ensure that they be reinvested and used as "a source of collective capital accumulation and not as a form of personal income."

In Germany the new revisionism appealed to the Social Democratic Party (SPD), which was out of office for all of the 1950s. It was not a marked feature of parties that were in power either on their own or in coalition, such as the Scandinavian or the Belgian and Dutch. By the end of the 1950s, Marxist doctrine, which the SPD, along with many socialist parties had formally adopted at the end of the nineteenth century, was abandoned. The SPD's new *Basic Programme,* ratified at the Bad Godesberg Congress in November 1959, declared solemnly that "Democratic Socialism" in Europe was "rooted in Christian ethics, humanism and classical philosophy." Karl Marx was relegated to the attic. The new revisionists also made their peace with religion. Anticlericalism had been one of the driving forces of continental socialism. By the 1950s it had become apparent that this served no practical purpose beyond antagonizing those with religious convictions, hence the reference in the Bad Godesberg program to the Christian heritage of Social Democrats.

None of this was entirely new. Positive references to the social values of Christianity could be found in the declarations of various parties such as those of the SPD itself, the Austrian Socialist Party (SPÖ), and the Dutch Labor Party, and even the Belgian Socialists and the Italian Communists. The most important aspect of the new Bad Godesberg program was not the abandonment of Marxism—something most commentators emphasize—nor that the party committed itself to growth (a commitment made in previous party statements), nor in the acceptance of the market, but in the conflation between the party's immediate demands and its long-term aims. This classical distinction enabled the party to advance virtually any reformist short-term goals provided the final aim, the abolition of capitalism, was regularly and resolutely reaffirmed. The forsaking of Marxism was the symbolic representation of the abandonment of socialism as an "end state." The new goals were equally valid for both present and future: growth of prosperity, a just share of the national product, full employment, stable currency, increased productivity.

This model of social democracy was now dominant on the Left throughout northern Europe. In Sweden, where the longevity of Social Democrats in power was an example to the rest of the Western European Left, a more practical model of management of the capitalist economy emerged. Since equality had become social democracy's most important goal, the principle of equal wages for similar works was to be enforced throughout the Swedish economy, after negotiations between trade unions and employers had agreed on the various wage levels—the so-called solidaristic wages policy. The more efficient firms, able to pay higher-than-agreed wages, would make higher-than-average profits (and pay more taxes). Workers made redundant by the closure of the less efficient firms unable to pay the going rate would be retrained and redeployed in the more advanced sectors thanks to what was called an "active labor market policy." That way a virtuous circle was established and was operational throughout most of the 1960s: flexible labor markets, capitalist efficiency, and technological progress coexisted with high taxes and social equality.

In much of southern Europe, however, social democracy was still regarded by Socialists themselves as flawed by its excessive moderation toward capitalism. Even in Britain the return to power of a Labour government in 1964 did not satisfy either the trade unions nor the Labour Left (in 1960 the Labour revisionists had been unable to remove from the party constitution the famous Clause Four, which claimed as the party's ultimate goal the common ownership of the means of production, distribution, and exchange). The country's economic conditions were such that the main preoccupation of the Labour governments of 1964–1970 and 1974–1979 as well as of the intervening conservative administration was to quell the wage demands of trade unions, with varying degrees of success. In Italy and France, Socialists were forced by their conditions of inferiority with respect to the communist parties to pose the question of alliance above that of policies—the French resolved it by forging a difficult entente with the Communists, the Italians by the opposite but equality difficult task of compromising with the ruling Christian Democratic Party. In the rest of southern Europe in 1974–1975—with Portugal, Greece, and Spain finally emerging from dictatorships of various hues—Socialists were faced by apparently strong communist parties and had to take a socially radical stance.

The key event for the subsequent convergence of the entire European Left around the goals of social democracy was the victory of the Left in France in 1981. The platform on which it had been elected was a radical program of nationalizations and public spending aimed at overcoming capitalism. The ensuing economic reflation, under the presidency of François Mitterrand (1916–1996), occurring at a time (1981–1982) when the rest of Europe was deflating, caused a rise in prices in France as well as a massive balance-of-payment deficit. The lessons would not be easily forgotten: the European economies were by now so interconnected that even social democracy in one country—to adapt the famous slogan of Joseph Stalin (1879–1953)—had become less probable than ever.

THE THIRD WAY

Economic interdependence—the term most frequently used before *globalization* became more fashionable—appeared to make redundant the main economic tool used by social democracy. This was not Marx's theory (he had been, after all, the first great theorist of globalization) but Keynes's. The kind of macroeconomic management favored by social democracy assumed that each nation-state was in charge of its destiny. This, at least in Europe, was no longer the case. Deprived of their pathfinders, Social Democrats adopted, more or less overtly, a defensive strategy. Having been out of power for eighteen years (1979–1997), the British Labour Party under Tony Blair (b. 1953) was the most outspoken advocate of the new policy turn, labeled the "Third Way," but the rest of the European Left

pursued a similar course, albeit less enthusiastically. The fall of the Berlin Wall, it seemed, had not just heralded the tocsin bell for communism but also a further retreat for social democracy. A grand narrative—largely inspired by the successes of neoliberal economic concepts—emerged and was accepted by most Social Democrats. Its basic coordinates were: an acceptance that market forces should not be muzzled by excessive regulation; that such regulation had to be coordinated with other countries; that public spending should be kept under strict control; that the welfare state should be defended, if possible, but not extended; that privatization, when it eradicates monopolies, was desirable; that equality had to be tempered by the need to preserve incentives and competition; and that the power of international financial institutions—and, above all, of financial markets—may be contained—if at all—only by international agreement and not by unilateral state policies. Social Democrats of northern and southern Europe converged toward these precepts and were joined by the emerging democratic Left in the postcommunist states of central and Eastern Europe—even more enthusiastic about the new "third way."

Further indicators of political convergence were the generally positive attitude of the Left toward European integration—at least compared to the position of many of their opponents on the Right—a dilution of their previous commitment to state centralism and, consequently, a significant acceptance of the values of devolving power.

Differences remain. Political parties continue to respond overwhelmingly to a national electorate. They are inevitably constrained by the weight of their own traditions and those of their own countries. They react to the persisting differences in the levels of development and structural characteristics of their respective economies. The size of the working class may have been shrinking everywhere, but the rate of deindustrialization was highly uneven: higher in Sweden and in the United Kingdom than in Germany or Austria. Opposition to cuts in welfare spending were more significant in France and Germany than in Britain, where unemployment was lower under Tony Blair's Labour government. Ecology plays a far more important role in politics in Germany and Sweden than in France or Spain.

Feminism has greater strength in Western than in Eastern Europe.

The perception of globalization has brought convergence not only to the Left but also between Left and neoconservatism—and largely and unavoidably on the terms set by the latter. Such convergence, in reality, had existed previously; for most of the 1950s and the 1960s Social Democrats and Conservatives shared common values: full employment and the welfare state. In the 1970s there was a widespread acceptance (across the political spectrum) that it was not possible to rule a country against the trade unions. To some extent this was the consequence of interdependence. If national politics is increasingly constrained by a globalized economy, it is hardly surprising if these constraints force both sides toward similar policies. Social democracy now has modest ambitions. Its aims are defensive: to protect the achievements of the past, to continue to improve social life under capitalism, to promote an ethos of cooperation, and to enhance social and civil rights.

See also **Beveridge, William; Keynes, J. M.; Social Insurance; Socialism.**

BIBLIOGRAPHY

Anderson, Perry, and Patrick Camiller, eds. *Mapping the West European Left.* London, 1994.

Baldwin, Peter. *The Politics of Social Solidarity: Class Bases of the European Welfare State, 1875–1975.* Cambridge, U.K., 1990.

Cronin, James. *New Labour's Pasts: The Labour Party and Its Discontents.* New York, 2004.

Crosland, Anthony. *The Future of Socialism.* London, 1956.

Eley, Geoff. *Forging Democracy: The History of the Left in Europe, 1850–2000.* Oxford, U.K., 2002.

Esping-Andersen, Gøsta. *Politics against Markets: The Social Democratic Road to Power.* Princeton, N.J., 1985.

Galbraith, John Kenneth. *The Affluent Society.* Boston, 1958.

Giddens, Anthony. *The Third Way: The Renewal of Social Democracy.* Malden, Mass., 1999.

Glyn, Andrew, ed. *Social Democracy in Neoliberal Times: The Left and Economic Policy since 1980.* Oxford, U.K., 2001.

Judt, Tony. *Marxism and the French Left: Studies on Labour and Politics in France, 1830–1981.* Oxford, U.K., 1986.

Korpi, Walter. *The Working Class in Welfare Capitalism: Work, Unions, and Politics in Sweden.* London, 1978.

Marquand, David. *The Progressive Dilemma.* London, 1991.

Moschonas, Gerassimos. *In the Name of Social Democracy: The Great Transformation, 1945 to the Present.* Translated by Gregory Elliott. London, 2002.

Miller, Susanne, and Heinrich Potthoff, comps. *A History of German Social Democracy from 1848 to the Present.* Translated by J. A. Underwood. Leamington Spa, U.K., 1986.

Newman, Michael. *Socialism: A Very Short Introduction.* Oxford, U.K., 2005.

Sassoon, Donald. *One Hundred Years of Socialism: The West European Left in the Twentieth Century.* London, 1996.

Sassoon, Donald, ed. *Looking Left: European Socialism after the Cold War.* London, 1997.

Scharpf, Fritz W. *Crisis and Choice in European Social Democracy.* Translated by Ruth Crowley and Fred Thompson. Ithaca, N.Y., 1991.

DONALD SASSOON

SOCIAL INSURANCE. *Social insurance* is the term used to describe a wide range of schemes designed to protect large groups of people against commonplace risks, in particular sickness, prolonged disability, accident, old age, unemployment, or death of the breadwinner. They are normally designed to provide financial support—and sometimes other benefits such as health care—for all members of the scheme out of a fund to which members contribute regular sums. Both employers and the state may also contribute, the latter from general taxation. The system of funding has varied from place to place and from time to time over the history of social insurance. Contributions are normally calculated at a level that assumes equal risk among all members. Social insurance is to be distinguished from personal insurance, which protects the contributor against individual risk calculated in accordance with her or his personal circumstances (e.g., age, health, or employment status) and is financed by contributions proportionate to that risk that are calculated to cover this risk in full. Modern social insurance schemes normally include some element of redistribution from lower- to higher-risk groups or from richer to poorer individuals.

PRECURSORS

The precursors of the large-scale, government-directed social insurance schemes that developed from the later nineteenth century were voluntary, collective, mutual organizations, privately initiated and managed by groups of people who were exposed to specific risks against which they could not otherwise protect themselves, such as miners and other blue-collar workers who risked losing their livelihoods and their capacity to support their dependents due to accident, illness, old age, or unemployment. Such organizations emerged in most European countries during the process of industrialization during the nineteenth and early twentieth centuries, mainly among better and more regularly paid workers, when such workers were not wealthy enough to insure individually for episodes of crisis but were sufficiently well and regularly paid to make regular, normally weekly, contributions to a fund that made payments on an agreed basis to all members when in need. Spreading the risk over large numbers of individuals of variable age and circumstances reduced the cost to each individual member. In most countries, the only other sources of support available to such people were charity or publicly funded poor relief. The former was highly variable in availability, quantity, and quality. Poor relief was normally minimal and granted on punitive terms. Workers sought to provide for themselves and their dependents greater certainty of support in times of crisis.

Examples of such institutions are the friendly societies that flourished in Britain between the late eighteenth and mid-twentieth centuries, and the miners' provident societies established in early nineteenth century Germany and Austria. Sometimes, as in German mining districts, employers established and contributed to such funds. They were motivated not only by concern for their workers' welfare but by the need to attract workers to, and to keep them in, often dangerous occupations in remote and inhospitable locations. Similar motives led national governments to provide pensions and other benefits for public servants, as in Britain and France where systematic pension schemes evolved out of older patronage systems in the later eighteenth and nineteenth centuries. Secure and healthy workers were perceived to be more efficient workers, and pensions enabled governments to dismiss workers rendered inefficient by advancing age without consigning them to destitution. Such benefits were financed from public funds because efficient public service was regarded as a public good.

In most countries there was a long tradition, which continued well into the twentieth century, of employers providing such support as care in sickness or a pension in old age to loyal and favored employees. Soldiers, sailors, and servants in royal households had long received pensions, though often unsystematically, at the grace and favor of royal or other official authorities. Their discretionary character makes these practices different in kind from social insurance. From the later nineteenth century, as business firms grew in scale, bureaucratized occupational provision—normally financed by the business—became more widespread and systematic, though generally confined to better-paid, more senior workers. Again, employers perceived that safeguarding key workers against hazards encouraged loyalty and efficiency.

THE INVENTION OF SOCIAL INSURANCE

Nation-states began to legislate for social insurance schemes from the 1880s. Since that time, most European countries have introduced such schemes, though with considerable variability in timing and structure. In 1884, German Chancellor Otto von Bismarck (1815–1898) introduced the world's first system of compulsory national insurance against disability due to accidents at work and sickness. This covered wage earners in most occupations who earned no more than 2,000 marks (about $500) per year. Pensions were funded by contributions from employers and workers. Both contributions and pensions were related to workers' earnings and subsidized from national taxation.

Most regularly employed German blue-collar workers thereafter paid weekly contributions into a national fund and received, when needed, health care and weekly benefits, though the amounts were low and accident compensation was especially difficult to obtain due to difficulty of proof and lack of employer cooperation. In 1889 the scheme was extended to include old age pensions, payable at age sixty-five, financed by further contributions.

Like workers' mutual schemes, the German system was open only to those in regular employment, because only they could afford the required regular contributions. Hence it excluded some of the poorest men, because they were irregularly employed or too low-paid to afford contributions, and the great majority of women, for similar reasons. Hence classical contributory social insurance is not an effective means of alleviating severe poverty. Alleviating poverty was not, however, Bismarck's chief concern. His explicit aim was to prevent the spread of socialism among German workers by demonstrating that their needs could be met by the liberal state, and socialism was most appealing to those male workers whose lives were not dominated by grinding poverty. Bismarck's actions stood in a long-established Prussian tradition. Since the late eighteenth century, Prussia had provided certain social benefits—for example, social insurance for miners—while vigorously suppressing labor dissidence. The German social insurance scheme was extended in 1911 to include white-collar workers. This again mainly benefited males.

The next national scheme to be introduced, in Denmark (the wealthiest of the Nordic countries at this time) in 1891, was quite different in being targeted at the poorest. It aimed to reform the poor relief system by removing older people from it and providing them with an old age pension as a less punitive alternative. The pension was funded wholly from taxation. It was means-tested and granted to full citizens aged sixty or above who had records of socially acceptable behavior (i.e., no record of crime, drunkenness, or failure to work). Denmark was predominantly rural and most workers were too poorly paid for contributory insurance to be an option, especially for those at risk of greatest need in old age. The amount of the pension was locally determined, according to local needs. Similar schemes were introduced in the United Kingdom in 1908 and in the Netherlands and Sweden in 1913. All of these were nationally administered and paid uniform pension rates, though they differed in such details as pension ages, which varied between sixty and seventy. They were "non-contributory" (that is, paid from public taxation rather than social insurance payments) and targeted at the poorest, hence they

generally particularly benefited women, who tended to outlive men and to suffer greater poverty in old age. It was common, as in Denmark, to confine benefits to naturalized citizens (or in the case of Britain, subjects of the Crown, including those born throughout the British Empire). In Britain, non-naturalized residents and their British-born wives were excluded from pensions and later from health and unemployment insurance. Initially this excluded mainly Jewish immigrants, whose protests forced some modification of the scheme, although as the twentieth century went on and flows of international migration intensified, the range of excluded groups grew. By the end of the twentieth century, the issue of the entitlement of migrants to benefits was a source of tension throughout Europe and most countries became more restrictive.

SOCIAL INSURANCE SPREADS THROUGH EUROPE, 1900–1914

In 1907 the government of Denmark, where the trade union movement was strong, began to subsidize trade union unemployment funds. Britain was the first country, in 1911, to introduce national unemployment insurance, along with national health insurance, funded by contributions from workers and their employers and subsidized by the state. British unemployment insurance was restricted to five skilled trades with normally moderate levels of unemployment. Health insurance provided cash benefits during sickness and free access to a doctor for insured workers. It also provided a small maternity benefit for insured women and the wives of insured men; after a battle by representatives of working class women, this was paid directly to the wives. It was the only benefit paid to a family member of an insured worker. Everywhere, except in Norway from the beginning of its health insurance scheme in 1909, family members were excluded from health insurance benefits, which were designed to keep workers, rather than their families, fit and active. In most west European countries families began to be included between the wars, though not until 1948 in Britain and 1955 in Italy. Neither of the British national insurance schemes could accommodate low or irregularly paid workers, so, again, they benefited mainly the more secure skilled workers. Nonetheless, European labor and socialist movements, which mainly represented such workers, generally opposed contributory insurance because they resented paying compulsory contributions from relatively low incomes and it did not benefit the poorest. They argued instead for redistributive social benefits financed by taxing the rich.

Existing voluntary providers, chiefly trade unions and friendly societies, administered British health insurance, which increased trade union support for the system. Many governments preferred to subsidize voluntary health insurance schemes, as in Denmark from 1892 to 1933, Sweden from 1891 to 1947, and Switzerland from 1911 to the present. All of these covered high proportions of the male workforce. Elsewhere similar subsidized schemes were restricted to specific occupations and generally excluded workers in agriculture, as in Belgium from 1894 to 1944 and in Italy from 1886 to 1928. Levels of state subsidy varied, as did the proportion of the population covered and also levels of regulation to ensure probity and minimum standards of benefit.

Various social insurance schemes spread through Europe. In Norway, national accident insurance was provided for fishermen in 1908 and for seamen in 1911 (both groups important to the Norwegian economy). In 1909, health insurance became compulsory for regular earners of manual wages in that country. No country except Britain introduced compulsory national unemployment insurance before 1914, although in Germany twenty municipalities had introduced unemployment insurance schemes by 1914, as had Ghent in Belgium in 1901 and St. Gall in Switzerland in the 1890s. Most countries proceeded cautiously with regard to the unpredictable risk of unemployment, generally preferring to subsidize voluntary, often trade union-run, schemes of varying degrees of generosity. This was true of Belgium between 1907 and 1944, the Netherlands between 1906 and 1949, Norway between 1906 and 1938, France between 1905 and 1967, and Switzerland between 1924 and 1976, all of which introduced earnings-related, state regulated schemes. This is still the case in Denmark, Finland, and Switzerland.

Attempts to introduce any form of social insurance in France faced resistance from socialists, trade unionists, and employers, and also the problems of covering a highly fragmented labor force with a large, self-employed peasant component. In 1910, compulsory sickness and old age insurance was introduced for eight million urban and rural workers, but a legal decision in 1912 questioning the legality of compulsion enabled a high proportion of employers and workers to evade the law. In Russia in 1912, accident and sickness insurance was introduced but it was restricted to the minority of industrial workers in large firms, which were seen as essential to the economic advance of the country. The great mass of poor peasantry was excluded. Insurance was financed by workers' contributions and grants from employers, and administered (as in Britain) by representatives of workers and employers. These were the only near-autonomous workers' organizations in tsarist Russia and between 1912 and the revolutions of 1917; the Bolsheviks used them with some success not only to improve the welfare of workers but as fronts for political organization.

The relatively poor countries of southern Europe—Spain, Portugal, Greece—could least afford state provision for their mainly rural populations and had few workers able to establish and benefit from voluntary mutual organizations before World War I.

WORLD WAR I AND AFTER

It is essential to understand the situation in Europe before 1914 to appreciate what happened later, since the basic principles that have continued to frame social insurance throughout Europe into the twenty-first century were established at that time. An effect of World War I was to extend the coverage of such schemes rather than to change the principles on which they were based. Extension resulted both from regime change, as in Russia, Germany, and the new nations formerly within the Austro-Hungarian Empire; or from the fear of it, as in Britain, where the apprehension that mass postwar unemployment would bring about revolution led to the immediate extension of unemployment insurance to most manual workers and the temporary provision of non-contributory benefits to everyone who was unemployed due to the effects of transition from peace to war and, unusually, to their dependents. There were frequent amendments to the unemployment insurance system through the Depression years, which in Britain lasted from 1920 to 1940, and the inquisitorial nature of its administration was much hated, but it provided a historically unprecedented safety-net for all unemployed workers through the interwar years. The British health insurance system remained basically unchanged until 1948, and in 1925 was extended to provide contributory old age pensions at age sixty-five for workers already falling within the system, and for the widows and orphans of insured men.

Similarly, in 1919 in Italy (during the "red years" following World War I), compulsory old age, health, and unemployment insurance was introduced for industrial workers. However, it was effectively emasculated by opposition from the Church and business interests, and little was achieved before the fascist takeover in 1920. The Italian state had subsidized limited voluntary schemes of sickness and old age insurance since 1886 and 1898, respectively.

Also after World War I, the League of Nations, and especially the International Labour Office (ILO) established under its auspices, encouraged the development of social insurance among member nations. It had most influence in the poor countries of southern Europe. Most other west European countries were in process of attaining the modest minimum standards the ILO sought. The Portuguese government (brought to power in 1910 following the revolution that ended the monarchy) apparently believed that the introduction of social insurance was a necessary condition for Portugal's admission to the League. Also, a Socialist minister of labor believed that there were votes to be gained if the state subsidized and expanded the limited number of existing mutual organizations. In 1919, Portugal introduced compulsory insurance through voluntary institutions covering sickness, workplace accidents, invalidity, and old age. But because only a tiny proportion of the largely rural and poor population could afford to belong to such institutions, the effects were slight before the dictator Antonio de Oliveira Salazar (1889–1970) took over in 1926.

The situation was similar in Spain, for similar reasons. Old age insurance was notionally compulsory from 1919, but few could afford to qualify. The Constitution of the Second Republic, in 1931, declared it the responsibility of the state to create a full system of compulsory social insurance, but plans to implement this were disrupted by the outbreak of civil war in 1936.

In Greece, the Liberal government of Eleutherios Venizelos (1864–1936) aimed to improve the security of the population, and Greece ratified the International Conventions of the first World Labour Conference in 1919 that prioritized labor protection. But with Greece's greatly expanded, largely agricultural postwar population, many of them refugees, there was little realistically that the government could do. In particular, social insurance—which best fitted the needs of urban, industrial populations—was not feasible. In 1922, a Conservative government introduced legislation compelling workers in industry, transport, commerce, and building to join subsidized workers' or employers' insurance schemes, while vigorously purging left-wing trade unions. But membership was not enforced, and by 1925 only seventeen thousand workers were insured, although, increasingly, higher paid professionals such as doctors and lawyers took advantage of state subsidies and established such schemes for themselves. When the Liberals returned to government in 1928 they sought, with the aid of the ILO, to provide improved health care and to coordinate and impose minimum standards upon voluntary insurance associations. Coverage among urban workers improved, but the problem of the rural masses remained.

In central Europe, compulsory unemployment insurance for industrial workers was introduced in post-Habsburg Austria in 1920. Austria had since the 1880s followed the German model of social insurance, building on preexisting schemes for state workers and for miners. Compulsory industrial accident insurance was introduced in 1887, compulsory sickness insurance in 1886, and compulsory pensions insurance in 1906, all on Bismarckian lines, covering mainly industrial labor. These measures applied throughout the Austrian part of the Dual Monarchy and, from 1907, in the Hungarian part, the latter fuelled by the fear of contagion from the 1905 revolution in Russia. This was the legacy inherited by the new states of Czechoslovakia and Hungary after World War I. The social insurance systems of the two countries then diverged for reasons largely linked to their economic structures. Industrialized Czechoslovakia, faced with unemployment and political unrest, established basic non-contributory unemployment assistance in 1918. From 1924 the state paid half the cost of trade union–run unemployment insurance, which covered about half of all blue- and white-collar employees. As elsewhere, better-paid workers could afford schemes that provided superior benefits. The state subsidy built in an element of redistributive subsidy for the lower paid. In Czechoslovakia, which had a relatively small rural workforce, agricultural workers were included in compulsory sickness and old age insurance. This was not so in Hungary, as in other countries with large, poor rural populations, who could not easily be fitted into a contributory system (such as France). By 1939 Hungary had a highly developed social insurance system, but it applied only to the urban minority. There was extensive poverty in the countryside.

In the Soviet Union, social insurance remained under the administration of trade unions, though their independence was extremely limited. This, again, restricted its coverage to those in regular industrial work and excluded the peasantry, though in time they were awarded basic non-contributory benefits, along with collectivization and the loss of independence. Social insurance included wage-related sickness, invalidity, and old-age benefits, but none for unemployment. Instead there was compulsory retraining and compulsory movement of unemployed labor to available jobs. Officially, unemployment could not exist in Soviet Russia. One outcome was extensive overmanning.

In Weimar Germany, the Social Democratic government in 1918 established unemployment insurance benefits that were locally administered. The scheme was frequently adjusted under the pressure of mounting unemployment, but it remained resilient and in 1927 became nationally uniform. One outcome of Adolf Hitler (1889–1945) coming to power in 1933 was the introduction of new forms of discrimination in the insurance system as access to social insurance was denied to "undesirables," chiefly Jews and gypsies, even when they were German citizens. For the remainder of the population, the health, accident, and unemployment insurance schemes were extended as the economy expanded under pressure of war production in the later 1930s. The Nazis left intact the structure of national and local administration of social insurance, although the social insurance fund was drained to help finance the war. After the war, the governments both of East and West Germany were able to build upon the structures put in place earlier in the century.

In Italy under Benito Mussolini (1883–1945), health insurance was introduced in 1929 and state support for voluntary institutions increased, again overwhelmingly benefiting urban workers. In 1943, in a desperate attempt to consolidate support for the regime, unification and rationalization of the mass of mutual associations was proposed, but it came too late, as the fascist state crumbled. In Spain under Francisco Franco (1892–1975) in 1939, minimum pensions were established, financed by employers and the state through subsidies to workers' mutual associations; as elsewhere, these could only assist the regularly employed urban minority. In Salazar's Portugal, the term *social insurance* disappeared from official discourse, as implying a degree of collectivism that the regime rejected. Unusually in Europe, Salazar's state discouraged workers' mutual associations for fear of their subversive potential. Instead, company and occupational funds were encouraged but not regulated, mainly for white-collar and skilled workers and artisans.

Sweden expanded its system of extensive, state-subsidized voluntary health insurance in 1931, partly under pressure of the severe slump of 1929–1931. This also helped the Social Democrats to power in 1932, promising social reform. They remained in office for forty-four years. They almost immediately increased expenditure on unemployment benefits and, more gradually, expanded government funding to voluntary sickness and pensions insurance. In Norway, the slump was followed by the election of a Labor government that introduced health insurance and compulsory pension insurance in 1936, again giving priority to seamen and fishermen; in 1938, the government introduced compulsory unemployment insurance for other regularly employed workers.

In France, state-subsidized sickness and old age insurance became compulsory in 1930 for workers in industry, commerce, and agriculture, and similar, separate schemes were established for other blue-collar and public employees. Contributions from workers and employers were mandatory.

SOCIAL INSURANCE IN WESTERN EUROPE, WORLD WAR II TO 2004

During, and in some cases before (such as in Sweden) World War II, some countries were reevaluating their social insurance systems, mainly in the direction of rationalizing and integrating the complex variety of schemes that had grown up over the preceding half-century. In Britain in 1942, the Beveridge Report recommended the integration of the existing old age, widows', sickness, and unemployment insurance schemes and their extension to the whole working population, providing flat rate benefits in return for flat rate contributions from workers and employers, subsidized and administered by the state. Since the beginning of the century, William Beveridge (1879–1963) had advocated social insurance as a means both to eliminate severe poverty and to reinforce social solidarity, because it entailed collective mutual responsibility for risk across classes. For the same reason he had long advocated that all workers—white- as well as blue-collar—should be members of the same insurance scheme and subject to the same conditions, rather than divided by occupation as in so many other European countries. Beveridge opposed benefits targeted on the poorest, partly for this reason, but also because he believed them to be more costly to administer than universal insurance and inefficient because suitably qualified people often did not apply, due to ignorance or fear of stigma. Beveridge did not, however, believe that social insurance benefits should provide more than a minimum income adequate for survival. Those who wished to supplement insurance benefits in order to raise their living standards in periods of personal crisis should do so in the private sector, preferably through nonprofit mutual associations such as friendly societies.

For a short period after the war, the Beveridge Report was inspirational elsewhere in Europe. It was implemented in Britain from 1948 by the country's first majority Labour government, providing, however, such low benefits that, ever since, many thousands of poorer people have required targeted state supplements. Britain has never quite escaped from its centuries-old Poor Law tradition of public responsibility to prevent destitution but

to do little more from collective funds. Between 1974 and 1986, a minimal income-related element was added to the state pension. Otherwise from the 1950s the state provided tax incentives to encourage employers to provide supplements to social insurance for their workers mainly through commercial rather than nonprofit insurance. These activities were regulated by the state, and workers in the large public and nationalized industrial sector received subsidized pensions, until the 1980s when Conservative governments of Margaret Thatcher (b. 1925) relaxed regulation of private insurance, denationalized extensively (for example, the railways), and reduced the size of the public sector, without safeguarding workers' benefits. The Conservatives also reduced the coverage of some state benefits, notably unemployment insurance, and reduced the real value of others such as pensions. Between 1997 and 2004, scandals in the private sector and increased poverty led Labour governments to reimpose regulation on the private sector and to increase state benefits, but through targeted assistance rather than improvements in social insurance.

The minimal British approach to social insurance was unusual in postwar Europe, with the exception of Ireland, which kept until 1952 the pre-1914 British system that had been in place when Ireland gained independence in 1920. This poor, largely agricultural country excluded agricultural workers from the insurance scheme until the 1950s. In 1952 the various insurance schemes were integrated on the postwar British model, but excluded the self-employed (including many independent small farmers) and better-paid white-collar workers. Only with entry to the European Union and the great expansion of the Irish economy from the 1980s did Irish social insurance reach the standards prevailing elsewhere in northern Europe.

Most other countries reassessed and overhauled their social insurance systems in the decade following World War II. Some, such as Germany, Italy, and the countries of what became communist Eastern Europe, did so in response to regime change. But even Portugal, which remained under Salazar's authoritarian dictatorship, sought in 1946 to harmonize and rationalize its variety of occupational and local schemes and to extend them to cover a larger proportion of the population.

Coverage was further extended in the early 1960s to include most of the population, though benefits were low. The Marcello Caetano (1906–1980) government that succeeded Salazar between 1969 and 1973 increased benefits as part of an unsuccessful attempt to preserve the regime. Francoist Spain, similarly, in 1942 introduced comprehensive health insurance for low-income workers and their dependents, to which was added old age and invalidity insurance in 1947. These schemes ran alongside trade union funds. Benefits were low and the state contribution minimal, but coverage improved as part of the attempt by the Francoist state to achieve legitimacy with its opponents, and as the economy improved from the late 1950s. In 1963, the state sought to establish common principles for the plethora of independent occupational and local insurance schemes, and a non-contributory pension was introduced targeted at the poorest people over age seventy. By Franco's death in 1975 there was a high level of coverage of social insurance in Spain but the organization remained fragmented and benefits highly variable. The democratic constitution of 1978 introduced the principle of universal social security, although in 1982, 14.4 percent of the population was still excluded from social insurance. Thereafter, as the economy expanded, coverage and level of benefits improved until by the late 1990s it matched the rest of Europe.

The three poor states of southern Europe—Portugal, Spain, and Greece—all emerged from right-wing rule in 1974–1975. Thereafter they sought to improve and standardize their social insurance systems as an indicator of their new democratic principles and to signify their suitability for partnership with the rest of Western Europe. Also, as their economies expanded, they could better afford to do so, although the international recession and mounting unemployment of the later 1970s and 1980s there, as elsewhere in Europe, led governments to expand insurance schemes more cautiously than they had hoped and to rely extensively on employer and employee contributions. Also as elsewhere in Europe, the need to provide for mounting unemployment diverted potential state funds from other sources of risk. And social insurance standards in southern Europe came increasingly under pressure from the European Union as, one by

one, they joined it. The European Union set out to ensure high standards of social insurance and assistance provision among member states. It could not, however, insist that its guidelines were followed: Britain, for example, continued to the end of the period to provide state pensions well below the level (50 percent of average earnings) recommended by the European Union.

Elsewhere in Western Europe, all states introduced universal social protection after World War II, some more quickly than others. Italy did not achieve a universal system until the 1970s. It had a large, poor, rural southern population that could not easily fit into a classical social insurance system. Attempts after the war to unify and rationalize the variety of occupationally based schemes surviving from before the war, and to supplement them with state-financed benefits for the poorest (the system which developed from the 1970s), also were opposed by employers and professional organizations.

Throughout Western Europe, social insurance systems varied in their mix of public and private, contributory and non-contributory schemes, but all except Britain and Ireland gave a large role to occupationally based schemes, managed by representatives of workers and employers and, in the case of Germany and Sweden, the state, with benefits related to incomes and to perceived needs in each occupation. An important effect of this approach was to ensure that potential beneficiaries were kept informed by their representatives about their rights under social insurance and about potential changes to the schemes. Hence, when governments such as those of France, Germany, and Sweden sought to cut benefits from the 1980s as they experienced economic recession while public expenditure mounted, following rapid growth from the 1950s to early 1970s, strong and effective resistance was quickly mobilized. In Britain, by contrast, where the administration of social insurance was wholly in the hands of the state, the real value and coverage of insurance benefits was eroded in the 1980s after reaching a peak in the late 1970s and the population seemed hardly to notice, until the early years of the twenty-first century when the collapse of a number of commercial and occupational pension schemes, combined with the low level of state pensions, at last caused public protest from pensioner groups and trade unions. The country in mainland Europe most similar to Britain in this respect was Denmark, which had a similar tradition of minimal state-controlled social security. There also benefits were eroded by right-wing governments in the 1980s.

Throughout the postwar period, the state played a larger role in regulating and subsidizing occupationally based insurance schemes in the Nordic countries than elsewhere in mainland Western Europe. Immediately after the war Sweden introduced universal flat-rate pensions, family allowances, and sickness insurance similar to those recommended by Beveridge in Britain. But in 1959 Sweden shifted to higher, income related benefits, under pressure from blue-collar workers who wanted more in terms of coverage and levels of benefits. Similarly, shortly after the war, Norway expanded and integrated its system on Beveridge-style lines, but from 1966 moved to an income-related system. Norway, unlike Sweden and Denmark, had not entered the European Union by 2004, but, with its oil-rich economy, it maintained high standards of social benefits without external pressure. Denmark, like Norway, recovered slowly from wartime occupation and only in the 1950s did a Social Democratic government introduce a universal, and initially modest, social insurance system.

EASTERN EUROPE FROM COMMUNISM TO TRANSITION

In Eastern Europe from 1948 a fairly uniform welfare system was introduced throughout the Soviet bloc. Notions of insurance and of statutory rights were replaced by provision of benefits by the state, paid either directly through state agencies or through the workplace or trade unions. Because unemployment was deemed not to exist, neither did unemployment benefits, though these were introduced in Hungary in the late 1980s, when the extent of unemployment became impossible to ignore. The schemes were universal and so included those, such as independent farmers in Czechoslovakia, who previously had been excluded. In general, elite groups and key workers such as miners received higher benefits. After 1989, East Germany was absorbed into the West German system. Elsewhere, often encouraged by the World Bank, governments shifted to variable mixes of privatization and marketization of social insurance,

retaining, at least in principle, basic, targeted, safety nets of social assistance. These were often very basic and steadily eroded, as in Russia and Hungary. The more prosperous Czech Republic retained a minimum income guarantee and relatively high levels of benefit for its poorest people. The entry of the major countries of East-Central Europe into the European Union in 2004 may be a step to greater harmonization of social insurance across the whole of Europe. However, as has been seen, national political, social, and economic differences have always profoundly shaped social insurance systems. Such differences are unlikely wholly to disappear.

See also **Old Age; Public Health; Welfare State.**

BIBLIOGRAPHY

Baldwin, Peter. *The Politics of Social Solidarity: Class Bases of the European Welfare State, 1875–1975.* Cambridge, U.K., 1990.

Flora, Peter, and Arnold J. Heidenheimer, eds. *The Development of Welfare States in Europe and America.* New Brunswick, N.J., 1981.

Gordon, Margaret S. *Social Security Policies in Industrial Countries: A Comparative Analysis.* Cambridge, U.K., 1988.

Hennock, E. P. *British Social Reform and German Precedents: The Case of Social Insurance, 1880–1914.* Oxford, U.K., 1987.

Palier, Bruno. ed. *Comparing Social Welfare Systems in Southern Europe.* Paris, 1997.

Thane, Pat. *Foundations of the Welfare State.* 2nd ed. London, 1996.

———. *Old Age in English History: Past Experiences, Present Issues.* Oxford, UK, 2000.

PAT THANE

SOCIALISM. *Socialism* is a generic term attributed to movements, persons, and parties committed to some forms of nonmarket ways of allocating resources. The definition of *socialism* itself has been a terrain keenly contested by socialists themselves—from social democrats to communists. Since key aspects of socialism have constantly undergone adaptation and change by the political parties that have been its main proponents, it is preferable to examine how these parties have evolved historically and politically rather than to attempt to provide a watertight definition of the concept.

ORIGINS

The doctrine emerged in the course of the nineteenth century claiming some continuity with the republican traditions of the French Revolution and the democratic ethos of equality and human rights. Socialists distinguished themselves from anarchists by insisting that the abolition of the state could not be the immediate objective of the movement and by accepting the necessity of intermediate objectives within capitalism. By the end of the century, throughout Europe, the majority of workers organized in trade unions regarded themselves as committed to the long-term of goal of socialism understood as an "end state" following the abolition of capitalism and of the private property of the means of producing wealth.

By 1914 socialist parties—almost all inspired by some variant of Marxism—had succeeded in obtaining considerable electoral support in much of western Europe, particularly in the Nordic countries, where Socialists had polled 29 percent in Denmark (1913), 47 percent in Finland (1916), 36 percent in Sweden (1914), and 32 percent in Norway (1915). They were also strong in German-speaking Europe, with 35 percent in Germany (1912) and 25 percent in Austria. In Belgium the Socialist Party had reached 30 percent, thanks largely to the Francophone industrial belt. In France and Italy the highly factionalized socialist movement had succeeded in obtaining the support of almost 20 percent of the electorate. Great Britain, though one of the most advanced industrial countries in Europe with a large working class, constituted a special case, since the Labour Party before 1914 was neither electorally significant nor Marxist.

Continental socialist parties based their outlook on some variant of the Erfurt Program jointly drafted by Karl Kautsky and Eduard Bernstein and adopted by the German Social Democratic Party (SPD) in 1891. This distinguished the long-term aim of the movement—the abolition of capitalism—from objectives that could be achieved under capitalism, such as universal suffrage, social reforms, and the eight-hour day.

Socialists assumed that the working class, organized by the trade unions and the Socialist or Social Democratic Party (the names were then interchangeable), would be the central agency that could achieve both the long-term and the immediate aims of the movement. The development of capitalism itself would bring about the circumstances for a rapid transition toward socialism. The form of this transition was uncertain and debated at length within the movement. Some, such as the French Socialist leader Jules Guesde (1845–1922), thought that it would require a revolutionary upheaval along the pattern of the French Revolution, others, such as Rosa Luxemburg (1870–1919), assumed that a mass general strike would paralyze society and force the bourgeoisie to abdicate power, and others yet—such as the German Social Democratic theorist Eduard Bernstein (1850–1932) and, less forcefully, Guesde's French rival Jean Jaurès (1859–1914)—believed that universal suffrage would provide the working class with the peaceful means of gaining a parliamentary majority and legislating socialism into existence. Bernstein, in particular, since the 1890s, suggested that the party should abandon the prospect of a final goal of socialism and dedicate itself to incremental reforms.

Socialism, however, was a complex mélange of ideas and conceptions reflecting the social and political structure of the countries within which it was operating. In countries where political democracy was not extant—such as the Russian Empire—a more combative and insurrectionist ethos prevailed. In others, such as Germany, Socialists built up parallel organizations, from choral societies to public libraries, that formed a powerful alternative network.

The outbreak of the First World War found the majority of socialist parties patriotically rallying round their national state, notably in France and Germany. In Italy, however, only a small minority, led by Benito Mussolini (1883–1945), then a Socialist, supported the war. In Russia all the factions of the Russian Social Democratic Labor Party, from the Mensheviks to the Bolsheviks, refused to approve the war credits.

In spite of their original pacifist position most European Socialists supported the war because it was difficult for any mass organization to resist pressure from their own supporters, who were, at

Members of the Popular Front rally on Bastille Day at the Place de la Republic, Paris, 14 July 1936. A portrait of socialist leader Léon Blum can be seen at center. GETTY IMAGES

least initially, swept up in the general enthusiasm for what had seemed a short conflict.

The October Revolution of 1917 and the birth of the modern communist movement further exacerbated—and made final—the split in the socialist movement. Under pressure from the newly formed Communist International—or Comintern (1919)—communist parties supportive of the Bolshevik Revolution were formed, usually, but not always, by seceding from the main Socialist Party. In all instances, however, socialist parties were able to hold on to the support of the majority of the left electorate. In France, for instance, the Communists who seceded at the Tours Congress (1920) captured a majority of the Section Française de l'Internationale Ouvrière (SFIO)—as the French Socialist Party was called—

but had the support of only a fraction of the SFIO electorate.

THE INTERWAR YEARS

A wave of radicalism swept throughout Europe after 1918 without producing either new communist regimes or a major upsurge of support for socialist parties except in the Scandinavian countries and to a lesser extent in Britain, where the Labour Party supplanted the Liberal Party as the Conservatives' main opponents.

Such situations led most Socialists to reject their previous policy of noncollaboration with "bourgeois" parties. The British Labour Party formed its first government (1923) with the support of the Liberal Party, the French Socialists found themselves in de facto alliance with the Radicals, the Spanish with the Republicans, the Swedish with the Liberal Party (1917) and then with the Agrarian Party (1936), the Norwegians with the Farmers' Party (1935), and the Germans with the Center Party (among others).

Socialists did not just change their alliance strategy, they also saw the capitalist economy under a new light. The First World War had provided some parties, notably the French and the German, with some experience of government. After the war many Socialists recognized that, as a consequence of the growing role of the state during the war, traditional liberal economic policies were being challenged even by some on the right of the political spectrum who advocated a "corporatist" cooperation of the main social forces, especially the employers' associations and trade unions. Under the threat of working-class unrest, the interwar years witnessed a blossoming of employer-union pacts such as the Stinnes-Legien pact of 1918, which established in Germany a joint labor-management board for economic regulation; the albeit ineffectual "Whitley Councils" in Britain; the Matignon Accords of 1936 following the victory of the Popular Front in France; and the employers-employee pacts in the Nordic countries such as the Saltsjöbaden agreements in Sweden (1938) and the so-called Main Agreement in Norway (1935). Even the British trade unions, notoriously hostile to any corporatist approach, began, under the dominant influence of Ernest Bevin (1881–1951), to be systematically included in Royal Commissions and committees of inquiry alongside employers and government representatives.

That some sort of agreement between employers and trade unions was necessary had been first recognized in Germany by the SPD during the 1920s. What this pact amounted to was a "class compromise" whereby the labor movement "traded" growth and productivity in exchange for social reforms along the lines advocated by Rudolf Hilferding, the Social Democratic minister of finance in 1923 and 1928–1929, in a number of essays and speeches on the theory of "organized capitalism."

Such trends led to a further bout of confrontation between the mainstream socialist parties and the communist parties that, prompted by the Soviet Union, denounced the Socialists as "social traitors" (1928), a policy known as the "Third Period" of "class against class," hoping that the forthcoming economic crisis would bring about a final confrontation resulting in a communist revolution. Such policies further divided the Left just at a time when the threat of fascism accelerated—above all in Germany.

Sparked by the collapse of the New York stock exchange in 1929, the long-awaited crisis finally arrived, bringing about massive unemployment in Europe but no political dividends for either Socialists or Communists, since it accelerated the Nazi takeover. During the whole of the interwar period only two western European communist parties had developed a significant electoral base: the Kommunistische Partei Deutschlands (KPD) and the Parti Communiste Français (PCF). The advent of Nazism destroyed the KPD along with all the other parties. In France, however, the PCF, after the advent of Nazism, adopted a less sectarian position, abandoned the Third Period policies and, encouraged by Moscow, joined the Socialists in a pact. A similar understanding was reached in Spain. It was the birth of the Popular Front. In 1936 the Popular Front, led by the Socialists, obtained a significant electoral victory in both countries. The consequences, however, were far from positive in Spain, where the reformist policies of the Popular Front unclenched a counteroffensive by the military establishment, acting on behalf of landed and church interests. The ensuing bloody civil war resulted in the victory of Francisco Franco (1892–1975), whose authoritarian regime lasted until his death in 1975. In France the first Socialist government—led by Léon Blum (1872–1950) and supported by the Communists—although short-lived, established thanks to a wave of strikes the working week of forty hours, paid holidays, compulsory arbitration of labor disputes, and the nationalization of the Bank of France. Between 1922 and 1926 Blum had developed a conceptual distinction between the *conquest of power* and the *exercise of power*. The former was a revolutionary, though not necessarily violent, act that led to socialism. The second meant pursuing limited reformist goals without challenging existing property relations. Such a distinction was used in 1936 to explain and legitimize the new Popular Front government.

In spite of the relative success of many such reforms, most Socialists still conceived of socialism as a "model of society," that is, as a "final goal."

There were exceptions, notably in Scandinavia and especially in Sweden. The Swedish Social Democrats (Socialdemokratiska Arbetarepartiet, or SAP), were able to combat unemployment more effectively than the German SPD and the British Labour Party. In so doing, between 1932 and 1938 they laid the foundation for what would become the modern Western European conception of social democracy after the Second World War: the compromise between labor and capital, with a welfare state and full employment.

Between the war and 1932 the SAP had repeatedly been in government, either in coalition with the Liberal Party (October 1917–March 1918) or as a minority government (March–October 1920, October 1921–April 1923, and October 1924–June 1926). Coalition with a bourgeois party had become acceptable on the grounds that Sweden had a politically backward bourgeoisie that could not be relied on to carry out the democratization of society. The Swedish Social Democrats did not put forward any plans for constitutional reform or for abolishing the monarchy and had dropped from their 1932 electoral manifesto all references to socialism and to socialization of the means of production. There were to be no major nationalizations. Instead the SAP established a successful "corporative" structure for permanent negotiations between employers, trade unions, and government on labor-market and social policies. In the 1930s the Swedish Social Democrats introduced employment-creation programs, a housing program to the benefit of large families, indexation of pensions, near-universal maternity benefits, paid holidays, and state loans to newly married couples. Similar policies were promulgated in Denmark and Norway, so that one could speak in broader terms of a Nordic model, harbinger of post–Second World War social democracy.

Less successful was the interwar experience of government of the British Labour Party. After 1923 its dependence on the parliamentary support of the Liberals made it impossible to contemplate the nationalization of the mines, railways, and electric power stations. Besides, it had no plans for dealing with unemployment. Defeated at the 1924 elections it was returned to power in 1929 to head another Liberal-supported minority government. The Labour leadership decided that economic responsibility entailed following the advice of the treasury (the "treasury view"). Faced with an increase in unemployment, the cabinet split. The resulting crisis led to the formation of a "National Government" dominated by the Conservatives but led by the former Labour prime minister, James Ramsay MacDonald (1866–1937). The Labour Party remained in opposition until 1940 during which time the ideas of John Maynard Keynes (1883–1946) on the causes of unemployment became influential within the Labour Party.

AFTER 1945

The Second World War provided European socialism with the chance of becoming a significant political force. In the aftermath of the conflict the Soviet model was extended to much of Eastern Europe but, in the democratic West, socialist parties became the main opposition to the Conservatives and Christian Democrats everywhere except in the Republic of Ireland and Switzerland. During the war the armed Resistance against the Nazis was dominated by the Communists, whose greater militancy and stronger organization proved far superior to that of the often-divided Socialists. Once the conflict was over, however, the Socialists turned out to be far more popular than the Communists (except in France and Italy)—a pattern that was repeated thirty years later, in the mid-1970s, when the dictatorships of southern Europe (Greece, Portugal, and Spain) collapsed, benefiting the Socialists rather than the Communists, even though the latter had a more important role in the Resistance.

Once the conflict was over, the socialist and social democratic parties were in power in virtually the whole of democratic Western Europe, though they shared power with other parties everywhere except in Britain, Sweden, and Norway, where they governed on their own. In Britain the Labour Party achieved a historic and unexpected victory in 1945. The Labour Party had prevailed because, unlike its Conservative opponents, it expressed the mood of the time: the egalitarian ethos of the war and the social solidarity enhanced by having to face a common enemy. The war enabled Labour to acquire a national-patriotic identity, something that Socialists had sought in vain before. The considerable social reforms that were promulgated in the successive five years, particularly the establishment of the National Health Service, offered noncommunist Socialists a

British Minister of Health and Housing Aneuran Bevan (third from left) and his wife, Jennie Lee (second from left) are escorted on a hospital tour, May 1948. Bevan's creation of the National Health Service was a centerpiece of the Labour Party's reform agenda during the immediate postwar period. GETTY IMAGES

powerful model of reform within capitalism, the welfare state. In one form or other the pursuit and development of this social model became the hallmark of the new variant of European socialism: social democracy.

Elsewhere socialism meant something different. In some Latin American countries, in parts of decolonized Africa, and in some Asian countries, notably India, socialism was seen as providing a model of state-led industrialization and modernization. In Eastern and central Europe socialism became subsumed by communism, and social development followed a pattern similar to that of the Soviet Union.

There is little doubt, however, that a centralized state was considered everywhere to be a useful instrument for the introduction of welfare socialism. The idea that reforms would have to be introduced from above could coexist perfectly well with the democratic rule that prescribed a prior electoral sanction.

Once this was achieved, politicians were entitled to implement their program using all instruments provided by the state. Thus a statist (economic planning and control by the state) mentality suited social reformers exceptionally well, and the temptation of social engineering was seldom resisted, especially in countries where there was little upheaval and considerable continuity and where socialists could realistically aspire to government.

The development of mass democratic politics had led these parties to formulate appeals that included the whole people and were no longer directed toward the "working class" as a separate group. The concept of working class itself was dramatically enlarged. It now included all "working people" and thus also many members of the employed middle classes without whose support electoral victory would be problematic. Even before deindustrialization had started with the consequent diminution in the size of the working class, Socialists were aware that the support of a considerable section of the middle classes was mandatory.

A remarkable radicalization of middle-class youth occurred toward the end of the 1960s, particularly in France (May 1968) and Italy (the "hot autumn") in conjunction with a revival of working-class militancy—strikes were at their highest in Europe in the years 1960–1965. The consequences for socialist parties were minimal, except in France, where the Socialist Party was entirely reorganized under the leadership of François Mitterrand (1916–1996), whose alliance with the Communist Party paved the way for the Socialist victory of 1981 and the eventual marginalization of the Communists.

The larger communist parties of Western Europe, mainly the French and the Italian, followed, in their practical policies, an orientation not dissimilar to other Socialists, while demarcating themselves substantially in foreign policy by maintaining a close link with the Soviet Union. This link grew less strong in the following decades, particularly in the 1970s, when the failures of central planning in the USSR became increasingly apparent. Even within the Soviet bloc, notably in Czechoslovakia, some Communists propounded a vision of "communism with a human face" by removing the more salient authoritarian and undemocratic features of communism and operating a rapprochement with Western socialism. Though this experiment was terminated by the Soviet invasion of Czechoslovakia in 1968 (condemned by the Italian Communist Party though not by the French), it was revived, paradoxically, in the USSR itself when Mikhail Gorbachev (b. 1931) became its leader in 1985 and started the process of renewal that would lead to the unintended dismantling of the USSR and the collapse of the communist bloc. Many of the ruling communist parties, notably in Hungary, Poland, and Romania, recycled themselves as social-democratic and socialist parties, winning elections without being able to stem the impetus of neoliberal economic policies.

By the new millennium the mainstream socialist parties in Europe had abandoned not just the hostility toward capitalist social relations that they had originally possessed but even the concepts and terminology associated with the doctrine of socialism. To all intents and purposes they had become, at most, the defenders of welfare reforms. The idea of subverting capitalism had been abandoned.

See also **Communism; Social Democracy.**

BIBLIOGRAPHY

Anderson, Perry, and Patrick Camiller, eds. *Mapping the West European Left.* London, 1994.

Berger, Stefan. *Social Democracy and the Working Class in Nineteenth and Twentieth Century Germany.* Harlow, U.K., 2000.

Eley, Geoff. *Forging Democracy: The History of the Left in Europe, 1850–2000.* Oxford, U.K., 2002.

Glyn, Andrew, ed. *Social Democracy in Neoliberal Times: The Left and Economic Policy since 1980.* Oxford, U.K., 2001.

Haupt, Georges. *Aspects of International Socialism, 1871–1914: Essays.* Translated by Peter Fawcett. Cambridge, U.K., 1986.

Jackson, Julian. *The Popular Front in France: Defending Democracy, 1934–38.* Cambridge, U.K., 1988.

Korpi, Walter. *The Working Class in Welfare Capitalism: Work, Unions, and Politics in Sweden.* London, 1978.

Miller, Susanne, and Heinrich Potthoff. *A History of German Social Democracy from 1848 to the Present.* Translated by J. A. Underwood. Leamington Spa, U.K., 1986.

Newman, Michael. *Socialism: A Very Short Introduction.* Oxford, U.K., 2005.

Sassoon, Donald. *One Hundred Years of Socialism: The West European Left in the Twentieth Century.* London, 1996.

Shaw, Eric. *The Labour Party since 1945: Old Labour, New Labour.* Oxford, U.K., 1996.

DONALD SASSOON

SOCIALIST REALISM.

Socialist realism was a Soviet doctrine developed in the early 1930s about literature and other branches of culture. Doctrine here means not simply an available school or method of art but rather a mandatory set of guidelines that all Soviet creative figures were required to follow. It came into being largely as way to end the ambivalences and ideological squabbling that went on in the Soviet Union all through the 1920s, but also as a means of curbing the more extreme self-described "proletarian movements" that escalated during the period of the first Five-Year Plan and the Cultural Revolution that accompanied it (c. 1929–1932). During the period of the New Economic Policy in the 1920s, cultural life had developed in a free-wheeling bazaar of conflicting tastes and canons. In most of the arts, roughly three positions were advanced and put into practice: traditionalism, harking back to prerevolutionary Europe and Russia; proletarian culture, stressing heroic themes of revolution, civil war, and factory life; and the avant-garde, borrowing freely from Western modernism and experimenting in its own Russian context as well as those of other nationalities. In addition to these, though minus any supporting argument, ordinary urban popular culture (pulp fiction, jazz, entertainment) flourished amid caustic criticism from the cultural and ideological elites. Much overlapping and many sub-movements produced an exceptionally rich tapestry of cultural expression—seen by some as a golden age of Soviet poetry, theater, film, music, and architecture. When the Cultural Revolution began, the leaders of the proletarian movement took command and tried to shut down all competing genres and styles—even including folk culture, seen as retrograde by the machine-loving urban enthusiasts.

1930S: DEFINING "SOVIET" ART

In 1932 the proletarian organizations themselves felt the power of the Communist Party, which closed them down in a resolution titled "On the

Reformation of Literary and Art Organizations." A new Union of Soviet Writers was called for and over the next two years literary circles around the country and a special commission of writers and political figures appointed by the Party Central Committee engaged in intense discussion on the future of Soviet literature. The first congress of the Union assembled in August 1934, presided over by the returned émigré Maxim Gorky. After much debate, the congress adopted the term *socialist realism,* vaguely defined as the representation of Soviet reality in its revolutionary development. Unions of writers and all the arts came into being with the mission of producing works in this category and condemning alternative styles. For narrative works, a master plot emerged, usually featuring a hot-headed young revolutionary or worker who encounters obstacles, either natural or the product of evildoers or slackers. The hero is tamed and mentored by an older and wiser character, and eventually the difficulties are resolved into a happy ending. Thus even stories of revolutionary victims and martyrs ended with an optimistic upswell of reverence and a promise of revolutionary immortality and the victory of socialism. Original models for this schema included Gorky's prerevolutionary novel *Mother* (1906) and Dmitri Furmanov's civil war epic *Chapaev* (1923), among others. Emphatically excluded were psychological nuances, existential angst, religion and mysticism, overt sexuality, and experimentalism in form and style. All works were required to be accessible to the toilers of the Soviet Union. The much-cited exemplar of this doctrine, Nikolai Ostrovsky's *How the Steel Was Tempered* (1932–1934), embodies all the limits and negative qualities of such a constrictive theory.

The enforcement of socialist realism does not explain all the physical casualties among creative figures of the era: Vladimir Mayakovsky committed suicide in 1930 before it emerged, and the great poet Osip Mandelstam died in the camps for an insulting verse about Stalin. Yet the theater director Vsevolod Meyerhold lost his life clearly because of a stubborn adherence to his art. Soviet plays followed the scenario of socialist realism with pious representations of civil war heroes, rehabilitated camp prisoners, and industrial production. They adhered to what was then conventional in staging, realist sets, and acting styles. Konstantin Stanislavsky, the main architect of these conventions before the revolution, reached the pinnacle of his career. Gone were the days of biomechanics (robotic movements of actors), flying lizards in the ballet, and the innovative stylized performances of the 1920s.

Cinema, a much more popular art, came under strict control in the early 1930s. The freedom and lyrical flights of Sergei Eisenstein and other directors of the 1920s gave way to the "iron script," censorship, and a demand for "movies for the millions" in the words of the chief movie bureaucrat, Boris Shumyatsky. Professional actors and "stars" replaced the mass scenes of nonactors from some of the 1920s films. Like fiction and drama, cinema took up themes of revolution and socialist construction. A lighter twist to the canons of socialist realism appeared in the well-received musical comedies of the 1930s, which borrowed domesticated forms of American jazz and Hollywood dance. The best examples featured the superstar of the era, Lyubov Orlova, and her director husband, Grigory Alexandrov. Their political correctness—though ever present—was submerged beneath the jolly good time had by all, complete with the mandatory happy ending. One important Eisenstein film appeared in this decade: *Alexander Nevsky* (1938), a lavishly produced story of the Novgorod prince's defense of Kievan Rus against the Teutonic invaders in the Middle Ages. The warning reference to the detested Adolf Hitler regime was lost on no one, though the film had to be withdrawn in 1939 with the signing of the Nazi-Soviet Pact.

From the perspective of ideological inspection, music came in two forms: opera and other story-filled works whose content was more easily monitored than the music that accompanied it; and purely instrumental music that was obviously much harder to check. Dmitri Shostakovich, the greatest Soviet composer, fell victim in both categories when his opera *Lady Macbeth of the Mtsensk District* was roundly attacked in 1936. Apparently the impetus was Stalin's dislike of the "immorality" displayed on stage. (The plot, from Nikolai Leskov's nineteenth-century story, revolves around adultery and murder.) But critics, taking the cue, also assaulted the music and set an example for

A scene from Sergei Eisenstein's film *Alexander Nevsky,* 1938. Bowing to the realities of government mandates, Eisenstein created an epic film celebrating the strength and patriotism of the Russian people. THE KOBAL COLLECTION

others to hound him again in the late 1930s and in 1948—on purely musical grounds. The still-raging debate over whether Shostakovich's vaunted Seventh ("Leningrad") Symphony (1941) was inspired by the composer's hatred for Hitler or for Stalin suggests how difficult it was and is to prove the political meanings of symphonic music. Other composers satisfied the demands of the regime by concocting song symphonies and cantatas with easily recognizable and audible paeans to Stalin, the factory, the Russian forest, or Red Cossacks, as in Ivan Dzerzhinsky's *Quiet Don* (1935), based on the novel *Quiet Flows the Don* by Mikhail Sholokhov.

POSTWAR SOVIET ART AND "HIGH STALINISM"

The definitive moment of persecution occurred after the war when the political chieftain and self-appointed critic Andrei Zhdanov assaulted one

well-known writer, Mikhail Zoshchenko, for satirizing Soviet society and another, Anna Akhmatova, for poetry that was too personal. In the field of music, Zhdanov scolded Vano Muradeli for using stylized instead of "authentic" Georgian folk dancing in his opera *The Great Friendship* (1947). Zhdanov blasted Shostakovich, Sergei Prokofiev, and others for failure to meet the standards of Soviet musical life. By this he meant producing accessible music with soaring melodies reflecting the greatness of the Russian people. By this time the experience of war had deepened the Russian nationalist and even chauvinist elements in socialist realism. Even so, beginning in the 1930s the regime had made a point of sponsoring and creating "national" music and dance in all the non-Russian republics, based loosely on collected folk materials and designed to pull the ethnic minorities into the larger Soviet culture. Although measuring the "socialist" content of music always remained problematic, on one matter clarity prevailed: the strict prohibition of twelve-tone, serial, and other modernist forms of composition that a few Soviet composers had supported and practiced in the early days of the revolution.

Socialist realist art—particularly painting—has often wrongly been equated with the realism of the so-called Travelers (*Peredvizhniki*) of the late nineteenth century. While the similarity of representational styles cannot be denied (such styles appear in many historical epochs), the realism of the Travelers was critical, not adulatory. In some of their works, they unveiled the maladies of their time and place: poverty, suicide, child labor, religious hypocrisy, alcoholism. The mandate of Soviet socialist realist painters pointed in the opposite direction: to use realist techniques to promote the values of the regime. This they did with great vigor and often with considerable skill. One may find the same themes in art as portrayed in fiction, drama, and film: the greatness of the Great Leader (particularly in the hands of the court painter, Alexander Gerasimov), comforting scenes of the new Moscow, the efficient productive factory, sinewy workers, and the fertile and joyous collective farm (reflecting Stalin's motto "Life has become happier"). As in the other arts, graphic production became both more skillful and more subservient to the doctrine in the postwar period of High Stalinism. Alexander Laktionov provides the prime example. He scored high with the nostalgic *Letter from the Front* (1947), a sweet and sad domestic scene of a family reading the missive from their loved one away at war. Family also dominates his famous painting *Moving into a New Flat* (1952), with the portrait of Stalin waiting to be hung. Even when not overtly political, official themes of the Soviet good life were embedded in his canvases, just as the idealized American dream was in the 1940s paintings by Norman Rockwell.

After World War II socialist realism migrated to the Soviet-controlled satellites of Eastern Europe and even to communist states in Asia. Local conditions often allowed for more latitude, but no real freedom of expression. In the post-Stalin USSR, certain strictures remained in force until the era of glasnost in the 1980s. But beside and within them, freer forms emerged and even flourished (the "thaw" novel, village prose, rock

Letter from the Front. Painting by Alexander Laktionov, 1947. BRIDGEMAN ART LIBRARY

music), bringing to Soviet readers and listeners much more "real" realism than ever was provided by the Stalinist doctrine of the 1930s.

See also **Akhmatova, Anna; Eisenstein, Sergei; Gorky, Maxim; New Economic Policy (NEP); Prokofiev, Sergei; Shostakovich, Dmitri; Stalin, Joseph; Zhdanov, Andrei.**

BIBLIOGRAPHY

Bown, Matthew Cullerne. *Socialist Realist Painting.* New Haven, Conn., 1998.

Clark, Katerina. *The Soviet Novel: History as Ritual.* 2nd ed. Chicago, 1985.

Dunham, Vera S. *In Stalin's Time.* Cambridge, U.K., 1976.

Günther, Hans, ed. *The Culture of the Stalin Period.* New York, 1990.

Papernyi, Vladimir. *Architecture in the Age of Stalin.* Translated by John Hill and Roann Barris in collaboration with the author. Cambridge, U.K., 2002.

Robin, Régine. *Socialist Realism: An Impossible Aesthetic.* Translated by Catherine Porter. Stanford, Calif., 1992.

Schwarz, Boris. *Music and Musical Life in Soviet Russia.* Enl. ed. Bloomington, Ind., 1983.

RICHARD STITES

SOLIDARITY. Conceived in 1980 as the first autonomous labor union in the Soviet bloc, the Independent Self-Governing Trade Union "Solidarity" (Niezależny Samoządny Związek Zawodowy "Solidarność") challenged the authority of the one-party state in Poland and the communist system at large.

HISTORICAL BACKGROUND

The direct origins of Solidarity date back to the 1970 workers' rising on the Baltic Sea coast and the birth of the democratic opposition in the mid-1970s. In broader terms, however, its emergence in Poland can be attributed to several essential features of twentieth-century Polish history. First, during the period of partitions (1795–1918), the Poles developed a strong sense of national identity, which included fervent nationalism, ardent Catholicism, and resistance to foreign domination. Second, the nation's cultural elite, the intelligentsia, enriched these values with the ethos of grassroots activism. Finally, it was the failure of the communist regime to win total control over society that led to a series of political upheavals and crises culminating in the birth of Solidarity.

At the end of World War II, Poland found itself in the sphere of Soviet influence. Border shifts, population transfers, and the destruction of Jews had made Poland an ethnically homogenous and predominantly Catholic country. Polish Communists benefited from the help of the Soviet army and quickly consolidated power. However, in contrast to other communist states, the Communist Party—the Polish United Workers' Party (PZPR)—never succeeded in conquering two vestiges of pluralism: private agriculture and the Roman Catholic Church. Recruited mostly from among peasants, the new industrial labor force held to its traditional customs including ardent religiosity, while the church preserved traditional values constituting an alternative community to the party-state.

The inability of the Communist Party to fully dominate society also stemmed from its internal divisions and relatively frequent changes of leadership. The immediate postwar period saw the ascent to power of Władysław Gomułka (1905–1982), a Communist leader who advocated the "Polish road to socialism," acknowledging the country's national and socioeconomic specificities rather than mimicking the Soviet model. Persecuted under Stalinism, Gomułka returned to power in 1956. He halted collectivization, reinstated religious tolerance, relaxed censorship, and passed economic reforms. From the mid-1960s, however, Gomułka grew increasingly authoritarian. Having antagonized liberal intellectuals, party reformers, and the clergy, the regime embraced aggressive nationalism to legitimize its flagging rule. In 1968 it launched an anti-Semitic campaign and brutally suppressed student protests. The ideological and moral bankruptcy of communism in Poland paved the way for the birth of the new democratic opposition, no longer interested in reforming the system, but rather determined to pursue alternative solutions.

THE ROOTS OF SOLIDARITY: 1970–1980

The Gomułka government was toppled by the workers' strikes against food price increases of December 1970. After the massacre of strikers in the coastal cities of Gdańsk, Gdynia, and Szczecin, the party politburo ousted Gomułka. The new party leader, Edward Gierek (1913–2001), believed that consumerism, not ideology and coercion, was the key to winning social compliance. Loans from Western banks facilitated his ambitious program of rapid modernization, helped to increase wages, and brought greater availability of consumer goods. But overheated investment combined with incompetent management and rampant corruption soon led to an economic slowdown. In June 1976, after the announcement of food price increases, strikes and social protests erupted in several cities, most notably in Radom, where demonstrators besieged and burned party buildings. The government rescinded its plans but suppressed the riots with utmost brutality. Hundreds of workers were beaten, jailed, and sacked from their jobs.

The pacification of protests mobilized dissident intellectuals, who in September 1976 formed the Komitet Obrony Robotników (Committee for the Defense of Workers, or KOR). The original task of assisting arrested workers soon broadened into the promotion of human and civil rights, underground publishing, and the creation of free trade unions. Among its leading activists were the dissidents Jacek Kuroń and Adam Michnik, the writer Jerzy Andrzejewski, the literary scholar Jan Józef Lipski, and the Catholic priest Jan Zieja.

Above all, the KOR sought to build a civil society and ensure an independent and democratic public active outside of state control. The group's agenda was elaborated in essays by the philosopher Leszek Kołakowski, Kuroń, and Michnik, who argued that while a socialist system would not be democratized from above, it could be transformed by pressure applied from below by self-organized social groups. Soon KOR members made forays into the working class helping to organize the Free Trade Unions of the Coast in Gdańsk in 1978. Among the union's most outspoken activists was a young electrician, Lech Wałęsa. An employee of the Lenin Shipyard, Wałęsa took part in the 1970 strike. In 1976 he was fired for vehement criticism of the state-sponsored unions, democratic agitation, and calls for the commemoration of fallen workers. Introduced to the Gdańsk opposition milieu by a KOR member, Bogdan Borusewicz, Wałęsa joined the Free Unions in 1978. In 1979 he was one of the signatories of the Charter of Workers' Rights, which called for the right to strike, independent labor unions, and just wages.

In addition to the KOR, other groups emerged, including the Movement for the Defense of Human and Civil Rights (ROPCiO), and the Confederation for an Independent Poland (KPN). The alliance of intelligentsia and workers that began to materialize under the tutelage of the KOR was boosted by the rapprochement between opposition intellectuals and the Roman Catholic Church, the strongest autonomous institution in the country. These developments coupled with the leniency of Gierek, who was careful not to alienate Western creditors by brutalizing dissidents, transformed Poland into a major center of opposition to communism in the Soviet bloc. As the opposition provided revolutionary cadres, the Roman Catholic Church offered spiritual mobilization. The naming of Cardinal Karol Wojtyła, archbishop of Kraków, as Pope John Paul II in 1978, followed by his visit to Poland in 1979, brought about sense of moral reawakening and transformed the Polish public. In his farewell address, the pope urged his compatriots to "have the courage to go the way no one has followed before" (Luxmoore and Babiuch, p. 217). It was not long before the country experienced a cataclysmic political upheaval in 1980.

FIRST SOLIDARITY: 1980–1981

Rising foreign debt, economic slowdown, and an alarming discrepancy between imports and exports prompted the Gierek regime to introduce radical price adjustments for inflation and to cut down meat supplies for domestic markets in the summer of 1980. As work stoppages spread across Poland, free trade union activists from the coast and KOR members decided to launch a strike in the Lenin Shipyard in Gdańsk. The shipyard went on strike on 14 August 1980. Workers combined economic demands with political postulates calling for the reinstatement of a free trade union activist, Anna Walentynowicz, and of Wałęsa; the erection of a monument to the victims of the 1970 shootings; and compensatory pay increases. Under the leadership of Wałęsa, the Międzyzakładowy Komitet Strajowy (Interfactory Strike Committee, MKS) was formed in the Baltic region, demanding independent trade unions, the right to strike, freedom of expression, the release of political prisoners, and various economic concessions. By the end of August, political strikes had swept the entire country. On 31 August, Wałęsa and Deputy Premier Mieczysław Jagielski signed the Gdańsk agreement, in which the government conceded to most of the strikers' demands, including the right to form independent labor unions. Similar accords were concluded in Szczecin and Jastrzębie.

The August accords brought down the Gierek regime. The Soviets perceived the agreements as a temporary compromise and expected that the Polish Communists would gradually dismantle the workers' movement. But on 17 September 1980, delegates of thirty-five regional strike committees and several opposition activists set up the national federation of trade unions, the Independent Self-Governing Trade Union "Solidarity," with Wałęsa

A demonstration by Solidarity members and supporters, 1 May 1982. ©BETTMANN/CORBIS

as its chairman. After the government blocked its registration, Solidarity launched a general warning strike. Yielding to popular pressure, the regime agreed to legalize the union in exchange for Solidarity's recognition of the party's leading role in the state in November 1980. In December 1980, private farmers founded Rural Solidarity. By the end of that year, Solidarity had nine million members, and by the following spring ten million. It was a nationwide social movement functioning outside the party's control and encompassing all sectors of society including people from a variety of political persuasions.

Throughout 1981 Solidarity underwent increasing radicalization. The national congress of Solidarity, held in September and October 1981, adopted the program of the "Self-Governing Republic," in which citizens would take responsibility for various political, social, and cultural matters. The government, led by General Wojciech Jaruzelski (b. 1923), grew intransigently hostile

toward the union. Subjected to pressure from Moscow and keen to reinstate the party's authority, Jaruzelski set about destroying Solidarity by force. On 13 December 1981 he imposed martial law. As the military and police took total control of the country, civil rights and all political and social organizations were suspended. Thousands of Solidarity activists, including most of its leaders, were arrested and detained. In October 1982 the Polish parliament formally dissolved the union.

1982–1989

After the imposition of martial law, Solidarity continued underground under the command of those leaders who had escaped arrest. The union launched political strikes, organized campaigns of civil disobedience, and built a framework of independent institutions. Still, the underground Solidarity failed to mobilize the weary population. The lifting of martial law in 1983 indicated the regime's self-confidence. However, in the same year the government suffered

Solidarity leader Lech Wałęsa makes the victory sign during the 1989 presidential campaign in Plock, Poland. ©REUTERS/CORBIS

a major blow when Wałęsa received the Nobel Peace Prize. Even more devastating was the brutal assassination of Father Jerzy Popiełuszko, a staunch supporter of Solidarity, by a group of security policemen. In a desperate face-saving gesture, Jaruzelski had the killers arrested, tried, and sentenced to prison terms. Following this period of immediate repression, the general softened his policies, releasing political prisoners, allowing channels of pluralism, and implementing economic reforms. With the accession of Mikhail Gorbachev (b. 1931) to power in the Soviet Union, Jaruzelski followed and at times expanded the Soviet pattern of perestroika in the hope of winning society's compliance and achieving economic recovery while preserving the power of the party.

During the 1980s neither the underground Solidarity nor the Communist regime had enough power to eliminate its opponents. This stalemate continued until 1988, when government austerity measures sparked a wave of strikes. But the strikers' major demand was the re-legalization of Solidarity. The Polish Roundtable Talks between Solidarity and the government that concluded in April 1989 legalized the union and provided for its participation in parliamentary elections. In June 1989 Solidarity won 99 of 100 seats in the Senate and all of the 169 freely contested seats in the Sejm (lower house). The formation of the Solidarity-led coalition government led by Tadeusz Mazowiecki in August 1989 marked the end of communism in Poland and sparked the 1989 revolutions in Eastern Europe.

1989–2005

In 1990 Solidarity underwent political fragmentation over the issues of free-market reforms, decommunization, and Wałęsa's bid for the presidency. During the presidential elections of that year,

Wałęsa defeated Mazowiecki, and the Solidarity parliamentary club split into new political parties. Solidarity continued as a trade union. Radicalized and discontented by rising unemployment and other side effects of the economic transition, the union brought down Hanna Suchocka's center-right coalition government in 1993, paving the way for the electoral victory of former Communists. In 1995 Wałęsa lost the presidential elections to Aleksander Kwaśniewski, a former Communist. Two years later, Solidarity helped to build the center-right Electoral Action "Solidarity," which won the 1997 election. However, in 2001 Solidarity gained only a fraction of the vote, failing to enter parliament.

Lech Wałęsa, whose popularity plummeted in the 1990s (in the 2000 presidential elections he received only 1 percent of the vote) reentered politics acting as a mediator in the Ukrainian political crisis in 2005. The parliamentary elections of September 2005 saw the victory of two center-right parties, partly recruited from former Solidarity members, the Law and Justice Party (PiS) and the Civic Platform (PO). In the October 2005 presidential election, Lech Kaczyński, a former Solidarity activist, defeated Donald Tusk, another veteran of the democratic opposition.

See also **Gierek, Edward; Gomułka, Władysław; Jaruzelski, Wojciech; John Paul II; Perestroika; Poland; Wałęsa, Lech.**

BIBLIOGRAPHY

Garton Ash, Timothy. *The Polish Revolution: Solidarity, 1980–82.* London, 1983.

Kubik, Jan. *The Power of Symbols against the Symbols of Power: The Rise of Solidarity and the Fall of State Socialism in Poland.* University Park, Pa., 1994.

Laba, Roman. *The Roots of Solidarity.* Princeton, N.J., 1991.

Lipski, Jan Józef. *KOR: A History of the Workers' Defense Committee in Poland, 1976–1981.* Translated by Olga Amsterdamska and Gene M. Moore. Berkeley, Calif., 1985.

Luxmoore, Janathan, and Jolanta Babiuch. *The Vatican and the Red Flag: The Struggle for the Soul of Eastern Europe.* London, 1999.

Ost, David. *Solidarity and the Politics of Anti-Politics: Opposition and Reform in Poland since 1968.* Philadelphia, 1990.

Paczkowski, Andrzej. *The Spring Will Be Ours: Poland and the Poles from Occupation to Freedom.* Translated by Jane Cave. University Park, Pa., 2003.

MIKOLAJ KUNICKI

SOLZHENITSYN, ALEXANDER

(b. 1918), Russian novelist and winner of the 1970 Nobel Prize for literature.

Alexander Solzhenitsyn was born in Kislovodsk, a small town in southern Russia. Brought up by his mother and other relatives in very straitened circumstances, Solzhenitsyn attended school and university in Rostov-on-Don, by the age of sixteen or seventeen abandoning the traditional beliefs of his home for the new Marxist verities. He graduated from Rostov State University in 1941 with a degree in mathematics and physics, but his plans to pursue postgraduate work in Moscow's Institute of History, Philosophy, and Literature (MIFLI) were dashed by the outbreak of the war. Called up for service in the Red Army, he rose to the rank of captain in command of a sound-ranging battery but in early 1945 was arrested for disparaging comments about Joseph Stalin, who, in Solzhenitsyn's opinion, had strayed from the true revolutionary path. The writer was sentenced to eight years of "corrective labor" to be followed by "perpetual exile" in a remote area of the USSR.

Solzhenitsyn served his sentence in work camps in the Moscow region, in prison research institutes, and finally in a "special regime" camp in Ekibastuz, Kazakhstan. At the conclusion of his eight-year-long incarceration (1953) he was directed to settle in Kok Terek, a tiny settlement in southeastern Kazakhstan, where he began teaching in the local secondary school. An abdominal swelling was here diagnosed as terminal cancer, but the writer was successfully treated in Tashkent, Uzbekistan, in 1954–1955. Meanwhile major political changes were under way in the Soviet Union. In his campaign to repudiate Stalin's legacy, Nikita Khrushchev disbanded the entire exile system in 1956, enabling Solzhenitsyn to leave Central Asia. This was followed in 1957 by the writer's "rehabilitation," with the original sentence against him formally annulled.

Alexander Solzhenitsyn photographed at his hotel in Switzerland shortly after his arrival there in 1974. ©James Andanson/Sygma/Corbis

Solzhenitsyn was now teaching school in the European part of Russia, first in a village east of Moscow, then in Ryazan, a provincial city south of the capital. But every moment free of teaching responsibilities was dedicated to writing. By 1957 he had in fact been writing in deep secrecy for more than a decade, having produced a substantial volume of poetry, drama, and prose, much of it involving a reexamination of his former beliefs in view of the radical insight he had gained into the essence of Soviet ideology by virtue of his prison experience. But it was not until 1961, at the height of Khrushchev's anti-Stalinist campaign, that Solzhenitsyn risked submitting his short novel *One Day in the Life of Ivan Denisovich* (*Odin den Ivana Denisovicha*) for Soviet publication. It appeared in 1962 in *Novy Mir*, the leading Soviet literary magazine of the day, thanks to the personal intervention of Khrushchev, who deemed the depiction of a Stalin-era forced-labor camp—heretofore an absolutely taboo subject—useful for his anti-Stalinist purposes. To be sure,

Ivan Denisovich is much more than a political statement and its impact derives mainly from the astonishingly understated and morally lucid viewpoint expressed by the main protagonist (who provides the dominant narrative voice) despite the obvious fact that he is immersed in an irredeemably unnatural and corrupt social environment. The novel became an instant sensation both inside and outside the Soviet Union, and the writer received hundreds of letters from former Soviet prison-camp inmates wishing to share their specific experiences with the writer. This led to meetings and testimonies later used by Solzhenitsyn in composing *The Gulag Archipelago* (*Arkhipelag GULag*).

Solzhenitsyn was not long in the good graces of the regime, and was able to publish only a small number of other short works before Soviet journals closed their doors to him. Things became more ominous when Khrushchev was toppled in a coup in 1964, with the new regime headed by Leonid Brezhnev taking an actively hostile attitude toward the writer. Uncowed, Solzhenitsyn turned to samizdat, a method of self-publication whereby opposition-minded individuals retyped and distributed officially prohibited texts in chain-letter fashion. Disseminated in this manner, the writer's combative statements, such as his eloquent appeal against censorship (1967), became widely known both in the Soviet Union and abroad, making him an iconic figure in the dissident movement (even though Solzhenitsyn never identified himself in that way).

The 1968 publication in the West of Solzhenitsyn's novels *The First Circle (V kruge pervom)* and *Cancer Ward (Rakovy korpus)* was met with high critical acclaim. *The First Circle* is based on Solzhenitsyn's stint in a prison research institute in the late 1940s and traces the intellectual evolution of the main protagonist as he attempts to define his philosophical identity in contrast to, and in philosophical conflict with, other inmates. *Cancer Ward* has a similarly autobiographical dimension in that it reflects Solzhenitsyn's radiation treatment in Tashkent and touches upon ultimate metaphysical questions of life, disease, and death. The reaction of the Soviet authorities to Solzhenitsyn's unsanctioned publications was belligerently hostile, and when Solzhenitsyn was awarded the Nobel Prize for Literature in 1970 the harassment escalated to a KGB-directed assassination attempt by means of a poisoned needle. The plot failed, miraculously, but when the first volume of *The Gulag Archipelago*, Solzhenitsyn's searing account of the Soviet punitive system, appeared in Paris at the end of 1973, the regime decided to act openly. On 12 February 1974 Solzhenitsyn was arrested, charged with treason, and expelled to the West, where his family was soon allowed to join him.

The term *gulag* in the title is the Soviet acronym for Main Administration of Corrective-Labor Camps (*Glavnoe upravlenie ispravitelno-trudovykh lagerei*), but it is used by Solzhenitsyn as a generic—and phonetically memorable—designation of the entire system of camps and prisons. (The metaphor of an archipelago is added to suggest the scattered and isolated location of the camps within the Soviet Union.) Based on the testimony of more than two hundred former prisoners, not least Solzhenitsyn himself, *The Gulag Archipelago* is a massive, and massively powerful, indictment of the ideological system that generated and encouraged this vast inhuman enterprise. The book is also a disarmingly honest account of the author's struggle with his weaknesses and philosophical quandaries. The political impact of *Gulag* is difficult to overestimate, and for many left-leaning Western intellectuals it proved to be the decisive text in their view of the Soviet Union.

After his expulsion, Solzhenitsyn lived for a time in Zurich, Switzerland, moving to Cavendish, Vermont, in 1976. At the beginning of his Western sojourn the writer engaged in numerous statements and public appearances, most memorably at the Harvard Commencement in 1978, but he soon chose to concentrate on what he considered the major task of his life—the series of historical narratives ("knots") tracing Russia's catastrophic slide toward the Bolshevik Revolution. Between 1983 and 1991 he completed four "knots" (entitled *August 1914, November 1916, March 1917,* and *April 1917* respectively) comprising ten volumes and more than six thousand pages, with the entire series named *The Red Wheel (Krasnoe koleso)*.

With the collapse of the Soviet Union in 1991 and the cancellation of the treason charges against him, Solzhenitsyn prepared to return to Russia, making his move in 1994. He settled in a Moscow suburb and resisted efforts to draw him into the political process, preferring to make public statements of his own choosing. The outflow of works continued unabated after his return, among them serialized reminiscences of his years in the West (1998–2003), a two-volume study of Russian-Jewish relations (2001–2002), several short stories with an unusual "binary" structure, and a large number of essays on Russian and Soviet writers.

The reception of Solzhenitsyn's works and statements has been a study in extremes. Praised at first in both East and West, Solzhenitsyn soon came to be vituperated in the Soviet Union for his criticisms while being extolled in the West as a courageous truth-teller. But the prevailing Western sympathy changed sharply at the realization that Solzhenitsyn was no admirer of modern secular liberalism. Endless attacks on his moderate traditionalism followed, producing a major decline in his Western reputation, particularly in the United States. Meanwhile Solzhenitsyn's star rose in Russia as the Soviet regime crumbled, and his long-banned works filled Russian journals. But the boom was short lived here as well, as the writer refused to share the fashionable enthusiasm for the chaotic reforms that characterized the Yeltsin years.

See also **Dissidence; Gulag; Russia; Samizdat; Soviet Union.**

BIBLIOGRAPHY

Primary Sources

Solzhenitsyn, Alexander. *The First Circle.* Translated by Thomas P. Whitney. New York, 1968. Translation of *V kruge pervom,* 1968.

———. *Cancer Ward.* Translated by Nicholas Bethell and David Burg. New York and London, 1968. Translation of *Rakovy korpus,* 1968.

———. *The Gulag Archipelago, 1918–1956.* 3 vols. Translated by Thomas P. Whitney (vols. 1 and 2) and H. T. Willetts (vol. 3). New York and London, 1974–1978. Translation of *Arkhipelag GULag,* 1973–1975.

———. *Sobranie sochinenii.* 20 vols. Paris and Vermont, 1978–1991. Collected works.

———. *The Oak and the Calf.* Translated by H. T. Willetts. New York and London, 1980. Translation of *Bodalsia telenok s dubom,* 1975.

———. *August 1914.* Translated by H. T. Willetts. New York and London, 1989. Translation of *Avgust chetyrnadtsatogo,* 1983. Not to be confused with the incomplete 1971 edition.

———. *One Day in the Life of Ivan Denisovich.* Translated by H. T. Willetts. New York, 1991. The most reliable translation of *Odin den Ivana Denisovicha,* 1962.

———. *Invisible Allies.* Translated by Alexis Klimoff and Michael Nicholson. Washington, D.C., 1995. Translation of *Nevidimki,* 1991.

———. *November 1916.* Translated by H. T. Willetts. New York and London, 1999. Translation of *Oktiabr shestnadtsatogo,* 1984.

Secondary Sources

Dunlop, John B., Richard S. Haugh, and Alexis Klimoff, eds. *Aleksandr Solzhenitsyn: Critical Essays and Documentary Materials.* 2nd ed. New York, 1975. Contains more than thirty essays.

Dunlop, John B., Richard S. Haugh, and Michael Nicholson, eds. *Solzhenitsyn in Exile: Critical Essays and Documentary Materials.* Stanford, Calif., 1985. Includes surveys of the reception of Solzhenitsyn in Europe.

Ericson, Edward E., Jr. *Solzhenitsyn and the Modern World.* Washington, D.C., 1993. A detailed reception study, focused mainly on English-language articles and reviews.

Nivat, Georges. *Soljénitsyne.* Paris, 1980. This French translation is the best introduction to Solzhenitsyn's life and works in any language.

Pearce, Joseph. *Solzhenitsyn: A Soul in Exile.* Grand Rapids, Mich., 2001. Includes information bearing on Solzhenitsyn's life after his 1994 return to Russia.

Scammell, Michael. *Solzhenitsyn: A Biography.* New York, 1984. A massive study.

Scammell, Michael, ed. *The Solzhenitsyn Files: Secret Soviet Documents Reveal One Man's Fight against the Monolith.* Translated under supervision of Catherine A. Fitzpatrick. Chicago, 1995. Reports received and resolutions made by the Soviet leadership in connection with Solzhenitsyn between 1965 and 1980.

ALEXIS KLIMOFF

SOVIET-GERMAN NONAGGRESSION PACT. *See* Molotov-Von Ribbentrop Pact.

SOVIET UNION.

The single most important fact in Russia's social history was serfdom, an institution that developed later than it did in western Europe, but existed until 1861. At the time of the Revolution of 1917, there were still people alive who had been born serfs, and a large majority had parents who had not been full-fledged citizens of their country. Serfdom was both the consequence of the poverty of the land and also the cause of lack of economic development. The land, not blessed by good climate and soil, had hardly produced enough for subsistence. The vast majority of the Russian people in early modern times lived in poorer material circumstances than people in the rest of Europe.

While in Europe competing social forces such as the aristocracy, royal power, and independent cities fought each other to reach a standstill and therefore concluded compromises, in Russia autocracy succeeded in defeating the nobility time and again, and cities, after the earliest stage of history, never became important. While in Europe the struggle between the papacy and the empire ended in compromise, Russia from Byzantium inherited a theory according to which the church was glad to serve the state. Prerevolutionary Russia was authoritarian, although it had just introduced some political reforms as a consequence of a revolution in 1905. The Russian parliament, the Duma, was elected on the basis of restricted, estate-based suffrage and therefore did not genuinely represent the political will of the nation. The government, which was not responsible to the legislature, itself in its struggle against the powerful revolutionary movement, did not always observe its own laws. Only in retrospect, in comparison with Stalinist practice, could tsarist legal order be considered civilized.

When the serfs were liberated, the reform plan was not drawn up in such a way as to bring about maximum economic development, but to protect the social order, including the economic interests of the landowning class. Nevertheless, since the beginning of the 1890s Russia experienced impressive economic growth. Indeed, arguably what led to social tensions was not the antiquated social and political order, but the changes that were the consequence of industrialization, such as the growth of the proletariat and urbanization in circumstances that produced great misery. Prerevolutionary society was deeply split between the privileged, who were able to participate in a European culture and civilization, and the rest of society.

WAR AND REVOLUTION

After the events of 1905 the regime stabilized itself and the revolutionary movement was in retreat. However, after 1912 the number of strikes once again started to increase, and arguably at the time of the outbreak of World War I Russia was once again facing a revolutionary situation that was only retarded temporarily by the war. It has been a passionately debated issue among historians whether the country was heading toward a revolution before 1914, and the momentary patriotic enthusiasm simply delayed the outbreak, or, on the contrary, the tsarist regime was capable of reforming itself and it was the accident of the war that led to its demise. It is, however, self-evident that the tsarist regime, based on antiquated principles, proved incapable of mobilizing society for a modern war. The soldiers were increasingly tired of fighting, the logistical system broke down, and the cities could not be sufficiently supplied. On 8 March 1917, International Women's Day, when demonstrators expressed their anger, soldiers, unlike in the Revolution of 1905, proved unwilling to disperse the crowds, and the three-hundred-year-old Romanov monarchy collapsed with astonishing ease.

Two centers of power emerged. One was a provisional government that was self-appointed and based on the Duma. Strictly speaking, it lacked legitimacy because it came into being after Nicholas II (r. 1894–1917), the tsar, had prorogued the parliament. The new government represented liberal Russia. The other center of power was the soviets (*soviet,* meaning council) spontaneously created by workers and soldiers to take care of the organizational needs of the moment. The power of the Petrograd Soviet was considerable because it could call on the workers of the capital and of the soldiers stationed there to demonstrate. For some months moderate socialists dominated the soviets. This dual system of power, in which one center had the responsibility for governing and the other had a following among the masses of citizens but no responsibility, was inherently unstable. Indeed in the course of 1917 the country lurched from one crisis to another of increasing severity.

The government ultimately failed because on the basis of principles in which the ministers believed it was impossible to govern the country at that historical moment. The first unresolved issue was the war. The moderate socialists in the soviets were still willing to support a defensive war, although soldiers were increasingly tired of the struggle. When in May, a letter became public in which the foreign minister Pavel Milyukov, a prominent leader of the liberal Constitutional Democratic Party, spoke of the continuation of the war to a victorious end and claimed significant territorial gains for Russia, a public demonstration forced his removal, and the entire government moved to the left. The government did not wish to end the war, but in retrospect it is clear that even if it did, it could not have received terms from the Germans acceptable to the majority of Russians.

The second irresolvable issue was land reform. The peasants after serf liberation did not receive all the lands that they believed should have been theirs and clamored for more. The ministers of the provisional government did not altogether oppose land reform, but on the basis of their liberal principles

Volunteers sign up for the people's militia at the Taurida palace, Petrograd, Russia, March 1917. The people's militia replaced the police under the provisional government established in Petrograd following the abdication of Tsar Nicholas II. ©MARY EVANS PICTURE LIBRARY/THE IMAGE WORKS

took it for granted that the landlords had to be compensated, and the country lacked the resources. Even more importantly, they considered that carrying out a land reform during wartime would contribute to the disintegration of the army, since the peasant soldiers would want to return to their villages in order to claim their share. The government decided to postpone this difficult and contentious issue until a constituent assembly could be convened. The problem was that the authority of the government did not extend to the thousands of villages. The peasants took matters into their own hands; they chased away landlords and occupied land. The government did not have the power to prevent this lawlessness on the one hand and on the other was unable satisfy the desire of the peasants. By the summer of 1917 the country was descending into anarchy.

The third problem the government faced was the increased national consciousness of the minorities. Imperial Russia was a multinational empire, but as long as it was powerful the nationalism of the minorities could be controlled and suppressed. However, now that the center was obviously weak, not only historical nations such as Poles and Finns, but also Ukrainians claimed if not independence, at least autonomy. The government had neither the will to satisfy these demands nor the ability to repress.

In July the government was able to fend off a rising from disgruntled soldiers who did not want to go to battle. At this point Alexander Kerensky, a moderate socialist, became prime minister. In August it was the turn of the Right to attempt to change the status quo. General Lavr Kornilov, recently named commander of the army, organized a coup. The regime prevailed once again; however, the cost of these "victories" was that the government's base of support evaporated. In September the Bolsheviks, uncompromising Marxist revolutionaries—led by Vladimir Lenin (Vladimir Ilyich Ulyanov; 1870–1924)—who at the time of the March revolution made up only a tiny minority within the soviets, won majorities both in Petrograd and in Moscow. Unlike the moderate socialists, who were willing to compromise, the Bolsheviks were ready to take power. At this time they could count on the support of the majority of the workers in the two major cities and also on the support of the soldiers stationed in the rear. Workers and soldiers supported the Bolsheviks because they alone were not compromised by collaboration with the increasingly hated provisional government. Lenin decided to take power before a scheduled congress of soviets because he wanted the congress to legitimize his action. The Bolsheviks did not so much overthrow the provisional government as that government disintegrated and the revolutionaries were there to take advantage.

Bolshevik action on 7 November initiated a civil war that lasted for three years. At the outset both sides were weak, but as time went on each succeeded in organizing their forces. The Bolsheviks were able and willing to satisfy the desire of the majority—ending the international war by accepting highly unfavorable terms from the Germans, and giving land to the peasants, that is, legitimizing land grabs. Consequently the majority of the people, while not attracted to Marxist ideas and programs, nevertheless opposed the Bolsheviks less vigorously than they opposed their opponents, the Whites, whom they associated with the old regime. Tsarist officers led the forces of the counterrevolutionaries, and their numerically smaller armies were better led. The Whites also enjoyed the support of the Orthodox Church.

The end of the war in Europe had far-reaching consequences for the course of the civil war in Russia. As long as the Allies and the Central Powers were fighting one another, they looked at their involvement in Russia as far less important. Although the Allied governments regarded the Bolsheviks and everything they stood for with fear and loathing, had the Bolsheviks continued the war against the Germany, they could have received Allied support. The Allies first assisted the Whites with the illusory hope that the anti-German front might be reconstructed. The British and the Americans, who in early 1918 sent small detachments to the far north in Murmansk and Archangel and to the far east in Vladivostok, justified their intervention in Russian affairs in terms of their need to fight the Germans. Once World War I ended, any rationale for the intervention fell away, while the opportunities for practical aid to the anti-Bolsheviks vastly improved. Immediately after the defeat of the Germans, French troops landed in Odessa, and shortly after in the Crimea. The British sent small detachments to the Caucasus and to Central Asia, and soon began the delivery of valuable military hardware to Kolchak and to Anton Denikin, the commander of the volunteer White Army.

By 1920 it was fairly certain that the Reds would ultimately win. Poland, which became an independent country at the end of the war, had great territorial ambitions at Russia's expense. The Polish leader, Józef Piłsudski, believing he could get a better deal from the Bolsheviks than from the victorious Whites, waited until the defeat of the main White forces and then started his campaign. The Russo-Polish War, which inspired nationalist passions on both sides, saw changing military fortunes; at one point the victorious Red Army threatened the Polish capital. The war ultimately ended in the compromise peace of Riga in March 1921. Following the decisive phase of the Polish campaign, the Red Army defeated the commander of the volunteer White Army, Peter Wrangel, and forced him and the remnants of his army into exile. By the end of 1920 the Bolsheviks had defeated all their enemies with the exception of a few scattered peasant bands.

Ultimately, after changing fortunes, the Bolsheviks emerged victorious. However, the cost was horrendous. During the world war and in the bitter civil conflict millions died; the destruction was extraordinary, and the reconstruction therefore had to be slow and painful. Famine ravaged the land. The civil war changed the Bolsheviks from underground revolutionaries to administrators and rulers. They had never been liberals; they believed that their knowledge of Marxism enabled them to interpret past, present, and future. They took it for granted that they were acting in the interest the of the people even if the "people" did not understand their own interests. The repression of ideas and opponents started at the very moment of the creation of the regime. The Bolsheviks did not recoil

Workers drive tractors at Gigant, a Soviet state farm near the town of Rostov-na-Donu, c. 1920. ©UNDERWOOD & UNDERWOOD/CORBIS

from introducing terror, though it must be said that they were neither better nor worse in this respect than their enemies, the Whites.

NEW ECONOMIC POLICY (NEP)

At the end of the civil war the country was exhausted. The Bolsheviks in order to supply their armies and feed the cities had resorted to requisitioning from the peasants. They had suspended all free economic activities, most importantly among them free trade in grain. In 1921 at the Tenth Party Congress Lenin introduced a system that came to be called the New Economic Policy (NEP). From the Bolshevik point of view, this was a step backward, away from the dream of classless society, and a concession given to the "class enemy," but circumstances forced the revolutionaries to give concessions. NEP was indeed a hybrid of Marxist ideology and capitalism. In practice it meant that peasants regained their ability to sell their products in the market, and small-scale

industry was allowed to operate. Socially it meant that the regime decided to tolerate economic conditions that would allow some peasants at least to become reasonably prosperous and to coexist with the "Nepman," an obnoxious (from the regime's point of view) petty capitalist. Culturally it meant that while the regime preserved its monopoly of interpreting politics, it allowed a considerable degree of heterogeneity and contacts of intellectuals and artists with the outside world. Consequently, the notorious turning point in Soviet intellectual history should be dated not in 1917, but in 1930. NEP was indeed successful to the extent of allowing recovery after dreadful devastation.

Against the background of mixed economy and flourishing intellectual life took place the struggle for succession to Lenin's mantle. The struggle was bound to be contentious. Lenin, after all, was the founder of the movement, his charisma was such that his fellow leaders naturally deferred to him and he could be magnanimous enough to take them back time and again when they "erred." There could be no natural successor. Ultimately it was Joseph Stalin (1878–1953) who emerged victorious. This was because while he may not have been the equal of a Leon Trotsky (1879–1940), a great organizer and eloquent speaker, or a Nikolai Bukharin (1888–1938) as a theorist, he was better as a politician. He prevailed over better-known politicians not only because as general secretary since 1922 he had been able to place his followers in crucial positions, but also because he managed to convey the impression to a wide circle of activists, ironically, that he was a safer choice, one who would pursue an internationally less adventurous policy than Trotsky.

The NEP system was internally self-contradictory and from the outset doomed to failure. The regime needed the services of private entrepreneurs and kulaks (well-to-do peasants) but on the other hand feared these people as possible opposition and therefore hampered their activities. At the end of the 1920s the country faced a crisis. The government set the price of grain too low in order to save money for its ambitious industrialization project. The predictable consequence was that the peasants switched to other products, which promised better return, and suddenly the government could not feed the cities. The Stalinist solution was to cut the Gordian knot by returning to the system of forced collection of grain used at the time of the civil war. This action violated the fundamental principle of NEP, and there was no return. If the peasants could not be certain that they would be fairly compensated for their labor, they had no incentive to produce. Stalin started a war against the peasantry by forcing them to join collective farms. The country once again experienced a revolution. It was from this point on in 1929 that we can properly talk of the age of Stalin.

THE AGE OF STALIN

Collectivization was the most extraordinary, most dangerous act of the regime and would also have the most far-reaching consequences. While in the 1920s the regime had maintained only a weak hold on the countryside, by forcing the peasants into collective farms against their will, the regime created an institution that enabled it to control every aspect of peasant life. Most immediately, it enabled the regime to take hold of the products of the collective farms cheaply, thereby enabling the government to proceed with its ambitious industrialization plans for which it had lacked capital. The great Soviet industrialization that took place in the course of the First and Second Five-Year Plans and that transformed society was primarily financed by the extraordinarily low standard of living of the peasantry that in the years 1932–1933 led to mass famine with millions of victims. Industrialization was unbalanced; scarce resources were devoted disproportionately to heavy industry, while the production of consumer goods suffered. Waste in human lives and in material was extraordinary, and the unquestionably great achievements were accomplished at a very high price in terms of human suffering. On the other hand, it is hard to contradict the proposition that it was this industrialization that allowed the Soviet economy to produce weapons, which were later needed to defeat the German army of World War II.

During the First Five-Year Plan the population of Soviet cities almost doubled. What this meant in terms of living conditions can be easily imagined. The Soviet state was determined to invest in heavy industry and was not about to be diverted by spending scarce resources on social overhead, meaning construction of apartment buildings and provision of various city amenities such as transportation and water. Living conditions became appalling: usually several families had to share a kitchen, and often a family could not even have a single room to itself. It would take a long time for the Soviet Union to make up for this dreadful neglect. The vast social transformation of the 1930s created a Soviet urban working class.

The terror of the 1930s defies rational explanation. It is possible to point out that the soil had been well prepared: the extraordinary human losses in World War I, followed by a murderous civil war, followed by a man-made famine, gave a sense to the rulers that life was cheap. Hundreds of thousands of people were sentenced to death, without exception on trumped up charges, and millions died in concentration camps. Obviously, Stalin and his comrades could not possibly choose all the victims; nevertheless they created an atmosphere in which denunciations for revenge and for personal benefit became the rule of the day. Although all segments of the population suffered, there were particular groups that were especially victimized. Intellectuals, foreign Communists, people who had had contact with foreigners, and former Communists were most likely to be hard hit.

This period of terror and privation was also a time of genuine achievements. The regime finally succeeded in enlarging the educational system, above all on the primary level, and by the end of the decade, for the first time in Russian history, the country was able to make good on its promise to provide at least some schooling for all children. Thousands of new schools opened in the countryside, and tens of thousands of teachers, willingly or unwillingly, left the cities to teach village children. The circumstances in which the teachers had to work were extremely primitive and difficult, and many had to be compelled to give up their relatively comfortable lives in the cities. Only a dictatorial regime could have forced people to undertake such jobs and accept such unattractive transfers. The great expansion of the educational system was a major step in transforming backward Russia into an industrial Soviet Union. To be sure, village schools remained much inferior to what was available in the cities; nevertheless, it was a remarkable achievement of Stalinist industrialization that every child was able to spend at least some years in school. It was the general availability of primary schools that enabled the regime finally to take decisive steps toward the elimination of illiteracy.

The bodies of twelve people killed by the Soviet secret police, the Cheka, lie in a street in Petrograd, November 1921. ©BETTMANN/CORBIS

By the end of the decade, four out of five Soviet citizens under the age of fifty could read and write.

In between the civil war and the mid-1930s the Soviet Union was not genuinely threatened by a foreign power. Even Adolf Hitler's rise to power in January 1933 did not particularly concern the Soviet leadership. However, German rearmament and Hitler's boundlessly aggressive policies, aside from his explicit anticommunism and low regard for Slavs, made it clear to Stalin and his advisors that they were facing a new and dangerous international environment. The first Soviet response to the new threat was to reorient its foreign policy and attempt to find allies among democratic countries. Such a policy line also necessitated directing the communist parties to support the policy of "popular fronts," meaning willingness to cooperate with socialist and liberal parties. The pusillanimity of the governments of England and France to Nazi aggression, concerning the remilitarization of the Rhineland, the open German and Italian intervention in the Spanish civil war (1936–1939), and

finally the abandonment of Czechoslovakia, convinced the Soviet government that the West was not a reliable ally in deterring the Nazis. When the German army was ready to move against Poland in August 1939, the Nazis, to avoid a two-front war, concluded a nonaggression pact with Stalin, which enabled the Soviet dictator to reclaim lands that Russia had lost at the end of the First World War: the eastern half of the interwar Polish state, the Baltic republics, and Bessarabia. Stalin's thinking in concluding this pact, an act that demoralized the world communist movement, was that the Western Allies and Germany would fight each other to a standstill and his country would greatly benefit. Of course, we know it did not turn out that way. In the summer of 1940 France collapsed, on 22 June 1941 the Germans invaded the Soviet Union, and for three dreadful years the Red Army for all intents and purposes had to face the brunt of the German attacking forces alone.

Stalin had every reason to fear that the long-suffering peoples of the Soviet Union would not show loyalty to a regime that had mistreated so many of them so badly. Indeed, in the newly occupied territories the Nazis were often received as liberators, however, ultimately, the Russian people persevered. The government, out of necessity, changed its policy line: instead of speaking of international solidarity of the working classes, it called on the Russian people to demonstrate their love of the motherland.

Perhaps the most significant battle of the war took place in December 1941 at the gates of Moscow. The Soviet Union, taking advantage of its recently signed nonaggression pact with Japan, was able to bring up fresh troops and prevent the Germans from occupying the capital. Once the myth of German invincibility was broken, time was on the side of the Red Army. The Soviet Union was able to mobilize its entire industry for the needs of the war to a far greater extent than any other belligerent country. Its industry had always been centralized, essentially on a wartime footing. The Soviet Union, under extraordinarily difficult circumstances, was able to move its industry from the war zone to the Ural Mountains or into Siberia, where the factories continued to produce tanks, airplanes, and guns. The turning point was, of course, the enormous battle of Stalingrad, where the extent of German defeat was such as to make it clear to the rest of the world that Germany could not win this war. Although the Red Army still suffered occasional reverses and the death of millions of its soldiers, ultimate victory was only a matter of time.

The Soviet Union emerged from the war with its prestige greatly heightened, a prestige it had not enjoyed since Russia's victory over Napoleon in 1812. On the other hand, it was greatly weakened: the human and material losses were horrendous; it is estimated that over twenty-six million citizens of the Soviet Union died. Among the dead there were disproportionate numbers of Jews, Ukrainians, Byelorussians, and citizens of the Baltic states. In 1946–1947 the Soviet people suffered the ravages of yet another famine. Reconstruction was bound to be slow and painful. The regime returned to the economic policies that it had followed since collectivization: it invested scarce resources in the rebuilding of heavy industry, neglecting agriculture and light industry.

The government in order to win the war had had to allow a degree of loosening of social discipline. During the war, peoples of the Soviet Union believed that by showing their loyalty the regime would reciprocate and allow a freer life. This was not to be. The Stalinists could not conceive a regime in which they did not have total control. They feared that contact with the West, which had been inevitable during the war, would have subversive consequences. In 1946 the regime once again tightened the screws: harsh discipline was imposed on the collective farms, the degree of intellectual heterogeneity that had been allowed during the struggle against the Nazis was suspended, and a deadly uniformity was imposed on the cultural life of the nation that was even worse than what had existed before 1939. Concentration camps once again came to be filled. Liberated prisoners of war were often not allowed to settle in their previous domicile. Culture was poisoned by an exaggerated form of Russian nationalism, xenophobia, and for the first time in Soviet history, an almost explicit anti-Semitism. Stalin's last years (1945–1953) were the darkest, intellectually most barren years of Soviet history.

The Red Army liberated most of Eastern Europe from the Nazis and in between 1945 and 1947 the Soviet Union established satellite regimes in this region. As the wartime alliance between the Soviet Union and the Western Allies came to an end it was unlikely that friendly relations could continue. From the Soviet point of view the West with its immeasurably higher standard of living represented a subversive force. The Soviet Union, after the great destruction of the war could not afford another, but on the other hand, in the perception of the leadership, neither could it afford good relations. Stalin's foreign policy was cautious in the sense that he made sure that Soviet expansion would not involve the country in an armed conflict. On the other hand, in countries where the Red Army was already present, Soviet-type regimes were imposed. The Cold War was the result.

DEALING WITH THE STALINIST LEGACY
Stalin died on 5 March 1953. On the one hand, it seemed impossible that anyone could take his place, but on the other many people could not imagine the system functioning without a dictator.

A tank leads Soviet troops into Nazi gunfire along the northern sector of the Russian front, winter 1941–1942.
©BETTMANN/CORBIS

Stalin's closest comrades, Georgy Malenkov, Vyacheslav Molotov, Lavrenty Beria, and Nikita Khrushchev agreed on "collective leadership." Those who had served Stalin unquestioningly now immediately agreed that substantial liberalization was needed. Collective leadership did not last long. Malenkov, who became premier, seemed in the strongest position to emerge on the top, but Khrushchev, who shortly after Stalin's death assumed leadership of the party, succeeded in outmaneuvering him by gaining the support of the army leadership and of those who wanted to preserve the primacy of heavy industry. In 1955 Khrushchev removed Malenkov from his position. Only at this point did he associate himself with a more liberal policy and then went even further than Malenkov had advocated.

The Twentieth Party Congress in February 1956 was a major turning point in Soviet history. The frozen intellectual life began to thaw almost immediately after Stalin's death, and some of Stalin's policies were implicitly repudiated.

Nevertheless the explicit criticisms of Stalin in Khrushchev's so-called secret speech still had an extraordinary impact. Khrushchev was in a difficult position: he wanted to separate his policies from that of the dead tyrant because he believed that society could no longer tolerate the burden placed on it by Stalin. At the same time any repudiation of Stalin had to be limited, for the institutions that he had created, the collective farms, the highly centralized economy, a centralized party organization, continued to be the defining characteristics of Soviet polity and society. Khrushchev's compromise was to argue that Stalin had lost the correct path before World War II as he became affected by a "cult of personality." He of course made no attempt to explain how a nominally Marxist society could fall victim to a personality cult. Furthermore, by calling attention to Stalin's crimes he exposed himself to the danger of people pointing out that he himself was deeply implicated in the terror. It is to Khrushchev's credit that he was willing to run the risk. Probably he believed that his fellow leaders were even guiltier than he was and therefore he was safe from being attacked by them.

The consequences of the revelations were far reaching. An attack on Stalinism, however moderate and limited, was bound to create a contradictory situation in a country such as Hungary, where the Hungarian Stalin, Mátyás Rákosi (1892–1971), remained in office yet was in no position to oppose this new turn of Soviet politics. In October 1956 the Polish government was tottering and on the brink of collapse, while Hungary in the same month experienced an anti-Soviet, anticommunist revolution. After some hesitation the Soviet leadership decided to intervene for it feared that its entire hold on Eastern Europe might unravel, and its enemies would perceive a lack of response as a sign of weakness.

The international communist movement received a major blow: communists up to that point could deny the obvious, but this strategy worked no longer. This was a serious loss. The Soviet Union had benefited in the past from the support of people in the West who saw in it an example of attempting to overcome inequality and economic irrationality that supposedly was inherent in capitalism. In the 1930s antifascists regarded the Soviet Union as the best hope of confronting Hitler. At the time of World War II millions were rightly impressed by the Soviet achievement of overcoming a fearsome adversary. The foreign friends of the Soviet Union at times could influence the policies of their countries.

Most of the people who had an unrealistic opinion of the Soviet Union in fact were unhappy with their own societies and therefore looked for an alternative. After Khrushchev's revelations of the real Stalin, Western idealists had to look elsewhere for a "better society," than the Soviet Union, such as China, Cuba, or North Vietnam.

It is understandable that Khrushchev's colleagues blamed him for the problems in the Soviet bloc. In June 1957 they made an attempt to remove him from his position. On this occasion, however, the wily Khrushchev prevailed. The following four or five years were the most optimistic period in the history of the Soviet Union. Khrushchev made serious attempts to raise the pitifully low level of standard of living of the Soviet people. He increased investment in agriculture both in order to lessen the wide gap between the cities and the countryside and also to provide better nourishment for all the people. The most significant reform he introduced was the simplest, namely paying higher prices for agricultural products. He also encouraged bringing new lands under cultivation, mostly in Central Asia. He dissolved the machine tractor stations, institutions coeval with the collective farms, which compelled the farms to share agriculture machinery. Because it did not divide responsibility for agricultural work this was a sensible move, although in the short run it caused problems, for the farms were not in the position to pay for the machinery. The government was willing to make major investments to improve the dreadful housing situation. Although the buildings were poorly constructed and maintained, nevertheless it immeasurably improved the quality of life for many, in that they could have more or less decent living space.

In Khrushchev's days the Soviet Union was an authoritarian state where dissent was not tolerated, and the authorities were capricious, one day allowing the publication of significant criticism of the system, the next day arresting an unfortunate artist for saying much less. On the other hand, unlike in the days of Stalin, people were arrested for what they wrote, said, or did, and rarely for no reason at all. It was at this point that dissent became possible. The dissenters were people who for the sake of their beliefs were willing to accept often very heavy punishment. The authoritarian as opposed to totalitarian state allowed the revival of the arts. Once again it was possible to publish worthwhile articles and books and make interesting films. Alexander Solzhenitsyn, for example, obtained permission to publish his stories including descriptions of living conditions in the camps. Honest, first rate films could be made, reminiscent of the golden age of the 1920s.

Khrushchev also introduced major changes in Soviet foreign policy. Stalin had been a cautious leader: he took control over the countries when he could without involving the Soviet Union in a major war. He established a system where a sharp line was drawn between areas in which the Soviet domination was unquestioned and the rest of the world. However much hostility existed between the two sides, the international system in fact was remarkably stable. Khrushchev by contrast wanted to ameliorate the Cold War and spoke of the

An instructor works with young female gymnasts at the Dynamo Children's Sports School, Kiev, Ukraine, 1957.
Following World War II, the Soviet Union sought to demonstrate its superiority to the West in all areas, especially the skill of its athletes. Young people who showed promise were drafted to attend state-sponsored schools; these were later criticized for their harsh treatment of students. ©JERRY COOKE/CORBIS

peaceful coexistence between the two social systems. He also aimed to reform the socialist bloc by allowing a degree of autonomy to the various countries. But at the same time he hoped to extend Soviet influence in regions of the world where before the Soviet Union had shown no interest. Ironically, Khrushchev's desire to lessen tensions ended by creating a more dangerous world. He obviously did not foresee the decisiveness of the American response to his placing nuclear missiles in Cuba, and at that point the world was closer to a nuclear war than ever before or since. His greatest foreign policy disaster, however, was not the humiliation that he had to suffer by bowing to American threats and withdrawing the missiles, but allowing the deterioration of relations with the other communist giant, China.

Khrushchev's successes and failures came from the same source. He believed in the superiority of the communist system and when he saw failures he attempted to remedy them by experimenting. Some of his experiments were successful, but most of them were not well thought out and actually created confusion. Also, because of his belief in communism he was dismayed to see that social equality remained an empty promise and that the privileged were able to transmit their advantages to the next generation. His reforms that aimed to curb privilege made a greater contribution to his ultimate fate than his failures in foreign policy and his inability to reform Soviet economy. On 15 October 1964 the top leaders successfully conspired against him and he was removed from office.

DECLINE

Once against the Soviet leaders called for collective leadership and once again it lasted only for a short time. This time it was Leonid Brezhnev (1906–

1982) who emerged at the top. For some time the regime was able to further increase the standard of living of the people and at the same time make great investment in military hardware. The Soviet Union was, or at least seemed to be, the equal of the United States in military power. Soviet power and therefore influence now for the first time extended to every part of the globe. Gradually, however, decline set in. Methods that had enabled the economy to function reasonably well, at a different stage of development in a different international environment, failed to produce results. The autarky (an economy that does not trade with other countries) that had made sense in the 1930s and 1940s was no longer possible; the economic system, which was able to produce a great deal of steel—however poor in quality—and cement, was not very efficient in creating software for computers. It had been possible in earlier decades to cut off the Soviet Union from the rest of the world, but in the age of modern communications that no longer worked.

The regime deteriorated into senescence. As time passed the leadership became increasingly conservative: turnover in important positions slowed down, and the incompetent were not removed. Brezhnev and his comrades saw in the process of liberalization above all a danger that change might lead to disintegration. During roughly the last five years of Brezhnev's life there were constant rumors of his failing health. His comrades in the Politburo, almost all of them as old as he, were also tired, unimaginative people. The Soviet leadership became the butt of jokes at home and abroad.

Publicists of the Brezhnev era described the political and social system of their country as "real, existing socialism." This phrase well described the difference between Khrushchev's and Brezhnev's Soviet Union. The new leaders felt uncomfortable with a utopian ideology, unconsciously realizing that the promise of a just and affluent society in the distant future had outlived its usefulness: people were tired of waiting. The publicists simply declared that "socialism" had arrived. The implication was that constant experimentation, mass mobilization, and exhortation for new and ambitious campaigns would largely be abandoned. The era was one of complacency and conservatism.

Brezhnev died in 1982 and was followed by two short-term first secretaries, Yuri Andropov (1914–1984) and Konstantin Chernenko (1911–1985). Andropov was intelligent, but was ill during most of his tenure, and Chernenko was a man of limited vision. Consequently the period between 1982 and 1985 could be regarded as an interregnum when the problems facing the Soviet Union not only were not addressed but were allowed to worsen. At this point even in the highest circle of leadership there was an understanding that some sort of change was inevitable, and that made it possible for the relatively youthful and obviously intelligent Mikhail Gorbachev (b. 1931) to be elected general secretary in 1985.

DISINTEGRATION

The recognition that reforms were needed of course did not mean that the new leader had a mandate to alter the fundamental institutions of the regime. Indeed, it is clear that Gorbachev himself had no such intention. He obviously believed that it was possible to eliminate the flaws within a fundamentally healthy system: workers had to work better and more efficiently, alcoholism had to be checked, corruption stopped. The first series of reforms, which came to be called "acceleration" (*uskorenie*), were simply tinkering, and it soon became obvious that these did not eliminate the problems but if anything made them worse. It was at that point and also partially as a result of the obviously mishandled Chernobyl disaster in April 1986 (the largest nuclear accident so far in history) that impelled Gorbachev to take the second and ultimately crucial step, calling for openness (*glasnost*) in discussing the problems facing the country. Indeed, in order to remedy what ailed the country, the problems had to be honestly examined. Probably no one foresaw the consequences.

At least for a time, among the intelligentsia the possibility to speak, to write openly, and to organize produced euphoria. For a while it seemed that there was a national unity, in opposition to the crimes of the Stalin era, not seen since World War II. This unity, however, was only apparent. Discussions led to proposals for reorganization and changes (*perestroika*, literally "restructuring"), and as economic and political reforms were introduced it became clear that society was far from

A sculptor works on a large statue of Soviet cosmonaut Yuri Gagarin, Moscow, 1962.
Gagarin became the first human to orbit the earth in a spacecraft in 1961 and as such became a powerful symbol of Soviet prowess during the so-called space race of the 1960s. ©YEVGENY KHALDEI/CORBIS

united. No conceivable set of reforms could have both improved standards of living and at the same time remedied the profound, structural problems of the economy. Nor was it possible to introduce a degree of democracy and openness and at the same time to preserve the privileged role of the Communist Party. It turned out that there was no constituency for change that required sacrifice. By 1990 the steam from the reformist impulse ran out. The economy further deteriorated, and the country was foundering. Just as in 1917, as the center weakened, the national minorities increasingly asserted themselves not only against the dominant Russians, but also against one another. The Soviet Union was falling apart. The decisive moment came in August 1991. The opponents of the reforms—all put into office by Gorbachev himself—conspired to carry out a coup and attempt to return to the prereform era. That was not possible. They were not only incompetent, but they also lacked a constituency. Not merely did they fail to achieve their goal, but they gave a coup de grace to the Soviet Union itself.

In the post-Soviet era after the dissolution of the Soviet Union in December 1991, Gorbachev had no role to play. The man of the moment was Boris Yeltsin (b. 1931), a maverick and populist former Communist, whose achievement was the destruction of the political and economic institutions of the Soviet state.

The last decade of the twentieth century turned out to be a painful and troubled one for the people of Russia. The introduction of the market economy and privatization led to great injustices and profound social inequality, and the majority of the people found that capitalism, at least in the short run, did not benefit them, but on the contrary, made their misery greater. The demise of the Soviet state did not mean the introduction of a genuinely democratic political system, for example, in 1993 Yeltsin forcefully dissolved the Russian parliament. The newly successful and enormously rich businessmen acquired considerable political power that they used for their own benefit. Corruption came to assume extraordinary proportions.

It is impossible to say to what extent the problems of contemporary Russia are the consequence of the legacy of seventy-four years of communism or to mismanaged reforms. The two, of course, are not mutually exclusive. It must be recognized, however, that the Soviet Union was unreformable, and the country had no choice but to take a different path.

See also **Bolshevism; Chernobyl; Cold War; Collectivization; Commonwealth of Independent States; Communism; Destalinization; Dissidence; Eastern Bloc; Five-Year Plan; Gulag; Molotov-Von Ribbentrop Pact; Moscow; New Economic Policy (NEP); Perestroika; Purges; Russia; Russian Civil War; Russian Revolutions of 1917; Samizdat; Stakhanovites; Terror; Totalitarianism; Warsaw Pact.**

BIBLIOGRAPHY

Heller, Mikhail, and Aleksandr Nekrich. *Utopia in Power: The History of the Soviet Union from 1917 to the Present.* New York, 1986.

Hosking, Geoffrey. *First Socialist Society: A History of the Soviet Union from Within.* 2nd ed. Cambridge, Mass., 1993.

Kenez, Peter. *A History of the Soviet Union from the Beginning to the End.* New York, 1999.

Malia, Martin. *The Soviet Tragedy: A History of Socialism in Russia, 1917–1991.* New York, 1994.

McCauley, Martin. *The Soviet Union: 1917–1991.* 2nd ed. London, 1993.

Service, Robert. *Russia: Experiment with a People.* Cambridge, Mass., 2003.

Suny, Ronald Grigor. *The Soviet Experiment: Russia, the USSR, and the Successor States.* New York, 1998.

Thompson, John. *A Vision Unfulfilled: Russia and the Soviet Union in the Twentieth Century.* Lexington, Mass., 1996.

PETER KENEZ

SPACE PROGRAMS.

Imagining space travel may be said to have begun in Europe in the late sixteenth century when the great German astronomer Johannes Kepler wrote *The Dream,* a tale in which Kepler sends a witch to the moon on a broomstick that follows mathematically accurate trajectories. Within the next three hundred years other European writers contributed to the space-travel bookshelf, including France's Jules Verne, England's H. G. Wells, and Russia's Konstantin Tsiolkovsky. Tsiolkovsky (1857–1935), a mathematician as well as a science-fiction writer, published a paper in 1903, "Exploration of Space with a Rocket Device," that accurately calculated the escape velocity of his proposed spacecraft. By the second decade of the twentieth century Tsiolkovsky had been honored by the new Soviet government and installed as a member of the Academy of Sciences. He inspired young Russians to design rockets and fulfill his prophecy when he wrote, "The Earth is the cradle of humanity, but mankind cannot stay in the cradle forever." By the early twenty-first century Europeans had orbited Earth in space stations and shuttles, sent robotic explorers to Mars and the moons of Saturn, and established an agency in which they could work together.

INTO ORBIT, 1920–1959

This cooperation was a long time coming. From the 1920s through the 1950s, each European nation that looked to space worked independently. It was only after the launch of *Sputnik 1* in 1957 and the ensuing space race between the United States and the Soviet Union that the rest of Europe realized that they could not compete with the extraordinary budgets of the superpowers. At first France, Britain, and Germany made separate arrangements with both the Soviets and the Americans, but none proved altogether satisfactory. In the early 1970s, those governments that were interested reached an agreement that allowed them to maintain national space programs, work with the United States and Russia, and work together as members of the European Space Agency (ESA) when joint interests warranted it. Alone and together west Europeans worked with the American space agency, NASA; with their neighbor to the east, the Soviet Union; and launched their own exploratory flights.

As early as 1924 young Germans and Soviets had formed rocket clubs with an eye to exploring space. A decade later, as both nations prepared for war, their governments drafted these rocket-builders into weapons research. The purges that swept the Soviet Union in the late 1930s destroyed many scientists. But scientist and engineer Sergei Korolev survived the gulag and forced labor during World War II without losing his patriotism or devotion to space exploration. Meanwhile the Nazis enlisted their rocket scientists in the war effort that resulted in the V-2 rocket-propelled bombs that devastated British cities and in the process ushered in the space age.

As Allied troops closed in on Germany in 1945, Wernher von Braun, head of the rocket program, surrendered with a hundred of his engineers to Americans who flew them almost immediately overseas. When Soviet troops reached Peenemünde, a fishing village on the island of Usedom in the Baltic Sea where the rockets had been built, most of the German rocket team was gone. They found one top guidance expert and several hundred rocket engineers as well as leftover hardware and shipped them all east. The British also retained twenty-three German engineers with whose help, in October 1945, they fired three left-over V-2s for an audience of American experts and one Soviet engineer. But Korolev, out of prison and recently rehabilitated, was prevented from watching the demonstration. Nonetheless, he was able to use the purloined German personnel and rocket detritus to kick-start the Soviet space effort.

The political map changed in the next five years, with Western Europe allied with the United States and facing a bloc of communist states dominated and occupied by the Soviet Union. In the Cold War that had quietly begun, each side stockpiled nuclear weapons and explored ways of developing intercontinental ballistic missiles (ICBMs) to deliver them. The leading missile designers were alumni of rocket clubs: von Braun had joined the Americans in Huntsville, Alabama, and Korolev headed a design bureau in Moscow. Both men successfully lobbied their governments for the wherewithal to launch satellites that would have military, scientific, and propaganda value while personally holding to visions of space travel as an adventure in its own right.

The Cold War did not stop scientific exchanges. The International Council of Scientific Unions declared the first International Geophysical Year (IGY), eighteen months between July 1957 and December 1958, devoted to peaceful cooperation and competition even during this difficult period. Scientists on both sides of the Iron Curtain pursued rocketry and it was in 1957 that both the Soviets and Americans launched their first vehicles into orbit. Although there had been "chatter" for a long time about sending a scientific instrument into orbit, the Soviet launch of *Sputnik 1*, the first artificial satellite, on 4 October 1957, caught the world by surprise.

THE SOVIETS ENTER SPACE

The Soviet space program, in contrast with the West's, operated in secret under the leadership of Korolev with the blessings of Soviet premier Nikita Khrushchev. After *Sputnik 1*, Korolev launched *Sputnik 2* carrying a live dog. The shock of *Sputnik* spurred the United States to create NASA, the National Aeronautics and Space Administration, in 1958. Within a year NASA selected the first American astronauts, which the Soviets matched in 1960 with their first cosmonauts. Then in April 1961, the Soviets startled the world again with the launch of the first human being into orbit. What was already a race heated up in May when President John F. Kennedy raised the ante by proclaiming that the United States would send a man to the Moon before the decade was out. The following year John Glenn became the first astronaut in orbit and soon astronauts and cosmonauts followed each other into space. In 1963 the Soviets broke the gender barrier by launching Valentina Tereshkova. She would be the only woman to travel into orbit until 1982. This was not Korolev's vision. He had anticipated seeing whole families traveling into space and planned to launch three other women. But his sudden death in 1966 left that dream

The Soviet Soyuz 19 space capsule, as seen from the Apollo command module during the 1975 Apollo-Soyuz test project. DIGITAL IMAGE ©1996 CORBIS; ORIGINAL IMAGE COURTESY OF NASA/CORBIS

unfulfilled and the entire Soviet program rudderless. After the loss of three cosmonauts in 1971, the Soviets quietly withdrew from the race to the Moon.

SENDING SCIENTIFIC INSTRUMENTS INTO ORBIT

The Soviets and NASA launched rockets carrying three kinds of payload into orbit: the first, like *Sputnik,* were satellites that travel in Earth orbit carrying the instruments, military, commercial and scientific, that revolutionized telecommunications, weather, Earth observations and military surveillance; the second kind, with great fanfare, sent people into space; the third, with as much attention, sent exploratory vehicles on missions to the

Moon, Venus, Mars, comets and the outer planets in the solar system.

France, Great Britain, Germany and the rest of the world watched as Soviets and Americans vied for space firsts, including the first photographs of the dark side of the Moon, and followed the first space disaster when the three American astronauts on *Apollo 1* died in a fire on the launch pad in 1967. Keenly aware that they were on the sidelines, Western European nations, alone and in concert, planned their own launch facility even as they negotiated with Soviets and Americans to rent theirs.

France was especially eager to be independent. As early as 1950 the first international astronautical conference met in Paris. After *Sputnik* in 1958, Charles de Gaulle led France as it chartered the Centre National d'Etudes Spatiales (CNES). That same year France launched its *Veronique* rocket from its temporary base at Hamaguir, a desert plateau in Algeria, where it had three launch pads, storage space, and housing for six hundred people. In 1960 France began its own rocket program and initiated a collaborative space effort with its neighbors that resulted, in 1964, in the formation of the European Space Research Organization (ESRO) with ten members: Belgium, Britain, Denmark, France, Germany, Italy, the Netherlands, Spain, Sweden, and Switzerland. The same year a second agreement between Australia, Belgium, Britain, France, Germany, Italy, and the Netherlands gave birth to the European Launcher Development Organization (ELDO). As part of the settlement following the Algerian War, France agreed to evacuate its North African launch site. In 1964 the French government selected Kourou in French Guiana for its new base.

In 1973 these organizations gave way to the European Space Agency (ESA), whose original members were Germany, Belgium, Denmark, Spain, France, Britain, Switzerland, the Netherlands, Italy, and Sweden. Member nations continued to run their own programs, some still do, but ESA gradually assumed more power as it negotiated with the Soviet (now Russian) Space Agency and with NASA. The 1970s were hard for NASA. Their post-Apollo plans ran into the congressional obstacles of reduced funding and demands for redesigns for the proposed space shuttle and space station. As NASA endured postponements, the Soviets launched a series of space stations, which, beginning with *Salyut 6* in 1977, could maintain at least two cosmonauts working productively for up to 175 days. Then in 1979, France, with ESA participation, launched *Ariane 1* from Kourou and celebrated the end of America's commercial launch monopoly. Within a few years the company Arianespace (a French-led European company that tried, unsuccessfully, to compete with NASA) included thirty-six industrial partners and thirteen banks.

American budgetary problems led NASA to negotiate an agreement with ESA in 1973. In exchange for delivering one flight-ready *Spacelab*, a modular laboratory built to fit inside the space shuttle's cargo hold, Europe would share half of the payload for the first mission, which NASA would launch without charge. At least one European would fly on that mission. Later astronaut assignments would be negotiated. After the first mission, NASA would own the module but agreed to order another *Spacelab* in the future on which ESA could fly additional experiments and astronauts but for which ESA would pay launch costs. The first *Spacelab* flew at the end of 1983 with seventy-two experiments and German scientist-astronaut Ulf Merbold representing ESA. *Spacelab* missions continued through 1998, carrying ten ESA astronauts in fifteen years.

France, especially, felt short-changed with this arrangement and in 1985 began planning Hermes, a space-plane that would carry a crew of two to four scientists or a five-ton payload for thirty days, or ninety days if docked to a space station. Hermes would have made ESA independent of the Soviets and NASA, but it proved much more expensive than anticipated, gradually lost financial support from ESA members, and disappeared from the scene in the early 1990s.

In order to upstage NASA in the early 1980s, the Soviets secretly selected a group of scientifically trained women cosmonauts and chose Svetlana Savitskaya to fly to the *Salyut 7* space station in August 1982, eight months ahead of Sally Ride's mission for NASA in April 1983. Two years later, when NASA announced that Katherine Sullivan would be the first woman to do a spacewalk, the Soviets flew Savitskaya a second time. A Russian woman would be the first to walk in space. Savitskaya, however, decried Soviet chauvinism at her press conferences. The Soviets never flew a planned all-female crew, and the third and last Soviet/Russian woman cosmonaut to date, Elena Kondakova, flew in 1994. By 2003 NASA had launched thirty-six women into orbit.

Also in the 1980s, with a functioning space station, the Soviets were following a new agenda that included scientific experimentation, not the least of which involved monitoring the health of its cosmonauts, who gradually increased the length of their missions to over a year. They also used the station to host visiting cosmonauts for diplomatic, financial, and propaganda purposes. Visitors came from the communist states of Czechoslovakia, Poland, East Germany, Bulgaria, Hungary, Romania, and Cuba, and from France and Britain as well. After the USSR gave way to the Russian Federation, the Russian Federal Space Agency (RKA) signed an agreement with NASA in 1992 for a program called Shuttle-Mir. NASA considered this the first stage of what became the International Space Station. American astronauts would learn about space stations by flying on *Mir* for a sum that would rescue the Russian space program as it made the transition to a free-market economy. At the millennium Russia was one of sixteen nations sharing the International Space Station (ISS), along with the members of ESA, Canada, Japan, Brazil, and, of course, the United States.

Mir fell to a fiery end in 2001, and astronauts and cosmonauts began occupying the still incomplete International Space Station. The loss of the shuttle *Columbia* in 2003 grounded NASA, halting work on the Station. In the interim NASA reconsidered its space priorities and turned its focus to human missions to the Moon and Mars. ESA and the other partners in the ISS assumed that the shuttle program would resume sooner than it did and would complete the International Space Station, a task totally dependent on the shuttles' ability to carry the completed segments of the station's infrastructure into space. However, in reviewing the shuttles' problems NASA estimated that the remaining shuttles might not be able to fulfill this promise before the program is phased out in 2010.

With the future of the ISS uncertain, robotic exploration of Mars has continued with great success. Europe triumphed in January 2005 when its *Huygens* probe separated from NASA's *Cassini* orbiter, and as programmed, penetrated the clouds covering Titan, one of Saturn's moons, and touched down on land, sending back images of what looks like a lake and volcano on its surface. *Huygens* continued to send back data for about ninety minutes after landing. Europeans are also thinking again of going it alone in privately financed projects. The winning of the Ansari X Prize, given to the first privately financed team to orbit a spacecraft with passengers and return it safely and ready to fly again, by an American

millionaire in 2004 kindled hope of a future of perhaps less costly private ventures that would include space tourism, independent scientific research, and private launch pads for telecommunication satellites.

Although Europe continues to support astronauts who may fly on one of NASA's remaining shuttles or work on the ISS, Europeans look with pride to the success of robotic explorers like *Huygens*. Unlike NASA, the ESA also supports sending art projects, if not artists, into orbit as part of an effort to explore the cultural impact of space exploration. European art works have flown on the Russian space station *Mir*. The London-based Arts Catalyst Science-Art Agency has sent artists from France and Slovenia, as well as Britain, on parabolic flights on which they have created a variety of space-centered art projects.

EUROPE'S FUTURE IN SPACE

After the terrorist attacks in 2001, Europeans, on the whole, did not change course on the purpose and value of space exploration. It is unclear how long they will continue to depend on NASA's launch facilities and its robotic spacecraft as a joint international effort. Europe may turn to private companies or to its own military establishments. The exploration of space is poised between the forces of the global market and terrorist acts, forces that vie with each other in directing how Europe and the rest of the world utilize space in the decades ahead.

See also **Aviation; Braun, Wernher von; Cold War; Gagarin, Yuri; Science; Sputnik.**

BIBLIOGRAPHY

Cassutt, Michael. *Who's Who in Space: The International Space Station Edition.* New York, 1999.

Collins, Guy. *Europe in Space.* Houndmills, U.K., 1990.

Crouch, Tom D. *Aiming for the Stars: The Dreamers and Doers of the Space Age.* Washington, D.C., 1999.

Harvey, Brian. *Europe's Space Programme: To Ariane and Beyond.* London, 2003.

Kevles, Bettyann Holtzmann. *Almost Heaven: The Story of Women in Space.* New York, 2003.

BETTYANN HOLTZMANN KEVLES

SPAIN.

SPAIN. Spain entered the twentieth century as one of the two most underdeveloped countries in Western Europe, its political and military elite traumatized by defeat at the hands of the United States in 1898, a disaster that cost Spain all the remnants of its former world empire. The new slogan in Spanish affairs would be "regenerationism," an all-embracing term that could refer to political development, economic growth, educational expansion, social reform, or any possible combination of these goals.

INSTABILITY AND RAPID CHANGE

During the nineteenth century Spain had adapted with some difficulty to the institutions of modern liberalism, after introducing the first new liberal constitution of that century in 1812. Political conflict was profound both between traditionalists and liberals and among varying sectors of the liberal elite. The result was the "era of pronunciamentos, (1820–1874) in which sectors of the military provided the strength either for stability or for further change. In addition, Spain spent more time at war during that period than any other European country, engaging in three international wars, two major civil wars, numerous political insurgencies, and thirteen years of costly colonial campaigns in Cuba. The economy grew but at a comparatively modest rate, so that the gap between Spain and advanced northwestern Europe was proportionately as great in 1900 as it had been in 1800. The economy remained largely agricultural and underdeveloped, the society predominantly rural and still partially illiterate. Political stability was achieved only after the restoration of the Bourbon dynasty in 1874. A two-party system of Liberals and Conservatives, led by Antonio Cánovas del Castillo, ruled the country with a system of restricted suffrage. Universal male suffrage was restored in 1890 but participation was limited and elections largely controlled by established elites.

Alfonso XIII assumed the throne at the age of sixteen in 1902 and reigned until 1931, a period in which the country underwent decisive change. Although political fragmentation increased, a process of greater mobilization and incipient democratization began, challenging the entrenched elites.

Spain was the largest of the European countries to remain neutral during World War I but was also strongly affected by the tidal wave of political and social change after the war ended. Labor organization became important for the first time, the chief protagonist being the anarchosyndicalist movement of the CNT (Confederación Nacional del Trabajo, or National Confederation of Labor). Three prime ministers were assassinated by anarchists between 1897 and 1921, and from 1919 on labor strife intensified and turned very violent.

While all-Spanish nationalism was weak, a further challenge appeared in the form of the movements of "peripheral nationalism" that were gaining strength in Catalonia and the Basque country. Added to these domestic conflicts was the increasingly disruptive impact of a long, bloody, intractable colonial war in Morocco, where a Spanish Protectorate had been established over the northern 10 percent of the country in 1912–1913.

DICTATORSHIP AND THE SECOND REPUBLIC

By 1923 political and social relations had reached an impasse. Although the nineteenth-century elites retained control of the two-party system, challenges mounted on every side, with severe conflict over political, social, and colonial issues. In September, General Miguel Primo de Rivera (1870–1930) intervened to institute the first direct military dictatorship in Spanish history. With military assistance from France, he crushed the revolt in Morocco and also presided over a great wave of economic prosperity. Primo de Rivera was nonetheless bereft of concrete political ideas and failed to offer any long-term political alternative. The king forced him to resign in January 1930, but by that time half a century of stable parliamentary government had come to an end and could not readily be restored. Between 1910 and 1930, while experiencing political failure, Spain enjoyed the greatest economic growth in all its history to that time, and prosperity began to transform the country. During the 1920s the country had one of the highest growth rates in the world. Industrialization, urbanization, per capita income, and educational opportunities all expanded rapidly. By 1930 the agricultural share of the labor force had declined to 45.5 percent, dropping below half for the first time. Yet these dramatic improvements were not sufficient to turn Spain within one generation into a fully developed and modernized country, and their political and social effects were profoundly destabilizing. They produced the most fundamental of all revolutions—the revolution of rising expectations.

The new government appointed by the Crown in 1930 to succeed the dictatorship moved very slowly toward holding elections, having found that the old ruling class had been displaced. In the minds of many, Alfonso XIII was identified with Primo de Rivera, and a republican movement gained strength for the first time in more than half a century. The municipal elections held in April 1931 were won by an alliance of republican parties and Socialists, who demanded that the king abdicate. No longer enjoying support even from the armed forces, Alfonso XIII chose to avoid conflict and left the country. The Second Republic was proclaimed on 14 April 1931.

This introduced a directly democratic political system to Spain for the first time, but it had to cope with the combined effects of the Great Depression, mounting political radicalization, and the more distant influence of the Soviet Union and the rise of fascist and rightist dictatorships abroad. The first Republican cabinets between 1931 and 1933 were dominated by a coalition of middle-class left Republicans and Socialists. They prepared a left Republican constitution that established the separation of church and state and also instituted a militant anticlerical policy. Religious orders were banned from teaching and a series of social, economic, and political reforms were enacted, including a highly controversial agrarian reform, laws strongly favoring organized labor that increased both wages and prices in the midst of the Depression, and extensive autonomy for Catalonia. At the same time, the new regime restricted certain civil rights more severely than the monarchy had done.

REVOLUTION AND COUNTERREVOLUTION

For the next elections, in November 1933, an electoral law that heavily favored coalitions allowed an alliance between the center and the Catholic Right to win control of Parliament. The displaced

leftist parties, which had written the electoral law, rejected the results and insisted the election be voided. The Socialist Party, a major force for the first time, had adopted a position of social democratic reformism in 1931, but by 1934 veered toward violent revolution. The anarchosyndicalist CNT attempted three different revolutionary insurrections during 1932 and 1933, and in October 1934 the Socialists undertook a more extensive one of their own, which was suppressed.

The Republic tended increasingly toward polarization between the revolutionary Left and a counterrevolutionary Right. Since all insurrections had failed, the leftist parties formed a popular front for the elections of February 1936. They won a narrow victory but the electoral law gave them a decisive majority in parliament. The leftist Republicans of Manuel Azaña then formed a minority government in the face of the Socialists' refusal to collaborate, and the revolutionary forces reopened the revolutionary process, seizing farmland, burning churches, forcibly closing Catholic schools, initiating the largest series of strikes in Spanish history, and launching a wave of violence. By-elections in two provinces in May were marked by strong police repression and the denial of civil rights, which skewed the results.

There were also revolutionary activists among the police, and they participated in the kidnapping and murder of José Calvo Sotelo, the leader of the monarchist parliamentary opposition, on 13 July 1936. This was the Spanish equivalent of the Matteotti affair in Italy twelve years earlier. In each case the major source of political violence—the Fascists in Italy, the Socialists in Spain—was responsible for the assassination, with traumatic consequences. Five days later, part of the military revolted, beginning the civil war of 1936–1939.

The left Republican government responded by "arming the people," that is, distributing weapons to the revolutionary groups, who then seized power in most of what became known as the "Republican zone." This produced the most extensive worker revolution in modern European history, as worker groups seized control of most of the economy and the greater share of farmland, effecting a much more extensive direct worker revolution than the one that had occurred in Russia in 1917. The first months were violent in

Republican soldiers march in the streets of Madrid, July 1936. ©BETTMANN/CORBIS

the extreme, as both sides carried out tens of thousands of political executions.

The weakness of the Spanish revolution lay, however, in its internal fragmentation and relative international isolation. The anarchists, revolutionary Socialists, and independent communists insisted on *révolution à l'outrance* (all-out revolution), whereas left Republicans, more moderate Socialists, and the Spanish Communist Party called for a more disciplined policy that would emphasize unity and the military strength necessary to win the civil war.

After Britain and France instituted a formal policy of nonintervention, the only state to support the Spanish revolution was the Soviet Union. It began to send large-scale military assistance in September 1936, and for the first time the Spanish Communist Party became a major force. A more effective Republican government began to be reestablished, and, together with the extensive Comintern propaganda apparatus, sought to present the image abroad of a middle-class democracy rather than a violent revolutionary regime.

Internally, the Comintern policy dictated that the Spanish revolution eschew extreme collectivist policies for the duration of the war in order to win over the lower middle class and adopt an economic program equivalent to the Soviets' New Economic Policy (NEP) during the 1920s. Resistance from the anarchists was crushed in May 1937 and the new government, under the Socialist Juan Negrín, came to rely heavily on the Communists, concentrating on military resistance. The new Spanish Republican People's Army sought to emulate the Soviet Red Army of twenty years earlier but lacked its great numbers and relative strength, while international complications led Joseph Stalin to reduce assistance to the Republic.

THE FRANCO REGIME

The military rebels soon chose General Francisco Franco (1892–1975) as commander-in-chief. He assumed dictatorial powers in the "Nationalist zone" on 1 October 1936 and received extensive military assistance from Fascist Italy and Nazi Germany. Franco proved an effective leader, slowly building a preponderance of military strength based on a more effective army and foreign assistance. He won complete victory in the civil war and total control of Spain by 1 April 1939.

Franco organized a semipluralist rightist dictatorship that was concerned to avoid the limitations of the Primo de Rivera regime by codifying an ideology and building a new institutional structure. In April 1937 he took control of Spain's native fascist party, Falange Española (Spanish phalanx), merging it with a sector of the extreme Right to create a new state political organization. The other main pole of support came from conservative Catholicism, which built a broad base for the regime but also generated a certain internal contradiction and tension.

Although Spanish legend enshrined the myth of *un millón de muertos* (a million dead), the civil war in fact produced approximately 300,000 violent deaths, of which about 100,000 were political executions by both sides. Militarily, it had been a relatively low-intensity conflict punctuated by a number of high-intensity battles. It borrowed a strange combination of tactics and weapons from both World War I and World War II, the principal innovation being the effective employment of air-to-ground support. The Germans accurately gauged the military lessons of the civil war, but it was the Soviet Red Army that studied it most intensively, sometimes drawing the wrong conclusions.

Franco's Nationalist regime pursued an effective economic policy, avoiding inflation and maintaining full production, the opposite of the situation in the Republican zone. In general, however, economic deprivation became more severe in Spain during the years of World War II, when vital imports were in short supply, international markets were either badly skewed or disrupted, and a rigidly statist policy by the new regime had the effect of discouraging production.

Franco's foreign policy was oriented toward the fascist powers that had helped him achieve victory, but, as ruler of a gravely weakened country, he at first declared neutrality in the European war that began in September 1939. After the fall of France nine months later, Franco became convinced that Germany would win the war and changed his government's policy to official "nonbelligerence,"

with a tilt toward the Axis. Spain later sent a division of volunteers, the "Blue Division," to fight alongside the Germans on the eastern front, but never entered the war. Franco demanded that Germany provide massive economic and military assistance and also hand over much of French northwest Africa to Spain. This was a price that Hitler refused to pay.

In August 1943, one month after the fall of Benito Mussolini in Italy, the Franco regime began a tenuous process of "defascistization," downgrading the Falange. In postwar Europe the regime was diplomatically ostracized as a residue of the fascist era, but it tried to recast its structure and alter its image through a "cosmetic constitutionalism." A referendum in 1947 ratified Spain's future form of government as that of a monarchy, with Franco a sort of regent for life, holding all power to choose the king who would succeed him.

The regime also wrapped itself in the banner of Catholic corporatism, stressing its identity as the most Catholic regime in the world. The onset of the Cold War ended the ostracism, and Franco was partially rehabilitated in 1953 when he signed a pact to establish American military bases in Spain and also finally managed to negotiate an official concordat with the Vatican. A unique feature of Spanish society during the 1940s and 1950s was the temporary revival of neotraditionalist Catholicism, a revival unprecedented in twentieth-century Western countries, paralleled only by the later growth of Islamist neotraditionalism in certain Muslim societies.

After midcentury the dictatorship increasingly abandoned its initial economic nationalism, stressing rapid growth, foreign investment, mass tourism, and an increasing openness to the international market. This policy worked, and by the 1960s Spain had regained its ranking of the 1920s, possessing one of the highest economic growth rates in the world. This new "economic miracle" started at a higher level than the previous one, converting Spain into a developed, educated, and urbanized country, with a middle-class society that was increasingly independent and secularized. Thus Franco achieved the secular Spanish dream of "regeneration," but at the cost of eroding the conservative Catholic society and culture on which he had based his regime. Even before Franco's death in November 1975, Spanish society had developed characteristics and aspirations similar to those of social democratic Western Europe.

Although the fundamentally authoritarian character of the Franco regime was never altered, its policies and procedures grew steadily more moderate. The goal of an empire in Africa had to be abandoned altogether. The Moroccan Protectorate was relinquished in 1956, Equatorial Guinea was granted independence in 1968, and the Spanish Sahara was handed over to Morocco in 1975–1976. The aftermath of these last two transfers was grim, resulting in dictatorship and genocide in Guinea and bloody repression by the Moroccan government in the Sahara.

Franco was intent on creating a new system, not just a temporary dictatorship, that would survive his death, but the profound changes that took place in Spanish society and culture under his rule made this unlikely. Spain had become increasingly integrated into the economy and culture of Western Europe.

DEMOCRATIZATION IN POST-FRANCO SPAIN

Franco's successor as chief of state, King Juan Carlos, the grandson of Alfonso XIII, therefore had no illusion that the system of personal dictatorship could continue. He instituted a process of democratization in 1976 under the leadership of Adolfo Suárez, whose Unión de Centro Democrático presided over democratic elections in the following year and the writing of a new constitution that established a democratic parliamentary monarchy. In the process, there emerged a new "Spanish model" of democratization that eschewed overt rupture and violence but achieved peaceful reform from the inside out, using the legal mechanisms of the old authoritarian system to achieve democracy without major strife. Aspects of the Spanish model would be adopted a few years later by newly democratizing systems in Latin America, South Africa, and Eastern Europe. The new system also provided for extensive regional autonomy, and by the 1980s a de facto federalism had developed, known to the Spanish as "the state of the autonomies."

A charismatic new Socialist leader, Felipe González, changed his party from an ideologically Marxist-collectivist organization into a Western European–style social democratic party, and on that basis won an absolute majority in the elections of 1982. González enjoyed the longest tenure of any premier under the system, heading the government for nearly fourteen years, until the spring of 1996. Under the Socialists economic growth resumed and further social and cultural transformation took place, facilitated by entry into the European Union at the beginning of 1986. Spain had joined NATO five years earlier (a privilege always denied to the Franco regime) and benefited considerably from the transfer payments of the European Union. Yet the Socialist government was never able to overcome the highest rate of unemployment in Western Europe and struggled with recession in the early 1990s. Moreover, during their long tenure in power, González's Socialists succumbed to the temptations of office and became highly corrupt. A long series of scandals played a major role in the electoral loss that drove González from power in 1996.

After the death of Franco, a new generation of Spaniards made a major effort to put the civil war behind them without further recrimination, and largely succeeded. A culture of secularization and radical individualism expanded rapidly, with the result that Spain changed more during the second half of the twentieth century than any other Western European country save Ireland. Its birth rate became one of the lowest in the world.

The new Spanish democracy rested on a broad consensus that faced only one major political problem, the continuing demands of the more extreme "peripheral nationalisms," especially that of the Basques, who demanded outright independence. Whereas Catalan nationalists were generally more cooperative, the most radical Basque organization, ETA (for "Basqueland and Liberty"), adopted a policy of violence and terrorism, causing nearly a thousand deaths during the first twenty-five years of democracy. Painful though this was, it was a much lower rate of violence than during the Second Republic in 1931–1936; under the democratic monarchy, all the major Spanish parties remained united in a consensus to reject violence and uphold the democratic constitution.

A progressive and democratic form of Spanish conservatism came to power in 1996, when José

The Guggenheim Museum in Bilbao, Spain, designed by American architect Frank O. Gehry, opened in 1997. ©BEN WOOD/CORBIS

María Aznar's People's Party formed its first government, going on to win an absolute majority in the elections of 2000. The greatest success of the Aznar government was its growth-oriented economic policy, which by the beginning of the twenty-first century had achieved the highest growth rate of any large country in Western Europe. Spain's per capita income was more than 80 percent of the average in Western Europe overall. The public debt, the budget deficit, and tax rates were reduced, and the country's social security and pension accounts became more solidly grounded. Unemployment declined considerably for the first time in years. Terrorism was reduced and new reforms in education were introduced.

Aznar proved a strong leader, supporting the U.S. invasion of Iraq in 2003, despite massive domestic opposition on this issue. The People's Party nonetheless seemed to retain predominant support, based on its impressive performance in most aspects of domestic affairs. Aznar became the first prime minister in more than a century to retire voluntarily from political life at the height of his success, even though he was only fifty-two. Conversely, the massive attacks on two Madrid commuter trains by Moroccan Islamists in March 2004, three days before general elections, had a major impact on public opinion, returning the Socialists to power.

Unsolved problems during the early twenty-first century included the continuing tension with Basques and Catalans, a new concern about Spain's southern flank—given the influx of Muslim immigrants and the instability in the Islamic world—and the common European dilemma of a rapidly aging population that had failed to reproduce itself.

See also **Alfonso XIII; Basques; ETA; Falange; Franco, Francisco; Garzón, Baltasar; González, Felipe; Spanish Civil War.**

BIBLIOGRAPHY

Balfour, Sebastian. *The End of the Spanish Empire, 1898–1923.* Oxford, U.K., 1997.

Balfour, Sebastian, and Paul Preston, eds. *Spain and the Great Powers in the Twentieth Century.* London, 1999.

Ben-Ami, Shlomo. *Fascism from Above: The Dictatorship of Primo de Rivera in Spain, 1923–1930.* Oxford, U.K., 1983.

Carr, Raymond. *Spain, 1808–1975.* Oxford, U.K., 1982.

Conversi, Daniele. *The Basques, the Catalans, and Spain: Alternative Routes to Nationalist Mobilisation.* London, 1997.

Heywood, Paul. *The Government and Politics of Spain.* London, 1995.

Hooper, John. *The New Spaniards.* London, 1995.

Payne, Stanley G. *The Franco Regime 1936–1975.* Madison, Wis., 1987.

———. *Spain's First Democracy: The Second Republic, 1931–1936.* Madison, Wis., 1993.

———. *The Spanish Civil War, the Soviet Union, and Communism.* New Haven, Conn., 2004.

Preston, Paul. *Franco: A Biography.* London, 1993.

Shubert, Adrian. *A Social History of Modern Spain.* London, 1990.

Thomas, Hugh. *The Spanish Civil War.* 3rd rev. ed. New York, 1986.

STANLEY G. PAYNE

SPANISH CIVIL WAR. The Spanish civil war (July 1936–April 1939) was a brutal fratricidal struggle. Representing the clash between diametrically opposed views of Spain, it was a battle to settle crucial issues that had divided Spaniards for generations: agrarian reform, recognition of the identity of the historical regions (Catalonia, the Basque Country), and the roles of the Catholic Church and the armed forces in a modern state.

Spain's tragedy, however, cannot be separated from the wider European picture. The London *Times* noted in September 1936 that the "Spanish Cockpit" was the distorting mirror in which Europe could see a reflection of its own tensions. In an interwar period marked by massive political polarization, the Spanish conflict became the fiercest battle in a European civil war that had included, among other events, the consolidation of Soviet Russia, the rise of fascism, and the establishment of authoritarian dictatorships throughout central and eastern Europe. However, Spain was exceptional. It aroused an unprecedented level of popular passion, and all of Europe's political leaders—Adolf Hitler, Benito Mussolini, Joseph Stalin, Neville Chamberlain, Léon Blum—played a crucial role.

There had been other conflicts in which the occasional volunteer or adventurer had taken part, but in Spain, the high number of intellectuals and, above all, ordinary citizens prepared to do so was startling. Some two thousand foreigners joined the rebels in the belief that theirs was the cause of Christian civilization against communist barbarism. Additionally, over thirty-five thousand volunteers fought for a republic that they regarded as the last-ditch stand against the seemingly invincible forces of fascism.

SEEDS OF THE CONFLICT

The Spanish civil war is deeply rooted in that country's history. Its religious fanaticism was borrowed from the legendary Reconquista, the almost eight-hundred-year struggle to expel the Moors from the peninsula. The clash between state centralism and peripheral nationalisms evoked the War of Succession of the early eighteenth century when Catalan autonomy was crushed. The cruelty displayed by both sides mirrored the brutality of the nineteenth-century civil wars fought between the supporters of the absolute monarchy (Carlists) and the Liberals. More recently, the origins of the war can be found in the political and social polarization of the Restoration Monarchy (1874–1931) and the Second Republic (1931–1936).

Despite all its democratic trappings, the regime ushered in by the restoration of the Bourbons in December 1874 was an oligarchic system in which two monarchist parties (Conservatives and Liberals) alternated in power by systematically rigging the ballot. By failing to initiate reform from within, this elitist order faced, as elsewhere in Europe, the mass mobilization and revolutionary upheaval that followed World War I and the Bolshevik Revolution of 1917. With the southern countryside in revolt and the cities paralyzed by industrial unrest, the military, also involved in a cruel colonial adventure in Morocco, began to assume the role of "saviors" of social order and finally, with the consent of King Alfonso XIII, seized power in September 1923.

The military coup was Spain's authoritarian solution to the crisis of elitist politics in an era of mass mobilization. However, in contrast to other

European dictatorships, the Spanish dictator, General Miguel Primo de Rivera, failed to create a viable order. His downfall brought about the collapse of the monarchy and made possible the advent of democracy. Following the adverse result of the municipal elections of April 1931, and with the officers unwilling to play again the role of the regime's praetorian guard, Alfonso XIII was forced into exile.

The Second Republic handed power to a coalition of Socialists, Republicans, and Catalans committed to a wide range of reform that included the long-awaited agrarian reform, far-reaching social legislation, Catalan home rule, the reconversion of the armed forces into an apolitical institution, and the secularization of society by curbing the privileged status of the Catholic Church. Unfortunately, against a background of world economic depression and political reaction, the Republic's reformist program led to the worst of both worlds. While lack of capital to finance the reforms produced disenchantment among aggrieved sectors of society, the traditional vested interests sought to overthrow a regime that endangered their previous unchallenged hegemony.

Sporadic revolutionary outbursts carried out by anarchosyndicalist groups as well as right-wing attempts to oust democracy by violent or legal means marked the Republican period. In August 1932 General José Sanjurjo rebelled in Seville. Following the rapid quelling of the coup, a new right-wing political coalition, the Spanish Confederation of Right-Wing Autonomous Groups (CEDA) emerged in February 1933. Embracing a legalist route, the CEDA's objective was to build a mass party with which to win elections and then once in government destroy the political system from within. Well-financed by the rural oligarchy and counting on the church's enthusiastic support, the CEDA sought to attract the officer corps, the urban middle classes, and the many Catholic farmers in northern and central Spain.

The CEDA's strategy appeared to be vindicated. After returning the largest parliamentary minority in the elections of November 1933, its demands to be represented in government triggered a revolution in October 1934. The example of Mussolini in 1922 and Hitler in 1933, who had joined governmental coalitions and then destroyed democracy from within, fueled widespread fear that Spain was heading a similar way. The subsequent crushing of the Socialist-led revolution resulted in a period of CEDA supremacy. About forty thousand left-wing militants languished in prisons, wages were slashed, trade unions were disbanded, peasants were evicted, the church was restored to its prominent position, and Catalan autonomy was suspended. Unexpectedly, in the autumn of 1935 a series of financial scandals involving the Radical Party, the CEDA's main governmental partner, led to the dissolution of parliament and the summoning of new elections in February 1936.

The victory at the polls of the Popular Front (the electoral coalition including Liberal Republicans, Socialists, and Communists) shattered the CEDA's legalist strategy. Having lost the political argument, the Spanish Right saw no alternative but to resort to a military insurrection that began on 17 July 1936.

THE PLOTTERS' MISCALCULATION

Confident that in a country with a long tradition of military intervention their uprising would lead to a relatively swift takeover, the conspirators had not anticipated massive popular resistance. The insurgents (Nationalists) gained control of roughly one-third of the country. It contained the traditionally conservative areas (Galicia, Old Castile, and Navarre), all the colonies, the Canary Islands, and the Balearics (with the exception of Minorca) as well as a few working-class strongholds such as Zaragoza and Oviedo and a small but vital strip of land in Andalusia that included Seville, Granada, Córdoba, and Cádiz.

However, in the rest of the country the determination of the trade unions and the loyalty of large numbers of the peninsular troops, police forces, and many senior officers resulted in the crushing of the insurrection. This territory was the most densely populated, including the main industrial areas of northern and eastern Spain (Madrid, Barcelona, Valencia, Bilbao, and so on), the entire Mediterranean coast as far south as Málaga, and the vast rural areas of Estremadura, Murcia, New Castile, and Eastern Andalusia. Furthermore, Spain's air force (albeit tiny) and the country's huge gold reserves (the fourth-largest

Republican soldiers who have surrendered are escorted by Loyalists, Sierra de Guadarrama, Spain, November 1936. ©Hulton-Deutsch Collection/Corbis

in the world) remained in the hands of the government. The Army of Africa, containing the fierce Foreign Legion and the *regulares* (indigenous Moorish troops commanded by Spanish officers), Spain's most battle-hardened professional military force, was unable to cross the Strait of Gibraltar after sailors stayed loyal to the Republic, overpowered their officers, and retained control of the fleet.

FRATRICIDAL TERROR

Describing Spain in the summer of 1936 as a country fiercely divided into two polarized camps is largely misleading. The overwhelming majority of Spaniards did not welcome the war but regarded the unfolding tragedy with horror. It was often geography that dictated the side for which people would fight. Nevertheless, the rebellion opened the gates to innate social hatreds, and Spain embarked upon an era of darkness and violence.

In Nationalist Spain, members of the Popular Front parties, trade union activists, and anybody deemed to be "red" were rounded up and executed. In turn, right-wingers, landowners, and

employers were hunted down in Republican Spain. The Catholic Church, identified as the institution that had blessed the glaring social injustices of the past, was particularly singled out for popular hatred.

Nobody could plead total innocence in the slaughter. However, there existed an essential difference between the two sides. In Republican Spain, the orgy of killing was largely produced by the collapse of governmental authority. Popular crowds ran amok, unleashing their anger against those associated with years of oppression. Certainly all Popular Front groups contained *exaltés* who were convinced that the physical liquidation of class enemies was necessary. However, the atrocities were never condoned, let alone encouraged, by the Republican authorities. On the contrary, from the start they sought to end this indiscriminate system of mob justice, and eventually terror diminished proportionally to the gradual reconstruction of the Republican state. By contrast, there was very little spontaneity to the bloodbath taking place in Nationalist Spain. Most vigilantism could have been effectively limited, if not eliminated altogether, by the military commanders. They not only failed to do so but even encouraged the violence. The rebel leadership merely implemented the brutal methods that they had learned from years of vicious campaigns against the "heathen natives" in Morocco: the enemy had to be exterminated and the potentially hostile population paralyzed by sheer terror.

THE TWO SPAINS AT WAR

For weeks the war remained a series of disparate and fierce local clashes. The Nationalists had not prepared for a long conflict and soon found themselves without leadership. On 20 July the coup's nominal head, General Sanjurjo, died in a plane crash in Portugal; other leading rebel generals were also killed and most of the prewar right-wing political leaders were imprisoned, dead, or overwhelmed by events. Unclear as to whether it stood for a "rectified" Republic under the tutelage of a military junta, a monarchist restoration, or the establishment of a fascist order, the rebel camp was, in the summer of 1936, a motley collection of different warlords, separated geographically and supported by disparate paramilitary militias.

In turn, with the state machinery swept away by the ongoing revolutionary tide and the forces of public order outnumbered by armed militants, the Republican government's authority hardly reached beyond its ministerial offices. A myriad of popular committees took over the running of local economies, trade unions collectivized significant tracts of land and large sectors of industry and public services, and militias patrolled the streets. However, although badly mauled, the legitimacy of the Republican state was never in dispute. A bolshevik party seeking to generate an alternative revolutionary source of authority never existed.

As the war dragged on, both camps realized that total victory could only be achieved through a strong state in full control of a coordinated military strategy, diplomacy, public order, and war economy. Therefore, Francisco Largo Caballero and General Francisco Franco were catapulted to power in September 1936. Largo Caballero, the leader of the largest trade union, the Socialist General Union of Workers (UGT), formed the "government of victory," which included all the forces fighting for the Republic (Liberal Republicans, Basque and Catalan nationalists, socialists, communists, and anarchosyndicalists). In turn, the Nationalist generals appointed Franco, in charge of the Army of Africa, as commander in chief and head of state. With the endorsement of the church, he adopted the title of *caudillo* (leader), a name borrowed from the Christian medieval chieftains.

Historical and ideological reasons made it easier for the Nationalists to collaborate. They all shared a similar authoritarian and ultra-Catholic program, had participated in the military conspiracy, and readily accepted their subordination to the military command. Without much difficulty Franco created a dictatorial regime in which a militarized state, modern fascist values, and arcane religious traditions were the dominant features.

By contrast, the bickering that had traditionally marked the Republican forces was exacerbated by the new wartime framework: the central administration was faced with Catalan and Basque nationalist aspirations; bourgeois Republicans were overwhelmed by the leading role of the working-class organizations (themselves bitterly divided between socialists and anarchosyndicalists) and facing the rapid growth of the Communist Party. Even if the fear of defeat led them to rally around the Largo Caballero government, tensions persisted and often degenerated into violent clashes. An armed confrontation in Barcelona in May 1937 exploded into a mini civil war. The outcome of the May events represented a victory for those who demanded greater centralization of authority and welcomed the downfall of Largo Caballero and his replacement by another Socialist, Juan Negrín. Political infighting persisted until the end of the conflict. However, to explain the Republic's ultimate defeat in terms of its own internal squabbling only provides part of the story.

INTERNATIONALIZATION OF THE WAR

Lacking any important armament industry, both sides looked abroad for diplomatic and military support. The international response proved crucial in determining the course and outcome of the conflict.

Postrevolutionary Mexico was the only state that supported the Republic wholeheartedly from the beginning. It shipped arms and food and represented in many countries the diplomatic interests of

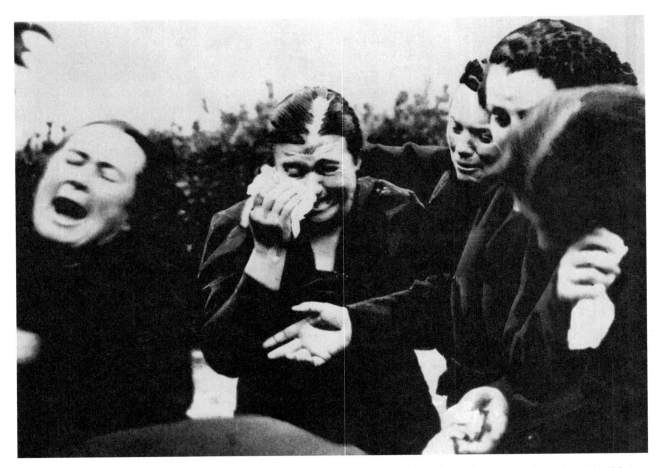

Mothers weep after identifying the bodies of their children, who were killed in the bombing of a school, Lerida, Spain, November 1937. ©Bettmann/Corbis

the Spanish government. Nevertheless, geographical distance and scarcity of resources hampered Mexico's ability to play a major role. In fact, the Republic's hopes of foreign support rested on the Western democracies, particularly its sister Popular Front government in France.

Led by the Socialist Léon Blum, the French administration responded positively to the Republic's pleas for military aid. That decision was a result of ideological solidarity and the need for France to have a friendly state on its southern border. However, the initial French stance was to alter due to pressures both domestic—the fears within some government circles that intervention in Spain could widen the conflict to France—and foreign, chiefly the attitude of France's ally, Britain, toward the Spanish war.

The instructions given by the Conservative prime minister, Stanley Baldwin, to his foreign minister, Anthony Eden, described eloquently the British position: "On no account, French or other, must you bring us into the fight on the side of the Russians!" Indeed, Baldwin's administration and, from May 1937, that of Neville Chamberlain, were committed to the appeasement of the fascist dictators and regarded communism as the main enemy. Class, upbringing, and their vast financial interests in Spain led the British ruling elites to sympathize with the insurgents. The problem for British diplomacy was that the counterrevolution remained formally illegitimate. Consequently, since intervention in favor of the rebellion was unthinkable, the British government maintained for the home audience an image of scrupulous neutrality that was designed to harm the Republic.

Unlike the international ostracism faced by the Spanish government, from the start the rebels could rely on the support of the Portuguese dictator, Antonio Salazar. Portugal's proximity to the battleground was of inestimable value, particularly as a conduit for the delivery of foreign aid. Still more vital contributions came from the fascist powers.

Both Italy and Germany initially rebuffed the pleas of the Spanish rebels. However, realizing the potential advantages of the Spanish conflict, they soon reversed that decision. After meeting Franco's emissaries, Hitler concluded that backing the Nationalists was a limited risk that was worth taking: it would lead to France, Germany's continental enemy, being surrounded by potentially hostile neighbors. Furthermore, Spain's raw materials were a blessing to a Germany bent on rearming, and the war offered the perfect testing ground not only for men and equipment but also for the resolution of the Allies.

Mussolini's ego was flattered by being the recipient of pleas for help, and he was eager to assist the establishment of a potential ally in the Mediterranean. Knowledge of British hostility toward the Spanish government, including its opposition to French involvement, appeared to indicate that Britain would not object to discreet intervention in favor of the insurgents. Also, he was aware that the divided French cabinet had drawn back from open military support, leaving the Republic badly equipped. Finally, Italian diplomats in Morocco advised that once the rebels' colonial troops landed in the peninsula the war would soon be over.

Thus, fascist aid, together with British acquiescence and French paralysis, altered dramatically the course of the war. In August 1936 Italian and German transport planes carried out the first successful airlift of troops in modern warfare, enabling Franco's elite Army of Africa to land in the peninsula and initiate its inexorable advance toward Madrid. When in October they reached the gates of the capital, the war seemed to be reaching its end.

THE EUROPEAN CIVIL WAR
In late July 1936 the secrecy surrounding fascist involvement foundered when two Italian planes crash-landed in French North Africa. With Britain warning of an end to the alliance if French intervention led to continental war, the Blum government proposed that all European powers should accept a Non-Intervention Agreement (NIA) in Spain.

Twenty-seven European nations adhered to NIA in August 1936, and a working committee (NIC) was established in London one month later. In turn, the United States introduced a moral arms embargo on both Spanish parties in August 1936, formalized by the Spanish Embargo Act and the Neutrality Act of January and May 1937 respectively. Blum thought that an arms embargo offered the Republic a chance to crush the rebellion. In fact, nonintervention became a diplomatic farce. A legal government was on an equal footing with seditious generals while its military efforts were hindered by an arms embargo; for the fascist powers it provided a perfect cloak to conceal their flagrant involvement.

Awareness of fascist intervention cemented the Republic's romantic appeal. In the democratic nations there were huge rallies demanding the Spanish government's right to purchase weapons freely, and aid committees were established to raise money, medicines, and clothes to help the beleaguered Spanish people. Nurses, doctors, ambulance drivers, and others volunteered to travel to Spain.

Initially the Soviet Union adopted a cautious strategy. The Spanish war presented a dilemma: Stalin could not allow the emergence of another fascist state; however, a Republican victory, encompassing a social revolution, could result in driving the Allies away from the Soviet Union. He welcomed NIA, but its continual flouting by Germany and Italy changed his initial prudence. From mid-September, under the utmost secrecy, the Soviets began to dispatch weapons while the Communist International organized the recruitment and transport of volunteers (the International Brigades). Ensuring the Republic's survival (albeit a Republic in which revolutionary fervor was restrained) became central to Soviet designs to woo the Western democracies into an alliance with the Soviet Union against Nazi aggression.

The arrival of the first Soviet supplies and International Brigades in October 1936 proved crucial. Against all expectations Franco's troops were held at the gates of Madrid, crushing all hopes for the quick Nationalist victory upon which the fascist states had bet. In fact, with their elite troops badly crippled by casualties, the insurgents even contemplated defeat. In light of these new circumstances, Franco turned again to his fascist friends. Aware of NIC ineffectualness, Germany and Italy committed further reinforcements, thus attaching their prestige to the Spanish adventure.

Nearly twenty thousand German troops served in the Condor Legion, an air force that included the most modern bomber and fighter squadrons in the Nazi arsenal. Still, in 1936 Hitler was not prepared to frighten the Allies through excessive involvement and was happy to let Italy bear the brunt of the effort. Indeed, Mussolini was all but in name at war with the Republic, dispatching some eighty thousand troops (the Corpo di Truppe Volontarie) organized into mechanized divisions, with a permanent contingent of three hundred aircraft (La Aviazione Legionaria). In turn, Russia increased its military aid, and the flow of foreign volunteers continued unabated. By 1937 Spain was a veritable European battlefield, yet NIC continued to turn a blind eye to the flagrant violations of the agreement. Blum himself connived in the smuggling of armaments over the frontier in what was called "relaxed nonintervention."

THE REPUBLIC'S DEFEAT

Buoyed by the Axis reinforcements, the Nationalists captured throughout 1937 the key northern industrial provinces of Asturias, Vizcaya, and Santander and in the spring of 1938 stormed through Aragon, reaching the Mediterranean and splitting the Republic in two. By then the chaotic Republican militias of the first months had been transformed into an efficient Popular Army capable of mounting well-planned offensives. However, small gains in the battlefields, followed by bloody stalemates and painful losses, revealed that the sheer material superiority of the Nationalists ultimately prevailed over the Republicans' courage and even tactical cunning. Furthermore, as Franco held the agrarian heartland, the Republic's population suffered from growing food shortages. However, defeat was above all the result of NIC's crippling embargo, unevenly enforced, which prevented the Republic from engaging on an equal military footing with the Axis-equipped enemy.

Nearly eighty thousand Moroccan mercenaries and thousands of German and Italian professional soldiers, constantly reequipped with the best available matériel, joined the Nationalists. By contrast, excluding the two thousand Soviet pilots and technicians, the Republican foreign troops were genuine volunteers who had to be armed, trained, and fed. While Franco always obtained promptly and on credit crucial oil deliveries from the main Anglo-American companies and weapons from the dictatorships, the Spanish government had to send its gold reserves abroad (to France and the Soviet Union) to finance the war effort and, due to the international boycott, had to rely on the intrigues and inflated prices of the black market for mostly obsolete equipment. Unlike the reliability of the Nationalist supplies, the long distance between the Soviet Union and Spain and the dependence on contraband meant irregular deliveries. Furthermore, the deadly attacks of Italian submarines and aviation effectively closed the Mediterranean supply route. From late 1937 the Republic depended on deliveries to French Atlantic ports that then had to be smuggled into Spain.

Negrín's slogan—"resisting is winning"—encapsulated alternative strategies. At best, victory could be achieved by linking the Spanish conflict with a European war or by persuading the Allies either to enforce nonintervention or to abandon it altogether and give the Republic the military supplies to defend itself; at worst, the mounting of an effective war effort would force Franco to negotiate a compromise peace. Negrín's calls for resistance appeared justified as Nazi aggression in central Europe seemed to be about to plunge the Continent into an all-out confrontation.

Indeed, the worsening of the international situation offered the Republic some glimmer of hope. On 12 March 1938 Germany annexed Austria (the Anschluss) and made plans for the next prize, the Sudetenland in Czechoslovakia. It was an opportunity for the Republic to embark upon a parallel diplomatic and military offensive. On 1 May, Negrín published a thirteen-point declaration stating his government's desire both to reach a negotiated peace and to attain a democratic postwar Spain independent of foreign interference. On 25 July the Republican army crossed the river Ebro, taking the Nationalists by surprise

Spanish refugees fleeing the civil war arrive in the French town of Perthus, 1939. ©HULTON-DEUTSCH COLLECTION/CORBIS

and establishing a bridgehead forty kilometers into enemy territory. The Battle of the Ebro became the longest and bloodiest of the entire war. However, the ultimate fate of the conflict was decided in the European chancelleries rather than on the blood-soaked sierras of eastern Spain.

On 21 September 1938 Negrín traveled to the League of Nations in Geneva to announce the unilateral withdrawal of foreign soldiers. The loss of the remaining twelve thousand International Brigadiers was not of any serious military consequence. However, it could bring about international pressure to force the Nationalists to follow suit. Of course, Franco, if bereft of Axis aid, could not pursue the war. As Republican optimism surged, the other camp was plagued by gloom. After much hesitation, on 27 September Franco reassured the Allies of his neutrality in the event of a European conflict. However, the Allies could

not ignore the vast amount of Axis matériel and troops in Spain. Franco's headquarters could not but dread that as soon as hostilities broke out on the Continent the Republic would declare war on Germany and link its fortune to that of the Western democracies. The insurgents would then find themselves geographically isolated from their friends and starved of military supplies, if not at war with the Allies.

In fact the international situation could not have evolved more favorably for Franco. On 29 September the British and French prime ministers, Neville Chamberlain and Édouard Daladier, agreed in Munich to browbeat the Czechs into surrendering the Sudetenland. It was the final nail in the Republic's coffin.

On 16 November 1938 the Battle of the Ebro concluded. It had taken the Nationalists almost four months to regain the territory lost in July. Despite their material inferiority the Republicans had avoided being routed, but morale had plummeted. Hopes of being rescued by the Western democracies—or, at the very least, of the implementation of genuine nonintervention—had been shattered in Munich. While the Republic could never replace its massive losses, the Nationalists, promptly rearmed by Germany, conquered Catalonia in two months. Despite all military adversities, Negrín was determined to hold onto the 30 percent of Spain still in Republican hands. However, spurred by a combination of irresponsibility, delusion, and treachery, several political and military figures revolted against the government. Their leader, the Republican commander in the central zone, Colonel Segismundo Casado, claimed he could deliver a honorable peace. Instead his coup led to clashes between rival Republican forces and ruined the possibility of further resistance. Franco, who had always insisted on unconditional surrender, ordered a new offensive against Madrid on 26 March 1939. The war officially concluded on 1 April.

After thirty-three months of steadfast struggle, the Republic collapsed. A red but democratic Spain was sacrificed on the altar of Western appeasement before fascist aggression. However, Western appeasement only made war in Europe more likely. During their common Spanish adventure, Germany and Italy sealed the Axis Pact, perfected their military techniques, and were emboldened by the impunity with which they acted despite the existence of NIA. Its Spanish experience also encouraged the Soviet Union to play the appeasement game, which led to the Non-Aggression Pact with Germany in August 1939. As Spain was immersed in Franco's brutal pacification, Europe was about to be plunged into the horrors of World War II.

See also **Antifascism; Appeasement; Fascism; Franco, Francisco; Spain.**

BIBLIOGRAPHY

Alpert, Michael. *A New International History of the Spanish Civil War.* Basingstoke, U.K., 1994.

Esenwein, George, and Adrian Shubert. *Spain at War: The Spanish Civil War in Context, 1931–1939.* London, 1995.

Graham, Helen. *The Spanish Republic at War, 1936–1939.* Cambridge, U.K., 2002.

———. *The Spanish Civil War: A Very Short Introduction.* Oxford, U.K., 2005.

Howson, Gerald. *Arms for Spain: The Untold Story of the Spanish Civil War.* London, 1998.

Jackson, Gabriel. *The Spanish Republic and the Civil War, 1931–1939.* Princeton, N.J., 1972.

Moradiellos, Enrique. *1936: Los mitos de la guerra civil.* Barcelona, 2004.

Preston, Paul. *The Coming of the Spanish Civil War: Reform, Reaction and Revolution in the Second Republic.* 2nd ed. London, 1994.

———. *A Concise History of the Spanish Civil War.* London, 1996.

Romero Salvadó, Francisco J. *The Spanish Civil War: Origins, Course, and Outcomes.* Basingstoke, U.K., 2005.

Thomas, Hugh. *The Spanish Civil War.* 3rd ed. Harmondsworth, U.K., 1986.

FRANCISCO J. ROMERO SALVADÓ

SPARTACISTS. The Spartacists amounted to a small group of radical socialists who split off from the German Social Democratic Party (SPD) during World War I to agitate against the war and prepare workers for a revolution against the imperial state. The Spartacus League derived its name from Spartacus, the Roman slave who led a revolt of gladiators against the Roman Empire from 73 to 71 B.C.E.

Rosa Luxemburg and Karl Liebknecht, two figures who have become hallowed names in the history of the European Left, officially founded the Spartacus League in January 1916. Luxemburg, born of Jewish ancestry in Russian Poland in 1870, was a brilliant social theorist who moved to Berlin in 1898 and worked diligently to instill a revolutionary consciousness in the German working class. Early on she backed the SPD's efforts to achieve political and economic reforms, but she always insisted that "reformism" could never bring true socialism: a revolution was required. As a humanistic socialist, however, she hoped that the revolution could be achieved with minimal bloodshed. Liebknecht, whose father, Wilhelm, had helped found the SPD, shared Luxemburg's

Spartacist guards gather in the street in Berlin, Germany, January 1919. ©Hulton-Deutsch Collection/Corbis

commitment to revolution without her reservations about spilling blood. Like her, he bitterly opposed the SPD's decision to support the German war effort in 1914. The two of them, along with other radicals such as Clara Zetkin and Franz Mehring, distributed revolutionary materials they called "Spartacus Letters." The group's inability to reorient mainstream German socialism prompted the decision to establish the Spartacus League as a radical alternative voice on the German Left.

On May Day 1916 the Spartacus League organized an antiwar demonstration in the center of Berlin. The demonstration was nonviolent and not very large. Nevertheless, the government felt sufficiently threatened to arrest Luxemburg and Liebknecht and pack them off to jail. There they remained until almost the end of the war. In their absence the Spartacist movement floundered.

The Spartacists reemerged as one of the contending factions on the Left in October 1918, on the eve of Germany's military defeat and imperial collapse. Liebknecht, recently released from jail, drew up a program inspired by the Bolshevik model; it called for the transfer of power to workers' and soldiers' councils without regard for parliamentary elections and the nationalization of land and property. When the new SPD-dominated republican regime chose instead to postpone a socialization of the economy and to institutionalize parliamentary democracy, the Spartacists claimed that the revolution was being betrayed. In December 1918 they backed a brief and abortive revolt in Berlin by the People's Naval Division, a band of mutinous sailors with which they had ties. The government's suppression of the sailors prompted the Spartacists and their allies to reconstitute themselves as the Communist Party of Germany.

The real moment of truth for the Spartacists came in January 1919, when, in alliance with yet another radical faction, the Revolutionary Shop Stewards, they launched a violent insurgency in Berlin. The action, inspired by the dismissal of Emil Eichhorn, the radical leftist chief of police in Berlin, came over the objections of Luxemburg, who argued that the time was not ripe for such a move. She proved to be right. The radicals managed to seize a few buildings, but they failed to gain control of the city. After a few days government forces, backed by paramilitary Free Corps, put down the rebellion. Liebknecht and Luxemburg went into hiding but were quickly run down and subjected to summary justice. Liebknecht was shot "while trying to escape," while Luxemburg was clubbed to death and thrown into the Landwehr canal.

Few Germans at the time lamented the defeat of the Spartacists, whose goals were too extreme for most of the Left, let alone the rest of the population. The brutal slayings of Liebknecht and Luxemburg, however, shocked even jaded Berlin, and in retrospect it becomes evident that the killings helped to make political murder an acceptable way of doing business in postwar Germany. The Spartacist uprising also sharpened divisions within the German Left, because radical leftists blamed the SPD-dominated government for the bloodletting. The division in the leftist camp persisted throughout the Weimar Republic, making genuine cooperation impossible in the face of the Nazi challenge.

With the exception of some historians of the former German Democratic Republic, who hailed the Spartacists as part of their state's pedigree, the scholarly assessment of the Spartacist enterprise has been largely critical. While Luxemburg has received due regard for her theoretical brilliance, the group as a whole is considered to have been dogmatic in its ideology and irresponsible in its actions. The Spartacist uprising helped discredit the German revolution and the young Weimar Republic.

See also Germany; Liebknecht, Karl; Luxemburg, Rosa; Social Democracy.

BIBLIOGRAPHY

Ettinger, Elzbieta. *Rosa Luxemburg.* Boston, 1986.

Kluge, Ulrich. *Die deutsche Revolution, 1918–1919: Staat, Politik, und Gesellschaft zwischen Weltkrieg und Kapp-Putsch.* Frankfurt, 1985.

Ryder, A. J. *The German Revolution of 1918.* Cambridge, U.K., 1967.

Waldman, Eric. *The Spartacist Uprising of 1919 and the Crisis of the German Socialist Movement.* Milwaukee, Wis., 1958.

DAVID CLAY LARGE

SPEER, ALBERT (1905–1981), best-known architect of Adolf Hitler's National Socialist regime.

Albert Speer operated at the intersection of architecture, urbanism, Third Reich political propaganda, and, beginning in 1942, large-scale armaments production and industrial organization. Born on 19 March 1905 in Mannheim, Germany, Speer rose to become one of the key figures in the short-lived but immensely powerful and destructive twelve-year Third Reich. Albert Speer studied under the influential architect and popular professor Heinrich Tessenow at the Charlottenburg Technical University in Berlin, absorbing his teacher's interest in a restrained neoclassicism. This historical bent, combined with Speer's considerable charisma and gifts for communication and organization, appealed immensely to the rising dictator Adolf Hitler, himself a frustrated architect inclined toward megalomania in matters architectural as well as political. Speer's close friendship, or at the very least close professional association with Hitler, began after the death of the Nazi architect Paul Ludwig Troost in 1934; it led to a string of large-scale commissions for Nazi Party rallying grounds and stadia in Nuremberg, along with an outsized, imperial replanning of Berlin as "Germania," the new capital of the Nazis' vaunted "Thousand-Year Reich."

Together, Hitler and Speer developed detailed models of a new Berlin city center, complete with a domed Great Hall to accommodate rallies of up to 180,000 people; the quarter-mile-long Reich Chancellery on Vossstrasse (constructed 1937–1939); projects for an array of new ministries; a

FÜHRER- PALAST

GROSSER PLATZ—BERLIN
1938–1940

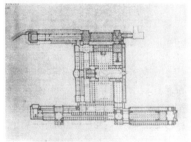

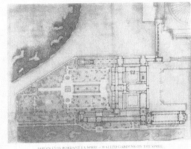

Plans for a palace for Adolf Hitler by German architect Albert Speer c. 1938-1940. PRIVATE COLLECTION/ARCHIVES CHARMET/
THE BRIDGEMAN ART LIBRARY

gigantic triumphal arch known as "Bauwerk T"; and, at the end of a monumental north-south axis through the heart of the city, a new railway station adjacent to the new Tempelhof Airport. Realized only in part, the plans and models nevertheless figured centrally in Hitler's and Speer's reconceptualizations of Berlin and Munich as ideal Nazi cities, embodiments of a new German community (*Volksgemeinschaft*). Among the führer's and General Building Inspector Speer's favorite topics of discussion were the ruins left by ancient empires at Karnak and Ur, which in turn inspired plans for the use of huge amounts of marble and granite in Berlin, so that the "Thousand-Year Reich" would one day leave similarly inspiring ruins as well.

Speer's proximity to the führer, coupled with his organizational talents and political skills, enabled him to rise as a very young man to the pinnacle of power in the Nazi hierarchy. Having successfully maneuvered to succeed Fritz Todt (1891–1942) as minister of armaments production in 1942, at the age of thirty-seven, Speer used German and prisoner-of-war labor to erect monuments, Nazi Party rallying grounds, and industrial buildings throughout the Third Reich while overseeing the Reich's immense infrastructure and its industrial and military supply chain. Speer, whom Karl Hettlage, one of his subordinates, called a "rational man *par excellence*" (Sereny, p. 296) credited much of his organizational success to the innovations of Fritz Todt and, before him, to "the real originator of [the] idea of industrial 'self-responsibility,'" Walther Rathenau (Speer to Rudolf Wolters, 1953; quoted in Sereny, p. 296).

Because of Speer's polish, sophistication, and qualified admissions of war guilt at the Nuremberg war trials of 1946, he received an unusually lenient sentence of twenty years in jail; many other members of the Nazi leadership were executed for their crimes. From jail in Spandau, near Berlin, Speer released sanitized versions of his immensely readable, informative memoirs. These helped make him an important, if still controversial, celebrity in West Germany right up to his release on 30 September

1966 and his death in 1981. Making the hardly believable claim that he was ignorant to the end about the Nazis' Final Solution, the genocide of Europe's Jews, the charming and enigmatic Speer combined the qualities of an haut bourgeois architect and master executive technocrat with the ideological relativism and willingness to compromise that snared so many during the darkest years of modern German history.

Speer's architectural legacy has been to inoculate many German architects and government authorities against overt expressions of monumental, modern classicism, deemed too close to Hitler's megalomaniacal visions. In reunified, post–Cold War Berlin, such official projects as Axel Schultes's and Charlotte Frank's modernist master plan for the government quarter of the early 1990s, their highly sculptural chancellery building (2000), and Sir Norman Foster's high-tech renovation of the Reichstag building (1999) reflect this aversion to direct classical quotation. Instead, these buildings express the German government's ambition to erect modern symbols of a new "Berlin Republic," leader of a modern European nation that is perceived to be simultaneously open, democratic, and progressive.

See also **Architecture; Hitler, Adolf; Nazism.**

BIBLIOGRAPHY

Primary Sources

Speer, Albert. *Inside the Third Reich: Memoirs.* Translated by Richard Winston and Clara Winston. New York, 1970.

———. *Spandau: The Secret Diaries.* Translated by Richard Winston and Clara Winston. New York, 1976.

Secondary Sources

Bärnreuther, Andrea. "Berlin in the Grip of Totalitarian Planning: Functionalism in Urban Design between Hostility to the City, Megalomania and Ideas of Order on a New Scale." In *City of Architecture/Architecture of the City: Berlin 1900–2000,* edited by Thorsten Scheer et al., 200–211. Berlin, 2000.

Lane, Barbara Miller. *Architecture and Politics in Germany, 1918–1945.* Cambridge, Mass., 1968.

Sereny, Gitta. *Albert Speer: His Battle with Truth.* London, 1995.

JOHN V. MACIUIKA

SPUTNIK. Sputnik, or satellite, after the Russian word for "companion in travel" or "satellite," is the name of the world's first artificial satellite. Sputnik 1, launched by the Soviet Union on 4 October 1957, awed the world, ushered the space age, and had global political repercussions.

The team of Soviet engineers behind Sputnik included the chief designer, Sergei Korolyov (1907–1966), and the rocket engine specialist Valentin Glushko (1908–1989). Their work on rocketry started in the 1920s, inspired by writings of Konstantin Tsiolkovsky (1857–1935), a visionary of space travel, science fiction author, and amateur inventor, many of whose ideas, including Sputnik, they later managed to realize. After a short honeymoon around 1930 with revolutionary utopian projects, rocket engineers were forced by the hard realities of Soviet history—the looming war threat from Nazi Germany and Stalinist purges—to switch to more useful and down-to-earth designs with short-range missiles and aircraft. Meanwhile, in Germany, the military pursued a much more ambitious project headed by Walter Dornberger (1895–1980) and Wernher von Braun (1912–1977), which by the end of World War II developed a long-range guided missile, A-4 (better known as V-2). Although at that stage of development still a failure as a military weapon, V-2 constituted a great engineering breakthrough and, after the Nazi defeat, inspired subsequent missile projects in the United States, Soviet Union, and United Kingdom.

The best of the "war bounty"—the core of the German missile team (along with most of the surviving V-2s)—was brought to the United States in Operation Paperclip to work on ballistic missiles for the Department of Defense. Having acquired much less, the Soviet military relied mostly on its own engineers, who were first gathered in occupied Germany to study the remaining equipment and documentation and in 1946 moved to a secret research center, NII-88, in Kaliningrad near Moscow. Despite an initial disadvantage, the Soviet team eventually surpassed its German-American rivals in developing intercontinental ballistic missiles (ICBMs). The Soviet project's chief military motivations were rooted in the asymmetrical strategic balance. American bombers from air bases in Europe and Asia could target cities deep inside the Soviet territory, while the Soviet Union lacked forward bases from which aircraft could reach American shores. Without ICBMs, atomic bombs alone did not provide deterrence against the American nuclear threat. In an attempt to accelerate the development of a delivery system, Soviet officials set their target payload in 1953, before they actually knew the exact mass of the hydrogen bomb, on the basis of a higher estimate of three tons. The assignment led Korolyov's team to leapfrog several incremental stages and develop the powerful two-stage missile R-7 with a seven-thousand-kilometer reach.

Some of the engineers still remembered their youthful dreams about space travel, and Mikhail Tikhonravov's (1901–1974) small group started working on parallel designs for sputniks and manned space missions. In 1956, having impressed the Soviet leader Nikita Khrushchev with the progress of work on R-7, Korolyov obtained permission to use one of the future missiles for a sputnik launch, on the condition that the all-important military assignment would not be deterred. Information about the first successful test of R-7 in August 1957 and a few predictions of imminent space launches appeared in the Soviet press. Concerned about possible U.S. competitors, Korolyov decided to go ahead with a simple sputnik—an 83.6 kilogram aluminum sphere, 58 centimeters in diameter, with a radio transmitter and four antennas—without waiting for more sophisticated equipment. Launched in the early morning of 4 October from the Baykonur site in Kazakhstan, Sputnik orbited Earth every ninety-eight minutes for the next three months at the altitude of 230 to 940 kilometers. It could be seen from ground with the naked eye, and its beeping signal was heard by radio amateurs around the world. Overnight it became a public sensation and world media fixation.

Only after the fact did authorities in the Soviet Union and the United States understand the full political and symbolic importance of Sputnik. Soviet propaganda quickly started promoting the achievement nationally and internationally as the demonstration of socialism's superiority over capitalism. The U.S. leadership initially tried to downplay Sputnik's importance but also worried about the changed dynamics in Cold War technological

competition: in 1945 the Soviets had been viewed as backward, but they had "caught up" in the development of the atomic bomb, then had come even with thermonuclear weapons and had actually surpassed the Americans in missile design. After Sputnik, the idea of space travel captivated the minds of millions and became a chief political priority for existing and aspiring superpowers. The space race began in earnest.

Khrushchev asked Korolyov for further spectacular achievements pegged to two major forthcoming Soviet holidays, 7 November 1957 and 1 May 1958. Sputnik 2 (508 kilograms), carrying the dog Layka, followed on 3 November 1957. The United States, having earlier announced its plans to launch satellites during the International Geophysical Year 1957–1958, tried hastily to catch up, which resulted in a public embarrassment with Vanguard ("Flopnik") on 6 December 1957 and eventual success with Explorer 1 (14 kilograms) on 31 January 1958, lifted up by von Braun's Jupiter missile. The Soviet Sputnik 3, delayed until 15 May 1958 by a launching failure, weighed 1.3 tons and contained an array of scientific instruments. Subsequent Soviet probes in the Sputnik and Luna series brought further achievements, including recovering dogs alive from space, circumnavigating the moon, and for the first time photographing its far side. But the ultimate prize was claimed on 12 April 1961, when a modified three-stage version of R-7 carried the capsule Vostok 1 with the cosmonaut Yuri Gagarin (1934–1968), who orbited the earth once and landed safely after the 108-minute flight. In the Soviet Union and also in present-day Russia, the victory of the first manned flight was valued higher than any other human achievement in space, including Sputnik, and celebrated annually as Cosmonautics Day. In the United States, the defeat in the space race led President John F. Kennedy to proclaim sending man to the moon as the nation's major goal. The National Aeronautics and Space Administration (NASA) had been created in 1958 as a response to Sputnik by the National Aeronautics and Space Act to provide a U.S. space program with centralized government management in the way the Soviets were thought to have their work organized. Granted national priority and unrestricted funds, NASA accomplished its main task on 20 July 1969 with the successful moon landing of Apollo 11. Other

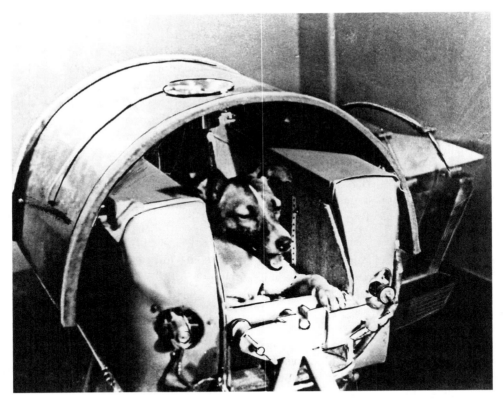

Layka sits inside Sputnik II in preparation for her flight into space, 1957. ©BETTMANN/
CORBIS

countries followed with their own satellites: United Kingdom and Canada (1962), Italy (1964), France (1965), Australia (1967), Germany (1969), and Japan and China (1970). A collaborative European Space Research Organization (ESRO) was established in 1964, which launched its first satellite in 1968.

Sputnik's aftereffects spread far beyond space policy, although they remain considerably understudied. The technological achievement proved its practical usefulness almost immediately, with spy, meteorological, and communications satellites. Whereas manned space missions remained important as propaganda but of little economic benefit, without sputniks, modern global economy and communications would have been unimaginable. Like the atomic bomb twelve years earlier, Sputnik influenced major changes in general science and technology policy. In the United States, overall spending on research and development jumped to a new high, and government funding agencies adopted the originally Marxist approach of not making a sharp distinction between pure and applied research. The National Defense Education Act of 1958 was intended to increase government involvement in mathematics and science education in order to catch up with the Soviets in the mass training of engineers and scientists. It proved easier, however, to import qualified personnel from abroad. Changes in U.S. immigration laws toward preferential acceptance of professional and technical workers with degrees led in the 1960s to the serious problem of brain drain, first for Western Europe and later for many third world countries, but the same process made American science multiracial, diverse, and less American.

For the Soviet Union, Sputnik was a propaganda and diplomatic coup that changed the country's international image to that of a technologically advanced superpower roughly equal to the United States and increased the attractiveness of the Soviet model, especially in the developing world. From a military perspective, as the visible tip of the ICBM program, Sputnik signified the start of a more symmetrical stage in the Cold War, in which both opposing alliances possessed efficient deterrence against the other. The transition was hard to swallow for the United States, producing the dangerous Cuban missile crisis of 1962, but eventually resulted in a more stable state of growing mutual awareness that a thermonuclear war could not be won in principle. Indeed, Khrushchev's acquaintance with the progress of nuclear and missile development was a major factor in his proclamation of "peaceful coexistence" as the official Soviet strategy in 1956. Soviet leaders felt they needed real nuclear parity—catching up with the United States in the actual numbers of missiles and warheads rather than in the militarily and economically useless moon race—which became their first priority in the post-Sputnik period and was accomplished during the rest of the 1960s. It also can be argued that their pride in the space victory and the effects of their own bombastic propaganda contributed to the dominance of a self-congratulatory mood among Soviet leaders in later years, which made them less competitive and less willing to strive for changes. At least chronologically, Sputnik and Gagarin coincided with the acme of Soviet civilization, before it entered stagnation and decline. They thus remain in public perception the symbols of its greatest accomplishments and contributions to world culture.

See also **Cold War; Gagarin, Yuri; Space Programs.**

BIBLIOGRAPHY

Barsdale Clowse, Barbara. *Brainpower for the Cold War: The Sputnik Crisis and the National Defense Education Act of 1958.* Westport, Conn., 1981.

Chertok, Boris E. *Rakety i liudi.* 4 vols. Moscow, 1999–2002.

Dickson, Paul. *Sputnik: The Shock of the Century.* New York, 2001.

Golovanov, Yaroslav. *Korolyov: Fakty i mify.* Moscow, 1994.

McDougall, Walter A. *The Heavens and the Earth: A Political History of the Space Age.* New York, 1985.

Siddiqi, Asif A. *Sputnik and the Soviet Space Challenge.* Gainesville, Fla., 2003.

———. *The Soviet Space Race with Apollo.* Gainesville, Fla., 2003.

ALEXEI KOJEVNIKOV

SREBRENICA. Srebrenica is the name of a town in East Bosnia (six thousand inhabitants in 1990), which has become a synonym for the largest single act of genocide in post–World War II Europe. In April 1993 the United Nations Security Council proclaimed the town and its surroundings (an area of nine by ten miles) a "safe area." Thus, Srebrenica was a Muslim enclave within a region that Bosnian Serb armed forces had ethnically cleansed. In July 1995, after almost two years of siege, the Bosnian Serb Army conquered the enclave. A small force of UN peacekeepers proved to be unable to defend the area, or at least prevent the wholesale massacre of between seventy-five hundred and eight thousand captured Muslim men, both military and civilians, by the Bosnian Serbs.

The war in Bosnia had broken out in April 1992, as a part of the violent disintegration of the Socialist Federal Republic of Yugoslavia. Political leaders exploited ethnic differences in the face of possible independence for Bosnia-Herzegovina. As this new state was proclaimed, ethnic Serbs in Bosnia refused to be part of it. Their political leadership decided to found a Serb Republic in Bosnia. Their armed forces and militias launched an offensive, with the operational and logistical support of the Yugoslav Army. They laid siege before Sarajevo and quickly secured important areas and towns in Central and Eastern Bosnia. Among these was Srebrenica, where a majority of the population was Muslim. The Bosnian Serb militias subjected the conquered areas to ethnic cleansing by means of systematic terror, torture, and killings.

THE ENCLAVE

In May 1992 Muslim units from the area managed to recapture Srebrenica and take control once again. Now the town became a refuge for large numbers of Muslim refugees from surrounding rural areas. A continuous series of bloody skirmishes began. In one particular case, Bosnian Serb paramilitaries killed at least four hundred captured men to avenge the death of their leader, Goran Zekič. The Bosnian Serb Army (BSA) cut off the enclave from outside supplies and shelled the town while Muslim units undertook raids to secure food and to gain tactical progress. All this produced extreme hardship for the civilians. In the enclave, thirty-two thousand inhabitants out of a total population of an estimated total of forty-four thousand were refugees. A humanitarian crisis developed and attracted the attention of international relief agencies and the United Nations.

Diplomatic intervention from the international community remained only partially successful. In June 1992 the United Nations deployed its peacekeeping force for former Yugoslavia (UNPROFOR, or United Nations Protection Force) to Bosnia. The purpose was to facilitate humanitarian aid and, generally, to prevent the warring parties from acts of aggression. As a result of political reluctance, the actual mandate for UNPROFOR remained rather limited and more directed toward peacekeeping while there was an actual need for more robust peace enforcement. This gap was bridged by the expectation that UN presence in itself would deter the warring parties from acts of aggression. Srebrenica in particular would prove this assumption to be completely untrue.

When confronted, early in 1993, with the hardship and desperation of the local population, the French UN General Philippe Morillon (b. 1935) told them in front of television cameras that from now on, Srebrenica was under the protection of the United Nations. The Security Council then declared Srebrenica a United Nations–protected "safe area" (UN Security Council Resolution 819). Consequently, Canadian peacekeepers were deployed to protect the enclave. It still remained unclear if the mandate for this solution, taken on an ad hoc basis, included military defense of the area. "To deter by presence" was the strategy, which—with hindsight—produced a false sense of security among the people in the enclave, who initially were happy to believe that they would actually be defended by UN forces.

In February 1994 the Canadians were relieved by a battalion from the Netherlands (Dutchbat). The Canadian government felt that Canbat had been deployed to the enclave by chance and it remained strongly critical of the whole concept of "safe area." Moreover, the Canadians were very unhappy about their lack of influence in the

international process of decision-making about the former Yugoslavia.

UNPROFOR found itself more and more caught between two fires. The Bosnian Serbs blocked supplies, forcing Dutchbat to negotiate all traffic of personnel and supplies with local BSA commanders. This undermined both Dutchbat's effectiveness and standing with the warring parties. From their side, the Muslim army in the enclave refused to implement disarmament, which they had agreed upon when the "safe area" was established. UNPROFOR's mandate and rules of engagement did not allow for a strong military response to the BSA's shelling of the town or for searching the enclave for caches of arms and ammunition. The blockade continuously undermined Dutchbat's operational capacity, a matter that the UN Headquarters could not solve. "Deterrence by presence" proved illusory while life in the enclave grew more and more difficult for tens of thousands of idle, deprived, and starving people.

In early July 1995 the BSA command launched a new offensive to brace the blockade of Srebrenica. As the operation progressed easily, they decided to go for the whole of the enclave. The UN forces had not developed a strategy for dealing with such an eventuality. Moreover, on the highest level there was much political unwillingness to use robust force to stop these offensive actions. Airstrikes were supposed to undermine the peace process in general. Limited close-air support was considered but applied only once, without any effect. Thus, Dutchbat, being unprepared and unable to defend the area, was actually overrun without difficulty by General Ratko Mladić's (b. 1942) troops, who took the town of Srebrenica on 11 July 1995.

THE MASS KILLINGS

All the confusion blurred the judgement of Dutchbat's command. A division of the Muslim army disappeared with a large number of men and boys from the enclave, in an effort to reach Muslim-controlled territory on foot. BSA units quickly hunted down this column of about fifteen thousand people; many of them were captured and killed. Moreover, the conquering BSA units entered the enclave, pushing panicking refugees toward Dutchbat's compound. These people thought to find protection, but their hope proved to be an illusion too. The intimidating BSA presence around the compound posed a constant threat of shelling and massacre. Therefore, lieutenant-colonel Thom Karremans (b. 1948), Dutchbat's commander, entered negotiations with Mladić.

Under the circumstances, Karremans and his staff decided that a quick evacuation of the Muslim population was preferable. BSA commanders called for buses to collect them, but would not allow the men to depart before they had been "screened." BSA units were already committing revenge-killings in the enclave, claiming several hundred victims. The first wave of killings in the enclave seem to have been inspired by the fact that the BSA command gave their men free rein to avenge small-scale attacks directed against Serb villages in 1992 and 1993. These killings and other forms of violence against the Bosniaks in the enclave, including the rape of women, created an atmosphere of utter horror. Owing to their failing communications, Dutchbat's commanding officers did not realize what was happening. They felt compelled to accept the separation of about five thousand men and their deportation to places unknown. The remaining twenty-three thousand women, children, and elderly men were deported to Muslim-occupied territories. Karremans took care to organize the evacuation of his own men. In the whole process, he allowed himself to be bullied and belittled by Mladić before the eyes of the world press. His reputation suffered even more when he gave a first press conference after reaching the UN headquarters, telling journalists that from an operational point of view, Mladić had done a very professional job.

At the moment, little was known about the fate of the column that had tried to escape and of the thousands of men deported by the BSA from the enclave. Still, neither the Dutch nor the UN force command or political leadership took steps to enquire about what was going on, where these people were, and what their condition was. What actually had happened was a dreadful series of improvised mass killings, probably ordered by the Bosnian Serb military leadership. The captured men were brought to places outside the former enclave, some as close as neighboring Bratunac, some far as sixty miles away, and summarily executed. This killing of unarmed prisoners, civilian and military, was evidently motivated by intense feelings of revenge and ethnic hatred, giving evidence of a genocidal mentality among the BSA. Moreover, the conquerors felt the urge to take quick countermeasures against the breakout of the Muslim army, to which they had to adapt their own strategic plan. Much evidence shows that they had not prepared, and did not wish to prepare, to treat the Bosniaks as prisoners of war.

AFTERMATH

The fall of Srebrenica and other developments in the summer of 1995 produced a shift in the international community toward a stronger policy in Bosnia-Herzegovina. A Bosnian Serb attack on another Muslim enclave, Gorazde, was countered. The shelling of a marketplace in Sarajevo, allegedly by Bosnian Serbs, on 28 August provoked harsh reactions from both the United Nations and NATO. Heavy airstrikes, under the name of "Operation Deliberate Force," compelled the Bosnian Serbs to resume negotiations. On 21 November 1995 the Dayton Agreement produced a political compromise that none of the parties in the conflict could afford to reject.

In the aftermath, the punishment of those suspected of war crimes and genocide was given to a newly founded International Criminal Tribunal for the Former Yugoslavia (ICTY) in The Hague. Meanwhile, international public opinion started to discuss the United Nations' strategies and policies, both in the field and in the diplomatic spheres. The fact that UNPROFOR did not made a firm stand against the occupation of the "safe area" and the subsequent mass murder have provoked many penetrating questions. Especially in the Netherlands, the whole affair produced collective soul-searching and political commotion for years to come. Controversies about the historical interpretation may continue for decades.

See also **Balkans; Bosnia-Herzegovina; Ethnic Cleansing; Genocide; Yugoslavia.**

BIBLIOGRAPHY

Blom, J. C. H., and P. Romijn, eds. *A "Safe" Area: Reconstruction, Background, Consequences and Analyses of the Fall of a Safe Area.* Amsterdam, 2003. Full text in English available at http://www.srebrenica.nl. The

Dutch Government commissioned the Netherlands Institute for War Documentation (NIOD) in late 1996 to write a full-scale report on what had happened.

Documents d'Information de l'Assemblée National, no. 62/2002. Paris, 2001. Available at http://www.assemblee-nationale.fr/11/dossiers/srebrenica.asp. An investigative committee of the French Assemblée Nationale reported about the French implication in the affair.

Honig, Jan Willem, and Norbert Both. *Srebrenica: Record of a War Crime*. London, 1996.

International Criminal Tribunal for the Former Yugoslavia (ICTF) in The Hague. Available at http://www.un.org/icty.

Rohde, David. *Endgame: The Betrayal and Fall of Srebrenica, Europe's Worst Massacre since World War II.* New York, 1997.

Secretary-General of the United Nations report in 1999 to the General Assembly, pursuant to General Assembly Resolution 53/35. Available at http://www.un.org/peace/srebrenica.

Silber, Laura, and Allan Little. *The Death of Yugoslavia.* London, 1995.

PETER ROMIJN

SS (SCHUTZSTAFFEL). The SS was founded in 1925 as a security organization for Adolf Hitler (1889–1945) and the Nazi Party. Its early years converge with those of the SA (Sturmabteilung); however, in 1929 its history was fundamentally altered when Heinrich Himmler was named its third SS Reichsführer (chief for the Reich). Once nominated to the post, Himmler launched a systematic expansion policy that entailed intense yet still highly elite recruiting. By 1932 the SS was a powerful, fifty-two thousand-man-strong organization whose numbers would quadruple in the next year alone. After the Nazis assumed power, its rise was unstoppable, becoming consolidated solely under Himmler's direction and assuming authority for itself to intervene in ever larger domains. As the regime's elite ideological corps it furnished an officer reserve, was a laboratory for ideas, and assumed responsibility for the fundamental axes of Nazi thinking and planning.

The SS was first and foremost a tool used to accomplish the acquisition of power in Germany and of empire in Europe. Secondarily it was one of the primary mechanisms for implementing policies of administering and exploiting occupied territories. Finally it was the almost sole agent responsible for carrying out the policies of repression and extermination that constituted the heart of Nazi praxis.

ACQUISITION OF POWER AND EMPIRE

From 1929 to 1932, the SS was primarily an underground SA appendage group. The SA was a mass movement dedicated as much to winning the battle with Communists and other opponents for the streets as to winning at the ballot box. When the SA did so, they organized torch-lit marches in Berlin on 30 January 1933, the day Hitler was named chancellor of Germany. The SS, on the other hand, at that time seemed to be relegated to playing a more subordinate role. Himmler had been appointed Munich chief of police, and had little else in his portfolio. However he used his post to heavily influence virtually all the other police forces in Germany and began to compete with the SA, which was brutally eliminated on 30 June 1934 in the "Night of the Long Knives." Hitler and Himmler then moved into a period of relative calm following the "revolutionary phase" that occurred during the first year of Nazi rule.

The SS was the primary agent for carrying out the SA's dismantlement: it assumed direct responsibility for the execution of its officers, as well as the murder of other figures targeted because they were likely to support it. To facilitate this purge, the SS was given official status as an organism independent of the party, and Himmler, now appointed chief of the Prussian political police, was at last able to assume overt control of all German police forces. After the SA's elimination Himmler reorganized the SS by splitting it into paramilitary units called the Emergency Troops (Verfuegungstruppen, or SSVT), and the Death's Head Formations (Totenkopfverbände), charged with running the concentration camps. Now the shape of SS power emerged. It rested on elite militarized units, soon to grow in number, and on a monopoly on police and intelligence services.

In 1936 when Himmler was finally certain of his control over all the police forces in Germany, he appointed Paul Hausser as chief inspector of the Emergency Troops, charging him with militarizing

Members of the SS march during the Nuremberg rally of 1933, carrying standards with swastikas and the motto "Germany Awake." ©CORBIS

its units. After undergoing intensive military training, the SSVT's three regiments would take part in the invasions of Austria, the Sudetenland, and Bohemia and Moravia. Finally in 1939 the Waffen SS (Armed SS) were created and deployed in the Polish September Campaign, marking an even more unexpected expansion in the SS's armed forces. By erecting these two pillars, Himmler had built between 1929 and 1939 what was destined to become the most powerful organization in the Third Reich. However in the eyes of Hitler, as in those of his SS Reichsführer, external conquest inaugurated a new era, destined to be followed by the Germanization and exploitation of occupied territories.

OCCUPIED TERRITORIES: 1939–1945

In the fall of 1939 the SS spawned new institutions that reflected its ongoing evolution. On 1 October the Security Service (Sicherheitsdienst, or SD) was established along with the Reich Central Security Office (Reichssicherheitshauptamt, or RSHA), the central SS department designed to coordinate the political and criminal police forcesHimmler and his chief deputy Reinhard Heydrich had just acquired a highly adaptable police force that would eventually assume responsibility for all repressive actions that took place in Europe, while continuing to maintain its function as a brain trust and authority for Nazi ideology. On 6 October Hitler announced he had decided to reorganize "interethnic" relations in Europe. The following day Himmler set up a Reich Commission for the Strengthening of Germandom (Reichskommissariat für die Festigung deutschen Volkstums, or RKFdV), charged with coordinating Germanization programs in the occupied territories.

The RKFdV brought together several already seasoned SS institutions under one umbrella organization, including the Race and Resettlement Main Office (Rasse- und Siedlungshauptamt, or RuSHA), which was especially responsible for racial matters, and the Ethnic German Aid Office (Volksdeutsche Mittelstelle, or VoMi), an organism that both provided material assistance to ethnic German communities and engaged in clandestine political activities. These preexisting institutions coincided with new ones created in response to needs generated by further conquests. For example a Central Office for Racial Germans (Volksdeutsche Mittelstelle) was created, responsible for making the necessary arrangements to relocate the *Volksdeutsche,* or racially pure Germans, in newly acquired lands, as well as for the expulsion of "racially undesirable" communities, primarily Jews and Poles. The result was a thorough policy of Germanization, designed to subject the Slavic communities to a "process of depopulation." This department was responsible for the starvation policies in occupied countries developed to meet the economic needs of the Wehrmacht (German army), in addition to the predatory forced labor practices the SS operated in concert with the civilian administrations in areas of the occupied Soviet Union. The last of these plans, laid out in January 1943, envisioned the deaths of more than thirteen million Slavs in total, and the deportation of another thirty-five million to the "Asiatic Section" of the conquered Soviet Union.

REPRESSION AND EXTERMINATION
The SS plans for deportation reflected the murderous drives at the heart of its institutional structure. However the same plans were also carried out through the short-term planning arm of the RSHA, its Amt IV B4 (office 4, subsection B4) led by Karl Adolf Eichmann, a specialist on Jewry and other "cults." Beginning in 1939 Eichmann's agencies operated a policy of population displacement that carried with it Poles, Jews trapped in the ghettos and nearly starved by devastating rationing policies, and *Volksdeutsche* repatriated in that same year. The economic chaos that ensued caused the death by starvation of tens of thousands of Jews. Then the field of action grew enormously after the Nazi invasion of the Soviet Union.

The various phases of the Reich's aggrandizement had been accompanied by seizing control over policing duties, henceforth carried out by the mobile commandos of the Gestapo and the SD, designated together by the name Einsatzgruppen,

or rear guard action groups. It was in Poland that these groups committed mass murder when they eliminated ten thousand people, mostly members of the Polish elites. However it was in the Soviet Union that they progressively slid into a violent war whose aim was the complete annihilation of its Jewish communities. From June to August 1941 these four groups limited themselves to executing men (mostly Jews) old enough to bear arms. However they soon began to add women to their target population, and, probably under Himmler's Heydrich's [*sic*] orders, began to kill children starting in mid-August 1941. By September and October the Einsatzgruppens' aim of completely eliminating Soviet Jewish communities was at last put into full practice, leaving practically no Jewish survivors in its wake.

During this same period the SS officials charged with carrying out programs for the persecution and deportation of the Jews were examining the means available to them for resolving the difficulties engendered by population displacement. The solution envisioned during the fall of 1941 entailed the indirect elimination of Eastern Europe's Jewish communities via deportation above the Arctic Circle. However by the summer of 1941 local occupation authorities were asking for the direct elimination of those contingents of Jews in their ghettos who were unfit for work. The Reichschancellery, which had implemented the initial programs for gassing the mentally and chronically ill in the fall of 1939, sent specialists in these techniques to the Warthegau, a part of Poland congruent to Lodz, which was to be incorporated into the Reich, as well as to the Lublin District.

In this way two extermination programs were implemented based on regional initiatives. The first, which was based on the techniques used in the mobile gas units, was erected in a manor house in Chelmno known as the Castle. The second, at the initiative of the Lublin SS commander Odilo Globocnik, culminated in the construction of the death camps at Belzec, Sobibor, and Treblinka. At the same time Eichmann, the official responsible for the RSHA's anti-Jewish and deportation policies, began to search for a location to accommodate permanent death camp installations. He ended up choosing Auschwitz because it was a central rail crossroads and because it already had a vast

Jurgen Stroop, the SS general in charge of the Warsaw ghetto, questions Jewish men, 1939. ©CORBIS

concentration camp, intended for Soviet prisoners of war. Here was a site amenable to further enlargement. Eichmann and Rudolf Höss, the camp's commander, agreed to proceed with gassing tests using Zyklon B, already in widespread use in the camps to kill lice on Soviet prisoners of war.

Thus by the fall of 1941 the three primary modes of direct extermination—firing squads, carbon monoxide, and Zyklon B—were fully operational. However only the firing squads had been utilized in the process of mass killings, in particular for the massacre of Kiev's 33,371 Jews in the Babi Yar Ravine. Although a few incidents of gassings . had taken place in the fall of 1941, the truly murderous drive emerged only after the United States entered the war, and most likely after Hitler took the decision to exterminate all of Europe's Jews. At the Wannsee Conference on 20 January 1942 this decision was transformed into a Europe-wide plan, which Himmler set in motion during the summer of 1942, issuing an order stipulating that the lion's share of extermination would be completed before the year's end.

Beginning in the spring of 1942 the exterminations proceeded at an almost frenetic pace, culminating in the gassing of some 275,000 Hungarian Jews in the massive gas chambers at Auschwitz in the summer of 1944. By that date those who were "unfit to work" were gassed upon their arrival at camp, whereas the SS Main Economic and Administration Office (Hauptamt Verwaltung und Wirtschaft, or WVHA), in charge of the immense network of camps that by then covered the entire eastern portion of Europe, had innovated a form of extermination-by-work as a tool for economically useful murder. Indeed extermination-by-work condemned the majority of the detainees who peopled the vast concentration camp universe to a slow but certain death, situating it at the crux of the Nazi policies of economic predatory behavior and repression in Europe, henceforth carried out in all directions.

The extermination of the Hungarian Jews took place in 1944 even though the Reich's fortunes had taken a definitive turn for the worse: by the fall of 1944 the Soviets had annihilated the German Heeresgruppe Mitte (Army Group Center) in a massive encirclement maneuver around Minsk, liberating nearly all of central Europe. With the SS at the forefront, the Germans mounted their final defense, as desperate as it was fierce. The SS therefore was the final holdout in the Battle of Berlin, but was not composed of the Nordic avant-garde, since from 1942 it had begun to integrate Ukrainian, Baltic, and western European contingents, and it was the French SS that defended the chancellor's bunker until the morning of 2 May 1945.

Himmler was captured by the British in the Flensburg region and committed suicide several days later. The top rung of SS officials, including the RSHA and WVHA in particular, were condemned to death and executed, with the notable exception of the authorities responsible for the population displacement policies. The organization itself was outlawed during the Nuremberg War Crimes Trials.

The SS was an elite organization entrusted with safeguarding the monstrous dystopian dimension of Nazism, not only because it represented the ideals of Nordic racial purification and the policies of Germanizing the occupied territories, but also because it spearheaded programs for exterminating undesirable populations. Mass murder constituted, from the Nazi viewpoint, the condition sine qua non for the realization of their utopia. In this sense the SS was not merely the executor of the Nazi Party's murderous plans, it was the quintessence of Nazism itself.

See also **Babi Yar; Concentration Camps; Einsatzgruppen; Heydrich, Reinhard; Himmler, Heinrich; Holocaust; Nazism.**

BIBLIOGRAPHY

Kohel, Robert Lewis. *The Black Corps: The Structure and Power Struggles of the Nazi SS.* Madison, Wis., 1983.

Wegner, Bernd. *Hilter Politische Soldaten: Die Waffen SS 1933–1945.* Paderborn, Germany, 1982.

CHRISTIAN INGRAO

STAKHANOVITES. *Stakhanovite* was the term applied to Soviet workers and peasants who set production records or otherwise demonstrated mastery of their assigned tasks. The term was derived from the name of one Alexei Stakhanov, a thirty-year-old miner in the Donets Basin, who on 31 August 1935 mined 102 tons of coal in a six-hour shift, an amount representing fourteen times his quota. Within a few days Stakhanov's feat was hailed by *Pravda* as a world record. The Stakhanovite movement was launched by the Communist Party in a spirit of technological nationalism and to intensify pressure on managers and workers alike to raise labor productivity. Initially, it was characterized by the setting of production records first in coal mining and then in other industries—automobile production, shoe manufacturing, textiles, and so forth. Workers who met or exceeded their work quotas previously had been known as "shock workers" (*udarniki*); with the implementation of the Stakhanovite movement, the title of Stakhanovite quickly superseded that of shock worker. The campaign culminated in an All-Union Conference of Stakhanovites in industry and transportation, which met in the Kremlin in late November 1935. Here, the most celebrated Stakhanovites recounted how they managed to overcome the skepticism of fellow workers and supervisors in pioneering new methods of production and achieving amazing results. Amazing too were their monetary and in-kind rewards. Joseph Stalin captured the optimism of the conference when, by way of explaining how such records were only possible in the "land of socialism," he uttered the phrase that would become the movement's motto, "Life has become better, and happier too."

In quantitative terms, the Stakhanovite movement seems to have been most widespread in the extractive industries, power generation, and railroad transportation, where upward of 40 percent of all workers were designated as Stakhanovites by August 1936. Young male workers who had passed technical training courses, were classified as at least semiskilled, and had an average of three to five years experience were overrepresented among Stakhanovites. However, what was characteristic in industry was not the case in agriculture, where, among collective and state farm workers who were Stakhanovites, the most prominent were women, such as the tractor-driving Pasha Angelina and the sugar-beet cultivator Maria Demchenko.

The Stakhanovite movement provided lessons not only on how to work but also on how to live. Many of the same attributes Stakhanovites were supposed to exhibit on the shop floor—neatness, punctuality, preparedness, and a keenness for learning—they were also expected to show outside of work hours. Stakhanovites in this way came to exemplify the New Soviet Man or Woman, and the quality of being cultured (*kulturnost*). The wives of male Stakhanovites also had an important role in this scenario by preparing nutritious meals, ensuring that their husbands got plenty of rest, and otherwise creating a cultured evvironment in the home. The publicity surrounding Stakhanovites' domestic lives—replete with objects such as phonograph records, motorcycles, and even automobiles—was intended to convey the message that the Soviet Union would be a society of abundance in the future.

Quite a few Stakhanovites received special educational training, followed by promotion into the ranks of management; others were sent on tours of work sites, where they demonstrated their skills. Some served as models for artists' renderings of the quintessentially socialist-realist worker, and in the case of the textile weaver Maria Vinogradova, for the heroine in the film *The Radiant Path*, a musical comedy from 1940.

Stakhanovites were portrayed as being admired by their workmates, yet this was not necessarily true. Even before output norms were raised in early 1936, workers who had not been favored with the best conditions and who consequently had to struggle to fulfill their norms expressed resentment of Stakhanovites through verbal and sometimes physical abuse. Foremen and engineers, only too well aware that a craze for setting records and the provision of special conditions for Stakhanovites created disruptions in production and bottlenecks in supplies, also on occasion "sabotaged" the movement. Or at least, when the Stakhanovite movement failed to unleash the productive forces of the country as promised, sabotage was blamed.

Thus, in an indirect way, the Stakhanovite movement fed the Great Terror of 1936–1938. However, the inertia of the movement carried it into World War II when workers who took over the jobs of inductees were celebrated. The movement even enjoyed something of a revival in the years after the war, when it was exported to Eastern Europe.

See also **Communism; Socialist Realism; Soviet Union; Stalin, Joseph.**

BIBLIOGRAPHY

Labour in the Land of Socialism: Stakhanovites in Conference. Moscow, 1936.

Siegelbaum, Lewis H. *Stakhanovism and the Politics of Productivity in the USSR, 1935–1941.* New York, 1988.

LEWIS H. SIEGELBAUM

STALIN, JOSEPH (Iosif Vissarionovich Dzhugashvili; 1878–1953), Soviet leader.

Born in the Georgian town of Gori, Joseph Stalin (Iosif Dzhugashvili) rose from humble beginnings as the son of a shoemaker to become one of the most powerful men in the world at the time of his death. His dissolute father, Bessarion Dzhugashvili, and his religious mother, Yekaterina (Keke) Geladze, fought over their son's education, and the mother ultimately triumphed, sending the boy to a religious seminary. But after reaching the cosmopolitan city of Tiflis (Tbilisi), young Joseph (Soso) turned away from the church toward Marxism and a career as a professional revolutionary. Somewhat romantic as a youth—he wrote nationalist poetry in his native Georgian language—Soso Dzhugashvili identified with the hero of a Georgian novella named Koba and went by that name among his closest friends and comrades. As a member of the Marxist Social Democratic Party, he organized workers in the port town of Batumi, but his impetuous nature led to a reckless strike that ended with the police killing protestors. Arrested and sent into exile to Siberia, Dzhugashvili gravitated toward the more militant wing of the party, the Bolsheviks, and thereby broke with most of his fellow Georgian revolutionaries, who preferred the more moderate Mensheviks.

Moving on to the oil-producing center at Baku, Dzhugashvili engaged in underground party work rather than the open labor movement. Taking the name "Stalin," from the Russian word *stal* (steel), he met the Bolshevik leader Vladimir Lenin, whom he likened to a "mountain eagle." Lenin commissioned Stalin to write a pamphlet on the problem of non-Russian peoples in the Russian Empire, the so-called national question, and in 1913 he published his first major work, *Marxism and the National Question,* thus earning a reputation as an expert on that issue.

After stints in prison and several escapes, Stalin was liberated by the revolution of February 1917. He returned to the Russian capital, Petrograd (formerly St. Petersburg), and soon became a leading figure in the Bolshevik Party. At first his positions on key issues of the day were more moderate than Lenin's, but Stalin soon readjusted his views to conform to the party line. After the Bolshevik seizure of power in October 1917, Stalin was named people's commissar of nationalities, responsible for the policies of the new Soviet state toward the non-Russians. While he was active on the southern front along the Volga River, Stalin's rivalry with the head of the Red Army, Leon Trotsky, contributed to the growing fractures in the party. Just before a stroke incapacitated him in March 1923, Lenin fought with Stalin over the formation of the new Soviet Union. Lenin preferred a genuine federation with some autonomy left for the non-Russian republics, but Stalin pressed for a more centralized state with greater power in Moscow. Lenin was furious with Stalin and wrote to his comrades:

> Comrade Stalin, having become Secretary General, has unlimited authority concentrated in his hands, and I am not sure whether he will always be capable of using that authority with sufficient caution. … Stalin is too rude, and this defect, though quite tolerable in our midst and in dealings among us Communists, becomes intolerable in a General Secretary. That is why I suggest that the comrades think of a way to remove Stalin from that post and appoint in his place another man who in all respects differs from Comrade Stalin in his superiority, that is, more loyal, more courteous and more considerate of the comrades, less capricious, etc. (Lenin, vol. 45, p. 346; author's translation)

Lenin's comrades did not heed his warning, and most of them paid with their lives a decade and a half later.

THE ACCUMULATION OF POWER

Even before Lenin died, Stalin had accumulated enormous power within the party, and though he was not generally recognized outside party circles as one of the most influential leaders, his authority grew steadily. Within the party, political manipulation, Machiavellian intrigues, and a willingness to resort to ruthlessness were certainly part of Stalin's repertoire, but he also managed to position himself in the immediately post-Lenin years as a pragmatic and cautious man of the center, a person who supported the compromises and concessions of Lenin's moderate, state capitalist New Economic Policy (NEP) and was unwilling to risk Soviet power to pursue elusive revolutions abroad. Like other high party leaders, he took on a wide range of assignments—from people's commissar of nationalities (1917–1923) and people's commissar of state control (from 1919) and worker-peasant inspection (1920–1922) to membership in the Military-Revolutionary Council of the Republic, the Politburo (the Political Bureau, the highest party council), and the Orgburo (Organizational Bureau, in charge of party workers), to political commissar of various fronts in the civil war and participant in a variety of commissions set up to solve specific problems. In what at the time seemed to many to be a trivial appointment, the Eleventh Party Congress in the spring of 1922 elected Stalin a member of the party secretariat with the title "general secretary."

By the time of Lenin's incapacitation in 1923, Stalin was fast becoming indispensable to many powerful figures. He combined with his political allies Grigory Zinoviev and Lev Kamenev to prevent the growth of Leon Trotsky's influence. On the eve of Politburo meetings, this troika would meet, at first in Zinoviev's apartment and later in Stalin's Central Committee office, to decide what positions they would take on specific issues and what roles each would play in the meeting. In 1924–1925 the group was expanded to seven, with the additions of Nikolai Bukharin, Alexsei Rykov, Mikhail Tomsky, and Valerian Kuibyshev. Power within the party steadily moved upward to the very institutions in which Stalin played key roles. He was the only person who was a member of all of the important committees. With his complete dominance over the Orgburo, Stalin was able to use this institution to make appointments throughout the party and to work out his own policies. He built up his own staff, which soon amounted to a personal chancellery. Despite his suspicious nature and his intellectual limitations (certainly exaggerated by political rivals and opponents), Stalin was able to attract a number of loyal subordinates, whose fortunes would rise with him.

Stalin was a master politician, able to win over supporters while disarming his enemies. Not only did he control the machinery of the Communist Party, appointing loyalists to various positions around the country, but he also positioned himself as a loyal follower of the revered Lenin, despite his principled disagreements with the leader. On 21 January 1924 Lenin died, and immediately a cult developed around his memory. The city of Petrograd was renamed Leningrad and, against the wishes of his widow, the party ordered Lenin's body mummified and placed in a marble mausoleum in Red Square, like a religious relic to be viewed by the faithful. In April and May Stalin gave a series of lectures at Sverdlov University that were soon published as *Foundations of Leninism,* wrapping himself in the mantle of Lenin. More than any past service, association with the dead Lenin gave a political leader legitimacy and authority in the post-Lenin years. In the new political environment in which loyalty to Lenin was the touchstone of political orthodoxy, Stalin, who had seldom differed openly with Lenin, flourished, while Trotsky, whose prerevolutionary writings had often polemicized against Lenin, withered.

The sphere of political decision making had steadily narrowed since 1917—from the open brawls among political parties and between state and society to the internal factional fights within the Communist Party and finally to the bureaucratic intrigues of a few powerful men at the very top of the party. The growth of bureaucracy within the party and state aided a man like Stalin who controlled appointments and patronage. Almost unnoticed, Stalin accumulated enormous power through the 1920s. Trotsky protested the bureaucratization of the party, but as a latecomer to the party he remained isolated among the Bolsheviks.

In 1924 Stalin and his close comrade Nikolai Bukharin adopted a moderate course, favoring the concessions to the peasantry that Lenin had inaugurated in 1921 with the New Economic Policy. But Bukharin's pro-peasant policies went further than other Leninist stalwarts, like Zinoviev and Kamenev, thought appropriate for a proletarian dictatorship. Stalin proclaimed that the Communists would build "socialism in one country," even though Lenin had always maintained that socialism could not be achieved in backward peasant Russia alone but required support from an international revolution in more developed, industrial countries. When Zinoviev and Kamenev balked at his cautious policies and the growing bureaucratization of the party, Stalin broke with them and formed a new bloc with Bukharin.

The NEP combined state control of heavy industry with a modified market system for agricultural products and consumer goods. The program restored the Soviet economy, which had been devastated by seven years of world war, revolution, and civil war. But when peasants found that the state prices for their grain were low, or industrial goods were scarce and high priced, they withheld their grain in anticipation of higher prices in the future. While some leaders saw this peasant hoarding as rational market activity, others like Stalin conceived of their actions as sabotage, a "grain strike." Bukharin advocated continuing the NEP, but as the moderate pro-peasant policy faltered at the end of the 1920s, Stalin broke with Bukharin and launched his own radical restructuring of the Soviet economy and society.

THE STALIN REVOLUTION AND THE GREAT PURGES

The years 1928–1932 have been dubbed the "Stalin revolution" or the "revolution from above," a five-year period of massive violence against the countryside and state-driven industrialization. The party/state forced the millions of peasants into collective farms, seized their grain without adequate compensation, and exiled or killed the most productive peasants, the so-called kulaks. Peasants did not go quietly into collectives but resisted, and armed clashes broke out with the Communist organizers. Overzealous grain collectors left many farmers without food or grain, and in Ukraine some five million people perished in a

Joseph Stalin (right) with Vladimir Lenin, August 1922.
©Hulton-Deutsch Collection/Corbis

powers. "One feature of the history of old Russia," he said,

> was the continual beatings she suffered because of her backwardness. She was beaten by the Mongol khans. She was beaten by the Turkish beys. She was beaten by the Swedish feudal lords. She was beaten by the Polish and Lithuanian gentry. She was beaten by the British and French capitalists. She was beaten by the Japanese barons. All beat her—because of her backwardness, because of her military backwardness, cultural backwardness, agricultural backwardness. . . . Such is the law of the exploiters—to beat the backward and the weak. It is the law of capitalism. . . . That is why we must no longer lag behind. (*Pravda*, February 5, 1931; author's translation)

By linking forced-pace economic development to national security, Stalin construed any hesitation or foot-dragging as "wrecking" or treason, crimes with heavy penalties. When the headlong rush to industrialization generated waste or breakdowns, rather than blaming the policy or the leaders, the police "uncovered" conspiracies or saboteurs. Contrived show trials imposed harsh sentences on innocent people.

In a few short years the Soviet government had initiated a massive transformation of society and the economy, founding the first modern nonmarket, state-run economy. Yet the Stalin revolution destroyed the regime's fragile relationship with the great majority of the population and created a new repressive apparatus that Stalin could use to consolidate his personal rule over the party and state. Stalin's rise was unexpected by most of his fellow Communists. He had little charisma, possessed no oratorical skills like Zinoviev, was neither a Marxist theorist like Trotsky nor a likeable comrade like Bukharin. Short in stature and reticent in meetings, Stalin did not project an image of a leader—until it was created for him (and by him) through the "personality cult." For his closest associates, however, Stalin was indispensable, the solid center of the bureaucratic state and party apparatus, a generous patron, and a stern master. He turned the revolution inward, emphasizing the building of a strong state and an industrial economy and playing down international revolution. His ideology was a radically revised Marxism that grafted onto it a pro-Russian nationalism and a great-power statism. As long as the country was surrounded by hostile capitalist states, it was claimed, state

famine that was directly caused by misguided state policies. When the regime itself seemed threatened by peasant rebellion, Stalin called a halt to the headlong rush into collectivization. In an article published in March 1930, "Dizzy from Success," he announced that "the basic turn of the village to socialism may be considered already secured." For a while collectivization was delayed, but the peasants' joy was short-lived, and a less frenetic campaign resumed. Hundreds of thousands of peasants fled to industrial sites; mammoth plants, dams, and towns were built; the number of workers swelled; and ordinary men and women, hastily educated, rose into the managerial and administrative ranks.

Stalinist industrialization had its own unique characteristics, its own language, slogans, strategies, and costs. It was carried out as a massive military campaign, along "fronts," scaling heights, conquering the steppe, and vanquishing backwardness, all while being encircled by capitalism. All obstacles, natural and technical, were to be overcome. Stalin spoke of human will as the essential force to achieve the economic plan, proclaiming that "there are no fortresses Bolsheviks cannot capture!" For him the need to industrialize rapidly was connected with the dangers that the USSR faced from the great capitalist and imperialist power had to be built up. When Stalin declared the Soviet Union to be socialist in 1936, the positive achievement of reaching a stage of history higher than the rest of the world was tempered by the constant reminders that the enemies of socialism existed both within and outside the country, that they were deceptive and concealed, and had to be "unmasked." Repeated references to dangers and insecurity and to the need for "vigilance" justified the enormous reliance on the secret police.

Stalin turned a political oligarchy into a personal dictatorship by the late 1930s. But as he rose to the pinnacle of power in the USSR, he became increasingly isolated. He narrowed his circle of friends and close comrades to those most loyal to him: his sometime prime minister and foreign minister Vyacheslav Molotov, the industrializer Sergo Orjonikidze, the economically savvy Anastas Mikoyan, the policeman and executioner Lavrenty Beria, and those loyal party workers ready to do his bidding—Lazar Kaganovich, Georgy Malenkov, Andrei Zhdanov, and Nikita Khrushchev. Suspicious even of these men, Stalin's personal life withered, especially after his young wife, Nadezhda Alliluyeva, killed herself in November 1932. Outside of his work, late-night dinners with his cronies, and the little time he spent with his daughter, Svetlana, Stalin had no personal life. His suspicions of others matched their fear of him.

Stalin can be considered a "conservative revolutionary." Earlier, more radical tendencies in Bolshevism were shelved: instead of equalization of wages, Stalin promoted greater differentials between skilled and unskilled workers; instead of attacking "Great Russian chauvinism," Stalin encouraged a new form of Soviet patriotism based on reverence for Russia's imperial past. Peter the Great, even Ivan the Terrible, became models of rulership. Stalin provided for a new Soviet middle class with its own "bourgeois values." Exemplary workers were rewarded with scarce consumer goods, like bicycles and wristwatches, while the wives of managers promoted a new form of cultural behavior and etiquette. Instead of greater political participation by working people, the characteristics of Stalinism were increased state power; the use of police terror to discipline the population; a state monopoly over mass media, culture, and education; the promotion of simple workers into positions of power and influence; and emotional campaigns, initiated from above, stirring up popular enthusiasm for the "building of socialism."

The height of Stalinist terror was reached in the Great Purges of 1937–1938, when approximately seven hundred thousand people were executed and millions more were exiled, imprisoned, or died in labor camps. Among the victims were thousands of Communists, including Lenin's closest associates—Zinoviev, Kamenev, and Bukharin. Angry and upset at the turn that Soviet policy under Stalin had taken, Orjonikidze shot himself. By the end of the 1930s 3,593,000 people were under the jurisdiction of the secret police, 1,360,000 of whom were in labor camps. Stalin personally initiated, guided, and prodded the arrests, as well as the show trials of 1936–1938, and he required his lieutenants to sign off on executions. The bloodletting defies rational explanation. Here personality and politics merged, and this excessive repression appears to be dictated by the peculiar demands of Stalin himself, who could not tolerate limits on his will set by the very ruling elite that he had brought to power. The purges eliminated all rivals and potential rivals to Stalin's autocracy and produced a new, younger, Soviet-educated political elite loyal to and dependent on the master. By 1938 the killings had so destabilized government and society that the regime gradually brought them to a halt, but the long arm of Stalin's police reached to Mexico, where in 1940 a secret agent murdered his rival Trotsky. Particularly devastating for the country on the eve of war was the decimation of the highest ranks of the military.

WORLD WAR II

By the outbreak of World War II the central government, the military, the republics and local governments, and the economic infrastructure had all been brutally disciplined. Obedience and conformity had eliminated most initiative and originality. After destroying the high command of the armed forces, Stalin's control over his military was greater than Hitler over his, at least at the beginning of the war. His control over politics was so complete that he was able to reverse completely the USSR's "collective security" foreign policy that favored allying with Western capitalist democracies against the fascist states and sign a nonaggression pact with Nazi Germany in August 1939.

Yet for all the human and material costs of Stalin's industrialization and state building, the Soviet Union was not prepared for the onslaught of the German invasion of June 1941. Stalin did not expect Hitler to attack before subduing Britain, and he was stunned when informed that German troops had crossed the border. Rallying himself and his countrymen to the colossal effort against the Nazis and their allies, Stalin stood at the center of all strategic, logistical, and political decisions. He was chairman of the State Defense Committee, which included the highest party officials (Molotov, Beria, Malenkov, Kliment Voroshilov, Lazar Kaganovich, and later Nikolai Voznesensky and Mikoyan); chairman of Stavka, the supreme military headquarters; general secretary of the party and chairman of the Politburo; chairman of the Council of Ministers and people's commissar of defense. Real business often took place in late-night meetings at Stalin's apartment or dacha (country house), where he attended to the most minute details of the war effort. Stalin was extraordinarily brutal in dealing with his commanders.

Like Hitler, Stalin made major miscalculations early in the war. In anticipation of the German invasion, the Soviet General Staff in September 1940 had argued that the Nazi attack would be concentrated in the center toward Moscow and in the north toward Leningrad, but Stalin overruled his commanders and ordered deployment in the south, believing that the Germans would make a major effort to capture Ukraine. When the German army surrounded five Soviet armies on the southwestern front, Stalin's generals urged withdrawal, but Stalin refused to give up the Ukrainian capital, Kiev. On 19 September 1941 Kiev fell, and the Germans captured over half a million prisoners and annihilated the Soviet southwestern front. But when in October 1941 the Germans approached Moscow and many Muscovites panicked and fled the city, Stalin demonstrably stayed in Moscow and encouraged the resistance with a speech blending the heroic military traditions of the Russian Empire with the cause of Lenin and the Soviet Union. Ultimately the war was won by the tenacity and enormous sacrifice of the Soviet people, but Stalin provided both inspiration for

Joseph Stalin (left) shakes hands with German foreign minister Joachim von Ribbentrop during their meeting to finalize the August 1939 nonaggression pact. ©HULTON-DEUTSCH COLLECTION/CORBIS

many and fear that one step backward would end in death. In time Stalin proved to be more willing to rely on his generals, as long as they did not question his ultimate authority.

During the war years Western governments feted Stalin, and journalists lionized him in the press. An American film, *Mission to Moscow* (1943), presented audiences with an avuncular, wise Stalin, complete with mischievous smile and an ever present pipe. For his part Stalin moderated the image of the USSR to attract the West. In 1943 he dissolved the Communist International (Comintern), the union of Communist parties founded by Lenin. He made overtures to religious leaders and eased Soviet policy toward the churches. Commissariats became ministries, and the Soviet anthem, the revolutionary *Internationale*, was replaced by a nationalist hymn to the Soviet Union that celebrated the role of historic Russia. Yet the infamous murder of captured Polish officers in the Katyn forest, along with the general secretiveness of the Kremlin, only fed Western suspicions of Stalin.

The Soviets bore the heaviest burdens of the war against fascism and lost some twenty-seven million people, but in the end they could take pride that they were the major force that thwarted Hitler's imperial ambitions. The triumph over fascism provided the Communists with a new source of legitimation and Stalin with a new, uncontested authority. Now Russia and the Soviet Union were melded into a single image. Patriotism and accommodation with established religious and national traditions, along with the toning down of revolutionary radicalism, contributed to a powerful ideological amalgam that outlasted Stalin himself. In the postwar decades the war became the central moment of Soviet history, eclipsing the revolution and the Stalin revolution of the early 1930s.

THE POSTWAR PERIOD

Stalin's postwar policies were repressive at home and expansive abroad. There were sporadic uses of repression and terror against individuals or groups (the "Leningrad Affair" of 1948, the "Doctors' Plot" of 1953), as well as a series of ethnic deportations of peoples from newly annexed territories (the Baltic republics, western Ukraine, and Byelorussia) and repatriations of Armenians, Kurds, Meskhetian Turks, and others, but no massive terror on the scale of 1937 was employed after the war. Intellectuals suffered from the cultural crackdown known as the *Zhdanovshchina*, and a campaign against "cosmopolitanism" was directed against Soviet Jews. In dealing with his former allies during the Cold War, Stalin attempted to maintain the grand alliance with the Western great powers while at the same time holding onto a sphere of influence in Eastern and Central Europe where he could impose "friendly" governments. Western leaders like President Harry S. Truman and the British prime minister Winston Churchill refused to acquiesce in the expansion of Soviet influence over Poland, Czechoslovakia, Hungary, Romania, and Bulgaria, and the cooperation of the war years disintegrated into two camps, each armed with atomic weapons.

In his last years, enfeebled by strokes, Stalin was arguably the most powerful man in the world.

He controlled not only the USSR and much of Eastern Europe but also was deferred to by the Communist leaders of China, North Korea, and Vietnam. In 1950 he agreed that the Korean leader Kim Il Sung could invade South Korea, thus opening the way to the Korean War. As he deteriorated physically and mentally, the entire country—its foreign policy, internal politics, cultural life, and economic slowdown—reflected the moods of its leader and was affected by his growing isolation, arbitrariness, and inactivity. No one could feel secure. The ruling elite was concerned with plots, intrigues, the rivalries among Stalin's closest associates, and the rise and fall of clients and patrons. "All of us around Stalin," wrote Khrushchev, "were temporary people. As long as he trusted us to a certain degree, we were allowed to go on living and working. But the moment he stopped trusting you, Stalin would start to scrutinize you until the cup of his distrust overflowed." In his last years Stalin turned against Molotov and Mikoyan, grew suspicious of Beria, Voroshilov, Kaganovich, and Malenkov. Khrushchev overheard him say, "I'm finished. I trust no one, not even myself." He died of a massive stroke on 5 March 1953.

Stalin's legacy was a powerful state with a crudely industrialized economy, a country in which millions had died to build his idea of socialism and other millions to defend their country against the enemies of communism. Almost immediately after his death, his successors began to dismantle many of the pillars of Stalinism. They ended the mass terror, closed down the slave-labor camps, introduced a degree of "socialist legality," and opened the country to the West. In 1956 Khrushchev denounced Stalin's crimes, and eventually Stalin's body was removed from its place of honor in Lenin's mausoleum.

See also **Bolshevism; Bukharin, Nikolai; Collectivization; Destalinization; Gulag; Hitler, Adolf; Khrushchev, Nikita; Lenin, Vladimir; Molotov-Von Ribbentrop Pact; Mussolini, Benito; New Economic Policy (NEP); Purges; Soviet Union; Stakhanovites; Terror; Trotsky, Leon; Zhdanov, Andrei.**

BIBLIOGRAPHY

Primary Sources

Getty, J. Arch, and Oleg V. Naumov, eds. *The Road to Terror: Stalin and the Self-Destruction of the*

Bolsheviks, 1932–1939. Translated by Benjamin Sher. New Haven, Conn., 1999. A collection of documents on the Stalin Terror and the Great Purges.

Siegelbaum, Lewis, and Andrei Sokolov. *Stalinism as a Way of Life: A Narrative in Documents.* Translated by Thomas Hoisington and Steven Shabad. New Haven, Conn., 2000. A collection of Soviet archival documents with insightful commentary on social life in Stalin's USSR.

Stalin, Joseph. *Works.* 13 vols. Moscow, 1952. The basic collection of Stalin's writings.

Secondary Sources

Fitzpatrick, Sheila. *Stalin's Peasants: Resistance and Survival in the Russian Village after Collectivization.* Oxford, U.K., 1994. An extraordinary social-historical study of peasants and their strategies in the wake of collectivization.

———. *Everyday Stalinism: Ordinary Life in Extraordinary Times: Soviet Russia in the 1930s.* Oxford, U.K., 1999. A sensitive reconstruction of life in Soviet towns and cities during Stalinism's first decade.

Fitzpatrick, Sheila, ed. *Stalinism: New Directions.* London and New York, 2000. A collection of essays using the archival materials available after the disintegration of the USSR.

Gorlizki, Yoram, and Oleg Khlevniuk. *Cold Peace: Stalin and the Soviet Ruling Circle, 1945–1953.* Oxford, U.K., 2004. An archivally based account of the inner workings of Stalin's postwar government.

Holloway, David. *Stalin and the Bomb: The Soviet Union and Atomic Energy, 1939–1956.* New Haven, Conn., and London, 1994. A brilliant reconstruction of Stalin's foreign policy in the early atomic age.

Kershaw, Ian, and Moshe Lewin, eds. *Stalinism and Nazism: Dictatorships in Comparison.* Cambridge, U.K., 1997. Exercises in comparative history.

Lenin, Vladimir. *Polnoe sobranie sochinenii.* 5th ed. Moscow, 1958–1965.

Lewin, Moshe. *The Making of the Soviet System: Essays in the Social History of Interwar Russia.* New York, 1985. A classic social history of Stalin's transformation of Soviet society and economy.

Montefiore, Simon Sebag. *Stalin: The Court of the Red Tsar.* London, 2003.

Service, Robert. *Stalin, A Biography.* Cambridge, Mass., 2005.

Suny, Ronald Grigor. "Beyond Psychohistory: The Young Stalin in Georgia." *Slavic Review* 50 (spring 1991): 48–58. An exploration of Stalin's early life that contests the psychoanalytic approach to biography.

Suny, Ronald Grigor, and Terry Martin, eds. *A State of Nations: Empire and Nation-Making in the Age of*

Lenin and Stalin. New York, 2001. A collection of essays on the construction of nations in interwar USSR.

Tucker, Robert C. *Stalin as Revolutionary, 1879–1929: A Study in History and Personality.* New York, 1973. A psychoanalytical biography of the young Stalin.

Tucker, Robert C. *Stalin in Power: The Revolution from Above, 1928–1941.* New York, 1990. The story of Stalin's revolution retold.

RONALD GRIGOR SUNY

STALINGRAD, BATTLE OF. A series of defensive and offensive operations from 7 July 1942 to 2 February 1943, the Battle of Stalingrad produced a hard-won Soviet victory and marked a turning point in World War II on the eastern front. Fought in and around the city (present-day Volgograd) on the Volga that bore Joseph Stalin's name, the confrontation at Stalingrad evoked memories both of the savagery at Verdun in 1916 and of the Prussian encirclement of the French at Sedan in 1870.

The circumstances that produced Stalingrad flowed from imperfect execution of Operation Blau, a German strategic offensive that was intended to win for Adolf Hitler the oil-rich Caucasus by the fall of 1942. However, the offensive suffered from delay, inadequate forces and resources, overextended logistics, and clumsy command arrangements. Although the Soviets were initially uncertain over the location of the Wehrmacht's main blow, by the summer of 1942 they had learned to give ground while punishing the Germans and mobilizing a steady procession of new formations. Meanwhile, as the Germans revealed their design for 1942 by doggedly advancing south, they exposed a long and vulnerable left flank, the security of which rested on control of the Don River bend near Stalingrad. As the Soviet high command rushed reinforcements to the city, Hitler, grasping its industrial and namesake significance, directed General Friedrich Paulus's reinforced German Sixth Army to secure this new objective, thereby perhaps fatally dividing the entire German strategic effort.

Beginning in July with hard fighting across the land bridge between the Don and Volga, Paulus

Soviet soldiers fire from the shelter of a ruined building during the battle of Stalingrad, January 1943. ©BETTMANN/
CORBIS

reached the outskirts of Stalingrad by early September. However, the Soviets had by now strengthened the city's defenses, with the tenacious General V. I. Chuikov commanding its main force, the Soviet Sixty-second Army. Almost simultaneously, the Soviet high command began planning for a counteroffensive, Operation Uranus, the objective of which was to encircle and destroy the German Sixth Army even as it bled itself dry inside the city.

Meanwhile, as both sides threw additional assets directly into the urban fray, the battle for the city soon assumed a particularly vicious form of close-quarters combat. Intense fighting swirled everywhere above and below ground, producing heavy losses among attackers and defenders. At one point, it was even remarked that the city's dogs swam across the Volga to escape the torment. Although Paulus had originally assumed that Stalingrad might fall in late September, by mid-November his Sixth Army was running short of manpower, ammunition, and supplies. Two months of incessant urban combat had left it exhausted and several hundred meters short of the Volga. Soviet commanders, meanwhile, continued to press often raw troops off Volga ferryboats into battle, only to watch them virtually evaporate in the maelstrom.

It was at this point, on 19 November 1942, with Soviet defenders barely clinging to the industrial sprawl along the Volga, that General A. M. Vasilevsky, representative of Stavka (headquarters of the supreme high command) launched Operation Uranus. With pincers from the north (the southwest and Don fronts) and south (the Stalingrad front) of Stalingrad, Soviet armored and mechanized formations easily broke through Romanian forces on the Sixth Army's soft flanks to link up near Kalach on the Don, encircling Paulus. Subsequent and complementary Soviet offensives (Mars south of Leningrad and Saturn and Little Saturn in the middle and upper Don) proved overly ambitious, but did exact losses and divert German attention and reserves from the encirclement at Stalingrad. However, the situation there remained in doubt until late December, because Paulus arguably retained sufficient combat power to fight his way out, especially in the event of timely assistance from Field Marshal Erich von Manstein's newly formed Army Group Don. However, Hitler ordered Paulus to hold at all costs, while Reichsmarschall Hermann Goering unrealistically vowed that his Luftwaffe might resupply Paulus from the air. Meanwhile, Manstein's effort to open a corridor to Stalingrad failed on 24 December, fifty kilometers short of the objective. Until the complete surrender of now Field Marshal Paulus's forces on 2 February 1943, the Soviets continued to conduct two sets of subsidiary offensive operations, one to reduce the cauldron at Stalingrad itself, the other to reinforce the outer ring of the encirclement, with an eye to exploitation that Manstein's skill largely foiled.

Losses on both sides were substantial. Paulus surrendered some 91,000 troops, while losing another 150,000 in combat for Stalingrad. Later Soviet and Russian estimates would place Hitler's total casualties for the entire campaign at 1.5 million, or approximately one-fourth of Germany's combat manpower on the eastern front. Post-1991 Russian figures place Soviet casualties at slightly more than a million, including 480,000 dead or missing.

The historiography on Stalingrad is voluminous, ranging from the reminiscences of survivors to various official histories in search of either explanation, lessons learned, or national military justification. Some blame the dictators for all the mistakes and bloodletting, while others emphasize the impact of the battle on national psyches, while still others focus on the purely military aspects that revealed a Wehrmacht and its blitzkrieg clearly on the wane and a Red Army and its deep battle operations just coming into its own. Within larger strategic content, Stalingrad ended any prospect that Hitler might consider the eastern front as an economy-of-force effort. In Soviet perspective, the battle indicated that Stalin might place growing confidence in his seasoned commanders and their increasingly resilient and capable military formations. Although the Nazi propaganda machine attempted to put the best sacrificial face on the battle's outcome, the German advance to Stalingrad gradually came to represent the high water mark of an increasingly futile effort to subjugate Stalin's Soviet Union. For the Soviets, meanwhile, Stalingrad won its own place alongside two other prominent "hero cities," Moscow and Leningrad, to symbolize tenacious defense of the motherland.

See also **Soviet Union; World War II.**

BIBLIOGRAPHY

Beevor, Antony. *Stalingrad*. London, 1998.

Chuikov, V. I. *The Battle for Stalingrad*. New York, 1964.

Erickson, John. *The Road to Stalingrad*. New York, 1975.

———. *The Road to Berlin*. Boulder, Colo., 1983.

Glantz, David M., and Jonathan M. House. *When Titans Clashed: How the Red Army Stopped Hitler*. Lawrence, Kans., 1995.

Rotundo, Louis C., ed. *Battle for Stalingrad: The 1943 Soviet General Staff Study*. Washington, D.C., 1989.

Ziemke, Earl F., and Magna E. Bauer. *Moscow to Stalingrad: Decision in the East*. Washington, D.C., 1987.

BRUCE W. MENNING

STANISLAVSKY, KONSTANTIN

(pseudonym of Konstantin Alekseyev; 1863–1938), Russian director, actor, and author.

Konstantin Sergeyevich Stanislavsky was a director, actor, and author whose founding of the Moscow Art Theatre and writings about the actor's craft established him as one of the most influential theater artists of the twentieth century. He was the son of a prominent industrialist in whose factory he worked after quitting school in 1881. At age fourteen, in 1877, he began organizing amateur theatricals. In 1888 he helped to launch an amateur group in Moscow, the Society of Art and Literature, where he became an accomplished actor and debuted as a director in 1889 with Pyotr Gnedich's (1855–1925) *Burning Letters*. The German Meiningen company, whose highly realistic, historically accurate performances Stanislavsky saw in Moscow in 1885 and 1890, was a major influence on his artistic development. He was inspired by the troupe's ability to express the spiritual essence of the plays it performed.

In a legendary encounter, Stanislavsky met with playwright Vladimir Nemirovich-Danchenko (1858–1943) at the Slavyansky Bazaar restaurant in Moscow on 22 June 1897 to discuss the state of Russian theater, which they believed was divorced from real life and burdened by histrionics. The company that emerged from this meeting, originally the Moscow Art Accessible Theatre, later the Moscow Art Theatre, debuted in Moscow on 14 October 1898 with an elaborate performance of Alexei Tolstoy's (1817–1875) historical chronicle *Tsar Fyodor Ioannovich*. Five more productions followed in six weeks. The seventh, Anton Chekhov's (1860–1904) *The Seagull* (17 December 1898), established the theater as Russia's most progressive venue. Chekhov famously was irritated by the meticulous realism incorporated by Stanislavsky, who codirected with Nemirovich-Danchenko and played the role of Trigorin, but Chekhov, Stanislavsky, and the Art Theatre forever remained linked in people's minds. Chekhov wrote *Three Sisters* (1901) and *The Cherry Orchard* (1904) specifically for the Art Theatre.

Emboldened by his success with Chekhov, Stanislavsky (with Nemirovich-Danchenko or others) staged plays by other famous contemporaries. In 1902 he directed Leo Tolstoy's (1828–1910) *The Power of Darkness* and Maxim Gorky's (Alexei Peshkov, 1868–1936) *The Petty Bourgeoisie* and *The Lower Depths*. These plays signaled Stanislavsky's desire to create a theater of social conscience. The popularity of *The Lower Depths*, performed 1,788 times, indicated the Russian public was ready for this kind of art. But Stanislavsky wished to experiment with many styles and in 1913 he created the First Studio for this purpose. Throughout the 1910s he staged fewer productions at the Art Theatre but worked on theories that eventually developed into his books about acting and gave rise to what became known as the Stanislavsky system of acting.

Following the Russian Revolution in 1917, Stanislavsky and the Moscow Art Theatre entered a crisis, producing no new shows until 1920. This changed when a three-month tour of Berlin, Zagreb, Prague, and Paris in 1922 turned into a fifteen-month traveling residence in the United States lasting to May 1924. Europeans and Americans were astonished by the exquisite detail of the direction, the lifelike manner of the actors, and the care with which writers' themes were revealed. The fascination of Americans with Stanislavsky's work encouraged him to write his ideas down. The English translation of his first book on acting (*An Actor Prepares,* 1936) appeared before the first Russian edition (1938). Other translations were published in German and Dutch in 1940, in Japanese in 1949, and in Italian in 1956.

Stanislavsky's ideas—he never considered them a precise system or regarded himself as a theorist—had an enormous impact worldwide. His notions of "emotional memory" (also known as "affective memory"), "experiencing," and "through action," to name a few, provided vague but valuable tools for actors, allowing them to harness personal experience in the creation of disparate roles. The Group Theatre, an influential New York ensemble founded in 1931, was openly modeled after Stanislavsky's theater. At the Actors Studio in New York, Lee Strasberg (1901–1982) became the leading proponent of "method acting," the American version of the so-called Stanislavsky system.

By the late 1920s Stanislavsky was officially canonized as a figure for Soviet theater artists to emulate. He thus avoided the persecution that affected many of his colleagues but was left to work in an uneasy atmosphere of protected isolation. Aided by various directors, he supervised several important productions, including Mikhail Bulgakov's (1891–1940) *Days of the Turbins* (1926), Beaumarchais's (Pierre-Augustin Caron, 1732–1799) *The Marriage of Figaro* (1927), Vsevolod Ivanov's (1895–1963) *Armored Train 14–69* (1927), and Nikolai Gogol's (1809–1852) *Dead Souls* (1932). Hampered after 1928 by a bad heart and increasingly at odds with Nemirovich-Danchenko, Stanislavsky devoted much of his time to studio experiments in the nature of acting. His pupils included some of the greatest figures of twentieth-century theater, including Vsevolod Meyerhold (1874–1940), Yevgeny Vakhtangov (1883–1922), and Mikhail (Michael) Chekhov (1891–1955), whose influence as an actor and teacher in Europe and Hollywood from the 1930s to the 1950s expanded Stanislavsky's fame abroad.

See also **Gorky, Maxim; Russia; Soviet Union; Theater.**

BIBLIOGRAPHY

Primary Sources

Stanislavsky, Konstantin. *My Life in Art.* Translated by J. J. Robbins. Boston, 1924.

———. *An Actor Prepares.* Translated by Elizabeth Reynolds Hapgood. New York, 1936.

———. *Building a Character.* Translated by Elizabeth Reynolds Hapgood. New York, 1949.

———. *Creating a Role.* Translated by Elizabeth Reynolds Hapgood. New York, 1961.

Secondary Sources

Carnicke, Sharon M. *Stanislavsky in Focus.* Amsterdam, 1998.

Merlin, Bella. *Konstantin Stanislavsky.* New York, 2003.

Strasberg, Lee. *A Dream of Passion: The Development of The Method.* Boston, 1987. See pp. 36–62.

JOHN FREEDMAN

STASI

STASI. East Germany's intelligence and security service, known as "the Stasi," was formally titled the Ministry for State Security (Ministerium für Staatsicherheit or MfS). Set up in 1950, it was dissolved, prior to German unity, in 1989–1990.

The Stasi was a highly professional secret service, perhaps the best in the Soviet bloc. Its spiritual father was Vladimir Lenin (1870–1924), who held that terror and violence against real and potential opponents could underpin the state power won by communists in 1917 and accordingly, created the Cheka (the Soviet secret police) in that same year. Following the establishment of a Soviet zone of occupation in the eastern part of Germany in 1945, the imposition of communism there became a major priority. The Red Army and Soviet secret police began the task but after the formation of the East German state in October 1949 it became a German activity. The Stasi quite openly dedicated itself to core Chekist principles of "aggression through conspiracy." The MfS's one thousand officers (some from a Nazi background) assumed the role of "the executive organ of the dictatorship of the proletariat" articulated through the East German Communist Party (the Socialist Unity Party or SED). The fusion between the Stasi and the SED was so effective that the question of who controlled whom was never raised. The Stasi was the backbone of the party, ending up one and a half times the size of the East German army. It doubled in size between 1972 and 1989, increasing its numbers by about three thousand each year. By 1989 the service consisted of more than 90,000 official personnel and as many as 150,000 to 170,000 agents, known as IMs or "co-opted workers." It comprised both a security service and a secret foreign intelligence service called the HVA (Hauptverwaltung Aufklärung), which was the largest single unit within the Stasi, working almost exclusively in the West. It had 3,819 officers, led until 1986 by Markus Wolf (b. 1923).

The Stasi's size and its huge financial assets (most of which were never recovered) provide some clues as to the extent of the repression it sustained. In the German Democratic Republic, there was one officer to 188 inhabitants. If the IMs are added to the officers, the result is astonishing: one Stasi member for every seventy people. At the height of Joseph Stalin's terror in the 1930s, there was one Soviet secret police officer to every 5,830 inhabitants—eighty-three times fewer than Stasi members per head of population. Some two million individuals, almost 12 percent of the East German population, had collaborated with the Stasi.

At home the Stasi attacked and persecuted all internal opposition to communism, often displaying great cruelty and sadism. Over the years, sheer brute force was usually replaced by psychological intimidation but repression remained the goal. From 1945 until 1989 some two hundred thousand Germans died either directly or indirectly as a result of communist policies, most deaths occurring before 1949. Even so, from 1950 to 1989 some 250,000 people were imprisoned, of whom 10 percent perished. This was the Stasi's work. Almost three million East Germans fled to the West to escape the police state. Those who resisted but stayed showed enviable courage. Ultimately, they vanquished the Stasi.

Abroad, the MfS sought secrets about the West's military and political strategy. It also supported international terror by training terrorists, particularly from the Middle East. West Germany and the United States were the primary targets of Stasi subversion. The former was riddled with thirty thousand spies who manipulated politics, foreign affairs, the media, academe, and sport. But the Stasi targeted all of Western Europe in its attempts to spy on, and steer, organizations and individuals whose activities involved them with domestic dissidents. Frequently it won as assets sympathetic left-wing Western intellectuals who regarded East Germany as "progressive" (and turned a blind eye to its abuses). The Stasi, always wholly within the KGB's orbit, increasingly became its surrogate, with some 50 percent of its intelligence going to the Soviet Union

The "ministry" called itself, and it *was*, "the sword and the shield of East German communism." Its militancy drove its readiness to fight its own people and its unquenchable thirst for secret intelligence. Historians agree that the Stasi made East Germany a real-life example of British writer

George Orwell's fictional totalitarian state of *1984,* able to exploit the most pervasive and efficient secret police in the history of the world. What remains in the early twenty-first century are 178 kilometers of its files—and the trauma of its persistent inhumanity toward Germans in the East.

See also **Berlin; Eastern Bloc; Espionage/Spies; Germany; Soviet Union.**

BIBLIOGRAPHY

Gauck, Joachim, with Margarethe Steinhausen and Hubertus Knabe. *Die Stasi-Akten: Das Unheimliche Erbe der DDR.* Reinbek, Germany, 1992.

Glees, Anthony. *The Stasi Files: East Germany's Secret Operations against Britain.* New York and London, 2003.

Grieder, Peter. *The East German Leadership 1946–1973—Conflict and Crisis.* Manchester, U.K., 1999.

Knabe, Hubertus. *West-Arbeit des MfS: Das Zusammenspiel von "Aufklärung und Abwehr."* Berlin, 1999.

McAdams, A. James. *Judging the Past in Unified Germany.* Cambridge, U.K., 2001.

Naimark, Norman M. *The Russians in Germany: A History of the Soviet Zone of Occupation, 1945–1949.* Cambridge Mass., and London, 1995.

ANTHONY GLEES

STAUFFENBERG, CLAUS VON

(1907–1944), German soldier and conspirator in the plot to assassinate Adolf Hitler.

The leading figure in the failed plot to assassinate Adolf Hitler on 20 July 1944, Stauffenberg was then a thirty-six-year-old career officer who had risen to the rank of colonel. He was raised in an aristocratic Catholic family, and one of his ancestors, August von Gneisenau, was a legendary leader in the Prussian struggle against Napoleon. A century later, Claus von Stauffenberg gave his life to rid Germany of Hitler and his tyranny.

He was a very unlikely revolutionary and assassin. Raised to take on the aristocratic calling of serving his country, Claus joined his family's Seventeenth Cavalry Regiment in 1926 and followed the conventional path toward military leadership others in his family had forged. Hitler's ascent to power in 1933 and restoration of German national pride were initially attractive to Stauffenberg, but the glow of the early days of the regime wore off quickly. In September 1934 he walked out of an anti-Semitic party lecture to which his men were obliged to go. By 1938 and the *Kristallnacht,* the first organized nationwide pogrom against Jews in Germany, Stauffenberg registered his disgust at the vulgarity and stupidity of the regime and its cruelties. His cousin Count Helmuth James von Moltke drew a number of those hostile to the regime together in the Kreisau circle, named after his estate, in which they debated the future of Germany after the Nazi regime had gone.

In 1936 Stauffenberg had graduated first in his class from the Army Staff College and had been promoted to the rank of captain. With the rest of his regiment, he joined the Sixth Panzer Division, which occupied the Sudentenland in 1939. He served in Poland and France during the first two years of the war.

Transferred to North Africa, Stauffenberg, now a colonel, was severely wounded in early 1943. He lost his left eye, his right hand, and the fourth and fifth fingers of his left hand. After his convalescence he was posted to the reserve army in Berlin, from which vantage point he began actively to plan the murder of Hitler and the overthrow of the regime.

Stauffenberg knew his fellow conspirators well. They represented the Germany he loved and for which he was prepared to lay down his life. His attitude toward the regime could not be doubted. It stood for everything he detested, as a soldier and as a Catholic. But armed resistance was another matter. Like every other officer in the German army, Stauffenberg had taken a personal oath to Hitler. By 1944 he was ready to strike. But in order to decapitate the regime, he and his fellow officers in the resistance had to offer the German army an alternative—a set of prominent officers who would seize power in Berlin after the death of Hitler. Stauffenberg was in an ideal place to do that, since one of his military responsibilities was to fashion an emergency plan in the event of a break in communication between Berlin and the high command.

The plotters set their plan in motion in July 1944, when the war was already lost. On 20 July in

Hitler's military headquarters in Rastenburg in East Prussia, Stauffenberg placed an attaché case with an explosive charge in the room where Hitler and two dozen staff officers and aides were surveying the military situation. The case was moved slightly away from Hitler, and when it exploded, he survived. Eleven men were wounded, of whom four were killed. Stauffenberg had made his escape and returned to Berlin to gather military units to seize power. He initially thought that Hitler was dead, but the failure of co-conspirators to cut the radio lines from Rastenburg allowed Hitler to broadcast to the nation, making his survival both undeniable and fatal to the plot. Stauffenberg continued to try to rally support, but it was futile to do so. He was arrested after a brief exchange of fire and, after a summary court-martial, shot by firing squad.

What sort of Germany did he envision after the overthrow of Hitler? There are indications that Stauffenberg saw the force of a social democratic approach to the future of Germany. But his cast of mind bore all the traces of his aristocratic and military bearing and background. He was a leader on horseback with a bomb in his damaged hand, a man of Christian conscience whose sense of a calling brought him to try to strike the blow that would kill Hitler and his circle and thereby end Germany's (and the world's) nightmare. His failure is less significant than the courage and dignity of the attempt.

See also **Germany; July 20th Plot.**

BIBLIOGRAPHY

Baigent, Michael, and Richard Leigh. *Secret Germany: Claus von Stauffenberg and the Mystical Crusade against Hitler.* London, 1994.

Bentzien, Hans. *Claus Schenk Graf von Stauffenberg: Zwischen Soldateneid und Tyrannenmord.* Hannover, 1997.

Hoffmann, Peter. *Stauffenberg: A Family History, 1905–1944.* 2nd ed. Ithaca, N.Y., 2003.

Kramarz, Joachim. *Stauffenberg, the Architect of the Famous July 20th Conspiracy to Assassinate Hitler.* Translated by R. H. Barry. Introduction by H. R. Trevor-Roper. New York, 1967.

Venohr, Wolfgang. *Stauffenberg: Symbol der deutschen Einheit: Eine politische Biographie.* Frankfurt, 1986.

Zeller, Eberhard. *Oberst Claus Graf Stauffenberg: Ein Lebensbild.* Paderborn, Germany, 1994.

JAY WINTER

STAVISKY AFFAIR.

In 1934 a resounding scandal shook the already-contested regime of interwar France, the Third Republic, to its foundations. The Stavisky affair combined the financial scams of a swindler and his accomplices, the weaknesses and susceptibilities of government regulators and elected representatives, the perversion of a free press, and a violent explosion of popular anger that assumed the seditious form of an antiparliamentary riot. The Republic survived. But by how much? And how corrupt a regime did the scandal reveal?

Serge Stavisky (1886–1934), known as "Sacha" or "handsome Serge," was a Ukrainian Jew who arrived in France at the age of three. Nothing in his background or upbringing predisposed him to a life of crime; he grew up in comfortable surroundings and attended one of the Republic's best secondary schools. But by early adulthood he had migrated forever into a marginal milieu of theft, counterfeiting, and confidence games. A stint in prison from 1926 to 1927 left him with an enduring terror of confinement and a determination just as enduring to protect himself from the vengeance of the law by a carapace of personal connections.

Stavisky wove his web of influence assiduously, placing generals and ambassadors on the boards of shaky corporations and insinuating himself by virtue of their goodwill and his own charm into the company of naive and impecunious politicians. Sometimes he retained deputies from the Chamber as legal counsel, granting them handsome honoraria; sometimes he enlisted the support of ministers by wheeling out his hard-won friends from the lesser daily newspapers and the scandal sheets of a chronically indigent press; and sometimes he discouraged the attentions of the law through his ostensible celebrity. Few asked him questions about the source of his riches.

His house of cards finally collapsed on Christmas Eve 1933, when Treasury Department officials uncovered an elaborate system of forged savings bonds that Stavisky had orchestrated behind the innocuous facade of a Basque country bank, the Crédit Municipal de Bayonne. The revelation, coupled with the fleeing swindler's death in a chalet in the Alps as police closed in, set off a scandal that quickly engulfed the country's representative institutions, its free press, its judiciary, and its police. Stavisky, the outcry went, had corrupted the deputies, the magistrates, the journalists; he had purchased influence and immunity; he had paid, in the end, with his life for knowing too much and too many. In fact, he had compromised perhaps six deputies and senators, and then mostly by retaining their legal services; had delayed rather than subverted the hand of justice; had bought a few friends only in the lesser press; and had committed suicide rather than face the renewed prospect of a lonely incarceration. But few wished to believe such mundane truths, and from their incredulity sprang scandal.

The most strident outcry came from the far right, from the xenophobic and anti-Semitic newspapers *Action Française* and *Je Suis Partout,* but also from veterans organizations such as the Croix de Feu and from a less incendiary right wing that deplored the weaknesses of the parliamentary regime and yearned for a strong executive branch. The affair did not so much create as intensify such yearnings, but the varied laments at the lost victory of World War I, economic stagnation, and diplomatic impotence made for a powerful mix that finally exploded on the night of 6 February 1934, after six weeks of almost daily headlines about Sacha Stavisky and his accomplices. A violent antiparliamentary riot on and around the Place de la Concorde left 15 dead and 1,435 wounded. For the only time in the history of the Third Republic, sedition forced out a sitting government, that of the Radical Édouard Daladier.

So strong was the belief in the "Republic of cronies," as Robert de Jouvenel had called it in his pamphlet of 1914, that when a magistrate who had once investigated Stavisky, Albert Prince, was found dead the following month on the railroad tracks near Dijon, the cry of murder rang out again. He too had committed suicide. But his death relaunched the affair, which finally petered out in the longest trial in French history, the prosecution of twenty of Stavisky's accomplices, in the winter of 1935–1936.

Stavisky had revealed a gray world of influence rather than a black one of corruption, but in the deteriorating climate of the 1930s fancy trumped fact and invective drove out discussion. When Léon Blum formed his Popular Front government in 1936, he endured some of the calumny that the affair had injected into the body politic. Later, Vichy propaganda resurrected the swindler's memory to poison that of the defunct regime. The Third Republic had not been perfect. But it had never been as vile as Stavisky had briefly and unwittingly allowed its enemies to paint it.

See also **Daladier, Édouard; France.**

BIBLIOGRAPHY

Charlier, Jean-Michel, and Marcel Montarron. *Stavisky: Les secrets du scandale.* Paris, 1974.

Garçon, Maurice. *Histoire de la justice sous la Troisième République.* 3 vols. Paris, 1957.

Jankowski, Paul F. *Stavisky: A Confidence Man in the Republic of Virtue.* Ithaca, N.Y., 2002.

Jeanneney, Jean-Noël. *L'argent caché. Milieux d'affaires et pouvoirs politiques dans la France au XXe siècle.* Paris, 1982.

PAUL JANKOWSKI

STEIN, GERTRUDE (1874–1946), American writer.

The life of Gertrude Stein, author of the famous "A rose is a rose is a rose," is indissociable from that of Alice B. Toklas (1877–1967) and from Paris, where she and Toklas lived for a large part of her life. As a couple, the two women were for many years the rallying point for American intellectuals and artists in Paris, and they were in all respects intermediaries between French and North American culture. They were also each other's foremost biographers and observers. Gertrude Stein's masterpiece is falsely titled *The Autobiography of Alice B. Toklas* (1933), and the latter published her memories of Stein thirty years later in *What Is Remembered.* These works are also mutual declarations of love, even though the erotic dimension of their relationship is carefully dissimulated in them.

Gertrude Stein came from an upper-middle-class Jewish family on the East Coast. In 1893, after spending her childhood and adolescence in France and Austria, and in Baltimore, Oakland, and San Francisco, she entered Radcliffe College (then known as Harvard Annex), where she studied

Gertrude Stein arriving in New York, 1935. ©BETTMANN/
CORBIS

psychology. She published her first article in a psychology journal. She enrolled in medical school but failed her exams in 1901. In 1903 she wrote her first book, *Q.E.D.* (the story of a homosexual love triangle between three young women, finished in 1903 and published in 1950 under the title *The Things as They Are*). The following year she went to Paris to join her brother Leo, with whom she was very close, at 27, rue de Fleurus, which very quickly became a meeting place for the toast of literary and artistic Paris. As one of the first buyers of modern French painters of the era, notably Henri Matisse (1869–1954) and Pablo Picasso (1881–1973)— she posed for him in 1906—she contributed to their renown in France and across the Atlantic. She completed two other books in Paris before the war: *Three Lives* (portraits of three women, finished in 1906 and published in 1909) and *The Making of Americans* (a 925-page panorama, finished in 1911 and published in 1925).

In 1912 her first texts were published in Alfred Stieglitz's journal *Camera Work*. Fittingly, they were dedicated to Picasso and Matisse. Shortly before the war she quarreled with her brother and left the apartment. In 1914 she published *Tender Buttons,* her most famous collection of poems.

When the war broke out the two women initially left Paris, then returned and in 1916 joined the war effort via the American Fund for the French Wounded. In an automobile imported from the United States they toured hospitals to bring aid to the wounded. The start of the war was also when the "Lost Generation"—in Gertrude Stein's own expression—of literary Americans settled in France, often in contempt for their country of origin. It was thus in Paris that Gertrude Stein met the writers Ernest Hemingway, F. Scott Fitzgerald, and Thornton Wilder. Hemingway, moreover, recalls her in the second chapter of *A Moveable Feast* (1964). In 1922 she published *Geography and Plays,* a collection of dramatic works, prose pieces, and poetry.

In 1933 success finally came with *The Autobiography of Alice B. Toklas.* The following year, she made a triumphant lecture tour of the United States. During the Second World War, the two women took refuge in the hamlet of Bilignin in the district of Belley in the department of the Ain, where they were protected by neighbors and friends who concealed the women's Jewish background. Evicted from their house, they experienced some difficult years and were forced to sell part of their collection of paintings. They returned to Paris in 1944 and recovered the rest of the collection intact. They subsequently intervened on behalf of Bernard Faÿ, a homosexual friend whom they had met in 1926, and who had been condemned for collaboration; he had also no doubt protected them during the war and was Gertrude Stein's French translator. Gertrude Stein died of colon cancer in 1946.

A guiding force and emblematic figure for feminist and homosexual demands, Gertrude Stein brought her way of life to the fore simply by living it. She also figured as a cultural mediator between the United States and France and played a leading role in cultural exchanges between the two continents. She willingly embraced this role, which stemmed from her love of France, throughout her life.

See also Paris; Picasso, Pablo; Toklas, Alice B.

BIBLIOGRAPHY

Primary Sources

Stein, Gertrude. *Writings.* 2 vols. New York, 1998.

Toklas, Alice B. *What Is Remembered.* New York, 1963.

Secondary Sources

Hobhouse, Janet. *Everybody Who Was Anybody: A Biography of Gertrude Stein.* London, 1975.

Hoffman, Michael J. *Gertrude Stein.* Boston, 1976.

Mellow, James R. *Charmed Circle: Gertrude Stein and Company.* New York, 1974.

Sutherland, Donald. *Gertrude Stein: A Biography of Her Work.* New Haven, Conn., 1951.

"tenderbuttons: gertrude stein online." Available at http://www.tenderbuttons.com.

NICOLAS BEAUPRÉ

STRAUSS, RICHARD (1864–1949), German composer and conductor.

The long life and career of Richard Georg Strauss spanned Germany's formal unification and post–World War II division, its accelerated industrialization and urbanization, and two world wars. He began composing as a child, showing extraordinary promise, and wrote his last compositions in 1948. His oeuvre was distinguished by a flexible style in which the form of each work was unique and often generated by extramusical ideas; dissonance was used liberally and freely; melodies were released from the strictures of predetermined phrase lengths; and instrumental techniques were extended to depict an array of extramusical sounds.

In 1889, when Strauss was only twenty-five, critical and audience response to his tone poem (a symphonic work structured according to a literary program) *Don Juan* catapulted him to national recognition as the premier German composer of his time and established his credentials internationally as a musical modernist. He continued to write tone poems steadily, premiering six more over the next fourteen years. All of them remain in today's orchestral repertory, although they were often the objects of controversy in their time because of their subject matter (for example, Strauss as antihero),

overwrought pictorial techniques, or jarring dissonances and abrupt shifts in tonality.

After the turn of the century, Strauss became renowned as an operatic composer with the 1905 premiere of *Salome,* which caused an international sensation. This highly chromatic, compact, one-act opera was based on Oscar Wilde's play, a stylized, decadent work that focused on the princess Salome's sexual obsession with her stepfather's prisoner, John the Baptist. *Elektra,* a highly dissonant one-act tragedy, followed in 1909. Based on the play by Hugo von Hofmannsthal (1874–1929), *Elektra* marked the beginning of a fruitful collaboration between them, in which Hofmannsthal served as Strauss's librettist until Hofmannsthal died. Strauss was never to return to the dissonance, jagged vocal lines, atonal passages, and extreme orchestral effects of these two operas. His next opera, *Der Rosenkavalier* (The cavalier of the rose), which premiered in 1911, was a bittersweet comedy set in eighteenth-century Vienna that, in the view of many commentators, marked a retreat to the lushness, elegant melodies, and orchestral beauty seen more often in the nineteenth century. *Rosenkavalier* was nevertheless his most popular opera and remains so in the early twenty-first century. Ten more operas followed, and his final opera, *Capriccio,* was completed in 1941.

Strauss was also one of Germany's most important conductors, holding positions in Munich, Weimar, Berlin, and Vienna and appearing as guest conductor in numerous venues throughout Europe. His fame led to his appointment as director of the Reichsmusikkammer (National Music Chamber) under the National Socialists (1933–1935), a position that he was forced to resign after authorities intercepted a letter in which he criticized the treatment of his librettist at the time, the Jewish author Stefan Zweig. The extent of Strauss's involvement with the National Socialist government remains unclear to this day, although most scholars agree that Strauss never held strong allegiances to any political movement or regime.

Strauss's career has provoked scholarly controversy for both musical and political reasons. After *Elektra,* contemporaries and commentators through most of the twentieth century (most notably Theodor Adorno) thought that he failed to fulfill his promise as a modernist because he never embraced the move to atonality, and later composition based on twelve tones, that was promoted by other composers of his era such as Arnold Schoenberg, Alban Berg, and Anton Webern.

Since the 1990s, however, scholars and critics have offered a revised and expanded assessment of Strauss that began essentially with two major collections of scholarly essays edited by Bryan Gilliam, published in 1992. Studies have been produced on such topics as the relationship between German literary modernism and Strauss's musical style; the influences of Arthur Schopenhauer and Friedrich Nietzsche on Strauss's work; and detailed musical analyses of his operas, tone poems, and art songs. Especially noteworthy is Leon Botstein's reassessment (in Gilliam, *Richard Strauss and His World*) of Strauss's post-*Elektra* musical style as a precursor to postmodernism, with its use of parody, irony, and the juxtaposition of musically and dramatically disparate elements in such operas as *Ariadne auf Naxos* (1911–1912; revised 1916) and *Rosenkavalier*. In addition, whereas Strauss's role in Germany's National Socialist government had been deemphasized in earlier twentieth-century writings, work by such commentators as Pamela Potter (in Gilliam, *Richard Strauss: New Perpectives*) and Matthew Boyden has brought to light a number of details about Strauss's involvement with the Nazis and his motivations for accepting the position of director of the Reichsmusikkammer.

See also **Adorno, Theodor; Berg, Alban; Germany; Schoenberg, Arnold.**

BIBLIOGRAPHY

Adorno, Theodor W. "Richard Strauss: Born June 11, 1864." Translated by Samuel Weber and Shierry Weber. *Perspectives of New Music* 4, no. 1–2 (1965–1966): 14–32, 113–129.

Ashley, Tim. *Richard Strauss.* London, 1999.

Boyden, Matthew. *Richard Strauss.* Boston, 1999.

Del Mar, Norman. *Richard Strauss, a Critical Commentary on His Life and Works.* 3 vols. Ithaca, N.Y., 1986.

Gilliam, Bryan. *Richard Strauss and His World.* Princeton, N.J., 1992.

———. *Richard Strauss: New Perspectives on the Composer and His Work, Sources of Music and Their Interpretation.* Durham, N.C., 1992.

———. *The Life of Richard Strauss.* Cambridge, U.K., 1999.

Kennedy, Michael. *Richard Strauss: Man, Musician, Enigma.* Cambridge, U.K., 1999.

Schmid, Mark-Daniel, ed. *The Richard Strauss Companion.* Westport, Conn., 2003.

Schuh, Willi. *Richard Strauss: A Chronicle of the Early Years, 1864–1898.* Translated by Mary Whittall. Cambridge, U.K., 1982.

Wilhelm, Kurt. *Richard Strauss: An Intimate Portrait.* Translated by Mary Whittall. New York, 2000.

SUZANNE M. LODATO

STRAVINSKY, IGOR (1882–1971, Russian composer.

Igor Stravinsky was one of the most cosmopolitan Russian artists of the twentieth century. Born into a family of opera singers, he started studying music at the age of twenty. He spent the first thirty years of his life in tsarist Russia. In 1910 he moved to Europe, settling in Paris in 1914. In 1939, as the Nazi army was advancing on France, he moved to the United States. He become a U.S. citizen in 1945; until that time he had been considered a stateless person.

Stravinsky's musical heritage encompasses different eras, places, musical forms, and genres, constituting a virtual encyclopedia of world classical music. His first ballets, performed in Paris by the Russian Seasons company before Russia's October Revolution, explored his country's pre-Christian past (*The Rite of Spring*, 1913) and folk culture (*Petrushka*, 1911; *Firebird*, 1910). His choreographic cantata *The Wedding* (1923) was based on Russian folk poetry. In it the composer created an original style that advanced music one step beyond the work of his teacher Nikolay Rimsky-Korsakov and that of two titans of nineteenth-century music, Modest Mussorgsky (who embraced nationalism) and Peter Tchaikovsky (who was cosmopolitan in his outlook). Everyday urban music was reflected in his ballet pantomime *Histoire du Soldat* (1918; *A Soldier's Story*), which merged the archaic and the contemporary. Stravinsky established a new type of performance that influenced twentieth-century theater art, creating, in effect, the multimedia show: singing elements in ballet, the reader's participation in symphonies, and so on.

Igor Stravinsky conducting, December 1958. ©HULTON-DEUTSCH COLLECTION/CORBIS

During his European period, he continued working on ballet. Having been separated from his native soil, Russian influences started to wane. His singing ballet *Pulcinella* (1920) marked a transition to seventeenth- and eighteenth-century neoclassicist forms. His total break with the militantly atheist Bolshevik Russia led him to embrace biblical texts and ancient Greek mythology. His vocal music also drew its inspiration from Latin texts. Some of the best works of this period are the opera-oratorio *Oedipus Rex* (1927), *Symphony of Psalms* (1930), two other symphonies, and a violin concerto (1931).

The years in the New World brought out different facets of his talent, thanks to his use of the modernist technique of dodecaphony, twelve-tone music in which all notes are treated as equal. Stravinsky's thematic range became increasingly religious and profoundly contemplative. This tendency began with *Mass* (1948), the cantata

Canticum sacrum (1955), and *Requiem Canticles* (1966).

Stravinsky left an impressive collection of writings: *Themes and Episodes* (1966), *Dialogues and a Diary* (1963), *Expositions and Developments* (1962), *Memories and Commentaries* (1960), *Conversations with Igor Stravinsky* (1959), and *Themes and Conclusions* (1972), all written in cooperation with his advisor and confidant Robert Craft. This need for verbal self-expression began with the publication of his *Chronicle of My Life* (Paris, 1935).

Although Stravinsky was not involved in politics and did not write politically engaged works like his Soviet contemporaries (Sergei Prokofiev and Dmitri Shostakovich), he advocated artistic freedom, expressed his abhorrence of censorship, and hailed the recognition of human rights. His life and work, together with those of fellow Russian émigré writer Vladimir Nabokov and the painter Marc Chagall, showed what artists might have produced had not the October Revolution unleashed the Great Terror, the reign of censorship and intimidation, and ultimately the liquidation of the Russian intelligentsia as a class.

Stravinsky's work was progressively criticized, censored, and banned in his native country. It was only with Nikita Khrushchev's Thaw and destalinization policy that orchestras and musicians were slowly allowed to reintegrate some of Stravinsky's works, primarily those of his Russian period, into their repertoires. The religious, mythical, and so-called decadent and modernist works were still not performed or recorded.

In 1962, marking his eightieth birthday, Stravinsky for the first and last time returned to Soviet Russia. He was not granted the stature of other great Russian and Soviet composers, however. The stigma of being an emigrant and non-Soviet artist always remained. Nevertheless, even during the years of the Cold War and the confrontation between East and West, his work, like that of Shostakovich on the other side of the Iron Curtain, formed a bridge between two worlds and became an unrivaled twentieth-century cross-cultural experience.

After the collapse of the communist regime in the USSR, Stravinsky's work was widely performed and academic and archival publications, along with conferences and seminars on his life and work, proliferated. His widow, Vera Stravinsky, and Robert Craft published an in-depth album commemorating the hundredth anniversary of his birth, and Craft later published selections from Stravinsky's correspondence with his wife.

In the early twenty-first century, his music was being played less than it had been during his lifetime. That was a reflection of a trend aimed at conclusively understanding the tragic experiences of the twentieth century, marred by the Holocaust, the gulag, two world wars, and cultural revolutions. In this search for understanding, audience preferences sometimes shifted toward content in the arts at the expense of form. Thus the public preferred to listen to the music of Prokofiev, and above all Shostakovich.

See also **Chagall, Marc; Prokofiev, Sergei; Shostakovich, Dmitri.**

BIBLIOGRAPHY

Primary Sources

Stravinsky, Igor. *Chronicle of My Life*. Translated from the French. London, 1936.

Stravinsky, Igor, and Robert Craft. *Memories and Commentaries*. London, 2002.

Secondary Sources

Craft, Robert. *Stravinsky: Glimpses of a Life*. London, 1992.

———. *Stravinsky. Chronicle of a Friendship*. Rev. and expanded ed. Nashville, Tenn., 1994.

Stravinsky, Vera, and Robert Craft. *Stravinsky in Pictures and Documents*. New York, 1978.

Taruskin, Richard. *Stravinsky and the Russian Traditions: A Biography of the Works through Mavra*. 2 vols. Berkeley, Calif., 1996.

Leonid Maximenkov

STRESEMANN, GUSTAV (1878–1929),
German chancellor (1923) and foreign minister (1923–1929).

Gustav Stresemann was the most important German statesman of the Weimar period. In recognition for his contribution to the stabilization of postwar Europe, he was awarded, along with his French counterpart Aristide Briand, the Nobel Peace Prize in 1926.

The son of a Berlin publican and neighborhood beer distributor, Stresemann grew up in modest circumstances and was the only member of his family to receive a university education. He wrote his doctoral dissertation on the Berlin beer business, analyzing its transformation into a modern industry by the emergence of big bottling companies. For the rest of his life, he retained a soft spot for old-fashioned craftwork and the interests of small-scale producers. In 1903 he joined the National Liberal Party, fully embracing that group's advocacy of a strong German Empire. He pushed for the creation of a high seas fleet and backed the pan-German aspirations of the German Colonial League. At the same time, however, his championship of social welfare legislation antagonized those of his National Liberal colleagues who opposed governmental interference in the prerogatives of big business. Attacks against him by the right wing of the National Liberal Party in the imperial period anticipated the challenges he would face in the Weimar era from unreconstructed nationalists.

In 1907, at age twenty-eight, Stresemann became the youngest member in the Reichstag (parliament). Like most Germans of the educated middle class, he greeted the outbreak of war in 1914 with enthusiasm, and though ill health kept him out of uniform he used his position in the Reichstag to push Germany's ambitious war aims. As an advocate of unrestricted submarine warfare he played a key role in the overthrow of Chancellor Theobald von Bethmann Hollweg, who opposed the use of U-boats against neutral shipping. Confident of German victory almost to the bitter end, Stresemann was appalled by Germany's defeat in 1918.

Stresemann did not become a convert to the new republican order immediately—and the depth of that conversion remained questionable. He opposed the Weimar constitution and profoundly resented the Treaty of Versailles. Nevertheless, with the young republic buffeted by putsch attempts from right and left, political assassinations, and the collapse of the currency, he came to view the new constitutional democracy as the only practical alternative to prolonged chaos. Having helped found the center-right German People's Party in 1920, he became chancellor in August 1923, heading a "grand coalition" embracing his own party, the Social Democratic Party, the Center Party, and the German Democratic Party. Although he held the chancellorship only from 13 August to 23 November 1923, he managed during those turbulent months to end Germany's policy of "passive resistance" to the French occupation of the Ruhr Valley, which was a prerequisite for Germany's economic recovery and a necessary first step toward reconciliation with France. Less laudably, on the domestic front Stresemann adopted a lenient line toward Adolf Hitler's abortive Beer Hall Putsch of November 1923, thereby helping the Nazi leader avoid the career-ending punishment he deserved.

Stresemann is best known for his six-year tenure as German foreign minister. In 1924 he orchestrated Germany's acceptance of the American-sponsored Dawes Plan, which by reorganizing German war reparations payments helped to stabilize the German currency. In 1925 Stresemann helped negotiate the Treaties of Locarno, which confirmed the inviolability of Germany's western borders and the demilitarization of the Rhineland. With respect to Germany's eastern borders with Poland and Czechoslovakia, Stresemann agreed that Berlin would not attempt changes without arbitration, but he did not formally endorse those borders. This caveat reflected Stresemann's, and Germany's, enduring opposition to the eastern settlement. A year after Locarno, Germany joined the League of Nations, a step that Stresemann had actively promoted. The German foreign minister also saw to it that Germany subscribed to the Kellogg-Briand Pact (1928), which outlawed war as an instrument of national policy.

Stresemann, who died in 1929, did not live to see how quickly the peace-and-arbitration edifice he had helped to construct collapsed into rubble. The fragility of his internationalist project constitutes part of the ambiguity of his legacy. Another part derives from the fact that his pursuit of international reconciliation was designed to promote Germany's reemergence as a major European power. Given the primacy of his German nationalism, many historians question whether he can legitimately be considered a forefather of the post–World War II European integrationist project. On the other hand, his understanding that Germany's national revival could be accomplished only within the broader framework of a stable and peaceful Europe certainly anticipated the later ideals of Konrad Adenauer and Helmut Kohl.

See also **Briand, Aristide; Germany; League of Nations.**

BIBLIOGRAPHY

Bessel, Richard. *Germany after the First World War.* Oxford, U.K., 1993.

Grathwol, Robert P. *Stresemann and the DNVP.* Lawrence, Kans., 1980.

Turner, Henry Ashby. *Stresemann and the Politics of the Weimar Republic.* Princeton, N.J., 1963.

Wright, Jonathan. *Gustav Stresemann: Weimar's Greatest Statesman.* Oxford, U.K., 2002.

DAVID CLAY LARGE

STRIKES. Strikes are temporary withdrawals of labor by more than one person. Those striking intend to return to work with better pay and/or improved conditions of work or to have made an emphatic political point. Sometimes employers refuse to permit the return of strikers and in these cases the strike terminates the employment.

In industrial disputes strikes can be a last resort by employees, whether unionized or not. They can also be a bargaining move in collective bargaining, intended to secure a better offer (whether of additional benefits or of less severe reductions). Strikes are but one symptom of dissatisfaction in workplaces, others ranging from sabotage to exit. Strikes occur most often when there is an upturn in the economy and workers are in a relatively strong position in the labor market or when economic conditions are deteriorating and workforces are trying to hold on to existing pay and other conditions of employment.

WORLD WAR I AND THE INTERWAR PERIOD

Except in revolutionary situations, political strikes have usually been short and clearly focused on a major issue. During the First World War demand for key war materials and widespread shortages of food, fuel, and consumer goods led to industrial unrest in some countries and revolution in others. In Russia, in the Vyborg district of Petrograd before the February 1917 revolution metalworkers repeatedly went on strike, and most of the strikes were political. These workers played a crucial role in the overthrow of the tsarist regime. Thereafter, until the Bolshevik Revolution, the numbers of people on strike increased but most demands were economic. However, by September and October 1917 a sizable minority of strikes were intended to express dissatisfaction with private ownership of industry. However, as Diane Koenker and William G. Rosenberg have commented, at that time all strikes in Russia were essentially political: "Regardless of goals . . . the act of striking was itself part of the process of developing political consciousness in 1917" (p. 17). In Germany strikes became increasingly political as the war went on. Dick Geary has written of Berlin that "as early as 1916 food riots could turn into strikes and vice versa" (1993, p. 32). In Leipzig and elsewhere in April 1917 strikers demanded peace, a more democratic electoral system, the ending of censorship and martial law, and the release of political prisoners as well as more pay.

After the end of the First World War political strikes were part of the challenges of labor in a period of economic boom and political uncertainty. In Germany in 1919 a series of armed insurrections and strikes sought to secure a more revolutionary social order. These occurred in Berlin, Bremen, Brunswick, and Cuxhaven in January, in Mannheim in February, in Berlin again in March, and in Munich in April. A general strike in Berlin in 1920 broke the Kapp putsch, a counterrevolutionary attempt to seize power. In Italy "direct action" in September 1920 took the form of occupation strikes in engineering factories in Milan and Turin. These were in response to employers' lockouts. Many of the participants felt that they were preparing the way for major political change.

In the "Red Years" of 1917–1921 the division between political and industrial strikes was often blurred. The sheer volume of disputes and the accompanying revolutionary rhetoric made many strikes appear political, aimed at redistributing wealth and power, and brought a feeling of insecurity to many of the propertied classes.

Organized labor had less chance of success when economies were not in upturns. While German labor had defeated the Right in 1920, in the early 1930s deflation and mass unemployment undercut its ability to take strike action to prevent the Nazis securing power. In Britain the trade union movement was on the defensive during and after the 1921–1922 recession. The Trades Union Congress, the central organization for the unions, called a general strike in May 1926. This was intended to be a solidarity strike in support of coal miners, who were faced with substantial pay reductions and increases in work hours, and to secure a subsidy for the industry from the government. This was not achieved. The strike was called off after nine days, though the coal strike ran on until late in the year. Whereas the average number of days lost in industrial disputes in the United Kingdom in the previous three years had been 9 million, in 1926 the total exceeded 162 million, with the coal dispute accounting for more than 90 percent.

During the boom years of 1915–1920, in many European countries the most strike-prone sectors were those crucial to the war: notably engineering, from armaments to shipbuilding, steel production, and coal mining. In Britain substantial engineering disputes took place in 1915–1917. In 1915, when there was a major coal strike in South Wales, coal accounted for 56 percent of all working days lost in disputes. Bad industrial relations were one reason for state control of the industry, but even after it was controlled, coal disputes accounted for just over 20 percent of all working days lost in 1917 and 1918. In Italy more than 90 percent of working days lost through disputes were in the regions of Lombardy, Piedmont, Liguria, and Compania. During the war Italian strikes were short and sharp. Metalworkers were often militant, and they became prominent in strike statistics in 1918–1920 and 1921–1922. In France trade unionism was weak, but in the face of inflation and war weariness substantial strikes by Renault and other factory workers occurred in Paris as well as in Toulouse and elsewhere in 1917 and 1918. In June 1919 a very militant engineering strike in Paris failed, and after 1920 metalworkers were not prominent again in French disputes until 1936. French industrial militancy suffered a great setback in 1920 with the failure of a major rail strike, which was widened into an unsuccessful general strike.

In most countries the great majority of strikes were not directly politically motivated but related to wages and conditions of work. Some sectors of economies stood out as having notably bad industrial relations. With recovery from the 1931–1933 international recession came an increasing number of strikes in many democratic European countries. In France considerable support for May Day rallies in 1936 was followed by some 1.85 million French workers on strike in June alone. The strikes of 1936 were notable for predominantly being in poorly unionized sectors and led to rapid trade union growth, including among women. The strikers were usually enthusiastic supporters of the Popular Front (a leftist coalition against fascism). Hence the case has been made for seeing these strikes as political. In Spain a wave of strikes in April–June 1936 followed the Popular Front victory. These were aimed at reversing a recent decline in living standards.

WORLD WAR II AND THE POSTWAR PERIOD

For much of the Second World War strikes were a safe possibility only in Britain because much of the rest of Europe was under German occupation. In Britain they were formally illegal (as they had been in the First World War under the Munitions of War Act of 1915) under Order 1305. The loss of days through industrial disputes increased during the war, with wage issues being attributed as the cause for 60 percent of those going on strike during 1940–1944. Strikes were overwhelmingly in coal mining (where 56 percent of days were lost), with engineering (19 percent) and shipbuilding (9 percent) as the next most strike-prone sectors.

After the Second World War strikes were often seen as an obstacle to economic reconstruction and then to competitiveness. In Britain strike levels remained low under the postwar Labour government (1945–1951) and its efforts to boost economic recovery from the war. A one-day engineering strike in 1953 was the first national strike since a 1933 strike in cotton textiles. Thereafter strike waves characterized the periods 1957–1962, 1968–1974, and 1977–1979, much of the unrest being brought about by stagnating or even declining real wages. In the 1957–1962 wave an average of 4,442,000 working days per year were lost; in 1968–1974 the average reached 11,703,000 per year and 16,340,000 in 1977–1979. In the early 1960s wildcat strikes caused considerable political anxiety, leading to the establishment of a Royal Commission (1965–1968) to investigate British industrial relations, while subsequent unrest contributed to the destabilization of two Labour governments (in 1969–1970 and 1979) and a Conservative government (in 1974).

In Britain during this period there was much talk of wildcat strikes, and then strikes generally, being "the English disease" (or British disease) and providing an explanation for the relatively poor performance of Britain's economy compared to those of its major industrial rivals. However, when British strike statistics are compared with those for other industrialized countries the British level of strikes drops as other countries' levels drop and rises as others' levels rise. (Some clear deterioration took place in Britain in 1968–1974, but this was insufficient to change Britain's rank order at a time when there were strikes across Europe.) Hence it

Strikers leave the Renault automobile factory in Paris following their six-day occupation of the facility, which resulted in concessions by owners, June 1936. ©BETTMANN/CORBIS

appears that changes in international economic circumstances affected strike levels in free-market economies, with particular governments and policies having an impact but not as great as is sometimes thought.

In Britain the rise in the days lost through strikes in 1968–1974 was partly due to the politicization of industrial relations, with trade unions holding strikes against the 1971 Industrial Relations Act. In the early 1980s the British level of days lost through strikes remained relatively high because of Prime Minister Margaret Thatcher's confrontations with steelworkers in 1980 and coal miners in 1984–1985. Yet, while the strike statistics dipped in the late 1980s after the government felt it had "tamed the trade unions," so did those for other countries. The 1984–1985 miners' dispute was one of the greatest in British history, with a total of 27,135,000 working days lost in 1984.

While strikes were not a peculiarly British phenomenon, with Australia, Canada, and the United States having higher levels for 1946–1976, Britain had a higher number of days lost through strike action than some of its European competitors. Apart from the early 1980s, Italy and Finland consistently had worse records, as did Ireland until the 1980s and France in the late 1940s and early 1960s. By contrast West Germany, the Netherlands, and Sweden had low numbers of days lost through industrial disputes.

In France there were widespread strikes after the Communist Party (CPF) left the postwar government in May 1947. The Confédération Générale du Travail (CGT) was dominated by the CPF after the liberation and was notably militant. In June 1947 alone, 6,416,000 working days were lost due to strikes over economic issues. In late

1947 a general strike involved up to 3 million workers, with 7,546,000 and 6,967,000 days lost in November and December. In 1948 troops were used during a major coal strike that lasted from 4 October to 29 November, with a lost output of 5.5 million tons of coal. A further wave of strikes came in 1950, aimed at substantial wage increases in the Paris metallurgical industry and others. Communist calls for political strikes in 1952 resulted in some riots but no substantial mass strike. In the 1950s the numbers of days lost through strikes fell markedly from 1947 to 1950, when the annual average was 13,393,000, but rose to a little above the British level in the early 1960s. The most dramatic strikes came in the summer of 1968, alongside mass demonstrations, and shook Charles de Gaulle's government. It seems likely that six to seven million people went on strike in France in May–June 1968.

In Italy in 1947 a communist-backed wave of strikes included a general strike in Rome in December. A national strike followed the attempted assassination of the Communist Party leader Palmiro Togliatti on 14 July 1948, with many factories in the north occupied. Although called off on 16 July, it led to a split in the Confederazione Generale del Lavoro (CGIL). The numerous strikes of the 1950s, such as a major rail strike in January 1953, generally sought higher wages. In September and December 1953 employers were forced to the bargaining table by two national general strikes, followed by strikes in individual industries in early 1954. National collective bargaining in this period helped avoid major national strikes, but dissatisfaction with wages led to a wave of major strikes in 1959 in metallurgical and other industries, followed by a general strike in June–July 1960.

Italy, France, and Britain were all part of Western European strike waves in 1960–1964 (which omitted Belgium) and 1968–1972 (which omitted Austria). The strikes of the early 1960s were associated with labor's demands in a period of full employment, perhaps in response to inflation, while the later strikes may have been responding to anti-inflation measures by governments. Among the most militant workers were the Italians in 1969, as radical factory councils mushroomed. West Germany experienced widespread unofficial strikes in 1969, in contrast to the country's hitherto stable postwar industrial relations (though official strikes had taken place, as in 1963 and 1966–1967).

In 1973 the oil crisis marked the end of a quarter-century's international economic boom and was followed by rising unemployment. Labor was increasingly on the defensive, with more and more strikes aimed at defending existing wages and conditions. In the 1990s and early 2000s strike levels in Britain and elsewhere were low.

In Eastern Europe strikes were often part of a broader movement seeking to limit or end communist rule. In East Germany a workers' uprising in 1953 began with a strike by a group of building workers, with a general strike on 11 June. It was put down by armed force. In Hungary in October 1956 a general strike was called in support of creating a more liberal regime and declaring Hungarian neutrality in the Cold War. In Czechoslovakia elected workers' councils were one element of the Prague Spring of 1968, with demonstrators leaving work to protest when Warsaw Pact troops invaded in August. In Poland, the trade union organization Solidarity was set up by Lech Wałęsa, an electrician in the Lenin Shipyard in Gdansk, after a strike in August 1980. Supported by the Catholic Church, Solidarity was recognized and soon had some three million supporters. Following strikes in 1988 in the Baltic cities and Silesian coalfields, Solidarity was allowed to campaign as a political party in 1989. It won all but one of the seats it could contest, and in December, Wałęsa was elected president of Poland.

See also **General Strike (Britain); Labor Movements; May 1968; Solidarity; Unemployment.**

BIBLIOGRAPHY

Alexander, Martin S., and Helen Graham. *The French and Spanish Popular Fronts: Comparative Perspectives.* Cambridge, U.K., 1989.

Charlesworth, Andrew, et al. *An Atlas of Industrial Protest in Britain, 1750–1990.* London, 1996.

Church, Roy, and Quentin Outram. *Strikes and Solidarity: Coalfield Conflict in Britain 1889–1966.* Cambridge, U.K., 1998.

Cronin, James. *Industrial Conflict in Modern Britain.* London, 1979.

Crouch, Colin. *Industrial Relations and European State Traditions.* Oxford, U.K., 1993.

Durcan, J. W., W. E. J. McCarthy, and G. P. Redman. *Strikes in Post-War Britain: A Study of Stoppages of Work Due to Industrial Disputes, 1946–73.* London and Boston, 1983.

Geary, Dick. *European Labour Politics from 1900 to the Depression.* London, 1991.

———. "Revolutionary Berlin, 1917–20." In *Challenges of Labour: Central and Western Europe 1917–1920*, edited by Chris Wrigley, 24–50. London, 1993.

Haimson, Leopold H., and Charles Tilly, eds. *Strikes, Wars, and Revolutions in an International Perspective: Strike Waves in the Late Nineteenth and Early Twentieth Centuries.* Cambridge, U.K., 1989.

Horowitz, Daniel L. *The Italian Labor Movement.* Cambridge, Mass., 1963.

Hyman, Richard. *Strikes.* 4th ed. London, 1989.

Knowles, K. G. J. *Strikes: A Study in Industrial Conflict.* Oxford, U.K., 1952.

Koenker, Diane P., and William G. Rosenberg. *Strikes and Revolution in Russia, 1917.* Princeton, N.J., 1989.

Magraw, Roger. *A History of the French Working Class.* Vol. 2: *Workers and the Bourgeois Republic 1871–1939.* Oxford, U.K., 1992.

Sassoon, Donald. *One Hundred Years of Socialism: The West European Left in the Twentieth Century.* London, 1996.

Shorter, Edward, and Charles Tilly. *Strikes in France 1830 to 1968.* Cambridge, Mass., 1974.

Wrigley, Chris, ed. *A History of British Industrial Relations.* Vol. 2: *1914–1939.* Brighton, U.K., 1987.

———. *Challenges of Labour: Central and Western Europe 1917–1920.* London, 1993.

———. *A History of British Industrial Relations.* Vol. 3: *1939–1979.* Cheltenham, U.K., 1996.

CHRIS WRIGLEY

STUDENT MOVEMENTS.

Student movements have frequently altered the history of twentieth-century Europe, from the assassination of Archduke Francis Ferdinand (1863–1914) by a nineteen-year-old Bosnian student to the efforts of young people in Leipzig to bring about the fall of communism in 1989. The causes of these youth movements are many and no single theory has been found to explain the political and social activism endemic among young people. By reviewing the history of student movements, some general trends can be discerned.

During the nineteenth century, student activists tended to support the nascent ideas of nationalism. German students heeded nationalist writer Johann Gottlieb Fichte's "Address to the German Nation" given at the University of Berlin in 1806. Italian students similarly followed the call of Giuseppe Mazzini (1805–1872) for a united Italy and joined the Young Italy clubs. Russian students turned more frequently to violence and successfully assassinated Tsar Alexander II in 1881. The politically active youth of the turn of the century tended to champion nationalist or liberal causes in defiance of the internationalist tendencies of the old aristocracy.

EARLY TWENTIETH CENTURY AND WORLD WAR I

Not all students of the early twentieth century were swept up in the growing nationalist sentiment. Instead, many young people joined outdoor movements such as the German Wandervögel (Migrating birds), founded in 1901, or the Boy Scouts, founded in Britain in 1907. Both groups stressed hiking, camping, and sports, but the Wandervögel later adopted a more nationalist message stressing Germany's Teutonic roots. At the university level, students began to become politically active through the organization of student unions. In 1907, French students founded the Union Nationale des Etudiants de France (UNEF) at Lille. Overall, these youth and student groups remained patriotic in their sentiments and supported the war efforts during World War I. It should be noted that a few small organizations of young socialists existed that opposed the war, but their voices were drowned out by the drums and bugles that sounded Europe's call to arms in 1914.

World War I was ignited by a nineteen-year-old Bosnian student named Gavrilo Princip (1895–1918) who had been studying in Belgrade. Princip had become deeply involved with nationalist groups that sought to rid the Balkans of their Habsburg overlords. Like the Russian students of the nineteenth century, Princip's youthful activism drifted into the realm of regicide and historians agree that Princip became a tool of the more militaristic Serbian nationalist group, the Black Hand.

A generation of student activism was cut short by machine-gun fire and barbed wire as Europe lost a significant percentage of its young adult males. The British lost fewer young men overall, but lost a high percentage of their future leaders as boys from Oxford and Eton enlisted in large numbers and were granted officer status due to their social standing. England's Siegfried Sassoon (1886–1967) and Germany's Erich Maria Remarque (1898–1970) would both immortalize this "Lost Generation" in stirring poetry and literature that would alter the politics of the postwar generation.

INTERWAR PERIOD

Student movements in the interwar era became far more diversified than those of the prewar period. In Germany, Ernst Toller (1893–1939), a former dueling club member who became a socialist and a pacifist after witnessing the slaughter of the trenches, founded the Cultural and Political League of German Youth in 1917. Toller and his young comrades would later support the socialist coup d'état in Munich led by Kurt Eisner (1867–1919) that created the short-lived Bavarian Republic in 1919 (Boren, p. 59). Others who opposed war after 1918 turned to the church as an outlet for their youth activism. In 1925, Joseph Cardijn (1882–1965), a Belgian priest, created the Young Christian Workers (JOC) organization promoting health and Christianity among young workers. Although the JOC certainly sought to combat the growing influence of socialism, the organization also helped instill Christian values among young people and later spread to eighty-seven countries.

Despite the proliferation of socialist, pacifist, and Christian activism among European youth after World War I, nationalist and militarist organizations thrived as well. In 1919, German university students organized the Deutsche Studentenschaft (German Students' Association), an umbrella organization to which all university students belonged. The association had been founded on democratic principles and its first leaders came from liberal and democratic students, but later drifted to the right and became dominated by Nazi students. By the 1930s, leaders of the Deutsche Studentenschaft were organizing the first book burnings. Italian students also moved to the right after the war.

Listening to the laments of veterans who bemoaned the "mutilated victory" of 1918, these angry students tended to sympathize with nationalist politicians like Benito Mussolini (1883–1945). Many restless and unemployed young Italians enlisted with Mussolini's thugs, the Blackshirts, whose motto *Me ne frego* ("I don't give a damn") appealed to the angst of Italian youth. The Italian Fascists were one of the first parties to recognize the power of youth activism and devoted significant propaganda efforts to its youth affiliates, the "Sons of the She-Wolf" and "Avanguardista" (Vanguardist).

In France, the large UNEF battled with students who had affiliated with the radical French Right and formed the nationalist Etudiants Action Français (EAF) The EAF became so aggressive that they staged *cahuts,* disrupting classes and harassing left-leaning and republican professors. At one point, the EAF even forced the government to close the University of Paris's Law School over the hiring of Georges Scelle (1878–1961), a member of the Masons and suspected socialist. On the eve of World War II, student movements had clearly moved to either the extreme left or right.

WORLD WAR II AND POSTWAR YEARS

As in World War I, student activism subsided as universities closed down and Europe's youth directed its energies to the war effort or took part in resistance movements. Although some resistance groups like Germany's White Rose drew their primary members from college students, most resistance organizations were multigenerational. Sadly, the majority of "youth activists" in Germany and Italy during the 1930s became enthusiastic supporters of the war effort.

The years following World War II marked an abrupt change in the character of student activism. Stunned by the atrocities committed during the war and the revelations of the Nazi genocide, youth activists tended to define their politics in direct opposition to those of the previous generation. The postwar baby boom of the late 1940s ensured that a significant demographic bubble of young people would burst upon the universities in the 1960s. Unlike their parents who had survived war and economic depression, those born after 1945 knew only peace, prosperity, and a growing sense of internationalism. As the Cold War descended upon Europe, student activists chose to define their politics in opposition to their governing elders—West European students embraced Marxism in the form of the New Left, and East European students rejected Soviet communism in favor of democratic reforms such as those espoused by Alexander Dubček (1921–1992), the leader of Czechoslovakia.

THE 1960S

The roots of the great student rebellion of the late 1960s can be traced to the previous decade. The first major event to politicize students on both sides of the Atlantic was the U.S. civil rights movement. Led by African American leaders such as the Reverend Martin Luther King Jr. (1929–1968), the civil rights struggle served to inspire and teach Europe's future activists the tactics of civil disobedience and nonviolent protest. Thousands of young people, led by key intellectuals such as Bertrand Russell (1872–1970), joined the "Ban the Bomb" movement to protest the installation of nuclear missiles in England, and the protesters mimicked the tactics used by U.S. civil rights activists. In the early 1960s, French students took up the banner of decolonization and protested the war in Algeria. The French students received inspiration from the words of the great existentialist writers Albert Camus (1913–1960) and Jean-Paul Sartre (1905–1980). Such protests signaled the beginning of a youth movement to remove General Charles de Gaulle from power.

Most historians agree that the great issue of the 1960s was the United States' war in Vietnam. To students in Europe, the U.S. invasion of a third world country in the name of freedom and democracy revealed the hypocrisy of U.S. foreign policy. Along with the war's galvanizing of youth politics, a group of scholars known as the Frankfurt School, including the sociologist Herbert Marcuse (1898–1979), proposed a critique of not only the Cold War world but also the dehumanizing nature of the consumer society that had been created by the economic boom years following World War II. The students not only turned away from Western consumer-oriented capitalism but also rejected Joseph Stalin's brand of communism ruling in the Soviet Union and Eastern Europe. They instead supported a "New Left," choosing Marxist revolutionaries like Ernesto (Che) Guevara (1928–1967), Mao Zedong (1893–1976), and Ho Chi Minh (1890–1967) to be their heroes. Ultimately, the established socialist and communist parties in Western Europe would expel the members of their student affiliates during the peak years of student protest in 1967 and 1968.

Local issues also goaded the baby boomers into student movements in the late 1960s. For the French, German, and Italian students who flooded their outdated universities in the 1960s, serious problems of overcrowding, inadequate dormitories, authoritarian professors, and outdated curriculums served as flashpoints for activism. Left-wing student organizations such as West Germany's Socialist German Student Union (SDS) and Italy's Union of Italian University Students (UGI) quickly became the vanguard for university reforms and took control of student governments in their respective countries. Problems within the university rapidly blended with larger national issues and outrage against the Vietnam War to create a potent cocktail of student activism. West German students protested against the deficiencies in their universities and the war in Vietnam. Drawing upon their own past, the German students claimed that U.S. troops were committing atrocities that were little different than those carried out by the Nazis during World War II. In Italy, student movements burst on the scene after a fascist student group threw a left-wing student from a balcony, reigniting old debates about fascism in Italy. In France, student activism reached its height when a small group of students at Nanterre led by Daniel Cohn-Bendit called into question the entire university system and the near monopoly of de Gaulle upon French politics. More so than anywhere else in Western Europe, the student movements in France touched off a much larger series of general strikes that essentially shut down the country in May 1968. Students also rose in rebellion on the other side of the Iron Curtain, as students in Warsaw and Budapest cheered on their comrades in Prague. The so-called Prague Spring that had been initiated by the democratizing reforms of Dubček was perhaps the only example in which a European student movement actually demonstrated in support of their government.

Ultimately, none of the 1968 student movements succeeded in their radical goals of toppling governments and re-creating a new society, but political and cultural changes did occur. The sexual revolution and feminism altered gender relationships and by the 1970s, Italy and West Germany had changed their laws regulating divorce and abortion. The gay rights movement and environmentalism also sprang from the student movements of the 1960s and the first Earth Day occurred in 1970. Although the universities were slow to change their ways, access for working-class students was increased and changes in pedagogy did begin to allow students a greater role in university governance.

FOLLOWING 1968

The 1973–1974 oil embargo ended the Western world's long period of economic prosperity following World War II, and the U.S. withdrawal from Vietnam signaled a rapid decline in the student movements that had shaken the world in the 1960s. Declining economic fortunes meant fewer job possibilities for college graduates and the end of the war in Vietnam subsequently removed one of the driving forces behind student activism. Nevertheless, the European "68ers" had learned their lessons well and by their middle years would provide cadres who became leaders of the Green Party that would play a major role in European politics in the 1980s and 1990s.

The movements to end communist rule in Eastern Europe would be multigenerational struggles that placed those who remembered Hungary's ill-fated revolution of 1956 and the Prague Spring of 1968 beside those who grew up with the Berlin Wall. In the old university and market town of Leipzig, East Germany, thousands of students joined their parents, clergy, and an orchestra for Monday night peace vigils in 1989. The youth of East Germany, who had never known a time when their country had been united, chanted, *"Wir sind das Volk!"* ("We are the people!"). By November 1989, the East German government had lost its right to rule and young Germans on both sides of the crumbling wall heralded the unification of their country.

As in the past, student movements around the turn of the twenty-first century have continued to be an expression of the times and student activists continue to play a heavy role in nuclear disarmament, environmental protests, and the struggle against globalization. In 2001, thousands of students from all over the European Union converged on Genoa to protest globalization at a G8 meeting of industrialized countries. Sadly, street battles ensued and the police killed a Genoese student.

See also **Cohn-Bendit, Daniel; Dissidence; May 1968; 1968; Prague Spring.**

BIBLIOGRAPHY

Boren, Mark Edelman. *Student Resistance: A History of the Unruly Subject.* New York, 2001.

Feuer, Lewis S. *The Conflict of Generations; The Character and Significance of Student Movements.* New York, 1969.

Statera, Gianni. *Death of a Utopia: The Development and Decline of Student Movements in Europe.* New York, 1975.

STUART J. HILWIG

SUÁREZ, ADOLFO (b. 1932), Spanish political leader.

Adolfo Suárez was born in the town of Cebreros, Spain, in Ávila province. After studying law in Madrid, he began a career in the administration of Francisco Franco, during which he held a large number and wide range of positions of increasing rank and importance. These included director of Spanish state television's Channel 1, civil governor of Segovia, director general of Spanish Radio and Television, and secretary general of the National Movement, the official party of the Franco regime, which also carried the rank of cabinet minister.

Given this orthodox background, there was great surprise when King Juan Carlos I named him prime minister in July 1976 and charged him with moving Spain from a dictatorship to a constitutional monarchy. The opposition saw Suárez as a Francoist, while the people within the regime who were known to advocate reform saw him as an inexperienced lightweight. One well-known political figure publicly described the choice as a "terrible mistake."

As it turned out, Suárez surprised everybody, and within two years Spain had become a democratic state. The keys to this success were his commitment to steady reform and his willingness to engage the main leaders of the democratic opposition—and their willingness to compromise on key issues, such as the monarchy. In November 1976 he got the last Francoist Cortes (parliament) to approve his Law of Political Reform, which called for democratic elections and a large number of public rights and freedoms. The law was overwhelmingly approved in a referendum held on 15 December 1976. Suárez was also prepared to take the occasional risk to highlight his sincerity: the most significant was his decision to legalize the Communist Party so it could take part in the first democratic elections, on 15 June 1977.

Suárez also succeeded in building a political party that could distance itself from too close an association with the Franco regime and reasonably claim to occupy the center ground of the political spectrum. The Union of the Democratic Center (Unión de Centro Democrático, or UCD) was a coalition of a number of political figures from diverse political currents: Christian Democrats, liberals, and even social democrats. A number of these figures were "notables" in their own right, and the party was always very fragile, held together primarily by Suárez's charisma and his ability to win elections.

Suárez's party comfortably won the first democratic elections, and this legislature saw the drafting and approval, on 6 December 1978, of a new democratic constitution. This marked the end of what was called the period of consensus. Competition among the political parties became more intense, and as the country's economic situation deteriorated markedly, social conflict also increased. UCD again won elections in March 1979, but by then the party's internal cohesion was under severe strain, with many deputies even leaving the party.

Suárez's position at the center of Spain's political life came to a sudden, unexpected, and highly dramatic end in early 1981. Faced with strong criticism from the opposition as well as from within his own party, and amidst rumors of a possible military coup, he resigned as prime minister. On 23 February, as parliament was voting on his successor, Leopoldo Calvo Sotelo, a group of Civil Guard burst into the legislature and held the entire parliament to ransom. The attempted coup, which was captured live on television, failed the next day.

By 1982, the conflicts within UCD had reached such a point that Suárez left the party he had founded and led to power to create a new party, the Democratic and Social Center. Suárez himself was elected to parliament in 1982, 1986, and 1989, and his party briefly appeared as if it would become a major force, winning nineteen deputies in 1986, but it declined quickly thereafter. Suárez himself retired from politics in 1991 and returned to practicing law. In 1996 he was awarded the Prince of Asturias Award for Concord, Spain's equivalent to the Nobel Peace Prize.

See also **Franco, Francisco; Spain.**

BIBLIOGRAPHY

Aguilar, Paloma. "The Opposition to Franco, the Transition to Democracy, and the New Political System." In *Spanish History since 1808,* edited by José Alvarez Junco and Adrian Shubert, 303–314. London, 2000.

Gunther, Richard, Giacomo Sani, and Goldie Shabad. *Spain after Franco: The Making of a Competitive Party System.* Berkeley, Calif., 1986.

Preston, Paul. *The Triumph of Democracy in Spain.* London, 1986.

ADRIAN SHUBERT

SUDETENLAND. Originally a geographic expression used for the central parts of the Sudeten mountain range that stretches along the northeastern border of what in the early twenty-first century is the Czech Republic and Poland, the term *Sudetenland* became highly political when after the Munich treaty of 30 September 1938 most of the German-speaking parts of the former Czechoslovakia were ceded to Nazi Germany. Signed by the British premier Neville Chamberlain (1869–1940), the French prime minister Édouard Daladier (1884–1970), and the fascist dictators Benito Mussolini (1883–1945) and Adolf Hitler (1889–1945), the Munich Treaty stipulated that the so-called Sudeten Germans should become part of the Third Reich, where they were incorporated under the official political and administrative status of Reichsgau Sudetenland. The Munich

Treaty lost validity only six months later, when Adolf Hitler reneged on its terms by occupying the remainder of Czechoslovakia, which was broken up into the Protectorate of Bohemia and Moravia and the Nazi puppet state of Slovakia. Referred to in historical circles as the "Rape of Czechoslovakia," the Hitler government's conquest of this industrialized and well-armed nation opened the path to the official outbreak of World War II on 1 September 1939, when German forces invaded Poland. After the defeat of Nazi Germany in 1945 the Reichsgau Sudetenland was returned to Czechoslovakia, and the largest part of the German-speaking population was expelled. Although this action was sanctioned by the Allied leaders in the Potsdam Treaty of August 1945, spokesmen for the Sudeten German Homelands Associations (Sudetendeutsche Landsmannschaft) in the early 2000s continued to insist on the validity of the Munich Treaty, adding to the instability then undermining the process of political consolidation within the European Union.

NATIONALITY AND ETHNICITY

The term *Sudeten Germans,* like *Sudetenland,* was highly politicized. Its origins go back to the peacemaking process after World War I, when nationalism and the demand for "nation-states" was at its height, and when political thought, demands, and ambitions had to be couched in nationalistic terms. It was then that the German-speaking people of the former Kingdom of Bohemia, the Duchy of Silesia, and the Margravate of Moravia, who had all been part of the Cisleithanian part of the now defunct Austro-Hungarian Empire, were confronted by the fact that the peace treaty following World War I made them "minority citizens" in the newly founded nation of Czechoslovakia. To counter the sudden creation of a Czechoslovak nationality, a new concept with little historical tradition behind it, these German people—or rather their political leaders and spokesmen—created from their diverse regionalism their own artificial nationality: that of the "Sudeten Germans." Until then, in addition of course to being subjects of the Habsburg Monarchy, the dialects and customs of the *Nordböhmer,* for example, or the *Egerländer,* or the *Südmährer,* or people from the tiny *Kuhländchen,* all related culturally and ethnically

more closely to their Austrian and German neighbors than to one another.

Before the catastrophes and tragedies of the twentieth century, Czechs and Germans had been living together harmoniously in a bilingual community sometimes referred to as a *Zweivölkerland*—a two-peoples' country—or a *Zweivölkerstaat*—a two-peoples' state. The Bohemian and Moravian lands, of course, were not spared the great turbulence that marked late-medieval/early-modern European history, but—with the partial exception of the fifteenth-century Hussite Rebellion—conflicts were not fought on ethnic grounds. The religious, political, and socioeconomic conflicts that characterized the Reformation period in the sixteenth and seventeenth centuries saw Czechs and Germans fighting for or against Catholicism. And ethnic rivalry played little part in the confrontations between the estates and the centralized government, the nobility and the Crown, or the towns and aristocratic landholders that put their stamp on the beginnings of modernity. Ethnic rivalry did not arise in any significant way until the nineteenth century with the spread of modern nationalism that arose from the French Revolution of 1789 and which seems to have gripped many sections of the educated middle classes throughout Europe, including the multi-ethnic Austro-Hungarian Empire. Attempts by the Habsburg rulers to stem the tide fell on deaf ears. And so did voices warning that the end of the transnational community might only too readily have fatal consequences.

Notwithstanding the bickering and rampaging of political extremists, however, parties advocating the dissolution of the empire were by 1914 still a small minority in the Bohemian lands. This did change as the war, which had a devastating impact on the people of the Habsburg Monarchy, dragged on into its final phase. In the end the chief advocates for Czech independence, Tomáš Garrigue Masaryk (1850–1937) and Edvard Beneš (1884–1948), managed to rally the support of the majority of the Czech population behind the creation of Czechoslovakia, a step that was sanctioned by the Allied Powers in the peace treaty signed at St. Germain on 10 September 1919.

For the German people in the Bohemian lands the collapse of the Habsburg Empire led to a loss of identity, and they felt apprehensive about their

German troops enter the Sudetenland in 1939. ©BETTMANN/CORBIS

minority role in the newly formed Czechoslovak Republic. They had hoped to become part of Germany or Austria, but these hopes had no chance of becoming reality. Having fought the German Empire for four years and having sustained horrendous losses, the last thing the Allied Powers would have agreed to was an enlarged Germany. Moreover, loss of the German-settled part of Bohemia and Moravia would have rendered the newly formed state nonviable. But the attempt to create nation-states in the checkered multiethnic landscape of east-central and southeastern Europe was bound to run into stumbling blocks. In Czechoslovakia the Czechs and Slovaks became the "Staatsvolk"; they constituted the actual "nationality" while the other ethnic groups— including approximately 3.3 million German-speaking people—became "minority citizens."

These "minority citizens" had minority rights—a lopsided concept that found little appeal among the non-Czechoslovaks. Prague governments throughout the 1920s were coy to tackle this issue, that is, to take steps that would bring the "minority citizens" closer to the state. Yet the Czechoslovak Republic granted its citizens full civil rights—political and legal equality, liberty of expression, and freedom of association, press, and religion. This meant that if the large German minority would unite behind a single movement or party, the state's democratic setup would ensure that they could wield enormous political power.

OCCUPATION

For a short time it looked as though the post–World War I setup for the Bohemian lands might have a chance of survival. More favorable economic conditions meant that by the mid-1920s so-called activist parties—parties that advocated a cooperative approach and that participated in the Czechoslovak Republic's political life—found the support of the majority of the Sudeten Germans, as they were now starting to be called. Regrettably this process was not able to consolidate itself. By the mid-1930s, when Czechoslovak governments did attempt to bring in legislation that addressed the country's German population, the tide had already turned. The calamitous economic instability that followed the 1929 Wall Street stock market collapse and the rise to power of the Nazi Party in Germany led to a huge election victory of the fascist and irredentist Sudeten-German Party (Sudetendeutsche Partei, or SdP) under the leadership of Konrad Henlein in May 1935. With two-thirds of the Germans' vote, the SdP became the largest party in the Czechoslovak parliament. For the next three years Henlein and Hitler worked toward the destruction of the country, which was achieved with the *Einmarsch* (entry) of German troops in March 1939.

For the Czechs, who were hurled together in the "Protectorate of Bohemia and Moravia," this meant six bitter years of brutal Nazi occupation. For the Germans, who in their Reichsgau Sudetenland became now part of the Third Reich, it was the first step toward final catastrophe. They soon became aware that they were not accepted by the Reichsdeutsche on equal terms, economically their position improved little, and above all, a year after the creation of the Reichsgau Sudetenland they found themselves at war. But now there was no way back. Neither the fact that close to two hundred thousand of their men had died at the front nor the first dropping of Allied Powers bombs on Sudeten territory in December 1944, nor the appalling sight of refugees fleeing from the advancing Czech army, could entice the Sudeten Germans to change course. Added now to the traditional dislike of the Czechs, whether due to a belief in German superiority or to a conviction, however justifiable, that the German community had been victimized under Czech rule, was a new fear of reprisals for events leading up to and since Munich. With news coming in from London of plans for large-scale expulsion, it is not surprising that the Sudeten Germans were the last to leave the sinking ship. It was not until Soviet and U.S.

troops literally had arrived at their doorstep that the people realized their Reichsgau Sudetenland was little more than a bursting bubble.

When the dream of an Aryan "Thousand Year Empire" had finally ended, a terrible punishment descended on many German people, including three million Sudeten Germans. Intense far-embracing Germanophobia, coupled with an equally staunch determination on the part of the victorious Allied Powers to once and for all eliminate the threat of future attempts to establish German hegemony in Europe, saw millions lose their homes and subjected to pitiless and often savage ejections from their *Heimat* (homeland). About thirty thousand Sudetens lost their life. Yet accounts of these tragedies that fail to highlight the carnage inflicted on Europe by Nazi Germans during the World War II as the chief reason for the postwar catastrophe lack credence.

The immediate post–World War II governments of the Federal Republic (West Germany) under Chancellor Konrad Adenauer (1876–1967) supported the demands of the Sudeten German Homelands Associations and other expellee organizations to have the "stolen lands" returned—but this was only for domestic consumption. Internationally the victorious Allied Powers never left any doubt that the Potsdam agreement of August 1945 between the Soviet leader Joseph Stalin (1879–1953), the U.S. president Harry S. Truman (1884–1972), and the British prime minister Clement Richard Attlee (1883–1967), which had officially sanctioned the expulsion of eleven million Germans from their homelands, would remain unaltered. When the center-left government of Willy Brandt (1913–1992) in the late 1960s ended conservative rule in West Germany, there were also far-reaching changes in foreign policies. By entering into treaties with the Soviet Union, Poland, and Czechoslovakia the Brandt government officially accepted the post–World War II political setup, a decision that by now had the support of the majority of the country's population.

POST-SOVIET DEVELOPMENTS

By the late 1980s the "Sudeten issue" had seemingly run its course. The slender hope on part of the Sudeten German associations' officials and some members that the return of a center-right government in 1982 would reverse the previous *Ostpolitik* (eastern politics) proved illusory. There were still strongly worded articles in the associations' periodicals and equally strong speeches at their annual gatherings, but only in Bavaria did the Sudetenland issue arouse any significant interest. Most Sudeten Germans had settled there and the ruling CSU in this state was greatly critical of the normalization process between Germany and the Czech Republic that commenced after the collapse of the Soviet Empire. The Bavarian premier Edmund Stoiber has voiced strong demands for Sudeten German compensation. If his intention to become German foreign minister in a center-right government under Chancellor Angela Merkel had succeeded, he indeed would have been in a position to present the demands of the Sudetens more forcefully. As German-Polish relations were already under great strain in the early 2000s, Stoiber's partisanship would have placed Germany's policy toward its eastern neighbors under additional pressure. His plans were thwarted by the outcome of the 2005 federal election, which led him to remain in Munich.

Understandably, Czech governments and the majority of the Czech population have been greatly irritated by the relentless attempts on part of the Sudeten German associations and their supporters to have the alleged injustices of the postwar era corrected, the more so as the leaders and spokesmen of these associations bar out the years from 1938 to 1945 from their accounts. It is true that the Czechs tend to overlook that there is much more to Germany in the early twenty-first century than Bavaria and that German foreign policies are made in Berlin and not Munich. But Bavaria is economically and politically one of the most influential German states, and so the ghost of Sudetenland and Sudeten Germans is likely to haunt European politics for some time.

See also **Czechoslovakia; Germany; Minority Rights; Munich Agreement; World War II.**

BIBLIOGRAPHY

Cordell, Karl, and Stefan Wolff. *Germany's Foreign Policy towards Poland and the Czech Republic: Ostpolitik Revisited.* New York, 2005.

Tampke, Jürgen. *Czech-German Relations and the Politics of Central Europe: From Bohemia to the EU.* Houndmills, U.K., 2003.

JÜRGEN TAMPKE

SUEZ CRISIS. The Suez Crisis was a major international confrontation that started when the Egyptian government nationalized the Suez Canal in July 1956 and climaxed in November when the British and French, in league with Israel, invaded Egypt. International pressure, especially from the United States, forced the invaders to withdraw, leaving Egypt still in control of the canal. The debacle hastened the decline of European influence in the Middle East and drew the superpowers more deeply into the region.

ORIGINS

Since its opening in 1869, the Suez Canal had been owned and operated by an Anglo-French company. To protect this important link to its Indian empire, the British occupied Egypt in 1882, running the country as a client state until the Free Officers, a nationalist military group, seized control in July 1952. Under intense pressure from the leader of the coup, Colonel Gamal Abdel Nasser (1918–1970), the British signed an agreement in October 1954 for a twenty-month phased withdrawal from the canal zone, a vast area of military bases roughly the size of Wales. The position of the Suez Canal Company remained unaffected, however, and, with Western Europe now reliant on the Middle East for 80 percent of its oil, the canal assumed a new strategic importance.

Despite the 1954 agreement, Nasser's position was fragile. In the spring of 1955, Iraq, Turkey, and Britain joined together in what became known as the Baghdad Pact. Intended by the British as an anti-Soviet bulwark in the Middle East, the pact was seen by Nasser as a threat to his own aspirations as regional leader. Tit-for-tat raids across Egypt's long border with Israel were a constant reminder of the unresolved legacy of Israel's war for independence in 1948, and the Americans, British, and French sought to reduce the violence by rationing arms supplies to the Middle East. Feeling increasingly encircled, Nasser concluded an arms deal with the Soviet bloc, announced in September 1955, whereupon Washington and London froze their financial support for the Aswan High Dam, centerpiece of his program of modernization.

The British hoped to let the offer of aid wither on the vine, but pressure from Congress and determination to teach Nasser a lesson prompted John Foster Dulles, the U.S. secretary of state, to end the project publicly and bluntly on 19 July 1956. A week later, on 26 July, Nasser announced that the Suez Canal Company would be nationalized, with Egypt taking over the running of the waterway. Revenue from the canal would help pay for the dam; more fundamentally, economic independence would make possible full political independence.

CONSPIRACY

Anthony Eden, the British prime minister, was furious and, as the architect of the 1954 agreement, also felt betrayed. Likening Nasser to Mussolini, he was convinced that appeasement would be as disastrous as in the 1930s and that Nasser must now be removed. The British and French began plans for an invasion of Egypt. The problem was that Nasser had promised to compensate shareholders and maintain freedom of navigation; on 15 September, the canal reopened under Egyptian management. Frustrated, the British took the issue to the United Nations, and by mid-October negotiations were under way between Egypt and an association of user nations about future Egyptian operation of the canal. It seemed that the crisis could be resolved peacefully.

For Britain and France, however, the stakes had now become much higher than simply the canal. The British regarded Nasser as a destabilizing force throughout the Middle East; the abrupt dismissal in March 1956 of Sir John Glubb, commander of the Jordanian army, was taken as another sign of his insidious influence. The French, for their part, believed Nasser was behind the escalating rebellion against their rule in Algeria. Both governments were under strong domestic pressure to be tough, with the lessons of appeasement regularly cited. But the successful Egyptian operation of the canal denied them a pretext for military action. That was where the Israelis came in.

For months the Israeli military had been agitating for a preemptive war against Egypt, but Prime Minister David Ben-Gurion would not go ahead without great-power support. In the summer of 1956 the Israelis opened up contacts with Guy Mollet, the French prime minister and a longstanding supporter of Israel, who drew in Eden. Increasingly desperate, the British prime minister worked behind the backs of most of the Foreign Office, mounting what was almost an alternative foreign policy using the intelligence service, MI6.

At a series of secret meetings on 22–24 October in the fashionable Paris suburb of Sèvres, representatives of the three governments confirmed their conspiracy. The Israelis would invade the Sinai peninsula to destroy Palestinian guerrilla bases and wreck the Egyptian military machine. Their thrust would threaten the canal and give the British and French a pretext to invade—ostensibly to separate the belligerents and safeguard their property, more fundamentally to kill Nasser and install a pro-Western regime.

The cover plan was, of course, transparently specious; so much so that Eden was appalled to learn of a written record, the Protocol of Sèvres, and had all the British copies destroyed. Moreover, the underlying set of alliances ran counter to national traditions. Eden, a consistent Arabist all his life, was now allied with the Arabs' greatest enemy. France, anxious for British support, was willing to abandon its cherished precept of independence and place French forces under British command. Above all, in turning to France, the British were violating the cardinal principle of their postwar policy, namely to keep in step with the United States. This proved the fatal mistake. President Dwight D. Eisenhower shared their view that Nasser was a threat to Western interests, but he was equally sure that the canal was "not the issue on which to try to downgrade Nasser," smacking as it did of old-fashioned European imperialism. On several occasions he made this clear to Eden but the British went ahead with the conspiracy, cutting Washington completely out of the loop, though American intelligence soon divined what was going on.

CONFLICT

On 29 October—the day that Britain, France, and Egypt were scheduled to open discussions in

Geneva about the operation of the canal—the Israeli Defense Forces invaded Sinai. Enjoying complete surprise, they made rapid gains. The following day the British and French issued their ultimatum to the belligerents; on the 31st their planes started bombing Egyptian bases. On 5 November, British and French paratroops landed around Port Said, at the Mediterranean end of the canal, followed the next day by amphibious troops. It was Nasser's turn to be wrong-footed. Back in July he had assumed that the chances of war would diminish every week and that "if we succeed in gaining two months by politics, we shall be safe." Now, in a fatalistic mood, he prepared to die with his troops in a last-ditch defense of the capital, Cairo.

But then Eisenhower came to his rescue. The president was incensed at the Anglo-French deception and also embarrassed by its timing—just before the presidential election on 6 November and at the height of the Red Army's suppression of Hungary's revolt against Soviet rule. Just when he wanted to demonstrate the moral distance between East and West in the Cold War, his allies seemed to be behaving as badly as his adversaries. "I've never seen great powers make such a complete *mess* and *botch* of things," he fumed. The United States therefore took the lead in sponsoring a ceasefire resolution in the United Nations, where Britain and France were virtually isolated—an unprecedented shock for two of the UN's founders. In Britain, public opinion was deeply and passionately divided. The Soviets threatened military action against the belligerents unless the fighting stopped. Most serious of all, the Americans refused to help stop the wartime run on sterling unless a ceasefire was implemented.

Eden, seriously ill with a damaged gall bladder and running a high temperature, watched aghast as the fragile coalition of support unravelled. As early as 3–4 November the Egyptians and Israelis were talking about a ceasefire in Sinai, undercutting the case for sending in British and French troops. And at home, Harold Macmillan, his chancellor of the exchequer, panicked about the sterling crisis. Having previously ignored warnings from Treasury officials about the vulnerability of the pound, this previously ferocious hawk turned almost overnight into a flapping dove.

On the morning of 6 November, the British cabinet agreed to an immediate ceasefire and Mollet, bitterly, was forced to follow suit. Ben-Gurion, also ill and overwrought, agreed to pull back from Sinai. All three powers still hoped to exploit their territorial gains as diplomatic leverage but the Americans kept up the political and financial pressure. On 18 November, Eden's doctors advised a complete rest; five days later he flew to Jamaica, leaving his colleagues to negotiate the denouement. Here Macmillan took the lead, persuading the cabinet to accept an unconditional withdrawal, devoid of the strings Eden had wanted, in return for American support of sterling. This was announced on 3 December. British and French troops completed their pull-out on 22 December and a United Nations force took their place, in a pioneering example of this kind of peacekeeping operation.

CONSEQUENCES

Eden returned to London on 14 December, hopeful of remaining prime minister. But his performances in the House of Commons did not reassure his party. Under severe pressure about reports of "collusion" with Israel, he lied blatantly to the members of Parliament on 20 December, insisting that "there were no plans got together to attack Egypt" and that "there was not foreknowledge that Israel would attack Egypt." Eden remained seriously ill and on 9 January 1957 he resigned as prime minister. After soundings of the cabinet, the Queen appointed Macmillan, the main architect of his political downfall, as Eden's successor.

In France, opinion had been less polarized by the war and Mollet continued in power until May 1957. But the French were bitter at their betrayal yet again, as they saw it, by "perfidious Albion." Konrad Adenauer, the West German chancellor, told Mollet that "Europe will be your revenge," and it was no accident that the winter of 1956–1957 saw increased French interest in plans for European integration, culminating in the Treaty of Rome signed in March 1957. The new nationalism often ascribed to the era of Charles de Gaulle actually had its roots in the mood of 1956–1957.

Of the three unlikely allies, the biggest beneficiary was Israel. The damage it had inflicted on Egypt and the Palestinians kept the country safe from attack for a decade. But it was Nasser, of course, who gained most from the crisis. Egypt, a British protectorate till only five years before, had humiliated the two greatest powers of Europe. Nasser's stock soared at home and abroad, as his example emboldened other nationalist leaders, particularly in the Middle East and Africa, to intensify their agitation against colonial rule.

Meanwhile, the United States moved hurriedly to fill the vacuum created by the Anglo-French collapse and the growing Soviet influence in Egypt. On 5 January 1957 the so-called Eisenhower Doctrine declared that the United States would use its armed forces in the event of Soviet or communist aggression in the Middle East. Thus, the Suez crisis proved a turning point both in Europe's retreat from empire and also in the progressive globalization of the Cold War.

See also **British Empire; British Empire, End of; Cold War; Colonialism; Eden, Anthony; Egypt.**

BIBLIOGRAPHY

Primary Sources

Gorst, Anthony, and Lewis Johnman. *The Suez Crisis.* London, 1997. Useful short introduction, with extensive documents.

U.S. Department of State. *Foreign Relations of the United States, 1955–1957.* Vol. 16: *Suez Crisis July 26–December 31, 1956.* Washington, D.C., 1990. The crisis as seen in American documents.

Secondary Sources

Carlton, David. *Britain and the Suez Crisis.* Oxford, U.K., 1988. A short account, with numerous British documents.

Kelly, Saul, and Anthony Gorst, eds. *Whitehall and the Suez Crisis.* London, 2000. Essays on key British policymakers, updating Carlton.

Kyle, Keith. *Suez.* London, 1991. A massive, detailed history.

Louis, William Roger, and Roger Owen, eds. *Suez 1956: The Crisis and Its Consequences.* Oxford, U.K., 1989. A truly international view, with essays on all the major players.

DAVID REYNOLDS

SUFFRAGE. Although women had campaigned for suffrage since the mid-nineteenth century, voting rights remained a controversial question well into the twentieth. By the outbreak of World War I in 1914 only two European countries, Finland (1906) and Norway (1913), had introduced legislative measures in favor of women's suffrage. And yet during and immediately after World War I women gained the right to vote in a variety of European countries, including Britain, Germany, Denmark, Sweden, Austria, Czechoslovakia, and the Republic of Ireland. Why did so many women achieve the vote in this period? What was the impact of war? What role did the suffrage movement play and to what extent was the political context of individual countries responsible for the timing and nature of women's enfranchisement?

IDEOLOGICAL DEBATES

During the early twentieth century women's enfranchisement was the subject of passionate debate. Opposition to it remained strong: it was suggested, for example, that their role within the family made women ill-suited to take part in national politics, in particular foreign affairs, and also that activity in the public world "unsexed" women, made them less feminine. Suffragists, however, argued on the grounds of individual rights, natural justice, and women's common humanity with men that women should be allowed to vote. At the same time, in particular after 1900, they also used women's difference from men as a basis for their claim to the franchise. It was argued that women, as nurturers and moral guardians of the family, would bring new qualities into political life and would work for peace, social reforms, and a moral regeneration of society.

These ideological debates were entangled with pragmatic political strategies that proved to be among the main barriers to women's enfranchisement before 1914. As Gisela Bock has argued, it was difficult for women to make a breakthrough in their demands when in most countries not all men had the vote and when democratization was associated with manhood suffrage. In Austria, for example, socialists refused to put their weight behind women's claims for the vote until manhood

WOMEN'S SUFFRAGE IN SELECTED COUNTRIES IN EUROPE

1906 Finland
1913 Norway
1915 Denmark, Iceland
1917 Russia
1918 Austria, Germany, Hungary (restricted
    1921), Czechoslovakia, Britain (women over
    thirty), Republic of Ireland
1919 The Netherlands
1921 Sweden

1928 Britain (all women over twenty-one)
1931 Portugal (restricted to women with
    secondary or higher education); Spain
    (lost in 1936)
1944 Bulgaria, France
1945 Italy, Hungary
1948 Belgium
1971 Switzerland
1976 Portugal, Spain

suffrage had been achieved in 1907. In Britain only two thirds of adult males were entitled to vote even after the franchise was extended in 1884. Thus, when women called for suffrage on the same terms as men, groups that might have been expected to support them on principle—socialists, liberals, and radicals—were suspicious that propertied, middle-class women would be the ones to gain the vote and that they would support conservative groups. For male-dominated parties of the Center and Left, therefore, the needs of class were seen to override those of gender.

WAR, THE CONTEXT FOR CHANGE

The upheavals caused by "total war" did provide the context for change in political, social, and gender structures and relationships. Women were encouraged to support the war effort through employment in nursing, munitions, and other essential war industries as well as through voluntary welfare work. This has led to the common assumption that women subsequently gained the vote as a reward for their war service. Indeed, many prewar suffrage activists believed that women's cooperation in the war effort would demonstrate that they could be as "patriotic" as men and that they were worthy of exercising the franchise. Nonetheless, the notion of reward for war service does not provide a sufficient or convincing explanation for women's enfranchisement. In

Britain, for example, only women over the age of thirty were enfranchised in 1918, and yet it was younger women who had been most involved in war work. Frenchwomen, who had played a role similar to that of their counterparts in Britain, did not gain the right to vote until 1944. Indeed, war raised arguments that tended toward the exclusion, rather than the inclusion, of women since patriotic duty was sometimes equated with fighting for one's country. In Britain, for example, it was suggested that military service should be the basis for the franchise, an argument that alarmed male conscientious objectors as well as women suffragists. In France a measure was put forward in 1916 that would have enabled a woman who had lost a close male relative in the war to vote in his place, but it was never adopted. In Belgium, however, the mothers and widows of soldiers were enfranchised in 1919.

What does seem to be crucial is the extent to which the disruption of war led to the introduction of more democratic political systems or opened up wider franchise debates. New spaces were created for women to be included as full citizens. Women gained the vote in states that were created after the war when the old European empires were dismantled, including Hungary, Poland, Estonia, and Czechoslovakia. They were also enfranchised in Germany and Austria, where democratic republics replaced more authoritarian systems of government. Here pragmatic rather than idealistic reasons were at play. The new governments felt threatened by Bolshevik revolutionaries on the left and conservative, nationalist groups on the right, and "moderate" political parties assumed that women would prove to be a force for stability. In Britain the government's decision to introduce a new franchise reform act to ensure that returning soldiers and sailors would be able to vote provided the occasion for the inclusion of women over thirty. The government was reluctant to accept equal voting rights in a context in which women would have outnumbered men and thought that the enfranchisement of "mothers" would pose far fewer risks. Suffrage campaigners accepted this compromise—even though it undermined their long-standing demand for voting rights for women on the same terms as for men—on the grounds that it was crucial that the principle of women's right, and ability, to vote be acknowledged.

THE ROLE OF THE SUFFRAGE MOVEMENT

Although it was difficult for women to gain the vote when the political context was unfavorable, it is important not to lose sight of the role played by the suffrage movement in contributing toward women's enfranchisement. By itself a strong suffrage movement could not ensure success; for instance, there was an active suffrage campaign in the republics of France and Switzerland, but in both countries women had to wait several decades before they were enfranchised. Conversely, in many countries women had managed to push the suffrage question to the forefront of the political agenda before the war. The campaign had gained momentum in the immediate prewar years as new suffrage organizations were formed and the basis of support widened. In Britain in particular, the development of militant methods attracted publicity to the cause, and the willingness of suffragettes to flout conventions inspired women from across the world to challenge their unequal status. Thus, by the outbreak of war it was claimed by many contemporaries that the argument for women's suffrage had been won—all that was needed was a changed political context in which it could be implemented. Indeed, in the countries noted above there was little opposition when women's suffrage was finally introduced. In Czechoslovakia, for

example, women had taken part in the prewar nationalist movement and gained support for women's suffrage from a wide range of political groups, including the liberal nationalist leader Tomáš Masaryk, who was to become president of the postwar republic. In Britain there is no guarantee that women would have been included in the Franchise Bill of 1918 if they had not continued to lobby the government after 1916. It then took sustained pressure from the women's movement before an equal franchise was finally achieved in 1928.

WOMEN'S DIFFERENCE AND POLITICAL SYSTEMS

Throughout all the franchise debates, political parties constantly raised the issue of women's difference from men to suggest that suffrage could pose a risk. On the one hand, women were viewed by conservatives as likely to be a radical force in politics, and it was feared that a greater public role would disrupt "traditional" family relationships. These fears were fueled by suffragists who had joined the peace movement during the war, since they argued that women needed the vote to have an influence on foreign affairs and that they would work to ensure a peaceful solution to national conflicts. On the other hand, radicals, liberals, and socialists feared that women, largely because of their domestic role, would be a force for conservatism. This was a key issue in France, which alone among the Allied nations failed to enfranchise women at the end of World War I. Although the Chamber of Deputies debated the question and passed a measure of support in 1919, the Senate procrastinated and in 1922 voted against women's suffrage. Many radicals and socialists feared that women would vote for the monarchy, conservatism, and the Catholic Church, and a significant proportion of women suffragists also thought that female voters might endanger the Republic. Again, Bock argues that in France and Switzerland, where all men had enjoyed the vote since the nineteenth century, there was little interest in forming alliances with women to extend the franchise and therefore this also set back the women's cause.

The disruption of gender roles during wartime led to fears that the "traditional" family would be undermined, and it was widely believed that male authority needed to be consolidated in the face of the modern woman, who sought an active role in the public sphere. At the same time, anxieties about population decline and its impact on the state led to a new focus on the importance of motherhood and domesticity. In the interwar years, mass unemployment, the development of conservative and fascist regimes, and the threat of war made it difficult for women who were not enfranchised to achieve the vote, and for others to hold on to, and to extend, the gains that had already been made. Indeed, the right to vote enjoyed by both sexes sometimes disappeared with the introduction of totalitarian political systems. In Russia, for example, women who had been enfranchised during the first revolution of 1917 lost this right when the Bolsheviks seized power later in the year. Women were also disenfranchised in Germany when National Socialism replaced the Weimar Republic. In Italy women's suffrage had been discussed during the war and Benito Mussolini was initially sympathetic to the demand, but by 1925 he had dissolved Parliament and all elections were suspended.

In some cases, however, women were able to hold on to voting rights, or even to acquire them for the first time, but under very restrictive circumstances designed to ensure that they would exert a conservative influence. In Hungary, for example, women received the vote on the same terms as men after the war when a new liberal constitution was established, though the suffrage movement itself had always been weak. Yet the successful counterrevolution by the conservative wing of the nationalist movement disenfranchised women in 1920. Voting rights were reestablished in 1921, but only for women over the age of thirty who met educational and economic qualifications. Similarly, in Portugal the authoritarian regime of Antonio Salazar granted women the vote in 1931 but they had to have completed secondary or higher education, whereas male voters had only to be able to read and write. This, however, was in the context of a single-party system where there was no real choice.

Women stood a greater chance of gaining the franchise when more constitutional governments were formed, if only for brief periods. In Spain women's groups and socialist feminists debated

women's emancipation during the 1920s when the military dictator General Miguel Primo de Rivera was in power. The introduction of the Second Republic in 1931 stimulated women to demand political rights. During discussions of the new constitution, two women, Victoria Kent and Clara Campoamor, who were both attorneys and had been elected deputies in 1931, debated the question of women's suffrage. Kent opposed the measure on the grounds that women were not yet ready and might endanger the Republic, whereas Campoamor claimed that it was a matter of principle and that the criticisms raised could also apply to men. In the event, the new constitution of 1931 did enfranchise all men and women over the age of twenty-three, but after the civil war of 1936–1939 and the introduction of General Franco's dictatorship, universal suffrage was suppressed.

THE IMPACT OF WORLD WAR II

It was after World War II that women in a number of the participant countries achieved the vote, most notably in France and Italy. In France women's enfranchisement was part of the ordinance of 21 April 1944, issued by General Charles de Gaulle as leader of the Free French in Algiers. This ordinance proposed constitutional arrangements for France once the country had been liberated. The short-term reasons for this included de Gaulle's need to reassure the Resistance within France, and also his British and American allies, that he was committed to restoring republican democracy in France. It is also likely that he assumed that women would vote for conservative and clerical parties. Within the Resistance itself there were divisions between socialists and communists who favored women's suffrage and radicals who opposed it. The National Resistance Council, which commented on the constitutional proposals, was interested in the idea, put forward ironically by the Vichy government, that heads of household should have extra votes to reflect the number of children in the family. This was, however, rejected in favor of the principle of one person, one vote. Nonetheless, it is important to note that these changes were not introduced in a vacuum. Women's suffrage had been widely debated for many decades, and during the interwar years the campaign for the vote continued to attract support; the French Union for Women's Suffrage, for example, extended its organization beyond Paris and into the provinces and had ten thousand members in 1929. It is significant that when the decision to enfranchise women was taken, it was broadly welcomed in the popular press and encountered little opposition.

By the end of World War II, therefore, most European women living in countries with some form of democratic government were enfranchised. (Many others, living under authoritarian or military governments, had to wait until representative political systems were introduced, as in Portugal and Spain in 1976, or until the Soviet Union and Communist regimes collapsed in the late twentieth century.) The main exception was Switzerland, which had a well-established republican government and yet did not grant women the vote until 1971. Here again, men had little incentive to support women's suffrage since they had long enjoyed the right to vote. There was a complex political system that required a referendum on proposed constitutional changes, while the local autonomy of cantons limited the power of the bicameral National Assembly. It was not until 1957, in the context of growing international pressure, that a national referendum was held on the subject of women's suffrage. Despite support from both chambers of the Assembly, male voters still opposed it. Women continued to campaign for the vote, but it was Switzerland's membership in the Council of Europe in 1963 that exposed the anomalies in its constitutional position. It was unable, for example, to sign the European Convention on Human Rights in 1968 and, when its petition for an exemption was turned down, a referendum on women's suffrage at last received the necessary majority in 1971.

THE VOTE AS AN AGENT OF POWER

The controversies and passions roused by the demand for women's suffrage indicate the importance attached to the vote as an agent of power in political democracies from the mid-nineteenth century onward. Women believed that their inclusion in the franchise would enable them to exert an influence on government policies, in particular social reforms. They also saw the vote as having considerable symbolic importance. Without voting rights, women could not be full citizens and therefore their inferior social status would be confirmed.

Since the nature and timing of women's enfranchisement was linked to political developments in individual countries and also to terms on which men had the vote, class was always an important factor in the debates. Conversely, women's own agency played an important part in bringing women's suffrage to the forefront of politics and in creating a climate in which it became an acceptable measure to adopt.

The achievement of the vote, however, certainly did not mark the end of women's long struggle for emancipation. Only a small proportion of women were elected to representative assemblies, and in the context of the interwar years it was difficult for women to gain, or hold onto, equal rights. Feminists themselves were divided about what they hoped to achieve, with some emphasizing equal rights and others focusing on the welfare needs of mothers and women's social duties to the state. Once the suffrage struggle was over, the women's movement became more fragmented and less visible, making it difficult to exert pressure for change in gender relations. It was recognized that deep-seated structural issues around women's position in the family and the workforce needed to be tackled alongside formal equal rights. At the beginning of the twenty-first century there was greater skepticism among both men and women about the extent to which the vote enables any group to exercise real political influence. Nonetheless, inclusion in the franchise was a vital first step for women in their campaign to be treated as full citizens with an equal right to take part in all areas of public life alongside men.

See also **Citizenship; Feminism; Suffrage Movements.**

BIBLIOGRAPHY

Bartley, Paula. *Votes for Women*. London, 1998. A useful overview of the British suffrage campaign and a guide to further reading.

Bock, Gisela. *Women in European History*. Translated by Allison Brown. Malden, Mass., 2001.

Evans, Richard J. *The Feminists: Women's Emancipation Movements in Europe, America, and Australasia, 1840–1920*. London, 1977. An early comparative study that emphasizes the importance of liberal nationalism in Europe.

Foley, Susan K. *Women in France since 1789: The Meanings of Difference*. New York, 2004.

Frevert, Ute. *Women in German History: From Bourgeois Emancipation to Sexual Liberation.* Translated by Stuart McKinnon-Evans in association with Terry Bond and Barbara Norden. Oxford, U.K., 1990.

Griffin, Gabriele, and Rosi Braidotti, eds. *Thinking Differently: A Reader in European Women's Studies.* London, 2002. Brief articles on individual countries.

Holton, Sandra Stanley. *Feminism and Democracy: Women's Suffrage and Reform Politics in Britain, 1900–1918.* Cambridge, U.K., 1986. Contains a detailed analysis of the impact of war on the British suffrage movement.

Keene, Judith. "'Into the Clean Air of the Plaza': Spanish Women Achieve the Vote in 1931." In *Constructing Spanish Womanhood: Female Identity in Modern Spain,* edited by Victoria Lorée Enders and Pamela Beth Radcliff, 325–347. Albany, N.Y., 1999.

Law, Cheryl. *Suffrage and Power: The Women's Movement, 1918–1928.* London, 1997. A detailed account of the struggle for an equal franchise in Britain after World War I.

Legates, Marlene. *In Their Time: A History of Feminism in Western Society.* London, 2001. A clear discussion of the interwar context and debates around women's suffrage across Europe.

Offen, Karen M. *European Feminisms, 1700–1950: A Political History.* Stanford, Calif., 2000. A key text that explores the suffrage campaign in a range of European countries.

Reynolds, Siân. *France between the Wars: Gender and Politics.* London, 1996. Stimulating discussion of why women gained the vote in 1944.

Smith, Harold L., ed. *British Feminism in the Twentieth Century.* Amherst, Mass., 1990. Focuses on the complex arguments around equality and difference among British feminists.

Summerfield, Penny. "Women and War in the Twentieth Century." In *Women's History: Britain, 1850–1945: An Introduction,* edited by June Purvis, 307–322. London, 1995.

Thane, Pat. "What Difference Did the Vote Make?" In *Women, Privilege, and Power: British Politics, 1750 to the Present,* edited by Amanda Vickery, 253–288. Stanford, Calif., 2001.

Ward, Margaret. "'Suffrage First—Above All Else!' An Account of the Irish Suffrage Movement." *Feminist Review* 10 (1982): 21–36.

JUNE HANNAM

SUFFRAGE MOVEMENTS. Conservative governments had generally resisted universal manhood suffrage during the nineteenth century, and consequently many of those governments were still chosen by limited manhood suffrage in 1914. France and Germany both practiced forms of universal suffrage, but Britain retained some limits on manhood suffrage (such as a residency requirement that disfranchised migrant workers). Societies as diverse as Spain, Italy, Belgium, Norway, and Denmark also practiced limited suffrage in 1914. Denmark and Italy only allowed the franchise at age thirty; Italy added a disqualification of illiterates who had not performed military service. Norway and Belgium excluded men under twenty-five plus paupers and bankrupts. The trend, however, was toward universal suffrage. Such traditionally autocratic governments as the Russian and Austrian empires had granted forms of universal suffrage—Russia in elections for the Duma in 1906, Austria in an electoral reform of 1907.

Social conservatives more firmly resisted democratic reforms such as women's suffrage and proportional representation. Few states had accepted these reforms before World War I. In 1906 Finland, an autonomous province after the Russian Revolution of 1905, became the first European state to grant women's suffrage in national elections. Norway became the first independent country to do so, in 1913. When the war began in 1914 none of the Great Powers had extended the national vote to women. Britain had, however, allowed the right to vote in local elections in 1869.

Women's suffrage movements existed in virtually all of Europe in 1914, actively campaigning in many countries. In England, Ireland, and France, "suffragettes" (such as the Pankhursts [Emmeline and her daughters Christabel and Sylvia] in England and Hubertine Auclert in France) used violent tactics in their campaign to overcome male single-sex political systems. Tens of thousands of women had signed petitions or marched in demonstrations by 1914, and most expected victory within the near future.

Systems of voting in which minorities received representation comparable to their share of the electorate—typically called "proportional representation"—had achieved slightly more success by 1914. Belgium became the first state to adopt this form of the suffrage in 1899, and before 1914 variants were being used in the Netherlands, Sweden, Finland, Portugal, and

Suffragists march in London, 1914. ©HULTON-DEUTSCH COLLECTION/CORBIS

Bulgaria—but not in the Great Powers, although it was being seriously considered in France.

WORLD WAR I AND POSTWAR DEMOCRATIZATION

The beginning of World War I in 1914 led many suffrage movements to suspend activities, but a few suffrage reforms were introduced during the war. Denmark granted a greater degree of universal suffrage in 1915, including women's suffrage; the Netherlands introduced universal suffrage with proportional representation in 1917; the Russian Revolution of 1917 produced (at least on paper) universal suffrage including women.

By 1920 it appeared that democracy had triumphed in most of Europe. The breakup of empires produced new constitutions, most of them granting universal suffrage, women's suffrage, and proportional representation. The constitution of Weimar Germany granted women the vote on the same basis as men and allowed a generous degree of proportional representation, which encouraged minority parties. Women's suffrage similarly arrived in new constitutions in Austria, Hungary, Ireland, and Poland in 1918 and then in Czechoslovakia in 1920. Belgian electoral laws of 1919 granted full manhood suffrage at age twenty-one and partial women's suffrage; the Dutch granted full women's suffrage in parallel laws. Italy introduced universal manhood suffrage with proportional representation that same year. The Swiss adopted proportional representation in 1919 but denied women the vote until late in the twentieth century.

The postwar record of the western European democracies was less democratic than the achievements in the new constitutions adopted in central Europe. The British adopted a new Representation of the People Act in 1918, with a greater measure of manhood suffrage and a first attempt at women's suffrage, but not granting full democracy.

Men still faced a residency requirement (reduced to six months) and women were enfranchised only at age thirty. The French adopted proportional representation but rejected women's suffrage in 1922 when traditionalists in the French Senate rejected the women's suffrage bill that had passed the French Chamber of Deputies in 1919.

Militant suffragists protested in both Britain and France, but the postwar mood in both countries was conservative. British women disbanded their suffrage union (National Union of Women's Suffrage Societies) and the most prominent suffragette organization (Women's Social and Political Union), but they witnessed the gradual success of women in politics (eight women members of Parliament were elected in 1924), which would culminate in the government of the first woman prime minister, Margaret Thatcher, in 1979. In France the postwar conservative government felt so strongly that it denied suffragists the right to hold protest marches. Militant suffragism revived in France when a new generation of women's rights advocates led by Louise Weiss emerged in the 1930s, but the French Senate continued to block women's suffrage by large margins.

THE STEADY VICTORY OF SUFFRAGISM
Great Britain adopted equal women's suffrage at age twenty-one in the Equal Franchise Act of 1928, but the 1930s saw democratic successes reversed in many countries. Truly universal suffrage, including women's suffrage, did not become the rule in Europe until after World War II. French women obtained the vote from Charles de Gaulle's government in exile in 1944; German and Italian women obtained it in postwar constitutions; Belgian women won equal suffrage in 1948. A few small states and autocracies remained bastions of masculine privilege into the late twentieth century. Monaco granted women the vote in 1962, Switzerland in 1971; Spain and Portugal democratized in the 1970s following the death of General Francisco Franco.

Proportional representation similarly became the standard of suffrage in Europe, encouraging the emergence of new political movements such as the Green Party and regional parties. By the start of the twenty-first century, proportional representation became the standard for the European Union's

elections, and in national elections only England practiced universal suffrage in the American style (the Scots and the Welsh both adopted proportional representation for their assemblies). And, in a final victory of suffragism, most European states granted the vote at age eighteen, as Britain did in the Representation of the People Act of 1969.

See also **Citizenship; Feminism; Minority Rights.**

BIBLIOGRAPHY

Daley, Caroline, and Melanie Nolan, eds. *Suffrage and Beyond: International Feminist Perspectives.* New York, 1994.

Joannou, Maraoula, and June Purvis, eds. *The Women's Suffrage Movement: New Feminist Perspectives.* Manchester, U.K., 1998.

Lijphart, Arend. *Electoral Systems and Party Systems: A Study of Twenty-Seven Democracies, 1945–1990.* Oxford, U.K., 1994.

Pugh, Martin. *Women and the Women's Movement in Britain, 1914–1959.* London, 1994.

Smith, Paul. *Feminism and the Third Republic: Women's Political and Civil Rights in France, 1918–1945.* Oxford, U.K. 1996.

STEVEN C. HAUSE

SURREALISM. In 1924 the French writer André Breton published his *Manifesto of Surrealism,* in which he defined the new movement:

> SURREALISM, *n.* Psychic automatism in its pure state, by which one proposes to express—verbally, by means of the written word, or in any other manner—the actual functioning of thought. Dictated by the thought, in the absence of any control exercised by reason, exempt from any aesthetic or moral concern. (translated from the French)

It was Breton's definition—as much as his authority—that in the 1920s brought together Louis Aragon, Antonin Artaud, Hans Bellmer, Victor Brauner, Salvador Dalí, Paul Delvaux, Giorgio De Chirico, Marcel Duchamp, Paul Éluard, Max Ernst, René Magritte, André Masson, Roberto Matta, Joan Miró, Francis Picabia, and Yves Tanguy, to mention only the best-known of the surrealists, thereby recognizing that surrealism was definitively not an aesthetic school, as is evident from the diversity of the artists' work, any more than it was a plastic formula with a given set of combinable and interchangeable elements.

Surrealism was a new path of artistic exploration that questioned the meaning of the real, beyond its materiality. The real thus became that of the innermost depths of being, a reality within. Although this principle was recurrent, its formal expressions, because they were those of the unconscious in a state of dream, anxiety, or hallucination, were at least as numerous as the artists themselves. And while the use of dreams as a source of inspiration had its origins in Romantic and, in particular, symbolist practices, the surrealists, in the light of psychoanalysis, were able to go beyond oneirism, a fantasized form of dream, and allow the unconscious to express itself freely.

Still, it was necessary to somehow liberate the unconscious, and it is precisely at this step of production that the different surrealist typologies were established. First is painting, in which the illusionist realism of the representation contrasts with, and thereby underscores, a surreality expressed by the improbable nature of the scene owing to the lack of normally logical congruence among the elements. Then there are the practices linked to automatism. Automatic drawings and other "exquisite corpses" are characterized by a practice of immediacy and decontextualization (in the case of the "exquisite corpse," a collection of words or images assembled by a group, the participants know neither what precedes nor what follows their contribution). At the limits of the unconscious and chance, such works escape any form of structuring and consequently any cultural referent. Finally there are mechanical processes such as Max Ernst's *grattages* (paint scrapings) and collages, or Man Ray's photograms (or "rayographs," as he called them), which excite the imagination and imply that which is beyond the mere appearance of things.

It should be noted that with the exception of Jacques-André Boiffard (described as an "absolute surrealist" in Breton's *Manifesto of Surrealism*), and apart from some known contacts, not a single photographer, even counting Man Ray, Dora Maar, Raoul Ubac, and Claude Cahun, was truly part of the surrealist group.

Exquisite Corpse. Drawing by André Breton, Max Morise, Yves Tanguy, and Man Ray. This is one of a number of drawings executed by the surrealists using a technique wherein each contributor created a section of an image without being able to see the other portions. CNAC/MNAM/DIST. RÉUNION DES MUSÉES NATRIONAUX/ART RESOURCE, NY

ORIGINS

Beyond a variety of approaches and forms, one characteristic remains fundamentally, immutably surrealist: the rejection of all constraints. Social and political constraints, in particular, were targeted, their rejection embodied in an extremely acerbic denunciation of work, prisons, asylums, the army, and the church. This stance engendered an art that was denounced for its cynicism, its anarchist aims, or its disillusioned individualism—a disillusionment that is entirely relative if one considers the paramount importance given to love, the only alternative to an imposed system, as subject matter in surrealist creations.

By liberating gesture and by incorporating multiple techniques, surrealism escaped from the historicity of art and thus from yet another constraint: it also questioned the very notion of the work of art. The means required to gain access to the surreal, linked to the practice of automatism, repudiated the qualities of artistic praxis. Certain characteristics that had traditionally been indissociable from a production such as art had already been challenged by Dada.

Many of those who joined the surrealist movement in 1923, or at least collaborated, did in fact come out of Dada. Some of the technical processes, notably collage and the photogram, and creative behaviors based on the refusal of constraints, whether political, social, or cultural, also came out of dadaism before being integrated into surrealism. Thus the first automatic text written by André Breton and Philippe Soupault, *Les champs magnétiques* (The magnetic fields), considered to be a surrealist work, was in fact written in 1920 in the spirit of dadaist spontaneity.

ANDRÉ BRETON, "POPE OF SURREALISM"

Breton participated in Dada sessions until 1921, when a rupture took place that would allow the surrealist group, already in gestation, to emerge and take shape. The open and dispersed format of Dada was succeeded by the elaboration of a unique and compact group under the leadership of the man who quickly came to be known as the "pope of surrealism."

Breton was charismatic and the true theoretician of surrealism. He was demanding, and he expected from members an unwavering adherence to the movement's ideals—its artistic ideals, but also, since they were inseparable, its moral and political ideals. Any offenders received a sentence with no concessions: expulsion. Fiercely protective of the purity of surrealist aims, Breton systematically proceeded to throw out, with varying degrees of courtesy, elements deemed to be parasitical. Thus, Antonin Artaud, André Masson, Philippe Soupault, and Roger Vitrac were violently expelled. Robert Desnos, Marcel Duchamp, and Francis Picabia were expelled with more circumspection.

MANIFESTOS AND REVIEWS

Breton nonetheless remained the federator of the surrealist group, if only because he was the author of the *Manifesto of Surrealism* and, along with Louis Aragon, Paul Éluard, Joan Miró, André Masson, and Yves Tanguy (from 1925), of *La révolution surréaliste*. This review was considered to be "the most scandalous in the world," notably because it published, on the cover of the first issue, a photo of Germaine Berton, who assassinated Marius Plateau, a member of the extreme-right party Action Française, surrounded by portraits of a number of the surrealists, including André Breton, and because it proclaimed, in the second issue, "Open the prisons! Fire the army!" About a dozen issues were published, ending in 1929.

The orientation of *La révolution surréaliste* was thus resolutely political, deliberately provocative, and intellectually violent. This, however, does not imply any amorality, as witness this question the review put to its readers: "Is suicide a solution?"—a question that most of the surrealists were to answer in the most absolute negative. Black humor and provocation should not conceal the way this review served as a tool for ethical and poetic reflection and as an aid to experimentation (issue 9–10, for example, was devoted to automatic writing).

Effective modes of dissemination, manifestos and periodicals, were an important part of surrealist activity. They also allowed for theoretical aims to be refined progressively over time. *La révolution surréaliste* enabled Breton, for example, between 1924 and 1928 to write a series of articles that would appear together in *Le surréalisme et la peinture* (1928; Surrealism and painting).

Succeeding *La révolution surréaliste*, six issues of *Le surréalisme au service de la révolution* were published between July 1930 and May 1933. Publication took place in a context of high tensions within the surrealist group. Indeed, 1929 had seen the release of Breton's new surrealist opus, the *Second Manifesto* (*Second Manifeste du surréalisme*), and with it the drastic operation of the dismissal of some members of the group. The ranks of the surrealists were partially decimated, even taking into account Dalí's arrival and Tristan Tzara's reintegration the same year; the excluded artists came together to produce an anti-Breton diatribe, *Un cadavre*.

The Key of Dreams. Painting by René Magritte, 1930. Magritte juxtaposes unrelated words and images to subvert the concept of objective reality. PHOTOTHÈQUE R. MAGRITTE-ADAGP/ART RESOURCE, NY

La révolution surréaliste and *Le surréalisme au service de la révolution* are good illustrations of surrealism's politico-artistic approach. That approach proved to be problematic, because it was based on a paradox, that is, the articulation of a fundamentally free and individualistic poetics together with a fundamentally collective revolutionary political engagement.

The difficulties did not curtail the movement's spread. Indeed, the 1930s saw the formation of a number of surrealist groups abroad. At the same time, the group's publishing activity ceased. Strictly speaking, since the folding of *Le surréalisme au service de la révolution,* and for the first time since 1924, no surrealist review was being published. However, in June 1933 the artists started collaborating on the first issue of *Minotaure.* Some ten issues later, *Minotaure* was completely in their control.

THE MOVEMENT'S EXPANSION AND DECLINE

Between 1933 and 1938, increasing numbers of surrealist exhibitions took place around the world. The first group show took place in 1925, and from 1926 to 1928 a surrealist gallery hosted regular events, ensuring the cohesion of a group that had been seriously destabilized by a crisis in 1926.

The year 1936 attested to the movement's outward expansion: the first major international surrealist exhibition was held in London. However, the 1938 exhibition, held in Paris, marked the start of an irreversible decline of a group whose apparent mobilization could not conceal the ruptures that had taken place or those that were imminent (Éluard and Ernst took their places in the surrealist cortege for the last time). The exhibition also marked the decline of surrealist ideology by renouncing its long-held obscurantism and giving way to facilitating explanation to the public.

The misunderstanding of surrealist ideas in the context of the exhibitions often provoked public reactions of irony or anger. The show of 1938 was not completely exempt from this rule: Dalí's *Taxi pluvieux* (Rainy taxi) featured a blond mannequin in a car, caught in a downpour of real vegetables and real snails; a "Surrealist Street" was peopled with wax mannequins signed by Dalí, Duchamp, Ernst, Masson, and J. Miró. But this was not the whole story. In this case, a tempering of visitors' reactions was facilitated by the publication of a sort of user's manual, a *Dictionnaire abrégé du surréalisme* (Abridged dictionary of surrealism) compiled by Breton and Éluard. This overture to the public was a renunciation of the occult character of surrealism. The dictionary itself was proof that the movement had turned back upon itself, evidence of an introspective gaze whose aims were undoubtedly historicizing.

The Second World War then hit like a bombshell. Many surrealists, including Breton, Dalí, Matta, and Tanguy, left France for the United States. Their exile, while others such as Éluard, Pablo Picasso, Bellmer, Desnos, and Artaud, remained in France, led to the breakup of the movement. Destinies were split; the experience of those who had stayed behind was too distant from that of the dreamers across the ocean. During the global conflict some of the most representative personalities of the group came together, mainly in New York,

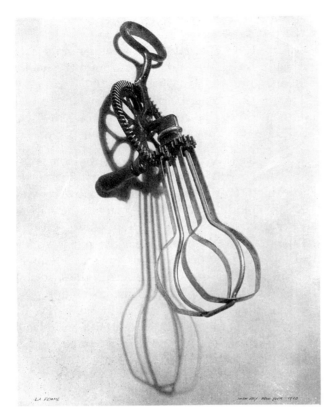

La femme (Woman). Photograph by Man Ray, 1920. CNAC/MNAM/Dist. Réunion des Musées Nationaux/Art Resource, NY

BIBLIOGRAPHY

Primary Sources

Breton, André. *Manifestoes of Surrealism.* Translated by Richard Seaver and Helen R. Lane. Ann Arbor, Mich., 1969.

Secondary Sources

Caws, Mary Ann, ed. *Surrealist Painters and Poets: An Anthology.* Cambridge, Mass., 2001.

Matthews, J. H. *The Imagery of Surrealism.* Syracuse, N.Y., 1977.

Melly, George. *Paris and the Surrealists.* London, 1991.

Passeron, René. *Surrealism.* Paris, 2001.

Rosemont, Franklin. *André Breton and the First Principles of Surrealism.* London, 1978.

Strom, Kirsten. *Making History: Surrealism and the Invention of a Political Culture.* Lanham, Md., 2002.

ALEXANDRA KOENIGUER

where they continued their surrealist oeuvre, produced the periodicals *Views* and *VVV*, and organized exhibitions such as *First Papers of Surrealism* (New York, 1942). When they returned, they brought with them a desire to revitalize the movement and to prescribe a more occult system for surrealist creations, in direct contrast to the change in direction begun in 1938, whereas the surrealists who had remained in occupied Europe sought to establish contacts with revolutionary political movements.

Despite ongoing surrealist activity in painting, as evidenced in the 1947 exhibit at the Galerie Maeght in Paris, surrealism virtually disappeared after 1945. But its presence continued in particular because its incursions into the realm of the unconscious and its theoretical investments with regard to the work of art as *object* had lasting effects on twentieth-century art as a whole.

See also **Aragon, Louis; Artaud, Antonin; Avant-Garde; Breton, André; Dada; Dalí, Salvador; Duchamp, Marcel; Éluard, Paul; Ernst, Max; Miró, Joan.**

SWEDEN. Sweden democratized relatively late. Not until after World War I did Sweden, swayed by the political and social turbulence that characterized Europe at that time, introduce universal suffrage for men and women. A two-chamber parliamentary system was established and the role of the monarch substantially curtailed. Nonetheless, the king formally remained head of the cabinet until 1974 and was formally responsible for work connected with changes of government. In 1970 a single-chamber system was introduced.

The Swedish party system is characterized by marked continuity. The same five parties were represented in the Riksdag in the early 1920s and in the late 1980s: on the left, the Social Democratic Workers' Party and the Communist Party (today the Left Party); on the right, the Liberal Party, the Farmers' Party (now the Center Party), and the Conservative Party (today's Moderate Party).

The 1920s were years of shifting and unstable political majorities, which caused frequent changes of government. In the Riksdag elections of 1932, however, the Social Democrats gained a powerful lead due to a Keynesian-inspired anti-unemployment program. Since then the Social Democratic Party has held a unique position in Swedish politics. During only nine of the seventy-three years between 1932 and 2005 did the bourgeois (i.e., nonsocialist) parties hold government power. On the other hand, the Social Democrats have seldom enjoyed absolute parliamentary majorities.

Sweden has not been at war since 1814. The country remained neutral throughout World War I. During the interwar period Sweden supported a policy of neutrality and national security that gave the League of the Nations a central role. Sweden significantly reduced its defense establishment, and not until the late 1930s did a limited rearmament take place against the backdrop of impending war.

When war broke out in 1939 Sweden issued a declaration of neutrality. Immediately thereafter, a coalition government—excluding only the Communists—was formed under the leadership of Per Albin Hansson. It succeeded in keeping Sweden out of the war, but only at the cost of concessions to Germany. These included, among other things, the extensive transport of German soldiers to and from occupied Norway and, in connection with the German attack on the Soviet Union in 1941, the transit conveyance of an entire, fully equipped military division to the eastern front. The extensive Swedish export to Germany of, among other things, iron ore and ball bearings was important both to the Swedish economy and to the German war industry. Sweden's refugee policy was initially very restrictive, not least toward Jewish immigrants. After the war the government's policy was generally defended as a small nation's realistic and successful adaptation to existing circumstances, an interpretation that has subsequently been questioned and criticized.

SWEDEN DURING THE POSTWAR ERA
Sweden entered the postwar era under exceptionally favorable conditions. Its industrial infrastructure was unharmed by war. Sweden topped the international charts of prosperous nations throughout this era. The export industry was the most expansive part of the Swedish economy, and exports quadrupled during the 1950s and 1960s. Production within the technically most advanced and knowledge-intensive part of the engineering industry expanded particularly rapidly. Sweden's classic industries, based on the country's raw materials—the manufacture of wood products, paper, pulp, and iron ore—also expanded significantly.

During the favorable economic conditions of the postwar era, the particular features of what had become known as the *Swedish model* became more firmly established. The questions of whether such a Swedish model really existed, and if so, the nature of its distinguishing characteristics, are among those that have dominated modern research on twentieth-century history. The following elements have been emphasized. First, institutionalized cooperation between employers and trade unions, codified in the Saltsjöbaden Agreement of 1938. This agreement consisted of a mutual expression of support for efforts to avoid labor disputes through a well-functioning and centralized negotiation process. This proved successful; the number of strikes diminished significantly, and politicians, trade union representatives, and employers from all over the world arranged educational visits in order to study the calm Swedish labor market.

Second, a vigorous state economic policy. Sweden belonged to those nations which as early as the 1930s had employed Keynesian-inspired economic policies against unemployment. During the postwar era, however, economic policy makers were usually faced with the opposite problem: economic overheating, inflation, high profits and wages, and labor shortages. This, in its turn, made it difficult to achieve rationalization and increased efficiency. For two decades the so-called Rehn-Meidner model (named for Gösta Rehn and Rudolf Meidner, the two leading trade union economists who formulated it) was used to guide the government's economic policy.

One of this model's premises was the use of wage policies to rationalize the economy. Implementation of the so-called solidaristic wage policy was to ensure that wage developments in economically less sound companies did not lag behind those of more expansive branches. At the same time, those employed in the export industries were to restrain their demands for increased wages. Those workers who lost their jobs because many of the less profitable companies risked folding were to be reemployed in those parts of the economy where labor shortages tended to be a growing problem. Government subsidies were to encourage mobility among the unemployed, and there was extensive investment in active labor-market policies. This resulted in very low rates of open unemployment by international standards.

Third, extensive social reforms, starting with family policy and health insurance. The pension reform of the 1950s, ATP, became an issue of great symbolic importance; it also caused one the great political battles of the postwar era. The reform established a trend toward a universalist welfare system that benefited all citizens, not just those with special needs. The Swedish welfare system is further distinguished by its primarily tax-based financing and by its administration by the state.

Fourth, a relatively extensive political consensus, including certain corporative decision-making structures. A distinctive trait of the Swedish model is the strong position of interest organizations. Spokespeople for Swedish industry, the trade unions, cooperative organizations, and established social movements were well represented in, for example, government committees and on the boards of civil service departments and in informal deliberations with the government. This phenomenon was often termed *Harpsund democracy*—Harpsund being the prime minister's country estate, where the nation's political and economic elite sometimes gathered for informal discussions.

The Social Democrats were in uninterrupted control of the government until 1976, usually receiving between 45 and 50 percent of the vote. Tage Erlander was prime minister from 1946 to 1969. The Social Democratic Party's influence extends far beyond the parliamentary sphere. It exercises great influence over, for example, the powerful Swedish Trade Union Confederation and the widespread consumers' cooperative movement. The party has generally ruled without an absolute majority in the Riksdag. It entered into a political coalition with the Farmers' Party between 1951 and 1957; during other periods it has usually depended on support from the small Communist Party (now Left Party). The three bourgeois parties have alternated as leading opposition parties; between 1948 and 1968 the Liberal Party assumed that role, the Center Party from 1968 to 1979, and the Moderate Party from 1979 onward.

Swedish postwar foreign policy has been primarily oriented toward nonalignment, directed toward neutrality in war. Its security policies have presupposed active participation in the United Nations and its agencies. There was an attempt, in 1948, to create a common Scandinavian defensive alliance. As it turned out, Denmark and Norway preferred an alliance with NATO, something ruled out by Sweden's neutrality. However, Sweden did initiate covert cooperation with the West in order to obtain military reinsurance should the nation be drawn into war; this policy of secret cooperation also made it possible to import armaments. There was, in addition, a significant exchange of military information between Sweden and the western defense alliance. Both the United States and the Soviet Union were well aware of the duplicity of Swedish foreign policy, while the Swedish people were informed of the true state of affairs only much later. Sweden's policy of neutrality also affected its collaboration with Europe. Sweden took part in establishing the European Free Trade Association, but the government long felt that Sweden's neutrality made it impossible for it to join the European Economic Community.

SWEDEN SINCE THE 1970S

Swedish society was radicalized during the 1970s. The newly elected prime minister, Olof Palme, was associated with a critical attitude toward the U.S. war in Vietnam and with a growing Swedish commitment to Third World development. Palme's sharp criticism of the war, which received international attention, periodically strained diplomatic relations with the United States. Extensive youth radicalization led to the emergence of new social movements, of which the women's movement and the environmental movement were to gain considerable influence. A series of highly visible strikes marked the end of the long period of industrial peace. The Social Democratic government's decision to pursue union-friendly legislation led to growing tension between the two labor-market parties. Especially important was the decision to introduce wage earners' investment funds, which were designed gradually to transfer part of the industries' profits to funds controlled by the trade unions. A diluted version of the funds was introduced during the 1980s amid vehement protests from the bourgeois parties.

During the 1970s a series of new social reforms were implemented, especially in areas that concerned family policy and equality between the sexes. These included an extensive expansion of the system of day-care centers, which facilitated women's wage employment.

At the same time, however, the long international boom came to an end. The subsequent economic crises, including growing unemployment, helped to defeat the Social Democrats in the elections of 1976. There had also been complaints about Social Democracy's bureaucratization and autocratic style, both associated with the party's long stint in power. Nuclear power was another central election issue, as the Center Party's nuclear-critical attitude gained it votes at the cost of the Social Democrats.

At first the new bourgeois three-party coalition government continued with Keynesian-style policies. In 1980, however, there was a sudden change. For the first time since World War II steps were taken—in accordance with the decade's neoliberal trends—to increase Sweden's market adaptability and to cut back the welfare system.

When, in 1982, the Social Democrats again took power, after being in opposition for two electoral terms, they continued in part—to the surprise of many Swedes—down the same path. The party's economic policies have essentially followed the international trend toward deregulation of the credit and exchange market, increased exposure to competition and privatization of the public sector, an independent National Bank and high prioritization of anti-inflation measures. Swedish unemployment rates have also approached those of Europe as a whole.

Except for an interval of bourgeois government in 1991–1994, the Social Democrats have held power since 1982. Around 1990 several new parliamentary parties emerged, and the Green Party and the Swedish Christian Democrats assumed a permanent place in the Riksdag. The Social Democrats are still the largest party, although their parliamentary power has diminished to around 40 percent of the electorate. Since 1979 the Moderate Party has been the leading bourgeois party with, as a rule, between 20 and 25 percent of the votes.

The flare-up of Cold War tensions in the 1980s also affected Swedish domestic policy. The question of whether and to what extent Soviet submarines systematically trespassed on Swedish territorial waters was extensively debated. Despite government investigatory commissions and Swedish protests to the Soviet Union, the question of what actually took place remains basically unanswered.

Since 1990, Swedish foreign policy has become markedly Europeanized. In 1991, after the fall of the Berlin Wall, Sweden applied for membership in the European Union (EU). A referendum was held in 1994 and a small majority—52 percent—voted for membership. The Swedish population is among the most EU-skeptical in the union and in 2003 a clear majority voted against membership in the European Monetary Union.

The international economic crisis of the early 1990s adversely affected the Swedish economy, with large-scale industrial shutdowns and growing unemployment. The resulting budgetary crisis resulted in far-reaching cuts in the social sector. However, in spite of these cuts, Sweden continued to have an extensive, publicly financed system of social insurance and a high taxation rate. Surveys clearly demonstrate that these systems enjoy considerable support, even from right-wing voters. During the early years of the twenty-first century the Swedish economy again became stable.

See also **Norway; Palme, Olof; Welfare State.**

BIBLIOGRAPHY

Ekman, Stig, and Nils Edling, eds. *War Experience, Self-Image and National Identity: The Second World War as Myth and History.* Stockholm, 1997.

Florin, Christina, and Bengt Nilsson. "'Something in the Nature of a Bloodless Revolution': How New Gender Relations Became Gender Equality Policy in Sweden in the Nineteen-Sixties and Seventies." In *State Policy and Gender System in the Two German States and Sweden, 1945–1989,* edited by Rolf Torstendahl, 11–78. Uppsala, Sweden, 1999.

Hadenius, Stig. *Swedish Politics during the 20th Century: Conflict and Consensus.* Stockholm, 1999.

Misgeld, Klaus, Karl Molin, and Klas Åmark, eds. *Creating Social Democracy: A Century of the Social Democratic Labor Party in Sweden.* University Park, Pa., 1992.

Thullberg, Per, and Kjell Östberg. *Den svenska modellen.* Lund, Sweden, 1994.

KJELL ÖSTBERG

SWITZERLAND. The war years 1914 to 1918 were a time of profound political, cultural, and economic change in Switzerland although the country avoided being involved in acts of war. The concept of its "permanent neutrality" (*immerwährende Neutralität*) imposed by the Congress of Vienna (1815) only provided a superficial protection against severe internal and external tensions.

Internally, the differences between the culturally and economically Germany-oriented and German-speaking majority and the France or Italy-oriented French, Italian, and Romanic-speaking minorities threatened to tear the country apart, along the borders of its four language regions. This conflict, which biased the political climate during the entire war and postwar years, became obvious when a general known for his support of Prussian militarism was elected commander-in-chief. The secret attempts to bring about a separate peace between Germany and revolutionary Russia in 1917 led to the resignation of the foreign minister. To calm the Allies as well as the non-German-speaking and less German-friendly Swiss, the foreign minister was replaced by a "Romand," as the French-speaking Swiss are called. Ever since his election, the Romands have had the right to appoint two federal councillors to the government, a seven-man executive elected by both chambers of parliament and supposed to represent all major parties and regions.

SOCIAL TENSIONS
In addition to these tensions bearing upon foreign relations, social unrest among the population proved a burden domestically because the government did not have an effective economic policy: some entrepreneurs profited by the export of war goods, and the farmers gained from inflation, whereas others— especially industrial workers—suffered from a rise in prices and shortages of everyday goods. As there was, moreover, still no financial support for the families of the soldiers serving at the borders, violent demonstrations and strikes became more and more frequent. In July 1918 the Swiss Workers' Congress gave the Olten Action Committee, a union consisting of leading figures of the Social Democratic Party (SPS) and the unions, the go-ahead to threaten a national strike. The situation escalated in late autumn of 1918, when the Federal Council, irritated and

alarmed by the class struggle, was misled into mobilizing army units for a precautionary occupation of Zurich. The Olten Action Committee reacted with protest strikes that expanded to a nationwide general strike from 12 November until 14 November 1918. The strikers' demands included key political and social conditions, such as the introduction of a proportional representation of the electorate and of women's right to vote, a forty-eight-hour work week, and an old-age, disability, and survivors' social security system. Given the mobilization of about one hundred thousand soldiers, the Olten Action Committee stopped the strike, fearing it would cause a civil war.

The interpretation of the conflict as a revolutionary attempt, controlled by outside forces (Soviet Union), to overthrow the regime hampered social reform and determined the domestic climate until the 1930s. From among the political objectives of the national strike, only proportional representation was implemented. In 1919 this led, during the first elections based on the new system, to a shifting of the parliamentarian balance of power: the Liberals lost their traditional predominance, the Social Democrats improved their position and won 20 percent of the seats, though their gains were offset by the newly founded Agrarian Party, which won 14 percent and thus again strengthened the Liberal-Conservative alliance. The result of these elections can be taken as a sign of the rather contradictory situation and self-image of Switzerland. By the end of the nineteenth century, the country was highly industrialized. The fact that Switzerland grew to be an international financial center soon became an additional key element of modern economic growth. But although nearly half the inhabitants lived in urban surroundings and worked in industry, the self-image of Switzerland and especially that of its political elite was deeply rooted in a conservative belief in the value of an idealized peasantry. Part of this contradictory ideology was a conservative definition of women's role and the family. Attempts to introduce women's suffrage in the 1920s at least on a cantonal level were doomed to fail because of its rejection by male voters.

The economic depression of the 1930s hit Switzerland comparatively late, but lasted until 1936. Fascist tendencies had been latent in

Switzerland since the suppression of the general strike of 1918. Advocates of fascism received support by the Nazis' takeover in Germany in 1933. Federal authorities were slow to react and even showed some sympathy for these tendencies. Swiss Nazi groups—the so-called Fronten (fronts)—were founded and right-wing Conservatives made plans to remodel the state along corporative lines. The threat of war, however, caused the general population to turn away from right-wing ideologies.

WORLD WAR II AND AFTER

Switzerland's war preparations were influenced by the experience of World War I and the fear of social unrest. The election of the first Social Democratic federal councillor in 1943 was considered as much a token of social unity as the election of a general from the French-speaking Canton of Vaud as commander-in-chief was considered a sign of national unity. In September 1939 the country quickly mobilized. After the fall of France in 1940, when Switzerland was completely surrounded by the Axis Powers, the defense strategy was reduced to the Alps. The "Reduit National" (Alpine Redoubt), a huge system of fortresses in the Alps, was expanded to offer a place of retreat for the army and the government in case of a German attack, robbing civilians of any protection. Nevertheless, the commander-in-chief managed to maintain the image of a country ready to defend itself to the last. This defense strategy allowed a partial demobilization in order to use all forces for production, not least for the export of goods deemed important to the war effort. Despite an affirmation of neutrality, the Axis Powers profited more from Swiss exports than did the Allies. Modern historians hold that Switzerland was most likely spared during the war not only because of its army but because a neutral and largely cooperative Switzerland—with its railways, Alpine passes, engineering resources, and banking services—was useful to the Third Reich.

In 1938, when Adolf Hitler annexed Austria, the stream of refugees into Switzerland, which had begun immediately after the Nazi takeover in Germany in 1933, started to swell. By the time the war began, Switzerland played host to seven or eight thousand emigrants, among them five thousand Jews. The refugee policy was restrictive; victims of racial persecution were not granted the status of refugees. It became the official policy of the federal government and administration to deny sanctuary to Jews for fear of "over-foreignization" (*Überfremdung*). Some of the cantons and several private organizations and individuals dodged these restrictive policies. During the war, about 53,000 civilians (about half of them Jews) and 104,000 soldiers (deserters, prisoners of war, soldiers of the French army) were taken in. The number of people turned back and physically prevented from crossing the borders is estimated to have been about twenty thousand. Restrictions were loosened as late as 1944.

Once the war was over, Switzerland was internationally isolated. Trade with Germany had undermined the credibility of Swiss neutrality. Relations with the United States were normalized only after painstaking negotiations (Washington Accord of 1946). But the country was soon integrated into the anticommunist American-dominated postwar order. At the end of the Cold War, Switzerland was again confronted with its role during World War II, when the question of Jewish assets and looted gold threatened to damage the credibility and image of the Swiss financial market. In 1996 this led to the appointment of the Independent Commission of Experts Switzerland (IEC) to study the relations between Switzerland and Nazi Germany. The research results confirmed that Swiss banks had been serving as a repository for Nazi gold and cash, stolen in part from murdered Jews, and had been responsible for retaining dormant Jewish accounts. The banks had to pay back 1.2 million dollars. The Swiss government expressed its deep regret for the repulsion of refugees but, in the end, did not acknowledge responsibility for the policy in general.

The postwar political system proved to be stable but also extremely rigid. This was because important decisions and change had to be accepted by a majority of voters (for laws that were to be changed) or, in addition, by a majority of all cantons (for changes of the constitution). Thus, women's right to vote, put to a vote for the first time on the federal level in 1959 but then rejected, was only accepted in 1971. Voters proved even less flexible concerning the renewal of civil rights: the extremely long periods of residence required from foreigners (twelve years) were maintained, and voters several times denied foreigners a right to be naturalized. Thus the high share of foreigners (which increased from 5.1 percent in 1950 to 15.9 percent in 1970 and 20 percent in 2004) is partly a result of these inflexible and rigid naturalization provisions. The first system of social security was created in 1948 and has been expanded gradually ever since.

The Swiss government, composed of all larger political parties, was based on the so-called Zauberformel or magic formula of 1959: two Liberals, two Christian Democrats, two Social Democrats, and one representative of the People's (or Farmer's) Party. For the first time ever, it was not adhered to in 2004, when a second representative of the populist, right-wing People's Party was elected to the detriment of the Christian Democrats.

Economically, Switzerland developed in the second half of the twentieth century from an industrial society into a society dominated by the service sector. In 2004, two-thirds of all employees worked for the service industry and about one-quarter for trade and industry. By the early twenty-first century, agriculture was of marginal significance.

Switzerland avoided the international alliances of the postwar period because of its definition of neutrality: several times, the Swiss said "nay" to joining the United Nations; it finally joined in 2004. The country also remained reserved in the face of European political integration efforts; it did, however, join the European Free Trade Association (EFTA) and established a political and socioeconomic system largely conforming to the European Union ("autonomous adjustment"). The end of the Cold War saw Switzerland once again face the issue of whether and how neutrality was still a viable position in the world of the twenty-first century.

See also **Germany; Nazism.**

BIBLIOGRAPHY

Fahrni, Dieter. *An Outline History of Switzerland: From the Origins to the Present Day.* 8th enl. ed. Zurich, 2003.

Hettling, Manfred von, et al. *Eine Kleine Geschichte der Schweiz: der Bundesstaat und seine Traditionen.* Frankfurt, 1998.

Imhof, Ulrich, et al. *Geschichte der Schweiz und der Schweizer.* 3rd ed. Basel, 2004

Independent Commission of Experts Switzerland–Second World War. *Switzerland, National Socialism, and the Second World War. Final Report.* Zurich, 2002.

Joris, Elisabeth, and Heidi Witzig, eds. *Frauengeschichte(n): Dokumente aus zwei Jahrhunderten zur Situation der Frauen in der Schweiz.* 4 vols. Zurich, 2001.

Steinberg, Jonathan. *Why Switzerland?* 2nd ed. Cambridge, U.K., and New York, 2002.

REGINA WECKER

For Reference

Not to be taken from this room